Introduction to Psychology

PGS101 - Szeli

Dennis Coon | John O. Mitterer

CENGAGE
Learning™

Australia • Brazil • Japan • Korea • Mexico • Singapore • Spain • United Kingdom • United States

CENGAGE
Learning™

Introduction to Psychology: PGS101 - Szeli

Dennis Coon | John O. Mitterer

Executive Editors:
 Maureen Staudt
 Michael Stranz

Senior Project Development Manager:
Linda DeStefano

Marketing Specialist:
 Sara Mercurio
 Lindsay Shapiro

Senior Production / Manufacturing Manager:
 Donna M. Brown

PreMedia Supervisor:
 Joel Brennecke

Rights & Permissions Specialist:
 Kalina Hintz
 Todd Osborne

Cover Image:
 Getty Images*

* Unless otherwise noted, all cover images used by Custom Solutions, a part of Cengage Learning, have been supplied courtesy of Getty Images with the exception of the Earthview cover image, which has been supplied by the National Aeronautics and Space Administration (NASA).

ISBN-13: 978-1-4266-3360-7

ISBN-10: 1-4266-3360-2

Cengage Learning
5191 Natorp Boulevard
Mason, Ohio 45040
USA

Cengage Learning is a leading provider of customized learning solutions with office locations around the globe, including Singapore, the United Kingdom, Australia, Mexico, Brazil, and Japan. Locate your local office at:
international.cengage.com/region

Cengage Learning products are represented in Canada by Nelson Education, Ltd.

For your lifelong learning solutions, visit **www.cengage.com/custom**

Visit our corporate website at **www.cengage.com**

Printed in the United States of America

Table of Contents

(*Note – this is a "custom" textbook that has been designed specifically for this course in a joint effort between your instructor and the publisher. Please note that some chapters have been removed intentionally and some pages may be black & white as dictated by the changes.)

From "Psychology", Coon/Mitterer

From "Study Guide, With Language Development Guide", Coon/Mitterer

Contents

Introduction The Psychology of Studying 1

1 Introducing Psychology and Research Methods 12

2   Brain and Behavior   56

3 Human Development 96

4 Sensation and Perception 148

5 States of Consciousness 202

6   Conditioning and Learning   246

7 Memory 286

8 Intelligence, Cognition, Language, and Creativity   326

9 Motivation and Emotion   370

10 Personality 412

11 Health, Stress, and Coping 456

12 Psychological Disorders 496

13   Therapies   540

14 Gender and Sexuality 582

15 Social Behavior 620

16 Applied Psychology 668

Preface

To the Student—An Invitation to Psychology

Psychology is an exciting field. It is at once familiar, exotic, surprising, and challenging. Most of all, psychology is ever changing. Indeed, this book is just a "snapshot" of a colorful passing scene. Yet, change makes psychology especially fascinating: What, really, could be more intriguing than our evolving knowledge of human behavior?

Psychology is about each of us. It asks us to adopt a reflective attitude as we ask, "How can we step outside of ourselves to look objectively at how we live, think, feel, and act?" Psychologists believe the answer is through careful thought, observation, and inquiry. Although that may seem simple, thoughtful reflection takes practice to develop. It is the guiding light for all that follows in this text.

Each chapter of this book will take you into a different realm of psychology, such as personality, abnormal behavior, memory, consciousness, and child development. Each realm is complex and fascinating in its own right, with many pathways, landmarks, and interesting detours to discover. *Psychology: Modules for Active Learning* is your passport to an adventure in learning. It is, in a very real sense, written about you, for you, and to you. Like any journey of discovery, your "tour" of psychology will help you better understand yourself, others, and the world around you. It's definitely a trip worth taking. In the pages that follow, we have done all that we could imagine to make your journey through psychology enjoyable and worthwhile.

Getting Started

None of us likes to start out a new adventure by reading the manual. We just want to get right into our new computer game, step off the plane and begin our vacation, or just start using our new camera or cell phone. You might be similarly tempted to just start reading this textbook.

Please be patient. Learning psychology depends on how you study this book, as well as how you read it. *Psychology: Modules for Active Learning* is your passport to an active adventure in learning, and not just passive reading. To help you get off to a good start, we strongly encourage you to read our short Introduction, which precedes Chapter 1. The Introduction describes study skills, including the SQ4R method, which you can use to get the most out of this text and your psychology course. It also tells how you can explore psychology through the Internet, electronic databases, and interactive CDs.

To the Instructor—A Concise Survey of Psychology

Psychology: Modules for Active Learning was written to provide a concise, but complete, first course in psychology. It is organized in modules, which are grouped into 16 chapters, to allow flexibility in assigning topics for your course. Throughout this text, we have tried to select only the very "best" material from the many topics that could be presented. Nevertheless, *Psychology* covers not only the heart of psychology, but also many topics at the cutting edge of current knowledge. New information, anecdotes, perspectives, and narratives appear throughout the Eleventh Edition. The result is a concise text that is readable, manageable, informative, and motivating.

Marcel Proust wrote, "The real voyage of discovery consists not in seeing new landscapes but in having new eyes." It is in this spirit that this book is designed to help you promote an interest in human behavior, including an appreciation of the practical applications of psychology, the richness of human diversity, the relationship between brain and behavior, and the field of positive psychology.

In this edition we have also updated the SQ4R method. The steps are now Survey, Question, Read, Recite, Reflect, Review. This update has allowed us to expand the Reflect step to strengthen the relationship between learning and doing the kinds of active, elaborative processing and critical thinking that characterize the reflective student (Gadzella, 1995). The end result is a more effective promotion of active learning, better long-term retention of ideas, and a reflective attitude that lies at the heart of critical thinking. Without such skills, students cannot easily go, as Jerome Bruner put it, "beyond the information given" (Bruner, 1973).

Readability and Narrative Emphasis

Selecting a textbook is half the battle in teaching a successful course. A good text does much of the work of imparting information to your students. This frees class time for discussions, extra topics, or media presentations. It also leaves students asking for more. When a book overwhelms students or cools their interest, teaching and learning suffer.

Many introductory psychology students are reluctant readers. No matter how interesting a text may be, its value is lost if students fail to read it. That's why we've worked hard to make this a clear, readable, and engaging text. We want students to read this book with genuine interest and enthusiasm, not merely as an obligation.

To encourage students to read, we made a special effort to weave narrative threads through every chapter. Everyone loves a good story, and the story of psychology is among the most compelling to be told. Throughout *Psychology*, we have used intriguing anecdotes and examples to propel reading and sustain interest. As students explore concepts, they are asked to think about ideas and relate them to their own experiences.

Practical Applications

Psychology: Modules for Active Learning is designed to give students a clear grasp of major concepts, without burying them in details. At the same time, it offers a broad overview that reflects psychology's rich heritage of ideas. We think students will find this book informative and intellectually stimulating. Moreover, we have emphasized the many ways that psychology relates to practical problems in daily life.

A major feature of this book is the *Psychology in Action* modules found at the end of each chapter. These high-interest discussions bridge the gap between theory and practical applications. We believe it is fair for students to ask, "Does this mean anything to me? Can I use it? Why should I learn it if I can't?" The Psychology in Action modules show students how to solve practical problems and manage their own behavior. This allows them to see the benefits of adopting new ideas, and it breathes life into psychology's concepts.

Modular Approach and Integrated Study Guide

The chapters of this text are divided into short, self-contained modules. Each module concludes with a summary and a feature called a *Knowledge Builder*. These "mini-study guides" challenge students to quiz themselves, relate concepts to their own experiences, and think critically about the principles they are learning. For this edition, we have reorganized the Knowledge Builders into *Recite* and *Reflect* sections, to better mirror the SQ4R method. Recite questions are similar in difficulty to in-class test questions, and they provide immediate feedback to students. If students would like more feedback and practice, an excellent new printed supplement, *Concept Modules with Note-Taking and Practice Exams,* is bundled with this text. Also, a traditional *Study Guide* is available.

Electronic Resources

To encourage further reflection, students will find a section called *Links* in each Knowledge Builder. The websites described there invite students to go beyond the text to explore a wealth of interesting information on topics related to psychology. In addition, the *Interactive Learning* section at the end of each chapter directs students to *ThomsonNOW,* a powerful online study tool that provides students with a rich assortment of interactive learning experiences, animations, and simulations.

ThomsonNOW is a Web-based, personalized study system that provides a pre-test and a post-test for each chapter and can also create personalized study plans that point students to areas in the text, as well as additional learning materials that will help them master course content.

On the Internet, students can visit this text's *Book Companion Website,* where they will find quizzes, a final exam, chapter-by-chapter Web links, flash cards, a glossary, and more (http://academic.cengage.com/psychology/coon).

At www.iChapters.com, students can select from over 10,000 print and digital study tools, inlcuding the option to buy individual e-chapters and e-books. The first e-chapter is free!

Human Diversity

Today's students reflect the multicultural, multifaceted nature of contemporary society. In *Psychology,* students will find numerous discussions of human diversity, including differences in race, ethnicity, culture, gender, abilities, sexual orientation, and age. Too often, such differences needlessly divide people into opposing groups. Our aim throughout this text is to discourage stereotyping, prejudice, discrimination, and intolerance. We've tried to make this book gender neutral and sensitive to diversity issues. All pronouns and examples involving females and males are equally divided by gender. In artwork, photographs, and examples, we have tried to portray the rich diversity of humanity. In addition, *Human Diversity* highlights appear throughout the book, providing students with examples of how to be more reflective about human diversity. Many topics and examples in this book encourage students to appreciate social, physical, and cultural differences and to accept them as a natural part of being human.

Positive Psychology

Over the past 100 years, psychologists have paid ample attention to the negative side of human behavior. This is easy to understand because we urgently need to find remedies for human problems. However, Martin Seligman and Mihaly Csikszentmihalyi have urged us to also study positive psychology. What do we know, for instance, about love, happiness, creativity, well-being, self-confidence, and achievement? Throughout this book, we have attempted to answer such questions for students. Our hope is that students who read this book will gain an appreciation for the potential we all have for optimal functioning. Also, of course, we hope that they will leave introductory psychology with emotional and intellectual tools they can use to enhance their lives.

How Module Features Support the SQ4R Method

Psychology: Modules for Active Learning uses an SQ4R, active-learning format to make studying psychology a rewarding experience. Notice how the steps of the SQ4R method—*survey, question, read, recite, reflect,* and *review*—are incorporated into the modular design.

Survey At the front of each chapter, several features help students build cognitive maps of upcoming topics. A short vignette arouses interest, provides a preview of the main topic of the chapter, and focuses attention. Next, a list of *Modules* and *Survey Questions* provides an overview of the chapter. To help students structure their learning, the same Survey Questions appear again in the modules, where they are used to introduce major topics. The Survey Questions also appear in the *Study Guide* to give students a consistent framework for learning.

Question Throughout each chapter, italicized *Guide Questions* serve as advance organizers that prompt students to look for important ideas as they read. These questions also establish a dialogue in which the concerns and reactions of students are anticipated. This ongoing dialogue clarifies difficult points—in a lively give-and-take between questions and responses.

Read We've made every effort to make this a clear, readable text. To further aid comprehension, we've used a full array of traditional learning aids. These include: boldface terms (with phonetic pronunciations), bullet summaries, a robust illustration program, summary tables, a name index, a subject index, and a detailed glossary. As an additional aid, figure and table references in the text are marked with small geometric shapes. These "placeholders" make it easier for students to return to reading after they have paused to view a table or figure.

An integrated Glossary aids reading comprehension by providing precise definitions directly in context. When important terms first appear, they are immediately defined. In this way, students get clear definitions when and where they need them—in the general text itself. In addition, a parallel Running Glossary defines key terms in the margins of pages.

The Running Glossary makes it easier for students to find, study, and review important terms.

In each chapter, several boxed highlights discuss high-interest topics related to human diversity, using psychology, and critical thinking. In addition, new *Discovering Psychology* highlights get students involved through in-text demonstrations and self-assessment exercises. Highlights are stimulating but nonintrusive supplements to the main text. They enrich the presentation and encourage students to think about the ideas they are learning.

Recite At the end of each module, the Knowledge Builder gives students a chance to test their understanding and recall of preceding topics. Knowledge Builders include an opportunity to *Recite* (a short, noncomprehensive quiz) in order to enhance learning. They also help students actively process information and assess their progress. Students who miss any items are asked to backtrack and clarify their understanding before reading more.

Reflect Cognitive psychology tells us that elaboration, the reflective processing of new information, is one of the best ways to actively foster understanding and form lasting memories (Gadzella, 1995). The more elaborated that processing, the richer the understanding and the better the resulting memory. To help students reflect, each Knowledge Builder includes a series of Reflect exercises.

Self-reference, a particularly powerful form of elaboration, makes new information more meaningful by relating it to what is already known (Klein & Kihlstrom, 1986). To help students elaborate their new understanding, each Knowledge Builder includes a series of *Relate* questions. These questions encourage students to associate new concepts with personal experiences and prior knowledge. New in this edition are the *Discovering Psychology* boxes. These "try-it" demonstrations allow students to observe interesting facets of their own behavior or do self-assessment exercises, thus linking new chapter information to the student's concrete experience.

A course in psychology naturally contributes to critical thinking abilities. To further facilitate critical thinking, each Knowledge Builder also includes one or more *Critical Thinking* questions. These stimulating questions challenge students to think critically and analytically about psychology. Each is followed by a brief answer with which students can compare their own thoughts. Many of these answers cite research findings and are informative in their own right.

In addition, several boxed highlights encourage other forms of reflective thought. The *Critical Thinking* features model a reflective approach to critical thinking in psychology. In addition, *Human Diversity* features encourage reflection on the variability of the human experience, *The Clinical File* features encourage reflection on the clinical applications of psychology, and *Brainwaves* features encourage reflection on the role of the brain in understanding psychological phenomena.

Review To help students consolidate their learning, each module concludes with a bulleted summary of major ideas presented in the unit. As noted previously, chapter-ending Psychology in Action modules show students how psychological concepts relate to practical problems, including problems in their own lives. The information found in the Psychology in Action modules helps reinforce learning by illustrating psychology's practicality. Also, as noted previously, all important terms appear in a Running Glossary throughout the book, which aids review.

Critical Thinking

The active, questioning nature of the SQ4R method is, in itself, an inducement to think critically. Many of the guide questions that introduce topics in the text serve as examples of critical thinking. Further, Chapter 1 contains a discussion of critical thinking skills and a rational appraisal of pseudo-psychologies. In addition, the discussion of research methods in Chapter 1 is actually a short course on how to think clearly about behavior. It is augmented by suggestions about how to critically evaluate claims in the popular media. Chapter 8, "Intelligence, Cognition, Language, and Creativity," includes many topics that focus on thinking skills. Throughout the text, many boxed highlights promote critical thinking about specific topics that students should approach with healthy skepticism. As mentioned earlier, every Knowledge Builder includes Critical Thinking questions. Taken together, these features will help students gain thinking skills of lasting value.

Psychology: Modules for Active Learning—What's New?

Thanks to psychology's vitality, this text is improved in many ways. The title has been changed to reflect our enhanced focus on active processing, reflection, and critical thinking. The two human development chapters of the previous edition have been combined, resulting in a 16-chapter book. Another notable change is the enhanced modular format of the Eleventh Edition. As mentioned earlier, topics are still grouped by chapters. However, modules are now more clearly defined within chapters. Many chapters have also been reorganized so that modules are more, well, modular.

Specifically, each numbered module begins on a separate page and concludes with a point-by-point summary and a Knowledge Builder, with Recite and Reflect exercises. Entire chapters or individual modules can be assigned with equal ease, and reading assignments can be closely integrated with your course syllabus.

The Eleventh Edition of *Psychology: Modules for Active Learning* features some of the most recent and interesting information in psychology, supported with many new and recent references. The following annotations highlight some of the new topics and features that appear in this edition.

Introduction: The Psychology of Studying

The Introduction shows students how to read effectively, study more efficiently, take good notes, prepare for tests, perform well on various types of tests, create study schedules, and avoid procrastination. The advice to students in this edition has been adapted to match the modular format of the text.

Chapter 1: Introducing Psychology and Research Methods

- This chapter has been extensively reorganized.
- A module is now specifically dedicated to critical thinking and the scientific method.
- Experimental and nonexperimental methods are now treated in thier own modules.
- A new highlight, *Testing Common-Sense Beliefs,* indicates why psychology's reliance on empirical methods is superior to a reliance on unreflective common sense.
- Three major modern perspectives are now outlined (biological, psychological, and sociocultural) and referred to throughout the remainder of the book.
- Brief research updates improve discussions of current trends in psychology, prescription privileges, mechanisms of the placebo effect, and self-fulfilling prophecies.

Chapter 2: Brain and Behavior

- This chapter has been lengthened and updated to reflect the growing importance of neuroscience to psychology today.
- This new focus on neuroscience is extended throughout the book, including *Brainwaves* features, which appear in various modules and highlight the growing importance of the biological perspective.
- Two new features have been added to this chapter, *A Stroke of Bad Luck* and *If You Change Your Mind, Do You Change Your Brain?*
- An old module has been split into two separate modules, *Neurons and the Nervous System* and *Brain Research,* resulting in a clearer organization of topics.

- The module *Hemispheres and Lobes of the Cerebral Cortex* has been extensively updated to better highlight differences between the primary areas and association areas. Mirror neurons are now discussed, as is the relationship between the prefrontal area and the sense of self.
- Many updates have been included in the chapter, including new material on neural networks, sidedness (along with handedness), and recent research on use of the fMRI as a lie detector.

Chapter 3: Human Development

- Chapters 3 and 4 of the previous edition have been combined and rewritten to create a single chapter that is organized chronologically.
- The opening module on heredity and environment has been rewritten and expanded to include a discussion of the concept of reaction range. It also eschews simple either/or discussions of the relationship between nature and nurture.
- Material on effective parenting is now collected in the chapter-closing Psychology in Action module.
- A new feature, *The Twixters,* introduces the phenomenon of delayed adulthood.

Chapter 4: Sensation and Perception

- This chapter has been reorganized so that the opening module, *Sensory Systems and Selective Attention,* now draws together in one place information about the general functioning of sensory systems. Vision is now treated in its own module, as is material on the other senses.
- A new Brainwaves feature, *The Matrix: Do Phantoms Live Here?* introduces students to the neuromatrix theory of phantom limb pain.
- Another new feature, *The Boiled Frog Syndrome,* explores the dangers to humankind of failing to encode life-threatening sensory information.
- The highlight, *Staying in Touch with Reality,* updates a previous highlight to explain the concept of reality testing, to better explain when hallucinations can be regarded as a symptom of mental disorders, and to describe how "sane hallucinations" can occur.

Chapter 5: States of Consciousness

- A new Brainwaves feature, *How Addictive Drugs Affect the Brain,* better explains synaptic mechanisms underlying drug effects.

- A new feature, *What Is It Like to Be a Bat?* invites students to reflect on the difference between subjective and objective perspectives on consciousness.
- A new feature, *Abducted by Space Aliens?* explores hypnopompic imagery.
- References and statistics (drug abuse rates, accidents due to sleepiness or drug use, and so forth) have been updated throughout the chapter.
- Several sections have been updated, including *Sleep Patterns, Types and Causes of Insomnia,* and a number of subsections about drugs.
- The treatment of hypnosis now includes coverage of Hilgard's dissociation theory and the hidden observer.
- The new section, *Hypnosis, Meditation, and Sensory Deprivation,* combines information on sensory deprivation with a discussion of meditation and gives both topics a fuller treatment, rather than implying that they are only helpful for relaxation.
- The College Alcohol Problems Scale is used to help students recognize problem drinking.
- More recent work suggesting that marijuana can produce physical dependence is now included.
- The questions in the Probing Dreams section now reflect the Hall–Van de Castle system of dream content analysis.

Chapter 6: Conditioning and Learning

- The *Classical Conditioning* module has been reorganized to clarify the basic classical conditioning model.
- A new highlight, *Are Animals Stuck In Time?* explores a method for studying time perception by animals.
- A new highlight, *Coping with Chemo,* discusses the role of classical conditioning in conditioned nausea during chemotherapy.
- A new highlight, *You Mean Video Games Might Be Bad for Me?* is part of a reworked treatment of the role of media in fostering aggressive behavior.

Chapter 7: Memory

- Material on exceptional memory has been combined with a discussion about how to improve memory, resulting in a new module, *Exceptional Memory and Improving Memory.* Methods of measuring memory are now treated in their own module.
- Mnemonic memory strategies are more clearly distinguished from meaning-based memory improvement.
- A new highlight, *Telling Wrong from Right in Forensic Memory,* combines information on the use of hypnosis and the cognitive interview to clarify the impor-

tance of reducing false memories in eye-witness testimony.

- A new highlight, *Do You Like Jam With Your Memory?* explores the memory-jamming theory of advertising.

Chapter 8: Intelligence, Cognition, Language, and Creativity

- The chapter title has been changed to reflect both an extensive reorganization and a recognition of the importance of human language.
- The chapter-opening vignette focuses on the autistic savant Kim Peek.
- The opening module is now *Intelligence*.
- The distinction between intelligence as "g" and multiple intelligences is given more prominence, and the section on multiple intelligences has been lengthened.
- Artificial intelligence is now given a different emphasis and is included in the *Intelligence* module. The material on expertise is now in the section on problem solving.
- A new highlight on bilingualism introduces the benefits of additive bilingualism.
- A new highlight, *Have You Ever Thin Sliced Your Teacher?* discusses the potential importance of rapid cognition and impressions gained from minimal information.
- A new highlight, *Intelligence—How Would a Fool Do It?* focuses on cross-cultural definitions of intelligence.
- A new highlight, *You Mean Video Games Might Be Good for Me?* offers a counterpoint as it explores the possibility that popular culture is raising IQs.
- The Psychology in Action module now focuses on race, intelligence, and IQ.

Chapter 9: Motivation and Emotion

- An engaging new vignette on alexythymia opens this chapter, to promote interest in the modules that follow.
- The material on circadian rhythms was moved to the opening section of the book. The discussion of *Stimulus Drives* was restructured as a result.
- The section on hunger was restructured into major sections on internal and external factors, and the section on eating disorders now includes information about eating disorders among men.

- A new highlight, *Xtreme!* upgrades the discussion of sensation seeking.
- Material on fat set points is now treated as a Brainwaves highlight.
- A new highlight, *To Catch a Terrorist*, presents some new approaches to lie detection.

Chapter 10: Personality

- The opening module now offers an overview of personality, the role of heredity, and theories of personality, while the second module focuses exclusively on trait theories.
- A new highlight, *Telling Stories about Ourselves*, discusses narrative psychology and personality change.
- The highlight on identical twins has been updated.
- Direct and indirect aggression has been differentiated in the section on personality and gender, highlighting the rising rate of female aggression.

Chapter 11: Health, Stress, and Coping

- The module on stress, frustration, and conflict now includes the general adaptation syndrome. The module on stress and health has been rewritten accordingly.
- An updated table now lists the most common sources of stress at work.
- A new highlight, *Acculturative Stress—Stranger in a Strange Land*, focuses on the stresses of immigrants.
- A new highlight, *It's All in Your Mind*, distinguishes between the medical model and the biopsychosocial model.
- The discussion of burnout has been highlighted.

Chapter 12: Psychological Disorders

- Mental health statistics have been updated throughout the chapter, as have many case study examples.
- A new Brainwaves highlight, *The Schizophrenic Brain*, stresses the role of neuroscience in understanding psychological disorders.
- A new highlight, *Sick of Being Sick*, introduces the interesting topic of Munchausen syndrome by proxy.
- The discussion of culturally defined maladies and the politics of mental illness has been updated.

Chapter 13: Therapies

- A new section on interpersonal psychotherapy has been added.
- The section on cybertherapy has been rewritten.

- A new highlight, *Ten Irrational Beliefs—Which Do You Hold?* concretely connects students with key ideas in rational-emotive therapy.
- A new highlight on gambling addiction has been added.
- The treatment of cultural issues in therapy has been updated.

Chapter 14: Gender and Sexuality

- In view of the controversy surrounding John Money's research on gender assignment, the entire discussion of intersexual infants has been revised.
- The updated highlight, *Bruce or Brenda—Can Sex Be Assigned?* discusses one of the most famous, yet failed, cases of sex reassignment.
- Statistics on sexuality and sexually transmitted diseases have been updated.
- A new highlight asks if we are oversexualizing young girls.
- Material on the role of genetics, the brain, and sexual orientation has been upgraded into a Brainwaves feature.
- Information about HIV and AIDS reflects the latest findings.

Chapter 15: Social Behavior

- The chapter has been reorganized so that social influence topics are treated in increasing order of directness from conformity to compliance to obedience.
- Material on self-assertiveness now follows the presentation of the three major forms of social influence.
- The explanation of the role of chance conditioning in forming attitudes has been integrated with the concept of direct contact.
- A new highlight box, *Is America Purple?* describes how oversimplification contributes to stereotyping and prejudice.
- The material on media violence has been rewritten and updated.

Chapter 16: Applied Psychology

- The module on industrial/organizational psychology has been extensively rewritten. Leadership is now the lead-off topic.
- A new highlight on women as corporate leaders has been added.
- The treatment of flextime has been expanded into a discussion of flexible work in general.

- A new highlight offers practical tips about how to prepare for a job interview.
- The module on evironmental psychology has been updated and reorganized.
- The concepts of ecological footprints and carbon footprints are now discussed and characterized as important souces of feedback for fostering environmentally friendly behaviors.
- The Psychology in Action module is new and now focuses on human factors psychology, including the design of human-computer interfaces and the role of human factors in space psychology.

A Complete Course—Teaching and Learning Supplements

A rich array of supplements accompanies *Psychology: Modules for Active Learning,* including several that make use of the latest technologies. These supplements are designed to make teaching and learning more effective. Many are available free to professors or students. Others can be packaged with this text at a discount. For more information on any of the listed resources, please call the Thomson Learning™ Academic Resource Center at 800-423-0563.

Student Support Materials

Introductory students must learn a multitude of abstract concepts, which can make a first course in psychology difficult. The materials listed here will greatly improve students' chances for success.

Concept Modules with Note Taking and Practice Exams Created by Claudia Cochran of El Paso Community College and Shawn Talbot of Kellogg Community College, this booklet includes key concepts in each chapter, a place to take notes, and a practice exam of 20 multiple-choice questions. (ISBN: 0-495-50709-1)

Study Guide with Language Development Guide The *Study Guide,* prepared by Steven Hoekstra of Kansas Wesleyan University, is an invaluable student resource. It contains a variety of study tools, including: Chapter Overviews, Recite and Review (fill-in-the-blank), Connections (matching), Check your Memory (true-false), Final Survey and Review (fill-in-the-blank), and Mastery Test. A language development section clarifies idioms, special phrases, cultural and historical allusions, and difficult vocabulary. New to this edition is a Critical Thinking feature. Study Guide content is keyed to Learning Objectives to help students master important concepts. (ISBN: 0-495-50711-3)

Careers in Psychology: Opportunities in a Changing World This informative booklet, written by Tara L. Kuther and Robert D. Morgan, is a Wadsworth exclusive. The pamphlet describes the field of psychology, as well as how to prepare for a career in psychology. Career options and resources are also discussed. *Careers in Psychology* can be packaged with this text at no additional cost to students. (ISBN 0-495-09078-6)

Multimedia CD-ROMs

Interactive CD-ROMs make it possible for students to directly experience some of the phenomena they are studying. The following CDs from Wadsworth provide a wealth of engaging modules and exercises.

Sniffy™ the Virtual Rat, Lite Version 2.0 There's no better way to master the basic principles of learning than working with a real laboratory rat. However, this is usually impractical in introductory psychology courses. *Sniffy the Virtual Rat* offers a fun, interactive alternative to working with lab animals. This innovative and entertaining software teaches students about operant and classical conditioning by allowing them to condition a virtual rat. Users begin by training Sniffy to press a bar to obtain food. Then they progress to studying the effects of reinforcement schedules and simple classical conditioning. In addition, special "Mind Windows" enable students to visualize how Sniffy's experiences in the Skinner Box produce learning. The Sniffy CD-ROM includes a Lab Manual that shows students how to set up various operant and classical conditioning experiments. *Sniffy™ the Virtual Rat, Lite Version 2.0* may be packaged with this text for a discount. (ISBN: 0-534-63357-9)

Internet Resources

The Internet is providing new ways to exchange information and enhance education. In psychology, Wadsworth is at the forefront in making use of this exciting technology.

Book Companion Website As users of this text, you and your students will have access to the companion site for *Psychology: Modules for Active Learning* (http://academic.cengage.com/psychology/coon). Access is free and no pincode is required. This outstanding site features Learning Objectives, Tutorial Quizzes, Essay Questions, Glossary, Web Links, Flash Cards, Crossword Puzzles, and more!

ThomsonNow™ This Web-based program helps your students discover the areas of text where they need to focus their efforts through a series of diagnostic pre-tests and post-tests (written by Christopher Mayhorn of North Carolina State University), personalized study plans with learning modules that parallel the modules in the book, eBook files, and other integrated media elements. While students can use ThomsonNow™ without any instructor setup or involvement, an Instructor Gradebook is available for you to monitor student progress.

Printed Access Card: 0-495-59502-0
Instant Access Card: 0-495-59503-9

Psychology Resource Center The new Psychology Resource Center features powerful teaching and learning tools, bringing psychology to life with a full library of original and classic video clips plus interactive learning modules tied to all of the topics covered in an Introductory Psychology course. Organized by topic, the Resource Center is easy to navigate by students to find learning resources, and instructors will also find it an amazing lecture resource to easily stream multimedia into their classrooms. For more information, please contact your representative.

InfoTrac® College Edition *InfoTrac College Edition* is a powerful online learning resource, consisting of thousands of full-text articles from hundreds of journals and periodicals. Students using *Psychology: Modules for Active Learning* receive four months of free access to the *InfoTrac College Edition*. This fully searchable database offers over 20 years' worth of full-text articles from thousands of scholarly and popular sources—updated daily, and available 24 hours a day from any computer with Internet access. By doing a simple keyword search, students can quickly generate a list of relevant articles from thousands of possibilities. Then they can select full-text articles to read, explore, and print for reference or further study. *InfoTrac College Edition's* collection of articles can be useful for doing reading and writing assignments that reach beyond the pages of this text. Students also have access to *InfoWrite,* which provides extensive resources for writing papers, including suggested topics, APA guidelines, and more. (*InfoTrac College Edition* is at http://www.infotrac-college.com.)

WebTutor™ WebTutor™ course cartridges provide an easy, fast, and reliable way to integrate and customize rich text-specific content into your on-campus course management system. For students, *WebTutor* offers real-time access to a full array of study tools, including flash cards, practice quizzes and tests, online tutorials, exercises, asynchronous discussion, a whiteboard, and an integrated e-mail system. Students will also have integrated access to *InfoTrac College Edition,* the online library.

Professors can use *WebTutor* to offer virtual office hours, to post syllabi, to set up threaded discussions, to track student progress on quizzes, and more. You can customize the content of *WebTutor* in any way you choose, including uploading images and other resources, adding Web links, and creating course-specific practice materials. (*Web Tutor* on *WebCT*, ISBN: 0-495-59563-2; on *Blackboard*, ISBN: 0-495-59564-0)

Thomson Audio Study Tools Audio Study Tools provides audio reinforcement of key concepts that students can listen to from their personal computer or MP3 player. Created specifically for *Psychology: Modules for Active Learning*, Audio Study Tools provides approximately 10 minutes of audio content for each chapter, giving students a quick and convenient way to master key concepts. Audio content allows students to test their knowledge with quiz questions, listen to a brief overview reflecting the major themes of each chapter, and review key terminology. Order Audio Study Tools directly at www.ichapters.com.

Essential Teaching Resources

As every professor knows, teaching an introductory psychology course is a tremendous amount of work. Not only should the supplements listed here make life easier for you, they should also make it possible for you to concentrate on the more creative and rewarding facets of teaching.

Instructor's Resource Manual The *Instructor's Manual*, by Susan Weldon of Henry Ford Community College, contains resources designed to streamline and maximize the effectiveness of your course preparation. In a three-ring binder, this IRM is a treasure trove—from the introduction section, which includes grading rubrics, a sample syllabus, and a Resource Integration Guide, to a full array of chapter resources. Each chapter includes learning objectives, discussion questions, lecture enhancements, role-playing scenarios, "one-minute motivators," broadening our cultural horizons exercises, journal questions, suggestions for further reading, media suggestions, Web links, and more. (ISBN 0-495-50707-5)

Test Bank The *Test Bank* was prepared by Jeannette Murphey of Meridian Community College. It includes over 5,000 questions. The multiple-choice questions are correlated to learning objectives and are labeled with question-type, difficulty, and main text page reference. Essay questions and true-false questions are also included. All questions new to this edition are marked with an asterisk. (ISBN: 0-495-50708-3)

PowerLecture CD-ROM (with JoinIn™ on TurningPoint® and ExamView®) This one-stop lecture and class preparation tool, prepared by Corinne McNamara of Kennesaw State University, contains ready-to-use Microsoft® PowerPoint® slides and allows you to assemble, edit, publish, and present custom lectures for your course. PowerLecture lets you bring together text-specific lecture outlines and art from Coon's text, along with videos or your own materials-culminating in a powerful, personalized, media-enhanced presentation. The CD-ROM also includes TurningPoint® software that lets you pose book-specific questions and display students' answers seamlessly within the Microsoft PowerPoint slides of your own lecture, in conjunction with the "clicker" hardware of your choice, as well as the ExamView® assessment and tutorial system, which guides you step by step through the process of creating tests. (ISBN: 0-495-50777-6)

Videotapes and Films

Wadsworth offers a variety of videotapes and films to enhance classroom presentations. Many video segments in the Wadsworth collection pertain directly to major topics in this text, making them excellent lecture supplements.

Wadsworth Film and Video Library for Introductory Psychology Adopters can select from a variety of continually updated film and video options. The Wadsworth Film and Video Library includes selections from the *Discovering Psychology* series, the *Annenberg* series, and *Films for Humanities*. It also includes the exclusive ABC offerings described below. Contact your local sales representative or Wadsworth Marketing at 877-999-2350 for details.

ABC® Videos for Introductory Psychology These one- to four-minute video clips, a Wadsworth exclusive, allow you to integrate the newsgathering and programming power of ABC into the classroom to show students the relevance of psychology to daily life. Organized by course topics, these compelling clips are ideal for launching lectures and encouraging discussion. Adopters receive one new, updated video each year. A Wadsworth/Thomson Learning Exclusive!

Topics covered in the videos include:

- **New Brain Scan** A new brain scan using adapted MRI technology gives doctors a more detailed look at the brain, enabling them to treat brain injuries more effectively.
- **Artificial Eye** New artificial eye technology enables spatial recognition and navigation in the blind.
- **Curing Insomnia** An alternative treatment to prescription sleep drugs for insomnia patients using cognitive behavioral therapy to retrain the body and induce sleep.
- **Weight Loss Hypnosis** Hypnosis helps one woman find the motivation to eat healthier and exercise. A look at the scientific side of hypnosis, how it can help, and its limitations.

- **Gay Teens** Gay teens talk about coming out to their families and friends, and the difficulties they encountered along the way.
- **Rules of Attraction** Dating criteria are evaluated through a test to determine the level of shallowness in the dating pool.
- **Suicide Bomber Profile** An in-depth look at the background of the suicide bomber who killed a group of civilians at an Israeli night club.

Contact your sales representative to order.

Wadsworth Psychology: Research in Action Videos The Wadsworth Psychology: Research in Action Videos offer students a look at cutting-edge research in psychology, illustrating real-life applications of concepts they're learning in their textbook and classroom. Authored and produced by Roger Klein, Associate Professor of Educational Psychology at the University of Pittsburgh, the videos feature established and up-and-coming researchers from leading research institutions around the country. Volume I (0-495-59520-9, available for Spring 2008) presents 25 segments, and Volume II (available for Fall 2008) presents 23; together, the volumes comprise more than 2½ hours of stimulating research video. For more information, please contact your representative.

Wadsworth Media Guide for Introductory Psychology This essential instructor resource, edited by Russell J. Watson, contains hundreds of video and feature film recommendations for all major topics in Introductory Psychology. (ISBN: 0-534-17585-6)

Supplementary Books

No text can cover all of the topics that might be included in an introductory psychology course. If you would like to enrich your course, or make it more challenging, the Wadsworth titles listed here may be of interest.

Challenging Your Preconceptions: Thinking Critically about Psychology, Second Edition This paperbound book (ISBN: 0-534-26739-4), written by Randolph Smith, helps students strengthen their critical thinking skills. Psychological issues such as hypnosis and repressed memory, statistical seduction, the validity of pop psychology, and other topics are used to illustrate the principles of critical thinking.

Writing Papers in Psychology: A Student Guide The Seventh Edition of *Writing Papers in Psychology* (ISBN: 0-534-53331-0), by Ralph L. Rosnow and Mimi Rosnow, is a valuable "how-to" manual for writing term papers and research reports. This edition has been updated to reflect the latest APA guidelines. The book covers each task with examples,

hints, and two complete writing samples. Citation ethics, how to locate information, and new research technologies are also covered.

Cross-Cultural Perspectives in Psychology How well do the concepts of psychology apply to various cultures? What can we learn about human behavior from cultures different from our own? These questions lie behind a collection of original articles written by William F. Price and Rich Crapo. The Fourth Edition of *Cross-Cultural Perspectives in Psychology* (ISBN: 0-534-54653-6) contains articles on North American ethnic groups as well as cultures from around the world.

Culture and Psychology, Fourth Edition David Matsumoto and Linda Juang's unique book (ISBN: 0-495-09787-X) discusses similarities and differences in research findings in the United States and other cultures. By doing so, it helps students see psychology and their own behavior from a broader, more culturally aware perspective.

Summary

We sincerely hope that teachers and students will consider this book and its supporting materials a refreshing change from the ordinary. Creating it has been quite an adventure. In the pages that follow, we think students will find an attractive blend of the theoretical and the practical, plus many of the most exciting ideas in psychology. Most of all, we hope that students using this book will discover that reading a college textbook can be entertaining and enjoyable.

Acknowledgments

Psychology is a cooperative effort requiring the talents and energies of a large community of scholars, teachers, researchers, and students. Like most endeavors in psychology, this book reflects the efforts of many people. We deeply appreciate the contributions of the following professors, whose sage advice helped improve the Eleventh Edition of *Psychology: Modules for Active Learning:*

Kimberly Glackin, Blue River Community College
Gene Indenbaum, SUNY–Farmingdale
Patricia Lanzon, Henry Ford Community College
Andrea Macari, Suffolk County Community College
J. Mark McKellop, Juniata College
Dan Patanella, John Jay College of Criminal Justice
Pete Peterson, Johnson County Community College
Thomas Weatherly, Georgia Perimeter College
Tammi Wynn, Rowan-Cabarrus Community College

We would like to thank the following reviewers of the previous editions: Judith Balcerzak, Ventura College; Bakhtawar Bhadha, Glendale College; LeAnn Binger, Richard Bland College; John Dilworth, Kellogg Community College; Patricia Donat, Mississippi University for Women; Cindy Lehar, York County Community College; Katherine McNellis, Lakeshore Technical College; Bill Roe, Phoenix College; James Scepansky, Cedar Crest College; Dawn Strongin, California State University at Stanislaus; Shawn Talbot, Kellogg Community College; Lisa Wood, Ouchita Technical College; Brian R. Bate, Cuyahoga Community College; James R. Bean, Lock Haven University; Gary A. Biel, Schreiner University; Martin Bourgeois, University of Wyoming; T. L. Brink, Crafton Hills Community College; Lucy Capuano-Brewer, Ventura College; Roy Cohen, Mesa Community College; Robert S. Coombs, Southern Adventist University; Beatrice M. de Oca, Western New Mexico University; Linda DiDesidero, Capitol College; David N. Entwistle, Malone College; Christopher J. Frost, Southwest Texas State University; Adrienne Garro, Kean University; Gordon Hammerle, Adrian College; Mark L. Harmon, Reedley College–North Centers; Robert A. Hayes, Westfield State College; Diedra T. Hayman, Virginia Western Community College; William R. Holt, University of Massachusetts–Dartmouth; Lawrence Jesky, Seton Hill College; Diana Jimeno, University of Illinois–Urbana/Champaign; James J. Johnson, Illinois State University; William G. LaChappelle, Brevard Community College; Fred Leavitt, California State University at Hayward; John F. Lindsay, Jr., Georgia College and State University; Britton L. Mace, Southern Utah University; Denise McClung, West Virginia University–Parkersburg; Michael McVay, Colby Community College; Sandra Merryman, Southwest Texas State University; Robert L. Moore, Marshalltown Community College; Colleen Moran, Gloucester County College; Donna Webster Nelson, Winthrop University; Caroline Olko, Nassau Community College–SUNY; Randall E. Osborne, Southwest Texas State University; Michelle L. Pilati, Rio Hondo College; Kathy Pillow-Price, Arkansas State University–Beebe; Beth Robinson, Lubbock Christian University; Cynthia Ross, Las Positas College; Edward Samulewicz, Rosemont College; Karen K. Saules, Eastern Michigan University; Donna Love Seagle, Chattanooga State Technical Community College; Barbara Biondo Sloan, Marshalltown Community College; Steven M. Specht, Utica College; Martha S. Spiker, University of Charleston; Elizabeth Swenson, John Carroll University; Inger Thompson, Glendale Community College; Robert J. Wood, Las Positas College.

Producing *Psychology: Modules for Active Learning* and its supplements was a formidable task. We are especially indebted to each of the following individuals, for supporting this book:

Susan Badger

Sean Wakely

Eve Howard and Michele Sordi

We also wish to thank the individuals at Wadsworth who so generously shared their knowledge and talents over the past year. These are the people who made it happen: Vernon Boes, Chris Caldeira, Jerilyn Emori, Jeremy Judson, Magnolia Molcan, Rachel Guzman, Wilson Co, Sara Swangard, and Margaret Parks.

It has been a pleasure to work with such a gifted group of professionals and many others at Wadsworth. We are grateful to Jaime Perkins for his wisdom, creativity, humor, and unflagging support. We especially want to thank Jeremy Judson for his unstintingly invaluable editorial assistance.

Up in St. Catharines, Barbara Kushmier, Kayleigh Hagerman, and Heather Mitterer pitched in to lend a hand. Last of all, we would like to thank our wives, Sevren and Heather, for making the journey worthwhile.

The Psychology of Studying

Introduction

You're actually reading this! As your authors, we're impressed. Too often, students just jump in and read a textbook from the first assigned chapter to the last one. As far as we're concerned, that's a shame because a textbook needs to be studied, not just read. Think about it: How much do you typically remember after you've read straight through a whole textbook chapter? If the answer is "Nada," "Zilch," or simply "Not enough," it may be because reading a chapter is not really the same as studying it. Even if you're an excellent student, you may be able to improve your study skills. Students who get good grades tend to work *smarter*, not just longer or harder (Santrock & Halonen, 2007). To help you get a good start, let's look at several ways to improve studying.

The SQ4R Method—How To Tame a Textbook

What's the difference between reading a textbook and studying it? You have probably spent the occasional evening just vegging out in front of the TV set. According to psychologist Donald Norman (1993), you were engaging in *experiential cognition*, more or less passively letting the experience happen to you. There is nothing at all wrong with merely experiencing entertainment. But have you ever noticed that the morning after one of those evenings you often have trouble remembering just exactly what you watched the night before?

In contrast, suppose one of those programs was about, say, global warming and it really got you thinking. You might have wondered how global warming will affect your own future plans. You might have questioned some of the program's more dire projections for the future. You might have thought back to another program on global warming and remembered some different perspectives. Now you are "going beyond the information given" (Bruner, 1973). For Norman (1993), this is *reflective cognition*: not just experiencing something, but also actively thinking *about* what you have just experienced. The next morning you may well forget most of what you watched the night before, but the odds are you will remember the program on global warming. To use Norman's terms, then, studying a textbook involves not just experiencing it; it also involves actively reflecting on what you have just read.

One way to be more reflective while reading a textbook is to use the **SQ4R method.** SQ4R stands for *survey, question, read, recite, reflect,* and *review.* These six steps can help you learn as you read and reflect, remember more, and review effectively:

S = *Survey.* Skim through a chapter before you begin reading it. Start by looking at topic headings, figure captions, and summaries. Try to get an overall picture of what lies ahead. Because this textbook is organized into short modules, you can survey just one module at a time if you prefer.

Q = *Question.* As you read, turn each topic heading into one or more questions. For example, when you read the heading "Stages of Sleep" you might ask: "Is there more than one stage of sleep?" "What are the stages of sleep?" "How do they differ?" Asking questions helps you read with a purpose.

R1 = *Read.* The first R in SQ4R stands for *read.* As you read, look for answers to the questions you asked. Read in short "bites," from one topic heading to the next, then stop. For difficult material you may want to read only a paragraph or two at a time.

SQ4R method An active study-reading technique based on these steps: survey, question, read, recite, reflect, and review.

R2 = *Recite*. After reading a small amount, you should pause and recite or rehearse. That is, try to mentally answer your questions. Better yet, summarize what you just read in brief notes. Making notes will show you what you know and don't know, so you can fill gaps in your knowledge (Peverly et al., 2003).

If you can't summarize the main ideas, skim over each section again. Until you can remember what you just read, there's little point to reading more. After you've studied a short "bite" of text, turn the next topic heading into questions. Then read to the following heading. Remember to look for answers as you read and to recite or take notes before moving on. Ask yourself repeatedly, "What is the main idea here?"

Repeat the question-read-recite cycle until you've finished an entire chapter (or just one module if you want to read shorter units).

R3 = *Reflect*. As you read, try to reflect on what you are reading. One powerful way to do this is to relate new facts, terms, and concepts to information you already know well or to your own experiences. You've probably noticed that it is especially easy to remember ideas that are personally meaningful, so try to relate the ideas you encountered to your own life. This may be the most important step in the SQ4R method. The more genuine interest you can bring to your reading, the more you will learn (Hartlep & Forsyth, 2000).

R4 = *Review*. When you're done reading, skim back over a module or the entire chapter, or read your notes. Then check your memory by reciting and quizzing yourself again. Try to make frequent, active review a standard part of your study habits (See ● Fig. I.1.)

Does this really work? Yes. Using a reflective reading strategy improves learning and course grades (Taraban, Rynearson, & Kerr, 2000). Simply reading straight through a chapter can give you "intellectual indigestion." That's why it's better to stop often to think, question, recite, reflect, review, and "digest" information as you read.

How to Use *Psychology: Modules for Active Learning*

You can apply the SQ4R method to any textbook. However, we have specifically designed this textbook to help you actively learn psychology.

Survey Each chapter opens with a chapter survey that includes a *Preview* as well as a list of *Modules* and *Survey Questions* that will be covered. You can use these features to identify important ideas as you begin reading. The Preview should help you get interested in the topics you will be reading about, and the Survey Questions are a good guide to the kinds of information to look for as you read. After you've studied these features, take a few minutes to do your own survey of the chapter. Doing so will help you build a "mental map" of upcoming topics.

Question *How can I use the SQ4R method to make reading more interesting and effective?* One of the key steps is to ask yourself lots of questions while you read. The Survey Questions are repeated throughout each chapter to help you recognize key topics. In addition, questions like the one that began this paragraph appear throughout each module. They will help you focus on seeking information as you read. However, be sure to ask your own questions, too. Try to actively interact with your textbooks as you read.

Read As an aid to reading, important terms are printed in **boldface type** and defined where they first appear. (Some are followed by pronunciations—capital letters show which syllables are accented.) You'll also find a *running glossary* on the page you are reading, so you never have to guess about the meaning of technical terms. If you need to look up a term from lecture or another module, check the main *Glossary*. This "mini-dictionary" is located near the end of the book. Perhaps you should take a moment to find it now.

Recite and Reflect To help you study in smaller "bites," each module in this textbook ends with a study guide called a *Knowledge Builder*. Knowledge Builders provide opportuni-

● **FIGURE I.1** The SQ4R method promotes active learning and information processing. You should begin with a survey of the chapter or module, depending on how much you plan to read. Then you should proceed through cycles of questioning, reading, reflecting, and relating, and conclude with a review of the module or the entire chapter.

ties to check your memory for what you just read. They also invite you to think more deeply by presenting critical thinking questions as well as questions designed to help you relate material to your own life and web links leading to more information on topics of particular interest. (Don't forget to also take notes or recite and reflect on your own.)

This book also provides other opportunities for you to reflect more deeply about what you are reading. Each chapter ends with a *Psychology in Action* module. These discussions are filled with practical ideas you can relate to your own life. *Discovering Psychology* boxes also invite you to relate psychology to your own life. The *Critical Thinking* boxes will help you reflect on intriguing questions and apply critical thinking skills to psychology. In addition, *Human Diversity* boxes encourage you to reflect on the rich variability of human experience, *Brainwaves* boxes invite you to reflect on how the brain relates to psychology, and *The Clinical File* encourages you to reflect on ways that psychology can be applied to treat clinical problems.

Review Each module concludes with a point-by-point *Summary* to help you identify important ideas to remember. These summaries are organized around the same Survey Questions you read at the beginning of the module. You can also return to the glossary items throughout each module for further review.

● Table I.1 summarizes how this text helps you apply the SQ4R method. Even with all this help, there is still much more you can do on your own.

The LISAN Method—How To Tame a Lecture

Reading strategies may be good for studying, but what about taking notes in class? Sometimes it's hard to know what's important. Just as studying a textbook is best done reflectively, so too is attending class (Norman, 1993). Like effective reading, good notes come from actively seeking information. People who are **active listeners** avoid distractions and skillfully gather ideas. Here's a listening/note-taking plan that works for many students. The letters LISAN, pronounced like the word *listen,* will help you remember the steps.

L = *Lead. Don't follow.* Try to anticipate what your teacher will say by asking yourself questions. If your teacher provides course notes or PowerPoint overheads before lecture, review them before coming to class. Reflective questions can come from those materials or from study guides, reading assignments, or your own curiosity.

I = *Ideas.* Every lecture is based on a core of ideas. Usually, an idea is followed by examples or explanations. Ask yourself often, "What is the main idea now? What ideas support it?"

S = *Signal words.* Listen for words that tell you what direction the instructor is taking. For instance, here are some signal words:

There are three reasons why . . .   Here come ideas
Most important is . . .   Main idea
On the contrary . . .   Opposite idea
As an example . . .   Support for main idea
Therefore . . .   Conclusion

■ TABLE I.1   Using the SQ4R Method

Survey
- Preview
- List of Modules
- Survey Questions
- Figure Captions
- Module Summaries

Question
- Topic Headings
- Survey Questions
- In-Text Dialogue Questions

Read
- Topic Headings
- Boldface Terms
- Running Glossary (in margins)
- Figures and Tables

Recite
- Recite Questions (in Knowledge Builders)
- Practice Quizzes (online)
- Notes (make them while reading)

Reflect
- Reflect Questions and Web Links (in Knowledge Builders)
- Boxed Features (throughout the text)

Review
- Modules Summaries
- Boldface Terms
- Running Glossary (in margins)
- Tables
- Practice Quizzes (online)
- Study Guide

Active listener A person who knows how to maintain attention, avoid distractions, and actively gather information from lectures.

A = *Actively listen.* Sit where you can get involved and ask questions. Bring questions you want answered from the last lecture or from your text. Raise your hand at the beginning of class or approach your professor before the lecture. Do anything that helps you stay active, alert, and engaged.

N = *Note taking.* Students who take accurate lecture notes tend to do well on tests (Williams & Eggert, 2002). However, don't try to be a tape recorder. Listen to everything, but be selective and write down only key points. If you are too busy writing, you may not grasp what your professor is saying. When you're taking notes, it might help to think of yourself as a reporter who is trying to get a good story (Ryan, 2001).

Actually, most students take reasonably good notes—and then don't use them! Many students wait until just before exams to review. By then, their notes have lost much of their meaning. If you don't want your notes to seem like "chicken scratches," it pays to review them every day (Rowe, 2007).

Using and Reviewing Your Notes

When you review, you will learn more if you take the extra steps listed here (Knaus & Ellis, 2002; Rowe, 2007; Santrock & Halonen, 2007).

- As soon as you can, reflect on and improve your notes by filling in gaps, completing thoughts, and looking for connections among ideas.
- Remember to link new ideas to what you already know.
- Summarize your notes. Boil them down and *organize* them.
- After each class session, write down at least seven major ideas, definitions, or details that are likely to become test questions. Then, make up questions from your notes and be sure you can answer them.

Summary The letters LISAN are a guide to active listening, but listening and good note taking are not enough. You must also review, organize, reflect, extend, and think about new ideas. Use active listening to get involved in your classes and you will undoubtedly learn more (Rowe, 2007).

Study Strategies—Making a Habit of Success

Grades depend on effort. However, don't forget that good students work more *efficiently,* not just harder. Many study practices are notoriously poor, such as recopying lecture notes, studying class notes but not the textbook (or the textbook but not class notes), outlining chapters, answering study questions with the book open, and "group study" (which often becomes a party). The best students emphasize *quality:* They study their books and notes in depth and attend classes regularly. It's a mistake to blame poor grades on events "beyond your control." Students who are motivated to succeed usually get better grades (Perry et al., 2001). Let's consider a few more things you can do to improve your study habits.

Study in a Specific Place Ideally, you should study in a quiet, well-lighted area free of distractions. If possible, you should also have at least one place where you *only study.* Do nothing else at that spot: Keep magazines, MP3 players, friends, cell phones, pets, posters, video games, puzzles, food, lovers, sports cars, elephants, pianos, televisions, YouTube, and other distractions out of the area. In this way, the habit of studying will become strongly linked with one specific place. Then, rather than trying to force yourself to study, all you have to do is go to your study area. Once there, you'll find it is relatively easy to get started.

Use Spaced Study Sessions It is reasonable to review intensely before an exam. However, you're taking a big risk if you are only "cramming" (learning new information at the last minute). Spaced practice is much more efficient (Anderson, 2005). **Spaced practice** consists of a large number of relatively short study sessions. Long, uninterrupted study sessions are called **massed practice.** (If you "massed up" your studying, you probably messed it up too.)

Cramming places a big burden on memory. Usually, you shouldn't try to learn anything new about a subject during the last day before a test. It is far better to learn small amounts every day and review frequently (Anderson, 2005).

Try Mnemonics Learning has to start somewhere, and memorizing is often the first step. Let's consider just one technique here.

A **mnemonic** (nee-MON-ik) is a memory aid. Most mnemonics link new information to ideas or images that are easy to remember. For example, what if you want to remember that the Spanish word for duck is *pato* (pronounced POT-oh)? To use a mnemonic, you could picture a duck in a pot or a duck wearing a pot for a hat. Likewise, to remember that the cerebellum controls coordination, you might picture someone named "Sarah Bellum" who is very coordinated. For best results, make your mnemonic images exaggerated or bizarre, vivid, and interactive (Macklin & McDaniel, 2005). There are many ways to create mnemonics. If you would like to learn more about memory strategies, see Chapter 7, especially Modules 7.5 and 7.6.

Mnemonics make new information more familiar and memorable. Forming an image of a duck wearing a pot for a hat might help you remember that *pato* is the Spanish word for duck.

Test Yourself A great way to improve grades is to take practice tests before the real one in class. In other words, studying should include **self-testing,** in which you pose questions to yourself. You can use flash cards, "Learning Check" questions, online quizzes, a study guide, or other means. As you study, ask many questions and be sure you can answer them. Studying without self-testing is like practicing for a basketball game without shooting any baskets.

For more convenient self-testing, your professor may make a *Study Guide* or a separate booklet of *Practice Quizzes* available. You can use either to review for tests. Practice quizzes are also available on the *Book Companion Website*, as described later. However, don't use practice quizzes as a substitute for studying your textbook and lecture notes. Trying to learn from quizzes alone will probably *lower* your grades. It is best to use quizzes to find out what topics you need to study more (Brothen & Wambach, 2001).

Overlearn Many students *underprepare* for exams, and most *overestimate* how well they will do. A solution to both problems is **overlearning,** in which you continue studying beyond your initial mastery of a topic. In other words, plan to do extra study and review *after* you think you are prepared for a test. One way to overlearn is approach all tests as if they will be essays. That way, you will learn more completely, so you really "know your stuff."

Self-Regulated Learning— Academic All-Stars

Think of a topic you are highly interested in, such as music, sports, fashion, cars, cooking, politics, or movies. Whatever the topic, you have probably learned a lot about it— painlessly. How could you make your college work more like voluntary learning? An approach called self-regulated learning might be a good start. **Self-regulated learning** is deliber-

ately reflective and active self-guided study (Hofer & Yu, 2003). Here's how you can change passive studying into reflective, goal-oriented learning.

1. *Set specific, objective learning goals.* Try to begin each learning session with specific goals in mind. What knowledge or skills are you trying to master? What do you hope to accomplish (Knaus & Ellis, 2002)?

2. *Plan a learning strategy.* How will you accomplish your goals? Make daily, weekly, and monthly plans for learning. Then put them into action.

3. *Be your own teacher.* Effective learners silently give themselves guidance and ask themselves questions. For example, as you are learning, you might ask yourself, "What are the important ideas here? What do I remember? What don't I understand? What do I need to review? What should I do next?"

4. *Monitor your progress.* Self-regulated learning depends on self-monitoring. Exceptional learners keep records of their progress toward learning goals (pages read, hours of studying, assignments completed, and so forth). They quiz themselves, use study guides, make sure they follow the SQ4R system, and find other ways to check their understanding while learning.

5. *Reward yourself.* When you meet your daily, weekly, or monthly goals, reward your efforts in some way, such as going to a movie or downloading some new music. Be aware that self-praise also rewards learning. Being able to say "Hey, I did it!" or "Good work!" and knowing that you deserve it can be very rewarding. In the long run, success, self-improvement, and personal satisfaction are the real payoffs for learning.

6. *Evaluate your progress and goals.* It is a good idea to frequently evaluate your performance records and goals. Are there specific areas of your work that need improvement? If you are not making good progress toward long-range goals, do you need to revise your short-term targets?

7. *Take corrective action.* If you fall short of your goals, you may need to adjust how you budget your time.

Spaced practice Practice spread over many relatively short study sessions.
Massed practice Practice done in a long, uninterrupted study session.
Mnemonic A memory aid or strategy.
Self-testing Evaluating learning by posing questions to yourself.
Overlearning Continuing to study and learn after you think you've mastered a topic.
Self-regulated learning Deliberately reflective and active self-guided study.

You may also need to change your learning environment, to deal with distractions such as watching TV, daydreaming, talking to friends, or testing the structural integrity of the walls with your stereo system.

If you discover that you lack necessary knowledge or skills, ask for help, take advantage of tutoring programs, or look for information beyond your courses and textbooks. Knowing how to regulate and control learning can be a key to lifelong enrichment and personal empowerment.

Procrastination—Avoiding the Last-Minute Blues

All these study techniques are fine. But what can I do about procrastination? A tendency to procrastinate is almost universal. (When campus workshops on procrastination are offered, many students never get around to signing up!) Even when procrastination doesn't lead to failure, it can cause much suffering. Procrastinators work only under pressure, skip classes, give false reasons for late work, and feel ashamed of their last-minute efforts. They also tend to feel frustrated, bored, and guilty more often (Blunt & Pychyl, 2005).

Why do so many students procrastinate? Many students equate grades with their *personal worth.* That is, they act as if grades tell whether they are good, smart people who will succeed in life. By procrastinating they can blame poor work on a late start, rather than a lack of ability (Beck, Koons, & Milgrim, 2000). After all, it wasn't their best effort, was it?

Perfectionism is a related problem. If you expect the impossible, it's hard to start an assignment. Students with high standards often end up with all-or-nothing work habits (Onwuegbuzie, 2000).

Time Management

Most procrastinators must eventually face the self-worth issue. Nevertheless, most can improve by learning study skills and better time management. We have already discussed general study skills, so let's consider time management in a little more detail.

A **weekly time schedule** is a written plan that allocates time for study, work, and leisure activities. To prepare your schedule, make a chart showing all the hours in each day of the week. Then fill in times that are already committed: sleep, meals, classes, work, team practices, lessons, appointments, and so forth. Next, fill in times when you will study for various classes. Finally, label the remaining hours as open or free times.

Each day, you can use your schedule as a checklist. That way you'll know at a glance which tasks are done and which still need attention (Knaus & Ellis, 2002).

You may also find it valuable to make a **term schedule** that lists the dates of all quizzes, tests, reports, papers, and other major assignments for each class.

The beauty of sticking to a schedule is that you know you are making an honest effort. It will also help you avoid feeling bored while you are working or guilty when you play.

Be sure to treat your study times as serious commitments, but respect your free times, too. And remember, students who study hard and practice time management *do* get better grades (Rau & Durand, 2000).

Goal Setting

As mentioned earlier, students who are active learners set **specific goals** for studying. Such goals should be clear-cut and measurable (Knaus & Ellis, 2002). If you find it hard to stay motivated, try setting goals for the semester, the week, the day, and even for single study sessions. Also, be aware that more effort early in a course can greatly reduce the "pain" and stress you will experience later. If your professors don't give frequent assignments, set your own day-by-day goals. That way, you can turn big assignments into a series of smaller tasks that you can actually complete (Ariely & Wertenbroch, 2002). An example would be reading, studying, and reviewing 8 pages a day to complete a 40-page chapter in 5 days. For this textbook, reading one module a day might be a good pace. Remember, many small steps can add up to an impressive journey. (See ● Fig. I.2 for a summary of study skills.)

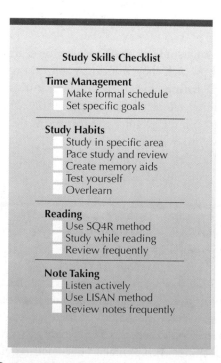

Study Skills Checklist

Time Management
- ☐ Make formal schedule
- ☐ Set specific goals

Study Habits
- ☐ Study in specific area
- ☐ Pace study and review
- ☐ Create memory aids
- ☐ Test yourself
- ☐ Overlearn

Reading
- ☐ Use SQ4R method
- ☐ Study while reading
- ☐ Review frequently

Note Taking
- ☐ Listen actively
- ☐ Use LISAN method
- ☐ Review notes frequently

● **FIGURE I.2** Study skills checklist.

Make Learning an Adventure

A final point to remember is that you are most likely to procrastinate if you think a task will be unpleasant (Pychyl et al., 2000). Learning can be hard work. Nevertheless, many students find ways to make schoolwork interesting and enjoyable. Try to approach your schoolwork as if it were a game, a sport, an adventure, or simply a way to become a better person. The best educational experiences are challenging, yet fun (Ferrari & Scher, 2000).

Virtually every topic is interesting to someone, somewhere. You may not be particularly interested in the sex life of South American tree frogs. However, a biologist might be fascinated. (Another tree frog might be, too.) If you wait for teachers to "make" their courses interesting, you are missing the point. Interest is a matter of *your attitude.*

Taking Tests—Are You "Test Wise"?

If I read and study effectively, is there anything else I can do to improve my grades? You must also be able to show what you know on tests. Here are some suggestions for improving your test-taking skills.

General Test-Taking Skills

You'll do better on all types of tests if you observe the following guidelines (Wood & Willoughby, 1995).

1. Read all directions and questions carefully. They may give you good advice or clues.
2. Quickly survey the test before you begin.
3. Answer easy questions before spending time on more difficult ones.
4. Be sure to answer all questions.
5. Use your time wisely.
6. Ask for clarification when necessary.

Objective Tests Several additional strategies can help you do better on objective tests. Objective tests (multiple-choice and true-false items) require you to recognize a correct answer among wrong ones or a true statement versus a false one. Here are some strategies for taking objective tests.

1. First, relate the question to what you know about the topic. Then, read the alternatives. Does one match the answer you expected to find? If none match, reexamine the choices and look for a *partial* match.
2. Read *all* the choices for each question before you make a decision. Here's why: If you immediately think that *a* is correct and stop reading, you might miss seeing a better answer like "both *a* and *d*."

3. Read rapidly and skip items you are unsure about. You may find "free information" in later questions that will help you answer difficult items.
4. Eliminate certain alternatives. With a four-choice multiple-choice test, you have one chance in four of guessing right. If you can eliminate two alternatives, your guessing odds improve to 50-50.
5. Unless there is a penalty for guessing, be sure to answer any skipped items. Even if you are not sure of the answer, you may be right. If you leave a question blank, it is automatically wrong. When you are forced to guess, don't choose the longest answer or the letter you've used the least. Both strategies lower scores more than random guessing does.
6. There is a bit of folk wisdom that says "Don't change your answers on a multiple-choice test. Your first choice is usually right." This is *false*. If you change answers, you are more likely to gain points than to lose them. This is especially true if you are uncertain of your first choice or it was a hunch, and if your second choice is more reflective (Higham & Gerrard, 2005).
7. Remember, you are searching for the one *best* answer to each question. Some answers may be partly true, yet flawed in some way. If you are uncertain, try rating each multiple-choice alternative on a 1-to-10 scale. The answer with the highest rating is the one you are looking for.
8. Few circumstances are *always* or *never* present. Answers that include superlatives such as *most, least, best, worst, largest,* or *smallest* are often false.

Essay Tests Essay questions are a weak spot for students who lack organization, don't support their ideas, or don't directly answer the question (Rowe, 2007). When you take an essay exam, try the following:

1. Read the question carefully. Be sure to note key words, such as *compare, contrast, discuss, evaluate, analyze,* and *describe.* These words all demand a certain emphasis in your answer.
2. Answer the question. If the question asks for a definition and an example, make sure you provide both. Providing just a definition or just an example will

Weekly time schedule A written plan that allocates time for study, work, and leisure activities during a 1-week period.

Term schedule A written plan that lists the dates of all major assignments for each of your classes for an entire semester or quarter.

Specific goal A goal with a clearly defined and measurable outcome.

get you half marks. Giving three examples instead of the one asked for will not earn you any extra marks.

3. Think about your answer for a few minutes and list the main points you want to make. Just write them as they come to mind. Then rearrange the ideas in a logical order and begin writing. Elaborate plans or outlines are not necessary.

4. Don't beat around the bush or pad your answer. Be direct. Make a point and support it. Get your list of ideas into words.

5. Look over your essay for errors in spelling and grammar. Save this for last. Your *ideas* are of first importance. You can work on spelling and grammar separately if they affect your grades.

Short-Answer Tests   Tests that ask you to fill in a blank, define a term, or list specific items can be difficult. Usually, the questions themselves contain little information. If you don't know the answer, you won't get much help from the questions.

The best way to prepare for short-answer tests is to overlearn the details of the course. As you study, pay special attention to lists of related terms.

Again, it is best to start with the questions you're sure you know. Follow that by completing items you think you probably know. Questions you have no idea about can be left blank.

Again, for your convenience, Figure I.2 provides a checklist summary of the main study skills we have covered.

Using Digital Media—Netting New Knowledge

Google any psychological term ranging from *amnesia* to *zoophobia* and you will find a vast library of information, from serious websites like that maintained by the American Psychological Association to Wikipedia entries to personal blogs. Even if you don't own a computer, you can usually use one on campus to learn more about psychology. However, be aware that information on the Internet is not always accurate. It is wise to approach all websites with a healthy dose of skepticism.

Digital Journeys

The **Internet** is a network of interlinked computers. An important subpart of the Internet is the **World Wide Web (WWW)** or just plain "web," an interlinked system of information "sites" or "pages." If you know the URL, the "address" of a website, you can view the information it contains. Al-

most all web pages also have links to other websites. These **links** let you "jump" from one site to the next to find more information.

Google It   To find psychological information on the Internet you'll need a computer and an Internet connection. If you don't own a computer, you can usually use one on campus. Various software browsers make it easier to navigate around the web. A **browser** allows you to see text, images, sounds, and video clips stored on other computers. Browsers also keep lists of your favorite URLs so that you can return to them.

The Book Companion Website

How would I find information about psychology on the Internet? Your first stop on the Internet should be the *Book Companion Website.* Here's what you'll find there:

Online Quizzes. You can use these chapter-by-chapter multiple choice quizzes to practice for tests and check your understanding.

Interactive Activities. The demonstrations and mini-experiments in this feature allow you to directly experience various psychological principles.

Internet Resources. This area is a "launching pad" that will take you to other psychology-related sites on the Internet. If a site sounds interesting, a click of the mouse will link you to it.

Online Flash Cards. These online flash cards allow you to practice terms and concepts interactively.

Psych in the News. This section features a news item or current event that is explored from a psychological perspective. After you've thought about a topic, you can share your opinions with others in an online discussion.

Discussion Forum. In the Discussion Forum you'll have a chance to share your ideas with those of psychology students from all over the country.

Research and Teaching Showcase. Here you'll find regularly updated summaries of presentations, articles, or other teaching and research materials.

Archives. Using the Archives, you can quickly search for current and past articles from Psych in the News and the Research and Teaching Showcase.

Meet the Author. Meet the author of your text in an interactive, multimedia presentation.

The Book Companion Website is located at **www.thomsonedu.com/psychology/coon.** Be sure to visit this site for valuable information about how to improve your grades and enhance your appreciation of psychology.

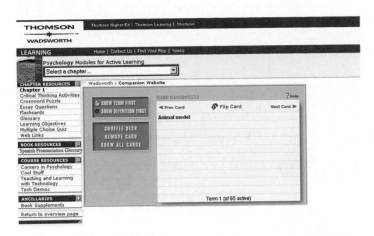

The *Book Companion Website* gives you online access to a variety of valuable learning aids and interesting materials.

ThomsonNOW

Students can also make use of *ThomsonNOW for Coon/Mitterer's Psychology: Modules for Active Learning 11e,* a web-based, personalized study system that provides a pre-test and a post-test for each chapter and separate chapter quizzes. *ThomsonNOW,* located at **www.thomsonedu.com,** can also create personalized study plans—which include rich media such as videos, animations, and learning modules—that point students to areas in the text that will help them master course content (● Fig. I.3). An additional set of integrative questions helps students pull all the material together.

Psych Sites

You'll find a list of interesting websites you may want to explore at the end of each module in this book, including this one. The best way to reach these sites is through the Book

Companion Website. We have not included website addresses in the book because they often change or may become inactive. At the website you'll find up-to-date links for websites listed in this book. The sites we've listed are generally of high quality. However, be aware that information on the Internet is not always accurate. It is wise to approach all Websites with a healthy dose of skepticism.

PsycINFO Psychological knowledge can also be found through specialized online databases. One of the best is PsycINFO, offered by the American Psychological Association. **PsycINFO** provides summaries of the scientific and scholarly literature in psychology. Each record in PsycINFO consists of an abstract (short summary), plus notes about the author, title, source, and other details (● Fig. I.4). All entries are indexed using key terms. Thus, you can search for various topics by entering words such as *drug abuse, postpartum depression,* or *creativity.*

You can gain access to PsycINFO in several ways. Almost every college and university subscribes to PsycINFO. If this is the case, you can usually search PsycINFO from a terminal in your college library or computer center—for free. PsycINFO can also be directly accessed (for a fee) through the Internet via APA's PsycINFO Direct service. For more information on how to gain access to PsycINFO, check this website: **www.apa.org/psycinfo.**

The APA Website The APA also maintains an online library of general interest articles on aging, anger, children and families, depression, divorce, emotional health, kids and the media, sexuality, stress, testing issues, women and men, and other topics. They are well worth consulting when you have questions about psychological issues. You'll find them at **www.apa.org.** For links to recent articles in newspapers and magazines, be sure to check the APA's PsycPORT page at **www.psycport.com.**

Please do take some of the "digital journeys" described here. You might be surprised by the fascinating information that awaits you. Investigating psychology on your own is one of the best ways to enrich an already valuable course.

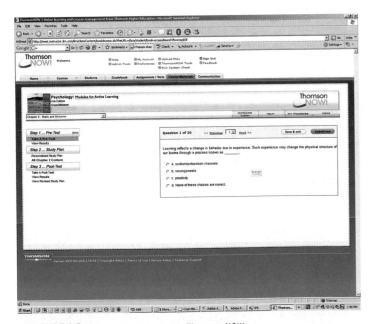

● **FIGURE I.3** A sample screen from *ThomsonNOW.*

Internet An electronic network of interlinked computers.

World Wide Web (WWW) A system of information "sites" accessible through the Internet.

Links Connections built into Internet sites that let you "jump" from one site to the next.

Browser Software that facilitates access to text, images, sounds, video, and other information stored in formats used on the Internet.

PsycINFO A searchable, online database that provides brief summaries of the scientific and scholarly literature in psychology.

● **FIGURE I.4** This is a sample abstract from the PsycINFO database. If you search for the term *study skills*, you will find this article and many more in PsycINFO. (This record is reprinted with permission of the American Psychological Association, publisher of the PsycINFO Database, all rights reserved. May not be reproduced without prior permission.)

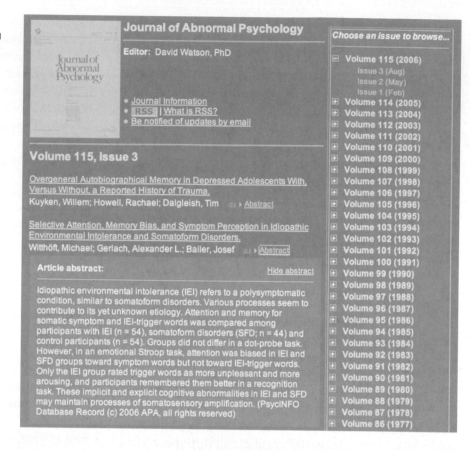

KNOWLEDGE BUILDER

Study Skills

Recite

1. The four R's in SQ4R stand for "read, recite, reflect, and review." T or F?

2. When using the LISAN method, students try to write down as much of a lecture as possible so that their notes are complete. T or F?

3. Spaced study sessions are usually superior to massed practice. T or F?

4. According to research, you should almost always stick with your first answer on multiple-choice tests. T or F?

5. To use the technique known as overlearning, you should continue to study after you feel you have begun to master a topic. T or F?

6. Setting learning goals and monitoring your progress are important parts of _____ _____ learning.

7. Procrastination is related to seeking perfection and equating self-worth with grades. T or F?

Reflect
Critical Thinking

8. How are the SQ4R method and the LISAN method related?

Reflect

Which study skills do you think would help you the most? Which techniques do you already use? Which do you think you should try? To what extent do you already engage in self-regulated learning? What additional steps could you take to become a more active, goal-oriented learner?

Link

Internet addresses frequently change. To find the sites listed here, visit **http://www.thomsonedu.com/psychology/coon** for an updated list of Internet addresses and direct links to relevant sites.

- **How to Succeed as a Student** Advice on how to be a college student. Topics from studying to housing to preparation for work are included.

- **Library Research in Psychology** Hints on how to do library research in psychology.

- **Psychology Glossary** You can use this glossary to get additional definitions for common psychological terms.

- **Study Skills** More information on SQ4R, taking tests, note taking, and time management.

ANSWERS

1. T 2. F 3. T 4. F 5. T 6. self-regulated 7. T 8. Both encourage people to be reflective and to actively seek information as a way of learning more effectively.

A Final Word

There is a distinction in Zen between "live words" and "dead words." Live words come from personal experience; dead words are "about" a subject. This book can only be a collection of dead words unless you accept the challenge of making an intellectual journey. You will find many helpful, useful, and exciting ideas in the pages that follow. To make them yours, you must set out to *actively* learn as much as you can. The ideas presented here should get you off to a good start. Good luck!

For more information, consult any of the following books.

Hettich, P. I. (2005). *Connect college to career: Student guide to work and life transition*. Belmont, CA: Wadsworth.

Knaus, W. J., & Ellis, A. (2002). *The procrastination workbook: Your personalized program for breaking free from the patterns that hold you back*. Oakland, CA: New Harbinger Press.

Rosnow, R. L. (2006). *Writing papers in psychology: A student guide to research papers, essays, proposals, posters, and handouts* (7th Ed.). Belmont, CA: Wadsworth.

Rowe, B. (2007). *College awareness guide: What students need to know to succeed in college*. Upper Saddle River, NJ: Prentice Hall.

Santrock, J. W., & Halonen, J. S. (2007). *Connections to college success*. Belmont, CA: Wadsworth.

Introducing Psychology and Research Methods

1

MODULE 1.1 The Science of Psychology
SURVEY QUESTIONS: What is psychology? What are its goals?

MODULE 1.2 Critical Thinking and the Scientific Method in Psychology
SURVEY QUESTION: What is critical thinking?
SURVEY QUESTION: How does psychology differ from false explanations of behavior?
SURVEY QUESTION: Why is the scientific method important to psychologists?

MODULE 1.3 History and Contemporary Perspectives
SURVEY QUESTION: How did the field of psychology emerge?
SURVEY QUESTION: What are the contemporary perspectives in psychology?

MODULE 1.4 Psychologists and Their Specialties
SURVEY QUESTION: What are the major specialties in psychology?

MODULE 1.5 The Psychology Experiment
SURVEY QUESTION: How is an experiment performed?

MODULE 1.6 Nonexperimental Research Methods
SURVEY QUESTION: What other research methods do psychologists use?

MODULE 1.7 Psychology in Action: Psychology in the Media
SURVEY QUESTION: How good is psychological information found in the popular media?

The Mysteries of Human Behavior

Your authors are often asked, "Why did you become a psychologist?" Because we are just getting acquainted, let us answer this way:

> You are a universe, a collection of worlds within worlds. Your brain is arguably the most complicated system in existence. Through its action you are capable of love, science, art, music, philosophy, hatred, and charity. You are the most challenging riddle ever written, a mystery even to yourself at times. Your thoughts, emotions, and actions—and those of your family and friends—are the most fascinating subject we can imagine. We chose to study psychology because almost everything of interest and importance in the world is ultimately related to human behavior.

Look around you: The Internet, television, newspapers, radio, and magazines are brimming with psychological topics. Psychology is an ever-changing panorama of people and ideas. You really can't call yourself educated without knowing something about it. And, although we might envy those who have walked on the moon or explored the ocean's depths, the ultimate frontier lies much closer to home. Psychology can help you better understand yourself and others. This book is a guided tour of human behavior. We hope you enjoy the adventure.

The Science of Psychology

PSYCHOLOGY touches our lives in many ways. Psychology is about memory, stress, therapy, love, persuasion, hypnosis, perception, death, conformity, creativity, learning, personality, aging, intelligence, sexuality, emotion, happiness, wisdom, and much more. Psychologists use critical thinking and scientific investigation to achieve the goals of describing, understanding, predicting, and controlling human behavior.

Psychology—Spotlight on Behavior

SURVEY QUESTIONS: *What is psychology? What are its goals?*

Psychology is both a *science* and a *profession.* As scientists, some psychologists do research to discover new knowledge. Others are teachers who pass this knowledge on to students. Still others apply psychology to solve problems in mental health, education, business, sports, law, and medicine. Later we will return to the profession of psychology. For now, let's focus on how knowledge is created. Whether they work in a lab, a classroom, or a clinic, all psychologists rely on critical thinking and information gained from scientific research.

Defining Psychology

The word *psychology* comes from the roots *psyche,* which means "mind," and *logos,* meaning "knowledge or study." However, when did you last see or touch a "mind"? Because the mind can't be studied directly, **psychology** is now defined as the scientific study of behavior and mental processes.

Psychologists are highly trained professionals. In addition to the psychological knowledge they possess, psychologists learn specialized skills in counseling and therapy, measurement and testing, research and experimentation, statistics, diagnosis, treatment, and many other areas.

What does behavior *refer to in the definition of psychology?* Anything you do—eating, emailing, sleeping, talking, or sneezing—is a behavior. So are snowboarding, gambling, watching television, picking your nose, learning Spanish, and reading this book. Naturally, we are interested in *overt behaviors* (directly observable actions and responses). But psychologists also study *covert behaviors.* These are private, internal activities, such as thinking, dreaming, remembering, and other mental events (Jackson, 2008).

Empiricism

Many people regard themselves as expert "people watchers." "Common-sense" theories abound. However, you may be surprised to learn how often self-appointed authorities and common-sense beliefs about human behavior are wrong. Take a moment and read "Testing Commonsense Beliefs" for more information.

Because of the limitations of common sense, psychologists have a special respect for *empirical evidence* (information gained from direct observation), especially when it is collected systematically. We study behavior directly and collect data (observed facts) so that we can draw valid conclusions. Would you say it's true, for instance, that "You can't teach an old dog new tricks"? Why argue about it? As psychologists, we would simply get some "old" dogs and some "new" dogs (and some "borrowed" dogs and some "blue" dogs?) and then try to teach them all a new trick to find out!

Basically, the empirical approach says, "Let's take a look" (Stanovich, 2007). Have you ever wondered if people become more hostile when it's blazing hot outside? John Simister and Cary Cooper (2005) decided to find out. They obtained data on temperatures and criminal activity in Los Angeles over a 4-year period. When air temperature and the frequency of aggravated assaults was graphed, a clear relationship emerged. (See ● Fig. 1.1.) Temperatures and crime rates rise and fall more or less in parallel (so there may be something to the phrase "hot under the collar").

Isn't the outcome of this study fairly predictable? Sometimes the results of studies are consistent with common knowledge, and sometimes they come as a surprise. In this instance, you may have guessed the outcome. However, hostile actions that require more extreme physical exertion, such as fistfights, become *less* likely at very high temperatures. Without systematically gathering data, we wouldn't know for sure if overheated Angelenos become more lethargic or more aggressive. Thus, the study tells us something interesting about frustration, discomfort, and aggression.

CRITICAL THINKING

Testing Commonsense Beliefs

It may appear that psychological research "discovers" what we already know from everyday experience. Why waste time and money confirming the obvious? Actually, commonsense beliefs are often wrong. See if you can tell which of the following commonsense beliefs are true and which are false (Landau & Bavaria, 2003).

• Babies love their mothers because mothers fulfill their babies' physiological need for food. True or False?

• Most humans use only 10 percent of their potential brainpower. True or False?

• Blind people have unusually sensitive organs of touch. True or False?

• The more motivated you are, the better you will do at solving a complex problem. True or False?

• The weight of evidence suggests the major cause of forgetting is that memory traces decay as time passes. True or False?

• Psychotherapy has its greatest success in the treatment of psychotic patients who have lost touch with reality. True or False?

• Personality tests reveal your basic motives, including those you may not be aware of. True or False?

• To change people's behavior toward members of ethnic minority groups, we must first change their attitudes. True or False?

It turns out that research has shown that *all* these commonsense beliefs are false. Yet in a survey, *all* the beliefs were accepted as true by a large number of college students (Landau & Bavaria, 2003). How did you do?

We can all benefit from being more reflective in evaluating our beliefs. It's valuable to apply your critical thinking skills by asking whether a belief makes logical sense. Can it be explained by any of the concepts in this book? Can you imagine what sort of study you could do that might yield evidence to get you closer to the truth? *Critical Thinking* boxes like this one will help you be more reflective and think critically about human behavior.

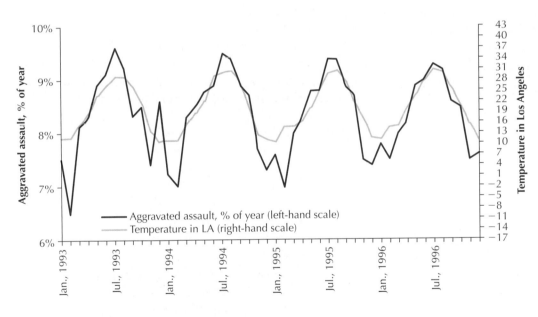

● **FIGURE 1.1** Results of an empirical study. The graph shows that aggravated assaults in Los Angeles become more likely as air temperature increases. This suggests that physical discomfort is associated with interpersonal hostility. (Data from Simister & Cooper, 2005.)

Psychological Research

Many fields, such as history, law, art, and business, are interested in human behavior. How is psychology different? Psychology's great strength is that it uses **scientific observation** to systematically answer questions about behavior (Stanovich, 2007).

Of course, some topics can't be studied because of ethical or practical concerns. More often, questions go unanswered for lack of a suitable **research method** (a systematic process for answering scientific questions). In the past, for example, we had to take the word of people who say they never dream. Then the EEG (electroencephalograph, or brain-wave ma-

chine) was invented. Certain EEG patterns, and the presence of eye movements, can reveal that a person is dreaming. People who "never dream," it turns out, dream frequently. If they are awakened during a dream, they vividly remember it. Thus, the EEG helped make the study of dreaming more scientific.

Psychology The scientific study of behavior and mental processes.

Scientific observation An empirical investigation that is structured so that it answers questions about the world.

Research method A systematic approach to answering scientific questions.

Research Specialties *What kinds of topics do psychologists study?* Here's a sample of what various psychologists might say about their work.

"In general, *developmental psychologists* study the course of human growth and development, from conception until death. I'm especially interested in the transition from the teenage years to early adulthood."

"Like other *learning theorists,* I study how and why learning occurs in humans and animals. Right now I'm investigating how patterns of punishment affect learning."

"I'm a *personality theorist.* I study personality traits, motivation, and individual differences. I am especially interested in the personality profiles of highly creative college students."

"As a *sensation and perception psychologist,* I investigate how we discern the world through our senses. I am using a perceptual theory to study how we are able to recognize faces in a crowd."

"*Comparative psychologists* study and compare the behavior of different species, especially animals. Personally, I'm fascinated by the communication abilities of porpoises."

"*Biopsychologists* are interested in how behavior relates to biological processes, especially activities in the nervous system. I've been doing some exciting research on how the brain controls hunger."

"*Cognitive psychologists* are primarily interested in thinking. I want to know how reasoning, problem solving, memory, and other mental processes relate to computer game playing."

"*Gender psychologists* study differences between females and males. I want to understand how gender differences are influenced by biology, child rearing, education, and stereotypes."

"*Social psychologists* explore human social behavior, such as attitudes, persuasion, riots, conformity, leadership, racism, and friendship. My own interest is interpersonal attraction. I place two strangers in a room and analyze how strongly they are attracted to each other."

"*Cultural psychologists* study the ways in which culture affects human behavior. The language you speak, the foods you eat, how your parents disciplined you, what laws you obey, who you regard as 'family,' whether you eat with a spoon or your fingers—these and countless other details of behavior are strongly influenced by culture."

"*Evolutionary psychologists* are interested in how our behavior is guided by patterns that evolved during the long history of humankind. I am studying some interesting trends in male and female mating choices that don't seem to be merely learned or based on culture."

"*Forensic psychologists* apply psychological principles to legal issues. I am interested in improving the reliability of eyewitness testimony during trials."

This small sample should give you an idea of the diversity of psychological research. It also hints at some of the kinds of information we will explore in this book.

Animals and Psychology *Research involving animals was mentioned in some of the preceding examples. Why is that?*

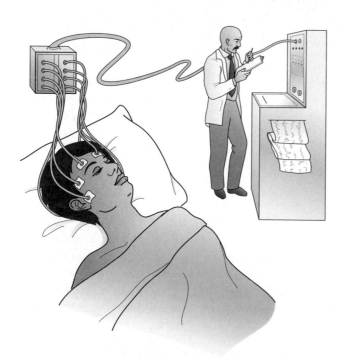

The scientific study of dreaming was made possible by use of the EEG, a device that records the tiny electrical signals generated by the brain as a person sleeps. The EEG converts these electrical signals to a written record of brain activity. Certain shifts in brain activity, coupled with the presence of rapid eye movements, are strongly related to dreaming. (See Module 5.1 for more information.)

The Gorilla Foundation

Some of the most interesting research with animals has focused on attempts to teach primates to communicate with sign language. Psychologist Penny Patterson has spent 25 years teaching Koko more than 1,000 signs. One of Koko's favorite signs ("stink") is shown here. (For more, google The Gorilla Foundation.) Such research has led to better methods for teaching language to aphasic children (children with serious language impairment).

The variety and complexity of human behavior make psychological investigation challenging. How would you explain the behaviors shown here?

You may be surprised to learn that psychologists are interested in the behavior of *any* living creature—from flatworms to humans. Indeed, some comparative psychologists spend their entire careers studying rats, cats, dogs, turtles, or chimpanzees.

Although only a small percentage of psychological studies involve animals, they include many different types of research (Ord et al., 2005). Some psychologists use **animal models** to discover principles that apply to humans. For instance, animal studies have helped us understand stress, learning, obesity, aging, sleep, and many other topics. Psychology also benefits animals. For example, caring for domestic animals, as well as endangered species in zoos, relies on behavioral studies.

Psychology's Goals

What do psychology's goals mean in practice? Imagine that we would like to answer questions such as these: What happens when the right side of the brain is injured? Why are some people risk seekers while others avoid risk at all costs? Do autistic children react abnormally to their parents?

Description Answering psychological questions requires a careful description of behavior. **Description,** or naming and classifying, is typically based on making a detailed record of behavioral observations.

But a description doesn't explain anything, does it? Right. Useful knowledge begins with accurate description, but descriptions fail to answer the important "why" questions. *Why* do more women attempt suicide, and *why* do more men complete it? *Why* are people more aggressive when they are uncomfortable? *Why* are bystanders often unwilling to help in an emergency?

Understanding We have met psychology's second goal when we can explain an event. That is, **understanding** usually

Animal model In research, an animal whose behavior is used to derive principles that may apply to human behavior.

Description In scientific research, the process of naming and classifying.

Understanding In psychology, understanding is achieved when the causes of a behavior can be stated.

means we can state the causes of a behavior. Take our last "why" question as an example: Research on "bystander apathy" reveals that people often fail to help when *other* possible helpers are nearby. Why? Because a "diffusion of responsibility" occurs. Basically, no one feels personally obligated to pitch in. As a result, the more potential helpers there are, the less likely it is that anyone will help (Darley, 2000; Darley & Latané, 1968). Now we can explain a perplexing problem.

Prediction Psychology's third goal, **prediction,** is the ability to forecast behavior accurately. Notice that our explanation of bystander apathy makes a prediction about the chances of getting help. If you've ever been stranded on a busy freeway with car trouble, you'll recognize the accuracy of this prediction: Having many potential helpers nearby is no guarantee that anyone will stop to help.

Control *Description, explanation, and prediction seem reasonable, but is control a valid goal?* Control may seem like a threat to personal freedom. However, to a psychologist, **control** simply refers to altering conditions that affect behavior. If you suggest changes in a classroom that help children learn better, you have exerted control. If a clinical psychologist helps a person overcome a terrible fear of heights, control is involved. Control is also involved in designing airplanes to keep pilots from making fatal errors. Clearly, psychological control must be used wisely and humanely.

In summary, psychology's goals are a natural outgrowth of our desire to understand behavior. Basically, they boil down to asking the following questions:

What is the nature of this behavior? (description)

Why does it occur? (understanding and explanation)

Can we forecast when it will occur? (prediction)

What conditions affect it? (control)

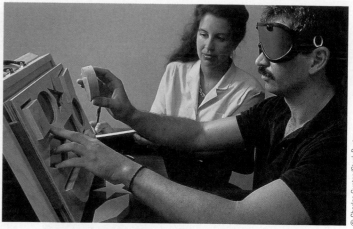

© Charles Gupton/Stock Boston

Some psychologists specialize in administering, scoring, and interpreting psychological tests, such as tests of intelligence, creativity, personality, or aptitude. This specialty, which is called psychometrics, is an example of using psychology to predict future behavior.

MODULE **1.1** Summary

What is psychology? What are its goals?

- Psychology is the scientific study of behavior and mental processes.

- Psychologists engage in critical thinking as they gather and analyze empirical evidence to answer questions about behavior.

- Some major areas of research in psychology are comparative psychology, learning, sensation, perception, personality, biopsychology, motivation and emotion, social psychology, cognitive psychology, developmental psychology, the psychology of gender, cultural psychology, evolutionary psychology, and forensic psychology.

- Some psychologists are directly interested in animal behavior. Others study animals as models of human behavior.

- As a science, psychology's goals are to describe, understand, predict, and control behavior.

KNOWLEDGE BUILDER

The Science of Psychology

Recite

To check your memory, see if you can answer these questions. If you miss any, skim over the preceding material before continuing, to make sure you understand what you just read.

1. Psychology is the _____ study of _____ and _____ processes.

2. Information gained through direct observation and measurement is called _____ evidence.

3. In psychological research, animal _____ may be used to discover principles that apply to human behavior.

4. Which of the following questions relates most directly to the goal of *understanding* behavior?

   a. Do the scores of men and women differ on tests of thinking abilities?

   b. Why does a blow to the head cause memory loss?

   c. Will productivity in a business office increase if room temperature is raised or lowered?

   d. What percentage of college students suffer from test anxiety?

Match the following research areas with the topics they cover.

____ 5. Developmental psychology

____ 6. Learning

____ 7. Personality

____ 8. Sensation and perception

____ 9. Biopsychology

____ 10. Social psychology

____ 11. Comparative psychology

A. Attitudes, groups, leadership

B. Conditioning, memory

C. The psychology of law

D. Brain and nervous system

E. Child psychology

F. Individual differences, motivation

G. Animal behavior

H. Processing sensory information

Reflect
Critical Thinking

12. All sciences are interested in controlling the phenomena they study. True or false?

Relate

At first, many students think that psychology is primarily about abnormal behavior and psychotherapy. Did you? How would you describe the field now?

Link

Internet addresses frequently change. To find the sites listed here, visit **http://www .thomsonedu.com/psychology/coon** for an updated list of Internet addresses and direct links to relevant sites.

- **Definition of "Psychology"** Provides definitions of *psychology* and *psychologist*.

- **Self-Quiz on Psychology and Science** A 10-item online test (with answers) about psychology and science.

- **What Is Psychology?** Discusses psychology as a science, with links to other articles about various branches of psychology.

ANSWERS

1. scientific, behavior, mental 2. empirical 3. models 4. *b* 5. E 6. B 7. F 8. H 9. D 10. A 11. G 12. False. Astronomy and archaeology are examples of sciences that do not share psychology's fourth goal.

Prediction An ability to accurately forecast behavior.

Control Altering conditions that influence behavior.

1.3 History and Contemporary Perspectives

STARTING WITH PHILOSOPHY and continuing through psychology's history, various viewpoints have helped us understand and interpret human behavior. Today, three complementary perspectives guide research and theorizing in psychology. These are the biological perspective, the psychological perspective, and the sociocultural perspective.

A Brief History of Psychology— Psychology's Family Album

SURVEY QUESTION: *How did the field of psychology emerge?*

People have been informally observing about human behavior and speculating about it for thousands of years. In contrast, psychology's short history as a science dates back only about 130 years. Of course, to some students any history is "not short enough!" Nevertheless, to understand psychology today, we need to explore its past.

Psychology's history as a science began in 1879 in Leipzig, Germany. There, the "father of psychology," Wilhelm Wundt (VILL-helm Voont), set up the first psychological laboratory to study conscious experience. What happens, he wondered, when we have sensations, images, and feelings? To find out, Wundt systematically observed and measured stimuli of various kinds (lights, sounds, weights). A **stimulus** is any physical energy that affects a person and evokes a response (stimulus: singular; stimuli [STIM-you-lie]: plural). Wundt then used **introspection,** or "looking inward," and careful measurement to probe his reactions to various stimuli. (If you carefully examine your thoughts, feelings, and sensations for a moment, you will have done some introspecting.) Over the years, Wundt studied vision, hearing, taste, touch, memory, time perception, and many other topics. By insisting on systematic observation and measurement, he asked some interesting questions and got psychology off to a good start (Schultz & Schultz, 2008).

Structuralism

Wundt's ideas were carried to the United States by a man named Edward Titchener (TICH-in-er). Titchener called Wundt's ideas **structuralism** and tried to analyze the structure of mental life into basic "elements" or "building blocks."

How could they do that? You can't analyze experience like a chemical compound, can you? Perhaps not, but the structuralists tried, mostly by using introspection. For instance, an observer might heft an apple and decide that she had experienced the elements "hue" (color), "roundness," and "weight." Another example of a question that might have interested a structuralist is, What basic tastes mix together to create complex flavors as different as liver, lime, bacon, and burnt-almond fudge?

Introspection proved to be a poor way to answer most questions. Why? Because no matter how systematic the observations, the structuralists frequently *disagreed*. And when they did, there was no way to settle differences. Think about it. If you and a friend both introspect on your perceptions of an apple and end up listing different basic elements, who would be right? Despite such limitations, "looking inward" is still used in studies of hypnosis, meditation, problem solving, moods, and many other topics.

Functionalism

William James, an American scholar, broadened psychology to include animal behavior, religious experience, abnormal behavior, and other interesting topics. James's brilliant first book, *Principles of Psychology* (1890), helped establish the field as a separate discipline (Hergenhahn, 2005).

The term **functionalism** comes from James's interest in how the mind functions to help us adapt to the environment. James regarded consciousness as an ever-changing *stream* or

Wilhelm Wundt, 1832–1920. Wundt is credited with making psychology an independent science, separate from philosophy. Wundt's original training was in medicine, but he became deeply interested in psychology. In his laboratory, Wundt investigated how sensations, images, and feelings combine to make up personal experience.

Stimulus Any physical energy sensed by an organism.

Introspection To look within; to examine one's own thoughts, feelings, or sensations.

Structuralism The school of thought concerned with analyzing sensations and personal experience into basic elements.

Functionalism The school of psychology concerned with how behavior and mental abilities help people adapt to their environments.

William James, 1842–1910. William James was the son of philosopher Henry James, Sr., and the brother of novelist Henry James. During his long academic career, James taught anatomy, physiology, psychology, and philosophy at Harvard University. James believed strongly that ideas should be judged in terms of their practical consequences for human conduct.

flow of images and sensations—not a set of lifeless building blocks, as the structuralists claimed.

The functionalists admired Charles Darwin, who deduced that creatures evolve in ways that favor survival. According to Darwin's principle of **natural selection,** physical features that help animals adapt to their environments are retained in evolution. Similarly, the functionalists wanted to find out how the mind, perception, habits, and emotions help us adapt and survive.

What effect did functionalism have on modern psychology? Functionalism brought the study of animals into psychology. It also promoted *educational psychology* (the study of learning, teaching, classroom dynamics, and related topics). Learning makes us more adaptable, so the functionalists tried to find ways to improve education. For similar reasons, functionalism spurred the rise of *industrial psychology,* the study of people at work.

Behaviorism

Functionalism and structuralism were soon challenged by **behaviorism,** the study of observable behavior. Behaviorist John B. Watson objected strongly to the study of the "mind" or "conscious experience." He believed that introspection is unscientific because there is no way to settle disagreements between observers. Watson realized that he could study the overt behavior of animals even though he couldn't ask them

John B. Watson, 1878–1958. Watson's intense interest in observable behavior began with his doctoral studies in biology and neurology. Watson became a psychology professor at Johns Hopkins University in 1908 and advanced his theory of behaviorism. He remained at Johns Hopkins until 1920 when he left for a career in the advertising industry!

questions, or know what they were thinking (Watson, 1913/1994). He simply observed the relationship between *stimuli* (events in the environment) and an animal's **responses** (any muscular action, glandular activity, or other identifiable behavior). These observations were objective because they did not involve introspecting on subjective experience. Why not, he asked, apply the same objectivity to human behavior?

Watson soon adopted Russian physiologist Ivan Pavlov's (ee-VAHN PAV-lahv) concept of *conditioning* to explain most behavior. (A *conditioned response* is a learned reaction to a particular stimulus.) Watson eagerly claimed, "Give me a dozen healthy infants, well-formed, and my own special world to bring them up in and I'll guarantee to take any one at random and train him to become any type of specialist I might select—doctor, lawyer, artist, merchant-chief, and yes, beggarman and thief" (Watson, 1913/1994).

Would most psychologists agree with Watson's claim? No, today it is regarded as an overstatement. Just the same, behaviorism helped make psychology a natural science, rather than a branch of philosophy (Benjafield, 2004).

One of the best-known behaviorists, B. F. Skinner (1904–1990), believed that our actions are controlled by rewards and punishments. To study learning, Skinner created his famous conditioning chamber, or "Skinner box." With it, he could present stimuli to animals and record their responses

B. F. Skinner, 1904–1990. Skinner studied simple behaviors under carefully controlled conditions. The "Skinner Box" you see here has been widely used to study learning in simplified animal experiments. In addition to advancing psychology, Skinner hoped that his radical brand of behaviorism would improve human life.

(see Module 6.2, "Operant Conditioning"). Many of Skinner's ideas about learning grew out of work with rats and pigeons. Nevertheless, he believed that the same laws of behavior apply to humans. As a "radical behaviorist," Skinner also believed that mental events, such as thinking, are not needed to explain behavior (Schultz & Schultz, 2008).

Skinner was convinced that a "designed culture" based on positive reinforcement could encourage desirable behavior. (Skinner disliked the use of punishment because it doesn't teach correct responses.) Too often, he believed, misguided rewards lead to destructive actions that create problems such as overpopulation, pollution, and war.

Cognitive Behaviorism   Radical behaviorists have been criticized for ignoring the role that thinking plays in our lives. One critic even charged that Skinnerian psychology had "lost consciousness"! However, many criticisms have been answered by **cognitive behaviorism,** a view that combines cognition (thinking) and conditioning to explain behavior (Zentall, 2002). As an example, let's say you frequently visit a particular website because it offers free streaming videos. A behaviorist would say that you visit the site because you are rewarded by the pleasure of watching interesting videos each time you go there. A cognitive behaviorist would add that, in addition, you *expect* to find free videos at the site. This is the cognitive part of your behavior.

Behaviorists deserve credit for much of what we know about learning, conditioning, and the proper use of reward and punishment. Behaviorism is also the source of behavior therapy, which uses learning principles to change problem behaviors such as overeating, unrealistic fears, or temper tantrums. (See Modules 13.3 and 13.4 for more information.)

Gestalt Psychology

Imagine that you just played "Happy Birthday" on a low-pitched tuba. Next, you play it on a high-pitched clarinet. The clarinet duplicates none of the tuba's sounds. Yet, we notice something interesting: The melody is still recognizable—as long as the *relationship* between notes remains the same.

Now, what would happen if you played the notes of "Happy Birthday" in the correct order, but at a rate of one per hour? What would we have? Nothing! The separate notes would no longer be a melody. Perceptually, the melody is somehow more than the individual notes that define it.

It was observations like these that launched the Gestalt school of thought. The German word *Gestalt* means form, pattern, or whole. **Gestalt psychologists** studied thinking, learning, and perception as whole units, not by analyzing experiences into parts. Their slogan was, "The whole is greater than the sum of its parts." (See ● Fig. 1.4.)

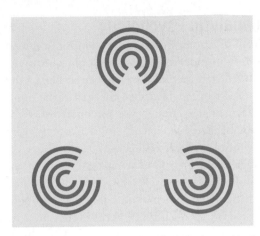

● **FIGURE 1.4**   The design you see here is entirely made up of broken circles. However, as the Gestalt psychologists discovered, our perceptions have a powerful tendency to form meaningful patterns. Because of this tendency, you will probably see a triangle in this design, even though it is only an illusion. Your whole perceptual experience exceeds the sum of its parts.

In Germany, Max Wertheimer (VERT-hi-mer) was the first psychologist to advance the Gestalt viewpoint. It is a mistake, he said, to analyze psychological events into pieces, or "elements," as the structuralists did. Like a melody, many experiences cannot be broken into smaller units, as the Structuralists proposed. For this reason, studies of perception and personality have been especially influenced by the Gestalt viewpoint.

Archives of the History of American Psychology, University of Akron

Max Wertheimer, 1880–1941. Wertheimer first proposed the Gestalt viewpoint to help explain perceptual illusions. He later promoted Gestalt psychology as a way to understand not only perception, problem solving, thinking, and social behavior, but also art, logic, philosophy, and politics.

Natural selection   Darwin's theory that evolution favors those plants and animals best suited to their living conditions.

Behaviorism   The school of psychology that emphasizes the study of overt, observable behavior.

Response   Any muscular action, glandular activity, or other identifiable aspect of behavior.

Cognitive behaviorism   An approach that combines behavioral principles with cognition (perception, thinking, anticipation) to explain behavior.

Gestalt psychology   A school of psychology emphasizing the study of thinking, learning, and perception in whole units, not by analysis into parts.

Psychoanalytic Psychology

As American psychology grew more scientific, an Austrian doctor named Sigmund Freud was developing his own theories. Freud believed that mental life is like an iceberg: Only a small part is exposed to view. He called the area of the mind that lies outside of personal awareness the **unconscious.** According to Freud, our behavior is deeply influenced by unconscious thoughts, impulses, and desires—especially those concerning sex and aggression. Freud's ideas opened new horizons in art, literature, and history, as well as psychology (Jacobs, 2003).

Freud theorized that many unconscious thoughts are **repressed** (held out of awareness) because they are threatening. But sometimes, he said, they are revealed by dreams, emotions, or slips of the tongue. ("Freudian slips" are often humorous, as when a student who is tardy for class says, "I'm sorry I couldn't get here any later.")

Freud believed that all thoughts, emotions, and actions are *determined*. In other words, nothing is an accident: If we probe deeply enough we will find the causes of every thought or action. Freud was also among the first to appreciate that childhood affects adult personality ("The child is father to the man"). Most of all, perhaps, Freud is known for creating **psychoanalysis,** the first "talking cure." Freud's method of psychotherapy explores unconscious conflicts and emotional problems (see Module 13.1).

It wasn't very long before some of Freud's students began to promote their own theories. Several who modified Freud's ideas became known as neo-Freudians (*neo* means "new" or "recent"). **Neo-Freudians** accept much of Freud's theory but revise parts of it. Many, for instance, place less emphasis on sex and aggression and more on social motives and relationships. Some well-known neo-Freudians are Alfred Adler, Anna Freud (Freud's daughter), Karen Horney (HORN-eye), Carl Jung (yoong), Otto Rank (rahnk), and Erik Erikson. Today, Freud's ideas have been altered so much that few

strictly psychoanalytic psychologists are left. However, his legacy is still evident in various **psychodynamic theories,** which continue to emphasize internal motives, conflicts, and unconscious forces (Gedo, 2002).

Humanistic Psychology

Humanism is a view that focuses on subjective human experience. Humanistic psychologists are interested in human problems, potentials, and ideals.

How is the humanistic approach different from others? Carl Rogers, Abraham Maslow, and other humanists rejected the Freudian idea that we are ruled by unconscious forces. They were also uncomfortable with the behaviorist emphasis on conditioning. Both views have a strong undercurrent of **determinism** (the idea that behavior is determined by forces beyond our control). Instead, the humanists stress **free will,** our ability to make voluntary choices. Of course, past experiences do affect us. Nevertheless, humanists believe that people can freely *choose* to live more creative, meaningful, and satisfying lives.

Humanists are interested in psychological needs for love, self-esteem, belonging, self-expression, creativity, and spirituality. Such needs, they believe, are as important as our biological urges for food and water. For example, newborn infants deprived of human love may die just as surely as they would if deprived of food.

How scientific is the humanistic approach? Initially, humanists were less interested in treating psychology as a science. They stressed more subjective factors, such as one's self-image, self-evaluation, and frame of reference. (*Self-image* is your perception of your own body, personality, and capabilities. *Self-evaluation* refers to appraising yourself as good or bad. A *frame of reference* is a mental perspective used to interpret events.) Today, humanists still seek to understand how we perceive ourselves and experience the world. However, most now do research to test their ideas, just as other psychologists do (Schneider, Bugental, & Pierson, 2001).

Maslow's concept of self-actualization is a special feature of humanism. **Self-actualization** refers to developing one's potential fully and becoming the best person possible. According to humanists, everyone has this potential. Humanists

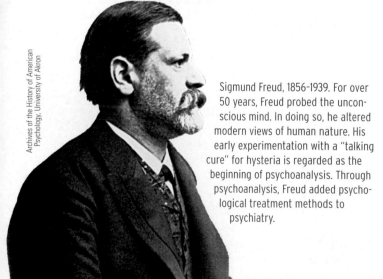

Sigmund Freud, 1856-1939. For over 50 years, Freud probed the unconscious mind. In doing so, he altered modern views of human nature. His early experimentation with a "talking cure" for hysteria is regarded as the beginning of psychoanalysis. Through psychoanalysis, Freud added psychological treatment methods to psychiatry.

Archives of the History of American Psychology, University of Akron

Abraham Maslow, 1908-1970. As a founder of humanistic psychology, Maslow was interested in studying people of exceptional mental health. Such self-actualized people, he believed, make full use of their talents and abilities. Maslow offered his positive view of human potential as an alternative to the schools of behaviorism and psychoanalysis.

Bettmann/Corbis

■ TABLE 1.2	The Early Development of Psychology	
PERSPECTIVE	**DATE**	**NOTABLE EVENTS**
Experimental psychology	1875	• First psychology course offered by William James
	1878	• First American Ph.D. in psychology awarded
	1879	• Wilhelm Wundt opens first psychology laboratory in Germany
	1883	• First American psychology lab founded at Johns Hopkins University
	1886	• First American psychology textbook written by John Dewey
Structuralism	1898	• Edward Titchener advances psychology based on introspection
Functionalism	1890	• William James publishes *Principles of Psychology*
	1892	• American Psychological Association founded
Psychodynamic psychology	1895	• Sigmund Freud publishes first studies
	1900	• Freud publishes *The Interpretation of Dreams*
Behaviorism	1906	• Ivan Pavlov reports his research on conditioned reflexes
	1913	• John Watson presents behavioristic view
Gestalt psychology	1912	• Max Wertheimer and others advance Gestalt viewpoint
Humanistic psychology	1942	• Carl Rogers publishes *Counseling and Psychotherapy*
	1943	• Abraham Maslow publishes "A Theory of Human Motivation"

seek ways to help it emerge. (See ■ Table 1.2 for a summary of psychology's early development.)

The Role of Women in Psychology's Early Days

Were all the early psychologists men? Even though most of the early psychologists were men, women have contributed to psychology from the beginning (Minton, 2000). By 1906, in America, about 1 psychologist in 10 was a woman. Who were these "foremothers" of psychology? Three who became well known are Mary Calkins, Christine Ladd-Franklin, and Margaret Washburn.

Mary Calkins did valuable research on memory. She was also the first woman president of the American Psychological Association, in 1905. Christine Ladd-Franklin studied color vision. In 1906 she was ranked among the 50 most important psychologists in America. In 1908 Margaret Washburn published an influential textbook on animal behavior, titled *The Animal Mind.*

Archives of the History of American Psychology, University of Akron

Mary Calkins, 1863-1930.

The first woman to be awarded a Ph.D. in psychology was Margaret Washburn, in 1894. Over the next 15 years many more women followed her pioneering lead. Today, two out of three graduate students in psychology are women. And, in recent years, nearly 75 percent of all college graduates with a major in psychology have been women. Clearly, psychology has become fully open to both men and women (Hyde, 2004).

Archives of the History of American Psychology, University of Akron

Archives of the History of American Psychology, University of Akron

Christine Ladd-Franklin, 1847-1930.

Margaret Washburn, 1871-1939.

Unconscious Contents of the mind that are beyond awareness, especially impulses and desires not directly known to a person.

Repression The unconscious process by which memories, thoughts, or impulses are held out of awareness.

Psychoanalysis A Freudian approach to psychotherapy emphasizing the exploration of unconscious conflicts.

Neo-Freudian A psychologist who accepts the broad features of Freud's theory but has revised the theory to fit his or her own concepts.

Psychodynamic theory Any theory of behavior that emphasizes internal conflicts, motives, and unconscious forces.

Humanism An approach to psychology that focuses on human experience, problems, potentials, and ideals.

Determinism The idea that all behavior has prior causes that would completely explain one's choices and actions if all such causes were known.

Free will The idea that human beings are capable of freely making choices or decisions.

Self-actualization The ongoing process of fully developing one's personal potential.

Psychology Today—Three Complementary Perspectives on Behavior

SURVEY QUESTION: *What are the contemporary perspectives in psychology?*

At one time, loyalty to each school of thought was fierce, and clashes were common. Today, viewpoints such as functionalism and Gestalt psychology have blended into newer, broader perspectives. Also, some early systems, such as structuralism, have disappeared entirely while new ones have gained prominence. Certainly, loyalties and specialties still exist. But today, many psychologists are *eclectic* (ek-LEK-tik), because they re-

alize that a single perspective is unlikely to fully explain complex human behavior. As a result, psychologists commonly draw insight from a variety of perspectives, insights from one complementing insights from the other. The three broad views that shape modern psychology are the *biological, psychological,* and *sociocultural* perspectives (■ Table 1.3).

The Biological Perspective

The **biological perspective** seeks to explain behavior in terms of biological principles such as brain processes, evolution, and genetics. By using new techniques, *biopsychologists* are producing exciting insights about how the brain relates to thinking, feelings, perception, abnormal behavior, and other topics. Biopsychologists and others who study the brain and nervous system, such as biologists and biochemists, are part

■ **TABLE 1.3   Contemporary Ways to Look at Behavior**

BIOLOGICAL PERSPECTIVE

Biopsychological View

Key Idea: *Human and animal behavior is the result of internal physical, chemical, and biological processes.*

Seeks to explain behavior through activity of the brain and nervous system, physiology, genetics, the endocrine system, and biochemistry; neutral, reductionistic, mechanistic view of human nature.

Evolutionary View

Key Idea: *Human and animal behavior is the result of the process of evolution.*

Seeks to explain behavior through evolutionary principles based on natural selection; neutral, reductionistic, mechanistic view of human nature.

PSYCHOLOGICAL PERSPECTIVE

Behavioristic View

Key Idea: *Behavior is shaped and controlled by one's environment.*

Emphasizes the study of observable behavior and the effects of learning; stresses the influence of external rewards and punishments; neutral, scientific, somewhat mechanistic view of human nature.

Cognitive View

Key Idea: *Much human behavior can be understood in terms of the mental processing of information.*

Concerned with thinking, knowing, perception, understanding, memory, decision making, and judgment; explains behavior in terms of information processing; neutral, somewhat computer-like view of human nature.

Psychodynamic View

Key Idea: *Behavior is directed by forces within one's personality that are often hidden or unconscious.*

Emphasizes internal impulses, desires, and conflicts—especially those that are unconscious; views behavior as the result of clashing forces within personality; somewhat negative, pessimistic view of human nature.

Humanistic View

Key Idea: *Behavior is guided by one's self-image, by subjective perceptions of the world, and by needs for personal growth.*

Focuses on subjective, conscious experience, human problems, potentials, and ideals; emphasizes self-image and self-actualization to explain behavior; positive, philosophical view of human nature.

SOCIOCULTURAL PERSPECTIVE

Sociocultural View

Key Idea: *Behavior is influenced by one's social and cultural context.*

Emphasizes that behavior is related to the social and cultural environment within which a person is born, grows up, and lives from day to day; neutral, interactionist view of human nature.

of the broader field of *neuroscience. Evolutionary psychologists* look at how human evolution and genetics might explain our current behavior.

The Psychological Perspective

The **psychological perspective** takes the view that behavior is shaped by psychological processes occurring within each person. While it continues the objective observation championed by the *behavioristic view*, the psychological perspective now includes cognitive behaviorism and cognitive psychology, which acknowledge that mental processes underlie much of our behavior.

Over the last 50 years, a "cognitive revolution" has taken place as *cognitive psychologists* have successfully applied objective observation to study covert mental behaviors, such as thinking, memory, language, perception, problem solving, consciousness, and creativity. Cognitive psychologists and other researchers interested in cognition, such as computer scientists and linguists, form the broader field of *cognitive science*. With a renewed interest in thinking, it can be said that psychology has finally "regained consciousness" (Robins, Gosling, & Craik, 1998).

Freudian psychoanalysis continues to evolve into the broader *psychodynamic view*. Although many of Freud's ideas have been challenged, psychodynamic psychologists continue to trace human behavior to unconscious processes. They also seek to develop therapies to help people lead happier, fuller lives. Humanistic psychologists do, too, although they stress subjective, conscious experience and the positive side of human nature, rather than unconscious processes.

Positive Psychology Psychologists have always paid attention to the negative side of human behavior. This is easy to understand because of the pressing need to solve human problems. However, inspired by the humanists, more and more psychologists have recently begun to ask, What do we know about love, happiness, creativity, well-being, self-confidence, and achievement? Together, such topics make up **positive psychology,** the study of human strengths, virtues, and optimal behavior (Compton, 2005; Seligman & Csikszentmihalyi, 2000). Many topics from positive psychology can be found in this book. Ideally, they will help make your own life more positive and fulfilling (Simonton & Baumeister, 2005).

The Sociocultural Perspective

As you can see, it is helpful to view human behavior from more than one perspective. This is also true in another sense. The **sociocultural perspective** stresses the impact that social and cultural contexts have on our behavior. We are rapidly becoming a multicultural society, made up of people from many different nations. How has this affected psychology? Let us introduce you to Jerry, who is Japanese American and is married to an Irish Catholic American. Here is what Jerry, his wife, and their children did one New Year's Day:

> We woke up in the morning and went to Mass at St. Brigid's, which has a black gospel choir. . . . Then we went to the Japanese-American Community Center for the Oshogatsu New Year's program and saw Buddhist archers shoot arrows to ward off evil spirits for the year. Next, we ate traditional rice cakes as part of the New Year's service and listened to a young Japanese-American storyteller. On the way home, we stopped in Chinatown and after that we ate Mexican food at a taco stand. (Njeri, 1991)

Jerry and his family reflect a new social reality: Cultural diversity is becoming the norm. About one third of the population in the United States is now African American, Hispanic, Asian American, Native American, or Pacific Islander. In some large cities "minority" groups are already the majority (Schmitt, 2001).

In the past, psychology was based mostly on the cultures of North America and Europe. Now, we must ask, Do the principles of Western psychology apply to people in all cultures? Are some psychological concepts invalid in other cultures? Are any universal? As psychologists have probed such

To fully understand human behavior, personal differences based on age, race, culture, ethnicity, gender, and sexual orientation must be taken into account.

Biological perspective The attempt to explain behavior in terms of underlying biological principles.

Psychological perspective The traditional view that behavior is shaped by psychological processes occurring at the level of the individual.

Positive psychology The study of human strengths, virtues, and effective functioning.

Sociocultural perspective The focus on the importance of social and cultural contexts in influencing the behavior of individuals.

questions, one thing has become clear: Most of what we think, feel, and do is influenced in one way or another by the social and cultural worlds in which we live (Lehman, Chiu, & Schaller, 2004).

Cultural Relativity Imagine that you are a psychologist. Your client, Linda, who is a Native American, tells you that spirits live in the trees near her home. Is Linda suffering from a delusion? Is she abnormal? Obviously, you will misjudge Linda's mental health if you fail to take her cultural beliefs into account. **Cultural relativity** (the idea that behavior must be judged relative to the values of the culture in which it occurs) can greatly affect the diagnosis and treatment of mental disorders (Draguns, Gielen, & Fish, 2004). Cases like Linda's teach us to be wary of using narrow standards when judging others or comparing groups.

A Broader View of Diversity In addition to cultural differences, age, ethnicity, gender, religion, disability, and sexual orientation all affect the **social norms** that guide behavior. Social norms are rules that define acceptable and expected behavior for members of various groups. All too often, the unstated standard for judging what is "average," "normal," or "correct" has been the behavior of white, middle-class males (Reid, 2002). To fully understand human behavior, psychologists need to know how people differ, as well as the ways in which we are all alike (APA, 2003). For the same reason, an appreciation of human diversity can enrich your life, as well as your understanding of psychology (Denmark, Rabinowitz, & Sechzer, 2005).

MODULE 1.3 Summary

How did the field of psychology emerge?

- Historically, psychology is an outgrowth of philosophy. Psychology first became a science when researchers began to directly study and observe psychological events.
- The first psychological laboratory was established in Germany by Wilhelm Wundt, who studied conscious experience.
- The first school of thought in psychology was structuralism, a kind of "mental chemistry" based on introspection.
- Structuralism was followed by functionalism, behaviorism, and Gestalt psychology.
- Psychodynamic approaches, such as Freud's psychoanalytic theory, emphasize the unconscious origins of behavior.
- Humanistic psychology accentuates subjective experience, human potentials, and personal growth.

What are the contemporary perspectives in psychology?

- Three complementary streams of thought in modern psychology are the biological perspective, including biopsychology and evolutionary psychology; the psychological perspective, including behaviorism, cognitive psychology, the psychodynamic approach, and humanism; and the sociocultural perspective.
- Psychologists have recently begun to formally study positive aspects of human behavior, or positive psychology.
- Most of what we think, feel, and do is influenced by the social and cultural worlds in which we live.

KNOWLEDGE BUILDER

History and Contemporary Perspectives

Recite

Match:

1. ____ Philosophy
2. ____ Wundt
3. ____ Structuralism
4. ____ Functionalism
5. ____ Behaviorism
6. ____ Gestalt
7. ____ Psychodynamic
8. ____ Humanistic
9. ____ Cognitive
10. ____ Washburn
11. ____ Biopsychology

A. Against analysis; studied whole experiences
B. "Mental chemistry" and introspection
C. Emphasizes self-actualization and personal growth
D. Interested in unconscious causes of behavior
E. Interested in how the mind aids survival
F. First woman Ph.D. in psychology
G. Studied stimuli and responses, conditioning
H. Part of psychology's "long past"

I. Concerned with thinking, language, problem solving
J. Used introspection and careful measurement
K. Relates behavior to the brain, physiology, and genetics
L. Also known as engineering psychology

12. Who among the following was not a historic woman psychologist?

   a. Calkins *b.* Ladd-Franklin *c.* Washburn *d.* Watson

13. A psychotherapist is working with a person from an ethnic group other than her own. She should be aware of how cultural relativity and _____ affect behavior.

   a. the anthropomorphic error *b.* operational definitions *c.* biased sampling *d.* social norms

Reflect

Critical Thinking

14. Modern sciences like psychology are built on observations that can be verified by two or more independent observers. Did structuralism meet this standard? Why or why not?

Relate

Which school of thought most closely matches your own view of behavior? Do you think any of the early schools offers a complete explanation of why we behave as we do? What about the three contemporary perspectives? Can you explain why so many psychologists are eclectic?

Link

Internet addresses frequently change. To find the sites listed here, visit **http://www.thomsonedu.com/psychology/coon** for an updated list of Internet addresses and direct links to relevant sites.

- **Today in the History of Psychology** Events in the history of psychology by the date, including podcasts.
- **Classics in the History of Psychology** Original articles by a wide range of psychologists from Allport to Yerkes, including Sigmund Freud, B. F. Skinner, and Carl Rogers.
- **Women's Intellectual Contributions to the Field of Psychology** Information about women's contributions to the field of psychology from a historical perspective.

ANSWERS

1. H 2. J 3. B 4. E 5. G 6. A 7. D 8. C 9. I 10. F 11. K 12. d 13. d 14. No, it did not. The downfall of structuralism was that each observer examined the contents of his or her own mind—which is something that no other person can observe.

Cultural relativity The idea that behavior must be judged relative to the values of the culture in which it occurs.

Social norms Rules that define acceptable and expected behavior for members of a group.

1.5 The Psychology Experiment

PSYCHOLOGISTS want to be able explain *why* we act the way we do. Many different research strategies may be used to investigate human behavior. However, we must usually do an experiment to discover the *causes* of behavior. Experiments bring cause-and-effect relationships into sharp focus.

The Psychology Experiment—Where Effect Meets Cause

SURVEY QUESTION: *How is an experiment performed?*

The most powerful scientific research tool is the **experiment** (a formal trial undertaken to confirm or disconfirm a hypothesis about the causes of behavior). Psychologists carefully control conditions in experiments to identify cause-and-effect relationships. To perform an experiment you would do the following:

1. Directly vary a condition you think might affect behavior.
2. Create two or more groups of subjects. These groups should be alike in all ways *except* the condition you are varying.
3. Record whether varying the condition has any effect on behavior.

Assume that you want to find out if hunger affects creativity. First, you would form two groups of people. Then you could give the members of one group a test of creativity while they are hungry. The second group would take the same test after eating a meal. By comparing average creativity scores for the two groups, you could tell if hunger affects creative thinking.

As you can see, the simplest psychological experiment is based on two groups of **experimental subjects** (animals or people whose behavior is investigated; human subjects are also commonly called **participants**). One group is called the *experimental group;* the other becomes the *control group.* The control group and the experimental group are treated exactly alike except for the condition you intentionally vary. This condition is called the *independent variable.*

Variables and Groups

A **variable** is any condition that can change and that might affect the outcome of the experiment. Identifying causes and effects in an experiment involves three types of variables:

1. **Independent variables** are conditions altered or varied by the experimenter, who sets their size, amount, or value. Independent variables are suspected *causes* for differences in behavior.
2. **Dependent variables** measure the results of the experiment. That is, they reveal the *effects* that independent variables have on *behavior.* Such effects are often revealed by measures of performance, such as test scores.
3. **Extraneous variables** are conditions that a researcher wishes to prevent from affecting the outcome of the experiment.

We can apply these terms to our hunger/creativity experiment in this way: Creativity is the independent variable—we want to know if hunger affects creativity. Creativity (defined by scores on the creativity test) is the dependent variable—we want to know if the ability to think creatively depends on how creative a person is. All other variables that could affect creativity scores are extraneous. Examples are the number of hours slept the night before the test, intelligence, or difficulty of the questions.

As you can see, an **experimental group** consists of participants exposed to the independent variable (creativity in the preceding example). Members of the **control group** are exposed to all conditions except the independent variable.

Let's examine another simple experiment. Suppose you notice that you seem to study better while listening to your iPod. This suggests the hypothesis that music improves learning. We could test this idea by forming an experimental

Experiment A formal trial undertaken to confirm or disconfirm a hypothesis about cause and effect.

Experimental subjects Humans (also referred to as **subjects** or **participants**) or animals whose behavior is investigated in an experiment.

Variable Any condition that changes or can be made to change; a measure, event, or state that may vary.

Independent variable In an experiment, the condition being investigated as a possible cause of some change in behavior. The values that this variable takes are chosen by the experimenter.

Dependent variable In an experiment, the condition (usually a behavior) that is affected by the independent variable.

Extraneous variables Conditions or factors excluded from influencing the outcome of an experiment.

Experimental group In a controlled experiment, the group of subjects exposed to the independent variable or experimental condition.

Control group In a controlled experiment, the group of subjects exposed to all experimental conditions or variables *except* the independent variable.

CONTROL GROUP   OUT OF CONTROL GROUP

Courtesy of Peter S. Mueller

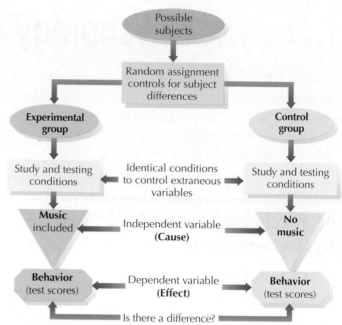

● **FIGURE 1.6** Elements of a simple psychological experiment to assess the effects of music during study on test scores.

group that studies with music. A control group would study without music. Then we could compare their scores on a test.

Is a control group really needed? Can't people just study while listening to their iPods to see if they do better? Without a control group it would be impossible to tell if music had any effect on learning. The control group provides a *point of reference* for comparison with the scores in the experimental group. If the average test score of the experimental group is higher than the average of the control group, we can conclude that music improves learning. If there is no difference, it's obvious that the independent variable had no effect on learning.

In this experiment, the amount learned (indicated by scores on the test) is the *dependent variable*. We are asking, Does the independent variable *affect* the dependent variable? (Does music affect, or influence, learning?)

Experimental Control *How do we know that the people in one group aren't more intelligent than those in the other group?* It's true that personal differences might affect the experiment. However, they can be controlled by randomly assigning people to groups. **Random assignment** means that a participant has an equal chance of being in either the experimental group or the control group. Randomization evenly balances personal differences in the two groups. In our musical experiment, this could be done by simply flipping a coin for each participant: Heads, and the participant is in the experimental group; tails, it's the control group. This would result in few average differences in the number of people in each group who are women or men, geniuses or dunces, hungry, hung over, tall, music lovers, or whatever.

Other *extraneous,* or outside, variables—such as the amount of study time, the temperature in the room, the time of day, the amount of light, and so forth—must also be prevented from affecting the outcome of an experiment. But how? Usually this is done by making all conditions (except the independent variable) *exactly* alike for both groups. When all conditions are the same for both groups—*except* the presence or absence of music—then a difference in the amount learned *must* be caused by the music (● Fig. 1.6). (Psychology

experiments sometimes raise ethical questions. See "That's Interesting, But Is It Ethical" for more information.)

Cause and Effect Now let's summarize. In an experiment two or more groups of subjects are treated differently with respect to the independent variable. In all other ways they are treated the same. That is, extraneous variables are equalized for all groups. The effect of the independent variable (or variables) on some behavior (the dependent variable) is then measured. In a carefully controlled experiment, the independent variable is the only possible *cause* for any *effect* noted in the dependent variable. This allows clear cause-and-effect connections to be identified (● Fig. 1.7).

Placebo Effects, Sugar Pills, and Saltwater

Now let's do an experiment to see if the drug amphetamine (a stimulant) affects learning: Before studying, members of our experimental group take an amphetamine pill. Control group members get nothing. Later, we assess how much each participant learned. Does this experiment seem valid? Actually, it is seriously flawed.

Why? The experimental group took the drug and the control group didn't. Differences in the amount they learned must have been caused by the drug, right? No, because the drug wasn't the only difference between the groups. People in the experimental group swallowed a pill, and control participants did not. Without using a placebo (plah-SEE-bo), it is impossible to

CRITICAL THINKING

That's Interesting, But Is It Ethical?

Three areas of ethical concern in behavioral research are the use of *deception, invasion of privacy,* and the risk of *lasting harm.* Deception and potential harm are illustrated by a classic study of obedience. Participants were ordered to give what they thought were painful electric shocks to another person (no shocks were actually given) (Milgram, 1974). Believing that they had hurt someone, many people left the experiment shaken and upset. A few suffered guilt and distress for some time afterward.

Such experiments raise serious ethical questions. Did the information gained justify the emotional costs? Was deception really necessary? As a reply to such questions, American Psychological Association guidelines state that "Psychologists must carry out investigations with respect for the people who participate and with concern for their dignity and welfare." Similar guidelines apply to animals, where investigators are expected to "ensure the welfare of animals and treat them humanely" (APA, 2002). (See ■ Table 1.5.) To ensure this, most university psychology departments have ethics committees that oversee research. Nevertheless, no easy answers exist for the ethical questions raised by psychology, and debate about specific experiments is likely to continue.

■ **TABLE 1.5**   Basic Ethical Guidelines for Psychological Researchers
Do no harm.
Accurately describe risks to potential participants.
Ensure that participation is voluntary.
Minimize any discomfort to participants.
Maintain confidentiality.
Do not unnecessarily invade privacy.
Use deception only when absolutely necessary.
Remove any misconceptions caused by deception (debrief).
Provide results and interpretations to participants.
Treat participants with dignity and respect.

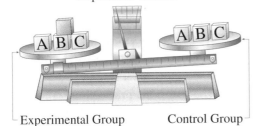

Dependent Variable

Experimental Group   Control Group

☐ Extraneous Variables
▨ Independent Variable

● **FIGURE 1.7** Experimental control is achieved by balancing extraneous variables for the experimental group and the control group. For example, the average age (A), education (B), and intelligence (C) of group members could be made the same for both groups. Then we could apply the independent variable to the experimental group. If their behavior (the dependent variable) changes (in comparison with the control group), the change must be caused by the independent variable.

tell if the drug affects learning. It could be that those who swallowed a pill *expected* to do better. This alone might have affected their performance, even if the actual pill didn't.

What is a placebo? Why would it make a difference? A **placebo** is a fake drug. Inactive substances such as sugar pills and saline (saltwater) injections are commonly used as placebos. If a placebo has any effect, it must be based on suggestion, rather than chemistry (Thompson, 2005).

The **placebo effect** (changes in behavior caused by belief that one has taken a drug) can be powerful. For instance, a saline injection is 70 percent as effective as morphine in reducing pain. That's why doctors sometimes prescribe placebos—especially for complaints that seem to have no physical basis. Placebos have been shown to affect pain, anxiety, depression, alertness, tension, sexual arousal, cravings for alcohol, and many other processes (Wampold et al., 2005).

How could an inert substance have any effect? Placebos alter our expectations about our own emotional and physical reactions. Because we associate taking medicine with feeling better, we expect placebos to make us feel better, too (Stewart-Williams, 2004). After a person takes a placebo, there is a reduction in brain activity linked with pain, so the effect is not imaginary (Wager et al., 2004).

Random assignment The use of chance (for example, flipping a coin) to assign subjects to experimental and control groups.

Placebo An inactive substance given in the place of a drug in psychological research or by physicians who wish to treat a complaint by suggestion.

Placebo effect Changes in behavior due to expectations that a drug (or other treatment) will have some effect.

The placebo effect is a major factor in medical treatments. Would you also expect the placebo effect to occur in psychotherapy? (It does, which complicates studies on the effectiveness of new psychotherapies.)

Controlling Placebo Effects To control for placebo effects, we could use a **single-blind experiment.** In this case, participants do not know if they are receiving a real drug or a placebo. All subjects get a pill or injection. People in the experimental group get a real drug and the control group gets a placebo. Because participants are *blind* as to whether they received the drug or not, their expectations are the same. Any difference in their behavior must be caused by the drug. Even this is not enough because researchers themselves sometimes affect experiments by influencing the behavior of their participants. Let's see how this occurs.

The Experimenter Effect

How could a researcher influence participants? The **experimenter effect** (changes in behavior caused by the unintended influence of an experimenter) is a common problem in psychological research. In essence, experimenters run the risk of finding what they expect to find. This occurs because humans are very sensitive to hints about what is expected of them (Rosenthal, 1994).

The experimenter effect even applies outside the laboratory. Psychologist Robert Rosenthal (1973) reports a classic example of how expectations can influence people: At the U.S. Air Force Academy Preparatory School, 100 airmen were randomly assigned to five different math classes. Their teachers did not know about this random placement. Instead, each teacher was told that his or her students had unusually high or low ability. Students in the classes labeled "high ability" improved much more in math scores than those in "low-ability" classes. Yet, initially all the classes had students of equal ability.

Apparently, the teachers subtly communicated their expectations to students. Most likely, they did this through tone of voice, body language, and by giving encouragement or criticism. Their "hints," in turn, created a self-fulfilling proph-

ecy that affected the students. A **self-fulfilling prophecy** is a prediction that prompts people to act in ways that make the prediction come true. In short, people sometimes become what we prophesy for them. It is wise to remember that others tend to live *up* or *down* to our expectations for them (Jussim & Harber, 2005).

Because of the experimenter effect, it is common to keep both participants and researchers "blind." In a **double-blind experiment** neither participants nor experimenters know who has received a drug and who has taken a placebo. This also keeps researchers from unconsciously influencing participants. Typically, someone else prepares the pills or injections so that experimenters don't know until after testing who got what.

Double-blind testing has shown that about 50 percent of the effectiveness of antidepressant drugs, such as the "wonder drug" Prozac, is due to the placebo effect (Kirsch & Sapirstein, 1998). It's very likely that much of the current popularity of herbal health remedies is also based on the placebo effect (Seidman, 2001). Some psychologists have even suggested replacing the term *placebo effect* with the term *meaning response*, to better reflect just how important people's beliefs are to influencing their behavior (Moerman, 2002).

MODULE 1.5 Summary

How is an experiment performed?

- Experiments involve two or more groups of subjects that differ only with regard to the independent variable.

- Effects on the dependent variable are then measured. All other conditions (extraneous variables) are held constant.

- Because experiments are set up so the independent variable is the only possible cause of a change in the dependent variable, clear cause-and-effect connections can be identified.

- The placebo effect is a problem in some studies, especially in experiments involving drugs, but double-blind testing allows us to draw valid conclusions. The placebo effect is also referred to as the *meaning response.*

- A related problem is the experimenter effect (a tendency for experimenters to unconsciously influence the outcome of an experiment). Researcher expectations can create a self-fulfilling prophecy, in which a participant changes in the direction of the expectation.

- Psychological research must be done ethically, in order to protect the rights, dignity, and welfare of participants.

KNOWLEDGE BUILDER

The Psychology Experiment

Recite

1. To understand cause and effect, a simple psychological experiment is based on creating two groups: the _____ group and the _____ group.

2. There are three types of variables to consider in an experiment: _____ variables (which are manipulated by the experimenter); _____ variables (which measure the outcome of the experiment); and _____ variables (factors to be excluded in a particular experiment).

3. A researcher performs an experiment to learn if room temperature affects the amount of aggression displayed by college students under crowded conditions in a simulated prison environment. In this experiment, the independent variable is which of the following?

   a. room temperature *b.* the amount of aggression *c.* crowding *d.* the simulated prison environment

4. A procedure used to control both the placebo effect and the experimenter effect in drug experiments is the

   a. correlation method *b.* extraneous prophecy *c.* double-blind technique *d.* random assignment of subjects

Reflect
Critical Thinking

5. There is a loophole in the statement, "I've been taking Echinacea tablets, and I haven't had a cold all year. Echinacea is great!" What is the loophole?

6. People who believe strongly in astrology have personality characteristics that actually match, to a degree, those predicted by their astrological signs. Can you explain why this occurs?

Relate

In a sense, we all conduct little experiments to detect cause-and-effect connections. If you are interested in gardening, for example, you might try adding plant food to one bed of flowers but not another. The question then becomes, Does the use of plant food (the independent variable) affect the size of the flowers (the dependent variable)? By comparing unfed plants (the control group) to those receiving plant food (the experimental group) you could find out if plant food is worth using.

Can you think of at least one informal experiment you've run in the last month? What were the variables? What was the outcome?

Link

Internet addresses frequently change. To find the sites listed here, visit **http://www .thomsonedu.com/psychology/coon** for an updated list of Internet addresses and direct links to relevant sites.

- **The Experimental Method** An introduction to experimental research methods.

- **The Simple Experiment** A description of a basic two-group experimental design.

- **Ethical Principles of Psychologists and Code of Conduct** The full text of the ethical principles that guide professional psychologists.

ANSWERS

1. experimental, control 2. independent, dependent, extraneous 3. *a* 4. *c* 5. The statement implies that Echinacea prevented colds. However, not getting a cold could just be a coincidence. A controlled experiment with a group given Echinacea and a control group not taking Echinacea would be needed to learn if Echinacea actually has any effect on susceptibility to colds. 6. Belief in astrology can create a self-fulfilling prophecy in which people alter their behaviors and self-concepts to match their astrological signs (Van Rooij, 1994).

Single-blind experiment An arrangement in which participants remain unaware of whether they are in the experimental group or the control group.

Experimenter effect Changes in subjects' behavior caused by the unintended influence of an experimenter's actions.

Self-fulfilling prophecy A prediction that prompts people to act in ways that make the prediction come true.

Double-blind experiment An arrangement in which both participants and experimenters are unaware of whether participants are in the experimental group or the control group.

WHILE THE EXPERIMENT is frequently used by psychologists, many questions cannot be answered without the aid of nonexperimental methods. For example, psychologists who want to study behavior in natural settings use a technique called naturalistic observation. Psychologists who are looking for interesting relationships between events often rely on the correlational method. It can be difficult or impossible to study mental disorders, such as depression or psychosis, with the experimental method. In such cases, the clinical method may be used. Likewise, questions about the behavior of large groups of people are often best answered with the survey method.

Psychological Research—Different Strokes

SURVEY QUESTION: *What other research methods do psychologists use?*

Determining cause-and-effect relationships between variables lies at the heart of explaining not just *what* we do, but *why* we do it. For this reason, psychologists place a special emphasis on controlled experimentation **(experimental method).** However, because it is not always possible to conduct experiments, psychologists gather evidence and test hypotheses in many others ways: They observe behavior as it unfolds in natural settings **(naturalistic observation);** they make measurements to discover relationships between events **(correlational method);** they study psychological problems and therapies in clinical settings **(clinical method);** and they use questionnaires to poll large groups of people **(survey method).** Let's see how each of these is used to advance psychological knowledge.

Naturalistic Observation—Psychology Steps Out!

Psychologists sometimes actively observe behavior in a *natural setting* (the typical environment in which a person or animal lives). The work of Jane Goodall provides a good example. She and her staff have been observing chimpanzees in Tanzania since 1960. A quote from her book, *In the Shadow of Man,* captures the excitement of a scientific discovery:

> Quickly focusing my binoculars, I saw that it was a single chimpanzee, and just then he turned my direction . . . . He was squatting beside the red earth

mound of a termite nest, and as I watched I saw him carefully push a long grass stem into a hole in the mound. After a moment he withdrew it and picked something from the end with his mouth. I was too far away to make out what he was eating, but it was obvious that he was actually using a grass stem as a tool (● Fig. 1.8). (Van Lawick-Goodall, 1971)

Notice that naturalistic observation only provides *descriptions* of behavior. In order to *explain* observations we may need information from other research methods. Just the same, Goodall's discovery showed that humans are not the only tool-making animals (Nakamichi, 2004).

Chimpanzees in zoos use objects as tools. Doesn't that demonstrate the same thing? Not necessarily. Naturalistic observation allows us to study behavior that hasn't been tampered with or altered by outside influences. Only by observing chimps in their natural environment can we tell if they use tools without human interference.

Limitations

Doesn't the presence of human observers affect the animals' behavior? Yes. The observer effect is a major problem. The **observer effect** refers to changes in a subject's behavior caused by an awareness of being observed. Naturalists must be very careful to keep their distance and avoid "making friends" with the animals they are watching. Likewise, if you are interested in why automobile drivers have traffic accidents, you can't simply get in people's cars and start taking notes. As a stranger, your presence would probably change the driver's behaviors. When possible, this problem can be minimized by concealing the observer. Another solution is to use hidden recorders. For example, a naturalistic study of traffic accidents was done with video cameras installed in 100 cars (Dingus et al., 2006). It turns out that most accidents are caused by failing to look at the traffic in front of the car (eyes forward!).

Observer bias is a related problem in which observers see what they expect to see or record only selected details. For instance, teachers in one study were told to watch normal elementary school children who had been labeled (for the study) as "learning disabled," "mentally retarded," "emotionally disturbed," or "normal." Sadly, teachers gave the children very different ratings, depending on the labels used (Foster & Ysseldyke, 1976). In some situations, observer bias can have serious consequences (Jackson, 2008). For example, psychotherapists tend to get better results with the type of therapy they favor (Lambert, 1999).

● **FIGURE 1.8** A special moment in Jane Goodall's naturalistic study of chimpanzees. A chimp uses a grass stem to extract a meal from a termite nest. Goodall's work also documented the importance of long-term emotional bonds between chimpanzee mothers and their offspring, as well as fascinating differences in the behavior and "personalities" of individual chimps (Goodall, 1990). (Photo by Baron Hugo van Lawick. © National Geographic Society.)

The Anthropomorphic Error A special mistake to avoid while observing animals is the **anthropomorphic** (AN-thro-po-MORE-fik) **error.** This is the error of attributing human thoughts, feelings, or motives to animals—especially as a way of explaining their behavior (Wynne, 2004). The temptation to assume that an animal is "angry," "jealous," "bored," or "guilty" can be strong. If you have pets at home, you probably already know how difficult it is to avoid anthropomorphizing. But it can lead to false conclusions. For example, if your dog growls at your girlfriend every time she visits, you might assume the dog doesn't like her. But maybe she wears a perfume that irritates the dog's nose.

Recording Observations

Psychologists doing naturalistic studies make a special effort to minimize bias by keeping an **observational record,** or detailed summary of data and observations. As suggested by the study of traffic accidents, video recording often provides the most objective record of all.

Despite its problems, naturalistic observation can supply a wealth of information and raise many interesting questions. In most scientific research it is an excellent starting point.

Correlational Studies—In Search of the Perfect Relationship

Let's say a psychologist notes an association between the IQs of parents and their children, or between beauty and social popularity, or between anxiety and test performance, or even between crime and the weather. In each case, two observations or events are **correlated** (linked together in an orderly way).

A **correlational study** finds the degree of relationship, or correlation, between two existing traits, behaviors, or events. First, two factors are measured. Then a statistical technique is used to find their degree of correlation. (See the Appendix near the end of this book for more information.) For example, we could find the correlation between the number of hours spent practicing and sports performance during competitions. If the correlation is large, knowing how much a person practices would allow us to predict his or her success in competition. Likewise, success in competition could be used to predict the amount of practice.

Correlation Coefficients

How is the degree of correlation expressed? The strength and direction of a relationship can be expressed as a **coefficient of correlation.** This is simply a number falling somewhere between +1.00 and −1.00. (See the Appendix.) If the number is zero or close to zero, the association between two measures is weak or nonexistent. For example, the correlation between shoe size and intelligence is zero. (Sorry, size 12 readers.) If the correlation is +1.00, a perfect positive relationship exists; if it is −1.00, a perfect negative relationship has been discovered.

Correlations in psychology are rarely perfect. But the closer the coefficient is to +1.00 or −1.00, the stronger the relationship. For example, identical twins tend to have almost

Experimental method Investigating causes of behavior through controlled experimentation.

Naturalistic observation Observing behavior as it unfolds in natural settings.

Correlational method Making measurements to discover relationships between events.

Clinical method Studying psychological problems and therapies in clinical settings.

Survey method Using questionnaires and surveys to poll large groups of people.

Observer effect Changes in a person's behavior brought about by an awareness of being observed.

Observer bias The tendency of an observer to distort observations or perceptions to match his or her expectations.

Anthropomorphic error The error of attributing human thoughts, feelings, or motives to animals, especially as a way of explaining their behavior.

Observational record A detailed summary of observed events or a videotape of observed behavior.

Correlation The existence of a consistent, systematic relationship between two events, measures, or variables.

Correlational study A nonexperimental study designed to measure the degree of relationship (if any) between two or more events, measures, or variables.

Coefficient of correlation A statistical index ranging from −1.00 to +1.00 that indicates the direction and degree of correlation.

identical IQs. In contrast, the IQs of parents and their children are only generally similar. The correlation between the IQs of parents and children is .35; between identical twins it's .86.

What do the terms "positive" and "negative" correlation mean? A **positive correlation** shows that increases in one measure are matched by increases in the other (or decreases correspond with decreases). For example, there is a positive correlation between high school grades and college grades; students who do well in high school tend to do well in college (and the reverse). In a **negative correlation,** increases in the first measure are associated with decreases in the second (● Fig. 1.9). We might observe, for instance, that students who play many hours of computer games get lower grades than those who play few hours. (This is the well-known computer-game-zombie effect.)

Wouldn't that show that playing computer games too much causes lower grades? It might seem so, but we cannot be sure without performing an experiment.

Correlation and Causation Correlational studies help us discover relationships and make predictions. However, correlation *does not* demonstrate **causation** (a cause-effect relationship) (Elder, 2006). It could be, for instance, that students who aren't interested in their classes have more time for computer games. If so, then their lack of study and lower grades would *both* result from disinterest, not from excess game playing. Just because one thing *appears* to be related to another does not mean that a cause-and-effect connection exists.

Here is another example of mistaking correlation for causation: What if a psychologist discovers that the blood of patients with schizophrenia contains a certain chemical not found in the general population? Does this show that the chemical *causes* schizophrenia? It may seem so, but schizophrenia could cause the chemical to form. Or, both schizophrenia and the chemical might be caused by some unknown third factor, such as the typical diet in mental hospitals. Just because one thing *appears* to cause another does not *confirm* that it does. The best way to be confident that a cause-and-effect relationship exists is to perform a controlled experiment.

The Clinical Method—Data by the Case

It can be difficult or impossible to use the experimental method to study mental disorders, such as depression or psychosis. Many experiments are impractical, unethical, or impossible to do. In such instances, a **case study** (an in-depth focus on a single subject) may be the best source of information. Clinical psychologists rely heavily on case studies, especially as a way to investigate rare or unusual problems.

Case studies may sometimes be thought of as **natural clinical tests** (accidents or other natural events that provide psychological data). Gunshot wounds, brain tumors, accidental poisonings, and similar disasters provide much information about the human brain. One remarkable case from the history of psychology is reported by Dr. J. M. Harlow (1868). Phineas Gage, a young foreman on a work crew, had a 13-pound steel rod blown through the front of his brain by a dynamite explosion (● Fig. 1.10). Amazingly, he survived the accident. Within 2 months Gage could walk, talk, and move normally. But the injury forever changed his personality. Instead of the honest and dependable worker he had been before, Gage became a surly, foul-mouthed liar. Dr. Harlow carefully recorded all details of what was perhaps the first in-depth case study of an accidental frontal lobotomy (the destruction of front brain matter).

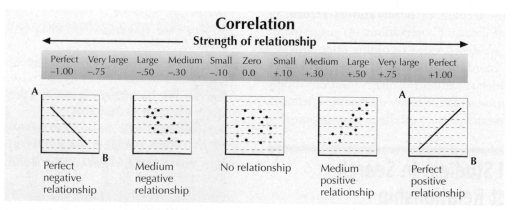

● **FIGURE 1.9** The correlation coefficient tells how strongly two measures are related. These graphs show a range of relationships between two measures, A and B. If a correlation is negative, increases in one measure are associated with decreases in the other. (As B gets larger, A gets smaller.) In a positive correlation, increases in one measure are associated with increases in the other. (As B gets larger, A gets larger.) The center-left graph ("medium negative relationship") might result from comparing anxiety level (B) with test scores (A): Higher anxiety is associated with lower scores. The center graph ("no relationship") would result from plotting a person's shoe size (B) and his or her IQ (A). The center-right graph ("medium positive relationship") could be a plot of grades in high school (B) and grades in college (A) for a group of students: Higher grades in high school are associated with higher grades in college.

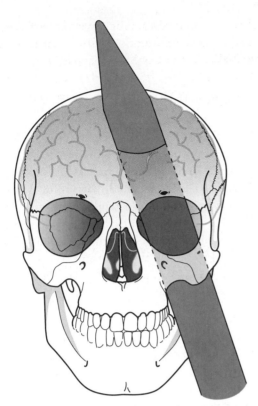

● **FIGURE 1.10** Some of the earliest information on the effects of damage to frontal areas of the brain came from a case study of the accidental injury of Phineas Gage.

When a Los Angeles carpenter named Michael Melnick suffered a similar injury, he recovered completely, with no sign of lasting ill effects. Melnick's very different reaction to a similar injury shows why psychologists prefer controlled experiments and often use lab animals for studies of the brain. Case studies lack formal control groups. This, of course, limits the conclusions that can be drawn from clinical observations. Nonetheless, case studies are especially valuable for studying rare events, such as unusual mental disorders, childhood "geniuses," or "rampage" school shootings (Harding, Fox, & Mehta, 2002). Also, case studies of psychotherapy have provided many useful ideas about how to treat emotional problems (Wedding & Corsini, 2005).

Case studies can provide special opportunities to answer interesting questions. For instance, a classic case study in psychology concerns four identical quadruplets, known as the Genain sisters. In addition to having identical genes, all four women became schizophrenic before age 25 (Rosenthal & Quinn, 1977). The Genains, who have been studied for more than 40 years, were in and out of mental hospitals most of their lives. The fact that they share identical genes suggests that mental disorders are influenced by heredity. The fact that some of the sisters are more disturbed than others suggests that environmental conditions also affect mental illness. Indeed, Myra, the least ill of the four, was the only sister who

was able to avoid her father, an alcoholic who terrorized, spied on, and sexually molested the girls. (See Module 12.3 for more information about the causes of schizophrenia.)

The chances of four identical quads all becoming schizophrenic are about 1 in 1.5 billion. Thus, cases like theirs provide insights that can't be obtained by any other means (Mirsky et al., 2000).

Survey Method—Here, Have a Sample

Sometimes psychologists would like to ask everyone in the world a few well-chosen questions: "Do you drink alcoholic beverages? How often per week?" "What form of discipline did your parents use when you were a child?" "What is the most creative thing you've done?" Honest answers to such questions can reveal much about behavior. But because it is impossible to question everyone, doing a survey is often more practical.

In the **survey method,** public polling techniques are used to answer psychological questions (Tourangeau, 2004). Typically, people in a representative sample are asked a series of carefully worded questions. A **representative sample** is a small group that accurately reflects a larger population. A good sample must include the same proportion of men, women, young, old, professionals, blue-collar workers, Republicans, Democrats, whites, African Americans, Native Americans, Latinos, Asians, and so on, as found in the population as a whole.

A **population** is an entire group of animals or people belonging to a particular category (for example, all college students or all single women). Ultimately, we are interested in entire populations. But by selecting a smaller sample, we can draw conclusions about the larger group without polling each and every person. Representative samples are often ob-

Positive correlation A statistical relationship in which increases in one measure are matched by increases in the other (or decreases correspond with decreases).

Negative correlation A statistical relationship in which increases in one measure are matched by decreases in the other.

Causation The act of causing some effect.

Case study An in-depth focus on all aspects of a single person.

Natural clinical test An accident or other natural event that allows the gathering of data on a psychological phenomenon of interest.

Survey method The use of public polling techniques to answer psychological questions.

Representative sample A small, randomly selected part of a larger population that accurately reflects characteristics of the whole population.

Population An entire group of animals or people belonging to a particular category (for example, all college students or all married women).

tained by *randomly* selecting who will be included (● Fig. 1.11). (Notice that this is similar to randomly assigning participants to groups in an experiment.)

How accurate is the survey method? Modern surveys like the Gallup and Harris polls are quite accurate. The Gallup poll has erred in its election predictions by only 1.5 percent since 1954. However, if a survey is based on a biased sample, it may paint a false picture. A *biased sample* does not accurately reflect the population from which it was drawn. Surveys done by magazines, websites, and online information services can be quite biased. Surveys on the use of guns done by *O: The Oprah Magazine* and *Guns and Ammo* magazine would probably produce very different results—neither of which would represent the general population. That's why psychologists using the survey method go to great lengths to ensure that their samples are representative. Fortunately, people can often be polled by telephone, which makes it easier to obtain large samples. Even if one person out of three refuses to answer survey questions, the results are still likely to be valid (Hutchinson, 2004).

Internet Surveys
Recently, psychologists have started doing surveys and experiments on the Internet. Web-based research has the advantage of low cost, and it can reach very large groups of people. Internet studies have provided interesting information about topics such as anger, decision-making, racial prejudice, what disgusts people, religion, sexual attitudes, and much more. Biased samples can limit web-based research (because it isn't easy to control who actually answers

your online questionnaire), but psychologists are finding ways to gather valid information with it (Birnbaum, 2004; Whitaker, 2007).

Social Desirability
Even well-designed surveys may be limited by another problem. If a psychologist were to ask you detailed questions about your sexual history and current sexual behavior, how accurate would your replies be? Would you exaggerate? Would you be embarrassed? Replies to survey questions are not always accurate or truthful. Many people show a distinct *courtesy bias* (a tendency to give "polite" or socially desirable answers). For example, answers to questions concerning sex, drinking or drug use, income, and church attendance tend to be less than truthful. Likewise, the week after an election, more people will say they voted than actually did (Hutchinson, 2004).

Summary
Despite their limitations, surveys frequently produce valuable information. For instance, the survey method has been used to find out about the attitudes of Muslims in the Middle East toward U.S. policies in the region and to clarify the debate about Islam and violence that has arisen since the terrorist attacks of 9/11 (Haddad, 2003). To sum up, the survey method can be a powerful research tool. Like other methods, it has limitations, but new techniques and strategies are providing valuable information about our behavior (Kahneman et al., 2004). ■ Table 1.6 summarizes many of the important ideas we have covered.

● **FIGURE 1.11** If you were conducting a survey in which a person's height might be an important variable, the upper, nonrandom sample would be very unrepresentative. The lower sample, selected using a table of random numbers, better represents the group as a whole.

■ TABLE 1.6   Comparison of Psychological Research Methods

	ADVANTAGES	DISADVANTAGES
Naturalistic Observation	Behavior is observed in a natural setting; much information is obtained, and hypotheses and questions for additional research are formed	Little or no control is possible; observed behavior may be altered by the presence of the observer; observations may be biased; causes cannot be conclusively identified
Correlational Method	Demonstrates the existence of relationships; allows prediction; can be used in lab, clinic, or natural setting	Little or no control is possible; relationships may be coincidental; cause-and-effect relationships cannot be confirmed
Experimental Method	Clear cause-and-effect relationships can be identified; powerful controlled observations can be staged; no need to wait for natural event	May be somewhat artificial; some natural behavior not easily studied in laboratory (field experiments may avoid these objections)
Clinical Method	Takes advantage of "natural clinical trials" and allows investigation of rare or unusual problems or events	Little or no control is possible; does not provide a control group for comparison, subjective interpretation is often necessary, a single case may be misleading or unrepresentative
Survey Method	Allows information about large numbers of people to be gathered; can address questions not answered by other approaches	Obtaining a representative sample is critical and can be difficult to do; answers may be inaccurate; people may not do what they say or say what they do

MODULE 1.6 Summary

What other research methods do psychologists use?

- Unlike controlled experiments, nonexperimental methods usually cannot demonstrate cause-and-effect relationships.
- Naturalistic observation is a starting place in many investigations.
- Two problems with naturalistic observation are the effects of the observer on the observed and observer bias.
- In the correlational method, relationships between two traits, responses, or events are measured.

- A correlation coefficient is computed to gauge the strength of the relationship. Correlations allow prediction but do not demonstrate cause-and-effect.
- Case studies and natural clinical tests provide insights into human behavior that can't be gained by other methods.
- In the survey method, people in a representative sample are asked a series of carefully worded questions.
- Obtaining a representative sample of people is crucial when the survey method is used to study large populations.

KNOWLEDGE BUILDER

Nonexperimental Research Methods

Recite

1. Two major problems in naturalistic observation are the effects of the observer and observer bias. T or F?

2. Correlation typically does not demonstrate causation. T or F?

3. Which correlation coefficient represents the strongest relationship?

   a. −0.86 b. +0.66 c. +0.10 d. +0.09

4. Case studies can often be thought of as natural tests and are frequently used by clinical psychologists. T or F?

5. For the survey method to be valid, a representative sample of people must be polled. T or F?

6. Amnesia would most likely be investigated by use of

   a. a representative sample b. field experiments c. the double-blind procedure d. case studies

Reflect
Critical Thinking

7. Adults who often ate Frosted Flakes cereal as children now have half the cancer rate seen in adults who never ate Frosted Flakes. What do you think explains this strange correlation?

8. A psychologist conducting a survey at a shopping mall (The Gallery of Wretched Excess) flips a coin before stopping passersby. If the coin shows heads, he interviews the person; if it shows tails, he skips that person. Has the psychologist obtained a random sample?

9. Attributing mischievous motives to a car that is not working properly is a thinking error similar to anthropomorphizing. T or F?

Relate

Have you ever been asked to complete a survey, either in person or via the telephone or the Internet? Did you do it or did you refuse? If you refused, do you think your refusal influenced the final results of the survey? What would it say about accuracy if lots of people refused to complete the survey? If you completed the survey, were you honest about your answers? What would it say about accuracy if lots of people refused to answer accurately?

Link

Internet addresses frequently change. To find the sites listed here, visit **http://www .thomsonedu.com/psychology/coon** for an updated list of Internet addresses and direct links to relevant sites.

- **Psychological Research on the Net** Find and complete a survey study.

- **The Jane Goodall Institute** Information about Goodall's work at Gombe, in Tanzania, where she has studied and protected wild chimpanzees for more than 40 years.

- **Research Methods and the Correlation** Explore different research methods in psychology.

3 Human Development

A Star Is Born—Here's Amy!

Olivia has just given birth to her first child, Amy. Frankly, at the moment Amy looks something like a pink prune, with pudgy arms, stubby legs, and lots of wrinkles. She also has the face of an angel—at least in her parents' eyes. As Olivia and her husband Tom look at Amy they wonder, "How will her life unfold? What kind of a person will she be?"

What if we could skip ahead through Amy's life and observe her at various ages? What could we learn? Seeing the world through her eyes would be fascinating and instructive. For example, a child's viewpoint can make us more aware of things we take for granted. Younger children, in particular, are very literal in their use of language. When Amy was 3, she thought her bath was too hot and said to Tom, "Make it warmer, daddy." At first,

Tom was confused. The bath was already fairly hot. But then he realized that what she really meant was, "Bring the water closer to the temperature we call *warm*." It makes perfect sense if you look at it that way.

Tom and Olivia can only hope that by the time Amy is 83, she will have lived a full and satisfying life. Research done by developmental psychologists tells a fascinating story about human growth and development. Let's let Olivia, Tom, and Amy represent parents and children everywhere, as we see what psychology can tell us about the challenges of growing up, maturing, aging, and facing death. Tracing Amy's development might even help you answer two very important questions, How did I become the person I am today? and Who will I become tomorrow?

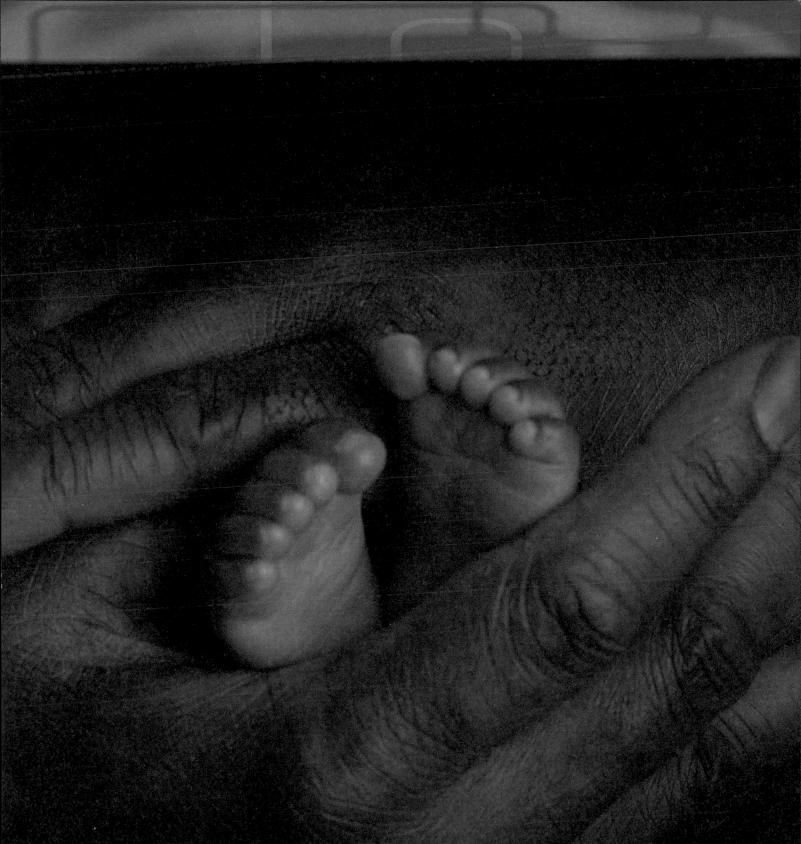

3.1 The Interplay of Heredity and Environment

HEREDITY influences development during the entire human growth sequence. Prenatal risks, sensitive periods, and conditions of deprivation or enrichment all show how the environment can influence development. Ultimately, the person you are today reflects a continuous interplay between the forces of nature and nurture. Even young infants have inborn differences in personality.

Nature and Nurture—It Takes Two to Tango

SURVEY QUESTION: *How do heredity and environment affect development?*

When we think of development we naturally think of children "growing up" into adults. But even as adults we never really stop changing. **Developmental psychology,** the study of progressive changes in behavior and abilities, involves every stage of life from conception to death (or "the womb to the tomb"). Heredity and environment also affect us throughout life. Some events, such as when Amy achieves sexual maturity, are mostly governed by heredity. Others, such as when Amy learns to swim, read, or drive a car, are primarily a matter of environment.

But which is more important, heredity or environment? Actually, neither. Biopsychologist D. O. Hebb (1904–1985) once offered a useful analogy: To define the area of a rectangle, what is more important, height or width? Of course, both dimensions are absolutely essential. If either is reduced to zero, there is no rectangle. Similarly, if Amy grows up to become a prominent civil rights lawyer, her success will be due to both heredity and environment.

While heredity gives each of us a variety of potentials and limitations, these are, in turn, affected by environmental influences, such as learning, nutrition, disease, and culture. Thus, the person you are today reflects a constant *interaction,* or interplay, between the forces of nature and nurture (Kalat, 2007). Let's look in more detail at this dance.

Heredity

Heredity ("nature") refers to the genetic transmission of physical and psychological characteristics from parents to their children. An incredible number of personal features are set at conception, when a sperm and an ovum (egg) unite.

How does heredity operate? The nucleus of every human cell contains **DNA,** deoxyribonucleic acid (dee-OX-see-RYE-bo-new-KLEE-ik). DNA is a long, ladder-like chain of pairs of chemical molecules (● Fig. 3.1). The order of these molecules, or organic bases, acts as a code for genetic information. The DNA in each cell contains a record of all the instructions needed to make a human—with room left over to spare. A major scientific milestone was reached with the completion in 2003 of the Human Genome Project, an effort to completely identify the sequence of all 3 billion chemical base pairs in human DNA (U.S. Department of Energy Office of Science, 2005).

● **FIGURE 3.1** *(Top left)* Linked molecules (organic bases) make up the "rungs" on DNA's twisted "molecular ladder." The order of these molecules serves as a code for genetic information. The code provides a genetic blueprint that is unique for each individual (except identical twins). The drawing shows only a small section of a DNA strand. An entire strand of DNA is composed of billions of smaller molecules. *(Bottom left)* The nucleus of each cell in the body contains chromosomes made up of tightly wound coils of DNA. (Don't be misled by the drawing: Chromosomes are microscopic, and the chemical molecules that make up DNA are even smaller.)

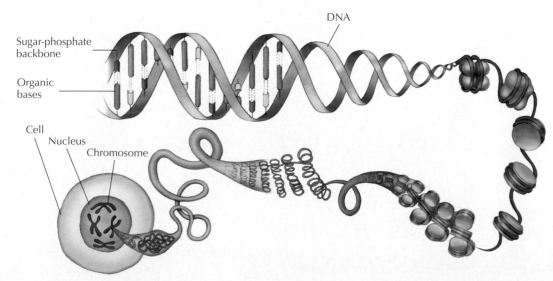

DNA

Sugar-phosphate backbone

Organic bases

Cell

Nucleus

Chromosome

Human DNA is organized into 46 **chromosomes.** (The word *chromosome* means "colored body.") These thread-like structures hold the coded instructions of heredity (● Fig. 3.2). A notable exception is sperm cells and ova, which contain only 23 chromosomes. Thus, Amy received 23 chromosomes from Olivia and 23 from Tom. This is her genetic heritage.

Genes are small areas of DNA that affect a particular process or personal characteristic. Sometimes, a single gene is responsible for an inherited feature, such as Amy's eye color. Genes may be dominant or recessive. When a gene is **dominant,** the feature it controls will appear every time the gene is present. When a gene is **recessive,** it must be paired with a second recessive gene before its effect will be expressed. For example, if Amy got a blue-eye gene from Tom and a brown-eye gene from Olivia, Amy will be brown-eyed, because brown-eye genes are dominant.

If brown-eye genes are dominant, why do two brown-eyed parents sometimes have a blue-eyed child? If one or both parents have two brown-eye genes, the couple's children can only be brown-eyed. But what if each parent has one brown-eye gene and one blue-eye gene? In that case, both parents would have brown eyes. Yet there is 1 chance in 4 that their children will get two blue-eye genes and have blue eyes (● Fig. 3.3).

In actuality, few of our characteristics are controlled by single genes. Instead, most are **polygenic** (pol-ih-JEN-ik), or controlled by many genes working in combination. Through the expression of genes, heredity determines eye color, skin color, and susceptibility to some diseases. Also, genes can switch on (or off) at certain ages or developmental stages. In this way, heredity continues to exert a powerful influence throughout maturation, the unfolding of the *human growth sequence.* (See ■ Table 3.1.) To a degree, genetic instructions affect body size and shape, height, intelligence, athletic potential, personality traits, sexual orientation, and a host of other details (Cummings, 2006).

Environment

Our environment also exerts a profound influence on our development. For example, the brain of a newborn baby has fewer *dendrites* (nerve cell branches) and *synapses* (connections between nerve cells) than an adult brain (● Fig. 3.4).

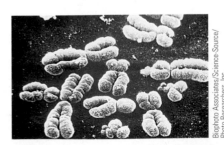

● **FIGURE 3.2** This image, made with a scanning electron microscope, shows several pairs of human chromosomes. (Colors are artificial.)

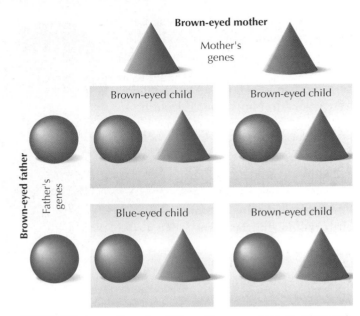

● **FIGURE 3.3** Gene patterns for children of brown-eyed parents, where each parent has one brown-eye gene and one blue-eye gene. Because the brown-eye gene is dominant, 1 child in 4 will be blue-eyed. Thus, there is a significant chance that two brown-eyed parents will have a blue-eyed child.

However, the newborn brain is highly *plastic* (capable of being altered by experience). During the first 3 years of life, millions of new connections form in the brain every day. At the same time, unused connections disappear. As a result, early learning environments literally shape the developing brain, through "blooming and pruning" of synapses (Nelson, 1999).

Environment ("nurture") refers to the sum of all external conditions that affect a person. The environments in which a child grows up can have a powerful impact on development. Humans today are genetically very similar to cave

Developmental psychology The study of progressive changes in behavior and abilities from conception to death.

Heredity ("nature") The transmission of physical and psychological characteristics from parents to offspring through genes.

DNA Deoxyribonucleic acid, a molecular structure that contains coded genetic information.

Chromosomes Thread-like "colored bodies" in the nucleus of each cell that are made up of DNA.

Genes Specific areas on a strand of DNA that carry hereditary information.

Dominant gene A gene whose influence will be expressed each time the gene is present.

Recessive gene A gene whose influence will be expressed only when it is paired with a second recessive gene.

Polygenic characteristics Personal traits or physical properties that are influenced by many genes working in combination.

Environment ("nurture") The sum of all external conditions affecting development, including especially the effects of learning.

dwellers who lived 30,000 years ago. Nevertheless, a bright baby born today could learn to become almost anything—a ballet dancer, an engineer, a gangsta rapper, or a biochemist who likes to paint in watercolors. But an Upper Paleolithic baby could have only become a hunter or food gatherer.

Prenatal Influences The interplay of nature and nurture actually starts before birth. Although the intra-uterine environment (interior of the womb) is highly protected, environmental conditions can affect the developing child. For example, when Olivia was pregnant, Amy's fetal heart rate and movements in-

Identical twins. Twins who share identical genes (identical twins) demonstrate the powerful influence of heredity. Even when they are reared apart, identical twins are strikingly alike in motor skills, physical development, and appearance. At the same time, twins are less alike as adults than they were as children, which shows environmental influences are at work (Larsson, Larsson, & Lichtenstein, 2004).

Myrleen Ferguson Cate/PhotoEdit

creased when loud sounds or vibrations penetrated the womb (Kisilevsky et al., 2004).

If Olivia's health or nutrition had been poor, or if she had German measles, syphilis, or HIV, or used drugs, or was exposed to X-rays or atomic radiation, Amy's growth sequence might have been harmed. In such cases babies can suffer from **congenital problems,** or "birth defects." These environmental problems affect the developing fetus and become apparent at birth. In contrast, **genetic disorders** are inherited from parents. Examples are sickle-cell anemia, hemophilia, cystic fibrosis, muscular dystrophy, albinism, and some types of mental retardation.

■ **TABLE 3.1 Human Growth Sequence**

PERIOD	DURATION	DESCRIPTIVE NAME
Prenatal Period	From conception to birth	
Germinal period	First 2 weeks after conception	Zygote
Embryonic period	2-8 weeks after conception	Embryo
Fetal period	From 8 weeks after conception to birth	Fetus
Neonatal Period	From birth to a few weeks after birth	Neonate
Infancy	From a few weeks after birth until child is walking securely; some children walk securely at less than a year, while others may not be able to until age 17-18 months	Infant
Early Childhood	From about 15-18 months until about 2-2½ years	Toddler
	From age 2-3 to about age 6	Preschool child
Middle Childhood	From about age 6 to age 12	School-age child
Pubescence	Period of about 2 years before puberty	
Puberty	Point of develoment at which biological changes of pubescence reach a climax marked by sexual maturity	
Adolescence	From the beginning of pubescence until full social maturity is reached (difficult to fix duration of this period)	Adolescent
Adulthood Young adulthood (19-25) Adulthood (26-40) Maturity (41 plus)	From adolescence to death; sometimes subdivided into other periods as shown at left	Adult
Senescence	No defined limit that would apply to all people; extremely variable; characterized by marked physiological and psychological deterioration	Adult (senile), "old age"

Note: There is no exact beginning or ending point for various growth periods. The ages are approximate, and each period may be thought of as blending into the next. (Table courtesy of Tom Bond.)

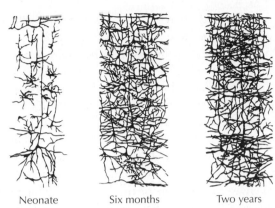

Neonate   Six months   Two years

● **FIGURE 3.4** A rapid increase in brain synapses continues until about age 4. At that point, children actually have more brain synapses than adults do. Then, after age 10, the number slowly declines, reaching adult levels at about age 16. (Reprinted by permission of the publisher from *The Postnatal Development of the Human Cerebral Cortex, Vols. I–III* by Jesse LeRoy Conel, Cambridge, Mass.: Harvard University Press, Copyright © 1935, 1975 by the President and Fellows of Harvard College.)

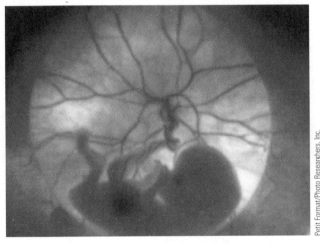

Because of the rapid growth of basic structures, the developing fetus is sensitive to a variety of diseases, drugs, and sources of radiation. This is especially true during the first trimester (3 months) of gestation (pregnancy).

How is it possible for the embryo or the fetus to be harmed? No direct intermixing of blood takes place between a mother and her unborn child. Yet some substances—especially drugs—do reach the fetus. Anything capable of directly causing birth defects is called a **teratogen** (teh-RAT-uh-jen). Sometimes women are exposed to powerful teratogens, such as radiation, lead, pesticides, or polychlorinated biphenyls (PCBs), without knowing it. But pregnant women do have direct control over many teratogens. For example, a woman who takes cocaine runs a serious risk of injuring her fetus (Schuetze & Eiden, 2006). In short, when a pregnant woman takes drugs, her unborn child does too.

Unfortunately, in the United States this is one of the greatest risk factors facing unborn children (Coles & Black, 2006). If a mother is addicted to morphine, heroin, or methadone, her baby may be born with an addiction. Re-

Some of the typical features of children suffering from fetal alcohol syndrome (FAS) include a small nonsymmetrical head, a short nose, a flattened area between the eyes, oddly shaped eyes, and a thin upper lip. Many of these features become less noticeable by adolescence. However, mental retardation and other problems commonly follow the FAS child into adulthood. The child shown here represents a moderate example of FAS.

peated heavy drinking during pregnancy causes *fetal alcohol syndrome (FAS)*. Affected infants have low birth weight, a small head, body defects, and facial malformations. Many also suffer from emotional, behavioral, and mental handicaps (Golden, 2005).

Tobacco is also harmful. Smoking during pregnancy greatly reduces oxygen to the fetus. Heavy smokers risk miscarrying or having premature, underweight babies who are more likely to die soon after birth. Children of smoking mothers score lower on tests of language and mental ability (Huijbregts et al., 2006). In other words, an unborn child's future can go "up in smoke." That goes for marijuana as well (Viveros et al., 2005).

Sensitive Periods Early experiences can have particularly lasting effects. For example, children who are abused may suffer lifelong emotional problems (Goodwin, Fergusson, & Horwood, 2005). At the same time, extra care can sometimes reverse the effects of a poor start in life (Bornstein & Tamis-LeMonda, 2001). In short, environmental forces guide human development, for better or worse, throughout life.

Congenital problems Problems or defects that originate during prenatal development in the womb.

Genetic disorders Problems caused by defects in the genes or by inherited characteristics.

Teratogen Radiation, a drug, or other substance capable of altering fetal development in nonheritable ways that cause birth defects.

Why do some experiences have more lasting effects than others? Part of the answer lies in **sensitive periods.** These are times when children are more susceptible to particular types of environmental influences. Events that occur during a sensitive period can permanently alter the course of development (Bruer, 2001). For example, forming a loving bond with a caregiver early in life seems to be crucial for optimal development. Likewise, babies who don't hear normal speech during their first year may have impaired language abilities (Thompson & Nelson, 2001).

Deprivation and Enrichment

Some environments can be described as *enriched* or *deprived*. **Deprivation** refers to a lack of normal nutrition, stimulation, comfort, or love. **Enrichment** exists when an environment is deliberately made more stimulating, loving, and so forth.

What happens when children suffer severe deprivation? Tragically, a few mistreated children have spent their first years in closets, attics, and other restricted environments. When first discovered, these children are usually mute, retarded, and emotionally damaged. Fortunately, such extreme deprivation is unusual.

Nevertheless, milder perceptual, intellectual, or emotional deprivation occurs in many families, especially those that must cope with poverty. Poverty can effect the development of children in at least two ways (Sobolewski & Amato, 2005). First, poor parents may not be able to give their children needed resources such as nutritious meals, health care, or learning materials (Bradley & Corwyn, 2002). As a result, impoverished children tend to be sick more often, their cognitive development lags, and they do poorly at school. Second, the stresses of poverty can also be hard on parents, leading to marriage problems, less positive parenting, and poorer parent-child relationships. The resulting emotional turmoil can damage a child's socioemotional development. In the extreme, it may increase the risk of mental illness and delinquent behavior (Bradley & Corwyn, 2002).

Adults who grew up in poverty often remain trapped in a vicious cycle of continued poverty. Because one in seven American families fall below the poverty line, this grim reality plays itself out in millions of American homes every day (Sobolewski & Amato, 2005).

Can an improved environment enhance development? To answer this question, psychologists have created *enriched environments* that are especially novel, complex, and stimulating. Enriched environments may be the "soil" from which brighter children grow. To illustrate, let's consider the effects of raising rats in a sort of "rat wonderland." The walls of their cages were decorated with colorful patterns, and each cage was filled with platforms, ladders, and cubbyholes. As adults, these rats were superior at learning mazes. In addition, they had larger, heavier brains, with a thicker cortex (Benloucif, Bennett, & Rosenzweig, 1995). Of course, it's a long leap from rats to people, but an actual increase in brain size is impressive. If extra stimulation can enhance the "intelligence" of a lowly rat, it's likely that human infants also benefit from enrichment. Many studies have shown that enriched environments improve abilities or enhance development. It would be wise for Tom and Olivia to make a point of nourishing Amy's mind, as well as her body (Beeber et al., 2007).

What can parents do to enrich a child's environment? They can encourage exploration and stimulating play by paying attention to what holds the baby's interest. It is better to "child-proof" a house than to strictly limit what a child can touch. There is also value in actively enriching sensory experiences. Infants are not vegetables. Babies should be surrounded by colors, music, people, and things to see, taste, smell, and touch. It makes perfect sense to take them outside, to hang mobiles over their cribs, to place mirrors nearby, to play music for them, or to rearrange their rooms now and then. Children progress most rapidly when they have responsive parents and stimulating play materials at home (Beeber et al., 2007). In light of this, it is wise to view all of childhood as a *relatively sensitive period* (Nelson, 1999).

Reaction Range

One way to visualize the interplay of heredity and environment is through the concept of **reaction range,** the limits that one's environment places on the effects of heredity (● Fig. 3.5). Let's suppose that Amy was born with genes for a normal level of intelligence. If Amy grows up in a deprived environment, she might well end up with lower than average adult intelligence. If Olivia and Tom provide her with an enriched environment, she will probably have normal, or even above normal, intelligence. While Amy might not be genetically capable of becoming a genius, the environment her parents provide for her will also determine her developmental path.

Anna Kaufman Moon/Stock, Boston

Children who grow up in poverty run a high risk of experiencing many forms of deprivation. There is evidence that lasting damage to social, emotional, and cognitive development occurs when children must cope with severe early deprivation.

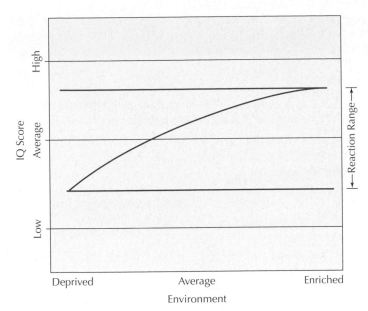

● **FIGURE 3.5** The effect of heredity on the development of human traits, such as intelligence, can often influenced by environmental circumstances. A child with average genes for intelligence growing up in an average environment might have an average IQ score as an adult. However, growing up in a deprived environment might result in a somewhat lower IQ score and growing up in an enriched environment might result in a somewhat higher IQ score. In this way, the environment sets a range within which our hereditary potential is actually expressed. This range is called the *reaction range.*

Reciprocal Influences Nurture often affects the expression of hereditary tendencies through ongoing reciprocal influences. A good example of such influences is the fact that growing infants influence their parents' behavior at the same time they are changed by it.

Newborn babies differ noticeably in **temperament.** This is the inherited, physical core of personality. It includes sensitivity, irritability, distractibility, and typical mood (Kagan, 2004). About 40 percent of all newborns are *easy children* who are relaxed and agreeable. Ten percent are *difficult children* who are moody, intense, and easily angered. *Slow-to-warm-up children* (about 15 percent) are restrained, unexpressive, or shy. The remaining children do not fit neatly into a single category (Chess & Thomas, 1986).

Because of differences in temperament, some babies are more likely than others to smile, cry, vocalize, reach out, or pay attention. As a result, babies rapidly become active participants in their own development. For example, Amy is an easy baby who smiles frequently and is easily fed. This encourages Olivia to touch, feed, and sing to Amy. Olivia's affection rewards Amy, causing her to smile more. Soon, a dynamic relationship blossoms between mother and child. Similarly, good parenting can reciprocally influence a very shy child who, in turn, becomes progressively less shy.

The reverse also occurs: Difficult children make parents unhappy and elicit more negative parenting (Parke, 2004).

Alternately, negative parenting can turn a moderately shy child into a very shy one. This suggests that inherited temperaments are dynamically modified by learning (Kagan, 2005).

A person's **developmental level** is his or her current state of physical, emotional, and intellectual development. To summarize, three factors combine to determine your developmental level at any stage of life. These are *heredity, environment,* and your *own behavior,* each tightly interwoven with the others.

MODULE 3.1 Summary

How do heredity and environment affect development?

- Heredity (nature) and environment (nurture) are interacting forces that are both necessary for human development. However, caregivers can only influence environment.

- Hereditary instructions are carried by the chromosomes and genes in each cell of the body. Most characteristics are polygenic and reflect the combined effects of dominant and recessive genes.

- Prenatal development is influenced by environmental factors, such as diseases, drugs, radiation, various teratogens, and the mother's diet, health, and emotions.

- During sensitive periods in development, infants are more sensitive to specific environmental influences.

- Early perceptual, intellectual, or emotional deprivation seriously retards development, whereas deliberate enrichment of the environment has a beneficial effect on infants.

- Temperament is hereditary. Most infants fall into one of three temperament categories: easy children, difficult children, and slow-to-warm-up children.

- A child's developmental level reflects heredity, environment, and the effects of the child's own behavior.

Sensitive period During development, a period of increased sensitivity to environmental influences. Also, a time during which certain events must take place for normal development to occur.

Deprivation In development, the loss or withholding of normal stimulation, nutrition, comfort, love, and so forth; a condition of lacking.

Enrichment In development, deliberately making an environment more stimulating, nutritional, comforting, loving, and so forth.

Reaction range The limits environment places on the effects of heredity.

Temperament The physical core of personality, including emotional and perceptual sensitivity, energy levels, typical mood, and so forth.

Developmental level An individual's current state of physical, emotional, and intellectual development.

KNOWLEDGE BUILDER

The Interplay of Heredity and Environment

Recite

1. Areas of the DNA molecule called genes are made up of dominant and recessive chromosomes. T or F?

2. Most inherited characteristics can be described as polygenic. T or F?

3. If one parent has a one dominant brown-eye gene and one recessive blue-eye gene and the other parent has two dominant brown-eye genes, what is the chance that their child will have blue eyes?

   a. 25 percent

   b. 50 percent

   c. 0 percent

   d. 75 percent

4. "Slow-to-warm-up" children can be described as restrained, unexpressive, or shy. T or F?

5. A _____ _____ is a time of increased reactivity to environmental influences.

6. As a child develops there is a continuous _____ between the forces of heredity and environment.

Reflect
Critical Thinking

7. Environmental influences can interact with hereditary programming in an exceedingly direct way. Can you guess what it is?

Relate

Can you think of clear examples of some ways in which heredity and environmental forces have combined to affect your development?

What kind of temperament did you have as an infant? How did it affect your relationship with your parents or caregivers?

What advice would you give a friend who has just become pregnant? Be sure to consider the prenatal environment and sensitive periods.

Link

Internet addresses frequently change. To find the sites listed here, visit **http://www.thomsonedu.com/psychology/coon** for an updated list of Internet addresses and direct links to relevant sites.

- **Heredity Versus Environment** Read more about the interplay of nature and nurture.

- **Diving into the Gene Pool** From the Exploratorium, this site teaches about modern genetics.

- **Human Genome Project** Learn more about your human genetic heritage.

ANSWERS

1. F 2. T 3. c 4. T 5. sensitive period 6. interaction 7. Environmental conditions sometimes turn specific genes on or off, thus directly affecting the expression of genetic tendencies (Gottlieb, 1998).

3.3 Social Development in Childhood

INFANTS begin to develop self-awareness and to become aware of others at about the same time they first form an emotional bond with an adult. Each of these developments is an important step toward entering the social world. Parents are the most important influences in early social development. Later, playing with other children begins to extend a child's social life beyond the family.

Social Development—Baby, I'm Stuck on You

SURVEY QUESTION: *Of what significance is a child's emotional bond with parents?*

Like all humans, babies are social creatures. Their early **social development** lays a foundation for relationships with parents, siblings, friends, and relatives. A first basic step into the social world involves becoming aware of oneself as a person. When you look in a mirror, you recognize the image staring back as your own—except, perhaps, early on Monday mornings. Like many such events, initial self-awareness depends on maturation of the nervous system. In a typical test of self-recognition, infants are shown images of themselves on a TV. Most infants have to be 18 months old before they recognize themselves (Nielsen & Dissanayake, 2004).

A sense of self, or self-awareness, develops at about age 18 months. Before children develop self-awareness, they do not recognize their own image in a mirror. Typically, they think they are looking at another child. Some children hug the child in the mirror or go behind it looking for the child they see there (Lewis, 1995).

Attachment

The real core of social development is found in the **emotional attachment,** or close emotional bond, that babies form with their primary caregivers. There is a sensitive period (roughly the first year of life) during which this must occur for optimal development. Returning to Amy's story, we find that attachment keeps her close to Olivia, who provides safety, stimulation, and a secure "home base" from which Amy can go exploring.

Mothers usually begin to feel attached to their baby before birth. For their part, as babies mature, they become more and more capable of bonding with their mothers. For the first few months, babies respond more or less equally to everyone. By 2 or 3 months, most babies prefer their mothers to strangers. By around 7 months, babies generally become truly attached to their mothers, crawling after her if they can. Shortly thereafter they also begin to form attachments to other people as well, such as father, grandparents, or siblings (Sigelman & Rider, 2006).

A direct sign that an emotional bond has formed appears around 8 to 12 months of age. At that time Amy will display **separation anxiety** (crying and signs of fear) when she is left alone or with a stranger. Mild separation anxiety is normal. When it is more intense, it may reveal a problem. At some point in their lives, about 1 in 20 children suffer from *separation anxiety disorder* (Dick-Niederhauser & Silverman, 2006). These children are miserable when they are separated

Most parents are familiar with the storm of crying that sometimes occurs when babies are left alone at bedtime. Bedtime distress can be a mild form of separation anxiety. As many parents know, it is often eased by the presence of "security objects," such as a stuffed animal or favorite blanket (Donate-Bartfield & Passman, 2004).

Social development The development of self-awareness, attachment to parents or caregivers, and relationships with other children and adults.

Emotional attachment An especially close emotional bond that infants form with their parents, caregivers, or others.

Separation anxiety Distress displayed by infants when they are separated from their parents or principal caregivers.

from their parents, whom they cling to or constantly follow. Some fear that they will get lost and never see their parents again. Many refuse to go to school, which can be a serious handicap. Children tend to grow out of the disorder (Kearney et al., 2003), but if separation anxiety is intense or lasts for more than a month, parents should seek professional help for their child (Masi, Mucci, & Millepiedi, 2001).

Attachment Quality According to psychologist Mary Ainsworth (1913–1999), the quality of attachment is revealed by how babies act when their mothers return after a brief separation. Infants who are **securely attached** have a stable and positive emotional bond. They are upset by the mother's absence and seek to be near her when she returns. **Insecure-avoidant** infants have an anxious emotional bond. They tend to turn away from the mother when she returns. **Insecure-ambivalent** attachment is also an anxious emotional bond. In this case, babies have mixed feelings: They both seek to be near the returning mother and angrily resist contact with her. (See ● Fig. 3.12.)

Attachment can have lasting effects. Infants who are securely attached at the age of 1 year show more resiliency, curiosity, problem-solving ability, and social skill in preschool (Collins & Gunnar, 1990). In contrast, attachment failures can be quite damaging. Consider, for example, the plight of children raised in severely overcrowded Romanian orphanages. These children got almost no attention from adults for the first year or two of their lives. Some have now been adopted by American and Canadian families, but many are poorly attached to their new parents. Some, for instance, will wander off with strangers; they are anxious and remote, and they don't like to be touched or make eye contact with others (O'Conner et al., 2003). In short, for some children, a lack of affectionate care early in life leaves a lasting emotional impact well into adulthood. (See "What's Your Attachment Style?")

Attachment Category

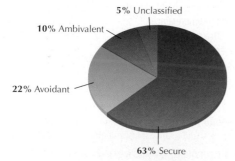

5% Unclassified
10% Ambivalent
22% Avoidant
63% Secure

● **FIGURE 3.12** In the United States, about two thirds of all children from middle-class families are securely attached. About 1 child in 3 is insecurely attached. (Percentages are approximate. From Kaplan, 1998.)

Promoting Secure Attachment The key to secure attachment is a mother who is accepting and sensitive to her baby's signals and rhythms. Poor attachment occurs when a mother's actions are inappropriate, inadequate, intrusive, over-stimulating, or rejecting. An example is the mother who tries to play with a drowsy infant or who ignores a baby who is looking at her and vocalizing. The link between sensitive caregiving and secure attachment appears to apply to all cultures (Posada et al., 2002).

What about attachment to fathers? Fathers of securely attached infants tend to be outgoing, agreeable, and happy in their marriage. In general, a warm family atmosphere—one that includes sensitive mothering *and* fathering—produces secure children (Belsky, 1996).

Day Care

Does commercial day care interfere with the quality of attachment? It depends on the quality of day care. Overall, *high-quality* day care does not adversely affect attachment to parents (National Institute of Child Health and Human Development, 1999). In fact, children in high-quality day care tend to have better relationships with their mothers and fewer behavior problems. They also have better cognitive skills and language abilities (Burchinal et al., 2000; Vandell, 2004). Thus, high-quality day care can actually improve children's social and mental skills (Mercer, 2006).

However, all the positive effects just noted are *reversed* for low-quality day care. Poor-quality day care can actually create behavior problems that didn't exist beforehand (Pierrehumbert et al., 2002). Parents are wise to carefully evaluate and monitor the quality of day care their children receive.

What should parents look for when they evaluate the quality of child care? Low-quality day care *is* risky and it *may* weaken attachment. Parents seeking quality should insist on *at least* the following: (1) a small number of children per caregiver, (2) small overall group size (12 to 15), (3) trained caregivers, (4) minimal staff turnover, and (5) stable, consistent care (Howes, 1997). (Also, avoid any child-care center with the words *zoo, menagerie,* or *stockade* in its name.)

Attachment and Affectional Needs

A baby's **affectional needs** (needs for love and affection) are every bit as important as more obvious needs for food, water, and physical care. All things considered, creating a bond of trust and affection between the infant and at least one other person is a key event during the first year of life. Parents are sometimes afraid of "spoiling" babies with too much attention, but for the first year or two this is nearly impossible. In fact, a later capacity to experience warm and loving relationships may depend on it.

DISCOVERING PSYCHOLOGY

What's Your Attachment Style?

Do our first attachments continue to affect us as adults? Some psychologists believe they do, by influencing how we relate to friends and lovers (Bridges, 2003; Sroufe et al., 2005). Read the following statements and see which best describes your adult relationships.

Secure Attachment Style

In general, I think most other people are well intentioned and trustworthy.

I find it relatively easy to get close to others.

I am comfortable relying on others and having others depend on me.

I don't worry much about being abandoned by others.

I am comfortable when other people want to get close to me emotionally.

Avoidant Attachment Style

I tend to pull back when things don't go well in a relationship.

I am somewhat skeptical about the idea of true love.

I have difficulty trusting my partner in a romantic relationship.

Other people tend to be too eager to seek commitment from me.

I get a little nervous if anyone gets too close emotionally.

Ambivalent Attachment Style

I have often felt misunderstood and unappreciated in my romantic relationships.

My friends and lovers have been somewhat unreliable.

I love my romantic partner but I worry that she or he doesn't really love me.

I would like to be closer to my romantic partner, but I'm not sure I trust her or him.

Do any of the preceding statements sound familiar? If so, they may describe your adult attachment style. Most adults have a secure attachment style that is marked by caring, supportiveness, and understanding. However, it's not unusual to have an avoidant attachment style that reflects a tendency to resist intimacy and commitment to others (Collins et al., 2002). An ambivalent attachment style is marked by mixed feelings about love and friendship (Tidwell, Reis, & Shaver, 1996). Do you see any similarities between your present relationships and your attachment experiences as a child?

Parental Influences—Life with Mom and Dad

SURVEY QUESTION: *How important are parenting styles?*

From the first few years of life, when caregivers are the center of a child's world, through to adulthood, the style and quality of mothering and fathering are very important.

Parenting Styles

Psychologist Diana Baumrind (1991, 2005) has studied the effects of three major **parental styles,** which are identifiable patterns of parental caretaking and interaction with children. See if you recognize the styles she describes.

Authoritarian parents enforce rigid rules and demand strict obedience to authority. Typically they view children as having few rights but adult-like responsibilities. The child is expected to stay out of trouble and to accept, without question, what parents regard as right or wrong. ("Do it because I say so.") The children of authoritarian parents are usually obedient and self-controlled. But they also tend to be emotionally stiff, withdrawn, apprehensive, and lacking in curiosity.

Overly permissive parents give little guidance, allow too much freedom, or don't hold children accountable for their actions. Typically, the child has rights similar to an adult's but few responsibilities. Rules are not enforced, and the child usually gets his or her way. ("Do whatever you want.") Per-missive parents tend to produce dependent, immature children who misbehave frequently. Such children are aimless and likely to "run amok."

Baumrind describes **authoritative parents** as those who supply firm and consistent guidance, combined with love and affection. Such parents balance their own rights with those of their children. They control their children's behavior in a caring, responsive, nonauthoritarian way. ("Do it for this reason.") Effective parents are firm and consistent, not harsh or rigid. In general, they encourage the child to act responsibly, to think, and to make good decisions. This style produces

---

Secure attachment A stable and positive emotional bond.

Insecure-avoidant attachment An anxious emotional bond marked by a tendency to avoid reunion with a parent or caregiver.

Insecure-ambivalent attachment An anxious emotional bond marked by both a desire to be with a parent or caregiver and some resistance to being reunited.

Affectional needs Emotional needs for love and affection.

Parental styles Identifiable patterns of parental caretaking and interaction with children.

Authoritarian parents Parents who enforce rigid rules and demand strict obedience to authority.

Overly permissive parents Parents who give little guidance, allow too much freedom, or do not require the child to take responsibility.

Authoritative parents Parents who supply firm and consistent guidance combined with love and affection.

Close to Home

© 1993 John McPherson/Distributed by Universal Press Syndicate 3-20

"All right now, give Mommy the super-glue."

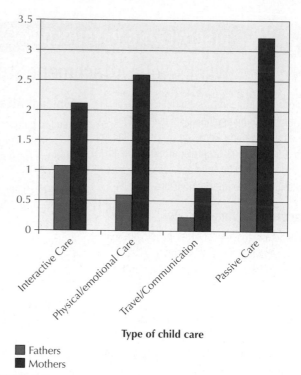

● **FIGURE 3.13** Mother-child and father-child interactions. This graph shows what occurred on routine days in a sample of more than 1,400 Australian homes. Mothers spend about twice as long each day on child care, compared with fathers. Further, mothers spend more time on physical and emotional care (e.g., feeding, bathing, soothing) than on interactive care (e.g., playing, reading, activities); fathers show the reverse pattern. Finally, mothers spend more time on travel (e.g., driving children to sports or music lessons), communication (e.g., talking to teachers about their children), and passive care (e.g., supervising children while they play). (Adapted from Craig, 2006.)

children who are *resilient* (good at bouncing back after bad experiences) and develop the strengths they need to thrive even in difficult circumstances (Kim-Cohen et al., 2004; Masten, 2001). The children of authoritative parents are competent, self-controlled, independent, assertive, and inquiring. They know how to manage their emotions and use positive coping skills (Eisenberg et al., 2003; Lynch et al., 2004). To read more about effective parenting, see this chapter's "Psychology in Action" module.

Maternal and Paternal Influences

Don't mothers and fathers parent differently? Yes. Although **maternal influences** (all the effects a mother has on her child) generally have a greater impact, fathers do make a unique contribution to parenting (Santrock, 2007). Although fathers are spending more time with their children, mothers still do most of the nurturing and caretaking, especially of young children (Craig, 2006).

Studies of **paternal influences** (the sum of all effects a father has on his child) reveal that fathers are more likely to play with their children and tell them stories. In contrast, mothers are typically responsible for the physical and emotional care of their children (● Fig. 3.13).

It might seem that the father's role as a playmate makes him less important. Not so. Amy's playtime with Tom is actually very valuable. From birth onward, fathers pay more visual attention to children than mothers do. Fathers are much more tactile (lifting, tickling, and handling the baby), more physically arousing (engaging in rough-and-tumble play),

and more likely to engage in unusual play (imitating the baby, for example) (Crawley & Sherrod, 1984; Paquette et al., 2003). In comparison, mothers speak to infants more, play more conventional games (such as peekaboo), and, as noted, spend much more time in care giving. Young children

Fathering typically makes a contribution to early development that differs in emphasis from mothering.

who spend a lot of time playing with their fathers tend to be more competent in many ways (Tamis-LeMonda, et al., 2004).

Overall, fathers can be as affectionate, sensitive, and responsive as mothers are. Nevertheless, infants and children tend to get very different views of males and females. Females, who offer comfort, nurturance, and verbal stimulation, tend to be close at hand. Males come and go, and when they are present, action, exploration, and risk-taking prevail. It's no wonder, then, that the parental styles of mothers and fathers have a major impact on children's gender role development (Lindsay, Mize, & Pettit, 1997; Videon, 2005).

Ethnic Differences: Four Flavors of Parenting

Do ethnic differences in parenting affect children in distinctive ways? Diana Baumrind's work provides a good overall summary of the effects of parenting. However, her conclusions are probably most valid for families whose roots lie in Europe. Child-rearing in other ethnic groups often reflects different customs and beliefs. Cultural differences are especially apparent with respect to the meaning attached to a child's behavior. Is a particular behavior "good" or "bad"? Should it be encouraged or discouraged? The answer will depend greatly on parents' cultural values (Leyendecker et al., 2005).

Making generalizations about groups of people is always risky. Nevertheless, some typical differences in child-rearing patterns have been observed in North American ethnic communities (Kaplan, 1998; Parke, 2004).

African-American Families Traditional African-American values emphasize loyalty and interdependence among family members, security, developing a positive identity, and not giving up in the face of adversity. African-American parents typically stress obedience and respect for elders. Child discipline tends to be fairly strict (Parke, 2004), but many African-American parents see this as a necessity, especially if they live in urban areas where safety is a concern. Self-reliance, resourcefulness, and an ability to take care of oneself in difficult situations are also qualities that African-American parents seek to promote in their children.

Hispanic Families Like African-American parents, Hispanic parents tend to have relatively strict standards of discipline. They also place a high value on family values, family pride, and loyalty. Hispanic families are typically affectionate and indulgent toward younger children. However, as children grow older, they are expected to learn social skills and to be calm, obedient, courteous, and respectful. In fact, such social skills may be valued more than cognitive skills (Delgado & Ford, 1998). In addition, Hispanic parents tend to stress co-operation more than competition. Such values can put Hispanic children at a disadvantage in highly competitive, European-American culture.

Asian-American Families Asian cultures tend to be group oriented, and they emphasize interdependence among individuals. In contrast, Western cultures value individual effort and independence. This difference is often reflected in Asian-American child-rearing practices (Chao & Tseng, 2002). Asian-American children are taught that their behavior can bring either pride or shame to the family. Therefore, they are obliged to set aside their own desires when the greater good of the family is at stake (Parke, 2004). Parents tend to act as teachers who encourage hard work, moral behavior, and achievement. For the first few years, parenting is lenient and permissive. However, after about age 5, Asian-American parents begin to expect respect, obedience, self-control, and self-discipline from their children.

In other ethnic communities, norms for effective parenting often differ in subtle ways from parenting styles in Euro-American culture.

Maternal influences The aggregate of all psychological effects mothers have on their children.

Paternal influences The aggregate of all psychological effects fathers have on their children.

Arab-American Families In Middle Eastern cultures, children are expected to be polite, obedient, disciplined, and conforming. Punishment generally consists of spankings, teasing, or shaming in front of others. Arab-American fathers tend to be strong authority figures who demand obedience so that the family will not be shamed by a child's bad behavior. Success, generosity, and hospitality are highly valued in Arab-American culture. The pursuit of family honor encourages hard work, thrift, conservatism, and educational achievement. The welfare of the family is emphasized over individual identity. Thus, Arab-American children are raised to respect their parents, members of their extended family, and other adults as well (Erickson & Al-Timimi, 2001; Medhus, 2001).

Implications Child-rearing is done in a remarkable variety of ways around the world. In fact, many of the things we do in North America, such as forcing young children to sleep alone, would be considered odd or wrong in other cultures. In the final analysis, parenting can only be judged if we know what culture or ethnic community a child is being prepared to enter (Leyendecker et al., 2005).

MODULE **3.3 Summary**

Of what significance is a child's emotional bond with parents?

- Opportunities for social interaction increase as infants develop self-awareness and they begin to actively seek guidance from adults.

- Emotional attachment of human infants is a critical early event.
- Infant attachment is reflected by separation anxiety. The quality of attachment can be classified as secure, insecure-avoidant, or insecure-ambivalent.
- Secure attachment is fostered by consistent care from parents who are sensitive to a baby's signals and rhythms.
- High-quality day care is not harmful and can even be helpful to preschool children. Low-quality care can be risky.
- Meeting a baby's affectional needs is as important as meeting needs for physical care.

How important are parenting styles?

- Studies suggest that parental styles have a substantial impact on emotional and intellectual development.
- Three major parental styles are authoritarian, permissive, and authoritative (effective). Authoritative parenting appears to benefit children the most.
- Whereas mothers typically emphasize care giving, fathers tend to function as playmates for infants. Both care-giving styles contribute to the competence of young children.
- The ultimate success of various parenting styles depends on what culture or ethnic community a child will enter.
- Parenting styles vary across cultures.

KNOWLEDGE BUILDER

Social Development in Childhood

Recite

1. Clear signs of self-awareness or self-recognition are evident in most infants by the time they reach 8 months of age. T or F?

2. The development of separation anxiety in an infant corresponds to the formation of an attachment to parents. T or F?

3. High-quality day care can actually improve children's social and mental skills. T or F?

4. Fathers are more likely to act as playmates for their children, rather than caregivers. T or F?

5. According to Diana Baumrind's research, effective parents are authoritarian in their approach to their children's behavior. T or F?

6. Asian-American parents tend to be more individually oriented than parents whose ethnic roots are European. T or F?

Reflect
Critical Thinking

7. Can you think of another way to tell if infants have self-awareness?

8. Can emotional bonding begin before birth?

9. If power assertion is a poor way to discipline children, why do so many parents use it?

Relate

Do you think that your experiences as a child, such as your early attachment pattern, really affect your life as an adult? Can you think of any examples from your own life?

Do you know any parents who have young children and who are authoritarian, permissive, or authoritative? What are their children like?

Do you think parenting depends on ethnicity? If so, why? If not, why not?

Link

Internet addresses frequently change. To find the sites listed here, visit **http://www .thomsonedu.com/psychology/coon** for an updated list of Internet addresses and direct links to relevant sites.

- **I'm Embarrassed!** Read more about the development of self-awareness in young children.

- **Attachment Theory** Read more on attachment styles.

- **How to Choose a Daycare That's Right for Your Child** An information resource about day care options.

ANSWERS

1. F 2. T 3. T 4. T 5. F 6. F 7. Another successful method is to secretly rub a spot of rouge on an infant's nose. The child is then placed in front of a mirror. The question is, Will the child touch the red spot, showing recognition of the mirror image as his or her own? The probability that a child will do so jumps dramatically during the second year. 8. It certainly can for parents. When a pregnant woman begins to feel fetal movements, she becomes aware that a baby is coming to life inside of her. Likewise, prospective parents who hear a fetal heartbeat at the doctor's office or see an ultrasound image of the fetus begin to become emotionally attached to the unborn child (Santrock, 2007). 9. Most parents discipline their children in the same ways that they themselves were disciplined. Parenting is a responsibility of tremendous importance, for which most people receive almost no training.

3.5 Cognitive Development in Childhood

JEAN PIAGET provided some of the first great insights into how children develop thinking abilities. Piaget proposed that children's cognitive skills progress through a series of maturational stages. Although Piaget's theory has been very valuable, psychologists continue to update his ideas. Also, many psychologists have become interested in how children learn the intellectual skills valued by their culture. Typically, children do this with guidance from skilled "tutors" (parents and others).

Cognitive Development—How Do Children Learn to Think?

SURVEY QUESTION: *How DO children learn to think?*

Now that we have Amy talking, let's move on to a broader view of intellectual development. Jean Piaget (Jahn pea-ah-ZHAY) provided some of the first great insights into how children develop thinking abilities.

How different is a child's understanding of the world from that of an adult? Generally speaking, their thinking is less abstract. Children use fewer generalizations, categories, and principles. They also tend to base their understanding on particular examples and objects they can see or touch.

Before the age of 6 or 7, thinking is very concrete. Younger children cannot make **transformations** in which they must mentally change the shape or form of a substance (such as clay or water). Let's visit Amy at age 5: If you show her a short, wide glass full of milk and a taller, narrow glass (also full), she will most likely tell you that the taller glass contains more milk (even if it doesn't). Amy will tell you this even if she watches you pour milk from the short glass into an empty, tall glass. She is not bothered by the fact that the milk appears to be transformed from a smaller to a larger amount. Instead, she responds only to the fact that *taller* seems to mean *more.* (See ● Fig. 3.15.) After about age 7, children are no longer fooled by this situation. Perhaps that's why 7 has been called the "age of reason." From age 7 on, we see a definite trend toward more logical, adult-like thought (Flavell, 1992).

Is there any pattern to the growth of intellect in childhood? According to the Swiss psychologist and philosopher Jean Piaget (1951, 1952), there is.

Piaget's Theory of Cognitive Development

Jean Piaget believed that all children mature through a series of distinct stages in intellectual development. Many of his ideas came from observing his own children as they solved

● **FIGURE 3.15** Children under age 7 intuitively assume that a volume of liquid increases when it is poured from a short, wide container into a taller, thinner one. This boy thinks the tall container holds more than the short one. Actually each holds the same amount of liquid. Children make such judgments based on the height of the liquid, not its volume.

various thought problems. (It is tempting to imagine that Piaget's illustrious career was launched one day when his wife said to him, "Watch the children for a while, will you, Jean?")

Mental Adaptations Piaget was convinced that intellect grows through processes he called assimilation and accommodation. **Assimilation** refers to using existing mental patterns in new situations. Let's say that a plastic hammer is the favorite toy of a boy named Benjamin, who pounds on blocks with it. For his birthday Benjamin gets an oversized toy wrench. If he uses the wrench for pounding, it has been assimilated to an existing knowledge structure.

Jean Piaget—philosopher, psychologist, and keen observer of children.

In **accommodation,** existing ideas are modified to fit new requirements. For instance, a younger child might think that a dime is worth less than a (larger) nickel. However, as children begin to spend money, they must alter their ideas about what "more" and "less" mean. Thus, new situations are assimilated to existing ideas, and new ideas are created to accommodate new experiences.

Piaget's ideas have deeply affected our view of children (Feldman, 2004). The following is a brief summary of what he found.

The Sensorimotor Stage (0–2 Years) In the first 2 years of life, Amy's intellectual development will be largely nonverbal. She will be mainly concerned with learning to coordinate information from her senses with her motor movements. Also, **object permanence** (an understanding that objects continue to exist when they are out of sight) emerges at this time. Sometime during their first year, babies begin to actively pursue disappearing objects. By age 2, they can anticipate the movement of an object behind a screen. For example, when watching an electric train, Amy will look ahead to the end of a tunnel, rather than staring at the spot where the train disappeared.

In general, developments in this stage indicate that the child's conceptions are becoming more *stable.* Objects cease to appear and disappear magically, and a more orderly and predictable world replaces the confusing and disconnected sensations of infancy.

The Preoperational Stage (2–7 Years) During this period, children begin to think *symbolically* and use language. But the child's thinking is still very **intuitive** (it makes little use of reasoning and logic). (Do you remember thinking as a child that the sun and the moon followed you when you took a walk?) In addition, the child's use of language is not as sophisticated as it might seem. Children have a tendency to confuse words with the objects they represent. If Benjamin calls a toy block a "car" and you use it to make a "house," he may be upset. To children, the name of an object is as much a part of the object as its size, shape, and color. This seems to underlie a preoccupation with name calling. To the preoperational child, insulting words may really hurt. Consider one rather protected youngster who was angered by her older brother. Searching for a way to retaliate against her larger and stronger foe, she settled on, "You panty-girdle!" It was the worst thing she could think of saying.

During the preoperational stage, the child is also quite **egocentric** (unable to take the viewpoint of other people). The child's ego seems to stand at the center of his or her world. To illustrate, show Amy a two-sided mirror. Then hold it between you and her, so she can see herself in it. If you ask her what she thinks *you* can see, she imagines that you see *her* face reflected in the mirror, instead of your own. Such egocentrism explains why children can seem exasperatingly selfish or uncooperative at times. If Benjamin blocks your view by standing in front of the TV, he assumes that you can see it if he can. If you ask him to move so you can see better,

Crossing a busy street can be dangerous for the preoperational child. Because their thinking is still egocentric, younger children cannot understand why the driver of a car can't see them if they can see the car. Children under the age of 7 also cannot consistently judge speeds and distances of oncoming cars. Adults can easily overestimate the "street smarts" of younger children. It is advisable to teach children to cross with a light, in crosswalks, or with assistance.

he may move so that he can see better! Benjamin is not being selfish in the ordinary sense. He just doesn't realize that your view differs from his.

The Concrete Operational Stage (7–11 Years) An important development during this stage is mastery of **conservation** (the concept that mass, weight, and volume remain un-

---

Transformation The mental ability to change the shape or form of a substance (such as clay or water) and to perceive that its volume remains the same.

Assimilation In Piaget's theory, the application of existing mental patterns to new situations (that is, the new situation is assimilated to existing mental schemes).

Accommodation In Piaget's theory, the modification of existing mental patterns to fit new demands (that is, mental schemes are changed to accommodate new information or experiences).

Sensorimotor stage Stage of intellectual development during which sensory input and motor responses become coordinated.

Object permanence Concept, gained in infancy, that objects continue to exist even when they are hidden from view.

Preoperational stage Period of intellectual development during which children begin to use language and think symbolically, yet remain intuitive and egocentric in their thought.

Intuitive thought Thinking that makes little or no use of reasoning and logic.

Egocentric thought Thought that is self-centered and fails to consider the viewpoints of others.

Concrete operational stage Period of intellectual development during which children become able to use the concepts of time, space, volume, and number, but in ways that remain simplified and concrete, rather than abstract.

Conservation In Piaget's theory, mastery of the concept that the weight, mass, and volume of matter remains unchanged (is conserved) even when the shape or appearance of objects changes.

changed when the shape of objects changes). Children have learned conservation when they understand that rolling a ball of clay into a "snake" does not increase the amount of clay. Likewise, pouring liquid from a tall, narrow glass into a shallow dish does not reduce the amount of liquid. In each case the volume remains the same despite changes in shape or appearance. The original amount is *conserved.* (See Fig. 3.15.)

During the concrete operational stage, children begin to use concepts of time, space, and number. The child can think logically about very concrete objects or situations, categories, and principles. Such abilities explain why children stop believing in Santa Claus when they reach this stage. Because they can conserve volume, they realize that Santa's sack couldn't possibly hold enough toys for millions of girls and boys.

Another important development at this time is the ability to *reverse* thoughts or mental operations. A 4-year-old boy in the preoperational stage might have a conversation like this (showing what happens when a child's thinking *lacks* reversibility):

"Do you have a brother?"

"Yes."

"What's his name?"

"Sam."

"Does Sam have a brother?"

"No."

Reversibility of thought allows children in the concrete operational stage to recognize that if $4 \times 2 = 8$, then 2×4 does, too. Younger children must memorize each relationship separately. Thus, a preoperational child may know that $4 \times 9 = 36$, without being able to tell you what 9×4 equals.

The Formal Operations Stage (11 Years and Up) After about the age of 11, children begin to break away from concrete objects and specific examples. Thinking is based more on abstract principles, such as "democracy," "honor," or "correlation." Children who reach this stage can think about their thoughts, and they become less egocentric. Older children and young adolescents also gradually become able to consider hypothetical possibilities (suppositions, guesses, or projections). For example, if you ask a younger child, "What do you think would happen if it suddenly became possible for people to fly?" the child might respond, "People can't fly." Older children are able to consider such possibilities.

Full adult intellectual ability is attained during the stage of formal operations. Older adolescents are capable of inductive and deductive reasoning, and they can comprehend math, physics, philosophy, psychology, and other abstract systems. They can learn to test hypotheses in a scientific manner. Of course, not everyone reaches this level of thinking. Also, many adults can think formally about some topics, but their thinking becomes concrete when the topic is unfamiliar.

This implies that formal thinking may be more a result of culture and learning than maturation. In any case, after late adolescence, improvements in intellect are based on gaining specific knowledge, experience, and wisdom, rather than on any leaps in basic thinking capacity.

How can parents apply Piaget's ideas? Piaget's theory suggests that the ideal way to guide intellectual development is to provide experiences that are only slightly novel, unusual, or challenging. Remember, a child's intellect develops mainly through accommodation. It is usually best to follow a *one-step-ahead strategy,* in which your teaching efforts are aimed just beyond a child's current level of comprehension (Brainerd, 2003).

Parents should avoid *forced teaching,* or "hothousing," which is like trying to force plants to bloom prematurely. Forcing children to learn reading, math, gymnastics, swimming, or music at an accelerated pace can bore or oppress them. True intellectual enrichment respects the child's interests. It does not make the child feel pressured to perform (Alvino et al., 1996).

For your convenience, ■ Table 3.2 briefly summarizes each Piagetian stage. To help you remember Piaget's theory, the table describes what would happen at each stage if we played a game of *Monopoly* with the child. You'll also find brief suggestions about how to relate to children in each stage.

Piaget Today

Piaget's theory is a valuable "road map" for understanding how children think. However, many psychologists are convinced that Piaget gave too little credit to the effects of the learning environment. For example, children who grow up in villages where pottery is made can correctly answer questions about the conservation of clay at an earlier age than Piaget would have predicted.

According to learning theorists, children continuously gain specific knowledge; they do not undergo stage-like leaps in general mental ability (Siegler, 2004). On the other hand, the growth in connections between brain cells occurs in waves that parallel some of Piaget's stages. (See ● Fig. 3.16.) Thus, the truth may lie somewhere between Piaget's stage theory and modern learning theory.

On a broad scale, many of Piaget's *observations* have held up well. However, his *explanations* of childhood thinking abilities continue to be debated (Feldman, 2004). Where early infancy is concerned, even Piaget's observations may need updating. It looks like Piaget greatly underestimated the mental abilities of infants.

Infant Cognition *What evidence is there that Piaget underestimated infant abilities?* Piaget believed that infants under the age of 1 year cannot think. Babies, he said, have no memory

■ TABLE 3.2 Piaget—A Guide for Parents

PIAGET	*MONOPOLY* GAME	GUIDELINES FOR PARENTS
Sensorimotor Stage (0–2 Years) The stage during which sensory input and motor responses become coordinated.	The child puts houses, hotels, and dice in her mouth and plays with "Chance" cards.	Active play with a child is most effective at this stage. Encourage explorations in touching, smelling, and manipulating objects. Peekaboo is a good way to establish the permanence of objects.
Preoperational Stage (2–7 Years) The period of cognitive development when children begin to use language and think symbolically, yet remain intuitive and egocentric.	The child plays *Monopoly*, but makes up her own rules and cannot understand instructions.	Specific examples and touching or seeing things continues to be more useful than verbal explanations. Learning the concept of conservation may be aided by demonstrations with liquids, beads, clay, and other substances.
Concrete Operational Stage (7–11 Years) The period of cognitive development during which children begin to use concepts of time, space, volume, and number, but in ways that remain simplified and concrete.	The child understands basic instructions and will play by the rules but is not capable of hypothetical transactions dealing with mortgages, loans, and special pacts with other players.	Children are beginning to use generalizations, but they still require specific examples to grasp many ideas. Expect a degree of inconsistency in the child's ability to apply concepts of time, space, quantity, and volume to new situations.
Formal Operations Stage (11 Years and Up) The period of intellectual development marked by a capacity for abstract, theoretical, and hypothetical thinking.	The child no longer plays the game mechanically; complex and hypothetical transactions unique to each game are now possible.	It is now more effective to explain things verbally or symbolically and to help children master general rules and principles. Encourage the child to create hypotheses and to imagine how things could be.

3 to 6 years

7 to 15 years

16 to 20 years

Growth

Pruning

● **FIGURE 3.16** Between the ages of 3 and 6 a tremendous wave of growth occurs in connections among neurons in the frontal areas of the brain. This corresponds to the time when children make rapid progress in their ability to think symbolically. Between ages 7 and 15, peak synaptic growth shifts to the temporal and parietal lobes. During this period children become increasingly adept at using language, a specialty of the temporal lobes. In the late teens, the brain actively destroys unneeded connections, especially in the frontal lobes. This pruning of synapses sharpens the brain's capacity for abstract thinking (Restak, 2001).

of people and objects that are out of sight. Yet, we now know that infants begin forming representations of the world very early in life. For example, babies as young as 3 months of age appear to know that objects are solid and do not disappear when out of view (Baillargeon, 2004).

Why did Piaget fail to detect the thinking skills of infants? Most likely, he mistook babies' limited *physical* skills for *mental* incompetence. Piaget's tests required babies to search for objects or reach out and touch them. Newer, more sensitive methods are uncovering abilities Piaget missed. One such method takes advantage of the fact that babies, like adults, act surprised when they see something "impossible" or unexpected occur. To use this effect, psychologist Renee Baillargeon (1991, 2004) puts on little "magic shows" for infants. In her "theater," babies watch as possible and impossible events occur with toys or other objects. Some 3-month-old infants act surprised and gaze longer at impossible events. An example is seeing two solid objects appear to pass through each other. By the time they are 8 months old, babies can remember where objects are (or should be) for at least 1 minute (● Fig. 3.17).

Formal operations stage Period of intellectual development characterized by thinking that includes abstract, theoretical, and hypothetical ideas.

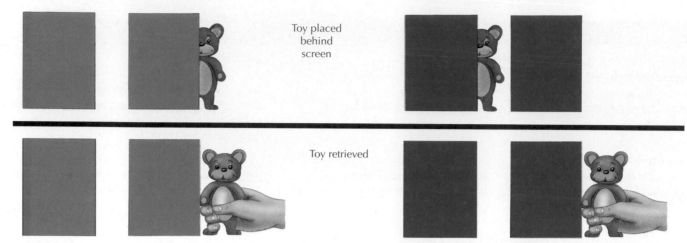

● **FIGURE 3.17** The panels on the left show a possible event, in which an infant watches as a toy is placed behind the right of two screens. After a delay of 70 seconds, the toy is brought into view from behind the right screen. In the two panels on the right, an impossible event occurs. The toy is placed behind the left screen and retrieved from behind the right. (A duplicate toy was hidden there before testing.) Eight-month-old infants react with surprise when they see the impossible event staged for them. Their reaction implies that they remember where the toy was hidden. Infants appear to have a capacity for memory and thinking that greatly exceeds what Piaget claimed is possible during the sensorimotor period. (Adapted from Baillargeon et al., 1989.)

Piaget believed that abilities like those described in Figure 3.17 emerge only after a long period of sensorimotor development. However, it's clear that babies quickly acquire the capacity to form concepts about the world (Eimas, Quinn, & Cowan, 1994). It looks as if further study is likely to refine and amend the ideas that grew from Piaget's fateful decision to "watch the children for a while."

Another criticism of Piaget is that he underestimated the impact of culture on mental development. The next section tells how Amy will master the intellectual tools valued by her culture.

Vygotsky's Sociocultural Theory

Whereas Piaget stressed the role of maturation in cognitive development, Russian scholar Lev Vygotsky (1896–1934) focused on the impact of sociocultural factors. Vygotsky's key insight is that children's thinking develops through dialogues with more capable persons (Vygotsky, 1962, 1978).

How does that relate to intellectual growth? So far, no one has ever published *A Child's Guide to Life on Earth.* Instead, children must learn about life from various "tutors," such as parents, teachers, and older siblings. Even if *A Child's Guide to Life on Earth* did exist, we would need a separate version for every culture. It is not enough for children to learn how to think. They must also learn specific intellectual skills valued by their culture.

Like Piaget, Vygotsky believed that children actively seek to discover new principles. However, Vygotsky emphasized that many of a child's most important "discoveries" are guided by skillful tutors. Psychologist David Shaffer (2002) offers the following example:

Annie, a 4-year-old, has just received her first jigsaw puzzle as a birthday present. She attempts to work the puzzle but gets nowhere until her father comes along, sits down beside her, and gives her some tips. He suggests that it would be a good idea to put together the corners first, points to the pink area at the edge of one corner piece and says, "Let's look for another pink piece." When Annie seems frustrated, he places two interlocking pieces near each other so that she will notice them, and when Annie succeeds, he offers words of encouragement. As Annie gradually gets the hang of it, he steps back and lets her work more and more independently. (p. 260.)

Interactions like this are most helpful when they take place within a child's **zone of proximal development.**

What did Vygotsky mean by that? The word *proximal* means close or nearby. Vygotsky realized that, at any given time, some tasks are just beyond a child's reach. The child is close to having the mental skills needed to do the task, but it is a little too complex to be mastered alone. However, children working within this zone can make rapid progress if they receive sensitive guidance from a skilled partner (LeBlanc & Bearison, 2004).

Vygotsky also emphasized a process he called **scaffolding.** A scaffold is a framework or temporary support. Vygotsky believed that adults help children learn how to think by "scaffolding," or supporting, their attempts to solve problems or discover principles (Daniels, 2005). To be most effective, scaffolding must be responsive to a child's needs. For example, as Annie's father helped her with the puzzle, he tailored his hints and guidance to match her evolving abilities. The two of them worked together, step by step, so that Annie could better understand how to assemble a puzzle. In a sense, Annie's father set up a series of temporary bridges that helped her move into new mental territory. As predicted by Vygotsky's theory, the reading skills of 8- to 10-year-old children are closely related to the amount of verbal scaffolding their mothers provided at ages 3 and 4 (Dieterich et al., 2006).

During their collaborations with others, children learn important cultural beliefs and values. For example, imagine that a boy wants to know how many baseball cards he has. His mother helps him stack and count the cards, moving each card to a new stack as they count it. She then shows him how to write the number on a slip of paper so he can remember it. This teaches the child not only about counting, but also that writing is valued in our culture. In other parts of the world, a child learning to count might be shown how to make notches on a stick or tie knots in a cord.

Implications Vygotsky saw that grown-ups play a crucial role in what children know. As they try to decipher the world, children rely on adults to help them understand how things work. Vygotsky further noticed that adults unconsciously adjust their behavior to give children the information they need to solve problems that interest the child. In this way, children use adults to learn about their culture and society (Gopnik, Meltzoff, & Kuhl, 2000; LeBlanc & Bearison, 2004).

MODULE 3.5 Summary

How do children learn to think?

- The intellect of a child is less abstract than that of an adult. Jean Piaget theorized that intellectual growth occurs through a combination of assimilation and accommodation.
- Piaget also held that children mature through a fixed series of cognitive stages. The stages and their approximate age ranges are sensorimotor (0–2), preoperational (2–7), concrete operational (7–11), and formal operations (11–adult).
- Caregivers should offer learning opportunities that are appropriate for a child's level of cognitive development.
- Learning principles provide an alternate explanation that assumes cognitive development is continuous; it does not occur in stages.
- Recent studies of infants under the age of 1 year suggest that they are capable of thought well beyond that observed by Piaget.
- Lev Vygotsky's sociocultural theory emphasizes that a child's mental abilities are advanced by interactions with more competent partners. Mental growth takes place in a child's zone of proximal development, where a more skillful person may scaffold the child's progress. As children rely on adults to help them discover new skills and principles, they learn cultural beliefs and values.

Zone of proximal development Refers to the range of tasks a child cannot yet master alone, but that she or he can accomplish with the guidance of a more capable partner.

Scaffolding The process of adjusting instruction so that it is responsive to a beginner's behavior and supports the beginner's efforts to understand a problem or gain a mental skill.

KNOWLEDGE BUILDER

Cognitive Development in Childhood

Recite

Match each item with one of the following stages.

A. Sensorimotor B. Preoperational C. Concrete operational D. Formal operations

1. ____ egocentric thought
2. ____ abstract or hypothetical
3. ____ purposeful movement
4. ____ intuitive thought
5. ____ conservation
6. ____ reversibility thought
7. ____ object permanence
8. ____ nonverbal development
9. *Assimilation* refers to applying existing thought patterns or knowledge to new situations. T or F?
10. Newer methods for testing infant thinking abilities frequently make note of whether

an infant is _____ by seemingly _____ events.

11. Vygotsky called the process of providing a temporary framework of supports for learning new mental abilities

_____.

Reflect
Critical Thinking

12. Using Piaget's theory as a guide, at what age would you expect a child to recognize that a Styrofoam cup has weight?

Relate

You are going to make cookies with children of various ages. See if you can name each of Piaget's stages and give an example of what a child in that stage might be expected to do.

You have been asked to help a child learn to use a pocket calculator to do simple addi-

tion. How would you go about identifying the child's zone of proximal development for this task? How would you scaffold the child's learning?

Link

Internet addresses frequently change. To find the sites listed here, visit **http://www .thomsonedu.com/psychology/coon** for an updated list of Internet addresses and direct links to relevant sites.

- **Jean Piaget Archives: Biography** The life of Jean Piaget, plus five photos from birth to old age.
- **Jean Piaget and Cognitive Development** Read a fuller account of Piaget's theory.
- **Scaffolding as a Teaching Strategy** Download a paper on the application of Vygotsky's idea of scaffolding to teaching.

ANSWERS

1. B 2. D 3. A 4. B 5. C 6. C 7. A 8. A 9. T 10. surprised, impossible 11. scaffolding 12. Seventy-five percent of 4- to 6-year-olds say that a Styrofoam cup has no weight after lifting it! Most children judge weight intuitively (by the way an object feels) until they begin to move into the concrete operational stage (Smith, Carey, & Wiser, 1985).

3.6 Adolescence, Young Adulthood, and Moral Development

ADOLESCENCE and young adulthood is a time of change, exploration, exuberance, and youthful searching. It can also be a time of worry and problems, especially in today's world. It might even be fair to describe this period as "the best of times, the worst of times." During adolescence, a person's identity and moral values come into sharper focus even as the transition to adulthood is occurring at ever-later ages.

Adolescence and Young Adulthood— The Best of Times, the Worst of Times

SURVEY QUESTION: *Why is development during adolescence and young adulthood especially challenging?*

Adolescence is the culturally defined period between childhood and adulthood. Socially, the adolescent is no longer a child, yet not quite an adult. Almost all cultures recognize this transitional status. However, the length of adolescence varies greatly from culture to culture. For example, most 14-year-old girls in North America live at home and go to school. In contrast, many 14-year-old females in rural villages of many poorer countries are married and have children. In our culture, 14-year-olds are adolescents. In others, they may be adults.

Is marriage the primary criterion for adult status in North America? No, it's not even one of the top three criteria. Today, the most widely accepted standards are (1) taking responsibility for oneself, (2) making independent decisions, and (3) becoming financially independent. In practice, this typically means breaking away from parents by taking a job and setting up a separate residence (Arnett, 2001).

Puberty

Many people confuse adolescence with puberty. However, puberty is a *biological* event, not a social status. During **puberty,** hormonal changes promote rapid physical growth and sexual maturity. Biologically, most people reach reproductive maturity in the early teens. Social and intellectual maturity, however, may lie years ahead. Young adolescents often make decisions that affect their entire lives, even though they are immature mentally and socially. The tragically high rates of teenage pregnancy and drug abuse are prime examples. Despite such risks, most people do manage to weather adolescence without developing any serious psychological problems (Steinberg, 2001).

How much difference does the timing of puberty make? For boys, maturing early is generally beneficial. Typically, it enhances their self-image and gives them an advantage socially and athletically. Early-maturing boys tend to be more relaxed, dominant, self-assured, and popular. However, early puberty does carry some risks because early-maturing boys are also more likely to get into trouble with drugs, alcohol, and antisocial behavior (Steinberg, 2001).

For girls, the advantages of early maturation are less clear-cut. In elementary school, fast-maturing girls are *less* popular and have poorer self-images, perhaps because they are larger and heavier than their classmates (Alsaker, 1992). By junior high, however, early development includes sexual features. This leads to a more positive body image, *greater* peer prestige, and adult approval (Brooks-Gunn & Warren, 1988). Early-maturing girls tend to date sooner and are more independent and more active in school. However, like their male counterparts, they are also more often in trouble at school and more likely to engage in early sex (Flannery, Rowe, & Gulley, 1993).

As you can see, there are costs and benefits associated with early puberty. One added cost of early maturation is that it may force premature identity formation. When a teenager begins to look like an adult, she or he may be treated like an adult. Ideally, this change can encourage greater maturity and independence. However, if the search for identity ends too soon, it may leave the person with a distorted, poorly formed sense of self (● Fig. 3.18).

The Search for Identity

Identity formation is a key task of adolescence. Of course, problems of identity occur at other times too. But in a very real sense, puberty signals that it's time to begin forming a new, more mature self-image (Douvan, 1997). Many problems stem from unclear standards about the role adolescents should play within society. Are they adults or children? Should they be autonomous or dependent? Should they work or play? Such ambiguities make it difficult for young people to form clear images of themselves and of how they should act (Alsaker, 1995).

Adolescence The culturally defined period between childhood and adulthood.

Puberty The biologically defined period during which a person matures sexually and becomes capable of reproduction.

HUMAN DIVERSITY

Ethnic Diversity and Identity

For adolescents of ethnic descent, the question is often not just "Who am I?" Rather, it is "Who am I at home? Who am I at school? Who am I with friends from my neighborhood?"

Ethnic heritage can have a powerful influence on personal identity (Weisskirch, 2005). Yet, at a time when teens are trying to find their place in society, they may feel rejected or excluded because of their ethnic heritage. In America, popular culture is loaded with images that dismiss anyone who doesn't look like Scarlett Johansson or Orlando Bloom. Also,

ethnic adolescents often face degrading stereotypes concerning their intelligence, sexuality, social status, manners, and so forth. The result can be lowered self-esteem and confusion about roles, values, and personal identity (de las Fuentes & Vasquez, 1999).

In forming an identity, adolescents of ethnic descent face the question of how they should think of themselves. Is Lori an American or a Chinese American or both? Is Jaime a Latino, a Chicano, or a Mexican American? The answer typically depends on how strongly ado-

lescents identify with their family and ethnic community. Teens who take pride in their ethnic heritage have higher self-esteem, a better self-image, and a stronger sense of personal identity (Roberts et al., 1999; Tse, 1999). They are also less likely to engage in drug use (Marsiglia et al., 2004) or violent behavior (French, Kim, & Pillado, 2006).

Group pride, positive models, and a more tolerant society could do much to keep a broad range of options open to *all* adolescents.

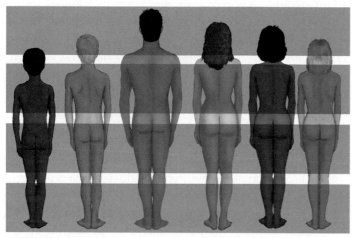

● **FIGURE 3.18** Dramatic differences in physical size and maturity are found in adolescents of the same age. The girls pictured are all 13, the boys 16. Maturation that occurs earlier or later than average can affect the "search for identity." (Adapted from "Growing Up" by J. M. Tanner. Copyright © September 1973 by Scientific American, Inc. All rights reserved.)

Answering the question "Who am I?" is also spurred by cognitive development. After adolescents have attained the stage of formal operations, they are better able to ask questions about their place in the world and about morals, values, politics, and social relationships. Then too, being able to think about hypothetical possibilities allows the adolescent to contemplate the future and ask more realistically, "Who will I be?" (Suls, 1989). (See "Ethnic Diversity and Identity.")

The Transition to Adulthood

Today the challenge of identity formation is further complicated by the fact that more and more young people are deferring young adulthood, preferring to prolong identity explorations into their 20s before they commit to long-term choices in love and work (Arnett, 2000, 2004; Arnett & Tanner, 2006). According to sociologist James Côté, western industrialized societies, like the United States and Canada, are becoming increasingly tolerant of this period of extended adolescence (Côté, 2006). (See "The Twixters.")

CRITICAL THINKING

The Twixters

As you read these modules, we encourage you to reflect on new ideas and concepts by thinking critically about them. Consider, for example, the term *adulthood*. Is becoming an adult strictly a biological event? Meet 22-year old Kirsten:

"When our mothers were our age, they were engaged. . . . They at least had some idea what they were going to do with their lives. . . . I, on the other hand, will have a dual degree in majors that are ambiguous at best and impractical at worst (English and political science), no ring on my finger and no idea who I am, much less what I want to do. . . . I realize that having nothing ahead to count on means I now have to count on myself; that having no direction means forging one of my own." (Page, 1999).

Kirsten is a "twixter": twentysomething, still living at home, not yet married, with no children, and no settled career. In England, twixters are called "kippers" (Kids In Parents' Pockets Eroding Retirement Savings). In Australia they are "boomerang kids" (they always come back home). And in Germany they are "Nesthocker" (nest squatters). Are twixters adolescents who are taking longer to find their identity? Or are they young adults avoiding their need to enter the adult world? Are they self-indulgent individuals trapped in a "maturity gap" (Galambos, Barker, & Tilton-Weaver, 2003)? Or are they part of a new social status that could be called "emerging adulthood" (Arnett & Tanner, 2006)?

According to psychologist Jeffrey Arnett, emerging adulthood is increasingly common in affluent Westernized cultures that allow young people to take longer to settle into their adult roles (Arnett, 2000, 2004). However, in less affluent countries, as in poorer parts of America, most adolescents continue to "become adults" at much younger ages (Arnett & Galambos, 2003). Thus, words like *adolescent* or *adulthood* cannot be defined solely in terms of physical maturation. Sociocultural factors also play a role in defining when we stop being children or become adults (Arnett, 2004).

Amy may live with Olivia and Tom until her mid-20s, delaying her transition to adulthood. Alternately, she may make the transition to young adulthood during the traditional 18-to-21 period. Regardless, she will eventually face the primary adult issues of marriage, children, and career. How she manages, especially in her core relationships, will determine whether she feels a sense of intimacy or feels isolated from others.

In many ways adolescence and young adulthood are more emotionally turbulent than midlife or old age. This is borne out by a national survey in which younger adults reported feeling more negative emotions than older adults did. Likewise, older adults are more likely than younger adults to say they often feel happy, truly alive, and peaceful (● Fig. 3.19). One important aspect of the emotional turbulence of adolescence and young adulthood is the struggle with right and wrong—in other words, the need to develop moral values.

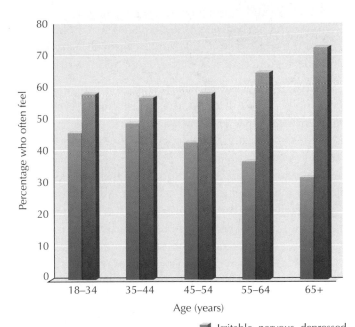

● **FIGURE 3.19** Negative emotions are more common before age 50 than after. The frequency of positive feelings tends to increase from midlife on into old age.

Moral Development— Growing a Conscience

SURVEY QUESTION: *How do we develop morals and values?*

A person with a terminal illness is in great pain. She is pleading for death. Should extraordinary medical efforts be made to keep her alive? A friend of yours desperately needs to pass a test and asks you to help him cheat. Will you do it? These are *moral* questions, or questions of conscience.

Moral development starts in childhood and continues into adulthood (Turiel, 2006). Through this process, we acquire values, beliefs, and thinking patterns that guide responsible behavior. Moral values are especially likely to come into sharper focus during adolescence and the transition to adulthood, as capacities for self-control and abstract thinking increase (Hart & Carlo, 2005). Let's take a brief look at this interesting aspect of personal development.

Levels of Moral Development

How are moral values acquired? In an influential account, psychologist Lawrence Kohlberg (1981) held that we learn moral values through thinking and reasoning. To study moral development, Kohlberg posed dilemmas to children of different ages. The following is one of the moral dilemmas he used (Kohlberg, 1969, adapted).

> A woman was near death from cancer, and there was only one drug that might save her. It was discovered by a druggist who was charging 10 times what it cost to make the drug. The sick woman's husband could only pay $1,000, but the druggist wanted $2,000. He asked the druggist to sell it cheaper or to let him pay later. The druggist said no. So the husband became desperate and broke into the store to steal the drug for his wife. Should he have done that? Was it wrong or right? Why?

Each child was asked what action the husband should take. Kohlberg classified the reasons given for each choice and identified three levels of moral development. Each is based not so much on the choices made, but on the reasoning used to arrive at a choice.

At the lowest, **preconventional level,** moral thinking is guided by the consequences of actions (punishment, reward, or an exchange of favors). For example, a person at this level might reason that "The man shouldn't steal the drug because he could get caught and sent to jail" (avoiding punishment) or "It won't do him any good to steal the drug because his wife will probably die before he gets out of jail" (self-interest).

At the second, or **conventional level,** reasoning is based on a desire to please others or to follow accepted authority, rules, and values. For example, a person at this intermediate level might say "He shouldn't steal the drug because others will think he is a thief. His wife would not want to be saved by thievery" (avoiding disapproval) or "Although his wife needs the drug, he should not break the law to get it. Everyone has to obey the law. His wife's condition does not justify stealing" (traditional morality of authority).

At the highest, or **postconventional level,** moral behavior is directed by self-chosen ethical principles that tend to be general, comprehensive, or universal. People at this level place high value on justice, dignity, and equality. For example, a highly principled person might say "He should steal the drug and then inform the authorities that he has done so. He will have to face a penalty, but he will have saved a human life" (self-chosen ethical principles).

Does everyone eventually reach the highest level? People advance at different rates, and many fail to reach the postconventional level of moral reasoning. In fact, many do not even reach the conventional level. For instance, one English survey revealed that 11 percent of men and 3 percent of women would commit murder for $1 million if they could be sure of getting away with the crime ("They'd kill," 1991).

The preconventional level is most characteristic of young children and delinquents (Forney, Forney, & Crutsinger, 2005). Conventional, group-oriented morals are typical of older children and most adults. Kohlberg estimated that only about 20 percent of the adult population achieves postconventional morality, representing self-direction and higher principles. (It would appear that few of these people enter politics!)

Developing a "moral compass" is an important part of growing up. Many of the choices we make every day involve fundamental questions of right and wrong. Being able to think clearly about such questions is essential to becoming a responsible adult.

Justice or Caring? Carol Gilligan (1982) pointed out that Kohlberg's system is concerned mainly with *justice*. Based on studies of women who faced real-life dilemmas, Gilligan argued that there is also an ethic of *caring* about others. As one illustration, Gilligan presented the following story to 11- to 15-year-old American children.

> **THE PORCUPINE AND THE MOLES**
> Seeking refuge from the cold, a porcupine asked to share a cave for the winter with a family of moles. The moles agreed. But because the cave was small, they soon found they were being scratched each time the porcupine moved about. Finally, they asked the porcupine to leave. But the porcupine refused, saying, "If you moles are not satisfied, I suggest that you leave."

Boys who read this story tended to opt for justice in resolving the dilemma: "It's the moles' house. It's a deal. The porcupine leaves." In contrast, girls tended to look for solutions that would keep all parties happy and comfortable, such as "Cover the porcupine with a blanket."

Gilligan's point is that male psychologists have, for the most part, defined moral maturity in terms of justice and autonomy. From this perspective, a woman's concern with relationships can look like a weakness rather than a strength.

(A woman who is concerned about what pleases or helps others would be placed at the conventional level in Kohlberg's system.) But Gilligan believes that caring is also a major element of moral development, and she suggests that males may lag in achieving it (Botes, 2000; Gilligan & Attanucci, 1988).

Does the evidence support Gilligan's position? Several studies have found little or no difference in men's and women's overall moral reasoning abilities (Glover, 2001; Wilson, 1995). Indeed, both men and women may use caring *and* justice to make moral decisions. The moral yardstick they use appears to depend on the situation they face (Wark & Krebs, 1996). Just the same, Gilligan deserves credit for identifying a second major way in which moral choices are made. It can be argued that our best moral choices combine justice and caring, reason and emotion—which may be what we mean by wisdom (Pasupathi & Staudinger, 2001).

MODULE 3.6 Summary

Why is development during adolescence and young adulthood especially challenging?

- Transitioning from childhood to adulthood requires the formation of a personal identity; the major life task of adolescence. Identity formation is even more challenging for adolescents of ethnic descent.

- In western industrialized societies the transition into adulthood is further complicated as it is increasingly delayed well into the 20s.

How do we develop morals and values?

- Lawrence Kohlberg identified preconventional, conventional, and postconventional levels of moral reasoning.

- Most people function at the conventional level of morality, but some never get beyond the selfish, preconventional level. Only a minority of people attain the highest, or postconventional level, of moral reasoning.

Moral development The development of values, beliefs, and thinking abilities that act as a guide regarding what is acceptable behavior.

Preconventional moral reasoning Moral thinking based on the consequences of one's choices or actions (punishment, reward, or an exchange of favors).

Conventional moral reasoning Moral thinking based on a desire to please others or to follow accepted rules and values.

Postconventional moral reasoning Moral thinking based on carefully examined and self-chosen moral principles.

KNOWLEDGE BUILDER

Adolescence, Young Adulthood, and Moral Development

Recite

1. In North America the primary criterion for the transition from adolescence to adulthood is marriage. T or F?

2. Identify formation is spurred by _____ and _____ _____.

3. According to Jeffrey Arnett, the trend in affluent Westernized cultures towards allowing young people to take longer to settle into their adult roles is best referred to as
   a. emerging adulthood
   b. hurried childhood
   c. a maturity gap
   d. extended adolescence

4. According to Kohlberg, the conventional level of moral development is marked by a reliance on outside authority. T or F?

5. Self-interest and avoiding punishment are elements of postconventional morality. T or F?

6. About 80 percent of all adults function at the postconventional level of moral reasoning. T or F?

7. Gilligan regards gaining a sense of justice as the principal basis of moral development. T or F?

Reflect
Critical Thinking

8. Are labels like "adolescent" or "young adult" reflective of heredity or environment?

Relate

To what extent does the concept of identity formation apply to your own experience during adolescence?

Do you know any twixters? (Are you one?) Do you think twixters are adolescents taking longer to find their identity or young adults avoiding their need to establish themselves in the world of adults?

At what stage of moral development do you think most terrorists function?

Link

Internet addresses frequently change. To find the sites listed here, visit **http://www .thomsonedu.com/psychology/coon** for an updated list of Internet addresses and direct links to relevant sites.

- **A Positive Approach to Identity Formation of Biracial Children** Join the debate about multiethnicity and identity formation.

- **Delayed Adulthood** Read two articles about delayed adulthood.

- **Kohlberg Dilemmas** Try your hand at answering several moral dilemmas.

ANSWERS

1. F 2. puberty, cognitive development 3. a 4. T 5. F 6. F 7. F 8. Environment, rather than heredity, is the better answer. Even better, the meanings of terms like "adolescence" or "adult" vary considerably from culture to culture indicating that it is really a matter a matter of definition (Côté, 2006).

3.7 Challenges Across the Lifespan

ERIK ERIKSON'S psychosocial theory provides a good overview of the major psychological conflicts that occur during a "typical" life. In later adulthood we all face many additional challenges, including physical aging. Regardless, it is possible to age successfully. We also must face our own mortality and inevitable death.

■ TABLE 3.3 Erikson's Psychosocial Dilemmas	
AGE	**CHARACTERISTIC DILEMMA**
Birth to 1 year	Trust versus mistrust
1 to 3 years	Autonomy versus shame and doubt
3 to 5 years	Initiative versus guilt
6 to 12 years	Industry versus inferiority
Adolescence	Identity versus role confusion
Young adulthood	Intimacy versus isolation
Middle adulthood	Generativity versus stagnation
Late adulthood	Integrity versus despair

The Story of a Lifetime— Rocky Road or Garden Path?

SURVEY QUESTION: *What are the typical tasks and dilemmas through the lifespan?*

Every life is marked by a number of developmental milestones. These are notable events, markers, or turning points in personal development. Some examples include graduating from school, voting for the first time, getting married, watching a child leave home (or move back!), the death of a parent, becoming a grandparent, retirement, and one's own death. Thus far, we have traced Amy's progress through childhood, adolescence, and young adulthood. What challenges lie ahead for her?

Erikson's Psychosocial Theory

Perhaps the best way to get a preview of Amy's life is to consider some of the major psychological challenges she is likely to encounter. Broad similarities can be found in the life stages of infancy, childhood, adolescence, young adulthood, middle adulthood, and old age. Each stage confronts a person with new **developmental tasks** that must be mastered for optimal development. Examples are learning to read in childhood, adjusting to sexual maturity in adolescence, and establishing a vocation as an adult.

In an influential book titled *Childhood and Society* (1963), personality theorist Erik Erikson (1903–1994) suggests that we face a specific *psychosocial dilemma,* or "crisis," at each stage of life. A **psychosocial dilemma** is a conflict between personal impulses and the social world. Resolving each dilemma creates a new balance between a person and society. A string of "successes" produces healthy development and a satisfying life. Unfavorable outcomes throw us off balance, making it harder to deal with later crises. Life becomes a "rocky road," and personal growth is stunted. ■ Table 3.3 lists Erikson's dilemmas.

What are the major developmental tasks and life crises? A brief description of each psychosocial dilemma follows.

Stage One, First Year of Life: Trust versus Mistrust During
the first year of life, children are completely dependent on

Personality theorist Erik Erikson (1903-1994) is best known for his life-stage theory of human development.

Developmental task Any skill that must be mastered, or personal change that must take place, for optimal development.

Psychosocial dilemma A conflict between personal impulses and the social world.

others. Erikson believes that a basic attitude of trust or mistrust is formed at this time. **Trust** is established when babies are given warmth, touching, love, and physical care. **Mistrust** is caused by inadequate or unpredictable care and by parents who are cold, indifferent, or rejecting. Basic mistrust may later cause insecurity, suspiciousness, or an inability to relate to others. Notice that trust comes from the same conditions that help babies become securely attached to their parents.

Stage Two, 1–3 Years: Autonomy versus Shame and Doubt

In stage two, children express their growing self-control by climbing, touching, exploring, and trying to do things for themselves. Tom and Olivia fostered Amy's sense of **autonomy** by encouraging her to try new skills. However, her first efforts were sometimes crude, involving spilling, falling, wetting, and other "accidents." If Tom and Olivia had ridiculed or overprotected Amy, they might have caused her to **doubt** her abilities and feel **shameful** about her actions.

Stage Three, 3–5 Years: Initiative versus Guilt

In stage three, children move beyond simple self-control and begin to take initiative. Through play, children learn to make plans and carry out tasks. Parents reinforce **initiative** by giving children freedom to play, ask questions, use imagination, and choose activities. Feelings of **guilt** about initiating activities are formed if parents criticize severely, prevent play, or discourage a child's questions.

Stage Four, 6–12 Years: Industry versus Inferiority

Many events of middle childhood are symbolized by that fateful day when you first entered school. With dizzying speed your world expanded beyond your family, and you faced a whole series of new challenges.

The elementary school years are a child's "entrance into life." In school, children begin to learn skills valued by society, and success or failure can affect a child's feelings of adequacy. Children learn a sense of **industry** if they win praise for productive activities, such as building, painting, cooking, reading, and studying. If a child's efforts are regarded as messy, childish, or inadequate, feelings of **inferiority** result. For the first time, teachers, classmates, and adults outside the home become as important as parents in shaping attitudes toward oneself.

Stage Five, Adolescence: Identity versus Role Confusion

As we have noted, adolescence is often a turbulent time Erikson considers a need to answer the question "Who am I?" the primary task during this stage of life. As Amy matures mentally and physically, she will have new feelings, a new body, and new attitudes. Like other adolescents, she will need to build a consistent **identity** out of her talents, values, life history and relationships and the demands of her culture (Côté

& Levine, 2002). Her conflicting experiences as a student, friend, athlete, worker, daughter, lover, and so forth must be integrated into a unified sense of self. Persons who fail to develop a sense of identity suffer from **role confusion,** an uncertainty about who they are and where they are going.

Stage Six, Young Adulthood: Intimacy versus Isolation

What does Erikson believe is the major conflict in early adulthood? In stage six, the individual feels a need for *intimacy* in his or her life. After establishing a stable identity, a person is prepared to share meaningful love or deep friendship with others. By **intimacy,** Erikson means an ability to care about others and to share experiences with them. In line with Erikson's view, 75 percent of college-age men and women rank a good marriage and family life as important adult goals (Bachman & Johnson, 1979). And yet, marriage or sexual involvement is no guarantee of intimacy: Many adult relationships remain shallow and unfulfilling. Failure to establish intimacy with others leads to a deep sense of **isolation** (feeling alone and uncared for in life). This often sets the stage for later difficulties.

Stage Seven, Middle Adulthood: Generativity versus Stagnation

According to Erikson, an interest in guiding the next generation provides emotional balance in mature adulthood. Erikson called this quality **generativity.** It is expressed by caring about oneself, one's children, and future generations. Generativity may be achieved by guiding one's own children or by helping other children (as a teacher or coach, for ex-

According to Erikson, an interest in future generations characterizes optimal adult development.

ample). Productive or creative work can also express generativity. In any case, a person's concerns and energies must broaden to include the welfare of others and society as a whole. Failure to do this is marked by a **stagnant** concern with one's own needs and comforts. Life loses meaning, and the person feels bitter, dreary, and trapped (Friedman, 2004).

Stage Eight, Late Adulthood: Integrity versus Despair
What does Erikson see as the conflicts of old age? Old age is a time of reflection. According to Erikson, when Amy grows old it would be best if she were able to look back over her life with acceptance and satisfaction. People who have lived richly and responsibly develop a sense of **integrity** (self-respect). This allows them to face aging and death with dignity. If previous life events are viewed with regret, the elderly person experiences **despair** (heartache and remorse). In this case, life seems like a series of missed opportunities. The person feels like a failure and knows it's too late to reverse what has been done. Aging and the threat of death then become sources of fear and depression.

The Lifespan in Perspective
To squeeze a lifetime into a few pages, we had to ignore countless details. Although much is lost, the result is a clearer picture of an entire life cycle. Is Erikson's description, then, an exact map of Amy's past and her future—or your own? Probably not. Still, psychosocial dilemmas are major events in many lives. Knowing about them may allow you to anticipate typical trouble spots in your own life. You may also be better prepared to understand the problems and feelings of friends and relatives at various points in the life cycle.

Later Adulthood: Will You Still Need Me When I'm 64?

SURVEY QUESTION: *What issues arise during later adulthood?*

Although Erikson's dilemmas extend into adulthood, they are not the only challenges adults face. Others are all too familiar: marital strife, divorce, career difficulties, unemployment, health problems, financial pressures, legal conflicts, and personal tragedies—to name but a few. How do people maintain a state of well-being as they run the gauntlet of modern life? Psychologist Carol Ryff (1995; Ryff, Singer, & Palmersheim, 2004) believes that well-being during adulthood has six elements:

1. Self-acceptance
2. Positive relations with others
3. Autonomy (personal freedom)
4. Environmental mastery
5. A purpose in life
6. Continued personal growth

Ryff found that for many older adults, age-related declines are offset by positive relationships and greater mastery of life's demands (Ryff & Keyes, 1995). Thus, sharing life's joys and sorrows with others, coupled with a better understanding of how the world works, can help carry people through midlife and into their later years (Ryff & Singer, 2000; Ryff, Singer, & Palmersheim, 2004). Despite the emphasis on youth in our culture, middle age and beyond can be a rich period of life in which people feel secure, happy, and self-confident (Rubenstein, 2002).

A Midlife Crisis?
But don't people face a "midlife crisis" at this point in their lives? Yes and no. Serious difficulties at the midpoint of life are certainly not universal. Most people thrive during middle adulthood and have no special problems. Only about a quarter of men and women believe they have experienced a midlife crisis (Wethington, Kessler, & Pixley, 2004).

Nevertheless, midlife does pose special challenges. According to Roger Gould (1975), a psychiatrist interested in adult personality, North American adults actually experience two "crisis" points in their development.

Crisis of Questions
According to Gould, around the age of 30 many people experience a minor life crisis. The heart of this crisis is a serious questioning of what life is all about. People tend to ask themselves, "Is this it?" and confidence in previous choices and values can waver. Unsettled by these developments, the person actively searches for a style of living that will bring more meaning to life. Marriages are particularly vulnerable during this time of dissatisfaction. Extramarital affairs and divorces are common symptoms of the "crisis of questions."

Trust versus mistrust A conflict early in life about learning to trust others and the world.

Autonomy versus shame and doubt A conflict created when growing self-control (autonomy) is pitted against feelings of shame or doubt.

Initiative versus guilt A conflict between learning to take initiative and overcoming feelings of guilt about doing so.

Industry versus inferiority A conflict in middle childhood centered around lack of support for industrious behavior, which can result in feelings of inferiority.

Identity versus role confusion A conflict of adolescence, involving the need to establish a personal identity.

Intimacy versus isolation The challenge of overcoming a sense of isolation by establishing intimacy with others.

Generativity versus stagnation A conflict of middle adulthood in which self-interest is countered by an interest in guiding the next generation.

Integrity versus despair A conflict in old age between feelings of integrity and the despair of viewing previous life events with regret.

"Follow that dream!"

Crisis of Urgency People in their late 30s and 40s are typically beginning to become more aware of the reality of death. Having a limited number of years to live begins to exert pressure on the individual. Intensified attempts are made to succeed at a career or to achieve one's life goals. Generativity, in the form of nurturing, teaching, or serving others, helps alleviate many of the anxieties of this stage.

If a midlife crisis does occur, what does it look like? Psychologist Daniel Levinson carried out a classic in-depth study of adulthood and identified several periods when people typically make major transitions. A **transition period** ends one life pattern and opens the door to new possibilities (Levinson, 1986). At such times, people address concerns about their identity, their work, and their relationships to others.

Levinson's first study focused on men. As they approached the midlife transition (between the ages of 37 and 41), most men went through a period of instability, anxiety, and change. (Notice that this corresponds closely to Gould's crisis-of-urgency period.) In a later study, Levinson found that most of what he learned about men also applies to women (Levinson & Levinson, 1996).

Of the men Levinson studied, roughly half defined the midlife period as a "last chance" to achieve their goals. Such goals were often stated as a key event, such as reaching a certain income or becoming a supervisor, a full professor, a shop steward, and so forth. For these men the midlife period was stressful but manageable.

A smaller percentage of men experienced a serious midlife decline. Many of these men had to face the fact that they had chosen a dead-end job or lifestyle. Others had achieved financial success but felt that what they were doing was pointless.

In a third pattern, a few hardy individuals appeared to "break out" of a seriously flawed life structure. For them, a decision to "start over" was typically followed by 8 to 10 years of rebuilding.

In what ways does the midlife transition differ for women? Compared with men, women were less likely to enter adulthood with specific "goals." As a result, they were less likely to define "success" in terms of some key event. Rather than focusing on external goals, women tended to seek changes in personal identity at midlife. For example, a woman might become more self-reliant and independent—qualities she might have regarded as "masculine" earlier in life (Levinson & Levinson, 1996). But make no mistake, midlife can be challenging for women, too (Wethington, 2000). In another survey of middle-aged women, two thirds said they made major changes in their lives between ages 37 and 43 (Stewart & Vandewater, 1999).

Midcourse Corrections In summary, people tend to move through cycles of stability and transition in their adult lives (Ornstein & Isabella, 1990). However, it is more common to make a "midcourse correction" at midlife than it is to survive a "crisis" (Lachman, 2004). Ideally, the midlife transition involves reworking old identities, achieving valued goals, finding one's own truths, and preparing for old age. Taking stock may be especially valuable at midlife, but reviewing past choices to prepare for the future is helpful at any age (Lewchanin & Zubrod, 2001). For some people, difficult turning points in life can serve as "wake-up calls" that create opportunities for personal growth (Wethington, 2003).

Old Age

After the late 50s, personal development is complicated by physical aging. However, it is wrong to believe that most elderly people are sickly, infirm, or senile. (Nowadays, 60 is the new 40, an idea both of your authors whole-heartedly agree with!) Only about 5 percent of those older than 65 are in nursing homes. Mentally, many elderly persons are at least as capable as the average young adult. On intellectual tests, top scorers over the age of 65 match the average for men younger than 35. What sets these silver-haired stars apart? Typically they are people who have continued to work and remain intellectually active (Salthouse, 2004). Gerontologist Warner Schaie (1994, 2005) found that you are most likely to stay mentally sharp in old age if:

1. You remain healthy.
2. You live in a favorable environment. (You are educated and have a stimulating occupation, an above-average income, and an intact family.)

3. You are involved in intellectually stimulating activities (reading, travel, cultural events, continuing education, clubs, professional associations).

4. You have a flexible personality.

5. You are married to a smart spouse.

6. You maintain your perceptual processing speed.

7. You were satisfied with your accomplishments in midlife.

A shorter summary of this list is "Those who live by their wit die with their wits."

Successful Aging *What are the keys to successful aging?* They are not unlike the elements of well-being at midlife. Four psychological characteristics shared by the healthiest, happiest older people are (de Leon, 2005; Vaillant, 2002):

Optimism, hope, and an interest in the future

Gratitude and forgiveness; an ability to focus on what is good in life

Empathy; an ability to share the feelings of others and see the world through their eyes

Connection with others; an ability to reach out, to give and receive social support

Actually, these are excellent guidelines for well-being at any stage of adulthood.

In summary, enlightened views of aging call for an end to the forced obsolescence of the elderly. As a group, older people represent a valuable source of skill, knowledge, and energy that we can't afford to cast aside. As we face the challenges of this planet's uncertain future, we need all the help we can get!

At age 77, John Glenn became the oldest person to fly into space, in October 1998. Glenn was also the first American astronaut to orbit Earth, in 1962. As Glenn's space adventure shows, aging does not inevitably bring an end to engaging in challenging activities.

Tony Ranze/AFP/Getty Images

Aging and Ageism You have almost certainly encountered ageism in one way or another. **Ageism,** which refers to discrimination or prejudice based on age, can oppress the young as well as the old. For instance, a person applying for a job may just as well be told "You're too young" as "You're too old." In some societies ageism is expressed as respect for the elderly. In Japan, for instance, aging is seen as positive, and greater age brings more status and respect. In most Western nations, however, ageism tends to have a negative impact on older individuals (Ng, 2002).

Ageism is often expressed through patronizing language. Older people are frequently spoken to in an overly polite, slow, loud, and simple way implying that they are infirm, even when they are not (Nelson, 2005). Popular stereotypes of the "dirty old man," "meddling old woman," "senile old fool," and the like also help perpetuate myths about aging. But such stereotypes are clearly wrong: A tremendous diversity exists among the elderly—ranging from the infirm to aerobic-dancing grandmothers.

In many occupations, older workers perform well in jobs that require *both* speed and skill. Of course, people do experience a gradual loss of *fluid abilities* (those requiring speed or rapid learning) as they age but often this can be offset by many *crystallized abilities* (learned knowledge and skills), such as vocabulary and stored-up facts, which may actually improve—at least into the 60s (Schaie, 2005). Overall, very little loss of job performance occurs as workers grow older. In the professions, wisdom and expertise can usually more than compensate for any loss of mental quickness (Ericsson, 2000). Basing retirement solely on a person's age makes little sense.

Death and Dying—The Final Challenge

SURVEY QUESTION: *How do people typically react to death?*

DEAR ABBY: Do you think about dying much? *(signed)* CURIOUS

DEAR CURIOUS: No, it's the last thing I want to do.

"I'm not afraid of dying. I just don't want to be there when it happens." Woody Allen

"Why not? Why not?" LSD guru Timothy Leary (his last words before dying)

Transition period Time span during which a person leaves an existing life pattern behind and moves into a new pattern.

Ageism Discrimination or prejudice based on a person's age.

THE STATISTICS ON DEATH are very convincing: One out of one dies. In spite of this, most of us are poorly informed about a process that is as basic as birth. We have seen through the modules in this chapter that it is valuable to understand major trends in the course of development. With this in mind, let us now explore emotional responses to death, the inevitable conclusion of every life. For many people, to die well is no less an accomplishment than to live well.

It might seem that as people grow older they would fear death more. However, older persons actually have fewer death fears than younger people. Older people more often fear the *circumstances* of dying, such as pain or helplessness, rather than death itself (Thorson & Powell, 1990). These findings seem to show a general lack of death fears, but they may actually reflect a widespread denial of death. Notice how denial is apparent in the language used to talk about death: Often we speak of a dead person as having "passed away," "expired," "gone to God," or "breathed one's last."

Many people have little direct experience with death until they, themselves, are fairly old. The average person's exposure to death consists of the artificial and unrealistic portrayals of death on TV. By the time the average person is 17 years old, she or he will have witnessed thousands of TV deaths. With few exceptions these are *homicides*, not deaths due to illness or aging.

Reactions to Impending Death

A direct and highly influential account of emotional responses to death comes from the work of Elisabeth Kübler-Ross (1926–2004). Kübler-Ross was a **thanatologist** (THAN-ah-TOL-oh-jist: one who studies death). Over the years she spent hundreds of hours at the bedsides of the ter-

minally ill, where she observed five basic emotional reactions to impending death (Kübler-Ross, 1975).

1. **Denial and isolation.** A typical first reaction is to deny death's reality and isolate oneself from information confirming that death is really going to occur. Initially the person may be sure that "It's all a mistake." "Surely," she or he thinks, "the lab reports have been mixed up or the doctor made an error." This sort of denial may proceed to attempts to avoid any reminder of the situation.

2. **Anger.** Many dying individuals feel anger and ask, "Why me?" As they face the ultimate threat of having life torn away, their anger may spill over into rage toward the living. Even good friends may temporarily evoke anger because their health is envied.

3. **Bargaining.** In another common reaction, the terminally ill bargain with themselves or with God. The dying person thinks, "Just let me live a little longer and I'll do anything to earn it." Individuals may bargain for time by trying to be "good" ("I'll never smoke again"), by righting past wrongs, or by praying that if they are granted more time they will dedicate themselves to their religion.

4. **Depression.** As death draws near and the person begins to recognize that it cannot be prevented, feelings of futility, exhaustion, and deep depression may set in. The person realizes she or he will be separated from friends, loved ones, and the familiar routines of life, and this causes a profound sadness.

5. **Acceptance.** If death is not sudden, many people manage to come to terms with dying and accept it calmly. The person who accepts death is neither happy nor sad, but at peace with the inevitable. Acceptance usually signals that the struggle with death has been resolved. The need to talk about death ends, and silent companionship from others is frequently all the person desires.

Not all terminally ill persons display all these reactions, nor do they always occur in this order. Individual styles of dying vary greatly. Generally, there does tend to be a movement from initial shock, denial, and anger toward eventual acceptance. However, some people who seem to have accepted death may die angry and raging against the inevitable. Conversely, the angry fighter may let go of the struggle and die peacefully. In general, one's approach to dying will mirror his or her style of living (Yedidia & MacGregor, 2001).

It is a mistake, then, to think that Kübler-Ross's list is a series of stages to go through in order or that there is something wrong if a person does not show all these emotions. Rather, the list describes typical reactions to impending

Death may be inevitable, but it can be faced with dignity and, sometimes, even humor. Mel Blanc's famous sign-off, "That's all folks," is engraved on a marble headstone over his grave. Blanc was the voice of Bugs Bunny, Porky Pig, and many other cartoon characters.

Michael Newman/PhotoEdit

death. Note, as well, that many of the same reactions accompany any major loss, be it divorce, loss of a home due to fire, death of a pet, or loss of a job.

Implications   *How can I make use of this information?* First, it can help both the dying and survivors to recognize and cope with periods of depression, anger, denial, and bargaining. Second, it helps to realize that close friends or relatives may feel many of the same emotions before or after a person's death because they, too, are facing a loss.

Perhaps the most important thing to recognize is that the dying person needs to share feelings with others and to discuss death openly. Too often, dying persons feel isolated and separated from others. Adults tend to "freeze up" with someone who is dying. For such people, thanatologist Kirsti Dyer (2001) has this advice:

- Be yourself and relate person to person.
- Be ready to listen again and again.
- Be respectful.
- Be aware of feelings and nonverbal cues.
- Be comfortable with silence.
- Be genuine.
- Most of all, be there.

Understanding what the dying person is going through may make it easier for you to offer support at this important time. A simple willingness to be with the person and to honestly share his or her feelings can help bring dignity, acceptance, and meaning to death (Holstein, 1997).

MODULE **3.7** Summary

What are the typical tasks and dilemmas through the lifespan?

- Erik Erikson identified a series of challenges that occur across the lifespan. These range from a need to gain trust in infancy to the need to live with integrity in old age.

What issues arise during later adulthood?

- Well-being during adulthood consists of six elements: self-acceptance, positive relations with others, autonomy, environmental mastery, having a purpose in life, and continued personal growth.

- Only a minority of people have a midlife crisis, but midlife course corrections are more common.

- Even if no crisis occurs, people tend to move through repeated cycles of stability and transition throughout adulthood.

- Intellectual declines associated with aging are limited, at least through one's 70s. This is especially true of individuals who remain mentally active.

- *Ageism* refers to prejudice, discrimination, and stereotyping on the basis of age. It affects people of all ages but is especially damaging to older people. Most ageism is based on stereotypes, myths, and misinformation.

How do people typically react to death?

- Death is a natural part of life. There is value in understanding it and accepting it.

- Typical emotional reactions to impending death include denial, anger, bargaining, depression, and acceptance, but not necessarily in that order or in every case.

Thanatologist   A specialist who studies emotional and behavioral reactions to death and dying.

KNOWLEDGE BUILDER

Challenges Across the Lifespan

Recite

As a way to improve your memory, you might find it helpful to summarize Erikson's eight life stages. Complete this do-it-yourself summary and compare your answers to those given below.

Stage	Crisis	Favorable Outcome
First year of life	1. _____ vs.	Faith in the environment and in others
	2. _____	
Ages 1-3	Autonomy vs.	Feelings of self-control and adequacy
	3. _____	
Ages 3-5	4. _____ vs. guilt	Ability to begin one's own activities
Ages 6-12	Industry vs.	Confidence in productive skills, learning how to work
	5. _____	
Adolescence	6. _____ vs. role confusion	An integrated image of oneself as a unique person
Young adulthood	Intimacy vs.	Ability to form bonds of love and friendship with others
	7. _____	
Middle adulthood	Generativity vs.	Concern for family, society, and future generations
	8. _____	
Late adulthood	9. _____ vs.	Sense of dignity and fulfillment, willingness to face death
	10. _____	

11. Nearly everyone experiences a midlife crisis sometime around age 40. T or F?

12. After age 65, a large proportion of older people show significant signs of mental disability and most require special care. T or F?

13. Job performance tends to decline rapidly in older workers. T or F?

14. In the reaction that Kübler-Ross describes as bargaining, the dying individual asks, "Why me?" T or F?

Reflect
Critical Thinking

15. Trying to make generalizations about development throughout life is complicated by at least one major factor. What do you think it is?

Relate

See if you can think of a person you know who is facing one of Erikson's psychosocial dilemmas. Now see if you can think of specific people who seem to be coping with each of the other dilemmas.

See if you can describe three instances of ageism you have witnessed.

Link

Internet addresses frequently change. To find the sites listed here, visit **http://www.thomsonedu.com/psychology/coon** for an updated list of Internet addresses and direct links to relevant sites.

• **Welcome to Middle Age** Home page of middleage.org.

• **The AARP** Home page of the American Association of Retired Persons.

• **Hospice** A website of information about death, bereavement, and hospices.

ANSWERS

1. Trust 2. mistrust 3. shame or doubt 4. Initiative 5. inferiority 6. Identity 7. isolation 8. stagnation 9. Integrity 10. despair 11. F 12. F 13. F 14. F 15. Different cohorts (groups of people born in various decades may have very different life experiences. People born in different historical times. This makes it difficult to identify universal patterns (Stewart & Ostrove, 1998).

6 Conditioning and Learning

What Did You Learn in School Today?

When one of your authors was in college, he and other students discovered an intriguing flaw in the dorm plumbing: Flush a toilet while someone was taking a shower and the cold water pressure would suddenly drop. This caused the shower to become scalding hot. Naturally, the shower victim screamed in terror as his reflexes caused him to leap backward in pain. Soon it was discovered that if *all* the toilets were flushed at once, the effects were multiplied many times over!

A toilet has to be one of the world's most uninspiring stimuli. But for a time, a whole flock of college students twitched involuntarily whenever they heard a toilet flush. Their reactions were the result of classical conditioning, a basic type of learning. Classical conditioning is one of the topics of this chapter.

Now, let's say that you are at school and you feel like you are "starving to death." You locate a vending machine and deposit your last bit of change to buy a candy bar. Then you press the button, and . . . nothing happens. Being civilized and in complete control, you press the other buttons, try the coin return, and look for an attendant. Still nothing. Your stomach growls. Impulsively, you give the machine a little kick (just to let it know how you feel). Then, as you turn away, out pops a candy bar plus 75 cents change. Once this happens, chances are good that you will repeat the "kicking response" in the future. If it pays off several times more, kicking vending machines may become a regular feature of your behavior. In this case, learning is based on operant conditioning (also called instrumental learning).

Classical and operant conditioning reach into every corner of our lives. Are you ready to learn more about learning? If so, read on!

MODULE
6.1 Learning and Classical Conditioning

MOST BEHAVIOR is learned. Imagine if you suddenly lost all you had ever learned. What could you do? You would be unable to read, write, or speak. You couldn't feed yourself, find your way home, drive a car, play the bassoon, or "party." Needless to say, you would be totally incapacitated. (Dull, too!) How do the most fundamental types of learning occur?

What Is Learning—Does Practice Make Perfect?

SURVEY QUESTION: *What is learning?*

Learning is a relatively permanent change in behavior due to experience (Domjan, 2006). Notice that this definition excludes temporary changes caused by motivation, fatigue, maturation, disease, injury, or drugs. Each of these can alter behavior, but none qualifies as learning.

Isn't learning the result of practice? It depends on what you mean by practice. Merely repeating a response will not necessarily produce learning. You could close your eyes and swing a tennis racket hundreds of times without learning anything about tennis. Reinforcement is the key to learning. **Reinforcement** refers to any event that increases the probability that a response will occur again. A response is any identifiable behavior. Responses may be observable actions, such as blinking, eating a piece of candy, or turning a doorknob. They can also be internal, such as having a faster heartbeat.

To teach a dog a trick, we could reinforce correct responses by giving the dog some food each time it sits up. Similarly, you could teach a child to be neat by praising him for picking up his toys. Learning can also occur in other ways. For instance, if a girl gets stung by a bee, she may learn to associate pain with bees and to fear them. In this case, the girl's fear is reinforced by the discomfort she feels immediately after seeing the bee. Later, you'll discover how such varied experiences lead to learning.

Antecedents and Consequences Unlocking the secrets of learning begins with noting what happens before and after a response. Events that precede a response are called **antecedents.** For example, Ashleigh, who is 3, has learned that when she hears a truck pull into the driveway, it means that daddy is home. Ashleigh runs to the front door, where she gets a hug from her father. Effects that follow a response are **consequences.** The hug is what reinforces Ashleigh's tendency to run to the door. As this suggests, paying careful attention to the "before and after" of learning is a key to understanding it.

Classical Conditioning

Classical conditioning is based on what happens before we respond. It begins with a stimulus that reliably triggers a response. Imagine, for example, that a puff of air (the stimulus) is aimed at your eye. The air puff will make you blink (a response) every time. The eye blink is a **reflex** (automatic, nonlearned response).

Now, assume that we sound a horn (another stimulus) just before each puff of air hits your eye. If the horn and the air puff occur together many times, what happens? Soon, the horn alone will make you blink. Clearly, you've learned something. Before, the horn didn't make you blink. Now it does. Similarly, if your mouth waters each time you eat a cookie, you may learn to salivate when you merely *see* a cookie, a picture of cookies, a cookie jar, or other stimuli that preceded salivation.

In **classical conditioning,** an antecedent stimulus that doesn't produce a response is linked with one that does (a horn is associated with a puff of air to the eye, for example). We can say that learning has occurred when the new stimulus will also *elicit* (bring forth) responses (● Fig. 6.1).

Operant Conditioning

In **operant conditioning,** learning is based on the consequences of responding. A response may be followed by a reinforcer (such as food). Or by punishment. Or by nothing.

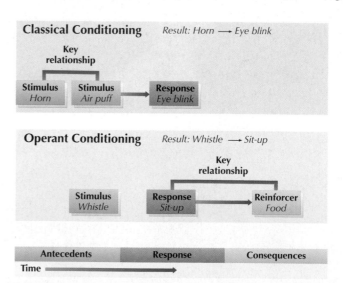

● **FIGURE 6.1** In classical conditioning, a stimulus that does not produce a response is paired with a stimulus that does elicit a response. After many such pairings, the stimulus that previously had no effect begins to produce a response. In the example shown, a horn precedes a puff of air to the eye. Eventually the horn alone will produce an eye blink. In operant conditioning, a response that is followed by a reinforcing consequence becomes more likely to occur on future occasions. In the example shown, a dog learns to sit up when it hears a whistle.

These results determine whether a response is likely to be made again. (See Fig. 6.1.) For example, if you wear a particular hat and get lots of compliments (reinforcement), you are likely to wear it more often. If people snicker, insult you, call the police, or scream (punishment), you will probably wear it less often.

Now that you have an idea of what happens in the two basic kinds of learning, let's look at classical conditioning in more detail.

Classical Conditioning—Does the Name Pavlov Ring a Bell?

SURVEY QUESTION: *How does classical conditioning occur?*

At the beginning of the twentieth century, something happened in the lab of Russian physiologist Ivan Pavlov that brought him the Nobel Prize: Pavlov's subjects drooled at him.

Actually, Pavlov was studying digestion. To observe salivation, he placed meat powder or some tidbit on a dog's tongue. After doing this many times, Pavlov noticed that his dogs were salivating *before* the food reached their mouths (Schultz & Schultz, 2005). Later, the dogs even began to salivate when they saw Pavlov enter the room. Was this misplaced affection? Pavlov knew better. Salivation is normally a reflex. For the animals to salivate at the mere sight of food, some type of learning must have occurred. Pavlov called it conditioning (● Fig. 6.2). Because of its importance in psychology's history, it is now called classical conditioning (also known as *Pavlovian conditioning* or *respondent conditioning*) (Mackintosh, 2003).

Pavlov's Experiment

How did Pavlov study conditioning? After Pavlov observed that food made his dogs salivate, he began his classic experiments. (See Fig. 6.2.) To begin, he rang a bell. At first, the bell was a

● **FIGURE 6.2** An apparatus for Pavlovian conditioning. A tube carries saliva from the dog's mouth to a lever that activates a recording device (far left). During conditioning, various stimuli can be paired with a dish of food placed in front of the dog. The device pictured here is more elaborate than the one Pavlov used in his early experiments.

neutral stimulus (the dogs did not respond to it by salivating). Immediately after Pavlov rang the bell, he placed meat powder on the dog's tongue, which caused reflex salivation. This sequence was repeated a number of times: bell, meat powder, salivation; bell, meat powder, salivation. Eventually (as conditioning took place), the dogs began to salivate when they heard the bell (● Fig. 6.3). By association, the bell, which before had no effect, began to evoke the same response that food did. This was shown by sometimes ringing the bell alone. Then the dog salivated even though no food had been placed in its mouth.

Psychologists use several terms to describe these events. The meat powder is an **unconditioned stimulus (US)** (a stimulus innately capable of producing a response; salivation in this case). Notice that the dog did not have to learn to respond to the US. Such stimuli naturally trigger reflexes or emotional reactions. Because a reflex is innate, or "built in," it is called an **unconditioned** (nonlearned) **response (UR).** Reflex salivation was the UR in Pavlov's experiment.

The bell starts out as a **neutral stimulus (NS).** In time, the bell becomes a **conditioned stimulus (CS)** (a stimulus that, because of learning, will elicit a response). When Pavlov's bell also produced salivation, the dog was making a new response. Thus, salivation had also become a **conditioned** (learned) **response (CR).** (See Fig. 6.3.) ■ Table 6.1 summarizes the important elements of classical conditioning.

Are all these terms really necessary? Yes, because they help us recognize similarities in various instances of learning. Let's summarize the terms, using an earlier example:

BEFORE CONDITIONING	EXAMPLE
US → UR	Puff of air → eye blink
NS → no effect	Horn → no effect
AFTER CONDITIONING	**EXAMPLE**
CS → CR	Horn → eye blink

Learning Any relatively permanent change in behavior that can be attributed to experience.

Reinforcement Any event that increases the probability that a particular response will occur.

Antecedents Events that precede a response.

Consequences Effects that follow a response.

Reflex An innate, automatic response to a stimulus; for example, an eye blink.

Classical conditioning A form of learning in which reflex responses are associated with new stimuli.

Operant conditioning Learning based on the consequences of responding.

Unconditioned stimulus A stimulus innately capable of eliciting a response.

Unconditioned response An innate reflex response elicited by an unconditioned stimulus.

Neutral stimulus A stimulus that does not evoke a response.

Conditioned stimulus A stimulus that evokes a response because it has been repeatedly paired with an unconditioned stimulus.

Conditioned response A learned response elicited by a conditioned stimulus.

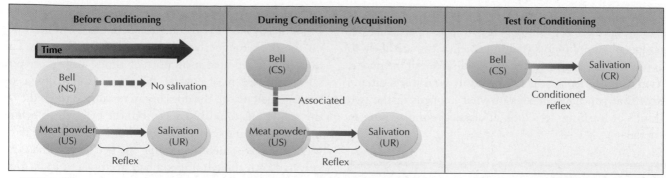

● **FIGURE 6.3** The classical conditioning procedure.

ELEMENT	SYMBOL	DESCRIPTION	EXAMPLE
TABLE 6.1 Elements of Classical Conditioning			
Unconditioned stimulus	US	A stimulus innately capable of eliciting a response	Meat powder
Unconditioned response	UR	An innate reflex response elicited by an unconditioned stimulus	Reflex salivation
Neutral stimulus NS		A stimulus that does not evoke a response	Bell
Conditioned stimulus	CS	A stimulus that evokes a response because it has been repeatedly paired with an unconditioned stimulus	Bell
Conditioned response	CR	A learned response elicited by a conditioned stimulus	Salivation

Now let's see if we can explain the shower and flushing toilet example described earlier. The unconditioned, or non-learned, response (UR) was a reflex jump from the hot water. The unconditioned stimulus (US) was the hot water. The conditioned stimulus (CS) was the sound of a flushing toilet. That is, the flushing sound was at first neutral. But as a result of conditioning, it became capable of triggering a learned reflex. See "Coping with Chemo" for an example of how classical conditioning is being used to solve a clinical problem.

Principles of Classical Conditioning— The Boy and the Bell

Imagine a boy named Johnny. To observe conditioning, you could ring a bell and squirt lemon juice into Johnny's mouth. By repeating this procedure several times, you could condition Johnny to salivate to the bell. Johnny might then be used to explore other aspects of classical conditioning. Let's see how conditioning occurs.

Acquisition

During **acquisition,** or training, a conditioned response must be reinforced (strengthened) (● Fig. 6.4). Classical conditioning is *reinforced* when the CS is followed by, or paired with, an unconditioned stimulus. This type of reinforcement is known as **respondent reinforcement**. For Johnny, the bell

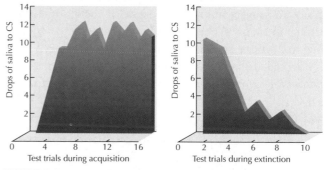

● **FIGURE 6.4** Acquisition and extinction of a conditioned response. (Adapted from Pavlov, 1927.)

is the CS, salivating is the UR, and the sour lemon juice is a US. To reinforce salivating to the bell, we must link the bell with the lemon juice. Conditioning will be most rapid if the US (lemon juice) follows *immediately* after the CS (the bell). With most reflexes, the optimal delay between CS and US is from one-half second to about 5 seconds (Chance, 2006).

Higher Order Conditioning Once a response is learned, it can bring about **higher order conditioning.** In this case, a well-learned CS is used to reinforce further learning. That is, the CS has become strong enough to be used like an unconditioned stimulus. Let's illustrate again with our salivating child.

As a result of earlier learning, the bell now makes Johnny salivate. (No lemon juice is needed.) To go a step further, you

THE CLINICAL FILE

Coping with Chemo

Our hearts go out to children with cancer. Even the treatment, chemotherapy, makes them miserable because it causes nausea and vomiting. In a cruel twist, after a few treatments, nausea can occur even when no chemotherapy is scheduled. Typically, it is triggered by certain sights or tastes, like the sight of the treatment center or the taste of a food the child ate before an earlier chemotherapy session.

In classical conditioning terms, chemotherapy is a US that leads to nausea, which is a UR. The sight of the treatment center or the taste of food eaten before treatment is initially a neutral stimulus that becomes associated with nausea and vomiting, making it a CS. These sights or tastes can now elicit anticipatory nausea (a CR) even at times when the child doesn't receive chemotherapy (Chance, 2006).

In nature, many species are *biologically prepared* to associate specific locations and tastes with nausea. If animals eat contaminated food and then get sick and vomit, later the same locations or tastes may trigger anticipatory nausea and vomiting. These reactions discourage animals from eating potentially dangerous food. Unfortunately, conditioned nausea only complicates treatment for young cancer patients. If Gita eats pepperoni pizza, her favorite meal, before she has a chemotherapy session, the taste of pizza may come to make her feel sick.

Is there any way to prevent conditioned nausea? No, but classical conditioning can provide some relief (Taylor, 2002). Meals eaten before chemotherapy can be strongly flavored with an unusual taste, such as peppermint. The unique flavor overshadows other tastes, which don't become linked with nausea (Bovbjerg et al., 1992). In this way, Gita can continue to enjoy her pepperoni pizza, because the nausea becomes conditioned to the unusual taste.

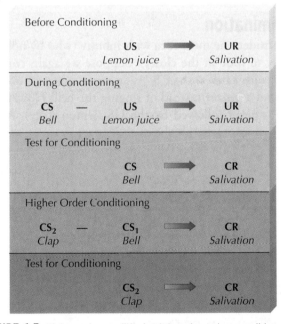

● **FIGURE 6.5** Higher order conditioning takes place when a well-learned conditioned stimulus is used as if it were an unconditioned stimulus. In this example, a child is first conditioned to salivate to the sound of a bell. In time, the bell will elicit salivation. At that point, you could clap your hands and then ring the bell. Soon, after repeating the procedure, the child would learn to salivate when you clapped your hands.

could clap your hands and then ring the bell. (Again, no lemon juice would be used.) Through higher order conditioning, Johnny would soon learn to salivate when you clapped your hands (● Fig. 6.5). (This little trick could be a real hit with friends and neighbors.)

Higher order conditioning extends learning one or more steps beyond the original conditioned stimulus. Many adver-

tisers use this effect by pairing images that evoke good feelings (such as people smiling and having fun) with pictures of their products. They hope that you will learn, by association, to feel good when you see their products (Priluck & Till, 2004).

Expectancies

Many psychologists believe that classical conditioning is related to information that might aid survival. According to this **informational view,** we look for associations among events. Doing so creates new mental **expectancies,** or expectations about how events are interconnected.

How does classical conditioning alter expectancies? Notice that the conditioned stimulus reliably precedes the unconditioned stimulus. Because it does, the CS *predicts* the US (Rescorla, 1987). During conditioning, the brain learns to *expect* that the US will follow the CS. As a result, the brain prepares the body to respond to the US. Here's an example: When you are about to get a shot with a hypodermic needle,

Acquisition The period in conditioning during which a response is reinforced.

Respondent reinforcement Reinforcement that occurs when an unconditioned stimulus closely follows a conditioned stimulus.

Higher order conditioning Classical conditioning in which a conditioned stimulus is used to reinforce further learning; that is, a CS is used as if it were a US.

Informational view Perspective that explains learning in terms of information imparted by events in the environment.

Expectancy An anticipation concerning future events or relationships.

your muscles tighten and there is a catch in your breathing. Why? Because your body is preparing for pain. You have learned to expect that getting poked with a needle will hurt. This expectancy, which was acquired during classical conditioning, changes your behavior.

Extinction and Spontaneous Recovery

After conditioning has occurred, what would happen if the US no longer followed the CS? If the US never again follows the CS, conditioning will extinguish, or fade away. Let's return to the boy and the bell. If you ring the bell many times and do not follow it with lemon juice, Johnny's expectancy that "bell precedes lemon juice" will weaken. As it does, he will lose his tendency to salivate when he hears the bell. Thus, we see that classical conditioning can be weakened by removing the connection between the conditioned and unconditioned stimulus. (See Fig. 6.4.) This process is called **extinction.**

If conditioning takes a while to build up, shouldn't it take time to reverse? Yes. In fact, it may take several extinction sessions to completely reverse conditioning. Let's say that we ring the bell until Johnny quits responding. It might seem that extinction is complete. However, Johnny will probably respond to the bell again on the following day, at least at first (Rescorla, 2004). The return of a learned response after apparent extinction is called **spontaneous recovery.** It explains why people who have had car accidents may need many slow, calm rides before their fear of driving extinguishes.

Generalization

After conditioning, other stimuli similar to the CS may also trigger a response. This is called **stimulus generalization.** For example, we might find that Johnny salivates to the sound of a ringing telephone or doorbell, even though they were never used as conditioning stimuli.

It is easy to see the value of stimulus generalization. Consider the child who burns her finger while playing with matches. Most likely, lighted matches will become conditioned fear stimuli for her. But will she fear only matches? Because of stimulus generalization, she may also have a healthy fear of flames from lighters, fireplaces, stoves, and so forth. It's fortunate that generalization extends learning to related situations. Otherwise, we would all be far less adaptable.

As you may have guessed, stimulus generalization has limits. As stimuli become less like the original CS, responding decreases. If you condition a person to blink each time you play a particular note on a piano, blinking will decline as you play higher or lower notes. If the notes are *much* higher or lower, the person will not respond at all (● Fig. 6.6). Stimulus generalization explains why many stores carry imitations of nationally known products. For many customers, positive attitudes conditioned to the real products tend to generalize to the cheaper knockoffs (Till & Priluck, 2000).

Discrimination

Let's consider one more idea with Johnny (who by now must be ready to hide in the closet). Suppose we again condition Johnny, with a bell as the CS. As an experiment, we occasionally sound a buzzer instead of ringing the bell. However, the buzzer is never followed by the US (lemon juice). At first, Johnny salivates when he hears the buzzer (because of generalization). But after we sound the buzzer several times more, Johnny will stop responding to it. Why? In essence, Johnny's generalized response to the buzzer has extinguished. As a result, he has learned to *discriminate,* or respond differently, to the bell and the buzzer.

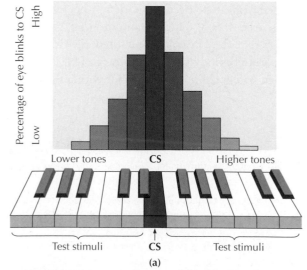

● **FIGURE 6.6** *(a)* Stimulus generalization. Stimuli similar to the CS also elicit a response. *(b)* This cat has learned to salivate when it sees a cat food box. Because of stimulus generalization, it also salivates when shown a similar-looking detergent box.

Stimulus discrimination is the ability to respond differently to various stimuli. As an example, you might remember the feelings of anxiety or fear you had as a child when your mother's or father's voice changed to its you're-in-a-heap-of-trouble tone. (Or the dreaded give-me-that-Wii-controller tone.) Most children quickly learn to discriminate voice tones associated with punishment from those associated with praise or affection.

Classical Conditioning in Humans— An Emotional Topic

SURVEY QUESTION: *Does conditioning affect emotions?*

How much human learning is based on classical conditioning? At its simplest, classical conditioning depends on unconditioned reflex responses. As mentioned earlier, a reflex is a dependable, inborn stimulus-and-response connection. For example, your hand reflexively draws back from pain. Bright light causes the pupil of the eye to narrow. A puff of air directed at your eye will make you blink. Various foods elicit salivation. Any of these reflexes, and others as well, can be associated with a new stimulus. At the very least, you have probably noticed how your mouth waters when you see or smell a bakery. Even pictures of food may make you salivate (a photo of a sliced lemon is great for this).

Conditioned Emotional Responses

In addition to simple reflexes, more complex *emotional,* or "gut," responses may be linked to new stimuli. For instance, if your face reddened when you were punished as a child, you may blush now when you are embarrassed or ashamed. Or think about the effects of associating pain with a dentist's office during your first visit. On later visits, did your heart pound and your palms sweat *before* the dentist began?

Many *involuntary,* autonomic nervous system responses ("fight-or-flight" reflexes) are linked with new stimuli and situations by classical conditioning. For example, learned reactions worsen many cases of hypertension (high blood pressure). Traffic jams, arguments with a spouse, and similar situations can become conditioned stimuli that trigger a dangerous rise in blood pressure (Reiff, Katkin, & Friedman, 1999).

Of course, emotional conditioning also applies to animals. One of the most common mistakes people make with pets (especially dogs) is hitting them if they do not come when called. Calling the animal then becomes a conditioned stimulus for fear and withdrawal. No wonder the pet disobeys when called on future occasions. Parents who belittle, scream at, or physically abuse their children make the same mistake.

Learned Fears Some phobias (FOE-bee-ahs) are also based on emotional conditioning. A *phobia* is a fear that persists even when no realistic danger exists. Fears of animals, water, heights, thunder, fire, bugs, elevators, and the like are common. Psychologists believe that many phobias begin as **conditioned emotional responses** (**CERs**), learned emotional reactions to a previously neutral stimulus. People who have phobias can often trace their fears to a time when they were frightened, injured, or upset by a particular stimulus, especially in childhood (King, Muris, & Ollendick, 2005). Just one bad experience in which you were frightened or disgusted by a spider may condition fears that last for years (de Jong & Muris, 2002).

Stimulus generalization and higher order conditioning can spread CERs to other stimuli (Gewirtz & Davis, 1998). As a result, what began as a limited fear may become a disabling phobia (● Fig. 6.7). However, a therapy called *desensitization* is now widely used to extinguish fears, anxieties, and phobias. This is done by gradually exposing the phobic person to feared stimuli while she or he remains calm and relaxed. For example, people have been desensitized for acrophobia (fear of heights) through *virtual reality exposure*, the use of computers to safely simulate, in this case, the experience of heights (Wiederhold & Wiederhold, 2005). (See Modules 13.3 & 13.4 for more information about therapies based on learning principles.)

Undoubtedly, we acquire many of our likes, dislikes, and fears as conditioned emotional responses. As noted before, advertisers try to achieve the same effect by pairing products with pleasant images and music. So do many students on a first date.

Vicarious, or Secondhand, Conditioning

Conditioning also occurs indirectly, which adds to its impact on us. Let's say, for example, that you watch another person get an electric shock. Each time, a signal light comes on before the shock is delivered. Even if you don't receive a shock yourself, you will soon develop a CER to the light. Children who learn to fear thunder by watching their parents react to it have un-

---

Extinction The weakening of a conditioned response through removal of reinforcement.

Spontaneous recovery The reappearance of a learned response after its apparent extinction.

Stimulus generalization The tendency to respond to stimuli similar to, but not identical to, a conditioned stimulus.

Stimulus discrimination The learned ability to respond differently to similar stimuli.

Conditioned emotional response (CER) An emotional response that has been linked to a previously nonemotional stimulus by classical conditioning.

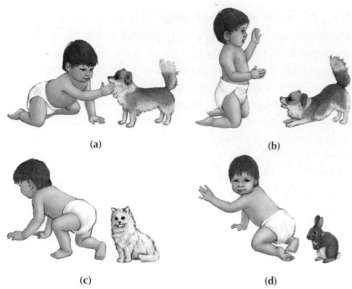

(a)

(b)

(c)

(d)

● **FIGURE 6.7** Hypothetical example of a CER becoming a phobia. Child approaches dog (a) and is frightened by it (b). Fear generalizes to other household pets (c) and later to virtually all furry animals (d).

dergone similar conditioning. Many Americans were traumatized as a consequence of watching media coverage of the September 11 terrorist attacks in New York and Washington (Blanchard et al., 2004). Similarly, people who counsel traumatized victims of sexual abuse can themselves develop vicarious trauma (Rothschild & Rand, 2006; Way et al., 2004).

Vicarious classical conditioning occurs when we learn to respond emotionally to a stimulus by observing another person's emotional reactions. Such "secondhand" learning affects feelings in many situations. For example, "horror" movies filled with screaming actors probably add to fears of snakes, caves, spiders, heights, and other terrors. If movies can affect us, we might expect the emotions of parents, friends, and relatives to have even more impact. How, for instance, does a city child learn to fear snakes and respond emotionally to mere pictures of them? Being told that "snakes are dangerous" may not explain the child's *emotional* response. More likely, the child has observed others reacting fearfully to the word *snake* or to snake images on television (King, Muris, & Ollendick, 2005).

The emotional attitudes we develop toward foods, political parties, ethnic groups, escalators—whatever—are probably conditioned not only by direct experiences, but vicariously as well. No one is born prejudiced—all attitudes are learned. Parents may do well to look in a mirror if they wonder how or where a child "picked up" a particular fear or emotional attitude.

What is learning?

- Learning is a relatively permanent change in behavior due to experience. Learning depends on reinforcement, which increases the probability that a particular response will occur.
- Classical conditioning and operant conditioning are responsible for basic learning capacity in humans and animals.
- In classical conditioning, a neutral stimulus is followed by an unconditioned stimulus. With repeated pairings, the neutral stimulus begins to elicit a response.
- In operant conditioning, responses that are followed by reinforcement occur more frequently.

How does classical conditioning occur?

- Classical conditioning, studied by Pavlov, occurs when a neutral stimulus (NS) is associated with an unconditioned stimulus (US).
- The US triggers a reflex called the unconditioned response (UR). If the NS is consistently paired with the US, it becomes a conditioned stimulus (CS). After conditioning, a CS is capable of producing a conditioned (learned) response (CR).
- When the conditioned stimulus is followed by the unconditioned stimulus, conditioning is reinforced (strengthened).
- When the CS is repeatedly presented alone, conditioning is extinguished (weakened or inhibited).
- In classical conditioning, the CS creates an expectancy that the US will follow, which alters behavior.
- In higher order conditioning, a well-learned conditioned stimulus is used as if it were an unconditioned stimulus, which leads to further learning.
- Through stimulus generalization, stimuli similar to the conditioned stimulus will also produce a response. Stimulus discrimination occurs when we learn to respond to a particular stimulus, but not to others that are similar.

Does conditioning affect emotions?

- Conditioning applies to visceral or emotional responses as well as simple reflexes. As a result, conditioned emotional responses (CERs) also occur.
- Irrational fears called phobias may begin as CERs. Conditioning of emotional responses can occur vicariously (secondhand) as well as directly.

KNOWLEDGE BUILDER

Learning and Classical Conditioning

Recite

1. The concept of reinforcement applies to both
   a. antecedents and consequences
   b. neutral stimuli and rewards
   c. classical and operant conditioning
   d. acquisition and spontaneous recovery

2. Classical conditioning, studied by the Russian physiologist _____, is also referred to as _____ conditioning.

3. You smell the odor of cookies being baked and your mouth waters. Apparently, the odor of cookies is a _____ and your salivation is a _____.
   a. CR, CS
   b. CS, CR
   c. consequence, neutral stimulus
   d. reflex, CS

4. The informational view says that classical conditioning is based on changes in mental _____ about the CS and US.

5. After you have acquired a conditioned response, it may be weakened by
   a. spontaneous recovery
   b. stimulus generalization
   c. removing reinforcement
   d. following the CS with a US

6. When a conditioned stimulus is used to reinforce the learning of a second conditioned stimulus, higher order conditioning has occurred. T or F?

7. Psychologists theorize that many phobias begin when a CER generalizes to other, similar situations. T or F?

8. Three-year-old Josh sees his 5-year-old sister get chased by a neighbor's dog. Now Josh is as afraid of the dog as his sister is. Josh's fear is a result of
   a. stimulus discrimination
   b. vicarious conditioning
   c. spontaneous recovery
   d. higher order conditioning

Reflect
Critical Thinking

9. Lately you have been getting a shock of static electricity every time you touch a door handle. Now there is a hesitation in your door-opening movements. Can you analyze this situation in terms of classical conditioning?

Relate

US, CS, UR, CR—How will you remember these terms? First, you should note that we are interested in either a stimulus (S) or a response (R). What else do we need to know? Each S or R can be either conditioned (C) or unconditioned (U).

Can a stimulus provoke a response before any learning has occurred? If it can, then it's a US. Do you have to learn to respond to the stimulus? Then it's a CS.

Does a response occur without being learned? Then it's a UR. If it has to be learned, then it's a CR.

Link

Internet addresses frequently change. To find the sites listed here, visit **http://www .thomsonedu.com/psychology/coon** for an updated list of Internet addresses and direct links to relevant sites.

- **Ivan Pavlov** Read a short biography of the man who discovered classical conditioning.
- **Classical Conditioning Experiment** Try this demonstration of classical conditioning.
- **Conditioned Emotional Responses** Read the classic 1920 paper on Little Albert.

ANSWERS

1. c 2. Pavlov, respondent 3. b 4. expectancies 5. c 6. T 7. T 8. b 9. Door handles have become conditioned stimuli that elicit the reflex withdrawal and muscle tensing that normally follows getting a shock. This conditioned response has also generalized to other handles.

Vicarious classical conditioning Classical conditioning brought about by observing another person react to a particular stimulus.

6.2 Operant Conditioning

THE PRINCIPLES of operant learning are among the most powerful tools in psychology. You won't regret learning how to use them. Operant conditioning applies to all living creatures and explains much day-to-day behavior. Operant conditioning can be used to alter the behavior of pets, children, and other adults, and your own behavior, too.

Operant Conditioning—Can Pigeons Play Ping-Pong?

SURVEY QUESTION: *How does operant conditioning occur?*

As stated earlier, in **operant conditioning** (or instrumental learning) we associate responses with their consequences. The basic principle is simple: Acts that are reinforced tend to be repeated (Mazur, 2006). Pioneer learning theorist Edward L. Thorndike called this the **law of effect**; the probability of a response is altered by the effect it has (Schultz & Schultz, 2005). Learning is strengthened each time a response is followed by a satisfying state of affairs. Think of the earlier example of the vending machine. Because kicking the machine had the effect of producing food and money, the odds of repeating the "kicking response" increased. Likewise, if you like jokes, you are much more likely to tell a joke to several different friends if each of them laughs at it. If the first three people frown when they hear the joke, you may not tell it again.

Classical conditioning is passive. It simply "happens to" the learner when a US follows a CS. In operant conditioning, the learner actively "operates on" the environment. Thus, operant conditioning refers mainly to learning *voluntary* responses. For example, pushing buttons on a TV remote control is a learned operant response. Pushing a particular button is reinforced by gaining the consequence you desire, such as changing channels or muting an obnoxious commercial. (See ■ Table 6.2 for a further comparison of classical and operant conditioning.)

Positive Reinforcement

The idea that reward affects learning is certainly nothing new to parents (and other trainers of small animals). However, parents, as well as teachers, politicians, supervisors, and even you, may use reward in ways that are inexact or misguided. A case in point is the term *reward*. To be correct, it is better to say *reinforcer*. Why? Because rewards do not always increase responding. If you try to give licorice candy to a child as a "reward" for good behavior, it will work only if the child likes licorice. What is reinforcing for one person may not be for another. As a practical rule of thumb, psychologists define an **operant reinforcer** as any event that follows a response and increases its probability of occurring again (● Fig. 6.8).

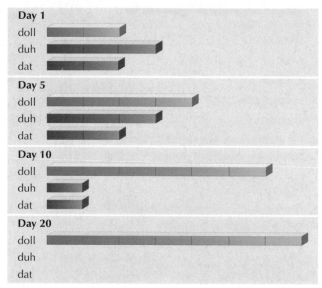

● FIGURE 6.8 Assume that a child who is learning to talk points to her favorite doll and says either "doll," "duh," or "dat" when she wants it. Day 1 shows the number of times the child uses each word to ask for the doll (each block represents one request). At first, she uses all three words interchangeably. To hasten learning, her parents decide to give her the doll only when she names it correctly. Notice how the child's behavior shifts as operant reinforcement is applied. By day 20, saying "doll" has become the most probable response.

■ **TABLE 6.2** Comparison of Classical and Operant Conditioning		
	CLASSICAL CONDITIONING	**OPERANT CONDITIONING**
Nature of response	Involuntary, reflex	Spontaneous, voluntary
Reinforcement	Occurs *before* response (CS paired with US)	Occurs *after* response (response is followed by reinforcing stimulus or event)
Role of learner	Passive (response is *elicited* by US)	Active (response is emitted)
Nature of learning	Neutral stimulus becomes a CS through association with a US	Probability of making a response is altered by consequences that follow it
Learned expectancy	US will follow CS	Response will have a specific effect

Acquiring an Operant Response

Many studies of instrumental learning have been done in a conditioning chamber, an apparatus designed to study operant conditioning in animals (Skinner, 1938). This device is also called a Skinner box, after B. F. Skinner, who invented it (● Fig. 6.9). A look into a typical Skinner box will clarify the process of operant conditioning.

THE ADVENTURES OF EINSTEIN THE RAT

A hungry (but smart) rat is placed in a small cage-like chamber. The walls are bare except for a metal lever and a tray into which food pellets can be dispensed. (See Fig. 6.9.)

Frankly, there's not much to do in a Skinner box. This increases the chances that our subject will make the response we want to reinforce, which is pressing the bar. Also, hunger keeps the animal motivated to seek food and actively *emit,* or freely give off, a variety of responses. Now let's take another look at our subject.

FURTHER ADVENTURES OF EINSTEIN THE RAT

For a while our subject walks around, grooms, sniffs at the corners, or stands on his hind legs—all typical rat behaviors. Then it happens. He places his paw on the lever to get a better view of the top of the cage. *Click!* The lever depresses, and a food pellet drops into the tray. The rat walks to the tray, eats the pellet, and then grooms himself. Up and exploring the cage again, he leans on the lever. *Click!* After a trip to the food tray, he returns to the bar and sniffs it, then puts his foot on it. *Click!* Soon the rat settles into a smooth pattern of frequent bar pressing.

Notice that the rat did not acquire a new skill in this situation. He was already able to depress the bar. Reinforcement only alters how *frequently* he presses the bar. In operant conditioning, new behavior patterns are molded by changing the probability that various responses will be made.

Information and Contingency Like classical conditioning, operant learning is based on information and expectancies. In operant conditioning, *we learn to expect that a certain response will have a certain effect at certain times* (Pierce & Cheney, 2004). That is, we learn that a particular response is associated with reinforcement (Hergenhahn & Olson, 2005). Further, operant reinforcement works best when it is *response contingent* (kon-TIN-jent). That is, it must be given only after a desired response has occurred. From this point of view, a reinforcer tells a person or an animal that a response was "right" and worth repeating.

● Figure 6.10 shows how operant reinforcement can change behavior. The results are from an effort to teach a severely disturbed 9-year-old child to say "Please," "Thank you," and "You're welcome." As you can see, during the initial, baseline period, the child rarely used the word *please.* Typically, he just grabbed objects and became angry if he couldn't have them. However, when he was reinforced for saying "Please," he soon learned to use the word nearly every time he wanted something. When the child said "Please" he was reinforced in three ways: He received the object he asked for (a crayon, for example); he was given a small food treat, such as a piece of candy, popcorn, or a grape; and he was praised for his good behavior (Matson et al., 1990).

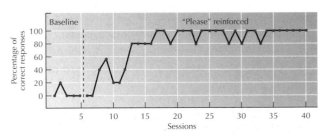

● **FIGURE 6.10** Reinforcement and human behavior. The percentage of times that a severely disturbed child said "Please" when he wanted an object was increased dramatically by reinforcing him for making a polite request. Reinforcement produced similar improvements in saying "Thank you" and "You're welcome," and the boy applied these terms in new situations as well. (Adapted from Matson et al., 1990.)

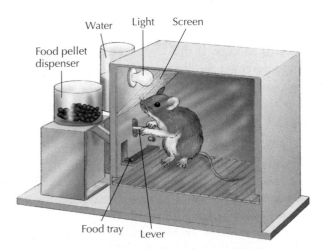

● **FIGURE 6.9** The Skinner box. This simple device, invented by B. F. Skinner, allows careful study of operant conditioning. When the rat presses the bar, a pellet of food or a drop of water is automatically released. (A photograph of a Skinner box appears in Module 1.3.)

Operant conditioning Learning based on the consequences of responding.

Law of effect Responses that lead to desirable effects are repeated; those that produce undesirable results are not.

Operant reinforcer Any event that reliably increases the probability or frequency of responses it follows.

The Timing of Reinforcement

Operant reinforcement is most effective when it rapidly follows a correct response (Mazur, 2006). For rats in a Skinner box, little learning occurs, if any, when the delay between bar pressing and receiving food exceeds 50 seconds (● Fig. 6.11). In general, you will be most successful if you present a reinforcer *immediately* after a response you wish to change. Thus, a child who is helpful or courteous should be immediately praised for her good behavior.

Let's say I work hard all semester in a class to get an A grade. Wouldn't the delay in reinforcement keep me from learning anything? No, for several reasons. First, as a mature human you can anticipate future reward. Second, you get reinforced by quiz and test grades all through the semester. Third, a single reinforcer can often maintain a long *response chain* (a linked series of actions that lead to reinforcement). A classic example of **response chaining** is provided by Barnabus, a rat trained by psychologists at Brown University.

THE GREAT BARNABUS

By carefully working from the last response to the first, Barnabus was trained to make an ever-longer chain of responses to obtain a single food pellet. When in top form, Barnabus was able to climb a spiral staircase, cross a narrow bridge, climb a ladder, pull a toy car with a chain, get into the car, pedal it to a second staircase, climb the staircase, wriggle through a tube, climb onto an elevator and descend to a platform, press a lever to receive a food pellet, and . . . start over! (Pierrel & Sherman, 1963)

Many of the things we do every day involve similar response chains. The long series of events necessary to prepare a meal is rewarded by the final eating. A violinmaker may carry out thousands of steps for the final reward of hearing a

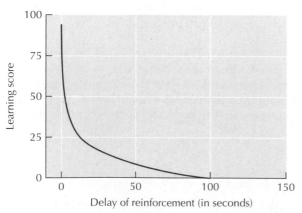

● **FIGURE 6.11** The effect of delay of reinforcement. Notice how rapidly the learning score drops when reward is delayed. Animals learning to press a bar in a Skinner box showed no signs of learning if food reward followed a bar press by more than 100 seconds (Perin, 1943).

first musical note. And as a student, you have built up a long response chain for the final reward of a good grade (right?).

Are You Superstitious? Reinforcers affect not only the specific response they follow but also other responses that occur shortly before. This helps explain many human superstitions. If a golfer taps her club on the ground three times and then hits a great shot, what happens? The successful shot reinforces not only the correct swing but also the three taps. During operant training, animals often develop similar unnecessary responses. If this happens a few times more, the golfer may superstitiously tap her club three times before every shot. Some examples of actual superstitious behaviors of professional baseball players include drawing four lines in the dirt before getting in the batter's box, eating chicken before each game, and always playing in the same athletic supporter—for 4 years (phew!) (Burger & Lynn, 2005).

Superstitious behaviors are repeated because they appear to produce reinforcement, even though they are actually unnecessary (Burger & Lynn, 2005). If you walk under a ladder and then break a leg, you may avoid ladders in the future. Each time you avoid a ladder and nothing bad happens, your superstitious action is reinforced. Belief in magic can also be explained along such lines. Rituals to bring rain, ward off illness, or produce abundant crops very likely earn the faith of participants because they occasionally appear to succeed. Besides, better safe than sorry.

Shaping

How is it possible to reinforce responses that rarely occur? Even in a barren Skinner box, it could take a long time for a rat (even one as smart as Einstein) to accidentally press the bar and get a food pellet. We might wait forever for more complicated responses to occur. For example, you would have to wait a long time for a duck to accidentally walk out of its cage, turn on a light, play a toy piano, turn off the light, and walk back to its cage. If this is what you wanted to reward, you would never get the chance.

Then how are the animals on TV and at amusement parks taught to perform complicated tricks? The answer lies in **shaping,** which is the gradual molding of responses to a desired pattern. Let's look again at our subject, Einstein.

EINSTEIN THE RAT SHAPES UP

Assume that Einstein has not yet learned to press the bar. He also shows no signs of interest in the bar. Instead of waiting for the first accidental bar press, we can shape his behavior. At first, we settle for just getting him to face the bar. Any time he turns toward the bar, he is reinforced with a bit of food. Soon Einstein spends much of his time facing the bar. Next, we reinforce him every time he takes a step toward the bar. If he turns toward the bar and walks away, nothing happens. But when he faces the bar and takes a step forward, *click!* His responses are being shaped.

By changing the rules about what makes a successful response, we can gradually train the rat to approach the bar and press it. In other words, *successive approximations* (ever-closer matches) to a desired response are reinforced during shaping. B. F. Skinner once taught two pigeons to play Ping-Pong in this way (● Fig. 6.12). Shaping applies to humans, too. Let's say you want to study more, clean the house more often, or exercise more. In each case, it would be best to set a series of gradual, daily goals. Then you can reward yourself for small steps in the right direction (Watson & Tharp, 2007).

Operant Extinction

Would a rat stop bar pressing if no more food arrived? Yes, but not immediately. Through **operant extinction,** learned responses that are not reinforced gradually fade away. Just as acquiring an operant response takes time, so does extinction. For example, if a TV program repeatedly bores you, watching the program will probably extinguish over time.

Even after extinction seems complete, the previously reinforced response may return. If a rat is removed from a Skinner box after extinction and given a short rest, the rat will press the bar again when returned to the box. Similarly, a few weeks after they give up on buying state lottery tickets, many people are tempted to try again.

Does extinction take as long the second time? If reinforcement is still withheld, a rat's bar pressing will extinguish again, usually more quickly. The brief return of an operant response after extinction is another example of spontaneous recovery (mentioned earlier regarding classical conditioning). Spontaneous recovery is very adaptive. After a rest period, the rat responds again in a situation that produced food in the past: "Just checking to see if the rules have changed!"

Marked changes in behavior occur when reinforcement and extinction are combined. For example, parents often unknowingly reinforce children for *negative attention seeking* (using misbehavior to gain attention). Children are generally ignored when they are playing quietly. They get attention when they become louder and louder, yell "Hey, Mom!" at the top of their lungs, throw tantrums, show off, or break something. Granted, the attention they get is often a scolding, but attention is a powerful reinforcer, nevertheless. Parents report dramatic improvements when they *ignore* their children's disruptive behavior and praise or attend to a child who is quiet or playing constructively.

Negative Reinforcement

Until now, we have stressed **positive reinforcement,** which occurs when a pleasant or desirable event follows a response. How else could operant learning be reinforced? The time has come to consider **negative reinforcement,** which occurs when making a response removes an unpleasant event. Don't be fooled by the word *negative.* Negative reinforcement also increases responding. However, it does so by ending (negating) discomfort.

Let's say that you have a headache and take an aspirin. Your aspirin taking will be negatively reinforced if the headache stops. Likewise, a rat could be taught to press a bar to get food (positive reinforcement), or the rat could be given a continuous mild shock (through the floor of its cage) that is turned off by a bar press (negative reinforcement). Either way, the rat will learn to press the bar more often. Why? Because it leads to a desired state of affairs (food or an end to pain). Here are two additional examples of negative reinforcement:

While walking outside, your hands get so cold they hurt. You take a pair of gloves out of your backpack and put them on, ending the pain. (Putting on the gloves is negatively reinforced.)

A politician who irritates you is being interviewed on the evening news. You change channels so you won't have to listen to him. (Channel changing is negatively reinforced.)

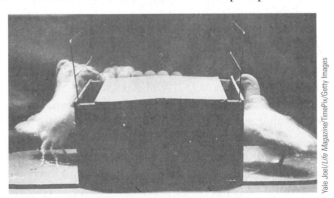

Yale Joel/*Life Magazine*/TimePix/Getty Images

● **FIGURE 6.12** Operant conditioning principles were used to train these pigeons to play Ping-Pong.

Response chaining The assembly of separate responses into a series of actions that lead to reinforcement.

Superstitious behavior A behavior repeated because it seems to produce reinforcement, even though it is actually unnecessary.

Shaping Gradually molding responses to a final desired pattern.

Operant extinction The weakening or disappearance of a nonreinforced operant response.

Positive reinforcement Occurs when a response is followed by a reward or other positive event.

Negative reinforcement Occurs when a response is followed by an end to discomfort or by the removal of an unpleasant event.

Punishment

Many people mistake negative reinforcement for punishment. However, **punishment** refers to following a response with an *aversive* (unpleasant) consequence. Punishment *decreases* the likelihood that the response will occur again. As noted, negative reinforcement *increases* responding. The difference can be seen in a hypothetical example. Let's say you live in an apartment and your neighbor's stereo is blasting so loudly that your ears hurt. If you pound on the wall and the volume suddenly drops (negative reinforcement), future wall pounding will be more likely. But if you pound on the wall and the volume increases (punishment) or if the neighbor comes over and pounds on you (more punishment), wall pounding becomes less likely. Here are two more examples of punishment, in which an unpleasant result follows a response:

> You are driving your car too fast. You are caught in a radar trap and given a speeding ticket. Henceforth, you will be less likely to speed. (Speeding was punished by a fine.)

> Every time you give advice to a friend she suddenly turns cold and distant. Lately, you've stopped offering her advice. (Giving advice was punished by rejection.)

Isn't it also punishing to have privileges, money, or other positive things taken away for making a particular response? Yes. Punishment also occurs when a reinforcer or positive state of affairs is removed, such as losing privileges. This second type of punishment is called **response cost.** Parents who "ground" their teenage children for misbehavior are applying response cost. Parking tickets and other fines are also based on response cost. For your convenience, ■ Table 6.3 summarizes four basic consequences of making a response.

Operant Reinforcers— What's Your Pleasure?

SURVEY QUESTION: *Are there different kinds of operant reinforcement?*

For humans, learning may be reinforced by anything from an M&M candy to a pat on the back. In categorizing reinforcers, useful distinctions can be made between *primary reinforcers, secondary reinforcers,* and *feedback.* Operant reinforcers of all types have a large impact on our lives. Let's examine them in more detail.

Primary Reinforcers

Primary reinforcers are natural, nonlearned, and rooted in biology: They produce comfort, end discomfort, or fill an immediate physical need. Food, water, and sex are obvious examples. Every time you open the refrigerator, walk to a drinking fountain, turn up the heat, or order a double latte, your actions reflect primary reinforcement.

In addition to obvious examples, there are other, less obvious, primary reinforcers, such as psychoactive drugs. One of the most powerful is *intracranial self-stimulation* (ICS). ICS involves the direct activation of "pleasure centers" in the brain. (See "Tickling Your Own Fancy.")

Secondary Reinforcers

Much human learning is still strongly tied to food, water, and other primary reinforcers. Regardless, humans also respond to a much broader range of rewards and reinforcers. Money, praise, attention, approval, success, affection, grades, and the like all serve as learned or **secondary reinforcers.**

How does a secondary reinforcer gain its ability to promote learning? Some secondary reinforcers are simply associated with a primary reinforcer. For example, if you would like to train a dog to follow you ("heel") when you take a walk, you could reward the dog with small food treats for staying near you. If you praise the dog each time you give it a treat, praise will become a secondary reinforcer. In time, you will be able to skip giving treats and simply praise your pup for doing the right thing. The same principle applies to children. One reason that parents' praise becomes a secondary reinforcer is because it is frequently associated with food, candy, hugs, and other primary reinforcers.

Tokens Secondary reinforcers that can be *exchanged* for primary reinforcers gain their value more directly (Mazur, 2006). Printed money obviously has little or no value of its own. You can't eat it, drink it, or sleep with it. However, it can be exchanged for food, water, lodging, and other necessities.

A **token reinforcer** is a tangible secondary reinforcer, such as money, gold stars, poker chips, and the like. In a series of classic experiments, chimpanzees were taught to work for tokens. The chimps were first trained to put poker chips into a "Chimp-O-Mat" vending machine. Each chip dispensed a few grapes or raisins. Once the animals had learned to exchange tokens for food, they would learn new tasks to earn the chips. To maintain the value of the tokens, the chimps were occasionally allowed to use the "Chimp-O-Mat" (● Fig. 6.14) (Cowles, 1937; Wolfe, 1936).

A major advantage of tokens is that they don't lose reinforcing value as quickly as primary reinforcers do. For instance, if you use candy to reinforce a developmentally disabled child for correctly naming things, the child might lose interest once he is satiated (fully satisfied) or no longer hungry. It would be better to use tokens as immediate rewards for learning. Later, the child can exchange his tokens for candy, toys, or other treats.

BRAINWAVES

Tickling Your Own Fancy

Suppose you could have an electrode permanently implanted in your brain and connected to an iPod-style controller. Twirl the controller and electrical impulses stimulate one of your brain's "pleasure centers." The very few humans who have ever had a chance to try direct brain stimulation report feeling intense pleasure that is better than food, water, sex, drugs, or any other primary reinforcer (Heath, 1963). (See ● Fig. 6.13.)

Most of what we know about intracranial self-stimulation comes from studying rats with similar implants (Olds & Fobes, 1981). A rat "wired for pleasure" can be trained to press the bar in a Skinner box to deliver electrical stimulation to its own limbic system. (Refer back to Fig. 2.27.) Some rats will press the bar thousands of times per hour to obtain brain stimulation. After 15 or 20 hours of constant pressing, animals sometimes collapse from exhaustion. When they revive, they begin pressing again. If the reward circuit is not turned off,

an animal will ignore food, water, and sex in favor of bar pressing.

Many natural primary reinforcers activate the same pleasure pathways in the brain that make ICS so powerful (McBride, Murphy, & Ikemoto, 1999). So do psychoactive drugs, such as alcohol and cocaine (Eisler, Justice, Jr., & Neill, 2004; Rodd et al., 2005). In fact, rats will also self-administer nicotine. When they do, they are even more likely to engage in ICS (Kenny & Markou, 2006). Apparently, nicotine further increases the sensitivity of pleasure pathways in the brain.

One shudders to think what might happen if brain implants were easy and practical to do. (They are not.) Every company from Playboy to Microsoft would have a device on the market, and we would have to keep a closer watch on politicians than usual!

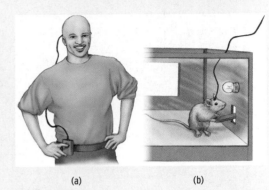

(a)   (b)

● **FIGURE 6.13** Humans have been "wired" for brain stimulation, as shown in (a). However, in humans, this has been done only as an experimental way to restrain uncontrollable outbursts of violence. Implants have not been done merely to produce pleasure. Most research has been carried out with rats. Using the apparatus shown in (b), the rat can press a bar to deliver mild electric stimulation to a "pleasure center" in the brain.

	CONSEQUENCE OF MAKING A RESPONSE	EXAMPLE	EFFECT ON RESPONSE PROBABILITY
Positive reinforcement	Positive event begins	Food given	Increase
Negative reinforcement	Negative event ends	Pain stops	Increase
Punishment	Negative event begins	Pain begins	Decrease
Punishment (response cost)	Positive event ends	Food removed	Decrease
Nonreinforcement	Nothing	———	Decrease

■ **TABLE 6.3   Behavioral Effects of Various Consequences**

Tokens have been used with troubled children and adults in special programs, and even in ordinary elementary school classrooms (Spiegler & Guevremont, 2003) (● Fig. 6.15). In each case the goal is to provide an immediate reward for learning. Typically, tokens may be exchanged for food, special privileges, or trips to movies, amusement parks, and so forth. Many parents find that tokens greatly reduce discipline problems with younger children. For example, children can earn points or gold stars during the week for good behavior. If they earn enough tokens, they are allowed on Sunday to choose one item out of a "grab bag" of small prizes.

Punishment Any event that follows a response and *decreases* its likelihood of occurring again.

Response cost Removal of a positive reinforcer after a response is made.

Primary reinforcers Nonlearned reinforcers; usually those that satisfy physiological needs.

Secondary reinforcer A learned reinforcer; often one that gains reinforcing properties by association with a primary reinforcer.

Token reinforcer A tangible secondary reinforcer such as money, gold stars, poker chips, and the like.

Chimp-O-Mat, Yukes Regional Primate Research Center, Emory University

● **FIGURE 6.14** Poker chips normally have little or no value for chimpanzees, but this chimp will work hard to earn them once he learns that the "Chimp-O-Mat" will dispense food in exchange for them.

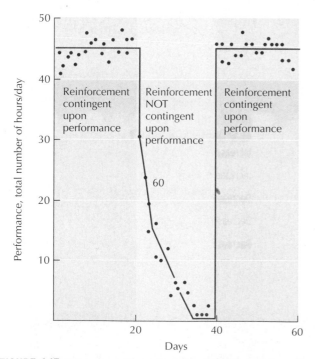

● **FIGURE 6.15** Reinforcement in a token economy. This graph shows the effects of using tokens to reward socially desirable behavior in a mental hospital ward. Desirable behavior was defined as cleaning, making the bed, attending therapy sessions, and so forth. Tokens earned could be exchanged for basic amenities such as meals, snacks, coffee, game-room privileges, or weekend passes. The graph shows more than 24 hours per day because it represents the total number of hours of desirable behavior performed by all patients in the ward. (Adapted from Ayllon & Azrin, 1965.)

Social Reinforcers As we have noted, learned desires for attention and approval, which are called **social reinforcers,** often influence human behavior. This fact can be used in a classic, if somewhat mischievous, demonstration.

SHAPING A TEACHER

For this activity, about one half (or more) of the students in a classroom must participate. First, select a target behavior. This should be something like "lecturing from the right side of the room." (Keep it simple, in case your teacher is a slow learner.) Begin training in this way: Each time the instructor turns toward the right or takes a step in that direction, participating students should look *really* interested. Also, smile, ask questions, lean forward, and make eye contact. If the teacher turns to the left or takes a step in that direction, participating students should lean back, yawn, check out their split ends, close their eyes, or generally look bored. Soon, without being aware of why, the instructor should be spending most of his or her time each class period lecturing from the right side of the classroom.

This trick has been a favorite of psychology graduate students for decades. For a time, one of your author's professors delivered all her lectures from the right side of the room while toying with the cords on the window shades. (We added the cords the second week!) The point to remember from this example is that attention and approval can change the behavior of children, family members, friends, roommates, and co-workers. Be aware of what you are reinforcing.

Feedback

His eyes, driven and blazing, dart from side to side. His left hand twitches, dances, rises, and strikes, hitting its target again and again. At the same time, his right hand furiously spins in circular motions. Does this describe some strange neurological disorder? Actually, it depicts 10-year-old Vikram as he plays his favorite video game, an animated skateboarding adventure!

How did Vikram learn the complex movements needed to excel at virtual skateboarding? After all, he was not rewarded with food or money. The answer lies in the fact that Vikram's favorite video game provides *feedback,* a key element that underlies learning. **Feedback** (information about the effect a response had) is particularly important in human learning (Lefrançois, 2006).

Every time a player moves, a video game responds instantly with sounds, animated actions, and a higher or lower score. The machine's responsiveness and the information flow it provides can be very motivating if you want to win. The

DISCOVERING PSYCHOLOGY

Conditioning and Conservation

Psychologists enjoy seeing behavioral principles used to solve practical problems. One area of behavior very much in need of attention is our "throw-away" society. We burn fossil fuels; destroy forests; use chemical products; and strip, clear, and farm the land. In doing so, we alter the very face of the Earth. What can be done? One approach involves changing the *consequences* of wasteful energy use, polluting, and the like. For example, energy taxes can be used to increase the cost of using fossil fuels (response cost). On the reinforcement side of the equation, rebates can be offered for installing insulation, or buying energy-efficient appliances or cars, and tax breaks can be given to companies that take steps to preserve the environment.

On a daily level, people can help recycle materials such as paper, steel, glass, aluminum, and plastic. Again, behavioral principles come into play. For instance, people who set their own goals for recycling tend to meet them. Likewise, when families, work groups, factories, and dorms receive feedback, on a weekly basis, about how much they recycled, they typically recycle more. Recycling is also more effective when entire families participate, with some family members (usually mom, of course) reinforcing the recycling behavior of other family members (Meneses & Beerlipalacio, 2005). We also know that people are more likely to continue recycling if they feel a sense of satisfaction from helping protect the environment (Ewing, 2001). Is such satisfaction sufficiently reinforcing to encourage more people to reduce, reuse, and recycle? We certainly hope so.

same principle applies to many other learning situations: If you are trying to learn to use a computer, to play a musical instrument, to cook, or to solve math problems, reinforcement comes from feedback that you achieved a desired result.

The adaptive value of feedback helps explain why much human learning occurs in the absence of obvious reinforcers, such as food or water. Humans readily learn responses that merely have a desired effect or that bring a goal closer. Let's explore this idea further.

Knowledge of Results Imagine that you are asked to throw darts at a target. Each dart must pass over a screen that prevents you from telling if you hit the target. If you threw 1,000 darts, we would expect little improvement in your performance because no feedback is provided. Vikram's video game did not explicitly reward him for correct responses. Yet, because it provided feedback, rapid learning took place.

How can feedback be applied? Increased feedback (also called **knowledge of results, or KR**) almost always improves learning and performance (Horn et al., 2005). If you want to learn to play a musical instrument, to sing, to speak a second language, or to deliver a speech, recorded feedback can be very helpful. In sports, videos replays are used to provide feedback on everything from tennis serves to pick-off moves in baseball. Whenever you are trying to learn a complex skill, it pays to get more feedback (Wulf et al., 2002). (Also, see "Conditioning and Conservation.")

Learning Aids

How do these techniques make use of feedback? Feedback is most effective when it is *frequent, immediate,* and *detailed.* *Programmed instruction* teaches students in a format that presents information in small amounts, gives immediate practice, and provides continuous feedback to learners. Frequent feedback keeps learners from practicing errors. It also lets students work at their own pace. (A small sample of programmed instruction is shown in ● Figure 6.16 so that you can see what the format looks like.) Programmed learning can be done in book form, presented on a CD-ROM or through the web (Emurian, 2005; McDonald, Yanchar, & Osguthorpe, 2005).

In *computer-assisted instruction (CAI),* learning is aided by computer-presented information and exercises. In addition to giving learners immediate feedback, the computer can give hints about why an answer was wrong and what is needed to correct it (Timmerman & Kruepke, 2006). Although the final level of skill or knowledge gained is not necessarily higher, CAI can save much time and effort. In addition, people often do better with feedback from a computer because they can freely make mistakes and learn from them (Luyben, Hipworth, & Pappas, 2003; Norton, 2003). For example, CAI can give medical students unlimited practice at diagnosing diseases from symptoms, such as "acute chest pain" (Papa, Aldrich, & Schumacker, 1999).

Some CAI programs, called *serious games,* make use of instructional games in which stories, competition with a partner, sound effects, and game-like graphics increase interest and motivation (Michael & Chen, 2006) (● Fig. 6.17). Educational simulations allow students to explore an imagi-

Social reinforcer Reinforcement based on receiving attention, approval, or affection from another person.

Feedback Information returned to a person about the effects a response has had; also known as knowledge of results.

Knowledge of results (KR) Informational feedback.

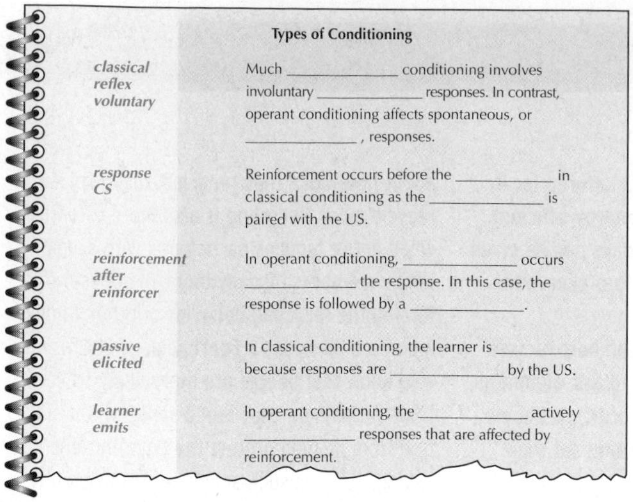

Types of Conditioning

classical reflex voluntary	Much _____ conditioning involves involuntary _____ responses. In contrast, operant conditioning affects spontaneous, or _____ , responses.
response CS	Reinforcement occurs before the _____ in classical conditioning as the _____ is paired with the US.
reinforcement after reinforcer	In operant conditioning, _____ occurs _____ the response. In this case, the response is followed by a _____ .
passive elicited	In classical conditioning, the learner is _____ because responses are _____ by the US.
learner emits	In operant conditioning, the _____ actively _____ responses that are affected by reinforcement.

● **FIGURE 6.16** To sample a programmed instruction format, try covering the terms on the left with a piece of paper. As you fill in the blanks, uncover one new term for each response. In this way, your correct (or incorrect) responses will be followed by immediate feedback.

nary situation or "microworld" that simulates real-world problems. By seeing the effects of their choices, students discover basic principles of physics, biology, psychology, or other subjects (Grabe, 2006).

As psychologists fully explore the value and limits of computer-assisted instruction, it seems likely that their efforts will improve not only education but our understanding of human learning as well. Let's pause now for some learning exercises so that you can get some feedback about your mastery of the preceding ideas.

MODULE 6.2 Summary

How does operant conditioning occur?

- To understand why people behave as they do, it is important to identify how their responses are being reinforced.

- Operant conditioning occurs when a voluntary action is followed by a reinforcer, which increases the frequency of the response. Operant learning is based on the law of effect.

- Delaying reinforcement greatly reduces its effectiveness, but long chains of responses may be maintained by a single reinforcer.

- Superstitious behaviors often become part of response chains because they *appear* to be associated with reinforcement.

- By rewarding successive approximations to a particular response, behavior can be shaped into desired patterns.

- If an operant response is not reinforced, it may extinguish (disappear). But after extinction seems complete, it may temporarily reappear (spontaneous recovery).

- Both positive reinforcement and negative reinforcement increase the likelihood that a response will be repeated. Punishment decreases the likelihood that the response will occur again.

Are there different kinds of operant reinforcement?

- Operant learning may be based on primary reinforcers or secondary reinforcers.

- Feedback, or knowledge of results, also aids learning and improves performance.

- Programmed instruction breaks learning into a series of small steps and provides immediate feedback. Computer-assisted instruction (CAI) does the same but has the added advantage of providing alternative exercises and information when needed.

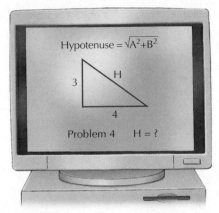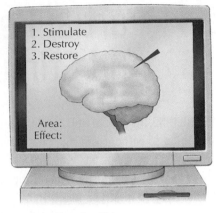

● **FIGURE 6.17** Computer-assisted instruction. The screen on the left shows a typical drill-and-practice math problem, in which students must find the hypotenuse of a triangle. The center screen presents the same problem as an instructional game to increase interest and motivation. In the game, a child is asked to set the proper distance on a ray gun in the hovering space ship to "vaporize" an attacker. The screen on the right depicts an educational simulation. Here, students place a "probe" at various spots in a human brain. They then "stimulate," "destroy," or "restore" areas. As each area is altered, it is named on the screen and the effects on behavior are described. This allows students to explore basic brain functions on their own.

KNOWLEDGE BUILDER

Operant Conditioning

Recite

1. Responses in operant conditioning are _____ or _____, whereas those in classical conditioning are passive, _____, or _____ responses.

2. Changing the rules in small steps so that an animal (or person) is gradually trained to respond as desired is called _____.

3. Extinction in operant conditioning is also subject to _____ of a response.
   a. successive approximations
   b. shaping
   c. automation
   d. spontaneous recovery

4. Positive reinforcers increase the rate of responding, and negative reinforcers decrease it. T or F?

5. Primary reinforcers are those learned through classical conditioning. T or F?

6. Which is a correct match?
   a. social reinforcer-primary reinforcement
   b. token reinforcer-secondary reinforcement
   c. ICS-secondary reinforcement
   d. negative reinforcer-punishment

7. Superstitious responses are those that are
   a. shaped by secondary reinforcement
   b. extinguished
   c. prepotent
   d. unnecessary to obtain reinforcement

8. Knowledge of results, or KR, is also known as _____.

9. CAI is based on the same principles as
   a. negative reinforcement
   b. programmed instruction
   c. higher order conditioning
   d. stimulus generalization

Reflect
Critical Thinking

10. How might operant conditioning principles be used to encourage people to pick up litter? (What rewards could be offered, and how might the cost of rewards be kept low?)

Relate

How have your thoughts about the effects of "rewards" changed now that you've read about operant conditioning? Can you explain the difference between positive reinforcement, negative reinforcement, and punishment? Can you give an example of each concept from your own experience?

A friend of yours punishes his dog all the time. What advice would you give him about how to use reinforcement, extinction, and shaping, instead of punishment?

Link

Internet addresses frequently change. To find the sites listed here, visit **http://www.thomsonedu.com/psychology/coon** for an updated list of Internet addresses and direct links to relevant sites.
- **B.F. Skinner** Read about the life and work of B. F. Skinner in his own words.
- **Clicker Training for Animals** One approach to using operant conditioning to train animals.
- **Hardwired for Happiness** Are our brains hardwired for happiness?

ANSWERS

1. voluntary or emitted, involuntary or elicited 2. shaping 3. d 4. F 5. F 6. b 7. d 8. feedback 9. b 10. A strategy that has been used with some success is to hold drawings for various prizes, such as movie or concert passes. Each time a person turns in a specific amount of litter, he or she receives one chance (a token) to enter in the drawing. Giving refunds for cans and bottles is another way to reinforce recycling of litter.

6.3 Partial Reinforcement and Stimulus Control

ANYONE WISHING TO INFLUENCE operant learning would be ill equipped to do so without knowing how various patterns of reinforcement affect behavior. Imagine, for example, that a mother wants to reward her child for turning off the lights when he leaves a room. Contrary to what you might think, she would be well advised to reinforce only some of her son's correct responses. Why would this be so? You'll find the answer in this module. You'll also learn how antecedent stimuli control our behavior in a stop-and-go fashion.

Partial Reinforcement—Las Vegas, a Human Skinner Box?

SURVEY QUESTION: *How are we influenced by patterns of reward?*

Until now, we have treated operant reinforcement as if it were continuous. *Continuous reinforcement* means that a reinforcer follows every correct response. This is fine for the lab, but it has little to do with the real world. Most of our responses are more inconsistently rewarded. In daily life, learning is usually based on **partial reinforcement,** in which reinforcers do not follow every response. Partial reinforcement can be given in several patterns, called **schedules of reinforcement** (plans for determining which responses will be reinforced). Each has a distinct effect on behavior. In addition to these (which will be explored in a moment), there is a general effect: Responses acquired by partial reinforcement are highly resistant to extinction (Svartdal, 2003). For some obscure reason, lost in the lore of psychology, this is called the **partial reinforcement effect.**

How does getting reinforced part of the time make a habit stronger? If you have ever visited Las Vegas or a similar gambling mecca, you have probably seen row after row of people playing slot machines. To gain insight into partial reinforcement, imagine that you are making your first visit to Las Vegas. You put a dollar in a slot machine and pull the handle. Ten dollars spills into the tray. Using one of your newly won dollars, you pull the handle again. Another payoff! Let's say this continues for 15 minutes. Every pull is followed by a payoff. Suddenly each pull is followed by nothing. Obviously, you would respond several times more before giving up. However, when continuous reinforcement is followed by extinction, the message soon becomes clear: No more payoffs.

The one-armed bandit (slot machine) is a dispenser of partial reinforcement.

Christoph Wilhelm/Getty Images

Contrast this with partial reinforcement. Again, imagine that this is your first encounter with a slot machine. You put a dollar in the machine five times without a payoff. You are just about to quit, but decide to play once more. Bingo! The machine returns $20. After this, payoffs continue on a partial schedule; some are large, and some are small. All are unpredictable. Sometimes you hit 2 in a row, and sometimes 20 or 30 pulls go unrewarded.

Now let's say the payoff mechanism is turned off again. How many times do you think you would respond this time before your handle-pulling behavior extinguished? Because you have developed the expectation that any play may be "the one," it will be hard to resist just one more play . . . and one more . . . and one more. Also, because partial reinforcement includes long periods of nonreward, it will be harder to discriminate between periods of reinforcement and extinction. It is no exaggeration to say that the partial reinforcement effect has left many people penniless. Even psychologists visiting Las Vegas may get "cleaned out" (not your authors, of course!).

Schedules of Partial Reinforcement

Partial reinforcement can be given in many different patterns (Domjan, 2006). Let's consider the four most basic, which have some interesting effects on us. Typical responses to each pattern are shown in ● Figure 6.18. Results such as these are obtained when a cumulative recorder is connected to a Skinner box. The device consists of a moving strip of paper and a mechanical pen that jumps upward each time a response is made. Rapid responding causes the pen to draw a steep line; a horizontal line indicates no response. Small tick marks on the lines show when a reinforcer was given.

Fixed Ratio (FR)

What would happen if a reinforcer followed only every other response? Or what if we followed every third, fourth, fifth, or other number of responses with reinforcement? Each of these patterns is a **fixed ratio (FR) schedule** (a set number of correct responses must be made to obtain a reinforcer). Notice that in an FR schedule the ratio of reinforcers to responses is fixed: FR-2 means that every other response is rewarded; FR-3 means that every third response is reinforced; in an FR-10 schedule, exactly 10 responses must be made to obtain a reinforcer.

Fixed ratio schedules produce *very high response rates.* (See Fig. 6.18.) A hungry rat on an FR-10 schedule will quickly run off 10 responses, pause to eat, and then run off 10 more. A similar situation occurs when factory or farm workers are paid on a piecework basis. When a fixed number of items must be produced for a set amount of pay, work output is high.

Variable Ratio (VR)

In a **variable ratio (VR) schedule** a varied number of correct responses must be made to get a reinforcer. Instead of reinforcing every fourth response (FR-4), for example, a person or animal on a VR-4 schedule gets rewarded *on the average* every fourth response. Sometimes 2 responses must be made to obtain a reinforcer; sometimes it's 5, sometimes 4, and so on. The actual number varies, but it averages out to 4 (in this example). Variable ratio schedules also produce high response rates.

VR schedules seem less predictable than FR. Does that have any effect on extinction? Yes. Because reinforcement is less predictable, VR schedules tend to produce greater resistance to extinction than fixed ratio schedules. Playing a slot machine is an example of behavior maintained by a variable ratio schedule. Another would be a child asking for a "treat" at the supermarket. The number of times the child must ask before getting reinforced varies, so the child becomes quite persistent. Golf, tennis, baseball, and many other sports are also reinforced on a variable ratio basis: Even the best batters in baseball rarely hit more than an average of 3 out of every 10 balls pitched to them.

Fixed Interval (FI)

In another pattern, reinforcement is given only when a correct response is made after a fixed amount of time has passed. This time interval is measured from the last reinforced response. Responses made during the time interval are not reinforced. In a **fixed interval (FI) schedule** the first correct response made after the time period has passed is reinforced. Thus, a rat on an FI-30-second schedule has to wait 30 seconds after the last reinforced response before a bar press will pay off again. The rat can press the bar as often as it wants during the interval, but it will not be rewarded.

Fixed interval schedules produce *moderate response rates.* These are marked by spurts of activity mixed with periods of inactivity. Animals working on an FI schedule seem to develop a keen sense of the passage of time (Eckerman, 1999). (See "Are Animals Stuck in Time?") For example:

EINSTEIN THE RAT TAKES A BREAK

Einstein, trained on an FI-60-second schedule, has just been reinforced for a bar press. What does he do? He saunters around the cage, grooms himself, hums, whistles, reads magazines, and polishes his

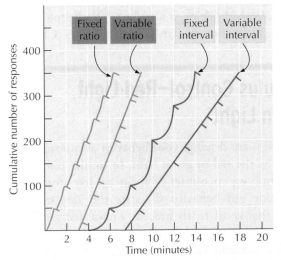

● **FIGURE 6.18** Typical response patterns for reinforcement schedules.

Partial reinforcement A pattern in which only a portion of all responses are reinforced.

Schedule of reinforcement A rule or plan for determining which responses will be reinforced.

Partial reinforcement effect Responses acquired with partial reinforcement are more resistant to extinction.

Fixed ratio (FR) schedule A set number of correct responses must be made to get a reinforcer. For example, a reinforcer is given for every four correct responses.

Variable ratio (VR) schedule A varied number of correct responses must be made to get a reinforcer. For example, a reinforcer is given after three to seven correct responses; the actual number changes randomly.

Fixed interval (FI) schedule A reinforcer is given only when a correct response is made after a set amount of time has passed since the last reinforced response. Responses made during the time interval are not reinforced.

CRITICAL THINKING

Are Animals Stuck in Time?

We humans are *cognitive time travelers*, regularly zooming back and forth through time in our minds. You can, for example, think about past events, such as what you had for breakfast this morning. We can also imagine events in the future. Brides-to-be are famous for planning their weddings down to the last detail. But what about animals? Are they cognitive time travelers or are they "stuck in time" (Roberts, 2002; Zentall, 2005)? Do dogs ever think about how hot it was yesterday or what they plan to do tomorrow? To answer such questions, psychologists have used operant conditioning as a research tool.

Conditioning studies have repeatedly shown that animals are sensitive to the passage of time (Zentall, 2005). For example, pigeons and rats reinforced on fixed interval schedules stop responding immediately after they receive a reinforcer and do not start again until just before the next scheduled reinforcement (Roberts, 2002). In one study, pigeons were put in a Skinner box with a pecking key

on each wall. They quickly learned to peck only at Key 1 if it was 9:30 in the morning and at Key 3 if it was 4:00 in the afternoon (Saksida & Wilkie, 1994).

Another study focused on scrub jays. These birds are hoarders; they store excess food at different locations and then go back later to eat it. Scrub jays were allowed to hoard some nuts in one location and some worms in another. If they were released 4 hours later, they went directly to the worms. However, if they are released 5 days later, they went straight for the nuts. Worms are a scrub jay's favorite food, which explains their choice after 4 hours. But worms decay after a day or so, while nuts stay edible. It seems that the jays knew exactly where they stored each type of food and how much time had passed (Clayton, Yu, & Dickinson, 2001).

While these studies are suggestive, they are part of an ongoing debate about whether or not animals are stuck in time (Roberts & Roberts, 2002). Nevertheless, be careful if you

Florida scrub jays are food hoarders. Does their food hoarding behavior prove they are not "trapped in time"?

forget to feed your beloved dog, Rover, at his usual mealtime. If he has been conditioned to think it's time to eat, he may settle for your favorite flip-flops instead of dog food!

---

nails. After 50 seconds, he walks to the bar and gives it a press—just testing. After 55 seconds, he gives it two or three presses, but there's still no payoff. Fifty-eight seconds, and he settles down to rapid pressing, 59 seconds, 60 seconds, and he hits the reinforced press. After one or two more presses (unrewarded), he wanders off again for the next interval.

Is getting paid weekly an FI schedule? Pure examples of fixed interval schedules are rare, but getting paid each week at work does come close. Notice, however, that most people do not work faster just before payday, as an FI schedule predicts. A closer parallel would be having a report due every 2 weeks for a class. Right after turning in a paper, your work would probably drop to zero for a week or more (Chance, 2006).

Variable Interval (VI) **Variable interval (VI)** schedules are a variation on fixed intervals. Here, reinforcement is given for the first correct response made after a varied amount of time. On a VI-30-second schedule, reinforcement is available after an interval that *averages* 30 seconds.

VI schedules produce *slow, steady response rates* and tremendous resistance to extinction (Lattal, Reilly, & Kohn, 1998). When you dial a phone number and get a busy signal, reward (getting through) is on a VI schedule. You may have to wait 30 seconds or 30 minutes. If you are like most people, you will doggedly dial over and over again until you get a connection. Success in fishing is also on a VI schedule—which may explain the bulldog tenacity of many anglers (Chance, 2006).

Stimulus Control—Red Light, Green Light

When you are driving, your behavior at intersections is controlled by the red or green light. In similar fashion, many of the stimuli we encounter each day act like stop or go signals that guide our behavior. To state the idea more formally, stimuli that consistently precede a rewarded response tend to influence when and where the response will occur. This effect is called **stimulus control.** Notice how it works with our friend Einstein.

LIGHTS OUT FOR EINSTEIN THE RAT
While learning the bar-pressing response, Einstein has been in a Skinner box illuminated by a bright light. During several training sessions, the light is alternately turned on and off. When the light is on, a bar press will produce food. When the light is off, bar pressing goes unrewarded. We soon observe that the rat presses vigorously when the light is on and ignores the bar when the light is off.

In this example, the light signals what consequences will follow if a response is made. Evidence for stimulus control could be shown by turning the food delivery *on* when the light is *off*. A well-trained animal might never discover that the rules had changed. A similar example of stimulus control would be a child learning to ask for candy when her mother is in a good mood, but not asking at other times. Likewise, we pick up phones that are ringing, but rarely answer phones that are silent. Thus, a simplified summary of stimulus control is: Notice something, do something, get something (Powell, Symbaluk, & Macdonald, 2005).

Generalization Two important aspects of stimulus control are generalization and discrimination. Let's return to the example of the vending machine (from the chapter preview) to illustrate these concepts. First, generalization.

Is generalization the same in operant conditioning as it is in classical conditioning? Basically, yes. **Operant stimulus generalization** is the tendency to respond to stimuli similar to those that preceded operant reinforcement. That is, a reinforced response tends to be made again when similar antecedents are present. Assume, for instance, that you have been reliably rewarded for kicking one particular vending machine. Your kicking response tends to occur in the presence of that machine. It has come under stimulus control. Now let's say that there are three other machines on campus identical to the one that pays off. Because they are similar, your kicking response may well transfer to them. If each of these machines also pays off when kicked, your kicking response may *generalize* to other machines only mildly similar to the original. Similar generalization explains why children may temporarily call all men *daddy*—much to the embarrassment of their parents.

Discrimination Meanwhile, back at the vending machine. . . . As stated earlier, to discriminate means to respond differently to varied stimuli. Because one vending machine reinforced your kicking response, you began kicking other identical machines (generalization). Because these also paid off, you began kicking similar machines (more generalization). If kicking these new machines has no effect, the kicking response that generalized to them will extinguish because of nonreinforcement. Thus, your response to machines of a particular size and color is consistently rewarded, whereas the same response to different machines is extinguished. Through **operant stimulus discrimination** you have learned to differentiate between antecedent stimuli that signal reward and nonreward. As a result, your response pattern will shift to match these **discriminative stimuli** (stimuli that precede reinforced and nonreinforced responses).

A discriminative stimulus that most drivers are familiar with is a police car on the freeway. This stimulus is a clear signal that a specific set of reinforcement contingencies applies. As you have probably observed, the presence of a police car brings about rapid reductions in driving speed, lane changes, and tailgating.

The role of discriminative stimuli may be clarified by an interesting feat achieved by Jack, a psychologist friend of one of your authors. Here is his account of what Jack did:

Jack decided to teach his cat to say its name. To begin, he gave the cat a pat on the back. If the cat meowed in a way that sounded anything like its name, Jack immediately gave the cat a small amount of food. If the cat made this unusual meow at other times, it received nothing. This process was repeated many times each day.

By gradual shaping, the cat's meow was made to sound very much like its name. Also, this peculiar meow came under stimulus control: When it received a pat on the back, the cat said its name; without the pat, it remained silent or meowed normally.

I should add at this point that I was unaware that Jack had a new cat or that he had trained it. I went to visit him one night and met the cat on the front steps. I gave the cat a pat on the back and said, "Hi kitty, what's your name?" Imagine my surprise when the cat immediately replied, "Ralph"!

Variable interval (VI) schedule A reinforcer is given for the first correct response made after a varied amount of time has passed since the last reinforced response. Responses made during the time interval are not reinforced.

Stimulus control Stimuli present when an operant response is acquired tend to control when and where the response is made.

Operant stimulus generalization The tendency to respond to stimuli similar to those that preceded operant reinforcement.

Operant stimulus discrimination The tendency to make an operant response when stimuli previously associated with reward are present and to withhold the response when stimuli associated with nonreward are present.

Discriminative stimuli Stimuli that precede rewarded and nonrewarded responses in operant conditioning.

Carleton Ray/Photo Researchers, Inc.

Stimulus control. Operant shaping was used to teach this whale to "bow" to an audience. Fish were used as reinforcers. Notice the trainer's hand signal, which serves as a discriminative stimulus to control the performance.

Psychologists symbolize a stimulus that precedes reinforced responses as an S+. Discriminative stimuli that precede unrewarded responses are symbolized as S— (Chance, 2006). Thus, ● Figure 6.19 summarizes Ralph's training.

Stimulus discrimination is also aptly illustrated by the "sniffer" dogs that locate drugs and explosives at airports and border crossings. Operant discrimination is used to teach these dogs to recognize contraband. During training, they are reinforced only for approaching containers baited with drugs or explosives.

Stimulus discrimination clearly has a tremendous impact on human behavior. Learning to recognize different automobile brands, birds, animals, wines, types of music, and even the answers on psychology tests all depends, in part, on operant discrimination learning.

Antecedent	Response	Consequence
S+ ⟶	"Ralph" ⟶	Food
S− ⟶	"Ralph" ⟶	Nothing
S+ ⟶	"Meow" ⟶	Nothing

● **FIGURE 6.19** A diagram of Ralph the cat's discrimination training.

MODULE 6.3 Summary

How are we influenced by patterns of reward?

- Reward or reinforcement may be given continuously (after every response) or on a schedule of partial reinforcement. Partial reinforcement produces greater resistance to extinction.

- Five basic schedules of reinforcement are continuous, fixed ratio, variable ratio, fixed interval, and variable interval. Each schedule produces a different pattern of responding.

- Stimuli that precede a reinforced response tend to control when and where operant responses occur (stimulus control). Two aspects of stimulus control are generalization and discrimination.

- In generalization, an operant response tends to occur when stimuli similar to those preceding reinforcement are present.

- In discrimination, responses are given in the presence of discriminative stimuli associated with reinforcement (S+) and withheld in the presence of stimuli associated with nonreinforcement (S–).

KNOWLEDGE BUILDER

Partial Reinforcement and Stimulus Control

Recite

1. Two aspects of stimulus control are
_____ and
_____.

2. Responding tends to occur in the presence of discriminative stimuli associated with reinforcement and tends not to occur in the presence of discriminative stimuli associated with nonreinforcement. T or F?

3. *Stimulus generalization* refers to making an operant response in the presence of stimuli similar to those that preceded reinforcement. T or F?

4. Moderate response rates that are marked by spurts of activity and periods of inactivity are characteristic of
a. FR schedules
b. VR schedules
c. FI schedules
d. VI schedules

5. Partial reinforcement tends to produce slower responding and reduced resistance to extinction. T or F?

6. The schedule of reinforcement associated with playing slot machines and other types of gambling is
a. fixed ratio
b. variable ratio
c. fixed interval
d. variable interval

Reflect
Critical Thinking

7. A business owner who pays employees an hourly wage wants to increase productivity. How could the owner make more effective use of reinforcement?

8. How could you use conditioning principles to teach a dog or a cat to come when called?

Relate

Think of something you do that is reinforced only part of the time. Do you pursue this activity persistently? How have you been affected by partial reinforcement?

See if you can think of at least one everyday example of the five basic schedules of reinforcement.

Doors that are meant to be pushed outward have metal plates on them. Those that are meant to be pulled inward have handles. Do these discriminative stimuli affect your behavior? (If they don't, how's your nose doing?)

Link

Internet addresses frequently change. To find the sites listed here, visit **http://www .thomsonedu.com/psychology/coon** for an updated list of Internet addresses and direct links to relevant sites.

- **Schedules of Reinforcement** Read more about partial reinforcement schedules.

- **Stimuli** Explore the different functions stimuli can serve.

- **Positive and Negative Discriminative Stimuli in Animal Training** Read about the application of discriminative stimuli in animal training.

ANSWERS

1. generalization, discrimination 2. T 3. T 4. c 5. F 6. b 7. Continuing to use fixed interval rewards (hourly wage or salary) would guarantee a basic level of income for employees. To reward extra effort, the owner could add some fixed ratio reinforcement (such as incentives, bonuses, commissions, or profit sharing) to employees' pay. 8. An excellent way to train a pet is to give a distinctive call or whistle each time you feed the animal. This makes the signal a secondary reinforcer and a discriminative stimulus for reward (food). Of course, it also helps to directly reinforce an animal with praise, petting, or food for coming when called.

SPANKINGS, reprimands, fines, jail sentences, firings, failing grades, and the like are commonly used to control behavior. Clearly, the story of learning is unfinished without a return to the topic of punishment.

Punishment—Putting the Brakes on Behavior

SURVEY QUESTION: *What does punishment do to behavior?*

Recall that **punishment** lowers the probability that a response will occur again. To be most effective, punishment must be given contingently (only after an undesired response occurs). Punishers, like reinforcers, are defined by observing their effects on behavior. A **punisher** is any consequence that reduces the frequency of a target behavior. It is not always possible to know ahead of time what will act as a punisher for a particular person. For example, when Jason's mother reprimanded him for throwing toys, he stopped doing it. In this instance, the reprimand was a punisher. However, Chris is starved for attention of any kind from his parents, who both work full-time. For Chris, a reprimand, or even a spanking, might actually reinforce toy throwing. Remember, too, that a punisher can be either the onset of an unpleasant event or the removal of a positive state of affairs (response cost).

Variables Affecting Punishment

How effective is punishment? Although many people assume that punishment stops unacceptable behavior, the effectiveness of punishers depends greatly on their *timing, consistency,* and *intensity.* Punishment works best when it occurs as the response is being made or *immediately* afterward (timing), and when it is given *each time* a response occurs (consis-

tency). Thus, you could effectively (and humanely) punish a dog that barks incessantly by spraying water on its nose each time it barks. About 10 to 15 such treatments are usually enough to greatly reduce barking. This would not be the case if you applied punishment haphazardly or long after the barking stopped. If you discover that your dog dug up a tree and ate it while you were gone, punishing the dog hours later will do little good. Likewise, the commonly heard childhood threat, "Wait 'til your father comes home, then you'll be sorry," just makes the father a feared brute; it doesn't effectively punish an undesirable response.

Severe punishment (following a response with an intensely aversive or unpleasant stimulus) can be extremely effective in stopping behavior. If 3-year-old Beavis sticks his finger in a light socket and gets a shock, that may be the last time he *ever* tries it. However, mild punishment only temporarily *suppresses* a response. If the response is still reinforced, punishment may be particularly ineffective.

This fact was demonstrated by slapping rats on the paw as they were bar pressing in a Skinner box. Two groups of well-trained rats were placed on extinction. One group was punished with a slap for each bar press, and the other group was not. It might seem that the slap would cause bar pressing to extinguish more quickly. Yet, this was not the case, as you can see in ● Figure 6.20. Punishment temporarily slowed responding, but it did not cause more rapid extinction. Slapping the paws of rats or children has little permanent effect on a reinforced response.

Similarly, if 7-year-old Alissa sneaks a snack from the refrigerator before dinner and is punished for it, she may pass up snacks for a short time. But because snack sneaking was also rewarded by the sneaked snack, she will probably try

Punishers are consequences that lower the probability that a response will be made again. Receiving a traffic citation is directly punishing because the driver is delayed and reprimanded. Paying a fine and higher insurance rates add to the punishment in the form of response cost.

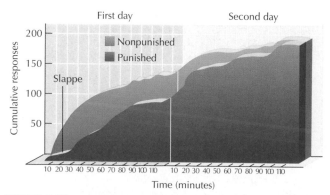

● **FIGURE 6.20** The effect of punishment on extinction. Immediately after punishment, the rate of bar pressing is suppressed, but by the end of the second day, the effects of punishment have disappeared. (From B. F. Skinner, *The Behavior of Organisms.* © 1938. D. Appleton-Century Co., Inc. Reprinted by permission of Prentice-Hall, Inc.)

sneaky snacking again, sometime later (the sneaky little devil). But seriously, to reiterate, intense punishment may permanently suppress responding, even for actions as basic as eating. Animals severely punished while eating may never eat again (Bertsch, 1976).

Side Effects of Punishment

Are there drawbacks to using punishment? There are several, all of which become more of a problem as punishment increases in severity. Basically, punishment is *aversive* (painful or uncomfortable). As a result, people and situations associated with punishment tend, through classical conditioning, to become feared, resented, or disliked. The aversive nature of punishment makes it especially poor to use when teaching children to eat politely or in toilet training.

Escape and Avoidance A second major problem is that aversive stimuli encourage escape and avoidance learning (Brennan, Beck, & Servatius, 2003). In **escape learning** we learn to make a response in order to end an aversive stimulus. For example, if you work with a loud and obnoxious person, you may at first escape from conversations with him to obtain relief. (Notice that escape learning is based on negative reinforcement.) Later you may dodge him altogether. This is an example of **avoidance learning** (making a response in order to postpone or prevent discomfort). Each time you sidestep him, your avoidance is again reinforced by a sense of relief. In many situations involving frequent punishment, similar desires to escape and avoid are activated. For example, children who run away from punishing parents (escape) may soon learn to lie about their behavior (avoidance) or to spend as much time away from home as possible (also an avoidance response).

Aggression A third problem with punishment is that it can greatly increase *aggression*. Animals react to pain by attacking whomever or whatever else is around. A common example is the faithful dog that nips its owner during a painful procedure at the veterinarian's office. Likewise, humans who are in pain have a tendency to lash out at others.

We also know that one of the most common responses to frustration is aggression. Generally speaking, punishment is painful, frustrating, or both. Punishment, therefore, sets up a powerful environment for learning aggression. When spanked, a child may feel angry, frustrated, and hostile. What if that child then goes outside and hits a brother, a sister, or a neighbor? The danger is that aggressive acts may feel good because they release anger and frustration. If so, aggression has been rewarded and will tend to occur again in other frustrating situations.

One study found that children who are physically punished are more likely to engage in aggressive, impulsive, antisocial behavior (Thomas, 2004). Similarly, a classic study of angry adolescent boys found that they were severely punished

at home. This suppressed their misbehavior at home but made them more aggressive elsewhere. Parents were often surprised to learn that their "good boys" were in trouble for fighting at school (Bandura & Walters, 1959). Fortunately, at least for younger children, if parents change to less punitive parenting, their children's levels of aggression will decline (Thomas, 2004).

In the classroom, physical punishment, yelling, and humiliation are also generally ineffective. Positive reinforcement, in the form of praise, approval, and reward, is much more likely to quell classroom disruptions, defiance, and inattention (Alberto & Troutman, 2006).

Using Punishment Wisely

In light of its limitations and drawbacks, should punishment be used to control behavior? Parents, teachers, animal trainers, and the like have three basic tools to control simple learning: (1) Reinforcement strengthens responses; (2) nonreinforcement causes responses to extinguish; (3) punishment suppresses responses. (Consult ● Figure 6.21 to refresh your

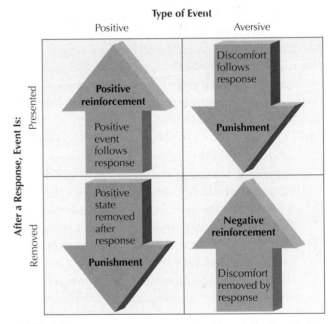

● **FIGURE 6.21** Types of reinforcement and punishment. The impact of an event depends on whether it is presented or removed after a response is made. Each square defines one possibility: Arrows pointing upward indicate that responding is increased; downward-pointing arrows indicate that responding is decreased.

Punishment The process of suppressing a response.

Punisher Any event that decreases the probability or frequency of responses it follows.

Escape learning Learning to make a response in order to end an aversive stimulus.

Avoidance learning Learning to make a response in order to postpone or prevent discomfort.

memory about the different types of reinforcement and punishment.) These tools work best in combination. It is usually best to begin by making liberal use of positive reinforcement, especially praise, to encourage good behavior. Also, try extinction first: See what happens if you ignore a problem behavior, or shift attention to a desirable activity and then reinforce it with praise. Remember, it is much more effective to strengthen and encourage desirable behaviors than it is to punish unwanted behaviors (Gershoff, 2002). When all else fails, it may be necessary to use punishment to help manage the behavior of an animal, child, or even another adult. For those times, here are some tips to keep in mind:

1. *Apply punishment during, or immediately after, misbehavior.* Of course, immediate punishment is not always possible. With older children and adults, you can bridge the delay by clearly stating what act you are punishing. If you cannot punish an animal or young child immediately, wait for the next instance of misbehavior.

2. *Be consistent.* Be very clear about what you regard as misbehavior. Punish every time the misbehavior occurs. Don't punish for something one day and ignore it the next. If you are usually willing to give a child three chances, don't change the rule and explode without warning after a first offense. Both parents should try to punish their children for the same things and in the same way.

3. *Use the minimum punishment necessary to suppress misbehavior.* If punishment is used at all, it should always be mild. In a situation that poses immediate danger, such as when a child reaches for something hot or a dog runs into the street, mild punishment may prevent disaster. Punishment in such cases works best when it produces actions *incompatible* with the response you want to suppress. Let's say a child reaches toward a stove burner. Would a swat on the bottom serve as an effective punisher? Probably so. It would be better, however, to slap the child's outstretched hand so that it will be *withdrawn* from the source of danger. Taking away privileges or other positive reinforcers (response cost) is usually best for older children and adults. Often, a verbal rebuke or a scolding is enough.

4. *Avoid harsh punishment.* Harsh or excessive punishment has serious negative drawbacks (never slap a child's face, for instance). "Sparing the rod" will not spoil a child. In fact, the reverse is true. As we just discussed, harsh punishment can lead to negative emotional reactions, avoidance and escape behaviors, and increased aggression (Aucoin, Frick, & Bodin, 2006). It can even lead to long-term mental health problems (Afifi et al., 2006).

What about spanking? Parents should minimize spanking or avoid it entirely (Gershoff, 2002). Although most children show no signs of long-term damage from spanking if it is backed up by supportive parenting, emotional damage does occur if spankings are severe, frequent, or coupled with harsh parenting (Baumrind, Larzelere, & Cowan, 2002). Like all harsh punishment, frequent spanking tends to increase aggression and leads to more problem behaviors, not fewer (McLoyd & Smith, 2002; Saadeh, Rizzo, & Roberts, 2002). In fact, antispanking laws have been passed in a number of countries around the world.

5. *Don't rely exclusively on punishment.* Mild punishment tends to be ineffective if reinforcers are still available in the situation. That's why it is best to also reward an alternate, desired response. For example, a child who has a habit of taking toys from her sister should not just be reprimanded for it. She should also be praised for cooperative play and sharing her toys with others. Besides, punishment only tells a person or an animal that a response was "wrong." Punishment does not say what the "right" response is, so it *does not teach new behaviors.* If reinforcement is missing, punishment becomes less effective (Gershoff, 2002).

6. *Expect anger from a punished person.* Briefly acknowledge this anger but be careful not to reinforce it. Be willing to admit your mistake if you wrongfully punish someone or if you punished too severely.

7. *Punish with kindness and respect.* Allow the punished person to retain self-respect. For instance, do not punish a person in front of others, if possible. A strong, trusting relationship tends to minimize behavior problems. Ideally, others should want to behave well to get your praise, not because they fear punishment.

To summarize, the most common error in using punishment is to over-rely on it for training or discipline. The overall emotional adjustment of a child or pet disciplined mainly by reward is usually superior to one disciplined mainly by punishment. Frequent punishment makes a person or an animal unhappy, confused, anxious, aggressive, and fearful.

Parents and teachers should also be aware that using punishment can be "habit forming." When children are being noisy, messy, disrespectful, or otherwise misbehaving, the temptation to punish them can be strong. The danger is that punishment often works. When it does, a sudden end to the adult's irritation acts as a negative reinforcer. This encourages the adult to use punishment more often in the future (Alberto & Troutman, 2006). Immediate silence may be "golden," but its cost can be very high in terms of a child's emotional health.

MODULE 6.4 Summary

What does punishment do to behavior?

- Punishment decreases responding. Punishment occurs when a response is followed by the onset of an aversive event or by the removal of a positive event (response cost).
- Punishment is most effective when it is immediate, consistent, and intense.

- Although severe punishment can virtually eliminate a particular behavior, mild punishment usually only temporarily suppresses responding. Reinforcement must be used to make lasting changes in the behavior of a person or an animal.
- Punishment tends to produce escape and avoidance learning, and it encourages the learning of aggressive responses.

KNOWLEDGE BUILDER

Punishment

Recite

1. Negative reinforcement increases responding; punishment suppresses responding. T or F?

2. Three factors that greatly influence the effects of punishment are timing, consistency, and _____.

3. Mild punishment tends to only temporarily _____ a response that is also reinforced.

   a. enhance

   b. aggravate

   c. replace

   d. suppress

4. Three undesired side effects of punishment are (1) conditioning of fear and resentment, (2) encouragement of aggression, and (3) the learning of escape or _____ responses.

5. Using punishment can be "habit forming" because putting a stop to someone else's irritating behavior can _____ _____ the person who applies the punishment.

Reflect
Critical Thinking

6. Using the concept of partial reinforcement, can you explain why inconsistent punishment is especially ineffective?

7. Escape and avoidance learning have been applied to encourage automobile seat belt use. Can you explain how?

Relate

Think of how you were punished as a child. Was the punishment immediate? Was it consistent? What effect did these factors have on your behavior? Was the punishment effective? Which

of the side effects of punishment have you witnessed or experienced?

Link

Internet addresses frequently change. To find the sites listed here, visit **http://www .thomsonedu.com/psychology/coon** for an updated list of Internet addresses and direct links to relevant sites.

- **Ten Reasons Not to Hit Your Kids** Read more about the limitations of spanking.

- **Guidelines for Using Time Out with Children and Preteens** Read about the use of response cost as an effective form of punishment.

- **Reinforcement vs Punishment in the Training of Animals** Learn why punishment should be avoided in the training of animals.

ANSWERS

1. T 2. intensity 3. d 4. avoidance 5. negatively reinforce 6. An inconsistently punished response will continue to be reinforced on a partial schedule, which makes it even more resistant to extinction. 7. Many automobiles have an unpleasant buzzer that sounds if the ignition key is turned before the driver's seat belt is fastened. Most drivers quickly learn to fasten the belt to stop the annoying sound. This is an example of escape conditioning. Avoidance conditioning is evident when a driver learns to buckle up before the buzzer sounds.

6.5 Cognitive Learning and Imitation

MUCH LEARNING can be explained by classical and operant conditioning. But, as we have seen, even basic conditioning has "mental" elements. As a human, you can anticipate future reward or punishment and react accordingly. (You may wonder why this doesn't seem to work when a doctor or dentist says, "This won't hurt a bit." Here's why: They lie!). In this module we will move beyond conditioning into the realm of cognitive learning.

© Ed Arno/SCIENCE 80. Reprinted by permission.

Cognitive Learning—Beyond Conditioning

SURVEY QUESTION: *What is cognitive learning?*

There is no doubt that human learning includes a large *cognitive,* or mental, dimension (Lefrançois, 2006). As humans, we are greatly affected by information, expectations, perceptions, mental images, and the like. Loosely speaking, **cognitive learning** refers to understanding, knowing, anticipating, or otherwise making use of information-rich higher mental processes. Cognitive learning extends beyond basic conditioning into the realms of memory, thinking, problem solving, and language. Because these topics are covered in later chapters, our discussion here is limited to a first look at learning beyond conditioning.

Cognitive Maps

How do you navigate around the town you live in? Have you constructed an overall mental picture of how the town is laid out. This *cognitive map* acts as a guide even when you must detour or take a new

It's easy to get lost when visiting a new city if you don't have a cognitive map of the area. Printed maps help, but they may still leave you puzzled until you begin to form a mental representation of major landmarks and directions.

Peter Cade/Getty Images

route (Foo et al., 2005). A **cognitive map** is an internal representation of an area, such as a maze, city, or campus. Even the lowly rat—not exactly a mental giant (well, except for Einstein the rat)—learns *where* food is found in a maze, not just which turns to make to reach the food (Tolman, Ritchie, & Kalish, 1946). If you have ever learned your way through some of the levels found in many video games, you will have a good idea of what a cognitive map is. In a sense, cognitive maps also apply to other kinds of knowledge. For instance, it could be said that you have been developing a "map" of psychology while reading this book. That's why students sometimes find it helpful to draw pictures or diagrams of how they envision concepts fitting together.

Latent Learning

Cognitive learning is also revealed by latent (hidden) learning. **Latent learning** occurs without obvious reinforcement and remains hidden until reinforcement is provided (Davidson, 2000). Here's an example from a classic animal study: Two groups of rats were allowed to explore a maze. The animals in one group found food at the far end of the maze. Soon, they learned to rapidly make their way through the maze when released. Rats in the second group were unrewarded and showed no signs of learning. But later, when the "uneducated" rats were given food, they ran the maze as quickly as the rewarded group (Tolman & Honzik, 1930). Although there was no outward sign of it, the unrewarded animals had learned their way around the maze. Their learning, therefore, remained latent at first (● Fig. 6.22).

How did they learn if there was no reinforcement? Just satisfying curiosity can be enough to reward learning (Harlow

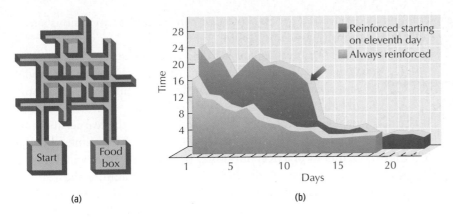

● **FIGURE 6.22** Latent learning. *(a)* The maze used by Tolman and Honzik to demonstrate latent learning by rats. *(b)* Results of the experiment. Notice the rapid improvement in performance that occurred when food was made available to the previously unreinforced animals. This indicates that learning had occurred but that it remained hidden or unexpressed. (Adapted from Tolman & Honzik, 1930.)

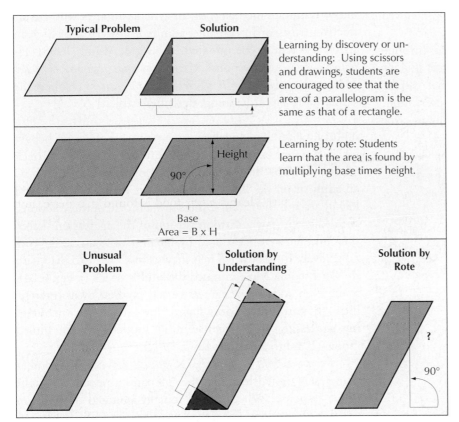

● **FIGURE 6.23** Learning by understanding and by rote. For some types of learning, understanding may be superior, although both types of learning are useful. (Adapted from Wertheimer, 1959.)

people *discover* facts and principles on their own. In **discovery learning,** skills are gained by insight and understanding instead of by rote (Swaak, de Jong, & van Joolingen, 2004).

As long as learning occurs, what difference does it make if it is by discovery or by rote?
● Figure 6.23 illustrates the difference. Two groups of students were taught to calculate the area of a parallelogram by multiplying the height by the length of the base. Some were encouraged to see that a "piece" of a parallelogram could be "moved" to create a rectangle. Later, they were better able to solve unusual problems in which the height times base formula didn't seem to work. Students who simply memorized a rule were confused by the same problems (Wertheimer, 1959). As this implies, discovery can lead to a better understanding of new or unusual problems. When possible, people should try new strategies and discover new solutions during learning. However, this doesn't mean that students are supposed to stumble around and rediscover the principles of math, physics, or chemistry. The best teaching strategies are based on *guided discovery,* in which students are

& Harlow, 1962). In humans, latent learning is related to higher-level abilities, such as anticipating future reward. For example, if you give an attractive classmate a ride home, you may make mental notes about how to get to his or her house, even if a date is only a remote future possibility.

Discovery Learning Much of what is meant by cognitive learning is summarized by the word *understanding*. Each of us has, at times, learned ideas by **rote** (repetition and memorization). Although rote learning is efficient, many psychologists believe that learning is more lasting and flexible when

Cognitive learning Higher level learning involving thinking, knowing, understanding, and anticipation.

Cognitive map Internal images or other mental representations of an area (maze, city, campus, and so forth) that underlie an ability to choose alternative paths to the same goal.

Latent learning Learning that occurs without obvious reinforcement and that remains unexpressed until reinforcement is provided.

Rote learning Learning that takes place mechanically, through repetition and memorization, or by learning rules.

Discovery learning Learning based on insight and understanding.

given enough freedom to actively think about problems and enough guidance so that they gain useful knowledge (Mayer, 2004).

Modeling—Do as I Do, Not as I Say

SURVEY QUESTION: *Does learning occur by imitation?*

Many skills are learned by what Albert Bandura (1971) calls *observational learning,* or *modeling.* **Observational learning** is achieved by watching and imitating the actions of another person or by noting the consequences of the person's actions. In other words, modeling is any process in which information is imparted by example, before direct practice is allowed (Lefrançois, 2006).

The value of learning by observation is obvious: Imagine trying to *tell* someone how to tie a shoe, do a dance step, or play a guitar. Bandura believes that anything that can be learned from direct experience can be learned by observation. Often, this allows a person to skip the tedious trial-and-error stage of learning.

Observational Learning

It seems obvious that we learn by observation, but how does it occur? By observing a **model** (someone who serves as an example), a person may (1) learn new responses, (2) learn to carry out or avoid previously learned responses (depending on what happens to the model for doing the same thing), or

(3) learn a general rule that can be applied to various situations (Lefrançois, 2006).

For observational learning to occur, several things must take place. First, the learner must pay *attention* to the model and *remember* what was done. (A beginning auto mechanic might be interested enough to watch an entire tuneup but unable to remember all the steps.) Next, the learner must be able to *reproduce* the modeled behavior. (Sometimes this is a matter of practice, but it may be that the learner will never be able to perform the behavior. We may admire the feats of world-class gymnasts, but most of us could never reproduce them, no matter how much we practiced.) If a model is *successful* at a task or *rewarded* for a response, the learner is more likely to imitate the behavior. In general, models who are attractive, trustworthy, capable, admired, powerful, or high in status also tend to be imitated (Brewer & Wann, 1998). Finally, once a new response is tried, *normal reinforcement determines whether it will be repeated thereafter.* (Notice the similarity to latent learning, described earlier.)

Imitating Models Modeling has a powerful effect on behavior. In a classic experiment, children watched an adult attack a large blowup "Bo-Bo the Clown" doll. Some children saw an adult sit on the doll, punch it, hit it with a hammer, and kick it around the room. Others saw a movie of these actions. A third group saw a cartoon version of the aggression. Later, the children were frustrated by having some attractive toys taken away from them. Then they were allowed to play with the Bo-Bo doll. Most imitated the adult's attack (● Fig. 6.24). Some even added new aggressive acts of their own! Interestingly, the cartoon was only slightly less effective in encouraging aggression than the live adult model and the filmed model (Bandura, Ross, & Ross, 1963).

Then do children blindly imitate adults? No. Remember that observational learning only prepares a person to duplicate a response. Whether it is actually imitated depends on whether the model was rewarded or punished for what was done. Nevertheless, when parents tell a child to do one thing but model a completely different response, children tend to imitate what the parents *do,* and *not* what they *say.* Thus, through modeling, children learn not only attitudes, gestures, emotions, and personality traits, but fears, anxieties, and bad habits as well. A good example is the adolescent smoker, who is much more likely to begin smoking if her parents, siblings, and friends smoke (Wilkinson & Abraham, 2004).

Now, consider a typical situation: Little Raymond has just been interrupted at play by his older brother, Robert.

Bambu Productions/Getty Images

Observational learning often imparts large amounts of information that would be difficult to obtain by reading instructions or memorizing rules.

● **FIGURE 6.24** A nursery school child imitates the aggressive behavior of an adult model he has just seen in a movie. (Photos courtesy of Albert Bandura.)

Angry and frustrated, he screams at Robert. This behavior interrupts his father Frank's TV watching. Father promptly spanks little Raymond, saying, "This will teach you to hit your big brother." And it will. Because of modeling effects, it is unrealistic to expect a child to "Do as I say, not as I do." The message Frank has given the child is clear: "You have frustrated me; therefore, I will hit you." The next time little Raymond is frustrated, it won't be surprising if he imitates his father and hits his brother (so why does everybody love Raymond, anyway?).

Modeling and the Media

Does television promote observational learning? Today's 8- to 18-year-olds spend an average of 44.5 hours a week engaged with various media, including television, video games, movies, the Internet, music, and print media (Roberts, Foehr, & Rideout, 2005). Although overall use is falling, television still consumes the lion's share of media attention, averaging 21 hours every week.

By the time the average person has graduated from high school, she or he will have viewed some 15,000 hours of TV, compared with only 11,000 hours spent in the classroom. In that time, viewers will have seen some 18,000 murders and countless acts of robbery, arson, bombing, torture, and beatings. Even G-rated cartoons average 10 minutes of violence per hour (Yokota & Thompson, 2000). In short, typical TV viewers are exposed to a massive dose of media violence, which tends to promote observational learning of aggression (Bushman & Anderson, 2001).

Televised Aggression The last finding comes as no surprise. Studies show conclusively that if large groups of children watch a great deal of televised violence, they will be more prone to behave aggressively (Anderson et al., 2003; Bushman & Anderson, 2001). In other words, not all children will become more aggressive, but many will. More ominously, the effect can last into early adulthood. A group of primary school students with known television viewing habits were

later contacted in early adulthood (Huesmann et al., 2003). Those who watched more violence on television as elementary schoolers were more aggressive as adults 15 years later (● Fig. 6.25).

Does the same conclusion apply to video games? Oh, yes. Children tend to imitate what they observe in all media. From professional wrestling (Bernthal, 2003) to rap music (Wing-

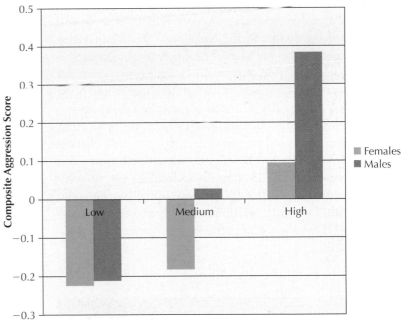

● **FIGURE 6.25** This graph shows that preschoolers who watched low levels of television violence were less aggressive than average as young adults when contacted 15 years later. In contrast, preschoolers who watched high levels of television violence were more aggressive than average as young adults. The composite aggression score includes measures of indirect aggression (e.g., verbal abusiveness) and direct aggression (physical aggression). (Data adapted from Huesmann et al., 2003.)

Observational learning Learning achieved by watching and imitating the actions of another or noting the consequences of those actions.

Model A person who serves as an example in observational learning.

CRITICAL THINKING

You Mean Video Games Might Be Bad for Me?

Today's kids can experience more gore in a day than most people used to experience in a lifetime, even during military combat. For example, in one video game you can kill an entire marching band with a flamethrower. Some of your victims won't die right away. They will just writhe in pain, begging you to finish them off.

What effects do such experiences have on people who play violent video games? Reviews have concluded that violent video games increase aggressive behavior in children and young adults (Anderson & Bushman, 2001; Anderson, 2004). As with TV, young children are especially susceptible to fantasy violence in video games (Anderson et al., 2003; Bensley & Van Eenwyk, 2001).

One study illustrates the impact of video game violence. First, college students played a violent (Mortal Kombat) or nonviolent (PGA Tournament Golf) video game. Next, they competed with another student (actually an actor) in a task that allowed aggression and retaliation to take place. Students who played Mortal Kombat were much more likely to aggress, by punishing their competitor (Bartholow & Anderson, 2002). (Don't mess with someone who just played Mortal Kombat!)

How does video game violence increase aggressive behavior? One possibility is that repeated exposure to violence desensitizes players, making them less likely to react negatively to violence and, hence, more prone to engage in it (Bartholow, Sestir, & Davis, 2005; Funk, 2005). Another possibility is that by practicing violence against other people, players may learn to be aggressive in real life (Unsworth & Ward, 2001). (Before you write off video games altogether, read "You Mean Video Games Might Be Good For Me?" in Module 9.1.)

ood et al., 2003) to video games (Carnagey & Anderson, 2004), children have plenty of opportunity to observe and imitate both the good and the bad. (See "You Mean Video Games Might Be Bad for Me?" for some recent evidence.)

Is it fair to say, then, that media violence causes aggression in consumers, especially children? Fortunately, that would be an exaggeration (Kirsh, 2005). Media violence can make aggression more *likely,* but it does not invariably "cause" it to occur for any given child. Many other factors affect the chances that hostile thoughts will be turned into actions. Youngsters who believe that aggression is an acceptable way to solve problems, who believe that TV violence is realistic, and who identify with TV characters are most likely to copy televised aggression (Huesmann et al., 2003). It is particularly troubling to find media *heroes* behaving aggressively, as well as villains. Younger children, in particular, are more likely to be influenced because they don't fully recognize that media characters and stories are fantasies (McKenna & Ossoff, 1998).

In view of such findings, it is understandable that countries like Canada, Norway, and Switzerland have restricted the amount of permissible violence on television. Should all countries do the same?

A Look Ahead Conditioning principles are often derived from animal experiments. However, it should be apparent that the same principles apply to human behavior. Perhaps the best way to appreciate this fact is to observe how reinforcement affects your own behavior. With this in mind, the upcoming Psychology in Action section proposes a personal experiment in operant conditioning. Don't miss this coming attraction!

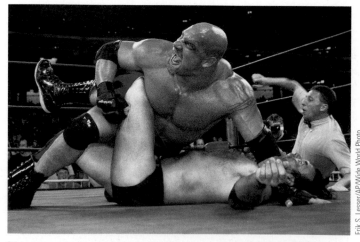

Erik S. Lesser/AP/Wide World Photo

TV heroes can act as powerful models for observational learning of aggression.

MODULE **6.5** Summary

What is cognitive learning?

- Cognitive learning involves higher mental processes, such as memory, thinking, problem solving, understanding, knowing, and anticipating.
- Even in relatively simple learning situations, animals and people seem to form cognitive maps (internal representations of relationships).
- In latent learning, learning remains hidden or unseen until a reward or incentive for performance is offered.
- Discovery learning emphasizes insight and understanding, in contrast to rote learning.

Does learning occur by imitation?

- Learning can occur by merely observing and imitating the actions of another person or by noting the consequences of the person's actions.

- Observational learning is influenced by the personal characteristics of the model and the success or failure of the model's behavior. Aggression is readily learned and released by modeling.

- Television characters can act as powerful models for observational learning. Televised violence increases the likelihood of aggression by viewers.

KNOWLEDGE BUILDER

Cognitive Learning and Imitation

Recite

1. An internal representation of relationships is referred to as a _____ _____.

2. Learning that suddenly appears when a reward or incentive for performance is given is called
   a. discovery learning
   b. latent learning
   c. rote learning
   d. reminiscence

3. Psychologists use the term _____ to describe observational learning.

4. If a model is successful, rewarded, attractive, or high in status, his or her behavior is
   a. difficult to reproduce
   b. less likely to be attended to
   c. more likely to be imitated
   d. subject to positive transfer

5. Children who observed a live adult behave aggressively became more aggressive; those who observed movie and cartoon aggression did not. T or F?

6. Children are most likely to imitate TV characters with whom they identify. T or F?

7. Children who watch a great deal of televised violence are more prone to be aggressive, an effect that is best explained by
   a. negative reinforcement
   b. shaping and successive approximations
   c. observational learning
   d. vicarious classical conditioning

Reflect
Critical Thinking

8. Draw a map of your school's campus as you picture it now. Draw a map of the campus as you pictured it after your first visit. Why do the maps differ?

9. Children who watch many aggressive programs on television tend to be more aggressive than average. Why doesn't this observation prove that televised aggression causes aggressive behavior?

Relate

Try to think of at least one personal example of each of these concepts: cognitive map, latent learning, discovery learning.

Describe a skill you have learned primarily through observational learning. How did modeling help you learn?

What entertainment or sports personalities did you identify with when you were a child? How did it affect your behavior?

Link

Internet addresses frequently change. To find the sites listed here, visit **http://www .thomsonedu.com/psychology/coon** for an updated list of Internet addresses and direct links to relevant sites.

- **Social Learning Theory and Criminality** Explore the hypothesis that cognitive learning underlies much criminal behavior.

- **Mirror Neurons and Imitation Learning** Read about a possible neural basis for imitation learning.

- **Media Violence** How much do children learn by imitating what they see in the media?

ANSWERS

7.1 Memory Systems

DO YOU REMEMBER what you had for breakfast this morning? The last friend you instant messaged? Or what happened on September 11, 2001? Of course you do. But how is it possible for us to so easily travel back in time? Let's begin with a look at basic memory systems. An interesting series of events must occur before we can say "I remember."

Stages of Memory—Do You Have a Mind Like a Steel Trap? or a Sieve?

SURVEY QUESTION: *Is there more than one type of memory?*

Many people think of memory as "a dusty storehouse of facts." In reality, **memory** is an active system that receives, stores, organizes, alters, and recovers information (Lieberman, 2004). In some general ways memory acts like a computer (● Fig. 7.1). Incoming information is first **encoded,** or changed into a usable form. This step is like typing data into a computer. Next, information is **stored,** or held, in the system. (As we will see in a moment, human memory can be pictured as three separate storage systems.) Finally, memories must be **retrieved,** or taken out of storage to be useful. If you're going to remember all the 9,856 new terms on your next psychology exam, you must successfully encode, store, and retrieve them.

What are the three separate memory systems just mentioned? Psychologists have identified three stages of memory in a model known as the *Atkinson-Schiffrin model* (Atkinson &

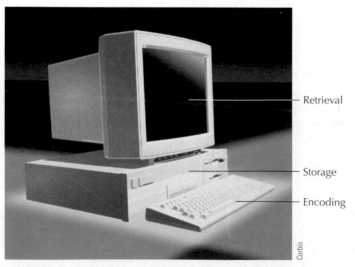

● **FIGURE 7.1** In some ways, a computer acts like a mechanical memory system. Both systems process information, and both allow encoding, storage, and retrieval of data.

Retrieval

Storage

Encoding

Schiffrin, 1968; Goldstein, 2008). To be stored for a long time, information must pass through all three stages (● Fig. 7.2).

Sensory Memory

Let's say a friend asks you to pick up several things at a market. How will you remember them? Information first enters **sensory memory,** which can hold an exact copy of what you see or hear, for a few seconds or less. We are normally unaware of the functioning of our sensory memories. For instance, look at a flower and then quickly close your eyes. If you are lucky, you might just notice that an **iconic** (eye-KON-ick) **memory,** or fleeting mental image, of the flower will persist for about one-half second (Keysers et al., 2005). Similarly, when you hear information, sensory memory stores it as an *echoic memory* for up to 2 seconds (Haenschel et al., 2005). (An **echoic memory** is a brief flurry of activity in the auditory system.) In general, sensory memory holds information just long enough to move it to the second memory system, short-term memory (Neath & Surprenant, 2003).

Short-Term Memory

Not everything we see or hear stays in memory. Imagine that a radio is playing in the background as your friend reads her shopping list. Will you remember what the announcer says, too? Probably not, because *selective attention* (focusing on a selected portion of sensory input) controls what information moves on to short-term memory. **Short-term memory (STM)** holds small amounts of information in conscious awareness for a dozen seconds or so. By paying attention to your friend, you will place her shopping list in short-term memory (while you ignore the voice on the radio saying, "Buy Burpo Butter").

How are short-term memories encoded? Short-term memories can be stored as images. But more often they are stored *phonetically* (by sound), especially in recalling words and letters (Page et al., 2007). If you are introduced to Tim at a party and you forget his name, you are more likely to call him by a name that sounds like Tim (Jim, Kim, or Slim, for instance), rather than a name that sounds different, such as Bob or Mike. Your friend with the shopping list may be lucky if you don't bring home jam instead of ham and soap instead of soup!

Short-term memory briefly stores small amounts of information. When you dial a phone number or briefly remember a shopping list, you are using STM. Notice that information is quickly "dumped" from STM and forever lost. Short-term memory prevents our minds from storing useless names, dates, telephone numbers, and other trivia.

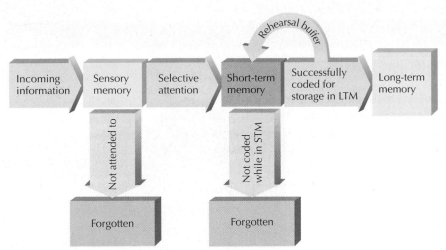

● **FIGURE 7.2** The Atkinson-Schiffrin model. Remembering is thought to involve at least three steps. Incoming information is first held for a second or two by sensory memory. Information selected by attention is then transferred to temporary storage in short-term memory (STM). If new information is not rapidly encoded, or rehearsed, it is forgotten. If it is transferred to long-term memory (LTM), it becomes relatively permanent, although retrieving it may be a problem. The preceding is a useful, but highly simplified, *model* of memory; it may not be literally true of what happens in the brain (Atkinson & Schiffrin, 1968; Goldstein, 2008).

As you may have noticed when dialing a telephone, STM is very sensitive to *interruption,* or *interference.* You've probably had something like this happen: Someone leaves a phone number on your answering machine. You repeat the number to yourself as you start to dial. Then the doorbell rings and you rush to see who is there. When you return to the phone, you have completely forgotten the number. You listen to the message again and memorize the number. This time as you begin to dial, someone asks you a question. You answer, turn to the phone, and find that you have forgotten the number. Notice again that STM can handle only small amounts of information. It is very difficult to do more than one task at a time in STM (Miyake, 2001; Oberauer & Göthe, 2006).

Working Memory Short-term memory is often used for more than just storing information. When STM is combined with other mental processes, it provides an area of **working memory** where we do much of our thinking. Working memory acts as a sort of "mental scratchpad." It briefly holds the information we need when we are thinking and solving problems (Holmes & Adams, 2006). Whenever you do mental arithmetic, put together a puzzle, plan a meal, follow directions, or read a book, you are using working memory (Baddeley, 2003).

Long-Term Memory

If STM is so limited, how do we remember for longer periods? Information that is important or meaningful is transferred to **long-term memory (LTM)**, which acts as a lasting store-

house for knowledge. LTM contains everything you know about the world—from aardvark to zucchini, math to *Desperate Housewives,* facts to fantasy. Yet, there appears to be no danger of running out of room. LTM can hold nearly limitless amounts of information. In fact, the more you know, the easier it becomes to add new information to memory. This is the reverse of what we would expect if LTM could be "filled up" (Goldstein, 2008). It is also one of many reasons for getting an education.

Are long-term memories also encoded as sounds? They can be. But typically, long-term memories are stored on the basis of *meaning,* not sound. If you make an error in LTM, it will probably be related to meaning. For example, if you are trying to recall the word *barn* from a memorized list, you are more likely to mistakenly say *shed* or *farm* than *yarn* or *darn.* If you can link information in STM to knowledge already stored in LTM, it gains meaning. This makes it easier to remember. As an example, try to memorize this story:

> With hocked gems financing him, our hero bravely defied all scornful laughter. "Your eyes deceive," he had said. "An egg, not a table, correctly typifies this unexplored planet." Now three sturdy sisters sought proof. Forging along, days became weeks as many doubters spread fearful rumors about the edge. At last from nowhere welcome winged creatures appeared, signifying momentous success. (Adapted from Dooling & Lachman, 1971.)

Memory The mental system for receiving, encoding, storing, organizing, altering, and retrieving information.

Encoding Converting information into a form in which it will be retained in memory.

Storage Holding information in memory for later use.

Retrieval Recovering information from storage in memory.

Sensory memory The first, normally unconscious, stage of memory, which holds an exact record of incoming information for a few seconds or less.

Iconic memory A mental image or visual representation.

Echoic memory A brief continuation of sensory activity in the auditory system after a sound is heard.

Short-term memory (STM) The memory system used to hold small amounts of information in our conscious awareness for about a dozen seconds.

Working memory Another name for short-term memory, especially as it is used for thinking and problem solving.

Long-term memory (LTM) The memory system used for relatively permanent storage of meaningful information.

HUMAN DIVERSITY

Cows, Memories, and Culture

If you were on a farm and saw 20 cows walk by, do you think you could remember the age, color, gender, and condition of all of them? Unless you are a dairy farmer, doing so would be quite a feat of memory. As noted, we are most likely to remember information that is personally important or meaningful. However, for a Maasai person from East Africa, it would be easier. Livestock are very important in Maasai culture; a Maasai's wealth is measured by the number of cattle owned. Thus, the Maasai are prepared to encode and store information about cattle that would be difficult for most people in the United States to remember.

Culture affects our memories in other interesting ways. For example, American culture emphasizes individuals, whereas Chinese culture emphasizes membership in groups. In one study, European-American and Chinese adults were asked to recall 20 memories from any time in their lives. As expected, American memories tended to be self-centered: Most people remembered surprising events and what they did during the events. Chinese adults, in contrast, remembered important social or historical events and their own interactions with family members, friends, and others (Wang & Conway, 2004). Thus, in the United States, personal memories tend to be about "me"; in China they tend to be about "us."

This odd story emphasizes the impact that meaning has on memory. People given the title of the story were able to remember it far better than those not given a title. See if the title helps you as much as it did them: "Columbus Discovers America."

Dual Memory Although sensory memory is involved every time we use our memory, we are most likely to notice STM and LTM. To summarize their connection, picture short-term memory as a small desk at the front of a huge warehouse full of filing cabinets (LTM). As information enters the warehouse, it is first placed on the desk. Because the desk is small, it must be quickly cleared off to make room for new information. Unimportant items are simply tossed away. Meaningful or personally important information is placed in the files (LTM). (See "Cows, Memories, and Culture.")

When we want to use knowledge from LTM to answer a question, the information is returned to STM. Or, in our analogy, a folder is taken out of the files (LTM) and moved to the desk (STM), where it can be used. Now that you have a general picture of memory it is time to explore STM and LTM in more detail. But first, here's a chance to rehearse what you've learned.

MODULE 7.1 Summary

Is there more than one type of memory?

- Memory systems allow us to encode, store, and retrieve information.
- The three stages of memory (sensory memory, short-term memory, and long-term memory) hold information for increasingly longer periods.
- The best way to remember depends, to an extent, on which memory system you are using.
- Sensory memories are encoded as iconic memories or echoic memories. Short-term memories tend to be encoded by sound, and long-term memories by meaning.

KNOWLEDGE BUILDER

Memory Systems

Recite
Learning Check

Match: **A.** Sensory memory **B.** STM **C.** LTM

1. ____ Information tends to be stored phonetically

2. ____ Holds information for a few seconds or less

3. ____ Stores an iconic memory or echoic memory

4. ____ Permanent, unlimited capacity

5. ____ Temporarily holds small amounts of information

6. ____ Selective attention determines its contents

7. STM is improved by interruption, or interference, because attention is more focused at such times. T or F?

Reflect
Critical Thinking

8. Why is sensory memory important to filmmakers?

Relate

Wave a pencil back and forth in front of your eyes while focusing on something in the distance. The pencil's image looks transparent. Why? (Because sensory memory briefly holds an image of the pencil. This image persists after the pencil passes by.)

Think of a time today when you used short-term memory (such as briefly remembering a phone number, an Internet address, or someone's name). How long did you retain the information? How did you encode it? How much do you remember now?

How is long-term memory helping you read this sentence? If the words weren't already stored in LTM, could you read at all? How else have you used LTM today?

Link

Internet addresses frequently change. To find the sites listed here, visit **http://www.thomsonedu.com/psychology/coon** for an updated list of Internet addresses and direct links to relevant sites.

- **Playing Games With Memory** Try some activities to test your memory.

- **The Atkinson-Schiffrin model** Further explore the three-store model of memory.

- **Working Memory, Language and Reading** Use the concept of working memory to better understand the process or reading.

ANSWERS

1. B 2. A 3. A 4. C 5. B 6. B 7. F 8. Without sensory memory, a movie would look like a series of still pictures. The split-second persistence of visual images helps blend one motion-picture frame into the next.

7.2 STM and LTM

TO MAKE GOOD USE OF YOUR MEMORY, it is valuable to know more about the quirks and characteristics of both STM and LTM. It's time to dig deeper into the inner workings of our dual memory system.

Short-Term Memory—Do You Know the Magic Number?

SURVEY QUESTION: *What are the features of short-term memory?*

How much information can be held in short-term memory? For an answer, read the following numbers once. Then close the book and write as many as you can in the correct order.

8 5 1 7 4 9 3

This is called a digit-span test. It is a measure of attention and short-term memory. If you were able to correctly repeat 7 digits, you have an average short-term memory. Now try to memorize the following list, again reading it only once.

7 1 8 3 5 4 2 9 1 6 3 4

This series was probably beyond your short-term memory capacity. Psychologist George Miller found that short-term memory is limited to the "magic number" 7 (plus or minus 2) **information bits** (Miller, 1956). A bit is a single meaningful "piece" of information, such as a digit. It is as if short-term memory has 7 "slots" or "bins" into which separate items can be placed. Actually, a few people can remember up to 9 bits, and for some types of information 5 bits is the limit. Thus, an *average* of 7 information bits can be held in short-term memory (Neath & Surprenant, 2003).

When all of the "slots" in STM are filled, there is no room for new information. Picture how this works at a party: Let's say your hostess begins introducing everyone who is there, "Chun, Dasia, Marco, Roseanna, Cholik, Shawn, Kyrene. . . ." "Stop," you think to yourself. But she continues, "Nelia, Jay, Efren, Frank, Marietta, Jorge, Patty, Amit, Ricky." The hostess leaves, satisfied that you have met everyone. And you spend the evening talking with Chun, Dasia, and Ricky, the only people whose names you remember!

Chunking

Before we continue, try your short-term memory again, this time on letters. Read the following letters once, then look away and try to write them in the proper order.

T V I B M U S N Y M C A

Notice that there are 12 letters, or "bits" of information. This should be beyond the 7-item limit of STM. However, because the letters are in four groups, or *chunks* of information, many students are able to memorize them. **Information chunks** are made up of bits of information grouped into larger units.

How does chunking help? Chunking *recodes* (reorganizes) information into units that are already in LTM. For example, you may have noticed that NY is the abbreviation for New York. If so, the two bits N and Y became one chunk. In a classic experiment that used lists like this one, people remembered best when the letters were read as familiar meaningful chunks: TV, IBM, USN, YMCA (Bower & Springston, 1970). If you recoded the letters this way, you probably remembered the entire list.

Chunking suggests that STM holds about 5 to 7 of whatever units we are using. A single chunk could be made up of numbers, letters, words, phrases, or familiar sentences. Picture STM as a small desk again. Through chunking, we combine several items into one "stack" of information. This allows us to place 7 stacks on the desk, where before there was only room for 7 separate items. While you are studying, try to find ways to link 2, 3, or more separate facts or ideas into larger chunks, and your short-term memory will improve. Psychologist Nelson Cowan (2001, 2005) believes that STM may actually hold only 4 items, unless some chunking has occurred. The clear message is that creating information chunks is the key to making good use of your short-term memory (Gobet, 2005).

Rehearsing Information

How long do short-term memories last? They disappear very rapidly. However, you can prolong a memory by silently repeating it, a process called **maintenance rehearsal.** You have probably briefly remembered an address or telephone number this way. In a sense, rehearsing information allows you to "hear" it many times, not just once (Nairne, 2002). The more times a short-term memory is rehearsed, the greater its chances of being stored in LTM (Goldstein, 2008).

What if rehearsal is prevented, so a memory cannot be recycled or moved to LTM? Without maintenance rehearsal, STM is quite brief. In one experiment, subjects heard meaningless syllables like XAR followed by a number like 67. As soon as subjects heard the number, they began counting backward by threes (to prevent them from repeating the syllable). After a delay of between 12 and 18 seconds, their memory for the syllables fell to zero (Peterson & Peterson, 1959).

After *12 to 18 seconds* without rehearsal, the short-term memories were gone forever! Part of this rapid loss can be explained by the testing procedures used (Goldstein, 2008). In daily life, short-term memories usually last longer. Just the same, if you are introduced to someone, and the name slips out of STM, it is gone forever. To escape this awkward situation you might try saying something like, "I'm curious, how do you spell your name?" Unfortunately, the response is often an icy reply like, "B-O-B S-M-I-T-H, it's really not too difficult." To avoid embarrassment, pay careful attention to the name, repeat it to yourself several times, and try to use it in the next sentence or two—before you lose it (Neath & Surprenant, 2003).

Elaborative rehearsal, which makes information more meaningful, is a far better way to form lasting memories. Elaborative rehearsal links new information to memories that are already in LTM. When you are studying, you will remember more if you elaborate, extend, and reflect about the meaning of the information. As you read, try to reflect frequently. Ask yourself "why" questions, such as "Why would that be true?" (Toyota & Kikuchi, 2005; Willoughby et al., 1997). Also, try to relate new ideas to your own experiences and knowledge (Hartlep & Forsyth, 2000).

Long-Term Memory— Where the Past Lives

SURVEY QUESTIONS: *What are the features of long-term memory? Is there more than one type of long-term memory?*

An electrode touched the patient's brain. Immediately she said, "Yes, sir, I think I heard a mother calling her little boy somewhere. It seemed to be something happening years ago. It was somebody in the neighborhood where I live." A short time later the electrode was applied to the same spot. Again the patient said, "Yes, I hear the same familiar sounds, it seems to be a woman calling, the same lady" (Penfield, 1958). A woman undergoing brain surgery made these statements. There are no pain receptors in the brain, so the patient was awake as her brain was electrically stimulated (● Fig. 7.3). When activated, some brain areas seemed to produce vivid memories of long-forgotten events.

Permanence *Are all our experiences permanently recorded in memory?* Results like those described led neurosurgeon Wilder Penfield to claim that the brain records the past like a "strip of movie film, complete with sound track" (Penfield, 1957). But as you know, this is an exaggeration. Many events never get past short-term memory. Also, brain stimulation produces memory-like experiences in only about 3 percent of cases. Most reports resemble dreams more than memories,

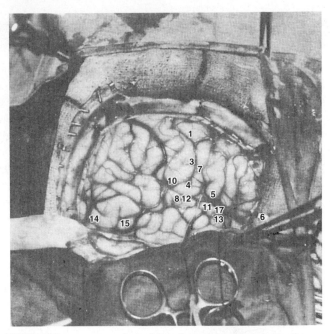

● **FIGURE 7.3** Exposed cerebral cortex of a patient undergoing brain surgery. Numbers represent points that reportedly produced "memories" when electrically stimulated. A critical evaluation of such reports suggests that they are more like dreams than memories. This fact raises questions about claims that long-term memories are permanent. (From Penfield, 1958. Courtesy of the author and Charles C Thomas, Publisher, Springfield, Illinois.)

and many are clearly imaginary. Memory experts now believe that long-term memories are only *relatively* permanent (Goldstein, 2008). Perfect, eternal memories are a myth.

TRY IT YOURSELF: HOW'S YOUR MEMORY?
To better appreciate the next topic, pause for a moment and read the words you see here. Read through the list once. Then continue reading the next section of this module.

bed dream blanket doze pillow nap
snore mattress alarm clock rest slumber
nod sheet bunk cot cradle groggy

Constructing Memories

There's another reason for doubting that all our experiences are permanently recorded. As new long-term memories are stored, older memories are often updated, changed, lost, or

Information bits Meaningful units of information, such as numbers, letters, words, or phrases.

Information chunks Information bits grouped into larger units.

Maintenance rehearsal Silently repeating or mentally reviewing information to hold it in short-term memory.

Elaborative rehearsal Rehearsal that links new information with existing memories and knowledge.

CRITICAL THINKING

Do You Like Jam With Your Memory?

Have you ever wondered why famous companies, which already sell huge amounts of familiar products (such as soft drinks or beer), continue to advertise as heavily as they do? If you believe the point of the advertising is to familiarize people with a product or to inform them about it, this *is* a mystery. But if you think about the constructive nature of memory, the mystery is solved. According to economist Jesse Shapiro (2006), the intent of much advertising is to "jam" your memory with positive impressions of a product.

How does "memory jamming" work? How many times have you had a bottle or can of

your favorite beer or soft drink? And how many commercials for those beverages have you watched? Every extra commercial adds one more positive memory of the beverage to your long-term memory. Here's a typical commercial: Boy goes to cool party, sees hot girl, flashes favorite beer, gets girl. (Yes, beer commercials mainly target young men.) Because we cannot easily tell which recollection is fact and which is fiction, storing enough of these commercials can eventually create "memories" that never happened. For example, you might remember enjoying a particular beverage more than you actually did, in fact.

According to Shapiro (2006), the more positive fictional commercials we see, the less likely we are to remember an actual negative experience with a product. In effect, the positive, fictional memories "jam," or block, our ability to remember actual negative memories when deciding whether to buy a product. Braun-LaTour & LaTour (2004) add that long-term advertising campaigns create a "brand" memory that can be remarkably strong. This appears to be especially true when the ads are first viewed in early childhood. So perhaps you have been having jam with your memories ever since you were a baby.

---

revised (Lieberman, 2004). To illustrate this point, Elizabeth Loftus and John Palmer (1974) showed people a filmed automobile accident. Afterward, some participants were asked to estimate how fast the cars were going when they "smashed" into each other. For others the words "bumped," "contacted," or "hit" replaced "smashed." One week later, each person was asked, "Did you see any broken glass?" Those asked earlier about the cars that "smashed" into each other were more likely to say yes. (No broken glass was shown in the film.) The new information ("smashed") was included in memories and altered them.

Eyewitness memories are notoriously inaccurate. By the time witnesses are asked to testify in court, information they learned after an incident may blend into their original memories.

TRY IT YOURSELF: OLD OR NEW?
Now, without looking back to the list of words you read a few minutes ago, see if you can tell which of the following are "old" words (items from the list you read) and which are "new" words (items that weren't on the list). Mark each of the following words as old or new:

sofa   sleep   lamp   kitchen

Updating memories is called **constructive processing.** Gaps in memory, which are common, may be filled in by logic, guessing, or new information (Schacter, Norman, & Koutstaal, 1998). Indeed, it is possible to have "memories" for things that never happened (such as remembering broken glass at an accident when there was none) (Loftus, 2003a, 2003b). In one study, people who had visited a Disney resort were shown several fake ads for Disney that featured Bugs Bunny. Later, about 16 percent of the people who saw these fake ads claimed that they had met Bugs at Disneyland. This is impossible, of course, because Bugs Bunny is a Warner Brothers character that would never be found at Disneyland (Braun, Ellis, & Loftus, 2002).

Could constructive processing be used to deliberately manipulate memory? Bingo. According to one theory, advertisers do it all the time. See "Do You Like Jam With Your Memory?" for more information.

TRY IT YOURSELF: AND NOW, THE RESULTS
Return now and look at the labels you wrote on the "old or new" word list. Contrary to what you may think you "remembered," all of the listed words are "new." None was on the original list!

Index Stock Imagery

CRITICAL THINKING

Telling Wrong from Right in Forensic Memory

Imagine that you are a forensic psychologist, investigating a crime. Unfortunately, your witness can't remember much of what happened. As a "memory detective," what can you do to help?

Could hypnosis improve the witness's memory? It might seem so. In one case in California, 26 children were abducted from a school bus and held captive for ransom. Under hypnosis, the bus driver recalled the license plate number of the kidnappers' van. This memory helped break the case. Such successes seem to imply that hypnosis can improve memory. But does it?

Research has shown that hypnosis increases false memories more than it does true ones. Eighty percent of the new memories produced by hypnotized subjects in one classic experiment were *incorrect* (Dywan & Bowers, 1983). This is in part because a hypnotized person is more likely than normal to use imagination to fill in gaps in memory. Also, if a questioner asks misleading or suggestive questions, hypnotized persons tend to weave the information into their memories (Scoboria et al., 2002). To make matters worse, even when a memory is completely false, the hypnotized person's confidence in it can be unshakable (Burgess & Kirsch, 1999).

Thus, hypnosis sometimes uncovers more information, as it did with the bus driver (Schreiber & Schreiber, 1999). However, in the absence of corroborating evidence, there is no sure way to tell which of these memories are false and which are true (Newman & Thompson, 2001).

Is there a better way to improve eyewitness memory? To help police detectives, R. Edward Geiselman and Ron Fisher created the **cognitive interview,** a technique for jogging the memory of eyewitnesses (Fisher & Geiselman, 1987). The key to this approach is recreating the crime scene. Witnesses revisit the scene in their imaginations or in person. That way, aspects of the crime scene, such as sounds, smells, and objects, provide helpful retrieval cues (stimuli associated with a memory). Back in the context of the crime, the witness is encouraged to recall events in different orders and from different viewpoints. Every new memory, no matter how trivial it may seem, can serve as a cue to trigger the retrieval of yet more memories. (Later, in Module 7.4, we will see why such cues are so effective for jogging memories.)

When used properly, the cognitive interview produces 35 percent more correct information than standard questioning (Davis, McMahon, & Greenwood, 2005; Geiselman et al., 1986). This improvement comes without adding to the number of false memories elicited, as occurs with hypnosis. The result is a procedure that is more effective in actual police work (Ginet & Py, 2001; Kebbell & Wagstaff, 1998) and in different cultures (Stein & Memon, 2006).

Some police detectives, following the advice of psychologists, recreate crime scenes to help witnesses remember what they saw. Typically, people return to the scene at the time of day the crime occurred. They are also asked to wear the same clothing they wore and go through the same motions as they did before the crime. With so many memory cues available, witnesses sometimes remember key items of information they hadn't recalled before.

If you thought you "remembered" that "sleep" was on the original list, you had a false memory. The word *sleep* is associated with most of the words on the original list, which creates a strong impression that you saw it before (Roediger & McDermott, 1995).

As the preceding examples show, thoughts, inferences, and mental associations may be mistaken for true memories (Loftus, 2003a, 2003b). People in Elizabeth Loftus's experiments who had these *pseudomemories* (false memories) were often quite upset to learn they had given false "testimony" (Loftus & Ketcham, 1994).

False long-term memories are a common problem in police work. For example, a witness may select a photo of a suspect from police files or see a photo in the news. Later, the witness identifies the suspect in a lineup or in court.

Did the witness really remember the suspect from the scene of the crime? Or was it from the more recently seen photograph?

Does new information "overwrite" existing memories? No, the real problem is that we often can't remember the *source* of a memory (Simons et al, 2004). This can lead witnesses to "remember" a face that they actually saw somewhere other than the crime scene (Ruva, McEvoy, & Bryant, 2007). Many tragic cases of mistaken identity occur this way. One famous example involved memory expert Donald Thomson.

Constructive processing Reorganizing or updating memories on the basis of logic, reasoning, or the addition of new information.

Cognitive interview Use of various cues and strategies to improve the memory of eyewitnesses.

After appearing live on Australian television, he was accused of rape. It turns out that the victim was watching him on TV when the actual rapist broke into her apartment (Schacter, 1996, 2001).

Is there any way to avoid such problems? Forensic psychologists have tried a variety of techniques to help improve the memory of witnesses. "Telling Wrong from Right in Forensic Memory" examines research on this important question.

To summarize, forming and using long-term memories is an active, creative, highly personal process. Our memories are colored by emotions, judgments, and quirks of personality. If you and a friend were joined at the hip and you went through life side-by-side, you would still have different memories. What we remember depends on what we pay attention to, what we regard as meaningful or important, and what we feel strongly about (Schacter, 2000).

Organizing Memories

Long-term memory stores huge amounts of information during a lifetime. How are we able to quickly find specific memories? The answer is that each person's "memory index" is highly organized.

Do you mean that information is arranged alphabetically, as in a dictionary? Not a chance! If we ask you to name a black-and-white animal that lives on ice, is related to a chicken, and cannot fly, you don't have to go from aardvark to zebra to find the answer. You will probably only think of black-and-white birds living in the Antarctic. *Voila,* the answer is penguin.

Information in LTM may be arranged according to rules, images, categories, symbols, similarity, formal meaning, or personal meaning (Lieberman, 2004). In recent years, psy-

chologists have begun to develop a picture of the *structure,* or organization, of memories. *Memory structure* refers to the pattern of associations among items of information. For example, assume that you are given two statements, to which you must answer yes or no: (1) *A canary is an animal.* (2) *A canary is a bird.* Which do you answer more quickly? Most people can say that *A canary is a bird* faster than they can recognize that *A canary is an animal* (Collins & Quillian, 1969). Why should this be so? Psychologists believe that a **network model** of memory explains why. According to this view, LTM is organized as a network of linked ideas (● Fig. 7.4). When ideas are "farther" apart, it takes a longer chain of associations to connect them. The more two items are separated, the longer it takes to answer. In terms of information links, *canary* is probably "close" to *bird* in your "memory files." *Animal* and *canary* are farther apart. Remember though, this has nothing to do with alphabetical order. We are talking about a system of linked meanings.

Redintegrative Memories Networks of associated memories may also help explain a common experience: Imagine finding a picture taken on your sixth birthday or tenth Christmas. As you look at the photo, one memory leads to another, which leads to another, and another. Soon you have unleashed a flood of seemingly forgotten details. This process is called redintegration (ruh-DIN-tuh-GRAY-shun).

Redintegrative memories seem to spread through the "branches" of memory networks. Many people find that such memories are also touched off by distinctive odors out of the past—from a farm visited in childhood, Grandma's kitchen, the seashore, a doctor's office, the perfume or aftershave of a former lover, and so on. The key idea in redintegration is that

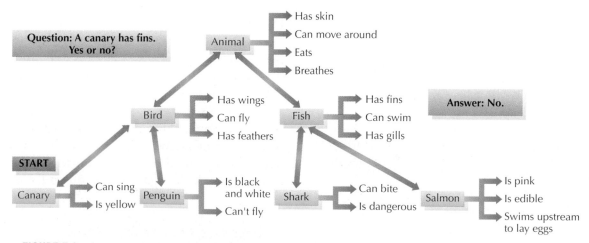

● **FIGURE 7.4** A hypothetical network of facts about animals shows what is meant by the structure of memory. Small networks of ideas such as this are probably organized into larger and larger units and higher levels of meaning. (Adapted from Collins & Quillian, 1969.)

one memory serves as a cue to trigger another. As a result, an entire past experience may be reconstructed from one small recollection.

Skill Memory and Fact Memory

How many types of long-term memory are there? It is becoming clear that more than one type of long-term memory exists. For example, a curious thing happens to many people who develop amnesia. Amnesic patients may be unable to learn a telephone number, an address, or a person's name. Yet, the same patients can learn to solve complex puzzles in a normal amount of time (Cavaco et al., 2004) (● Fig. 7.5). These and other observations have led many psychologists to conclude that long-term memories fall into at least two categories. One is called *procedural memory* (or skill memory). The other is *declarative memory* (also sometimes called fact memory).

Skills **Procedural memory** includes basic conditioned responses and learned actions, such as those involved in typing, driving, or swinging a golf club. Memories such as these can be fully expressed only as actions (or "know-how"). It is likely that skill memories register in "lower" brain areas, especially the cerebellum. They represent the more basic "automatic" elements of conditioning, learning, and memory (Hermann et al., 2004).

Facts **Declarative memory** stores specific factual information, such as names, faces, words, dates, and ideas. Declarative memories are expressed as words or symbols. For example, knowing that Peter Jackson directed both the *Lord of the Rings* trilogy and the latest remake of *King Kong* is a declarative memory. This is the type of memory that a person with amnesia lacks and that most of us take for granted. Declara-tive memory can be further divided into *semantic memory* and *episodic memory* (Tulving, 2002).

Semantic Memory Most of our basic factual knowledge about the world is almost totally immune to forgetting. The names of objects, the days of the week or months of the year, simple math skills, the seasons, words and language, and other general facts are all quite lasting. Such impersonal facts make up a part of LTM called **semantic memory.** Semantic memory serves as a mental dictionary or encyclopedia of basic knowledge.

Episodic Memory Semantic memory has no connection to times or places. It would be rare, for instance, to remember when and where you first learned the names of the seasons. In contrast, **episodic** (ep-ih-SOD-ik) **memory** is an "auto-biographical" record of personal experiences. It stores life events (or "episodes") day after day, year after year. Can you remember your seventh birthday? Your first date? An accident you witnessed? What you did yesterday? All are episodic memories. Note that episodic memories are about the "what," "where," and "when" of our lives. More than a simple ability to store information, they make it possible for us to mentally travel back in time and *re-experience* events (Tulving, 2002).

Are episodic memories as lasting as semantic memories? In general, episodic memories are more easily forgotten than semantic memories. In fact, it is the forgetting of episodic information that results in the formation of semantic memories. At first, you remembered when and where you were when you learned the names of the seasons. Over time you forgot the episodic details but will likely remember the names for the rest of your life.

New information constantly pours into episodic memory. Stop for a moment and remember where and when you

● **FIGURE 7.5** The tower puzzle. In this puzzle, all the colored disks must be moved to another post without ever placing a larger disk on a smaller one. Only one disk may be moved at a time, and a disk must always be moved from one post to another (it cannot be held aside). An amnesic patient learned to solve the puzzle in 31 moves, the minimum possible. Even so, each time he began, he protested that he did not remember ever solving the puzzle before and that he did not know how to begin. Evidence like this suggests that memories for skills are distinct from memories for facts. (Adapted from Squire & Zola-Morgan, 1988.)

Network model A model of memory that views it as an organized system of linked information.

Redintegrative memories Memories that are reconstructed or expanded by starting with one memory and then following chains of association to other, related memories.

Procedural memory Long-term memories of conditioned responses and learned skills.

Declarative memory That part of long-term memory containing specific factual information.

Semantic memory A subpart of declarative memory that records impersonal knowledge about the world.

Episodic memory A subpart of declarative memory that records personal experiences that are linked with specific times and places.

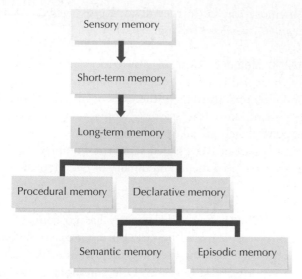

● **FIGURE 7.6** In the model shown here, long-term memory is divided into procedural memory (learned actions and skills) and declarative memory (stored facts). Declarative memories can be either semantic (impersonal knowledge) or episodic (personal experiences associated with specific times and places).

first met your best friend. That was an episodic memory. Notice that you now remember that you just remembered something. You have a new episodic memory in which you remember that you remembered while reading this text! It's easy to see how much we ask of our memory.

How Many Types of Memory? In answer to the question posed at the beginning of this section, it is very likely that three kinds of long-term memories exist: procedural memory and two types of declarative memory, semantic and episodic (Lieberman, 2004) (● Fig. 7.6). Although other types of memory may be discovered, it appears that some pieces of the puzzle are falling into place.

MODULE **7.2 Summary**

What are the features of short-term memory?

- Selective attention determines what information moves from sensory memory, which is exact but very brief, on to STM.
- STM has a capacity of about 5 to 7 bits of information, but this limit can be extended by chunking. Short-term memories are brief and very sensitive to interruption or interference. However, they can be kept alive by maintenance rehearsal.

What are the features of long-term memory?

- LTM serves as a general storehouse for meaningful information. Elaborative rehearsal helps us form lasting, long-term memories.
- Long-term memories are relatively permanent. LTM seems to have an almost unlimited storage capacity.
- Constructive processing tends to alter memories. Remembering is an active process. Our memories are frequently lost, altered, revised, or distorted.
- LTM is highly organized. The structure of memory networks is the subject of current research.
- Redintegrative memories are reconstructed, as one bit of information leads to others, which then serve as cues for further recall.

Is there more than one type of long-term memory?

- LTM contains procedural (skill) and declarative (fact) memories. Declarative memories can be semantic or episodic.

KNOWLEDGE BUILDER

STM and LTM

Recite

1. Information is best transferred from STM to LTM when a person engages in

    a. maintenance chunking

    b. maintenance recoding

    c. elaborative networking

    d. elaborative rehearsal

2. Constructive processing is often responsible for creating pseudomemories. T or F?

3. Electrical stimulation of the brain has shown conclusively that all memories are stored permanently but not all memories can be retrieved. T or F?

4. Memories elicited under hypnosis are more vivid, complete, and reliable than normal. T or F?

5. The existence of redintegrative memories is best explained by _____ models of memory.

    a. network

    b. integrative

    c. implicit

    d. chunking

6. Which of the following is a synonym for skill memory?

    a. semantic memory

    b. declarative memory

    c. episodic memory

    d. procedural memory

Reflect
Critical Thinking

7. Parents sometimes warn children not to read comic books, fearing that they will learn less in school if they "fill their heads up with junk." Why is this warning unnecessary?

Relate

Telephone numbers are divided into an area code (3 digits) and a 7-digit number that is divided into 3 digits, plus 4 more. Can you relate this practice to STM? How about to chunking and recoding?

Think about how you've used your memory in the last hour. See if you can identify an example of each of the following: a procedural memory, a declarative memory, a semantic memory, and an episodic memory.

Link

Internet addresses frequently change. To find the sites listed here, visit **http://www.thomsonedu.com/psychology/coon** for an updated list of Internet addresses and direct links to relevant sites.

- **The Magical Number Seven, Plus or Minus Two** Read George Miller's original paper on capacity limits in short-term memory.

- **Questions and Answers about Memories of Childhood Abuse** Read a summary of the repressed memory issue from the American Psychological Association.

- **False Memory Syndrome Foundation** This site provides information about false memory and its devastating effects, explanations of how it works, and aid to those who are affected.

ANSWERS

1. d 2. T 3. F 4. F 5. a 6. d 7. Because the more information you have in long-term memory, the greater the possibilities for linking new information to it. Generally, the more you know, the more you can learn—even if some of what you know is "junk."

7.3 Measuring Memory

WHETHER YOU HAVE "REMEMBERED" depends on how you are tested. Also, various types of testing have revealed much of what is known about memory. For example, unconscious memories are revealed by a special technique called priming. In this module we will consider various ways of measuring memory.

Measuring Memory—The Answer Is on the Tip of My Tongue

SURVEY QUESTION: *How is memory measured?*

You either remember something or you don't, right? Wrong. Partial memories are common. For instance, have you ever tried to remember something only to find yourself stuck in a **tip-of-the-tongue (TOT) state?** This is the feeling that a memory is available but not quite retrievable (Schwartz, 2002). It is as if an answer or a memory is just out of reach—on the "tip of your tongue." In a classic TOT study, university students read the definitions of words such as *sextant, sampan,* and *ambergris.* Students who "drew a blank" and couldn't name a defined word were asked to give any other information they could. Often, they could guess the first and last letter and the number of syllables of the word they were seeking. They also gave words that sounded like or meant the same thing as the defined word (Brown & McNeill, 1966). In another study, people listened to theme music from popular TV shows. Then they tried to name the program the tune came from. This produced TOT experiences for about 1 out of 5 tunes (Riefer, Keveri, & Kramer, 1995).

The items listed next may induce the TOT state. See if you can name the defined words. (*Answers are at the bottom of this page.)

WHAT´S ON THE TIP OF YOUR TONGUE?

1. A person who collects and studies postage stamps
2. To officially renounce a throne
3. A nylon strip surfaced with tiny hooks that fasten to another strip surfaced with uncut pile
4. Produced by humans rather than natural
5. The pictorial system of writing used in ancient Egypt
6. A small fish that attaches itself to a shark

Closely related to the TOT state is the fact that people can often tell beforehand if they are likely to remember some-

thing. This is called the **feeling of knowing** (Widner, Jr., Otani, & Winkelman, 2005). Feeling-of-knowing reactions are easy to observe on TV game shows, where they occur just before contestants are allowed to answer. *Déjà vu,* the experience that you have previously experienced a new situation, is yet another example of partial retrieval. A déjà vu experience likely occurs when a new experience triggers the retrieval of a past experience without yielding *any* of the details (Brown, 2004).

Because memory is not an all-or-nothing event, there are several ways of measuring it. Three commonly used *memory tasks* (tests of memory) are recall, recognition, and relearning. Let's see how they differ.

Recalling Information

What is the name of the first song on your favorite CD? Who won the World Series last year? Who wrote *Hamlet?* If you can answer these questions you are using **recall,** a direct retrieval of facts or information. Tests of recall often require *verbatim* (word-for-word) memory. If you study a poem until you can recite it without looking at it, you are recalling it. If you complete a fill-in-the-blank question, you are using recall. When you answer an essay question by providing facts and ideas, you are also using recall, even though you didn't learn your essay verbatim.

The order in which information is memorized has an interesting effect on recall. To experience it, try to memorize the following list, reading it only once:

> bread, apples, soda, ham, cookies, rice, lettuce, beets, mustard, cheese, oranges, ice cream, crackers, flour, eggs

If you are like most people, it will be hardest for you to recall items from the middle of the list. ● Figure 7.7 shows the results of a similar test. Notice that most errors occur with middle items of an ordered list. This is the **serial position effect.** You can remember the last items on a list because they are still in STM. The first items are also remembered well because they entered an "empty" short-term memory. This allows you to rehearse the items so they move into long-term memory (Addis & Kahana, 2004). The middle items are neither held in short-term memory nor moved to long-term memory, so they are often lost.

Recognizing Information

Try to write down everything you can remember learning from a class you took last year. If you actually did this, you might conclude that you had learned very little. However, a

---

* 1. philatelist 2. abdicate 3. Velcro 4. artificial
5. hieroglyphics 6. remora

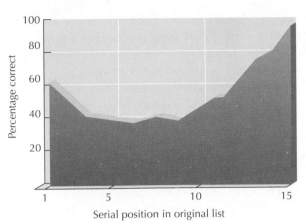

● FIGURE 7.7 The serial position effect. The graph shows the percentage of subjects correctly recalling each item in a 15-item list. Recall is best for the first and last items. (Data from Craik, 1970.)

more sensitive test based on recognition could be used. In **recognition memory,** previously learned material is correctly identified. For instance, you could take a multiple-choice test on facts and ideas from the course. Because you would only have to recognize correct answers, you would probably find that you had learned a lot.

Recognition memory can be amazingly accurate for pictures and photographs (Whitehouse, Maybery, & Durkin, 2006). In one classic study, the investigator showed people 2,560 photographs at a rate of one every 10 seconds. Each person was then shown 280 pairs of photographs. Each pair included an "old" picture (from the first set of photos) and a similar "new" image. Subjects could tell 85 to 95 percent of the time which photograph they had seen before (Haber, 1970). This finding may explain why we rarely need to see our friends' vacation photos more than once.

Recognition is usually superior to recall. That's why people so often say, "I may forget a name, but I never forget a face." (You recall the name but recognize the face.) That's also why police departments use photographs or a lineup to identify criminal suspects. Witnesses who disagree when they try to recall a suspect's height, weight, age, or eye color often agree completely when they merely need to recognize the person.

Is recognition always superior? It depends greatly on the kind of *distractors* used (Flowe & Ebbese, 2007). These are false items included with an item to be recognized. If distractors are very similar to the correct item, memory may be poor. A reverse problem occurs when only one choice looks like it could be correct. This can produce a *false positive,* or false sense of recognition, like the false memory you had earlier when you thought you remembered seeing the word *sleep.*

There have been instances in which witnesses described a criminal as black, tall, or young. Then a lineup was held in which a suspect was the only African American among whites, the only tall suspect, or the only young person. In such cases a false identification is very likely. A better method is to have *all* the distractors look like the person witnesses described. Also, to reduce false positives, witnesses should be warned that the culprit *may not be present.* Many hundreds of people have been put in jail on the basis of mistaken eyewitness memories (Wells, Memon, & Penrod, 2006). To avoid tragic mistakes, it's far better to show witnesses one photo at a time (a sequential lineup). For each photo, the witness must decide whether the person is the culprit before another photo is shown (Wells, 2001; Wells & Olsen, 2003).

Relearning Information

In another classic experiment, a psychologist read a short passage in Greek to his son every day when the boy was between 15 months and 3 years of age. At age 8, the boy was asked if he remembered the Greek passage. He showed no evidence of recall. He was then shown selections from the passage he heard and selections from other Greek passages. Could he recognize the one he heard as an infant? "It's all Greek to me!" he said, indicating a lack of recognition (and drawing a frown from everyone in the room).

Had the psychologist stopped, he might have concluded that no memory of the Greek remained. However, the child was then asked to memorize the original quotation and oth-

Police lineups make use of the sensitivity of recognition memory. However, unless great care is taken, false identifications are still possible (Wells, 2001).

Tip-of-the-tongue (TOT) state The feeling that a memory is available but not quite retrievable.

Feeling of knowing The ability to predict beforehand whether one will be able to remember something.

Recall To supply or reproduce memorized information with a minimum of external cues.

Serial position effect The tendency to make the most errors in remembering the middle items of an ordered list.

Recognition memory An ability to correctly identify previously learned information.

ers of equal difficulty. This time his earlier learning became evident. The boy memorized the passage he had heard in childhood 25 percent faster than the others (Burtt, 1941). As this experiment suggests, **relearning** is typically the most sensitive measure of memory.

When a person is tested by relearning, how do we know a memory still exists? As with the boy described, relearning is measured by a *savings score* (the amount of time saved when relearning information). Let's say it takes you 1 hour to memorize all the names in a telephone book. (It's a small town.) Two years later you relearn them in 45 minutes. Because you "saved" 15 minutes, your savings score would be 25 percent (15 divided by 60 times 100). Savings of this type are a good reason for studying a wide range of subjects. It may seem that learning algebra, history, or a foreign language is wasted if you don't use the knowledge immediately. But when you do need such information, you will be able to relearn it quickly.

Implicit and Explicit Memories

Many memories remain outside of conscious awareness. For example, if you know how to type, it is apparent that you know where the letters are on the keyboard. But how many typists could correctly label blank keys in a drawing of a keyboard? Many people find that they cannot directly remember such information, even though they "know" it.

Who were the last three presidents of the United States? What did you have for breakfast today? What is the title of The Black Eyed Peas' latest album? Explicit memory is used in answering each of these questions. **Explicit memories** are past experiences that are consciously brought to mind. Recall, recognition, and the tests you take in school rely on explicit memories. In contrast, **implicit memories** lie outside of awareness (Roediger & Amir, 2005). That is, we are not aware that a memory exists. Nevertheless, implicit memories—such as unconsciously knowing where the letters are on a keyboard—greatly influence our behavior (Neath & Surprenant, 2003).

Priming *How is it possible to show that a memory exists if it lies outside of awareness?* Psychologists first noticed implicit memory while studying memory loss caused by brain injuries.

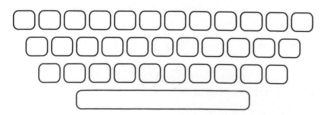

Can you label the letter keys on this blank keyboard? If you can, you probably used implicit memory to do it.

Let's say, for example, that a patient is shown a list of common words, such as *chair, tree, lamp, table,* and so on. A few minutes later, the patient is asked to recall words from the list. Sadly, he has no memory of the words.

Now, instead of asking the patient to explicitly recall the list, we could "prime" his memory by giving him the first two letters of each word. "We'd like you to say a word that begins with these letters," we tell him. "Just say whatever comes to mind." Of course, many words could be made from each pair of letters. For example, the first item (from *chair*) would be the letters *CH.* The patient could say "child," "chalk," "chain," "check," or many other words. Instead, he says "chair," a word from the original list. The patient is not aware that he is remembering the list, but as he gives a word for each letter pair, almost all are from the list. Apparently, the letters **primed** (activated) hidden memories, which then influenced his answers.

Similar effects have been found for people with normal memories. As the preceding example implies, implicit memories are often revealed by giving a person limited cues, such as the first letter of words or partial drawings of objects. Typically, the person believes that he or she is just saying whatever comes to mind. Nevertheless, information previously seen or heard affects his or her answers (Rueckl & Galantucci, 2005). Some nutritionists like to say, "You are what you eat." In the realm of memory it appears that we are what we experience—to a far greater degree than once realized.

MODULE 7.3 Summary

How is memory measured?

- The tip-of-the-tongue state shows that memory is not an all-or-nothing event. Memories may therefore be revealed by recall, recognition, relearning, or priming.

- In recall, memories are retrieved without explicit cues, as in an essay exam. Recall of listed information often reveals a serial position effect.

- A common test of recognition is the multiple-choice question.

- In relearning, material that seems to be forgotten is learned again, and memory is revealed by a savings score.

- Recall, recognition, and relearning mainly measure explicit memories. Other techniques, such as priming, are necessary to reveal implicit memories.

KNOWLEDGE BUILDER

Measuring Memory

Recite

Unless you have a memory like Mr. S's, it might be a good idea to see if you can answer these questions before reading on.

1. Four techniques for measuring or demonstrating memory are _____, _____, _____, _____.

2. Essay tests require _____ of facts or ideas.

3. As a measure of memory, a savings score is associated with
   a. recognition
   b. eidetic images
   c. relearning
   d. reconstruction

4. The two most sensitive tests of memory are
   a. recall and redintegration
   b. recall and relearning
   c. recognition and relearning
   d. recognition and digit-span

5. Priming is used to reveal which type of memories?
   a. explicit
   b. sensory
   c. skill
   d. implicit

Reflect
Critical Thinking

6. When asked to explain why they may have failed to recall some information, people often claim it must be because the information is no longer in their memory. Why does the existence of implicit memories challenge this explanation?

Relate

Have you experienced the TOT state recently? Were you able to retrieve the word you were searching for? If not, what could you remember about it?

Do you prefer tests based primarily on recall or recognition? Have you observed a sav-

ings effect while relearning information you studied in the past (such as in high school)?

Can you think of things you do that are based on implicit memories? For instance, how do you know which way to turn various handles in your house, apartment, or dorm? Do you have to explicitly think, "Turn it to the right," before you act?

Link

Internet addresses frequently change. To find the sites listed here, visit **http://www .thomsonedu.com/psychology/coon** for an updated list of Internet addresses and direct links to relevant sites.

- **What is Déjà Vu?** Links to more information on this fascinating form of partial retrieval.

- **A New Theoretical Framework for Explicit and Implicit Memory** An excellent article exploring a new framework for understanding and measuring explicit and implicit memory functions.

- **Free Recall Test** Test your free recall ability.

ANSWERS

1. recall, recognition, relearning, priming 2. recall 3. c 4. c 5. d 6. It is possible to have an implicit memory that cannot be consciously recalled. Memories like these (*available* in memory even though they are not consciously *accessible*) show that failing to recall something does not mean it is no longer in memory (Allik, 2000). The *feeling of knowing* is related. Have you ever left an examination unable to recall the correct answer to a question *knowing* that you know the answer? That's because the answer was available but not accessible at the time of the exam.

Relearning Learning again something that was previously learned. Used to measure memory of prior learning.

Explicit memory A memory that a person is aware of having; a memory that is consciously retrieved.

Implicit memory A memory that a person does not know exists; a memory that is retrieved unconsciously.

Priming Facilitating the retrieval of an implicit memory by using cues to activate hidden memories.

MODULE
7.4 Forgetting

WHY ARE SOME MEMORIES lost so quickly? For example, why is it hard to remember information a week or two after taking a test in class? Forgetting is one of the more vexing aspects of memory. Why do we forget? Again, the more you know about how we "lose" memories, the better you will be able to hang on to them.

Forgetting—Why We, Uh, Let's See; Why We, Uh . . . Forget!

SURVEY QUESTION: *What causes forgetting?*

Most forgetting tends to occur immediately after memorization. Herman Ebbinghaus (1885) famously tested his own memory at various intervals after learning. Ebbinghaus wanted to be sure he would not be swayed by prior learning, so he memorized *nonsense syllables*. These are meaningless three-letter words such as CEF, WOL, and GEX. The importance of using meaningless words is shown by the fact that OMO, FAB, and DUZ are no longer used on memory tests. People who recognize these words as detergent names find them very easy to remember. This is another reminder that relating new information to what you already know can improve memory.

By waiting various lengths of time before testing himself, Ebbinghaus plotted a **curve of forgetting.** This graph shows the amount of information remembered after varying lengths of time (● Fig. 7.8). Notice that forgetting is rapid at first and is then followed by a slow decline (Hintzman, 2005). The same applies to meaningful information, but the forgetting curve is stretched over a longer time. As you might expect,

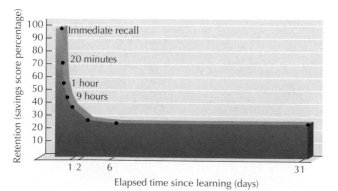

● **FIGURE 7.8** The curve of forgetting. This graph shows the amount remembered (measured by relearning) after varying lengths of time. Notice how rapidly forgetting occurs. The material learned was nonsense syllables. Forgetting curves for meaningful information also show early losses followed by a long gradual decline, but overall, forgetting occurs much more slowly. (Adapted from Ebbinghaus, 1885.)

recent events are recalled more accurately than those from the remote past (O'Connor et al., 2000). Thus, you are more likely to remember that *The Departed* won the "Best Picture" Academy Award for 2006 than you are to remember that *A Beautiful Mind* was the 2001 winner.

As a student, you should note that a short delay between studying and taking a test minimizes forgetting. However, this is no reason for cramming. Most students make the error of only cramming. If you cram, you don't have to remember for very long, but you may not learn enough in the first place. If you use short, daily study sessions and review intensely before a test, you will get the benefit of good preparation and a minimum time lapse.

The Ebbinghaus curve shows less than 30 percent remembered after only 2 days have passed. Is forgetting really that rapid? No, not always. Meaningful information is not lost nearly as quickly as nonsense syllables. After 3 years, students who took a university psychology had forgotten about 30 percent of the facts they learned. After that, little more forgetting occurred (Conway, Cohen, & Stanhope, 1992). Actually, as learning grows stronger, some knowledge may become nearly permanent (Berntsen & Thomsen, 2005).

"I'll never forget old, old . . . oh, what's his name?" Forgetting is both frustrating and embarrassing. Why *do* we forget? The Ebbinghaus curve gives a general picture of forgetting, but it doesn't explain it. For explanations, we must search further. Before we do, look at "Card Magic!" where you will find an interesting demonstration.

When Encoding Fails

Whose head is on a U.S. penny? Which way is it facing? What is written at the top of a penny? Can you accurately draw and label a penny? In an interesting experiment, Ray Nickerson and Marilyn Adams (1979) asked a large group of students to draw a penny. Few could. Well then, could the students at least recognize a drawing of a real penny among fakes? (See ● Fig. 7.11.) Again, few could.

The most obvious reason for forgetting is also the most commonly overlooked. Obviously, few of us ever encode the details of a penny. In many cases, we "forget" because of **encoding failure.** That is, a memory was never formed in the first place (the card trick you just saw is another example). If you are bothered by frequent forgetting or absentmindedness, it is wise to ask yourself, "Have I been storing the information in the first place?" (Schacter, 2001). When 140 college professors were asked what they do to improve their memory, the favorite technique was to *write things down* (Park, Smith, & Cavanaugh, 1990). Making notes prevents

DISCOVERING PSYCHOLOGY

Card Magic!

● FIGURE 7.9

Pick a card from the six shown in ● Figure 7.9 above. Look at it closely and be sure you can remember which card is yours. Now, snap your fingers and look at the cards in Figure 7.10, below. Poof! Only five cards remain, and the card you chose has disappeared. Obviously, you could have selected any one of the six cards in Figure 7.9. How did we know which one to remove?

This trick is based entirely on an illusion of memory. Recall that you were asked to concentrate on one card among the six cards in Figure 7.9. That prevented you from paying attention to the other cards, so they weren't stored in your memory (Mangels, Picton, & Craik, 2001; Naveh-Benjamin, Guez, & Sorek, 2007). The five cards you see below are all new (none is shown above in Figure 7.9). Because you couldn't find your card in the "remaining five," it looked like your card disappeared. What looked like "card magic" is actually memory magic. Now return to "When Encoding Fails" and continue reading to learn more about forgetting.

● **FIGURE 7.10**

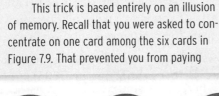

● **FIGURE 7.11** Some of the distractor items used in a study of recognition memory and encoding failure. Penny A is correct but was seldom recognized. Pennies G and J were popular wrong answers. (Adapted from Nickerson & Adams, 1979.)

information from slipping out of short-term memory before you can review it and store it more permanently. By the way, if you like to study while watching television or instant messaging, beware. Dividing your attention like that also leads to encoding failure (Naveh-Benjamin, Guez, & Sorek, 2007).

College Students: They're All Alike! Encoding failures also affect our memories of people. Imagine yourself in this situation: As you are walking on campus, a young man who looks like a college student approaches you and asks for directions. While you are talking, two workers carrying a door pass between you and the young man. While your view is blocked by the door, another man takes the place of the first. Now you are facing a different person than the one who was there just seconds earlier. If this happened to you, do you think you would notice the change? Remarkably, only half the people tested in this way noticed the switch (Simons & Levin, 1998)!

How could anyone fail to notice that one stranger had been replaced by another? The people who didn't remember the first man were all older adults. College students weren't fooled by the switch. Apparently, older adults encoded the first man in very general terms as a "college student." As a result, that's all they remembered about him. Because his replacement also looked like a college student, they thought he was the same person (Simons & Levin, 1998).

Curve of forgetting A graph that shows the amount of memorized information remembered after varying lengths of time.

Encoding failure Failure to store sufficient information to form a useful memory.

Actually, we all tend to categorize strangers in general terms: Is the person young or old, male or female, a member of my ethnic group or another? This tendency is one reason why eyewitnesses are better at identifying members of their own ethnic group than persons from other groups (Burgess & Weaver, 2003; Michel, Caldara, & Rossion, 2006). It may seem harsh to say so, but during brief social contacts, people really do act as if members of other ethnic groups "all look alike." Of course, this bias disappears when people get acquainted and learn more about one another as individuals (McKone et al., 2007).

Memory Decay

One view of forgetting holds that **memory traces** (changes in nerve cells or brain activity) decay (fade or weaken) over time. **Memory decay** appears to be a factor in the loss of sensory memories. Such fading also applies to short-term memory. Information stored in STM seems to initiate a brief flurry of activity in the brain that quickly dies out. Short-term memory therefore operates like a "leaky bucket": New information constantly pours in, but it rapidly fades away and is replaced by still newer information. Let's say that you are trying to remember a short list of letters, numbers, or words after seeing or hearing them once. If it takes you more than 4 to 6 seconds to repeat the list, you will forget some of the items (Dosher & Ma, 1998).

Disuse Is it possible that the decay of memory traces also explains long-term forgetting? That is, could long-term memory traces fade from **disuse** (infrequent retrieval) and eventually become too weak to retrieve? There is evidence that memories not retrieved and "used" or rehearsed become weaker over time (Schacter, 2001). However, disuse alone cannot fully explain forgetting.

Disuse doesn't seem to account for our ability to recover seemingly forgotten memories through redintegration, relearning, and priming. It also fails to explain why some unused memories fade, whereas others are carried for life. A third contradiction will be recognized by anyone who has spent time with the elderly. People growing senile may become so forgetful that they can't remember what happened a week ago. Yet at the same time your Uncle Oscar's recent memories are fading, he may have vivid memories of trivial and long-forgotten events from the past. "Why, I remember it as clearly as if it were yesterday," he will say, forgetting that the story he is about to tell is one he told earlier the same day. In short, disuse offers no more than a partial explanation of long-term forgetting.

If decay and disuse don't fully explain forgetting from long-term memory, what does? Let's briefly consider some additional possibilities.

Cue-Dependent Forgetting

Often, memories appear to be *available* but not *accessible*. An example is having an answer on the "tip of your tongue." You know the answer is there (it is available), but it remains just "out of reach" (it is inaccessible). This suggests that many memories are "forgotten" because **memory cues** (stimuli associated with a memory) are missing when the time comes to retrieve information. For example, if you were asked, "What were you doing on Monday afternoon of the third week in May 2 years ago?" your reply might be, "Come on, how should I know?" However, if you were reminded, "That was the day the courthouse burned," or "That was the day Stacy had her automobile accident," you might remember immediately.

The presence of appropriate cues almost always enhances memory (Nairne, 2002). In theory, for instance, memory will be best if you study in the same room where you will be tested. Because this is often impossible, when you study, try to visualize the room where you will be tested. Doing so can enhance memory later (Jerabek & Standing, 1992). Similarly, people remember better if the same odor (such as lemon or lavender) is present when they study and are tested (Parker, Ngu, & Cassaday, 2001). If you wear a particular perfume or cologne while you prepare for a test, it might be wise to wear it when you take the test.

State-Dependent Learning Have you heard the story about the drunk who misplaced his wallet and had to get drunk again to find it? Although this tale is often told as a joke, it is not too far-fetched. The bodily state that exists during learn-

External cues like those found in a photograph, in a scrapbook, or during a walk through an old neighborhood often aid recall of seemingly lost memories. For many veterans, finding a familiar name engraved in the Vietnam Veterans Memorial unleashes a flood of memories.

ing can be a strong cue for later memory, an effect known as **state-dependent learning** (Neath & Surprenant, 2003). Being very thirsty, for instance, might prompt you to remember events that took place on another occasion when you were thirsty. Because of such effects, information learned under the influence of a drug is best remembered when the drugged state occurs again (Slot & Colpaert, 1999).

A similar effect applies to emotional states (Wessel & Wright, 2004). For instance, Gordon Bower (1981) found that people who learned a list of words while in a happy mood recalled them better when they were again happy. People who learned while they felt sad remembered best when they were sad (● Fig. 7.12). Similarly, if you are in a happy mood, you are more likely to remember recent happy events. If you are in a bad mood, you will tend to have unpleasant memories. Such links between emotional cues and memory could explain why couples who quarrel often end up remembering—and rehashing—old arguments.

Interference

Further insight into forgetting comes from a classic experiment in which college students learned lists of nonsense syllables. After studying, students in one group slept for 8 hours and were then tested for memory of the lists. A second group stayed awake for 8 hours and went about business as usual. When members of the second group were tested, they remembered *less* than the group that slept (● Fig. 7.13). This difference is based on the fact that new learning can interfere with previous learning. **Interference** refers to the tendency for new memories to impair retrieval of older memories (and the reverse). It seems to apply to both short-term and long-term memory (Lustig, May, & Hasher, 2001; Nairne, 2002).

It is not completely clear if new memories alter existing memory traces or if they make it harder to "locate" (retrieve)

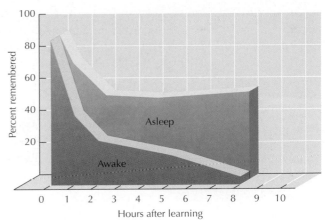

● **FIGURE 7.13** The amount of forgetting after a period of sleep or of being awake. Notice that sleep causes less memory loss than activity that occurs while one is awake. (Adapted from Jenkins & Dallenbach, 1924.)

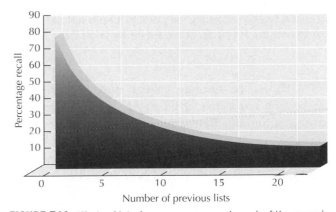

● **FIGURE 7.14** Effects of interference on memory. A graph of the approximate relationship between percentage recalled and number of different word lists memorized. (Adapted from Underwood, 1957.)

earlier memories. In any case, there is no doubt that interference is a major cause of forgetting (Neath & Surprenant, 2003). College students who memorized 20 lists of words (one list each day) were able to recall only 15 percent of the last list. Students who learned only one list remembered 80 percent (Underwood, 1957) (● Fig. 7.14).

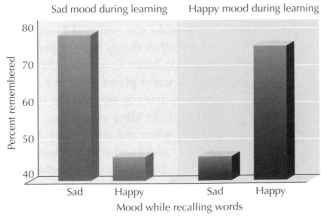

● **FIGURE 7.12** The effect of mood on memory. Subjects best remembered a list of words when their mood during testing was the same as their mood was when they learned the list. (Adapted from Bower, 1981.)

Memory traces Physical changes in nerve cells or brain activity that take place when memories are stored.

Memory decay The fading or weakening of memories assumed to occur when memory traces become weaker.

Disuse Theory that memory traces weaken when memories are not periodically used or retrieved.

Memory cue Any stimulus associated with a particular memory. Memory cues usually enhance retrieval.

State-dependent learning Memory influenced by one's bodily state at the time of learning and at the time of retrieval. Improved memory occurs when the bodily states match.

Interference The tendency for new memories to impair retrieval of older memories, and the reverse.

Spencer Grant/Photo Researchers, Inc.

How could anyone lose something as large as a car? If you park your car in a different place every day, you may have experienced forgetting caused by interference. Today's memory about your car's location is easily confused with memories from yesterday, and the day before, and the day before that.

Order Effects The sleeping college students remembered more because retroactive (RET-ro-AK-tiv) interference was held to a minimum. **Retroactive interference** refers to the tendency for new learning to inhibit retrieval of old learning. Avoiding new learning prevents retroactive interference. This doesn't exactly mean you should hide in a closet after you study for an exam. However, you should avoid studying other subjects until the exam. Sleeping after study can help you retain memories, and reading, writing, or even watching TV may cause interference.

Retroactive interference is easily demonstrated in the laboratory by this arrangement:

Experimental group:	Learn A	Learn B	Test A
Control group:	Learn A	Rest	Test A

Imagine yourself as a member of the experimental group. In task A, you learn a list of telephone numbers. In task B, you learn a list of Social Security numbers. How do you score on a test of task A (the telephone numbers)? If you do not remember as much as the control group that learns *only* task A, then retroactive interference has occurred. The second thing learned interfered with memory of the first thing learned; the interference went "backward," or was "retroactive" (● Fig. 7.15).

Proactive (pro-AK-tiv) interference is a second basic source of forgetting. **Proactive interference** occurs when prior learning inhibits recall of later learning. A test for proactive interference would take this form:

Experimental group:	Learn A	Learn B	Test B
Control group:	Rest	Learn B	Test B

Let's assume that the experimental group remembers less than the control group on a test of task B. In that case, learning task A interfered with memory for task B.

Then proactive interference goes "forward"? Yes. For instance, if you cram for a psychology exam and then later the same night cram for a history exam, your memory for the second subject studied (history) will be less accurate than if you had studied only history. (Because of retroactive interference, your memory for psychology would probably also suffer.) The greater the similarity in the two subjects studied, the more interference takes place. The moral, of course, is don't procrastinate in preparing for exams. The more you can avoid competing information, the more likely you are to recall what you want to remember (Anderson & Bell, 2001; Wixted, 2004).

The interference effects we have described apply primarily to memories of verbal information, such as the contents of this chapter. When you are learning a skill, similarity can sometimes be beneficial, rather than disruptive. The next section explains how this occurs.

Transfer of Training Two people begin mandolin lessons. One already plays the violin. The other is a trumpet player. All other things being equal, which person will initially do better in learning the mandolin? If you chose the violin player, you have an intuitive grasp of what positive transfer is. (The strings on a mandolin are tuned the same as a violin.) **Positive transfer** takes place when mastery of one task aids mastery of a second task. Another example would be learning to balance and turn on a bicycle before learning to ride a motorcycle or motor scooter. Likewise, surfing and skateboarding skills transfer to snowboarding.

Is there such a thing as negative transfer? There is indeed. In **negative transfer,** skills developed in one situation con-

Retroactive   *Interference*   Learn A   Learn B   Memory loss for A   New learning interferes with old memory

Proactive   *Interference*   Learn A   Learn B   Memory loss for B   Old learning interferes with new memory

Order of Events

● **FIGURE 7.15** Retroactive and proactive interference. The order of learning and testing shows whether interference is retroactive (backward) or proactive (forward).

flict with those required to master a new task. Learning to back a car with a trailer attached to it is a good example. Normally, when you are backing a car, the steering wheel is turned in the direction you want to go, the same as when moving forward. However, when backing a trailer, you must turn the steering wheel *away* from the direction you want the trailer to go. This situation results in negative transfer and often creates comical scenes at campgrounds and boat launching ramps.

On a more serious note, many tragic crashes caused by negative transfer finally led to greater standardization of airplane cockpits. Fortunately, negative transfer is usually brief, and it occurs less often than positive transfer. Negative transfer is most likely to occur when a new response must be made to an old stimulus (Besnard & Cacitti, 2005). If you have ever encountered a pull-type handle on a door that must be pushed open, you will appreciate this point.

Repression and Suppression of Memories

Take a moment and scan over the events of the last few years of your life. What kinds of things most easily come to mind? Many people remember happy, positive events better than disappointments and irritations (Moore & Zoellner, 2007). A clinical psychologist would call this tendency **repression,** or motivated forgetting. Through repression, painful, threatening, or embarrassing memories are held out of consciousness (Anderson et al., 2004). An example is provided by soldiers who have repressed some of the horrors they saw during combat (Karon & Widener, 1997).

The forgetting of past failures, upsetting childhood events, the names of people you dislike, or appointments you don't want to keep may reveal repression. People prone to repression tend to be extremely sensitive to emotional events. As a result, they use repression to protect themselves from threatening thoughts (McNally, Clancy, & Barrett, 2004). See "The Recovered Memory/False Memory Debate" for further cautions.

If I try to forget a test I failed, am I repressing it? No. Repression can be distinguished from **suppression,** an active, conscious attempt to put something out of mind. By not thinking about the test, you have merely suppressed a memory. If you choose to, you can remember the test. Clinicians consider true repression an *unconscious* event. When a memory is repressed we may be unaware that forgetting has even occurred.

Although some psychologists have questioned whether repression exists (Court & Court, 2001), evidence suggests that we can choose to actively suppress remembering upsetting information (Anderson, 2001). If you have experienced a painful emotional event, you will probably avoid all thoughts associated with it. This tends to keep cues out of

It is highly likely that you have a flashbulb memory about where you were when you first learned about the terrorist attack on the World Trade Center in New York. If someone alerted you about the news, you will remember that person's call and you will have clear memories about how you reacted to seeing the collapse of the towers.

mind that could trigger a painful memory. In time, your active suppression of the memory may become true repression (Anderson & Green, 2001).

Flashbulb Memories

Why are some traumatic events vividly remembered, whereas others are repressed? Psychologists use the term **flashbulb memories** to describe images that seem to be frozen in

---

Retroactive interference The tendency for new memories to interfere with the retrieval of old memories.

Proactive interference The tendency for old memories to interfere with the retrieval of newer memories.

Positive transfer Mastery of one task aids learning or performing another.

Negative transfer Mastery of one task conflicts with learning or performing another.

Repression Unconsciously pushing unwanted memories out of awareness.

Suppression A conscious effort to put something out of mind or to keep it from awareness.

Flashbulb memories Memories created at times of high emotion that seem especially vivid.

THE CLINICAL FILE

The Recovered Memory/False Memory Debate

Many sexually abused children develop problems that persist into adulthood. In some instances, they repress all memory of the abuse. According to some psychologists, uncovering these hidden memories can be an important step toward regaining emotional health (Palm & Gibson, 1998).

Although the preceding may be true, the search for repressed memories of sexual abuse has itself been a problem. Cases have surfaced in which families were torn apart by accusations of sexual abuse that later turned out to be completely false (Porter et al., 2003). For example, Gary Ramona lost his marriage and his $400,000-a-year job when his daughter Holly alleged that he molested her throughout her childhood. To prove to Holly that her memories were true, the therapists gave her the drug Amytal, and told her that it was a "truth drug." (Amytal is a hypnotic drug that induces a twilight state of consciousness. People do not automatically tell the truth while under its influence.) Ramona sued Holly's therapists, claiming that they had been irresponsible. After reviewing the evidence, a jury awarded Gary Ramona $500,000 in damages. In a way, Gary Ramona was lucky. Most people who are falsely accused have no way to prove their innocence (Loftus & Ketcham, 1994).

Why would anyone have false memories about such disturbing events? Several popular

Gary Ramona's life was shattered by "recovered" memories that turned out to be false.

AP/Wide World Photos

books and a few misguided therapists have actively encouraged people to find repressed memories of abuse. Hypnosis, guided visualization, suggestion, age regression, and similar techniques can elicit fantasies that are mistaken for real memories. As we saw in Module 7.2, it is easy to create false memories, especially by using hypnosis (Loftus, 2003b; Loftus & Bernstein, 2005).

In an effort to illustrate how easy it is to create false memories, and to publicize *false*

memory syndrome, memory expert Elizabeth Loftus once deliberately implanted a false memory in actor Alan Alda. As the host of the television series *Scientific American Frontiers*, he was scheduled to interview Loftus. Before the interview, Alda was asked to fill out a questionnaire about his tastes in food. When he arrived, Loftus told Alda that his answers revealed that he must once have gotten sick after eating hard-boiled eggs (which was false). Later that day, at a picnic, Alda would not eat hard-boiled eggs (Loftus, 2003a).

Certainly, some memories of abuse that return to awareness are genuine and must be dealt with. However, there is little doubt that some "recovered" memories are pure fantasy. No matter how real a recovered memory may seem, it could be false, unless it can be verified by others or by court or medical records (Olio, 2004).

A few years ago, an "epidemic" of recovered memories took place. Today, psychologists have developed new guidelines for therapists to minimize the risk of influencing clients' memories. Nevertheless, false claims about childhood abuse still occasionally make the news. The saddest thing about such claims is that they deaden public sensitivity to actual abuse. Childhood sexual abuse is widespread. Awareness of its existence must not be repressed.

---

memory at times of personal tragedy, accident, or other emotionally significant events (Niedzwienska, 2004).

Depending on your age, you may have a "flashbulb" memory for the assassinations of John F. Kennedy and Martin Luther King, the *Challenger* or *Columbia* space shuttle disasters, or the terrorist attack on the World Trade Center in New York (Curci & Luminet, 2006). Flashbulb memories are most often formed when an event is surprising, important, or emotional (Paradis et al., 2004). They are frequently associated with public tragedies, but memories of positive events may also have "flashbulb" clarity.

Flashbulb memories seem to be very detailed. Often, they focus primarily on how you reacted to the event. ■ Table 7.1 lists some memories that had "flashbulb" clarity for at least 50 percent of a group of college students. How vivid are

the memories they trigger for you? (Note again that both positive and negative events are listed.)

The term *flashbulb memories* was first used to describe recollections that seemed to be unusually vivid and permanent. It has become clear, however, that flashbulb memories are not always accurate (Greenberg, 2004). More than anything else, what sets flashbulb memories apart is that we tend to place great *confidence* in them—even when they are wrong (Niedzwienska, 2004). Perhaps that's because we review emotionally charged events over and over and tell others about them. Also, public events such as wars, earthquakes, and assassinations reappear many times in the news, which highlights them in memory. Over time, flashbulb memories tend to crystallize into consistent, if not entirely accurate, landmarks in our lives (Schmolck, Buffalo, & Squire, 2000).

■ TABLE 7.1   Bright Flashes of Memory

MEMORY CUE	PERCENTAGE OF STUDENTS WITH FLASHBULB MEMORIES
A car accident you were in or witnessed	85
When you first met your college roommate	82
The night of your high school graduation	81
The night of your senior prom (if you went or not)	78
An early romantic experience	77
A time you had to speak in front of an audience	72
When you first got your college admissions letter	65
Your first date–the moment you met him/her	57

Source: From Rubin, 1985.

Memory and the Brain—Some "Shocking" Findings

SURVEY QUESTION: *What happens in the brain when memories are formed?*

One possibility overlooked in our discussion of forgetting is that memories may be lost as they are being formed (Papanicolaou, 2006). For example, a head injury may cause a "gap" in memories preceding the accident. **Retrograde amnesia,** as this is called, involves forgetting events that occurred before an injury or trauma. In contrast, **anterograde amnesia** involves forgetting events that follow an injury or trauma (Behrend, Beike, & Lampinen, 2004). (An example of this type of amnesia is discussed in a moment.)

Consolidation

Retrograde amnesia can be understood if we assume that it takes a certain amount of time to form a lasting memory through a process called **consolidation** (Vogel, Woodman, & Luck, 2006). You can think of consolidation as being somewhat like writing your name in wet concrete. Once the concrete is set, the information (your name) is fairly lasting. But while it is setting, it can be wiped out (amnesia) or scribbled over (interference).

Consider a classic experiment on consolidation, in which a rat is placed on a small platform. The rat steps down to the floor and receives a painful electric shock. After one shock, the rat can be returned to the platform repeatedly, but it will not step down. Obviously, the rat remembers the shock. Would it remember if consolidation were disturbed?

Interestingly, one way to prevent consolidation is to give a different kind of shock called electroconvulsive shock (ECS). ECS is a mild electric shock to the brain. It does not harm the animal, but it does destroy any memory that is being formed. If each painful shock (the one the animal remembers) is followed by ECS (which wipes out memories during consolidation), the rat will step down over and over. Each time, ECS will erase the memory of the painful shock. (ECS is employed as a psychiatric treatment for severe depression in humans.)

What would happen if ECS were given several hours after the learning? Recent memories are more easily disrupted than older memories. If enough time is allowed to pass between learning and ECS, the memory will be unaffected because consolidation is already complete. That's why people with mild head injuries lose only memories from just before the accident and older memories remain intact (Lieberman, 2004). Likewise, you would forget more if you studied, stayed awake 8 hours, and then slept 8 hours than you would if you studied, slept 8 hours, and were awake for 8 hours. Either way, 16 hours would pass. However, less forgetting would occur in the second instance because more consolidation would occur before interference begins (Wixted, 2005).

Where does consolidation take place in the brain? Actually, many parts of the brain are responsible for memory, but the **hippocampus** is particularly important (Sutherland et al., 2006). The hippocampus acts as a sort of "switching station" between short-term and long-term memory (Squire, 2004). The hippocampus does this, in part, by growing new neurons and by making new connections within the brain (Eichenbaum & Fortin, 2005). If the memory in question is particularly emotional, as are many flashbulb memories, activity in the *amygdala,* another part of the limbic system, appears to intensify the process of consolidation (McGaugh, 2004).

Humans who have hippocampal damage usually develop anterograde amnesia, showing a striking inability to consolidate new memories (Zola & Squire, 2001). A patient described by Brenda Milner provides a vivid example. Two years after an operation damaged his hippocampus, the 29-year-old patient continued to give his age as 27. He also reported that it seemed as if the operation had just taken place

Retrograde amnesia Loss of memory for events that preceded a head injury or other amnesia-causing event.

Anterograde amnesia Loss of the ability to form or retrieve memories for events that occur after an injury or trauma.

Consolidation Process by which relatively permanent memories are formed in the brain.

Hippocampus A brain structure associated with emotion and the transfer of information from short-term memory to long-term memory.

(Milner, 1965). His memory of events before the operation remained clear, but he found forming new long-term memories almost impossible. When his parents moved to a new house a few blocks away on the same street, he could not remember the new address. Month after month, he read the same magazines over and over without finding them familiar. If you were to meet this man, he would seem fairly normal because he still has short-term memory. But if you were to leave the room and return 15 minutes later, he would act as if he had never seen you before. Years ago his favorite uncle died, but he suffers the same grief anew each time he is told of the death. Lacking the ability to form new lasting memories, he lives eternally in the present (Corkin, 2002).

The Brain and Long-Term Memory

Somewhere within the 3-pound mass of the human brain lies all we know: ZIP codes, faces of loved ones, history, favorite melodies, the taste of an apple, and much, much more. Where is this information? According to neuroscientist Richard Thompson (2005), many parts of the brain can become active when we learn and form long-term memories, but usually one area is more critical for each particular form of memory.

Some areas of the cerebral cortex *are* more important to long-term memory than others. Patterns of blood flow in the cerebral cortex (the wrinkled outer layer of the brain) can be used to map brain activity. ● Figure 7.16 shows the results of measuring blood flow while people were thinking about a semantic memory *(a)* or an episodic memory *(b)*. In the map, green indicates areas that are more active during semantic thinking. Reds show areas of greater activity during episodic thinking. The brain in view *c* shows the difference in activity between views *a* and *b*. The resulting pattern indicates that the front of the cortex is related to episodic memory. Back areas are more associated with semantic memory (Tulving, 2002).

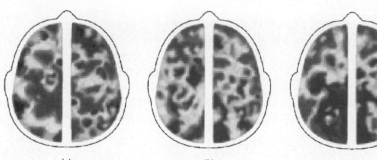

An *aplysia*. The relatively simple nervous system of this sea animal allows scientists to study memory as it occurs in single nerve cells.

Jeffrey L. Rotman/Corbis

● **FIGURE 7.16** Patterns of blood flow in the cerebral cortex associated with semantic memories and episodic memories. (© Tulving, E. (1989). Remembering and knowing the past. *American Scientist*, 77(4), 361-367.)

To summarize (and simplify greatly), the hippocampus handles memory consolidation (Zola & Squire, 2001). Once declarative long-term memories are formed, they appear to be stored in the cortex of the brain (Squire, 2004). In contrast, long-term procedural (skill) memories are likely stored in the cerebellum (Hermann et al., 2004).

How are memories recorded in the brain? Scientists are beginning to identify the exact ways in which nerve cells record information. For example, Eric Kandel and his colleagues have studied learning in the marine snail *aplysia* (ah-PLEEZ-yah). Kandel found that learning in *aplysia* occurs when certain nerve cells in a circuit alter the amount of transmitter chemicals they release (Bailey & Kandel, 2004). Learning also alters the activity, structure, and chemistry of brain cells. Such changes determine which connections get stronger and which become weaker. This "reprograms" the brain and records information (Abel & Lattal, 2001; Squire, 2004).

Scientists continue to study various chemicals, especially neurotransmitters, that affect memory. If their research succeeds, it may be possible to help the millions of persons who suffer from memory impairment (Elli & Nathan, 2001). (See "The Long-Term Potential of a Memory Pill.")

MODULE **7.4 Summary**

What causes forgetting?

- Herman Ebbinghaus found that forgetting is most rapid immediately after learning, as shown by the curve of forgetting.
- Failure to encode information is a common cause of "forgetting."

CRITICAL THINKING

The Long-Term Potential of a Memory Pill

At long last, scientists may have found the chemical "signature" that records memories in everything from snails to rats to humans. If two or more interconnected brain cells become more active at the same time, the connections between them grow stronger (Squire & Kandel, 2000). This process is called *long-term potentiation*. After it occurs, an affected brain cell will respond more strongly to messages from the other cells. The brain appears to use this mechanism to form lasting memories (García-Junco-Clemente, Linares-Clemente, & Fernández-Chacón, 2005).

How has that been demonstrated? Electrically stimulating parts of the brain involved in memory, such as the hippocampus, can decrease long-term potentiation (Ivanco & Racine, 2000). For example, using electroconvulsive shock to overstimulate memory areas in the brains of rats interferes with long-term potentiation (Trepel & Racine, 1999). It also causes memory loss—just as it does when humans are given ECS for depression.

Will researchers ever produce a "memory pill" for people with normal memory? It's a growing possibility. Drugs that *increase* long-term potentiation also tend to improve memory (Shakesby, Anwyl, & Rowan, 2002). For example, rats administered such drugs could remember the correct path through a maze better than rats not given the drug (Service, 1994). Such findings suggest that memory can be and will be artificially enhanced (Schacter, 2000). However, the possibility of something like a "physics pill" or a "math pill" still seems remote.

- Forgetting in sensory memory and STM probably reflects a weakening (decay) of memory traces. Decay of memory traces may also explain some LTM losses.

- Forgetting is often based on a lack of memory cues. State-dependent learning is related to the effects of memory cues.

- Much forgetting in STM and LTM is caused by interference.

- In retroactive interference, new learning interferes with the ability to remember earlier learning.

- Proactive interference occurs when old learning interferes with new learning.

- Memories can be consciously suppressed and they may be unconsciously repressed.

What happens in the brain when memories are formed?

- It takes time to consolidate memories. Lasting memories are recorded by changes in the activity, structure, and chemistry of brain cells.

- In the brain, memory consolidation takes place in the hippocampus. After memories have been consolidated, they appear to be stored in the cortex of the brain.

KNOWLEDGE BUILDER

Forgetting

Recite

1. According to the Ebbinghaus curve of forgetting, we forget slowly at first and then a rapid decline occurs. T or F?

2. Which explanation seems to account for the loss of short-term memories?

   a. decay

   b. disuse

   c. repression

   d. interference

3. When memories are available but not accessible, forgetting may be cue dependent. T or F?

4. When learning one thing makes it more difficult to recall another, forgetting may be caused by _____.

5. You are asked to memorize long lists of telephone numbers. You learn a new list each day for 10 days. When tested on list 3, you remember less than a person who only learned the first three lists. Your larger memory loss is probably caused by

   a. disuse

   b. retroactive interference

   c. regression

   d. proactive interference

6. If you consciously succeed at putting a painful memory out of mind, you have used

   a. redintegration

   b. suppression

   c. negative rehearsal

   d. repression

7. Flashbulb memories could be thought of as the reverse of

   a. repressed memories

   b. proactive memories

   c. retroactive memories

   d. episodic memories

8. Retrograde amnesia results when consolidation is speeded up. T or F?

Reflect
Critical Thinking

9. Based on state-dependent learning, why do you think that music often strongly evokes memories?

10. You must study French, Spanish, psychology, and biology in one evening. What do you think would be the best order in which to study these subjects so as to minimize interference?

11. There may be another way to explain why flashbulb memories are so long lasting. Can you think of one?

Relate

Which of the following concepts best explain why you have missed some answers on psychology tests: encoding failure, decay, disuse, memory cues, interference?

Do you know someone whose name you have a hard time remembering? Do you like or dislike that person? Do you think your difficulty is an instance of repression? Suppression? Interference? Encoding failure?

Have you had a flashbulb memory? How vivid is the memory today? How accurate do you think it is?

Here's a mnemonic tip: Elephants are supposed to have good memories, but a *hippo campus* is the place to go if you want to learn to consolidate memories.

Link

Internet addresses frequently change. To find the sites listed here, visit **http://www .thomsonedu.com/psychology/coon** for an updated list of Internet addresses and direct links to relevant sites.

- **Memory: A Contribution to Experimental Psychology** Read Hermann Ebbinghaus' original article.

- **About Education: Fundamental Concepts of Forgetting and Learning** Relate ideas about forgetting to education.

- **Memory Loss & the Brain** Read issues of a free newsletter.

ANSWERS

1. F 2. a and d 3. T 4. interference 5. b 6. b 7. a 8. F 9. Music tends to affect the mood that a person is in, and moods tend to affect memory (Miranda & Kihlstrom, 2005). 10. Any order that separates French from Spanish and psychology from biology would work (for instance: French, psychology, Spanish, biology). 11. Memories of emotionally significant events may be unusually strong because such memories are rehearsed more frequently. People usually mentally review emotionally charged events many times.

7.5 Exceptional Memory and Improving Memory

IN THIS MODULE we explore exceptional memories. Is superior memory a biological gift, such as having a "photographic" memory? Or do excellent memorizers merely make better-than-average use of normal memory capacities? Regardless of how good your memory may be, there are probably times when you wish it were better. While we're waiting around for the arrival of a memory pill, this module also describes some ways to immediately improve your memory skills.

Exceptional Memory—Wizards of Recall

SURVEY QUESTION: *What are "photographic" memories?*

Can you remember how many doors there are in your house or apartment? To answer a question like this, many people form **mental images** (mental pictures) of each room and count the doorways they visualize. As this example implies, many memories are stored as mental images (Roeckelein, 2004).

Stephen Kosslyn, Thomas Ball, and Brian Reiser (1978) found an interesting way to show that memories do exist as images. Participants first memorized a sort of treasure map similar to the one shown in ● Figure 7.17*a*. They were then asked to picture a black dot moving from one object, such as one of the trees, to another, such as the hut at the top of the island. Did people really form an image to do this task? It seems they did. As shown in Figure 7.17*b*, the time it took to "move" the dot was directly related to actual distances on the map.

Is the "treasure map" task an example of photographic memory? In some ways, internal memory images do have "photographic" qualities. However, the term *photographic memory* is more often used to describe a memory ability called eidetic imagery.

Eidetic Imagery

Eidetic (eye-DET-ik) **imagery** occurs when a person has visual images clear enough to be "scanned" or retained for at least 30 seconds. Internal memory images can be "viewed" mentally with the eyes closed. In contrast, eidetic images are "projected" out in front of a person. That is, they are best "seen" on a plain surface, such as a blank piece of paper. In this respect, eidetic images are somewhat like the afterimages you might have after looking at a flashbulb or a brightly lit neon sign (Haber & Haber, 2000).

Eidetic memory is more common in childhood, with about 8 children in 100 having eidetic images. In one series of tests, children were shown a picture from *Alice's Adventures in Wonderland* (● Fig. 7.18). To test your eidetic imagery, look at the picture and read the instructions there.

Now, let's see how much you remember. Can you say (without looking again) which of Alice's apron strings is longer? Are the cat's front paws crossed? How many stripes are on the cat's tail? After the picture was removed from view, one 10-year-old boy was asked what he saw. He replied, "I see the tree, gray tree with three limbs. I see the cat with stripes around its tail." Asked to count the stripes, the boy replied, "There are about 16" (a correct count!). The boy then went

---

Mental images Mental pictures or visual depictions used in memory and thinking.

Eidetic imagery The ability to retain a "projected" mental image long enough to use it as a source of information.

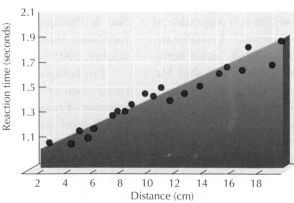

● **FIGURE 7.17** *(a)* "Treasure map" similar to the one used by Kosslyn, Ball, and Reiser (1978) to study images in memory. *(b)* This graph shows how long it took subjects to move a visualized spot various distances on their mental images of the map. (See text for explanation.)

(a) (b)

● **FIGURE 7.18** A test picture like that used to identify children with eidetic imagery. To test your eidetic imagery, look at the picture for 30 seconds. Then look at a blank surface and try to "project" the picture onto it. If you have good eidetic imagery, you will be able to see the picture in detail. Return now to the text and try to answer the questions there. (Redrawn from an illustration in Lewis Carroll's *Alice's Adventures in Wonderland*.)

on to describe the remainder of the picture in striking detail (Haber, 1969).

Don't be disappointed if you didn't do too well when you tried your eidetic skills. Most eidetic imagery disappears during adolescence and becomes rare by adulthood (Haber & Haber, 2000).

A Case of Photographic Memory

Let's return now to the concept of mental images. In rare instances, such images may be so vivid that it is reasonable to say that a person has "photographic memory." A notable example was reported by Aleksandr Luria (1968) in his book, *The Mind of a Mnemonist*. Luria studied a man he called Mr. S, who had practically unlimited memory for visual images. Mr. S could remember almost everything that ever happened to him with incredible accuracy. Luria tried to test Mr. S's memory by using longer and longer lists of words or numbers. However, he soon discovered that no matter how long the list, Mr. S was able to recall it without error. Mr. S could memorize, with equal ease, strings of digits, meaningless con-

sonants, mathematical formulas, and poems in foreign languages. His memory was so powerful that he had to devise ways to *forget*—such as writing information on a piece of paper and then burning it.

Mr. S's abilities might seem fantastic to any college student. However, Mr. S remembered so much that he couldn't separate important facts from trivia or facts from fantasy (Neath & Surprenant, 2003). For instance, if you asked him to read this chapter, he might remember every word. Yet, he might also recall all the images each word made him think of and all the sights, sounds, and feelings that occurred as he was reading. Therefore, finding the answer for a specific question, writing a logical essay, or even understanding a single sentence was very difficult for him. If you didn't have selective memory, you would recall all the ingredients on your cereal box, every street number you've seen, and countless other scraps of information.

Few people in history have possessed memory abilities like Mr. S's. Instead most people with good memories have learned effective strategies for remembering. Let's investigate further.

Strategies for Remembering

At first, a student volunteer named Steve could remember 7 digits—a typical score for a college student. Could he improve with practice? For 20 months Steve practiced memorizing ever-longer lists of digits. Ultimately, he was able to memorize approximately 80 digits, like this sample:

92842048050842268953990190252912807999970
66065747173106010805852697260263573 32135

How did Steve do it? Basically, he worked by chunking digits into meaningful groups containing 3 or 4 digits each. Steve's avid interest in long-distance running helped greatly. For instance, to him the first 3 digits above represented 9 minutes and 28 seconds, a good time for a 2-mile run. When running times wouldn't work, Steve used other associations, such as ages or dates, to chunk digits (Ericsson & Chase, 1982). It seems apparent that Steve's success was based on learned strategies. By using similar memory systems, other people have trained themselves to equal Steve's feat (Bellezza, Six, & Phillips, 1992). In fact, the ability to organize information into chunks underlies expertise in many fields (Gobet, 2005).

Psychologist Anders Ericsson believes that most exceptional memory is merely a learned extension of normal memory (Ericsson et al., 2004). As evidence, he notes that Steve's short-term memory did not improve during months of practice. For example, Steve could still memorize only 7 consonants. Steve's phenomenal memory for numbers grew as he figured out new ways to chunk digits at encoding and store them in LTM.

Researchers studying Rajan Mahadevan have drawn similar conclusions about his spectacular memory for long strings of digits. In 1981 Rajan earned a place in the *Guinness Book of World Records* by reciting the first 31,811 digits of *pi!* Yet, like Steve, Rajan's memory for most other types of information is average. His exceptional memory seems to be based on highly practiced strategies for encoding and storing digits (Thompson, Cowan, & Frieman, 1993). By using similar memory systems, college students have even managed to duplicate some of Mr. S's feats, such as memorizing a 50-digit matrix in 3 minutes (Higbee, 1997).

Steve and Rajan began with normal memory for digits. Both extended their memory abilities by diligent practice. Clearly, exceptional memory can be learned (Ericsson et al., 2004). However, we still have to wonder, do some people have naturally superior memories?

Memory Champions

Each year the World Memory Championship is held in England. Contestants must rapidly memorize daunting amounts of information, such as long lists of unrelated words and numbers. Psychologists John Wilding and Elizabeth Valentine saw this event as an opportunity to study exceptional memory and persuaded the contestants to take some additional memory tests. These ranged from ordinary (recall a story), to challenging (recall the telephone numbers of 6 different people), to diabolical (recall 48 numerals arranged in rows and columns; recognize 14 previously seen pictures of snowflakes among 70 new photos) (Maguire et al., 2003; Wilding & Valentine, 1994).

Exceptional memorizers were found to:

- Use memory strategies and techniques
- Have specialized interests and knowledge that make certain types of information easier to encode and recall
- Have naturally superior memory abilities, often including vivid mental images
- Not have superior intellectual abilities or different brains

87379268
20117495
01758783
19476069
36168154
45240297

This number matrix is similar to the ones contestants in the World Memory Championship had to memorize. To be scored as correct, digits had to be recalled in their proper positions (Wilding & Valentine, 1994).

The first two points confirm what we learned from Steve's acquired memory ability. Many of the contestants, for example, actively used memory strategies, including special memory "tricks" called *mnemonics* (nee-MON-iks). Specialized interests and knowledge also helped for some tasks. For example, one contestant, who is a mathematician, was exceedingly good at memorizing numbers (Wilding & Valentine, 1994).

Several of the memory contestants were able to excel on tasks that prevented the use of learned strategies and techniques. This observation implies that superior memory ability can be a "gift" as well as a learned skill. Wilding and Valentine conclude that exceptional memory may be based on either natural ability or learned strategies. Usually it requires both.

Improving Memory— Keys to the Memory Bank

SURVEY QUESTION: *How can I improve my memory?*

Most super memorizers use strategies to augment whatever natural talents they have. Some of their strategies are described in the remainder of this module. Further, mnemonics are explored in this chapter's Psychology in Action section. Please do remember to read it.

Memory Strategies

As we have seen in this chapter, memory is not like a tape recorder or a video camera. Information is frequently lost, and memories change as they are stored and retrieved. This can be frustrating at times, but it's also a good thing. The flexibility of human memory allows us to focus on what's important and meaningful, even though it also contributes to some inaccuracies. Making full use of memory requires effort and practice. Let's see how you can improve your memory.

Knowledge of Results Learning proceeds best when feedback, or knowledge of results, allows you to check your progress. Feedback can help you identify ideas that need extra practice. In addition, knowing that you have remembered or answered correctly is rewarding. A prime way to provide feedback for yourself while studying is *recitation*.

Recitation If you are going to remember something, eventually you will have to retrieve it. *Recitation* refers to summarizing aloud while you are learning. Recitation forces you to practice retrieving information. When you are reading a text, you should stop frequently and try to remember what you have just read by restating it in your own words. In one classic experiment, the best memory score was earned by a group of students who spent 80 percent of their time reciting and only 20 percent reading (Gates, 1958). Maybe students who talk to themselves aren't crazy after all.

Rehearsal The more you *rehearse* (mentally review) information as you read, the better you will remember it. But remember that maintenance rehearsal alone is not very effective. Elaborative rehearsal, in which you look for connections to existing knowledge, is far better. Thinking about facts helps link them together in memory. To learn college-level information, you must make active use of more reflective rehearsal strategies (Santrock & Halonen, 2007).

Selection The Dutch scholar Erasmus said that a good memory should be like a fish net: It should keep all the big fish and let the little ones escape. If you boil down the paragraphs in most textbooks to one or two important terms or ideas, your memory chores will be more manageable. Practice very selective marking in your texts and use marginal notes to further summarize ideas. Most students mark their texts too much instead of too little. If everything is underlined, you haven't been selective. And, very likely, you didn't pay much attention in the first place (Peterson, 1992).

Organization Assume that you must memorize the following list of words: north, man, red, spring, woman, east, autumn, yellow, summer, boy, blue, west, winter, girl, green, south. This rather difficult list could be reorganized into *chunks* as follows: north-east-south-west, spring-summer-autumn-winter, red-yellow-green-blue, man-woman-boy-girl. Organizing class notes and summarizing chapters can be quite helpful (Hettich, 2005). You may even want to summarize your summaries, so that the overall network of ideas becomes clearer and simpler. Summaries improve memory by encouraging better encoding of information (Hadwin, Kirby, & Woodhouse, 1999).

Whole Versus Part Learning If you have to memorize a speech, is it better to try to learn it from beginning to end? Or in smaller parts like paragraphs? Generally it is better to practice whole packages of information rather than smaller parts (*whole learning*). This is especially true for fairly short, organized information. An exception is that learning parts may be better for extremely long, complicated information. In *part learning*, subparts of a larger body of information are studied (such as sections of a textbook chapter). To decide which approach to use, remember to study the *largest meaningful amount of information* you can at one time.

For very long or complex material, try the *progressive part method,* by breaking a learning task into a series of short sections. At first, you study part A until it is mastered. Next, you study parts A and B; then A, B, and C; and so forth. This is a good way to learn the lines of a play, a long piece of music, or a poem (Ash & Holding, 1990). After the material is learned, you should also practice by starting at points other than A (at C, D, or B, for example). This helps prevent getting "lost" or going blank in the middle of a performance.

Serial Position Whenever you must learn something in *order,* be aware of the serial position effect. As you will recall, this is the tendency to make the most errors in remembering the middle of a list. If you are introduced to a long line of people, the names you are likely to forget will be those in the middle, so you should make an extra effort to attend to them. You should also give extra practice to the middle of a list, poem, or speech. Try to break long lists of information into short sublists, and make the middle sublists the shortest of all.

Cues The best memory cues (stimuli that aid retrieval) are those that were present during encoding (Anderson, 2005). For example, students in one study had the daunting task of trying to recall a list of 600 words. As they read the list (which they did not know they would be tested on), the students gave three other words closely related in meaning to each listed word. In a test given later, the words each student supplied were used as cues to jog memory. The students recalled an astounding 90 percent of the original word list (Mantyla, 1986). Now read the following sentence:

The fish bit the swimmer.

If you were tested a week from now, you would be more likely to recall the sentence if you were given a memory cue. And, surprisingly, the word *shark* would work better as a reminder than *fish* would. The reason for this is that most people think of a shark when they read the sentence. As a result, *shark* becomes a potent memory cue (Schacter, 2000).

The preceding example shows, once again, that it often helps to *elaborate* information as you learn. When you study, try to use new names, ideas, or terms in several sentences. Also, form images that include the new information, and relate it to knowledge you already have. Your goal should be to knit meaningful cues into your memory code to help you retrieve information when you need it (● Fig. 7.19).

Overlearning Numerous studies have shown that memory is greatly improved when you *overlearn.* That is, when study is continued beyond bare mastery. After you have learned material well enough to remember it once without error, you should continue studying. Overlearning is your best insurance against going blank on a test because of being nervous.

Spaced Practice To keep boredom and fatigue to a minimum, try alternating short study sessions with brief rest periods. This pattern, called **spaced practice,** is generally supe-

● **FIGURE 7.19** Actors can remember large amounts of complex information for many months, even when learning new roles in between. During testing, they remember their lines best when they are allowed to move and gesture as they would when performing. Apparently their movements supply cues that aid recall (Noice & Noice, 1999).

rior to **massed practice,** in which little or no rest is given between learning sessions. By improving attention and consolidation, three 20-minute study sessions can produce more learning than 1 hour of continuous study. There's an old joke that goes, "How do you get to Carnegie Hall?" The answer is, "Practice, practice, practice." A better answer would be "Practice, wait awhile, practice, wait awhile, practice" (Neath & Surprenant, 2003).

Perhaps the best way to make use of spaced practice is to *schedule* your time. To make an effective schedule, designate times during the week before, after, and between classes when you will study particular subjects. Then treat these times just as if they are classes you have to attend.

Sleep and Memory Remember that sleeping after study reduces interference. However, unless you are a "night person," late evening may not be a very efficient time for you to study. Also, you obviously can't sleep after every study session or study everything just before you sleep. That's why your study schedule should include ample breaks between subjects as described earlier. (See "Spaced Practice.") The breaks and free time in your schedule are as important as your study periods.

Hunger and Memory People who are hungry almost always score lower on memory tests. So, mother was right—it's a good idea to make sure you've had a good breakfast or lunch before you take tests at school (Smith, Clark, & Gallagher, 1999). And a coffee won't hurt your test performance, either (Smith, 2005).

Extend How Long You Remember When you are learning new information, test yourself repeatedly. As you do, gradually lengthen the amount of time that passes before you test yourself again. For example, if you are studying German words on flash cards, look at the first card and then move it a few cards back in the stack. Do the same with the next few cards. When you get to the first "old" card, test yourself on it and check the answer. Then, move it farther back in the stack. Do the same with other "old" cards as they come up. When "old" cards come up for the third time, put them clear to the back of the stack (Cull, Shaughnessy, & Zechmeister, 1996).

Review If you have spaced your practice and overlearned, review will be like icing on your study cake. Reviewing shortly before an exam cuts down the time during which you must remember details that may be important for the test. When reviewing, hold the amount of new information you try to memorize to a minimum. It may be realistic to take what you have actually learned and add a little more to it at the last minute by cramming. But remember that more than a little new learning may interfere with what you already know.

Using a Strategy to Aid Recall Successful recall is usually the result of a planned *search* of memory (Herrmann et al., 2006). For example, one study found that students were most likely to recall names that eluded them if they made use of partial information (Reed & Bruce, 1982). The students were trying to answer questions such as, "He is best remembered as the scarecrow in the Judy Garland movie *The Wizard of Oz*." (The answer is Ray Bolger.) Partial information that helped students remember included impressions about the length of the name, letter sounds within the name, similar names, and related information (such as the names of other characters in the movie). A similar helpful strategy is to go through the alphabet, trying each letter as the first sound of a name or word you are seeking.

The *cognitive interview* described in Module 7.2 (see "Telling Wrong from Right in Forensic Memory") offers some further hints for recapturing context and jogging memories:

1. Say or write down *everything* you can remember that relates to the information you are seeking. Don't worry about how trivial any of it seems; each bit of information you remember can serve as a cue to bring back others.

Spaced practice A practice schedule that alternates study periods with brief rests.

Massed practice A practice schedule in which studying continues for long periods, without interruption.

2. Try to recall events or information in different orders. Let your memories flow out backward or out of order, or start with whatever impressed you the most.

3. Recall from different viewpoints. Review events by mentally standing in a different place. Or try to view information as another person would remember it. When taking a test, for instance, ask yourself what other students or your professor would remember about the topic.

4. Mentally put yourself back in the situation where you learned the information. Try to mentally recreate the learning environment or relive the event. As you do, include sounds, smells, details of weather, nearby objects, other people present, what you said or thought, and how you felt as you learned the information (Fisher & Geiselman, 1987; Milne & Bull, 2002).

A Look Ahead Psychologists still have much to learn about the nature of memory and how to improve it. For now, one thing stands out clearly: People who have good memories excel at organizing information and making it meaningful. Sometimes, however, you are faced with the need to memorize information without much inherent meaning. For example, a shopping list is just a list of more or less unrelated items. There isn't much of a meaningful relationship between carrots, toilet paper, TV dinners, and Twinkies except that you need more of them. With this in mind, the Psychology in Action discussion for this chapter tells how you can use mnemonics to better memorize when meaning-based memory strategies, like those described in this module, are not helpful.

MODULE 7.5 Summary

What are "photographic" memories?

- Eidetic imagery (photographic memory) occurs when a person is able to project an image onto a blank surface.
- Eidetic imagery is rarely found in adults. However, many adults have internal memory images, which can be very vivid.
- Exceptional memory may be based on natural ability or learned strategies. Usually it involves both.

How can I improve my memory?

- Excellent memory abilities are based on using strategies and techniques that make learning efficient and that compensate for natural weaknesses in human memory.
- Some people have naturally superior memories, but even they find it beneficial to use memory strategies.
- Memory can be improved by using feedback, recitation, and rehearsal, by selecting and organizing information, and by using the progressive part method, spaced practice, overlearning, and active search strategies.
- When you are studying or memorizing, you should also keep in mind the effects of serial position, sleep, review, cues, and elaboration.

KNOWLEDGE BUILDER

Exceptional Memory and Improving Memory

Recite

1. Children with eidetic imagery typically have no better than average long-term memory. T or F?

2. For most people, having an especially good memory is based on

   a. maintenance rehearsal

   b. constructive processing

   c. phonetic imagery

   d. learned strategies

3. To improve memory, it is reasonable to spend as much or more time reciting as reading. T or F?

4. Organizing information while studying has little effect on memory because long-term memory is already highly organized. T or F?

5. The progressive part method of study is best suited to long and complex learning tasks. T or F?

6. As new information is encoded and rehearsed it is helpful to elaborate on its meaning and connect it to other information. T or F?

7. The cognitive interview helps people remember more by providing

   a. memory cues

   b. a serial position effect

   c. phonetic priming

   d. massed practice

Reflect
Critical Thinking

8. Mr. S had great difficulty remembering faces. Can you guess why?

9. What advantages would there be to taking notes as you read a textbook, as opposed to underlining words in the text?

Relate

What kinds of information are you good at remembering? Why do you think your memory is better for those topics?

Return to the topic headings in the preceding pages that list techniques for improving memory. Place a check mark next to those that you have used recently. Review any you didn't mark and think of a specific example of how you could use each technique at school, at home, or at work.

Link

Internet addresses frequently change. To find the sites listed here, visit **http://www .thomsonedu.com/psychology/coon** for an updated list of Internet addresses and direct links to relevant sites.

- **Does No One Have a Photographic Memory?** A discussion of the impossibility of photographic memory.

- **Famous Mnemonists** Read about some of history's most famous memorizers.

- **Memory Strategies** Read about a useful list of memory strategies for studying.

ANSWERS

1. T 2. d 3. T 4. F 5. T 6. T 7. a 8. Mr. S's memory was so specific that faces seemed different and unfamiliar if he saw them from a new angle or if a face had a different expression on it than when Mr. S last saw it. 9. Note-taking is a form of recitation; it encourages elaborative rehearsal and facilitates the organization and selection of important ideas, and your notes can be used for review.

MODULE
8.1 Intelligence

WHAT DO WE MEAN when we say that a person is "bright" or "smart"? Can intelligence be measured? Can intelligence tests predict success in life? What are the consequences of having extremely high or low intelligence? These questions and others concerning intelligence have fascinated psychologists for more than 100 years. Let's see what has been learned and what issues are still debated.

Human Intelligence—The IQ and You

SURVEY QUESTION: *How is human intelligence defined and measured?*

Like many important concepts in psychology, intelligence cannot be observed directly. Nevertheless, we feel certain it exists. Let's compare two children:

> When she was 14 months old, Anne H. wrote her own name. She taught herself to read at age 2. At age 5, she astounded her kindergarten teacher by bringing a notebook computer to class—on which she was reading an encyclopedia. At 10 she breezed through an entire high school algebra course in 12 hours.

> Billy A., who is 10 years old, can write his name and can count, but he has trouble with simple addition and subtraction problems and finds multiplication impossible. He has been held back in school twice and is still incapable of doing the work his 8-year-old classmates find easy.

Anne is considered a genius; Billy, a slow learner. There seems little doubt that they differ in intelligence.

Wait! Anne's ability is obvious, but how do we know that Billy isn't just lazy? This is the same question that Alfred Binet faced in 1904 (Jarvin & Sternberg, 2003). The minister of education in Paris had asked Binet to find a way to distinguish slower students from the more capable (or the capable but lazy). In a flash of brilliance, Binet and an associate created a test made up of "intellectual" questions and problems. Next, they learned which questions an average child could answer at each age. By giving children the test, they could tell if a child was performing up to his or her potential (Kaufman, 2000).

Binet's approach gave rise to modern intelligence tests. At the same time, it launched nearly 100 years of heated debate. Part of the debate is related to the basic difficulty of defining intelligence (Sternberg, Grigorenko, & Kidd, 2005).

James D. Wilson/Getty Images

The power of intelligence is beautifully expressed by Stephen W. Hawking, a theoretical physicist and one of the best-known scientific minds of modern times. Hawking has suffered since age 13 from Lou Gehrig's disease. Today, he can only control his left hand, and he cannot speak. Nevertheless, his brain remains fiercely active. With courage and determination, he has used his intellect to advance our understanding of the universe.

Defining Intelligence

Isn't there an accepted definition of intelligence? Yes, **intelligence** is the global capacity to act purposefully, to think rationally, and to deal effectively with the environment. The core of intelligence consists of *general mental abilities* (called the **g-factor**) in the areas of reasoning, problem solving, knowledge, memory, and successful adaptation to one's surroundings (Sternberg, 2004). Beyond this there is much disagreement. In fact, many psychologists simply accept an *operational definition* of

Bob Daemmrich/Stock, Boston/PictureQuest

Modern intelligence tests are widely used to measure intellectual abilities. When properly administered, such tests provide an operational definition of intelligence.

HUMAN DIVERSITY

Intelligence—How Would a Fool Do It?

You have been asked to sort some objects into categories. Wouldn't it be smart to put the clothes, containers, implements, and foods in separate piles? Not necessarily. When members of the Kpelle culture in Liberia were asked to sort objects, they grouped them together by function. For example, a potato (food) would be placed together with a knife (implement). When the Kpelle were asked why they grouped the objects this way, they often said that's how a wise man would do it. The researchers finally asked the Kpelle, "How would a fool do it?"

Only then did the Kpelle sort the objects into the nice, neat categories we Westerners prefer.

This anecdote, related by cultural psychologist Patricia Greenfield (1997), raises serious questions about general definitions of intelligence. For example, among the Cree of Northern Canada, "smart" people are the ones who have visual skills needed to find food on the frozen tundra (Darou, 1992). For the Puluwat people in the South Pacific, being smart means having ocean-going navigation skills necessary

to get from island to island (Sternberg, 2004). And so it goes, as each culture teaches its children the kinds of "intelligence" valued in that culture—how the wise man would do it, not a fool (Correa-Chávez, Rogoff, & Arauz, 2005).

In view of such differences, psychologists have tried to create "culture-fair" intelligence tests. Some have even questioned the value of intelligence testing itself. We'll discuss both these ideas in this chapter's "Psychology in Action" module.

intelligence by spelling out the procedures they use to measure it. Thus, by selecting items for an intelligence test, a psychologist is saying in a very direct way, "This is what I mean by intelligence." A test that measures memory, reasoning, and verbal fluency offers a very different definition of intelligence than one that measures strength of grip, shoe size, length of the nose, or the person's best *Too Human* video game score. (For a glimpse at how other cultures define "intelligent" behavior, see "Intelligence—How Would a Fool Do It?")

Intelligence Tests

American psychologists quickly saw the value of Alfred Binet's test. In 1916, Lewis Terman and others at Stanford University revised it for use in North America. After more revisions, the *Stanford-Binet Intelligence Scales, Fifth Edition* continues to be widely used. The original Stanford-Binet assumed that a child's intellectual abilities improve with each passing year. Today, the Stanford-Binet (or SB5) is still primarily made up of age-ranked questions. Naturally, these questions get a little harder at each age level. The SB5 is appropriate for people from age 2 to 85+ years (Roid, 2003).

The SB5 measures five cognitive factors (types of mental abilities) that make up general intelligence. These are *fluid reasoning, knowledge, quantitative reasoning, visual-spatial processing,* and *working memory.* Each factor is measured with verbal questions (those involving words and numbers) and nonverbal questions (items that use pictures and objects). Let's see what each factor looks like.

Fluid Reasoning

Fluid Reasoning tests reasoning ability with questions like the following:

> How are an apple, a plum, and a banana different from a beet?

An apprentice is to a master as a novice is to an

_____.

"I knew my bag was going to be in the last place I looked, so I looked there first." What is silly or impossible about that?

Other items ask people to fill in the missing shape in a group of shapes and to tell a story that explains what's going on in a series of pictures.

Knowledge

The Knowledge factor assesses the person's knowledge about a wide range of topics.

> Why is yeast added to bread dough?
> What does cryptic mean?
> What is silly or impossible about this picture?
> (For example, a bicycle has square wheels.)

Quantitative Reasoning

Test items for Quantitative Reasoning measure a person's ability to solve problems involving numbers. Here are some samples:

> If I have six marbles and you give me another one, how many marbles will I have?
> Given the numbers 3, 6, 9, 12, what number would come next?
> If a shirt is being sold for 50 percent of the normal price, and the price tag is $60, what is the cost of the shirt?

Intelligence An overall capacity to think rationally, act purposefully, and deal effectively with the environment.

g-factor A general ability factor or core of general intellectual ability that involves reasoning, problem-solving ability, knowledge, memory, and successful adaptation to one's surroundings.

Visual-Spatial Processing People who have visual-spatial skills are good at putting picture puzzles together and copying geometric shapes (such as triangles, rectangles, and circles). Visual-Spatial Processing questions ask test takers to reproduce patterns of blocks and choose pictures that show how a piece of paper would look if it were folded or cut. Verbal questions can also require visual-spatial abilities:

> Suppose that you are going east, then turn right, then turn right again, then turn left. In what direction are you facing now?

Working Memory The Working Memory part of the SB5 measures the ability to use short-term memory. Some typical memory tasks include the following:

> Correctly remember the order of colored beads on a stick.
> After hearing several sentences, name the last word from each sentence.
> Repeat a series of digits (forward or backward) after hearing them once.

If you were to take the SB5, it would yield a score for your general intelligence, verbal intelligence, nonverbal intelligence, and each of the five cognitive factors (Bain & Allin, 2005).

Intelligence Quotients

Imagine that a child named Yuan can answer questions that an average 7-year-old can answer. How smart is she? Actually, we can't say yet, because we don't know how old Yuan is. If she is 10, she's not very smart. If she's 5, she is very bright. Thus, to estimate a child's intelligence we need to know both her **mental age** (average intellectual performance) and her **chronological age** (age in years).

Mental age is based on the level of age-ranked questions a person can answer. For example, at ages 8 or 9, very few children can define the word *connection*. At age 10, 10 percent can. At age 13, 60 percent can. Thus, a 13-year-old of average ability can define *connection*. If we had only this one item to test children with, those who answered correctly would be given a mental age of 13. When scores from many such items are combined, a child's overall mental age can be found. ■ Table 8.1 is a sample of items that persons of average intelligence can answer at various ages.

Mental age is a good measure of actual ability. But mental age says nothing about whether overall intelligence is high or low compared with other people of the same age. To find out what a particular mental age means, we must relate mental age to actual age. This yields an **intelligence quotient**, or **IQ.** A quotient results from dividing one number into another. When the Stanford-Binet was first used, IQ was de-

■ TABLE 8.1	Sample Items from the Stanford-Binet Intelligence Scale
2 years old	On a large paper doll, points out the hair, mouth, feet, ears, nose, hands, and eyes. When shown a tower built of four blocks, builds one like it.
3 years old	When shown a bridge built of three blocks, builds one like it. When shown a drawing of a circle, copies it with a pencil.
4 years old	Fills in the missing word when asked, "Brother is a boy; sister is a _____." "In daytime it is light; at night it is _____." Answers correctly when asked, "Why do we have houses?" "Why do we have books?"
5 years old	Defines *ball*, *hat*, and *stove*. When shown a drawing of a square, copies it with a pencil.
9 years old	Answers correctly when examiner says, "In an old graveyard in Spain they have discovered a small skull which they believe to be that of Christopher Columbus when he was about 10 years old. What is foolish about that?" Answers correctly when asked, "Tell me the name of a color that rhymes with head." "Tell me a number that rhymes with tree."
Adult	Can describe the difference between laziness and idleness, poverty and misery, character and reputation. Answers correctly when asked, "Which direction would you have to face so your right hand would be toward the north?"

(From L. Terman & M. Merrill, *Stanford-Binet Intelligence Scale*, 1937. Revised edition, 1960. Houghton Mifflin Co. Used with permission.)

fined as mental age (MA) divided by chronological age (CA) and multiplied by 100. (Multiplying by 100 changes the IQ into a whole number, rather than a decimal.)

$$\frac{\text{MA}}{\text{CA}} \times 100 = \text{IQ}$$

An advantage of the original IQ calculation was that intelligence could be compared among children with different chronological and mental ages. For instance, 10-year-old Justin has a mental age of 12. Thus, his IQ is 120:

$$\frac{(\text{MA})\ 12}{(\text{CA})\ 10} \times 100 = 120\ (\text{IQ})$$

Justin's friend Suke also has a mental age of 12. However, Suke's chronological age is 12, so his IQ is 100:

$$\frac{(\text{MA})\ 12}{(\text{CA})\ 12} \times 100 = 100\ (\text{IQ})$$

The IQ shows that 10-year-old Justin is brighter than his 12-year-old friend Suke, even though their intellectual skills are about the same. Notice that a person's IQ will be 100 when mental age equals chronological age. An IQ score of 100 is therefore defined as average intelligence.

Then does a person with an IQ score below 100 have below average intelligence? Not unless the IQ is well below 100. An IQ of 100 is the *mathematical* average (or mean) for such scores. However, average intelligence is usually defined as any score from 90 to 109. The important point is that IQ scores will be over 100 when mental age is higher than age in years (● Fig. 8.1). IQ scores below 100 occur when a person's age in years exceeds his or her mental age. An example of the second situation would be a 15-year-old with an MA of 12:

$$\frac{12}{15} \times 100 = 80 \; (IQ)$$

Deviation IQs The preceding examples may give you insight into IQ scores. However, it's no longer necessary to directly calculate IQs. Instead, modern tests use **deviation IQs.** These scores are based on a person's relative standing in his or her age group. That is, they tell how far above or below average the person's score falls. (For more information, see the Statistics appendix near the end of this book.) Tables supplied with the test are then used to convert a person's relative standing in the group to an IQ score. For example, if you score at the fiftieth percentile, half the people your age who take the test score higher than you and half score lower. In this case, your IQ score is 100. If you score at the eighty-fourth percentile, your IQ score is 115. If you score at the ninety-seventh percentile, your IQ score is 130.

● **FIGURE 8.1** With a score of 230, Marilyn vos Savant has the highest IQ ever officially recorded. When she was only 7 years and 9 months old, vos Savant could answer questions that the average 13-year-old can answer. At ages 8, 9, and 10, she got perfect scores on the Stanford-Binet scale. Now in her 60s, she is a well-published author and recently became the host of an *Ask Marilyn* segment for CBS TV News.

The Wechsler Tests

Is the Stanford-Binet the only intelligence test? A widely used alternative is the *Wechsler Adult Intelligence Scale–Third Edition* (WAIS-III). A version for children is called the *Wechsler Intelligence Scale for Children–Fourth Edition* (WISC-IV) (Baron, 2005).

The Wechsler tests are similar to the Stanford-Binet but differ in important ways. For one thing, the WAIS-III was specifically designed to test adult intelligence. The original Stanford-Binet was better suited for children and adolescents. The latest Stanford-Binet (the SB5) can now be used for all ages, but the WAIS was the first "adult" IQ test. Like the Stanford-Binet, the Wechsler tests yield a single overall IQ. In addition, the WAIS and WISC give separate scores for **performance** (nonverbal) **intelligence** and **verbal** (language- or symbol-oriented) **intelligence**. (Note that this feature was also recently added to the SB5.) The abilities measured by the Wechsler tests and some sample test items are listed in ■ Table 8.2.

Group Tests

The SB5 and the Wechsler tests are **individual intelligence tests,** which must be given to a single person by a trained specialist. In contrast, **group intelligence tests** can be given to large groups of people with minimal supervision. Group tests usually require people to read, to follow instructions, and to solve problems of logic, reasoning, mathematics, or spatial skills. If you're wondering if you have ever taken an intelligence test, the answer is probably yes. The well-known *Scholastic Assessment Test* (SAT) measures aptitudes for language, math, and reasoning. The SAT is designed to predict your chances for success in college. Because it measures a number of different mental aptitudes, it can also be used to estimate general intelligence (Frey & Detterman, 2004).

Mental age The average mental ability people display at a given age.

Chronological age A person's age in years.

Intelligence quotient (IQ) An index of intelligence defined as a person's mental age divided by his or her chronological age and multiplied by 100.

Deviation IQ An IQ obtained statistically from a person's relative standing in his or her age group; that is, how far above or below average the person's score was relative to other scores.

Performance intelligence Intelligence measured by solving puzzles, assembling objects, completing pictures, and other nonverbal tasks.

Verbal intelligence Intelligence measured by answering questions involving vocabulary, general information, arithmetic, and other language- or symbol-oriented tasks.

Individual intelligence test A test of intelligence designed to be given to a single individual by a trained specialist.

Group intelligence test Any intelligence test that can be administered to a group of people with minimal supervision.

■ **TABLE 8.2** Sample Items Similar to Those Used on the WAIS-III

VERBAL SUBTESTS	SAMPLE ITEMS
Information	How many wings does a bird have? Who wrote *Paradise Lost*?
Digit span	Repeat from memory a series of digits, such as 3 1 0 6 7 4 2 5, after hearing it once.
General comprehension	What is the advantage of keeping money in the bank? Why is copper often used in electrical wires?
Arithmetic	Three men divided 18 golf balls equally among themselves. How many golf balls did each man receive? If 2 apples cost 15¢, what will be the cost of a dozen apples?
Similarities	In what way are a lion and a tiger alike and/or unalike? In what way are a saw and a hammer alike and/or unalike?
Vocabulary	What is a guitar? What does "robin" mean?
Letter-number sequencing	Repeat a list of mixed numbers and letters, numbers first, in numerical order, and letters second, in alphabetical order.
PERFORMANCE SUBTESTS	DESCRIPTION OF ITEM
Picture arrangement	Arrange a series of cartoon panels to make a meaningful story.
Picture completion	What is missing from these pictures?
Block design	Copy designs with blocks.
Object assembly	Put together a jigsaw puzzle.
Digit symbol	Fill in the symbols.
Matrix reasoning	Select the item that completes the matrix.
Symbol search	Match symbols appearing in separate groups.

Picture Arrangement

Matrix Reasoning

1   2   3   4   5

Symbol Search

Wechsler Adult Intelligence Scale®–Third Edition. Copyright © 2007 by Harcourt Assessment, Inc. Reproduced with permission. All rights reserved.

Variations in Intelligence—Curved like a Bell

SURVEY QUESTION: *How much does intelligence vary from person to person?*

IQ scores are classified as shown in ■ Table 8.3. A look at the percentages reveals a definite pattern. The distribution (or scattering) of IQ scores approximates a **normal** (bell-shaped) **curve.** That is, most scores fall close to the average and very few are found at the extremes. ● Figure 8.2 shows this characteristic of measured intelligence.

■ **TABLE 8.3** Distribution of Adult IQ Scores on WAIS-III

IQ	DESCRIPTION	PERCENT
Above 130	Very superior	2.2
120-129	Superior	6.7
110-119	Bright normal	16.1
90-109	Average	50.0
80-89	Dull normal	16.1
70-79	Borderline	6.7
Below 70	Intellectual disabled	2.2

The Mentally Gifted

How high is the IQ of a genius? Only 2 people out of 100 score above 130 on IQ tests. These bright individuals are usually described as "gifted." Less than one-half of 1 percent of the population scores above 140. These people are certainly gifted or perhaps even "geniuses." However, some psychologists reserve the term *genius* for people with even higher IQs or those who are exceptionally creative (Hallahan & Kauffman, 2006).

Gifted Children *Do high IQ scores in childhood predict later ability?* To directly answer this question, Lewis Terman selected 1,500 children with IQs of 140 or more. Terman followed this gifted group (the "Termites" as he called them) into adulthood and found that most were quite successful. A majority finished college, earned advanced degrees, or held professional positions, and many had written books or scientific articles (Terman & Oden, 1959).

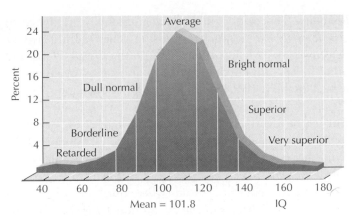

● **FIGURE 8.2** Distribution of Stanford-Binet Intelligence Test scores for 3,184 children. (Adapted from Terman & Merrill, 1960.)

In general, the correlation between IQ scores and school grades is 0.50, a sizable association. The link would be even stronger, but motivation, special talents, off-campus learning, and many other factors also affect grades. The same is true of "real world" success beyond school. IQ is not at all good at predicting success in art, music, writing, dramatics, science, and leadership. Creativity is much more strongly related to doing well in these areas (Preckel, Holling, & Wiese, 2006; Runco, 2004). Regardless, when people score in the gifted range, their chances for high achievement do seem to rise (Shurkin, 1992).

Were all the gifted children superior as adults? No. Some had committed crimes, were unemployable, or were emotionally troubled. Remember that a high IQ reveals *potential.* It does not guarantee success. Marilyn vos Savant, with an IQ of 230, has contributed little to science, literature, or art. Nobel prize–winning physicist Richard Feynman, whom many regarded as a genius, had an IQ of 122 (Michalko, 1998).

How did Terman's more successful Termites differ from the less successful? Most of them had educated parents who taught them to value learning. They also had *intellectual determination,* which is a desire to know, to excel, and to persevere (Winner, 2003). Thus, successful gifted persons tend to be *persistent* and *motivated* to learn. No one is paid to sit around being *capable* of achievement. What you do is always more important than what you should be able to do. That's why a child's talents are most likely to blossom when they are nurtured with support, encouragement, education, and effort (Callahan, 2006).

Identifying Gifted Children How might a parent spot an unusually bright child? Early signs of giftedness are not always purely "intellectual." **Giftedness** can be either the possession of a high IQ or special talents or aptitudes, such as creativity. Remember, Kim Peek is remarkably gifted *in some ways.*

The following signs may reveal that a child is gifted: A tendency to seek out older children and adults; an early fascination with explanations and problem solving; talking in complete sentences as early as 2 or 3 years of age; an unusually good memory; precocious talent in art, music, or number skills; an early interest in books, along with early reading (often by age 3); showing of kindness, understanding, and cooperation toward others (Alvino & Editors, 1996; Distin, 2006).

Notice that this list goes beyond straight g-factor, or "academic" intelligence. In fact, if artistic talent, mechanical aptitude, musical aptitude, athletic potential, and so on are considered, many children have a special "gift" of one kind or another. Limiting giftedness to high IQ can shortchange children with special talents. This is especially true of ethnic minority children, who may be the victims of subtle biases in standardized intelligence tests. These children, as well as children with physical disabilities, are less likely to be recognized as gifted (Ford & Moore, 2006; Robinson & Clinkenbeard, 1998).

Intellectual Disability

A person with mental abilities far below average is termed **intellectually disabled** (a related term, **mentally retarded,** is seen by many as offensive). Intellectual disability begins at an IQ of approximately 70 or below. However, a person's ability

It is wise to remember that there are many ways in which a child may be gifted. Many schools now offer Gifted and Talented Education programs for students with a variety of special abilities—not just for those who score well on IQ tests.

Normal curve A bell-shaped curve characterized by a large number of scores in a middle area, tapering to very few extremely high and low scores.

Giftedness The possession of a high IQ or special talents or aptitudes.

Intellectual disability (formerly mental retardation) The presence of a developmental disability, a formal IQ score below 70, or a significant impairment of adaptive behavior.

TABLE 8.4 Levels of Intellectual Disability

IQ RANGE	DEGREE OF INTELLECTUAL DISABILITY	EDUCATIONAL CLASSIFICATION	REQUIRED LEVEL OF SUPPORT
50-55 to 70	Mild	Educable	Intermittent
35-40 to 50-55	Moderate	Trainable	Limited
20-25 to 35-40	Severe	Dependent	Extensive
Below 20-25	Profound	Life support	Pervasive

(DSM-IV-TR, 2000; Hodapp, 1994.)

to perform *adaptive behaviors* (basic skills such as dressing, eating, communicating, shopping, and working) also figures into evaluating this disability (DSM-IV-TR, 2000; Hallahan & Kauffman, 2006). (See ■ Table 8.4.)

It's important to realize that intellectually disabled persons have no handicap where feelings are concerned. They are easily hurt by rejection, teasing, or ridicule. Likewise, they respond warmly to love and acceptance. They have a right to self-respect and a place in the community (AAIDD, 2004). This is especially important during childhood, when support from others adds greatly to the person's chances of becoming a well-adjusted member of society.

Causes of Intellectual Disability *What causes intellectual disability?* About half of all cases of intellectual disability are *organic,* or related to physical disorders (Das, 2000). These include *fetal damage* (prenatal damage from teratogens such as disease, infection, or drugs) and *birth injuries* (such as lack of oxygen during delivery). *Metabolic disorders,* which affect energy production and use in the body, also cause intellectual

These youngsters are participants in the Special Olympics—an athletic event for the intellectually disabled. It is often said of the Special Olympics that "everyone is a winner—participants, coaches, and spectators."

disability. Some forms of intellectual disability are linked to *genetic abnormalities,* such as missing genes, extra genes, or defective genes. Malnutrition and exposure to lead, PCBs, and other toxins early in childhood can also cause organic intellectual disability (Beirne-Smith, Patton, & Shannon, 2006).

In 30 to 40 percent of cases, no known biological problem can be identified. In many such instances, the degree of intellectual disability is mild, in the 50 to 70 IQ range. Often, other family members are also mildly intellectually disabled. *Familial intellectual disability,* as this is called, occurs mostly in very poor households where nutrition, intellectual stimulation, medical care, and emotional support may be inadequate. This suggests that familial intellectual disability is based largely on an impoverished environment. Thus, better nutrition, education, and early childhood enrichment programs could prevent many cases of intellectual disability (Beirne-Smith, Patton, & Shannon, 2006).

Questioning Intelligence—How Intelligent Are Intelligence Tests?

SURVEY QUESTION: *What are some controversies in the study of intelligence?*

Defining intelligence as a g-factor (general ability) has been controversial. As we noted earlier in our discussion of "intelligent" behavior in other cultures, there are many ways to be smart. For example, consider William, a grade-school student 2 years behind in reading, who shows his teacher how to solve a difficult computer-programming problem. Or what about his classmate, Malika, who performs poorly in math but plays intricate pieces of piano music? Both these children show clear signs of intelligence. And yet, each might score below average on a traditional IQ test. And, as we have seen, autistic savants like Kim Peek have even more extreme intellectual strengths and weaknesses. Such observations have convinced many psychologists that it is time to forge new, broader definitions of intelligence. Their basic goal is to better predict "real-world" success—not just the likelihood of success in school (Sternberg & Grigorenko, 2006).

Multiple Intelligences

One such psychologist is Howard Gardner of Harvard University. Gardner (2003, 2004) theorizes that there are actually eight distinctly different kinds of intelligence. These are different mental "languages" that people use for thinking. Each is listed below, with examples of pursuits that make use of them.

1. *Language* (linguistic abilities)—writer, lawyer, comedian

2. *Logic and math* (numeric abilities)—scientist, accountant, programmer
3. *Visual and spatial* (pictorial abilities)—engineer, inventor, artist
4. *Music* (musical abilities)—composer, musician, music critic
5. *Bodily-kinesthetic* (physical abilities)—dancer, athlete, surgeon
6. *Intrapersonal* (self-knowledge)—poet, actor, minister
7. *Interpersonal* (social abilities)—psychologist, teacher, politician
8. *Naturalist* (an ability to understand the natural environment)—biologist, medicine man, organic farmer

To simplify a great deal, people can be "word smart," "number smart," "picture smart," "musically smart," "body smart," "self smart," "people smart," and/or "nature smart."

Most of us are probably strong in only a few types of intelligence. In contrast, geniuses like Albert Einstein seem to be able to use nearly all of the intelligences, as needed, to solve problems.

If Gardner's theory of **multiple intelligences** is correct, traditional IQ tests measure only a part of real-world intelligence—namely, linguistic, logical-mathematical, and spatial abilities. A further implication is that our schools may be wasting a lot of human potential (Campbell, Campbell, & Dickinson, 2003). For example, some children might find it easier to learn math or reading if these topics were tied into art, music, dance, drama, and so on. Already, many schools are using Gardner's theory to cultivate a wider range of skills and talents (Campbell, Campbell, & Dickinson, 2003; Kornhaber & Gardner, 2006). Before we return to human intelligence, let's see what we can learn from some smart machines.

Artificial Intelligence: I Compute, Therefore I Am

How smart are computers and robots? Just as people like Kim Peek challenge our understanding of general intelligence, so too does the prospect of creating intelligent machines. Let's say you are exchanging instant messages over the Internet with someone you don't know. You are allowed to make any comments and ask any questions you like, for as long as you like. In reality, the "person" you are communicating with is a computer. Do you think a computer could fool you into believing it was human? If it did, wouldn't that qualify it as "intelligent"? You may be surprised to learn that, to date, no machine has come close to passing this test (Moor, 2003).

The problem computers face is that we humans can mentally "shift gears" from one topic to another with incredible flexibility. In contrast, machine "intelligence" is currently "blind" outside its underlying set of rules. As a tiny example, u cann understnd wrds thet ar mizpeld. Computers are very literal and easily stymied by such errors.

Regardless, artificial intelligence has been successful at very specific tasks. **Artificial intelligence (AI)** usually refers

According to Howard Gardner's theory, bodily-kinesthetic skills reflect one of eight distinct types of intelligence.

Two composers. The one on the left was a genius who wrote sublime, multi-voiced harmonies. The one on the right has created reasonably good, if uninspired, music. Computer models of thought can approximate intelligent human behavior. However, rule-based computer "thinking" still lacks the flexibility, creativity, and common sense of human intelligence.

Multiple intelligences Howard Gardner's theory that there are several specialized types of intellectual ability.

Artificial intelligence Any artificial system (often a computer program) that is capable of human-like problem solving or intelligent responding.

to computer programs capable of doing things that require intelligence when done by people (Russell & Norvig, 2003). For example, listeners sometimes mistake music created by Kemal Ebcioglu for that written by Johann Sebastian Bach, the eighteenth-century German composer. Ebcioglu wrote a computer program that creates harmonies remarkably similar to Bach's. By analyzing Bach's music, Ebcioglu came up with 350 rules that govern harmonization. The result is a program that displays artificial intelligence in a specific area.

Much of current artificial intelligence is based on the fact that many tasks—from harmonizing music to diagnosing disease—can be reduced to a set of rules applied to a collection of information. AI is valuable in situations where speed, vast memory, and persistence are required. In fact, AI programs are better at some tasks than humans are. An example is world chess champion Garry Kasparov's loss, in 1997, to a computer called Deep Blue.

AI and Cognition

AI and Cognition Although AI is a long way from duplicating general human intelligence, artificial intelligence offers a way to probe some of our specific cognitive skills, or intelligences. For instance, computer simulations and expert systems provide good examples of how AI is being used as a research tool.

Computer simulations are programs that attempt to duplicate specific human behaviors, especially thinking, decision making, or problem solving. Here, the computer acts as a "laboratory" for testing models of cognition. If a computer program behaves as humans do (including making the same errors), then the program may be a good model of how we think.

Expert systems are computer programs that respond as a human expert would (Giarratano & Riley, 2005). They have demystified some human abilities by converting complex skills into clearly stated rules a computer can follow. Expert systems can predict the weather, analyze geological formations, diagnose disease, play chess, read, tell when to buy or sell stocks, and perform many other tasks.

Eventually, AI will almost certainly lead to robots that recognize voices and that speak and act "intelligently" in specific areas of ability. To achieve this, should intelligence be directly programmed into computers? Or should computers be designed to learn from experience, like the human brain does (McClelland & Rogers, 2003)? Only time will tell. For now, it's interesting to note that these questions mirror another area of controversy—whether human intelligence is inherited or learned from experience.

Heredity, Environment, and Intelligence

Is intelligence inherited? Most people are aware that there is a moderate similarity in the intelligence of parents and their children, or between brothers and sisters. As ● Figure 8.3

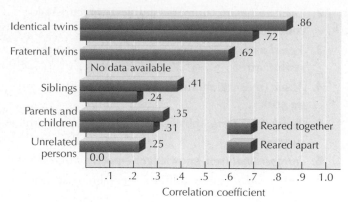

● **FIGURE 8.3** Approximate correlations between IQ scores for persons with varying degrees of genetic and environmental similarity. Notice that the correlations grow smaller as the degree of genetic similarity declines. Also note that a shared environment increases the correlation in all cases. (Estimates from Bouchard, 1983; Henderson, 1982.)

shows, the similarity in IQ scores among relatives grows in proportion to how close they are on the family tree.

Does this indicate that intelligence is hereditary? Not necessarily. Brothers, sisters, and parents share similar environments as well as similar heredity. To separate nature and nurture, **twin studies** may be done. Such studies compare the IQs of twins who were raised together or separated at birth. This allows us to estimate how much heredity and environment affect intelligence.

Twin Studies Notice in Figure 8.3 that the IQs of fraternal twins are more alike than the IQs of ordinary siblings. *Fraternal twins* come from two separate eggs fertilized at the same time. Genetically, they are no more alike than ordinary siblings. Why, then, should the twins' IQs be more similar? The reason is environmental: Parents treat twins more alike than ordinary siblings, resulting in a closer match in IQs.

More striking similarities are observed with *identical twins,* who develop from a single egg and have identical genes. At the top of Figure 8.3 you can see that identical twins who grow up in the same family have highly correlated IQs. This is what we would expect with identical heredity and very similar environments. Now, let's consider what happens when identical twins are reared apart. As you can see, the correlation drops, but only from 0.86 to 0.72. Psychologists who emphasize genetics believe these figures show that adult intelligence is roughly 50 percent hereditary (Grigorenko & Sternberg, 2003).

How do environmentalists interpret the figures? They point out that the IQs of some separated twins differ by as much as 20 points. Such IQ gaps occur when the twins grow up with big educational and environmental differences. It is more common for separated twins to be placed in homes socially and educationally similar to their biological parents. This fact

CRITICAL THINKING

You Mean Video Games Might Be Good for Me?

Although rapidly rising Western IQ scores suggest that environmental factors influence intelligence (Schooler, 1998), we are left with the question, Which factors? Writer Steven Johnson (2005) believes that popular culture is responsible. Although he agrees that much popular media content is too violent or sexual in nature, he points out that video games, the Internet, and even television are becoming more complex. As a result, they demand ever-greater cognitive effort from us. In other words, it is as important to understand *how* we experience the environment as it is to understand *what* we experience.

For example, early video games, such as Pong or Pac Man, offered simple, repetitive visual experiences. In contrast, today's popular games, such as The World of Warcraft or Second Life, offer rich, complicated experiences that can take many hours of intense problem solving to complete. Furthermore, players must usually figure out the rules by themselves. Instructions that fans have written for popular games are typically much longer than chapters in this book. Only a complex and engaging game would prompt players to use such instructions, much less write them for others to use (Johnson, 2005).

According to Johnson, other forms of popular culture have also become more complex, including the Internet, computer software, and even popular television. For example, compared with television dramas of the past, modern dramas weave plot lines and characters through an entire season of programs. In the end, popular culture may well be inviting us to read, reflect, and problem-solve more than ever before. (Before you uncritically embrace video games, read "You Mean Video Games Might Be Bad For Me?" in Module 6.5.)

---

would tend to inflate apparent genetic effects by making the separated twins' IQs more alike. Another frequently overlooked fact is that twins grow up in the same environment *before birth* (in the womb). If we take such environmental similarities into account, intelligence would seem to be less than 50 percent hereditary (Devlin, Daniels, & Roeder, 1997; Turkheimer et al., 2003).

IQ and Environment *How much can environment alter intelligence?* Strong evidence for an environmental view of intelligence comes from adoption studies. Consider families having one adopted child and one biological child. As ● Figure 8.4 shows, parents contribute genes *and* environment to their biological child. With an adopted child they contribute only environment. If intelligence is highly genetic, the IQs of biological children should be more like their parents' IQs than are the IQs of adopted children. However, one study found that children reared by the same mother tend to resemble her IQ to the same degree. It does not matter whether or not they share her genes (Kamin, 1981; Weinberg, 1989).

In another study, striking increases in IQ occurred in 25 children who were moved from an orphanage and were even-

tually adopted by parents who gave them love, a family, and a stimulating home environment. Once considered intellectually disabled and unadoptable, the children gained an average of 29 IQ points. A second group of initially less "intellectually disabled" children, who stayed in the orphanage, *lost* an average of 26 IQ points (Skeels, 1966)!

A particularly dramatic environmental effect is the fact that Westernized nations have shown average IQ gains of 15 points during the last 30 years (Dickens & Flynn, 2001). These IQ boosts occurred in far too short a time for genetics to explain them. It is more likely that the gains reflect environmental forces, such as improved education and nutrition and living in a technologically complex society (Johnson, 2005). If you've ever tried to play a computer game or set up a wireless network in your home, you'll understand why people may be getting better at answering IQ test questions. (See "You Mean Video Games Might Be Good for Me?")

Summary In the final analysis, intelligence reflects development as well as potential, nurture as well as nature (Grigorenko, 2005). Moreover, the fact that intelligence is partly determined by heredity tells us little of any real value. Genes are fixed at birth. Improving the environments in which children learn and grow is the main way in which we can assure that they reach their full potential (Grigorenko & Sternberg, 2003; White, 2006).

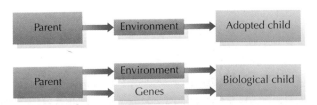

● **FIGURE 8.4** Comparison of an adopted child and a biological child reared in the same family. (Adapted from Kamin, 1981.)

Twin study A comparison of the characteristics of twins who were raised together or separated at birth; used to identify the relative impact of heredity and environment.

MODULE 8.1 Summary

How is human intelligence defined and measured?

- Intelligence refers to the general capacity (or g-factor) to act purposefully, think rationally, and deal effectively with the environment. In practice, intelligence is operationally defined by intelligence tests.

- The first intelligence test was assembled by Alfred Binet. A modern version of Binet's test is the *Stanford-Binet Intelligence Scale.*

- Intelligence is expressed as an intelligence quotient (IQ), defined as mental age divided by chronological age and then multiplied by 100. The distribution of IQ scores approximates a normal curve.

- Another major intelligence test is the *Wechsler Adult Intelligence Scale* (WAIS). The WAIS measures both verbal and performance intelligence. Group intelligence tests are also available.

How much does intelligence vary from person to person?

- People with IQs in the gifted or "genius" range of above 140 tend to be superior in many respects.

However, by criteria other than IQ, many children can be considered gifted or talented in one way or another.

- The term *intellectually disabled* is applied to those whose IQ falls below 70 or who lack various adaptive behaviors. About 50 percent of the cases of intellectual disability are organic. The remaining cases are of undetermined cause. Many of these cases are thought to reflect familial intellectual disability.

What are some controversies in the study of intelligence?

- Many psychologists have begun to forge new, broader definitions of intelligence. Howard Gardner's theory of multiple intelligences is a good example.

- *Artificial intelligence* refers to any artificial system that can perform tasks that require intelligence when done by people. Two principal areas of artificial intelligence research on particular human skills are computer simulations and expert systems.

- Intelligence is partially determined by heredity. However, environment is also important, as revealed by IQ increases induced by education and stimulating environments.

9.1 Overview of Motivation

WHAT DO YOU PLAN TO DO TODAY? What are your goals? Why do you pursue them? How vigorously do you try to reach them? When are you satisfied? When do you give up? These are all questions about motivation, or why we act as we do. Let's begin with a basic model of motivation and an overview of types of motives.

Motivation—Forces that Push and Pull

SURVEY QUESTIONS: *What is motivation? Are there different types of motives?*

Motivation refers to the dynamics of behavior—the ways in which our actions are *initiated, sustained, directed*, and *terminated* (Franken, 2007).

Can you clarify that? Yes. Imagine that Kendra is studying psychology in the library. Her stomach begins to growl and she can't concentrate. She grows restless and decides to buy an apple from a vending machine. The machine is empty, so she goes to the cafeteria. Closed. Kendra drives home, where she cooks a meal and eats it. At last her hunger is satisfied, and she resumes studying. Notice how Kendra's food seeking was *initiated* by a bodily need. Her search was *sustained* because her need was not immediately met, and her actions were *directed* by possible sources of food. Finally, her food seeking was *terminated* by achieving her goal.

A Model of Motivation

Many motivated activities begin with a **need,** or internal deficiency. The need that initiated Kendra's search was a shortage of key substances in her body. Needs cause a **drive** (an energized motivational state) to develop. The drive was hunger, in Kendra's case. Drives activate a **response** (an action or series of actions) designed to attain a **goal** (the "target" of motivated behavior). Reaching a goal that satisfies the need will end the chain of events. Thus, a simple model of motivation can be shown in this way:

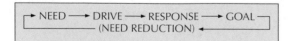

Aren't needs and drives the same thing? No, because the strength of needs and drives can differ (Franken, 2007). If you begin fasting today, your bodily need for food will increase every day. However, you would probably feel less "hungry" on the seventh day of fasting than you did on the first. Whereas your need for food steadily increases, the hunger drive comes and goes.

Now let's observe Kendra again. It's Saturday night: For dinner, Kendra has soup, salad, a large steak, a baked potato, four pieces of bread, two pieces of cheesecake, and three cups of coffee. After dinner, she complains that she is "too full to move." Soon after, Kendra's roommate arrives with a strawberry pie. Kendra exclaims that strawberry pie is her favorite dessert and eats three large pieces! Is this hunger? Certainly, Kendra's dinner satisfied her biological needs for food.

How does that change the model of motivation? Kendra's "pie lust" illustrates that motivated behavior can be energized by the "pull" of external stimuli, as well as by the "push" of internal needs.

Incentives The "pull" of a goal is called its **incentive value** (the goal's appeal beyond its ability to fill a need). Some goals are so desirable (strawberry pie, for example) that they can motivate behavior in the absence of an internal need. Other goals are so low in incentive value that they may be rejected even if they meet the internal need. Fresh, live grubworms, for instance, are highly nutritious. However, it is doubtful that you would eat one no matter how hungry you might be.

Usually, our actions are energized by a mixture of internal needs *and* external incentives. That's why a strong need may change an unpleasant incentive into a desired goal. Perhaps you've never eaten a grubworm, but we'll bet you've eaten some pretty horrible leftovers when the refrigerator was bare. The incentive value of goals also helps explain motives that don't seem to come from internal needs, such as drives for success, status, or approval (● Fig. 9.1).

Types of Motives For our purposes, motives can be divided into three major categories:

1. **Primary motives** are based on biological needs that must be met for survival. The most important primary motives are hunger, thirst, pain avoidance, and needs for air, sleep, elimination of wastes, and regulation of body temperature. Primary motives are innate.

2. **Stimulus motives** express our needs for stimulation and information. Examples include activity, curiosity, exploration, manipulation, and physical contact. Although such motives also appear to be innate, they are not strictly necessary for survival.

3. **Secondary motives** are based on learned needs, drives, and goals. Learned motives help explain many human activities, such as making music, blogging, or trying to win the skateboarding finals in the

● **FIGURE 9.1** Needs and incentives interact to determine drive strength *(left)*. *(a)* Moderate need combined with a high-incentive goal produces a strong drive. *(b)* Even when a strong need exists, drive strength may be moderate if a goal's incentive value is low. It is important to remember, however, that incentive value lies "in the eye of the beholder" *(photo)*. No matter how hungry, few people would be able to eat the pictured grubworms.

X Games. Many secondary motives are related to learned needs for power, affiliation (the need to be with others), approval, status, security, and achievement. Fear and aggression also appear to be greatly affected by learning.

Primary Motives and Homeostasis

How important is air in your life? Water? Sleep? Food? Temperature regulation? Finding a public rest room? For most of us, satisfying biological needs is so routine that we tend to overlook how much of our behavior they direct. But exaggerate any of these needs through famine, shipwreck, poverty, near drowning, bitter cold, or drinking 10 cups of coffee, and their powerful grip on behavior becomes evident. We are, after all, still animals in many ways.

Biological drives are essential because they maintain *homeostasis* (HOE-me-oh-STAY-sis), or bodily equilibrium (Cannon, 1932).

What is homeostasis? The term **homeostasis** means "standing steady," or "steady state." Optimal levels exist for body temperature, for chemicals in the blood, for blood pressure, and so forth (Levin, 2006). When the body deviates from these "ideal" levels, automatic reactions begin to restore equilibrium (Deckers, 2005). Thus, it might help to think of homeostasis as being similar to a thermostat set at a particular temperature.

A (VERY) SHORT COURSE ON THERMOSTATS

The thermostat in your house constantly compares the actual room temperature to a *set point,* or ideal temperature, which you can control. When room temperature falls below the set point, the heat is automatically turned on to warm the room. When the heat equals or slightly exceeds the set point, it is automatically turned off or the air conditioning is turned on. In this way room temperature is kept in a state of equilibrium hovering around the set point.

The first reactions to disequilibrium in the human body are also automatic. For example, if you become too hot, more blood will flow through your skin and you will begin to perspire, thus lowering body temperature. Usually, we are not aware of such changes, unless continued disequilibrium drives us to seek shade, warmth, food, or water.

Motivation Internal processes that initiate, sustain, and direct activities.

Need An internal deficiency that may energize behavior.

Drive The psychological expression of internal needs or valued goals—for example, hunger, thirst, or a drive for success.

Response Any action, glandular activity, or other identifiable behavior.

Goal The target or objective of motivated behavior.

Incentive value The value of a goal above and beyond its ability to fill a need.

Primary motives Innate motives based on biological needs.

Stimulus motives Innate needs for stimulation and information.

Secondary motives Motives based on learned needs, drives, and goals.

Homeostasis A steady state of body equilibrium.

Circadian Rhythms

Our needs and drives can change from moment to moment. After eating, our motivation to eat more food tends to diminish, and a few minutes in the hot sun can leave us feeling thirsty. But our motivation can also vary over longer cycles. Scientists have long known that body activity is guided by internal "biological clocks." Every 24 hours, your body undergoes a cycle of changes called **circadian** (SUR-kay-dee-AN) **rhythms** (*circa*: about; *diem*: a day) (Beersma & Gordijn, 2007). Throughout the day, activities in the liver, kidneys, and endocrine glands undergo large changes. Body temperature, blood pressure, and amino acid levels also shift from hour to hour. These activities, and many others, peak once a day (● Fig. 9.2). People are usually more motivated and alert at the high point of their circadian rhythms (Antle & Mistlberger, 2005).

Shift Work and Jet Lag Circadian rhythms are most noticeable after a major change in time schedules. Businesspersons, athletes, and other time zone travelers tend to perform poorly when their body rhythms are disturbed. If you travel great distances east or west, the peaks and valleys of your circadian rhythms will be out of phase with the sun and clocks. For example, you might be wide awake at midnight and feel like you're sleepwalking during the day. (Return to Fig. 9.2.) Shift work has the same effect, causing fatigue, irritability, upset stomach, and depression (Garbarino, 2002; Shen et al., 2006).

How fast do people adapt to rhythm changes? For major time zone shifts (5 hours or more) it can take up to 2 weeks

to resynchronize. The *direction* of travel also affects adaptation (Herxheimer & Waterhouse, 2003). If you fly west, adapting is relatively easy; if you fly east, adapting takes much longer (● Fig. 9.3). When you fly east, the sun comes up *earlier* relative to your "home" time. Let's say that you live in Seattle and fly to Washington. If you get up at 7 A.M. in Washington, it's 4 A.M. back in Seattle—and your body knows it. If you fly west, the sun comes up later. In this case, it is easier for people to "advance" (stay up later and sleep in) than it is to shift backward.

Adjusting to jet lag is slowest when you stay indoors, where you can sleep and eat on "home time." Getting outdoors speeds adaptation. A few intermittent 5-minute periods of exposure to bright light early in the morning are also helpful for resetting your circadian rhythm (Duffy & Wright, Jr., 2005).

How does this affect those of us who are not world travelers? There are few college students who have not at one time or another "burned the midnight oil," especially for final exams. At such times it is wise to remember that departing from your regular schedule usually costs more than it's worth. You may be motivated to do as much during 1 hour in the morning as you could have done in 3 hours of work after midnight. You might just as well go to sleep 2 hours earlier.

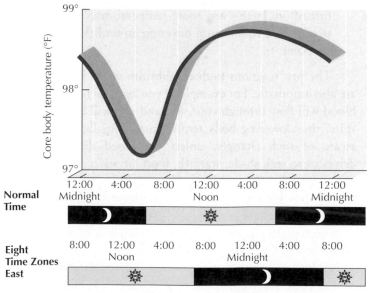

● **FIGURE 9.2** Core body temperature is a good indicator of a person's circadian rhythm. Most people reach a low point 2 to 3 hours before their normal waking time. It's no wonder that both the Chernobyl and Three Mile Island nuclear power plant accidents occurred around 4 A.M. Rapid travel to a different time zone, shift work, depression, and illness can throw sleep and waking patterns out of synchronization with the body's core rhythm. Mismatches of this kind are very disruptive (Hauri & Linde, 1990).

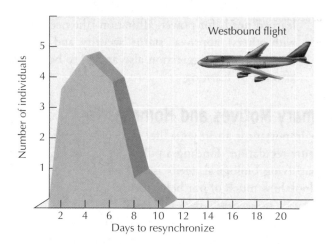

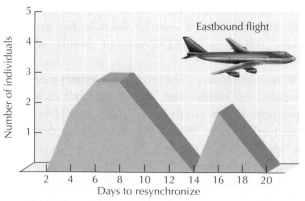

● **FIGURE 9.3** Time required to adjust to air travel across six time zones. The average time to resynchronize was shorter for westbound travel than for eastbound flights. (Data from Beljan et al., 1972; cited by Moore-Ede et al., 1982.)

In general, if you can anticipate an upcoming body rhythm change, it is best to preadapt to your new schedule. *Preadaptation* refers to gradually matching your sleep–waking cycle to a new time schedule. Before traveling, for instance, you should go to sleep 1 hour later (or earlier) each day until your sleep cycle matches the time at your destination.

MODULE 9.1 Summary

What is motivation?

- Motives initiate, sustain, and direct activities. Many motives involve the following sequence: need, drive, goal, and goal attainment (need reduction).

- Behavior can be activated either by needs (push) or by goals (pull).
- The attractiveness of a goal and its ability to initiate action are related to its incentive value.

Are there different types of motives?

- Three basic categories of motives are primary motives, stimulus motives, and secondary motives.
- Most primary motives operate to maintain homeostasis.
- Circadian rhythms are closely tied to sleep, activity, and energy cycles. Time zone travel and shift work can seriously disrupt motivation, sleep, and bodily rhythms.

KNOWLEDGE BUILDER

Overview of Motivation

Recite

Classify the following needs or motives by placing the correct letter in the blank.

A. Primary motive B. Stimulus motive
C. Secondary motive

1. ____ curiosity
2. ____ status
3. ____ sleep
4. ____ thirst
5. ____ achievement
6. ____ physical contact

7. Motives _____, sustain, and _____ activities.

8. The maintenance of bodily equilibrium is called thermostasis. T or F?

9. Desirable goals are motivating because they are high in
   a. secondary value
   b. stimulus value
   c. homeostatic value
   d. incentive value

10. The term *jet lag* is commonly used to refer to disruptions of
    a. the inverted U function
    b. circadian rhythms
    c. any of the episodic drives
    d. the body's set point

Reflect
Critical Thinking

11. Many people mistakenly believe that they suffer from "hypoglycemia" (low blood sugar), which is often blamed for fatigue, difficulty concentrating, irritability, and other symptoms. Why is it unlikely that many people actually have hypoglycemia?

Relate

Motives help explain why we do what we do. See if you can think of something you do that illustrates the concepts of need, drive, response, and goal. Does the goal in your example vary in incentive value? What effects do high and low incentive value goals have on your behavior?

Mentally list some primary motives you have satisfied today. Then list some stimulus motives and secondary motives. How did each influence your behavior?

Link

Internet addresses frequently change. To find the sites listed here, visit **http://www.thomsonedu.com/psychology/coon** for an updated list of Internet addresses and direct links to relevant sites.

- **Theories of Motivation** Because no single theory can account for all aspects of biological aspects of motivation, this site examines the major approaches to understanding motivation and includes discussions of both the strengths and weaknesses of each theory.
- **Sleeplessness and Circadian Rhythm Disorder** Read what happens when your biological clock malfunctions and what you can do about it.
- **Drive Reduction Theory and Incentives in the Regulation of Food Intake** Using eating behavior as an example, explore the roles of drive reduction and incentives.

ANSWERS

1. b 2. c 3. a 4. a 5. c 6. b 7. initiate, direct 8. F 9. d 10. b 11. Because of homeostasis: Blood sugar is normally maintained within narrow bounds. Although blood sugar levels fluctuate enough to affect hunger, true hypoglycemia is an infrequent medical problem.

Circadian rhythms Cyclical changes in body functions and arousal levels that vary on a schedule approximating a 24-hour day.

9.3 Arousal, Achievement, and Growth Needs

ARE YOU FULL OF ENERGY RIGHT NOW? Are you feeling tired? Clearly, the level of arousal you are experiencing is closely linked with your motivation. Are there ideal levels of arousal for different people and different activities? Let's find out.

Stimulus Drives—Skydiving, Horror Movies, and the Fun Zone

SURVEY QUESTION: *How does arousal relate to motivation?*

Most people enjoy a steady "diet" of new movies, novels, tunes, fashions, games, news, web sites, and adventures. Yet stimulus drives, which reflect needs for information, exploration, manipulation, and sensory input, go beyond mere entertainment. Stimulus drives also help us survive. As we scan our surroundings, we constantly identify sources of food, danger, shelter, and other key details. The drive for stimulation is already present during infancy. By the time a child can walk, there are few things in the home that have not been tasted, touched, viewed, handled, or, in the case of toys, destroyed!

Stimulus drives are readily apparent in animals as well as humans. For example, monkeys will quickly learn to solve a mechanical puzzle made up of interlocking metal pins, hooks, and latches (Butler, 1954) (● Fig. 9.10). No food

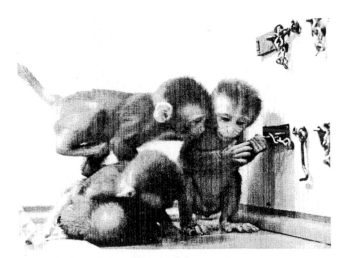

● **FIGURE 9.10** Monkeys happily open locks that are placed in their cage. Because no reward is given for this activity, it provides evidence for the existence of stimulus needs. (Photo courtesy of Harry F. Harlow.)

treats or other external rewards are needed to get them to explore and manipulate their surroundings. The monkeys seem to work for the sheer fun of it.

Arousal Theory

Are stimulus drives homeostatic? Yes. According to **arousal theory** we try to keep arousal at an optimal level (Franken, 2007; Hancock & Ganey, 2003). In other words, when your level of arousal is too low or too high, you will seek ways to raise or lower it.

What do you mean by arousal? Arousal refers to activation of the body and the nervous system. Arousal is zero at death; it is low during sleep; it is moderate during normal daily activities; and it is high at times of excitement, emotion, or panic. Arousal theory assumes that we become uncomfortable when arousal is too low ("I'm bored") or when it is too high, as in fear, anxiety, or panic ("The dentist will see you now"). Most adults vary their activities to maintain a comfortable level of activation. Music, parties, sports, conversation, sleep, surfing the web, and the like, are combined to keep arousal at moderate levels. The right mix of activities prevents boredom *and* overstimulation (Csikszentmihalyi, Abuhamdeh, & Nakamura, 2005).

Sensation Seekers *Do people vary in their needs for stimulation?* Picture a city dweller who is visiting the country. Before long, she begins to complain that it is "too quiet" and seeks some "action." Now imagine a country dweller who is visiting the city. Very soon, she finds the city "overwhelming" and seeks peace and quiet. These examples are extremes, but arousal theory also suggests that people learn to seek particular levels of arousal.

Sensation seeking is a trait of people who prefer high levels of stimulation (Gray & Wilson, 2007). Whether you are high or low in sensation seeking is probably based on how your body responds to new, unusual, or intense stimulation (Zuckerman, 2002). People high in sensation seeking tend to be bold and independent, and they value change. They also report more sexual partners than low scorers, they are more likely to smoke, and they prefer spicy, sour, and crunchy foods over bland foods. Low sensation seekers are orderly, nurturant, and giving, and they enjoy the company of others. Which are you? (Most people fall somewhere between the extremes. See "Xtreme!")

HUMAN DIVERSITY

Xtreme!

Where would you prefer to go on your next summer vacation? How about a week with your best friends at a cottage on a nearby lake? Or a shopping and museum trip to New York City? Better yet, how about cage diving with great white sharks in South Africa? If the shark adventure attracts you, you are probably high in sensation seeking and would be interested in a vacation that includes activities like bungee jumping, scuba diving, skiing, surfing, sky diving, or white-water rafting (Pizam et al., 2004).

Thrill seeking is an element of the sensation-seeking personality.

Marvin Zuckerman (1990, 2000) has devised a test to measure differences in sensation seeking. His *Sensation-Seeking Scale* (SSS) includes statements like the samples shown here (from Zuckerman, 1996):

Thrill and adventure seeking
- I would like to try parachute jumping.
- I think I would enjoy the sensations of skiing very fast down a high mountain slope.

Experience seeking
- I like to explore a strange city or section of town myself, even if it means getting lost.
- I like to try new foods that I have never tasted before.

Disinhibition
- I like wild, "uninhibited" parties.
- I often like to get high (drinking liquor or smoking marijuana).

Boredom susceptibility
- I can't stand watching a movie that I've seen before.
- I like people who are sharp and witty, even if they do sometimes insult others.

So who are the potential cage divers? Perhaps it's not surprising that SSS scores tend to be higher among men and younger people (Butkovic & Bratko, 2003; Roberti, 2004). SSS scores also vary across cultures. In one study of 11 different cultures, people from America, Israel, and Ireland scored higher on the SSS than people from South Africa, Slovakia, Sicily, or Gabon (Pizam et al., 2004).

Exciting lives aside, there is a dark side to sensation seeking as well. High sensation seekers are also more likely to engage in high-risk behaviors such as substance abuse (Horvath et al., 2004) and casual unprotected sex (Gullette & Lyons, 2005).

Levels of Arousal

Is there an ideal level of arousal for peak performance? If we set aside individual differences, most people perform best when their arousal level is *moderate.* Let's say that you have to take an essay exam. If you are feeling sleepy or lazy (arousal level too low), your performance will suffer. If you are in a state of anxiety or panic about the test (arousal level too high), you will also perform below par. Thus, the relationship between arousal and performance forms an *inverted* U function (a curve in the shape of an upside-down U) (● Fig. 9.11) (Hancock & Ganey, 2003).

The inverted U tells us that at very low levels of arousal you're not sufficiently energized to perform well. Performance will improve as your arousal level increases, up to the middle of the curve. Then it begins to drop off, as you become emotional, frenzied, or disorganized. For example, imagine trying to start a car stalled on a railroad track, with a speeding train bearing down on you. That's what the high-arousal end of the curve feels like.

Is performance always best at moderate levels of arousal? No, the ideal level of arousal depends on the complexity of a task. If a task is relatively simple, it is best for arousal to be high.

When a task is more complex, your best performance will occur at lower levels of arousal. (See Fig. 9.11.) This relationship is called the **Yerkes-Dodson law.** It applies to a wide variety of tasks and to measures of motivation other than arousal.

For example, at a track meet, it is almost impossible for sprinters to get too aroused for a race. The task is direct and simple: Run as fast as you can for a short distance. On the other hand, a golfer making a tournament-deciding putt faces a more sensitive and complex task. Excessive arousal is almost certain to hurt his or her performance. In school, most students have had experience with "test anxiety," a familiar example of how too much arousal can lower performance.

Arousal theory Assumes that people prefer to maintain ideal, or comfortable, levels of arousal.

Yerkes-Dodson law A summary of the relationships among arousal, task complexity, and performance.

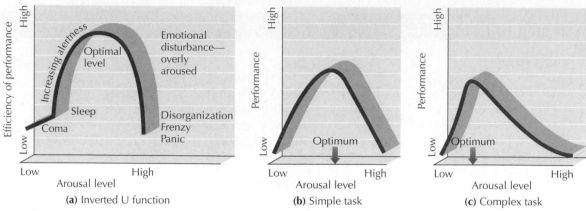

● **FIGURE 9.11** *(a)* The general relationship between arousal and efficiency can be described by an inverted U curve. The optimal level of arousal or motivation is higher for a simple task *(b)* than for a complex task *(c)*.

Coping with Test Anxiety

Then is it true that by learning to calm down, a person would do better on tests? Usually, but not always. To begin with, some arousal is healthy; it focuses us on the task at hand. It is only when arousal interferes with performance that we refer to anxiety. **Test anxiety** is a mixture of *heightened physiological arousal* (nervousness, sweating, pounding heart) and *excessive worry*. This combination—arousal plus worry—tends to distract students with a rush of upsetting thoughts and feelings (Stipek, 2001).

Also, studies show that students are typically most anxious when they don't know the material (Cassady, 2004). If this is the case, calming down simply means you will remain calm while failing. Here are some suggestions for coping with test anxiety:

Preparation *Hard work* is the most direct antidote for test anxiety. Many anxious students simply study too little, too late. That's why improving your study skills is a good way to reduce test anxiety (Cassady, 2004). The best solution is to *overprepare* by studying long before the "big day." Well-prepared students score higher, worry less, and are less likely to panic (Zohar, 1998).

Relaxation Learning to relax is another way to lower test anxiety (Ricketts & Galloway, 1984). You can learn self-relaxation skills by looking at Module 13.6, where a relaxation technique is described. Emotional support also helps (Stöber, 2004). If you are test anxious, discuss the problem with your professors or study for tests with a supportive classmate.

Rehearsal To reduce nervousness, rehearse how you will cope with upsetting events. Before taking a test, imagine yourself going blank, running out of time, or feeling panicked. Then calmly plan how you will handle each situation—by keeping your attention on the task, by focusing on one question at a time, and so forth (Watson & Tharp, 2007).

Restructuring Thoughts Another helpful strategy involves listing the upsetting thoughts you have during exams. Then you can learn to combat these worries with calming, rational replies (Jones & Petruzzi, 1995). (These are called *coping statements*; see Module 11.5 for more information.) Let's say you think, "I'm going to fail this test and everybody will think I'm stupid." A good reply to this upsetting thought would be to say, "If I prepare well and control my worries, I will probably pass the test. Even if I don't, it won't be the end of the world. My friends will still like me, and I can try to improve on the next test."

Students who cope well with exams usually try to do the best they can, even under trying circumstances. Becoming a more confident test taker can actually increase your scores, because it helps you remain calm. With practice, most people can learn to be less testy at test-taking time (Smith, 2002).

Social Motives—In Pursuit of Excellence

SURVEY QUESTIONS: *What are social motives? Why are they important?*

Some of your friends are more interested than others in success, achievement, competition, money, possessions, status, love, approval, grades, dominance, power, or belonging to groups—all of which are *social motives* or goals. We acquire **social motives** in complex ways, through socialization and cultural conditioning (Franken, 2007). The behavior of outstanding artists, scientists, athletes, educators, and leaders is best understood in terms of such learned needs, particularly the need for achievement.

The Need for Achievement

To many people, being "motivated" means being interested in achievement (Wigfield & Eccles, 2002). In a later chapter we will investigate aggression, helping, affiliation, seeking approval, and other social motives. For now, let us focus on the

need for achievement (nAch), which is a desire to meet an internal standard of excellence (McClelland, 1961). People with a high need for achievement strive to do well any time they are evaluated.

Is that like the aggressive businessperson who strives for success? Not necessarily. Needs for achievement may lead to wealth and prestige, but people who are high achievers in art, music, science, or amateur sports may excel without seeking riches. Such people typically enjoy challenges, and they relish a chance to test their abilities (Puca & Schmalt, 1999).

Power The need for achievement differs from the **need for power,** which is a desire to have impact or control over others (McClelland, 1975). People with strong needs for power want their importance to be visible: They buy expensive possessions, wear prestigious clothes, and exploit relationships. In some ways, the pursuit of power and financial success is the dark side of the American dream. People whose main goal in life is to make lots of money tend to be poorly adjusted and unhappy (Kasser & Ryan, 1993).

Characteristics of Achievers Using a simple measure, David McClelland (1917–1998) found that he could predict the behavior of high and low achievers. For instance, McClelland compared people's occupations with scores on an achievement test they took as college sophomores. Fourteen years later, those who scored high in nAch tended to have jobs that involved risk and responsibility (McClelland, 1965).

Here's a test: In front of you are five targets. Each is placed at an increasing distance from where you are standing. You are given a beanbag to toss at the target of your choice. Target A, anyone can hit; target B, most people can hit; target C, some people can hit; target D, very few people can hit; target E is rarely if ever hit. If you hit A, you will receive $2; B, $4; C, $8; D, $16; and E, $32. You get only one toss. Which one would you choose? McClelland's research suggests that if you have a high need for achievement, you will select C or perhaps D. Those high in nAch are *moderate* risk takers. When faced with a problem or a challenge, persons high in nAch avoid goals that are too easy.

Why do they pass up sure success? They do it because easy goals offer no sense of satisfaction. They also avoid long shots either because there is no hope of success or because "winning" will be due to luck rather than skill. Persons low in nAch select sure things or impossible goals. Either way, they don't have to take any responsibility for failure.

Desires for achievement and calculated risk taking lead to success in many situations. People high in nAch complete difficult tasks, they earn better grades, and they tend to excel in their occupations. College students high in nAch attribute success to their own ability, and failure to insufficient effort. Thus, high nAch students are more likely to renew their ef-

The person with high needs for achievement strives to do well in any situation in which evaluation takes place.

forts when they perform poorly. When the going gets tough, high achievers get going.

The Key to Success

What does it take to achieve extraordinary success? Psychologist Benjamin Bloom studied America's top concert pianists, Olympic swimmers, sculptors, tennis players, mathematicians, and research neurologists. Bloom (1985) found that drive and determination, not great natural talent, led to exceptional success.

The first steps toward high achievement began when parents exposed their children to music, swimming, scientific ideas, and so forth, "just for fun." At first, many of the children had very ordinary skills. One Olympic swimmer, for instance, remembers repeatedly losing races as a 10-year-old. At some point, however, the children began to actively cultivate their abilities. Before long, parents noticed the child's rapid progress and found an expert instructor or coach. After more successes, the youngsters began "living" for their talent and practiced many hours daily. This continued

Test anxiety High levels of arousal and worry that seriously impair test performance.

Social motives Learned motives acquired as part of growing up in a particular society or culture.

Need for achievement (nAch) The desire to excel or meet some internalized standard of excellence.

Need for power The desire to have social impact and control over others.

for many years before they reached truly outstanding heights of achievement.

The upshot of Bloom's work is that talent is nurtured by dedication and hard work (Beck, 2004). It is most likely to blossom when parents actively support a child's special interests and emphasize doing one's best at all times. Studies of child prodigies and eminent adults also show that intensive practice and expert coaching are common ingredients of high achievement. Elite performance in music, sports, chess, the arts, and many other pursuits typically requires at least 10 years of dedicated practice (Ericsson & Charness, 1994; Ross, 2006). The belief that talent will magically surface on its own is largely a myth.

Self-Confidence Achieving elite performance may be reserved for the dedicated few. Nevertheless, like elite athletes, you may be able to improve your motivation by increasing your self-confidence (Hanton, Mellalieu, & Hall, 2004). People with self-confidence believe they can successfully carry out an activity or reach a goal. To enhance self-confidence, it is wise to do the following (Druckman & Bjork, 1994):

- Set goals that are specific and challenging but attainable.
- Visualize the steps you need to take to reach your goal.
- Advance in small steps.
- When you first acquire a skill, your goal should be to make progress in learning. Later, you can concentrate on improving your performance, compared with other people.
- Get expert instruction that helps you master the skill.
- Find a skilled model (someone good at the skill) to emulate.
- Get support and encouragement from an observer.
- If you fail, regard it as a sign that you need to try harder, not that you lack ability.

Self-confidence affects motivation by influencing the challenges you will undertake, the effort you will make, and how long you will persist when things don't go well. You can be confident that self-confidence is worth cultivating.

Motives in Perspective— A View from the Pyramid

SURVEY QUESTION: *Are some motives more basic than others?*

As you may recall from Module 1.3, Abraham Maslow called the full use of personal potential *self-actualization.* Maslow also described a **hierarchy of human needs,** in which some needs are more basic or powerful than others. Think about the

needs that influence your own behavior. Which seem strongest? Which do you spend the most time and energy satisfying? Now look at Maslow's hierarchy (● Fig. 9.12). Note that physiological needs are at the base of the pyramid. Because these needs must be met if we are to survive, they tend to be *prepotent,* or dominant over the higher needs. It could be said, for example, that "to a starving person, food is god."

Maslow believed that higher, more fragile needs are expressed only after we satisfy our physiological needs. This is also true of needs for safety and security. Until they are met, we may have little interest in higher pursuits. For instance, a person who is extremely thirsty might have little interest in writing poetry or even talking with friends. For this reason, Maslow described the first four levels of the hierarchy as **basic needs.** Other basic needs include love and belonging (family, friendship, caring), and needs for esteem and self-esteem (recognition and self-respect).

All the basic needs are *deficiency* motives. That is, they are activated by a *lack* of food, water, security, love, esteem, or other basic needs. At the top of the hierarchy we find **growth needs,** which are expressed as a need for self-actualization. The need for self-actualization is not based on deficiencies. Rather, it is a positive, life-enhancing force for personal growth (Reiss & Havercamp, 2005). Like other humanistic psychologists, Maslow believed that people are basically good. If our basic needs are met, he said, we will tend to move on to actualizing our potentials.

How are needs for self-actualization expressed? Maslow called the less powerful but humanly important actualization motives **meta-needs** (Maslow, 1970). Meta-needs are an expression of tendencies to fully develop your personal potentials. The meta-needs are:

1. Wholeness (unity)
2. Perfection (balance and harmony)
3. Completion (ending)
4. Justice (fairness)
5. Richness (complexity)
6. Simplicity (essence)
7. Aliveness (spontaneity)
8. Beauty (rightness of form)
9. Goodness (benevolence)
10. Uniqueness (individuality)
11. Playfulness (ease)
12. Truth (reality)
13. Autonomy (self-sufficiency)
14. Meaningfulness (values)

According to Maslow, we tend to move up through the hierarchy of needs, toward the meta-needs. When the meta-needs are unfulfilled, people fall into a "syndrome of decay" marked by despair, apathy, and alienation.

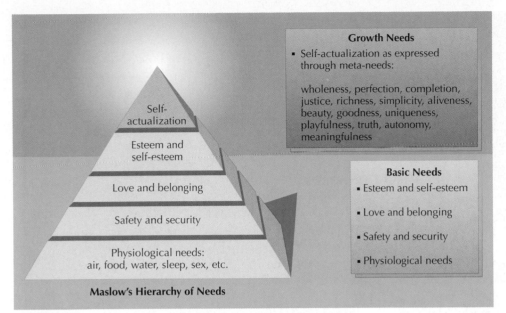

Growth Needs
- Self-actualization as expressed through meta-needs:

  wholeness, perfection, completion, justice, richness, simplicity, aliveness, beauty, goodness, uniqueness, playfulness, truth, autonomy, meaningfulness

Basic Needs
- Esteem and self-esteem
- Love and belonging
- Safety and security
- Physiological needs

Self-actualization

Esteem and self-esteem

Love and belonging

Safety and security

Physiological needs: air, food, water, sleep, sex, etc.

Maslow's Hierarchy of Needs

● **FIGURE 9.12** Maslow believed that lower needs in the hierarchy are dominant. Basic needs must be satisfied before growth motives are fully expressed. Desires for self-actualization are reflected in various meta-needs (see text).

Maslow's point is that mere survival or comfort is usually not enough to make a full and satisfying life. It's interesting to note, in this regard, that college students who are primarily concerned with money, personal appearance, and social recognition score lower than average in vitality, self-actualization, and general well-being (Kasser & Ryan, 1996).

Maslow's hierarchy is not well documented by research and parts of it are questionable. How, for instance, do we explain the actions of a person who fasts as part of a social protest? How can the meta-need for justice overcome the more basic need for food? (Perhaps the answer is that fasting is temporary and self-imposed.) Despite such objections, Maslow's views are a good way to understand and appreciate the rich interplay of human motives.

Are many people motivated by meta-needs? Maslow estimated that few people are primarily motivated by needs for self-actualization. Most of us are more concerned with esteem, love, or security. Perhaps this is because rewards in our society tend to encourage conformity, uniformity, and security in schools, jobs, and relationships. When was the last time you met a meta-need?

Intrinsic and Extrinsic Motivation

Some people cook for a living and consider it hard work. Others cook for pleasure and dream of opening a restaurant. For some people, mountain biking, gardening, writing, photography, or jewelry making is fun. For others the same activities are drudgery they must be paid to do. How can the same activity be "work" for one person and "play" for another?

When you do something for enjoyment or to improve your abilities, your motivation is usually *intrinsic*. **Intrinsic motivation** occurs when we act without any obvious external rewards. We simply enjoy an activity or see it as an opportunity to explore, learn, and actualize our potentials. In contrast, **extrinsic motivation** stems from external factors, such as pay, grades, rewards, obligations, and approval. Most of the activities we think of as "work" are extrinsically rewarded (Baard, Deci, & Ryan, 2004; Ryan & Deci, 2000).

Turning Play into Work

Don't extrinsic incentives strengthen motivation? Yes, they can, but not always. In fact, *excessive* rewards can decrease intrinsic motivation and spontaneous interest. For instance, in one classic study, children who were lavishly rewarded for drawing with felt-tip pens later showed little interest in playing with the

Reuters/Corbis

Wheelchair athletes engage in vigorous competition. Maslow considered such behavior an expression of the need for self-actualization.

Hierarchy of human needs Abraham Maslow's ordering of needs, based on their presumed strength or potency.

Basic needs The first four levels of needs in Maslow's hierarchy; lower needs tend to be more potent than higher needs.

Growth needs In Maslow's hierarchy, the higher level needs associated with self-actualization.

Meta-needs In Maslow's hierarchy, needs associated with impulses for self-actualization.

Intrinsic motivation Motivation that comes from within, rather than from external rewards; motivation based on personal enjoyment of a task or activity.

Extrinsic motivation Motivation based on obvious external rewards, obligations, or similar factors.

People who are intrinsically motivated feel free to explore creative solutions to problems. (*Left*, Dean Kaman, inventor of the Segway personal transportation device. *Right*, "Caffiends at the Beach," an entrant in the Great Arcata to Ferndale World Championship Cross Country Kinetic Sculpture Race.)

Rick Friedman/Corbis

Gregory A. Beaumont/© The Great Arcata to Ferndale World Championship Cross Country Kinetic Sculpture Race

pens again (Greene & Lepper, 1974). Apparently, "play" can be turned into "work" by *requiring* people to do something they would otherwise enjoy. When we are coerced or "bribed" to act, we tend to feel as if we are "faking it." Employees who lack initiative and teenagers who reject school and learning are good examples of such reactions (Ryan & Deci, 2000).

Creativity People are more likely to be creative when they are intrinsically motivated. On the job, for instance, salaries and bonuses may increase the amount of work done. However, work *quality* is affected more by intrinsic factors, such as personal interest and freedom of choice (Nakamura & Csikszentmihalyi, 2003). When a person is intrinsically motivated, a certain amount of challenge, surprise, and complexity makes a task rewarding. When extrinsic motivation is stressed, people are less likely to solve tricky problems and come up with innovative ideas (Amabile, Hadley, & Kramer, 2002).

How can the concept of intrinsic motivation be applied? Both types of motivation are necessary. But extrinsic motivation shouldn't be overused, especially with children. To summarize: (1) If there's no intrinsic interest in an activity to begin with, you have nothing to lose by using extrinsic rewards; (2) if basic skills are lacking, extrinsic rewards may be necessary at first; (3) extrinsic rewards can focus attention on an activity so real interest will develop; (4) if extrinsic rewards are used, they should be small and phased out as soon as possible (Cameron & Pierce, 2002; Greene & Lepper, 1974). It also helps to tell children they seem to be *really interested* in drawing, playing the piano, learning a language, or whatever activity you are rewarding (Cialdini et al., 1998).

At work, it is valuable for managers to find out what each employee's interests and career goals are. People are not solely motivated by money. A chance to do challenging, interesting, and intrinsically rewarding work is often just as important. In many situations it is important to encourage intrinsic motivation, especially when children are learning new skills.

MODULE 9.3 Summary

How does arousal relate to motivation?

- Many activities are related to needs for stimulation and our efforts to maintain desired levels of arousal.

- Drives for stimulation are partially explained by arousal theory, which states that people seek to maintain ideal levels of bodily arousal. People vary in their desired level of arousal or stimulation, as measured by the Sensation-Seeking Scale.

- Optimal performance usually occurs at moderate levels of arousal, as described by an inverted U function. The Yerkes-Dodson law further states that the ideal arousal level is higher for simple tasks and lower for complex tasks.

What are social motives? Why are they important?

- Social motives, which are learned, account for much of the diversity of human motivation.

- One prominent social motive is the need for achievement (nAch). High nAch is correlated with moderate risk taking and success in many situations.

- Self-confidence greatly affects motivation in everyday life.

Are some motives more basic than others?

- Maslow's hierarchy of motives categorizes needs as either basic or growth oriented. Lower needs are assumed to be prepotent (dominant) over higher needs. Self-actualization, the highest and most fragile need, is reflected in meta-needs.

- Meta-needs are closely related to intrinsic motivation. In some situations, external rewards can undermine intrinsic motivation, enjoyment, and creativity.

KNOWLEDGE BUILDER

Arousal, Achievement, and Growth Needs

Recite

1. Exploration, manipulation, and curiosity provide evidence for the existence of _____ drives.

2. People who score high on the SSS tend to be extroverted, independent, and individuals who value change. T or F?

3. Complex tasks, such as taking a classroom test, tend to be disrupted by high levels of arousal, an effect predicted by

   a. the Sensation-Seeking Scale

   b. the Yerkes-Dodson law

   c. studies of circadian arousal patterns

   d. studies of the need for achievement

4. Two key elements of test anxiety that must be controlled are _____ and excessive _____.

5. People high in nAch

   a. prefer long shots

   b. prefer sure things

   c. are moderate risk takers

   d. prefer change and high levels of stimulation

6. The highest level of Maslow's hierarchy of motives involves

   a. meta-needs

   b. needs for safety and security

   c. needs for love and belonging

   d. extrinsic needs

7. Intrinsic motivation is often undermined in situations in which obvious external rewards are applied to a naturally enjoyable activity. T or F?

8. Which of the following is *not* a characteristic of people who score high on the Sensation-Seeking Scale?

   a. boredom susceptibility

   b. experience seeking

   c. inhibition

   d. thrill seeking

Reflect
Critical Thinking

9. Many U.S. college freshmen say that "being well-off financially" is an essential life goal and that "making more money" was a very important factor in their decision to attend college. Which meta-needs are fulfilled by "making more money"?

Relate

Does arousal theory seem to explain any of your own behavior? Think of at least one time

when your performance was impaired by arousal that was too low or too high. Now think of some personal examples that illustrate the Yerkes-Dodson law.

In situations involving risk and skill, do you like to "go for broke"? Or do you prefer sure things? Do you think you are high, medium, or low in nAch?

Which levels of Maslow's hierarchy of needs occupy most of your time and energy?

Name an activity you do that is intrinsically motivated and one that is extrinsically motivated. How do they differ?

Link

Internet addresses frequently change. To find the sites listed here, visit **http://www.thomsonedu.com/psychology/coon** for an updated list of Internet addresses and direct links to relevant sites.

- **Sensation-Seeking Scale** Find out if you are high or low in sensation seeking.
- **The Yerkes-Dodson Law** Read more about the Yerkes-Dodson law.
- **Achievement Motivation in Business.** Find out if people high in the need for achievement make good managers.

ANSWERS

NEXT TO OUR OWN FEELINGS, the expressions of others are the most familiar aspect of emotion. In this module we will address such questions as: Are emotional expressions universal? Do they really reveal what others are feeling? How are they affected by culture and learning? In addition, we will explore several theories of emotion. Explanations of emotion are important because the better you understand your emotions, the better you will be able to manage them.

Expressing Emotions—Making Faces and Talking Bodies

SURVEY QUESTION: *How accurately are emotions expressed by the face and "body language"?*

Next to our own feelings, the expressions of others are the most familiar part of emotion. Are emotional expressions a carryover from human evolution? Charles Darwin thought so. Darwin (1872) observed that angry tigers, monkeys, dogs, and humans all bare their teeth in the same way. Psychologists believe that emotional expressions evolved to communicate our feelings to others, which aids survival. Such messages give valuable hints about what other people are likely to do next (Kalat & Shiota, 2007). For instance, in one study, people were able to detect angry and scheming faces faster than happy, sad, or neutral faces (● Fig. 9.17). Presumably, we are especially sensitive to threatening faces because they warn us of possible harm (Tipples, Atkinson, & Young, 2002).

Facial Expressions

Are emotional expressions the same for all people? Basic expressions appear to be fairly universal (● Fig. 9.18). Facial expressions of *fear, anger, disgust, sadness, surprise,* and *happiness*

● **FIGURE 9.18** Is anger expressed the same way in different cultures? Masks that are meant to be frightening or threatening are strikingly similar around the world. Most have an open, downward-curved mouth and diagonal or triangular eyes, eyebrows, nose, cheeks, and chin. (Keep this list in mind next Halloween.) Obviously, the pictured mask is not meant to be warm and cuddly. Your ability to "read" its emotional message suggests that basic emotional expressions have universal biological roots (Aronoff, Barclay, & Stevenson, 1988).

(enjoyment) are recognized around the world (Smith et al., 2005). *Contempt* and *interest* may also be universal, but researchers are less certain of these expressions (Ekman, 1993). Notice that this list covers most of the primary emotions described earlier. Children who are born blind have little opportunity to learn emotional expressions from others. Even so, they also display basic expressions in the same way sighted people do (Galati, Scherer, & Ricci-Bitti, 1997). It's also nice to note that a smile is the most universal and easily recognized facial expression of emotion.

Some facial expressions are shaped by learning and may be found only in specific cultures. Among the Chinese, for example, sticking out the tongue is a gesture of surprise, not of disrespect or teasing. If a person comes from another culture, it is wise to remember that you may easily misunderstand his or her expressions. At such times, knowing the social *context* in which an expression occurs helps clarify its meaning (Carroll & Russell, 1996; Kalat & Shiota, 2007).

Your face can produce some 20,000 different expressions, which makes it the most expressive part of your body. Most of these are *facial blends* (a mixture of two or more basic expressions). Imagine, for example, that you just received an F on an unfair test. Quite likely, your eyes, eyebrows, and forehead would reveal anger, and your mouth would be turned downward in a frown.

Most of us believe we can fairly accurately tell what others are feeling by observing their facial expressions. If thousands

| Angry | Sad | Happy | Scheming | Neutral |

● **FIGURE 9.17** When shown groups of simplified faces (without labels), the angry and scheming faces "jumped out" at people faster than sad, happy, or neutral faces. An ability to rapidly detect threatening expressions probably helped our ancestors survive. (Adapted from Tipples, Atkinson, & Young, 2002.)

of facial blends occur, how do we make such judgments? The answer is that facial expressions can be boiled down to three basic dimensions: *pleasantness-unpleasantness, attention-rejection,* and *activation* (or arousal) (Schlosberg, 1954). By smiling when you give a friend a hard time, you add an emotional message of acceptance to the verbal insult, which changes it's meaning. As they say in movie Westerns, it makes a big difference to "Smile when you say that, partner."

Cultural Differences in Emotion

How many times have you been angry this week? If it was more than once, you're not unusual. Anger is a very common emotion in Western cultures. Very likely this is because our culture emphasizes personal independence and a free expression of individual rights and needs. In North America, anger is widely viewed as a "natural" reaction to feeling that you have been treated unfairly.

In contrast, many Asian cultures place a high value on group harmony. In Asia, expressing anger in public is less common and anger is regarded as less "natural." The reason for this is that anger tends to separate people. Thus, being angry is at odds with a culture that values cooperation. Culture also influences positive emotions. In America, we tend to have positive feelings such as pride, happiness, and superiority, which emphasize our role as *individuals*. In Japan, positive feelings are more often linked with membership in groups (friendly feelings, closeness to others, and respect) (Kitayama, Markus, & Kurokawa, 2000; Markus et al., 2006).

It is common to think of emotion as an individual event. However, as you can see, emotion is shaped by cultural ideas, values, and practices (Mesquita & Markus, 2004).

Gender and Emotion *Women have a reputation for being "more emotional" than men. Are they?* Compared with women, men in Western cultures are more likely to have difficulty expressing their emotions. According to psychologist Ronald Levant, although male babies start out life more emotionally expressive than female babies, little boys soon learn to "toughen up," beginning in early childhood (Levant et al., 2006). As a result, men have learned to curtail the expression of most of their emotions, although not to the extent of Robert, the alexithymic man we met at the beginning of the chapter. Whereas girls are encouraged to express sadness, fear, shame, and guilt, boys are more likely to be allowed to express only anger and hostility (Fischer et al., 2004).

But does this mean that men experience emotions less than women? Ronald Levant believes that men who fail to express emotions become less aware of their own emotions. For many men, an inability to express feelings or to even be aware of them is a major barrier to having close, satisfying relation-

The expression of emotion is strongly influenced by learning. As you have no doubt observed, women cry more often, longer, and more intensely than men do. Men begin learning early in childhood to suppress crying—possibly to the detriment of their emotional health (Levant, 2003). Many men are especially unwilling to engage in public displays of emotion, in contrast to these women, who are grieving for the victims of a 2005 school siege in Beslan, Russia, which left nearly 200 children dead.

ships with others (Levant, 2003). Blunted emotions may even contribute to tragedies like the mass murders at Columbine High School in Littleton, Colorado. For many young males, anger is the only emotion they can freely feel and express.

Body Language

If a friend walked up to you and said, "Hey, ugly, what are you doing?" would you be offended? Probably not, because such remarks are usually delivered with a big grin. The facial and bodily gestures of emotion speak a language all their own and add to what a person says.

Kinesics (kih-NEEZ-iks) is the study of communication through body movement, posture, gestures, and facial expres-

Emotions are often unconsciously revealed by gestures and body positioning.

Kinesics Study of the meaning of body movements, posture, hand gestures, and facial expressions; commonly called "body language."

sions (Harrigan, 2006). Informally, we call it body language. To see a masterful use of body language, turn off the sound on a television and watch a popular entertainer or politician at work.

What kinds of messages are sent with body language? Again, it is important to realize that cultural learning affects the meaning of gestures. What, for instance, does it mean if you touch your thumb and first finger together to form a circle? In North America it means "Everything is fine" or "A-okay." In France and Belgium it means "You're worth zero." In southern Italy it means "You're an ass!" When the layer of culturally defined meanings is removed, it is more realistic to say that body language reveals an overall emotional tone (underlying emotional state).

The body telegraphs other feelings. The most general "messages" involve *relaxation* or *tension* and *liking* or *disliking.* Relaxation is expressed by casually positioning the arms and legs, leaning back (if sitting), and spreading the arms and legs. Liking is expressed mainly by leaning toward a person or object. Thus, body positioning can reveal feelings that would normally be concealed. Who do you "lean toward"?

Theories of Emotion—Several Ways to Fear a Bear

SURVEY QUESTION: *How do psychologists explain emotions?*

Is it possible to explain what takes place during emotion? How are arousal, behavior, cognition, expressions, and feelings interrelated? Theories of emotion offer different answers to these questions. Let's explore five views. Each appears to have a part of the truth, so we will try to put them all together in the end.

The James-Lange Theory

You're hiking in the woods when a bear suddenly steps out onto the trail. What will happen next? Common sense tells us that we will then feel fear, become aroused, and run (and sweat and yell). But is this the true order of events? In the 1880s, William James and Carl Lange (LON-geh) proposed that common sense had it backward. According to the **James-Lange theory,** bodily arousal (such as increased heart rate) does not *follow* a feeling such as fear. Instead, they argued, *emotional feelings follow bodily arousal.* Thus, we see a bear, run, are aroused, and *then* feel fear as we become aware of our bodily reactions (● Fig. 9.19).

To support his ideas, James pointed out that we often do not experience an emotion until after reacting. For example, imagine that you are driving. Suddenly a car pulls out in front of you. You swerve and skid to an abrupt halt at the side of the road. Only after you have come to a stop do you notice

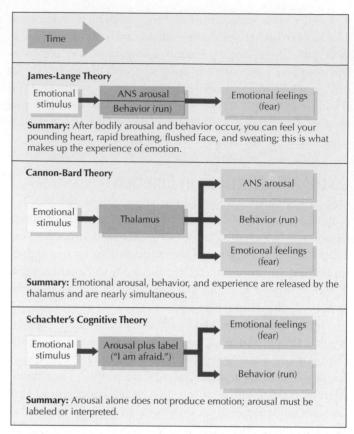

● **FIGURE 9.19** Earlier theories of emotion.

your pounding heart, rapid breathing, and tense muscles—and recognize your fear.

The Cannon-Bard Theory

Walter Cannon (1932) and Phillip Bard disagreed with the James-Lange theory. According to the **Cannon-Bard theory,** emotional feelings and bodily arousal *occur at the same time.* Cannon and Bard believed that seeing a bear activates the thalamus in the brain. The thalamus, in turn, alerts the cortex and the hypothalamus for action. The cortex produces our emotional feelings and emotional behavior. The hypothalamus triggers a chain of events that arouses the body. Thus, if you see a dangerous-looking bear, brain activity will simultaneously produce bodily arousal, running, and a feeling of fear. (See Fig. 9.19.)

Schachter's Cognitive Theory of Emotion

The previous theories are mostly concerned with our physical responses. Stanley Schachter realized that cognitive (mental) factors also enter into emotion. According to **Schachter's cognitive theory,** emotion occurs when we apply a particular *label* to general physical *arousal.* Schachter believed that when we are aroused, we have a need to interpret our feelings. Assume, for instance, that someone sneaks up behind you on a dark street and says "Boo!" No matter who the person is, your body will be aroused (pounding heart, sweating palms, and so on). If the person is a total stranger, you might interpret this arousal as fear; if the person is a close friend, the arousal may be labeled as surprise or delight. The label (such as anger, fear, or happiness) you apply to bodily arousal is influenced by your past experiences, the situation, and the reactions of others. (See Fig. 9.19.)

Support for the cognitive theory of emotion comes from an experiment in which people watched a slapstick movie (Schachter & Wheeler, 1962). Before viewing the movie, one third of the people received an arousing injection of adrenaline, one third got a placebo (salt water) injection, and one third were given a tranquilizer. People who received the adrenaline rated the movie funniest and laughed the most while watching it. In contrast, those given the tranquilizer were least amused. The placebo group fell in between.

According to the cognitive theory of emotion, individuals who received adrenaline had a stirred-up body but no explanation for what they were feeling. Consequently, they became happy when the movie implied that their arousal was due to amusement. This and similar experiments make it clear that emotion is much more than just an agitated body. Perception, experience, attitudes, judgment, and many other mental factors also affect the emotions we feel. Schachter's theory would predict, then, that if you met a bear, you would be aroused. If the bear seemed unfriendly, you would interpret your arousal as fear, and if the bear offered to shake your "paw," you would be happy, amazed, and relieved!

Attribution We now move from slapstick movies and fear of bear bodies to an appreciation of bare bodies. Researcher Stuart Valins (1967) added an interesting wrinkle to Schachter's theory of emotion. According to Valins, arousal can be attributed to various sources—a process that alters our perceptions of emotion. To demonstrate **attribution,** Valins

Michael Grecco/Stock, Boston/PictureQuest

Which theory of emotion best describes the reactions of these people? Given the complexity of emotion, each theory appears to possess an element of truth.

(1966) showed male college students a series of photographs of nude females. While watching the photographs, each student heard an amplified heartbeat that he believed was his own. In reality, students were listening to a recorded heartbeat carefully designed to beat *louder* and *stronger* when some (but not all) of the slides were shown.

After watching the slides, each student was asked to say which was most attractive. Students who heard the false heartbeat consistently rated slides paired with a "pounding heart" as the most attractive. In other words, when a student saw a slide and heard his heart beat louder, he attributed his "emotion" to the slide. His interpretation seems to have been, "Now that one I like!" His next reaction, perhaps, was "But why?" Later research suggests that subjects persuaded themselves that the slide really was more attractive in order to explain their apparent arousal (Truax, 1983).

That seems somewhat artificial. Does it really make any difference what arousal is attributed to? Yes. To illustrate attribution in the "real world," consider what happens when parents interfere with the budding romance of a son or daughter. Often, trying to separate a young couple *intensifies* their feelings. Meddling parents add frustration, anger, and fear or excitement (as in seeing each other "on the sly") to the couple's feelings. Because they already care for each other, they are likely to attribute all this added emotion to "true love" (Walster, 1971).

Attribution theory predicts that you are most likely to "love" someone who gets you stirred up emotionally (Foster et al., 1998). This is true even when fear, anger, frustration, or rejection is part of the formula. Thus, if you want to successfully propose marriage, take your intended to the middle of a narrow, windswept suspension bridge over a deep chasm and look deeply into his or her eyes. As your beloved's heart pounds wildly (from being on the bridge, not from your irresistible charms), say, "I love you." Attribution theory predicts that your companion will conclude, "Oh wow, I must love you, too."

The preceding is not as farfetched as it may seem. In an ingenious study, a female psychologist interviewed men in a park. Some were on a swaying suspension bridge 230 feet above a river. The rest were on a solid wooden bridge just 10 feet above the ground. After the interview, the psychologist

James-Lange theory States that emotional feelings follow bodily arousal and come from awareness of such arousal.

Cannon-Bard theory States that activity in the thalamus causes emotional feelings and bodily arousal to occur simultaneously.

Schachter's cognitive theory States that emotions occur when physical arousal is labeled or interpreted on the basis of experience and situational cues.

Attribution The mental process of assigning causes to events. In emotion, the process of attributing arousal to a particular source.

gave each man her telephone number, so he could "find out about the results" of the study. Men interviewed on the suspension bridge were much more likely to give the "lady from the park" a call (Dutton & Aron, 1974). Apparently, these men experienced heightened arousal, which they interpreted as attraction to the experimenter—a clear case of love at first fright!

The Facial Feedback Hypothesis

Schachter added thinking and interpretation (cognition) to our view of emotion, but the picture still seems incomplete. What about expressions? How do they influence emotion? As Charles Darwin observed, the face is very central to emotion—perhaps it is more than just an "emotional billboard."

Psychologist Carrol Izard (1977, 1990) was among the first to suggest that the face does, indeed, affect emotion. According to Izard, emotions cause innately programmed changes in facial expression. Sensations from the face then provide cues to the brain that help us determine what emotion we are feeling. This idea is known as the **facial feedback hypothesis** (Soussignan, 2002). Stated another way, it says that having facial expressions and becoming aware of them is what influences our private emotional experience. Exercise, for instance, arouses the body, but we don't experience this arousal as emotion because it does not trigger emotional expressions.

Psychologist Paul Ekman takes this idea one step further. He believes that "making faces" can actually cause emotion (Ekman, 1993). In one study, participants were guided as they arranged their faces, muscle by muscle, into expressions of surprise, disgust, sadness, anger, fear, and happiness (● Fig. 9.20). At the same time, each person's bodily reactions were monitored.

Contrary to what you might expect, "making faces" can affect the autonomic nervous system, as shown by changes in heart rate and skin temperature. In addition, each facial expression produces a different pattern of activity. An angry face, for instance, raises heart rate and skin temperature,

whereas disgust lowers both (Ekman, Levenson, & Friesen et al., 1983). Other studies have confirmed that posed expressions alter emotions and bodily activity (Duclos & Laird, 2001; Soussignan, 2002).

In a fascinating experiment on facial feedback, people rated how funny they thought cartoons were while holding a pen crosswise in their mouths. Those who held the pen in their teeth thought the cartoons were funnier than did people who held the pen in their lips. Can you guess why? The answer is that if you hold a pen with your teeth, you are forced to form a smile. Holding it with the lips makes a frown. As predicted by the facial feedback hypothesis, emotional experiences were influenced by the facial expressions that people made (Strack, Martin, & Stepper, 1988). Next time you're feeling sad, bite a pen!

It appears, then, that not only do emotions influence expressions, but expressions influence emotions, as shown here (Duclos & Laird, 2001).

Contracted Facial Muscles	Felt Emotion
Forehead	Surprise
Brow	Anger
Mouth (down)	Sadness
Mouth (smile)	Joy

This could explain an interesting effect you have probably observed. When you are feeling "down," forcing yourself to smile will sometimes be followed by an actual improvement in your mood (Kleinke, Peterson, & Rutledge, 1998).

If smiling can improve a person's mood, is it a good idea to inhibit negative emotions? For an answer, see "Suppressing Emotion—Don't Turn Off the Music."

Emotional Appraisal

According to Richard Lazarus (1991a, 1991b), the emotions you experience are greatly influenced by how you think about an event in the first place. **Emotional appraisal** refers to evaluating the personal meaning of a stimulus: Is it good/bad,

● **FIGURE 9.20** Facial feedback and emotion. Participants in Ekman's study formed facial expressions like those normally observed during emotion. When they did this, emotion-like changes took place in their body activity. (Adapted from Ekman et al., 1983.)

THE CLINICAL FILE

Suppressing Emotion—Don't Turn Off the Music

According to popular media, we are supposed to be happy all the time (Hecht, 2007). Thus, while sharing a beautiful day with friends, you can freely express your happiness. Yet real emotional life has its ups and downs. Often we try to appear less emotional than we really are, especially when we are feeling negative emotions. Have you ever been angry with a friend in public? Embarrassed by someone's behavior at a party? Disgusted by someone's table manners? In such circumstances, people are quite good at suppressing outward signs of emotion.

However, restraining emotion can actually increase activity in the sympathetic nervous system. In other words, hiding emotion requires a lot of effort. Suppressing emotions can also impair thinking and memory, as you devote energy to self-control. Thus, although suppressing emotion allows us to appear calm and collected on the outside, this cool appearance comes at a high cost (Richards & Gross, 2000). People who suppress emotions cope poorly with life and are prone to depression and other problems (Lynch et al., 2001).

Conversely, people who express their emotions generally experience better emotional and physical health (Lumley, 2004; Pennebaker, 2004). Paying attention to our negative emotions can also lead us to think more clearly about the positive *and* the negative. The end result is better decision making, which can increase our overall happiness in the long run (Norem, 2002). Usually, it's better to manage emotions than it is to suppress them. You will find some suggestions for managing emotions in the upcoming "Psychology in Action" section.

---

threatening/supportive, relevant/irrelevant, and so on. Some examples of emotional appraisals and the emotions they give rise to can be found in ■ Table 9.2.

A Contemporary Model of Emotion

To summarize, James and Lange were right that feedback from arousal and behavior adds to our emotional experiences. Cannon and Bard were right about the timing of events. Schachter showed us that cognition is important. In fact,

psychologists are increasingly aware that how you *appraise* a situation greatly affects your emotions (Strongman, 2003). Richard Lazarus stressed the importance of emotional appraisal. Let's put these ideas together in a single model of emotion (● Fig. 9.21).

Imagine that a large snarling dog lunges at you with its teeth bared. A modern view of your emotional reactions goes

■ TABLE 9.2 Appraisals and Corresponding Emotions	
APPRAISAL	**EMOTION**
You have been slighted or demeaned.	Anger
You feel threatened.	Anxiety
You have experienced a loss.	Sadness
You have broken a moral rule.	Guilt
You have not lived up to your ideals.	Shame
You desire something another has.	Envy
You are near something repulsive.	Disgust
You fear the worst but yearn for better.	Hope
You are moving toward a desired goal.	Happiness
You are linked with a valued object or accomplishment.	Pride
You have been treated well by another.	Gratitude
You desire affection from another person.	Love
You are moved by someone's suffering.	Compassion

Source: Adapted from Lazarus, 1991a.

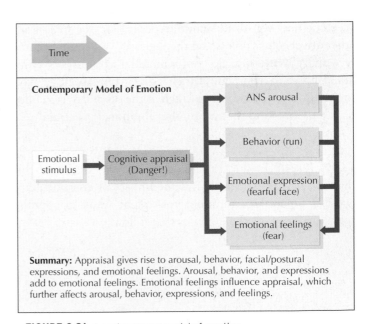

● **FIGURE 9.21** A contemporary model of emotion.

Facial feedback hypothesis States that sensations from facial expressions help define what emotion a person feels.

Emotional appraisal Evaluating the personal meaning of a stimulus or situation.

something like this: An *emotional stimulus* (the dog) is *appraised* (judged) as a threat or other cause for emotion. (You think to yourself, "Uh oh, big trouble!") Your appraisal gives rise to *ANS arousal* (your heart pounds, and your body becomes stirred up) and *cognitive labeling*. The appraisal also releases *innate emotional expressions*. (Your face twists into a mask of fear, and your posture becomes tense.) At the same time, your appraisal leads to *adaptive behavior*. (You run from the dog.) It also causes a change in consciousness that you recognize as the subjective experience of fear. (The intensity of this *emotional feeling* is directly related to the amount of ANS arousal taking place in your body.)

Each element of emotion—ANS arousal, labeling, adaptive behavior, subjective experience, and your emotional expressions—may further alter your emotional appraisal of the situation, as well as your thoughts, judgments, and perceptions. Thus, according to the facial feedback hypothesis, your facial expression will further influence your emotion. Such changes affect each of the other reactions, which again alters your appraisal and interpretation of events. Thus, emotion may blossom, change course, or diminish as it proceeds. Note too that the original emotional stimulus can be external, like the attacking dog, or internal, such as a memory of being chased by a dog, rejected by a lover, or praised by a friend. That's why mere thoughts and memories can make us fearful, sad, or happy (Strongman, 2003).

Our discussion suggests that emotion is greatly influenced by how you think about an event. For example, if another driver "cuts you off" on the highway, you could become very angry. But if you do, you will add 15 minutes of emotional upset to your day. By changing your appraisal, you could just as easily choose to laugh at the other driver's childish behavior—and minimize the emotional wear-and-tear (Gross, 2001).

A Look Ahead In the "Psychology in Action" section of this chapter we will look further at the impact of emotional appraisals. Before we continue, you might want to appraise your learning with the exercises that follow.

MODULE 9.5 Summary

How accurately are emotions expressed by the face and "body language"?

• Basic facial expressions of fear, anger, disgust, sadness, and happiness are universal. Contempt, surprise, and interest may be, too.

• Body gestures and movements (body language) express general emotional tone rather than specific universal messages.

• Facial expressions reveal pleasantness versus unpleasantness, attention versus rejection, and a person's degree of emotional activation. Body positioning expresses relaxation or tension and liking or disliking.

How do psychologists explain emotions?

• The James-Lange theory says that emotional experience follows bodily reactions. In contrast, the Cannon-Bard theory says that bodily reactions and emotional experiences occur at the same time.

• Schachter's cognitive theory emphasizes that labeling bodily arousal can determine what emotion you feel. Emotions are also influenced by attribution (ascribing arousal to a particular source).

• The facial feedback hypothesis holds that facial expressions help define the emotions we feel.

• Contemporary views of emotion emphasize the effects of cognitive appraisals. Also, our feelings and actions change as each element of emotion interacts with others. One of the best ways to manage emotion is to change your emotional appraisal of a situation.

KNOWLEDGE BUILDER

Emotional Expression and Theories of Emotion

Recite

1. Charles Darwin held that emotional expressions aid survival for animals. T or F?

2. A formal term for "body language" is

   _____.

3. Which three dimensions of emotion are communicated by facial expressions?

   a. pleasantness-unpleasantness

   b. complexity

   c. attention-rejection

   d. anger

   e. curiosity-disinterest

   f. activation

4. According to the James-Lange theory, emotional experience precedes physical arousal and emotional behavior. (We see a bear, are frightened, and run.) T or F?

5. The Cannon-Bard theory of emotion says that bodily arousal and emotional experience occur _____.

6. The idea that labeling arousal helps define what emotions we experience is associated with

   a. the James-Lange theory

   b. Schachter's cognitive theory

   c. the Cannon-Bard theory

   d. Darwin's theory of innate emotional expressions

7. Subjects in Valins's false heart rate study attributed increases in their heart rate to the action of a placebo. T or F?

8. As you try to wiggle your ears, you keep pulling the corners of your mouth back into a smile. Each time you do, you find yourself giggling. Which of the following provides the best explanation for this reaction?

   a. attribution

   b. the Cannon-Bard theory

   c. appraisal

   d. facial feedback

Reflect
Critical Thinking

9. People with high spinal injuries may feel almost no signs of physiological arousal from their bodies. Nevertheless they still feel emotion, which can be intense at times. What theory of emotion does this observation contradict?

Relate

Write a list of emotions that you think you can accurately detect from facial expressions. Does your list match Paul Ekman's? Would you be more confident in rating pleasantness-unpleasantness, attention-rejection, and activation? Why?

Which theory seems to best explain your own emotional experiences? Try frowning or smiling for 5 minutes. Did facial feedback have any effect on your mood? Cover the left column of Table 9.2. Read each emotional label in the right column. What appraisal do you think would lead to the listed emotion? Do the appraisals in the table match your predictions?

Link

Internet addresses frequently change. To find the sites listed here, visit **http://www .thomsonedu.com/psychology/coon** for an updated list of Internet addresses and direct links to relevant sites.

- **The Expression of the Emotions in Man and Animals** Read Charles Darwin's original book.

- **What's in a Face?** Read an APA article about facial expressions.

- **Controlling Anger** Discusses anger and some strategies for its control.

ANSWERS

1. T 2. kinesics 3. a, c, f 4. F 5. simultaneously 6. b 7. F 8. d 9. The James-Lange theory and Schachter's cognitive theory. The facial feedback hypothesis also helps explain the observation.

10.1 Overview of Personality

EACH PERSON HAS A UNIQUE PATTERN OF THINKING, behaving, and expressing feelings. In short, everyone has a unique personality. As psychologists, we would like to better understand Annette's personality. What concepts and theories can we use?

The Psychology of Personality— Do You Have Personality?

SURVEY QUESTIONS: *How do psychologists use the term* personality? *What core concepts make up the psychology of personality?*

"Annette has a very optimistic personality." "Ramiro's not handsome, but he has a great personality." "My father's business friends think he's a nice guy. They should see him at home where his real personality comes out." "It's hard to believe Tanya and Nikki are sisters. They have such opposite personalities."

It's obvious that we all frequently use the term *personality*. But if you think that personality means "charm," "charisma," or "style," you have misused the term. Psychologists regard **personality** as a person's unique pattern of thinking, emotions, and behavior (Burger, 2008; Mischel, 2004). In other words, *personality* refers to the consistency in who you are, have been, and will become. It also refers to the special blend of talents, values, hopes, loves, hates, and habits that makes each of us a unique person.

How is that different from the way most people use the term? Many people confuse personality with *character*. The term **character** implies that a person has been evaluated, not just described (Skipton, 1997). If, by saying someone has "personality," you mean the person is friendly, outgoing, and attractive, you are describing what we regard as good character in our culture. But in some cultures it is deemed good for people to be fierce, warlike, and cruel. So, whereas everyone in a particular culture has personality, not everyone has character—or at least not good character. (Do you know any good characters?)

Personality is also distinct from *temperament*, the "raw material" from which personalities are formed. **Temperament** refers to the hereditary aspects of your personality, such as your sensitivity, irritability, distractibility, and typical mood (Kagan, 2004). Judging from Annette's adult personality, you might guess that she was an active, happy baby.

Psychologists use a large number of terms to explain personality. It might be wise, therefore, to start with a few key concepts. These ideas should help you keep your bearings as you read this chapter.

Traits

We use the idea of traits every day to talk about personality. For instance, Dan is *sociable, orderly,* and *intelligent*. His sister Kayla is *shy, sensitive,* and *creative*. As we observed in our reunion with Annette, personality traits like these are usually quite stable (Gustavsson et al., 1997; Hergenhahn & Olson, 2007). Think about how little the traits of your best friends have changed in the last 5 years. It would be strange indeed to feel like you were talking with a different person every time you met a friend or an acquaintance. In general, then,

Neal Preston/Corbis

Does this man have personality? Do you?

Bill Bachman

Psychologists and employers are especially interested in the personality traits of individuals who hold high-risk, high-stress positions involving public safety, such as police, air-traffic controllers, and nuclear power plant employees.

CRITICAL THINKING

The Amazing Twins

Many reunited twins in the Minnesota study have displayed similarities far beyond what would be expected on the basis of heredity. The "Jim twins," James Lewis and James Springer, are one famous example. Both Jims had married and divorced women named Linda. Both had undergone police training. One named his firstborn son James Allan, the other named *his* firstborn son James Alan. Both drove Chevrolets and vacationed at the same beach each summer. Both listed carpentry and mechanical drawing among their hobbies. Both had built benches around trees in their yards. And so forth (Holden, 1980).

Are all identical twins so, well, identical? No, they aren't. Consider identical twins Carolyn Spiro and Pamela Spiro Wagner who, unlike the "Jim Twins," lived together throughout their childhood. While in sixth grade, they found out that President Kennedy had been assassinated. Carolyn wasn't sure why everyone was so upset. Pamela heard voices announcing that she was responsible for his death. After years of hiding her voices from everyone, Pamela tried to commit suicide while the twins were attending Brown University. She was diagnosed with schizophrenia. Never to be cured, she has gone on to write award-winning poetry. Carolyn eventually became a Harvard psychiatrist (Spiro Wagner & Spiro, 2005). Some twins

reared apart appear very similar; some reared together appear rather different.

So why are some identical twins, like the Jim Twins, so much alike even if they were reared apart? Although genetics is important, it is preposterous to suggest that there are child-naming genes and bench-building genes. How, then, do we explain the eerie similarities in some separated twins' lives? Imagine that you were separated at birth from a twin brother or sister. If you were reunited with your twin today, what would you do? Quite likely, you would spend the next several days comparing every imaginable detail of your lives. Under such circumstances it is virtually certain that you and your twin would notice and compile a long list of similarities. ("Wow! I use the same brand of toothpaste you do!") Yet, two unrelated persons of the same age, sex, and race could probably rival your list—*if* they were as motivated to find similarities.

In fact, one study compared twins to unrelated pairs of students. The unrelated pairs, who were the same age and sex, were almost as alike as the twins. They had highly similar political beliefs, musical interests, religious preferences, job histories, hobbies, favorite foods, and so on (Wyatt et al., 1984). Why were the unrelated students so similar? Basically, it's because people of the same age and sex live in

Identical twins Pam (left) and Carolyn (right) were raised together. Regardless, Carolyn became a psychiatrist while Pamela developed schizophrenia and went on to become an award-winning poet (Spiro Wagner & Spiro, 2005). Their story illustrates the complex interplay of forces which shape our adult personalities.

the same historical times and select from similar societal options. As just one example, in nearly every elementary school classroom you will find several children with the same first name.

It appears then that many of the seemingly "astounding" coincidences shared by reunited twins may be a special case of the fallacy of positive instances, described in Module 1.2. Reunited twins tend to notice the similarities and ignore the differences.

---

personality traits like these are stable qualities that a person shows in most situations (Matthews, Deary, & Whiteman, 2003).

Typically, traits are inferred from behavior. If you see Dan talking to strangers—first at a supermarket and later at a party—you might deduce that he is "sociable." Once personality traits are identified, they can be used to predict future behavior. For example, noting that Dan is outgoing might lead you to predict that he will be sociable at school or at work. In fact, such consistencies can span many years (McAdams & Pals, 2006). A study of women who appeared to be happy in their college yearbook photos (they had genuine smiles) found that most were still happy people 30 years later (Harker & Keltner, 2001).

At what age are personality traits firmly established? Personality starts to stabilize at around age 3 and continues to

"harden" though age 50 (Caspi, Roberts, & Shiner, 2005). Personality slowly matures during old age as most people continue to become more conscientious and agreeable. It appears that stereotypes of the "grumpy old man" and "cranky old woman" are largely unfounded (Roberts, Walton, & Viechtbauer, 2006; Srivastava et al., 2003).

Personality A person's unique and relatively stable behavior patterns.

Character Personal characteristics that have been judged or evaluated; a person's desirable or undesirable qualities.

Temperament The hereditary aspects of personality, including sensitivity, activity levels, prevailing mood, irritability, and adaptability.

Personality trait A stable, enduring quality that a person shows in most situations.

Do We Inherit Personality?

Does the stability of personality traits mean that they are affected by heredity? Some breeds of dogs have reputations for being friendly, aggressive, intelligent, calm, or emotional. Such differences fall in the realm of **behavioral genetics,** the study of inherited behavioral traits. We know that facial features, eye color, body type, and many other physical characteristics are inherited. So are many of our behavioral tendencies (Bouchard, 2004; Kalat, 2007). Genetic studies have shown that intelligence, some mental disorders, temperament, and other complex qualities are influenced by heredity. In view of such findings, we also might wonder, Do genes affect personality?

Wouldn't comparing the personalities of identical twins help answer the question? It would indeed—especially if the twins were separated at birth or soon after.

Twins and Traits For several decades, psychologists at the University of Minnesota have been studying identical twins who grew up in different homes. Medical and psychological tests reveal that reunited twins are very much alike, even when they are reared apart (Bouchard, 2004; Bouchard et al., 1990). They may even be similar in appearance, voice quality, facial gestures, hand movements, and nervous tics, such as nail biting. Separated twins also tend to have similar talents. If one twin excels at art, music, dance, drama, or athletics, the other is likely to as well—despite wide differences in childhood environment. However, as "The Amazing Twins" explains, it's wise to be cautious about some reports of extraordinary similarities in reunited twins.

Summary Studies of twins make it clear that heredity has a sizable effect on each of us. All told, it seems reasonable to conclude that heredity is responsible for about 25 to 50 percent of the variation in many personality traits (Caspi, Roberts, & Shiner, 2005; Loehlin et al., 1998). Notice, however, that the same figures imply that personality is shaped as much, or more, by environment as it is by heredity.

Each personality is a unique blend of heredity and environment, biology and culture. We are not—thank goodness—genetically programmed robots whose behavior and personality traits are "wired in" for life. Where you go in life is the result of the choices you make. Although these choices are influenced by inherited tendencies, they are not merely a product of your genes (Funder, 2006).

Types

Have you ever asked the question, "What type of person is she (or he)?" A **personality type** refers to people who have *several traits in common* (Larsen & Buss, 2005). Informally, your own thinking might include categories such as the executive type, the athletic type, the motherly type, the hip-hop type, the techno geek, and so forth. If you tried to define these informal types, you would probably list a different collection of traits for each one.

How valid is it to speak of personality "types"? Over the years, psychologists have proposed many ways to categorize personalities into types. For example, Swiss psychiatrist Carl Jung (yoong) proposed that people are either *introverts* or *extroverts.* An **introvert** is a shy, reserved person whose attention is focused inward. An **extrovert** is a bold, outgoing person whose attention is directed outward. These terms are so widely used that you may think of yourself and your friends as being one type or the other. However, the wildest, wittiest, most party-loving "extrovert" you know is introverted at times. Likewise, extremely introverted persons are assertive and sociable in some situations. In short, two categories (or even several) are often inadequate to fully capture differences in personality. That's why rating people on a list of traits tends to be more informative than classifying them into two or three types.

Even though types tend to oversimplify personality, they do have value. Most often, types are a shorthand way of labeling people who have several key traits in common. For example, in Module 11.4 we discuss Type A and Type B personalities. Type A's are people who have personality traits that increase their chance of suffering a heart attack; Type B's take a more laid-back approach to life (● Fig. 10.1). Similarly, you will read in

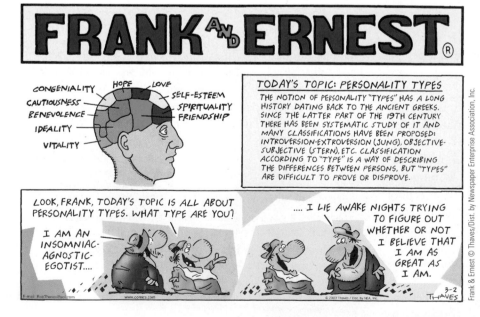

Frank & Ernest © Thaves/Dist. by Newspaper Enterprise Association, Inc.

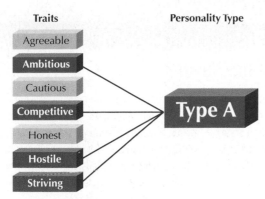

Traits   **Personality Type**

Agreeable
Ambitious
Cautious
Competitive
Honest
Hostile
Striving

Type A

● **FIGURE 10.1** Personality types are defined by the presence of several specific traits. For example, several possible personality traits are shown in the left column. A person who has a Type A personality typically possesses all or most of the highlighted traits. Type A persons are especially prone to heart disease. (See Module 11.4.)

Self-concepts can be remarkably consistent. In an interesting study, very old people were asked how they had changed over the years. Almost all thought they were essentially the same person they were when they were young (Troll & Skaff, 1997).

Module 12.2 about unhealthy personality types such as the paranoid personality, the dependent personality, and the antisocial personality. Each problem type is defined by a specific collection of maladaptive traits.

Self-Concept

Self-concepts provide another way of understanding personality. The rough outlines of your self-concept could be revealed by this request: "Please tell us about yourself." In other words, your **self-concept** consists of all your ideas, perceptions, stories, and feelings about who you are. It is the mental "picture" you have of your own personality (Swann, Chang-Schneider, & Larsen McClarty, 2007).

We creatively build our self-concepts out of daily experiences. Then we slowly revise them as we have new experiences. Once a stable self-concept exists, it tends to guide what we pay attention to, remember, and think about. Because of this, self-concepts can greatly affect our behavior and personal adjustment—especially when they are inaccurate (Ryckman, 2008). For instance, Alesha is a student who thinks she is stupid, worthless, and a failure, despite getting good grades. With such an inaccurate self-concept, she tends to be depressed regardless of how well she does.

Self-Esteem Note that in addition to having a faulty self-concept, Alesha has low **self-esteem** (a negative self-evaluation). A person with high self-esteem is confident, proud, and self-respecting. One who has low self-esteem is insecure, lacking in confidence, and self-critical. Like Alesha, people with low self-esteem are usually anxious and unhappy.

Self-esteem tends to rise when we experience success or praise. A person who is competent and effective and who is loved, admired, and respected by others will almost always

have high self-esteem (Baumeister et al., 2003). (The reasons for having high self-esteem can vary in different cultures. See "Self-Esteem and Culture" for more information.)

What if you "think you're hot," but you're not? Genuine self-esteem is based on an accurate appraisal of your strengths and weaknesses. A positive self-evaluation that is bestowed too easily may not be healthy (Twenge & Campbell, 2001). People who think very highly of themselves (and let others know it) may at first seem confident, but their arrogance quickly turns off other people (Paulhus, 1998).

Personality Theories

As you can already see, it would be easy to get lost without a framework for understanding personality. How do our thoughts, actions, and feelings relate to one another? How does personality develop? Why do some people suffer from psychological problems? How can they be helped? To answer such questions, psychologists have created a dazzling array of

Behavioral genetics The study of inherited behavioral traits and tendencies.

Personality type A style of personality defined by a group of related traits.

Introvert A person whose attention is focused inward; a shy, reserved, self-centered person.

Extrovert A person whose attention is directed outward; a bold, outgoing person.

Self-concept A person's perception of his or her own personality traits.

Self-esteem Regarding oneself as a worthwhile person; a positive evaluation of oneself.

HUMAN DIVERSITY

Self-Esteem and Culture–Hotshot or Team Player?

You and some friends are playing soccer. Your team wins, in part because you make some good plays. After the game, you bask in the glow of having performed well. You don't want to brag about being a hotshot, but your self-esteem gets a boost from your personal success.

In Japan, Shinobu and some of his friends are playing soccer. His team wins, in part because he makes some good plays. After the game Shinobu is happy because his team did well. However, Shinobu also dwells on the ways in which he let his team down. He thinks about how he could improve, and he resolves to be a better team player.

These sketches illustrate a basic difference in Eastern and Western psychology. In individualistic cultures such as the United States, self-esteem is based on personal success and outstanding performance (Lay & Verkuyten, 1999). For us, the path to higher self-esteem lies in self-enhancement. We are pumped up by our successes and tend to downplay our faults and failures (Ross et al., 2005).

Japanese and other Asian cultures place a greater emphasis on collectivism, or interdependence among people. For them, self-esteem is based on a secure sense of belonging to social groups. As a result, people in Asian cultures are more apt to engage in self-criticism (Ross et al., 2005). By correcting personal faults, they add to the well-being of the group (Kitayama, Markus, & Kurokawa, 2000). And when the *group* succeeds, individual members feel better about themselves, which raises their self-esteem.

Perhaps self-esteem is still based on success in both Eastern and Western cultures. However, it is fascinating that cultures define success in such different ways (Schmitt & Allik, 2005). The North American emphasis on winning is not the only way to feel good about yourself.

---

theories. A **personality theory** is a system of concepts, assumptions, ideas, and principles proposed to explain personality (● Fig. 10.2). In this chapter, we can only explore a few of the many personality theories. These are the four major perspectives we will consider:

1. **Trait theories** attempt to learn what traits make up personality and how they relate to actual behavior.

2. **Psychodynamic theories** focus on the inner workings of personality, especially internal conflicts and struggles.

3. **Behavioristic and social learning theories** place importance on the external environment and on the effects of conditioning and learning. Social learning theories attribute differences in personality to socialization, expectations, and mental processes.

4. **Humanistic theories** stress private, subjective experience, and personal growth.

Which personality theory is right? To date, each theory has added to our understanding by providing a sort of lens through which human behavior can be viewed. Nevertheless, theories can't be fully proved or disproved. We can only ask, Does the evidence tend to support this theory or disconfirm it? Yet, although theories are neither true nor false, their implications or predictions may be. The best way to judge a theory, then, is in terms of its *usefulness.* Does the theory adequately explain behavior? Does it stimulate new research? Does it suggest how to treat psychological disorders? Each theory has fared differently in these areas (Pervin, Cervone, & John, 2005). ■ Table 10.1 provides an overview of the four principal approaches to personality. In the final analysis, the challenge now facing

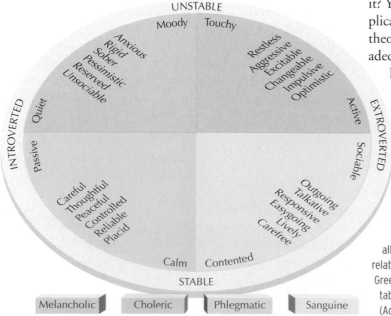

● **FIGURE 10.2** English psychologist Hans Eysenck (1916–1997) believed that many personality traits are related to whether you are mainly introverted or extroverted and whether you tend to be emotionally stable or unstable (highly emotional). These characteristics, in turn, are related to four basic types of temperament first recognized by the early Greeks. The types are: *melancholic* (sad, gloomy), *choleric* (hot-tempered, irritable), *phlegmatic* (sluggish, calm), and *sanguine* (cheerful, hopeful). (Adapted from Eysenck, 1981.)

■ **TABLE 10.1** Comparison of Personality Theories

	TRAIT THEORIES	PSYCHOANALYTIC THEORY	BEHAVIORISTIC AND SOCIAL LEARNING THEORIES	HUMANISTIC THEORY
View of human nature	Neutral	Negative	Neutral	Positive
Is behavior free or determined?	Determined	Determined	Determined	Free choice
Principal motives	Depends on one's traits	Sex and aggression	Drives of all kinds	Self-actualization
Personality structure	Traits	Id, ego, superego	Habits, expectancies	Self
Role of unconscious	Minimized	Maximized	Practically nonexistent	Minimized
Conception of conscience	Traits of honesty, etc.	Superego	Self-reinforcement, punishment history	Ideal self, valuing process
Developmental emphasis	Combined effects of heredity and environment	Psychosexual stages	Critical learning situations, identification, and imitation	Development of self-image
Barriers to personal growth	Unhealthy traits	Unconscious conflicts, fixations	Maladaptive habits, unhealthy environment	Conditions of worth, incongruence

personality theorists is how to integrate the four major perspectives into a unified, systematic explanation of personality (Mayer, 2005; McAdams & Pals, 2006). With these broad perspectives in mind, let's take a deeper look at personality.

MODULE 10.1 Summary

How do psychologists use the term personality? *What core concepts make up the psychology of personality?*

- *Personality* refers to a person's unique pattern of thinking, emotion, and behavior.
- Character is personality evaluated, or the possession of desirable qualities.
- *Temperament* refers to the hereditary aspects of one's emotional nature.

- Traits are lasting personal qualities that are inferred from behavior.
- Behavioral genetics and studies of identical twins show that heredity contributes significantly to personality traits.
- Personality types group people into categories on the basis of shared traits.
- Behavior is influenced by self-concept and self-esteem.
- Personality theories combine interrelated assumptions, ideas, and principles to explain personality.
- Four main types of personality theories are trait, psychodynamic, behavioristic and social learning, and humanistic.

Personality theory A system of concepts, assumptions, ideas, and principles used to understand and explain personality.

KNOWLEDGE BUILDER

Overview of Personality

Recite

1. When someone's personality has been evaluated, we are making a judgment about his or her

   a. temperament

   b. character

   c. extroversion

   d. self-esteem

2. A personality type is usually defined by the presence of

   a. all five personality dimensions

   b. a stable self-concept

   c. several specific traits

   d. a source trait

3. The research methods of _____ have been used to study the extent to which we inherit personality characteristics.

   a. behavioral genetics

   b. social learning theory

   c. factor analysis

   d. trait profiling

4. Heredity is more important than environment in shaping personality. T or F?

5. Our self-concept affects our behavior and _____.

   a. temperament

   b. extraversion

   c. personality type

   d. personal adjustment

Reflect
Critical Thinking

6. In what way would memory contribute to the formation of an accurate or inaccurate self-image?

Relate

See if you can define or describe the following terms in your own words: personality, character, temperament, trait, type, self-concept, self-esteem.

Meet with another student in your psychology class to explore your similarities. Did you find any similarities as surprising as those shared by the "Jim Twins"?

Link

Internet addresses frequently change. To find the sites listed here, visit **http://www .thomsonedu.com/psychology/coon** for an updated list of Internet addresses and direct links to relevant sites.

- **Personality Theories** Explore an electronic textbook about personality theories.

- **The Personality Project** Access a wide variety of information on personality.

- **Personality: Theory & Perspectives** An undergraduate psychology course about individual differences.

ANSWERS

1. b 2. c 3. a 4. F 5. D. 6. As discussed in Chapter 7, memory is highly selective, and long-term memories are often distorted by recent information. Such properties add to the moldability of self-concept.

10.2 Trait Theories

THE DOMINANT APPROACH to the study of personality is currently the trait approach. Trait theories seek to describe personality in terms of a small number of underlying personality traits or factors. Of the various trait theories, The Big Five is currently the most influential. According to this theory, all personalities can be described as varying along five key factors: *extroversion, agreeableness, conscientiousness, neuroticism,* and *openness to experience* (Costa & McCrae, 2006).

The Trait Approach—Describe Yourself in 18,000 Words or Less

SURVEY QUESTION: *Are some personality traits more basic or important than others?*

How many words can you think of to describe the personality of a close friend? Your list might be long: More than 18,000 English words refer to personal characteristics. As we have noted, traits are stable qualities that a person shows in most situations (Matthews, Deary, & Whiteman, 2003). For example, if you are usually friendly, optimistic, and cautious, these qualities are traits of your personality.

What if I am also sometimes shy, pessimistic, or uninhibited? The original three qualities are still traits as long as they are most *typical* of your behavior. Let's say our friend Annette approaches most situations with optimism but tends to expect the worst each time she applies for a job. If her pessimism is limited to this situation or just a few others, it is still accurate and useful to describe her as an optimistic person.

Predicting Behavior

As we have noted, separating people into broad types, such as "introvert" or "extrovert," may oversimplify personality. However, introversion/extroversion can also be thought of as a trait. Knowing how you rate on this single dimension would allow us to predict how you will behave in a variety of settings. Where, for example, do you prefer to meet people, face-to-face or through the Internet? Researchers have found that students high in the trait of introversion are more likely to prefer the Internet because they find it easier to talk with people online (Koch & Pratarelli, 2004). (Other interesting links exist between traits and behavior. See "What's Your Musical Personality?")

Describing People

In general, psychologists try to identify traits that best describe a person. Take a moment to check the traits in ■ Table 10.2 that describe your personality. Are the traits you checked

of equal importance? Are some stronger or more basic than others? Do any overlap? For example, if you checked "dominant," did you also check "confident" and "bold"? Answers to these questions would interest a trait theorist. To better understand personality, **trait theorists** attempt to analyze, classify, and interrelate traits.

Classifying Traits

Are there different types of traits? Yes, psychologist Gordon Allport (1961) identified several kinds. **Common traits** are characteristics shared by most members of a culture. Common traits tell us how people from a particular nation or culture are similar or which traits a culture emphasizes. In America, for example, competitiveness is a fairly common trait. Among the Hopi of Northern Arizona, however, it is relatively rare.

Of course, common traits don't tell us much about individuals. Although many people are competitive in American culture, various people you know may rate high, medium, or low in this trait. Usually we are also interested in **individual traits,** which describe a person's unique qualities.

■ TABLE 10.2 Adjective Checklist			
Check the traits you feel are characteristic of your personality. Are some more basic than others?			
aggressive	organized	ambitious	clever
confident	loyal	generous	calm
warm	bold	cautious	reliable
sensitive	mature	talented	jealous
sociable	honest	funny	religious
dominant	dull	accurate	nervous
humble	uninhibited	visionary	cheerful
thoughtful	serious	helpful	emotional
orderly	anxious	conforming	good-natured
liberal	curious	optimistic	kind
meek	neighborly	passionate	compulsive

Trait theorist A psychologist interested in classifying, analyzing, and interrelating traits to understand personality.

Common traits Personality traits that are shared by most members of a particular culture.

Individual traits Personality traits that define a person's unique individual qualities.

DISCOVERING PSYCHOLOGY

What's Your Musical Personality?

Even if you like all kinds of music, you probably prefer some styles to others. Of the styles listed here, which three do you enjoy the most? (Circle your choices.)

blues jazz classical folk rock alternative heavy metal country sound track religious pop rap/hip-hop soul/funk electronic/dance

In one study, Peter Rentfrow and Samuel Gosling found that the types of music people prefer tend to be associated with their personality characteristics. See if your musical tastes match their findings (Rentfrow & Gosling, 2003).

People who value aesthetic experiences, have good verbal abilities, and are liberal and tolerant of others tend to like music that is reflective and complex (blues, jazz, classical, and folk music).

People who are curious about new experiences, enjoy taking risks, and are physically active prefer intense, rebellious music (rock, alternative, and heavy metal music).

People who are cheerful, conventional, extroverted, reliable, helpful, and conservative tend to enjoy upbeat conventional music (country, sound track, religious, and pop music).

People who are talkative, full of energy, forgiving, and physically attractive and who reject conservative ideals tend to prefer energetic, rhythmic music (rap/hip-hop, soul/funk, and electronic/dance music).

Unmistakably, personality traits affect our everyday behavior.

Here's an analogy to help you separate common traits from individual traits: If you decide to buy a pet dog, you will want to know the general characteristics of the dog's breed (its common traits). In addition, you will want to know about the "personality" of a specific dog (its individual traits) before you decide to take it home.

Allport also made distinctions between *cardinal traits, central traits,* and *secondary traits.* **Cardinal traits** are so basic that all of a person's activities can be traced to the trait. For instance, compassion was an overriding trait of Mother Teresa's personality. Likewise, Abraham Lincoln's personality was dominated by the cardinal trait of honesty. According to Allport, few people have cardinal traits.

Central Traits

How do central and secondary traits differ from cardinal traits? **Central traits** are the basic building blocks of personality. A surprisingly small number of central traits can capture the essence of a person. For instance, just six traits would provide a good description of Annette's personality: dominant, sociable, honest, cheerful, intelligent, and optimistic. When college students were asked to describe someone they knew well, they mentioned an average of seven central traits (Allport, 1961).

Secondary traits are more superficial personal qualities, such as food preferences, attitudes, political opinions, musical tastes, and so forth. In Allport's terms, a personality description might therefore include the following items:

Name: Jane Doe

Age: 22

Cardinal traits: None

Central traits: Possessive, autonomous, artistic, dramatic, self-centered, trusting

Secondary traits: Prefers colorful clothes, likes to work alone, politically liberal, always late

Source Traits

How can you tell if a personality trait is central or secondary? Raymond B. Cattell (1906–1998) tried to answer this question by directly studying the traits of a large number of people. Cattell began by measuring visible features of personality, which he called **surface traits.** Soon, Cattell noticed that these surface traits often appeared together in groups. In fact, some traits appeared together so often that they seemed to represent a single, more basic trait. Cattell called these deeper characteristics, or dimensions, **source traits** (Cattell, 1965). They are the core of each individual's personality.

How do source traits differ from Allport's central traits? Allport classified traits subjectively, and it's possible that he was wrong at times. Cattell used *factor analysis* to look for connections among traits. **Factor analysis** is a statistical technique used to correlate multiple measurements and identify general underlying factors. For example, he found that imaginative people are almost always *inventive, original, curious, creative, innovative,* and *ingenious.* Thus, *imaginative* is a source trait. If you are an imaginative person, we automatically know that you have several other traits, too.

Cattell identified 16 source traits. According to him, all 16 are needed to fully describe a personality. Source traits are measured by a test called the *Sixteen Personality Factor Questionnaire* (often referred to as the 16 PF). Like many personality tests, the 16 PF can be used to produce a **trait profile,** or graph of a person's score on each trait. Trait profiles draw a "picture" of individual personalities, which makes it easier to compare them (● Fig. 10.3).

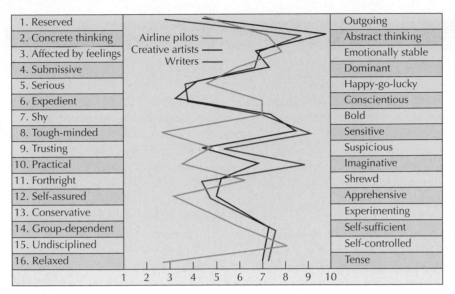

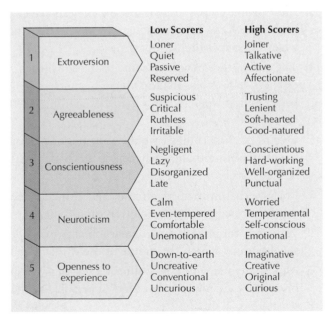

	1. Reserved	Outgoing
	2. Concrete thinking	Abstract thinking
	3. Affected by feelings	Emotionally stable
	4. Submissive	Dominant
	5. Serious	Happy-go-lucky
	6. Expedient	Conscientious
	7. Shy	Bold
	8. Tough-minded	Sensitive
	9. Trusting	Suspicious
	10. Practical	Imaginative
	11. Forthright	Shrewd
	12. Self-assured	Apprehensive
	13. Conservative	Experimenting
	14. Group-dependent	Self-sufficient
	15. Undisciplined	Self-controlled
	16. Relaxed	Tense

Airline pilots ——
Creative artists ——
Writers ——

1 2 3 4 5 6 7 8 9 10

● **FIGURE 10.3**   The 16 source traits measured by Cattell's 16 PF are listed beside the graph. Scores can be plotted as a profile for an individual or a group. The profiles shown here are group averages for airline pilots, creative artists, and writers. Notice the similarity between artists and writers and the difference between these two groups and pilots. (Cattell, R. B., "Personality Pinned Down," 1973. Reprinted by permission of Dr. R. B. Cattell.)

		Low Scorers	High Scorers
1	Extroversion	Loner Quiet Passive Reserved	Joiner Talkative Active Affectionate
2	Agreeableness	Suspicious Critical Ruthless Irritable	Trusting Lenient Soft-hearted Good-natured
3	Conscientiousness	Negligent Lazy Disorganized Late	Conscientious Hard-working Well-organized Punctual
4	Neuroticism	Calm Even-tempered Comfortable Unemotional	Worried Temperamental Self-conscious Emotional
5	Openness to experience	Down-to-earth Uncreative Conventional Uncurious	Imaginative Creative Original Curious

● **FIGURE 10.4**   The Big Five. According to the five-factor model, basic differences in personality can be "boiled down" to the dimensions shown here. The five-factor model answers these essential questions about a person: Is she or he extroverted or introverted? Agreeable or difficult? Conscientious or irresponsible? Emotionally stable or unstable? Smart or unintelligent? These questions cover a large measure of what we might want to know about someone's personality. (Trait descriptions adapted from McCrae & Costa, 2001.)

The Big Five

Noel is outgoing and friendly, conscientious, even-tempered, and curious. His brother Joel is reserved, hostile, irresponsible, temperamental, and disinterested in ideas. You will be spending a week in a space capsule with either Noel or Joel. Who would you choose? If the answer seems obvious, it's because Noel and Joel were described with the **five-factor model,** a system that identifies the five most basic dimensions of personality.

The "Big Five" factors listed in ● Figure 10.4 attempt to further reduce Cattell's 16 factors to just five universal dimensions, or source traits (Costa & McCrae, 2006). The Big Five may be the best answer of all to the question, What is the essence of human personality (McCrae & Terracciano, 2005)?

Five Key Dimensions   If you would like to compare the personalities of two people, try rating them informally on the five dimensions shown in Figure 10.4. For factor 1, *extroversion,* rate how introverted or extroverted each person is. Factor 2, *agreeableness,* refers to how friendly, nurturant, and caring a person is, as opposed to cold, indifferent, self-centered, or spiteful. A person who is *conscientious* (factor 3) is self-disciplined, responsible, and achieving. People low on this factor are irresponsible, careless, and undependable. Factor 4, *neuroticism,* refers to negative, upsetting emotions. People who are high in neuroticism tend to be anxious, emotionally "sour," irritable, and unhappy. Finally, people who rate high on factor 5, *openness to experience,* are intelligent and open to new ideas (McCrae & Costa, 2001).

The beauty of the Big-Five model is that almost any trait you can name will be related to one of the five factors. If you were selecting a college roommate, hiring an employee, or answering a singles ad, you would probably like to know all

Cardinal trait   A personality trait so basic that all of a person's activities relate to it.

Central traits   The core traits that characterize an individual personality.

Secondary traits   Traits that are inconsistent or relatively superficial.

Surface traits   The visible or observable traits of one's personality.

Source traits   Basic underlying traits, or dimensions, of personality; each source trait is reflected in a number of surface traits.

Factor analysis   A statistical technique used to correlate multiple measurements and identify general underlying factors.

Trait profile   A graph of the scores obtained on several personality traits.

Five-factor model   Proposes that there are five universal dimensions of personality.

THE CLINICAL FILE

Perfectly Miserable

Up to a point, conscientiousness is associated with high achievement. However, having impossibly high standards, a trait called perfectionism, can be a problem. As you might expect, college students who are perfectionists tend to get good grades. Yet some students cross the line into maladaptive perfectionism, which typically *lowers* performance at school and elsewhere (Accordino, Accordino, & Slaney, 2000).

People who suffer from unhealthy perfectionism set unattainably high standards for themselves. This causes them to feel as if they are always failing. Perfectionistic students are self-critical, terrified of making mistakes, and often seriously depressed (Grzegorek et al., 2004; Sumi & Kanda, 2002).

For many students, maladaptive perfectionism begins with harsh, perfectionistic parenting. There's nothing wrong with having parents who expect a lot of you–if they are also emotionally supportive. However, parents who are demanding and highly critical may leave a student feeling that nothing she or he does is ever quite good enough. As already noted, this is a recipe for self-doubt and depression.

Authentic Navajo rugs always have a flaw in their intricate designs. Navajo weavers intentionally make a "mistake" in each rug as a reminder that humans are not perfect. There is a lesson in this: It is not always necessary, or even desirable, to be "perfect." To learn from your experiences you must feel free to make mistakes (Castro & Rice, 2003). Success, in the long run, is more often based on seeking "excellence," rather than "perfection" (Enns, Cox, & Clara, 2005).

---

the personal dimensions covered by the Big Five. Such traits predict how people will act in various circumstances. For example, people who score high in conscientiousness tend to perform well at work, do well in school, and rarely have automobile accidents (Arthur & Doverspike, 2001; Barrick, Moun, & Judge, 2001; Chamorro-Premuzic & Furnham, 2003). They even live longer (Martin, Friedman, & Schwartz, 2007). (Is it possible to be too conscientious? See "Perfectly Miserable" for an answer.)

Before you read the next section, take a moment to answer the questions that follow. Doing so will add to your understanding of a long-running controversy in the psychology of personality.

Knowing where a person stands on the "Big Five" personality factors helps predict his or her behavior. For example, people who score high on conscientiousness tend to be safe drivers who are unlikely to have automobile accidents (Arthur & Doverspike, 2001).

Tony Freeman/PhotoEdit

Rate Yourself: How Do You View Personality?

1. My friends' actions are fairly consistent from day to day and in different situations. T or F?

2. Whether a person is honest or dishonest, kind or cruel, a hero or a coward depends mainly on circumstances. T or F?

3. Most people I have known for several years have pretty much the same personalities now as they did when I first met them. T or F?

4. The reason that people in some professions (such as teachers, lawyers, or doctors) seem so much alike is because their work requires that they act in particular ways. T or F?

5. One of the first things I would want to know about a potential roommate is what the person's personality is like. T or F?

6. I believe that immediate circumstances usually determine how people act at any given time. T or F?

7. To be comfortable in a particular job, a person's personality must match the nature of the work. T or F?

8. Almost anyone would be polite at a wedding reception; it doesn't matter what kind of personality the person has. T or F?

Now count the number of times you marked true for the odd-numbered items. Do the same for the even-numbered items.

If you agreed with most of the odd-numbered items, you tend to view behavior as strongly influenced by personality traits or lasting personal dispositions.

If you agreed with most of the even-numbered items, you view behavior as strongly influenced by external situations and circumstances.

What if I answered true about equally for odd and even items? Then you place equal weight on traits and situations as ways to explain behavior. This is the view now held by many personality psychologists (Funder, 2006; Mischel & Shoda, 1998).

Traits, Consistency, and Situations

Does that mean that to predict how a person will act, it is better to focus on both personality traits and external circumstances? Yes, it's best to take both into account. Personality traits are quite consistent. Also, they can predict such things as job performance, dangerous driving, or a successful marriage (Funder, 2006). Yet, *situations* also greatly influence our behavior. For instance, it would be unusual for you to dance at a movie or read a book at a football game. Likewise, few people sleep in roller coasters or tell off-color jokes at funerals. However, your personality traits may predict whether you choose to read a book, go to a movie, or attend a football game in the first place. Typically, traits *interact* with situations to determine how we will act (Mischel, 2004).

In a **trait-situation interaction,** external circumstances influence the expression of a personality trait. For instance, imagine what would happen if you moved from a church to a classroom to a party to a football game. As the setting changed, you would probably become louder and more boisterous. This change would show situational effects on behavior. At the same time, your personality traits would also be apparent: If you were quieter than average in church and class, you would probably be quieter than average in the other settings, too.

MODULE 10.2 Summary

Are some personality traits more basic or important than others?

- Trait theories identify lasting and consistent personal characteristics.
- Allport made distinctions between common traits and individual traits and among cardinal, central, and secondary traits.
- Cattell's theory attributes visible surface traits to the existence of 16 underlying source traits.
- The five-factor model identifies the following five universal dimensions of personality: extroversion, agreeableness, conscientiousness, neuroticism, and openness to experience.
- Traits and situations interact to determine how we behave.

Trait-situation interaction The influence that external settings or circumstances have on the expression of personality traits.

KNOWLEDGE BUILDER

Trait Theories

Recite

1. A trait can be used to describe someone's personality if that trait is _____ descriptive of his or her behavior.

   a. always

   b. typically

   c. occasionally

   d. rarely

2. Central traits are those shared by most members of a culture. T or F?

3. Cattell believes that clusters of _____ traits reveal the presence of underlying _____ traits.

4. Which of the following is *not* one of the Big Five personality factors?

   a. submissiveness

   b. agreeableness

   c. extroversion

   d. neuroticism

5. Conscientious people tend to be perfectionists. T or F?

6. To understand personality, it is wise to remember that traits and situations _____ to determine our behavior.

Reflect
Critical Thinking

7. Are situations equally powerful in their impact on behavior?

Relate

List six or seven traits that best describe your personality. Which system of traits seems to best match your list, Allport's, Cattell's, or the Big Five?

Choose a prominent trait from your list. Does its expression seem to be influenced by specific situations? Do you think that heredity contributed to the trait?

Link

Internet addresses frequently change. To find the sites listed here, visit **http://www.thomsonedu.com/psychology/coon** for an updated list of Internet addresses and direct links to relevant sites.

- **Raymond Cattell** Read about Raymond Cattell and his Sixteen Personality Factor Questionnaire.
- **Internet Personality Inventory** Test yourself on the Big Five.
- **The Big Five Dimensions** Provides additional information about the Big Five, with links to related sites.

ANSWERS

1. a or b 2. F 3. surface, source 4. a 5. interact 6. F 7. No. Circumstances can have a strong or weak influence. In some situations, almost everyone will act the same, no matter what their personality traits may be. In other situations, traits may be of greater importance.

10.3 Psychoanalytic Theory

PSYCHODYNAMIC THEORISTS are not content with studying traits. Instead, they try to probe under the surface of personality–to learn what drives, conflicts, and energies animate us. Psychodynamic theorists believe that many of our actions are based on hidden, or unconscious, thoughts, needs, and emotions.

Psychoanalytic Theory— Id Came to Me in a Dream

SURVEY QUESTION: *How do psychodynamic theories explain personality?*

Psychoanalytic theory, the best-known psychodynamic approach, grew out of the work of Sigmund Freud, a Viennese physician. As a doctor, Freud was fascinated by patients whose problems seemed to be more emotional than physical. From about 1890 until he died in 1939, Freud evolved a theory of personality that deeply influenced modern thought

(Jacobs, 2003). Let's consider some of its main features (Schultz & Schultz, 2005).

The Structure of Personality

How did Freud view personality? Freud's model portrays personality as a dynamic system directed by three mental structures, the **id,** the **ego,** and the **superego.** According to Freud, most behavior involves activity of all three systems. (Freud's theory includes a large number of concepts. For your convenience, they are defined in ■ Table 10.3 rather than in glossary boxes.)

The Id The id is made up of innate biological instincts and urges. It is self-serving, irrational, impulsive, and totally unconscious. The id operates on the **pleasure principle.** That is, it seeks to freely express pleasure-seeking urges of all kinds.

Psychoanalytic theory Freudian theory of personality that emphasizes unconscious forces and conflicts.

■ TABLE 10.3 Key Freudian Concepts

Anal stage The psychosexual stage corresponding roughly to the period of toilet training (ages 1 to 3).

Anal-expulsive personality A disorderly, destructive, cruel, or messy person.

Anal-retentive personality A person who is obstinate, stingy, or compulsive and who generally has difficulty "letting go."

Conscience The part of the superego that causes guilt when its standards are not met.

Conscious The region of the mind that includes all mental contents a person is aware of at any given moment.

Ego The executive part of personality that directs rational behavior.

Ego ideal The part of the superego representing ideal behavior; a source of pride when its standards are met.

Electra conflict A girl's sexual attraction to her father and feelings of rivalry with her mother.

Erogenous zone Any body area that produces pleasurable sensations.

Eros Freud's name for the "life instincts."

Fixation A lasting conflict developed as a result of frustration or overindulgence.

Genital stage Period of full psychosexual development, marked by the attainment of mature adult sexuality.

Id The primitive part of personality that remains unconscious, supplies energy, and demands pleasure.

Latency According to Freud, a period in childhood when psychosexual development is more or less interrupted.

Libido In Freudian theory, the force, primarily pleasure oriented, that energizes the personality.

Moral anxiety Apprehension felt when thoughts, impulses, or actions conflict with the superego's standards.

Neurotic anxiety Apprehension felt when the ego struggles to control id impulses.

Oedipus conflict A boy's sexual attraction to his mother and feelings of rivalry with his father.

Oral stage The period when infants are preoccupied with the mouth as a source of pleasure and means of expression.

Oral-aggressive personality A person who uses the mouth to express hostility by shouting, cursing, biting, and so forth. Also, one who actively exploits others.

Oral-dependent personality A person who wants to passively receive attention, gifts, love, and so forth.

Phallic personality A person who is vain, exhibitionistic, sensitive, and narcissistic.

Phallic stage The psychosexual stage (roughly ages 3 to 6) when a child is preoccupied with the genitals.

Pleasure principle A desire for immediate satisfaction of wishes, desires, or needs.

Preconscious An area of the mind containing information that can be voluntarily brought to awareness.

Psyche The mind, mental life, and personality as a whole.

Psychosexual stages The oral, anal, phallic, and genital stages, during which various personality traits are formed.

Reality principle Delaying action (or pleasure) until it is appropriate.

Superego A judge or censor for thoughts and actions.

Thanatos The **death instinct** postulated by Freud.

Unconscious The region of the mind that is beyond awareness, especially impulses and desires not directly known to a person.

If we were solely under control of the id, the world would be chaotic beyond belief.

The id acts as a well of energy for the entire **psyche** (sigh-KEY), or personality. This energy, called **libido** (lih-BEE-doe), flows from the **life instincts** (or **Eros**). According to Freud, libido underlies our efforts to survive, as well as our sexual desires and pleasure seeking. Freud also described a **death instinct. Thanatos,** as he called it, produces aggressive and destructive urges. Freud offered humanity's long history of wars and violence as evidence of such urges. Most id energies, then, are aimed at discharging tensions related to sex and aggression.

The Ego The ego is sometimes described as the "executive," because it directs energies supplied by the id. The id is like a blind king or queen whose power is awesome but who must rely on others to carry out orders. The id can only form mental images of things it desires. The ego wins power to direct behavior by relating the desires of the id to external reality.

Are there other differences between the ego and the id? Yes. Recall that the id operates on the pleasure principle. The ego, in contrast, is guided by the **reality principle.** The ego is the system of thinking, planning, problem solving, and deciding. It is in conscious control of the personality and often delays action until it is practical or appropriate.

The Superego *What is the role of the superego?* The superego acts as a judge or censor for the thoughts and actions of the

Freud considered personality an expression of two conflicting forces: life instincts and the death instinct. Both are symbolized in this drawing by Allan Gilbert. (If you don't immediately see the death symbolism, stand farther from the drawing.)

ego. One part of the superego, called the **conscience,** reflects actions for which a person has been punished. When standards of the conscience are not met, you are punished internally by *guilt* feelings.

A second part of the superego is the **ego ideal.** The ego ideal reflects all behavior one's parents approved of or rewarded. The ego ideal is a source of goals and aspirations. When its standards are met, we feel *pride.*

The superego acts as an "internalized parent" to bring behavior under control. In Freudian terms, a person with a weak superego will be a delinquent, criminal, or antisocial personality. In contrast, an overly strict or harsh superego may cause inhibition, rigidity, or unbearable guilt.

The Dynamics of Personality

How do the id, ego, and superego interact? Freud didn't picture the id, ego, and superego as parts of the brain or as "little people" running the human psyche. Instead, they are conflicting mental processes. Freud theorized a delicate balance of power among the three. For example, the id's demands for immediate pleasure often clash with the superego's moral restrictions. Perhaps an example will help clarify the role of each part of the personality.

FREUD IN A NUTSHELL
Let's say you are sexually attracted to an acquaintance. The id clamors for immediate satisfaction of its sexual desires but is opposed by the superego (which finds the very thought of sex shocking). The id says, "Go for it!" The superego icily replies, "Never even think that again!" And what does the ego say? The ego says, "I have a plan!"

Of course, this is a drastic simplification, but it does capture the core of Freudian thinking. To reduce tension, the ego could begin actions leading to friendship, romance,

courtship, and marriage. If the id is unusually powerful, the ego may give in and attempt a seduction. If the superego prevails, the ego may be forced to *displace* or *sublimate* sexual energies to other activities (sports, music, dancing, push-ups, cold showers). According to Freud, internal struggles and rechanneled energies typify most personality functioning.

Is the ego always caught in the middle? Basically yes, and the pressures on it can be intense. In addition to meeting the conflicting demands of the id and superego, the overworked ego must deal with external reality.

According to Freud, you feel anxiety when your ego is threatened or overwhelmed. Impulses from the id cause **neurotic anxiety** when the ego can barely keep them under control. Threats of punishment from the superego cause **moral anxiety.** Each person develops habitual ways of calming these anxieties, and many resort to using *ego-defense mechanisms* to lessen internal conflicts. Defense mechanisms are mental processes that deny, distort, or otherwise block out sources of threat and anxiety. (The ego defense mechanisms that Freud identified are used as a form of protection against stress, anxiety, and threatening events. See Module 11.3.)

Levels of Awareness Like other psychodynamic theorists, Freud believed that our behavior often expresses unconscious (or hidden) forces. The **unconscious** holds repressed memories and emotions, plus the instinctual drives of the id. Interestingly, modern scientists have found that the brain's limbic system does, in fact, seem to trigger unconscious emotions and memories (LeDoux, 1996).

Even though they are beyond awareness, unconscious thoughts, feelings, or urges may slip into behavior in disguised or symbolic form. For example, if you meet someone you would like to know better, you may unconsciously leave a book or a jacket at that person's house to ensure another meeting.

Are the actions of the ego and superego also unconscious, like the id? At times, yes, but they also operate on two other levels of awareness (● Fig. 10.5). The **conscious** level includes everything you are aware of at a given moment, including thoughts, perceptions, feelings, and memories. The **preconscious** contains material that can be easily brought to awareness. If you stop to think about a time when you felt angry or rejected, you will be moving this memory from the preconscious to the conscious level of awareness.

The superego's activities also reveal differing levels of awareness. At times we consciously try to live up to moral codes or standards. Yet, at other times a person may feel guilty without knowing why. Psychoanalytic theory credits such guilt to unconscious workings of the superego. Indeed, Freud believed that the unconscious origins of many feelings cannot be easily brought to awareness.

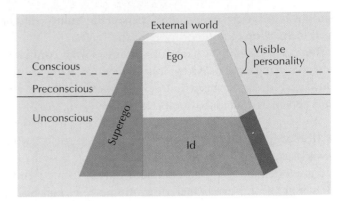

● **FIGURE 10.5** The approximate relationship between the id, ego, and super-ego, and the levels of awareness.

Personality Development

How does psychoanalytic theory explain personality development? Freud theorized that the core of personality is formed before age 6 in a series of **psychosexual stages.** Freud believed that erotic urges in childhood have lasting effects on development. As you might expect, this is a controversial idea. However, Freud used the terms *sex* and *erotic* very broadly to refer to many physical sources of pleasure.

A Freudian Fable? Freud identified four psychosexual stages, the **oral, anal, phallic,** and **genital.** (He also described a period of "latency" between the phallic and genital stages. Latency is explained in a moment.) At each stage, a different part of the body becomes a child's primary **erogenous zone** (an area capable of producing pleasure). Each area then serves as the main source of pleasure, frustration, and self-expression.

Was Freud's ever-present cigar a sign of an oral fixation? Was it a phallic symbol? Was it both? Or was it neither? An inability to say for sure is one of the shortcomings of psychoanalytic theory.

Freud believed that many adult personality traits can be traced to **fixations** in one or more of the stages.

What is a fixation? A fixation is an unresolved conflict or emotional hang-up caused by overindulgence or by frustration. As we describe the psychosexual stages you'll see why Freud considered fixations important.

The Oral Stage

During the first year of life, most of an infant's pleasure comes from stimulation of the mouth. If a child is overfed or frustrated, oral traits may be created. Adult expressions of oral needs include gum chewing, nail biting, smoking, kissing, overeating, and alcoholism.

What if there is an oral fixation? Fixation early in the oral stage produces an **oral-dependent** personality. Oral-dependent persons are gullible (they swallow things easily!) and passive and need lots of attention (they want to be mothered and showered with gifts). Frustrations later in the oral stage may cause aggression, often in the form of biting. Fixations here create cynical, **oral-aggressive** adults who exploit others. They also like to argue. ("Biting sarcasm" is their forte!)

The Anal Stage

Between the ages of 1 and 3, the child's attention shifts to the process of elimination. When parents attempt toilet training, the child can gain approval or express rebellion or aggression by "holding on" or by "letting go." Therefore, harsh or lenient toilet training can cause an anal fixation that may lock such responses into personality. Freud described the **anal-retentive** (holding-on) personality as obstinate, stingy, orderly, and compulsively clean. The **anal-expulsive** (letting-go) personality is disorderly, destructive, cruel, or messy.

The Phallic Stage

Adult traits of the **phallic personality** are vanity, exhibitionism, sensitive pride, and narcissism (self-love). Freud theorized that phallic fixations develop between the ages of 3 and 6. At this time, increased sexual interest causes the child to be physically attracted to the parent of the opposite sex. In males this attraction leads to an **Oedipus conflict.** In it, the boy feels a rivalry with his father for the affection of his mother. Freud believed that the male child feels threatened by the father (specifically, the boy fears castration). To ease his anxieties, the boy must *identify* with the father. Their rivalry ends when the boy seeks to become more like his father. As he does, he begins to accept the father's values and forms a conscience.

What about the female child? Girls experience an **Electra conflict.** In this case, the girl loves her father and competes with her mother. However, according to Freud, the girl identifies with the mother more gradually.

Freud believed that females already feel castrated. Because of this, they are less driven to identify with their mothers than boys are with their fathers. This, he said, is less effec-tive in creating a conscience. This particular part of Freudian thought has been thoroughly (and rightfully) rejected by modern experts in the psychology of women. It is probably best understood as a reflection of the male-dominated times in which Freud lived.

Latency

According to Freud there is a period of **latency** from age 6 to puberty. Latency is not actually a stage. Rather, it is a quiet time during which psychosexual development is dormant. Freud's belief that psychosexual development is "on hold" at this time is hard to accept. Nevertheless, Freud saw latency as a relatively quiet time compared with the stormy first 6 years of life.

The Genital Stage

At puberty an upswing in sexual energies activates all the unresolved conflicts of earlier years. This upsurge, according to Freud, is the reason why adolescence can be filled with emotion and turmoil. The genital stage begins at puberty. It is marked, during adolescence, by a growing capacity for responsible social-sexual relationships. The genital stage ends with a mature capacity for love and the realization of full adult sexuality.

Critical Comments

As bizarre as Freud's theory might seem, it has been influential for several reasons. First, it pioneered the idea that the first years of life help shape adult personality. Second, it identified feeding, toilet training, and early sexual experiences as critical events in personality formation. Third, Freud was among the first to propose that development proceeds through a series of stages. (Erik Erikson's psycho*social* stages, which cover development from birth to old age, are a modern offshoot of Freudian thinking. See Module 3.7.)

Is the Freudian view of development widely accepted? Few psychologists wholeheartedly embrace Freud's theory today. In some cases Freud was clearly wrong. His portrayal of the elementary school years (latency) as free from sexuality and unimportant for personality development is hard to believe. His idea of the role of a stern or threatening father in the development of a strong conscience in males has also been challenged. Studies show that a son is more likely to develop a strong conscience if his father is affectionate and accepting, rather than stern and punishing. Freud also overemphasized sexuality in personality development. Other motives and cognitive factors are of equal importance.

Freud has been criticized for his views of patients who believed they were sexually molested as children. Freud assumed that such events were merely childhood fantasies. This view led to a long-standing tendency to disbelieve children who have been molested and women who have been raped (Brannon, 1996).

Another important criticism is that Freud's concepts are almost impossible to verify scientifically. The theory provides numerous ways to explain almost any thought, action, or feeling *after* it has occurred. However, it leads to few predictions, which makes its claims difficult to test. Although more criticisms of Freud could be listed, the fact remains that there is an element of truth to much of what he said (Jacob, 2003). Because of this, some clinical psychologists continue to regard Freudian theory as a useful way to think about human problems.

MODULE **10.3** Summary

How do psychodynamic theories explain personality?

- Psychodynamic theories emphasize internal (and often unconscious) forces and mental activities.
- According to Sigmund Freud's psychoanalytic theory, personality consists of three mental systems: the id, the ego, and the superego.

- Libido, derived from the life instincts, is the primary source of energy within the personality.
- Internal conflicts may cause neurotic anxiety or moral anxiety and lead to the use of ego-defense mechanisms.
- Personal awareness operates on three levels: conscious, preconscious, and unconscious.
- According to Freud, personality development occurs in four psychosexual stages: oral, anal, phallic, and genital.
- Fixation at any stage of psychosexual development can leave a lasting imprint on adult personality.

KNOWLEDGE BUILDER

Psychoanalytic Theory

Recite

1. Freud stated that the mind functions on three levels: the conscious, the unconscious, and the
   a. psyche
   b. preconscious
   c. superego
   d. subconscious

2. List the three divisions of personality postulated by Freud. _____
   _____ _____

3. Which division is totally unconscious?
   _____

4. Which division is responsible for moral anxiety? _____

5. Freud proposed the existence of a life instinct known as Thanatos. T or F?

6. Freud's view of personality development is based on the concept of
   _____ stages.

7. Arrange these stages in the proper order: phallic, anal, genital, oral.
   _____

8. Freudian theory states that a person who is passive, dependent, and needs lots of attention has a fixation in the
   a. oral stage
   b. superego
   c. Oedipal stage
   d. genital stage

Reflect
Critical Thinking

9. Many adults would find it embarrassing or humiliating to drink from a baby bottle. Can you explain why?

Relate

Try to think of at least one time when your thoughts, feelings, or actions seemed to reflect the workings of each of the following: the id, the ego, and the superego.

Do you know anyone who seems to have oral, anal, or phallic personality traits? Do you think Freud's concept of fixation explains their characteristics?

Do any of your personal experiences support the existence of an Oedipus conflict or an Electra conflict? If not, is it possible that you have repressed feelings related to these conflicts?

Link

Internet addresses frequently change. To find the sites listed here, visit **http://www** **.thomsonedu.com/psychology/coon** for an updated list of Internet addresses and direct links to relevant sites.

- **Sigmund Freud and the Freud Archives** This site provides an extensive collection of links to Internet resources related to Sigmund Freud and his works. Included in this collection are libraries, museums, and biographical materials as well as materials in the Brill Library archives.

- **Freud & Women** Read about the controversy surrounding Freud's views on women.

- **Psychodynamic and Neo-Freudian Theories** Freud's followers did not always agree with his views. Read about their views on personality.

ANSWERS

1. b 2. id, ego, superego 3. id 4. superego 5. F 6. psychosexual 7. oral, anal, phallic, genital 8. a 9. A psychoanalytic theorist would say that it is because the bottle rekindles oral conflicts and feelings of vulnerability and dependence.

10.4 Behavioral and Social Learning Theories

UNLIKE PSYCHOANALYTIC THEORISTS, behavioral theorists explain personality through concepts such as learning, reinforcement, and imitation. Behavioral and social learning theories are based on scientific research, which makes them powerful ways of looking at personality.

Learning Theories of Personality— Habit I Seen You Before?

SURVEY QUESTION: *What do behaviorists and social learning theorists emphasize in personality?*

How do behaviorists approach personality? According to some critics, behaviorists approach personality as if people are robots like Data of *Star Trek* fame. Actually, the behaviorist position is not nearly that mechanistic, and its value is well established. Behaviorists have shown repeatedly that children can *learn* things like kindness, hostility, generosity, or destructiveness. What does this have to do with personality? Everything, according to the behavioral viewpoint.

Behavioral personality theories emphasize that personality is no more (or less) than a collection of learned behavior patterns. Personality, like other learned behavior, is acquired through classical and operant conditioning, observational learning, reinforcement, extinction, generalization, and discrimination. When Mother says, "It's not nice to make mud pies with Mommy's blender. If we want to grow up to be a

Freud believed that aggressive urges are "instinctual." In contrast, behavioral theories assume that personal characteristics such as aggressiveness are learned. Is this boy's aggression the result of observational learning, harsh punishment, or prior reinforcement?

big girl, we won't do it again, will we?" she serves as a model and in other ways shapes her daughter's personality.

Strict **learning theorists** reject the idea that personality is made up of traits. They would assert, for instance, that there is no such thing as a trait of "honesty" (Mischel, 2004).

Certainly some people are honest and others are not. How can honesty not be a trait? Learning theorists recognize that some people are honest *more often* than others. But knowing this does not allow us to predict whether a person will be honest in a specific situation. It would not be unusual, for example, to find that a person honored for returning a lost wallet had cheated on a test, bought a term paper, or broken the speed limit. If you were to ask a learning theorist, "Are you an honest person?" the reply might be, "In what situation?"

As you can see, learning theorists are interested in the **situational determinants** (external causes) of our actions. A good example of how situations can influence behavior is a study in which people were intentionally overpaid for doing an assigned task. Under normal circumstances, 80 percent kept the extra money without mentioning it. But as few as 17 percent were dishonest if the situation was altered. For instance, if people thought the money was coming out of the pocket of the person doing the study, far fewer were dishonest (Bersoff, 1999). Thus, situations always interact with our prior learning to activate behavior.

Situations vary greatly in their impact. Some are powerful. Others are trivial and have little effect on behavior. The more powerful the situation, the easier it is to see what is meant by *situational determinants.* For example, each of the following situations would undoubtedly have a strong influence on your behavior: an armed terrorist walks onto your bus; you accidentally sit on a lighted cigarette; you find your lover in bed with your best friend. Yet even these situations could provoke very different reactions from different personalities. That's why behavior is always a product of both prior learning and the situations in which we find ourselves (Mischel, Shoda, & Smith, 2004).

Ultimately, what is predictable about personality is that we respond in consistent ways to certain *types of situations.* Consider, for example, two people who are easily angered: One person might get angry when she is delayed (for example, in traffic or a checkout line) but not when she misplaces something at home; the other person might get angry whenever she misplaces things but not when she is delayed. Overall, the two women are equally prone to anger, but their anger tends to occur in different patterns and different types of situations.

Seventy-five percent of American college students admit that they have been academically dishonest in one way or another. What can be done about these high rates of dishonesty? The behavioral perspective holds that honesty is determined as much by circumstances as it is by personality. In line with this, simple measures like announcing in classes that integrity codes will be enforced can significantly reduce cheating. Using multiple forms of exams and web-based plagiarism software and educating students about plagiarism also tend to deter dishonesty (Altschuler, 2001; McKeever, 2006).

Personality = Behavior

How do learning theorists view the structure of personality? The behavioral view of personality can be illustrated with an early theory proposed by John Dollard and Neal Miller (1950). In their view, **habits** (learned behavior patterns) make up the structure of personality. As for the dynamics of personality, habits are governed by four elements of learning: *drive, cue, response,* and *reward.* A **drive** is any stimulus strong enough to goad a person to action (such as hunger, pain, lust, frustration, or fear). **Cues** are signals from the environment. These signals guide **responses** (actions) so that they are most likely to bring about **reward** (positive reinforcement).

How does that relate to personality? Let's say a child named Katrina is frustrated by her older brother Kelvin, who takes a toy from her. Katrina could respond in several ways: She could throw a temper tantrum, hit Kelvin, tell Mother, and so forth. The response she chooses is guided by available cues and the previous effects of each response. If telling Mother has paid off in the past and the mother is present, telling again may be her immediate response. If a different set of cues exists (if Mother is absent or if Kelvin looks particularly menacing), Katrina may select some other response. To an outside observer, Katrina's actions seem to reflect her personality. To a learning theorist, they simply express the combined effects of drive, cue, response, and reward.

Doesn't this analysis leave out a lot? Yes. Learning theorists first set out to provide a simple, clear model of personality.

But in recent years they have had to face a fact that they originally tended to overlook: People think. The new breed of behavioral psychologists—who include perception, thinking, expectations, and other mental events in their views—are called social learning theorists. Learning principles, modeling, thought patterns, perceptions, expectations, beliefs, goals, emotions, and social relationships are combined in **social learning theory** to explain personality (Mischel, Shoda, & Smith, 2004).

Social Learning Theory

The "cognitive behaviorism" of social learning theory can be illustrated by three concepts proposed by Julian Rotter: the psychological situation, expectancy, and reinforcement value (Rotter & Hochreich, 1975). Let's examine each.

Someone trips you. How do you respond? Your reaction probably depends on whether you think it was planned or an accident. It is not enough to know the setting in which a person responds. We also need to know the person's **psychological situation** (how the person interprets or defines the situation). As another example, let's say you score low on an exam. Do you consider it a challenge to work harder, a sign that you should drop the class, or an excuse to get drunk? Again, your interpretation is important.

Our actions are affected by an **expectancy,** or anticipation, that making a response will lead to reinforcement. To continue the example, if working harder has paid off in the past, it is a likely reaction to a low test score. But to predict your response, we would also have to know if you *expect* your efforts to pay off in the present situation. In fact, expected

Behavioral personality theory Any model of personality that emphasizes learning and observable behavior.

Learning theorist A psychologist interested in the ways that learning shapes behavior and explains personality.

Situational determinants External conditions that strongly influence behavior.

Habit A deeply ingrained, learned pattern of behavior.

Drive Any stimulus (especially an internal stimulus such as hunger) strong enough to goad a person to action.

Cue External stimuli that guide responses, especially by signaling the presence or absence of reinforcement.

Response Any behavior, either observable or internal.

Reward Anything that produces pleasure or satisfaction; a positive reinforcer.

Social learning theory An explanation of personality that combines learning principles, cognition, and the effects of social relationships.

Psychological situation A situation as it is perceived and interpreted by an individual, not as it exists objectively.

Expectancy Anticipation about the effect a response will have, especially regarding reinforcement.

Through self-reinforcement we reward ourselves for personal achievements and other "good" behavior.

reinforcement may be more important than actual past reinforcement. And what about the *value* you attach to grades, school success, or personal ability? The third concept of **reinforcement value** states that we attach different subjective values to various activities or rewards. This, too, must be taken into account to understand personality.

Self-Efficacy An ability to control your own life is the essence of what it means to be human. Because of this, Albert Bandura believes that one of the most important expectancies we develop concerns **self-efficacy** (EF-uh-keh-see: a capacity for producing a desired result). You're attracted to someone in your anthropology class. Will you ask him or her out? You're thinking about learning to snowboard. Will you try it this winter? You're beginning to consider a career in psychology. Will you take the courses you need to get into graduate school? You'd like to exercise more on the weekends. Will you join a hiking club? In these and countless other situations, efficacy beliefs play a key role in shaping our lives by influencing the activities and environments we choose (Bandura, 2001; Schultz & Schultz, 2005).

Self-Reinforcement One more idea deserves mention. At times, we all evaluate our actions and may reward ourselves with special privileges or treats for "good behavior." With this in mind, social learning theory adds the concept of self-reinforcement to the behavioristic view. **Self-reinforcement** refers to praising or rewarding yourself for having made a particular response (such as completing a school assignment). Thus, habits of self-praise and self-blame become an important part of personality (Schultz & Schultz, 2005). In fact, self-reinforcement can

be thought of as the social learning theorist's counterpart to the superego.

Rate Yourself: Self-Reinforcement
Check the statements in the list that apply to you.

___ I often think positive thoughts about myself.

___ I frequently meet standards that I set for myself.

___ I try not to blame myself when things go wrong.

___ I usually don't get upset when I make mistakes because I learn from them.

___ I can get satisfaction out of what I do even if it's not perfect.

___ When I make mistakes I take time to reassure myself.

___ I don't think talking about what you've done right is too boastful.

___ Praising yourself is healthy and normal.

___ I don't think I have to be upset every time I make a mistake.

___ My feelings of self-confidence and self-esteem stay pretty steady.

People who agree with most of these statements tend to have high rates of self-reinforcement (Heiby, 1983).

Self-reinforcement is closely related to high self-esteem. The reverse is also true: Mildly depressed college students tend to have low rates of self-reinforcement. It is not known if low self-reinforcement leads to depression, or the reverse. In either case, self-reinforcement is associated with less depression and greater life satisfaction (Seybolt & Wagner, 1997). From a behavioral viewpoint, there is value in learning to be "good to yourself."

Behavioristic View of Development

How do learning theorists account for personality development? Many of Freud's ideas can be restated in terms of learning theory. Dollard and Miller (1950) agree with Freud that the

first 6 years are crucial for personality development, but for different reasons. Rather than thinking in terms of psychosexual urges and fixations, they ask, "What makes early learning experiences so lasting in their effects?" Their answer is that childhood is a time of urgent drives, powerful rewards and punishments, and crushing frustrations. Also important is **social reinforcement,** which is based on praise, attention, or approval from others. These forces combine to shape the core of personality.

Critical Situations Dollard and Miller believe that during childhood four **critical situations** are capable of leaving a lasting imprint on personality. These are (1) feeding, (2) toilet or cleanliness training, (3) sex training, and (4) learning to express anger or aggression.

Why are these of special importance? Feeding serves as an illustration. If children are fed when they cry, it encourages them to actively manipulate their parents. The child allowed to cry without being fed learns to be passive. Thus, a basic active or passive orientation toward the world may be created by early feeding experiences. Feeding can also affect later social relationships because the child learns to associate people with pleasure or with frustration and discomfort.

Toilet and cleanliness training can be a particularly strong source of emotion for both parents and children. Rashad's parents were aghast the day they found him smearing feces about with joyful abandon. They reacted with sharp punishment, which frustrated and confused Rashad. Many attitudes toward cleanliness, conformity, and bodily functions are formed at such times. Studies have also long shown that severe, punishing, or frustrating toilet training can have undesirable effects on personality development (Christophersen & Mortweet, 2003). Because of this, toilet and cleanliness training demand patience and a sense of humor.

What about sex and anger? When, where, and how a child learns to express anger and sexual feelings can leave an imprint on personality. Specifically, permissiveness for sexual and aggressive behavior in childhood is linked to adult needs for power (McClelland & Pilon, 1983). This link probably occurs because permitting such behaviors allows children to get pleasure from asserting themselves. Sex training also involves learning socially defined "male" and "female" gender roles—which also affect personality (Pervin, Cervone, & John, 2005).

Personality and Gender From birth onward, children are labeled as boys or girls and encouraged to learn sex-appropriate behavior (Denmark, Rabinowitz, & Sechzer, 2005).

What does it mean to have a "masculine" or "feminine" personality? According to social learning theory, identification and imitation contribute greatly to personality development and to sex training. **Identification** refers to the child's emo-

Adult personality is influenced by identification with parents and imitation of their behavior.

tional attachment to admired adults, especially those who provide love and care. Identification typically encourages **imitation,** a desire to act like the admired person. Many "male" or "female" traits come from children's attempts to imitate a same-sex parent with whom they identify.

If children are around parents of both sexes, why don't they imitate behavior typical of the opposite sex as well as of the same sex? You may recall from Chapter 6 that learning takes place vicariously as well as directly. This means that we can learn

Reinforcement value The subjective value a person attaches to a particular activity or reinforcer.

Self-efficacy Belief in your capacity to produce a desired result.

Self-reinforcement Praising or rewarding oneself for having made a particular response (such as completing a school assignment).

Social reinforcement Praise, attention, approval, and/or affection from others.

Critical situations Situations during childhood that are capable of leaving a lasting imprint on personality.

Identification Feeling emotionally connected to a person and seeing oneself as like him or her.

Imitation An attempt to match one's own behavior to another person's behavior.

without direct reward by observing and remembering the actions of others. But the actions we choose to imitate depend on their outcomes. For example, boys and girls have equal chances to observe adults and other children acting aggressively. However, girls are less likely than boys to imitate directly aggressive behavior (shouting at or hitting). Instead, girls are more likely to rely on indirectly aggressive behavior (excluding others from friendship, spreading rumors). This may well be because the expression of direct aggression is thought to be inappropriate for girls. As a consequence, girls rarely see direct female aggression rewarded or approved (Richardson & Green, 1999). In others words, "girlfighting" is likely a culturally reinforced pattern (Brown, 2005). Intriguingly, over the last few years, girls have become more willing to engage in direct aggression as popular culture presents more and more images of directly aggressive women (Artz, 2005).

Historically, parents and other adults in Western countries like the United States tended to encourage boys to engage in **instrumental** (goal-directed) **behaviors,** to be directly aggressive, to hide their emotions, and to prepare for the world of work. Girls, on the other hand, were encouraged in **expressive** (emotion-oriented) **behaviors** and, to a lesser degree, were socialized for motherhood and to be indirectly aggressive. Thus, from an early age males and females tended to grow up in different, gender-defined cultures (Martin & Fabes, 2001). However, it is important to note that these differences are fading as more people redefine traditional male and female gender roles.

We have considered only a few examples of the links between social learning and personality. Nevertheless, the connection is unmistakable. When parents accept their children and give them affection, the children become sociable, positive, and emotionally stable, and they have high self-esteem. When parents are rejecting, punishing, sarcastic, humiliating, or neglectful, their children become hostile, unresponsive, unstable, and dependent and have impaired self-esteem (Triandis & Suh, 2002).

MODULE 10.4 Summary

What do behaviorists and social learning theorists emphasize in personality?

- Behavioral theories of personality emphasize learning, conditioning, and the situational determinants of behavior.

- Learning theorists John Dollard and Neal Miller consider habits the basic core of personality.

- Habits express the combined effects of drive, cue, response, and reward.

- To explain personality, social learning theory combines learning with thinking, expectations, and other mental processes.

- Social learning theory is exemplified by Julian Rotter's concepts of the psychological situation, expectancies, and reinforcement value.

- The behavioristic view of personality development holds that social reinforcement in four situations is critical: feeding, toilet or cleanliness training, sex training, and anger or aggression training.

- Identification and imitation are of particular importance in learning to be "male" or "female."

KNOWLEDGE BUILDER

Behavioral and Social Learning Theories

Recite

1. Learning theorists believe that personality "traits" really are _____ acquired through prior learning. They also emphasize _____ determinants of behavior.

2. Dollard and Miller consider cues the basic structure of personality. T or F?

3. To explain behavior, social learning theorists include mental elements, such as _____ (the anticipation that a response will lead to reinforcement).

4. Self-reinforcement is to behavioristic theory as superego is to psychoanalytic theory. T or F?

5. Which of the following is *not* a "critical situation" in the behaviorist theory of personality development?
   a. feeding
   b. sex training
   c. language training
   d. anger training

6. In addition to basic rewards and punishments, a child's personality is also shaped by _____ reinforcement.

7. Social learning theories of development emphasize the impact of identification and _____.

Reflect
Critical Thinking

8. Rotter's concept of *reinforcement value* is closely related to a motivational principle discussed in Module 9.1. Can you name it?

Relate

What is your favorite style of food? Can you relate Miller and Dollard's concepts of habit, drive, cue, response, and reward to explain your preference?

Some people love to shop. Others hate it. How have the psychological situation, expectancy, and reinforcement value affected your willingness to "shop 'til you drop"?

Who did you identify with as a child? What aspects of that person's behavior did you imitate?

Link

Internet addresses frequently change. To find the sites listed here, visit **http://www .thomsonedu.com/psychology/coon** for an updated list of Internet addresses and direct links to relevant sites.

- **Julian Rotter** Read about Julian Rotter and his social learning theory.
- **Information on Self-Efficacy** Read about Albert Bandura and the idea of self-efficacy.
- **Controlling Your Own Study Behavior** Apply the concept of self-reinforcement to your own studying.

ANSWERS

1. habits, situational 2. F 3. expectancies 4. T 5. c 6. social 7. imitation 8. Incentive value.

Instrumental behaviors Behaviors directed toward the achievement of some goal; behaviors that are instrumental in producing some effect.

Expressive behaviors Behaviors that express or communicate emotion or personal feelings.

10.5 Humanistic Theories

AT THE BEGINNING OF THIS CHAPTER you met Annette, an interesting personality. A few years ago, Annette and her husband spent a year riding mules across the country as a unique way to see America and get to know themselves better. Where do such desires for personal growth come from? Humanistic theories pay special attention to the fuller use of human potentials, and they help bring balance to our overall views of personality.

Humanistic Theory—Peak Experiences and Personal Growth

SURVEY QUESTION: *How do humanistic theories differ from other perspectives?*

Humanism focuses on human experience, problems, potentials, and ideals. It is a reaction to the rigidity of traits, the pessimism of psychoanalytic theory, and the mechanical nature of learning theory. At its core is a positive image of what it means to be human. Humanists reject the Freudian view of personality as a battleground for instincts and unconscious forces. Instead, they view human nature as inherently good. (**Human nature** consists of the traits, qualities, potentials, and behavior patterns most characteristic of the human species.) Humanists also oppose the machine-like overtones of behaviorism. We are not, they say, merely a bundle of moldable responses. Rather, we are creative beings capable of **free choice** (an ability to choose that is not determined by genetics, learning, or unconscious forces). In short, humanists seek ways to encourage our potentials to blossom.

To a humanist the person you are today is largely the product of all the choices you have made. Humanists also emphasize immediate **subjective experience** (private perceptions of reality), rather than prior learning. They believe that there are as many "real worlds" as there are people. To understand behavior, we must learn how a person subjectively views the world—what is "real" for her or him.

Who are the major humanistic theorists? Many psychologists have added to the humanistic tradition. Of these, the best known are Carl Rogers (1902–1987) and Abraham Maslow (1908–1970). Because Maslow's idea of self-actualization was introduced in Chapter 1, let's begin with a more detailed look at this facet of his thinking.

Maslow and Self-Actualization

Abraham Maslow became interested in people who were living unusually effective lives. How were they different? To find an answer, Maslow began by studying the lives of great men and women from history, such as Albert Einstein, William James, Jane Addams, Eleanor Roosevelt, Abraham Lincoln, John Muir, and Walt Whitman. From there he moved on to directly study living artists, writers, poets, and other creative individuals.

Along the way, Maslow's thinking changed radically. At first he studied only people of obvious creativity or high achievement. However, it eventually became clear that a housewife, clerk, student, or someone like our friend Annette could live a rich, creative, and satisfying life. Maslow referred to the process of fully developing personal potentials as **self-actualization** (Maslow, 1954). The heart of self-actualization is a continuous search for personal fulfillment (Ewen, 2003; Reiss & Havercamp, 2005).

Characteristics of Self-Actualizers A **self-actualizer** is a person who is living creatively and fully using his or her potentials. In his studies, Maslow found that self-actualizers share many similarities. Whether famous or unknown, well-schooled or uneducated, rich or poor, self-actualizers tend to fit the following profile.

1. **Efficient perceptions of reality.** Self-actualizers are able to judge situations correctly and honestly. They are very sensitive to the fake and dishonest.

2. **Comfortable acceptance of self, others, nature.** Self-actualizers accept their own human nature with all its flaws. The shortcomings of others and the contradictions of the human condition are accepted with humor and tolerance.

3. **Spontaneity.** Maslow's subjects extended their creativity into everyday activities. Actualizers tend to be unusually alive, engaged, and spontaneous.

4. **Task centering.** Most of Maslow's subjects had a mission to fulfill in life or some task or problem outside of themselves to pursue. Humanitarians such as Albert Schweitzer and Mother Teresa represent this quality.

5. **Autonomy.** Self-actualizers are free from reliance on external authorities or other people. They tend to be resourceful and independent.

6. **Continued freshness of appreciation.** The self-actualizer seems to constantly renew appreciation of life's basic goods. A sunset or a flower will be experienced as intensely time after time as it was at first. There is an "innocence of vision," like that of an artist or child.

7. **Fellowship with humanity.** Maslow's subjects felt a deep identification with others and the human situation in general.

8. **Profound interpersonal relationships.** The interpersonal relationships of self-actualizers are marked by deep, loving bonds (Hanley & Abell, 2002).

9. **Comfort with solitude.** Despite their satisfying relationships with others, self-actualizing persons value solitude and are comfortable being alone (Sumerlin & Bundrick, 1996).

10. **Nonhostile sense of humor.** This refers to the wonderful capacity to laugh at oneself. It also describes the kind of humor a man like Abraham Lincoln had. Lincoln probably never made a joke that hurt anybody. His wry comments were a gentle prodding of human shortcomings.

11. **Peak experiences.** All of Maslow's subjects reported the frequent occurrence of **peak experiences** (temporary moments of self-actualization). These occasions were marked by feelings of ecstasy, harmony, and deep meaning. Self-actualizers reported feeling at one with the universe, stronger and calmer than ever before, filled with light, beautiful and good, and so forth.

In summary, self-actualizers feel safe, nonanxious, accepted, loved, loving, and alive.

Maslow's choice of self-actualizing people for study seems pretty subjective. Is it really a fair representation of self-actualization? Although Maslow tried to investigate self-actualization empirically, his choice of people for study was subjective. Undoubtedly there are many ways to make full use of personal potential. Maslow's primary contribution was to draw our attention to the possibility of lifelong personal growth.

What steps can be taken to promote self-actualization? Maslow made few specific recommendations about how to proceed. There is no magic formula for leading a more creative life. Self-actualization is primarily a *process,* not a goal or an end point. As such, it requires hard work, patience, and commitment. Nevertheless, some helpful suggestions can be gleaned from his writings (Maslow, 1954, 1967, 1971). Here are some ways to begin:

1. **Be willing to change.** Begin by asking yourself, "Am I living in a way that is deeply satisfying to me and that truly expresses me?" If not, be prepared to make changes in your life. Indeed, ask yourself this question often and accept the need for continual change.

2. **Take responsibility.** You can become an architect of self by acting as if you are personally responsible for every aspect of your life. Shouldering responsibility in this way helps end the habit of blaming others for your own shortcomings.

3. **Examine your motives.** Self-discovery involves an element of risk. If your behavior is restricted by a desire for safety or security, it may be time to test some limits. Try to make each life decision a choice for growth, not a response to fear or anxiety.

4. **Experience honestly and directly.** Wishful thinking is another barrier to personal growth. Self-actualizers trust themselves enough to accept all kinds of information without distorting it to fit their fears and desires. Try to see yourself as others do. Be willing to admit, "I was wrong," or, "I failed because I was irresponsible."

5. **Make use of positive experiences.** Maslow considered peak experiences temporary moments of self-actualization. Therefore, you might actively repeat activities that have caused feelings of awe, amazement, exaltation, renewal, reverence, humility, fulfillment, or joy.

6. **Be prepared to be different.** Maslow felt that everyone has a potential for "greatness," but most fear becoming what they might. As part of personal growth, be prepared to trust your own impulses and feelings; don't automatically judge yourself by the standards of others. Accept your uniqueness.

7. **Get involved.** With few exceptions, self-actualizers tend to have a mission or "calling" in life. For these people, "work" is not done just to fill deficiency needs, but to satisfy higher yearnings for truth, beauty, community, and meaning. Get personally involved and committed. Turn your attention to problems outside yourself.

8. **Assess your progress.** There is no final point at which one becomes self-actualized. It's important to gauge your progress frequently and to renew your efforts. If you feel bored at school, at a job, or in a relationship, consider it a challenge. Have you been taking responsibility for your own personal growth? Almost any activity can be used as a chance for self-enhancement if it is approached creatively.

Humanism An approach that focuses on human experience, problems, potentials, and ideals.

Human nature Those traits, qualities, potentials, and behavior patterns most characteristic of the human species.

Free choice The ability to freely make choices that are not controlled by genetics, learning, or unconscious forces.

Subjective experience Reality as it is perceived and interpreted, not as it exists objectively.

Self-actualization The process of fully developing personal potentials.

Self-actualizer One who is living creatively and making full use of his or her potentials.

Peak experiences Temporary moments of self-actualization.

Positive Psychology: Positive Personality Traits

It could be said that self-actualizing people are thriving, not just surviving. In recent years, proponents of positive psychology have tried to scientifically study positive personality traits that contribute to happiness and well-being (Keyes & Haidt, 2003; Seligman, 2003). Although their work does not fall within the humanistic tradition, their findings are relevant here.

Martin Seligman, Christopher Peterson, and others have identified six human strengths that contribute to well-being and life satisfaction. Each strength is expressed by the positive personality traits listed here (Peterson & Seligman, 2004).

- **Wisdom and knowledge:** Creativity, curiosity, open-mindedness, love of learning, perspective
- **Courage:** Bravery, persistence, integrity, vitality
- **Humanity:** Love, kindness, social intelligence
- **Justice:** Citizenship, fairness, leadership
- **Temperance:** Forgiveness, humility, prudence, self-control
- **Transcendence:** Appreciation of beauty and excellence, gratitude, hope, humor, spirituality

Which of the positive personality traits are most closely related to happiness? A recent study found that traits of hope, vitality, gratitude, love, and curiosity are strongly associated with life satisfaction (Park, Peterson, & Seligman, 2004). These characteristics, in combination with Maslow's descriptions of self-actualizers, provide a good guide to the characteristics that help people live happy, meaningful lives.

Carl Rogers' Self Theory

Carl Rogers, another well-known humanist, also emphasized the human capacity for inner peace and happiness. The **fully functioning person,** he said, lives in harmony with his or her deepest feelings and impulses. Such people are open to their experiences, and they trust their inner urges and intuitions (Rogers, 1961). Rogers believed that this attitude is most likely to occur when a person receives ample amounts of love and acceptance from others.

Personality Structure and Dynamics Rogers' theory emphasizes the **self,** a flexible and changing perception of personal identity. Much behavior can be understood as an attempt to maintain consistency between our *self-image* and our actions. (Your **self-image** is a total subjective perception of your body and personality.) For example, people who think of themselves as kind tend to be considerate in most situations.

Let's say I know a person who thinks she is kind, but she really isn't. How does that fit Rogers' theory? According to

Humanists consider self-image a central determinant of behavior and personal adjustment.

Rogers, we allow experiences that match our self-image into awareness, where they gradually change the self. Information or feelings inconsistent with the self-image are said to be incongruent. Thus, a person who thinks she is kind but really isn't is in a state of **incongruence.** In other words, there is a discrepancy between her experiences and her self-image. As another example, it would be incongruent to believe that you are a person who "never gets angry" if you spend much of each day seething inside.

Experiences seriously incongruent with the self-image can be threatening and are often distorted or denied conscious recognition. Blocking, denying, or distorting experiences prevents the self from changing. This creates a gulf between the self-image and reality. As the self-image grows more unrealistic, the **incongruent person** becomes confused, vulnerable, dissatisfied, or seriously maladjusted (● Fig. 10.6). In line with Rogers' observations, a study of college students confirmed that being *authentic* is vital for healthy functioning. That is, we need to feel that our behavior accurately expresses who we are (Sheldon et al., 1997). Please note, however, that being authentic doesn't mean you can do whatever you want. Being true to yourself is no excuse for acting irresponsibly or ignoring the feelings of others.

When your self-image is consistent with what you really think, feel, do, and experience, you are best able to actualize your potentials. Rogers also considered it essential to have congruence between the self-image and the **ideal self.** The ideal self is similar to Freud's ego ideal. It is an image of the person you would most like to be.

Is it really incongruent not to live up to your ideal self? Rogers was aware that we never fully attain our ideals. Nevertheless, the greater the gap between the way you see yourself and the way you would like to be, the more tension and anxiety you will experience.

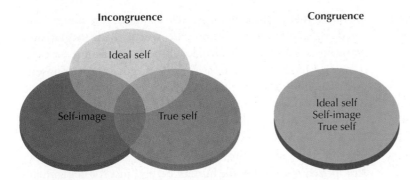

Incongruence   Congruence

Ideal self

Self-image   True self

Ideal self
Self-image
True self

● **FIGURE 10.6** Incongruence occurs when there is a mismatch between any of these three entities: the ideal self (the person you would like to be), your self-image (the person you think you are), and the true self (the person you actually are). Self-esteem suffers when there is a large difference between one's ideal self and self-image. Anxiety and defensiveness are common when the self-image does not match the true self.

THE CLINICAL FILE

Telling Stories about Ourselves

You know these two student types: the carefree party animal and the conscientious bookworm. Perhaps you even think of yourself as one or the other. Is there any truth to these (stereo)types? Can you change your type?

There is little doubt that college life creates a conflict between new opportunities for fun with friends and the need to study hard (McGregor, McAdams, & Little, 2006). In general, our personality traits are relatively stable lifelong characteristics (McAdams & Pals, 2006). As a result, a person high in the Big Five traits of extraversion and agreeableness will tend to embrace a carefree college lifestyle. In comparison, someone high in conscientiousness will find it easier to hit the books (McGregor, McAdams, & Little, 2006).

Does that mean a partyer can't become a bookworm (or vice versa)? It depends: Do you mean over a week? Or a lifetime? As we saw in Module 10.1, personality traits do slowly change as we age. In particular, we tend to become more agreeable and conscientious as we grow older (Roberts, Walton, & Viechtbauer, 2006).

Oh, you need to change by the end of the semester? That's a taller order. One promising approach is to tell yourself stories about possible selves you could become. The *narrative approach* to personality asserts that our personalities are shaped by the stories we tell about ourselves (Pals, 2006). In other words, alternate life stories are not just fantasies or daydreams. They actually influence who we are and who we become. Narratives may even underlie successful psychotherapy. Rather than trying to change personality traits, effective therapists help clients tell better stories about their lives (McAdams & Pals, 2006).

So, if you feel that you are being too careless and carefree at school, start imagining yourself studying more, getting to classes on time, and getting good grades. Listen to the stories of successful students and use them to revise your own story. Visit your campus counseling center to learn more about how to succeed at school. In other words, imagine yourself as a bit more of a bookworm. (Don't worry, your carefree nature won't desert you!)

If you feel you are too conscientious and working too hard, imagine yourself going out to socialize more often. Listen to the stories of your extraverted friends. Imagine the benefits of balancing work and play in your life. If you are shy or perfectionistic, visit your campus counseling center to learn how to become more social or relaxed. And, again, don't worry: Having more fun doesn't mean you will suddenly become irresponsible.

Whatever possible self you choose to pursue, you are more likely to become what you imagine if you elaborate your story, making it more detailed and "real" as you gradually adopt new patterns. You *can* create a new story for yourself, and you *can* make it yours.

Rogers emphasized that to maximize our potentials, we must accept information about ourselves as honestly as possible. In accord with his thinking, researchers have found that people with a close match between their self-image and ideal self tend to be socially poised, confident, and resourceful. Those with a poor match tend to be depressed, anxious, and insecure (Boldero et al., 2005).

According to psychologists Hazel Markus and Paula Nurius (1986), our ideal self is only one of a number of **possible selves** (persons we could become or are afraid of becoming). Annette, who was described earlier, is an interesting personality, to say the least. Annette is one of those people who seems to have lived many lives in the time that most of

Fully functioning person A person living in harmony with her or his deepest feelings, impulses, and intuitions.

Self A continuously evolving conception of one's personal identity.

Self-image Total subjective perception of one's body and personality (another term for self-concept).

Incongruence State that exists when there is a discrepancy between one's experiences and self-image or between one's self-image and ideal self.

Incongruent person A person who has an inaccurate self-image or whose self-image differs greatly from the ideal self.

Ideal self An idealized image of oneself (the person one would like to be).

Possible self A collection of thoughts, beliefs, feelings, and images concerning the person one could become.

us manage only one. Like Annette, you may have pondered many possible personal identities. (See "Telling Stories about Ourselves.")

Possible selves translate our hopes, fears, fantasies, and goals into specific images of who we *could* be. Thus, a beginning law student might picture herself as a successful attorney, an enterprising college student might imagine himself as an Internet entrepreneur, and a person on a diet might imagine both slim and grossly obese possible selves. Such images tend to direct our future behavior (Oyserman et al., 2004).

Of course, almost everyone over age 30 has probably felt the anguish of becoming aware that some cherished possible selves will never be realized. Nevertheless, there is value in asking yourself not just "Who am I?" but also "Who would I like to become?" As you do, remember Maslow's advice that everyone has a potential for "greatness," but most fear becoming what they might.

Humanistic View of Development

Why do mirrors, photographs, video cameras, and the reactions of others hold such fascination and threat for many people? Carl Rogers's theory suggests it is because they provide information about one's self. The development of a self-image depends greatly on information from the environment. It begins with a sorting of perceptions and feelings: my body, my toes, my nose, I want, I like, I am, and so on. Soon, it expands to include self-evaluation: I am a good person, I did something bad just now, and so forth.

How does development of the self contribute to later personality functioning? Rogers believed that positive and negative evaluations by others cause children to develop internal standards of evaluation called **conditions of worth.** In other words, we learn that some actions win our parents' love and approval whereas others are rejected. More important, parents may label some *feelings* as bad or wrong. For example, a child might be told that it is wrong to feel angry toward a brother or sister—even when anger is justified. Likewise, a little boy might be told that he must not cry or show fear, two very normal emotions.

Learning to evaluate some experiences or feelings as "good" and others as "bad" is directly related to a later capacity for self-esteem, positive self-evaluation, or **positive self-regard,** to use Rogers' term. To think of yourself as a good, lovable, worthwhile person, your behavior and experiences must match your internal conditions of worth. The problem is that this can cause incongruence by leading to the denial of many true feelings and experiences.

To put it simply, Rogers blamed many adult emotional problems on attempts to live by the standards of others. He believed that congruence and self-actualization are encouraged by replacing conditions of worth with **organismic valuing** (a natural, undistorted, full-body reaction to an experience). Organismic valuing is a direct, gut-level response to life that avoids the filtering and distortion of incongruence. It involves trusting one's own feelings and perceptions. Organismic valuing is most likely to develop, Rogers felt, when children (or adults) receive **unconditional positive regard** (unshakable love and approval) from others. That is, when they are "prized" as worthwhile human beings, just for being themselves, without any conditions or strings attached. Although this may be a luxury few people enjoy, we are more likely to move toward our ideal selves if we receive affirmation and support from a close partner (Drigotas et al., 1999).

MODULE 10.5 Summary

How do humanistic theories differ from other perspectives?

- Humanistic theories stress subjective experience, free choice, self-actualization, and positive models of human nature.

- Abraham Maslow's study of self-actualizers showed that they share traits that range from efficient perceptions of reality to frequent peak experiences.

- Self-actualization is best viewed as an ongoing process of personal growth, rather than a final destination.

- Positive psychologists have identified six human strengths that contribute to well-being and life satisfaction: wisdom and knowledge, courage, humanity, justice, temperance, and transcendence.

- Carl Rogers viewed the self as an entity that emerges from personal experience. Optimal functioning occurs when there is a good match between your true self, your self-image, and your ideal self.

- The incongruent person has an unrealistic self-image and/or a mismatch between the self-image and the ideal self. The congruent or fully functioning person is flexible and open to experiences and feelings.

- In the development of personality, humanists are interested in the emergence of a self-image and in self-evaluations.

- As parents apply conditions of worth to children's behavior, thoughts, and feelings, children begin to do the same. Internalized conditions of worth then contribute to incongruence.

- Positive self-regard is nurtured by organismic valuing and by receiving unconditional positive regard.

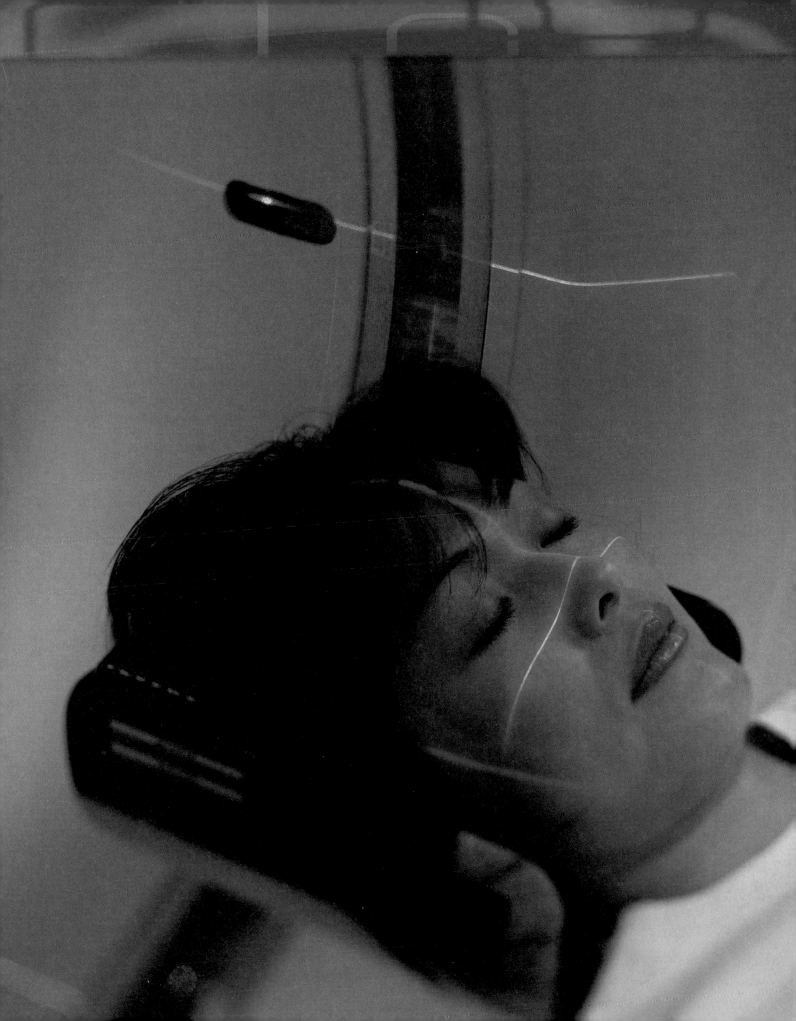

12.1 Normality and Psychopathology

DECIDING IF A PERSON'S BEHAVIOR is abnormal is harder than it might seem. The conservative, churchgoing housewife down the street might be flagrantly psychotic and a lethal danger to her children. The reclusive eccentric who hangs out at the park could be the sanest person in town. Let's begin our discussion with some basic factors that affect judgments of normality. Then in upcoming modules we'll survey some of the major disorders that psychologists diagnose and treat.

Normality—What Is Normal?

SURVEY QUESTIONS: *How is normality defined? What are the major psychological disorders?*

"That guy is really wacko. His porch lights are dimming." "Yeah, the butter's sliding off his waffle. He's ready to go postal." Informally, it's tempting to make such snap judgments about mental health. But to seriously classify people as psychologically unhealthy raises complex and age-old issues.

The scientific study of mental, emotional, and behavioral disorders is known as **psychopathology**. The term also refers to mental disorders themselves, such as schizophrenia or depression, and to behavior patterns that make people unhappy and impair their personal growth (Butcher, Mineka, & Hooley, 2007). Defining abnormality can be tricky. We might begin by saying that psychopathology is characterized by *subjective discomfort* (private feelings of pain, unhappiness, or emotional distress) like Carol North endured.

But couldn't a person be seriously disturbed without feeling discomfort? Yes. Psychopathology doesn't always cause personal anguish. A person suffering from mania might feel elated and "on top of the world." Also, a *lack* of discomfort may reveal a problem. For example, if you showed no signs of grief after the death of a close friend, we might suspect psychopathology. In practice, subjective discomfort explains most instances in which people voluntarily seek professional help.

Some psychologists use statistics to define normality more objectively. **Statistical abnormality** refers to scoring very high or low on some dimension, such as intelligence, anxiety, or depression. Anxiety, for example, is a feature of several psychological disorders. To measure it, we could create a test to learn how many people show low, medium, or high levels of anxiety. Usually, the results of such tests will form a *normal* (bell-shaped) *curve*. (*Normal* in this case refers only to the *shape* of the curve.) Notice that most people score near the middle of a normal curve; very few have extremely high

and low scores (● Fig. 12.1). A person who deviates from the average by being anxious all the time (high anxiety) might be abnormal. So, too, might a person who never feels anxiety.

Then statistical abnormality tells us nothing about the meaning of deviations from the norm? Right. It is as statistically "abnormal" (unusual) for a person to score above 145 on an IQ test as it is to score below 55. However, only the lower score is regarded as "abnormal" or undesirable. In the same sense, it is unusual for a person to speak four languages or to win an event at the Olympics, but these are desirable, if rare, accomplishments.

Statistical definitions also can't tell us *where to draw the line* between normality and abnormality. To take a new example, we could obtain the average frequency of sexual intercourse for persons of a particular age, sex, sexual orientation, and marital status. Clearly, a person who feels driven to have sex dozens of times a day has a problem. But as we move back toward the norm we face the problem of drawing lines. How often does normal behavior have to occur before it becomes abnormal? As you can see, statistical boundary lines tend to be somewhat arbitrary (Comer, 2005).

Atypical behavior or nonconformity may underlie some disorders. **Social nonconformity** refers to disobeying public standards for acceptable conduct. Extreme nonconformity can lead to destructive or self-destructive behavior. (Think, for instance, of a drug abuser or a prostitute.) However, we must be careful to separate unhealthy nonconformity from creative lifestyles. Many eccentric "characters" are charming and emotionally stable. Note, too, that strictly following social norms is no guarantee of mental health. In some cases, psychopathology involves rigid conformity. (See "Crazy for a Day.")

A young woman ties a thick rubber cord around her ankles, screams hysterically, and jumps head first off a bridge. Thirty years ago, the woman's behavior might have seemed

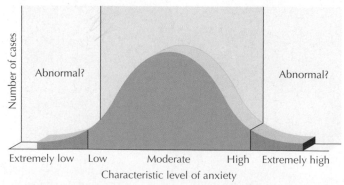

● **FIGURE 12.1** The number of people displaying a personal characteristic may help define what is statistically abnormal.

DISCOVERING PSYCHOLOGY

Crazy for a Day

Performing a mildly abnormal behavior is a good way to get a sense of how social norms define "normality" in daily life. Here's your assignment: Do something strange in public and observe how people react to you. (Please don't do anything dangerous, harmful, or offensive—and don't get arrested!) Here are some deviant behaviors that other students have staged:

• Sit in the dining area of a fast-food restaurant and loudly carry on a conversation with an imaginary companion.

• Stand in a busy hallway on campus and adopt a Kung Fu stance. Remain in that position for 10 minutes.

• Walk around campus on a sunny day while wearing a raincoat and carrying an open umbrella. Keep the umbrella over your head when you are inside buildings.

• Stick one finger in your nose and another in your ear. Walk through a busy shopping mall.

• Cover your head with aluminum foil for a day.

Does the idea of performing any of these actions make you uncomfortable? If so, you may not need to do anything more to appreciate how powerfully social norms constrain our actions. As we have noted, social nonconformity is just one facet of abnormal behavior. Nevertheless, actions that are regarded as "strange" within a particular culture are often the first sign to others that a person has a problem.

---

completely crazy. Today, it is a routine form of entertainment (called "bungee jumping"). Before any behavior can be defined as abnormal, we must consider the *situational context* (social situation, behavioral setting, or general circumstances) in which it occurs. Is it normal to stand outside and water a lawn with a hose? It depends on whether it is raining or not. Is it abnormal for a grown man to remove his pants and expose himself to another man or woman in a place of business? It depends on whether the other person is a bank clerk or a doctor!

Almost any imaginable behavior can be considered normal in some contexts. In 1972, an airplane carrying a rugby team crashed in the snow-capped Andes of South America. Incredibly, 16 of the 45 people onboard survived 73 days in deep snow and subfreezing temperatures. They were forced to use extremely grim measures to do so—they ate the bodies of those who died in the crash.

As implied by our earlier discussion of social norms, culture is one of the most influential contexts in which any be-

havior is judged (Fabrega, 2004). In some cultures it is considered normal to defecate or urinate in public or to appear naked in public. In our culture such behaviors would be considered unusual or abnormal. In Muslim cultures, women who remain completely housebound are considered normal or even virtuous. In Western cultures they might be diagnosed as suffering from a disorder called agoraphobia. (Agoraphobia is described later in this chapter.)

Thus, *cultural relativity* (the idea that judgments are made relative to the values of one's culture) can affect the diagnosis of psychological disorders. (See "A Disease Called Freedom.") Still, *all* cultures classify people as abnormal if they fail to communicate with others or are consistently unpredictable in their actions.

Core Features of Disordered Behavior

If abnormality is so hard to define, how are judgments of psychopathology made? Although the standards we have discussed are *relative*, abnormal behavior does have two core features. First, it is **maladaptive.** Rather than helping people cope successfully, abnormal behavior makes it more difficult for them to meet the demands of day-to-day life. Second, people suffering from psychological disorders *lose the ability to control* their thoughts, behaviors, or feelings adequately. For exam-

Social nonconformity does not automatically indicate psychopathology.

Rick Friedman/Corbis

Psychopathology The scientific study of mental, emotional, and behavioral disorders; also, abnormal or maladaptive behavior.

Statistical abnormality Abnormality defined on the basis of an extreme score on some dimension, such as IQ or anxiety.

Social nonconformity Failure to conform to societal norms or the usual minimum standards for social conduct.

Maladaptive behavior Behavior that makes it difficult to adapt to the environment and meet the demands of day-to-day life.

HUMAN DIVERSITY

A Disease Called Freedom

The year is 1840. You are a slave who has tried repeatedly to escape from a cruel and abusive master. You want to be free. An expert is consulted about your "abnormal" behavior. His conclusion? You are suffering from "drapeto-mania," a mental "disorder" that causes slaves to run away (Wakefield, 1992). Your "cure"? The expert will cut off your toes.

As this example suggests, psychiatric terms are easily abused. Historically, some have been applied to culturally disapproved behaviors that are not really disorders. Another of our personal favorites is the long-outdated diagnosis of "anarchia," a form of insanity that leads one to seek a more democratic society (Brown, 1990).

All of the following were also once considered disorders: childhood masturbation, lack of vaginal orgasm, self-defeating personality (applied mainly to women), homosexuality, and nymphomania (a woman with a healthy sexual appetite) (Wakefield, 1992). Even today, race, gender, and social class continue to affect the diagnosis of various disorders (Durand & Barlow, 2006; Poland & Caplan, 2004).

Gender is probably the most common source of bias in judging normality because standards tend to be based on males (Nolen-Hoeksema, 2007; Widiger, 2005). According to psychologist Paula Caplan (1995) and others, women are penalized both for conforming to female stereotypes and for ignoring them. If a woman is independent, aggressive, and unemotional, she may be considered "unhealthy." Yet at the same time, a woman who is vain, emotional, irrational, and dependent on others (all "feminine" traits in our culture) may be classified as having a personality disorder (Bornstein, 1996). Indeed, a majority of persons classified as having dependent personality disorder are women. In view of this, Paula Caplan asks, why isn't there a category called "delusional dominating personality disorder" for obnoxious men (Caplan, 1995)?

Because culture can influence perceptions of disorder and normality, it is worth being cautious before you leap to conclusions about the mental health of others (DSM-IV-TR, 2000). (They might be doing an assignment for their psychology class!)

---

ple, gambling is not a problem if people bet for entertainment and can maintain self-control. However, compulsive gambling is a sign of psychopathology. The voices that Carol North kept hearing are a prime example of what it means to lose control of one's thoughts. In the most extreme cases, people become a danger to themselves or others, which is clearly maladaptive (Hansell, 2007).

In practice, deciding that a person needs help usually occurs when the person *does something* (hits a person, hallucinates, stares into space, collects rolls of toilet paper, and so forth) that *annoys* or *gains the attention* of a person in a *position of power* in the person's life (an employer, teacher, parent, spouse, or the person himself or herself). That person then *does something* about it. (A police officer may be called, the person may be urged to see a psychologist, a relative may start commitment proceedings, or the person may voluntarily seek help.)

DSM-IV-TR is not the only system for classifying mental disorders. Nevertheless, most activities in mental health settings—from diagnosis to therapy to billing of insurance companies—are influenced by the *DSM*. *DSM-IV-TR* is both a scientific document and a social one. Major disorders are well-documented problems. Some problems, however, have little to do with "mental illness." Instead, they are primarily socially disapproved behaviors. (From the *Diagnostic and Statistical Manual of Mental Disorders, Fourth Edition, Text Revision*, © 2000 American Psychiatric Association.)

Classifying Mental Disorders— Problems by the Book

Psychological problems are classified by using the *Diagnostic and Statistical Manual of Mental Disorders* (DSM-IV-TR, 2000). The *DSM* helps psychologists correctly identify mental disorders and select the best therapies to treat them (First & Pincus, 2002).

A **mental disorder** is a significant impairment in psychological functioning. If you were to glance through the *DSM-IV-TR*, you would see many disorders described, including those in ■ Table 12.1. It's impossible here to discuss all of these problems. Major disorders are listed in the table so you can see the types of problems found in the *DSM*. (You don't need to memorize all of them.) The descriptions that follow will give you an overview of some selected problems.

▪ TABLE 12.1   Major *DSM-IV-TR* Categories

- Disorders usually first diagnosed in infancy, childhood, or adolescence
  Mental retardation
  Example: Mild mental retardation
  Learning disorders
  Example: Reading disorder
  Motor skills disorder
  Example: Developmental coordination disorder
  Communication disorders
  Example: Stuttering
  Pervasive developmental disorders
  Example: Autistic disorder
  Attention-deficit and disruptive behavior disorders
  Example: Attention-deficit/hyperactivity disorder
  Feeding and eating disorders of infancy or early childhood
  Example: Pica (eating inedible substances)
  Tic disorders
  Example: Tourette's disorder
  Elimination disorders
  Example: Enuresis (bedwetting)
  Other disorders of infancy, childhood, or adolescence
  Example: Separation anxiety disorder

- Delirium, dementia, amnestic, and other cognitive disorders
  Delirium
  Example: Delirium due to a general medical condition
  Dementia
  Example: Dementia of the Alzheimer's type
  Amnestic disorders (memory loss)
  Example: Amnestic disorder due to a general medical condition
  Cognitive disorder not otherwise specified

- Mental disorders due to a general medical condition not elsewhere classified
  Catatonic disorder due to a general medical condition
  Personality change due to a general medical condition
  Mental disorder not otherwise specified due to a general medical condition

- Substance-related disorders
  Example: Cocaine use disorders

- Schizophrenia and other psychotic disorders
  Schizophrenia
  Example: Schizophrenia, paranoid type
  Schizophreniform disorder
  Schizoaffective disorder
  Delusional disorder
  Example: Delusional disorder, grandiose type
  Brief psychotic disorder
  Shared psychotic disorder (folie á deux)
  Psychotic disorder due to a general medical condition
  Substance-induced psychotic disorder
  Psychotic disorder not otherwise specified

- Mood disorders
  Depressive disorders
  Example: Major depressive disorder
  Bipolar disorders
  Example: Bipolar I disorder
  Mood disorder due to a general medical condition
  Substance-induced mood disorder
  Mood disorder not otherwise specified

- Anxiety disorders
  Example: Panic disorder

- Somatoform disorders
  Example: Conversion disorder

- Factitious disorders (faked disability or illness)
  Example: Factitious disorder

- Dissociative disorders
  Example: Dissociative identity disorder

- Sexual and gender identity disorders
  Sexual dysfunctions
  Example: Sexual arousal disorders
  Paraphilias
  Example: Voyeurism
  Sexual disorder not otherwise specified
  Gender identity disorders
  Example: Gender identity disorder

- Eating disorders
  Example: Anorexia nervosa

- Sleep disorders
  Primary sleep disorders
  Dyssomnias
  Example: Primary insomnia
  Parasomnias
  Example: Sleep terror disorder
  Sleep disorders related to another mental disorder
  Example: Insomnia related to posttraumatic stress disorder
  Other sleep disorders
  Example: Substance-induced sleep disorder

- Impulse control disorders not elsewhere classified
  Example: Kleptomania

- Adjustment disorders
  Example: Adjustment disorder

- Personality disorders
  Example: Antisocial personality disorder

Mental disorder A significant impairment in psychological functioning.

An Overview of Psychological Disorders

People suffering from **psychotic disorders** have "retreated from reality." That is, they suffer from hallucinations and delusions and are socially withdrawn. Psychotic disorders are severely disabling and often lead to hospitalization. Typically, psychotic patients cannot control their thoughts and actions. For example, David often heard the voice of his Uncle Bill: "He told me to turn off the TV. He said, 'It's too damn loud, turn it down, turn it down.' Other times he talks about fishing. 'Good day for fishing. Got to go fishing'" (Durand & Barlow, 2006). Psychotic symptoms occur in schizophrenia, delusional disorders, and some mood disorders. Also, psychosis may be related to medical problems, drug abuse, and other conditions. (■ Table 12.2 provides a simplified list of major disorders.)

Organic mental disorders are problems caused by brain pathology; that is, by drug damage, diseases of the brain, injuries, poisons, and so on (● Fig. 12.2). A person with organic disorders may have severe emotional disturbances, impaired thinking, memory loss, personality changes, delirium, or psychotic symptoms (Nolen-Hoeksema, 2007).

In reality, almost all mental disorders are partly biological (Hansell, 2007). That's why *DSM-IV-TR* does not list "organic mental disorders" as a separate category. Nevertheless, all of the following problems are closely associated with organic damage: delirium, dementia, amnesia, and other cognitive disorders; mental disorders due to a general medical condition; and substance-related disorders (drug abuse).

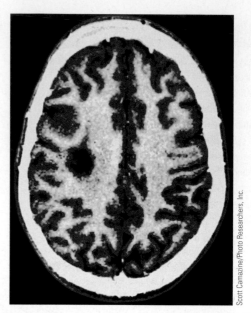

● **FIGURE 12.2** This MRI scan of a human brain (viewed from the top) reveals a tumor (dark spot). Mental disorders sometimes have organic causes of this sort. However, in many instances no organic damage can be found.

Mood disorders are primarily defined by the presence of extreme, intense, and long-lasting emotions. Afflicted persons may be *manic,* meaning agitated, elated, and hyperactive, or they may be *depressed.* Some people with mood disorders alternate between mania and depression, and they may have psychotic symptoms as well.

■ TABLE 12.2   Some Selected Categories of Psychopathology

PROBLEM	PRIMARY SYMPTOM	TYPICAL SIGNS OF TROUBLE
Psychotic disorders	Loss of contact with reality	You hear or see things that others don't; your mind has been playing tricks on you.
Mood disorders	Mania or depression	You feel sad and hopeless; or you talk too loud and too fast and have a rush of ideas and feelings that others think are unreasonable.
Anxiety disorders	High anxiety or anxiety-based	You have anxiety attacks and distortions of behavior; you feel like you are going to die; or you are afraid to do things that most people can do; or you spend unusual amounts of time doing things like washing your hands or counting your heartbeats.
Somatoform disorders	Bodily complaints without an organic (physical) basis	You feel physically sick, but your doctor says nothing is wrong with you; or you suffer from pain that has no physical basis; or you are preoccupied with thoughts about being sick.
Dissociative disorders	Amnesia, feelings of unreality, multiple identities	There are major gaps in your memory of events; you feel like you are a robot or a stranger to yourself; others tell you that you have done things that you don't remember doing.
Personality disorders	Unhealthy personality patterns	Your behavior patterns repeatedly cause problems at work, school, and in your relationships with others.
Sexual and gender identity disorders	Disturbed gender identity, deviant sexual behavior, problems in sexual adjustment	You feel that you are a man trapped in a woman's body (or the reverse); or you can only gain sexual satisfaction by engaging in highly atypical sexual behavior; or you have problems with sexual desire, arousal, or performance.
Substance-related disorders	Disturbances related to drug abuse or dependence	You have been drinking too much, using illegal drugs, or taking prescription drugs more often than you should.

The self-portraits shown here were painted by Andy Wilf between 1978 and 1981. During that time, Wilf is said to have increasingly abused drugs and alcohol. This dramatic series of images is a record of his self-destructive descent into a private hell. The third painting shows a shrouded skull—and foretells the artist's fate. Wilf died of a drug overdose. Drug abuse is but one of the many psychopathologies, or "problems in living," psychologists seek to alleviate. (Courtesy of Ulrike Kantor, Ulrike Kantor Gallery.)

Anxiety disorders are marked by fear or anxiety and by distorted behavior. Some anxiety disorders involve feelings of panic. Others take the form of phobias (irrational fears) or just overwhelming anxiety and nervousness. Two additional anxiety disorders are posttraumatic stress disorder and acute stress disorder. Obsessive-compulsive behavior patterns are also associated with high anxiety. (These problems are described later in this chapter.)

Somatoform (so-MAT-oh-form) **disorders** occur when a person has physical symptoms that mimic disease or injury (paralysis, blindness, illness, or chronic pain, for example), for which there is no identifiable physical cause. In such cases, psychological factors appear to explain the symptoms.

A person with a **dissociative disorder** may have temporary amnesia or multiple personalities. Also included in this category are frightening episodes of depersonalization, in which people feel like they are outside their bodies, are behaving like robots, or are lost in a dream world.

Personality disorders are deeply ingrained, unhealthy personality patterns. Such patterns usually appear in adolescence and continue through much of adult life. They include paranoid (overly suspicious), narcissistic (self-loving), dependent, borderline, and antisocial personality types, as well as others.

Sexual and gender identity disorders include any of a wide range of difficulties with sexual identity, deviant sexual behavior, or sexual adjustment. In gender identity disorders, sexual identity does not match a person's physical sex and the person may seek a sex-change operation. Deviations in sexual behavior known as *paraphilias* include exhibitionism, fetishism, voyeurism, and so on. Also found in this category are a variety of *sexual dysfunctions* (problems in sexual desire, arousal, or response). (Sexual dysfunctions are discussed in Module 14.4.)

Substance-related disorders involve abuse of, or dependence on, psychoactive drugs. Typical culprits include alcohol, barbiturates, opiates, cocaine, amphetamines, hallucinogens, marijuana, and nicotine. A person with a substance-related disorder cannot stop using the drug and may also suffer from withdrawal symptoms, delirium, dementia, amnesia, psychosis, emotional outbursts, sexual problems, and sleep disturbances. (Problems with drug abuse and dependence are discussed in Module 5.4.)

Shouldn't neurosis be listed here? Neurosis was once a recognized mental disorder. However, it is no longer included in the DSM because the term *neurosis* is too imprecise. Behavior that psychologists used to refer to as "neurotic" is now a part of anxiety, somatoform, or dissociative disorders. Even though **neurosis** is an outdated term, you may still hear it used to loosely refer to problems involving excessive anxiety.

In addition to the formal mental disorders we have reviewed, many cultures have names for "unofficial" psychological "disorders." See "Running Amok with Cultural Maladies" for some examples.

Psychotic disorder A severe mental disorder characterized by a retreat from reality, by hallucinations and delusions, and by social withdrawal.

Organic mental disorder A mental or emotional problem caused by brain diseases or injuries.

Mood disorder A major disturbance in mood or emotion, such as depression or mania.

Anxiety disorder Disruptive feelings of fear, apprehension, or anxiety, or distortions in behavior that are anxiety related.

Somatoform disorder Physical symptoms that mimic disease or injury for which there is no identifiable physical cause.

Dissociative disorder Temporary amnesia, multiple personality, or depersonalization.

Personality disorder A maladaptive personality pattern.

Sexual and gender identity disorders Any of a wide range of difficulties with sexual identity, deviant sexual behavior, or sexual adjustment.

Substance-related disorder Abuse of or dependence on a mood- or behavior-altering drug.

Neurosis An outdated term once used to refer, as a group, to anxiety disorders, somatoform disorders, dissociative disorders, and some forms of depression.

HUMAN DIVERSITY

Running Amok with Cultural Maladies

Every culture recognizes the existence of psychopathology, and most have at least a few folk names for afflictions you won't find in the *DSM-IV-TR*. Called *culture-bound syndromes*, here are some examples from around the world (Durand & Barlow, 2006; López & Guarnaccia, 2000; Sumathipala, Siribaddana, & Bhugra, 2004):

- **Amok** Men in Malaysia, Laos, the Philippines, and Polynesia who believe they have been insulted are sometimes known to go *amok*. After a period of brooding they erupt into an outburst of violent, aggressive, or homicidal behavior randomly directed at people and objects.

- **Susto** Among Latin Americans, the symptoms of susto include insomnia, irritability, phobias, and an increase in sweating and heart rate. Susto can result if someone is badly frightened by a black magic curse. In extreme cases, *voodoo death* can result, as the person is literally scared to death.

- **Ghost sickness** Among many American Indian tribes, people who become preoccupied

with death and the deceased are said to suffer from *ghost sickness*. The symptoms of ghost sickness include bad dreams, weakness, loss of appetite, fainting, dizziness, fear, anxiety, hallucinations, loss of consciousness, confusion, feelings of futility, and a sense of suffocation.

- **Koro** In southern and eastern Asia, a man may experience sudden and intense anxiety that his penis (or, in females, the vulva and nipples) will recede into the body. In addition to the terror this incites, victims also believe that advanced cases of *koro* can cause death. A similar fear of shrinking genitals has also been reported from West Africa (Dzokoto & Adams, 2005).

- **Zar** In North African and Middle Eastern societies, zar is said to occur when spirits possess an individual. Zar is marked by shouting, laughing, hitting the head against a wall, singing, or weeping. Victims may become apathetic or withdrawn and they may refuse to eat or carry out daily tasks.

- **Dhat** In Indian society, *dhat* is the fear of the loss of semen during nocturnal emissions. A man suffering from dhat will feel anxious and perhaps also guilty. He may also experience fatigue, loss of appetite, weakness, anxiety, and sexual dysfunction.

It's clear that people have a need to label and categorize disturbed behavior. As you can see, however, folk terminology tends to be vague. The terms listed here provide little guidance about the true nature of a person's problems or the best ways to treat them. That's why the *DSM* is based on empirical data and clinical observations. Otherwise, psychologists and psychiatrists would be no better than folk healers when making diagnoses (Ancis, Chen, & Schultz, 2004). By the way, culture-bound disorders occur in all societies. For example, American psychologists Pamela Keel and Kelly Klump believe that bulimia is primarily a syndrome of Western cultures, including the United States (Keel & Klump, 2003).

General Risk Factors

What causes psychological disorders like those listed in Table 12.2? We will soon explore the causes of some specific problems. For now, here are some general risk factors that contribute to psychopathology, including the following factors:

- **Social conditions:** poverty, stressful living conditions, homelessness, social disorganization, overcrowding
- **Family factors:** parents who are immature, mentally disturbed, criminal, or abusive; severe marital strife; extremely poor child discipline; disordered family communication patterns
- **Psychological factors:** stress, low intelligence, learning disorders, lack of control or mastery
- **Biological/physical factors:** genetic defects or inherited vulnerabilities, poor prenatal care, very low birth weight, chronic physical illness or disability, exposure to toxic chemicals or drugs, head injuries

Insanity

Which of the mental disorders causes insanity? None. **Insanity** is a legal term. It refers to an inability to manage one's affairs or foresee the consequences of one's actions. People who are declared insane are not legally responsible for their actions. If necessary, they can be involuntarily committed to a mental hospital.

Legally, insanity is established by testimony from *expert witnesses* (psychologists and psychiatrists) recognized by a court of law as being qualified to give opinions on a specific topic. Involuntary commitments happen most often when people are brought to emergency rooms. People who are involuntarily committed are usually judged to be a danger to themselves or to others, or they are severely mentally disabled (Luchins et al., 2004).

An Important Note—You're Okay, Really! In upcoming modules we will explore some selected problems in more detail, beginning with personality disorders. As your authors, we hope that you will not fall prey to "medical student's disease." Medical students, it seems, have a predictable tendency to notice in themselves the symptoms of each dreaded disease they study. As a psychology student you may notice what seem to be abnormal tendencies in your own behavior. If so, don't panic. In most instances, this only shows that pathological behavior is an *exaggeration* of normal defenses and reactions, not that your behavior is abnormal.

MODULE 12.1 Summary

How is normality defined, and what are the major psychological disorders?

- *Psychopathology* refers to maladaptive behavior and to the scientific study of mental disorders.
- Factors that typically affect judgments of abnormality include subjective discomfort, statistical abnormality, nonconformity, context, and culture.

- Two key elements of mental disorder are that abnormal behavior is maladaptive and it involves a loss of self-control.
- Judgments of normality are relative, but psychological disorders clearly exist and they need to be classified, explained, and treated.
- A widely used system for classifying mental disorders is found in the *Diagnostic and Statistical Manual of Mental Disorders (DSM)*.
- Major mental problems include psychotic disorders, organic disorders, mood disorders, anxiety disorders, somatoform disorders, dissociative disorders, personality disorders, sexual or gender identity disorders, and substance-related disorders.
- *Insanity* is a legal term defining whether a person may be held responsible for his or her actions. Sanity is determined in court on the basis of testimony by expert witnesses.

Insanity A legal term that refers to a mental inability to manage one's affairs or to be aware of the consequences of one's actions.

KNOWLEDGE BUILDER

Normality and Psychopathology

Recite

1. The core feature of abnormal behavior is that it is
   a. statistically unusual
   b. maladaptive
   c. socially nonconforming
   d. a source of subjective discomfort

2. One of the most powerful contexts in which judgments of normality and abnormality are made is
   a. the family
   b. occupational settings
   c. religious systems
   d. culture

3. Amnesia, multiple identities, and depersonalization are possible problems in
   a. mood disorders
   b. somatoform disorders
   c. psychosis
   d. dissociative disorders

4. Which among the following is not a major psychological problem listed in the DSM-IV-TR?
   a. mood disorders
   b. personality disorders
   c. insanity
   d. anxiety disorders

5. People are said to have "retreated from reality" when they suffer from
   a. psychotic disorders
   b. mood disorders
   c. somatoform disorders
   d. personality disorders

6. Koro and dhat are
   a. somatoform disorders
   b. forms of psychosis
   c. folk terminology
   d. organic mental disorders

7. Someone who engages in one of the paraphilias has what type of disorder?
   a. dissociative
   b. somatoform
   c. substance
   d. sexual

8. Which of the following is a legal concept?
   a. neurosis
   b. psychosis
   c. drapetomania
   d. insanity

Reflect
Critical Thinking

9. Brian, a fan of grunge rock, occasionally wears a skirt in public. Does Brian's cross-dressing indicate that he has a mental disorder?

10. Many states began to restrict use of the insanity defense after John Hinkley, Jr., who tried to murder former U.S. President Ronald Reagan, was acquitted by reason of insanity. What does this trend reveal about insanity?

Relate

Think of an instance of abnormal behavior you have witnessed. By what formal standards would the behavior be regarded as abnormal? In what way was the behavior maladaptive?

What disorders would the following sentences help you remember? An anxious psychotic in a bad mood asked for an organic substance. "First you have to fill out a somatoform and tell us what sex or gender you are," he was told. "Don't diss my personality," he replied.

Link

Internet addresses frequently change. To find the sites listed here, visit **http://www.thomsonedu.com/psychology/coon** for an updated list of Internet addresses and direct links to relevant sites.

- **Against All Odds** Read an article about Carol North, the psychiatrist who overcame schizophrenia.
- **The Insanity Defense** Follow some of the history of the insanity defense.
- **Psychiatric Disorders** Explore a complete listing of the DSM-IV-TR diagnostic categories.

ANSWERS

1. b 2. d 3. d 4. c 5. a 6. c 7. d 8. d 9. Probably not. Undoubtedly, Brian's cross-dressing is socially disapproved of by many people. Nevertheless, to be classified as a mental disorder it must cause him to feel disabling shame, guilt, depression, or anxiety. The cultural relativity of behavior like Brian's is revealed by the fact that it is fashionable and acceptable for women to wear men's clothing. 10. It emphasizes that insanity is a legal concept, not a psychiatric diagnosis. Laws reflect community standards. When those standards change, lawmakers may seek to alter definitions of legal responsibility.

12.2 Personality Disorders and Anxiety-Based Disorders

YOU PROBABLY KNOW SOMEONE whose personality characteristics make life difficult for her or him. Imagine that person's traits becoming even more extreme. If they did, the person would have a personality disorder, our first topic in this unit.

Now imagine that you are waiting to take an extremely important test, waiting to give a speech to a large audience, or waiting to find out if you or a loved one has a serious illness. You've almost certainly felt anxiety in similar situations. If so, then you will understand why anxiety-based disorders are so debilitating. People who suffer from extreme anxiety are miserable most of the time, and their behavior becomes distorted and self-defeating. In this module, we'll also discuss anxiety disorders and why they occur.

Personality Disorders—Blueprints for Maladjustment

SURVEY QUESTION: *What is a personality disorder?*

"Get out of here and leave me alone so I can die in peace," Judy screamed at her nurses in the seclusion room of the psychiatric hospital. On one of her arms, long dark red marks mingled with the scars of previous suicide attempts. Judy once bragged that her record was 67 stitches. Today, the nurses had to strap her into restraints to keep her from gouging her own eyes. She was given a sedative and slept for 12 hours. She woke calmly and asked for her therapist—even though her latest outburst began when he canceled a morning appointment and changed it to afternoon.

Judy has a condition called *borderline personality disorder.* Although she is capable of working, Judy has repeatedly lost jobs because of her turbulent relationships with other people. At times she can be friendly and a real charmer. At other times she is extremely unpredictable, moody, and even suicidal. Being a friend to Judy can be a fearsome challenge. Canceling an appointment, forgetting a special date, a wrong turn of phrase—these and similar small incidents may trigger Judy's rage or a suicide attempt. Like other people with borderline personality disorder, Judy is extremely sensitive to ordinary criticism, which leaves her feeling rejected and abandoned. Typically, she reacts with anger, self-hatred, and impulsive behavior. These "emotional storms" damage her personal relationships and leave her confused about who she is (Siever & Koenigsberg, 2000).

Maladaptive Personality Patterns

As stated earlier, a person with a personality disorder has maladaptive personality traits. For example, people with a paranoid personality disorder are suspicious, hypersensitive, and wary of others. Narcissistic persons need constant admiration, and they are lost in fantasies of power, wealth, brilliance, beauty, or love. Celebrities appear to more likely to be narcissistic than noncelebrities (Young & Pinsky, 2006). The dependent personality suffers from extremely low self-confidence. Dependent persons allow others to run their lives, and they place everyone else's needs ahead of their own. People with a histrionic personality disorder constantly seek attention by dramatizing their emotions and actions.

Typically, patterns such as the ones just described begin during adolescence or even childhood. Thus, personality disorders are deeply rooted and usually span many years. The list of personality disorders is long (■ Table 12.3), so let us focus on a single frequently misunderstood problem, the antisocial personality.

Antisocial Personality

What are the characteristics of an antisocial personality? A person with an **antisocial personality** lacks a conscience. Such people are impulsive, selfish, dishonest, emotionally shallow, and manipulative. Antisocial persons, who are sometimes called *sociopaths* or *psychopaths,* are poorly socialized and seem to be incapable of feeling guilt, shame, fear, loyalty, or love (DSM-IV-TR, 2000).

Are sociopaths dangerous? Sociopaths tend to have a long history of conflict with society. Many are delinquents or criminals who may be a threat to the general public (Ogloff, 2006). However, sociopaths are rarely the crazed murderers you may have seen portrayed on TV and in movies. In fact, many sociopaths are "charming" at first. Their "friends" only gradually become aware of the sociopath's lying and self-serving manipulation. One study found that psychopaths are "blind" to signs of disgust in others. This may add to their capacity for cruelty and their ability to use others (Kosson et al., 2002). Many successful businesspersons, entertainers, politicians, and other seemingly normal people have psycho-

Antisocial personality A person who lacks a conscience; is emotionally shallow, impulsive, selfish; and tends to manipulate others.

■ TABLE 12.3 Personality Disorders: Maladaptive Patterns and Degree of Impairment

MODERATE IMPAIRMENT

Dependent You lack confidence, and you are extremely submissive and dependent on others (clinging).

Histrionic You are dramatic and flamboyant; you exaggerate your emotions to get attention from others.

Narcissistic You think you are wonderful, brilliant, important, and worthy of constant admiration.

Antisocial You are irresponsible, lack guilt or remorse, and engage in antisocial behavior, such as aggression, deceit, or recklessness.

HIGH IMPAIRMENT

Obsessive-compulsive You demand order, perfection, control, and rigid routine at all times.

Schizoid You feel very little emotion and can't form close personal relationships with others.

Avoidant You are timid, uncomfortable in social situations, and fear evaluation.

SEVERE IMPAIRMENT

Borderline Your self-image, moods, and impulses are erratic, and you are extremely sensitive to any hint of criticism, rejection, or abandonment by others.

Paranoid You deeply distrust others and are suspicious of their motives, which you perceive as insulting or threatening.

Schizotypal You are a loner, you engage in extremely odd behavior, and your thought patterns are bizarre, but you are not actively psychotic.

Sources: DSM-IV-TR, 2000; Millon, 1981.

Studies show that more than 65 percent of all persons with antisocial personalities have been arrested, usually for crimes such as robbery, vandalism, or rape.

Again, this coldness seems to account for an unusual ability to calmly lie, cheat, steal, or take advantage of others.

Can sociopathy be treated? Antisocial personality disorders are rarely treated with success (Hare, 2006). All too often, sociopaths manipulate therapy, just like any other situation. If it is to their advantage to act "cured," they will do so. However, they return to their former behavior patterns as soon as possible. On a more positive note, antisocial behavior does tend to decline somewhat after age 40, even without treatment, because people tend to become more "mellow" as they age (Laub & Sampson, 2003).

pathic leanings. Basically, antisocial persons coldly use others and cheat their way through life (Ogloff, 2006).

Causes *What causes sociopathy?* Typically, people with antisocial personalities showed similar problems in childhood (Burt et al., 2007). Many were emotionally deprived and physically abused as children (Pollock et al., 1990). Adult sociopaths also display subtle neurological problems (● Fig. 12.3). For example, they have unusual brainwave patterns that suggest under-arousal of the brain. This may explain why sociopaths tend to be thrill seekers. Quite likely, they are searching for stimulation strong enough to overcome their chronic under-arousal and feelings of "boredom" (Hare, 2006).

In a revealing study, psychopaths were shown extremely grisly and unpleasant photographs of mutilations. The photos were so upsetting that they visibly startled normal people. The psychopaths, however, showed no startle response to the photos (Levenston et al., 2000). (They didn't "bat an eyelash.") Those with antisocial personalities might therefore be described as *emotionally cold.* They simply do not feel normal pangs of conscience, guilt, or anxiety (Blair et al., 2006).

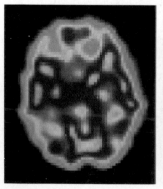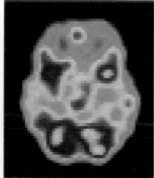

● **FIGURE 12.3** Using PET scans, Canadian psychologist Robert Hare found that the normally functioning brain *(left)* lights up with activity when a person sees emotion-laden words such as "maggot" or "cancer." But the brain of a psychopath *(right)* remains inactive, especially in areas associated with feelings and self-control. When Dr. Hare showed the bottom image to several neurologists, one asked, "Is this person from Mars?" (Images courtesy of Robert Hare.)

An individual with an antisocial personality feels very little anxiety. At the other end of the scale, people who have lots of anxiety also suffer from debilitating problems, as described next.

Anxiety-Based Disorders— When Anxiety Rules

SURVEY QUESTION: *What problems result when a person suffers high levels of anxiety?*

Anxiety refers to feelings of apprehension, dread, or uneasiness. We all feel anxiety, but anxiety that is out of proportion to a situation may reveal a problem. An example is a college student named Jian, who became unbearably anxious when he took exams. By the time Jian went to see a counselor, he had skipped several tests and was in danger of dropping out of school. In general, people with anxiety-related problems like Jian's display the following characteristics:

- High levels of anxiety and/or restrictive, self-defeating behavior patterns
- A tendency to use elaborate defense mechanisms or avoidance responses to get through the day
- Pervasive feelings of stress, insecurity, inferiority, and dissatisfaction with life

People with anxiety-related problems feel threatened and often can't do anything constructive about it. They struggle to control themselves, but they remain ineffective and unhappy (Rachman, 2004). In any given year, roughly 18 percent of the adult population suffers from an anxiety disorder (NIMH, 2006b).

If anxiety is a normal emotion, when does it signify a problem? A problem exists when intense anxiety prevents people from doing what they want or need to do. Also, their anxieties are out of control—they simply cannot stop worrying.

Adjustment Disorders

Do such problems cause a "nervous breakdown"? People suffering from anxiety-based problems may be miserable, but they rarely experience a "breakdown." Actually, the term *nervous breakdown* has no formal meaning. Nevertheless, a problem known as an *adjustment disorder* does come close to being something of a "breakdown."

Adjustment disorders occur when ordinary stresses push people beyond their ability to cope with life. Examples of such stresses are losing a job, intense marital strife, and chronic physical illness. People suffering from an adjustment disorder may be extremely irritable, anxious, apathetic, or depressed. They also have trouble sleeping, lose their appe-

tite, and suffer from various physical complaints. Often, their problems can be relieved by rest, sedation, supportive counseling, and a chance to "talk through" their fears and anxieties (DSM-IV-TR, 2000).

How is an adjustment disorder different from an anxiety disorder? The outward symptoms are similar. However, adjustment disorders disappear when a person's life circumstances improve. People suffering from anxiety disorders seem to generate their own misery, regardless of what's happening around them. They feel that they must be on guard against *future* threats that *could happen* at any time (Barlow, 2000).

Anxiety Disorders

In most anxiety disorders, distress seems greatly out of proportion to a person's circumstances. For example, consider the following description of Adrian H:

> She becomes very anxious that her children "might have been hurt or killed if they were out of the neighborhood playing and she hadn't heard from them in a couple of hours." She also worries all the time about her job performance and her relationships with men. Adrian believes that men rarely call back after a date or two because "They can sense I'm not a fun person." She never really relaxes, has difficulty focusing at work, has frequent headaches, and suffers from insomnia. (Adapted from Brown & Barlow, 2007.)

Distress like Adrian H's is a key ingredient in anxiety disorders. It also may underlie dissociative and somatoform disorders, where maladaptive behavior serves to reduce anxiety and discomfort. To deepen your understanding, let's first examine the anxiety disorders themselves (■ Table 12.4). Then we will see how anxiety contributes to other problems.

Generalized Anxiety Disorder A person with a **generalized anxiety disorder** has been extremely anxious and worried for at least 6 months. Sufferers typically complain of sweating, a racing heart, clammy hands, dizziness, upset stomach, rapid breathing, irritability, and poor concentration. Overall, more women than men have these symptoms (Brown & Barlow, 2007).

Adjustment disorder An emotional disturbance caused by ongoing stressors within the range of common experience.

Generalized anxiety disorder A chronic state of tension and worry about work, relationships, ability, or impending disaster.

TABLE 12.4 Anxiety Disorders

TYPE OF DISORDER	TYPICAL SIGNS OF TROUBLE
Generalized anxiety disorder	You have been extremely anxious or worried for 6 months.
Panic disorder (without agoraphobia)	You are anxious much of the time and have sudden panic attacks.
Panic disorder (with agoraphobia)	You have panic attacks and are afraid that they might occur in public places, so you rarely leave home.
Agoraphobia (without a history of panic disorder)	You fear that something extremely embarrassing will happen if you leave home (but you don't have panic attacks).
Specific phobia	You have an intense fear of specific objects, activities, or locations.
Social phobia	You fear social situations where people can watch, criticize, embarrass, or humiliate you.
Obsessive-compulsive disorder	Your thoughts make you extremely nervous and compel you to rigidly repeat certain actions or routines.
Acute stress disorder	You are tormented for less than a month by the emotional after effects of horrible events you have experienced.
Posttraumatic stress disorder	You are tormented for more than a month by the emotional aftereffects of horrible events you have experienced.

Source: DSM-IV-TR, 2000.

Was Adrian H's problem a generalized anxiety disorder? Yes. However, if she also experienced *anxiety attacks,* then she would likely be diagnosed with panic disorder.

Panic Disorder (without Agoraphobia)

In a **panic disorder** (**without agoraphobia**) people are highly anxious and also feel sudden, intense, unexpected panic. During a panic attack, victims experience chest pain, a racing heart, dizziness, choking, feelings of unreality, trembling, or fears of losing control. Many believe that they are having a heart attack, are going insane, or are about to die. Needless to say, this pattern leaves victims unhappy and uncomfortable much of the time. Again, the majority of people who suffer from panic disorder are women (Foot & Koszycki, 2004).

To get an idea of how a panic attack feels, imagine that you are trapped in your stateroom on a sinking ocean liner (the *Titanic*?). The room fills with water. When only a small air space remains near the ceiling and you are gasping for air, you'll know what a panic attack feels like.

Panic Disorder (with Agoraphobia)

In a **panic disorder** (**with agoraphobia**) people suffer from chronic anxiety and sudden panic. In addition, they have agoraphobia (ah-go-rah-FOBE-ee-ah), which is an intense *fear that a panic attack will occur* in a public place or unfamiliar situation. That is, agoraphobics intensely fear leaving their home and familiar surroundings. Typically, they find ways of avoiding places that frighten them—such as crowds, open roads, supermarkets, automobiles, and so on. As a result, some agoraphobics are prisoners in their own homes (DSM-IV-TR, 2000).

Agoraphobia The problem known as **agoraphobia** can also occur without panic. In this case, people *fear that something extremely embarrassing will happen* if they leave home or enter an unfamiliar situation. For example, an agoraphobic person may refuse to go outside because he or she fears having a sudden attack of dizziness, or diarrhea, or shortness of breath. Going outside the home alone, being in a crowd, standing in line, crossing a bridge, or riding in a car can be impossible for an agoraphobic person (DSM-IV-TR, 2000). About 4.2 percent of all adults suffer from agoraphobia (with or without panic) during their lifetime (Grant et al., 2006).

Specific Phobia As we noted earlier, phobias are intense, irrational fears that a person cannot shake off, even when there is no real danger. In a **specific phobia**, the person's fear, anxiety, and avoidance are focused on particular objects, activities, or situations. People affected by phobias recognize that their fears are unreasonable, but they cannot control them. For example, a person with a spider phobia would find it impossible to ignore a *picture* of a spider, even though a photograph can't bite anyone (Miltner et al., 2004). Specific phobias can be linked to nearly any object or situation. Many have been given names, such as these:

Acrophobia—fear of heights
Astraphobia—fear of storms, thunder, lightning
Arachnophobia—fear of spiders
Aviophobia—fear of airplanes
Claustrophobia—fear of closed spaces
Hematophobia—fear of blood
Microphobia—fear of germs
Nyctophobia—fear of darkness
Pathophobia—fear of disease
Triskaidekaphobia—fear of the number 13
Xenophobia—fear of strangers
Zoophobia—fear of animals

By combining the appropriate root word with the word *phobia,* any number of unlikely fears can be named. Some are *zemmiphobia,* fear of the great mole rat; *phobosophobia,* fear of fear; *arachibutyrophobia,* fear of peanut butter sticking to the roof of the mouth; and *hippopotomonstrosesquipedaliophobia,* fear of long words!

For a person with a strong fear of snakes (ophidiophobia), merely looking at this picture may be unsettling.

The severe obsessions and compulsions of billionaire Howard Hughes led him to live as a recluse for more than 20 years. Hughes had an intense fear of contamination. To avoid infection, he constructed sterile, isolated environments in which his contact with people and objects was strictly limited by complicated rituals. Before handling a spoon, for instance, Hughes had his attendants wrap the handle in tissue paper and seal it with tape. A second piece of tissue was then wrapped around the first before he would touch it (Hodgson & Miller, 1982). A spoon prepared as Hughes required is shown at right.

Almost everyone has a few mild phobias, such as fearing heights, closed spaces, or bugs and crawly things. A phobic disorder differs from such garden-variety fears in that it produces overwhelming fear. True phobias may lead to vomiting, wild climbing and running, or fainting. For a phobic disorder to exist, the person's fear must disrupt his or her daily life. Phobic persons are so threatened that they will go to almost any length to avoid the feared object or situation, such as driving 50 miles out of the way to avoid crossing a bridge. About 8 percent of all adults have phobic disorders during their lifetime (NIMH, 2006a).

Social Phobia In a **social phobia,** people fear situations in which they can be observed, evaluated, embarrassed, or humiliated by others. This leads them to avoid certain social situations, such as eating, writing, using the rest room, or speaking in public. When such situations cannot be avoided, people endure them with intense anxiety or distress. It is common for them to have uncomfortable physical symptoms, such as a pounding heart, shaking hands, sweating, diarrhea, mental confusion, and blushing. Social phobias greatly impair a person's ability to work, attend school, and form personal relationships (DSM-IV-TR, 2000). About 7 percent of all adults are affected by social phobias in a given year (NIMH, 2006b).

Obsessive-Compulsive Disorder People who suffer from **obsessive-compulsive disorder** are preoccupied with certain distressing thoughts and feel compelled to perform certain behaviors. You have probably experienced a mild obsessional thought, such as a song or stupid commercial jingle that repeats over and over in your mind. This may be irritating, but

it's usually not terribly disturbing. True obsessions are images or thoughts that force their way into awareness against a person's will. They are so disturbing that they cause intense anxiety. The most common obsessions are about violence or harm (such as poisoning one's spouse or being hit by a car), about being "dirty" or "unclean," about whether one has performed some action (such as turning off the stove), and about committing immoral acts (Barlow, 2002).

Obsessions usually give rise to compulsions. These are irrational acts that a person feels driven to repeat. Often, compulsive acts help control or block out anxiety caused by an obsession. For example, a minister who finds profanities popping into her mind might start compulsively counting her heartbeat. Doing this would prevent her from thinking "dirty" words.

Panic disorder (without agoraphobia) A chronic state of anxiety and also brief moments of sudden, intense, unexpected panic.

Panic disorder (with agoraphobia) A chronic state of anxiety and brief moments of sudden panic. The person fears that these panic attacks will occur in public places or unfamiliar situations.

Agoraphobia (without panic) The fear that something extremely embarrassing will happen if one leaves the house or enters unfamiliar situation.

Specific phobia An intense, irrational fear of specific objects, activities, or situations.

Social phobia An intense, irrational fear of being observed, evaluated, embarrassed, or humiliated by others in social situations.

Obsessive-compulsive disorder An extreme preoccupation with certain thoughts and compulsive performance of certain behaviors.

Many compulsive people are *checkers* or *cleaners*. For instance, a young mother who repeatedly pictures a knife plunging into her baby might check once an hour to make sure all the knives in her house are locked away. Doing so may reduce her anxieties, but it will probably also take over her life. Likewise, a person who feels "contaminated" from touching ordinary objects because "germs are everywhere" may be driven to wash his hands hundreds of times a day.

Of course, not all obsessive-compulsive disorders are so dramatic. Many simply involve extreme orderliness and rigid routine. Compulsive attention to detail and rigidly following rules helps keep activities totally under control and makes the highly anxious person feel more secure. (Notice that if such patterns are long-standing, but less intense, they are classified as a personality disorder.)

Stress Disorders

Stress disorders occur when people experience stresses outside the range of normal human experience, such as floods, tornadoes, earthquakes, or horrible accidents. They affect many political hostages; combat veterans; prisoners of war; victims of terrorism, torture, violent crime, child molestation, rape, or domestic violence; or people who have witnessed a death or serious injury (Brown & Barlow, 2007).

Symptoms of stress disorders include repeatedly reliving the traumatic event, avoiding reminders of the event, and blunted emotions. Also common are insomnia, nightmares, wariness, poor concentration, irritability, and explosive anger or aggression. If such reactions last *less* than a month after a traumatic event, the problem is called an **acute stress disorder.** If they last *more* than a month, the person is suffering from **posttraumatic stress disorder (PTSD)** (Nemeroff et al., 2006).

In December 2004 a tsunami killed more than 250,000 people in southern Asia. In the aftermath of such disasters, many survivors suffer from acute stress reactions. For some, the flare-up of anxiety and distress lasts for months or years after the stressful event, an example of a posttraumatic stress reaction.

If a situation causes distress, anxiety, or fear, we tend to avoid it in the future. This is a normal survival instinct. However, victims of PTSD fail to recover from these reactions. Military combat accounts for more than a quarter of the cases of PTSD among American men (Prigerson, Maciejewski, & Rosenheck, 2002). The constant threat of death and the gruesome sights and sounds of war take a terrible toll. Psychologists are already seeing high rates of PTSD among soldiers involved in combat in Iraq (Hoge et al., 2004). Sadly, 8 percent of military veterans still suffer from PTSD decades after they were in combat (Dirkzwager, Bramsen, & Van Der Ploeg, 2001). About 3.5 percent of adults suffer from posttraumatic stress in any given year (NIMH, 2006b).

Dissociative Disorders

In dissociative reactions we see striking episodes of *amnesia, fugue,* or *multiple identity.* **Dissociative amnesia** is an inability to recall one's name, address, or past. **Dissociative fugue** (FEWG) involves sudden, unplanned travel away from home and confusion about personal identity. Dissociations are often triggered by highly traumatic events (McLewin & Muller, 2006). In such cases, forgetting personal identity and fleeing unpleasant situations appear to be defenses against intolerable anxiety.

A person suffering from a **dissociative identity disorder** has two or more separate identities or personality states. (Note that identity disorders are not the same as schizophrenia. Schizophrenia, which is a psychotic disorder, is discussed later in this chapter.) One famous and dramatic example of multiple identities is described in the book *Sybil* (Schreiber, 1973). Sybil reportedly had 16 different personality states. Each identity had a distinct voice, vocabulary, and posture. One personality could play the piano (not Sybil), but the others could not.

When an identity other than Sybil was in control, Sybil experienced a "time lapse," or memory blackout. Sybil's amnesia and alternate identities first appeared during childhood. As a girl she was beaten, locked in closets, perversely tortured, sexually abused, and almost killed. Sybil's first dissociations allowed her to escape by creating another person who would suffer torture in her place. Identity disorders often begin with unbearable childhood experiences, like Sybil endured. A history of childhood trauma, especially sexual abuse, is found in a high percentage of persons whose personalities split into multiple identities (McLewin & Muller, 2006; Simeon et al., 2002).

Flamboyant cases like Sybil's have led some experts to question the existence of multiple personalities (Casey, 2001). However, a majority of psychologists continue to believe that multiple identity is a real, if rare, problem (Cormier & Thelen, 1998).

THE CLINICAL FILE

Sick of Being Sick

At 14, Ben was in the hospital again for his sinus problem. He had already undergone 40 surgeries since the age of 8. In addition, he had been diagnosed at various times with bipolar disorder, oppositional defiant disorder, and attention deficit disorder. Ben was taking 19 different medications, and his mother said she desperately wanted him to be "healed." She sought numerous tests and never missed an appointment. But at long last, it became clear that there was nothing wrong with Ben. Left alone with doctors, Ben revealed that he was "sick of being sick."

In reality, it was Ben's mother who was sick. She was eventually diagnosed as suffering from **Munchausen syndrome by proxy** (Awadallah, et al., 2005). This is a pattern in which a person fakes the medical problems of someone in his or her care. (In **Munchausen syndrome,** the person fakes his or her own medical problems.) As in Ben's case, most people with the syndrome are mothers who fabricate their children's illnesses. Sometimes they even deliberately harm their children. For example, one mother injected her son with 7-Up (Reisner, 2006).

But why? People who suffer from Munchausen syndrome and Munchausen by proxy appear to have a pathological need to seek attention and sympathy from medical professionals. They may also win praise for being health conscious or a good parent (DSM-IV-TR, 2000).

Munchausen by proxy illustrates another point about psychological disorders: Sam's mother was eventually diagnosed with several disorders, including Munchausen by proxy, schizoaffective disorder, and borderline personality disorder. As this suggests, many disturbed people are *comorbid.* That is, they suffer from more than one disorder at a time. Not only does comorbidity increase their misery, it makes it more difficult for health care providers to diagnose and treat them.

Therapy for dissociative identity disorders may make use of hypnosis, which allows contact with the various personality states. The goal of therapy is *integration* and *fusion* of the identities into a single, balanced personality. Fortunately, multiple identity disorders are far rarer in real life than they are in TV dramas!

Somatoform Disorders

Have you ever known someone who appeared to be healthy but seemed to constantly worry about disease? These people are preoccupied with bodily functions, such as their heartbeat or breathing or digestion. Minor physical problems—even a small sore or an occasional cough—may convince them that they have cancer or some other dreaded disease. Typically, they can't give up their fears of illness, even if doctors can find no medical basis for their complaints (Korol, Craig, & Firestone, 2003).

Are you describing hypochondria? Yes. In **hypochondriasis** (HI-po-kon-DRY-uh-sis), people interpret normal bodily sensations as proof that they have a terrible disease (see "Sick of Being Sick" for a related disorder with a curious twist). In a related problem called **somatization disorder** (som-ah-tuh-ZAY-shun), people express their anxieties through various bodily complaints. That is, they suffer from problems such as vomiting or nausea, shortness of breath, difficulty swallowing, or painful menstrual periods. Typically, the person feels ill much of the time and visits doctors repeatedly. Most sufferers take medicines or other treatments, but no physical cause can be found for their distress. Similarly, a person with **pain disorder** is disabled by pain that has no identifiable physical basis.

Stress disorder A significant emotional disturbance caused by stresses outside the range of normal human experience.

Acute stress disorder A psychological disturbance lasting up to 1 month following stresses that would produce anxiety in anyone who experienced them.

Posttraumatic stress disorder (PTSD) A psychological disturbance lasting more than 1 month following stresses that would produce anxiety in anyone who experienced them.

Dissociative amnesia Loss of memory (partial or complete) for important information related to personal identity.

Dissociative fugue Sudden travel away from home, plus confusion about one's personal identity.

Dissociative identity disorder The presence of two or more distinct personalities (multiple personality).

Hypochondriasis A preoccupation with fears of having a serious disease. Ordinary physical signs are interpreted as proof that the person has a disease, but no physical disorder can be found.

Somatization disorder Afflicted persons have numerous physical complaints. Typically, they have consulted many doctors, but no organic cause for their distress can be identified.

Pain disorder Pain that has no identifiable physical cause and appears to be of psychological origin.

Munchausen syndrome by proxy An affected person fakes the medical problems of someone in his or her care in order to gain attention.

Munchausen syndrome An affected person fakes his or her own medical problems in order to gain attention.

A rarer somatoform disorder ("body-form" disorder) is called a *conversion reaction.* In a **conversion disorder,** severe emotional conflicts are "converted" into symptoms that actually disturb physical functioning or closely resemble a physical disability. For instance, a soldier might become deaf or lame or develop "glove anesthesia" just before a battle.

What is "glove anesthesia"? "Glove anesthesia" is a loss of sensitivity in the areas of the skin that would normally be covered by a glove. Glove anesthesia shows that conversion symptoms often contradict known medical facts. The system of nerves in the hands does not form a glove-like pattern and could not cause such symptoms (● Fig. 12.4).

If symptoms disappear when a victim is asleep, hypnotized, or anesthetized, a conversion reaction must be suspected (Russo et al., 1998). Another sign to watch for is that victims of conversion reactions are strangely unconcerned about suddenly being disabled.

Uncontrollable sneezing, which may continue for days or weeks, is often a conversion disorder. In such cases, sneezing is atypical in rate and rhythm. In addition, the person's eyes do not close during a sneeze and sneezing does not occur during sleep. (A normal sneeze is shown here.) All these signs suggest that the cause of the sneezing is psychological, not physical (Fochtmann, 1995).

Anxiety and Disorder—Four Pathways to Trouble

SURVEY QUESTION: *How do psychologists explain anxiety-based disorders?*

What causes anxiety disorders? Susceptibility to anxiety-based disorders appears to be partly inherited (Rachman, 2004). Studies show that being high strung, nervous, or emotional runs in families. For example, 60 percent of children born to parents suffering from panic disorder have a fearful, inhibited temperament. Such children are irritable and wary as infants, shy and fearful as toddlers, and quiet and cautious introverts in elementary school. By the time they reach adulthood, they are at high risk for anxiety problems, such as panic attacks (Barlow, 2000; Durand & Barlow, 2006).

At least four major psychological perspectives on the causes of dissociative, anxiety-based, and somatoform disor-

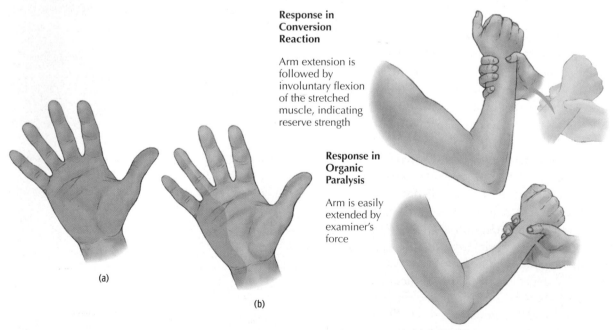

Response in Conversion Reaction

Arm extension is followed by involuntary flexion of the stretched muscle, indicating reserve strength

Response in Organic Paralysis

Arm is easily extended by examiner's force

(a)

(b)

● **FIGURE 12.4** *(left)* "Glove" anesthesia is a conversion reaction involving loss of feeling in areas of the hand that would be covered by a glove *(a)*. If the anesthesia were physically caused, it would follow the pattern shown in *(b)*. *(right)* To test for organic paralysis of the arm, an examiner can suddenly extend the arm, stretching the muscles. A conversion reaction is indicated if the arm pulls back involuntarily. (Adapted from Weintraub, 1983.)

ders exist. These are (1) the *psychodynamic* approach, (2) the *humanistic-existential* approach, (3) the *behavioral* approach, and (4) the *cognitive* approach.

Psychodynamic Approach

The term *psychodynamic* refers to internal motives, conflicts, unconscious forces, and other dynamics of mental life. Freud was the first to propose a psychodynamic explanation for what he called "neurosis." According to Freud, disturbances like those we have described represent a raging conflict among subparts of the personality—the id, ego, and superego.

Freud emphasized that intense anxiety can be caused by forbidden id impulses for sex or aggression that threaten to break through into behavior. The person constantly fears doing something "crazy" or forbidden. She or he may also be tortured by guilt, which the superego uses to suppress forbidden impulses. Caught in the middle, the ego is eventually overwhelmed. This forces the person to use rigid defense mechanisms and misguided, inflexible behavior to prevent a disastrous loss of control. (See Module 11.3.)

Humanistic-Existential Approaches

Humanistic theories emphasize subjective experience, human problems, and personal potentials. Humanistic psychologist Carl Rogers regarded emotional disorders as the end product of a faulty self-image or self-concept (Rogers, 1959). Rogers believed that anxious individuals have built up unrealistic mental images of themselves. This leaves them vulnerable to contradictory information. Let's say, for example, that an essential part of Cheyenne's self-image is the idea that she is highly intelligent. If Cheyenne does poorly in school, she may deny or distort her perceptions of herself and the situation. Should Cheyenne's anxiety become severe, she may resort to using defense mechanisms. A conversion reaction, anxiety attacks, or similar symptoms could also result from threats to her self-image. These symptoms, in turn, would become new threats that provoke further distortions. Soon, she would fall into a vicious cycle of maladjustment and anxiety that feeds on itself once started.

Existentialism focuses on the elemental problems of existence, such as death, meaning, choice, and responsibility. Psychologists who take a more existential view stress that unhealthy anxiety reflects a loss of *meaning* in one's life. According to them, we must show *courage* and *responsibility* in our choices if life is to have meaning. Too often, they say, we give in to "existential anxiety" and back away from life-enhancing choices. Existential anxiety is the unavoidable anguish that comes from knowing we are personally responsible for our lives. Hence, we have a crushing need to choose wisely and courageously as we face life's empty and impersonal void.

From the existential view, people who are anxious are living in "bad faith." That is, they have collapsed in the face of the awesome responsibility to choose a meaningful existence. In short, they have lost their way in life. From this point of view, making choices that don't truly reflect what you value, feel, and believe can make you sick.

Behavioral Approach

Behaviorist approaches emphasize overt, observable behavior and the effects of learning and conditioning. Behaviorists assume that the "symptoms" we have discussed are learned, just as other behaviors are. You might recall from Chapter 6, for instance, that phobias can be acquired through classical conditioning. Similarly, anxiety attacks may reflect conditioned emotional responses that generalize to new situations and the hypochondriac's "sickness behavior" may be reinforced by the sympathy and attention he or she gets. One point that all theorists agree on is that disordered behavior is ultimately self-defeating because it makes the person more miserable in the long run, even though it temporarily lowers anxiety.

But if the person becomes more miserable in the long run, how does the pattern get started? The behavioral explanation is that self-defeating behavior begins with avoidance learning (described in Chapter 6). Avoidance learning occurs when making a response delays or prevents the onset of a painful or unpleasant stimulus. Here's a quick review to refresh your memory:

An animal is placed in a special cage. After a few minutes a light comes on, followed a moment later by a painful shock. Quickly, the animal escapes into a second chamber. After a few minutes, a light comes on in this chamber, and the shock is repeated. Soon the animal learns to avoid pain by moving before the shock occurs. Once an animal learns to avoid the shock, it can be turned off altogether. A well-trained animal may avoid the nonexistent shock indefinitely.

The same analysis can be applied to human behavior. A behaviorist would say that the powerful reward of immediate relief from anxiety keeps self-defeating avoidance behaviors alive. This view, known as the **anxiety reduction hypothesis,** seems to explain why the behavior patterns we have discussed often look very "stupid" to outside observers.

Conversion disorder A bodily symptom that mimics a physical disability but is actually caused by anxiety or emotional distress.

Anxiety reduction hypothesis Explains the self-defeating nature of avoidance responses as a result of the reinforcing effects of relief from anxiety.

Cognitive Approach

The cognitive view is that distorted thinking causes people to magnify ordinary threats and failures, which leads to distress (Provencher, Dugas, & Ladouceur, 2004). For example, Bonnie, who is socially phobic, constantly has upsetting thoughts about being evaluated at school. One reason for this is that people with social phobias tend to be perfectionists. Like other social phobics, Bonnie is excessively concerned about mistakes. She also perceives criticism where none exists. Bonnie tends to avoid any social situation she perceives might focus too much attention on herself (Brown & Barlow, 2007). Even when socially phobic persons are successful, distorted thinking leads them to think they have failed (Barlow, 2002). In short, changing the thinking patterns of anxious individuals like Bonnie can greatly lessen their fears (Poulton & Andrews, 1996).

Implications All four psychological explanations probably contain a core of truth. For this reason, understanding anxiety-based disorders may be aided by combining parts of each perspective. Each viewpoint also suggests a different approach to treatment. Because many possibilities exist, therapy is discussed later, in Chapter 13.

MODULE 12.2 Summary

What is a personality disorder?

- Personality disorders are persistent, maladaptive personality patterns.
- Sociopathy is a common personality disorder. Antisocial persons lack a conscience, and they are emotionally cold, manipulative, shallow, and dishonest.

What problems result when a person suffers high levels of anxiety?

- Anxiety disorders, dissociative disorders, and somatoform disorders are characterized by high levels of anxiety, rigid defense mechanisms, and self-defeating behavior patterns.
- In an adjustment disorder, ordinary stresses push people beyond their ability to cope with life.
- Anxiety disorders include generalized anxiety disorder, panic disorder (with or without agoraphobia), agoraphobia, specific phobias, social phobia, obsessive-compulsive disorder, posttraumatic stress disorder, and acute stress disorder.
- High levels of anxiety also underlie the unhealthy distortions in behavior that occur in dissociative disorders and somatoform disorders.
- Dissociative disorders may take the form of amnesia, fugue, or multiple identities.
- Somatoform disorders center on physical complaints that mimic disease or disability. Four examples of somatoform disorders are hypochondriasis, somatization disorder, somatoform pain disorder, and conversion disorder.

How do psychologists explain anxiety-based disorders?

- Understanding anxiety-based disorders requires a combination of biological, psychodynamic, humanistic-existential, behavioral, and cognitive perspectives.

KNOWLEDGE BUILDER

Personality Disorders and Anxiety-Based Disorders

Recite

1. Which of the following personality disorders is associated with an inflated sense of self-importance and a constant need for attention and admiration?

   a. narcissistic

   b. antisocial

   c. paranoid

   d. manipulative

2. Antisocial personality disorders are difficult to treat, but there is typically a decline in antisocial behavior a year or two after adolescence. T or F? *False*

3. When prolonged unemployment, a bad marriage, or physical illness pushes a person beyond his or her ability to cope, it is most likely that which of the following problems will occur?

   a. a dissociative disorder

   b. agoraphobia

   c. an adjustment disorder

   d. a conversion disorder

4. Panic disorder can occur with or without agoraphobia, but agoraphobia cannot occur alone, without the presence of a panic disorder. T or F? *False*

5. Alice has a phobic fear of blood. What is the formal term for her fear?

   a. nyctophobia

   b. hematophobia

   c. pathophobia

   d. pyrophobia

6. A person who intensely fears eating, writing, or speaking in public suffers from _Social phobia_.

7. "Checkers" and "cleaners" suffer from which disorder?

   a. acarophobia

   b. panic disorder with agoraphobia

   c. generalized anxiety disorder

   d. obsessive-compulsive disorder

8. The symptoms of acute stress disorders last less than 1 month; posttraumatic stress disorders last more than 1 month. T or F? *True*

9. Which of the following is not a dissociative disorder?

   a. fugue

   b. amnesia

   c. conversion reaction

   d. multiple identity

10. According to the _____ view, anxiety disorders are the end result of a faulty self-image.

    a. psychodynamic

    b. humanistic

    c. behaviorist

    d. cognitive

Reflect
Critical Thinking

11. Many of the physical complaints associated with anxiety disorders are closely related to activity of what part of the nervous system?

12. How could someone get away with Munchausen syndrome by proxy? Wouldn't doctors figure out that something was fishy with Ben long before he had 40 surgeries for a faked sinus disorder? (See "Sick of Being Sick.")

Relate

Many of the qualities that define personality disorders exist to a minor degree in normal personalities. Try to think of a person you know who has some of the characteristics described for each type of personality disorder.

Which of the anxiety disorders would you *least* want to suffer from? Why?

What minor obsessions or compulsions have you experienced?

What is the key difference between a stress disorder and an adjustment disorder? (Review both discussions if you don't immediately know the answer.)

Which of the four psychological explanations of anxiety-based disorders do you find most convincing?

Link

Internet addresses frequently change. To find the sites listed here, visit **http://www.thomsonedu.com/psychology/coon** for an updated list of Internet addresses and direct links to relevant sites.

- **Personality Disorders** Read more about the 10 personality disorders.

- **Anxiety Disorders** The website of the Anxiety Disorders Association of America.

- **Famous People with Phobias** Find out more about famous phobias and how to live with them.

ANSWERS

1. a 2. F 3. c 4. F 5. b 6. social phobia 7. d 8. T 9. c 10. b 11. The autonomic nervous system (ANS), especially the sympathetic branch of the ANS. 12. No one doctor tolerates false symptoms for long. Once a doctor refuses further treatment, the Munchausen sufferer will move on to another. Also, sometimes more than one doctor is being seen at one time.

IMAGINE THAT A MEMBER OF YOUR FAMILY has been hearing voices, is talking strangely, has covered her head with aluminum foil, and believes that houseflies are speaking to her in code. If you observed such symptoms, would you be concerned? Of course you would, and rightly so. Psychotic disorders are among the most serious of all mental problems. They are also our next topic.

Psychotic Disorders—Life in the Shadow of Madness

SURVEY QUESTION: *What are the general characteristics of psychotic disorders?*

A person who is psychotic undergoes a number of striking changes in thinking, behavior, and emotion. Basic to all these changes is the fact that **psychosis** reflects a loss of contact with shared views of reality (psycho*sis*, singular; psycho*ses*, plural). The following comments, made by a psychotic patient, illustrate what is meant by a "split" from reality (Durand & Barlow, 2006):

> When you do the 25 of the clock, it means that you leave the house 25 after 1 to mail letters so they can check on you . . . and they know where you're at. That's the Eagle.

The Nature of Psychosis

What are the major features of psychotic disorders? Delusions and hallucinations are core features, but there are others as well.

People who suffer from **delusions** hold false beliefs that they insist are true, regardless of how much the facts contradict them. An example is a 43-year-old schizophrenic man who was convinced he was pregnant (Mansouri & Adityanjee, 1995).

Are there different types of delusions? Yes, some common types of delusions are: (1) *depressive* delusions, in which people feel that they have committed horrible crimes or sinful deeds; (2) *somatic* delusions, such as believing your body is "rotting away" or that it is emitting foul odors; (3) delusions of *grandeur,* in which people think they are extremely important; (4) delusions of *influence,* in which people feel they are being controlled or influenced by others or by unseen forces; (5) delusions of *persecution,* in which people be-

lieve that others are "out to get them"; and (6) delusions of *reference,* in which people give great personal meaning to unrelated events. For instance, delusional people sometimes think that television programs are giving them a special personal message (DSM-IV-TR, 2000).

Hallucinations are imaginary sensations, such as seeing, hearing, or smelling things that don't exist in the real world. The most common psychotic hallucination is hearing voices, like the voice that told Carol North to "Collide with the world." Sometimes these voices command patients to hurt themselves. Unfortunately, sometimes people obey (Barrowcliff & Haddock, 2006). More rarely, psychotic people may feel "insects crawling under their skin," taste "poisons" in their food, or smell "gas" their "enemies" are using to "get" them. Sensory changes, such as anesthesia (numbness, or a loss of sensation) or extreme sensitivity to heat, cold, pain, or touch, can also occur.

During a psychotic episode, emotions are often severely disturbed. For instance, the psychotic person may be wildly elated, depressed, hyperemotional, or apathetic. Sometimes psychotic patients display *flat affect,* a condition in which the face is frozen in a blank expression. Brain images from psychotic patients with "frozen faces" reveal that their brains process emotions abnormally (Fahim et al., 2005).

Some psychotic symptoms can be thought of as a primitive type of communication. That is, many patients can only

A psychotic individual in a state mental hospital.

use their actions to say "I need help" or "I can't handle it any more." Disturbed verbal communication is a nearly universal symptom of psychosis. In fact, psychotic speech tends to be so garbled and chaotic that it sometimes sounds like a "word salad."

Major disturbances such as those just described—as well as added problems with thinking, memory, and attention—bring about personality disintegration and a break with reality. *Personality disintegration* occurs when a person's thoughts, actions, and emotions are no longer coordinated. When psychotic disturbances and a fragmented personality are evident for weeks or months, the person has suffered a psychosis (DSM-IV-TR, 2000). (See ■ Table 12.5.)

Organic Psychosis   In a sense, all psychoses are partly organic, involving physical changes in the brain. However, the general term *organic psychosis* is usually reserved for problems involving clear-cut brain injuries or diseases. For example, poisoning by lead or mercury can damage the brain and cause hallucinations, delusions, and a loss of emotional control (● Fig. 12.5). A particularly dangerous situation is found in old buildings that contain leaded paints. Lead tastes sweet. Thus, young children may be tempted to eat leaded paint flakes as if they were candy. Children who eat leaded paint can become psychotic or intellectually disabled (Mielke, 1999).

Leaded paints also release powdered lead into the air. Children may breathe the powder or eat it after handling contaminated toys. Other sources of lead are soldered water pipes, old lead-lined drinking fountains, lead-glazed pottery, and lead deposited years ago from automobile exhaust. On a much larger scale, "poisoning" of another type, in the form of drug abuse, can also produce psychotic symptoms (DSM-IV-TR, 2000).

● **FIGURE 12.5**   The Mad Hatter, from Lewis Carroll's *Alice's Adventures in Wonderland*. History provides numerous examples of psychosis caused by toxic chemicals. Carroll's Mad Hatter character is modeled after an occupational disease of the eighteenth and nineteenth centuries. In that era, hatmakers were heavily exposed to mercury used in the preparation of felt. Consequently, many suffered brain damage and became psychotic, or "mad" (Kety, 1979).

The most common organic problem is **dementia** (duh-MEN-sha), a serious mental impairment in old age caused by deterioration of the brain. In dementia, we see major disturbances in memory, reasoning, judgment, impulse control, and personality. This combination usually leaves people con-

The soil and dust in cities and near busy streets is often heavily contaminated with lead. This lead came from automobile exhaust before leaded gasoline was banned. Young children frequently put objects and their hands in their mouths. This, then, is a major source of lead poisoning for many children. Paving play areas or covering them with clean soil can greatly reduce lead exposure (Mielke, 1999).

■ **TABLE 12.5**   Warning Signs of Psychotic Disorders and Major Mood Disorders
You express bizarre thoughts or beliefs that defy reality.
You have withdrawn from family members and other relationships.
You hear unreal voices or sees things others don't.
You are extremely sad, persistently despondent, or suicidal.
You are excessively energetic and have little need for sleep.
You lose your appetite, sleep excessively, and have no energy.
You exhibit extreme mood swings.
You believe someone is trying to get you.
You have engaged in antisocial, destructive, or self-destructive behavior.

Sources: Harvey et al., 1996; Sheehy & Cournos, 1992.

Psychosis   A withdrawal from reality marked by hallucinations and delusions, disturbed thought and emotions, and personality disorganization.

Delusion   A false belief held against all contrary evidence.

Hallucination   An imaginary sensation, such as seeing, hearing, or smelling things that don't exist in the real world.

Dementia   A serious mental impairment in old age caused by deterioration of the brain.

Former U.S. President Ronald Reagan was diagnosed with Alzheimer's disease in 1995. Like many Alzheimer's victims, Reagan slipped into a slow mental decline. He died in 2004.

fused, suspicious, apathetic, or withdrawn. Some common causes of dementia are circulatory problems, repeated strokes, or general shrinkage and atrophy of the brain. The majority of people who suffer from dementia slowly lose their mental abilities without becoming psychotic. However, some do develop delusions and lose contact with reality. The most common cause of dementia is *Alzheimer's disease.*

Alzheimer's disease (ALLS-hi-merz) is one of the most fearsome problems of aging. Alzheimer's victims slowly lose the ability to work, cook, drive, read, write, or do arithmetic. Eventually they are mute and bedridden. Alzheimer's disease appears to be caused by unusual webs and tangles in the brain that damage areas important for memory and learning (Ingram, 2003). Understandably, efforts to find a cure for Alzheimer's disease are expanding. For some of us, such efforts may be a race against time.

Are there specific kinds of psychotic disorders? Two major types of psychosis are *delusional disorders* and *schizophrenia.* As you will recall, mood disorders mainly involve emotional extremes. Nevertheless, psychotic symptoms can also occur in some mood disorders. You'll find information on each of these problems in upcoming discussions.

Delusional Disorders—An Enemy Behind Every Tree

SURVEY QUESTION: *What is the nature of a delusional disorder?*

People with delusional disorders usually do not suffer from hallucinations, emotional excesses, or personality disintegration. Even so, their break with reality is unmistakable. The main feature of **delusional disorders** is the presence of deeply held false beliefs, which may take the following forms (DSM-IV-TR, 2000):

- **Erotomanic type:** In this disorder, people have erotic delusions that they are loved by another person, especially by someone famous or of higher status.
- **Grandiose type:** In this case, people suffer from the delusion that they have some great, unrecognized talent, knowledge, or insight. They may also believe that they have a special relationship with an important person or with God or that they are a famous person. (If the famous person is alive, the deluded person regards her or him as an imposter.)
- **Jealous type:** An example of this type of delusion would be having an all-consuming, but unfounded, belief that your spouse or lover is unfaithful.
- **Persecutory type:** Delusions of persecution involve belief that you are being conspired against, cheated, spied on, followed, poisoned, maligned, or harassed.
- **Somatic type:** People suffering from somatic delusions typically believe that their bodies are diseased or rotting, or infested with insects or parasites, or that parts of their bodies are defective.

Although they are false, and sometimes far-fetched, all these delusions are about experiences that could occur in real life (Manschreck, 1996). In other types of psychosis, delusions tend to be more bizarre. For example, a person with schizophrenia might believe that space aliens have replaced all his internal organs with electronic monitoring devices. In contrast, people with ordinary delusions merely believe that someone is trying to steal their money, that they are being deceived by a lover, that the FBI is watching them, and the like (DSM-IV-TR, 2000).

Paranoid Psychosis

The most common delusional disorder, often called **paranoid psychosis,** centers on delusions of persecution. Many self-styled reformers, crank letter writers, conspiracy theorists, "UFO abductees," and the like suffer paranoid delusions. Paranoid individuals often believe that they are being cheated, spied on, followed, poisoned, harassed, or plotted against. Usually they are intensely suspicious, believing they must be on guard at all times.

The evidence such people find to support their beliefs usually fails to persuade others. Every detail of the paranoid person's existence is woven into a private version of "what's really going on." Buzzing during a telephone conversation may be interpreted as "someone listening"; a stranger who comes to the door asking for directions may be seen as "really trying to get information"; and so forth.

It is difficult to treat people suffering from paranoid delusions because it is almost impossible for them to accept that they need help. Anyone who suggests that they have a problem simply becomes part of the "conspiracy" to "persecute" them. Consequently, paranoid people frequently lead lonely, isolated, and humorless lives dominated by constant suspicion and hostility.

Although they are not necessarily dangerous to others, they can be. People who believe that the Mafia, "government agents," terrorists, or a street gang is slowly closing in on them may be moved to violence by their irrational fears. Imagine that a stranger comes to the door to ask a paranoid person for directions. If the stranger has his hand in his coat pocket, he could become the target of a paranoid attempt at "self-defense."

Delusional disorders are rare. By far, the most common form of psychosis is schizophrenia. Let's explore schizophrenia in more detail and see how it differs from a delusional disorder.

Schizophrenia—Shattered Reality

SURVEY QUESTIONS: *What forms does schizophrenia take? What causes it?*

Schizophrenia (SKIT-soh-FREN-ee-uh) is marked by delusions, hallucinations, apathy, thinking abnormalities, and a "split" between thought and emotion. In schizophrenia, emotions may become blunted or very inappropriate. For example, if a person with schizophrenia is told his mother just died, he might smile, or giggle, or show no emotion at all. Schizophrenic delusions may include the idea that the person's thoughts and actions are being controlled, that thoughts are being broadcast (so others can hear them), that thoughts have been "inserted" into the person's mind, or that thoughts have been removed. In addition, schizophrenia involves withdrawal from contact with others, a loss of interest in external activities, a breakdown of personal habits, and an inability to deal with daily events (Neufeld et al., 2003). One person in 100 has schizophrenia in any given year (NIMH, 2006b).

Many schizophrenic symptoms appear to be related to problems with *selective attention*. In other words, it is hard for people with schizophrenia to focus on one item of information at a time. Having an impaired "sensory filter" in their brains may be why they are overwhelmed by a jumble of thoughts, sensations, images, and feelings (Heinrichs, 2001).

Is there more than one type of schizophrenia? Schizophrenia appears to be a group of related disturbances. It has four major subtypes:

- **Disorganized type:** Schizophrenia marked by incoherence, grossly disorganized behavior, bizarre thinking, and flat or grossly inappropriate emotions.
- **Catatonic type:** Schizophrenia marked by stupor, rigidity, unresponsiveness, posturing, mutism, and, sometimes, agitated, purposeless behavior.
- **Paranoid type:** Schizophrenia marked by a preoccupation with delusions or by frequent auditory hallucinations related to a single theme, especially grandeur or persecution.
- **Undifferentiated type:** Schizophrenia in which there are prominent psychotic symptoms, but none of the specific features of catatonic, disorganized, or paranoid types.

Disorganized Schizophrenia

The disorder known as disorganized schizophrenia (sometimes called hebephrenic schizophrenia) comes close to matching the stereotyped images of "madness" seen in movies. In **disorganized schizophrenia,** personality disintegration is almost complete: Emotions, speech, and behavior are all highly disorganized. The result is silliness, laughter, and bizarre or obscene behavior, as shown by this intake interview of a patient named Edna:

Dr. I am Dr. _____. I would like to know something more about you.

Patient You have a nasty mind. Lord! Lord! Cats in a cradle.

Dr. Tell me, how do you feel?

Patient London's bell is a long, long dock. Hee! Hee! (Giggles uncontrollably.)

Dr. Do you know where you are now?

Patient D_____n! S_____t on you all who rip into my internals! The grudgerometer will take care of you all! (Shouting) I am the Queen, see my magic, I shall turn you all into smidgelings forever!

Dr. Your husband is concerned about you. Do you know his name?

Patient (Stands, walks to and faces the wall) Who am I, who are we, who are you, who are they, (turns) I . . . I . . . I . . . I! (Makes grotesque faces.)

Alzheimer's disease An age-related disease characterized by memory loss, mental confusion, and, in its later stages, a nearly total loss of mental abilities.

Delusional disorder A psychosis marked by severe delusions of grandeur, jealousy, persecution, or similar preoccupations.

Paranoid psychosis A delusional disorder centered especially on delusions of persecution.

Schizophrenia A psychosis characterized by delusions, hallucinations, apathy, and a "split" between thought and emotion.

Disorganized schizophrenia Schizophrenia marked by incoherence, grossly disorganized behavior, bizarre thinking, and flat or grossly inappropriate emotions.

Edna was placed in the women's ward where she proceeded to masturbate. Occasionally, she would scream or shout obscenities. At other times she giggled to herself. She was known to attack other patients. She began to complain that her uterus was attached to a "pipeline to the Kremlin" and that she was being "infernally invaded" by Communism. (Suinn, 1975*)

Disorganized schizophrenia typically develops in adolescence or young adulthood. Chances of improvement are limited, and social impairment is usually extreme (DSM-IV-TR, 2000).

Catatonic Schizophrenia

The catatonic person seems to be in a state of total panic (Fink & Taylor, 2003). **Catatonic schizophrenia** brings about a stuporous condition in which odd positions may be held for hours or even days. These periods of rigidity may be similar to the tendency to "freeze" at times of great emergency or panic. Catatonic individuals appear to be struggling desperately to control their inner turmoil. One sign of this is the fact that stupor may occasionally give way to agitated outbursts or violent behavior. The following excerpt describes a catatonic episode.

---

*All Suinn quotes in this chapter are from *Fundamentals of Behavior Pathology* by R. M. Suinn. Copyright © 1975. Reprinted by permission of John Wiley & Sons, Inc.

Manuel appeared to be physically healthy upon examination. Yet he did not regain his awareness of his surroundings. He remained motionless, speechless, and seemingly unconscious. One evening an aide turned him on his side to straighten out the sheet, was called away to tend to another patient, and forgot to return. Manuel was found the next morning, still on his side, his arm tucked under his body, as he had been left the night before. His arm was turning blue from lack of circulation, but he seemed to be experiencing no discomfort. (Suinn, 1975)

Notice that Manuel did not speak. *Mutism,* along with a marked decrease in responsiveness to the environment, makes patients with catatonic schizophrenia difficult to "reach." Fortunately, this bizarre disorder has become rare in Europe and North America (DSM-IV-TR, 2000).

Paranoid Schizophrenia

Paranoid schizophrenia is the most common schizophrenic disorder. As in paranoid delusional disorders, **paranoid schizophrenia** centers on delusions of grandeur and persecution. However, paranoid schizophrenics also hallucinate, and their delusions are more bizarre and unconvincing than those in a delusional disorder (Freeman & Garety, 2004).

Thinking that their minds are being controlled by God, the government, or "cosmic rays from space," or that someone is trying to poison them, people suffering from paranoid schizophrenia may feel forced into violence to "protect" themselves (● Fig. 12.6). An example is James Huberty, who brutally murdered 21 people at a McDonald's restaurant in

In disorganized schizophrenia, behavior is marked by silliness, laughter, and bizarre or obscene behavior.

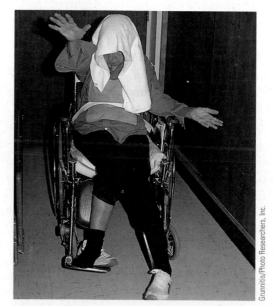

Can the catatonic's rigid postures and stupor be understood in terms of abnormal body chemistry? Environment? Heredity? As is true of other forms of schizophrenia, the answer appears to be all three factors.

CRITICAL THINKING

Are the Mentally Ill Prone to Violence?

News reports and television programs tend to exaggerate the connection between mental illness and violence (Corrigan et al., 2005). Such media reports both create and reflect deeply held beliefs about mental disorders in our society. Such beliefs are important because they affect laws and personal attitudes toward the mentally ill. For example, people who strongly believe that the mentally ill are prone to violence are typically afraid to have former mental patients as neighbors, coworkers, or friends (Corrigan & Watson, 2005).

The reality is just the opposite. According to the largest study ever conducted on this question, mentally ill individuals who are not also substance abusers are no more prone to violence than are normal individuals (Monahan et al., 2001). There are only a few exceptions to this conclusion, and in those cases the risk is not very large (Lidz, et al., 2007; Noble, 1997; Rice, 1997):

- Only persons who are also involved with *substance abuse* are more prone to violence than nonpatients.
- Only persons who are *actively psychotic* are more violence prone than nonpatients. That

is, if a person is experiencing delusions and hallucinations, the risk of violence is elevated. Other mental problems are unrelated to violence.

- Only persons *currently* experiencing psychotic symptoms are at increased risk for violence. Violent behavior is not related to having been a mental patient in the past or having had psychotic symptoms in the past.

Thus, most news stories give a false impression. Only a small minority of the actively mentally ill poses an increased risk. Even when we consider people who are actively psychotic,

we find that the vast majority are not violent. Former mental patients, in particular, are no more likely to be violent than people in general. No matter how disturbed a person may have been, she or he merits respect and compassion.

The risk of violence from mental patients is actually many times lower than that from persons who have the following attributes: young, male, poor, and intoxicated (Corrigan & Watson, 2005). Remember, people who are not mentally ill commit the overwhelming majority of violent crimes.

Many news stories give the impression that the mentally ill are dangerous. Consider, for example, the ghastly case of Jeffrey Dahmer, who killed, sexually molested, and then ate his victims. Like Dahmer, most of the mentally disordered persons who make the evening news have committed murder or some other horrible crime. This tends to give the impression that the mentally ill are violent and dangerous. Yet in reality, only a tiny percentage of all mentally disordered persons are more violent than average.

● **FIGURE 12.6** Over a period of years, Theodore Kaczynski mailed bombs to unsuspecting victims, many of whom were maimed or killed. As a young adult, Kaczynski was a brilliant mathematician. At the time of his arrest, he had become the Unabomber—a reclusive "loner" who deeply mistrusted other people and modern technology. After his arrest, Kaczynski was judged to be suffering from paranoid schizophrenia.

San Ysidro, California. Huberty, who had paranoid schizophrenia, felt persecuted and cheated by life. Shortly before he announced to his wife that he was "going hunting humans," Huberty had been hearing hallucinated voices.

How dangerous are the mentally ill? Horrific crimes, like the San Ysidro murders, lead many people to believe that the mentally ill are dangerous. Are they right? You might be surprised by the answer, found in "Are the Mentally Ill Prone to Violence?"

Catatonic schizophrenia Schizophrenia marked by stupor; rigidity; unresponsiveness; posturing; mutism; and, sometimes, agitated, purposeless behavior.

Paranoid schizophrenia Schizophrenia marked by a preoccupation with delusions or by frequent auditory hallucinations related to a single theme, especially grandeur or persecution.

Undifferentiated Schizophrenia

The three types of schizophrenia just described occur most often in textbooks. In reality, patients may shift from one pattern to another at different times. Many patients, therefore, are simply classified as suffering from **undifferentiated schizophrenia,** in which the specific features of catatonic, disorganized, or paranoid types are missing. Diagnosing schizophrenia is fairly subjective. All things considered, however, there is no doubt that schizophrenia is real or that its treatment is a major challenge.

The Causes of Schizophrenia

Former British Prime Minister Winston Churchill once described a question that perplexed him as "a riddle wrapped in a mystery inside an enigma." The same words might describe the causes of schizophrenia.

Environment *What causes schizophrenia?* An increased risk of developing schizophrenia may begin at birth or even before. Women who are exposed to the influenza (flu) virus or to rubella (German measles) during the middle of pregnancy have children who are more likely to become schizophrenic (Brown et al., 2001). Malnutrition during pregnancy and complications at the time of birth can have a similar impact. Possibly, such events disturb brain development, leaving people more vulnerable to a psychotic break with reality (Walker et al., 2004).

Early **psychological trauma** (a psychological injury or shock) may also add to the risk. Often, the victims of schizophrenia were exposed to violence, sexual abuse, death, divorce, separation, or other stresses in childhood (Walker et al., 2004). Living in a troubled family is a related risk factor. In a disturbed family environment, stressful relationships, communication patterns, and negative emotions prevail. Deviant communication patterns cause anxiety, confusion, anger, conflict, and turmoil. Typically, disturbed families interact in ways that are laden with guilt, prying, criticism, negativity, and emotional attacks (Bressi, Albonetti, & Razzoli, 1998; Davison & Neale, 2006).

Although they are attractive, environmental explanations alone are not enough to account for schizophrenia. For example, when the children of schizophrenic parents are raised away from their chaotic home environment, they are still more likely to become psychotic (Walker et al., 2004).

Heredity *Does that mean that heredity affects the risk of developing schizophrenia?* There is now little doubt that heredity is a factor in schizophrenia. It appears that some individuals inherit a potential for developing schizophrenia. They are, in other words, more vulnerable to the disorder than others are (Harrison & Weinberger, 2005; Walker et al., 2004).

How has that been shown? If one identical twin becomes schizophrenic (remember, identical twins have identical genes), then the other twin has a *48 percent* chance of also becoming schizophrenic (Lenzenweger & Gottesman, 1994). The figure for twins can be compared with the risk of schizophrenia for the population in general, which is about 1 percent. (See ● Fig. 12.7 for other relationships.) In general, schizophrenia is clearly more common among close relatives and it tends to run in families. There's even a case on record of *four* identical quadruplets *all* developing schizophrenia (Mirsky et al., 2000). In light of such evidence, researchers are now beginning to search for specific genes related to schizophrenia.

A problem exists with current genetic explanations of schizophrenia: Very few people with schizophrenia have children. How could a genetic defect be passed from one generation to the next if afflicted people don't reproduce? One possible answer is suggested by the fact that the older a man is (even if he doesn't suffer from schizophrenia) when he fathers a child, the more likely it is that the child will develop schizophrenia. Apparently, genetic mutations occur in aging

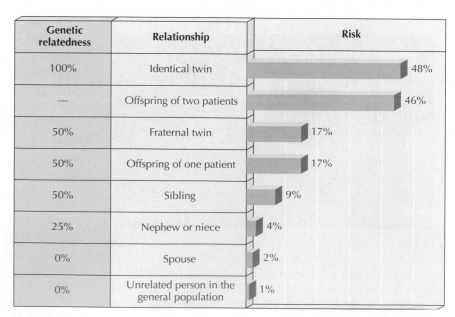

● **FIGURE 12.7** Lifetime risk of developing schizophrenia is associated with how closely a person is genetically related to a schizophrenic person. A shared environment also increases the risk. (Estimates from Lenzenweger & Gottesman, 1994.)

Genetic relatedness	Relationship	Risk
100%	Identical twin	48%
—	Offspring of two patients	46%
50%	Fraternal twin	17%
50%	Offspring of one patient	17%
50%	Sibling	9%
25%	Nephew or niece	4%
0%	Spouse	2%
0%	Unrelated person in the general population	1%

This series of paintings by Louis Wain reflects a troubled personality. Wain was a British illustrator who became schizophrenic in middle age. As Wain's psychosis progressed, his cat paintings became highly abstract and fragmented. In many ways, Wain's paintings resemble the perceptual changes caused by psychedelic drugs such as mescaline and LSD. Recent research suggests that psychosis may, in fact, be the result of mind-altering changes in brain chemistry.

male reproductive cells and increase the risk of schizophrenia (as well as other medical problems) (Malaspina et al., 2005; Sipos et al., 2004).

Brain Chemistry Amphetamine, LSD, PCP ("angel dust"), and similar drugs produce effects that partially mimic the symptoms of schizophrenia. Also, the same drugs (phenothiazines) used to treat LSD overdoses tend to alleviate psychotic symptoms. Facts such as these suggest that biochemical abnormalities (disturbances in brain chemicals or neurotransmitters) may occur in schizophrenic people. It is possible that the schizophrenic brain produces some substance similar to a *psychedelic* (mind-altering) drug. At present, one likely candidate is dopamine (DOPE-ah-meen), an important chemical messenger found in the brain.

Many researchers believe that schizophrenia is related to overactivity in brain dopamine systems (Durand & Barlow, 2006; Kapur & Lecrubier, 2003). Another possibility is that dopamine receptors become super-responsive to normal amounts of dopamine. Dopamine appears to trigger a flood of unrelated thoughts, feelings, and perceptions, which may account for the voices, hallucinations, and delusions of schizophrenia. The implication is that schizophrenic people may be on a sort of drug trip caused by their own bodies (• Fig. 12.8).

Dopamine is not the only brain chemical that has caught scientists' attention. The neurotransmitter glutamate also appears to be related to schizophrenia (van Elst et al., 2005). People who take the hallucinogenic drug PCP, which affects glutamate, have symptoms that closely mimic schizophrenia (Murray, 2002). This occurs because glutamate influences brain activity in areas that control emotions and sensory information (Tsai & Coyle, 2002). Another tantalizing connec-

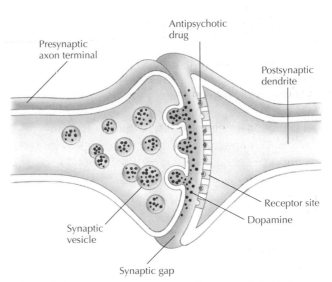

• **FIGURE 12.8** Dopamine normally crosses the synapse between two neurons, activating the second cell. Antipsychotic drugs bind to the same receptor sites as dopamine does, blocking its action. In people suffering from schizophrenia, a reduction in dopamine activity can quiet a person's agitation and psychotic symptoms.

tion is the fact that stress alters glutamate levels, which in turn alter dopamine systems (Moghaddam, 2002). The story is far from complete, but it appears that dopamine, glutamate, and other brain chemicals partly explain the devastating symptoms of schizophrenia (Walker et al., 2004). (See "The Schizophrenic Brain.")

Undifferentiated schizophrenia Schizophrenia lacking the specific features of catatonic, disorganized, or paranoid types.

Psychological trauma A psychological injury or shock, such as that caused by violence, abuse, neglect, separation, and so forth.

BRAINWAVES

The Schizophrenic Brain

Several brain imaging methods (remember Module 2.2?) have made it possible to directly observe the living schizophrenic brain. CT scans and MRI scans, which can reveal brain structure, suggest that the brains of schizophrenics have shrunk (atrophied). For example, ● Figure 12.9 shows a *CT scan* (*CT* stands for computed tomography, or computer-enhanced X-ray images) of the brain of John Hinkley, Jr., who shot former U.S. President Ronald Reagan and three other men in 1981. In the ensuing trial, Hinkley was declared insane. As you can see, his brain had wider-than-normal surface fissuring.

Similarly, *MRI* (magnetic resonance imaging) *scans* indicate that schizophrenic people tend to have enlarged ventricles (fluid-filled spaces within the brain), again suggesting that surrounding brain tissue has withered (Barkataki et al., 2006). One possible explanation is that the schizophrenic brain may be unable to continually create new neurons to replace old ones that have died (Toro & Deakin, 2007). Normal brains continue to produce new neurons (referred to as *neurogenesis*) throughout life (Toro & Deakin, 2007). It is telling that the af-

fected areas are crucial for regulating motivation, emotion, perception, actions, and attention (Gur et al., 1998; Walker et al., 2004).

Other methods provide images of brain activity, including PET scans. To make a *PET* (positron emission tomography) *scan*, a radioactive sugar solution is injected into a vein. When the sugar reaches the brain, an electronic device measures how much is used in each area. These data are then translated into a color map, or scan, of brain activity (● Fig. 12.10). Researchers are finding patterns in such scans that are consistently linked with schizophrenia, affective disorders, and other prob-

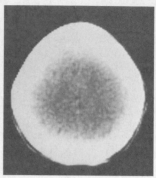

● **FIGURE 12.9** *(left)* CT scan of would-be presidential assassin John Hinkley, Jr., taken when he was 25. The X-ray image shows widened fissures in the wrinkled surface of Hinkley's brain. *(right)* CT scan of a normal 25-year-old's brain. In most young adults the surface folds of the brain are pressed together too tightly to be seen. As a person ages, surface folds of the brain normally become more visible. Pronounced brain fissuring in young adults may be a sign of schizophrenia, chronic alcoholism, or other problems.

lems. For instance, activity tends to be abnormally low in the frontal lobes of the schizophrenic brain (Durand & Barlow, 2006; Velakoulis & Pantelis, 1996). In the future, PET scans may be used to accurately diagnose schizophrenia. For now, such scans show that there is a clear difference in schizophrenic brain activity.

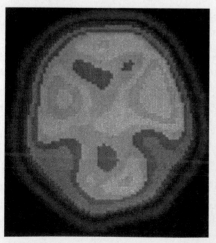

NORMAL

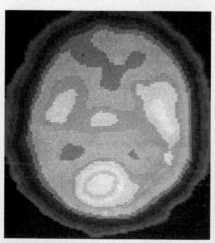

SCHIZOPHRENIC

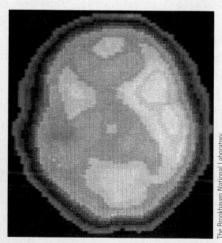

MANIC-DEPRESSIVE

● **FIGURE 12.10** Positron emission tomography produces PET scans of the human brain. In the scans shown here, red, pink, and orange indicate lower levels of brain activity; white and blue indicate higher activity levels. Notice that activity in the schizophrenic brain is quite low in the frontal lobes (top area of each scan) (Velakoulis & Pantelis, 1996). Activity in the manic-depressive brain is low in the left brain hemisphere and high in the right brain hemisphere. The reverse is more often true of the schizophrenic brain. Researchers are trying to identify consistent patterns like these to aid diagnosis of mental disorders.

Implications

In summary, the emerging picture of psychotic disorders such as schizophrenia takes this form: Anyone subjected to enough stress may be pushed to a psychotic break. (Battlefield psychosis is an example.) However, some people inherit a difference in brain chemistry or brain structure that makes them more susceptible—even to normal life stresses.

Thus, the right mix of inherited potential and environmental stress brings about mind-altering changes in brain chemicals and brain structure. This explanation is called a **stress-vulnerability model.** It attributes psychotic disorders to a blend of environmental stress and inherited susceptibility (Walker et al., 2004). The model seems to apply to other forms of psychopathology as well, such as depression (● Fig. 12.11).

Despite advances in our understanding, psychosis remains "a riddle wrapped in a mystery inside an enigma." Let us hope that recent progress toward a cure for schizophrenia will continue.

MODULE **12.3 Summary**

What are the general characteristics of psychotic disorders?

- Psychosis is a break in contact with reality that is marked by delusions, hallucinations, sensory changes, disturbed emotions, disturbed communication, and personality disintegration.
- An organic psychosis is based on known injuries or diseases of the brain.
- Some common causes of organic psychosis are poisoning, drug abuse, and dementia (especially Alzheimer's disease).

What is the nature of a delusional disorder?

- Delusional disorders are almost totally based on the presence of delusions of grandeur, persecution, infidelity, romantic attraction, or physical disease. The most common delusional disorder is paranoid psychosis.
- What forms does schizophrenia take? What causes it?
- Schizophrenia involves delusions, hallucinations, communication difficulties, and a split between thought and emotion.
- Disorganized schizophrenia is marked by extreme personality disintegration and silly, bizarre, or obscene behavior.
- Catatonic schizophrenia is associated with stupor, mutism, and odd postures. Sometimes violent and agitated behavior also occurs.
- In paranoid schizophrenia (the most common type), outlandish delusions of grandeur and persecution are coupled with psychotic symptoms and personality breakdown.
- Current explanations of schizophrenia emphasize a combination of prenatal injuries, early trauma, environmental stress, inherited susceptibility, and abnormalities in the brain.
- Heredity is a major factor in schizophrenia.
- Recent biochemical studies have focused on the brain transmitter dopamine and its receptor sites.
- The dominant explanation of schizophrenia, and other problems as well, is the stress-vulnerability model.

The Stress-Vulnerability Model

Vulnerability ☐
Stress ☐

Low   Medium   High
Degree of psychopathology

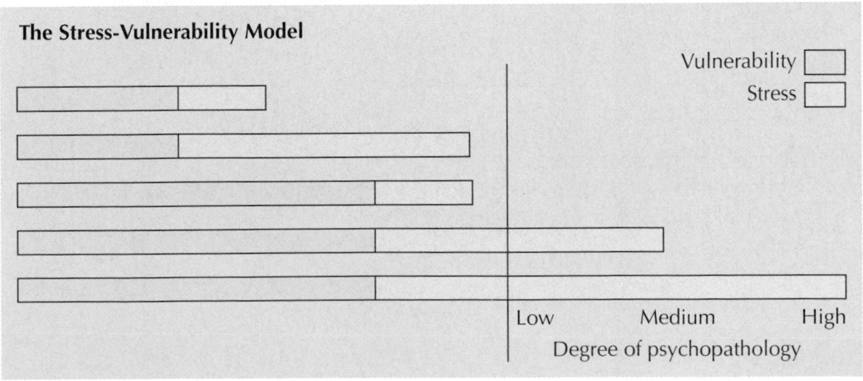

● **FIGURE 12.11** Various combinations of vulnerability and stress may produce psychological problems. The top bar shows low vulnerability and low stress. The result? No problem. The same is true of the next bar down, where low vulnerability is combined with moderate stress. Even high vulnerability (third bar) may not lead to problems if stress levels remain low. However, when high vulnerability combines with moderate or high stress (bottom two bars) the person "crosses the line" and suffers from psychopathology.

Stress-vulnerability model Attributes psychosis to a combination of environmental stress and inherited susceptibility.

KNOWLEDGE BUILDER

Psychosis, Delusional Disorders, and Schizophrenia

Recite

1. Carol wrongly believes that her body is "rotting away." She is suffering from
   a. depressive hallucinations
   b. a delusion
   c. flat affect
   d. Alzheimer's disease

2. Colin, who has suffered a psychotic break, is hearing voices. This symptom is referred to as
   a. flat affect
   b. hallucination
   c. a word salad
   d. organic delusions

3. A psychosis caused by lead poisoning would be regarded as an organic disorder. T or F? *True*

4. Hallucinations and personality disintegration are the principal features of paranoid psychosis. T or F? *False*

5. Which of the following is *not* one of the subtypes of schizophrenia?
   a. erotomanic type
   b. catatonic type
   c. paranoid type
   d. disorganized type

6. Environmental explanations of schizophrenia emphasize emotional trauma and
   a. manic parents
   b. schizoaffective interactions
   c. psychedelic interactions
   d. disturbed family relationships

7. The _identical twin_ of a schizophrenic person runs a 48 percent chance of also becoming psychotic.

8. Biochemical explanations of schizophrenia have focused on excessive amounts of _____ in the brain.
   a. radioactive sugar
   b. webs and tangles
   c. PCP
   d. dopamine and glutamate

9. The stress-vulnerability model of psychosis explains mental disorders as a product of environmental stresses and
   a. psychological trauma
   b. deviant communication
   c. exposure to the flu virus during pregnancy
   d. heredity

Reflect
Critical Thinking

10. Researchers have found nearly double the normal number of dopamine receptor sites in the brains of schizophrenics. Why might that be important?

11. Enlarged surface fissures and ventricles are frequently found in the brains of chronic schizophrenics. Why is it a mistake to conclude that such features cause schizophrenia?

Relate

What did you think psychosis was like before you read about it? How has your understanding changed? If you were writing a "recipe" for psychosis, what would the main "ingredients" be?

If you were asked to play the role of a paranoid person for a theater production, what symptoms would you emphasize?

You have been asked to explain the causes of schizophrenia to the parents of a schizophrenic teenager. What would you tell them?

Link

Internet addresses frequently change. To find the sites listed here, visit **http://www.thomsonedu.com/psychology/coon** for an updated list of Internet addresses and direct links to relevant sites.

- **Psychotic Disorders** Read more about the psychotic disorders.
- **William Utermohlen's Self-Portraits** View these remarkable paintings by a man descending into Alzheimer's disease.
- **Schizophrenia** Explore this extensive website, which includes brain images and videos about schizophrenia.

ANSWERS

12.4 Mood Disorders

FOR SOME PEOPLE, minor bouts of depression are as common as colds. But extreme swings of mood can be as disabling as a serious physical illness. In fact, depression can be deadly, because depressed persons may be suicidal. It is difficult to imagine how bleak and hopeless the world looks to a person who is deeply depressed, or how "crazy" it can be to ride a wave of mania. Let's explore mood disorders and their causes.

Mood Disorders—Peaks and Valleys

SURVEY QUESTIONS *What are mood disorders? What causes depression?*

Nobody loves you when you're down and out—or so it seems. Psychologists have come to realize that **mood disorders** (major disturbances in emotion) are among the most serious of all psychological conditions. In any given year, roughly 9.5 percent of the U.S. population suffers from a mood disorder (NIMH, 2006b).

Two general types of mood disorder are depressive disorders and bipolar disorders (Nevid & Greene, 2005). (See ■ Table 12.6.) In **depressive disorders,** sadness and despondency are exaggerated, prolonged, or unreasonable. Signs of a depressive disorder are dejection, hopelessness, and an inability to feel pleasure or to take interest in anything. Other common symptoms are fatigue, disturbed sleep and eating patterns, feelings of worthlessness, a very negative self-image, and thoughts of suicide. In **bipolar disorders,** people go both "up" and "down" emotionally (DSM-IV-TR, 2000).

Some mood disorders are long-lasting but relatively moderate problems. If a person is mildly depressed for at least 2 years, the problem is called a **dysthymic disorder** (dis-THY-mik). If depression alternates with periods when the person's mood is cheerful, expansive, or irritable, the problem is a **cyclothymic disorder** (SIKE-lo-THY-mik). Even at this level, mood disorders can be debilitating. However, major mood disorders are much more damaging.

Major Mood Disorders

Major mood disorders are characterized by emotional extremes. The person who only goes "down" emotionally suffers from a **major depressive disorder.** During major depressive episodes everything looks bleak and hopeless. The person has feelings of failure, worthlessness, and total despair. Suffering is intense, and the person may become extremely subdued, withdrawn, or intensely suicidal. Suicide attempted during a major depression is rarely a "plea for

In major depressive disorders, suicidal impulses can be intense and despair total.

help." Usually, the person intends to succeed and may give no prior warning.

In a **bipolar I disorder,** people experience both extreme mania and deep depression. During manic episodes, the person is loud, elated, hyperactive, grandiose, and energetic.

Mood disorder Major disturbances in mood or emotion, such as depression or mania.

Depressive disorders Emotional disorders primarily involving sadness, despondency, and depression.

Bipolar disorders Emotional disorders involving both depression and mania or hypomania.

Dysthymic disorder Moderate depression that persists for 2 years or more.

Cyclothymic disorder Moderate manic and depressive behavior that persists for 2 years or more.

Major mood disorders Disorders marked by lasting extremes of mood or emotion and sometimes accompanied by psychotic symptoms.

Major depressive disorder A mood disorder in which the person has suffered one or more intense episodes of depression.

Bipolar I disorder A mood disorder in which a person has episodes of mania (excited, hyperactive, energetic, grandiose behavior) and also periods of deep depression.

529

■ TABLE 12.6 Major *DSM-IV-TR* Categories

PROBLEM	PRIMARY SYMPTOM	TYPICAL SIGNS OF TROUBLE
Depressive Disorders		
Major depressive disorder	Extreme emotional depression for at least 2 weeks	You feel extremely sad, worthless, fatigued, and empty; you are unable to feel pleasure; you are having thoughts of suicide.
Dysthymic disorder	Moderately depressed mood on most days during the last 2 years	You feel down and depressed more days than not; your self-esteem and energy levels have been low for many months.
Bipolar Disorders		
Bipolar I disorder	Extreme mania and depression	At times you have little need for sleep, can't stop talking, your mind races, and everything you do is of immense importance; at other times you feel extremely sad, worthless, and empty.
Bipolar II disorder	Emotional depression and at least one episode of mild mania	Most of the time you feel extremely sad, worthless, fatigued, and empty; however, at times you feel unusually good, cheerful, energetic, or "high."
Cyclothymic disorder	Periods of moderate depression and moderate mania for at least 2 years	You have been experiencing upsetting emotional ups and downs for many months.

Manic patients may go bankrupt in a matter of days, get arrested, or go on a binge of promiscuous sex. During periods of depression, the person is deeply despondent and possibly suicidal.

In a **bipolar II disorder** the person is mostly sad and guilt ridden but has had one or more mildly manic episodes (called *hypomania*). That is, in a bipolar II disorder both elation and depression occur, but the person's mania is not as extreme as in a bipolar I disorder. Bipolar II patients who are hypomanic usually just manage to irritate everyone around them. They are excessively cheerful, aggressive, or irritable, and they may brag, talk too fast, interrupt conversations, or spend too much money (Nolen-Hoeksema, 2007).

In serious cases of depression it is impossible for a person to function at work or at school. Sometimes, depressed individuals cannot even feed or dress themselves. In cases of depression and/or mania that are even more severe, the person may also lose touch with reality and display psychotic symptoms.

How do major mood disorders differ from dysthymic and cyclothymic disorders? As mentioned, the major mood disorders involve more severe emotional changes. Also, major mood disorders more often appear to be **endogenous** (en-DODGE-eh-nus: produced from within) rather than a reaction to external events.

What Causes Mood Disorders?

Depression and other mood disorders have resisted adequate explanation and treatment. Some scientists are focusing on the biology of mood changes. They are interested in brain chemicals and transmitter substances, especially serotonin, noradrenaline, and dopamine levels. Their findings are incomplete, but progress has been made. For example, the chemical *lithium carbonate* can be effective for treating some cases of bipolar depression.

Other researchers seek psychological explanations. Psychoanalytic theory, for instance, holds that depression is caused by repressed anger. This rage is displaced and turned inward as self-blame and self-hate. As discussed in Chapter 11, behavioral theories of depression emphasize learned helplessness (LoLordo, 2001; Seligman, 1989). Cognitive psychologists believe that self-criticism and negative, distorted, or self-defeating thoughts underlie many cases of depression. (This view is discussed in Module 13.4.) Clearly, life stresses trigger many mood disorders (Maier, 2001). This is especially true for people who have personality traits and thinking patterns that make them vulnerable to depression (Dozois & Dobson, 2002).

Gender and Depression Overall, women are twice as likely as men to experience depression (Kuehner, 2003). Researchers believe that social and environmental conditions are the main reason for this difference (Winstead & Sanchez, 2005). Factors that contribute to women's greater risk of depression include conflicts about birth control and pregnancy, work and parenting, and the strain of providing emotional support for others. Marital strife, sexual and physical abuse, and poverty are also factors. Nationwide, women and children are most likely to live in poverty. As a result, poor women frequently suffer the stresses associated with single parenthood, loss of control over their lives, poor housing, and dangerous neighborhoods (Stoppard & McMullen, 2003). One study found that women in the United States were most likely to be depressed if they lacked education, were unmarried, were Latina, had high stress levels, and experienced feelings of hopelessness (Myers et al., 2002).

Postpartum Depression One source of women's depression is fairly easy to identify. After pregnancy and childbirth, many women face a high risk of becoming depressed.

Two weeks after her child was born, Makemba realized something was wrong. She could no longer ignore that she was extremely irritable, fatigued, tearful, and depressed. "Shouldn't I be happy?" she wondered. "What's wrong with me?"

Many women are surprised to learn that they face a risk of depression after giving birth. The two most common forms of the problem are maternity blues and postpartum depression. (The term *postpartum* refers to the time following childbirth.)

An estimated 25 to 50 percent of all women experience *maternity blues,* a mild depression that usually lasts from 1 to 2 days after childbirth. These "third-day blues" are marked by crying, fitful sleep, tension, anger, and irritability. For most women, such reactions are a normal part of adjusting to childbirth. The depression is usually brief and not too severe.

For some women, maternity blues can be the beginning of a serious depression. Roughly 13 percent of all women who give birth develop **postpartum depression,** a moderately severe depression that begins within 3 months following childbirth. Typical signs of postpartum depression are mood swings, despondency, feelings of inadequacy, and an inability to cope with the new baby. Depression of this kind may last anywhere from 2 months to about a year. Women are not the only ones to suffer when postpartum depression strikes. A depressed mother can seriously retard her child's rate of development (Cooper & Murray, 2001).

Stress and anxiety before birth and negative attitudes toward child rearing increase the risk of postpartum depression. A troubled marriage and lack of support from the father are also danger signs. Part of the problem may be hormonal: After a woman gives birth, her estrogen levels can drop, altering her mood (Bloch, Daly, & Rubinow, 2003).

Women who become depressed tend to see their husbands as unsupportive. Therefore, educating new parents about the importance of supporting one another may reduce the risk of depression. Groups where new mothers can discuss their feelings are also helpful. If depression is severe or long lasting, new mothers should seek professional help.

Biology and Depression *Does the fact that major mood disorders appear to be endogenous imply that heredity is involved?* Yes, especially in bipolar disorders (McGuffin et al., 2003). As a case in point, if one identical twin is depressed, the other has a 67 percent chance of suffering depression, too. For fraternal twins the probability is 19 percent. This difference may be related to the recent finding that people who have a particular version of a gene are more likely to become depressed when they are stressed (Caspi et al., 2003). As we have noted, psychological causes are important in many cases of depres-

sion. But for major mood disorders, biological factors seem to play a larger role. Surprisingly, one additional source of depression is related to the seasons.

Seasonal Affective Disorder Unless you have experienced a winter of "cabin fever" in the far north, you may be surprised to learn that the rhythms of the seasons underlie some depressions. Researcher Norman Rosenthal has found that some people suffer from **seasonal affective disorder (SAD),** or depression that only occurs during the fall and winter months. Almost anyone can get a little depressed when days are short, dark, and cold. But when a person's symptoms are lasting and disabling, the problem may be SAD. Here are some of the major symptoms of SAD (Rosenthal, 1993):

- **Oversleeping and difficulty staying awake:** Your sleep patterns may be disturbed, and waking very early in the morning is common.
- **Fatigue:** You feel too tired to maintain a normal routine.
- **Craving:** You hunger for carbohydrates and sweets, leading to overeating and weight gain.
- **Inability to cope:** You feel irritable and stressed.
- **Social withdrawal:** You become unsocial in the winter but are socially active during other seasons.

Starting in the fall, people with SAD sleep longer but more poorly. During the day they feel tired and drowsy, and they tend to overeat. With each passing day they become more sad, anxious, irritable, and socially withdrawn.

Although their depressions are not severe, many victims of SAD face each winter with a sense of foreboding. SAD is especially prevalent in northern latitudes, where days are very short during the winter (Michalak & Lam, 2002) (● Fig. 12.12). For instance, one study found that 13 percent of college students living in northern New England showed signs of suffering from SAD (Low & Feissner, 1998). The students most likely to be affected were those who had moved from the South to attend college!

Bipolar II disorder A mood disorder in which a person is mostly depressed (sad, despondent, guilt ridden) but has also had one or more episodes of mild mania (hypomania).

Endogenous depression Depression that appears to be produced from within (perhaps by chemical imbalances in the brain), rather than as a reaction to life events.

Postpartum depression A mild to moderately severe depression that begins within 3 months following childbirth.

Seasonal affective disorder (SAD) Depression that occurs only during fall and winter, presumably related to decreased exposure to sunlight.

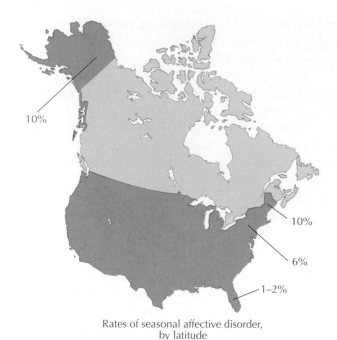

Rates of seasonal affective disorder,
by latitude

● **FIGURE 12.12** Seasonal affective disorder appears to be related to reduced exposure to daylight during the winter. SAD affects 1 to 2 percent of Florida's population, about 6 percent of the people living in Maryland and New York City, and nearly 10 percent of the residents of New Hampshire and Alaska (Booker & Hellekson, 1992).

Seasonal depressions are related to the release of more melatonin during the winter. This hormone, which is secreted by the pineal gland in the brain, regulates the body's response to changing light conditions (Wehr et al., 2001). That's why 80 percent of SAD patients can be helped by extra doses of bright light, a remedy called phototherapy (● Fig. 12.13). **Phototherapy** involves exposing SAD patients to one or more hours of very bright fluorescent light each day (Neumeister, 2004). This is best done early in the morning, where it simulates dawn in the summer (Avery et al., 2001). For many SAD sufferers a hearty dose of morning "sunshine" appears to be the next best thing to vacationing in the tropics.

Dan McCoy/Rainbow

● **FIGURE 12.13** An hour or more of bright light a day can dramatically reduce the symptoms of seasonal affective disorder. Treatment is usually necessary from fall through spring. Light therapy typically works best when it is used early in the morning (Lewy et al., 1998).

Disorders in Perspective—Psychiatric Labeling

As we conclude our survey of psychological disorders, a caution is in order. The terms we have reviewed in this chapter aid communication about human problems. But if used carelessly, they can hurt people. Everyone has felt or acted "crazy" during brief periods of stress or high emotion. People with psychological disorders have problems that are more severe or long lasting than most of us experience. Otherwise, they may not be that different from you or me.

A fascinating classic study carried out by psychologist David Rosenhan illustrates the impact of psychiatric labeling. Rosenhan and several colleagues had themselves committed to mental hospitals with a diagnosis of "schizophrenia" (Rosenhan, 1973). After being admitted, each of these "pseudo-patients" dropped all pretense of mental illness. Yet, even though they acted completely normal, none of the researchers was ever recognized by hospital *staff* as a phony patient. Real patients were not so easily fooled. It was not unusual for a patient to say to one of the researchers, "You're not crazy, you're checking up on the hospital!" or "You're a journalist."

To record his observations, Rosenhan took notes by carefully jotting things on a small piece of paper hidden in his hand. However, he soon learned that stealth was totally unnecessary. Rosenhan simply walked around with a clipboard, recording observations. No one questioned this behavior. Rosenhan's note taking was just regarded as a symptom of his "illness." This observation clarifies why staff members failed to detect the fake patients. Because they were in a mental ward and because they had been *labeled* schizophrenic, anything the pseudo-patients did was seen as a symptom of psychopathology.

As Rosenhan's study shows, it is far better to label *problems* than to label people. Think of the difference in impact between saying, "You are experiencing a serious psychological disorder" and saying, "You're a schizophrenic." Which statement would you prefer to have said about yourself?

Social Stigma

An added problem with psychiatric labeling is that it frequently leads to prejudice and discrimination. That is, the mentally ill in our culture are often *stigmatized* (rejected and disgraced). People who have been labeled mentally ill (at any time in their lives) are less likely to be hired. They also tend to be denied housing, and they are more likely to be falsely accused of crimes. Thus, people who are grappling with mental illness may be harmed as much by social stigma as they are by their immediate psychological problems (Corrigan & Penn, 1999).

A Look Ahead Treatments for psychological problems range from counseling and psychotherapy to mental hospitalization and drug therapy. Because they vary greatly, a complete discussion of therapies is found in the next chapter. For now, it's worth noting that many milder mental disorders can be treated successfully. Even major disorders may respond well to drugs and other techniques. It is wrong to fear "former mental patients" or to exclude them from work, friendships, and other social situations. A struggle with major depression or a psychotic episode does not inevitably lead to lifelong dysfunction. Too often, however, it does lead to unnecessary rejection based on groundless fears (Sarason & Sarason, 2005).

Let's conclude with a look at a widely misunderstood problem: By the time you finish reading this page, someone in the United States will have attempted suicide. What can be done about suicide? The upcoming "Psychology in Action" module provides some answers.

MODULE 12.4 Summary

What are mood disorders? What causes depression?

- Mood disorders primarily involve disturbances of mood or emotion, producing manic or depressive states. Severe mood disorders may include psychotic features.

- In a dysthymic disorder, depression is long lasting, though moderate. In a cyclothymic disorder, people suffer from long-lasting, though moderate, swings between depression and elation.

- Bipolar disorders combine mania and depression. In a bipolar I disorder the person swings between severe mania and severe depression. In a bipolar II disorder the person is mostly depressed but has had periods of mild mania.

- A major depressive disorder involves extreme sadness and despondency but no signs of mania.

- Major mood disorders are partially explained by genetic vulnerability and changes in brain chemistry. Other important factors are loss, anger, learned helplessness, stress, and self-defeating thinking patterns.

- Many women experience a brief period of depression, called the maternity blues, shortly after giving birth. Some women suffer from a more serious and lasting condition called postpartum depression.

- Seasonal affective disorder (SAD), which occurs during the winter months, is another common form of depression. SAD is typically treated with phototherapy.

Phototherapy A treatment for seasonal affective disorder that involves exposure to bright, full-spectrum light.

Psychotherapy and Psychoanalysis

FORTUNATELY, the odds are that you will *not* experience an emotional problem like Susan's. But if you did, what help is available? In most cases, it would be some form of psychotherapy. This module introduces several basic types of therapy and provides a brief history of mental health care. It concludes with a discussion of psychoanalysis, the first fully developed psychotherapy.

Psychotherapy—Getting Better by the Hour

SURVEY QUESTION: *How do psychotherapies differ?*

Psychotherapy refers to any psychological technique that can bring about positive changes in personality, behavior, or personal adjustment. In most cases, psychotherapy is based on a dialogue between therapists and their clients. Some therapists also use learning principles to directly alter troublesome behaviors.

Therapists have many approaches to choose from: psychoanalysis, desensitization, Gestalt therapy, client-centered therapy, cognitive therapy, and behavior therapy—to name but a few. As we will see, each therapy emphasizes different concepts and methods. For this reason, the best approach for a particular person or problem may vary (Trull, 2005).

Dimensions of Therapy

The terms listed here describe basic aspects of various therapies (Sharf, 2008). Notice that more than one term may apply to a particular therapy. For example, it is possible to have a directive, action-oriented group therapy or a nondirective, individual, insight-oriented therapy.

- **Individual therapy:** A therapy involving only one client and one therapist.
- **Group therapy:** A therapy session in which several clients participate at the same time.
- **Insight therapy:** Any psychotherapy whose goal is to lead clients to a deeper understanding of their thoughts, emotions, and behavior.
- **Action therapy:** Any therapy designed to bring about direct changes in troublesome thoughts, habits, feelings, or behavior, without seeking insight into their origins or meanings.
- **Directive therapy:** Any approach in which the therapist provides strong guidance.
- **Nondirective therapy:** A style of therapy in which clients assume responsibility for solving their own problems; the therapist assists but does not guide or give advice.
- **Time-limited therapy:** Any therapy begun with the expectation that it will last only a limited number of sessions.
- **Supportive therapy:** An approach in which the therapist's goal is to offer support, rather than to promote personal change. A person trying to get through an emotional crisis or one who wants to solve day-to-day problems may benefit from supportive therapy.
- **Positive therapy:** Techniques designed to enhance personal strengths, rather than "fix" weaknesses.

Myths Psychotherapy has been depicted as a complete personal transformation—a sort of "major overhaul" of the psyche. But therapy is *not* equally effective for all problems. Chances of improvement are fairly good for phobias, low self-esteem, some sexual problems, and marital conflicts. More complex problems can be difficult to solve. For many people, the major benefit of therapy is that it provides comfort, support, and a way to make constructive changes (Bloch, 2006; Hellerstein et al., 1998).

In short, it is often unrealistic to expect psychotherapy to undo a person's entire past. Yet even when problems are severe, therapy may help a person gain a new perspective or learn behaviors to better cope with life. Psychotherapy can be hard work for both clients and therapists. But when it succeeds, few activities are more worthwhile.

It's also a mistake to think that psychotherapy is only used to solve problems or end a crisis. Even if a person is already doing well, therapy can be a way to promote personal growth (Bloch, 2006). Therapists in the positive psychology movement are developing ways to help people make use of their personal strengths. Rather than trying to fix what is "wrong" with a person, they seek to nurture positive traits and actively solve problems (Compton, 2005). ■ Table 13.1 lists some of the elements of positive mental health that therapists seek to restore or promote.

Origins of Therapy—Bored Skulls and Hysteria on the Couch

SURVEY QUESTION: *How did psychotherapy originate?*

Early treatments for mental problems give good reasons to appreciate modern therapies (Sharf, 2008). Archaeological findings dating to the Stone Age suggest that most primitive

■ TABLE 13.1 Elements of Positive Mental Health

- Personal autonomy and independence
- A sense of identity
- Feelings of personal worth
- Skilled interpersonal communication
- Sensitivity, nurturance, and trust
- Genuine and honest with self and others
- Self-control and personal responsibility
- Committed and loving personal relationships
- Capacity to forgive others and oneself
- Personal values and a purpose in life
- Self-awareness and motivation for personal growth
- Adaptive coping strategies for managing stresses and crises
- Fulfillment and satisfaction in work
- Good habits of physical health

Source: Adapted from Bergin, 1991.

CIMMYT

(left) Supernatural explanations attributed abnormal behavior to the work of the devil or "possession" by demons. A modern analysis of "demonic possession" suggests that some victims were suffering from schizophrenia (Mirsky & Duncan, 2005). *(right)* Many other cases of "possession" in medieval Europe and "bewitchment" in colonial New England may be explained by the psychedelic effects of ergot fungus. An ear of rye infested with the fungus (dark areas) is shown here.

approaches were marked by fear and superstitious belief in demons, witchcraft, and magic. One of the more dramatic "cures" practiced by primitive "therapists" was a process called *trepanning* (treh-PAN-ing; also sometimes spelled *trephining*). In modern usage, trepanning is any surgical procedure in which a hole is bored in the skull. In the hands of primitive therapists it meant boring, chipping, or bashing holes into a patient's head. Presumably this was done to relieve pressure or release evil spirits (● Fig. 13.1). Actually, many "patients" didn't survive the "treatment," which sug-

gests that trepanning may have simply been an excuse to kill people who were unusual.

During the Middle Ages, treatments for mental illness in Europe focused on **demonology,** the study of demons and persons plagued by spirits. Medieval "therapists" commonly blamed abnormal behavior on supernatural forces, such as possession by the devil, or on curses from witches and wizards. As a cure, they used exorcism to "cast out evil spirits." For the fortunate, exorcism was a religious ritual. More often, physical torture was used to make the body an inhospitable place for the devil to reside. Modern analyses of "demonic possession" suggest that many victims were suffering from epilepsy, schizophrenia (Mirsky & Duncan, 2005), dissociative disorders (van der Hart, Lierens, & Goodwin, 1996), and depression (Thase, 2006).

One reason for the rise of demonology may lie in *ergotism* (AIR-got-ism), a psychotic-like condition caused by ergot poisoning. In the Middle Ages, rye (grain) fields were often infested with ergot fungus. Ergot, we now know, is a natural source of LSD and other mind-altering chemicals. Eating tainted bread could have caused symptoms that were easily mistaken for bewitchment or madness. Pinching sensations, muscle twitches, facial spasms, delirium, and hallucinations are all signs of ergot poisoning (Matossian, 1982). Thus, many people "treated" by demonologists may have been doubly victimized.

It wasn't until 1793 that the emotionally disturbed were regarded as "mentally ill" and given compassionate treatment. That was the year a French doctor named Philippe Pinel changed the Bicêtre Asylum in Paris from a squalid "madhouse" into a mental hospital by unchaining the inmates

Danielle Pellegrini/Photo Researchers, Inc.

● **FIGURE 13.1** Primitive "treatment" for mental disorders sometimes took the form of boring a hole in the skull. This example shows signs of healing, which means the patient survived the treatment. Many didn't.

Psychotherapy Any psychological technique used to facilitate positive changes in a person's personality, behavior, or adjustment.

Demonology In medieval Europe, the study of demons and the treatment of persons "possessed" by demons.

(left) Many early asylums were no more than prisons with inmates held in chains. *(right)* One late-nineteenth-century "treatment" was based on swinging the patient in a harness—presumably to calm the patient's nerves.

(Harris, 2003). Although it has been more than 200 years since Pinel began humane treatment, the process of improving care continues today.

When was psychotherapy developed? The first true psychotherapy was created by Sigmund Freud more than 100 years ago (Jacobs, 2003). As a physician in Vienna, Freud was intrigued by cases of *hysteria.* People suffering from hysteria have physical symptoms (such as paralysis or numbness) for which no physical causes can be found. (Such problems are now called somatoform disorders, as discussed in Module 12.2.) Slowly, Freud became convinced that hysteria was related to deeply hidden unconscious conflicts. Based on this insight, Freud developed a therapy called *psychoanalysis.* Because it is the "granddaddy" of more modern therapies, let us examine psychoanalysis in some detail.

Psychoanalysis—Expedition into the Unconscious

SURVEY QUESTION: *Is Freudian psychoanalysis still used?*

Isn't psychoanalysis the therapy where the patient lies on a couch? Freud's patients usually reclined on a couch during therapy, while Freud sat out of sight taking notes and offering interpretations. This procedure was supposed to encourage a free flow of thoughts and images from the unconscious. However, it is the least important element of psychoanalysis and many modern analysts have abandoned it.

How did Freud treat emotional problems? Freud's theory stressed that "neurosis" and "hysteria" are caused by repressed memories, motives, and conflicts—particularly those stemming

from instinctual drives for sex and aggression. Although they are hidden, these forces remain active in the personality, and they cause some people to develop rigid ego defenses and compulsive, self-defeating behavior. Thus, the main goal of **psychoanalysis** is to reduce internal conflicts that lead to emotional suffering (Marcus, 2002).

Freud developed on four basic techniques to uncover the unconscious roots of neurosis (Freud, 1949). These are *free association, dream analysis, analysis of resistance,* and *analysis of transference.*

Free Association Saying whatever comes to mind is the basis for **free association.** Patients must speak without worrying whether ideas are painful, embarrassing, or illogical. Thoughts are simply allowed to move freely from one idea to the next, without self-censorship. The purpose of free association is to lower defenses so that unconscious thoughts and feelings can emerge (Hoffer & Youngren, 2004).

Dream Analysis Freud believed that dreams provide a "royal road to the unconscious" because they freely express forbidden desires and unconscious feelings (Rock, 2004). Such feelings are found in the **latent content** (hidden, symbolic meaning) of dreams. Normally, we only remember a dream's **manifest content** (obvious, visible meaning), which tends to disguise information from the unconscious.

Freud was especially interested in unconscious messages revealed by **dream symbols** (images that have personal or

Pioneering psychotherapist Sigmund Freud's famous couch.

emotional meanings). Let's say a young man reports a dream in which he pulls a pistol from his waistband and aims at a target while his wife watches. The pistol repeatedly fails to discharge, and the man's wife laughs at him. Freud might have seen this as an indication of repressed feelings of sexual impotence, with the gun serving as a disguised image of the penis.

Analysis of Resistance When free associating or describing dreams, patients may *resist* talking about or thinking about certain topics. Such **resistances** (blockages in the flow of ideas) reveal particularly important unconscious conflicts. As analysts become aware of resistances, they bring them to the patient's awareness so the patient can deal with them realistically. Rather than being roadblocks in therapy, resistances can be challenges and guides (Engle & Arkowitz, 2006).

Analysis of Transference **Transference** is the tendency to "transfer" feelings to a therapist that match those the patient had for important persons in his or her past. At times, the patient may act as if the analyst is a rejecting father, an unloving or overprotective mother, or a former lover, for example. As the patient re-experiences repressed emotions, the therapist can help the patient recognize and understand them. Troubled persons often provoke anger, rejection, boredom, criticism, and other negative reactions from others. Effective therapists learn to avoid reacting as others do and playing the patient's habitual resistance and transference "games." This, too, contributes to therapeutic change (Marcus, 2002).

Psychoanalysis Today

What is the status of psychoanalysis today? Traditional psychoanalysis called for three to five therapy sessions a week, often for many years. Today, most patients are only seen once or twice per week, but treatment may still go on for years (Friedman et al., 1998). Because of the huge amounts of time and money this requires, psychoanalysts have become relatively rare. Nevertheless, psychoanalysis made a major contribution to modern therapies by highlighting the importance of unconscious conflicts (Friedman, 2006).

Many therapists have switched to doing **brief psychodynamic therapy**, which uses direct questioning to reveal unconscious conflicts (Binder, 2004). Modern therapists also actively provoke emotional reactions that will lower defenses and provide insights (Davanloo, 1995). Interestingly, brief therapy seems to accelerate recovery. Patients seem to realize that they need to get to the heart of their problems quickly (Messer & Kaplan, 2004).

Interpersonal Psychotherapy (IPT) One example of a brief dynamic psychotherapy is **interpersonal psychotherapy**, which was first developed to help people with depression by improving their relationships with others (Trull, 2005). Extensive empirical research has since confirmed the effectiveness of IPT in treating depressive disorders (de Mello, et al., 2005). It has also been used to help people with eating and substance abuse disorders, social phobias, and personality disorders (Hoffart, 2005; Markowitz, 2005; Trull, 2005).

Liona's therapy is a good example of IPT (Brown & Barlow, 2007). She was suffering from a depression that through her therapy she traced back to conflict between her mother and her father. When her father was absent, Liona adopted the role of her mother's protector and friend, but when her father was around she was expected to resume her role as "the daughter." She was angry with her father for abandoning her mother so frequently and upset at having to switch roles so often. Liona's IPT sessions (which sometimes included her mother) focused on clarifying Liona's family roles. She improved a lot after her mother urged her to stick to being "herself."

Is Traditional Psychoanalysis Effective? The development of newer, more streamlined dynamic therapies is in part due to questions about whether traditional psychoanalysis "works." In a classic criticism, Hans Eysenck (1994) suggested that psychoanalysis simply takes so long that patients experience a *spontaneous remission* of symptoms (improvement due to the mere passage of time). How could we tell if a particular therapy, or the passage of time, is responsible for a person's improvement? Typically, some patients are randomly assigned for treatment, and others are placed on a waiting list. If members of this *waiting-list control group*, who

---

Psychoanalysis A Freudian therapy that emphasizes the use of free association, dream interpretation, resistances, and transference to uncover unconscious conflicts.

Free association In psychoanalysis, the technique of having a client say anything that comes to mind, regardless of how embarrassing or unimportant it may seem.

Latent dream content The hidden or symbolic meaning of a dream, as revealed by dream interpretation and analysis.

Manifest dream content The surface, "visible" content of a dream; dream images as they are remembered by the dreamer.

Dream symbols Images in dreams whose personal or emotional meanings differ from their literal meanings.

Resistance A blockage in the flow of free association; topics the client resists thinking or talking about.

Transference The tendency of patients to transfer feelings to a therapist that correspond to those the patient had for important persons in his or her past.

Brief psychodynamic therapy A modern therapy based on psychoanalytic theory but designed to produce insights more quickly.

Interpersonal psychotherapy (IPT) A brief dynamic psychotherapy designed to help people by improving their relationships with other people.

receive no treatment, improve at the same rate as those in therapy, the therapy may be of little value.

How seriously should the possibility of spontaneous remission be taken? It's true that problems ranging from hyperactivity to anxiety improve with the passage of time. However, researchers have confirmed that psychoanalysis does, in fact, produce improvement in a majority of patients (Doidge, 1997).

The real value of Eysenck's critique is that it encouraged psychologists to try new ideas and techniques. Researchers began to ask: "When psychoanalysis works, why does it work? Which parts of it are essential and which are unnecessary?" Modern therapists have given surprisingly varied answers to these questions. Upcoming sections will acquaint you with some of the therapies currently in use.

MODULE 13.1 Summary

How do psychotherapies differ?

- Psychotherapy facilitates positive changes in personality, behavior, or adjustment.
- Psychotherapies may be classified as insight, action, directive, nondirective, supportive, or positive therapies or combinations of these.
- Therapies may be conducted either individually or in groups, and they may be time limited.

How did psychotherapy originate?

- Early approaches to mental illness were dominated by superstition and moral condemnation.
- Demonology attributed mental disturbance to supernatural forces, such as demonic possession, and prescribed exorcism as the cure.
- In some instances, the actual cause of bizarre behavior may have been ergot poisoning.
- More humane treatment began in 1793 with the work of Philippe Pinel in Paris.

Is Freudian psychoanalysis still used?

- As the first true psychotherapy, Freud's psychoanalysis gave rise to modern psychodynamic therapies.
- Psychoanalysis seeks to reveal unconscious thoughts, emotions, and conflicts.
- The psychoanalyst uses free association, dream analysis, and analysis of resistance and transference to reveal health-producing insights.
- Brief psychodynamic therapy (which relies on psychoanalytic theory but is brief and focused) is as effective as other major therapies. One example is interpersonal psychotherapy.
- Some critics argue that traditional psychoanalysis receives credit for spontaneous remissions of symptoms. However, psychoanalysis is successful for many patients.

KNOWLEDGE BUILDER

Psychotherapy and Psychoanalysis

Recite

Match:

U 1. Directive therapies
A 2. Action therapies
d 3. Insight therapies
B 4. Nondirective therapies

A. Change behavior
B. Place responsibility on the client
C. The client is guided strongly
D. Seek understanding

5. An approach that is incompatible with insight therapy is
   a. individual therapy
   b. action therapy
   c. nondirective therapy
   d. interpersonal psychotherapy

6. A scientific explanation of medieval "possessions" by "demons" is related to the effects of
   a. ergot poisoning
   b. trepanning
   c. exorcism
   d. unconscious transference

7. Pinel is famous for his use of exorcism. T or F? ✗ False

8. In psychoanalysis, an emotional attachment to the therapist is called:
   a. free association
   b. manifest association
   c. resistance
   d. transference

Reflect

Critical Thinking

9. Waiting-list control groups help separate the effects of therapy from improvement related to the mere passage of time. What other type of control group might be needed to learn if therapy is truly beneficial?

Relate

How has your understanding of psychotherapy changed? How many types of therapy can you name?

Make a list describing what you think it means to be mentally healthy. How well does your list match the items in Table 13.1?

The use of trepanning, demonology, and exorcism all implied that the mentally ill are "cursed." To what extent are the mentally ill rejected and stigmatized today?

Try to free associate (aloud) for 10 minutes. How difficult was it? Did anything interesting surface?

Can you explain, in your own words, the role of dream analysis, resistances, and transference in psychoanalysis?

Link

Internet addresses frequently change. To find the sites listed here, visit **http://www .thomsonedu.com/psychology/coon** for an updated list of Internet addresses and direct links to relevant sites.

- **Pre-Columbian Trephination** Read about the first psychosurgery as a treatment for mental illness.

- **Phillipe Pinel** Read about Pinel's contribution to the history of the treatment of mental illness.

- **Freud and Psychoanalysis** Read about the history of psychoanalysis.

ANSWERS

1. C 2. A 3. D 4. B 5. b 6. a 7. F 8. d 9. Placebo therapy is sometimes used to assess the benefits of real therapy. Placebo therapy superficially resembles the real thing but lacks key elements that are thought to be therapeutic.

13.2 Insight Therapies

WHEN MOST PEOPLE PICTURE CLINICAL PSYCHOLOGISTS at work, they probably imagine them doing insight therapy. As stated earlier, insight therapists help clients gain a deeper understanding of their thoughts, emotions, and behavior. Let's sample a variety of insight-oriented approaches, including therapies done at a distance (by telephone or over the Internet).

Humanistic Therapies— Restoring Human Potential

SURVEY QUESTION: *What are the major humanistic therapies?*

Better self-knowledge was the goal of traditional psychoanalysis. However, Freud claimed that his patients could expect only to change their "hysterical misery into common unhappiness"! Humanistic therapies are more optimistic. Most assume that it is possible for people to use their potentials fully and live rich, rewarding lives. Psychotherapy is seen as a way to give mental health a chance to emerge.

Client-Centered Therapy

What is client-centered therapy? How is it different from psychoanalysis? Psychoanalysts delve into the unconscious. Psychologist Carl Rogers (1902–1987) found it more beneficial to explore *conscious* thoughts and feelings. The psychoanalyst tends to take a position of authority, stating what dreams, thoughts, or memories "mean." In contrast, Rogers believed that what is right or valuable for the therapist may be wrong for the client. (Rogers preferred the term *client* to *patient* because *patient* implies that a person is "sick" and needs to be "cured.") Consequently, the client determines what will be discussed during each session. Thus, **client-centered therapy** (also called **person-centered therapy**) is nondirective and based on insights from conscious thoughts and feelings (Brodley, 2006; Schneider, 2002).

If the client runs things, what does the therapist do? The therapist's job is to create a safe "atmosphere of growth." The therapist provides opportunities for change, but the client must actively seek to solve his or her problems. The therapist cannot "fix" the client (Whitton, 2003).

Health-Promoting Conditions Rogers believed that effective therapists maintain four basic conditions. First, the therapist offers the client **unconditional positive regard** (unshakable personal acceptance). The therapist refuses to react with shock, dismay, or disapproval to anything the client says or feels. Total acceptance by the therapist is the first step to self-acceptance by the client.

Second, the therapist attempts to achieve genuine **empathy** by trying to see the world through the client's eyes and feeling some part of what the client is feeling.

As a third essential condition, the therapist strives to be **authentic** (genuine and honest). The therapist must not hide behind a professional role. Rogers believed that phony fronts destroy the growth atmosphere sought in client-centered therapy.

Fourth, the therapist does not make interpretations, propose solutions, or offer advice. Instead, the therapist **reflects** (rephrases, summarizes, or repeats) the client's thoughts and feelings. This allows the therapist to act as a psychological "mirror" so clients can see themselves more clearly. Rogers theorized that a person armed with a realistic self-image and greater self-acceptance will gradually discover solutions to life's problems.

Existential Therapy

According to the existentialists, "being in the world" (existence) creates deep anxiety. Each of us must deal with the realities of death. We must face the fact that we create our private world by making choices. We must overcome isolation on a vast and indifferent planet. Most of all, we must confront feelings of meaninglessness.

What do these concerns have to do with psychotherapy? **Existential therapy** focuses on the problems of existence, such as meaning, choice, and responsibility. Like client-centered therapy, it promotes self-knowledge. However, there are important differences. Client-centered therapy seeks to uncover a "true self" hidden behind a screen of defenses. In contrast, existential therapy emphasizes free will, the human ability to make choices. Accordingly, existential therapists believe you can *choose to become* the person you want to be.

Existential therapists try to give clients the *courage* to make rewarding and socially constructive choices. Typically, therapy focuses on *death, freedom, isolation,* and *meaninglessness,* the "ultimate concerns" of existence (van Deurzen & Kenward, 2005). These universal human challenges include

Psychotherapist Carl Rogers, who originated client-centered therapy.

an awareness of one's mortality, the responsibility that comes with freedom to choose, being alone in your own private world, and the need to create meaning in your life.

One example of existential therapy is Victor Frankl's logotherapy, which emphasizes the need to find and maintain meaning in life. Frankl (1904–1997) based his approach on experiences he had as a prisoner in a Nazi concentration camp. In the camp, Frankl saw countless prisoners break down as they were stripped of all hope and human dignity (Frankl, 1955). Those who survived with their sanity did so because they managed to hang on to a sense of meaning (logos). Even in less dire circumstances, a sense of purpose in life adds greatly to psychological well-being (Prochaska & Norcross, 2007).

What does the existential therapist do? The therapist helps clients discover self-imposed limitations in personal identity. To be successful, the client must fully accept the challenge of changing his or her life (Bretherton & Orner, 2004). Interestingly, Buddhists seek a similar state that they call "radical acceptance" (Brach, 2003). A key aspect of existential therapy is *confrontation,* in which clients are challenged to examine their values and choices and to take responsibility for the quality of their existence (Gerwood, 1998).

An important part of confrontation is the unique, intense, here-and-now *encounter* between two human beings. When existential therapy is successful, it brings about a renewed sense of purpose and a reappraisal of what's important in life. Some clients even experience an emotional rebirth, as if they had survived a close brush with death. As Marcel Proust wrote, "The real voyage of discovery consists not in seeing new landscapes but in having new eyes."

Gestalt Therapy

Gestalt therapy is based on the idea that perception, or *awareness,* is disjointed and incomplete in maladjusted persons. The German word *Gestalt* means "whole," or "complete." **Gestalt therapy** helps people rebuild thinking, feeling, and acting into connected wholes. This is achieved by expanding personal awareness; by accepting responsibility for one's thoughts, feelings, and actions; and by filling in gaps in experience (Joyce & Sills, 2001).

What do you mean by gaps in experience? Gestalt therapists believe that we often shy away from expressing or "owning" upsetting feelings. This creates a gap in self-awareness that may become a barrier to personal growth. For example, a person who feels anger after the death of a parent might go for years without fully expressing it. This and similar threatening gaps may impair emotional health.

The Gestalt approach is more directive than client-centered or existential therapy, and it emphasizes immediate experience. Working either one-to-one or in a group setting,

the Gestalt therapist encourages clients to become more aware of their moment-to-moment thoughts, perceptions, and emotions (Staemmler, 2004). Rather than discussing *why* clients feel guilt, anger, fear, or boredom, they are encouraged to have these feelings in the "here and now" and become fully aware of them. The therapist promotes awareness by drawing attention to a client's posture, voice, eye movements, and hand gestures. Clients may also be asked to exaggerate vague feelings until they become clear. Gestalt therapists believe that expressing such feelings allows people to "take care of unfinished business" and break through emotional impasses (O'Leary, 2006).

Gestalt therapy is often associated with the work of Frederick (Fritz) Perls (1969). In all his writings, Perls' basic message comes through clearly: Emotional health comes from knowing what you *want* to do, not dwelling on what you *should* do, *ought* to do, or *should want* to do (Rosenberg & Lynch, 2002). Another way of stating this idea is that emotional health comes from taking full responsibility for one's feelings and actions. For example, it means changing "I can't" to "I won't," or "I must" to "I choose to."

How does Gestalt therapy help people discover their real wants? Above all else, Gestalt therapy emphasizes *present* experience. Clients are urged to stop intellectualizing and talking *about* feelings. Instead, they learn to live now; live here; stop imagining; experience the real; stop unnecessary thinking; taste and see; express rather than explain, justify, or judge; give in to unpleasantness and pain just as to pleasure; and surrender to being as you are. Gestalt therapists believe that, paradoxically, the best way to change is to become who you really are (Joyce & Sills, 2001).

Client-centered (or person-centered) therapy A nondirective therapy based on insights gained from conscious thoughts and feelings; emphasizes accepting one's true self.

Unconditional positive regard An unqualified, unshakable acceptance of another person.

Empathy A capacity for taking another's point of view; the ability to feel what another is feeling.

Authenticity In Carl Rogers's terms, the ability of a therapist to be genuine and honest about his or her own feelings.

Reflection In client-centered therapy, the process of rephrasing or repeating thoughts and feelings expressed by clients so they can become aware of what they are saying.

Existential therapy An insight therapy that focuses on the elemental problems of existence, such as death, meaning, choice, and responsibility; emphasizes making courageous life choices.

Gestalt therapy An approach that focuses on immediate experience and awareness to help clients rebuild thinking, feeling, and acting into connected wholes; emphasizes the integration of fragmented experiences.

Because of their emphasis on verbal interaction, humanistic therapies may be conducted at a distance, by telephone, e-mail, or videoconferencing. Let's investigate this possibility.

Therapy at a Distance—Psych Jockeys and Cybertherapy

SURVEY QUESTION: *Can therapy be conducted at a distance?*

How valid are psychological services offered at a distance? For better or worse, high-tech psychotherapy and counseling are rapidly becoming commonplace (Ormay, 2006). Today, psychological services are available through radio, telephone, e-mail, Internet chat rooms, and videoconferencing (Maheu et al., 2004). What are the advantages and disadvantages of getting help at a distance?

Media Psychologists

By now you have probably heard a phone-in radio psychologist or watched one on television. On a typical program, participants describe problems arising from child abuse, loneliness, love affairs, phobias, sexual adjustment, or depression. The media psychologist then offers reassurance, advice, or suggestions for getting help. Such talk-radio and television programs may seem harmless, but they raise some important questions. For instance, is it reasonable to give advice without knowing anything about a person's background? Could the

Getty Images

Media psychologists have been urged to educate without actually doing therapy. Some overstep this boundary, however. Do you think popular TV psychologist Dr. Phil sometimes goes too far?

advice do harm? What good can a psychologist do in 3 minutes or even an hour?

In their own defense, media psychologists point out that listeners and viewers may learn solutions to their problems by hearing others talk. Many also stress that their work is educational, not therapeutic. Nevertheless, the question arises: When does advice become therapy? The American Psychological Association urges media psychologists to discuss problems only of a general nature, instead of actually counseling anyone. For example, if a caller complains about insomnia, the radio psychologist should talk about insomnia in general, not probe the caller's personal life.

By giving information, advice, and social support, media psychologists do help some people. The well-known media psychologist Dr. Phil McGraw has even been awarded a President's Citation from the American Psychological Association for his work in publicizing mental health issues (Meyers, 2006). Even so, a good guide for anyone tempted to call a radio psychologist or accept advice from a TV psychologist might be "let the consumer beware."

Telephone Therapists

The same caution applies to commercial telephone therapists. These "counselors" can be reached through 900-number services for $3 to $4 per minute. To date, there is no evidence that commercial telephone counseling is effective.

It's important to note, however, that legitimate therapists may use the phone to calm, console, or advise their clients between therapy sessions. Others are experimenting with actually doing therapy by telephone. For example, after the attack on the World Trade Center towers, many rescue personnel needed counseling. To fill the need, a phone network was created to link emergency workers with psychologists all over the country (Murray, 2001; Shore, 2003).

A key feature of successful face-to-face therapy is the establishment of a continuing *relationship* between two people. In this regard, telephone therapy is seriously limited by a lack of visual cues, such as facial expressions and body language (Haas, Benedict, & Kobos, 1996). Regardless, under the right circumstances, telephone therapy can be as successful as face-to-face therapy (Day & Schneider, 2002). For example, in one study, telephone counseling helped improve success rates for smokers who wanted to quit (Rabius et al., 2004). Other studies have shown that depressed people benefit from telephone therapy (Mohr et al., 2005; Simon et al., 2004).

Internet Therapy

The ever-evolving Internet has provided new communication tools, including voice, text, graphics, and video. All these tools are being used to deliver therapy. Psychological advice, support groups, self-help magazines, and even online therapy are available via the Internet. Some services, such as support groups, are free. Online counseling or advice, in contrast, is typically offered for a fee. Some online therapists will "discuss" problems with you through e-mail messages (Chester & Glass, 2006). Others merely answer questions or give advice concerning specific problems.

Online counseling and advice services do have some advantages. For one thing, clients can remain anonymous. Thus, a person who might hesitate to see a psychologist can seek help privately, online. Likewise, the Internet can link people who live in rural areas with psychologists living in large cities. And, compared with traditional office visits, Internet therapy is less expensive.

As with radio talk shows and telephone counselors, many objections can be raised about online psychological services. Clearly, brief e-mail messages are no way to make a diagnosis. And forget about facial expressions or body language—not even tone of voice reaches the online therapist. Typing emotional icons (called *emoticons*) like little smiley faces (☺) or frowns (☹) is a poor substitute for real human interaction. Another problem is that e-mail counseling may not be completely confidential and could be intercepted and misused. Of special concern is the fact that "cybershrinks" may or may not be trained professionals (Bloom, 1998). And even if they are, questions exist about whether a psychologist licensed in one state can legally do therapy in another state via the Internet. Despite such objections, psychologists have demonstrated success providing therapy over the Internet, at least for certain types of problems (Carlbring et al., 2007; Klein, Richards, & Austin, 2006).

Many of the drawbacks we have discussed can be solved with videoconferencing. A two-way audio-video link allows the client and therapist to see one another on computer monitors and to talk via speakerphones. Doing therapy this way still lacks the close personal contact of face-to-face interaction. However, it does remove many of the objections to doing therapy at a distance. It's very likely that distance services will continue to evolve (Riva & Wiederhold, 2006) and become a major source of mental health care in coming years (Schopp, Demiris, & Glueckauf, 2006).

Implications As you can see, psychological services that rely on electronic communication may serve some useful purposes. However, the value of therapy offered by commercial telephone "counselors" and Internet "therapists" remains open to question. The very best advice given by media psychologists, telephone "counselors," or Internet "therapists" may be, "If at all possible, you should consider discussing this problem with a psychologist or counselor in your own community."

MODULE 13.2 Summary

What are the major humanistic therapies?

- Client-centered (or person-centered) therapy is nondirective, based on insights gained from conscious thoughts and feelings, and dedicated to creating an atmosphere of growth.

- Unconditional positive regard, empathy, authenticity, and reflection are combined to give the client a chance to solve his or her own problems.

- Existential therapies focus on the end result of the choices one makes in life. Clients are encouraged through confrontation and encounter to exercise free will and to take responsibility for their choices.

- Gestalt therapy emphasizes immediate awareness of thoughts and feelings. Its goal is to rebuild thinking, feeling, and acting into connected wholes and to help clients break through emotional blockages.

Can therapy be conducted at a distance?

- Media psychologists, telephone counselors, and cybertherapists may, on occasion, do some good. However, each has drawbacks, and the effectiveness of telephone counseling and cybertherapy has not been unambiguously established.

- Therapy by videoconferencing shows more promise as a way to provide mental health services at a distance.

KNOWLEDGE BUILDER

Insight Therapies

Recite

Match:

____ 1. Client-centered therapy

____ 2. Gestalt therapy

____ 3. Existential therapy

____ 4. Internet therapy

A. Electronic advice

B. Unconditional positive regard

C. Gaps in awareness

D. Choice and becoming

5. The Gestalt therapist tries to *reflect* a client's thoughts and feelings. T or F?

6. Filling in gaps in immediate self-awareness is one of the principal goals of

a. supportive therapy

b. existential therapy

c. person-centered therapy

d. Gestalt therapy

7. Confrontation and encounter are concepts of existential therapy. T or F?

8. To date, the most acceptable type of "distance therapy" is

a. media psychology

b. commercial telephone counseling

c. Internet-based cybertherapy

d. based on videoconferencing

Reflect

Critical Thinking

9. How might using the term *patient* affect the relationship between an individual and a therapist?

Relate

Here's a mnemonic for the elements of client-centered therapy: Picture a therapist saying "I ear u" to a client. The *E* stands for empathy, *A* for authenticity, *R* for reflection, and *U* for unconditional positive regard.

What would an existential therapist say about the choices you have made so far in your life? Should you be choosing more "courageously"?

You are going to play the role of a therapist for a classroom demonstration. How would you act if you were a client-centered therapist? An existential therapist? A Gestalt therapist?

A neighbor of yours is thinking about getting counseling on the Internet. What would you tell her about the pros and cons of distance therapy?

Link

Internet addresses frequently change. To find the sites listed here, visit **http://www .thomsonedu.com/psychology/coon** for an updated list of Internet addresses and direct links to relevant sites.

• **Carl Rogers** Read Rogers' original article some observations on the organization of personality.

• **Existential Therapy** Explore this extensive website about existential therapy.

• **Dr. Phil** See for yourself how Dr. Phil publicizes mental health issues.

ANSWERS

1. B 2. C 3. D 4. A 5. F 6. d 7. T 8. d 9. The terms *doctor* and *patient* imply a large gap in status and authority between the individual and his or her therapist. Client-centered therapy attempts to narrow this gap by making the person the final authority concerning solutions to his or her problems. Also, the word *patient* implies that a person is "sick" and needs to be "cured." Many regard this as an inappropriate way to think about human problems.

13.3 Behavior Therapy

A BREAKTHROUGH OCCURRED when psychologists realized they could use learning principles to solve human problems. Behavior therapists directly change behavior patterns so that people can function more comfortably and effectively. This unit describes some innovative, and very successful, behavioral therapies.

Behavior Therapy—Healing by Learning

SURVEY QUESTIONS: *What is behavior therapy? How is behavior therapy used to treat phobias, fears, and anxieties?*

Jay repeatedly and vividly imagined himself going into a store to steal something. He then pictured himself being caught and turned over to the police, who handcuffed him and hauled him off to jail. Once there, he imagined calling his wife to tell her he had been arrested for shoplifting. He became very distressed as he faced her anger and his son's disappointment (Kohn & Antonuccio, 2002).

Why would anyone imagine such a thing? Jay's behavior is not as strange as it may seem. His goal was self-control: Jay is a *kleptomaniac* (a compulsive stealer). The method he chose (called *covert sensitization*) is a form of behavior therapy (Corsini, 2001). **Behavior therapy** is the use of learning principles to make constructive changes in behavior. Behavioral approaches include behavior modification, aversion therapy, desensitization, token economies, and other techniques (Forsyth & Savsevitz, 2002).

Behavior therapists believe that deep insight into one's problems is often unnecessary for improvement. Instead, they try to directly alter troublesome thoughts and actions. Jay didn't need to probe into his past or his emotions and conflicts; he simply wanted to break his shoplifting habit.

In general, how does behavior therapy work? Behavior therapists assume that people have *learned* to be the way they are. If they have learned responses that cause problems, then they can change them by *relearning* more appropriate behaviors. Broadly speaking, **behavior modification** refers to any use of classical or operant conditioning to directly alter human behavior (Miltenberger, 2008; Spiegler & Guevremont, 2003). (Some therapists prefer to call this approach *applied behavior analysis*.)

How does classical conditioning work? I'm not sure I remember. Classical conditioning is a form of learning in which simple responses (especially reflexes) are associated with new stimuli. Perhaps a brief review would be helpful. In classical conditioning, a neutral stimulus is followed by an *unconditioned stimulus (US)* that consistently produces an unlearned reaction, called the *unconditioned response (UR)*. Eventually, the previously neutral stimulus begins to produce this response directly. The response is then called a *conditioned response (CR)*, and the stimulus becomes a *conditioned stimulus (CS)*. Thus, for a child the sight of a hypodermic needle (CS) is followed by an injection (US), which causes anxiety or fear (UR). Eventually the sight of a hypodermic (the conditioned stimulus) may produce anxiety or fear (a conditioned response) *before* the child gets an injection. (For a more thorough review of classical conditioning, return to Module 6.1.)

What does classical conditioning have to do with behavior modification? Classical conditioning can be used to associate discomfort with a bad habit, as Jay did. More powerful versions of this approach are called aversion therapy.

Aversion Therapy

Imagine that you are eating an apple. Suddenly you discover that you just bit a large green worm in half. You vomit. Months later you cannot eat an apple again without feeling ill. It's apparent that you have developed a conditioned aversion to apples. (A *conditioned aversion* is a learned dislike or negative emotional response to some stimulus.)

How are conditioned aversions used in therapy? In **aversion therapy,** an individual learns to associate a strong aversion to an undesirable habit such as smoking, drinking, or gambling. Aversion therapy has been used to cure hiccups, sneezing, stuttering, vomiting, nail-biting, bed-wetting, compulsive hair-pulling, alcoholism, and the smoking of tobacco, marijuana, or crack cocaine. Actually, aversive conditioning happens every day. For example, not many physicians who treat lung cancer patients are smokers, nor do many emergency room doctors drive without using their seat belts (Eifert & Lejuez, 2000).

Puffing Up an Aversion
The fact that nicotine is toxic makes it easy to create an aversion that helps people give up smoking. Behavior therapists have found that electric shock, nauseating drugs, and similar aversive stimuli are not required to make smokers uncomfortable. All that is needed is for the smoker to smoke—rapidly, for a long time, at a forced pace.

Behavior therapy Any therapy designed to actively change behavior.

Behavior modification The application of learning principles to change human behavior, especially maladaptive behavior.

Aversion therapy Suppressing an undesirable response by associating it with aversive (painful or uncomfortable) stimuli.

During *rapid smoking*, clients are told to smoke continuously, taking a puff every 6 to 8 seconds. Rapid smoking continues until the smoker is miserable and can stand it no more. By then, most people are thinking, "I never want to see another cigarette for the rest of my life."

Rapid smoking has long been known as an effective behavior therapy for smoking (McRobbie & Hajek, 2007). Nevertheless, anyone tempted to try rapid smoking should realize that it is very unpleasant. Without the help of a therapist, most people quit too soon for the procedure to succeed. In addition, rapid smoking can be dangerous. It should only be done with professional supervision. (An alternative method that is more practical is described in the "Psychology in Action" module of this chapter.)

Aversive Therapy for Drinking Another excellent example of aversion therapy was pioneered by Roger Vogler and his associates (1977). Vogler works with alcoholics who were unable to stop drinking. For many clients, aversion therapy is a last chance. While drinking an alcoholic beverage, clients receive a painful (although not injurious) electric shock to the hand. Most of the time, these shocks occur as the client is beginning to take a drink of alcohol.

These *response-contingent shocks* (shocks that are linked to a response) obviously take the pleasure out of drinking. Shocks also cause the alcohol abuser to develop a conditioned aversion to drinking. Normally, the misery caused by alcohol abuse comes long after the act of drinking—too late to have much effect. But if alcohol can be linked with *immediate* discomfort, then drinking will begin to make the individual very uncomfortable.

Is it really acceptable to treat clients this way? People are often disturbed (shocked?) by such methods. However, clients usually *volunteer* for aversion therapy because it helps them overcome a destructive habit. Indeed, commercial aversion programs for overeating, smoking, and alcohol abuse have attracted many willing customers. More important, aversion therapy can be justified by its long-term benefits. As behaviorist Donald Baer put it, "A small number of brief, painful experiences is a reasonable exchange for the interminable pain of a lifelong maladjustment."

Desensitization

How is behavior therapy used to treat phobias, fears, and anxieties? Assume that you are a swimming instructor who wants to help a child named Jamie overcome fear of the high diving board. How might you proceed? Directly forcing Jamie off the high board could be a psychological disaster. Obviously, a better approach would be to begin by teaching her to dive off the edge of the pool. Then she could be taught to dive off the low board, followed by a platform 6 feet above the water, and then an 8-foot platform. As a last step, Jamie could try the high board.

Who's Afraid of a Hierarchy? This rank-ordered series of steps is called a **hierarchy**. The hierarchy allows Jamie to undergo *adaptation*. Gradually, she adapts to the high dive and overcomes her fear. When Jamie has conquered her fear, we can say that *desensitization* (dee-SEN-sih-tih-ZAY-shun) has occurred (Spiegler & Guevremont, 2003).

Desensitization is also based on **reciprocal inhibition** (using one emotional state to block another) (Heriot & Pritchard, 2004). For instance, it is impossible to be anxious and relaxed at the same time. If we can get Jamie onto the high board in a relaxed state, her anxiety and fear will be inhibited. Repeated visits to the high board should cause fear to disappear in this situation. Again we would say that Jamie has been desensitized. Typically, **systematic desensitization** (a guided reduction in fear, anxiety, or aversion) is attained by gradually approaching a feared stimulus while maintaining relaxation.

What is desensitization used for? Desensitization is primarily used to help people unlearn phobias (intense, unrealistic fears) or strong anxieties. For example, each of these people might be a candidate for desensitization: a teacher with stage fright, a student with test anxiety, a salesperson who fears people, or a newlywed with an aversion to sexual intimacy.

Performing Desensitization *How is desensitization done?* First, the client and the therapist *construct a hierarchy*. This is a list of fear-provoking situations, arranged from least disturbing to most frightening. Second, the client is taught *exercises that produce deep relaxation*. (See "Feeling a Little Tense? Relax!") Once the client is relaxed, she or he proceeds

Programs for treating fears of flying combine relaxation, systematic desensitization, group support, and lots of direct and indirect exposure to airliners. Many such programs conclude with a brief flight, so that participants can "test their wings."

DISCOVERING PSYCHOLOGY

Feeling a Little Tense? Relax!

The key to desensitization is relaxation. To inhibit fear, you must *learn* to relax. One way to voluntarily relax is by using the **tension-release method.** To achieve deep-muscle relaxation, try the following exercise.

Tense the muscles in your right arm until they tremble. Hold them tight as you slowly count to 10 and then let go. Allow your hand and arm to go limp and to relax completely. Repeat the procedure. Releasing tension two or three times will allow you to feel whether

or not your arm muscles have relaxed. Repeat the tension-release procedure with your left arm. Compare it with your right arm. Repeat until the left arm is equally relaxed. Apply the tension-release technique to your right leg; to your left leg; to your abdomen; to your chest and shoulders. Clench and release your chin, neck, and throat. Wrinkle and release your forehead and scalp. Tighten and release your mouth and

face muscles. As a last step, curl your toes and tense your feet. Then release.

Practice the tension-release method until you can achieve complete relaxation quickly (5 to 10 minutes). After you have practiced relaxation once a day for a week or two, you will begin to be able to tell when your body (or a group of muscles) is tense. Also, you will begin to be able to relax on command. This is a valuable skill that you can apply in any situation that makes you feel tense or anxious.

to the third step by trying to *perform the least disturbing item* on the list. For a fear of heights (acrophobia), this might be: "(1) Stand on a chair." The first item is repeated until no anxiety is felt. Any change from complete relaxation is a signal that clients must relax again before continuing. Slowly, clients move up the hierarchy: "(2) Climb to the top of a small stepladder"; "(3) Look down a flight of stairs"; and so on, until the last item is performed without fear: "(20) Fly in an airplane."

For many phobias, desensitization works best when people are directly exposed to the stimuli and situations they fear (Bourne, 2005). For something like a simple spider phobia, this exposure can even be done in groups. Also, for some fears (such as fear of riding an elevator) desensitization may be completed in a single session (Sturges & Sturges, 1998).

Vicarious Desensitization

I understand how some fears could be desensitized by a gradual approach—as in the case of the child on the high dive. But what if it's not practical to directly act out the steps of a hierarchy? For a fear of heights, the steps of the hierarchy might be acted out. However, if this is impractical, the problem can be handled by having clients observe *models* who are performing the feared behavior (Eifert & Lejuez, 2000) (● Fig. 13.2). A model is a person (either live or filmed) who serves as an example for observational learning. If such **vicarious desensitization** (secondhand learning) can't be used, there is yet another option. Fortunately, desensitization works almost as well when a person *vividly imagines* each step in the hierarchy (Yahnke, Sheikh, & Beckman, 2003). If the steps can be visualized without anxiety, fear in the actual situ-

● **FIGURE 13.2** Treatment of a snake phobia by vicarious desensitization. These classic photographs show models interacting with snakes. To overcome their own fears, phobic subjects observed the models (Bandura, Blanchard, & Ritter, 1969). (Photos courtesy of Albert Bandura.)

Hierarchy A rank-ordered series of higher and lower amounts, levels, degrees, or steps.

Reciprocal inhibition The presence of one emotional state can inhibit the occurrence of another, such as joy preventing fear or anxiety inhibiting pleasure.

Systematic desensitization A reduction in fear, anxiety, or aversion brought about by planned exposure to aversive stimuli.

Tension-release method A procedure for systematically achieving deep relaxation of the body.

Vicarious desensitization A reduction in fear or anxiety that takes place vicariously ("secondhand") when a client watches models perform the feared behavior.

ation is reduced. Because imagining feared stimuli can be done at a therapist's office, it is the most common way of doing desensitization.

Virtual Reality Exposure

Desensitization is an *exposure therapy*. Like other such therapies, it involves exposing people to feared stimuli until their fears extinguish. In an important new development, psychologists are using virtual reality to treat phobias. Virtual reality is a computer-generated, three-dimensional "world" that viewers enter by wearing a head-mounted video display. **Virtual reality exposure** presents computerized fear stimuli to clients in a realistic, yet carefully controlled fashion (Wiederhold & Wiederhold, 2005). It has already been used to treat fears of flying, driving, and public speaking as well as acrophobia (fear of heights), claustrophobia, and spider phobias (Arbona et al., 2004; Giuseppe, 2005; Hoffman et al., 2003; Lee et al., 2002; Wald and Taylor, 2000). (See ● Fig. 13.3.)

Desensitization has been one of the most successful behavior therapies. A second new technique may provide yet another way to lower fears, anxieties, and psychological pain.

Eye Movement Desensitization

Traumatic events produce painful memories. Disturbing flashbacks often haunts victims of accidents, disasters, molestations, muggings, rapes, or emotional abuse. Recently, Dr. Francine Shapiro developed **eye movement desensitization and reprocessing (EMDR)** to help ease traumatic memories and posttraumatic stress.

In a typical EMDR session, the client is asked to visualize the images that most upset her or him. At the same time, a pencil (or other object) is moved rapidly from side to side in front of the person's eyes. Watching the moving object causes the person's eyes to dart swiftly back and forth. After about 30 seconds, clients describe any memories, feelings, and thoughts that emerged and discuss them with the therapist. These steps are repeated until troubling thoughts and emotions no longer surface (Shapiro, 2001; Shapiro & Forrest, 2004).

A number of studies suggest that EMDR lowers anxieties and takes the pain out of traumatic memories (Seidler & Wagner, 2006; Silver et al., 2005). However, EMDR is highly controversial. Some studies, for example, have found that eye movements add nothing to the treatment. The apparent success of EMDR may simply be based on gradual exposure to upsetting stimuli, as in other forms of desensitization (Cahill, Carrigan, & Frueh, 1999; Davidson & Parker, 2001). On the other hand, some researchers continue to find that EMDR is superior to traditional therapies (Greenwald, 2006; Rogers & Silver, 2002).

Is EMDR a breakthrough? Given the frequency of traumas in modern society, it shouldn't be long before we find out.

MODULE **13.3 Summary**

What is behavior therapy? How is behavior therapy used to treat phobias, fears, and anxieties?

- Behavior therapists use the learning principles of classical or operant conditioning to directly change human behavior.
- In aversion therapy, classical conditioning is used to associate maladaptive behavior (such as smoking or drinking) with pain or other aversive events in order to inhibit undesirable responses.
- In desensitization, exposure to fear stimuli, adaptation, and reciprocal inhibition are used to break the link between fear and particular situations.

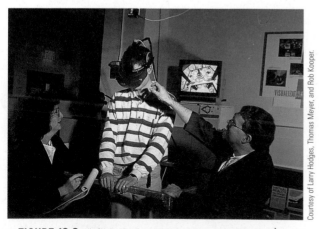
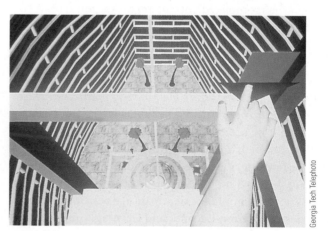

● **FIGURE 13.3** *(left)* Dr. Barbara Rothbaum and Dr. Larry Hodges show how a virtual reality system is used to expose people to feared stimuli. Many clients would rather face feared stimuli in a virtual environment than in a real physical environment. *(right)* A computer image from a virtual elevator. Over an 8-week period, clients who suffered from acrophobia "rode" in the elevator. Each session took them to greater heights.

- Typical steps in desensitization are: Construct a fear hierarchy, learn to produce total relaxation, and perform items on the hierarchy (from least to most disturbing).
- Desensitization may be carried out in real settings, or it may be done by vividly imagining feared stimuli or by watching models perform the feared responses.

- In some cases, virtual reality exposure can be used to present fear stimuli in a controlled manner.
- A technique called eye movement desensitization and reprocessing (EMDR) shows promise as a treatment for traumatic memories and stress disorders. At present, however, EMDR is highly controversial.

KNOWLEDGE BUILDER

Behavior Therapy

Recite

1. What two types of conditioning are used in behavior modification? _classical_ and _operant_

2. Shock, pain, and discomfort play what role in conditioning an aversion?
   a. conditioned stimulus
   b. unconditioned response
   c. unconditioned stimulus
   d. conditioned response

3. If shock is used to control drinking, it must be _response_ contingent.

4. What two principles underlie systematic desensitization? _adaption_ and _reciprocal_

5. When desensitization is carried out through the use of live or filmed models, it is called
   a. cognitive therapy
   b. flooding

c. covert desensitization
d. vicarious desensitization

6. The three basic steps in systematic desensitization are: construct a hierarchy, flood the person with anxiety, and imagine relaxation. T or F? _false_

7. In EMDR therapy, computer-generated virtual reality images are used to expose clients to fear-provoking stimuli. T or F? _false_

Reflect

Critical Thinking

8. Alcoholics who take a drug called Antabuse become ill after drinking alcohol. Why, then, don't they develop an aversion to drinking?

9. A natural form of desensitization often takes place in hospitals. Can you guess what it is?

Relate

Can you describe three problems for which you think behavior therapy would be an appropriate treatment?

A friend of yours has a dog that goes berserk during thunderstorms. You own an audiotape of a thunderstorm. How could you use the tape to desensitize the dog? (Hint: The tape player has a volume control.)

Have you ever become naturally desensitized to a stimulus or situation that at first made you anxious (for instance, heights, public speaking, or driving on freeways)? How would you explain your reduced fear?

Link

Internet addresses frequently change. To find the sites listed here, visit **http://www .thomsonedu.com/psychology/coon** for an updated list of Internet addresses and direct links to relevant sites.

- **Aversion therapy** Read more about aversion therapy.
- **Systematic Desensitization** Explore this self-administered procedure.
- **Virtual Reality Therapy** Learn more about VR therapy.

ANSWERS

1. classical (or respondent), operant 2. c 3. response 4. adaptation, reciprocal inhibition 5. d 6. F 7. F 8. Committed alcoholics may actually "drink through it" and learn to tolerate the nauseating effects. 9. Doctors and nurses learn to relax and remain calm at the sight of blood because of their frequent exposure to it.

Virtual reality exposure Use of computer-generated images to present fear stimuli. The virtual environment responds to a viewer's head movements and other inputs.

Eye movement desensitization and reprocessing (EMDR) A technique for reducing fear or anxiety; based on holding upsetting thoughts in mind while rapidly moving the eyes from side to side.

13.4 Operant Therapies and Cognitive Therapies

IN THE NEXT MODULE, we will consider two contrasting approaches to human problems. Operant therapies are very behavioral: They directly reinforce some behaviors and seek to extinguish others. In contrast, cognitive therapists help people change harmful thinking patterns.

Operant Therapies—All the World Is a Skinner Box?

SURVEY QUESTION: *What role does reinforcement play in behavior therapy?*

Aversion therapy and desensitization are based on classical conditioning. Where does operant conditioning fit in? As you may recall, *operant conditioning* refers to learning based on the consequences of making a response. The operant principles most often used by behavior therapists to deal with human behavior are:

1. **Positive reinforcement.** Responses that are followed by reward tend to occur more frequently. If children whine and get attention, they will whine more frequently. If you get A's in your psychology class, you may become a psychology major.
2. **Nonreinforcement.** A response that is not followed by reward will occur less frequently.
3. **Extinction.** If a response is not followed by reward after it has been repeated many times, it will go away. After winning three times, you pull the handle on a slot machine 30 times more without a payoff. What do you do? You go away. So does the response of handle pulling (for that particular machine, at any rate).
4. **Punishment.** If a response is followed by discomfort or an undesirable effect, the response will be suppressed (but not necessarily extinguished).
5. **Shaping.** Shaping means rewarding actions that are closer and closer approximations to a desired response. For example, to reward an intellectually disabled child for saying "ball," you might begin by rewarding the child for saying anything that starts with a *b* sound.
6. **Stimulus control.** Responses tend to come under the control of the situation in which they occur. If you set your clock 10 minutes fast, it may be easier to leave the house on time in the morning. Your departure is under the stimulus control of the clock, even though you know it is fast.
7. **Time out.** A time-out procedure usually involves removing the individual from a situation in which reinforcement occurs. Time out is a variation of nonreinforcement: It prevents reward from following an undesirable response. For example, children who fight with each other can be sent to separate rooms and allowed out only when they are able to behave more calmly. (For a more thorough review of operant learning, return to Modules 6.2, 6.3, and 6.4.)

As simple as these principles may seem, they have been used very effectively to overcome difficulties in work, home, school, and industrial settings. Let's see how.

Nonreinforcement and Extinction

An extremely overweight mental patient had a persistent and disturbing habit: She stole food from other patients. No one could persuade her to stop stealing or to diet. For the sake of her health, a behavior therapist assigned her a special table in the ward dining room. If she approached any other table, she was immediately removed from the dining room. Because her attempts to steal food went unrewarded, they rapidly disappeared. Additionally, any attempt to steal from others caused the patient to miss her own meal (Ayllon, 1963).

What operant principles did the therapist in this example use? The therapist used *nonreward* to produce *extinction*. The most frequently occurring human behaviors lead to some form of reward. An undesirable response can be eliminated by *identifying* and *removing* the rewards that maintain it. But people don't always do things for food, money, or other obvious rewards. Most of the rewards maintaining human behavior are subtler. *Attention, approval,* and *concern* are common yet powerful reinforcers for humans (● Fig. 13.4).

Nonreward and extinction can eliminate many problem behaviors, especially in schools, hospitals, and institutions. Often, difficulties center around a limited number of particularly disturbing responses. Time out is a good way to remove such responses, usually by refusing to pay attention to a person who is misbehaving. For example, 14-year-old Terrel periodically appeared in the nude in the activity room of a training center for disturbed adolescents. This behavior

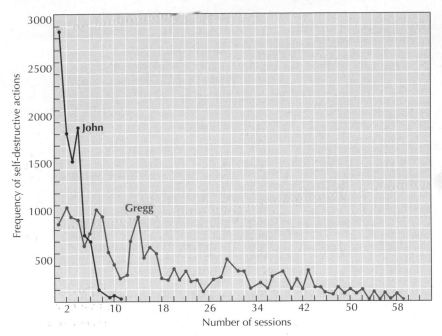

● **FIGURE 13.4** This graph shows extinction of self-destructive behavior in two autistic boys. Before extinction began, the boys received attention and concern from adults for injuring themselves. During extinction, the adults were taught to ignore the boys' self-damaging behavior. As you can see, the number of times that the boys tried to injure themselves declined rapidly. (Adapted from Lovaas & Simmons, 1969.)

tokens may be given for speaking a complete sentence. Later, the patient could gradually be required to speak more often, then to answer questions, and eventually to carry on a short conversation in order to receive tokens. In this way, deeply withdrawn patients have been returned to the world of normal communication.

Full-scale use of tokens in an institutional setting produces a *token economy*. In a **token economy,** patients are rewarded with tokens for a wide range of socially desirable or productive activities (Spiegler & Guevremont, 2003). They must *pay* tokens for privileges and for engaging in problem behaviors (● Fig. 13.5). For example, tokens are given to patients who get out of bed, dress themselves, take required medication, arrive for meals on time, and so on. Constructive activities, such as gardening, cooking, or cleaning, may also earn tokens. Patients must *exchange* tokens for meals and private rooms, movies, passes, off-ward activities, and other privileges. They are *charged* tokens for staying in bed, disrobing in public, talking to themselves, fighting, crying, and similar target behaviors (Morisse et al., 1996).

Token economies can radically change a patient's overall adjustment and morale. Patients are given an incentive to change, and they are held responsible for their actions. The use of tokens may seem manipulative, but it actually empowers patients. Many "hopelessly" intellectually disabled, mentally ill, and delinquent people have been returned to productive lives by means of token economies (Field et al., 2004).

By the time they are ready to leave, patients may be earning tokens on a weekly basis for maintaining sane, responsible, and productive behavior (Miltenberger, 2008). Typically, the most effective token economies are those that gradually switch from tokens to *social rewards* such as praise, recognition, and approval. Such rewards are what patients will receive when they return to family, friends, and community.

always generated a great deal of attention from staff and other patients. Usually Terrel was returned to his room and confined there. During this "confinement," he often missed doing his usual chores. As an experiment he was placed on time out. The next time he appeared nude, counselors and other staff members greeted him normally and then ignored him. Attention from other patients rapidly subsided. Sheepishly he returned to his room and dressed.

Reinforcement and Token Economies

A distressing problem therapists sometimes face is how to break through to severely disturbed patients who won't talk. Conventional psychotherapy offers little hope of improvement for such patients.

What can be done for them? One widely used approach is based on *tokens* (symbolic rewards, such as plastic chips, that can be exchanged for real rewards). Tokens may be printed slips of paper, check marks, points, or gold stars. Whatever form they take, tokens serve as rewards because they may be exchanged for candy, food, cigarettes, recreation, or privileges, such as private time with a therapist, outings, or watching TV. Tokens are used in mental hospitals, half-way houses, schools for the intellectually disabled, programs for delinquents, and ordinary classrooms. They usually produce improvements in behavior (Dickerson, Tenhula, & Green-Paden, 2005; Reitman et al., 2004).

By using tokens, a therapist can *immediately reward* positive responses. For maximum impact, therapists select specific *target behaviors* (actions or other behaviors the therapist seeks to modify). Target behaviors are then reinforced with tokens. For example, a mute mental patient might first be given a token each time he or she says a word. Next,

Token economy A therapeutic program in which desirable behaviors are reinforced with tokens that can be exchanged for goods, services, activities, and privileges.

Credit Card

OXNARD DAY TREATMENT CENTER CREDIT INCENTIVE SYSTEM			
EARN CREDITS BY		SPEND CREDITS FOR	
MONITOR DAILY	15	COFFEE	5
MENU PLANNING CHAIRMAN	50	LUNCH	10
PARTICIPATE	5	EXCEPT THURSDAY	15
BUY FOOD AT STORE	10	BUS TRIP	5
COOK FOR/PREPARE LUNCH	5	BOWLING	8
WIPE OFF KITCHEN TABLE	3	GROUP THERAPY	5
WASH DISHES	5-10	PRIVATE STAFF TIME	5
DRY AND PUT AWAY DISHES	5	DAY OFF	5-20
MAKE COFFEE AND CLEAN URN	15	WINDOW SHOPPING	5
CLEAN REFRIGERATOR	20	REVIEW WITH DR.	10
ATTEND PLANNING CONFERENCE	1	DOING OWN THING	1
OT PREPARATION	1-5	LATE 1 PER EVERY 10 MIN	
COMPLETE OT PROJECT	5	PRESCRIPTION FROM DR.	10
RETURN OT PROJECT	2		
DUST AND POLISH TABLES	5		
PUT AWAY GROCERIES	3		
CLEAN TABLE	5		
CLEAN 6 ASH TRAYS	2		
CLEAN SINK	5		
CARRY OUT CUPS & BOTTLES	5		
CLEAN CHAIRS	5		
CLEAN KITCHEN CUPBOARDS	5		
ASSIST STAFF	5		
ARRANGE MAGAZINES NEATLY	3		
BEING ON TIME	5		
MONITOR-ANN			

● **FIGURE 13.5** Shown here is a token used in one token economy system. In this instance the token is a card that records the number of credits eared by a patient. Also pictured is a list of credit values for various activities. Tokens may be exchanged for items or for privileges listed on the board. (Adapted from photographs by Robert P. Liberman.)

event applies to other, unrelated situations. An example would be considering yourself a total failure, or completely worthless, if you were to lose a part-time job or fail a test. To complete the picture, depressed persons tend to magnify the importance of undesirable events by engaging in **all-or-nothing thinking.** That is, they see events as completely good or bad, right or wrong, and themselves as either successful or failing miserably (Beck, 2002; Gilbert, 2001).

How do cognitive therapists alter such patterns? Cognitive therapists make a step-by-step effort to correct negative thoughts that lead to depression or similar problems. At first, clients are taught to recognize and keep track of their own thoughts. The client and therapist then look for ideas and beliefs that cause depression, anger, and avoidance. For example, here's how a therapist might challenge all-or-nothing thinking (Burns & Persons, 1982):

> **Client:** I'm feeling even more depressed. No one wants to hire me, and I can't even clean up my apartment. I feel completely incompetent!
>
> **Therapist:** I see. The fact that you are unemployed and have a messy apartment proves that you are completely incompetent?
>
> **Client:** Well . . . I can see that doesn't add up.

Next, clients are asked to gather information to test their beliefs. For instance, a depressed person might list his or her activities for a week. The list is then used to challenge all-or-nothing thoughts, such as "I had a terrible week" or "I'm a complete failure." With more coaching, clients learn to alter their thoughts in ways that improve their moods, actions, and relationships.

Cognitive therapy is as effective as drugs for treating many cases of depression. More important, people who have adopted new thinking patterns are less likely to become depressed again—a benefit that drugs can't impart (Dozois & Dobson, 2004).

In an alternate approach, cognitive therapists look for an

Cognitive Therapy—Think Positive!

SURVEY QUESTION: *Can therapy change thoughts and emotions?*

How would a behavior therapist treat a problem like depression? None of the techniques described seem to apply. As we have discussed, behavior therapists usually try to change troublesome actions. However, in recent years cognitive therapists have become interested in what people think, believe, and feel, as well as how they act. In general, **cognitive therapy** helps clients change thinking patterns that lead to troublesome emotions or behaviors (Hall, 2006). For example, compulsive hand-washing can be greatly reduced by changing a client's thoughts and beliefs about dirt and contamination (Jones & Menzies, 1998). Cognitive therapy has been used as a remedy for many problems, but it has been especially successful in treating depression (Chambless & Ollendick, 2001).

Cognitive Therapy for Depression

As you may recall from Module 12.4, cognitive psychologists believe that negative, self-defeating thoughts underlie depression. According to Aaron Beck (1991), depressed persons see themselves, the world, and the future in negative terms. Beck believes this occurs because of major distortions in thinking. The first is **selective perception,** which refers to perceiving only certain stimuli in a larger array. If five good things and three bad things happen during the day, depressed people focus only on the bad. A second thinking error in depression is **overgeneralization,** the tendency to think that an upsetting

DISCOVERING PSYCHOLOGY

Ten Irrational Beliefs—Which Do You Hold?

Rational-emotive behavior therapists have identified numerous beliefs that commonly lead to emotional upsets and conflicts. See if you recognize any of the following irrational beliefs:

1. I must be loved and approved by almost every significant person in my life or it's awful and I'm worthless.

   Example: "One of my roommates doesn't seem to like me. I must be a total zero."

2. I should be completely competent and achieving in all ways to be a worthwhile person.

   Example: "I don't understand my chemistry class. I guess I really am a stupid person."

3. Certain people I must deal with are thoroughly bad and should be severely blamed and punished for it.

   Example: "The old man next door is such a pain. I'm going to play my stereo even louder the next time he complains."

4. It is awful and upsetting when things are not the way I would very much like them to be.

   Example: "I should have gotten a B in that class. The teacher is unfair."

5. My unhappiness is always caused by external events; I cannot control my emotional reactions.

   Example: "You make me feel awful. I would be happy if it weren't for you."

6. If something unpleasant might happen, I should keep dwelling on it.

   Example: "I'll never forget the time my boss insulted me. I think about it every day at work."

7. It is easier to avoid difficulties and responsibilities than to face them.

   Example: "I don't know why my wife seems angry. Maybe it will just pass by if I ignore it."

8. I should depend on others who are stronger than I am.

   Example: "I couldn't survive if he left me."

9. Because something once strongly affected my life, it will do so indefinitely.

   Example: "My girlfriend dumped me during my junior year in college. I don't know if I can ever trust a woman again."

10. There is always a perfect solution to human problems, and it is awful if this solution is not found.

    Example: "I'm so depressed about politics in this country. It all seems hopeless."*

*Adapted from Beck, 2002; Ellis, 2004; Rohsenow & Smith, 1982.

If any of the listed beliefs sound familiar, you may be creating unnecessary emotional distress for yourself by holding on to unrealistic expectations.

---

absence of effective coping skills and thinking patterns, not for the *presence* of self-defeating thoughts (Dobson, Backs-Dermott, & Dozois, 2000). The aim is to teach clients how to cope with anger, depression, shyness, stress, and similar problems. Stress inoculation, which was described in Module 11.5, is a good example of this approach.

Cognitive therapy is a rapidly expanding specialty. Before we leave the topic, let's explore another widely used cognitive therapy.

Rational-Emotive Behavior Therapy

Rational-emotive behavior therapy (REBT) attempts to change irrational beliefs that cause emotional problems. According to Albert Ellis (1913–2007), the basic idea of rational-emotive behavior therapy is as easy as A-B-C (Ellis, 1995, 2004). Ellis assumes that people become unhappy and develop self-defeating habits because they have unrealistic or faulty *beliefs.*

How are beliefs important? Ellis analyzes problems in this way: The letter A stands for an *activating experience,* which the person assumes to be the cause of C, an *emotional consequence.* For instance, a person who is rejected (the activating experience) feels depressed, threatened, or hurt (the conse-

quence). Rational-emotive behavior therapy shows the client that the real problem is what comes between A and C: In between is B, the client's irrational and unrealistic *beliefs.* In this example, an unrealistic belief leading to unnecessary suffering is: "I must be loved and approved by everyone at all times." REBT holds that events do not *cause* us to have feelings. We feel as we do because of our beliefs (Kottler, 2004). (For some examples, see "Ten Irrational Beliefs—Which Do You Hold?").

Ellis (1979, 2004) says that most irrational beliefs come

Cognitive therapy A therapy directed at changing the maladaptive thoughts, beliefs, and feelings that underlie emotional and behavioral problems.

Selective perception Perceiving only certain stimuli among a larger array of possibilities.

Overgeneralization Blowing a single event out of proportion by extending it to a large number of unrelated situations.

All-or-nothing thinking Classifying objects or events as absolutely right or wrong, good or bad, acceptable or unacceptable, and so forth.

Rational-emotive behavior therapy (REBT) An approach that states that irrational beliefs cause many emotional problems and that such beliefs must be changed or abandoned.

THE CLINICAL FILE

Overcoming the Gambler's Fallacy

Seventeen-year-old Jonathan just lost his shirt again. This time he did it playing online Blackjack. Jonathan started out making $5 bets and then doubled his bet over and over. Surely, he thought, his luck would eventually change. However, he ran out of money after just eight hands, having lost more than $1,000. Last week he lost a lot of money playing Texas Hold 'Em and slot machines. Now Jonathan is in tears—he has lost most of his summer earnings, and he is worried about having to drop out of school and tell his parents about his losses. Jonathan has had to admit that he had joined the growing ranks of underage gambling addicts (LaBrie & Shaffer, 2007; Wilber & Potenza, 2006).

Like many problem gamblers, Jonathan suffers from several cognitive distortions related to gambling. Here are some of his mistaken beliefs (adapted from Toneatto, 2002):

Magnified gambling skill: You have exaggerated self-confidence despite losing persistently.

Attribution errors: You credit your skill for wins but blame losses on bad luck.

Gambler's fallacy: You believe that losses soon must be followed by wins.

Selective memory: You remember times when you won but forget your losses.

Overinterpretation of cues: You put too much faith in irrelevant cues such as bodily sensations or an intuition that your next bet will be a winner.

Luck as a trait: You believe that you are a "lucky" person in general.

Probability biases: You have incorrect beliefs about randomness and chance events.

Do you have any of these mistaken beliefs? Taken together, Jonathan's cognitive distortions created an "illusion of control." That is, he believed that if he worked hard enough, he could figure out how to win. Fortunately, a cognitive therapist helped Jonathan *cognitively restructure* his beliefs. He now no longer believes he can control chance events. Jonathan still gambles a bit, but he only does so recreationally, keeping his losses within his budget and enjoying himself in the process.

---

from three core ideas, each of which is unrealistic:

1. I *must* perform well and be approved of by significant others. If I don't, then it is awful, I cannot stand it, and I am a rotten person.

2. You *must* treat me fairly. When you don't, it is horrible, and I cannot bear it.

3. Conditions *must* be the way I want them to be. It is terrible when they are not, and I cannot stand living in such an awful world.

It's easy to see that such beliefs can lead to much grief and needless suffering in a less than perfect world. Rational-emotive behavior therapists are very directive in their attempts to change a client's irrational beliefs and "self-talk." The therapist may directly attack clients' logic, challenge their thinking, confront them with evidence contrary to their beliefs, and even assign "homework." Here, for instance, are some examples of statements that dispute irrational beliefs (after Kottler, 2004):

• "Where is the evidence that you are a loser just because you didn't do well this one time?"

• "Who said the world should be fair? That's your rule."

• "What are you telling yourself to make yourself feel so upset?"

• "Is it really terrible that things aren't working out as you would like? Or is it just inconvenient?"

Many of us would probably do well to give up our irrational beliefs. Improved self-acceptance and a better tolerance of daily annoyances are the benefits of doing so. (See "Overcoming the Gambler's Fallacy.")

The value of cognitive approaches is further illustrated by three techniques (*covert sensitization, thought stopping,* and *covert reinforcement*) described in this chapter's "Psychology in Action" module. A little later you can see what you think of them.

MODULE 13.4 Summary

What role does reinforcement play in behavior therapy?

• Behavior modification makes use of operant principles, such as positive reinforcement, nonreinforcement, extinction, punishment, shaping, stimulus control, and time out. These principles are used to extinguish undesirable responses and to promote constructive behavior.

• Nonreward can extinguish troublesome behaviors. Often this is done by simply identifying and eliminating reinforcers, particularly attention and social approval.

• To apply positive reinforcement and operant shaping, tokens are often used to reinforce selected target behaviors.

- Full-scale use of tokens in an institutional setting produces a token economy. Toward the end of a token economy program, patients are shifted to social rewards such as recognition and approval.

  Can therapy change thoughts and emotions?

- Cognitive therapy emphasizes changing thought patterns that underlie emotional or behavioral problems. Its goals are to correct distorted thinking and/or teach improved coping skills.

- Irrational beliefs are the core of many maladaptive thinking patterns. Changing such beliefs can have a positive impact on emotions and behavior.

- In a variation of cognitive therapy called rational-emotive behavior therapy (REBT), clients learn to recognize and challenge their irrational beliefs.

KNOWLEDGE BUILDER

Operant Therapies and Cognitive Therapies

Recite

1. Behavior modification programs aimed at extinction of an undesirable behavior typically make use of what operant principles?
   a. punishment and stimulus control
   b. punishment and shaping
   c. nonreinforcement and time out
   d. stimulus control and time out

2. Attention can be a powerful _____ for humans. *reinforcer*

3. Token economies depend on the time-out procedure. T or F? *false*

4. Tokens basically allow the operant shaping of desired responses or "target behaviors." T or F? *true*

5. According to Beck, selective perception, overgeneralization, and _____ thinking are cognitive habits that underlie depression. *all-or-nothing*

6. The B in the A-B-C of REBT stands for
   a. behavior
   b. belief

   c. being
   d. Beck

7. REBT teaches people to change the antecedents of irrational behavior. T or F? *false*

Reflect
Critical Thinking

8. In Aaron Beck's terms, a belief such as "I must perform well or I am a rotten person" involves two thinking errors. What are they?

Relate

See if you can give a personal example of how the following principles have affected your behavior: positive reinforcement, extinction, punishment, shaping, stimulus control, and time out.

You are setting up a token economy for troubled elementary school children. What target behaviors will you attempt to reinforce? For what behaviors will you charge tokens?

We all occasionally engage in negative thinking. Can you remember a time recently when you engaged in selective perception? Overgeneralization? All-or-nothing thinking?

Which of REBT's irrational beliefs have affected your feelings? Which beliefs would you like to change?

Link

Internet addresses frequently change. To find the sites listed here, visit **http://www .thomsonedu.com/psychology/coon** for an updated list of Internet addresses and direct links to relevant sites.

- **Token Economies** Read about the use of token economies with autistic children.

- **The Beck Institute** Read about cognitive therapy and visit the rest of the Beck Institute website.

- **Albert Ellis Institute** Read about Albert Ellis and his rational-emotive behavior therapy.

ANSWERS

1. c 2. reinforcer 3. F 4. T 5. all-or-nothing 6. b 7. F 8. Overgeneralization and all-or-nothing thinking.

15.1 Affiliation, Friendship, and Love

ALTHOUGH YOU MAY LIKE BEING ALONE AT TIMES, the fact is, humans are social animals. Imagine if you were deprived of all contact with your family and friends. You would probably find it painfully lonely and disorienting. In this first module, we will explore what brings people together in groups, in friendship, and in love.

Affiliation and Attraction— Come Together

SURVEY QUESTIONS: *Why do people affiliate? What factors influence interpersonal attraction?*

Social psychology is the scientific study of how individuals behave, think, and feel in social situations (that is, in the presence, actual or implied, of others) (Baron, Byrne, & Branscombe, 2007). Each of us is immersed in a complex social world of families, teams, crowds, tribes, companies, parties, troops, bands, sects, gangs, crews, clans, communities, and nations. But what brings us together in the first place? The *need to affiliate* (associate with other people) is based on basic human desires for approval, support, friendship, and information (Baumeister & Bushman, 2008). We also seek the company of others to alleviate fear or anxiety. A classic experiment in which college women were threatened with electric shock illustrates this point.

ZILSTEIN'S SHOCK SHOP
A man introduced as Dr. Gregor Zilstein ominously explained to arriving participants, "We would like to give each of you a series of electric shocks . . . these shocks will hurt, they will be painful." In the room was a frightening electrical device that seemed to verify Zilstein's plans. While waiting to be shocked, each woman was given a choice of waiting alone or with other participants. Women frightened in this way more often chose to wait with others; those who expected the shock to be "a mild tickle or tingle" were more willing to wait alone. (Schachter, 1959)

Apparently, the frightened women found it comforting to be with others. Should we conclude that "misery loves company"? Actually, that's not entirely correct. In a later experiment, women who expected to be shocked were given the choice of waiting with other future shock recipients, with women waiting to see their college advisers, or alone. Most women chose to wait with other future "victims." In short, misery seems to love miserable company! In general, we

prefer to be with people in circumstances similar to our own (Gump & Kulik, 1997).

Is there a reason for that? Yes. Other people provide information that helps us evaluate our own reactions. When a situation is threatening or unfamiliar, or when we are in doubt, *social comparisons* tend to guide our behavior (Kulik, Mahler, & Moore, 2003).

Social Comparison Theory

If you want to know how tall you are, you simply get out a tape measure. But how do you know if you are a good athlete, worker, parent, or friend? How do you know if your views on politics, religion, or hip-hop are unusual or widely shared? When there are no objective standards, the only available yardstick is provided by comparing yourself with others (Miller, 2006).

Social psychologist Leon Festinger (1919–1989) theorized that belonging to groups fills our needs for **social comparison** (comparing your own actions, feelings, opinions, or abilities with those of others). Have you ever "compared notes" with other students after taking an exam? ("How did you do?" "Wasn't that last question hard?") If you have, you were satisfying needs for social comparison (Festinger, 1957).

Typically, we don't make social comparisons randomly or on some absolute scale. Meaningful evaluations are based on

High school class reunions are notorious for the rampant social comparison they often encourage. Apparently it's hard to resist comparing yourself with former classmates to see how you are doing in life.

comparing yourself with people of similar backgrounds, abilities, and circumstances (Stapel & Marx, 2007). To illustrate, let's ask a student named Wendy if she is a good tennis player. If Wendy compares herself with a professional, the answer will be no. But this tells us little about her *relative* ability. Within her tennis group, Wendy is regarded as an excellent player. On a fair scale of comparison, Wendy knows she is good and she takes pride in her tennis skills. In the same way, thinking of yourself as successful, talented, responsible, or fairly paid depends entirely on whom you choose for comparison. Thus, a desire for social comparison provides a motive for associating with others and influences which groups we join (Franzoi & Klaiber, 2007).

Don't people also affiliate out of attraction for one another? They do, of course. Let's see why.

Interpersonal Attraction

"Birds of a feather flock together." "Familiarity breeds contempt." "Opposites attract." "Absence makes the heart grow fonder." Are these statements true? Actually, the folklore about friendship is, at best, a mixture of fact and fiction.

What does attract people to each other? **Interpersonal attraction** (affinity to another person) is the basis for most voluntary social relationships (Berscheid & Regan, 2005). As you might expect, we look for friends and lovers who are kind and understanding, who have attractive personalities, and who like us in return (Sprecher, 1998). Deciding whether you would like to know another person can happen very quickly, sometimes within just minutes of meeting (Sunnafrank, Ramirez, & Metts, 2004). In addition, several less obvious factors influence attraction.

Physical Proximity Our choice of friends (and even lovers) is based more on *physical proximity* (nearness) than we might care to believe. For example, the closer people live to each other, the more likely they are to become friends. Likewise, lovers like to think they have found the "one and only" person in the universe for them. In reality, they have probably found the best match in a 5-mile radius (Buss, 1985)! Marriages are not made in heaven—they are made in local schools, businesses, churches, bars, clubs, and neighborhoods.

Proximity promotes attraction by increasing the *frequency of contact* between people. In general, we are attracted to people we see often. (If you have a reluctant sweetheart, be careful not to send too many love letters—she or he might run off with the letter carrier!) In short, there does seem to be a "boy-next-door" or "girl-next-door" effect in romantic attraction, and a "folks-next-door" effect in friendship. Notice, however, that the Internet is making it increasingly easier to stay in constant "virtual contact," which is leading to more and more long-distance friendships and romances (Lawson & Leck, 2006; Ridings & Gefen, 2004).

What attracts people to each other? Proximity and frequency of contact have a surprisingly large impact.

Physical Attractiveness People who are *physically attractive* are regarded as good looking by others. Beautiful people are generally rated as more appealing than average. This is due, in part, to the *halo effect,* a tendency to generalize a favorable impression to unrelated personal characteristics. Because of it, we assume that beautiful people are also likable, intelligent, warm, witty, mentally healthy, and socially skilled. In reality, physical attractiveness has almost *no* connection to intelligence, talents, or abilities. Perhaps that's why beauty mainly affects our initial interest in getting to know others (Keller & Young, 1996). Later, more meaningful qualities

Social psychology The scientific study of how individuals behave, think, and feel in social situations.

Social comparison Making judgments about ourselves through comparison with others.

Interpersonal attraction Social attraction to another person.

Physical beauty can be socially advantageous because of the widespread belief that "what is beautiful is good." However, physical beauty is generally unrelated to actual personal traits and talents.

gain in importance (Berscheid, 2000; Miller, Perlman, & Brehm, 2007).

Competence People who are *competent* have knowledge, ability, or proficiency. All other things being equal, we are more attracted to people who are talented or competent. However, there's an interesting twist to this. In a revealing classic study, college students listened to audiotapes of candidates for a "college quiz bowl." Two of the candidates seemed to be highly intelligent. The other two were of average ability. In addition, one "intelligent" candidate and one "average" candidate could be heard to clumsily spill coffee on themselves. Later, students rated the intelligent candidate who blundered as *most* attractive. In contrast, the average person who blundered was rated *least* attractive (Aronson, 1969). Thus, the superior but clumsy person was more attractive than the person who was only superior. Apparently, we like people who are competent but imperfect—which makes them more "human."

Similarity Take a moment to make a list of your closest friends. What do they have in common (other than the joy of knowing you)? It is likely that their ages are similar to yours and you are of the same sex and ethnicity. There will be exceptions, of course. But similarity on these three dimensions is the general rule for friendships.

Similarity refers to how alike you are to another person in background, age, interests, attitudes, beliefs, and so forth. In everything from casual acquaintance to marriage, similar people are attracted to each other (Figueredo, Sefcek, & Jones, 2006; Miller, Perlman, & Brehm, 2007). And why not? It's reinforcing to see our beliefs and attitudes shared by others. It shows we are "right" and reveals that they are clever people as well (Alicke, Yurak, & Vredenburg, 1996)!

So similarity also influences mate selection? Yes, in choosing a mate we tend to marry someone who is like us in almost every way, a pattern called *homogamy* (huh-MOG-ah-me) (Blackwell & Lichter, 2004). Studies show that married couples are highly similar in age, education, ethnicity, and religion. To a lesser degree, they are also similar in attitudes and opinions, mental abilities, status, height, weight, and eye color. In case you're wondering, homogamy also applies to unmarried couples who are living together (Blackwell & Lichter, 2004). Homogamy is probably a good thing. The risk of divorce is highest among couples with sizable differences in age and education (Tzeng, 1992).

Self-Disclosure

How do people who are not yet friends learn if they are similar? To get acquainted you must be willing to talk about more than just the weather, sports, or nuclear physics. At some point you must begin to share private thoughts and feelings and reveal yourself to others. This process, which is called **self-disclosure,** is essential for developing close relationships. In general, as friends talk, they gradually deepen the level of liking, trust, and self-disclosure (Levesque, Steciuk, & Ledley, 2002).

We more often reveal ourselves to persons we like than to those we find unattractive. Disclosure also requires a degree of trust. Many people play it safe, or "close to the vest," with people they do not know well. Indeed, self-disclosure is governed by unspoken rules about what's acceptable. Moderate self-disclosure leads to *reciprocity* (a return in kind). In contrast, *overdisclosure* exceeds what is appropriate for a relationship or social situation, giving rise to suspicion and reducing attraction. For example, imagine standing in line at a store and having the stranger in front of you say, "Lately I've been

Excessive self-disclosure is a staple of many television talk shows. Guests frequently reveal intimate details about their personal lives, including private family matters, sex and dating, physical or sexual abuse, major embarrassments, and criminal activities. Viewers probably find such intimate disclosures entertaining, rather than threatening, because they don't have to reciprocate.

thinking about how I really feel about myself. I think I'm pretty well adjusted, but I occasionally have some questions about my sexual adequacy."

When self-disclosure proceeds at a moderate pace, it builds trust, intimacy, reciprocity, and positive feelings. When it is too rapid or inappropriate, we are likely to "back off" and wonder about the person's motives. It's interesting to note that on the Internet (and especially on social networking websites like Facebook and MySpace) people often feel freer to express their true feelings, which can lead to genuine, face-to-face friendships (Bargh, McKenna, & Fitzsimons, 2002). However, it can also lead to some very dramatic overdisclosure (George, 2006).

Loving and Liking—Dating, Rating, Mating

How does romantic attraction differ from interpersonal attraction? **Romantic love** is based on interpersonal attraction, but it also involves high levels of emotional arousal and/or sexual desire (Berscheid & Regan, 2005; Miller, Perlman, & Brehm, 2007). To get another angle on love, psychologist Zick Rubin (1973) chose to think of it as an attitude we hold toward another person. This allowed him to develop "liking" and "love" scales to measure each "attitude" (● Fig. 15.1). Next, he asked

dating couples to complete the scales twice, once with their lover in mind and once for a close friend of the same sex.

What were the results? Love for partners and friends differed more than liking did (■ Table 15.1). (**Liking** is affection without passion or deep commitment.) Basically, dating couples like *and* love their partners, but mostly they just like their friends. Women, however, were a little more "loving" of their friends than men were. Does this reflect real differences in the strength of male friendships and female friendships? Maybe not, because it is more acceptable in our culture for women to express love for one another than it is for men. Nevertheless, another study confirmed that dating couples feel a mixture of love and friendship for their partners. In fact, 44 percent of a group of dating persons named their romantic partner as their closest friend (Hendrick & Hendrick, 1993).

Love and friendship differ in another interesting way. Romantic love, in contrast to simple liking, usually involves deep *mutual absorption*. In other words, lovers (unlike friends) attend almost exclusively to one another. It's not surprising, then, that couples who score high on Rubin's love scale spend more time gazing into each other's eyes than do couples who score low on the scale. And what do lovers see when they gaze into each other's eyes? Generally, romantic partners tend to idealize each other, which helps keep relationships going, despite the fact that nobody's perfect (Murray, Holmes, & Griffin, 1996, 2003).

● **FIGURE 15.1** Sample love-scale and liking-scale items. The items shown here are similar to actual Rubin scale items. Scores on the 13-item Rubin scales correspond to other indications of love and liking.

Love Scale

1. I have a few secrets from _____ .
2. _____ has almost no faults.
3. I feel responsible for preventing _____ from feeling bad.

Liking Scale

1. If _____ were seeking work, I would gladly serve as a reference.
2. _____ and I often share the same moods.
3. I admire how well adjusted _____ is.

■ TABLE 15.1 Average Love and Liking Scores for Date and Same-Sex Close Friend

Attitude toward Dating Partner

	LOVE SCORE	LIKING SCORE
Women	89.5	88.5
Men	89.4	84.7

Attitude toward Close Friend

	LOVE SCORE	LIKING SCORE
Women	65.3	80.5
Men	55.0	79.1

Source: From Zick Rubin, "Measurement of Romantic Love," *Journal of Personality and Social Psychology,* © 1970 American Psychological Association. Reprinted by permission.

Self-disclosure The process of revealing private thoughts, feelings, and one's personal history to others.

Romantic love Love that is associated with high levels of interpersonal attraction, heightened arousal, mutual absorption, and sexual desire.

Liking A relationship based on intimacy, but lacking passion and commitment.

Sex, Evolution, and Mate Selection

Evolutionary psychology is the study of the evolutionary origins of human behavior patterns. Many psychologists believe that evolution left an imprint on men and women that influences everything from sexual attraction and infidelity to jealousy and divorce. According to David Buss, the key to understanding human mating patterns is to understand how evolved behavior patterns guide our choices (Buss, 2004, 2007).

In a study of 37 cultures on six continents, Buss found the following patterns: Compared with women, men are more interested in casual sex; they prefer younger, more physically attractive partners; and they get more jealous over real or imagined sexual infidelities than they do over a loss of emotional commitment. Compared with men, women prefer slightly older partners who appear to be industrious, higher in status, or economically successful; women are more upset by a partner who becomes emotionally involved with someone else, rather than one who is sexually unfaithful (Buss, 2000; Regan et al., 2000) (● Fig. 15.2).

Why do such differences exist? Buss and others believe that mating preferences evolved in response to the differing reproductive challenges faced by men and women. As a rule, women must invest more time and energy in reproduction and nurturing the young than men do. Consequently, women evolved an interest in whether their partners will stay with them and whether their mates have the resources to provide for their children (Buss, 2004, 2007; Regan et al., 2000).

In contrast, the reproductive success of men depends on their mates' fertility. Men, therefore, tend to look for health, youth, and beauty in a prospective mate, as signs of suitability for reproduction (Buss, 2007). This preference, perhaps, is why some older men abandon their first wives in favor of young, beautiful "trophy wives." Evolutionary theory further explains that the male emphasis on their mates' sexual fidelity is based on concerns about the paternity of offspring. From a biological perspective, men do not benefit from investing resources in children they did not sire (Buller, 2005).

Although some evidence supports the evolutionary view of mating, it is important to remember that evolved mating

According to evolutionary psychologists, women tend to be concerned with whether mates will devote time and resources to a relationship. Men place more emphasis on physical attractiveness and sexual fidelity.

tendencies are subtle at best and easily overruled by other factors. Some mating patterns may simply reflect the fact that men still tend to control the power and resources in most societies (Feingold, 1992). Also, early research may be misleading because women tend to give "polite" answers to questions about jealousy. Privately, they may be just as furious about a mate's sexual infidelity as any man would be (Harris, 2004).

Whatever the outcome of the debate about evolution and mate selection, it is important to remember this: Poten-

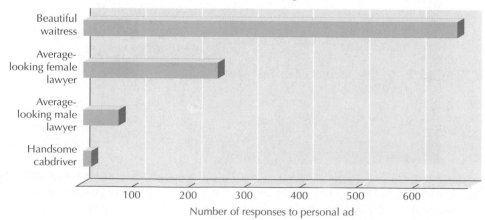

● **FIGURE 15.2** What do people look for when considering potential dating partners? Here are the results of a study in which personal ads were placed in newspapers. As you can see, men were more influenced by looks and women by success (Goode, 1996).

tial mates are rated as most attractive if they are kind, secure, intelligent, and supportive (Klohnen & Luo, 2003; Regan et al., 2000). These qualities are love's greatest allies.

Needs for affiliation and interpersonal attraction inevitably bring people together in groups. In the next section we will explore several interesting aspects of group membership. But first, here's a chance to review what you have learned.

MODULE 15.1 Summary

Why do people affiliate? What factors influence interpersonal attraction?

- Social psychology studies how we behave, think, and feel in social situations.
- We are attracted to other people for reasons that are fairly universal.
- Affiliation is tied to needs for approval, support, friendship, and information. Also, affiliation can reduce anxiety.

- Social comparison theory holds that we affiliate to evaluate our actions, feelings, and abilities.
- Interpersonal attraction is increased by proximity, frequent contact, beauty, and similarity.
- Mate selection is characterized by a large degree of similarity on many dimensions.
- Self-disclosure follows a reciprocity norm: Low levels of self-disclosure are met with low levels in return; moderate self-disclosure elicits more personal replies.
- In comparison with liking, romantic love involves higher levels of emotional arousal and it is accompanied by mutual absorption between lovers.
- Evolutionary psychologists attribute human mating patterns to the reproductive challenges men and women faced during the course of evolution.

KNOWLEDGE BUILDER

Affiliation, Friendship, and Love

Recite

1. Women threatened with electric shock in an experiment generally chose to wait alone or with other women not taking part in the experiment. T or F?

2. Interpersonal attraction is increased by all but one of the following. (Which does not fit?)

   a. physical proximity

   b. physical attractiveness

   c. similarity

   d. overdisclosure

3. High levels of self-disclosure are reciprocated in most social encounters. T or F?

4. Women rate their friends higher on the love scale than do men. T or F?

5. The most striking finding about marriage patterns is that most people choose mates whose personalities are quite unlike their own. T or F?

6. Compared with men, women tend to be more upset by sexual infidelity than by a loss of emotional commitment on the part of their mates. T or F?

Reflect
Critical Thinking

7. How has the Internet altered the effects of proximity on interpersonal attraction?

Relate

How has social comparison affected your behavior? Has it influenced who you associate with?

Think of three close friends. Which of the attraction factors described earlier apply to your friendships?

To what extent do Rubin's findings about love and liking match your own experiences?

Link

Internet addresses frequently change. To find the sites listed here, visit **http://www .thomsonedu.com/psychology/coon** for an updated list of Internet addresses and direct links to relevant sites.

- **Small World Project** Join Duncan Watt's online experiment to see if we are really all connected through six degrees of separation.

- **Social Psychology Network** Explore this massive website devoted to social psychology.

ANSWERS

1. F 2. d 3. F 4. T 5. F 6. F 7. As mentioned earlier, it is now possible to interact with another person through the Internet. This makes actual physical proximity less crucial in interpersonal attraction, because frequent contact is possible even at great distances. Internet romances are a good example of this possibility (Levine, 2000).

Evolutionary psychology Study of the evolutionary origins of human behavior patterns.

Groups, Social Influence, and Conformity

FAMILIES, TEAMS, CROWDS, TRIBES, COMPANIES, parties, troops, bands, sects, gangs, crews, clans, communities, nations. Participation in various groups is a basic fact of social life. How do groups influence our behavior? Because you are member of a group called "psychology class," it would be wise to find out.

Life in Groups—People, People, Everywhere

SURVEY QUESTION: *How does group membership affect our behavior?*

We all belong to many overlapping social groups, and in each we occupy a *position* in the *structure* of the group. **Social roles** are patterns of behavior expected of persons in various social positions (Breckler, Olson, & Wiggins, 2006). For instance, playing the role of mother, boss, or student involves different sets of behaviors and expectations. Some roles are *ascribed* (they are assigned to a person or are not under personal control): male or female, son, adolescent, inmate. *Achieved roles* are voluntarily attained by special effort: spouse, teacher, scientist, bandleader.

What effect does role playing have on behavior? Roles streamline daily interactions by allowing us to anticipate what others will do. When a person is acting as a doctor, mother, clerk, or police officer, we expect certain behaviors. However, roles have a negative side, too. Many people experience **role conflicts,** in which two or more roles make conflicting demands on them. Consider, for example, a teacher who must flunk a close friend's daughter; a mother who has

Roles have a powerful impact on social behavior. What kinds of behavior do you expect from your teachers? What behaviors do they expect from you? What happens if either of you fails to match the other's expectations?

a full-time job; and a soccer coach whose son is on the team but isn't a very good athlete. Likewise, the clashing demands of work, family, and school create role conflicts for many students (Hammer, Grigsby, & Woods, 1998; Senécal, Julien, & Guay, 2003). Role conflicts at work (such as being a good team player versus being a strong manager) lead to job burnout (Jawahar, Stone, & Kisamore, 2007) and negative health outcomes (Pomaki, Supeli, & Verhoeven, 2007).

Group Structure, Cohesion, and Norms

Are there other dimensions of group membership? Two important dimensions of any group are its structure and cohesiveness (Forsyth, 2006). **Group structure** consists of the network of roles, communication pathways, and power in a group. Organized groups such as an army or an athletic team have a high degree of structure. Informal friendship groups may or may not be very structured.

Group cohesiveness refers to the degree of attraction among group members or the strength of their desire to remain in the group. Members of cohesive groups literally stick together: They tend to stand or sit close together, they pay more attention to one another, and they show more signs of mutual affection. Also, their behavior tends to be closely coordinated (Chansler, Swamidass, & Cammann, 2003). Cohesiveness is the basis for much of the power that groups exert over us. Therapy groups, businesses, sports teams, and the like seek to increase cohesion because it helps people work together better (Craig & Kelly, 1999; Marmarosh, Holtz, & Schottenbauer, 2005).

In-groups Cohesiveness is particularly strong for **in-groups** (groups with which a person mainly identifies). Very likely, your own in-groups are defined by a combination of prominent social dimensions, such as nationality, ethnicity, age, education, religion, income, political values, gender, sexual orientation, and so forth. In-group membership helps define who we are socially. Predictably, we tend to attribute positive characteristics to our in-group and negative qualities to **out-groups** (groups with which we do not identify). We also tend to exaggerate differences between members of out-groups and our own groups. This sort of "us-and-them" thinking seems to be a basic fact of social life. It also sets the stage for conflict between groups and for racial and ethnic prejudice—topics we will explore in a later module.

Status In addition to defining roles, a person's social position within groups determines his or her **status,** or level of social power and importance. Higher status bestows special privileges and respect. For example, in one experiment, a man walked into a number of bakeries and asked for a croissant while claiming he did not have enough money to pay for it. Half the time he was well dressed and half the time he was poorly dressed. If the man was polite when he asked, he was equally likely to be given a free croissant no matter how he was dressed (95 versus 90 percent). But if he was impolite when he asked, he was much less likely to get a croissant if he was poorly dressed than if he was well dressed (75 versus 20 percent) (Guéguen & Pascual, 2003).

You don't have to be in a bakery for this to work. In most situations, we are more likely to comply with a request made by a high-status (well-dressed) person (Guéguen, 2002). Perhaps the better treatment given "higher status" persons, even when they are impolite, explains some of our society's preoccupation with expensive clothes, cars, and other status symbols.

Norms We are also greatly affected by group norms. A **norm** is a widely accepted (but often unspoken) standard for appropriate behavior. If you have the slightest doubt about the power of norms, try this test: Walk into a crowded supermarket, get in a checkout line, and begin singing loudly in your fullest voice. Are you the 1 person in 100 who could actually carry out these instructions?

The impact of norms is shown by an interesting study of littering. The question was, Does the amount of trash in an area affect littering? To find out, people were given flyers as they walked into a public parking garage. As you can see in ● Figure 15.3, the more litter there was on the floor, the more likely people were to add to it by dropping their flyer. Apparently, seeing that others had already littered implied a lax norm about whether littering is acceptable. The moral? The cleaner a public area is kept, the less likely people are to "trash" it (Cialdini, Reno, & Kallgren, 1990).

Making Attributions

Every day we must guess how people will act, often from small shreds of evidence. We do this through a process called **attribution.** As we observe others, we make inferences about them. Why did Vonda insult Sutchai? Why did Nick change his college major? Why does Kirti talk so fast when she's around men? In answering such questions we *attribute* people's behavior to various causes. Whether we are right or wrong about the causes of their behavior, our conclusions affect how *we* act. To learn how we fill in the "person behind the mask," let's explore the making of attributions.

Two people enter a restaurant and order different meals. Nell tastes her food, then salts it. Bert salts his food before he tastes it. How would you explain their behavior? In Nell's case, you might assume that the *food* needed salt. If so, you have attributed her actions to an *external cause* (one that lies outside a person). With Bert, you might be more inclined to conclude that he must really *like* salt. If so, the cause of his behavior is internal. *Internal causes,* such as needs, personality traits, and Bert's taste for salt, lie within the person.

What effects do such interpretations have? It is difficult to fully understand social behavior without considering the attributions that we make. For instance, let's say that at the last five parties you've been to, you've seen a woman named Macy. Based on this, you assume that Macy likes to socialize. You see Macy at yet another gathering and mention that she seems to like parties. She says, "Actually, I hate these parties, but I get invited to play my tuba at them. My music teacher says I need to practice in front of an audience, so I keep attending these dumb events. Want to hear a Sousa march?"

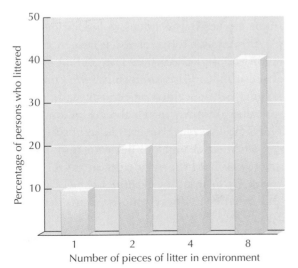

● **FIGURE 15.3** Results of an experiment on norms concerning littering. The prior existence of litter in a public setting implies that littering is acceptable. This encourages others to "trash" the area. (From Cialdini, Reno, & Kallgren, 1990.)

Social role Expected behavior patterns associated with particular social positions (such as daughter, worker, student).

Role conflict Trying to occupy two or more roles that make conflicting demands on behavior.

Group structure The network of roles, communication pathways, and power in a group.

Group cohesiveness The degree of attraction among group members or their commitment to remaining in the group.

In-group A group with which a person identifies.

Out-group A group with which a person does not identify.

Status An individual's position in a social structure, especially with respect to power, privilege, or importance.

Norm A widely accepted standard of conduct for appropriate behavior.

Attribution The process of making inferences about the causes of one's own behavior and that of others.

We seldom know the real reasons for others' actions. That is why we tend to infer causes from *circumstances*. However, in doing so, we often make mistakes like the one with Macy. The most common error is to attribute the actions of others to internal causes (Follett & Hess, 2002; Jones & Nisbett, 1971). This mistake is called the **fundamental attribution error.** We tend to think the actions of others have internal causes even if they are actually caused by external forces or circumstances. One amusing example of this error is the tendency of people to attribute the actions of actors in television programs to the personality of the actor rather than the obvious external cause (that they are playing a character) (Tal-Or & Papirman, 2007).

Where our own behavior is concerned, we are more likely to think that external causes explain our actions. In other words, there is an **actor-observer bias** in how we explain behavior. As *observers,* we attribute the behavior of others to their wants, motives, and personality traits (this is the fundamental attribution error). As *actors,* we tend to find external explanations for our own behavior (Gordon & Kaplar, 2002). No doubt you chose your major in school because of what it has to offer. Other students choose *their* majors because of the kind of people they are. Other people who don't leave tips in restaurants are cheapskates. If you don't leave a tip, it's because the service was bad. And, of course, other people are always late because they are irresponsible. You are late because you were held up by events beyond your control.

Ye Old Double Standard Attributions reveal an interesting double standard regarding the abilities of men and women. In a classic study by Kay Deaux and Tim Emswiller (1974),

Forest Whitaker won an Academy Award for his portrayal of dictator Idi Amin in the film *The Last King of Scotland.* Is Forest Whitaker a ruthless person or did he portray ruthlessness as a part of his role? According to Tal-Or & Papirman (2007), we are prone to attribute actors' screen actions to their personalities rather than to the personalities of the roles they are playing. Why do you think this occurs?

men and women overheard a male or female perform extremely well on a perception task. Each person was then asked to rate whether the test taker's success was due to ability, luck, or some combination of the two. Both men and women attributed men's success mainly to skill and women's performances mainly to luck! This was true even though male and female performances were identical.

As early as *kindergarten,* boys tend to take credit for successes. Girls tend to discount their own performances ("put themselves down") (Burgner & Hewstone, 1993). In general, there is a strong tendency to assume "He's skilled, she's lucky" when judging men and women (Swim & Sanna, 1996). Throughout life, such attributions no doubt haunt many talented and successful women.

Social Influence—Follow the Leader

SURVEY QUESTION: *What have social psychologists learned about conformity?*

No topic lies nearer the heart of social psychology than **social influence** (changes in behavior induced by the actions of others). When people interact, they almost always affect one another's behavior (Crano, 2000; Kassin, Fein, & Markus, 2008). For example, in a sidewalk experiment, various numbers of people stood on a busy New York City street. On cue they all looked at a sixth-floor window across the street. A camera recorded how many passersby also stopped to stare. The larger the influencing group, the more people were swayed to join in staring at the window (Milgram, Bickman, & Berkowitz, 1969).

Are there different kinds of social influence? Social influence ranges from *mere presence* (changing behavior just because other people are nearby) to intensive indoctrination (brainwashing). Three major forms of social influence are conformity, compliance, and obedience. The gentlest of these three forms of social influence is conformity. We **conform** when we bring our behavior into agreement with the actions, norms, or values of others in the absence of any direct pressure. Compliance is a more directed form of social influence. We *comply* when we change our behavior in response to another person who has little or no authority. Obedience is an even more direct form of social influence. We *obey* when we change our behavior in direct response to the demands of an authority.

Daily behavior is probably most influenced by group pressures for conformity (bringing your behavior into agreement with the actions, norms, or values of others) (Baron, Byrne, & Branscombe, 2007). We all conform to a degree. In fact, some uniformity is a necessity. Imagine being totally unable to anticipate the actions of others. In stores, schools, and homes this would be frustrating and disturbing. On the highways it would be lethal.

Conformity

When Fred first started working at the Fleegle Flange Factory, he found it easy to process 300 flanges an hour. Others around him averaged only 200. Fred's co-workers told him to slow down and take it easy. "I get bored," he said and continued to do 300 flanges an hour. At first Fred was welcomed, but now conversations broke up when he approached. Other workers laughed at him or ignored him when he spoke. Although he never made a conscious decision to conform, in another week Fred's output had slowed to 200 flanges an hour. Perhaps the most basic of all group norms is, as Fred discovered, "Thou shalt conform." Like it or not, life is filled with instances of conformity.

The Asch Experiment *How strong are group pressures for conformity?* One of the first experiments on conformity was staged by Solomon Asch (1907–1996). To fully appreciate it, imagine yourself as a subject. Assume that you are seated at a table with six other students. Your task is actually quite simple. On each trial you are shown three lines. Your job is to select the line that matches a "standard" line (● Fig. 15.4).

As the testing begins, each person announces an answer for the first card. When your turn comes, you agree with the others. "This isn't hard at all," you say to yourself. For several more trials your answers agree with those of the group. Then comes a shock. All six people announce that line 1 matches the standard, and you were about to say line 2 matches. Suddenly you feel alone and upset. You nervously look at the lines again. The room falls silent. Everyone seems to be staring at you. The experimenter awaits your answer. Do you yield to the group?

In this study the other "students" were all actors who gave the wrong answer on about a third of the trials to create

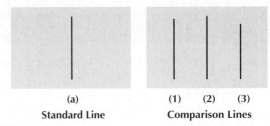

(a)
Standard Line

(1) (2) (3)
Comparison Lines

● **FIGURE 15.4** Stimuli used in Solomon Asch's conformity experiments.

group pressure (Asch, 1956). Real students conformed to the group in about one third of the critical trials. Of those tested, 75 percent yielded at least once. People tested alone erred in less than 1 percent of their judgments. Clearly, those who yielded to group pressures were denying what their eyes told them.

Are some people more susceptible to group pressures than others? People with high needs for structure or certainty are more likely to conform. So are people who are anxious, low in self-confidence, or concerned with the approval of others. People who live in cultures that emphasize group cooperation (such as many Asian cultures) are also more likely to conform (Bond & Smith, 1996; Fu et al., 2007).

In addition to personal characteristics, certain situations tend to encourage conformity—sometimes with disastrous results. "Groupthink—Agreement at Any Cost" offers a prime example.

Group Factors in Conformity *How do groups enforce norms?* In most groups, we have been rewarded with acceptance and approval for conformity and threatened with rejection or ridicule for nonconformity. These reactions are called *group sanctions.* Negative sanctions range from laughter, staring, or social disapproval to complete rejection or formal exclusion. If you've ever felt the sudden chill of disapproval by others, you will understand the power of group sanctions.

Wouldn't the effectiveness of group sanctions depend on the importance of the group? Yes. The more important group membership is to a person, the more he or she will be influenced by other group members. The risk of being rejected can be a threat to our sense of personal identity (Crano,

Roy Morsch/Corbis

Conformity is a subtle dimension of daily life. Notice the similarities in clothing and hairstyles among these couples.

Fundamental attribution error The tendency to attribute the behavior of others to internal causes (personality, likes, and so forth).

Actor-observer bias The tendency to attribute the behavior of others to internal causes while attributing one's own behavior to external causes (situations and circumstances).

Social influence Changes in a person's behavior induced by the presence or actions of others.

Conformity Bringing one's behavior into agreement or harmony with norms or with the behavior of others in a group in the absence of any direct pressure.

CRITICAL THINKING

Groupthink—Agreement at Any Cost

As we write this, debate continues to rage about the Iraq war. Why, for example, were no weapons of mass destruction found in Iraq, even though their existence was the major justification for the war in the first place? Was the decision to invade Iraq made by a small group of policymakers with little tolerance for dissenting views? Already, it has been suggested that this war may have been a result of **groupthink**—an urge by decision makers to maintain each other's approval, even at the cost of critical thinking (Porteus, 2004).

Groupthink has been blamed for many embarrassments, such as the *Columbia* space shuttle disaster in 2003 and the loss, in 1999, of the $165 million *Mars Climate Orbiter.* An analysis of 19 international crises found that groupthink contributed to most (Schafer & Crichlow,

1996). The core of groupthink is misguided loyalty. Group members are hesitant to "rock the boat" or question sloppy thinking. This self-censorship leads people to believe they agree more than they actually do (Henningsen et al., 2006; Whyte, 2000).

To prevent groupthink, group leaders should take the following steps:

- Define each group member's role as a "critical evaluator."
- Avoid revealing any personal preferences in the beginning.
- State the problem factually, without bias.
- Invite a group member or outside person to play devil's advocate.
- Make it clear that group members will be held accountable for decisions.

- Encourage open inquiry and a search for alternate solutions (Baron, 2005; Chen et al., 1996).

In addition, it is advisable to have a "second-chance" meeting to re-evaluate important decisions. That is, each decision should be reached twice.

In fairness to our decision makers, it is worth noting that the presence of too many alternatives can lead to *deadlock*, in which an inability to make a choice can delay taking necessary action (Kowert, 2002). Regardless, in an age clouded by the threat of war, global warming, and terrorism, even stronger solutions to the problem of groupthink would be welcome. Perhaps we should form a group to think about it!

2000). That's why the Asch experiments are impressive. Because these were only temporary groups, sanctions were informal and rejection had no lasting importance. Just the same, the power of the group was evident.

What other factors, besides importance of the group, affect the degree of conformity? In the sidewalk experiment described earlier, we noted that large groups had more influence. In Asch's face-to-face groups the size of the majority also made a difference, but a surprisingly small one. In other studies, the number of people who conformed increased dramatically as the majority grew from two to three people. However, a majority of three produced about as much yielding as a majority of eight. The next time you want to talk someone into (or out of) something, take two friends along and see what a difference it makes! (Sometimes it helps if the two are large and mean looking.)

Even more important than the size of the majority is its *unanimity* (total agreement). Having at least one person in your corner can greatly reduce pressures to conform. When Asch gave subjects an ally (who also opposed the majority by giving the correct answer), conformity was lessened. In terms of numbers, a unanimous majority of three is more powerful than a majority of eight with one dissenting. Perhaps this accounts for the rich diversity of human attitudes, beliefs, opinions, and lifestyles. If you can find at least one other person who sees things as you do (no matter how weird), you can be relatively secure in your opposition to other viewpoints. Incidentally, the Internet now makes it much easier to find that other like-minded person.

MODULE 15.2 Summary

How does group membership affect our behavior?

- To understand social behavior we must know what roles people play, their status, the norms they follow, and the attributions they make.
- Social roles are particular behavior patterns associated with social positions.
- Higher status within groups is associated with special privileges and respect.
- Norms are standards of conduct enforced (formally or informally) by groups.
- We attribute behavior to various causes. These attributions, in turn, affect how we act.
- The fundamental attributional error is to think that internal causes explain the actions of other people. In contrast, we tend to attribute our own behavior to external causes.

What have social psychologists learned about conformity, compliance, obedience, and self-assertion?

- *Social influence* refers to alterations in behavior brought about by the behavior of others.
- The famous Asch experiments demonstrated that people are likely to conform when they face social pressure from other group members.
- *Groupthink* refers to compulsive conformity in group decision making.

KNOWLEDGE BUILDER

Groups, Social Influence, and Conformity

Recite

1. *Status* refers to a set of expected behaviors associated with a social position. T or F?

2. The fundamental attribution error is to attribute the actions of others to internal causes. T or F?

3. The effect one person's behavior has on another is called _____

   _____.

4. In Solomon Asch's conformity experiment, participants yielded to group pressure on about _____ of the critical trials.

   a. 1 percent

   b. 10 percent

   c. one third

   d. two thirds

5. Nonconformity is punished by negative group _____ _____.

6. Groupthink is an example of the danger that lies in powerful pressures for group _____.

   a. cohesion

   b. conformity

   c. attribution

   d. reciprocity

Reflect
Critical Thinking

7. Is it possible to be completely nonconforming (that is, to not conform to some group norm)?

Relate

What are the most prominent roles you play? Which are achieved and which are ascribed? How do they affect your behavior? What conflicts do they create?

Do you commit the fundamental attribution error? Try to think of a specific example that illustrates the concept.

Identify a recent time when you conformed in some way. How did norms, group pressure, sanctions, and unanimity contribute to your tendency to conform?

Link

Internet addresses frequently change. To find the sites listed here, visit **http://www .thomsonedu.com/psychology/coon** for an updated list of Internet addresses and direct links to relevant sites.

- **Stanford Prison Study** Explore Phil Zimbardo's classic study of the power of social roles.

- **Conformity** Find out more about conformity and the Asch experiments.

- **Groupthink** Read about and download a PowerPoint presentation about groupthink.

ANSWERS

1. F 2. T 3. social influence 4. c 5. sanctions 6. b 7. A person who did not follow at least some norms concerning normal social behavior would very likely be perceived as extremely bizarre, disturbed, or psychotic.

MODULE
15.3 Compliance, Obedience, and Self-Assertion

WHAT ARE THE LIMITS of your willingness to comply with the requests of strangers or with the commands of authorities? You've probably seen a bumper sticker that says "Question Authority." Actually, that's not bad advice if it means "Think Critically." However, compliance and obedience are normal parts of social life. When is it appropriate to decline to comply or to resist authority? These are essential questions about how we are affected by social influence.

Compliance—A Foot in the Door

SURVEY QUESTION: *What have psychologists learned about compliance, obedience, and self-assertion?*

Pressures to "fit in" and conform are usually indirect. In contrast, the term **compliance** refers to situations in which one person bends to the requests of another person who has little or no authority. These more direct pressures to comply are quite common. For example, a stranger might ask you to borrow your cell phone so he can make a call; a saleswoman might suggest that you buy a more expensive watch than you had planned on; or a coworker might ask you for the money to buy a cappuccino.

What determines whether a person will comply with a request? Many factors could be listed, but three stand out as especially interesting.

The Foot-in-the-Door Effect People who sell door to door have long recognized that once they get a foot in the door, a sale is almost a sure thing. To state the **foot-in-the-door effect** more formally, a person who first agrees to a small request is later more likely to comply with a larger demand (Pascual & Guéguen, 2005). For instance, if someone asked you to put a large, ugly sign in your front yard to promote safe driving, you would probably refuse. If, however, you had first agreed to put a small sign in your window, you would later be much more likely to allow the big sign in your yard.

Apparently, the foot-in-the-door effect is based on observing one's own behavior. Seeing yourself agree to a small request helps convince you that you didn't mind doing what was asked. After that, you are more likely to comply with a larger request (Pascual & Guéguen, 2005).

The Door-in-the-Face Effect Let's say that a neighbor comes to your door and asks you to feed his dogs, water his plants, and mow his yard while he is out of town for a month. This is quite a major request—one that most people would probably turn down. Feeling only slightly guilty, you tell your neighbor that you're sorry but you can't help him. Now, what if the same neighbor returns the next day and asks if you would at least pick up his mail while he is gone. Chances are very good that you would honor this request, even if you might have originally turned it down, too.

Psychologist Robert Cialdini coined the term **door-in-the-face effect** to describe the tendency for a person who has refused a major request to agree to a smaller request. In other words, after a person has turned down a major request ("slammed the door in your face"), he or she may be more willing to comply with a lesser demand. This strategy works because a person who abandons a large request appears to have given up something. In response, many people feel that they must repay her or him by giving in to the smaller request (Cialdini & Goldstein, 2004). In fact, a good way to get another person to comply with a request is to first do a small favor for the person.

The Lowball Technique Anyone who has purchased an automobile will recognize a third way of inducing compliance. Automobile dealers are notorious for convincing customers to buy cars by offering "lowball" prices that undercut the competition. The dealer first gets the customer to agree to buy at an attractively low price. Then, once the customer is committed, various techniques are used to bump the price up before the sale is concluded.

The **lowball technique** consists of getting a person committed to act and then making the terms of acting less desirable (Guéguen, Pascual, & Dagot, 2002). Here's another example: A fellow student asks to borrow $25 for a day. This seems reasonable and you agree. However, once you have

DISCOVERING PSYCHOLOGY

How to Drive a Hard Bargain

Your local car lot is a good place to see compliance take place. Automobile salespersons play the compliance game daily and get very good at it. If you understand what they are up to, you will have a far better chance of resisting their tactics.

A Foot in the Door

The salesperson offers you a test drive. If you accept, you will have made a small commitment of time to a particular car and to the salesperson. The salesperson will then ask you to go to an office and fill out some papers "just to see what kind of a price" she or he can offer. If you go along, you will be further committed.

The Lowball Technique

To get things underway the salesperson will offer you a very good price for your trade-in or will ask you to make an offer on the new car,

"any offer, no matter how low." The salesperson will then ask if you will buy the car if she or he can sell it for the price you state. If you say yes, you have virtually bought the car. Most people find it very difficult to walk away once bargaining has reached this stage.

The Hook Is Set

Once buyers are "hooked" by a lowball offer, the salesperson goes to the manager to have the sale "approved." On returning, the salesperson will tell you with great disappointment that the dealership would lose money on the deal. "Couldn't you just take a little less for the trade-in or pay a little more for the car?" the salesperson will ask. At this point many people hesitate and grumble, but most give in and accept some "compromise" price or trade-in amount.

Evening the Odds

To combat all of the preceding, you must arm yourself with accurate information. In the past, salespeople had a great advantage in negotiating because they knew exactly how much the dealership paid for each car. Now, you can obtain detailed automobile pricing information on the Internet. With such information in hand, you will find it easier to challenge a salesperson's manipulative tactics.

After you've negotiated a final "best offer," get it in writing. Then walk out. Go to another dealer and see if the salesperson will better the price, in writing. When he or she does, return to the first dealership and negotiate for an even better price. Then decide where to buy. Now that you know some of the rules of the "Car Game," you might even enjoy playing it.

---

given your classmate the money, he explains that it would be easier to repay you after payday, in 2 weeks. If you agree, you've succumbed to the lowball technique. Here's another example: Let's say you ask someone to give you a ride to school in the morning. Only after the person has agreed do you tell her that you have to be there at 6 A.M.

Gaining Compliance To summarize, there are three basic ways to get people to voluntarily comply with a request.

- You can start with a small request that is easy for the person to agree to, and then make a bigger request. (This is the foot-in-the-door strategy.)

- You can make a major request that you know the person will turn down, and then make a smaller request (the one you actually wanted the person to comply with in the first place). (This is the door-in-the-face strategy.)

- You can make a request and get the person to agree to it. Then change the requirements for fulfilling the request to something the person probably wouldn't have otherwise agreed to do. (This is the lowball technique.)

One of the main benefits of knowing these strategies is that you can protect yourself from being manipulated by people using them. For example, "How to Drive a Hard Bargain" explains how car salespersons use compliance techniques on customers.

Obedience—Would You Electrocute a Stranger?

A person who has social power in one situation may have very little in another. In those situations where a person has power, she or he is described as an *authority*. Let's investigate **obedience,** a special type of conformity to the demands of an authority.

Groupthink A compulsion by members of decision-making groups to maintain agreement, even at the cost of critical thinking.

Compliance Bending to the requests of a person who has little or no authority or other form of social power.

Foot-in-the-door effect The tendency for a person who has first complied with a small request to be more likely later to fulfill a larger request.

Door-in-the-face effect The tendency for a person who has refused a major request to subsequently be more likely to comply with a minor request.

Lowball technique A strategy in which commitment is gained first to reasonable or desirable terms, which are then made less reasonable or desirable.

Obedience Conformity to the demands of an authority.

The question is this: If ordered to do so, would you shock a man with a heart condition who is screaming and asking to be released? Certainly, few people would obey. Or would they? In Nazi Germany, obedient soldiers (once average citizens) helped slaughter more than 6 million people in concentration camps. Do such inhumane acts reflect deep character flaws? Are they the acts of heartless psychopaths or crazed killers? Or are they simply the result of obedience to authority? What are the limits of obedience? These are questions that puzzled social psychologist Stanley Milgram (1965) when he began a provocative series of studies on obedience.

How did Milgram study obedience? As was true of the Asch experiments, Milgram's research is best appreciated by imagining yourself as a subject. Place yourself in the following situation.

Milgram's Obedience Studies

Imagine answering a newspaper ad to take part in a "learning" experiment at Yale University. When you arrive, a coin is flipped and a second person, a pleasant-looking man in his 50s, is designated the "learner." By chance you have become the "teacher."

Your task is to read a list of word pairs. The learner's task is to memorize them. You are to punish him with an electric shock each time he makes a mistake. The learner is taken to an adjacent room, and you watch as he is seated in an "electric chair" apparatus. Electrodes are attached to his wrists. You are then escorted to your position in front of a "shock generator." On this device is a row of 30 switches marked from 15 to 450 volts. Corresponding labels range from "Slight Shock" to "Extreme Intensity Shock" and finally "Danger Severe Shock." Your instructions are to shock the learner each time he makes a mistake. You must begin with 15 volts and then move one switch (15 volts) higher for each additional mistake (● Fig. 15.5).

The experiment begins, and the learner soon makes his first error. You flip a switch. More mistakes. Rapidly you

reach the 75-volt level. The learner moans after each shock. At 100 volts he complains that he has a heart condition. At 150 volts he says he no longer wants to continue and demands to be released. At 300 volts he screams and says he can no longer give answers.

At some point, you begin to protest to the experimenter. "That man has a heart condition," you say; "I'm not going to kill that man." The experimenter says, "Please continue." Another shock and another scream from the learner and you say, "You mean I've got to keep going up the scale? No, sir. I'm not going to give him 450 volts!" The experimenter says, "The experiment requires that you continue." For a time the learner refuses to answer any more questions and screams with each shock (Milgram, 1965). Then he falls chillingly silent for the rest of the experiment.

It's hard to believe many people would do this. What happened? Milgram also doubted that many people would obey his orders. When he polled a group of psychiatrists before the experiment, they predicted that less than 1 percent of those tested would obey. The astounding fact is that 65 percent obeyed completely by going all the way to the 450-volt level. Virtually no one stopped short of 300 volts ("Severe Shock") (● Fig. 15.6).

Was the learner injured? The time has come to reveal that the "learner" was actually an actor who turned a tape recorder on and off in the shock room. No shocks were ever administered, but the dilemma for the "teacher" was quite real. Subjects protested, sweated, trembled, stuttered, bit their lips, and laughed nervously. Clearly they were disturbed by what they were doing. Nevertheless, most obeyed the experimenter's orders.

Milgram's Follow-Up *Why did so many people obey?* Some have suggested that the prestige of Yale University added to subjects' willingness to obey. Could it be that they assumed the professor running the experiment would not really allow anyone to be hurt? To test this possibility, the study was rerun in a shabby office building in nearby Bridgeport, Connecti-

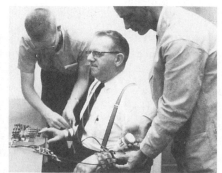

● **FIGURE 15.5** Scenes from Stanley Milgram's study of obedience: the "shock generator," strapping a "learner" into his chair, and a "teacher" being told to administer a severe shock to the learner. (Scenes from the film *Obedience*, by Stanley Milgram, The Pennsylvania State University, Audio Visual Services. Used by permission.)

DISCOVERING PSYCHOLOGY

Quack Like a Duck

Imagine your response to the following events. On the first day of class, your psychology professor begins to establish the basic rules of behavior for the course. Draw a line under the first instruction you think you would refuse to carry out.

1. Seats are assigned, and you are told to move to a new location.

2. You are told not to talk during class.

3. Your professor tells you that you must have permission to leave early.

4. You are told to bring your textbook to class at all times.

5. Your professor tells you to use only a pencil for taking notes.

6. You are directed to take off your watch.

7. The professor tells you to keep both hands on your desktop at all times.

8. You are instructed to keep both your feet flat on the floor.

9. You are told to stand up and clap your hands three times.

10. Your professor says, "Stick two fingers up your nose and quack like a duck."

At what point would you stop obeying such orders? In reality, you might find yourself obeying a legitimate authority long after that person's demands had become unreasonable (Aronson, Wilson, & Akert, 2007). What would happen, though, if a few students resisted orders early in the sequence? Would that help free others to disobey? For an answer, return to the discussion of Milgram's experiment for some final remarks.

---

cut. Under these conditions fewer people obeyed (48 percent), but the reduction was minor.

Milgram was disturbed by the willingness of people to knuckle under to authority and senselessly shock someone. In later experiments, he tried to reduce obedience. He found that the distance between the teacher and the learner was important. When subjects were in the *same room* as the learner, only 40 percent fully obeyed. When they were *face to face* with the learner and required to force his hand down on a simulated "shock plate," only 30 percent obeyed (● Fig. 15.7). Distance from the authority also had an effect. When the experimenter gave his orders over the phone, only 22 percent obeyed. You may doubt that Milgram's study of obedience applies to you. If so, take a moment to read "Quack Like a Duck."

Implications Milgram's research raises nagging questions about our willingness to commit antisocial or inhumane acts commanded by a "legitimate authority." The excuse so often

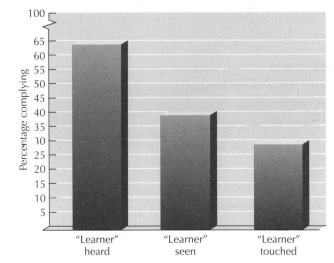

● **FIGURE 15.7** Physical distance from the "learner" had a significant effect on the percentage of subjects obeying orders.

given by war criminals—"I was only following orders"—takes on new meaning in this light. Milgram suggested that when directions come from an authority, people rationalize that they are not personally responsible for their actions. In locales as diverse as Vietnam, Rwanda, Bosnia, South Africa, Nicaragua, Sri Lanka, Laos, and Iraq, the tragic result has been "sanctioned massacres" of chilling proportions. Even in everyday life, crimes of obedience are common (Zimbardo, 2007). In order to keep their jobs, many people obey orders to do things that they know are dishonest, unethical, or harmful (Hamilton & Sanders, 1995).

Let us end on a more positive note. In one of his experiments, Milgram found that group support can greatly reduce destructive obedience. When real subjects saw two other "teachers" (both actors) resist orders and walk out of the ex-

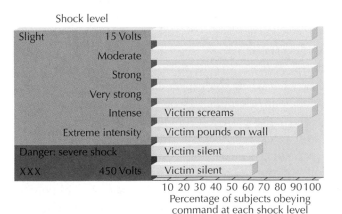

● **FIGURE 15.6** Results of Milgram's obedience experiment. Only a minority of subjects refused to provide shocks, even at the most extreme intensities. The first substantial drop in obedience occurred at the 300-volt level (Milgram, 1963).

Obedience to authority is often necessary and reasonable; however, it can also be destructive.

Associated Press photographer Jeff Widener snapped this timeless photo of a lone protester literally standing up on his own behalf while he halted a column of tanks during the 1989 pro-democracy rallies in Tiananmen Square in Beijing, China. How many of us would find the courage to assert ourselves against such direct expressions of authority?

periment, only 10 percent continued to obey. Thus, a personal assertion of courage or moral fortitude by one or two members of a group may free others to disobey misguided or unjust authority. Let's see how assertive people handle difficult social situations.

Assertiveness Training—Standing Up for Your Rights

Because we all face pressures to conform, comply, and obey, there is value in learning to assert yourself and stand up for your rights. Have you ever done any of the following?

- Hesitated to question an error on a restaurant bill because you were afraid of making a scene?
- Backed out of asking for a raise or a change in working conditions?
- Said yes when you wanted to say no?
- Been afraid to question a grade that seemed unfair?

If you've ever had trouble with similar situations, *assertiveness training* (instruction in how to be self-assertive) may offer a solution. In assertiveness training, people learn assertive behavior through group exercises, videotapes, and staged conflicts. They also learn to practice honesty, disagreeing, questioning authority, and assertive postures and gestures. As their self-confidence improves, nonassertive clients are taken on "field trips" to shops and restaurants where they practice what they have learned.

The first step in assertiveness training is to convince yourself of three basic rights: You have the right to refuse, to request, and to right a wrong. **Self-assertion** involves standing up for these rights by speaking out in your own behalf.

Is self-assertion just getting things your own way? Not at all. A basic distinction can be made between *self-assertion* and *aggressive* behavior. Self-assertion is a direct, honest expression of feelings and desires. It is not exclusively self-serving. People who are nonassertive are usually patient to a fault. Sometimes their pent-up anger explodes with unexpected fury, which can damage relationships. In contrast to assertive behavior, **aggression** involves hurting another person or achieving one's goals at the expense of another. Aggression does not take into account the feelings or rights of others. It is an attempt to get one's own way no matter what. Assertion techniques emphasize firmness, not attack (■ Table 15.2).

The basic idea in assertiveness training is that each assertive action is practiced until it can be repeated even under stress. For example, let's say it really angers you when a store clerk waits on several people who arrived after you did. To improve your assertiveness in this situation, you would begin by *rehearsing* the dialogue, posture, and gestures you would use to confront the clerk or the other customer. Working in front of a mirror can be very helpful. If possible, you should *role play* the scene with a friend. Be sure to have your friend take the part of a really aggressive or irresponsible clerk, as well as a cooperative one. Rehearsal and role playing should also be used when you expect a possible confrontation with someone—for example, if you are going to ask for a raise, challenge a grade, or confront a landlord.

Is that all there is to it? No. Another important principle is *overlearning* (practice that continues after initial mastery of a skill). When you rehearse or role-play assertive behavior, it is essential to continue to practice until your responses become almost automatic. This helps prevent you from getting flustered in the actual situation.

One more technique you may find useful is the *broken record*. This is a self-assertion technique involving repeating a

■ **TABLE 15.2** Comparison of Assertive, Aggressive, and Nonassertive Behavior

	ACTOR	RECEIVER OF BEHAVIOR
Nonassertive behavior	Self-denying, inhibited, hurt, and anxious; lets others make choices; goals not achieved	Feels sympathy, guilt, or contempt for actor; achieves goals at actor's expense
Aggressive behavior	Achieves goals at others' expense; expresses feelings, but hurts others; chooses for others or puts them down	Feels hurt, defensive, humiliated, or taken advantage of; does not meet own needs
Assertive behavior	Self-enhancing; acts in own best interests; expresses feelings; respects rights of others; goals usually achieved; self-respect maintained	Needs respected and feelings expressed; may achieve goal; self-worth maintained

request until it is acknowledged. A good way to prevent assertion from becoming aggression is to simply restate your request as many times and in as many ways as necessary. As an illustration, let's say you are returning a pair of shoes to a store. After two wearings the shoes fell apart, but you bought them 2 months ago and no longer have a receipt. The broken record could sound something like this:

Customer: I would like to have these shoes replaced.

Clerk: Do you have a receipt?

Customer: No, but I bought them here, and since they are defective, I would like to have you replace them.

Clerk: I can't do that without a receipt.

Customer: I understand that, but I want them replaced.

Clerk: Well, if you'll come back this afternoon and talk to the manager . . .

Customer: I've brought these shoes in because they are defective.

Clerk: Well, I'm not authorized to replace them.

Customer: Yes, well, if you'll replace these, I'll be on my way.

Notice that the customer did not attack the clerk or create an angry confrontation. Simple persistence is often all that is necessary for successful self-assertion.

Self-assertion does not supply instant poise, confidence, or self-assurance. However, it is a way of combating anxieties associated with life in an impersonal and sometimes intimidating society. If you are interested in more information, you can consult a book titled *Your Perfect Right* by Alberti and Emmons (2001).

MODULE **15.3 Summary**

What have psychologists learned about compliance, obedience, and self-assertion?

- Three strategies for gaining compliance are the foot-in-the-door technique, the door-in-the-face approach, and the lowball technique.
- Most people have a strong tendency to obey legitimate authority. Usually this is desirable, but it can be damaging when social power is used in misguided or unscrupulous ways.
- Obedience to authority in Milgram's studies decreased when the "teacher" and "learner" were close to one another, when the authority was absent, and when others refused to obey.
- Self-assertion helps people meet their needs without resorting to aggressive behavior.

Self-assertion A direct, honest expression of feelings and desires.

Aggression Hurting another person or achieving one's goals at the expense of another person.

KNOWLEDGE BUILDER

Compliance, Obedience, and Self-Assertion

Recite

1. The term *compliance* refers to situations in which a person complies with commands made by a person who has authority. T or F?

2. Which compliance technique involves getting a person committed to act and then making the terms of acting less desirable?

   a. foot in the door

   b. lowball

   c. door in the face

   d. groupthink

3. In Milgram's experiments, the lowest level of obedience occurred when subjects

   a. saw another person refuse to obey

   b. were in the same room with the "learner"

   c. were face to face with the "learner"

   d. received orders over the phone

4. By repeating his obedience experiment in a downtown office building, Milgram demonstrated that the prestige of Yale University was the main reason for subjects' willingness to obey in the original experiment. T or F?

5. "Achieving one's goals without taking into account the rights of others." This statement describes

   a. self-assertion

   b. overdisclosure

   c. cognitive dissonance

   d. aggression

Reflect
Critical Thinking

6. Modern warfare allows killing to take place impersonally and at a distance. How does this relate to Milgram's experiments?

Relate

You would like to persuade people to donate to a deserving charity. How, specifically, could you use compliance techniques to get people to donate?

Are you surprised that so many people obeyed orders in Milgram's experiments? Do you think you would have obeyed? How actively do you question authority?

Pick a specific instance when you could have been more assertive. How would you handle the situation if it occurs again? Think of a specific instance when you were angry and acted aggressively. How could you have handled the situation through self-assertion instead of aggression?

Link

Internet addresses frequently change. To find the sites listed here, visit **http://www.thomsonedu.com/psychology/coon** for an updated list of Internet addresses and direct links to relevant sites.

- **The Two Step** Dig down deeper into the foot-in-the-door and door-in-the-face compliance techniques.

- **Milgram's Study of Obedience** Listen to audio clips of this infamous experiment.

- **Assertiveness** Access a collection of virtual pamphlets on assertiveness.

ANSWERS

1. F 2. b 3. d 4. F 5. d 6. There is a big difference between killing someone in hand-to-hand combat and killing someone by lining up images on a video screen. Milgram's research suggests that it is easier for a person to follow orders to kill another human when the victim is at a distance and removed from personal contact.

15.4 Attitudes and Persuasion

WHAT IS YOUR ATTITUDE toward affirmative action, environmental groups, the death penalty, imported automobiles, junk food, psychology? The answers can have far-reaching effects on your behavior. Attitudes are intimately woven into our actions and views of the world. Our tastes, friendships, votes, preferences, and goals are all touched by attitudes. Let's see how attitudes are formed and changed.

Attitudes—Doomsday for the Seekers

HOW ARE ATTITUDES ACQUIRED AND CHANGED?

Hardly a year passes without a doomsday group of one kind or another making the news. In a classic example of such groups, a woman named Mrs. Keech claimed she was receiving messages from alien beings on a planet called Clarion. The aliens told Mrs. Keech that they had detected a fault in the earth's crust that would plunge North America into the ocean, causing an unimaginable disaster. The tragedy would occur on December 21. However, Mrs. Keech and her band of followers, who called themselves the Seekers, had no fear: On December 20 they expected to be met at midnight by a flying saucer and taken to safety in outer space.

The night of December 20 arrived, and the Seekers gathered at Mrs. Keech's house. Many had given up their jobs and possessions to prepare for departure. Expectations were high and commitment was total. But as midnight passed, the world continued to exist. It was a bitter and embarrassing disappointment for the Seekers.

Did the group break up then? Our story now takes an amazing twist—one that intrigued social psychologists. Instead of breaking up, the Seekers became *more* convinced than ever before that they had been right. At about 5 A.M. Mrs. Keech announced she had received a message explaining that the Seekers had saved the world.

Before December 20, the Seekers were uninterested in persuading other people that the world was coming to an end. Now they called newspapers and radio stations to convince others of their accomplishment.

How do we explain this strange turn in behavior? An answer may lie in the concept of *cognitive dissonance,* which also helps explain many aspects of attitude change. We will return to cognitive dissonance in a moment, but first let's answer some basic questions about attitudes.

Belief + Emotion + Action

Our tastes, friendships, votes, preferences, goals, and behavior in many other situations are all touched by attitudes (Baumeister & Bushman, 2008).

What specifically is an attitude? An **attitude** is a mixture of belief and emotion that predisposes a person to respond to other people, objects, or groups in a positive or negative way. Attitudes summarize your *evaluation* of objects (Oskamp & Schultz, 2005). As a result, they predict and direct future actions.

"Your attitude is showing" is sometimes said. Actually, attitudes are expressed through beliefs, emotions, and actions. The *belief component* of an attitude is what you believe about a particular object or issue. The *emotional component* consists of your feelings toward the attitudinal object. The *action component* refers to your actions toward various people, objects, or institutions. Consider, for example, your attitude toward gun control. You will have beliefs about whether gun control would affect rates of crime or violence. You will respond emotionally to guns, finding them either attractive and desirable or threatening and destructive. And you will have a tendency to seek out or avoid gun ownership. The action component of your attitude will probably also include support of organizations that urge or oppose gun control. As you can see, attitudes orient us to the social world. In doing so, they prepare us to act in certain ways (Albarracín, Johnson, & Zanna, 2005). (For another example, see ● Figure 15.8.)

Forming Attitudes

How do people acquire attitudes? Attitudes are acquired in several basic ways. Sometimes, attitudes come from *direct contact* (personal experience) with the object of the attitude—such as opposing pollution when a nearby factory ruins your favorite river (Ajzen, 2005). Some attitudes are simply formed through chance conditioning (learning that takes place by chance or coincidence) (Olson & Zanna, 1993). Let's say, for instance, that you have had three encounters in your lifetime with psychologists. If all three were negative, you might take an unduly dim view of psychology. In the same way, people often develop strong attitudes to-

---

Attitude A learned tendency to respond to people, objects, or institutions in a positive or negative way.

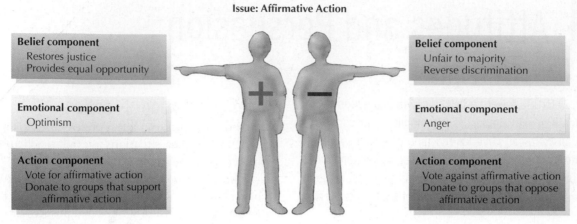

Issue: Affirmative Action

Belief component
Restores justice
Provides equal opportunity

Emotional component
Optimism

Action component
Vote for affirmative action
Donate to groups that support affirmative action

Belief component
Unfair to majority
Reverse discrimination

Emotional component
Anger

Action component
Vote against affirmative action
Donate to groups that oppose affirmative action

● **FIGURE 15.8** Elements of positive and negative attitudes toward affirmative action.

ward cities, foods, or parts of the country on the basis of one or two unusually good or bad experiences.

Attitudes are also learned through *interaction with others;* that is, through discussion with people holding a particular attitude. For instance, if three of your friends are volunteers at a local recycling center, and you talk with them about their beliefs, you will probably come to favor recycling, too. More generally, there is little doubt that many of our attitudes are influenced by *group membership*. In most groups, pressures to conform shape our attitudes, just as they do our behavior. *Child rearing* (the effects of parental values, beliefs, and practices) also affects attitudes (Bartram, 2006). For example, if both parents belong to the same political party, chances are that their children will belong to that party as adults.

Finally, there can be no doubt that attitudes are influenced by the *mass media* (all media, such as magazines and television, that reach large audiences). Every day we are coaxed, persuaded, and skillfully manipulated by messages in the mass media. Ninety-nine percent of North American homes have a television set, which is on an average of more than 7 hours a day (Steuer & Hustedt, 2002). The information thus channeled into homes has a powerful impact. For instance, frequent viewers mistrust others and overestimate their own chances of being harmed. This suggests that a steady diet of TV violence leads some people to develop a *mean worldview,* in which they regard the world as a dangerous and threatening place (Eschholz, Chiricos, & Gertz, 2003).

Attitudes and Behavior

Why are some attitudes acted on, whereas others are not? To answer this question, let's consider an example. Assume that a woman named Lorraine knows that automobiles add to air pollution, and she hates smog. Why would Lorraine continue to drive to work every day? Probably it is because the *immediate consequences* of our actions weigh heavily on the choices we make. No matter what Lorraine's attitude may be, it is difficult for her to resist the immediate convenience of driving. Our expectations of how *others will evaluate* our actions are also important. Lorraine may resist taking public transit to work for fear that her coworkers will be critical of her environmental stand. Finally, we must not overlook the effects of long-standing *habits* (Oskamp & Schultz, 2005). Let's say that after years of driving to work Lorraine finally vows to shift to public transit. Two months later it would not be unusual for her behavior to show the effects of habit rather than her good intentions.

In short, there are often large differences between attitudes and behavior—particularly between privately held attitudes and public behavior. However, barriers to action typically fall when a person holds an attitude with *conviction*. If you have *conviction* about an issue, it evokes strong feelings, you think about it and discuss it often, and you are knowledgeable about it. Attitudes held with passionate conviction often lead to major changes in personal behavior (Oskamp & Schultz, 2005).

THAT IS ENOUGH!!

OW!

OOH!

WE HAVE JUST BROUGHT A NEW BABY INTO THE WORLD. DO YOU WANT HER TO THINK THAT THIS IS WHAT LIFE IS ALL ABOUT?

WE WANT HER TO BELIEVE THAT PEOPLE ARE REASONABLE AND KIND, THAT THERE ARE OTHER WAYS OF RESOLVING DISPUTES WITHOUT VIOLENCE. WE WANT HER TO BELIEVE THAT THE WORLD IS A GOOD PLACE!

...AT LEAST UNTIL SHE STARTS WATCHING T.V.

4-13

Attitude Change—Why the "Seekers" Went Public

SURVEY QUESTION: *Under what conditions is persuasion most effective?*

Although attitudes are fairly stable, they do change. Some attitude change can be understood in terms of **reference groups** (any group an individual uses as a standard for social comparison). It is not necessary to have face-to-face contact with other people for them to be a reference group. It depends instead on whom you identify with or whose attitudes and values you care about (Ajzen, 2005).

In the 1930s, Theodore Newcomb studied real-life attitude change among students at Bennington College (Alwin, Cohen, & Newcomb, 1991). Most students came from conservative homes, but Bennington was a very liberal school. Newcomb found that most students shifted significantly toward more liberal attitudes during their 4 years at Bennington. Those who didn't change kept their parents and hometown friends as primary reference groups. This is typified by a student who said, "I decided I'd rather stick to my father's ideas." Those who did change identified primarily with the campus community. Notice that all students could count the college and their families as *membership* groups. However, one group or the other tended to become their point of reference.

Persuasion

What about advertising and other direct attempts to change attitudes? Are they effective? **Persuasion** is any deliberate attempt to change attitudes or beliefs through information and arguments (Brock & Green, 2005). Businesses, politicians, and others who seek to persuade us obviously believe that attitudes can be changed. Many billions of dollars are spent yearly on media advertising in the United States and Canada alone.

Do you exercise regularly? Like students in the Bennington study, your intentions to exercise are probably influenced by the exercise habits of your reference groups (Terry & Hogg, 1996).

Persuasion. Would you be likely to be swayed by this group's message? Successful persuasion is related to characteristics of the communicator, the message, and the audience.

Persuasion can range from the daily blitz of media commercials to personal discussion among friends. In most cases, the success or failure of persuasion can be understood if we consider the *communicator,* the *message,* and the *audience.*

At a community meeting, let's say you have a chance to promote an issue important to you (for or against building a nuclear power plant nearby, for instance). Whom should you choose to make the presentation, and how should that person present it? Research suggests that attitude change is encouraged when the following conditions are met.

1. The communicator is likable, expressive, trustworthy, an expert on the topic, and similar to the audience in some respect.

2. The message appeals to emotions, particularly to fear or anxiety.

3. The message also provides a clear course of action that will, if followed, reduce fear or produce personally desirable results.

4. The message states clear-cut conclusions.

5. The message is backed up by facts and statistics.

6. Both sides of the argument are presented in the case of a well-informed audience.

7. Only one side of the argument is presented in the case of a poorly informed audience.

8. The persuader appears to have nothing to gain if the audience accepts the message.

9. The message is repeated as frequently as possible (Aronson, 2008; Oskamp & Schultz, 2005).

Reference group Any group that an individual identifies with and uses as a standard for social comparison.

Persuasion A deliberate attempt to change attitudes or beliefs with information and arguments.

You should have little trouble seeing how these principles are applied to sell everything from underarm deodorants to presidents.

Cognitive Dissonance Theory

Cognitions are thoughts. *Dissonance* means clashing. The influential theory of **cognitive dissonance** states that contradicting or clashing thoughts cause discomfort. That is, we have a need for *consistency* in our thoughts, perceptions, and images of ourselves (Cooper, Mirabile, & Scher, 2005; Festinger, 1957).

What happens if people act in ways that are inconsistent with their attitudes or self-images? Typically the contradiction makes them uncomfortable. Such discomfort can motivate people to make their thoughts or attitudes agree with their actions (Tavris & Aronson, 2007). For example, smokers are told on every pack that cigarettes endanger their lives. They light up and smoke anyway. How do they resolve the tension between this information and their actions? They could quit smoking, but it may be easier to convince themselves that smoking is not really so dangerous. To do this, many smokers seek examples of heavy smokers who have lived long lives, they spend their time with other smokers, and they avoid information about the link between smoking and cancer. According to cognitive dissonance theory, we also tend to reject new information that contradicts ideas we already hold. We're all guilty of this "don't bother me with the facts, my mind is made up" strategy at times.

Now recall Mrs. Keech and her doomsday group. Why did their belief in Mrs. Keech's messages *increase* after the world failed to end? Why did the group suddenly become interested in convincing others that they were right? Cognitive dissonance theory explains that after publicly committing themselves to their beliefs, they had a strong need to maintain consistency (Tavris & Aronson, 2007). In effect, convincing others was a way of adding proof that they were correct (■ Table 15.3).

Acting contrary to one's attitudes doesn't always bring about change. How does cognitive dissonance explain that? The amount of justification for acting contrary to your attitudes and beliefs affects how much dissonance you feel. (*Justification* is the degree to which a person's actions are explained by rewards or other circumstances.) In a classic study, college students did an extremely boring task (turning wooden pegs on a board) for a *long* time. Afterward, they were asked to help lure others into the experiment by pretending that the task was interesting and enjoyable. Students paid $20 for lying to others did not change their own negative opinion of the task: "That was *really* boring!" Those who were paid only $1 later rated the task as "pleasant" and "interesting." How can we explain these results? Apparently, students paid $20

TABLE 15.3 Strategies for Reducing Cognitive Dissonance

Celia, who is a college student, has always thought of herself as an environmental activist. Recently, Celia "inherited" a car from her parents, who were replacing the family "barge." In the past, Celia biked or used public transportation to get around. Her parents' old car is an antiquated gas-guzzler, but she has begun to drive it every day. How might Celia reduce the cognitive dissonance created by the clash between her environmentalism and her use of an inefficient automobile?

STRATEGY	EXAMPLE
Change your attitude	"Cars are not really a major environmental problem."
Add consonant thoughts	"This is an old car, so keeping it on the road makes good use of the resources consumed when it was manufactured."
Change the importance of the dissonant thoughts	"It's more important for me to support the environmental movement politically than it is to worry about how I get to school and work."
Reduce the amount of perceived choice	"My schedule has become too hectic. I really can't afford to bike or take the bus anymore."
Change your behavior	"I'm only going to use the car when it's impossible to bike or take the bus."

Source: Adapted from Franzoi, 2002.

experienced no dissonance. These students could reassure themselves that anybody would tell a little white lie for $20. Those paid $1 were faced with the conflicting thoughts: "I lied" and " I had no good reason to do it." Rather than admit to themselves that they had lied, these students changed their attitude toward what they had done (Festinger & Carlsmith, 1959). (See ● Fig. 15.9.)

We are especially likely to experience dissonance after we cause an event to occur that we wish hadn't taken place. Let's

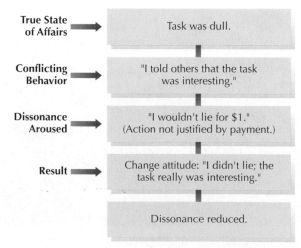

● **FIGURE 15.9** Summary of the Festinger and Carlsmith (1959) study from the viewpoint of a person experiencing cognitive dissonance.

say that you agree to help a friend move to a new apartment. The big day arrives and you feel like staying in bed. Actually, you wish you had never promised to help. To reduce dissonance, you may convince yourself that the work will actually be "good exercise," "sort of fun," or that your friend really deserves the help. We often make such adjustments in attitudes to minimize cognitive dissonance.

Before we leave the topic of attitudes, let's see what psychologists have learned about brainwashing and other high-pressure attempts to change attitudes.

Forced Attitude Change— Brainwashing and Cults

SURVEY QUESTIONS: *Is brainwashing actually possible? How are people converted to cult membership?*

If you're a history enthusiast, you may associate *brainwashing* with techniques used by the Communist Chinese on prisoners during the Korean War (Jowett, 2006). Through various types of "thought reform," the Chinese were able to coerce some of these prisoners to sign false confessions. More recently, the mass murder/suicide at Jonestown, the Branch Davidian tragedy at Waco, the Heaven's Gate group suicide in San Diego, and Osama bin Laden's al-Qaeda movement have heightened public interest in forced attitude change.

How does it differ from other persuasive techniques? Brainwashing, or forced attitude change, requires a captive audience. If you are offended by a television commercial, you can tune it out. Prisoners in POW camps are completely at the mercy of their captors. Complete control over the environment allows a degree of psychological manipulation that would be impossible in a normal setting.

Brainwashing

How does captivity facilitate persuasion? Brainwashing typically begins by making the target person feel completely helpless. Physical and psychological abuse, lack of sleep, humiliation, and isolation serve to *unfreeze*, or loosen, former values and beliefs. When exhaustion, pressure, and fear become unbearable, *change* occurs as the person begins to abandon former beliefs. Prisoners who reach the breaking point may sign a false confession or cooperate to gain relief. When they do, they are suddenly rewarded with praise, privileges, food, or rest. From that point on, a mixture of hope and fear, plus pressures to conform, serves to *refreeze* (solidify) new attitudes (Taylor, 2004).

How permanent are changes caused by brainwashing? In most cases, the dramatic shift in attitudes brought about by brainwashing is temporary. Most "converted" prisoners who returned to the United States after the Korean War eventually reverted to their original beliefs. Nevertheless, brainwashing can be powerful, as shown by the success of cults in recruiting new members.

Cults

Exhorted by their leader, some 900 members of the Reverend Jim Jones's People's Temple picked up paper cups and drank purple Kool-Aid laced with the deadly poison cyanide. Psychologically the mass suicide at Jonestown in 1978 is not so incredible as it might seem (Dein & Littlewood, 2005). The inhabitants of Jonestown were isolated in the jungles of Guyana, intimidated by guards, and lulled with sedatives. They were also cut off from friends and relatives and totally accustomed to obeying rigid rules of conduct, which primed them for Jones's final "loyalty test." Of greater psychological interest is the question of how people reach such a state of commitment and dependency.

Why do people join groups such as the People's Temple? The People's Temple was a classic example of a *cult*. A *cult* is an authoritarian group in which the leader's personality is more important than the beliefs she or he preaches. Cult members give their allegiance to this person, who is regarded as infallible, and they follow his or her dictates without question. Almost always, cult members are victimized by their leaders in one way or another. For example, in April 1993, David Koresh and members of his Branch Davidian group perished in a fire at their Waco, Texas, compound. Like Jim Jones had done years before in Jonestown, Koresh took nearly total control of his followers' lives. He told them what to eat, dictated sexual mores, and had errant followers paddled. Followers were persuaded to surrender money, property, and even their children and wives. Like Jones, Koresh also took mistresses and had children out of wedlock. And like other cult leaders, Jones and Koresh demanded absolute loyalty and obedience to themselves and to their cult, with tragic results (Dein & Littlewood, 2005; Reiterman, 1993).

Psychologist and pioneering brainwashing expert Margaret Singer (1921–2003) studied and aided hundreds of former cult members. Her interviews reveal that in recruiting new members, cults use a powerful blend of guilt, manipulation, isolation, deception, fear, and escalating commitment. In this respect, cults employ high-pressure indoctrination techniques not unlike those used in brainwashing (Singer, 2003; Singer & Addis, 1992). In the United States alone, an estimated 2 to 5 million people have succumbed to the lure of cults (Robinson, Frye, & Bradley, 1997).

Cognitive dissonance An uncomfortable clash between self-image, thoughts, beliefs, attitudes, or perceptions and one's behavior.

In April 1993, David Koresh and members of his Branch Davidian group perished in an inferno at their Waco, Texas, compound. Authorities believe the fire was set by a cult member, under the direction of Koresh. Like Jim Jones had done years before in Jonestown, Koresh took nearly total control of his followers' lives. He told them what to eat, dictated sexual mores, and directed the paddling of errant followers. Followers were persuaded to surrender money, property, and even their children and wives. Like Jones, Koresh also took mistresses and had children out of wedlock. Like other cult leaders, Jones and Koresh demanded absolute loyalty and obedience, with tragic results.

Recruitment Some people studied by Singer were seriously distressed when they joined a cult. Most, however, were simply undergoing a period of mild depression, indecision, or alienation from family and friends (Hunter, 1998). Cult members try to catch potential converts at a time of need—especially when a sense of belonging will be attractive to converts. For instance, many people were approached just after a romance had broken up, or when they were struggling with exams, or were trying to become independent from their families (Sirkin, 1990). At such times, people are easily persuaded that joining the group is all they need to do to be happy again (Hunter, 1998). Adolescents are especially vulnerable to recruitment into cults because they may be seeking a cause to conform to as a replacement for the parental authority they are rebelling against (Richmond, 2004).

Conversion *How is conversion achieved?* Often it begins with intense displays of affection and understanding ("love bombing"). Next comes isolation from non–cult members and drills, discipline, and rituals (all-night meditation or continuous chanting, for instance). These rituals wear down physical and emotional resistance, discourage critical thinking, and generate feelings of commitment (Langone, 2002).

Many cults make clever use of the foot-in-the-door technique described earlier. At first, recruits make small commitments (to stay after a meeting, for example). Then, larger commitments are encouraged (to stay an extra day, to call in sick at work, and so forth). Making a major commitment is usually the final step. The new devotee signs over a bank account or property to the group, moves in with the group, and

so forth. Making such major public commitments creates a powerful cognitive dissonance effect. Before long, it becomes virtually impossible for converts to admit they have made a mistake.

Once in the group, members are cut off from family and friends (former reference groups) and the cult can control the flow and interpretation of information to them. Members are isolated from their former value systems and social structures. Conversion is complete when they come to think of themselves more as group members than as individuals. At this point obedience is nearly total (Wexler, 1995).

Implications Behind the "throne" from which Jim Jones ruled Jonestown was a sign bearing these words: "Those who do not remember the past are condemned to repeat it." Sadly, another cult-related tragedy occurred in 2001. The terrorist attacks on the United States were carried out by followers of cult leader Osama bin Laden. At his direction, they learned hatred and contempt for everyone outside their band of true believers. If there is a lesson to be learned from such destructive cults, it is this: All true spiritual leaders have taught love and compassion. They also encourage followers to question their beliefs and to reach their own conclusions about how to live. In contrast, destructive cults show that it is dangerous to trade personal independence and critical thinking for security (Goldberg, 2001).

Aftermath of the mass suicide at Jonestown. How do cult-like groups recruit new devotees?

MODULE 15.4 Summary

How are attitudes acquired and changed?

- Attitudes are made up of a belief component, an emotional component, and an action component.
- Attitudes held with conviction are most likely to affect our behavior.
- Attitudes may be formed by direct contact, interaction with others, child-rearing practices, group pressures, peer group influences, reference group membership, the mass media, and chance conditioning.

Under what conditions is persuasion most effective?

- Effective persuasion must take into account characteristics of the communicator, the message, and the audience.

- In general, a likable and believable communicator who repeats a credible message that arouses emotion in the audience and states clear-cut conclusions will be persuasive.
- Cognitive dissonance theory explains many aspects of attitude change.

Is brainwashing actually possible? How are people converted to cult membership?

- Brainwashing is a form of forced attitude change. It depends on control of the target person's environment.
- Three steps in brainwashing are unfreezing, changing, and refreezing attitudes and beliefs.
- Many cults recruit new members with high-pressure indoctrination techniques.

KNOWLEDGE BUILDER

Attitudes and Persuasion

Recite

1. Attitudes have three parts:
   a ___emotional___ component,
   an ___behavioral belief___ component,
   and an ___cognitive action___ component.

2. Which of the following is associated with attitude formation?
   a. group membership
   b. mass media
   c. chance conditioning
   d. child rearing
   e. all of the preceding
   f. a and d only

3. If you are trying to persuade a well-informed audience, it is usually best to present
   a. one side of the argument
   b. both sides of the argument
   c. the unfreezing, change, refreezing cycle
   d. negative sanctions

4. The amount of cognitive dissonance a person feels is related to how much _____ exists for his or her actions.
   a. reciprocity
   b. justification

   c. chance conditioning
   d. reference

5. Brainwashing differs from other persuasive attempts in that brainwashing requires a ___captive audience___.

6. Cult members are almost always victimized by their leaders in one way or another.
   T or F? ___true.___

Reflect
Critical Thinking

7. Students entering a college gym are asked to sign a banner promoting water conservation. Later, the students shower at the gym. What effect would you expect signing the banner to have on how long students stay in the showers?

8. Cognitive dissonance theory predicts that false confessions obtained during brainwashing are not likely to bring about lasting changes in attitudes. Why?

Relate

Describe an attitude that is important to you. What are its three components?

Which of the various sources of attitudes best explain your own attitudes?

Who belongs to your most important reference group?

Imagine that you would like to persuade voters to support an initiative to preserve a small wilderness area by converting it to a park. Using research on persuasion as a guide, what could you do to be more effective?

How would you explain cognitive dissonance theory to a person who knows nothing about it?

Link

Internet addresses frequently change. To find the sites listed here, visit **http://www.thomsonedu.com/psychology/coon** for an updated list of Internet addresses and direct links to relevant sites.

- **General Persuasion Techniques** Explore a variety of persuasion techniques.
- **Cognitive Dissonance** Read an original article by Festinger and Carlsmith.
- **Heaven's Gate** Read more about the Heaven's Gate cult.

ANSWERS

1. belief, emotional, action 2. e 3. b 4. b 5. captive audience 6. T 7. Cognitive dissonance theory predicts that students who sign the banner will take shorter showers to be consistent with their publicly expressed support of water conservation. This is exactly the result observed in a study done by social psychologist Elliot Aronson. 8. Because there is strong justification for such actions. As a result, little cognitive dissonance is created when a prisoner makes statements that contradict his or her beliefs.

15.5 Prejudice and Intergroup Conflict

LOVE AND FRIENDSHIP bind people together. Prejudice, which is marked by suspicion, fear, or hatred, has the opposite effect. Prejudice is an all too common part of daily life. What are the origins of prejudice? How can prejudice and hurtful attitudes be reduced?

Prejudice—Attitudes That Injure

SURVEY QUESTION: *What causes prejudice and intergroup conflict?*

Prejudice is a negative emotional attitude held toward members of a specific social group. Prejudices may be reflected in the policies of police departments, schools, or government institutions (Dovidio, Glick, & Rudman, 2005). In such cases, prejudice is referred to as *racism, sexism, ageism,* or *heterosexism,* depending on the group affected. Because it is so prevalent and damaging, let's focus on racism.

Both racial prejudice and racism lead to **discrimination,** or unequal treatment of people who should have the same rights as others. Discrimination prevents people from doing things they should be able to do, such as buying a house, getting a job, voting, or attending a high-quality school. For example, in many cities, African-American drivers have been the target of "racial profiling" in which they are stopped by police without reason. Sometimes they are merely questioned, but many are cited for minor infractions, such as a cracked taillight or an illegal lane change. For many law-abiding citizens, being detained in this manner is a rude awakening (Plous, 2003). It's also one reason why many blacks and other persons of color in America distrust police and the legal system (Dovido et al., 2002).

Becoming Prejudiced

How do prejudices develop? One major theory suggests that prejudice is a form of *scapegoating* (blaming a person or a group for the actions of others or for conditions not of their making). Scapegoating, you may recall, is a type of *displaced aggression* in which hostilities triggered by frustration are redirected at "safer" targets (Nelson, 2006). One interesting classic test of this hypothesis was conducted at a summer camp for young men. The men were given a difficult test they were sure to fail. Additionally, completing the test caused them to miss a trip to the movies, which was normally the high point of their weekly entertainment. Attitudes toward Mexicans and Japanese were measured before the test and after the men had failed the test and missed the movie. Sub-

jects in this study, all European Americans, consistently rated members of the two ethnic groups lower after being frustrated (Miller & Bugelski, 1970). This effect has been easy to observe since the September 11, 2001, terrorist attacks in the United States, when people who looked "foreign" became targets for displaced anger and hostility.

At times, the development of prejudice (like other attitudes) can be traced to direct experiences with members of the rejected group. A child who is repeatedly bullied by members of a particular ethnic group might develop a lifelong dislike for all members of the group. Yet even subtle influences, such as parents' attitudes, the depiction of people in books and on TV, and exposure to children of other races can have an impact. By the time they are 3 years old, many children show signs of race bias (Katz, 2003). Sadly, once prejudices are established, they prevent us from accepting more positive experiences that could reverse the damage (Wilder, Simon, & Faith, 1996).

Distinguished psychologist Gordon Allport (1958) concluded that there are two important sources of prejudice. *Personal prejudice* occurs when members of another ethnic group are perceived as a threat to one's own interests. For example, members of another group may be viewed as competitors for jobs. *Group prejudice* occurs when a person conforms to group norms. Let's say, for instance, that you have no personal reason for disliking out-group members. Nevertheless, your friends, acquaintances, or co-workers expect it of you.

The Prejudiced Personality

Other research suggests that prejudice can be a general personality characteristic. Theodore Adorno and his associates (1950) carefully probed what they called the *authoritarian personality* (ah-thor-ih-TARE-ee-un). These researchers started out by studying anti-Semitism. In the process, they found that people who are prejudiced against one group tend to be prejudiced against *all* out-groups (Perreault & Bourhis, 1999).

What are the characteristics of the prejudice-prone personality? The **authoritarian personality** is marked by rigidity, inhibition, prejudice, and oversimplification (black-and-white thinking). Authoritarians also tend to highly value social conformity (Feldman, 2003) and hence to be very *ethnocentric.* **Ethnocentrism** refers to placing one's own group "at the center," usually by rejecting all other groups. Put more simply, authoritarians consider their own ethnic group superior to others. In fact, authoritarians think they are superior to everyone who is different, not just other ethnic groups (Altemeyer, 2004; Whitley, 1999).

In addition to rejecting out-groups, authoritarians are overwhelmingly concerned with power, authority, and obedience. To measure these qualities, the *F scale* was created (the *F* stands for "fascism"). This scale is made up of statements such as the ones that follow—to which authoritarians readily agree (Adorno et al., 1950).

Authoritarian Beliefs
- Obedience and respect for authority are the most important virtues children should learn.
- People can be divided into two distinct classes: the weak and the strong.
- If people would talk less and work more, everybody would be better off.
- What this country needs most, more than laws and political programs, is a few courageous, tireless, devoted leaders, in whom the people can put their faith.
- Nobody ever learns anything really important except through suffering.
- Every person should have complete faith in some supernatural power whose decisions are obeyed without question.
- Certain religious sects that refuse to salute the flag should be forced to conform to such patriotic action or else be abolished.

As you can see, authoritarians are rather close-minded (Butler, 2000). As children, authoritarians were usually severely punished. Most learned to fear authority (and to covet it) at an early age. Authoritarians are not happy people.

Even if we discount the obvious bigotry of the authoritarian personality, racial prejudice runs deep in many nations. Let's probe deeper into the roots of such prejudiced behavior.

Intergroup Conflict—The Roots of Prejudice

An unfortunate by-product of group membership is that it often limits contact with people in other groups. Additionally, groups themselves may come into conflict. Both events tend to foster hatred and prejudice toward the out-group. The bloody clash of opposing forces in Israel, Ireland, Iraq, Africa, and Hometown, U.S.A., are reminders that intergroup conflict is widespread. Daily, we read of jarring strife between political, religious, or ethnic groups.

Shared beliefs concerning *superiority, injustice, vulnerability,* and *distrust* are common triggers for hostility between groups. Pick almost any group in conflict with others and you will find people thinking along these lines: "We are special people who are superior to other groups, but we have

Ethnic pride is gradually replacing stereotypes and discrimination. For example, the African-American festival of Kwanzaa, a holiday celebrated late in December, emphasizes commitment to family, community, and African culture. However, despite affirmations of ethnic heritage, the problem of prejudice is far from solved.

been unjustly exploited, wronged, or humiliated [superiority and injustice]. Other groups are a threat to us [vulnerability]. They are dishonest and have repeatedly betrayed us [distrust]. Naturally, we are hostile toward them. They don't deserve our respect or cooperation" (Eidelson & Eidelson, 2003).

In addition to hostile beliefs about other groups, conflicts are almost always amplified by stereotyped images of out group members (Bar-Tal & Labin, 2001).

What exactly is a stereotype? **Social stereotypes** are oversimplified images of people in various groups. There is a good chance that you have stereotyped images of some of the following: African Americans, European Americans, Hispanics, Jews, women, Christians, old people, men, Asian Americans, blue-collar workers, rednecks, politicians, business executives, teenagers, and billionaires. In general, the top three categories on which most stereotypes are based are sex, age, and race (Fiske, 1993; Fiske et al., 2002).

Stereotypes tend to simplify people into "us" and "them" categories. Actually, aside from the fact that they always oversimplify, stereotypes often include a mixture of *positive* or

---

Prejudice A negative emotional attitude held against members of a particular group of people.

Discrimination Treating members of various social groups differently in circumstances where their rights or treatment should be identical.

Authoritarian personality A personality pattern characterized by rigidity, inhibition, prejudice, and an excessive concern with power, authority, and obedience.

Ethnocentrism Placing one's own group or race at the center—that is, tending to reject all other groups but one's own.

Social stereotypes Oversimplified images of the traits of individuals who belong to a particular social group.

● **FIGURE 15.10** Racial stereotypes are common in sports. For example, a study confirmed that many people actually do believe that "white men can't jump." This stereotype implies that black basketball players are naturally superior in athletic ability. White players, in contrast, are falsely perceived as smarter and harder working than black players. Such stereotypes set up expectations that distort the perceptions of fans, coaches, and sportswriters. The resulting misperceptions, in turn, help perpetuate the stereotypes (Stone, Perry, & Darley, 1997).

negative qualities (Fiske et al., 2002) (● Fig. 15.10). ■ Table 15.4 shows stereotyped images of various national and ethnic groups and their changes over a 34-year period. Notice that many of the qualities listed are desirable. Note too, that although the overall trend was a decrease in negative stereotypes, belief in the existence of some negative traits increased.

Even though stereotypes sometimes include positive traits, they are mainly used to control people. When a person is stereotyped, the easiest thing to do is to abide by others' expectations—even if they are demeaning. That's why no one likes to be stereotyped. Being forced into a small, distorted social "box" is limiting and insulting. Stereotypes rob people of their individuality (Maddox, 2004). Without stereotypes there would be far less hate, prejudice, exclusion, and conflict. (For a discussion of extreme stereotyping, see "Terrorists, Enemies, and Infidels.")

When a prejudiced person meets a pleasant or likable member of a rejected group, the out-group member tends to be perceived as "an exception to the rule," not as evidence against the stereotype. This prevents prejudiced persons from changing their stereotyped beliefs (Wilder, Simon, & Faith, 1996). In addition, some elements of prejudice are unconscious, which makes them difficult to change (Dovido et al., 2002).

■ **TABLE 15.4** University Students' Characterization of Ethnic Groups, 1933 and 1967

Trait	1933	1967	Trait	1933	1967	Trait	1933	1967
Americans			**Italians**			**Jews**		
Industrious	48	23	Artistic	53	30	Shrewd	79	30
Intelligent	47	20	Impulsive	44	28	Mercenary	49	15
Materialistic	33	67	Musical	32	9	Grasping	34	17
Progressive	27	17	Imaginative	30	7	Intelligent	29	37
Germans			**Irish**			**Blacks**		
Scientific	78	47	Pugnacious	45	13	Superstitious	84	13
Stolid	44	9	Witty	38	7	Lazy	75	26
Methodical	31	21	Honest	32	17	Ignorant	38	11
Efficient	16	46	Nationalistic	21	41	Religious	24	8

Source: M. Karlins, T. L. Coffman, and G. Walters, "On the fading of social stereotypes. Studies in three generations of college students," *Journal of Personality and Social Psychology* 13 (1969):116. Reprinted with permission of the American Psychological Association.

CRITICAL THINKING

Terrorists, Enemies, and Infidels

During times of war, normal people are called upon to kill other humans. How do they turn off their emotions and moral standards? Actually, they don't. Instead, they convince themselves that their actions are just. For example, violence may be seen as necessary to eradicate evil; to serve God; or to protect honor, virtue, justice, or freedom.

Whether it's Catholics and Protestants in Northern Ireland, Israelis and Palestinians, Serbs and Muslims in Bosnia, or al-Qaeda and the United States, each side believes that attack or counterattack is morally justified. And, whether they are right or wrong, both sides use the same psychological mechanisms to justify violence (Wilmot & Hocker, 2007). In violent conflicts between groups, "the enemy" is always portrayed as evil, monstrous, or less than human. Dehumanizing others makes it seem that they *deserve* hatred and even death. Undoubtedly, this provides a degree of emotional insulation that makes it easier for soldiers to harm other humans. However, it also makes terrorism, torture, murder, and genocide possible (Anderson & Bushman, 2002).

A danger in demonizing "the enemy" is that it can lead to misperceptions of the motives and actions of other nations or groups (Silverstein, 1989). Many of the bloodiest conflicts in history have been fueled, in part, by treating "the enemy" as evil and subhuman. Those who actually do hold the moral high ground must be careful not to succumb to the same kind of blind hatred that leads to wanton violence and terrorism. It is also wise to remember that ethnic jokes, racial stereotypes, degrading names, and out-group slurs are small-scale examples of the damage that "enemy" images can do.

Today's racism is often disguised by **symbolic prejudice.** That is, many people realize that crude and obvious racism is socially unacceptable. However, this may not stop them from expressing prejudice in thinly veiled forms when they state their opinions about affirmative action, busing, immigration, crime, and so on. In effect, modern racists find ways to rationalize their prejudice so that it seems to be based on issues other than raw racism. For instance, an African-American candidate and an European-American candidate apply for a job. Both are only moderately qualified for the position. If the person making the hiring decision is European-American, who gets the job? As you might guess, the European-American candidate is much more likely to be hired. In other words, the European-American candidate will be given "the benefit of the doubt" about his or her abilities, whereas the African-American candidate won't. People making such decisions often believe that they aren't being prejudiced, but they unconsciously discriminate against minorities (Dovido et al., 2002).

Two experiments, both in unlikely settings and both using children, offer some additional insights into how stereotypes and intergroup tensions develop.

Experiments in Prejudice

elementary school experiment

What is it like to be discriminated against? In a unique experiment, elementary school teacher Jane Elliot sought to give her pupils direct experience with prejudice. On the first day of the experiment, Elliot announced that brown-eyed children were to sit in the back of the room and that they could not use the drinking fountain. Blue-eyed children were given extra recess time and got to leave first for lunch. At lunch, brown-eyed children were prevented from taking second helpings because they would "just waste it." Brown-eyed and blue-eyed children were kept from mingling, and the blue-eyed children were told they were "cleaner" and "smarter" (Peters, 1971).

Eye color might seem like a trivial basis for creating prejudices. However, people primarily use skin color to make decisions about the race of another person (Brown, Dane, & Durham, 1998). Surely this is just as superficial a way of judging people as eye color is, especially given recent biological evidence that it does not even make genetic sense to talk about "races" (Bonham, Warshauer-Baker, & Collins, 2005). (See "Understand That Race Is a Social Construction" in Module 15.7.)

At first, Elliot made an effort to constantly criticize and belittle the brown-eyed children. To her surprise, the blue-eyed children rapidly joined in and were soon outdoing her in the viciousness of their attacks. The blue-eyed children began to feel superior, and the brown-eyed children felt just plain awful. Fights broke out. Test scores of the brown-eyed children fell.

How lasting were the effects of this experiment? The effects were short lived, because two days later the children's roles were reversed. Before long, the same destructive effects occurred again, but this time in reverse. The implications of this experiment are unmistakable. In less than one day it was possible to get children to hate each other because of eye color

Symbolic prejudice Prejudice that is expressed in disguised fashion.

based on eye color!

CRITICAL THINKING

Is America Purple?

As research shows, it is easy to create prejudice. Pick any simplistic way to divide a group of people into "us" and "them" and popularize it. That's what teacher Jane Elliott did when she divided her class into the brown-eyed kids and the blue-eyed kids. In no time at all, the groups were prejudiced against each other.

But that was just an experiment. It couldn't happen in the real world, right? According to psychologists Conor Seyle and Matthew Newman (2006), we are witnessing just such a real-world example in America today. In order to graphically convey the outcome of the presidential vote in the 2000 election, *USA Today* created a state-by-state map, color coded red and blue to denote states that had voted for the Republican candidate or the Democratic candidate.

Just a few years later, "red" and "blue" have become a national shorthand for dividing Americans into opposing camps. The "reds" are supposed to be Republican, conservative, middle-class, rural, religious, and live in the American heartland. The "blues" are supposed to be Democrat, liberal, upper class, urban, nonreligious, and live on the coasts. The end result is that the complex American social world is reduced to two oversimplified stereotypes, leading to an increase in between-group prejudice (Mundy, 2004).

This oversimplification ignores the fact that, in many states, the presidential votes are very close. Thus, a state that is "red" by 51 percent is nevertheless 49 percent "blue." Besides, many different combinations exist. Former President Bill Clinton is originally from Arkansas (a "red" state), identifies himself as a Southern Baptist, and worships in a Methodist church. Is he "blue"? How do you categorize someone from California (a "blue" state) who is an economic conservative, attends church occasionally, lives in San Francisco, supports gay marriage, and yet votes Republican?

According to Seyle & Newman (2006), a better approach is to recognize that America is made up of a full spectrum of political, social, religious, and economic views and that most Americans are "purple." Thinking this way also highlights the fact that Americans of all political persuasions share more similarities than they do differences when compared with the citizens of other countries. This more tolerant, less polarizing view of America is reflected in the "purple America" map (● Fig. 15.11) (Gastner, Shalizi, & Newman, 2005). Thinking purple just might result in a more productive national discussion about the important issues facing America today.

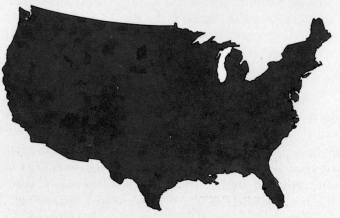

● **FIGURE 15.11** Purple America map. Counties within states voting more than 70 percent Republican appear in red; areas voting more than 70 percent Democratic appear in blue. Shades of purple represent intermediate percentages of voters. (Reprinted by permission of the authors, Michael Gastner, Cosma Shalizi, and Mark Newman, University of Michigan.)

and *status inequalities* (differences in power, prestige, or privileges). Certainly the effects of a lifetime of real racial or ethnic prejudice are infinitely more powerful and destructive (Clark et al., 1999). (See "Is America Purple?")

Equal-Status Contact *What can be done to combat prejudice?* Several lines of thought (including cognitive dissonance theory) suggest that more frequent *equal-status contact* between groups in conflict should reduce prejudice and stereotyping (Olson & Zanna, 1993; Wernet et al., 2003). *Equal-status contact* refers to interacting on an equal footing, without obvious differences in power or status. In various studies, mixed-race groups have been formed at work, in the laboratory, and at schools. The conclusion from such research is that personal contact with a disliked group tends to induce friendly behavior, respect, and liking. However, these benefits occur only when personal contact is cooperative and on an equal footing (Grack & Richman, 1996).

Superordinate Goals Let us now consider a revealing study done with 11-year-old boys. When the boys arrived at a summer camp, they were split into two groups and housed in separate cabins. At first the groups were kept apart to build up separate in-group identities and friendships. Soon each group had a flag and a name (the "Rattlers" and the "Eagles") and each had staked out its territory. At this point the two groups were placed in competition with each other. After a number of clashes, disliking between the groups bordered on hatred: The boys baited each other, started fights, and raided each other's cabins (Sherif et al., 1961).

Were they allowed to go home hating each other? As an experiment in reducing intergroup conflict, and to prevent the boys from remaining enemies, various strategies to reduce tensions were tried. Holding meetings between group leaders did nothing. When the groups were invited to eat together, the event turned into a free-for-all. Finally, emergencies that required *cooperation* among members of both groups were

Mary Kate Kenny/PhotoEdit

Many school districts in the United States have begun requiring students to wear uniforms. Appearance (including gang colors) is one of the major reasons why kids treat each other differently. Uniforms help minimize status inequalities and in-group/out-group distinctions. In Long Beach, California, a switch to uniforms was followed by a 91 percent drop in student assaults, thefts, vandalism, and weapons and drug violations (Ritter, 1998).

staged at the camp. For example, the water supply was damaged so that all the boys had to work together to repair it. Creating this and other *superordinate goals* helped restore peace between the two groups. (A **superordinate goal** exceeds or overrides other lesser goals.)

Cooperation and shared goals seem to help reduce conflict by encouraging people in opposing groups to see themselves as members of a single, larger group (Gaertner et al., 2000). Superordinate goals, in other words, have a "we're all in the same boat" effect on perceptions of group membership (Olson & Zanna, 1993). The power of superordinate goals can be seen in the unity that prevailed in the United States (and throughout much of the rest of the world) for months after the September 11 terrorist attacks. Superordinate goals are also an important factor in helping peacekeepers constructively engage with people from other nationalities (Boniecki & Britt, 2003).

Can such goals exist on a global scale? One example might be a desire to avoid nuclear holocaust. Another that comes to mind is the need to preserve the natural environment on a global scale. Still another is the continuing threat posed by terrorism and religious extremism. Politically, such goals may be far from universal. But their superordinate quality is clearly evident.

"Jigsaw" Classrooms Contrary to the hopes of many, integrating public schools often has little positive effect on racial prejudice. In fact, prejudice may be made worse, and the self-esteem of minority students frequently decreases (Aronson, 2008).

If integrated schools provide equal-status contact, shouldn't prejudice be reduced? Theoretically, yes. But in practice, minority group children often enter schools unprepared to compete on an equal footing. The competitive nature of schools almost guarantees that children will *not* learn to like and understand each other.

With the preceding in mind, social psychologist Elliot Aronson pioneered a way to apply superordinate goals to ordinary classrooms. According to Aronson, such goals are effective because they create **mutual interdependence.** That is, people must depend on one another to meet each person's goals. When individual needs are linked, cooperation is encouraged (Deutsch, 1993).

How has that idea been applied? Aronson has successfully created "jigsaw" classrooms that emphasize cooperation rather than competition. The term *jigsaw* refers to the pieces of a jigsaw puzzle. In a **jigsaw classroom,** each child is given a "piece" of the information needed to complete a project or prepare for a test.

In a typical session, children are divided into groups of five or six and given a topic to study for a later exam. Each child is given his or her "piece" of information and asked to

Jonathan Nourok/PhotoEdit/PictureQuest

In a "jigsaw" classroom, children help each other prepare for tests. As they teach each other on what they know, the children learn to cooperate and to respect the unique strengths of each individual.

Superordinate goal A goal that exceeds or overrides all others; a goal that renders other goals relatively less important.

Mutual interdependence A condition in which people must depend on one another to meet each person's needs or goals.

Jigsaw classroom A method of reducing prejudice; each student receives only part of the information needed to complete a project or prepare for a test.

learn it. For example, one child might have information on Thomas Edison's invention of the lightbulb; another, facts about his invention of the long-playing phonograph record; and a third, information about Edison's childhood. After the children have learned their parts, they teach them to others in the group. Even the most competitive children quickly realize that they cannot do well without the aid of everyone in the group. Each child makes a unique and essential contribution, so the children learn to listen to and respect each other.

Does the jigsaw method work? Compared with children in traditional classrooms, children in jigsaw groups are less prejudiced, they like their classmates more, they have more positive attitudes toward school, their grades improve, and their self-esteem increases (Aronson, 2008; Walker & Crogan, 1998). Such results are quite encouraging. As distinguished African-American psychologist Kenneth Clark said, "Racial prejudice . . . debases all human beings—those who are its victims, those who victimize, and in quite subtle ways, those who are merely accessories."

To summarize, prejudice will be reduced when:

- Members of different groups have equal status *within the situation* that brings them together.
- Members of all groups seek a common goal.
- Group members must cooperate to reach the goal.
- Group members spend enough time together for cross-group friendships to develop (Pettigrew, 1998).

Sports teams are an excellent example of a situation in which all these conditions apply. The close contact and interdependent effort required in team sports often create lifelong friendships and break down the walls of prejudice.

MODULE 15.5 Summary

What causes prejudice and intergroup conflict?

- Prejudice is a negative attitude held toward members of various out-groups.
- One theory attributes prejudice to scapegoating.
- Prejudices may be held for personal reasons (personal prejudice) or simply through adherence to group norms (group prejudice).
- Prejudiced individuals tend to have an authoritarian personality.
- Intergroup conflict gives rise to hostility and the formation of social stereotypes.
- Status inequalities tend to build prejudice.
- Equal-status contact, mutual interdependence, and superordinate goals tend to reduce prejudice.
- On a smaller scale, jigsaw classrooms have been shown to combat prejudice.

KNOWLEDGE BUILDER

Prejudice and Intergroup Conflict

Recite

1. Some expressions of prejudice can be thought of as scapegoating or
   a. displaced aggression
   b. empathic arousal
   c. reference group reversal
   d. external attribution

2. The authoritarian personality tends to be prejudiced against all out-groups, a quality referred to as ___ethnocentrism___

3. The stereotypes underlying racial and ethnic prejudice tend to evolve from the superordinate goals that often separate groups. T or F? *False*

4. The term *symbolic prejudice* refers to racism or prejudice that is expressed in disguised or hidden form. T or F? *True*

5. One of the reasons that superordinate goals tend to reduce prejudice is that they require cooperation and
   a. social stereotyping
   b. ethnocentrism
   c. unfreezing
   d. equal-status contact

6. Jigsaw classrooms use _____ to create mutual interdependence.
   a. social competition
   b. just-world beliefs
   c. self-fulfilling prophecies
   d. superordinate goals

Reflect
Critical Thinking

7. In court trials, defense lawyers sometimes try to identify and eliminate prospective jurors who have authoritarian personality traits. Can you guess why?

Relate

Mentally scan over the events of the last week. How would they have changed if prejudices of all types ceased to exist?

Think of the most rigid person you know. Does he or she match the profile of the authoritarian personality?

Stereotypes exist for many social categories, even ordinary ones such as "college student" or "unmarried young adult." What stereotypes do you think you face in daily life?

The director of a youth recreation center is concerned about the amount of conflict she is seeing between boys and girls from different racial and ethnic groups. What advice can you give the director?

Link

Internet addresses frequently change. To find the sites listed here, visit **http://www .thomsonedu.com/psychology/coon** for an updated list of Internet addresses and direct links to relevant sites.

- **Understanding Prejudice** Explore different activities that illuminate the causes and consequences of prejudice.

- **Authoritarian Personality** Take the F scale test.

- **Intergroup Conflict** Read an article on intergroup conflict.

ANSWERS

1. a 2. ethnocentrism 3. F 4. T 5. d 6. d 7. Because authoritarians tend to believe that punishment is effective, they are more likely to vote for conviction.

15.6 Aggression and Prosocial Behavior

AGGRESSION IS A HUMAN TRAGEDY. Helping others is a source of hope. It might seem that the horrors of war would lead to a worldwide revulsion for killing. In reality, homicide rates have increased in many countries in recent years. What causes aggression? Can violence be reduced? Can we promote prosocial behavior? More than ever, these are pressing questions.

Aggression—The World's Most Dangerous Animal

SURVEY QUESTION: *How do psychologists explain human aggression?*

> *"I know not with what weapons World War III will be fought, but World War IV will be fought with sticks and stones."*—Albert Einstein

For a time, the City Zoo of Los Angeles, California, had on display two examples of the world's most dangerous animal—the only animal capable of destroying the Earth and all other animal species. Perhaps you have already guessed which animal it was. In the cage were two college students, representing the species *Homo sapiens!*

The human capacity for aggression is staggering. It has been estimated that 58 million humans were killed by other

Ritualized human aggression. Violent and aggressive behavior is so commonplace it may be viewed as entertainment. How "natural" is aggressive behavior?

humans (an average of nearly one person per minute) during the 125-year period ending with World War II. War, homicide, riots, family violence, assassination, rape, assault, forcible robbery, and other violent acts offer sad testimony to the realities of human aggression.

What causes aggression? **Aggression** refers to any action carried out with the intention of harming another person. Aggression has many potential causes. Brief descriptions of some of the major possibilities follow.

Instincts

Some theorists argue that we are naturally aggressive creatures, having inherited a "killer instinct" from our animal ancestors. Ethologists theorize that aggression is a biologically rooted behavior observed in all animals, including humans (Blanchard & Blanchard, 2003). (An *ethologist* is a person who studies the natural behavior patterns of animals.) Noted ethologist Konrad Lorenz (1966, 1974) also believed that humans lack certain innate patterns that inhibit aggression in animals. For example, in a dispute over territory, two wolves may growl, lunge, bare their teeth, and fiercely threaten each other. In most instances, though, neither is killed or even wounded. One wolf, recognizing the dominance of the other, will typically bare its throat in a gesture of submission. The dominant wolf could kill in an instant, but it is inhibited by the other wolf's submissive gesture. In contrast, human confrontations of equal intensity almost always end in injury or death.

The idea that humans are "naturally" aggressive has an intuitive appeal, but many psychologists question it. Many of Lorenz's "explanations" of aggression are little more than loose comparisons between human and animal behavior. Just labeling a behavior as "instinctive" does little to explain it. More important, we are left with the question of why some individuals or human groups (the Arapesh, the Senoi, the Navajo, the Eskimo, and others) show little hostility or aggression. And, thankfully, the vast majority of humans *do not* kill or harm others.

Biology

Despite problems with the instinctive view, aggression may have biological roots. Physiological studies have shown that some brain areas are capable of triggering or ending aggressive behavior. Also, researchers have found a relationship between aggression and such physical factors as hypoglycemia (low blood sugar), allergy, and specific brain injuries and diseases. For both men and women, higher levels of the hormone testosterone may be associated with more aggressive behavior (Banks & Dabbs, 1996; Harris et al., 1996). Perhaps because of their higher testosterone levels, men are more likely to engage in physical aggression than women (Anderson & Bushman, 2002). However, none of these biological factors can be considered a direct *cause* of aggression (Moore, 2001; Popma et al., 2007). Instead, they probably lower the threshold for aggression, making hostile behavior more likely to occur.

The effects of alcohol and other drugs provide another indication of the role of the brain and biology in violence and aggression. A variety of studies show that alcohol is involved in large percentages of murders and violent crimes. Intoxicating drugs also seem to lower inhibitions to act aggressively—often with tragic results (Anderson & Bushman, 2002; Quigley & Leonard, 2000).

To summarize, the fact that we are biologically *capable* of aggression does not mean that aggression is inevitable or "part of human nature." Twenty eminent scientists who studied the question concluded that "Biology does not condemn humanity to war. . . . Violence is neither in our evolutionary legacy nor in our genes. The same species that invented war is capable of inventing peace" (Scott & Ginsburg, 1994; UNESCO, 1990). Humans are fully capable of learning to inhibit aggression. For example, American Quakers and Amish, who live in this country's increasingly violent culture, adopt nonviolence as a way of life (Bandura, 2001).

Frustration

Step on a cat's tail and you may get nipped. Frustrate a human and you may get insulted. The **frustration-aggression hypothesis** states that frustration tends to lead to aggression.

Does frustration always produce aggression? Although the connection is strong, a moment's thought will show that frustration does not *always* lead to aggression. Frustration, for instance, may lead to stereotyped responding or perhaps to a state of "learned helplessness." (See Modules 11.2 and 11.3.) Also, aggression can occur in the absence of frustration. This possibility is illustrated by sports spectators who start fights, throw bottles, and tear down goal posts after their team has *won*.

Aversive Stimuli Frustration probably encourages aggression because it is uncomfortable. Various *aversive stimuli*, which produce discomfort or displeasure, can heighten hostility and aggression (Anderson, Anderson, & Deuser, 1996; Morgan, 2005). (See ● Fig. 15.12.) Examples include insults, high

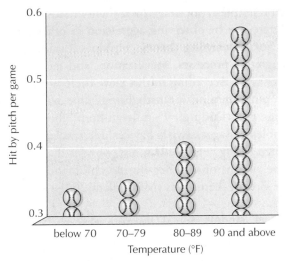

● **FIGURE 15.12** Personal discomfort caused by aversive (unpleasant) stimuli can make aggressive behavior more likely. For example, studies of crime rates show that the incidence of highly aggressive behavior, such as murder, rape, and assault, rises as the air temperature goes from warm to hot to sweltering (Anderson, 1989). The results you see here further confirm the heat-aggression link. The graph shows that there is a strong association between the temperatures at major league baseball games and the number of batters hit by a pitch during those games. When the temperature goes over 90°, watch out for that fastball (Reifman, Larrick, & Fein, 1991)!

Aggression Any action carried out with the intention of harming another person.

Frustration-aggression hypothesis States that frustration tends to lead to aggression.

Road rage and some freeway shootings may be a reaction to the stress and frustration of traffic congestion. The fact that automobiles provide anonymity, or a loss of personal identity, may also encourage aggressive actions that would not otherwise occur.

Harvey Schwartz/Index Stock/PictureQuest

temperatures, pain, and even disgusting scenes or odors. Such stimuli probably raise overall arousal levels so that we become more sensitive to *aggression cues* (signals that are associated with aggression) (Carlson, Marcus-Newhall, & Miller, 1990). Aversive stimuli also tend to activate ideas, memories, and expressions associated with anger and aggression (Morgan, 2005).

Some cues for aggression are internal (angry thoughts, for instance). Many are external: Certain words, actions, and gestures made by others are strongly associated with aggressive responses. A raised middle finger, for instance, is an almost universal invitation to aggression in North America. Weapons serve as particularly strong cues for aggressive behavior (Morgan, 2005). The implication of this *weapons effect* seems to be that the symbols and trappings of aggression encourage aggression. A prime example is the fact that murders are almost 3 times more likely to occur in homes where guns are kept. Nearly 80 percent of the victims in such homes are killed by a family member or acquaintance (Kellermann et al., 1993).

Social Learning

One of the most widely accepted explanations of aggression is also the simplest. Social learning theory holds that we learn to be aggressive by observing aggression in others (Bandura, 1973). **Social learning theory** combines learning principles with cognitive processes, socialization, and modeling to explain behavior. According to this view, there is no instinctive human programming for fistfighting, pipe bombing, knife wielding, gun loading, 95-mile-an-hour "bean balls," or other violent or aggressive behaviors. Hence, aggression must be learned (• Fig. 15.13). Is it any wonder that people who were the victims of violence during childhood are likely to become violent themselves (Macmillan, 2001)?

Aggressive Models Social learning theorists predict that people growing up in nonaggressive cultures will themselves be nonaggressive. Those raised in a culture with aggressive

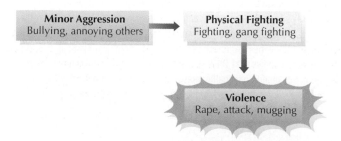

• **FIGURE 15.13** Violent behavior among delinquent boys doesn't appear overnight. Usually, their capacity for violence develops slowly as they move from minor aggression to increasingly brutal acts. Overall aggression increases dramatically in early adolescence as boys gain physical strength and more access to weapons (Loeber & Hay, 1997).

models and heroes will learn aggressive responses (Bandura, 2001). Considered in such terms, it is no wonder that America has become one of the most violent of all countries. A violent crime occurred every 23 seconds in the United States during 2005 (FBI, 2005). Approximately 40 percent of the population owns firearms. Nationally, 70 percent agree that "When a boy is growing up, it is very important for him to have a few fistfights." Children and adults are treated to an almost nonstop parade of aggressive models, in the media as well as in actual behavior. We are, without a doubt, an aggressive culture.

Media Violence Every day, mainstream media provide an endless stream of bad models, especially concerning violence. TV, movies, computer games, and even music lyrics all contain violence. According to the organization Adults and Children Against Violence Together, young children spend about 35 hours a week in front of TV or computer screens. By the end of elementary school, children will have seen about 8,000 murders and 100,000 other violent acts depicted on TV. Eighty percent of popular video games contain violent content. Many popular toys are also linked to violent media (ACT Against Violence, 2005a). And, of course, teenagers and young people are also chronically exposed to violence in the media.

How much does media violence affect children? As Albert Bandura showed in his studies of imitation (see Module 6.5), children may learn new aggressive actions by watching violent or aggressive behavior, or they may learn that violence is "okay." Either way, they are more likely to act aggressively. Heroes on TV are as violent as the villains, and they usually receive praise for their violence. There is now little doubt that widespread exposure to media violence contributes to aggression (Anderson et al., 2003; DeGaetano, 2005). Boys and girls who watch a lot of violence on TV are much more likely to be aggressive as adults (Huesmann et al., 2003). Violent video games are at least as problematic (Bartholow, Bushman, & Sestir, 2006), and even violent song lyrics increase aggressive tendencies (Anderson, Carnagey, & Eubanks, 2003).

In addition to teaching new antisocial actions, media such as TV and video games may disinhibit dangerous impulses that viewers already have. *Disinhibition* (the removal of inhibition) results in acting out behavior that normally would be restrained. For example, many TV programs give the message that violence is acceptable behavior that leads to success and popularity. For some people, this message can lower inhibitions against acting out hostile feelings (Anderson et al., 2003).

Another effect of media violence is that it tends to lower sensitivity to violent acts (Funk, 2005). As anyone who has seen a street fight or a mugging can tell you, TV violence is sanitized and unrealistic. The real thing is gross, ugly, and gut wrenching. Even when media violence is graphic, as it is in many video games, it is experienced in the relaxed and familiar setting of the home. For at least some viewers, this combination diminishes emotional reactions to violent scenes. More than 30 years ago, when Victor Cline and his associates showed a bloody fight film to a group of boys, they found that heavy TV viewers (averaging 42 hours a week) showed much less emotion than those who watched little or no TV (Cline, Croft, & Courrier, 1972). Media, it seems, can cause a *desensitization* (reduced emotional sensitivity) to violence (Huesmann et al., 2003).

Preventing Aggression

What can be done about aggression? Social learning theory implies that "aggression begets aggression." For example, children who are physically abused at home, those who suffer severe physical punishment, and those who merely witness violence in the community are more likely to be involved in fighting, aggressive play, and antisocial behavior at school (Bartholow, Sestir, & Davis, 2005; Margolin & Gordis, 2000).

According to social learning theorists, watching a prizefight, sporting event, or violent TV program may increase aggression, rather than drain off aggressive urges. A case in point is provided by psychologist Leonard Eron, who spent 22 years following more than 600 children into adulthood. Eron (1987) observes, "Among the most influential models for children were those observed on television. One of the best predictors of how aggressive a young man would be at age 19 was the violence of the television programs he preferred when he was 8 years old" (● Fig. 15.14). According to Eron, children learn aggressive strategies and actions from

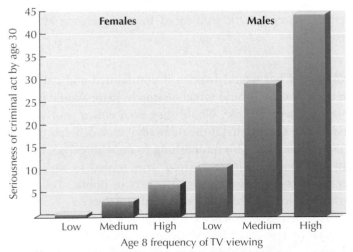

● **FIGURE 15.14** Although TV violence does not cause aggression, it can encourage it. The likelihood of committing criminal acts by age 30 is related to the amount of TV watching a person did when she or he was a child (Eron, 1987). (Graph © 1987 by the American Psychological Association, Inc. Reprinted by permission of the author.)

TV violence. Because of this, they are more prone to aggress when they face frustrating situations or cues. Others have found that viewers who experience violent media have more aggressive thoughts. As we have noted, violent thoughts often precede violent actions (Anderson, Carnagey, & Eubanks, 2003). Thus, the spiral of aggression might be broken if we did not so often portray it, reward it, and glorify it (Hughes & Hasbrouck, 1996).

Parents as TV Guides   As the preceding studies show, reducing exposure to violent media is one way to lower aggression. However, other than pulling the plug, what can parents do about media's negative effects on children? Actually, quite a lot. Parents can make a big difference if they do the following (ACT Against Violence, 2005b; Frydman, 1999).

1. Start by creating a safe, warm environment at home and school and by modeling positive ways of getting along in the world. Children typically model parents' behavior, including their media viewing habits, and they are guided by parents' reactions to media.

2. Limit total media time so that TV and computer games do not dominate your child's view of the world. If necessary, set schedules for when watching TV or playing video games is allowed. Don't use media as a babysitter.

3. Closely monitor what your child does experience. Change channels or turn off the TV if you object to a program. Be prepared to offer games and activities that stimulate your child's imagination and creativity.

4. Actively seek media your child will enjoy, especially those that model positive behavior and social attitudes.

5. Explore media with your child so that you can counter what is shown. Help your child distinguish between reality and fantasy in media. Reply to distortions and stereotypes as they appear on screen.

6. Discuss the social conflicts and violent solutions shown in media. Ask your child in what ways the situations are unrealistic and why the violence shown would not work in the real world. Encourage the child to propose more mature, realistic, and positive responses to situations.

7. Show by your own disapproval that violent TV and computer game heroes are not the ones to emulate. Remember, children who identify with media characters are more likely to be influenced by media aggression.

Social learning theory   Combines learning principles with cognitive processes, socialization, and modeling to explain behavior.

By following these guidelines you can help children learn to enjoy television and other media without being overly influenced by programs and advertisers. One study found that elementary school children become less aggressive when they decrease the amount of time they spend watching TV and playing video games (Robinson et al., 2001).

Beyond this, the question remains, how shall we tame the world's most dangerous animal? There is no easy answer, only a challenge of pressing importance (Lench, 2004). For the immediate future, it is clear that we need more people who are willing to engage in helpful, altruistic, **prosocial behavior** (actions that are constructive, altruistic, or helpful to others). In the next section we will examine some of the forces that prevent people from helping others and how prosocial behavior might be promoted.

Prosocial Behavior—Helping Others

SURVEY QUESTION: *Why are bystanders so often unwilling to help in an emergency?*

Late one night in 1964, tenants of a Queens, New York, apartment building watched and listened in horror as a young woman named Kitty Genovese was murdered on the sidewalk outside. From the safety of their rooms, no fewer than 38 people heard the agonized screams as her assailant stabbed her, was frightened off, and returned to stab her again.

Kitty Genovese's murder took more than 30 minutes, but none of her neighbors tried to help. None even called the police until after the attack had ended. Perhaps it is understandable that no one wanted to get involved. After all, it could have been a violent lovers' quarrel. Or helping might have meant risking personal injury. But what prevented these people from at least calling the police?

Does the person lying on the ground need help? What factors determine whether a person in trouble will receive help in an emergency? Surprisingly, more potential helpers tend to lower the chances that help will be given.

Robert Brenner/PhotoEdit, Inc.

Isn't this an example of the alienation of city life? News reports treated this incident as evidence of a breakdown in social ties caused by the impersonality of the city. Although it is true that urban living can be dehumanizing, this does not fully explain such *bystander apathy* (the unwillingness of bystanders to offer help during emergencies is also referred to as the *bystander effect*). According to landmark work by psychologists John Darley and Bibb Latané (1968), failure to help is related to the number of people present. Over the years many studies have shown that the *more* potential helpers present, the *less* likely people are to help (Latané, Nida, & Wilson, 1981; Miller, 2006).

Why would people be less willing to help when others are present? In Kitty Genovese's case, the answer is that everyone thought *someone else* would help. The dynamics of this effect are easily illustrated: Suppose that two motorists have stalled at roadside, one on a sparsely traveled country road and the other on a busy freeway. Who gets help first?

On the freeway, where hundreds of cars pass every minute, each driver can assume that someone else will help. Personal responsibility for helping is spread so thin that no one takes action. On the country road, one of the first few people to arrive will probably stop, because the responsibility is clearly theirs. In general, Darley and Latané assume that bystanders are not apathetic or uncaring; they are inhibited by the presence of others.

Bystander Intervention

People must pass through four decision points before giving help. First they must notice that something is happening. Next they must define the event as an emergency. Then they must take responsibility. Finally, they must select a course of action (● Fig. 15.15). Laboratory experiments have shown that each step can be influenced by the presence of other people.

Noticing What would happen if you fainted and collapsed on the sidewalk? Would someone stop to help? Would people think you were drunk? Would they even notice you? Darley and Latané suggest that if the sidewalk is crowded, few people will even see you. This has nothing to do with people blocking one another's vision. Instead, it is related to widely accepted norms against staring at others in public. People in crowds typically "keep their eyes to themselves."

Is there any way to show that this is a factor in bystander apathy? To test this idea, students were asked to fill out a questionnaire either alone or in a room full of people. While the students worked, a thick cloud of smoke was blown into the room through a vent.

Most students left alone in the room noticed the smoke immediately. Few of the people in groups noticed the smoke

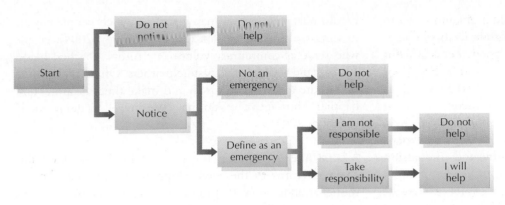

● **FIGURE 15.15** This decision tree summarizes the steps a person must take before making a commitment to offer help, according to Latané and Darley's model.

until it actually became difficult to see through it. Subjects working in groups politely kept their eyes on their papers and avoided looking at others (or the smoke). In contrast, those who were alone scanned the room from time to time.

Defining an Emergency The smoke-filled room also shows the influence others have on defining a situation as an emergency. When subjects in groups finally noticed the smoke, they cast sidelong glances at others in the room. Apparently, they were searching for clues to help interpret what was happening. No one wanted to overreact or act like a fool if there was no emergency. However, as subjects coolly surveyed the reactions of others, they were themselves being watched. In real emergencies, people sometimes "fake each other out" and underestimate the need for action because each person attempts to appear calm. In short, until someone acts, no one acts.

Taking Responsibility Perhaps the most crucial step in helping is assuming responsibility. In this case, groups limit helping by causing a *diffusion of responsibility* (spreading responsibility among several people).

Is that like the unwillingness of drivers to offer help on a crowded freeway? Exactly. It is the feeling that no one is personally responsible for helping. This problem was demonstrated in an experiment in which students took part in a group discussion over an intercom system. Actually, there was only one real subject in each group; the others were taperecorded actors. Each subject was placed in a separate room (supposedly to maintain confidentiality), and discussions of college life were begun. During the discussion, one of the "students" simulated an epileptic-like seizure and called out for help. In some cases, subjects thought they were alone with the seizure victim. Others believed they were members of three- or six-person groups.

Subjects who thought they were alone with the "victim" of this staged emergency reported it immediately or tried to help. Some subjects in the three-person groups failed to respond, and those who did were slower. In the six-person groups, more than a third of the subjects took no action at all. People in this experiment were obviously faced with a

conflict like that in many real emergencies: Should they be helpful and responsible, or should they mind their own business? Many were influenced toward inaction by the presence of others.

People do help in some emergencies. How are these different? It is not always clear what makes the difference. Helping behavior is complex and influenced by many variables. One naturalistic experiment staged in a New York City subway gives a hint of the kinds of things that may be important. When a "victim" (actor) "passed out" in a subway car, he received more help when carrying a cane than when carrying a liquor bottle. More important, however, was the fact that most people were willing to help in either case (Piliavin, Rodin, & Piliavin, 1969).

To better answer the question, we need to consider some factors not included in Darley and Latané's account of helping.

Who Will Help Whom?

Many studies suggest that when we see a person in trouble, it tends to cause *heightened arousal* (Dovidio et al., 2006). This aroused, keyed-up feeling can motivate us to give aid, but only if the rewards of helping outweigh the costs. Higher costs (such as great effort, personal risk, or possible embarrassment) almost always decrease helping. In addition to general arousal, potential helpers may also feel **empathic arousal.** This means they empathize with the person in need or feel some of the person's pain, fear, or anguish. Helping is much more likely when we are able to take the perspective of others and feel sympathy for their plight (Batson & Powell, 2003).

Empathic arousal is especially likely to motivate helping when the person in need seems to be similar to ourselves

Prosocial behavior Behavior toward others that is helpful, constructive, or altruistic.

Empathic arousal Emotional arousal that occurs when you feel some of another person's pain, fear, or anguish.

(Batson & Powell, 2003). In fact, a feeling of connection to the victim may be one of the most important factors in helping. This, perhaps, is why being in a good mood also increases helping. When we are feeling successful, happy, or fortunate, we may also feel more connected to others (Dovidio & Penner, 2001). In summary, there is a strong **empathy-helping relationship:** We are most likely to help someone in need when we "feel for" that person and experience emotions such as empathy, sympathy, and compassion (Batson, 2006).

Is there anything that can be done to encourage prosocial behavior? People who see others helping are more likely to offer help themselves. Also, persons who give help in one situation tend to perceive themselves as helpful people. This change in self-image encourages them to help in other situations. One more point is that norms of fairness encourage us to help others who have helped us (Dovidio & Penner, 2001). For all these reasons, helping others not only assists them directly, it encourages others to help too.

"De-victimize" Yourself If you should find yourself in need of help during an emergency, what can you do to avoid being a victim of bystander apathy? The work we have reviewed here suggests that you should make sure that you are noticed, that people realize there's an emergency, and that they need to take action. Being noticed can be promoted in some situations by shouting "Fire!" Bystanders who might run away from a robbery or an assault may rush to see where the fire is. At the very least, remember not to just scream. Instead, you should call out "Help" or "I need help right now." Whenever possible, define your situation for bystanders. Say, for instance, "I'm being attacked, call the police." Or, "Stop that man, he has my purse." You can also directly assign responsibility to a bystander by pointing to someone and saying, "You, call the police" or "I'm injured, I need you to call an ambulance" (Cummins, 1995).

Positive Psychology: Everyday Heroes

Every year awards are given to people who risk their lives while saving the lives of others. These heroes are typically honored for saving people from fires, drowning, animal attacks, electrocution, and suffocation. The majority of people who perform such heroic acts are men, perhaps because of the physical dangers involved. However, there are other heroic, prosocial acts that save lives and involve personal risk. Examples are kidney donors, Peace Corp volunteers, and Doctors of the World volunteers. In such endeavors, we find as many women as men, and often more. It is important to remember, perhaps, that sensational and highly visible acts of

heroism are only one of many ways in which people engage in selfless, altruistic behavior (Becker & Eagly, 2004). People who serve as community volunteers, tutors, coaches, blood donors, and the like don't just help others. Often, their efforts contribute to personal growth and make them healthier and happier. Thus, it can be said that "We do well by doing good" (Piliavin, 2003).

A Look Ahead The "Psychology in Action" module of this chapter returns to the topic of prejudice for some further thoughts about how to promote tolerance. Don't miss this interesting conclusion to our discussion of social psychology.

MODULE 15.6 Summary

How do psychologists explain human aggression?
- Aggression is a fact of life, but humans are not inevitably aggressive. The same factors that help explain aggression can form the basis for preventing it.
- Ethological explanations of aggression attribute it to inherited instincts.
- Biological explanations of aggression emphasize brain mechanisms and physical factors that lower the threshold for aggression.
- According to the frustration-aggression hypothesis, frustration and aggression are closely linked.
- Frustration is only one of many aversive stimuli that can arouse a person and make aggression more likely.
- Aggression is especially likely to occur when aggression cues are present.
- Social learning theory has focused attention on the role of aggressive models in the development of aggressive behavior.

Why are bystanders so often unwilling to help in an emergency?
- Four decision points must be passed before a person gives help: noticing, defining an emergency, taking responsibility, and selecting a course of action.
- Helping is encouraged by general arousal, empathic arousal, being in a good mood, low effort or risk, and perceived similarity between the victim and the helper.
- Prosocial behavior is most likely to occur when people feel sympathy or empathy for a person in need.
- For several reasons, giving help tends to encourage others to help, too.

KNOWLEDGE BUILDER

Aggression and Prosocial Behavior

Recite

false

1. The position of ethologists is that there is no biological basis for aggression. T or F?

2. Higher levels of testosterone are associated with more aggressive behavior. T or F? *true*

3. The *weapons effect* refers to the impact that _____ have on behavior.
   a. just-world beliefs
   b. aggression cues
   c. self-fulfilling prophecies
   d. televised models

4. The point of view most at odds with the idea that humans are instinctively aggressive is
   a. social learning theory
   b. the frustration-aggression hypothesis
   c. ethology
   d. the aversive stimuli effect

5. Heavy exposure to media results in lowered emotional sensitivity to violence. T or F? *true*

6. People are more likely to help another who is in trouble if
   a. many other helpers are present
   b. a diffusion of responsibility occurs
   c. they experience empathic arousal
   d. desensitization takes place

Reflect
Critical Thinking

7. If media violence contributes to aggressive behavior in our society, do you think it is possible that media could also promote prosocial behavior?

Relate

Most people have been angry enough at some time to behave aggressively. Which concepts or theories do you think best explain your own aggressive actions?

An elderly woman is at the side of the road, trying to change a flat tire. She obviously needs help. You are approaching her in your car. What must happen before you are likely to stop and help her?

Link

Internet addresses frequently change. To find the sites listed here, visit **http://www.thomsonedu.com/psychology/coon** for an updated list of Internet addresses and direct links to relevant sites.

- **Anger Management** Read about anger management.
- **The Frustration-Aggression Hypothesis** Read Neal Miller's original paper on the topic.
- **Media Violence** Explore the debate over media violence.

ANSWERS

1. F 2. T 3. b 4. a 5. T 6. c 7. Yes, media could be used to promote helping, charity, cooperation, and brotherhood in the same way that it has encouraged aggression. Numerous studies show, for example, that prosocial behavior on TV increases prosocial behavior by viewers.

Empathy-helping relationship Observation that we are most likely to help someone else when we feel emotions such as empathy and compassion.

Appendix Behavioral Statistics

MODULE A.1 Descriptive Statistics

SURVEY QUESTION: What are descriptive statistics?

SURVEY QUESTION: How are statistics used to identify an average score?

SURVEY QUESTION: What statistics do psychologists use to measure how much scores differ from one another?

MODULE A.2 Inferential Statistics

SURVEY QUESTION: What are inferential statistics?

SURVEY QUESTION: How are correlations used in psychology?

Statistics from "Heads" to "Tails"

Let's say a friend of yours invites you to try your hand at a "game of chance." He offers to flip a coin and pay you a dollar if the coin comes up heads. If the coin shows tails, you must pay him a dollar. He flips the coin: tails—you pay him a dollar. He flips it again: tails. Again: tails. And again: tails. And again: tails.

At this point you are faced with a choice. Should you continue the game in an attempt to recoup your losses? Or should you assume that the coin is biased and quit before you really get "skinned"? Taking out your trusty pocket calculator (and, of course, the statistics book you carry with you at all times), you compute the odds of obtaining 5 tails in a row from an unbiased coin. The probability is 0.031 (roughly 3 times out of 100).

If the coin really is honest, 5 consecutive tails is a rare event. Wisely, you decide that the coin is probably biased and refuse to play again. (Unless, of course, your "friend" is willing to take "tails" for the next 5 tosses!)

Perhaps a decision could have been made in this hypothetical example without using statistics. But notice how much clearer the situation becomes when it is expressed statistically.

Psychologists try to extract and summarize useful information from the observations they make. To do so, they use two major types of statistics. **Descriptive statistics** summarize or "boil down" numbers so they become more meaningful and easier to communicate to others. In comparison, **inferential statistics** are used for decision making, for generalizing from small samples, and for drawing conclusions. As was the case in the coin-flipping example, psychologists must often base decisions on limited data. Such decisions are much easier to make with the help of inferential statistics. Let's see how statistics are used in psychology.

A.1 Descriptive Statistics

LET'S SAY YOU HAVE COMPLETED A STUDY ON HUMAN BEHAVIOR. The results seem interesting, but can you really tell what your data reveal just by looking at a jumble of numbers? To get a clear picture of how people behaved, you will probably turn to descriptive statistics. By summarizing the results of your study, statistics will help you draw valid conclusions about what you observed.

Descriptive Statistics—Psychology by the Numbers

SURVEY QUESTION: *What are descriptive statistics?*

Statistics bring greater clarity and precision to psychological thought and research (Gravetter & Wallnau, 2007). To see how, let's begin by considering three basic types of descriptive statistics: *graphical statistics,* measures of *central tendency,* and measures of *variability.* Let's start with **graphical statistics,** which present numbers pictorially, so they are easier to visualize.

Graphical Statistics

■ Table A.1 shows simulated scores on a test of hypnotic susceptibility given to 100 college students. With such disorganized data, it is hard to form an overall "picture" of the differences in hypnotic susceptibility. But by using a *frequency distribution,* large amounts of information can be neatly organized and summarized. A **frequency distribution** is made by breaking down the entire range of possible scores into classes of equal size. Next, the number of scores falling into

each class is recorded. In ■ Table A.2, the raw data from Table A.1 have been condensed into a frequency distribution. Notice how much clearer the pattern of scores for the entire group becomes.

Frequency distributions are often shown *graphically* to make them more "visual." A **histogram,** or graph of a frequency distribution, is made by labeling class intervals on the *abscissa* (X axis or horizontal line) and frequencies (the number of scores in each class) on the *ordinate* (Y axis or vertical line). Next, bars are drawn for each class interval; the height of each bar is determined by the number of scores in each class (● Fig. A.1). An alternate way of graphing scores is the more familiar **frequency polygon** (● Fig. A.2). Here, points are placed at the center of each class interval to indicate the number of scores. Then the dots are connected by straight lines.

■ TABLE A.2 Frequency Distribution of Hypnotic Susceptibility Scores

CLASS INTERVAL	NUMBER OF PERSONS IN CLASS
0-19	10
20-39	20
40-59	40
60-79	20
80-99	10

■ TABLE A.1 RAW SCORES OF HYPNOTIC SUSCEPTIBILITY

55	86	52	17	61	57	84	51	16	64
22	56	25	38	35	24	54	26	37	38
52	42	59	26	21	55	40	59	25	57
91	27	38	53	19	93	25	39	52	56
66	14	18	63	59	68	12	19	62	45
47	98	88	72	50	49	96	89	71	66
50	44	71	57	90	53	41	72	56	93
57	38	55	49	87	59	36	56	48	70
33	69	50	50	60	35	67	51	50	52
11	73	46	16	67	13	71	47	25	77

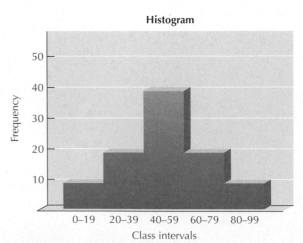

Histogram

● **FIGURE A.1** Frequency histogram of hypnotic susceptibility scores contained in Table A.2.

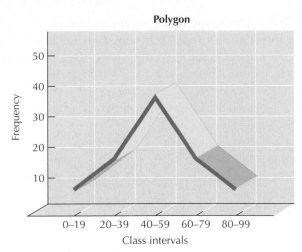

Polygon

● **FIGURE A.2** Frequency polygon of hypnotic susceptibility scores contained in Table A.2.

Measures of Central Tendency

SURVEY QUESTION: *How are statistics used to identify an average score?*

Notice in Table A.2 that more scores fall in the range 40–59 than elsewhere. How can we show this fact? A measure of **central tendency** is simply a number describing a "typical score" around which other scores fall. A familiar measure of central tendency is the mean, or "average." But as we shall see in a moment, other types of "averages" can be used. To illustrate each we need an example: Table A.3 shows the raw data for an imaginary experiment in which two groups of subjects were given a test of memory. Assume that one group was given a drug that might improve memory (let's call the drug Rememberine). The second group received a placebo. Is there a difference in memory scores between the two groups? It's difficult to tell without computing an average.

The Mean As one type of "average," the **mean** is calculated by adding all the scores for each group and then dividing by the total number of scores. Notice in ■ Table A.3 that the means reveal a difference between the two groups.

The mean is sensitive to extremely high or low scores in a distribution. For this reason it is not always the best

---

■ **TABLE A.3** Raw Scores on a Memory Test for Subjects Taking Rememberine or a Placebo

SUBJECT	GROUP 1 REMEMBERINE	GROUP 2 PLACEBO
1	65	54
2	67	60
3	73	63
4	65	33
5	58	56
6	55	60
7	70	60
8	69	31
9	60	62
10	68	61
Sum	650	540
Mean	65	54
Median	66	60

$$\text{Mean} = \frac{\Sigma X}{N} \text{ or } \frac{\text{Sum of all scores, X}}{\text{number of scores}}$$

$$\text{Mean Group 1} = \frac{65 + 67 + 73 + 65 + 58 + 55 + 70 + 69 + 60 + 68}{10}$$
$$= \frac{650}{10} = 65$$

$$\text{Mean Group 2} = \frac{54 + 60 + 63 + 33 + 56 + 60 + 60 + 31 + 62 + 61}{10}$$
$$= \frac{540}{10} = 54$$

Median = the middle score or the mean of the two middle scores*

Median Group 1 =   55 58 60 65 $\boxed{65\ 67}$ 68 69 70 73

$$= \frac{65 + 67}{2} = 66$$

Median Group 2 =   31 33 54 56 $\boxed{60\ 60}$ 60 61 62 63

$$= \frac{60 + 60}{2} = 60$$

*indicates middle score(s).

Descriptive statistics Mathematical tools used to describe and summarize numeric data.

Inferential statistics Mathematical tools used for decision making, for generalizing from small samples, and for drawing conclusions.

Graphical statistics Techniques for presenting numbers pictorially, often by plotting them on a graph.

Frequency distribution A table that divides an entire range of scores into a series of classes and then records the number of scores that fall into each class.

Histogram A graph of a frequency distribution in which the number of scores falling in each class is represented by vertical bars.

Frequency polygon A graph of a frequency distribution in which the number of scores falling in each class is represented by points on a line.

Central tendency The tendency for a majority of scores to fall in the midrange of possible values.

Mean A measure of central tendency calculated by adding a group of scores and then dividing by the total number of scores.

measure of central tendency. (Imagine how distorted it would be to calculate average yearly incomes from a small sample of people that happened to include a multimillionaire.) In such cases the middle score in a group of scores—called the *median*—is used instead.

The Median The **median** is found by arranging scores from the highest to the lowest and selecting the score that falls in the middle. In other words, half the values in a group of scores fall below the median and half fall above. Consider, for example, the following weights obtained from a small class of college students: 105, 111, 123, 126, 148, 151, 154, 162, 182. The median for the group is 148, the middle score. Of course, if there is an even number of scores, there will be no "middle score." This problem is handled by averaging the two scores that "share" the middle spot. This procedure yields a single number to serve as the median. (See the bottom panel of Table A.3.)

The Mode A final measure of central tendency is the *mode*. The **mode** is simply the most frequently occurring score in a group of scores. If you were to take the time to count the scores in Table A.3, you would find that the mode of Group l is 65 and the mode of Group 2 is 60. The mode is usually easy to obtain. However, the mode can be an unreliable measure, especially in a small group of scores. The mode's advantage is that it gives the score actually obtained by the greatest number of people.

Measures of Variability

SURVEY QUESTION: *What statistics do psychologists use to measure how much scores differ from one another?*

Let's say a researcher discovers two drugs that lower anxiety in agitated patients. However, let's also assume that one drug consistently lowers anxiety by moderate amounts, whereas the second sometimes lowers it by large amounts, sometimes has no effect, or may even increase anxiety in some patients. Overall, there is no difference in the *average* (mean) amount of anxiety reduction. Even so, an important difference exists between the two drugs. As this example shows, it is not enough to simply know the average score in a distribution. Usually, we would also like to know if scores are grouped closely together or scattered widely.

Measures of **variability** provide a single number that tells how "spread out" scores are. When the scores are widely spread, this number gets larger. When they are close together, it gets smaller. If you look again at the example in Table A.3, you will notice that the scores within each group vary widely. How can we show this fact?

The Range The simplest way would be to use the **range**, which is the difference between the highest and lowest scores. In Group 1 of our experiment the highest score is 73, and the lowest is 55; thus, the range is 18 (73 − 55 = 18). In Group 2 the highest score is 63, and the lowest is 31; this makes the range 32. Scores in Group 2 are more spread out (are more variable) than those in Group 1.

The Standard Deviation A better measure of variability is the **standard deviation** (an index of how much a typical score differs from the mean of a group of scores). To obtain the standard deviation, we find the deviation (or difference) of each score from the mean and then square it (multiply it by itself). These squared deviations are then added and averaged (the total is divided by the number of deviations). Taking the square root of this average yields the standard deviation (■ Table A.4). Notice again that the variability for Group 1 (5.4) is smaller than that for Group 2 (where the standard deviation is 11.3).

■ **TABLE A.4 Computation of the Standard Deviation**

GROUP 1 MEAN = 65

SCORE MEAN	DEVIATION (d)	DEVIATION SQUARED (d^2)
65 − 65 =	0	0
67 − 65 =	2	4
73 − 65 =	8	64
65 − 65 =	0	0
58 − 65 =	−7	49
55 − 65 =	−10	100
70 − 65 =	5	25
69 − 65 =	4	16
60 − 65 =	−5	25
68 − 65 =	3	9
		292

$$SD = \sqrt{\frac{\text{sum of } d^2}{n}} = \sqrt{\frac{292}{10}} = \sqrt{29.2} = 5.4$$

GROUP 2 MEAN = 54

SCORE MEAN	DEVIATION (d)	DEVIATION SQUARED (d^2)
54 − 54 =	0	0
60 − 54 =	6	36
63 − 54 =	9	81
33 − 54 =	−21	441
56 − 54 =	2	4
60 − 54 =	6	36
60 − 54 =	6	36
31 − 54 =	−23	529
62 − 54 =	8	64
61 − 54 =	7	49
		1276

$$SD = \sqrt{\frac{\text{sum of } d^2}{n}} = \sqrt{\frac{1276}{10}} = \sqrt{127.6} = 5.4$$

Standard Scores

A particular advantage of the standard deviation is that it can be used to "standardize" scores in a way that gives them greater meaning. For example, John and Heather both took psychology midterms, but in different classes. John earned a score of 118, and Heather scored 110. Who did better? It is impossible to tell without knowing what the average score was on each test, and whether John and Heather scored at the top, middle, or bottom of their classes. We would like to have one number that gives all this information. A number that does this is the *z-score*.

To convert an original score to a **z-score,** we subtract the mean from the score. The resulting number is then divided by the standard deviation for that group of scores. To illustrate, Heather had a score of 110 in a class with a mean of 100 and a standard deviation of 10. Therefore, her z-score is +1.0 (Table A.5). John's score of 118 came from a class having a mean of 100 and a standard deviation of 18; thus, his z-score is also +1.0. (See ■ Table A.5.) Originally it looked as if John did better on his midterm than Heather did. But we now see that relatively speaking, their scores were equivalent. Compared with other students, each was an equal distance above average.

The Normal Curve

When chance events are recorded, we find that some outcomes have a high probability and occur very often; others have a lower probability and occur infrequently; still others have little probability and occur rarely. As a result, the distribution (or tally) of chance events typically resembles a *normal curve* (● Fig. A.3). A **normal curve** is bell shaped, with a large number of scores in the middle, tapering to very few extremely high and low scores. Most psychological traits or events are determined by the action of a large number of factors. Therefore, like chance events, measures of psychological

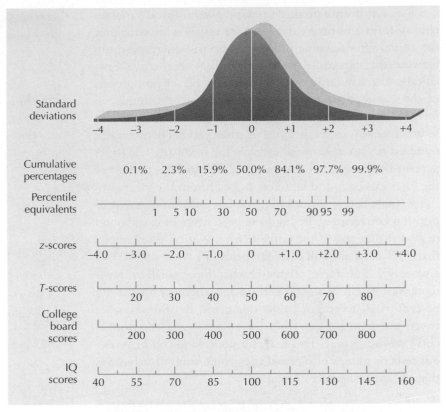

● **FIGURE A.3** The normal curve. The normal curve is an idealized mathematical model. However, many measurements in psychology closely approximate a normal curve. The scales you see here show the relationship of standard deviations, z-scores, and other measures to the curve.

variables tend to roughly match a normal curve. For example, direct measurement has shown such characteristics as height, memory span, and intelligence to be distributed approximately along a normal curve. In other words, many people have average height, memory ability, and intelligence. However, as we move above or below average, fewer and fewer people are found.

Median A measure of central tendency found by arranging scores from the highest to the lowest and selecting the score that falls in the middle. That is, half the values in a group of scores fall above the median and half fall below.

Mode A measure of central tendency found by identifying the most frequently occurring score in a group of scores.

Variability The tendency for a group of scores to differ in value. Measures of variability indicate the degree to which a group of scores differ from one another.

Range The difference between the highest and lowest scores in a group of scores.

Standard deviation An index of how much a typical score differs from the mean of a group of scores.

z-score A number that tells how many standard deviations above or below the mean a score is.

Normal curve A bell-shaped distribution, with a large number of scores in the middle, tapering to very few extremely high and low scores.

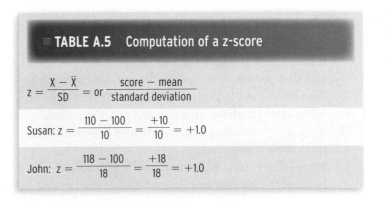

■ TABLE A.5   Computation of a z-score

$$z = \frac{X - \bar{X}}{SD} = \text{or } \frac{\text{score} - \text{mean}}{\text{standard deviation}}$$

Susan: $z = \dfrac{110 - 100}{10} = \dfrac{+10}{10} = +1.0$

John: $z = \dfrac{118 - 100}{18} = \dfrac{+18}{18} = +1.0$

It is very fortunate that so many psychological variables tend to form a normal curve, because much is known about the curve. One valuable property concerns the relationship between the standard deviation and the normal curve. Specifically, the standard deviation measures off set proportions of the curve above and below the mean. For example, in ● Figure A.4, notice that roughly 68 percent of all cases (IQ scores, memory scores, heights, or whatever) fall between one standard deviation above and below the mean (± 1 SD); 95 percent of all cases fall between ± 2 SD; and 99 percent of the cases can be found between ± 3 SD from the mean.

■ Table A.6 gives a more complete account of the relationship between z-scores and the percentage of cases found in a particular area of the normal curve. Notice, for example, that 93.3 percent of all cases fall below a z-score of +1.5. A z-score of 1.5 on a test (no matter what the original, or "raw," score was) would be a good performance, because roughly 93 percent of all scores fall below this mark. Relationships between the standard deviation (or z-scores) and the normal curve do not change. This makes it possible to compare various tests or groups of scores if they come from distributions that are approximately normal.

■ TABLE A.6	Computation of a z-score	
Z-SCORE	PERCENTAGE OF AREA TO THE LEFT OF THIS VALUE	PERCENTAGE OF AREA TO THE RIGHT OF THIS VALUE
−3.0 SD	00.1	99.9
−2.5 SD	00.6	99.4
−2.0 SD	02.3	97.7
−1.5 SD	06.7	93.3
−1.0 SD	15.9	84.1
−0.5 SD	30.9	69.1
0.0 SD	50.0	50.0
+0.5 SD	69.1	30.9
+1.0 SD	84.1	15.9
+1.5 SD	93.3	06.7
+2.0 SD	97.7	02.3
+2.5 SD	99.4	00.6
+3.0 SD	99.9	00.1

MODULE A.1 Summary

What are descriptive statistics?

- The results of psychological studies are often expressed as numbers, which must be summarized and interpreted before they have any meaning.
- Summarizing numbers visually, by using various types of graphs, makes it easier to see trends and patterns in the results of psychological investigations.
- Two basic questions about a group of numbers are: What is the average (central tendency)? How much do the numbers vary (variability)?
- Descriptive statistics organize and summarize numbers.
- Graphical statistics, such as histograms and frequency polygons, are used to represent numbers pictorially.

How are statistics used to identify an average score?

- Measures of central tendency define the "typical score" in a group of scores.
- The mean is found by adding all the scores in a group and then dividing by the total number of scores.
- The median is found by arranging a group of scores from the highest to the lowest and selecting the middle score.
- The mode is the score that occurs most frequently in a group of scores.

What statistics do psychologists use to measure how much scores differ from one another?

- Measures of variability provide a number that shows how how much scores vary.
- The range is the difference between the highest score and the lowest score in a group of scores.
- The standard deviation shows how much, on average, all the scores in a group differ from the mean.
- To change an original score into a standard score (or z-score), you must subtract the mean from the score and then divide the result by the standard deviation.
- Standard scores (z-scores) tell, in standard deviation units, how far above or below the mean a score is. This allows meaningful comparisons between scores from different groups.
- Scores that form a normal curve are easy to interpret because the properties of the normal curve are well known.

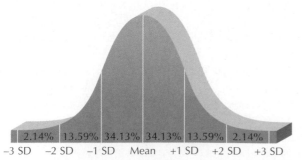

| 2.14% | 13.59% | 34.13% | 34.13% | 13.59% | 2.14% |
| −3 SD | −2 SD | −1 SD | Mean | +1 SD | +2 SD | +3 SD |

● **FIGURE A.4** Relationship between the standard deviation and the normal curve.

KNOWLEDGE BUILDER

Descriptive Statistics

Recite

1. _____ statistics summarize numbers so they become more meaningful or easier to communicate; _____ statistics are used for decision making, generalizing, or drawing conclusions.

2. Histograms and frequency polygons are graphs of frequency distributions. T or F?

3. Three measures of central tendency are the mean, the median, and the _____.

4. If scores are placed in order, from the smallest to the largest, the median is defined as the middle score. T or F?

5. As a measure of variability, the standard deviation is defined as the difference between the highest and lowest scores. T or F?

6. A z-score of −1 tells us that a score fell one standard deviation below the mean in a group of scores. T or F?

7. In a normal curve, 99 percent of all scores can be found between +1 and −1 standard deviations from the mean. T or F?

Reflect
Critical Thinking

8. You are asked to calculate the mean income of the following annual salaries: $2,000,000, $33,000, $27,000, $22,000, $21,000. Why might you refuse? What statistic might you propose to calculate instead?

Relate

Let's say you ask 100 people how long they sleep each night and record their answers. How could you show these scores graphically?

To find the average amount of sleep for your subjects, would you prefer to know the most frequent score (the mode), the middle score (the median), or the arithmetic average (the mean)?

How could you determine how much sleep times vary? That is, would you prefer to know the highest and lowest scores (the range) or the average amount of variation (the standard deviation)?

How would you feel about receiving your scores on classroom tests in the form of z-scores?

Do you think the distribution of scores in your study of sleep would form a normal curve? Why or why not?

Link

Internet addresses frequently change. To find the sites listed here, visit **http://www.thomsonedu.com/psychology/coon** for an updated list of Internet addresses and direct links to relevant sites.

- **Frequency Distribution of Tossing Coins and Dice** Automatically calculate frequency distributions for tossing coins or dice and plot the results as a frequency polygon.

- **Measures of Central Tendency** Work through another example of measures of central tendency.

- **Descriptive Statistics** Further explore descriptive statistics.

ANSWERS

1. Descriptive, inferential 2. T 3. mode 4. T 5. F 6. T 7. F 8. The single large salary in this small group will distort the mean. In cases like this, the median is a better measure of central tendency.

MODULE
A.2 Inferential Statistics

YOU WOULD LIKE TO KNOW if boys are more aggressive than girls. You observe a group of 5-year-old boys and girls on a playground. After collecting data for a week you find that the boys committed more aggressive acts than the girls. Could this difference just be a meaningless fluctuation in aggression? Or does it show conclusively that boys are more aggressive than girls? Inferential statistics were created to answer just such questions (Sprinthall, 2007).

Inferential Statistics— Significant Numbers

SURVEY QUESTION: *What are inferential statistics?*

Let's say that a researcher studies the effects of a new therapy on a small group of depressed individuals. Is she or he interested only in these particular individuals? Usually not, because except in rare instances, psychologists seek to discover general laws of behavior that apply widely to humans and animals. Undoubtedly the researcher would like to know if the therapy holds any promise for all depressed people. As stated earlier, **inferential statistics** are techniques that allow us to make inferences. That is, they allow us to generalize from the behavior of small groups of subjects to that of the larger groups they represent.

Samples and Populations

In any scientific study, we would like to observe the entire set, or **population,** of subjects, objects, or events of interest. However, this is usually impossible or impractical. Observing all terrorists, all cancer patients, or all mothers-in-law could be both impractical (because all are large populations) and impossible (because people change political views, may be unaware of having cancer, and change their status as relatives). In such cases, **samples** (smaller cross sections of a population) are selected, and observations of the sample are used to draw conclusions about the entire population.

For any sample to be meaningful, it must be **representative.** That is, the sample group must truly reflect the membership and characteristics of the larger population. In our earlier hypothetical study of a memory drug, it would be essential for the sample of 20 people to be representative of the general population. A very important aspect of representative samples is that their members are chosen at **random.** In other words, each member of the population must have an equal chance of being included in the sample.

Significant Differences

In our imaginary drug experiment, we found that the average memory score was higher for the group given the drug than it was for persons who didn't take the drug (the placebo group). Certainly this result is interesting, but could it have occurred by chance? If two groups were repeatedly tested (with neither receiving any drug), their average memory scores would sometimes differ. How much must two means differ before we can consider the difference "real" (not due to chance)?

Notice that the question is similar to one discussed earlier: How many tails in a row must we obtain when flipping a coin before we can conclude that the coin is biased? In the case of the coin, we noted that obtaining 5 tails in a row is a rare event. Thus, it became reasonable to assume that the coin was biased. Of course, it is possible to get 5 tails in a row when flipping an honest coin. But becaues this outcome is unlikely, we have good reason to suspect that something other than chance (a loaded coin, for instance) caused the results. Similar reasoning is used in tests of statistical significance.

Tests of **statistical significance** provide an estimate of how often experimental results could have occurred by chance alone. The results of a significance test are stated as a probability. This probability gives the odds that the observed difference was due to chance. In psychology, any experimental result that could have occurred by chance 5 times (or less) out of 100 (in other words, a probability of .05 or less) is considered *significant.* In our memory experiment, the probability is .025 ($p = .025$) that the group means would differ as much as they do by chance alone. This allows us to conclude with reasonable certainty that the drug actually did improve memory scores.

Correlation—Rating Relationships

SURVEY QUESTION: *How are correlations used in psychology?*

As we noted in Module 1.6, many of the statements that psychologists make about behavior do not result from the use of experimental methods. Rather, they come from keen observations and measures of existing phenomena. A psychologist might note, for example, that the higher a couple's socioeconomic and educational status, the smaller the number of children they are likely to have. Or that grades in high school are related to how well a person is likely to do in college. Or even that as rainfall levels increase within a given metropolitan area, crime rates decline. In these instances, we are dealing with the fact that two variables are **correlating** (varying together in some orderly fashion).

Relationships

Psychologists are very interested in detecting relationships between events: Are children from single-parent families more likely to misbehave at school? Is wealth related to happiness? Is there a relationship between childhood exposure to the Internet and IQ at age 20? Is the chance of having a heart attack related to having a hostile personality? All of these are questions about correlation (Howell, 2008).

The simplest way of visualizing a correlation is to construct a **scatter diagram.** In a scatter diagram, two measures (grades in high school and grades in college, for instance) are obtained. One measure is indicated by the X axis and the second by the Y axis. The scatter diagram plots the intersection (crossing) of each pair of measurements as a single point. Many such measurement pairs give pictures like those shown in ● Figure A.5.

Figure A.5 also shows scatter diagrams of three basic kinds of relationships between variables (or measures). Graphs

A, B, and C show *positive relationships* of varying strength. As you can see, in a **positive relationship,** increases in the X measure (or score) are matched by increases on the Y measure (or score). An example would be finding that higher IQ scores (X) are associated with higher college grades (Y). A **zero correlation** suggests that no relationship exists between two measures. (See graph D.) This might be the result of comparing subjects' hat sizes (X) to their college grades (Y). Graphs E and F both show a **negative relationship** (or correlation). Notice that as values of one measure increase, those of the second become smaller. An example might be the relationship between amount of alcohol consumed and scores on a test of coordination: Higher alcohol levels are correlated with lower coordination scores.

The Correlation Coefficient

The strength of a correlation can also be expressed as a **coefficient of correlation.** This coefficient is simply a number falling somewhere between +1.00 and –1.00. If the number is zero or close to zero, it indicates a weak or nonexistent relationship. If the correlation is +1.00, a **perfect positive relationship** exists; if the correlation is –1.00, a **perfect negative relationship** has been discovered. The most commonly used correlation coefficient is called the Pearson *r*.

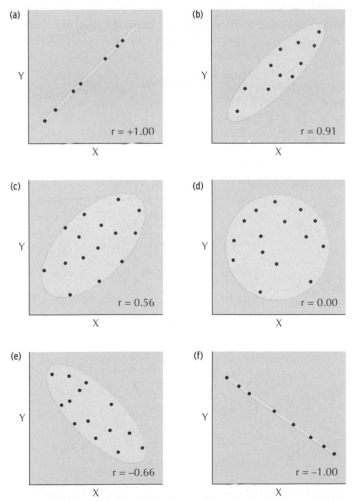

● **FIGURE A.5** Scatter diagrams showing various degrees of relationship for a positive, zero, and negative correlation.

Population An entire group of animals, people, or objects belonging to a particular category (for example, all college students or all married women).

Sample A smaller subpart of a population.

Representative sample A small, randomly selected part of a larger population that accurately reflects characteristics of the whole population.

Random selection Choosing a sample so that each member of the population has an equal chance of being included in the sample.

Statistical significance The degree to which an event (such as the results of an experiment) is unlikely to have occurred by chance alone.

Correlation The existence of a consistent, systematic relationship between two events, measures, or variables.

Scatter diagram A graph that plots the intersection of paired measures; that is, the points at which paired X and Y measures cross.

Positive relationship A mathematical relationship in which increases in one measure are matched by increases in the other (or decreases correspond with decreases).

Zero correlation The absence of a (linear) mathematical relationship between two measures.

Negative relationship A mathematical relationship in which increases in one measure are matched by decreases in the other.

Coefficient of correlation A statistical index ranging from –1.00 to +1.00 that indicates the direction and degree of correlation.

Perfect positive relationship A mathematical relationship in which the correlation between two measures is +1.00.

Perfect negative relationship A mathematical relationship in which the correlation between two measures is –1.00.

Calculation of the Pearson r is relatively simple, as shown in ■ Table A.7. (The numbers shown are hypothetical.)

As stated in Module 1.6, correlations in psychology are rarely perfect. Most fall somewhere between zero and plus or minus 1. The closer the correlation coefficient is to +1.00 or −1.00, the stronger the relationship. An interesting example of some typical correlations is provided by a study that compared the IQs of adopted children with the IQs of their biological mothers. At age 4, the children's IQs correlated .28 with their biological mothers' IQs. By age 7 the correlation was .35. And by age 13 it had grown to .38. Over time, the IQs of adopted children become more similar to the IQs of their biological mothers.

Prediction Correlations often provide highly useful information. For instance, it is valuable to know that there is a correlation between cigarette smoking and lung cancer rates. Another example is the fact that higher consumption of alcohol during pregnancy is correlated with lower birth weight and a higher rate of birth defects. There is a correlation between the number of recent life stresses experienced and the likelihood of emotional disturbance. Many more examples could be cited, but the point is, correlations help us to identify relationships that are worth knowing.

Correlations are particularly valuable for making *predictions*. If we know that two measures are correlated, and we know a person's score on one measure, we can predict his or her score on the other. For example, most colleges have formulas that use multiple correlations to decide which applicants have the best chances for success. Usually the formula includes such predictors as high school GPA, teacher ratings, extracurricular activities, and scores on the *Scholastic Assessment Test* (SAT) or some similar test. Although no single predictor is perfectly correlated with success in college, together the various predictors correlate highly and provide a useful technique for screening applicants.

There is an interesting "trick" you can do with correlations that you may find useful. It works like this: If you *square* the correlation coefficient (multiply r by itself), you will get a number telling the **percent of variance** (amount of variation in scores) accounted for by the correlation. For example, the correlation between IQ scores and college grade point average is .5. Multiplying .5 times .5 gives .25, or 25 percent. This means that 25 percent of the variation in college grades is accounted for by knowing IQ scores. In other words, with a correlation of .5, college grades are "squeezed" into an oval like the one shown in graph C, Figure A.5. IQ scores take away some of the possible variation in corresponding grade

---

■ TABLE A.7   IQ and Grade Point Average for Computing Pearson *r*

STUDENT NO.	IQ (X)	GRADE POINT AVERAGE (Y)	X SCORE SQUARED (X²)	Y SCORE SQUARED (Y²)	X TIMES Y (XY)
1	110	1.0	12,100	1.00	110.0
2	112	1.6	12,544	2.56	179.2
3	118	1.2	13,924	1.44	141.6
4	119	2.1	14,161	4.41	249.9
5	122	2.6	14,884	6.76	317.2
6	125	1.8	15,625	3.24	225.0
7	127	2.6	16,124	6.76	330.2
8	130	2.0	16,900	4.00	260.0
9	132	3.2	17,424	10.24	422.4
10	134	2.6	17,956	6.76	348.4
11	136	3.0	18,496	9.00	408.0
12	138	3.6	19,044	12.96	496.8
Total	1503	27.3	189,187	69.13	3488.7

$$r = \frac{\Sigma XY - \dfrac{(\Sigma X)(\Sigma Y)}{N}}{\sqrt{\left[\Sigma X^2 - \dfrac{(\Sigma X)^2}{N}\right]\left[\Sigma Y^2 - \dfrac{(\Sigma Y)^2}{N}\right]}}$$

$$= \frac{3488.7 - \dfrac{1503(27.3)}{12}}{\sqrt{\left[189,187 - \dfrac{(1503)^2}{122}\right]\left[69.13 - \dfrac{(27.3)^2}{12}\right]}}$$

$$= \frac{69.375}{81.088} = 0.856 = 0.86$$

point averages. If there were no correlation between IQ and grades, grades would be completely free to vary, as shown in Figure A.5, graph D.

Along the same line, a correlation of +1.00 or −1.00 means that 100 percent of the variation in the Y measure is accounted for by knowing the X measure: If you know a person's X score, you can tell exactly what the Y score is. An example that comes close to this state of affairs is the high correlation (.86) between the IQs of identical twins. In any group of identical twins, 74 percent of the variation in the "Y" twins' IQs is accounted for by knowing the IQs of their siblings (the "X's").

Squaring correlations to obtain the *percent variance* accounted for is a useful tool for interpreting the correlations encountered in the media and the psychological literature. For example, sweeping pronouncements about relationships are occasionally made on the basis of correlations in the .25 to .30 range even though the values mean that only 6 to 9 percent of the variance is accounted for by the observed correlation. Such correlations may document relationships worth noting, but they are rarely something to get excited about.

Correlation and Causation It is very important to reiterate that finding a correlation between two measures does not automatically mean that one causes the other: Correlation does not demonstrate **causation.** When a correlation exists, the best we can say is that two variables are related. Of course, this does not mean that it is impossible for two correlated variables to have a cause-and-effect relationship. Rather, it means that we cannot *conclude,* solely on the basis of correlation, that a causal link exists. To gain greater confidence that a cause-and-effect relationship exists, an experiment must be performed. (See Module 1.5.)

Often, two correlated measures are related as a result of the influence of a third variable. For example, we might observe that the more hours students devote to studying, the better their grades. Although it is tempting to conclude that more studying produces (causes) better grades, it is possible (indeed, it is probable) that grades and the amount of study

time are both related to the amount of motivation or interest a student has.

The difference between cause-and-effect data and data that reveal a relationship of unknown origin is one that should not be forgotten. Because we rarely run experiments in daily life, the information on which we act is largely correlational. This should make us more humble and more tentative in the confidence with which we make pronouncements about human behavior.

MODULE A.2 Summary

What are inferential statistics?

- Inferential statistics are used to make decisions, to generalize from samples, and to draw conclusions from data.

- Most studies in psychology are based on samples. Findings from representative samples are assumed to also apply to entire populations.

- In psychology experiments, differences in the average performance of groups could occur purely by chance. Tests of statistical significance tell us if the observed differences between groups are common or rare. If a difference is large enough to be improbable, it suggests that the results did not occur by chance alone.

How are correlations used in psychology?

- Pairs of scores that vary together in an orderly fashion are said to be correlated.

- Correlation is used to identify relationships between events or measures and to make predictions.

- The relationship between two variables or measures can be positive or negative.

- Correlation coefficients tell how strongly two groups of scores are related.

- Correlation alone does not demonstrate cause-and-effect links between variables or measures.

Percent of variance A portion of the total amount of variation in a group of scores.

Causation The act of causing some effect.

KNOWLEDGE BUILDER

Inferential Statistics

Recite

1. In inferential statistics, observations of a _____ are used to make inferences and draw conclusions about an entire _____.

2. A representative sample can be obtained by selecting members of the sample at _____.

3. If the results of an experiment could have occurred by chance alone less than 25 times out of 100, the result is considered statistically significant. T or F?

4. A scatter diagram can be used to plot and visualize a _____ between two groups of scores.

5. In a negative relationship, increases in X scores correspond to decreases in Y scores. T or F?

6. A perfect positive correlation exists when the correlation coefficient is 0.00. T or F?

7. It is important to remember that correlation does not demonstrate _____.

Reflect
Critical Thinking

8. Suppose it was found that sleeping with your clothes on is correlated with waking up with a headache. Could you conclude that sleeping with your clothes on causes headaches?

Relate

Informally, you have probably inferred something about a population of people based on the small sample you have observed directly. How could statistics improve the accuracy of your inferences?

If you were trying to test whether a drug causes birth defects, what level of statistical significance would you use? If you were doing a psychology experiment, what level would you be comfortable with?

See if you can identify at least one positive relationship and one negative relationship involving human behavior that you have observed. How strong do you think the correlation would be in each case? What correlation coefficient would you expect to see?

A woman you know drinks more coffee in the winter than she does in the summer. She also has more colds in the winter. She decides to reduce the amount of coffee she drinks to help prevent colds. What can you tell her about correlation and causation?

Link

Internet addresses frequently change. To find the sites listed here, visit **http://www.thomsonedu.com/psychology/coon** for an updated list of Internet addresses and direct links to relevant sites.

- **Concepts and Applications of Inferential Statistics** Browse this full online statistics textbook.

- **Scatter Diagram** Explore correlation by better understanding scatter diagrams.

- **Correlations** Vary the correlations and view the corresponding scatter diagram.

ANSWERS

1. sample, population 2. random 3. F 4. correlation 5. T 6. F 7. Causation 8. No. To reiterate, correlation does not prove causality. It is more likely here that a third factor is causing *both* the sleeping with the clothes on at night *and* the headaches (too much alcohol, anyone?).

Interactive Learning

Psychology: Active Learning Modules Book Companion Website

http://www.thomsonedu.com/psychology/coon
Visit your Book Companion Website, where you will find flash cards, practice quizzes, Internet links, and more to help you study.

ThomsonNOW™

Just what you need to know NOW!

Spend time on what you need to master rather than on information you already have learned. Take a pre-test for this chapter, and ThomsonNOW will generate a personalized study plan based on your results. The study plan will identify the topics you need to review and direct you to online resources to help you master those topics. You can then take a post-test to help you determine the concepts you have mastered and what you will need to work on. Try it out! Go to **www.thomsonedu.com/login** to sign in with an access code or to purchase access to this product.

Glossary

Ablation (ab-LAY-shun) Surgical removal of tissue.

Absolute threshold The minimum amount of physical energy necessary to produce a sensation.

Abstract principles Concepts and ideas removed from specific examples and concrete situations.

Accommodation In vision, changes in the shape of the lens of the eye.

Accommodation In Piaget's theory, the modification of existing mental patterns to fit new demands (that is, mental schemes are changed to accommodate new information or experiences).

Acculturative stress Stress caused by the many changes and adaptations required when a person moves to a foreign culture.

Acetylcholine The neurotransmitter released by neurons to activate muscles.

Acquaintance (date) rape Forced intercourse that occurs in the context of a date or other voluntary encounter.

Acquisition The period in conditioning during which a response is reinforced.

Action component How one tends to act toward the object of an attitude.

Action potential The nerve impulse.

Activation-synthesis hypothesis An attempt to explain how dream content is affected by motor commands in the brain that occur during sleep but are not carried out.

Active listener A person who knows how to maintain attention, avoid distractions, and actively gather information from lectures.

Activity theory Theory stating that the best adjustment to aging occurs when people remain active mentally, socially, and physically.

Actor-observer bias The tendency to attribute the behavior of others to internal causes while attributing one's own behavior to external causes (situations and circumstances).

Acute stress disorder A psychological disturbance lasting up to 1 month following stresses that would produce anxiety in anyone who experienced them.

Adaptation level An internal or mental "average" or "medium" point that is used to judge amounts.

Adaptive behaviors Actions that aid attempts to survive and adapt to changing conditions.

Adjustment disorder An emotional disturbance caused by ongoing stressors within the range of common experience.

Adolescence The culturally defined period between childhood and adulthood.

Adrenal glands Endocrine glands that arouse the body, regulate salt balance, adjust the body to stress, and affect sexual functioning.

Affectional needs Emotional needs for love and affection.

Ageism An institutionalized tendency to discriminate on the basis of age; prejudice based on age.

Aggression Any response made with the intent of causing harm or achieving one's goals at the expense of another person.

Aggression cues Stimuli or signals that are associated with aggression and that tend to elicit it.

Aggressive pornography Media depictions of sexual violence or of forced participation in sexual activity.

Agnosia An inability to grasp the meaning of stimuli, such as words, objects, or pictures.

Agoraphobia (ah-go-rah-FOBE-ee-ah) **(without panic)** The fear that something extremely embarrassing will happen if one leaves the house or enters unfamiliar situations.

Alarm reaction First stage of the GAS, during which bodily resources are mobilized to cope with a stressor.

Alcohol myopia Shortsighted thinking and perception that occurs during alcohol intoxication.

Algorithm A learned set of rules that always leads to the correct solution of a problem.

All-or-nothing thinking Classifying objects or events as absolutely right or wrong, good or bad, acceptable or unacceptable, and so forth.

Alpha waves Large, slow brain waves associated with relaxation and falling asleep.

Altered state of consciousness (ASC) A condition of awareness distinctly different in quality or pattern from waking consciousness.

Alzheimer's disease An age-related disease characterized by memory loss, mental confusion, and, in its later stages, a nearly total loss of mental abilities.

Ambivalence Mixed positive and negative feelings or simultaneous attraction and repulsion.

Amphetamine psychosis A loss of contact with reality due to repeated amphetamine use.

Ambivalent attachment An emotional bond marked by conflicting feelings of affection, anger, and emotional turmoil.

Amygdala (ah-MIG-dah-luh) A part of the limbic system associated with fear responses.

Anal stage The psychosexual stage corresponding roughly to the period of toilet training (ages 1 to 3).

Anal-expulsive personality A disorderly, destructive, cruel, or messy person.

Anal-retentive personality A person who is obstinate, stingy, or compulsive, and who generally has difficulty "letting go."

Androgen Any of a number of male sex hormones, especially testosterone.

Androgyny (an-DROJ-ih-nee) The presence of both "masculine" and "feminine" traits in a single person (as masculinity and femininity are defined within one's culture).

Andropause A gradual decline in testosterone levels in older men.

Anger control Personal strategies for reducing or curbing anger.

Anhedonia (an-he-DAWN-ee-ah) An inability to feel pleasure.

Anima An archetype representing the female principle.

Animal model In research, an animal whose behavior is used to derive principles that may apply to human behavior.

Animus An archetype representing the male principle.

Anorexia nervosa (AN-uh-REK-see-yah ner-VOH-sah) Active self-starvation or a sustained loss of appetite that has psychological origins.

Anosmia Loss or impairment of the sense of smell.

Antecedents Events that precede a response.

Anterograde amnesia Loss of the ability to form or retrieve memories for events that occur after an injury or trauma.

Anthropomorphic (AN-thro-po-MORE-fik) **error** The error of attributing human thoughts, feelings, or motives to animals, especially as a way of explaining their behavior.

Antidepressants Mood-elevating drugs.

Antipsychotics Drugs that, in addition to having tranquilizing effects, also tend to reduce hallucinations and delusional thinking. (Also called **major tranquilizers.**)

Antisocial personality A person who lacks a conscience; who is emotionally shallow, impulsive, selfish, and tends to manipulate others.

Anxiety Apprehension, dread, or uneasiness similar to fear but based on an unclear threat.

Anxiety disorder Disruptive feelings of fear, apprehension, or anxiety, or distortions in behavior that are anxiety related.

Anxiety reduction hypothesis Explains the self-defeating nature of avoidance responses as a result of the reinforcing effects of relief from anxiety.

Anxiolytics Drugs (such as Valium) that produce relaxation or reduce anxiety.

Aphasia (ah-FAZE-yah) A speech disturbance resulting from brain damage.

Apparent-distance hypothesis An explanation of the moon illusion stating that the horizon seems more distant than the night sky.

Applied psychology The use of psychological principles and research methods to solve practical problems.

Approach-approach conflict Choosing between two positive, or desirable, alternatives.

Approach-avoidance conflict Being attracted to and repelled by the same goal or activity.

Aptitude A capacity for learning certain abilities.

Aptitude test A test that rates a person's potential to learn skills required by various occupations.

Archetype A universal idea, image, or pattern, found in the collective unconscious.

Architectural psychology Study of the effects buildings have on behavior and the design of buildings using behavioral principles.

Arousal theory Assumes that people prefer to maintain ideal, or comfortable, levels of arousal.

Artificial intelligence Any artificial system (often a computer program) that is capable of human-like problem solving or intelligent responding.

Assertiveness training Instruction in how to be self-assertive.

Assessment center A program set up within an organization to conduct in-depth evaluations of job candidates.

Assimilation In Piaget's theory, the application of existing mental patterns to new situations (that is, the new situation is assimilated to existing mental schemes).

Association area (or cortex) All areas of the cerebral cortex that are not primarily sensory or motor in function.

Astigmatism (ah-STIG-mah-tiz-em) Defects in the cornea, lens, or eye that cause some areas of vision to be out of focus.

Attention Voluntarily focusing on a specific sensory input.

Attentional overload A stressful condition caused when sensory stimulation, information, and social contacts make excessive demands on attention.

Attention-deficit hyperactivity disorder (ADHD) A behavioral problem characterized by short attention span, restless movement, and impaired learning capacity.

Attitude A learned tendency to respond to people, objects, or institutions in a positive or negative way.

Attitude scale A collection of attitudinal statements with which respondents indicate agreement or disagreement.

Attribution The mental process of making inferences about the causes of events, one's own behavior, and that of others. In emotion, the process of attributing arousal to a particular source.

Authenticity In Carl Rogers's terms, the ability of a therapist to be genuine and honest about his or her own feelings.

Authoritarian parents Parents who enforce rigid rules and demand strict obedience to authority.

Authoritarian (ah-thor-ih-TARE-ee-un) **personality** A personality pattern characterized by rigidity, inhibition, prejudice, and an excessive concern with power, authority, and obedience.

Authoritative parents Parents who supply firm and consistent guidance combined with love and affection.

Autism A severe disorder involving mutism, sensory spin-outs, sensory blocking, tantrums, unresponsiveness to others, and other difficulties.

Autokinetic effect The apparent movement of a stationary pinpoint of light displayed in a darkened room.

Autonomic nervous system (ANS) The system of nerves carrying information to and from the internal organs and glands.

Autonomy versus shame and doubt A conflict created when growing self-control (autonomy) is pitted against feelings of shame or doubt.

Aversion therapy Suppressing an undesirable response by associating it with aversive (painful or uncomfortable) stimuli.

Aversive stimulus A stimulus that is painful or uncomfortable.

Avoidance learning Learning to make a response in order to postpone or prevent discomfort.

Avoidance-avoidance conflict Choosing between two negative, undesirable alternatives.

Avoidant attachment An emotional bond marked by a tendency to resist commitment to others.

Axon (AK-sahn) Fiber that carries information away from the cell body of a neuron.

Axon terminals Branching fibers at the ends of axons.

Babbling The repetition by infants of meaningless language sounds (including both vowel and consonant sounds).

Bait shyness An unwillingness or hesitation on the part of animals to eat a particular food.

Barnum effect The tendency to consider a personal description accurate if it is stated in very general terms.

Base rate The basic rate at which an event occurs over time; the basic probability of an event.

Basic anxiety A primary form of anxiety that arises from living in a hostile world.

Basic emotions The first distinct emotions to emerge in infancy.

Basic needs The first four levels of needs in Maslow's hierarchy; lower needs tend to be more potent than higher needs.

Basic suggestion effect The tendency of hypnotized persons to carry out suggested actions as if they were involuntary.

Behavior modification The application of learning principles to change human behavior, especially maladaptive behavior.

Behavior therapy Any therapy designed to actively change behavior.

Behavioral assessment Recording the frequency of various behaviors.

Behavioral contract A formal agreement stating behaviors to be changed and consequences that apply.

Behavioral dieting Weight reduction based on changing exercise and eating habits, rather than temporary self-starvation.

Behavioral genetics The study of inherited behavioral traits and tendencies.

Behavioral medicine The study of behavioral factors in medicine, physical illness, and medical treatment.

Behavioral personality theory Any model of personality that emphasizes learning and observable behavior.

Behavioral risk factors Behaviors that increase the chances of disease, injury, or premature death.

Behavioral setting A smaller area within an environment whose use is well defined, such as a bus depot, waiting room, or lounge.

Behaviorism The school of psychology that emphasizes the study of overt, observable behavior.

Belief component What a person thinks or believes about the object of an attitude.

Bereavement Period of emotional adjustment that follows the death of a loved one.

Beta waves Small, fast brain waves associated with being awake and alert.

Beta-endorphin A natural, painkilling brain chemical similar to morphine.

Biased sample A subpart of a larger population that does not accurately reflect characteristics of the whole population.

Bilingualism An ability to speak two languages.

Binge drinking Consuming five or more drinks in a short time.

Binocular depth cues Perceptual features that require two eyes and impart information about distance and three-dimensional space.

Biodata Detailed biographical information about a job applicant.

Biofeedback Information given to a person about his or her ongoing body activities; aids voluntary regulation of body states.

Biological aging Physiological changes that accompany growing older.

Biological biasing effect Hypothesized effect that prenatal exposure to sex hormones has on development of the body, nervous system, and later behavior patterns.

Biological perspective The attempt to explain behavior in terms of underlying biological principles.

Biological predisposition The presumed hereditary readiness of humans to learn certain skills, such as how to use language, or a readiness to behave in particular ways.

Biological rhythm Any repeating cycle of biological activity, such as sleep and waking cycles or changes in body temperature.

Bipolar disorders Emotional disorders involving both depression and mania or hypomania.

Bipolar I disorder A mood disorder in which a person has episodes of mania (excited, hyperactive, energetic, grandiose behavior) and also periods of deep depression.

Bipolar II disorder A mood disorder in which a person is mostly depressed (sad, despondent, guilt ridden) but

has also had one or more episodes of mild mania (hypomania).

Bisexual A person romantically and erotically attracted to both men and women.

Blind spot An area of the retina lacking visual receptors.

Bottom-up processing Organizing perceptions by beginning with low-level features.

Brainstem The lowest portions of the brain, including the cerebellum, medulla, pons, and reticular formation.

Brainstorming Method of creative thinking that separates the production and evaluation of ideas.

Brainwashing Engineered or forced attitude change involving a captive audience.

Brief psychodynamic therapy A modern therapy based on psychoanalytic theory but designed to produce insights more quickly.

Brightness constancy The apparent (or relative) brightness of objects remains the same as long as they are illuminated by the same amount of light.

Broca's (BRO-cahs) **area** A language area related to grammar and pronunciation.

Broken record A self-assertion technique involving repeating a request until it is acknowledged.

Browser Software that facilitates access to text, images, sounds, video, and other information stored in formats used on the Internet.

Bulimia (bue-LIHM-ee-yah) **nervosa** Excessive eating (gorging) usually followed by self-induced vomiting and/or taking laxatives.

Burnout A job-related condition of mental, physical, and emotional exhaustion.

Bystander apathy Unwillingness of bystanders to offer help during emergencies or to become involved in others' problems.

Caffeinism Excessive consumption of caffeine, leading to dependence and a variety of physical and psychological complaints.

Cannon-Bard theory States that activity in the thalamus causes emotional feelings and body arousal to occur simultaneously.

Carbon footprint The volume of greenhouse gases individual consumption adds to the atmosphere.

Cardinal trait A personality trait so basic that all of a person's activities relate to it.

Caregiving styles Identifiable patterns of parental caretaking and interaction with children.

Case study An in-depth focus on all aspects of a single person.

Castration Surgical removal of the testicles or ovaries.

Cataplexy (CAT-uh-plex-see) A sudden temporary paralysis of the muscles.

Catatonic schizophrenia Schizophrenia marked by stupor; rigidity; unresponsiveness; posturing; mutism; and, sometimes, agitated, purposeless behavior.

Causation The act of causing some effect.

Central nervous system (CNS) The brain and spinal cord.

Central tendency The tendency for a majority of scores to fall in the mid-range of possible values.

Central traits The core traits that characterize an individual personality.

Cerebellum (ser-ah-BEL-uhm) A brain structure that controls posture and coordination.

Cerebral cortex (seh-REE-brel or ser-EH-brel) The outer layer of the cerebrum.

Cervix (SER-vix) The lower end of the uterus that projects into the vagina.

Character Personal characteristics that have been judged or evaluated; a person's desirable or undesirable qualities.

Chromosomes Thread-like "colored bodies" in the nucleus of each cell that are made up of DNA.

Chronological age A person's age in years.

Circadian (SUR-kay-dee-AN) **rhythms** Cyclical changes in body functions and arousal levels that vary on a schedule approximating a 24-hour day.

Clairvoyance The purported ability to perceive events at a distance or through physical barriers.

Classical conditioning A form of learning in which reflex responses are associated with new stimuli.

Client-centered (or person-centered) therapy A nondirective therapy based on insights gained from conscious thoughts and feelings; emphasizes accepting one's true self.

Climacteric A point during late middle age when males experience a significant change in health, vigor, or appearance.

Clinical case study A detailed investigation of a single person, especially one suffering from some injury or disease.

Clinical method Studying psychological problems and therapies in clinical settings.

Clinical psychologist A psychologist who specializes in the treatment of psychological and behavioral disturbances or who does research on such disturbances.

Clinical study A detailed investigation of a single person, especially one suffering from some injury or disease.

Clitoris (KLIT-er-iss) Small, sensitive organ made up of erectile tissue; located above the vaginal opening.

Coefficient of correlation A statistical index ranging from −1.00 to +1.00 that indicates the direction and degree of correlation.

Coercive power Social power based on the ability to punish others.

Cognition The process of thinking or mentally processing information (images, concepts, words, rules, and symbols).

Cognitive behaviorism An approach that combines behavioral principles with cognition (perception, thinking, anticipation) to explain behavior.

Cognitive dissonance An uncomfortable clash between self-image, thoughts, beliefs, attitudes, or perceptions and one's behavior.

Cognitive interview Use of various cues and strategies to improve the memory of eyewitnesses.

Cognitive learning Higher-level learning involving thinking, knowing, understanding, and anticipation.

Cognitive map Internal images or other mental representations of an area (maze, city, campus, and so forth) that underlie an ability to choose alternative paths to the same goal.

Cognitive therapy A therapy directed at changing the maladaptive thoughts, beliefs, and feelings that underlie emotional and behavioral problems.

Collective unconscious A mental storehouse for unconscious ideas and images shared by all humans.

Color blindness A total inability to perceive colors.

Color weakness An inability to distinguish some colors.

Common traits Personality traits that are shared by most members of a particular culture.

Community health campaign A community-wide education program that provides information about how to lessen risk factors and promote health.

Community mental health center A facility offering a wide range of mental health services, such as prevention, counseling, consultation, and crisis intervention.

Comparison level A personal standard used to evaluate rewards and costs in a social exchange.

Compensation Counteracting a real or imagined weakness by emphasizing desirable traits or seeking to excel in the area of weakness or in other areas.

Compliance Bending to the requests of a person who has little or no authority or other form of social power.

Computer simulations Computer programs that mimic some aspect of human thinking, decision making, or problem solving.

Compressed workweek A work schedule that allows an employee to work fewer days per week by putting in more hours per day.

Concentrative meditation Mental exercise based on attending to a single object or thought.

Concept A generalized idea representing a category of related objects or events.

Concept formation The process of classifying information into meaningful categories.

Conceptual rule A formal rule for deciding if an object or event is an example of a particular concept.

Concrete operational stage Period of intellectual development during which children become able to use the concepts of time, space, volume, and number, but in ways that remain simplified and concrete, rather than abstract.

Condensation Combining several people, objects, or events into a single dream image.

Conditioned emotional response (CER) An emotional response that has been linked to a previously non-emotional stimulus by classical conditioning.

Conditioned response (CR) A learned response elicited by a conditioned stimulus.

Conditioned stimulus (CS) A stimulus that evokes a response because it has been repeatedly paired with an unconditioned stimulus.

Conditioning chamber (Skinner box) An apparatus designed to study operant conditioning in animals.

Conditions of worth Internal standards used to judge the value of one's thoughts, actions, feelings, or experiences.

Conduct disorder A pattern in which children consistently violate rules and behave aggressively and destructively.

Conductive hearing loss Poor transfer of sounds from the eardrum to the inner ear.

Cones Visual receptors for colors and daylight visual acuity.

Conflict A stressful condition that occurs when a person must choose between incompatible or contradictory alternatives.

Conformity Bringing one's behavior into agreement or harmony with norms or with the behavior of others in a group in the absence of any direct pressure.

Congenital problems Problems or defects that originate during prenatal development in the womb.

Conjunctive concept A class of objects that have two or more features in common. (For example, to qualify as an example of the concept an object must be both red *and* triangular.)

Connotative meaning The subjective, personal, or emotional meaning of a word or concept.

Conscience The part of the superego that causes guilt when its standards are not met.

Conscious The region of the mind that includes all mental contents a person is aware of at any given moment.

Consciousness Mental awareness of sensations, perceptions, memories, and feelings.

Consequences Effects that follow a response.

Conservation In Piaget's theory, mastery of the concept that the weight, mass, and volume of matter remain unchanged (are conserved) even when the shape or appearance of objects changes.

Consistency With respect to child discipline, the maintenance of stable rules of conduct.

Consolidation Process by which relatively permanent memories are formed in the brain.

Constructive processing Reorganizing or updating memories on the basis of logic, reasoning, or the addition of new information.

Contact comfort A pleasant and reassuring feeling human and animal infants get from touching or clinging to something soft and warm, usually their mother.

Context Information surrounding a stimulus.

Continuous reinforcement A schedule in which every correct response is followed by a reinforcer.

Control Altering conditions that influence behavior.

Control Where pain is concerned, refers to an ability to regulate the pain stimulus.

Control group In a controlled experiment, the group of subjects exposed to all experimental conditions or variables *except* the independent variable.

Control questions In a polygraph exam, questions that almost always provoke anxiety.

Conventional moral reasoning Moral thinking based on a desire to please others or to follow accepted rules and values.

Convergent thinking Thinking directed toward discovery of a single established correct answer; conventional thinking.

Conversion disorder A body symptom that mimics a physical disability but is actually caused by anxiety or emotional distress.

Conviction Beliefs that are important to a person and that evoke strong emotion.

Cooing Spontaneous repetition of vowel sounds by infants.

Cooperative play Play in which two or more children must coordinate their actions; if children don't cooperate, the game ends.

Coping statements Reassuring, self-enhancing statements that are used to stop self-critical thinking.

Correlation The existence of a consistent, systematic relationship between two events, measures, or variables.

Correlational method Making measurements to discover relationships between events.

Correlational study A nonexperimental study designed to measure the degree of relationship (if any) between two or more events, measures, or variables.

Corticalization (KORE-tih-kal-ih-ZAY-shun) An increase in the relative size of the cerebral cortex.

Counseling psychologist A psychologist who specializes in the treatment of milder emotional and behavioral disturbances.

Counselor A mental health professional who specializes in helping people with problems not involving serious mental disorder; for example, marriage counselors, career counselors, or school counselors.

Counterirritation Using mild pain to block more intense or long-lasting pain.

Covert reinforcement Using positive imagery to reinforce desired behavior.

Covert sensitization Use of aversive imagery to reduce the occurrence of an undesired response.

Cowper's glands Two small glands that secrete a clear fluid into the urethra during sexual excitement.

Cranial nerves Major nerves that leave the brain without passing through the spinal cord.

Creative self The "artist" in each of us that creates a unique identity and style of life.

Cretinism Stunted growth and intellectual disability caused by an insufficient supply of thyroid hormone.

Crisis intervention Skilled management of a psychological emergency.

Critical incidents Situations that arise in a job, with which a competent worker must be able to cope.

Critical situations Situations during childhood that are capable of leaving a lasting imprint on personality.

Critical thinking An ability to evaluate, compare, analyze, critique, synthesize, and reflect on information.

Cross-stimulation effect In group problem solving, the tendency of one person's ideas to trigger ideas from others.

Crowding A subjective feeling of being over-stimulated by a loss of privacy or by the nearness of others (especially when social contact with them is unavoidable).

Crystallized abilities Abilities that a person has intentionally learned; accumulated knowledge and skills.

CT scan Computed tomography scan; a computer-enhanced X-ray image of the brain or body.

Cue External stimuli that guide responses, especially by signaling the presence or absence of reinforcement.

Cult A group that professes great devotion to some person and follows that person almost without question; cult members are typically victimized by their leaders in various ways.

Cultural relativity The idea that behavior must be judged relative to the values of the culture in which it occurs.

Culture An ongoing pattern of life, characterizing a society at a given point in history.

Culturally skilled therapist A therapist who has the awareness, knowledge, and skills necessary to treat clients from diverse cultural backgrounds.

Culture-fair test A test (such as an intelligence test) designed to minimize the importance of skills and knowledge that may be more common in some cultures than in others.

Curve of forgetting A graph that shows the amount of memorized information remembered after varying lengths of time.

Curvilinear relationship A relationship that forms a curved line when graphed.

Cyclothymic (SIKE-lo-THY-mik) **disorder** Moderate manic and depressive behavior that persists for 2 years or more.

Dark adaptation Increased retinal sensitivity to light.

Daydream A vivid waking fantasy.

Death-qualified jury A jury composed of people who favor the death penalty or at least are indifferent to it.

Decay When referring to memory, the fading or weakening of memories assumed to occur when memory traces become weaker.

Declarative memory That part of long-term memory containing specific factual information.

Deductive thought Thought that applies a general set of rules to specific situations; for example, using the laws of gravity to predict the behavior of a single falling object.

Deep lesioning (LEE-zhun-ing) Removal of tissue within the brain by use of an electrode.

Deep sleep Stage 4 sleep; the deepest form of normal sleep.

Defense mechanism A habitual and often unconscious psychological process used to reduce anxiety.

Deinstitutionalization Reduced use of full-time commitment to mental institutions to treat mental disorders.

Delayed speech Speech that begins well after the normal age for language development has passed.

Delta waves Large, slow brainwaves that occur in deeper sleep (stages 3 and 4).

Delusion A false belief held against all contrary evidence.

Delusional disorder A psychosis marked by severe delusions of grandeur, jealousy, persecution, or similar preoccupations.

Dementia A serious mental impairment in old age caused by deterioration of the brain.

Demonology In medieval Europe, the study of demons and the treatment of persons "possessed" by demons.

Dendrites (DEN-drytes) Neuron fibers that receive incoming messages.

Denial Protecting oneself from an unpleasant reality by refusing to perceive it.

Denotative meaning The exact, dictionary definition of a word or concept; its objective meaning.

Density The number of people in a given space or, inversely, the amount of space available to each person.

Dependent variable In an experiment, the condition (usually a behavior) that is affected by the independent variable.

Depressant A substance that decreases activity in the body and nervous system.

Depression A state of despondency marked by feelings of powerlessness and hopelessness.

Depressive disorders Emotional disorders primarily involving sadness, despondency, and depression.

Deprivation In development, the loss or withholding of normal stimulation, nutrition, comfort, love, and so forth; a condition of lacking.

Depth cues Features of the environment and messages from the body that supply information about distance and space.

Depth perception The ability to see three-dimensional space and to accurately judge distances.

Description In scientific research, the process of naming and classifying.

Descriptive statistics Mathematical tools used to describe and summarize numeric data.

Desensitization A reduction in emotional sensitivity to a stimulus. Can be used to deliberately reduce fear or anxiety by repeatedly exposing a person to emotional stimuli while the person is deeply relaxed.

Determinism The idea that all behavior has prior causes that would completely explain one's choices and actions if all such causes were known.

Detoxification In the treatment of alcoholism, the withdrawal of the patient from alcohol.

Developmental level An individual's current state of physical, emotional, and intellectual development.

Developmental milestone A significant turning point or marker in personal development.

Developmental psychology The study of progressive changes in behavior and abilities from conception to death.

Developmental task Any skill that must be mastered, or personal change that must take place, for optimal development.

Deviation IQ An IQ obtained statistically from a person's relative standing in his or her age group; that is, how far above or below average the person's score was relative to other scores.

Diagnostic interview An interview used to find out how a person is feeling and what complaints or symptoms he or she has.

Difference threshold The minimum difference between two that is detectable to an observer.

Diffusion of responsibility Spreading the responsibility to act among several people; reduces the likelihood that help will be given to a person in need.

Direct instruction Presentation of factual information by lecture, demonstration, and rote practice.

Direct observation Assessing behavior through direct surveillance.

Discovery learning Learning based on insight and understanding.

Discrimination Treating members of various social groups differently in circumstances where their rights or treatment should be identical.

Discriminative stimuli Stimuli that precede rewarded and nonrewarded responses in operant conditioning.

Disease-prone personality A personality type associated with poor health; marked by persistent negative emotions, including anxiety, depression, and hostility.

Disengagement theory of aging Theory stating that it is normal for older people to withdraw from society and from roles they held earlier.

Dishabituation A reversal of habituation.

Disinhibition The removal of inhibition; results in acting out behavior that normally would be restrained.

Disjunctive concept A concept defined by the presence of at least one of several possible features. (For example, to qualify an object must be either blue *or* circular.)

Disorganized schizophrenia Schizophrenia marked by incoherence, grossly disorganized behavior, bizarre thinking, and flat or grossly inappropriate emotions.

Displaced aggression Redirecting aggression to a target other than the actual source of one's frustration.

Displacement Directing emotions or actions toward safe or unimportant dream images.

Dissociative amnesia Loss of memory (partial or complete) for important information related to personal identity.

Dissociative disorder Temporary amnesia, multiple personality, or depersonalization.

Dissociative fugue Sudden travel away from home, plus confusion about one's personal identity.

Dissociative identity disorder The presence of two or more distinct personalities (multiple personality).

Disuse The theory that memory traces weaken when memories are not periodically used or retrieved.

Divergent thinking Thinking that produces many ideas or alternatives; a major element in original or creative thought.

Divided attention Allotting mental space or effort to various tasks or parts of a task.

DNA Deoxyribonucleic acid, a molecular structure that contains coded genetic information.

Dogmatism An unwarranted positiveness or certainty in matters of belief or opinion.

Dominant gene A gene whose influence will be expressed each time the gene is present.

Dominant hemisphere A term usually applied to the side of a person's brain that produces language.

Door-in-the-face effect The tendency for a person who has refused a major request to subsequently be more likely to comply with a minor request.

Double approach-avoidance conflict Being simultaneously attracted to and repelled by each of two alternatives.

Double standard Applying different standards for judging the appropriateness of male and female sexual behavior.

Double-blind experiment An arrangement in which both participants and experimenters are unaware of whether participants are in the experimental group or the control group.

Down syndrome A genetic disorder caused by the presence of an extra chromosome; results in intellectual disability.

Downward comparison Comparing yourself with a person who ranks lower than you on some dimension.

Dream processes Mental filters that hide the true meanings of dreams.

Dream symbols Images in dreams that serve as visible signs of hidden ideas, desires, impulses, emotions, relationships, and so forth.

Dream symbols Images in dreams whose personal or emotional meanings differ from their literal meanings.

Drive The psychological expression of internal needs or valued goals strong enough to goad a person to action— for example, hunger, thirst, or a drive for success.

Drug interaction A combined effect of two drugs that exceeds the addition of one drug's effects to the other.

Drug tolerance A reduction in the body's response to a drug.

Dynamic touch Touch experienced when the body is in motion; a combination of sensations from skin receptors, muscles, and joints.

Dyslexia An inability to read with understanding, often caused by a tendency to misread letters (by seeing their mirror images, for instance).

Dyspareunia (DIS-pah-ROO-nee-ah) Genital pain before, during, or after sexual intercourse.

Dysthymic (dis-THY-mik) **disorder** Moderate depression that persists for 2 years or more.

Early childhood education program Programs that provide stimulating intellectual experiences, typically for disadvantaged preschoolers.

Echoic memory A brief continuation of sensory activity in the auditory system after a sound is heard.

Echolalia A compulsion, sometimes observed in autistic children, to repeat everything that is said.

Educational psychology The field that seeks to understand how people learn and how teachers instruct.

Ecological footprint The amount of land and water area required to replenish the resources that a human population consumes.

Ego The executive part of personality that directs rational behavior.

Ego ideal The part of the superego representing ideal behavior; a source of pride when its standards are met.

Egocentric thought Thought that is self-centered and fails to consider the viewpoints of others.

Eidetic (eye-DET-ik) **imagery** The ability to retain a "projected" mental image long enough to use it as a source of information.

Ejaculation The release of sperm and seminal fluid by the male at the time of orgasm.

Elaborative rehearsal Rehearsal that links new information with existing memories and knowledge.

Electra conflict A girl's sexual attraction to her father and feelings of rivalry with her mother.

Electrical stimulation of the brain (ESB) Direct electrical stimulation and activation of brain tissue.

Electroconvulsive shock (ECS) An electric current passed directly through the brain, producing a convulsion.

Electroconvulsive therapy (ECT) A treatment for severe depression, consisting of an electric shock passed directly through the brain, which induces a convulsion.

Electrode Any device (such as a wire, needle, or metal plate) used to electrically stimulate nerve tissue or to record its activity.

Electroencephalograph (ee-LEK-tro-in-SEF-ah-LOG-ruh-fee) **(EEG)** A device that detects, amplifies, and records electrical activity in the brain.

Emblems Gestures that have widely understood meanings within a particular culture.

Emotion A state characterized by physiological arousal, changes in facial expression, gestures, posture, and subjective feelings.

Emotional appraisal Evaluating the personal meaning of a stimulus or situation.

Emotional attachment An especially close emotional bond that infants form with their parents, caregivers, or others.

Emotional component One's feelings toward the object of an attitude.

Emotional expression Outward signs that an emotion is occurring.

Emotional feelings The private, subjective experience of having an emotion.

Emotional intelligence Emotional competence, including empathy, self-control, self-awareness, and other skills.

Emotion-focused coping Managing or controlling one's emotional reaction to a stressful or threatening situation.

Empathic arousal Emotional arousal that occurs when you feel some of another person's pain, fear, or anguish.

Empathy A capacity for taking another's point of view; the ability to feel what another is feeling.

Empathy-helping relationship Observation that we are most likely to help someone else when we feel emotions such as empathy and compassion.

Empty nest syndrome Psychological disturbance experienced by some women after their last child leaves home.

Encoding Converting information into a form in which it will be retained in memory.

Encoding failure Failure to store sufficient information to form a useful memory.

Encopresis A lack of bowel control; "soiling."

Encounter group A group experience that emphasizes intensely honest interchanges among participants regarding feelings and reactions to one another.

Endocrine (EN-duh-krin) **system** Glands whose secretions pass directly into the bloodstream or lymph system.

Endogenous (en-DODGE-eh-nus) **depression** Depression that appears to be produced from within (perhaps by chemical imbalances in the brain), rather than as a reaction to life events.

Engineering psychology (human factors engineering) A specialty concerned with making machines and work environments compatible with human perceptual and physical capacities.

Engram A "memory trace" in the brain.

Enrichment Deliberately making an environment more novel, complex, and perceptually or intellectually stimulating.

Enuresis An inability to control urination, particularly with regard to bed-wetting.

Enrichment In development, deliberately making an environment more stimulating, nutritional, comforting, loving, and so forth.

Environment ("nurture") The sum of all external conditions affecting development, including especially the effects of learning.

Environmental assessment Measurement and analysis of the effects an environment has on the behavior of people within that environment.

Environmental psychology The formal study of how environments affect behavior.

Epididymis (ep-ih-DID-ih-mus) A coiled structure at the top of the testes in which sperm are stored.

Epinephrine (ep-eh-NEF-rin) An adrenal hormone that tends to arouse the body; epinephrine is associated with fear. (Also known as adrenaline.)

Episodic (ep-ih-SOD-ik) **drive** A drive that occurs in distinct episodes.

Episodic (ep-ih-SOD-ik) **memory** A subpart of declarative memory that records personal experiences that are linked with specific times and places.

Equal-status contact Social interaction that occurs on an equal footing, without obvious differences in power or status.

Erectile disorder An inability to maintain an erection for lovemaking.

Erogenous (eh-ROJ-eh-nus) **zones** Areas of the body that produce pleasure and/or provoke erotic desire.

Erogenous zone Any body area that produces pleasurable sensations.

Eros Freud's name for the "life instincts."

Escape Reducing discomfort by leaving frustrating situations or by psychologically withdrawing from them.

Escape learning Learning to make a response in order to end an aversive stimulus.

Estrogen Any of a number of female sex hormones.

Estrus Changes in the sexual drives of animals that create a desire for mating; particularly used to refer to females in heat.

Ethnocentrism Placing one's own group or race at the center—that is, tending to reject all other groups but one's own.

Ethologist A person who studies the natural behavior patterns of animals.

Eugenics Selective breeding for desirable characteristics.

Evaluation fears Fears of being inadequate, embarrassed, ridiculed, or rejected.

Evolutionary psychology Study of the evolutionary origins of human behavior patterns.

Excitement phase The first phase of sexual response, indicated by initial signs of sexual arousal.

Existential therapy An insight therapy that focuses on the elemental problems of existence, such as death, meaning, choice, and responsibility; emphasizes making courageous life choices.

Expectancy An anticipation concerning future events or relationships, including anticipation about the effect a response will have, especially regarding reinforcement.

Experiential intelligence Specialized knowledge and skills acquired through learning and experience.

Experiment A formal trial undertaken to confirm or disconfirm a hypothesis about cause and effect.

Experimental group In a controlled experiment, the group of subjects exposed to the independent variable or experimental condition.

Experimental method Investigating causes of behavior through controlled experimentation.

Experimental subjects Humans (also referred to as **subjects** or **participants**) or animals whose behavior is investigated in an experiment.

Experimenter effect Changes in subjects' behavior caused by the unintended influence of an experimenter's actions.

Expert power Social power derived from possession of knowledge or expertise.

Expert systems Computer programs designed to respond as a human expert would; programs based on the knowledge and rules that underlie human expertise in specific topics.

Explicit memory A memory that a person is aware of having; a memory that is consciously retrieved.

Expressive behaviors Behaviors that express or communicate emotion or personal feelings.

External cause A cause of behavior that is assumed to lie outside a person.

External urethral orifice (yoo-REE-thral OR-ih-fis) The opening at the tip of the penis through which urine and semen pass.

Extinction The weakening of a conditioned response through removal of reinforcement.

Extracellular thirst Thirst caused by a reduction in the volume of fluids found between body cells.

Extraneous variables Conditions or factors excluded from influencing the outcome of an experiment.

Extrasensory perception (ESP) The purported ability to perceive events in ways that cannot be explained by known capacities of the sensory organs.

Extrinsic motivation Motivation based on obvious external rewards, obligations, or similar factors.

Extrovert A person whose attention is directed outward; a bold, outgoing person.

Eye movement desensitization and reprocessing (EMDR) A technique for reducing fear or anxiety; based on holding upsetting thoughts in mind while rapidly moving the eyes from side to side.

Facial agnosia (ag-KNOW-zyah) Inability to perceive familiar faces.

Facial feedback hypothesis States that sensations from facial expressions help define what emotion a person feels.

Factor analysis A statistical technique used to correlate multiple measurements and identify general underlying factors.

Fallacy of positive instances The tendency to remember or notice information that fits one's expectations, while forgetting discrepancies.

Fallopian tube (feh-LOPE-ee-en) One of two tubes that carry eggs from the ovaries to the uterus.

Familial intellectual disability Mild intellectual disability associated with homes that are intellectually, nutritionally, and emotionally impoverished.

Family therapy Technique in which all family members participate, both individually and as a group, to change destructive relationships and communication patterns.

Fantasy Fulfilling unmet desires in imagined achievements or activities.

Feedback Information returned to a person about the effects a response has had; also known as knowledge of results.

Feeling of knowing The ability to predict beforehand whether one will be able to remember something.

Female orgasmic disorder A persistent inability to reach orgasm during lovemaking.

Female sexual arousal disorder A lack of physical arousal to sexual stimulation.

Figure-ground organization Part of a stimulus appears to stand out as an object (figure) against a less prominent background (ground).

Five-factor model Proposes that there are five universal dimensions of personality.

Fixation A lasting conflict developed as a result of frustration or overindulgence.

Fixation In problem solving, a tendency to repeat wrong solutions or faulty responses, especially as a result of becoming blind to alternatives.

Fixed interval (FI) schedule A reinforcer is given only when a correct response is made after a set amount of time has passed since the last reinforced response. Responses made during the time interval are not reinforced.

Fixed ratio (FR) schedule A set number of correct responses must be made to get a reinforcer. For example, a reinforcer is given for every four correct responses.

Flashbulb memories Memories created at times of high emotion that seem especially vivid.

Flexibility In tests of creativity, flexibility is indicated by the number of different types of solutions produced.

Flextime A work schedule that allows flexible starting and quitting times.

Fluency In tests of creativity, fluency refers to the total number of solutions produced.

Fluid abilities Innate, nonlearned abilities based on perceptual, motor, or intellectual speed and flexibility.

fMRI scan Magnetic resonance imaging that records brain activity.

Foot-in-the-door effect The tendency for a person who has first complied with a small request to be more likely later to fulfill a larger request.

Forcible rape Sexual intercourse carried out against the victim's will, under the threat of violence or bodily injury.

Foreclosed identity The result of shutting down personal growth.

Formal operations stage Period of intellectual development characterized by thinking that includes abstract, theoretical, and hypothetical ideas.

Fovea An area at the center of the retina containing only cones.

Frame of reference An internal perspective relative to which events are perceived and evaluated.

Fragile X syndrome A genetic form of intellectual disability caused by a defect in the X chromosome.

Framing In thought, the terms in which a problem is stated or the way that it is structured.

Fraternal twins Twins conceived from two separate eggs.

Free association In psychoanalysis, the technique of having a client say anything that comes to mind, regardless of how embarrassing or unimportant it may seem.

Free choice The ability to freely make choices that are not controlled by genetics, learning, or unconscious forces.

Free will The idea that human beings are capable of freely making choices or decisions.

Frequency distribution A table that divides an entire range of scores into a series of classes and then records the number of scores that fall into each class.

Frequency polygon A graph of a frequency distribution in which the number of scores falling in each class is represented by points on a line.

Frequency theory Holds that tones up to 4,000 hertz are converted to nerve impulses that match the frequency of each tone.

Frontal lobes A brain area associated with movement, the sense of self, and higher mental functions.

Frustration A negative emotional state that occurs when one is prevented from reaching a goal.

Frustration-aggression hypothesis States that frustration tends to lead to aggression.

Fully functioning person A person living in harmony with her or his deepest feelings, impulses, and intuitions.

Functional fixedness A rigidity in problem solving caused by an inability to see new uses for familiar objects.

Functional MRI (fMRI) Functional magnetic resonance imaging that records brain activity.

Functional solution A detailed, practical, and workable solution.

Functionalism The school of psychology concerned with how behavior and mental abilities help people adapt to their environments.

Fundamental attribution error The tendency to attribute the behavior of others to internal causes (personality, likes, and so forth).

Galvanic skin response (GSR) A change in the electrical resistance (or inversely, the conductance) of the skin, due to sweating.

Gate control theory Proposes that pain messages pass through neural "gates" in the spinal cord.

Gender Psychological and social characteristics associated with being male or female; defined especially by one's gender identity and learned gender roles.

Gender bias (in research) A tendency for females and female issues to be under-represented in research, psychological or otherwise.

Gender identity One's personal, private sense of maleness or femaleness.

Gender role The pattern of behaviors that are regarded as "male" or "female" by one's culture; sometimes also referred to as a sex role.

Gender role socialization The process of learning gender behaviors considered appropriate for one's sex in a given culture.

Gender role stereotypes Oversimplified and widely held beliefs about the basic characteristics of men and women.

General adaptation syndrome (GAS) A series of bodily reactions to prolonged stress; occurs in three stages: alarm, resistance, and exhaustion.

General intelligence test A test that measures a wide variety of mental abilities.

General solution A solution that correctly states the requirements for success but not in enough detail for further action.

Generalized anxiety disorder A chronic state of tension and worry about work, relationships, ability, or impending disaster.

Generativity versus stagnation A conflict of middle adulthood in which self-interest is countered by an interest in guiding the next generation.

Genes Specific areas on a strand of DNA that carry hereditary information.

Genetic disorders Problems caused by defects in the genes or by inherited characteristics.

Genetic sex Sex as indicated by the presence of *XX* (female) or *XY* (male) chromosomes.

Genital sex Sex as indicated by the presence of male or female genitals.

Genital stage Period of full psychosexual development, marked by the attainment of mature adult sexuality.

Gerontologist One who scientifically studies aging and its effects.

Gestalt psychology A school of psychology emphasizing the study of thinking, learning, and perception in whole units, not by analysis into parts.

Gestalt therapy An approach that focuses on immediate experience and awareness to help clients rebuild thinking, feeling, and acting into connected wholes; emphasizes the integration of fragmented experiences.

g-factor A general ability factor or core of general intellectual ability that involves reasoning, problem-solving ability, knowledge, memory, and successful adaptation to one's surroundings.

Giftedness The possession of a high IQ or special talents or aptitudes.

Glans penis (glanz PEA-nis) The tip of the penis.

Goal The target or objective of motivated behavior.

Gonadal sex Sex as indicated by the presence of ovaries (female) or testes (male).

Gonads The primary sex glands—the testes in males and ovaries in females.

Grammar A set of rules for combining language units into meaningful speech or writing.

Graphical statistics Techniques for presenting numbers pictorially, often by plotting them on a graph.

Grief An intense emotional state that follows the death of a lover, friend, or relative.

Group cohesiveness The degree of attraction among group members or their commitment to remaining in the group.

In-group A group with which a person identifies.

Group intelligence test Any intelligence test that can be administered to a group of people with minimal supervision.

Group prejudice Prejudice held out of conformity to group views.

Group sanctions Rewards and punishments (such as approval or disapproval) administered by groups to enforce conformity among members.

Group structure The network of roles, communication pathways, and power in a group.

Group therapy Psychotherapy conducted in a group setting to make therapeutic use of group dynamics.

Groupthink A compulsion by members of decision-making groups to maintain agreement, even at the cost of critical thinking.

Growth hormone A hormone, secreted by the pituitary gland, that promotes body growth.

Growth needs In Maslow's hierarchy, the higher-level needs associated with self-actualization.

Growth spurt An often dramatic acceleration in physical growth that coincides with puberty.

Guided imagery Intentional visualization of images that are calming, relaxing, or beneficial in other ways.

Gustation The sense of taste.

Habit A deeply ingrained, learned pattern of behavior.

Habituation A decrease in perceptual response to a repeated stimulus.

Hair cells Receptor cells within the cochlea that transduce vibrations into nerve impulses.

Half-way house A community-based facility for individuals making the transition from an institution (mental hospital, prison, and so forth) to independent living.

Hallucination An imaginary sensation, such as seeing, hearing, or smelling things that don't exist in the real world.

Hallucinogen (hal-LU-sin-oh-jin) A substance that alters or distorts sensory impressions.

Halo effect The tendency to generalize a favorable or unfavorable first impression to unrelated details of personality.

Handedness A preference for the right or left hand in most activities.

Hardy personality A personality style associated with superior stress resistance.

Hassle (microstressor) Any distressing, day-to-day annoyance.

Health psychology Study of the ways in which behavioral principles can be used to prevent illness and promote health.

Heredity ("nature") The transmission of physical and psychological characteristics from parents to offspring through genes.

Heterosexism The belief that heterosexuality is better or more natural than homosexuality.

Heterosexual A person romantically and erotically attracted to members of the opposite sex.

Heuristic (hew-RIS-tik) Any strategy or technique that aids problem solving, especially by limiting the number of possible solutions to be tried.

Hidden observer A detached part of the hypnotized person's awareness that silently observes events.

Hierarchy A rank-ordered series of higher and lower amounts, levels, degrees, or steps.

Hierarchy of human needs Abraham Maslow's ordering of needs, based on their presumed strength or potency.

Higher-order conditioning Classical conditioning in which a conditioned stimulus is used to reinforce further learning; that is, a CS is used as if it were a US.

Hippocampus (HIP-oh-CAMP-us) A part of the limbic system associated with emotion and the transfer of information from short-term memory to long-term memory.

Histogram A graph of a frequency distribution in which the number of scores falling in each class is represented by vertical bars.

Homeostasis (HOE-me-oh-STAY-sis) A steady state of body equilibrium.

Homogamy Marriage of two people who are similar to one another.

Homosexual A person romantically and erotically attracted to same-sex persons.

Honesty test A paper-and-pencil test designed to detect attitudes, beliefs, and behavior patterns that predispose a person to dishonest behavior.

Hormonal sex Sex as indicated by a preponderance of estrogens (female) or androgens (male) in the body.

Hormone A glandular secretion that affects bodily functions or behavior.

Human factors psychology (ergonomics) A specialty concerned with making machines and work environments compatible with human perceptual and physical capacities.

Human growth sequence The pattern of physical development from conception to death.

Human nature Those traits, qualities, potentials, and behavior patterns most characteristic of the human species.

Human–computer interaction (HCI) The application of human factors to the design of computers and computer software.

Humanism An approach to psychology that focuses on human experience, problems, potentials, and ideals.

Hydrocephaly A buildup of cerebrospinal fluid within brain cavities.

Hyperopia (HI-per-OPE-ee-ah) Difficulty focusing on nearby objects (farsightedness).

Hypersomnia (hi-per-SOM-nee-ah) Excessive daytime sleepiness. This can result from depression, insomnia, narcolepsy, sleep apnea, sleep drunkenness (a very slow transition to waking), periodic limb movements, drug abuse, and other problems.

Hypnagogic images Vivid mental images that may occur just as one enters stage 1 sleep.

Hypnosis An altered state of consciousness characterized by narrowed attention and increased suggestibility.

Hypnotic susceptibility One's capacity for becoming hypnotized.

Hypoactive sexual desire A persistent, upsetting loss of sexual desire.

Hypochondriac (HI-po-KON-dree-ak) A person who complains about illnesses that appear to be imaginary.

Hypochondriasis (HI-po-kon-DRY-uh-sis) A preoccupation with fears of having a serious disease. Ordinary physical signs are interpreted as proof that the person has a disease, but no physical disorder can be found.

Hypothalamus (HI-po-THAL-ah-mus) A small area at the base of the brain that regulates many aspects of motivation and emotion, especially hunger, thirst, and sexual behavior.

Hypothesis (hi-POTH-eh-sis) The predicted outcome of an experiment or an educated guess about the relationship between variables.

Hypothetical possibilities Suppositions, guesses, or projections.

Iconic (EYE-kon-ick) **memory** A mental image or visual representation.

Id The primitive part of personality that remains unconscious, supplies energy, and demands pleasure.

Ideal self An idealized image of oneself (the person one would like to be).

Identical twins Twins who develop from a single egg and have identical genes.

Identification Feeling emotionally connected to a person and seeing oneself as like him or her. Taking on some of the characteristics of an admired person, usually as a way of compensating for perceived personal weaknesses or faults.

Identity versus role confusion A conflict of adolescence, involving the need to establish a personal identity.

Illogical thought Thought that is intuitive, haphazard, or irrational.

Illusion A misleading or distorted perception.

Illustrators Gestures people use to illustrate what they are saying.

Image Most often, a mental representation that has picture-like qualities; an icon.

Imagery rehearsal Mentally rehearsing and changing a nightmare in an attempt to prevent it from reoccurring.

Imaginary audience The group of people a person imagines is watching (or will watch) his or her actions.

I-message A message that states the effect someone else's behavior has on you.

Imitation An attempt to match one's own behavior to another person's behavior.

Immune system System that mobilizes the body's defenses (such as white blood cells) against invading microbes and other disease agents.

Implicit memory A memory that a person does not know exists; a memory that is retrieved unconsciously.

Imprinting A rapid and relatively permanent type of learning that occurs during a limited period early in life.

Inattentional blindness Failure to perceive a stimulus that is in plain view but not the focus of attention.

In-basket test A testing procedure that simulates the individual decision-making challenges that executives face.

Incentive value The value of a goal above and beyond its ability to fill a need.

Incongruence State that exists when there is a discrepancy between one's experiences and self-image or between one's self-image and ideal self.

Incongruent person A person who has an inaccurate self-image or whose self-image differs greatly from the ideal self.

Incremental problem solving Thinking marked by a series of small steps that lead to an original solution.

Independent variable In an experiment, the condition being investigated as a possible cause of some change in behavior. The values that this variable takes are chosen by the experimenter.

Individual intelligence test A test of intelligence designed to be given to a single individual by a trained specialist.

Individual traits Personality traits that define a person's unique individual qualities.

Individuating information Information that helps define a person as an individual, rather than as a member of a group or social category.

Inductive thought Thinking in which a general rule or principle is gathered from a series of specific examples; for instance, inferring the laws of gravity by observing many falling objects.

Industrial/organizational (I/O) psychology A field that focuses on the psychology of work and on behavior within organizations.

Industry versus inferiority A conflict in middle childhood centered around lack of support for industrious behavior, which can result in feelings of inferiority.

Inferential statistics Mathematical tools used for decision making, for generalizing from small samples, and for drawing conclusions.

Information bits Meaningful units of information, such as numbers, letters, words, or phrases.

Information chunks Information bits grouped into larger units.

In-group A group with which a person identifies.

Informational view Perspective that explains learning in terms of information imparted by events in the environment.

Initiative versus guilt A conflict between learning to take initiative and overcoming feelings of guilt about doing so.

Insanity A legal term that refers to a mental inability to manage one's affairs or to be aware of the consequences of one's actions.

Insecure-ambivalent attachment An anxious emotional bond marked by both a desire to be with a parent or caregiver and some resistance to being reunited.

Insecure-avoidant attachment An anxious emotional bond marked by a tendency to avoid reunion with a parent or caregiver.

Insight A sudden mental reorganization of a problem that makes the solution obvious.

Insomnia Difficulty in getting to sleep or staying asleep.

Inspection time The amount of time a person must look at a stimulus to make a correct judgment about it.

Instrumental behaviors Behaviors directed toward the achievement of some goal; behaviors that are instrumental in producing some effect.

Integrity versus despair A conflict in old age between feelings of integrity and the despair of viewing previous life events with regret.

Intellectual disability (formerly **mental retardation**) The presence of a developmental disability, a formal IQ score below 70, or a significant impairment of adaptive behavior.

Intellectualization Separating emotion from a threatening or anxiety-provoking situation by talking or thinking about it in impersonal "intellectual" terms.

Intelligence An overall capacity to think rationally, act purposefully, and deal effectively with the environment.

Intelligence quotient (IQ) An index of intelligence defined as a person's mental age divided by his or her chronological age and multiplied by 100.

Interference The tendency for new memories to impair retrieval of older memories, and the reverse.

Internal cause A cause of behavior assumed to lie within a person—for instance, a need, preference, or personality trait.

Internal images Mental images or visual depictions used in memory and thinking.

Internet An electronic network of interlinked computers.

Interpersonal attraction Social attraction to another person.

Interpretation Where pain is concerned, the meaning given to a stimulus.

Intersexual person A person who has genitals suggestive of both sexes.

Interview (personality) A face-to-face meeting held for the purpose of gaining information about an individual's personal history, personality traits, current psychological state, and so forth.

Intimacy versus isolation The challenge of overcoming a sense of isolation by establishing intimacy with others.

Intimate distance The most private space immediately surrounding the body (up to about 18 inches from the skin).

Intracellular thirst Thirst triggered when fluid is drawn out of cells due to an increased concentration of salts and minerals outside the cell.

Intrinsic motivation Motivation that comes from within, rather than from external rewards; motivation based on personal enjoyment of a task or activity.

Introspection To look within; to examine one's own thoughts, feelings, or sensations.

Introvert A person whose attention is focused inward; a shy, reserved, self-centered person.

Intuition Quick, impulsive thought that does not make use of formal logic or clear reasoning.

Intuitive thought Thinking that makes little or no use of reasoning and logic.

Ion (EYE-on) **channels** Tiny openings through the axon membrane.

Iris Circular muscle that controls the amount of light entering the eye.

Isolation Separating contradictory thoughts or feelings into "logic-tight" mental compartments so that they do not come into conflict.

James-Lange theory States that emotional feelings follow bodily arousal and come from awareness of such arousal.

Jigsaw classroom A method of reducing prejudice; each student receives only part of the information needed to complete a project or prepare for a test.

Job analysis A detailed description of the skills, knowledge, and activities required by a particular job.

Job enrichment Making a job more personally rewarding, interesting, or intrinsically motivating; typically involves increasing worker knowledge.

Job satisfaction The degree to which a person is comfortable with or satisfied with his or her work.

Just noticeable difference (JND) Any noticeable difference in a stimulus.

Just-world beliefs Belief that people generally get what they deserve.

Keyword method As an aid to memory, using a familiar word or image to link two items.

Kinesics (kih-NEEZ-iks) Study of the meaning of body movements, posture, hand gestures, and facial expressions; commonly called body language.

Kinesthetic senses The senses of body movement and positioning.

Knowledge of results (KR) Informational feedback.

Knowledge workers Workers who add value to their company by creating and manipulating information.

Labia majora (LAY-bee-ah mah-JOR-ah) The larger outer lips of the vulva.

Labia minora (LAY-bee-ah mih-NOR-ah) Inner lips of the vulva, surrounding the vaginal opening.

Language Words or symbols, and rules for combining them, that are used for thinking and communication.

Large-group awareness training Any of a number of programs (many of them commercialized) that claim to increase self-awareness and facilitate constructive personal change.

Latency According to Freud, a period in childhood when psychosexual development is more or less interrupted.

Latent dream content The hidden or symbolic meaning of a dream, as revealed by dream interpretation and analysis.

Latent learning Learning that occurs without obvious reinforcement and that remains unexpressed until reinforcement is provided.

Lateralization Differences between the two sides of the body; especially, differences in the abilities of the brain hemispheres.

Law of effect Responses that lead to desirable effects are repeated; those that produce undesirable results are not.

Leaderless group discussion A test of leadership that simulates group decision-making and problem solving.

Learned helplessness A learned inability to overcome obstacles or to avoid punishment; learned passivity and inaction to aversive stimuli.

Learning Any relatively permanent change in behavior that can be attributed to experience.

Learning disorder Any problem with thinking, perception, language, attention, or activity levels that tends to impair learning ability.

Learning theorist A psychologist interested in the ways that learning shapes behavior and explains personality.

Legitimate power Social power based on a person's position as an agent of an accepted social order.

Lexigram A geometric shape used as a symbol for a word.

Libido (lih-BEE-doe) In Freudian theory, the force, primarily pleasure oriented, that energizes the personality.

Life change units (LCUs) Numerical values assigned to each life event on the SRRS.

Life expectancy The average number of years a person of a given sex, race, and nationality can expect to live.

Life skills training A program that teaches stress reduction, self-protection, decision making, self-control, and social skills.

Life stages Widely recognized periods of life corresponding to broad phases of development.

Life-span perspective The study of continuity and change in behavior over a lifetime.

Lifestyle disease A disease related to health-damaging personal habits.

Light sleep Stage 1 sleep, marked by small, irregular brainwaves and some alpha waves.

Liking A relationship based on intimacy, but lacking passion and commitment.

Limbic system A system in the forebrain that is closely linked with emotional response.

Linear relationship A relationship that forms a straight line when graphed.

Links Connections built into Internet sites that let you "jump" from one site to the next.

Lobes of the cerebral cortex Areas on the cortex bordered by major fissures or defined by their functions.

Localization of function The research strategy of linking specific structures in the brain with specific psychological or behavioral functions.

Lock and key theory Holds that odors are related to the shapes of chemical molecules.

Logical consequences Reasonable consequences that are defined by parents.

Logical thought Drawing conclusions on the basis of formal principles of reasoning.

Logotherapy A form of existential therapy that emphasizes the need to find and maintain meaning in one's life.

Long sleeper A person averaging 9 hours of sleep or more per night.

Long-term memory (LTM) The memory system used for relatively permanent storage of meaningful information.

Lowball technique A strategy in which commitment is gained first to reasonable or desirable terms, which are then made less reasonable or desirable.

Lucid dream A dream in which the dreamer feels awake and capable of normal thought and action.

Magnetic resonance imaging (MRI) Magnetic resonance imaging; a three-dimensional image of the brain or body, based on its response to a magnetic field.

Maintenance rehearsal Silently repeating or mentally reviewing information to hold it in short-term memory.

Major depressive disorder A mood disorder in which the person has suffered one or more intense episodes of depression.

Major mood disorders Disorders marked by lasting extremes of mood or emotion and sometimes accompanied by psychotic symptoms.

Maladaptive behavior Behavior that makes it difficult to adapt to the environment and meet the demands of day-to-day life.

Male orgasmic disorder A persistent inability to reach orgasm during lovemaking.

Management by objectives A management technique in which employees are given specific goals to meet in their work.

Management techniques Combining praise, recognition, approval, rules, and reasoning to enforce child discipline.

Mandala A circular design representing balance, unity, and completion.

Manifest dream content The surface, "visible" content of a dream; dream images as they are remembered by the dreamer.

Massed practice A practice schedule in which studying continues for long periods, without interruption.

Mastery training Reinforcement of responses that lead to mastery of a threat or control over one's environment.

Masturbation Producing sexual pleasure or orgasm by directly stimulating the genitals.

Maternal influences The aggregate of all psychological effects mothers have on their children.

Maternity blues A brief and relatively mild state of depression often experienced by mothers 2 or 3 days after giving birth.

Maturation The physical growth and development of the body and nervous system.

Maximum life span The biologically defined maximum number of years humans can live under optimal conditions.

Mean A measure of central tendency calculated by adding a group of scores and then dividing by the total number of scores.

Means-ends analysis An analysis of how to reduce the difference between the present state of affairs and a desired goal.

Mechanical solution A problem solution achieved by trial and error or by a fixed procedure based on learned rules.

Median A central tendency found by arranging scores from the highest to the lowest and selecting the score that falls in the middle. That is, half the values in a group of scores fall above the median and half fall below.

Medicated birth The common practice in Western medicine of giving painkilling drugs during labor and birth.

Meditation A mental exercise for producing relaxation or heightened awareness.

Medulla (meh-DUL-ah) The structure that connects the brain with the spinal cord and controls vital life functions.

Melatonin (mel-ah-TONE-in) A hormone released by the pineal gland in response to daily cycles of light and dark.

Memory The mental system for receiving, encoding, storing, organizing, altering, and retrieving information.

Memory cue Any stimulus associated with a particular memory. Memory cues usually enhance retrieval.

Memory decay The fading or weakening of memories assumed to occur when memory traces become weaker.

Memory task Any task designed to test or assess memory.

Memory traces Physical changes in nerve cells or brain activity that take place when memories are stored.

Menopause The female "change of life" signaled by the end of regular monthly menstrual periods.

Mental age The average mental ability people display at a given age.

Mental disorder A significant impairment in psychological functioning.

Mental hospitalization Placing a person in a protected, therapeutic environment staffed by mental health professionals.

Mental images Mental pictures or visual depictions used in memory and thinking.

Mental practice Imagining a skilled performance to aid learning.

Mental set A predisposition to perceive or respond in a particular way.

Meta-analysis A statistical technique for combining the results of many studies on the same subject.

Meta-needs In Maslow's hierarchy, needs associated with impulses for self-actualization.

Metacognitive skills An ability to manage one's own thinking and problem-solving efforts.

Microcephaly A disorder in which the head and brain are abnormally small.

Microsleep A brief shift in brainwave patterns to those of sleep.

Mindfulness A state of open, nonjudgmental, awareness of current experience.

Mindfulness meditation Mental exercise based on widening attention to become aware of everything experienced at any given moment.

Minnesota Multiphasic Personality Inventory-2 (MMPI-2) One of the best-known and most widely used objective personality questionnaires.

Mirror neuron A neuron that becomes active when a motor action is carried out *and* when another organism is observed carrying out the same action.

Mirror technique Observing another person reenact one's own behavior, like a character in a play; designed to help persons see themselves more clearly.

MMPI-2 profile A graphic representation of an individual's scores on each of the primary scales of the MMPI-2.

Mnemonic (nee-MON-ik) Any kind of memory system or aid.

Mock jury A group that realistically simulates a courtroom jury.

Mode A measure of central tendency found by identifying the most frequently occurring score in a group of scores.

Model A person who serves as an example in observational learning.

Monocular depth cues Perceptual features that require just one eye and impart information about distance and three-dimensional space.

Mood A low-intensity, long-lasting emotional state.

Mood disorder A major disturbance in mood or emotion, such as depression or mania.

Moon illusion The apparent change in size that occurs as the moon moves from the horizon (large moon) to overhead (small moon).

Moral anxiety Apprehension felt when thoughts, impulses, or actions conflict with the superego's standards.

Moral development The development of values, beliefs, and thinking abilities that act as a guide regarding what is acceptable behavior.

Morphemes (MOR-feems) The smallest meaningful units in a language, such as syllables or words.

Motherese (parentese) A pattern of speech used when talking to infants, marked by a higher-pitched voice; short, simple sentences; repetition; slower speech; and exaggerated voice inflections.

Motivation Internal processes that initiate, sustain, and direct activities.

Motor cortex A brain area associated with control of movement.

Motor program A mental plan or model that guides skilled movement.

Motor skill A series of actions molded into a smooth and efficient performance.

MRI scan Magnetic resonance imaging; a computer-enhanced three-dimensional representation of the brain or body based on the body's response to a magnetic field.

Müller-Lyer (MEOO-ler-LIE-er) **illusion** Two equal-length lines tipped with inward or outward pointing V's appear to be of different lengths.

Multiculturalism Giving equal status, recognition, and acceptance to different ethnic and cultural groups.

Multimedia computerized test A test that uses a computer to present lifelike situations; test takers react to problems posed by the situations.

Multiple approach-avoidance conflict Being simultaneously attracted to and repelled by each of several alternatives.

Multiple aptitude test Test that measures two or more aptitudes.

Multiple intelligences Howard Gardner's theory that there are several specialized types of intellectual ability.

Mutual absorption With regard to romantic love, the nearly exclusive attention lovers give to each other.

Munchausen by proxy An affected person fakes the medical problems of someone in his or her care in order to gain attention.

Munchausen syndrome An affected person fakes his or her own medical problems in order to gain attention.

Mutual interdependence A condition in which two or more persons must depend on each other to meet each person's needs or goals.

Myelin (MY-eh-lin) A fatty layer coating some axons.

Myopia (my-OPE-ee-ah) Difficulty focusing on distant objects (nearsightedness).

Narcolepsy (NAR-koe-lep-see) Sudden, irresistible, daytime sleep attacks that may last anywhere from a few minutes to a half hour. Victims may fall asleep while standing, talking, or even driving.

Natural clinical test An accident or other natural event that allows the gathering of data on a psychological phenomenon of interest.

Natural consequences The effects that naturally tend to follow a particular behavior.

Natural design Human factors engineering that makes use of naturally understood perceptual signals.

Natural selection Darwin's theory that evolution favors those plants and animals best suited to their living conditions.

Naturalistic observation Observing behavior as it unfolds in natural settings.

Near-death experience (NDE) A pattern of subjective experiences that may occur when a person is clinically dead and then resuscitated.

Need An internal deficiency that may energize behavior.

Need for achievement (nAch) The desire to excel or meet some internalized standard of excellence.

Need for power The desire to have social impact and control over others.

Need to affiliate The desire to associate with other people.

Negative after-potential A drop in electrical charge below the resting potential.

Negative correlation A statistical relationship in which increases in one measure are matched by decreases in the other.

Negative instance In concept learning, an object or event that does not belong to the concept class.

Negative reinforcement Occurs when a response is followed by an end to discomfort or by the removal of an unpleasant event.

Negative relationship A mathematical relationship in which increases in one measure are matched by decreases in the other.

Negative self-statements Self-critical thoughts that increase anxiety and lower performance.

Negative transfer Mastery of one task conflicts with learning or performing another.

Neo-Freudian A psychologist who accepts the broad features of Freud's theory but has revised the theory to fit his or her own concepts.

Nerve A bundle of neuron fibers.

Network model A model of memory that views it as an organized system of linked information.

Neural intelligence The innate speed and efficiency of a person's brain and nervous system.

Neurilemma (NOOR-rih-LEM-ah) A layer of cells that encases many axons.

Neurological soft signs Subtle behavioral signs of brain dysfunction, including clumsiness, an awkward gait, poor hand-eye coordination, and other perceptual and motor problems.

Neurogenesis (noor-oh-JEN-uh-sis) The production of new brain cells.

Neuron (NOOR-on) An individual nerve cell.

Neuropeptides (NOOR-oh-PEP-tides) Brain chemicals, such as enkephalins and endorphins, that regulate the activity of neurons.

Neurosis An outdated term once used to refer, as a group, to anxiety disorders, somatoform disorders, dissociative disorders, and some forms of depression.

Neurotic anxiety Apprehension felt when the ego struggles to control id impulses.

Neurotransmitter (NOOR-oh-TRANS-mit-ers) Any chemical released by a neuron that alters activity in other neurons.

Neutral stimulus (NS) A stimulus that does not evoke a response.

Night blindness Blindness under conditions of low illumination.

Night terror A state of panic during NREM sleep.

Nightmare A bad dream that occurs during REM sleep.

Nightmare disorder Vivid, recurrent nightmares that significantly disturb sleep.

Noise pollution Stressful and intrusive noise; usually artificially generated by machinery, but also including noises made by animals and humans.

Noise-induced hearing loss Damage caused by exposing the hair cells to excessively loud sounds.

Nonhomeostatic drive A drive that is relatively independent of physical deprivation cycles or bodily need states

Non-REM (NREM) sleep Non–rapid eye movement sleep characteristic of stages 1, 2, 3, and 4.

Norepinephrine An adrenal hormone that tends to arouse the body; norepinephrine is associated with anger. (Also known as noradrenaline.)

Norm (social) A widely accepted (but often unspoken) standard of conduct for appropriate behavior.

Norm (testing) An average score for a designated group of people.

Normal curve A bell-shaped curve characterized by a large number of scores in a middle area, tapering to very few extremely high and low scores.

Obedience Conformity to the demands of an authority.

Object permanence Concept, gained in infancy, that objects continue to exist even when they are hidden from view.

Objective test A test that gives the same score when different people correct it.

Observational learning Learning achieved by watching and imitating the actions of another or noting the consequences of those actions.

Observational record A detailed summary of observed events or a videotape of observed behavior.

Observer bias The tendency of an observer to distort observations or perceptions to match his or her expectations.

Observer effect Changes in a person's behavior brought about by an awareness of being observed.

Obsessive-compulsive disorder An extreme preoccupation with certain thoughts and compulsive performance of certain behaviors.

Occipital (awk-SIP-ih-tal) **lobes** Portion of the cerebral cortex where vision registers in the brain.

Oedipus conflict A boy's sexual attraction to his mother and feelings of rivalry with his father.

Olfaction The sense of smell.

Open teaching Instruction based on active teacher-student discussion.

Open-ended interview An interview in which persons are allowed to freely state their views.

Operant conditioning (instrumental learning) Learning based on the consequences of responding.

Operant extinction The weakening or disappearance of a nonreinforced operant response.

Operant reinforcer Any event that reliably increases the probability or frequency of responses it follows.

Operant stimulus discrimination The tendency to make an operant response when stimuli previously associated with reward are present and to withhold the response when stimuli associated with nonreward are present.

Operant stimulus generalization The tendency to respond to stimuli similar to those that preceded operant reinforcement.

Operational definition Defining a scientific concept by stating the specific actions or procedures used to measure it. For example, "hunger" might be defined as "the number of hours of food deprivation."

Opponent-process theory With respect to emotions, a theory that states that strong emotions tend to be followed by an opposite emotional state; also, the strength of both emotional states changes over time.

Opponent-process theory Theory of color vision based on three coding systems (red or green, yellow or blue, black or white).

Oral stage The period when infants are preoccupied with the mouth as a source of pleasure and means of expression.

Oral-aggressive personality A person who uses the mouth to express hostility by shouting, cursing, biting, and so forth. Also, one who actively exploits others.

Oral-dependent personality A person who wants to passively receive attention, gifts, love, and so forth.

Organ of Corti (KOR-tee) Center part of the cochlea, containing hair cells, canals, and membranes.

Organic mental disorder A mental or emotional problem caused by brain diseases or injuries.

Organismic valuing A natural, undistorted, full-body reaction to an experience.

Organizational citizenship Making positive contributions to the success of an organization in ways that go beyond one's job description.

Organizational culture The social climate within an organization.

Orgasm A climax and release of sexual excitement.

Orientation response Bodily changes that prepare an organism to receive information from a particular stimulus.

Originality In tests of creativity, originality refers to how novel or unusual solutions are.

Out-group A group with which a person does not identify.

Ovary (OH-vah-ree) One of the two female reproductive glands; ovaries are the source of hormones and eggs.

Overgeneralization Blowing a single event out of proportion by extending it to a large number of unrelated situations.

Overlearning Continuing to study and learn after you think you've mastered a topic.

Overly permissive parents Parents who give little guidance, allow too much freedom, or do not require the child to take responsibility.

Pain disorder Pain that has no identifiable physical cause and appears to be of psychological origin.

Panic disorder (with agoraphobia) A chronic state of anxiety and brief moments of sudden panic. The person fears that these panic attacks will occur in public places or unfamiliar situations.

Panic disorder (without agoraphobia) A chronic state of anxiety and also brief moments of sudden, intense, unexpected panic.

Paranoid psychosis A delusional disorder centered especially on delusions of persecution.

Paranoid schizophrenia Schizophrenia marked by a preoccupation with delusions or by frequent auditory hallucinations related to a single theme, especially grandeur or persecution.

Paraphilias (PAIR-eh-FIL-ih-ahs) Compulsive or destructive deviations in sexual preferences or behavior.

Paraprofessional An individual who works in a near-professional capacity under the supervision of a more highly trained person.

Parapsychology The study of extra-normal psychological events, such as extrasensory perception.

Parasympathetic branch A part of the autonomic system that quiets the body and conserves energy.

Parasympathetic rebound Excess activity in the parasympathetic nervous system following a period of intense emotion.

Parasympathetic system A branch of the ANS that quiets the body.

Parental styles Identifiable patterns of parental caretaking and interaction with children.

Parentese A pattern of speech used when talking to infants, marked by a higher-pitched voice; short, simple sentences; repetition; slower speech; and exaggerated voice inflections.

Parietal (puh-RYE-ih-tal) **lobes** Area of the brain where body sensations register.

Partial hospitalization An approach in which patients receive treatment at a hospital during the day but return home at night.

Partial reinforcement A pattern in which only a portion of all responses are reinforced.

Partial reinforcement effect Responses acquired with partial reinforcement are more resistant to extinction.

Participants Humans (also referred to as **experimental subjects**) whose behavior is investigated in an experiment.

Participative management An approach to management that allows employees at all levels to participate in decision making.

Passive compliance Passively bending to unreasonable demands or circumstances.

Paternal influences The aggregate of all psychological effects fathers have on their children.

Peak experiences Temporary moments of self-actualization.

Peak performance A performance during which physical, mental, and emotional states are harmonious and optimal.

Peer counselor A nonprofessional person who has learned basic counseling skills.

Peer group A group of people who share similar social status.

Percent of variance A portion of the total amount of variation in a group of scores.

Pelvic bone One of the bones at the front of the pelvis (the pelvis connects the spine with the legs).

Perception The mental process of organizing sensations into meaningful patterns.

Perceptual construction A mental model of external events.

Perceptual defense Resistance to perceiving threatening or disturbing stimuli.

Perceptual expectancy (or **set**) A readiness to perceive in a particular manner, induced by strong expectations.

Perceptual features Important elements of a stimulus pattern, such as lines, shapes, edges, spots, and colors.

Perceptual hypothesis An initial guess regarding how to organize (perceive) a stimulus pattern.

Perceptual learning Changes in perception that can be attributed to prior experience; a result of changes in how the brain processes sensory information.

Perceptual reconstruction A mental model of external events.

Perfect negative relationship A mathematical relationship in which the correlation between two measures is −1.00.

Perfect positive relationship A mathematical relationship in which the correlation between two measures is +1.00.

Performance intelligence Intelligence measured by solving puzzles, assembling objects, completing pictures, and other nonverbal tasks.

Periodic limb movement syndrome Muscle twitches (primarily affecting the legs) that occur every 20 to 40 seconds and severely disturb sleep.

Peripheral nervous system (PNS) All parts of the nervous system outside the brain and spinal cord.

Peripheral vision Vision at the edges of the visual field.

Persona The "mask" or public self presented to others.

Personal distance The distance maintained when interacting with close friends (about 18 inches to 4 feet from the body).

Personal interview Formal or informal questioning of job applicants to learn their qualifications and to gain an impression of their personalities.

Personal prejudice Prejudicial attitudes held toward persons who are perceived as a direct threat to one's own interests.

Personal space An area surrounding the body that is regarded as private and subject to personal control.

Personal unconscious A mental storehouse for a single individual's unconscious thoughts.

Personality A person's unique and relatively stable behavior patterns.

Personality disorder A maladaptive personality pattern.

Personality questionnaire A paper-and-pencil test consisting of questions that reveal aspects of personality.

Personality theory A system of concepts, assumptions, ideas, and principles used to understand and explain personality.

Personality trait A stable, enduring quality that a person shows in most situations.

Personality type A style of personality defined by a group of related traits.

Personnel psychology Branch of industrial/organizational psychology concerned with testing, selection, placement, and promotion of employees.

Persuasion A deliberate attempt to change attitudes or beliefs with information and arguments.

PET scan Positron emission tomography; a computer-generated image of brain activity, based on glucose consumption in the brain.

Phallic personality A person who is vain, exhibitionistic, sensitive, and narcissistic.

Phallic stage The psychosexual stage (roughly ages 3 to 6), when a child is preoccupied with the genitals.

Phantom limb The illusory sensation that a limb still exists after it is lost through accident or amputation.

Pharmacotherapy (FAR-meh-koe-THER-eh-pea) The use of drugs to alleviate the symptoms of emotional disturbance.

Phenylketonuria (FEN-ul-KEET-uh-NUREee-ah) A genetic disease that allows phenylpyruvic acid to accumulate in the body.

Pheromone An airborne chemical signal.

Phonemes (FOE-neems) The basic speech sounds of a language.

Phototherapy A treatment for seasonal affective disorder that involves exposure to bright, full-spectrum light.

Physical dependence Physical addiction, as indicated by the presence of drug tolerance and withdrawal symptoms.

Physical environments Natural settings, such as forests and beaches, as well as environments built by humans, such as buildings, ships, and cities.

Physiological changes (in emotion) Alterations in heart rate, blood pressure, perspiration, and other involuntary responses.

Pica Eating or chewing on inedible objects or substances such as chalk, ashes, and the like.

Pictorial depth cues Monocular depth cues found in paintings, drawings, and photographs that impart information about space, depth, and distance.

Pineal (pin-EE-ul) **gland** A gland in the brain that helps regulate body rhythms and sleep cycles.

Pituitary gland The "master gland" whose hormones influence other endocrine glands.

Place theory A theory that higher and lower tones excite specific areas of the cochlea.

Placebo (plah-SEE-bo) An inactive substance given in the place of a drug in psychological research or by physicians who wish to treat a complaint by suggestion.

Placebo effect Changes in behavior due to expectations that a drug (or other treatment) will have some effect.

Plasticity The capacity of our brains to change in response to experience.

Plateau phase The second phase of sexual response, during which physical arousal is further heightened.

Pleasure principle A desire for immediate satisfaction of wishes, desires, or needs.

Polygenic (pol-ih-JEN-ik) **characteristics** Personal traits or physical properties that are influenced by many genes working in combination.

Polygraph A device for recording heart rate, blood pressure, respiration, and galvanic skin response; commonly called a "lie detector."

Pons An area on the brainstem that acts as a bridge between the medulla and other structures.

Population An entire group of animals or people belonging to a particular category (for example, all college students or all married women).

Positive correlation A statistical relationship in which increases in one measure are matched by increases in the other (or decreases correspond with decreases).

Positive instance In concept learning, an object or event that belongs to the concept class.

Positive psychology The study of human strengths, virtues, and effective functioning.

Positive reinforcement Occurs when a response is followed by a reward or other positive event.

Positive relationship A mathematical relationship in which increases in one measure are matched by increases in the other (or decreases correspond with decreases).

Positive self-regard Thinking of oneself as a good, lovable, worthwhile person.

Positive transfer Mastery of one task aids learning or performing another.

Possible self A collection of thoughts, beliefs, feelings, and images concerning the person one could become.

Postconventional moral reasoning Moral thinking based on carefully examined and self-chosen moral principles.

Postpartum depression A mild to moderately severe depression that begins within 3 months following childbirth.

Posttraumatic stress disorder (PTSD) A psychological disturbance lasting more than 1 month following stresses that would produce anxiety in anyone who experienced them.

Power assertion The use of physical punishment or coercion to enforce child discipline.

Precognition The purported ability to accurately predict future events.

Preconscious An area of the mind containing information that can be voluntarily brought to awareness.

Preconventional moral reasoning Moral thinking based on the consequences of one's choices or actions (punishment, reward, or an exchange of favors).

Prediction An ability to accurately forecast behavior.

Prefrontal area (cortex) The very front of the frontal lobes; involved in sense of self, reasoning, and planning.

Prejudice A negative emotional attitude held against members of a particular group of people.

Premack principle Any high-frequency response can be used to reinforce a low-frequency response.

Premature ejaculation Ejaculation that consistently occurs before the man and his partner want it to occur.

Preoperational stage A period of intellectual development during which children begin to use language and think symbolically, yet remain intuitive and egocentric in their thought.

Prepared childbirth A collection of techniques designed to manage discomfort and facilitate birth so that the use of painkilling drugs can be avoided or minimized.

Presbyopia (prez-bee-OPE-ee-ah) Farsightedness caused by aging.

Pressure A stressful condition that occurs when a person must meet urgent external demands or expectations.

Primary appraisal Deciding if a situation is relevant to oneself and if it is a threat.

Primary auditory area Part of the temporal lobe where auditory information is first registered.

Primary emotions According to Robert Plutchik's theory, the most basic emotions are fear, surprise, sadness, disgust, anger, anticipation, joy, and acceptance.

Primary motives Innate motives based on biological needs.

Primary motor area (or cortex) A brain area associated with control of movement.

Primary reinforcers Nonlearned reinforcers; usually those that satisfy physiological needs.

Primary sexual characteristics Sex as defined by the genitals and internal reproductive organs.

Primary somatosensory (SO-mat-oh-SEN-so-ree) **area (cortex)** A receiving area for body sensations.

Primary visual area The part of occipital lobe that first receives input from the eyes.

Priming Facilitating the retrieval of an implicit memory by using cues to activate hidden memories.

Private self-consciousness Preoccupation with inner feelings, thoughts, and fantasies.

Proactive (pro-AK-tiv) **interference** The tendency for old memories to interfere with the retrieval of newer memories.

Problem finding The active discovery of problems to be solved.

Problem-focused coping Directly managing or remedying a stressful or threatening situation.

Procedural memory Long-term memories of conditioned responses and learned skills.

Programmed instruction Any learning format that presents information in small amounts, gives immediate practice, and provides continuous feedback to learners.

Progressive relaxation A method for producing deep relaxation of all parts of the body.

Projection Attributing one's own feelings, shortcomings, or unacceptable impulses to others.

Projective tests Psychological tests making use of ambiguous or unstructured stimuli.

Prosocial behavior Behavior toward others that is helpful, constructive, or altruistic.

Prostate (PROSS-tate) A gland located at the base of the urinary bladder that supplies most of the fluid that makes up semen.

Prototype An ideal model used as a prime example of a particular concept.

Proxemics (prok-SEE-miks) Systematic study of the human use of space, particularly in social settings.

Pseudopsychology (SUE-doe-psychology) Any false and unscientific system of beliefs and practices that is offered as an explanation of behavior.

Psi (sigh) **phenomena** Events that seem to lie outside the realm of accepted scientific laws.

Psyche The mind, mental life, and personality as a whole.

Psychiatric social worker A mental health professional trained to apply social science principles to help patients in clinics and hospitals.

Psychiatrist A medical doctor with additional training in the diagnosis and treatment of mental and emotional disorders.

Psychoactive drug A substance capable of altering attention, memory, judgment, time sense, self-control, mood, or perception.

Psychoanalysis A Freudian therapy that emphasizes the use of free association, dream interpretation, resistances, and transference to uncover unconscious conflicts.

Psychoanalyst A mental health professional (usually a medical doctor) trained to practice psychoanalysis.

Psychoanalytic theory Freudian theory of personality that emphasizes unconscious forces and conflicts.

Psychodrama A therapy in which clients act out personal conflicts and feelings in the presence of others who play supporting roles.

Psychodynamic theory Any theory of behavior that emphasizes internal conflicts, motives, and unconscious forces.

Psychogenic Having psychological origins, rather than physical causes.

Psychokinesis The purported ability to mentally alter or influence objects or events.

Psychological dependence Drug dependence that is based primarily on emotional or psychological needs.

Psychological efficiency Maintenance of good morale, labor relations, employee satisfaction, and similar aspects of work behavior.

Psychological perspective The traditional view that behavior is shaped by psychological processes occurring at the level of the individual.

Psychological situation A situation as it is perceived and interpreted by an individual, not as it exists objectively.

Psychological trauma A psychological injury or shock, such as that caused by violence, abuse, neglect, separation, and so forth.

Psychologist A person highly trained in the methods, factual knowledge, and theories of psychology.

Psychology The scientific study of behavior and mental processes.

Psychology of law Study of the psychological and behavioral dimensions of the legal system.

Psychoneuroimmunology Study of the links among behavior, stress, disease, and the immune system.

Psychopathology The scientific study of mental, emotional, and behavioral disorders; also, abnormal or maladaptive behavior.

Psychophysics Study of the relationship between physical stimuli and the sensations they evoke in a human observer.

Psychosexual stages The oral, anal, phallic, and genital stages, during which various personality traits are formed.

Psychosis A withdrawal from reality marked by hallucinations and delusions, disturbed thought and emotions, and personality disorganization.

Psychosocial dilemma A conflict between personal impulses and the social world that affects development.

Psychosomatic (SIKE-oh-so-MAT-ik) **disorders** Illnesses in which psychological factors contribute to bodily damage or to damaging changes in bodily functioning.

Psychosurgery Any surgical alteration of the brain designed to bring about desirable behavioral or emotional changes.

Psychotherapy Any psychological technique used to facilitate positive changes in a person's personality, behavior, or adjustment.

Psychotic disorder A severe mental disorder characterized by a retreat from reality, by hallucinations and delusions, and by social withdrawal.

PsycINFO A searchable, online database that provides brief summaries of the scientific and scholarly literature in psychology.

Puberty The biologically defined period during which a person matures sexually and becomes capable of reproduction.

Public distance Distance at which formal interactions, such as giving a speech, occur (about 12 feet or more from the body).

Public self-consciousness Intense awareness of oneself as a social object.

Punisher Any consequence that reduces the frequency of a target behavior.

Punishment Any event that follows a response and *decreases* its likelihood of occurring again.

Pupil The opening at the front of the eye through which light passes.

Quality circle An employee discussion group that makes suggestions for improving quality and solving business problems.

Racism Racial prejudice that has become institutionalized (that is, it is reflected in government policy, schools, and so forth) and that is enforced by the existing social power structure.

Random assignment The use of chance (for example, flipping a coin) to assign subjects to experimental and control groups.

Random search strategy Trying possible solutions to a problem in a more or less random order.

Random selection Choosing a sample so that each member of the population has an equal chance of being included in the sample.

Range The difference between the highest and lowest scores in a group of scores.

Rape myths False beliefs about rape that tend to blame the victim and increase the likelihood that some men will think that rape is justified.

Rapid eye movements (REMs) Swift eye movements during sleep.

Rating scale A list of personality traits or aspects of behavior on which a person is rated.

Rational-emotive behavior therapy (REBT) An approach that states that irrational beliefs cause many emotional problems and that such beliefs must be changed or abandoned.

Rationalization Justifying your behavior by giving reasonable and "rational," but false, reasons for it.

Reaction formation Preventing dangerous impulses from being expressed in behavior by exaggerating opposite behavior.

Reaction range The limits environment places on the effects of heredity.

Readiness A condition that exists when maturation has advanced enough to allow the rapid acquisition of a particular skill.

Reality principle Delaying action (or pleasure) until it is appropriate.

Reality testing Obtaining additional information to check on the accuracy of perceptions.

Recall To supply or reproduce memorized information with a minimum of external cues.

Receptor sites Areas on the surface of neurons and other cells that are sensitive to neurotransmitters or hormones.

Recessive gene A gene whose influence will be expressed only when it is paired with a second recessive gene.

Reciprocal inhibition The presence of one emotional state can inhibit the occurrence of another, such as joy preventing fear or anxiety inhibiting pleasure.

Recoding Reorganizing or modifying information to assist storage in memory.

Recognition memory An ability to correctly identify previously learned information.

Rectum The lowest section of the large intestine.

Redintegrative memories Memories that are reconstructed or expanded by starting with one memory and then following chains of association to other, related memories.

Reference group Any group that an individual identifies with and uses as a standard for social comparison.

Referent power Social power gained when one is used as a point of reference by others.

Referred pain Pain that is felt in one part of the body but comes from another.

Reflection In client-centered therapy, the process of rephrasing or repeating thoughts and feelings expressed by clients so they can become aware of what they are saying.

Reflex An innate, automatic response to a stimulus; for example, an eye blink.

Reflective intelligence An ability to become aware of one's own thinking habits.

Reflex arc The simplest behavior, in which a stimulus provokes an automatic response.

Refractory period A short period after orgasm during which males are unable to again reach orgasm.

Refusal skills training Program that teaches youths how to resist pressures to begin smoking (can also be applied to other drugs and health risks).

Regression Retreating to an earlier level of development or to earlier, less demanding habits or situations.

Reinforcement Any event that increases the probability that a particular response will occur.

Reinforcement value The subjective value a person attaches to a particular activity or reinforcer.

Relational concept A concept defined by the relationship between features of an object or between an object and its surroundings (for example, "greater than," "lopsided").

Relaxation response The pattern of internal bodily changes that occurs at times of relaxation.

Relearning Learning again something that was previously learned. Used to measure memory of prior learning.

Reliability The ability of a test to yield the same score, or nearly the same score, each time it is given to the same person.

REM behavior disorder A failure of normal muscle paralysis, leading to violent actions during REM sleep.

REM rebound The occurrence of extra rapid eye movement sleep following REM sleep deprivation.

REM sleep Sleep marked by rapid eye movements and a return to stage 1 EEG patterns.

Reminding system Pain based on small nerve fibers; reminds the brain that the body has been injured.

Replicate To reproduce or repeat.

Representative sample A small, randomly selected part of a larger population that accurately reflects characteristics of the whole population.

Representativeness heuristic A tendency to select wrong answers because they seem to match pre-existing mental categories.

Repression The unconscious process by which memories, thoughts, or impulses are held out of awareness. Also referred to as motivated forgetting.

Research method A systematic approach to answering scientific questions.

Resistance A blockage in the flow of free association; topics the client resists thinking or talking about.

Resolution The fourth phase of sexual response, involving a return to lower levels of sexual tension and arousal.

Respondent reinforcement Reinforcement that occurs when an unconditioned stimulus closely follows a conditioned stimulus.

Response Any muscular action, glandular activity, or other identifiable aspect of behavior.

Response chaining The assembly of separate responses into a series of actions that lead to reinforcement.

Response cost Removal of a positive reinforcer after a response is made.

REST Restricted environmental stimulation therapy.

Resting potential The electrical charge of a neuron at rest.

Restless legs syndrome An irresistible urge to move the legs in order to relieve sensations of creeping, tingling, prickling, aching, or tension.

Restricted Environmental Stimulation Therapy (REST) A form of sensory deprivation that results in a variety of psychological benefits.

Reticular (reh-TICK-you-ler) **formation** A network within the medulla and brainstem; associated with attention, alertness, and some reflexes.

Reticular activating system (RAS) A part of the reticular formation that activates the cerebral cortex.

Retina The light-sensitive layer of cells at the back of the eye.

Retrieval Recovering information from storage in memory.

Retroactive (RET-ro-AK-tiv) **interference** The tendency for new memories to interfere with the retrieval of old memories.

Retrograde amnesia Loss of memory for events that preceded a head injury or other amnesia-causing event.

Reversibility of thought Recognition that relationships involving equality or identity can be reversed (for example, if A = B, then B = A).

Reward Anything that produces pleasure or satisfaction; a positive reinforcer.

Reward power Social power based on the capacity to reward a person for acting as desired.

Rhodopsin The light-sensitive pigment in the rods.

Rods Visual receptors for dim light that produce only black and white sensations.

Role conflict Trying to occupy two or more roles that make conflicting demands on behavior.

Role reversal Taking the role of another person to learn how one's own behavior appears from the other person's perspective.

Romantic love Love that is associated with high levels of interpersonal attraction, heightened arousal, mutual absorption, and sexual desire.

Rorschach Technique A projective test comprised of 10 standardized inkblots.

Rote learning Learning that takes place mechanically, through repetition and memorization, or by learning rules.

Run of luck A statistically unusual outcome (as in getting five heads in a row when flipping a coin) that could still occur by chance alone.

Sample A smaller subpart of a population.

Satisficing Engaging in behavior that achieves a minimum result, rather than maximizing the outcome of that behavior.

Scaffolding The process of adjusting instruction so that it is responsive to a beginner's behavior and supports the beginner's efforts to understand a problem or gain a mental skill.

Scapegoating Blaming a person or a group of people for conditions not of their making.

Scatter diagram A graph that plots the intersection of paired measures; that is, the points at which paired X and Y measures cross.

Schachter's cognitive theory States that emotions occur when physical arousal is labeled or interpreted on the basis of experience and situational cues.

Schedule of reinforcement A rule or plan for determining which responses will be reinforced.

Schizophrenia (SKIT-soh-FREN-ee-uh) A psychosis characterized by delusions, hallucinations, apathy, and a "split" between thought and emotion.

Scientific jury selection Using social science principles to choose members of a jury.

Scientific management (Theory X) An approach to managing employees that emphasizes work efficiency.

Scientific method A form of critical thinking based on careful measurement and controlled observation.

Scientific observation An empirical investigation that is structured so that it answers questions about the world.

Scrotum (SKROE-tehm) The sac-like pouch that holds the testes.

Seasonal affective disorder (SAD) Depression that occurs only during fall and winter; presumably related to decreased exposure to sunlight.

Secondary appraisal Deciding how to cope with a threat or challenge.

Secondary elaboration Making a dream more logical and complete while remembering it.

Secondary motives Motives based on learned needs, drives, and goals.

Secondary reinforcer A learned reinforcer; often one that gains reinforcing properties by association with a primary reinforcer.

Secondary sexual characteristics Sexual features other than the genitals and reproductive organs—breasts, body shape, facial hair, and so forth.

Secondary traits Traits that are inconsistent or relatively superficial.

Secure attachment A stable and positive emotional bond.

Selective attention Giving priority, usually voluntarily, to a particular incoming sensory message.

Selective perception Perceiving only certain stimuli among a larger array of possibilities.

Self A continuously evolving conception of one's personal identity.

Self archetype An unconscious image representing, unity, wholeness, completion, and balance.

Self-actualization The ongoing process of fully developing one's personal potential.

Self-actualizer One who is living creatively and making full use of his or her potentials.

Self-assertion A direct, honest expression of feelings and desires.

Self-concept A person's perception of his or her own personality traits.

Self-defeating bias A distortion of thinking that impairs behavior.

Self-disclosure The process of revealing private thoughts, feelings, and one's personal history to others.

Self-efficacy (EF-uh-keh-see) Belief in your capacity to produce a desired result.

Self-esteem Regarding oneself as a worthwhile person; a positive evaluation of oneself.

Self-fulfilling prophecy An expectation that prompts people to act in ways that make the expectation come true.

Self-handicapping Arranging to perform under conditions that usually impair performance, so as to have an excuse for a poor showing.

Self-help group A group of people who share a particular type of problem and provide mutual support to one another.

Self-image Total subjective perception of one's body and personality (another term for self-concept).

Self-managed team A work group that has a high degree of freedom with respect to how it achieves its goals.

Self-recording Self-management based on keeping records of response frequencies.

Self-regulated learning Deliberately reflective and active self-guided study.

Self-reinforcement Praising or rewarding oneself for having made a particular response (such as completing a school assignment).

Self-testing Evaluating learning by posing questions to yourself.

Semantic memory A subpart of declarative memory that records impersonal knowledge about the world.

Semantics The study of meanings in words and language.

Seminal vesicles (SEM-in-uhl VES-ih-kuhlz) These two small organs (one on each side of the prostate) supply fluid that becomes part of semen.

Sensate focus A form of therapy that directs a couple's attention to natural sensations of sexual pleasure.

Sensation The immediate response in the brain caused by excitation of a sensory organ; also, the process of detecting physical energies with the sensory organs.

Sensitive period During development, a period of increased sensitivity to environmental influences. Also, a time during which certain events must take place for normal development to occur.

Sensitivity group A group experience consisting of exercises designed to increase self-awareness and sensitivity to others.

Sensorimotor stage Stage of intellectual development during which sensory input and motor responses become coordinated.

Sensorineural hearing loss Loss of hearing caused by damage to the inner ear hair cells or auditory nerve.

Sensory adaptation A decrease in sensory response to an unchanging stimulus.

Sensory analysis Separation of sensory information into important elements.

Sensory coding Codes used by the sense organs to transmit information to the brain.

Sensory conflict theory Explains motion sickness as the result of a mismatch among information from vision, the vestibular system, and kinesthesis.

Sensory deprivation (SD) Any major reduction in the amount or variety of sensory stimulation.

Sensory gating Alteration of sensory messages in the spinal cord.

Sensory memory The first, normally unconscious, stage of memory, which holds an exact record of incoming information for a few seconds or less.

Sensory neuron A nerve cell that carries information from the senses toward the CNS.

Separation anxiety disorder Severe and prolonged distress displayed by children when they are separated from their parents or caregivers.

Serial position effect The tendency to make the most errors in remembering the middle items of an ordered list.

Set point The proportion of body fat that tends to be maintained by changes in hunger and eating.

Sex One's biological classification as female or male.

Sex drive The strength of one's motivation to engage in sexual behavior.

Sexism Institutionalized prejudice against members of either sex, based solely on their gender.

Sex-linked trait Traits other than sex that are influenced by genes carried on an X chromosome (or, rarely, on a Y chromosome).

Sexual and gender identity disorders Any of a wide range of difficulties with sexual identity, deviant sexual behavior, or sexual adjustment.

Sexual aversion Persistent feelings of fear, anxiety, or disgust about engaging in sex.

Sexual orientation One's degree of emotional and erotic attraction to members of the same sex, opposite sex, or both sexes.

Sexual script An unspoken mental plan that defines a plot, dialogue, and actions expected to take place in a sexual encounter.

Sexually transmitted disease (STD) A disease that is typically passed from one person to the next by intimate physical contact; a venereal disease.

Shape constancy The perceived shape of an object is unaffected by changes in its retinal image.

Shaping Gradually molding responses to a final desired pattern.

Shared leadership (participative management) A leadership approach that allows employees at all levels to participate in decision making.

Short sleeper A person averaging 5 hours of sleep or less per night.

Short-term memory (STM) The memory system used to hold small amounts of information in our conscious awareness for about a dozen seconds.

Shyness A tendency to avoid others, plus uneasiness and strain when socializing.

Sidedness A combination of preference for hand, foot, eye, and ear.

Signal In early language development, any behavior, such as touching, vocalizing, gazing, or smiling, that allows nonverbal interaction and turn-taking between parent and child.

Simultaneous color contrast Changes in perceived hue that occur when a colored stimulus is displayed on backgrounds of various colors.

Single-blind experiment An arrangement in which participants remain unaware of whether they are in the experimental group or the control group.

Situational demands Unstated expectations that define desirable or appropriate behavior in various settings and social situations.

Situational determinants External conditions that strongly influence behavior.

Situational judgment test Presenting realistic work situations to applicants in order to observe their skills and reactions.

Situational test Simulating real-life conditions so that a person's reactions may be directly observed.

Size constancy The perceived size of an object remains constant, despite changes in its retinal image.

Size-distance invariance The strict relationship between the distance an object lies from the eyes and the size of its image.

Skin receptors Sensory organs for touch, pressure, pain, cold, and warmth.

Skin senses The senses of touch, pressure, pain, heat, and cold.

Sleep apnea (AP-nee-ah) During sleep, breathing stops for 20 seconds or more until the person wakes a little, gulps in air, and settles back to sleep; this cycle may be repeated hundreds of times per night.

Sleep deprivation Being prevented from getting desired or needed amounts of sleep.

Sleep drunkenness A slow transition to clear consciousness after awakening; sometimes associated with irritable or aggressive behavior.

Sleep hormone A sleep-promoting substance found in the brain and spinal cord.

Sleep patterns The order and timing of daily sleep and waking periods.

Sleep spindles Distinctive bursts of brainwave activity that indicate a person is asleep.

Sleep stages Levels of sleep identified by brainwave patterns and behavioral changes.

Sleep terror disorder The repeated occurrence of night terrors that significantly disturb sleep.

Sleep-deprivation psychosis A major disruption of mental and emotional functioning brought about by sleep loss.

Sleeptalking Speaking that occurs during NREM sleep.

Sleep-wake schedule disorder A mismatch between the sleep-wake schedule demanded by a person's body rhythm and that demanded by the environment.

Sleepwalking disorder Repeated incidents of leaving bed and walking about while asleep.

Social anxiety A feeling of apprehension in the presence of others.

Social comparison Making judgments about ourselves through comparison with others.

Social competition Rivalry among groups, each of which regards itself as superior to others.

Social development The development of self-awareness, attachment to parents or caregivers, and relationships with other children and adults.

Social dilemma A social situation that tends to provide immediate rewards for actions that will have undesired effects in the long run.

Social distance Distance at which impersonal interaction takes place (about 4 to 12 feet from the body).

Social distance scale A rating of the degree to which a person would be willing to have contact with a member of another group.

Social environment An environment defined by a group of people and their activities or interrelationships (such as a parade, revival meeting, or sports event).

Social exchange Any exchange between two people of attention, information, affection, favors, or the like.

Social exchange theory A theory stating that rewards must exceed costs for relationships to endure.

Social influence Changes in a person's behavior induced by the presence or actions of others.

Social learning theory An explanation of personality that combines learning principles, cognition, and the effects of social relationships.

Social markers Visible or tangible signs that indicate a person's social status or role.

Social motives Learned motives acquired as part of growing up in a particular society or culture.

Social nonconformity Failure to conform to societal norms or the usual minimum standards for social conduct.

Social norms Unspoken rules that define acceptable and expected behavior for members of a group.

Social phobia An intense, irrational fear of being observed, evaluated, embarrassed, or humiliated by others in social situations.

Social power The capacity to control, alter, or influence the behavior of another person.

Social psychology The scientific study of how individuals behave, think, and feel in social situations.

Social Readjustment Rating Scale (SRRS) A scale that rates the impact of various life events on the likelihood of illness.

Social referencing Observing others in social situations to obtain information or guidance.

Social reinforcement Praise, attention, approval, and/or affection from others.

Social reinforcer Reinforcement based on receiving attention, approval, or affection from another person.

Social role Expected behavior patterns associated with particular social positions (such as daughter, worker, student).

Social skills Proficiency at interacting with others.

Social smile Smiling elicited by social stimuli, such as seeing a parent's face.

Social stereotypes Oversimplified images of the traits of individuals who belong to a particular social group.

Social support Close, positive relationships with other people.

Solitary play Playing alone.

Sociocultural perspective The focus on the importance of social and cultural contexts in influencing the behavior of individuals.

Soma (SOH-mah) The main body of a neuron or other cell.

Somatic nervous system The system of nerves linking the spinal cord with the body and sense organs.

Somatic therapy Any bodily therapy, such as drug therapy, electroconvulsive therapy, or psychosurgery.

Somatization (som-ah-tuh-ZAY-shun) **disorder** Afflicted persons have numerous physical complaints. Typically, they have consulted many doctors, but no organic cause for their distress can be identified.

Somatoform (so-MAT-oh-form) **disorder** Physical symptoms that mimic disease or injury for which there is no identifiable physical cause.

Somatosensory area A receiving area for bodily sensations.

Somesthetic sense Sensations produced by the skin, muscles, joints, viscera, and organs of balance.

Somnambulism (som-NAM-bue-liz-im) Sleepwalking; occurs during NREM sleep.

Source traits Basic underlying traits, or dimensions, of personality; each source trait is reflected in a number of surface traits.

Spaced practice Practice spread over many relatively short study sessions.

Special aptitude test A test to predict a person's likelihood of succeeding in a particular area of work or skill.

Specific goal A goal with a clearly defined and measurable outcome.

Specific phobia An intense, irrational fear of specific objects, activities, or situations.

Speed of processing The speed with which a person can mentally process information.

Spinal nerves Major nerves that carry sensory and motor messages in and out of the spinal cord.

Split-brain operation Cutting the corpus callosum.

Spontaneous recovery The reappearance of a learned response after its apparent extinction.

Sports psychology Study of the psychological and behavioral dimensions of sports performance.

SQ4R method An active study-reading technique based on these steps: survey, question, read, recite, reflect, and review.

Squeeze technique A method for inhibiting ejaculation by compressing the tip of the penis.

Stage ESP The simulation of ESP for the purpose of entertainment.

Stage hypnosis Use of hypnosis to entertain; often, merely a simulation of hypnosis for that purpose.

Stage of exhaustion The third stage of the GAS, at which time the body's resources are exhausted and serious health consequences occur.

Stage of resistance The second stage of the GAS, during which bodily adjustments to stress stabilize, but at a high physical cost.

Standard deviation An index of how much a typical score differs from the mean of a group of scores.

State-dependent learning Memory influenced by one's bodily state at the time of learning and at the time of retrieval. Improved memory occurs when the bodily states match.

Statistical abnormality Abnormality defined on the basis of an extreme score on some dimension, such as IQ or anxiety.

Statistical significance The degree to which an event (such as the results of an experiment) is unlikely to have occurred by chance alone.

Status An individual's position in a social structure, especially with respect to power, privilege, or importance.

Status inequalities Differences in the power, prestige, or privileges of two or more persons or groups.

Stereoscopic vision Perception of space and depth caused chiefly by the fact that the eyes receive different images.

Sterilization Medical procedures such as vasectomy or tubal ligation that make a man or a woman infertile.

Stimulant A substance that increases activity in the body and nervous system.

Stimulation hearing loss Damage caused by exposing the hair cells to excessively loud sounds.

Stimulus Any physical energy sensed by an organism.

Stimulus control Stimuli present when an operant response is acquired tend to control when and where the response is made.

Stimulus discrimination The learned ability to respond differently to similar stimuli.

Stimulus drives Drives based on needs for exploration, manipulation, curiosity, and stimulation.

Stimulus generalization The tendency to respond to stimuli similar to, but not identical to, a conditioned stimulus.

Stimulus motives Innate needs for stimulation and information.

Storage Holding information in memory for later use.

Stress The mental and physical condition that occurs when a person must adjust or adapt to the environment.

Stress disorder A significant emotional disturbance caused by stresses outside the range of normal human experience.

Stress inoculation Use of positive coping statements to control fear and anxiety.

Stress management The application of behavioral strategies to reduce stress and improve coping skills.

Stress reaction The physical response to stress, consisting mainly of bodily changes related to autonomic nervous system arousal.

Stressor A specific condition or event in the environment that challenges or threatens a person.

Stress-vulnerability model Attributes psychosis to a combination of environmental stress and inherited susceptibility.

Striving for superiority According to Adler, this basic drive propels us toward perfection.

Stroboscopic movement An illusion of movement in which an object is shown in rapidly changing series of positions.

Structuralism The school of thought concerned with analyzing sensations and personal experience into basic elements.

Structured interview An interview that follows a prearranged plan, usually a series of planned questions.

Stuttering Chronic hesitation or stumbling in speech.

Style of life The pattern of personality and behavior that defines the pathway each person takes through life.

Subcortex All brain structures below the cerebral cortex.

Subjective experience Reality as it is perceived and interpreted, not as it exists objectively.

Subjective well-being General life satisfaction combined with frequent positive emotions and relatively few negative emotions.

Sublimation Working off unmet desires, or unacceptable impulses, in activities that are constructive.

Subliminal perception Perception of a stimulus below the threshold for conscious recognition.

Substance-related disorder Abuse of or dependence on a mood- or behavior-altering drug.

Sudden infant death syndrome (SIDS) The sudden, unexplained death of an apparently healthy infant.

Superego A judge or censor for thoughts and actions.

Superordinate goal A goal that exceeds or overrides all others; a goal that renders other goals relatively less important.

Superstitious behavior A behavior repeated because it seems to produce reinforcement, even though it is actually unnecessary.

Suppression A conscious effort to put something out of mind or to keep it from awareness.

Surface traits The visible or observable traits of one's personality.

Surrogate mother A substitute mother (often an inanimate dummy in animal research).

Survey method Using questionnaires and surveys to poll large groups of people.

Syllogism A format for analyzing logical arguments.

Symbolic prejudice Prejudice that is expressed in disguised fashion.

Symbolization The nonliteral expression of dream content.

Sympathetic branch A part of the ANS that activates the body at times of stress.

Sympathetic system A branch of the ANS that arouses the body.

Synapse (SIN-aps) The microscopic space between two neurons, over which messages pass.

Synesthesia Experiencing one sense in terms normally associated with another sense; for example, "seeing" colors when a sound is heard.

Syntax Rules for ordering words when forming sentences.

Systematic desensitization (dee-SEN-sih-tih-ZAY-shun) A reduction in fear, anxiety, or aversion brought about by planned exposure to aversive stimuli.

Task analysis Breaking complex skills into their subparts.

Taste aversion An active dislike for a particular food.

Taste bud The receptor organ for taste.

Teaching strategy A plan for effective teaching.

Telecommuting An approach to flexible work that involves working from home but using a computer to stay connected to the office throughout the workday.

Telepathy The purported ability to directly know another person's thoughts.

Temperament The hereditary physical core of personality, including emotional and perceptual sensitivity, activity levels, prevailing mood, irritability, and adaptability.

Temporal lobes Areas that include the sites on each side of the brain where hearing registers in the brain.

Tension-release method A procedure for systematically achieving deep relaxation of the body.

Teratogen (teh-RAT-uh-jen) Radiation, a drug, or other substance capable of altering fetal development in nonheritable ways that cause birth defects.

Term schedule A written plan that lists the dates of all major assignments for each of your classes for an entire semester or quarter.

Terminal decline An abrupt decline in measured intelligence about 5 years before death.

Territorial behavior Any behavior that tends to define a space as one's own or that protects it from intruders.

Territorial markers Objects and other signals whose placement indicates to others the "ownership" or control of a particular area.

Test anxiety High levels of arousal and worry that seriously impair test performance.

Test battery A group of tests and interviews given to the same individual.

Test standardization Establishing standards for administering a test and interpreting scores.

Testis (TES-tis, singular; testes, plural) One of the two male reproductive glands; the testes are a source of hormones and sperm.

Testosterone (tes-TOSS-teh-rone) A male sex hormone, secreted mainly by the testes and responsible for the development of many male sexual characteristics.

Thalamus (THAL-uh-mus) A brain structure that relays sensory information to the cerebral cortex.

Thanatologist (THAN-ah-TOL-oh-jist) A specialist who studies emotional and behavioral reactions to death and dying.

Thanatos The death instinct postulated by Freud.

Thematic Apperception Test (TAT) A projective test consisting of 20 different scenes and life situations about which respondents make up stories.

Theory A system of ideas designed to interrelate concepts and facts in a way that summarizes existing data and predicts future observations.

Theory of mind A child's current understanding of the mind, including the desires, beliefs, intentions, and feelings of others.

Theory X leadership (scientific management) An approach to leadership that emphasizes work efficiency.

Theory Y leadership A leadership style that emphasizes human relations at work and that views people as industrious, responsible, and interested in challenging work.

Therapeutic alliance A caring relationship that unites a therapist and a client in working to solve the client's problems.

Therapy placebo effect Improvement caused not by the actual process of therapy but by a client's expectation that therapy will help.

Thought stopping Use of aversive stimuli to interrupt or prevent upsetting thoughts.

Threshold The point at which a nerve impulse is triggered.

Thyroid gland Endocrine gland that helps regulate the rate of metabolism.

Tip-of-the-tongue (TOT) state The feeling that a memory is available but not quite retrievable.

Token economy A therapeutic program in which desirable behaviors are reinforced with tokens that can be exchanged for goods, services, activities, and privileges.

Token reinforcer A tangible secondary reinforcer such as money, gold stars, poker chips, and the like.

Top-down processing Applying higher-level knowledge to rapidly organize sensory information into a meaningful perception.

Tragedy of the commons A social dilemma in which individuals, each acting in his or her immediate self-interest, overuse a scarce group resource.

Trait profile A graph of the scores obtained on several personality traits.

Trait theorist A psychologist interested in classifying, analyzing, and interrelating traits to understand personality.

Trait-situation interaction The influence that external settings or circumstances have on the expression of personality traits.

Tranquilizer A drug that lowers anxiety and reduces tension.

Transference The tendency of patients to transfer feelings to a therapist that correspond to those the patient had for important persons in his or her past.

Transformation The mental ability to change the shape or form of a substance (such as clay or water) and to perceive that its volume remains the same.

Transformation rules Rules by which a simple declarative sentence may be changed to other voices or forms (past tense, passive voice, and so forth).

Transition period Time span during which a person leaves an existing life pattern behind and moves into a new pattern.

Transsexual A person with a deep conflict between his or her biological sex and preferred psychological and social gender roles.

Traumatic stresses Extreme events that cause psychological injury or intense emotional pain.

Trichromatic (TRY-kro-MAT-ik) **theory** A theory of color vision based on three cone types: red, green, and blue.

Trust versus mistrust A conflict early in life about learning to trust others and the world.

Twin study A comparison of the characteristics of twins who were raised together or separated at birth; used to identify the relative impact of heredity and environment.

Two-way bilingual education A program in which English-speaking children and children with limited English proficiency are taught half the day in English and half in a second language.

Type A personality A personality type with an elevated risk of heart disease; characterized by time urgency, anger, and hostility.

Type B personality All personality types other than Type A; a low-cardiac-risk personality.

Unconditional positive regard An unqualified, unshakable acceptance of another person.

Unconditioned response (UR) An innate, unlearned, reflex response elicited by an unconditioned stimulus.

Unconditioned stimulus (US) A stimulus innately capable of eliciting a response.

Unconscious The region of the mind that is beyond awareness, especially impulses and desires not directly known to a person.

Uncritical acceptance The tendency to believe generally positive or flattering descriptions of oneself.

Understanding In problem solving, a deeper comprehension of the nature of the problem.

Understanding In psychology, understanding is achieved when the causes of a behavior can be stated.

Undifferentiated schizophrenia Schizophrenia lacking the specific features of catatonic, disorganized, or paranoid types.

Upward comparison Comparing yourself with a person who ranks higher than you on some dimension.

Unstructured interview An interview in which conversation is informal and topics are taken up freely as they arise.

Urethra (yoo-REE-thra) The tube through which urine drains as it leaves the body. In males, semen also passes through the urethra.

Urinary bladder The sac that collects urine before it is eliminated from the body.

Usability testing The empirical investigation of the ease with which users can learn and use a machine.

Uterus (YOO-ter-us) The pear-shaped muscular organ in which the fetus develops during pregnancy; also known as the womb.

Vagina (vah-JINE-ah) Tube-like structure connecting the external female genitalia with the uterus.

Vaginismus (VAJ-ih-NIS-mus) Muscle spasms of the vagina.

Validity The ability of a test to measure what it purports to measure.

Validity scales Scales that tell whether test scores should be invalidated for lying, inconsistency, or "faking good."

Variable Any condition that changes or can be made to change; a measure, event, or state that may vary.

Variable interval (VI) schedule A reinforcer is given for the first correct response made after a varied amount of time has passed since the last reinforced response. Responses made during the time interval are not reinforced.

Variable ratio (VR) schedule A varied number of correct responses must be made to get a reinforcer. For example, a reinforcer is given after three to seven correct responses; the actual number changes randomly.

Vas deferens (vaz DEH-fur-enz) The duct that carries sperm from the testes to the urethra.

Verbal intelligence Intelligence measured by answering questions involving vocabulary, general information, arithmetic, and other language- or symbol-oriented tasks.

Vestibular senses The senses of balance, position in space, and acceleration.

Vicarious classical conditioning Classical conditioning brought about by observing another person react to a particular stimulus.

Vicarious desensitization (dee-SEN-sih-tih-ZAY-shun) A reduction in fear or anxiety that takes place vicariously ("secondhand") when a client watches models perform the feared behavior.

Virtual reality exposure Use of computer-generated images to present fear stimuli. The virtual environment responds to a viewer's head movements and other inputs.

Visceral pain Pain originating in the internal organs.

Visible spectrum That part of the electromagnetic spectrum to which the eyes are sensitive.

Visual acuity The sharpness of visual perception.

Visual agnosia (ag-KNOW-zyah) Inability to identify seen objects.

Vocational interest test A paper-and-pencil test that assesses a person's interests and matches them to interests found among successful workers in various occupations.

Waking consciousness A state of normal, alert awareness.

Warning system Pain based on large nerve fibers; warns that bodily damage may be occurring.

Weapons effect The observation that weapons serve as strong cues for aggressive behavior.

Weber's law The just noticeable difference is a constant proportion of the original stimulus intensity.

Weekly time schedule A written plan that allocates time for study, work, and leisure activities during a 1-week period.

Wellness A positive state of good health; more than the absence of disease.

Wernicke's (VER-nick-ees) **area** A temporal lobe brain area related to language comprehension.

Wish fulfillment Freudian belief that many dreams express unconscious desires.

Withdrawal of love Withholding affection to enforce child discipline.

Withdrawal symptoms Physical illness and discomfort following the withdrawal of a drug.

Work efficiency Maximum output (productivity) at lowest cost.

Working memory Another name for short-term memory, especially as it is used for thinking and problem solving.

World Wide Web (WWW) A system of information "sites" accessible through the Internet.

X chromosome The female chromosome contributed by the mother; produces a female when paired with another X chromosome and a male when paired with a Y chromosome.

Y chromosome The male chromosome contributed by the father; produces a male when paired with an X chromosome. Fathers may give either an X or a Y chromosome to their offspring.

Yerkes-Dodson law A summary of the relationships among arousal, task complexity, and performance.

You-message A message that threatens, accuses, bosses, lectures, or criticizes another person.

Zener cards A deck of 25 cards bearing various symbols and used in early parapsychological research.

Zero correlation The absence of a (linear) mathematical relationship between two measures.

Zone of proximal development Refers to the range of tasks a child cannot yet master alone, but that she or he can accomplish with the guidance of a more capable partner.

z-score A number that tells how many standard deviations above or below the mean a score is.

References

AAIDD (2004). *Montreal declaration on intellectual disabilities.* Washington, DC: American Association on Mental Retardation. Retrieved June 25, 2007, from http://www.aaidd.org/pdf/DeclarationMTL.pdf.

Aamodt, M. G. (2007). *Industrial/organizational psychology: An applied approach* (5th ed.). Belmont, CA: Cengage Learning/Wadsworth.

Abel, G. G., & Harlow, N. (2001). *The stop child molestation book.* La Vergne, TN: Lightning Source.

Abel, G. G., Wiegel, M., & Osborn, C. A. (2007). Pedophilia and other paraphilias. In L. VandeCreek, F. L. Peterson. Jr., et al. (Eds.), *Innovations in clinical practice: Focus on sexual health. Innovations in clinical practice.* Sarasota: Professional Resource Press.

Abel, T., & Lattal, K. M. (2001). Molecular mechanisms of memory acquisition, consolidation and retrieval. *Current Opinion in Neurobiology, 11*(2), 180–187.

Abrahamse, W., Steg, L., Vlek, C., & Rothengatter, T. (2005). A review of intervention studies aimed at household energy conservation. *Journal of Environmental Psychology, 25*(3), 273–291.

Abrahamson, D. J., Barlow, D. H., & Abrahamson, L. S. (1989). Differential effects of performance demand and distraction on sexually functional and dysfunctional males. *Journal of Abnormal Psychology, 98*(3), 241–247.

Abrams, D. B., Brown, R., Niaura, R. S., Emmons, K., et al. (2003). *The tobacco dependence treatment handbook: A guide to best practices.* New York: Guilford.

Accordino, D. B., Accordino, M. P., & Slaney, R. B. (2000). An investigation of perfectionism, mental health, achievement, and achievement motivation in adolescents. *Psychology in the Schools, 37*(6), 535–545.

ACT Against Violence (2005a). *Facts related to media violence.* Washington, DC: Adults and Children Against Violence Together. Retrieved October 18, 2006, from http://www.actagainstviolence.com/materials/handouts/FamilyMV1.pdf.

ACT Against Violence (2005b). *Early violence prevention.* Washington, DC: Adults and Children Against Violence Together. Retrieved October 18, 2006, from http://www.actagainstviolence.com/violprevent/index.html.

Adams, J. (1988). *Conceptual blockbusting.* New York: Norton.

Adamson, K. (2004). *Kate's journey: Triumph over adversity.* Redondo Beach, CA: Nosmada Press.

Addis, K. M., & Kahana, M. J. (2004). Decomposing serial learning: What is missing from the learning curve? *Psychonomic Bulletin & Review, 11*(1), 118–174.

Adler, S. A., & Orprecio, J. (2006). The eyes have it: Visual pop-out in infants and adults. *Developmental Science, 9,* 189–206.

Adorno, T. W., Frenkel-Brunswik, E., Levinson, D. J., & Sanford, R. N. (1950). *The authoritarian personality.* New York: Harper.

Afifi, T. O., Brownridge, D. A., Cox, B. J., & Sareen, J. (2006). Physical punishment, childhood abuse and psychiatric disorders. *Child Abuse & Neglect, 30*(10), 1093–1103.

Ahima. R. S., & Osei, S. Y. (2004). Leptin signaling. *Physiology & Behavior, 81,* 223–241.

Ajzen, I. (2005). *Attitudes, personality and behaviour* (2nd ed.). New York: McGraw-Hill.

Akerstedt, T., Hume, K., Minors, D., & Waterhouse, J. (1993). Regulation of sleep and naps on an irregular schedule. *Sleep, 16*(8), 736–743.

Albarracín, D., Johnson, B. T., & Zanna, M. P. (Eds.) (2005). *The handbook of attitudes.* Mahwah, NJ: Erlbaum.

Alberti, R., & Emmons, M. (2001). *Your perfect right* (8th ed.). San Luis Obispo, CA: Impact.

Alberto, P. A., & Troutman, A. C. (2006). *Applied behavior analysis for teachers* (7th ed.). Englewood Cliffs, NJ: Prentice Hall.

Alcock, J. E. (2003). Give the null hypothesis a chance: Reasons to remain doubtful about the existence of psi. *Journal of Consciousness Studies, 10*(6–7), 29–50.

Alcock, J. E., Burns, J., & Freeman, A. (2003). *Psi wars: Getting to grips with the paranormal.* Exeter, UK: Imprint Academic Press.

Alicke, M. D., Yurak, T. J., & Vredenburg, D. S. (1996). Using personal attitudes to judge others. *Journal of Research in Personality, 30*(1), 103–119.

Allen, D., Carlson, D., & Ham, C. (2007). Well-being: New paradigms of wellness-inspiring positive health outcomes and renewing hope. *American Journal of Health Promotion, 21*(3), 1–9.

Allen, K., Blascovich, J., & Mendes, W. B. (2002). Cardiovascular reactivity in the presence of pets, friends, and spouses: The truth about cats and dogs. *Psychosomatic Medicine, 64*(5), 727–739.

Allen, M., Mabry, E., & McKelton, D. (1998). Impact of juror attitudes about the death penalty on juror evaluations of guilt and punishment: A meta-analysis. *Law & Human Behavior, 22*(6), 715–731.

Allgower, A., Wardle, J., & Steptoe, A. (2001). Depressive symptoms, social support, and personal health behaviors in young men and women. *Health Psychology, 20*(3), 223–227.

Allik, J. (2000). Available and accessible information in memory and vision. In E. Tulving (Ed.), *Memory, consciousness, and the brain: The Tallinn Conference.* Hove, UK: Psychology Press.

Allport, G. W. (1958). *The nature of prejudice.* Garden City, NY: Anchor Books, Doubleday.

Allport, G. W. (1961). *Pattern and growth in personality.* New York: Holt, Rinehart, & Winston.

Alsaker, F. D. (1992). Pubertal timing, overweight, and psychological adjustment. *Journal of Early Adolescence, 12*(4), 396–419.

Alsaker, F. D. (1995). Is puberty a critical period for socialization? *Journal of Adolescence, 18*(4), 427–444.

Altemeyer, B. (2004). Highly dominating, highly authoritarian personalities. *Journal of Social Psychology, 144*(4), 421–447.

Altman, L. K. (2002). AIDS threatens to claim 65M more lives by '20. *Arizona Daily Star,* July 3, A7.

Altschuler, G. C. (2001). Battling the cheats. *The New York Times: Education,* Jan. 7, 15.

Alvarado, N. (1994). Empirical validity of the Thematic Apperception Test. *Journal of Personality Assessment, 63*(1), 59–79.

Alvino, J., & the Editors of Gifted Children Monthly (1996). *Parents' guide to raising a gifted child.* New York: Ballantine.

Alwin, D. F., Cohen, R. L., & Newcomb, T. M. (1991). *Political attitudes over the life span: The Bennington women after fifty years.* Madison, WI: University of Wisconsin Press.

Amabile, T., Hadley, C. N., & Kramer, S. J. (2002). Creativity under the gun. *Harvard Business Review, 80*(8), 52–61.

Amato, P. R., & Fowler, F. (2002). Parenting practices, child adjustment, and family diversity. *Journal of Marriage & Family, 64*(3), 703–716.

Ambady, N., & Rosenthal, R. (1993). Half a minute: Predicting teacher evaluations from thin slices of nonverbal behavior and physical attractiveness. *Journal of Personality & Social Psychology, 64,* 431–441.

American Lung Association (2006). *Smokeless tobacco fact sheet.* Retrieved June 6, 2007, from http://www.lungusa.org/site/pp.asp?c=dvLUK9O0E&b=1694879.

Ancis, J. R., Chen, Y., & Schultz, D. (2004). Diagnostic challenges and the so-called culture-bound syndromes. In J. R. Ancis (Ed.), *Culturally responsive interventions: Innovative approaches to working with diverse populations.* New York: Brunner-Routledge.

Anderson, C. A. (1989). Temperature and aggression. *Psychological Bulletin, 106,* 74–96.

Anderson, C. A. (2004). An update on the effects of violent video games. *Journal of Adolescence, 27,* 113–122.

Anderson, C. A., & Bushman, B. J. (2001). Effects of violent video games on aggressive behavior, aggressive cognition, aggressive affect, physiological arousal, and prosocial behavior: A meta-analytic review of the scientific literature. *Psychological Science, 12*(5), 353–359.

Anderson, C. A., & Bushman, B. J. (2002). Human aggression. *Annual Review of Psychology, 53,* 27–51.

Anderson, C. A., Anderson, K. B., & Deuser, W. E. (1996). Examining an affective aggression framework. *Personality & Social Psychology Bulletin, 22*(4), 366–376.

Anderson, C. A., Berkowitz, L., Donnerstein, E., Huesmann, L. R., et al. (2003). The influence of media violence on youth. *Psychological Science in the Public Interest, 4,* 1–30.

Anderson, C. A., Carnagey, N. L., & Eubanks, J. (2003). Exposure to violent media: The effects of songs with violent lyrics on aggressive thoughts and feelings. *Journal of Personality & Social Psychology, 84*(5), 960–971.

Anderson, J. R. (2005). *Cognitive psychology and its implications* (6th ed.). New York: Worth.

Anderson, M. C. (2001). Active forgetting: Evidence for functional inhibition as a source of memory failure. *Journal of Aggression, Maltreatment & Trauma, 4*(2), 185–210.

Anderson, M. C., & Bell, T. (2001). Forgetting our facts: The role of inhibitory processes in the loss of propositional knowledge. *Journal of Experimental Psychology: General, 130*(3), 544–570.

Anderson, M. C., & Green, C. (2001). Suppressing unwanted memories by executive control. *Nature, 410*(6826), 366–369.

Anderson, M. C., Ochsner, K. N., Kuhl, B., Cooper, J., et al. (2004). Neural systems underlying the suppression of unwanted memories. *Science, 303*, 232–235.

Andrasik, F. (2003). Behavioral treatment approaches to chronic headache. *Neurological Sciences, 24*(Suppl 2), S80–S85.

André, C., Jaber-Filho, J. A., Carvalho, M., Jullien, C., et al. (2003). Predictors of recovery following involuntary hospitalization of violent substance abuse patients. *The American Journal on Addictions, 12*(1), 84–89.

Andresen, J. (2000). Meditation meets behavioural medicine: The story of experimental research on meditation. *Journal of Consciousness Studies, 7*(11–12), 17–73.

Annett, M. (2002). *Handedness and brain asymmetry: The right shift theory.* Hove, UK: Psychology Press.

Annett, M., & Manning, M. (1990). Arithmetic and laterality. *Neuropsychologia, 28*(1), 61–69.

Anshel, M. H. (1995). An examination of self-regulatory cognitive-behavioural strategies of Australian elite and non-elite competitive male swimmers. *Australian Psychologist, 30*(2), 78–83.

Antle, M. C., & Mistlberger, R. E. (2005). Circadian rhythms. In I. Q. Whishaw & B. Kolb (Eds.), *The behavior of the laboratory rat: A handbook with tests.* New York: Oxford University Press.

Antony, M. M. (2004). *10 simple solutions to shyness: How to overcome shyness, social anxiety & fear of public speaking.* Oakland, CA: New Harbinger.

APA. (2000). *2000 APA directory survey.* Washington, DC: American Psychological Association. Retrieved May 18, 2007, from http://research.apa.org/2000membershipt4.pdf.

APA. (2002). Ethical principles of psychologists and code of conduct. *American Psychologist, 57*, 1060–1073. Retrieved May 18, 2007, from http://www.apa.org/ethics/homepage.html.

APA. (2003). Guidelines on multicultural education, training, research, practice, and organizational change for psychologists. *American Psychologist, 58*(5), 377–402.

APA. (2004). *Sexual orientation and homosexuality.* Washington, DC: American Psychological Association. Retrieved July 29, 2007, from http://www.apahelpcenter.org/articles/article.php?id=31.

APA. (2005). *2005 APA directory survey.* Washington, DC: American Psychological Association. Retrieved May 18, 2007, from http://research.apa.org/profile2005t3.pdf.

APA. (2007). *Report of the APA Task Force on the sexualization of girls.* Washington, DC: American Psychological Association. Retrieved July 26, 2007, from http://www.apa.org/pi/wpo/sexualization.html.

Arbona, C. B., Osma, J., Garcia-Palacios, A., Quero, S., et al. (2004). Treatment of flying phobia using virtual reality: Data from a 1-year follow-up using a multiple baseline design. *Clinical Psychology & Psychotherapy, 11*(5), 311–323.

Ariely, D., & Wertenbroch, K. (2002). Procrastination, deadlines, and performance: Self-control by precommitment. *Psychological Science, 13*(3), 219–224.

Armeli, S., Gunthert, K. C., & Cohen, L. H. (2001). Stressor appraisals, coping, and post-event outcomes: The dimensionality and antecedents of stress-related growth. *Journal of Social & Clinical Psychology, 20*(3), 366–395.

Arnett, J. J. (2000). Emerging adulthood. *American Psychologist, 55*(5), 469–480.

Arnett, J. J. (2001). Conceptions of the transition to adulthood. *Journal of Adult Development, 8*(2), 133–143.

Arnett, J. J. (2004). *Emerging adulthood: The winding road from late teens through the twenties.* New York: Oxford University Press.

Arnett, J. J., & Galambos, N. L. (Eds.). (2003). *New directions for child and adolescent development: Exploring cultural conceptions of the transition to adulthood.* San Francisco: Jossey-Bass.

Arnett, J. J., & Tanner, J. L. (Eds.). (2006). *Emerging adults in America: Coming of age in the 21st century.* Washington, DC: American Psychological Association.

Aronoff, J., Barclay, A. M., & Stevenson, L. A. (1988). The recognition of threatening facial stimuli. *Journal of Personality & Social Psychology, 54*(4), 647–655.

Aronow, E., Altman Weiss, K., & Reznikoff, M. (2001). *A practical guide to the Thematic Apperception Test: The TAT in clinical practice.* New York: Brunner-Routledge.

Aronson, E. (1969). Some antecedents of interpersonal attraction. In W. J. Arnold & D. Levine (Eds.), *Nebraska Symposium on Motivation.* Lincoln: University of Nebraska Press.

Aronson, E. (2008). *The social animal* (10th ed.). New York: Worth.

Aronson, E., Wilson, T. D., & Akert, R. M. (2007). *Social psychology* (6th ed.). Englewood Cliffs, NJ: Prentice Hall.

Arthur, W., & Doverspike, D. (2001). Predicting motor vehicle crash involvement from a personality measure and a driving knowledge test. *Journal of Prevention & Intervention in the Community, 22*(1), 35–42.

Artz, S. (2005). To die for: Violent adolescent girls' search for male attention. In D. J. Pepler, K. C. Madsen et al. (Eds.), *The development and treatment of girlhood aggression.* Mahwah, NJ: Erlbaum.

Ary, D. V., Duncan, T. E., Biglan, A., Metzler, C. W., et al. (1999). Development of adolescent problem behavior. *Journal of Abnormal Child Psychology, 27*(2), 141–150.

Asch, S. E. (1956). Studies of independence and conformity: A minority of one against a unanimous majority. *Psychological Monographs, 70*(416).

Ash, D. W., & Holding, D. H. (1990). Backward versus forward chaining in the acquisition of a keyboard skill. *Human Factors, 32*(2), 139–146.

Ashby, F. G., & Maddox, W. T. (2005). Human category learning. *Annual Review of Psychology, 56*, 149–178.

Aslin, R. N., & Smith, L. B. (1988). Perceptual development. *Annual Review of Psychology, 39*, 435–473.

Asmundson, G. J. G., & Taylor, S. (2005). *It's not all in your head.* London: Psychology Press.

Assanand, S., Pinel, J. P. J., & Lehman, D. R. (1998). Personal theories of hunger and eating. *Journal of Applied Social Psychology, 28*(11), 998–1015.

Athenasiou, R., Shaver, P., & Tavris, C. (1970). Sex. *Psychology Today, 4*(2), 37–52.

Atkin, D. J., & Lau, T. Y. (2007). Information technology and organizational telework. In C. A. Lin & D. J Atkin (Eds.), *Communication technology and social change: Theory and implications.* Mahwah, NJ: Erlbaum.

Atkinson, R.C., & Schiffrin, R.M. (1968). Human memory: a proposed system and its control processes. In K. W. Spence & J. T. Spence (Eds.), *The psychology of learning and motivation* (Vol. 2). London: Academic Press.

Atwood, J. D. (2006). Mommy's little angel, daddy's little girl: Do you know what your pre-teens are doing? *American Journal of Family Therapy, 34*(5), 447–467.

Aucoin, K. J., Frick, P. J., & Bodin, S. D. (2006). Corporal punishment and child adjustment. *Journal of Applied Developmental Psychology, 27*(6), 527–541.

Avery, D. H., Eder, D. N., Bolte, M. A., Hellekson, C. J., et al. (2001). Dawn simulation and bright light in the treatment of SAD. *Biological Psychiatry, 50*(3), 205–216.

Awadallah, N., Vaughan, A., Franco, K., Munir, F., et al. (2005). Munchausen by proxy: A case, chart series, and literature review of older victims. *Child Abuse & Neglect, 29*(8), 931–941.

Ayers, L., Beaton, S., & Hunt, H. (1999). The significance of transpersonal experiences, emotional conflict, and cognitive abilities in creativity. *Empirical Studies of the Arts, 17*(1), 73–82.

Ayllon, T. (1963). Intensive treatment of psychotic behavior by stimulus satiation and food reinforcement. *Behavior Research & Therapy, 1,* 53–61.

Ayllon, T., & Azrin, N. H. (1965). The measurement and reinforcement of behavior of psychotics. *Journal of the Experimental Analysis of Behavior, 8,* 357–383.

Baard, P. P., Deci, E. L., & Ryan, R. M. (2004). Intrinsic need satisfaction: A motivational basis of performance and well-being in two work settings. *Journal of Applied Social Psychology, 34*(10), 2045–2068.

Bachman, J. G., & Johnson, L. D. (1979). The freshmen. *Psychology Today, 13,* 78–87.

Baddeley, A. D. (2003). Working memory: Looking back and looking forward. *Nature Reviews Neuroscience, 4*(10), 829–839.

Baer, J. M. (1993). *Creativity and divergent thinking.* Mahwah, NJ: Erlbaum.

Bagley, C., & Tremblay, P. (1998). On the prevalence of homosexuality and bisexuality, in a random community survey of 750 men aged 18 to 27. *Journal of Homosexuality, 36*(2), 1–18.

Bailey, C. H., & Kandel, E. R. (2004). Synaptic growth and the persistence of long-term memory: A molecular perspective. In M. S. Gazzaniga (Ed.), *The cognitive neurosciences* (3rd ed.). Cambridge, MA: MIT Press.

Bailey, L. M., & McKeever, W. F. (2004). A large-scale study of handedness and pregnancy/birth risk events: Implications for genetic theories of handedness. *Laterality: Asymmetries of Body, Brain & Cognition, 9*(2), 175–188.

Baillargeon, R. (1991). Reasoning about the height and location of a hidden object in 4.5- and 6.5-month-old infants. *Cognition, 38*(1), 13–42.

Baillargeon, R. (2004). Infants' reasoning about hidden objects: Evidence for event-general and event-specific expectations. *Developmental Science, 7*(4), 391–424.

Baillargeon, R., De Vos, J., & Graber, M. (1989). Location memory in 8-month-old infants in a non-search AB task. *Cognitive Development, 4,* 345–367.

Bain, S. K., & Allin, J. D. (2005). Stanford-Binet Intelligence Scales, Fifth Edition. *Journal of Psychoeducational Assessment, 23*(1), 87–95.

Bajracharya, S. M., Sarvela, P. D., & Isberner, F. R. (1995). A retrospective study of first sexual intercourse experiences among undergraduates. *Journal of American College Health, 43*(4), 169–177.

Baker, T. B., Brandon, T. H., & Chassin, L. (2004). Motivational influences on cigarette smoking. *Annual Review of Psychology, 55,* 463–491.

Bakich, I. (1995). Hypnosis in the treatment of sexual desire disorders. *Australian Journal of Clinical & Experimental Hypnosis, 23*(1), 70–77.

Baldo, O., & Eardley, I. (2005). Diagnosis and investigation of men with erectile dysfunction. *Journal of Men's Health & Gender, 2*(1), 79–86.

Balk, D. E., Lampe, S., Sharpe, B., Schwinn, S., et al. (1998). TAT results in a longitudinal study of bereaved college students. *Death Studies, 22*(1), 3–21.

Balsam, K. F., & Mohr, J. J. (2007). Adaptation to sexual orientation stigma: A comparison of bisexual and lesbian/gay adults. *Journal of Counseling Psychology, 54*(3), 306–319.

Baltes, B. B., Briggs, T. E., Huff, J. W., Wright, J. A., et al. (1999). Flexible and compressed workweek schedules. *Journal of Applied Psychology, 84*(4), 496–513.

Bandura, A. (1971). *Social learning theory.* New York: General Learning Press.

Bandura, A. (1973). *Aggression: A social learning analysis.* Englewood Cliffs, NJ: Prentice-Hall.

Bandura, A. (2001). Social cognitive theory: An agentic perspective. *Annual Review of Psychology, 52,* 1–26.

Bandura, A., & Walters, R. (1959). *Adolescent aggression.* New York: Ronald.

Bandura, A., Blanchard, E. B., & Ritter, B. (1969). Relative efficacy of desensitization and modeling approaches for inducing behavioral, affective, and attitudinal changes. *Journal of Personality & Social Psychology, 13*(1), 173–199.

Bandura, A., Ross, D., & Ross, S. A. (1963). Vicarious reinforcement and imitative learning. *Journal of*

Abnormal and Social Psychology, 67, 601–607.

Banich, M. T. (2004). *Cognitive neuroscience and neuropsychology* (2nd ed.). Boston: Houghton Mifflin.

Banks, A., & Gartrell, N. K. (1995). Hormones and sexual orientation: A questionable link. *Journal of Homosexuality, 28*(3–4), 247–268.

Banks, T., & Dabbs, Jr., J. M. (1996). Salivary testosterone and cortisol in delinquent and violent urban subculture. *Journal of Social Psychology, 136*(1), 49–56.

Barabasz, A. (2000). EEG markers of alert hypnosis. *Sleep & Hypnosis, 2*(4), 164–169.

Barber, T. X. (2000). A deeper understanding of hypnosis: Its secrets, its nature, its essence. *American Journal of Clinical Hypnosis, 42*(3–4), 208–272.

Bard, C., Fleury, M., & Goulet, C. (1994). Relationship between perceptual strategies and response adequacy in sport situations. *International Journal of Sport Psychology, 25*(3), 266–281.

Bargh, J. A., McKenna, K. Y. A., & Fitzsimons, G. M. (2002). Can you see the real me? Activation and expression of the "true self" on the Internet. *Journal of Social Issues, 58*(1), 33–48.

Barkataki, I., Kumari, V., Das, M., Taylor, P. et al. (2006). Volumetric structural brain abnormalities in men with schizophrenia or antisocial personality disorder. *Behavioural Brain Research, 169*(2), 239–247.

Barlow, D. H. (2000). Unraveling the mysteries of anxiety and its disorders from the perspective of emotion theory. *American Psychologist, 55,* 1247–1263.

Barlow, D. H. (2002). *Anxiety and its disorders* (2nd ed.). New York: Guilford.

Barlow, D. H. (2004). Psychological treatments. *American Psychologist, 59*(9), 869–878.

Barnett, J., Behnke, S. H., Rosenthal, S., & Koocher, G. (2007). In case of ethical dilemma, break glass: Commentary on ethical decision making in practice. *Professional Psychology: Research & Practice, 38*(1), 7–12.

Barnier, A. J., McConkey, K. M., & Wright, J. (2004). Posthypnotic amnesia for autobiographical episodes: Influencing memory accessibility and quality. *International Journal of Clinical and Experimental Hypnosis, 52*(3), 260–279.

Baron, R. A., Byrne, D., & Branscombe, N. R. (2007). *Mastering social psychology.* Boston, MA: Pearson/Allyn and Bacon.

Baron, R. S. (2005). So right it's wrong: Groupthink and the ubiquitous nature of polarized group decision making. In M. P. Zanna, (Ed.), *Advances in experimental so-*

cial psychology (Vol. 37). San Diego: Elsevier.

Baron, R. S. (2005). So right it's wrong: Groupthink and the ubiquitous nature of polarized group decision making. In M. P. Zanna (Ed.), *Advances in experimental social psychology* (Vol. 37). San Diego: Elsevier.

Barrett, D. (1993). The "committee of sleep": A study of dream incubation for problem solving. *Dreaming, 3*(2), 115–122.

Barrett, D., Greenwood, J. G., & McCullagh, J. F. (2006). Kissing laterality and handedness. *Laterality: Asymmetries of Body, Brain & Cognition, 11*(6), 573–579.

Barrick, M. R., Moun, M. K., & Judge, T. A. (2001). Personality and performance at the beginning of the new millennium. *International Journal of Selection & Assessment, 9*(1–2), 9–30.

Barron, F. (1958). The psychology of imagination. *Scientific American, 199*(3), 150–170.

Barrowcliff, A. L., & Haddock, G. (2006). The relationship between command hallucinations and factors of compliance: A critical review of the literature. *Journal of Forensic Psychiatry & Psychology, 17*(2), 266–298.

Bar-Tal, D., & Labin, D. (2001). The effect of a major event on stereotyping: Terrorist attacks in Israel and Israeli adolescents' perceptions of Palestinians, Jordanians and Arabs. *European Journal of Social Psychology, 31*(3), 265–280.

Bartholow, B. D., & Anderson, C. A. (2002). Effects of violent video games on aggressive behavior. *Journal of Experimental Social Psychology, 38*(3), 283–290.

Bartholow, B. D., Bushman, B. J., & Sestir, M. A. (2006). Chronic violent video game exposure and desensitization to violence: Behavioral and event-related brain potential data. *Journal of Experimental Social Psychology, 42*(4), 532–539.

Bartholow, B. D., Sestir, M. A., & Davis, E. B. (2005). Correlates and consequences of exposure to video game violence: Hostile personality, empathy, and aggressive behavior. *Personality and Social Psychology Bulletin, 31*(11), 1573–1586.

Bartlett, J. C., & Searcy, J. (1993). Inversion and configuration of faces. *Cognitive Psychology, 25*(3), 281–316.

Bartram, B. (2006). An examination of perceptions of parental influence on attitudes to language learning. *Educational Research, 48*(2), 211–222.

Basson, R., Brotto, L. A., Laan, E., Redmond, G., et al. (2005). Assessment and management of women's sexual dysfunctions: Prob-

lematic desire and arousal. *Journal of Sexual Medicine, 2*(3), 291–300.

Bastian, B., & Haslam, N. (2006). Psychological essentialism and stereotype endorsement. *Journal of Experimental Social Psychology, 42*(2), 228–235.

Bath, H. (1996). Everyday discipline or control with care. *Journal of Child & Youth Care, 10*(2), 23–32.

Batson, C. D. (2006). "Not all self-interest after all": Economics of empathy-induced altruism. In D. De Cremer, M. Zeelenberg, et al. (Eds.), *Social psychology and economics.* Mahwah, NJ: Erlbaum.

Batson, C. D., & Powell, A. A. (2003). Altruism and prosocial behavior. In T. Millon & M. J. Lerner (Eds.), *Handbook of psychology: Personality and social psychology* (Vol. 5). New York: Wiley.

Batterham, R. L., Cohen, M. A., Ellis, S. M., Le Roux, C. E., et al. (2003). Inhibition of food intake in obese subjects by peptide YY3–36. *New England Journal of Medicine, 349*(Sept. 4), 941–948.

Baum, A., & Davis, G. E. (1980). Reducing the stress of high-density living: An architectural intervention. *Journal of Personality & Social Psychology, 38,* 471–481.

Baum, A., & Posluszny, D. M. (1999). Health psychology. *Annual Review of Psychology, 50,* 137–163.

Baum, A., & Valins, S. (1979). Architectural mediation of residential density and control: Crowding and the regulation of social contact. *Advances in Experimental & Social Psychology, 12,* 131–175.

Baum, A., & Valins, S. (Eds.). (1977). *Human response to crowding: Studies of the effects of residential group size.* Mahwah, NJ: Erlbaum.

Bauman, L. J., Karasz, A., & Hamilton, A. (2007). Understanding failure of condom use intention among adolescents: Completing an intensive preventive intervention. *Journal of Adolescent Research, 22*(3), 248–274.

Baumeister, R. F., & Bushman, B. (2008). *Social psychology and human nature.* Belmont, CA: Cengage Learning/Wadsworth.

Baumeister, R. F., Campbell, J. D., Krueger, J. I., & Vohs, K. D. (2003). Does high self-esteem cause better performance, interpersonal success, happiness, or healthier lifestyles? *Psychological Science in the Public Interest, 4*(1), 1–44.

Baumrind, D. (1991). The influence of parenting style on adolescent competence and substance use. *Journal of Early Adolescence, 11*(1), 56–95.

Baumrind, D. (2005). Patterns of parental authority and adolescent autonomy. In J. Smetana (Ed.), *New directions for child development: Changes in parental authority dur-*

ing adolescence. San Francisco: Jossey-Bass.

Baumrind, D., Larzelere, R. E., & Cowan, P. A. (2002). Ordinary physical punishment: Is it harmful? *Psychological Bulletin, 128*(4), 580–589.

Beach, F. A. (Ed.). (1965). *Sex and behavior.* New York: Wiley.

Bearman, P. S., Moody, J., & Stovel, K. (2004). Chains of affection: The structure of adolescent romantic and sexual networks. *American Journal of Sociology, 110*(1), 44–91.

Beauchamp, P. H., Halliwell, W. R., Fournier, J. F., & Koestner, R. (1996). Effects of cognitive-behavioral psychological skills training on the motivation, preparation, and putting performance of novice golfers. *Sport Psychologist, 10*(2), 157–170.

Beaulieu, C. M. J. (2004). Intercultural study of personal space: A case study. *Journal of Applied Social Psychology, 34*(4), 794–805.

Beck, A. T. (1991). Cognitive therapy. *American Psychologist, 46*(4), 368–375.

Beck, A. T. (2004). Cognitive patterns in dreams and daydreams. In R. I. Rosner & W. J. Lyddon (Eds.), *Cognitive therapy and dreams.* New York: Springer.

Beck, A. T., & Greenberg, R. L. (1974). *Coping with depression.* Institute For Rational Living.

Beck, A. T., Brown, C., Berchick, R. J., Stewart, B. L., et al. (1990). Relationship between hopelessness and ultimate suicide. *American Journal of Psychiatry, 147*(2), 190–195.

Beck, B. L., Koons, S. R., & Milgrim, D. L. (2000). Correlates and consequences of behavioral procrastination. *Journal of Social Behavior & Personality, 15*(5), 3–13.

Beck, J. S. (2002). Beck therapy approach. In M. Hersen & W. H. Sledge (Eds.), *Encyclopedia of psychotherapy.* San Diego: Academic Press.

Beck, R. C. (2004). *Motivation: Theories and principles* (5th ed.). Englewood Cliffs, NJ: Prentice Hall.

Becker, S. W., & Eagly, A. H. (2004). The heroism of women and men. *American Psychologist, 59*(3), 163–178.

Beebe, B., Gerstman, L., Carson, B., Dolins, M., et al. (1982). Rhythmic communication in the mother–infant dyad. In M. Davis (Ed.), *Interaction rhythms, periodicity in communicative behavior.* New York: Human Sciences Press.

Beeber, L. S., Chazan-Cohen, R., Squires, J., Harden, B. J., et al. (2007). The Early Promotion and Intervention Research Consortium (E-PIRC): Five approaches to improving infant/toddler mental health in Early Head Start. *Infant*

Mental Health Journal, 28(2), 130–150.

Beeman, M. J., & Chiarello, C. (1998). Complementary right- and left-hemisphere language comprehension. *Current Directions in Psychological Science, 7*(1), 2–8.

Beersma, D. G. M., & Gordijn, M. C. M. (2007). Circadian control of the sleep-wake cycle. *Physiology & Behavior, 90*(2–3), 190–195.

Behrend, D. A., Beike, D. R., & Lampinen, J. M. (2004). *The self and memory.* Hove, UK: Psychology Press.

Beirne-Smith, M., Patton, J., & Shannon, K. (2006). *Mental retardation: An introduction to intellectual disability* (7th ed.). Englewood Cliffs, NJ: Prentice Hall.

Belenky, G., Wesensten, N. J., Thorne, D. R., Thomas, M. L., et al. (2003). Patterns of performance degradation and restoration during sleep restriction and subsequent recovery: A sleep dose-response study. *Journal of Sleep Research, 12*(1), 1–12.

Beljan, J. R., Rosenblatt, L. S., Hetherington, N. W., Layman, J., et al. (1972). Human performance in the aviation environment, *NASA Contract no 2-6657, Pt. Ia*, 253–259.

Bell, P. A., Greene, T., Fisher, J., & Baum, A. S. (2006). *Environmental psychology* (5th ed.). Mahwah, NJ: Erlbaum.

Bellezza, F. S., Six, L. S., & Phillips, D. S. (1992). A mnemonic for remembering long strings of digits. *Bulletin of the Psychonomic Society, 30*(4), 271–274.

Belsky, J. (1996). Parent, infant, and social-contextual antecedents of father–son attachment security. *Developmental Psychology, 32*(5), 905–913.

Bem, S. L. (1974). The measurement of psychological androgyny. *Journal of Consulting & Clinical Psychology, 42*(2), 155–162.

Bem, S. L. (1975). Androgyny vs. the tight little lives of fluffy women and chesty men. *Psychology Today,* Sept., 58–62.

Bem, S. L. (1981). Gender schema theory: A cognitive account of sex typing. *Psychological Review, 88,* 354–364.

Benbow, C. P. (1986). Physiological correlates of extreme intellectual precocity. *Neuropsychologia, 24*(5), 719–725.

Benjafield, J. G. (2004). *A history of psychology* (2nd ed.). Boston: Allyn & Bacon.

Benloucif, S., Bennett, E. L., & Rosenzweig, M. R. (1995). Norepinephrine and neural plasticity: The effects of xylamine on experience-induced changes in brain weight, memory, and behavior. *Neurobiology of Learning & Memory, 63*(1), 33–42.

Bensafi, M., Zelano, C., Johnson, B., Mainland, J., et al. (2004). Olfaction: From sniff to percept. In M. S. Gazzaniga (Ed.), *The cognitive neurosciences* (3rd ed.). Cambridge, MA: MIT Press.

Ben-Shakhar, G., & Dolev, K. (1996). Psychophysiological detection through the guilty knowledge technique: Effect of mental countermeasures. *Journal of Applied Psychology, 81*(3), 273–281.

Benski, C. (1998). Testing new claims of dermo-optical perception. *Skeptical Inquirer, 22*(1), 21–26.

Bensley, L., & Van Eenwyk, J. (2001). Video games and real-life aggression. *Journal of Adolescent Health, 29*(4), 244–257.

Benson, H. (1977). Systematic hypertension and the relaxation response. *The New England Journal of Medicine, 296,* 1152–1156.

Benson, J., Greaves, W., O'Donnell, M., & Taglialatela, J. (2002). Evidence for symbolic language processing in a Bonobo (Pan paniscus). *Journal of Consciousness Studies, 9*(12), 33–56.

Bergeron, S., & Lord, M. J. (2003). The integration of pelvi-perineal reeducation and cognitive-behavioral therapy in the multidisciplinary treatment of the sexual pain disorders, *Sexual & Relationship Therapy, 18,* 135–141.

Bergin, A. E. (1991). Values and religious issues in psychotherapy and mental health. *American Psychologist, 46*(4), 394–403.

Bernat, J. A., Calhoun, K. S., & Stolp, S. (1998). Sexually aggressive men's responses to a date rape analogue. *Journal of Sex Research, 35*(4), 41–348.

Berne, E. (1964). *Games people play.* New York: Grove.

Bernstein, H. J., Beale M. D., Burns C., & Kellner C. H. (1998). Patient attitudes about ECT after treatment. *Psychiatric Annals, 28*(9), 524–527.

Bernthal, M. J. (2003). The effects of professional wrestling viewership on children. *The Sport Journal, 6*(3). Retrieved June 6, 2007, from http://www.thesportjournal.org/2003Journal/Vol6-No3/wrestling.htm.

Berntsen, D., & Thomsen, D. K. (2005). Personal memories for remote historical events: Accuracy and clarity of flashbulb memories related to World War II. *Journal of Experimental Psychology: General, 134*(2), 242–257.

Berry, J. W. (1990). The psychology of acculturation. In R. A. Dienstbier & J. J. Berman (Eds.), *Nebraska Symposium on Motivation 1989: Cross-cultural perspectives, 37.* Lincoln: University of Nebraska Press.

Berry, J. W., Phinney, J. S, Sam, D. L., & Vedder, P. (2005). *Immi-*

grant youth in cultural transition. Mahwah, NJ: Erlbaum.

Berscheid, E. (2000). Attraction. In A. Kazdin (Ed.), *Encyclopedia of psychology.* Washington, DC: American Psychological Association.

Berscheid, E., & Regan, P. (2005). *The psychology of interpersonal relationships.* Englewood Cliffs, NJ: Prentice Hall.

Bersoff, D. M. (1999). Why good people sometimes do bad things: Motivated reasoning and unethical behavior. *Personality & Social Psychology Bulletin, 25*(1), 28–39.

Bertsch, G. J. (1976). Punishment of consummatory and instrumental behavior: A review. *Psychological Record, 26,* 13–31.

Besnard, D., & Cacitti, L. (2005). Interface changes causing accidents: An empirical study of negative transfer. *International Journal of Human-Computer Studies, 62*(1), 105–125.

Best, D. (2002). Cross-cultural gender roles. In J. Worell (Ed.), *Encyclopedia of women and gender.* New York: Oxford University Press.

Betancur, C., Velez, A., Cabanieu, G., le Moal, M., et al. (1990). Association between left-handedness and allergy: A reappraisal. *Neuropsychologia, 28*(2), 223–227.

Beyer, M., Gerlach, F. M., Flies, U., Grol, R., et al. (2003). The development of quality circles/peer review groups as a tool for quality improvement in Europe: Results of a survey in 26 European countries. *Family Practice, 20,* 443–451.

Bhushan, B., & Khan, S. M. (2006). Laterality and accident proneness: A study of locomotive drivers. *Laterality: Asymmetries of Body, Brain & Cognition, 11*(5), 395–404.

Bialystok, E. (2001). *Bilingualism in development: Language, literacy, and cognition.* New York: Cambridge.

Binder, J. L. (2004). *Key competencies in brief dynamic psychotherapy: Clinical practice beyond the manual.* New York: Guilford.

Binik, Y. M. (2005). Should dyspareunia be retained as a sexual dysfunction in DSM-V? A painful classification decision. *Archives of Sexual Behavior, 34*(1), 11–21.

Birch, J., & McKeever, L. M. (1993). Survey of the accuracy of new pseudoisochromatic plates. *Ophthalmic & Physiological Optics, 13*(1), 35–40.

Birnbaum, M. H. (2004). Human research and data collection via the Internet. *Annual Review of Psychology, 55,* 803–832.

Bisson, J. I., Ehlers, A., Matthews, R., Pilling, S., et al. (2007). Psychological treatments for chronic post-traumatic stress disorder: Systematic review and meta-analysis. *British Journal of Psychiatry, 190*(2), 97–104.

Blackmore, S. (2001). What can the paranormal teach us about consciousness? *Skeptical Inquirer, 25,* 22–27.

Blackmore, S. (2004). *Consciousness: An introduction.* New York: Oxford University Press.

Blackwell, D. L., & Lichter, D. T. (2004). Homogamy among dating, cohabiting, and married couples. *Sociological Quarterly, 45*(4), 719–737.

Blair, K. S., Richell, R. A., Mitchell, D. G. V., Leonard, A., et al. (2006). They know the words, but not the music: Affective and semantic priming in individuals with psychopathy. *Biological Psychology, 73*(2), 114–123.

Blakemore, C., & Cooper, G., (1970). Development of the brain depends on the visual environment. *Nature, 228,* 477–478.

Blanchard, D. C., & Blanchard, R. J. (2003). What can animal aggression research tell us about human aggression? *Hormones & Behavior, 44*(3), 171–177.

Blanchard, E. B., Kuhn, E., Rowell, D. L., Hickling, E. J., et al. (2004). Studies of the vicarious traumatization of college students by the September 11th attacks: Effects of proximity, exposure and connectedness. *Behaviour Research & Therapy, 42*(2), 191–205.

Blatner, A. (2006). Current trends in psychodrama. *International Journal of Psychotherapy, 10*(3), 43–53.

Bloch, M., Daly, R. C., & Rubinow, D. R. (2003). Endocrine factors in the etiology of postpartum depression. *Comprehensive Psychiatry, 44*(3), 234–246.

Bloch, S. (2006). *Introduction to the psychotherapies* (4th ed.). New York: Oxford University Press.

Blood, A. J., & Zatorre, R. J. (2001). Intensely pleasurable responses to music correlate with activity in brain regions implicated in reward and emotion. *Proceedings National Academy of Sciences, 98*(20) 11818–11823.

Bloom, B. (1985). *Developing talent in young people.* New York: Ballantine.

Bloom, C. M., & Lamkin, D. M. (2006). The Olympian struggle to remember the cranial nerves: Mnemonics and student success. *Teaching of Psychology, 33*(2), 128–129.

Bloom, G. W. (1998). The ethical practice of WebCounseling. *British Journal of Guidance & Counselling, 26*(1), 53–59.

Blunt, A., & Pychyl, T. A. (2005). Project systems of procrastinators: A personal project-analytic and action control perspective. *Personality & Individual Differences, 38*(8), 1771–1780.

Bockting, W. O., & Coleman, E. (Eds.). (2003). *Masturbation as a means of achieving sexual health.* New York: Haworth Press.

Boergers, J., Spirito, A., & Donaldson, D. (1998). Reasons for adolescent suicide attempts. *Journal of the American Academy of Child & Adolescent Psychiatry, 37*(12), 1287–1293.

Bohannon, J. N., & Stanowicz, L. B. (1988). The issue of negative evidence: Adult responses to children's language errors. *Developmental Psychology, 24*(5), 684–689.

Boivin, D. B., Czeisler, C. A., & Waterhouse, J. W. (1997). Complex interaction of the sleep-wake cycle and circadian phase modulates mood in healthy subjects. *Archives of General Psychiatry, 54*(2), 145–152.

Boldero, J. M., Moretti, M. M., Bell, R. C., & Francis, J. J. (2005). Self-discrepancies and negative affect: A primer on when to look for specificity, and how to find it. *Australian Journal of Psychology, 57*(3), 139–147.

Bonanno, G. A., Papa, A., Lalande, K., Westphal, M., et al. (2004). The importance of being flexible. *Psychological Science, 15*(7), 482–487.

Bond, R., & Smith, P. B. (1996). Culture and conformity: A meta-analysis of studies using Asch's (1952, 1956) line judgment task. *Psychological Bulletin, 119*(1), 111–137.

Bond, T., & Wooten, V. (1996). The etiology and management of insomnia. *Virginia Medical Quarterly, 123*(4), 254–255.

Bongard, S., al'Absi, M., & Lovallo, W. R. (1998). Interactive effects of trait hostility and anger expression on cardiovascular reactivity in young men. *International Journal of Psychophysiology, 28*(2), 181–191.

Bonham, V., Warshauer-Baker, E., & Collins, F. S. (2005). Race and ethnicity in the genome era: The complexity of the constructs. *American Psychologist, 60*(1), 9–15.

Boniecki, K. A., & Britt, T. W. (2003). Prejudice and the peacekeeper. In T. W. Britt & A. B Adler (Eds.), *The psychology of the peacekeeper: Lessons from the field.* Westport, CT: Praeger.

Bood, S., Sundequist, U., Kjellgren, A., Norlander, T., et al. (2006). Eliciting the relaxation response with the help of flotation-REST (Restricted Environmental Stimulation Technique) in patients with stress-related ailments. *International Journal of Stress Management, 13*(2), 154–175.

Booker, J. M., & Hellekson, C. J. (1992). Prevalence of seasonal affective disorder in Alaska. *American Journal of Psychiatry, 149*(9), 1176–1182.

Bootzin, R. R., & Epstein, D. R. (2000). Stimulus control. In K. L. Lichstein & C. M. Morin (Eds.), *Treatment of late life insomnia.* Thousand Oaks, CA: Sage.

Borlongan, C. V., Sanberg, P. R., & Freeman, T. B. (1999). Neural transplantation for neurodegenerative disorders. *Lancet, 353*(Suppl 1), S29–30.

Borman, W. C., Hanson, M. A., & Hedge, J. W. (1997). Personnel psychology. *Annual Review of Psychology, 48,* 299–337.

Bornstein, M. H., & Tamis-LeMonda, C. S. (2001). Mother–infant interaction. In A. Fogel & G. Bremmer (Eds.), *Blackwell handbook of infant development.* London: Blackwell.

Bornstein, R. F. (1996). Sex differences in dependent personality disorder prevalence rates. *Clinical Psychology: Science & Practice, 3*(1), 1–12.

Borod, J. C., Bloom, R. L., Brickman, A. M., Nakhutina, L., et al. (2002). Emotional processing deficits in individuals with unilateral brain damage. *Applied Neuropsychology, 9*(1), 23–36.

Botes, A. (2000). A comparison between the ethics of justice and the ethics of care. *Journal of Advanced Nursing, 32*(5), 1071–1075.

Bouchard, T. J., Jr. (1983). Twins—Nature's twice-told tale. In *Yearbook of science and the future.* Chicago: Encyclopedia Britannica.

Bouchard, T. J., Jr. (2004). Genetic influence on human psychological traits: A survey. *Current Directions in Psychological Science, 13*(4), 148–151.

Bouchard, T. J., Jr., Lykken, D. T., McGue, M., Segal, N. L., et al. (1990). Sources of human psychological differences: The Minnesota study of twins reared apart. *Science, 250,* 223–228.

Bourne, E. J. (2005). *The anxiety & phobia workbook* (4th ed.). Oakland, CA: New Harbinger.

Bovbjerg, D. H., Redd, W. H., Jacobsen, P. B., Manne, S. L., et al. (1992). An experimental analysis of classically conditioned nausea during cancer chemotherapy. *Psychosomatic Medicine, 54*(6), 623–637.

Bower, G. H. (1981). Mood and memory. *American Psychologist, 36,* 129–148.

Bower, G. H., & Springston, F. (1970). Pauses as recoding points in letter series. *Journal of Experimental Psychology, 83,* 421–430.

Bowker, A. (2006). The relationship between sports participation and self-esteem during early adolescence. *Canadian Journal of Behavioural Science, 38*(3), 214–229.

Boyle, S. H., Williams, R. B., Mark, D., Brummett, B. H., et al. (2004). Hostility as a predictor of survival in patients with coronary artery disease. *Psychosomatic Medicine, 66*(5), 629–632.

Brach, T. (2003). *Radical acceptance.* New York: Bantam Books.

Bradley, R. H., & Corwyn, R. F. (2002). Socioeconomic status and child development. *Annual Review of Psychology, 53,* 377–399.

Bradley, R., Greene, J., Russ, E., Dutra, L., et al. (2005). A multidimensional meta-analysis of psychotherapy for PTSD. *American Journal of Psychiatry, 162*(2), 214–227.

Bradshaw, S. D. (2006). Shyness and difficult relationships: Formation is just the beginning. In D. C. Kirkpatrick, D. S. Duck, et al. (Eds.), *Relating difficulty: The processes of constructing and managing difficult interaction.* Mahwah, NJ: Erlbaum.

Brainerd, C. J. (2003). Jean Piaget, learning research, and American education. In B. J. Zimmerman & D. H. Schunk (Eds.), *Educational psychology: A century of contributions.* Mahwah, NJ: Erlbaum.

Brannon, L. (1996). *Gender.* Boston: Allyn & Bacon.

Brannon, L., & Feist, J. (2007). *Health psychology: An introduction to behavior and health* (6th ed.). Belmont, CA: Cengage Learning/Wadsworth.

Bransford, J. D., & McCarrell, N. S. (1977). A sketch of cognitive approach to comprehension: Some thoughts about understanding what it means to comprehend. In P. N. Johnson-Laird & P. C. Wason (Eds.), *Thinking: Readings in cognitive science.* Cambridge, UK: Cambridge University Press.

Braun, A. R., Balkin, T. J., & Herscovitch, P. (1998). Dissociated pattern of activity in visual cortices and their projections during human rapid eye movement sleep. *Science, 279*(5347), 91–95.

Braun, K. A., Ellis, R., & Loftus, E. F. (2002). Make my memory: How advertising can change memories of the past. *Psychology and Marketing, 19,* 1–23.

Braun, S. (2001). Seeking insight by prescription. *Cerebrum, 3*(2), 10–21.

Braun-LaTour, K. A., & LaTour, M. S. (2004). Assessing the long-term impact of a consistent advertising campaign on consumer memory. *Journal of Advertising, 33*(2), 49–61.

Bray, S. R., & Widmeyer, W. N. (2000). Athletes' perceptions of the home advantage. *Journal of Sport Behavior, 23*(1), 1–10.

Breckler, S. J., Olson, J., & Wiggins, E. (2006). *Social psychology alive.* Belmont, CA: Cengage Learning/Wadsworth.

Breedlove, S. M., Cooke, B. M., & Jordan, C. L. (1999). The orthodox view of brain sexual differentiation. *Brain, Behavior & Evolution, 54*(1), 8–14.

Brennan, F. X., Beck, K. D., & Servatius, R. J. (2003). Lever press escape/avoidance conditioning in rats: Safety signal length and avoidance performance. *Integrative Physiological & Behavioral Science, 38*(1), 36–44.

Breslau, N., Johnson, E. O., Hiripi, E., & Kessler, R. (2001). Nicotine dependence in the United States. *Archives of General Psychiatry, 58*(9), 810–816.

Bressi, C., Albonetti, S., & Razzoli, E. (1998). "Communication deviance" and schizophrenia. *New Trends in Experimental & Clinical Psychiatry, 14*(1), 33–39.

Bretherton, R., & Orner, R. J. (2004). Positive psychology and psychotherapy: An existential approach. In P. A. Linley & S. Joseph (Eds.), *Positive psychology in practice.* New York: Wiley.

Brewer, J. S. (1981). Duration of intromission and female orgasm rates. *Medical Aspects of Human Sexuality, 15*(4), 70–71.

Brewer, K. R., & Wann, D. L. (1998). Observational learning effectiveness as a function of model characteristics. *Social Behavior & Personality, 26*(1), 1–10.

Brewer, N., & Wells, G. L. (2006). The confidence-accuracy relationship in eyewitness identification: Effects of lineup instructions, foil similarity, and target-absent base rates. *Journal of Experimental Psychology: Applied, 12*(1), 11–30.

Brewer, N., & Williams, K. D. (Eds.). (2005). *Psychology and law: An empirical perspective.* New York: Guilford.

Bridges, K. M. B. (1932). Emotional development in early infancy. *Child Development, 3,* 324–334.

Bridges, L. J. (2003). Trust, attachment, and relatedness. In M. H. Bornstein, L. Davidson, et al. (Eds.), *Well-being: Positive development across the life course.* Mahwah, NJ: Erlbaum.

Brief, A. P., & Weiss, H. M. (2002). Organizational behavior. *Annual Review of Psychology, 53,* 279–307.

Brigham, J. C., & Wasserman, A. W. (1999). The impact of race, racial attitude, and gender on reactions to the criminal trial of O. J. Simpson. *Journal of Applied Social Psychology, 29*(7), 1333–1370.

Bringing up baby. (1999). *Sierra,* Jan–Feb, 17.

Brinton, R. D., & Wang, J. M. (2006). Therapeutic potential of neurogenesis for prevention and recovery from Alzheimer's disease: Allopregnanolone as a proof of concept neurogenic agent. *Current Alzheimer Research, 3*(3), 185–190.

Brock, T. C., & Green, M. C. (Eds.). (2005). *Persuasion: Psychological in-*

sights and perspectives (2nd ed.). Thousand Oaks, CA: Sage.

Brodley, B. T. (2006). Non-directivity in client-centered therapy. *Person-Centered & Experiential Psychotherapies, 5*(1), 36–52.

Brooks-Gunn, J., & Warren, M. P. (1988). The psychological significance of secondary sexual characteristics in nine- to eleven-year-old girls. *Child Development, 59*(4), 1061–1069.

Brothen, T., & Wambach, C. (2001). Effective student use of computerized quizzes. *Teaching of Psychology, 28*(4), 292–294.

Brown, A. E., Jeffcott, Jr., H. A. (1970). *Absolutely mad inventions.* New York: Dover Publications.

Brown, A. M. (1990). Development of visual sensitivity to light and color vision in human infants: A critical review. *Vision Research, 30*(8), 1159–1188.

Brown, A. S. (2004). *The déjà vu experience.* New York: Psychology Press.

Brown, A. S., Cohen, P., Harkavy-Friedman, J., Babulas, V., et al. (2001). Prenatal rubella, premorbid abnormalities, and adult schizophrenia. *Biological Psychiatry, 49*(6), 473–486.

Brown, B. B., & Bentley, D. L. (1993). Residential burglars judge risk. *Journal of Environmental Psychology, 13*(1), 51–61.

Brown, K. W. & Ryan, R. M. (2003). The benefits of being present. *Journal of Personality and Social Psychology, 84*(4), 822–848.

Brown, L. M. (2005). *Girlfighting: Betrayal and rejection among girls.* New York: New York University Press.

Brown, R. L., Leonard, T., Saunders, L. A., & Papasouliotis, O. (1997). A two-item screening test for alcohol and other drug problems. *Journal of Family Practice, 44*(2), 151–160.

Brown, R., & McNeill, D. (1966). The "tip of the tongue" phenomenon. *Journal of Verbal Learning and Verbal Behavior, 5,* 325–337.

Brown, S. A., Tapert, S. F., Granholm, E., & Delis, D. C. (2000). Neurocognitive functioning of adolescents: Effects of protracted alcohol use. *Alcoholism: Clinical & Experimental Research, 24*(2), 164–171.

Brown, S. G., Roy, E., Rohr, L., & Bryden, P. (2006). Using hand performance measures to predict handedness. *Laterality: Asymmetries of Body, Brain & Cognition, 11*(1), 1–14.

Brown, T. A., & Barlow, D. H. (2007). *Casebook in abnormal psychology* (3rd ed.). Belmont, CA: Cengage Learning/Wadsworth.

Brown, T. D., Dane, F. C., & Durham, M. D. (1998). Perception of race and ethnicity. *Journal of Social*

Behavior & Personality, 13(2), 295–306.

Browne, B. A. (1998). Gender stereotypes in advertising on children's television in the 1990s. *Journal of Advertising, 27*(1), 83–96.

Browne, N., & Keeley, S. (2007). *Asking the right questions: A guide to critical thinking* (8th ed.). Englewood Cliffs, NJ: Prentice Hall.

Brownell, K. D. (2003). *Food fight.* New York: McGraw-Hill.

Bruch, M. A. (2001). Shyness and social interaction. In R. Crozier & L. Alden (Eds.), *International handbook of social anxiety.* Sussex, UK: Wiley.

Bruer, J. T. (2001). A critical and sensitive period primer. In D. B. Bailey, Jr., J. T. Bruer, et al. (Eds.), *Critical thinking about critical periods.* Baltimore, MD: Paul H. Brookes.

Bruner, J. (1973). *Going beyond the information given.* New York: Norton.

Bruner, J. (1983). *Child's talk.* New York: Norton.

Bryden, P. J., Bruyn, J., & Fletcher, P. (2005). Handedness and health: An examination of the association between different handedness classifications and health disorders. *Laterality: Asymmetries of Body, Brain & Cognition, 10*(5), 429–440.

Buchwald, A. (1965). Psyching out. *Washington Post,* June 20.

Buddie, A. M. (2004). Alternatives to twelvestep programs. *Journal of Forensic Psychology Practice, 4*(3), 61–70.

Budney, A. J., & Hughes, J. R. (2006). The cannabis withdrawal syndrome. *Current Opinion in Psychiatry, 19*(3), 233–238.

Buehner, M. J., & May, J. (2003). Rethinking temporal contiguity and the judgement of causality: Effects of prior knowledge, experience, and reinforcement procedure. *Quarterly Journal of Experimental Psychology: Human Experimental Psychology, 56A*(5), 865–890.

Buller, D. J. (2005). *Adapting minds: Evolutionary psychology and the persistent quest for human nature.* Cambridge, MA: MIT Press.

Bunde, J., & Suls, J. (2006). A quantitative analysis of the relationship between the cook-medley hostility scale and traditional coronary artery disease risk factors. *Health Psychology, 25*(4), 493–500.

Bunn, G. C. (2007). Spectacular science: The lie detector's ambivalent powers. *History of Psychology, 10*(2), 156–178.

Burchinal, M. R., Roberts, J. E., Riggins, R., Zeisel, S. A., et al. (2000). Relating quality of center-based child care to early cognitive and language development longitudinally. *Child Development, 71*(2), 339–357.

Burger, J. M. (2008). *Personality* (7th ed.). Belmont, CA: Cengage Learning/Wadsworth.

Burger, J. M., & Lynn, A. L. (2005). Superstitious behavior among American and Japanese professional baseball players. *Basic & Applied Social Psychology, 27*(1), 71–76.

Burgess, C. A., & Kirsch, I. (1999). Expectancy information as a moderator of the effects of hypnosis on memory. *Contemporary Hypnosis, 16*(1), 22–31.

Burgess, M. C. R., & Weaver, G. E. (2003). Interest and attention in facial recognition. *Perceptual & Motor Skills, 96*(2), 467–480.

Burgner, D., & Hewstone, M. (1993). Young children's causal attributions for success and failure. *British Journal of Developmental Psychology, 11*(2), 125–129.

Burlingame, G. M., & Davies, R. (2002). Self-help groups. In M. Hersen & W. H. Sledge (Eds.), *Encyclopedia of psychotherapy.* San Diego: Academic Press.

Burlingame, G. M., Fuhriman, A., & Mosier, J. (2003). The differential effectiveness of group psychotherapy: A meta-analytic perspective. *Group Dynamics: Theory, Research, & Practice, 7*(1), 3–12.

Burnett, R. C., Medin, D. L., Ross, N. O., & Blok, S. V. (2005). Ideal is typical. *Canadian Journal of Experimental Psychology, 59*(1), 3–10.

Burns, D. D., & Persons, J. (1982). Hope and hopelessness: A cognitive approach. In L. E. Abt & I. R. Stuart (Eds.), *The newer therapies: A sourcebook.* New York: Van Nostrand Reinhold.

Burns, T. (2004). *Community mental health teams: A guide to current practices.* New York: Oxford University Press.

Burt, S. A., McGue, M., Carter, L. A., & Iacono, W. G. (2007). The different origins of stability and change in antisocial personality disorder symptoms. *Psychological Medicine, 37*(1), 27–38.

Burton, C. M., & King, L. A. (2004). The health benefits of writing about intensely positive experiences. *Journal of Research in Personality, 38*(2), 150–163.

Burtt, H. E. (1941). An experimental study of early childhood memory: Final report. *Journal of General Psychology, 58,* 435–439.

Bushman, B. J., & Anderson, C. A. (2001). Media violence and the American public. *American Psychologist, 56*(6/7), 477–489.

Bushnell, L. W., Sai, F., & Mullin, L. T. (1989). Neonatal recognition of the mother's face. *British Journal of Developmental Psychology, 7*(1), 3–15.

Bushnell, M. C., Villemure, C., & Duncan, G. H. (2004). Psychophysical and neurophysiological studies of pain modulation by attention. In D. D. Price & M. C. Bushnell (Eds.), *Psychological methods of pain control: Basic science and clinical perspectives.* Seattle: IASP Press.

Buss, D. M. (1985). Human mate selection. *American Scientist, 73,* 47–51.

Buss, D. M. (2000). *The dangerous passion.* New York: Free Press.

Buss, D. M. (2004). *Evolutionary psychology: The new science of the mind* (2nd ed.). Boston: Allyn & Bacon.

Buss, D. M. (2007). The evolution of human mating. *Acta Psychologica Sinica, 39*(3), 502–512.

Butcher, J. N. (2005). *A beginner's guide to the MMPI-2* (2nd ed.). Washington, DC: American Psychological Association.

Butcher, J. N., Mineka, S., & Hooley, J. (2007). *Abnormal psychology and modern life* (13th ed.). Boston: Allyn & Bacon.

Butkovic, A., & Bratko, D. (2003). Generation and sex differences in sensation seeking: Results of the family study. *Perceptual and Motor Skills, 97*(3, Pt. 1), 965–970.

Butler, B. (2007). The role of death qualification in capital trials involving juvenile defendants. *Journal of Applied Social Psychology, 37*(3), 549–560.

Butler, J. C. (2000). Personality and emotional correlates of right-wing authoritarianism. *Social Behavior & Personality, 28*(1), 1–14.

Butler, M. G. (2001). *Overcoming social anxiety and shyness: A self-help guide using cognitive behavioral techniques.* New York: New York University Press.

Butler, R. (1954). Curiosity in monkeys. *Scientific American, 190*(18), 70–75.

Byrne, S. M., & McLean, N. J. (2002). The cognitive-behavioral model of bulimia nervosa: A direct evaluation. *International Journal of Eating Disorders, 31,* 17–31.

Cahill, S. P., Carrigan, M. H., & Frueh, B. C. (1999). Does EMDR work? and if so, why? *Journal of Anxiety Disorders, 13*(1–2), 5–33.

Cahn, B. R., & Polich, J. (2006). Meditation states and traits: EEG, ERP, and neuroimaging studies. *Psychological Bulletin, 132*(2), 180–211.

Calhoun, J. B. (1962). A "behavioral sink." In E. L. Bliss (Ed.), *Roots of behavior.* New York: Harper & Row.

Callahan, C. M. (2006). Giftedness. In G. G. Bear & K. M. Minke (Eds.), *Children's needs III: Development, prevention, and intervention.* Washington, DC: National Association of School Psychologists.

Camara, W. J., & Schneider, D. L. (1994). Integrity tests. *American Psychologist, 49*(2), 112–119.

Cameron, J. A., & Trope, Y. (2004). Stereotype-biased search and processing of information about group members. *Social Cognition, 22*(6), 650–672.

Cameron, J., & Pierce, W. D. (2002). *Rewards and intrinsic motivation: Resolving the controversy.* Westport, CO: Bergin & Garvey.

Campbell, L., Campbell, B., & Dickinson, D. (2003). *Teaching and learning through multiple intelligences* (3rd ed.). Boston: Allyn & Bacon.

Campion, M. A., & McClelland, C. L. (1993). Follow-up and extension of interdisciplinary costs and benefits of enlarged jobs. *Journal of Applied Psychology, 78*(3), 339–351.

Campion, M. A., Palmer, D. K., & Campion, J. E. (1998). Structuring employment interviews to improve reliability, validity and users' reactions. *Current Directions in Psychological Science, 7*(3), 77–82.

Canli, T., Desmond, J. E., Zhao, Z., Glover, G., et al. (1998). Hemispheric asymmetry for emotional stimuli detected with fMRI. *Neuroreport, 9*(14) 3233–3239.

Cannon, W. B. (1932). *The wisdom of the body.* New York: Norton.

Cannon, W. B. (1934). Hunger and thirst. In C. Murchinson (Ed.), *Handbook of general experimental psychology.* Worcester, MA: Clark University Press.

Cannon, W. B., & Washburn, A. L. (1912). An exploration of hunger. *American Journal of Physiology, 29,* 441–454.

Caplan, P. J. (1995). *They say you're crazy.* Reading, MA: Addison-Wesley.

Capuzzi, D. (2003). *Approaches to group counseling.* Englewood Cliffs, NJ: Prentice Hall.

Cardoso, S. H. (2000). Our ancient laughing brain. *Cerebrum, 2*(4), 15–30.

Carducci, B. J., & Fields, T. H. (2007). *The shyness workbook for teens.* Champaign, IL: Research Press.

Carlbring, P., Gunnarsdóttir, M., Hedensjö, L., Andersson, G., et al. (2007). Treatment of social phobia: Randomised trial of internet-delivered cognitive-behavioural therapy with telephone support. *British Journal of Psychiatry, 190*(2), 123–128.

Carlson, M., Marcus-Hewhall, A., & Miller, N. (1990). Effects of situational aggression cues: A quantitative review. *Journal of Personality & Social Psychology, 58*(4), 622–633.

Carlson, N. R. (2005). *Physiology of behavior* (8th ed.). Boston: Allyn & Bacon.

Carlson, N. R. (2007). *Physiology of behavior* (9th ed.). Boston: Allyn & Bacon.

Carnagey, N. L., & Anderson, C. A. (2004). Violent video game exposure and aggression: A literature review. *Minerva Psichiatrica, 45*(1), 1–18.

Carney, R. N., & Levin, J. R. (2001). Remembering the names of unfamiliar animals: Keywords as keys to their kingdom. *Applied Cognitive Psychology, 15*(2), 133–143.

Carney, R. N., & Levin, J. R. (2003). Promoting higher-order learning benefits by building lower-order mnemonic connections. *Applied Cognitive Psychology, 17*(5), 563–575.

Carroll, D. W. (2008). *Psychology of language* (5th ed.). Belmont, CA: Cengage Learning/Wadsworth.

Carroll, J. L. (2007). *Sexuality now: Embracing diversity* (2nd ed.). Belmont, CA: Cengage Learning/Wadsworth.

Carroll, J. M., & Russell, J. A. (1996). Do facial expressions signal specific emotions? Judging emotion from the face in context. *Journal of Personality & Social Psychology, 70*(2), 205–218.

Carskadon, M. A., Acebo, C., & Jenni, O. C. (2004). Regulation of adolescent sleep: Implications for behavior. *Annals of the New York Academy of Science, 1021,* 276–291.

Carter, D. A., Simkins, B. J., & Simpson, W. G. (2003). Corporate governance, board diversity, and firm value. *Financial Review, 38,* 33–53.

Cartwright, D. (2002a). *Psychoanalysis, violence and rage-type murder: Murdering minds.* New York: Brunner-Routledge.

Cartwright, D. (2002b). The narcissistic exoskeleton: The defensive organization of the rage-type murderer. *Bulletin of the Menninger Clinic, 66*(1), 1–18.

Cartwright, R., & Lamberg, L. (1992). *Crisis dreaming.* New York: HarperCollins.

Casey, P. (2001). Multiple personality disorder. *Primary Care Psychiatry, 7*(1), 7–11.

Caspi, A. Sugden, K., Moffitt, T. E., Taylor, A., et al. (2003). Influence of life stress on depression: Moderation by a polymorphism in the 5-HTT gene. *Science, 301*(5631), 386–389.

Caspi, A., Roberts, B. W., & Shiner, R. L. (2005). Personality development: Stability and change. *Annual Review of Psychology, 56,* 453–484.

Cassady, J. C. (2004). The influence of cognitive test anxiety across the learning-testing cycle. *Learning & Instruction, 14*(6), 569–592.

Castro, J. R., & Rice, K. G. (2003). Perfectionism and ethnicity: Implications for depressive symptoms and self-reported academic achieve-ment *Cultural Diversity & Ethnic Minority Psychology, 9*(1), 64–78.

Castro, J., Gila, A., Gual, P., Lahortiga, F., et al. (2004). Perfectionism dimensions in children and adolescents with anorexia nervosa. *Journal of Adolescent Health, 35*(5), 392–398.

Catalano, R., Novaco, R., & McConnell, W. (1997). A model of the net effect of job loss on violence. *Journal of Personality & Social Psychology, 72*(6), 1440–1447.

Cattell, R. B. (1949). *Culture Free Intelligence Test, Scale 1, Handbook.* Champaign, IL: Institute of Personality and Ability.

Cattell, R. B. (1965). *The scientific analysis of personality.* Baltimore: Penguin.

Cattell, R. B. (1973). Personality pinned down. *Psychology Today,* July, 40–46.

Cautela, J. R., & Kearney, A. J. (1986). *The covert conditioning handbook.* New York: Springer.

Cavaco, S., Anderson, S. W., Allen, J. S., Castro-Caldas, A., et al. (2004). The scope of preserved procedural memory in amnesia. *Brain: A Journal of Neurology, 127*(8), 1853–1867.

CDC. (2002). *Teenagers in the United States: sexual activity, contraceptive use, and childbearing, 2002.* Atlanta, GA: Centers for Disease Control and National Center for Health Statistics, National Vital Statistics System. Retrieved July 30, 2007, from http://0-www.cdc.gov.mill1.sjlibrary.org:80/nchs/data/series/sr_23/sr23_024.pdf.

CDC. (2002). *Overweight, obesity, and healthy weight among persons 20 years of age and over, according to sex, age, race, and Hispanic origin: United States, 1960–62, 1971–74, 1976–80, 1988–94, and 1999–2000.* Atlanta: Centers for Disease Control and Prevention. Retrieved July 8, 2007, from http://www.cdc.gov/nchs/data/hus/tables/2002/02hus070.pdf.

CDC. (2003). *Deaths, percent of total deaths, and death rates for 15 leading causes of death in 5-year age groups, by race and sex: United State, 2000.* Atlanta: Centers for Disease Control and National Center for Health Statistics, National Vital Statistics System. Retrieved July 25, 2007, from http://www.cdc.gov/nchs/datawh/statab/unpubd/mortabs/lcwk1_10.htm.

CDC. (2005). Annual smoking–attributable mortality, years of potential life lost, and productivity losses: United States, 1997–2001. *Centers for Disease Control and Prevention Morbidity and Mortality Weekly Report, 54*(25), 625–628.

CDC. (2007). *Sexual violence: Fact sheet.* Atlanta: National Center for Injury Prevention and Control.

Retrieved July 29, 2007, from http://www.cdc.gov/ncipc/factsheets/svfacts.htm.

Chabas, D., Taheri, S., Renier, C., & Mignot, E. (2003). The genetics of narcolepsy. *Annual Review of Genomics and Human Genetics, 4,* 459–483.

Chakos, M. H., Alvir, J. M. J., Woerner, M., & Koreen, A. (1996). Incidence and correlates of tardive dyskinesia in first episode of schizophrenia. *Archives of General Psychiatry, 53*(4), 313–319.

Chamberlin, J. (2004). Survey says: More Americans are seeking mental health treatment. *Monitor on Psychology,* July/Aug., 17.

Chamberlin, J., & Rogers, J. A. (1990). Planning a community-based mental health system. *American Psychologist, 45*(11), 1241–1244.

Chambers, R. A., Taylor, J. R., & Potenza, M. N. (2003). Developmental neurocircuitry of motivation in adolescence: A critical period of addiction vulnerability. *American Journal of Psychiatry, 160*(6), 1041–1052.

Chambless, D. L., & Ollendick, T. H. (2001). Empirically supported psychological interventions. *Annual Review of Psychology, 52,* 685–716.

Chamorro-Premuzic, T., & Furnham, A. (2003). Personality predicts academic performance. *Journal of Research in Personality, 37*(4), 319–338.

Chan, G. C.-K., Hinds, T. R., Impey, S., & Storm, D. R. (1998). Hippocampal neurotoxicity of _-sup-9-tetrahydrocannabinol. *Journal of Neuroscience, 18*(14), 5322–5332.

Chance, P. (2006). *Learning and behavior* (5th ed.). Belmont, CA: Cengage Learning/Wadsworth.

Chansler, P. A., Swamidass, P. M., & Cammann, C. (2003). Self-managing work teams: An empirical study of group cohesiveness in "natural work groups" at a Harley-Davidson Motor Company plant. *Small Group Research, 34*(1), 101–120.

Chao, R., & Tseng, V. (2002). Parenting of Asians. In M. H. Bornstein (Ed.), *Handbook of parenting* (Vol. 4): *Social conditions and applied parenting* (2nd ed.). Mahwah, NJ: Erlbaum.

Chapanis, A., & Lindenbaum, L. E. (1959). A reaction time study of four control-display linkages. *Human Factors, 1,* 1–7.

Chapman, R. A. (Ed.). (2006). *The clinical use of hypnosis in cognitive behavior therapy: A practitioner's casebook.* New York: Springer Publishing.

Chassin, L., Presson, C. C., Sherman, S. J., & Kim, K. (2003). Historical changes in cigarette

smoking and smoking-related beliefs after 2 decades in a midwestern community. *Health Psychology, 22*(4), 347–353.

Chaves, J. F. (2000). Hypnosis. In A. Kazdin (Ed.), *Encyclopedia of psychology.* Washington, DC: American Psychological Association.

Check, J. V. P., & Malamuth, N. M. (1983). Sex role stereotyping and reactions to depictions of stranger versus acquaintance rape. *Journal of Personality & Social Psychology, 45,* 344–356.

Cheek, J., & Buss, A. H. (1979). *Scales of shyness, sociability and self-esteem and correlations among them.* Unpublished research, University of Texas. (Cited by Buss, 1980.)

Chen, K., & Kandel, D. B. (1995). The natural history of drug use from adolescence to the mid-thirties in a general population sample. *American Journal of Public Health, 85*(1), 41–47.

Chen, Z., Lawson, R. B., Gordon, L. R., & McIntosh, B. (1996). Groupthink: Deciding with the leader and the devil. *Psychological Record, 46*(4), 581–590.

Chen, Z., Mo, L., & Honomichl, R. (2004). Having the memory of an elephant. *Journal of Experimental Psychology: General, 133*(3), 415–433.

Cheng, H., Cao, Y., & Olson, L. (1996). Spinal cord repair in adult paraplegic rats: Partial restoration of hind limb function. *Science, 273*(5274), 510.

Chess, S., & Thomas, A. (1986). *Know your child.* New York: Basic.

Chesson, A. L., Anderson, W. M., Littner, M., Davila. D., et al. (1999). Practice parameters for the nonpharmacologic treatment of chronic insomnia. *Sleep, 22,* 1128–1133.

Chester, A., & Glass, C. A. (2006). Online counselling: A descriptive analysis of therapy services on the internet. *British Journal of Guidance & Counselling, 34*(2), 145–160.

Cheyne, J. A. (2005). Sleep paralysis episode frequency and number, types, and structure of associated hallucinations. *Journal of Sleep Research, 14*(3), 319–324.

Cheyne, J. A., Rueffer, S. D., & Newby-Clark, I. R. (1999). Hypnagogic and hypnopompic hallucinations during sleep paralysis: Neurological and cultural construction of the nightmare. *Consciousness & Cognition, 8,* 319–337.

Chisolm, T. H., Willott, J. F., & Lister, J. J. (2003). The aging auditory system: Anatomic and physiologic changes and implications for rehabilitation. *International Journal of Audiology, 42*(Suppl 2), 2S3–2S10.

Chomsky, N. (1975). *Reflections on language.* New York: Pantheon.

Chomsky, N. (1986). *Knowledge of language.* New York: Praeger.

Christensen, A., & Jacobson, N. S. (1994). Who (or what) can do psychotherapy. *Psychological Science, 5*(1), 8–14.

Christian, K. M., & Thompson, R. F. (2005). Long-term storage of an associative memory trace in the cerebellum. *Behavioral Neuroscience, 119*(2), 526–537.

Christophersen, E. R., & Mortweet, S. L. (2003). *Parenting that works: Building skills that last a lifetime.* Washington, DC: American Psychological Association.

Chua, P., & Fujino, D. C. (1999). Negotiating new Asian-American masculinities: Attitudes and gender expectations. *Journal of Men's Studies, 7*(3), 391–413.

Cialdini, R. B., & Goldstein, N. J. (2004). Social influence: Compliance and conformity. *Annual Review of Psychology, 55,* 591–621.

Cialdini, R. B., Eisenberg, N., Green, B. L., Rhoads, K., et al. (1998). Undermining the undermining effect of reward on sustained interest. *Journal of Applied Social Psychology, 28*(3), 249–263.

Cialdini, R. B., Reno, R. R., & Kallgren, C. A. (1990). A focus theory of normative conduct: Recycling the concept of norms to reduce littering in public places. *Journal of Personality & Social Psychology, 58*(6), 1015–1026.

Ciarrochi, J., Dean, F. P., & Anderson, S. (2002). Emotional intelligence moderates the relationship between stress and mental health. *Personality & Individual Differences, 32*(2), 197–209.

Cinciripini, P. M., Wetter, D. W., & McClure, J. B. (1997). Scheduled reduced smoking. *Addictive Behaviors, 22*(6), 759–767.

Clark, D., Boutros, N., & Mendez, M. (2005). *The brain and behavior* (2nd ed.). Cambridge, UK: Cambridge University Press.

Clark, R., Anderson, N. B., Clark, V. R., & Williams, D. R. (1999). Racism as a stressor for African Americans. *American Psychologist, 54*(10), 805–816.

Clayton, N. S., Yu, K. S., & Dickinson, A. (2001). Scrub jays (Aphelocoma coerulescens) form integrated memories of the multiple features of caching episodes. *Journal of Experimental Psychology: Animal Behavior Processes, 27,* 17–29.

Clearfield, M. W., & Nelson, N. M. (2006). Sex differences in mothers' speech and play behavior with 6-, 9-, and 14-month-old infants. *Sex Roles, 54*(1–2), 127–137.

Clearwater, Y. (1985). A human place in outer space. *Psychology Today,* July, 34–43.

Clements, A. M., Rimrodt, S. L., Abel, J. R., Blankner, J. G. et al. (2006). Sex differences in cerebral

laterality of language and visuospatial processing. *Brain & Language, 98*(2), 150–158.

Click, P., Zion, C., & Nelson, C. (1988). What mediates sex discrimination in hiring decisions? *Journal of Personality & Social Psychology, 55*(2), 178–186.

Cline, V. B., Croft, R. G., & Courrier, S. (1972). Desensitization of children to television violence. *Journal of Personality & Social Psychology, 27,* 360–365.

Cnattingius, S., Signorello, L. B., Ammerén, G., Clausson, B., et al. (2000). Caffeine intake and the risk of first-trimester spontaneous abortion. *New England Journal of Medicine, 343*(25), 1839–1845.

Cochran, S. D. (2001). Emerging issues in research on lesbians' and gay men's mental health. *American Psychologist, 56*(11), 931–947.

Cohen, J. E. (1995). *How many people can the earth support?* New York: Norton.

Cohen, P., Cohen, J., Kasen, S., Velez, C. N., et al. (1993). An epidemiological study of disorders in late adolescence: I. Age- and gender-specific prevalence. *Journal of Child Psychology & Psychiatry, 6,* 851–867.

Cohen, S., Evans, G. W., Krantz, D. S., & Stokols, D. (1981). Cardiovascular and behavioral effects of community noise. *American Scientist, 69,* 528–535.

Colapinto, J. (2000). *As nature made him: The boy who was raised as a girl.* New York: HarperCollins.

Cole, J. (1995). *Pride and a daily marathon.* Cambridge, MA: MIT Press.

Coles, C. D., & Black, M. M. (2006). Introduction to the special issue. *Journal of Pediatric Psychology. Special Issue: Prenatal Substance Exposure: Impact on Children's Health, Development, School Performance, and Risk Behavior, 31*(1), 1–4.

Colin, A. K., Moore, K., & West, A. N. (1996). Creativity, oversensitivity, and rate of habituation. *EDRA: Environmental Design Research Association, 20*(4), 423–427.

Collins, A. M., & Quillian, M. R. (1969). Retrieval time from semantic memory. *Journal of Verbal Learning & Verbal Behavior, 8,* 240–247.

Collins, N. L., Cooper, M. L., Albino, A., & Allard, L. (2002). Psychosocial vulnerability from adolescence to adulthood: A prospective study of attachment style differences in relationship functioning and partner choice. *Journal of Personality, 70*(6), 965–1008.

Collins, W. A., & Gunnar, M. R. (1990). Social and personality development. *Annual Review of Psychology, 41,* 387–416.

Collop, N. A. (2005). Obstructive sleep apnea: treatment overview and controversies. In P. R. Carney, J. D. Geyer, & R. B. Berry (Eds.), *Clinical sleep disorders.* Philadelphia: Lippincott Williams & Wilkins.

Comer, R. J. (2005). *Fundamentals of abnormal psychology* (4th ed.). New York: Worth.

Compton, W. C. (2005). *An introduction to positive psychology.* Belmont, CA: Cengage Learning/Wadsworth.

Conway, A. R. A., Cowan, N., & Bunting, M. F. (2001). The cocktail party phenomenon revisited. *Psychonomic Bulletin & Review, 8*(2), 331–335.

Conway, M. A., Cohen, G., & Stanhope, N. (1992). Very long-term memory for knowledge acquired at school and university. *Applied Cognitive Psychology, 6*(6), 467–482.

Conyne, R. K., & Clack, R. J. (1981). *Environmental assessment and design.* New York: Praeger.

Cooper, J., Bennett, E. A., & Sukel, H. L. (1996). Complex scientific testimony: How do jurors make decisions? *Law & Human Behavior, 20*(4), 379–394.

Cooper, J., Mirabile, R., & Scher, S. J. (2005). Actions and attitudes: The theory of cognitive dissonance. In T. C. Brock & M. C. Green (Eds.), *Persuasion: Psychological insights and perspectives* (2nd ed). Thousand Oaks, CA: Sage.

Cooper, M. J. (2005). Cognitive theory in anorexia nervosa and bulimia nervosa: Progress, development and future directions. *Clinical Psychology Review, 25*(4), 511–531.

Cooper, P. J., & Murray, L. (2001). The treatment and prevention of postpartum depression and associated disturbances in child development. *Archives of Women's Mental Health, 3*(Suppl 2), 5.

Cooper, R. P., Abraham, J., Berman, S., & Staska, M. (1997). The development of infants' preference for motherese. *Infant Behavior & Development, 20*(4), 477–488.

Corballis, M. C. (2002). *From hand to mouth: The origins of language.* Princeton, NJ: Princeton University Press.

Corbin, W. R., & Fromme, K. (2002). Alcohol use and serial monogamy as risks for sexually transmitted diseases in young adults. *Health Psychology, 21*(3), 229–236.

Coren, S. (1992). *The left-hander syndrome.* New York: Free Press.

Coren, S. (1996). *Sleep thieves.* New York: Free Press.

Coren, S., Ward, L. M., & Enns, J. T. (2004). *Sensation and perception* (6th ed.). New York: Wiley.

Corey, G. (2008). *Theory and practice of group counseling* (7th ed.). Belmont, CA: Cengage Learning/Wadsworth.

Corkin, S. (2002). What's new with the amnesic patient H.M.? *Nature Reviews Neuroscience, 3,* 153–160.

Cormier, J. F., & Thelen, M. H. (1998). Professional skepticism of multiple personality disorder. *Professional Psychology: Research and Practice, 29*(2), 163–167.

Correa-Chávez, M., Rogoff, B., & Arauz, R. M. (2005). Cultural patterns in attending to two events at once. *Child Development, 76*(3), 664–678.

Corrigan, P. W., & Penn, D. L. (1999). Lessons from social psychology on discrediting psychiatric stigma. *American Psychologist, 54*(9), 765–776.

Corrigan, P. W., & Watson, A. C. (2005). Findings from the National Comorbidity Survey on the frequency of violent behavior in individuals with psychiatric disorders. *Psychiatry Research, 136*(2–3), 153–162.

Corrigan, P. W., Watson, A. C., Gracia, G., Slopen, N., et al. (2005). Newspaper stories as measures of structural stigma. *Psychiatric Services, 56*(5), 551–556.

Corsini, R. J. (2001). *Handbook of innovative therapy* (2nd ed.). New York: Wiley.

Costa, Jr., P. T., & McCrae, R. R. (2006). Trait and factor theories. In J. C. Thomas, D. L. Segal, et al. (Eds.), *Comprehensive handbook of personality & psychopathology* (Vol. 1): *Personality and everyday functioning.* New York: Wiley.

Côté, J. E. (2006). Emerging adulthood as an institutionalized moratorium: Risks and benefits to identity formation. In J. J. Arnett & J. L. Tanner (Eds.), *Emerging adults in America: Coming of age in the 21st century.* Washington, DC: American Psychological Association.

Côté, J. E., & Levine, C. (2002). *Identity formation, agency, and culture.* Mahwah, NJ: Erlbaum.

Cote, S. (1999). Affect and performance in organizational settings. *Current Directions in Psychological Science, 8*(2), 65–68.

Coulton, C. J., Korbin, J. E., & Su, M. (1996). Measuring neighborhood context for young children in an urban area. *American Journal of Community Psychology, 24*(1), 5–32.

Coursey, R. D., Ward-Alexander, L., & Katz, B. (1990). Cost-effectiveness of providing insurance benefits for posthospital psychiatric halfway house stays. *American Psychologist, 45*(10), 1118–1126.

Court, J. H., & Court, P. C. (2001). Repression: R. I. P. *Australian Journal of Clinical & Experimental Hypnosis, 29*(1), 8–16.

Cowan, G., Heiple, B., Marquez, C., Khatchadourian, D., et al. (2005). Heterosexuals' attitudes toward hate crimes and hate speech against gays and lesbians: Old-fashioned and modern heterosexism. *Journal of Homosexuality, 49*(2), 67–82.

Cowan, N. (2001). The magical number 4 in short-term memory. *Behavioral & Brain Sciences, 24*(1), 87–185.

Cowan, N. (2005). *Working memory capacity.* Hove, UK: Psychology Press.

Cowden, C. R. (2005). Worry and its relationship to shyness. *North American Journal of Psychology, 7*(1), 59–69.

Cowles, J. T. (1937). Food tokens as incentives for learning by chimpanzees. *Comparative Psychology,* Monograph, *14*(5, Whole no. 71).

Cox, R. H. (2007). *Sport psychology: Concepts and applications* (6th ed.). New York: McGraw-Hill.

Craig, L. (2006). Does father care mean fathers share?: A comparison of how mothers and fathers in intact families spend time with children. *Gender & Society, 20*(2), 259–281.

Craig, T. Y., & Kelly, J. R. (1999). Group cohesiveness and creative performance. *Group Dynamics, 3*(4), 243–256.

Craik, F. I. M. (1970). The fate of primary items in free recall. *Journal of Verbal Learning & Verbal Behavior, 9,* 143–148.

Craik, F. I. M., & Bialystok, E. (2005). Intelligence and executive control: Evidence from aging and bilingualism. *Cortex, 41*(2), 222–224.

Crano, W. D. (2000). Milestones in the psychological analysis of social influence. *Group Dynamics: Theory, Research, & Practice, 4*(1), 68–80.

Cravatt, B. F., Prospero-Garcia O., Siuzdak G., Gilula, N. B., et al. (1995). Chemical characterization of a family of brain lipids that induce sleep. *Science, 268*(5216), 1506–1509.

Crawley, S. B., & Sherrod, K. B. (1984). Parent–infant play during the first year of life. *Infant Behavior & Development, 7,* 65–75.

Crencavage, L. M., & Norcross, J. C. (1990). Where are the commonalities among the therapeutic common factors? *Professional Psychology: Research & Practice, 21*(5), 372–378.

Crisp, A., Gowers, S., Joughin, N., McClelland, L., et al. (2006). The enduring nature of anorexia nervosa. *European Eating Disorders Review, 14*(3), 147–152.

Cromdal, J. (1999). Childhood bilingualism and metalinguistic skills. *Applied Psycholinguistics, 20*(1), 1–20.

Crooks, R., & Baur, K. (2008). *Our sexuality* (10th ed.). Belmont, CA: Cengage Learning/Wadsworth.

Cropley, A. (2006). In praise of convergent thinking. *Creativity Research Journal, 18,* 391–404.

Crosby, R. A., & Yarber, W. L. (2001). Perceived versus actual knowledge about correct condom use among U.S. adolescents: results from a national study. *Journal of Adolescent Health, 28*(5), 415–420.

Crown, C. L., Feldstein, S., Jasnow, M. D., Beebe, B., et al. (2002). The cross-modal coordination of interpersonal timing. *Journal of Psycholinguistic Research, 31*(1), 1–23.

Crowther, J. H., Sanftner, J., Bonifazi, D. Z., & Shepherd, K. L. (2001). The role of daily hassles in binge eating. *International Journal of Eating Disorders, 29,* 449–454.

Csikszentmihalyi, M. (1997). *Creativity.* New York: HarperCollins.

Csikszentmihalyi, M. (1999). If we are so rich, why aren't we happy? *American Psychologist, 54*(10), 821–827.

Csikszentmihalyi, M., Abuhamdeh, S., Nakamura, J. (2005). Flow. In A. J. Elliot & C. S. Dweck (Eds.), *Handbook of competence and motivation.* New York: Guilford.

Cull, M. (2002). Treatment of intersex needs open discussion. *British Medical Journal, 324*(7342), 919.

Cull, W. L., Shaughnessy, J. J., & Zechmeister, E. B. (1996). Expanding understanding of the expanding-pattern-of-retrieval mnemonic. *Journal of Experimental Psychology: Applied, 2*(4) 365–378.

Cummings, M. R. (2006). *Human heredity: Principles and issues* (7th ed.). Belmont, CA: Cengage Learning/Wadsworth.

Cummins, D. D. (1995). *The other side of psychology.* New York: St. Martins.

Curci, A., & Luminet, O. (2006). Follow-up of a cross-national comparison on flashbulb and event memory for the September 11th attacks. *Memory, 14*(3), 329–344.

Czeisler, C. A., Duffy, J. F., Shanahan, T. L., Brown, E. N., et al. (1999). Stability, precision, and near-24-hour period of the human circadian pacemaker. *Science, 284*(5423), 2177–2181.

Czeisler, C. A., Richardson, G. S., Zimmerman, J. C., Moore-Ede, M. C., et al. (1981). Entrainment of human circadian rhythms by light-dark cycles: A reassessment. *Photochemistry, Photobiology, 34,* 239–247.

Dane, S., & Erzurumluoglu, A. (2003). Sex and handedness differences in eye-hand visual reaction times in handball players. *International Journal of Neuroscience, 113*(7), 923–929.

Daniels, H. (2005). Vygotsky and educational psychology: Some preliminary remarks. *Educational & Child Psychology, 22*(1), 6–17.

Danziger, N., Prkachin, K. M., & Willer, J.-C. (2006). Is pain the price of empathy? The perception of others' pain in patients with congenital insensitivity to pain. *Brain: A Journal of Neurology, 129*(9), 2494–2507.

Darley, J. M. (2000). Bystander phenomenon. In A. E. Kazdin (Ed.), *Encyclopedia of psychology* (Vol. 1). Washington, DC: American Psychological Association.

Darley, J. M., & Latané, B. (1968). Bystander intervention in emergencies: Diffusion of responsibility. *Journal of Personality & Social Psychology, 8,* 377–383.

Darling, C. A., Davidson, J. K., & Passarello, L. C. (1992). The mystique of first intercourse among college youth: The role of partners, contraceptive practices, and psychological reactions. *Journal of Youth & Adolescence, 21*(1), 97–117.

Darou, W. S. (1992). Native Canadians and intelligence testing. *Canadian Journal of Counselling, 26*(2), 96–99.

Daruna, J. H. (2004). *Introduction to psychoneuroimmunology.* Amsterdam: Elsevier.

Darwin, C. (1872). *The expression of emotion in man and animals.* Chicago: University of Chicago Press.

Das, J. P. (2000). Mental retardation. In A. Kazdin (Ed.), *Encyclopedia of psychology.* Washington, DC: American Psychological Association.

Dauvilliers, Y., Cervena, K, Carlander, B., Espa, F., et al. (2004). Dissociation in circadian rhythms in a pseudohypersomnia form of fatal familial insomnia. *Neurology, 63*(12), 2416–2418.

Davanloo, H. (1995). Intensive short-term dynamic psychotherapy. *International Journal of Short-Term Psychotherapy, 10*(3–4), 121–155.

Davidovitch, N., & Milgram, R. M. (2006). Creative thinking as a predictor of teacher effectiveness in higher education. *Creativity Research Journal, 18,* 385–390.

Davidson, P. R., & Parker, K. C. H. (2001). Eye movement desensitization and reprocessing (EMDR): A meta-analysis. *Journal of Consulting & Clinical Psychology, 69*(2), 305–316.

Davidson, R. J., Kabat-Zinn, J., Schumacher, J., Rosenkranz, M., et al. (2003). Alternations in brain and immune function produced by mindfulness meditation. *Psychosomatic Medicine, 65*(4), 564–570.

Davidson, T. L. (2000). Latent learning. In A. E. Kazdin (Ed.), *Encyclopedia of psychology* (Vol. 4). Washington, DC: American Psychological Association.

Davies, M., & McCartney, S. (2003). Effects of gender and sexuality on judgements of victim blame and rape myth acceptance in a depicted male rape. *Journal of Community & Applied Social Psychology, 13*(5), 391–398.

Davis, D., & Follette, W. C. (2002). Rethinking the probative value of evidence. *Law & Human Behavior, 26*(2), 133–158.

Davis, M. J., & Bibace, R. (1999). Dating couples and their relationships: Intimacy and contraceptive use. *Adolescence, 34*(133), 1–7.

Davis, M. R., McMahon, M., & Greenwood, K. M. (2005). The efficacy of mnemonic components of the cognitive interview: Towards a shortened variant for time-critical investigations. *Applied Cognitive Psychology, 19*(1), 75–93.

Davison, G. C., & Neale, J. M. (2006). *Abnormal psychology* (10th ed.). San Francisco: Jossey-Bass.

Dawson, G., & Toth, K. (2006). Autism spectrum disorders. In D. Cicchetti & D. J. Cohen (Eds.), *Developmental psychopathology* (Vol. 3): *Risk, disorder, and adaptation* (2nd ed.). Hoboken, NJ: Wiley.

de Jong, P. J., & Muris, P. (2002). Spider phobia. *Journal of Anxiety Disorders, 16*(1), 51–65.

de las Fuentes, C., & Vasquez, M. J. T. (1999). Immigrant adolescent girls of color. In N. G. Johnson, M. C. Roberts, et al. (Eds.), *Beyond appearance.* Washington, DC: American Psychological Association.

de Leon, C. F. M. (2005). Social engagement and successful aging. *European Journal of Ageing, 2*(1), 64–66.

de Mello, M. F., de Jesus Mari, J., Bacaltchuk, J., Verdeli, H., et al. (2005). A systematic review of research findings on the efficacy of interpersonal therapy for depressive disorders. *European Archives of Psychiatry & Clinical Neuroscience, 255*(2), 75–82.

de Rios, M. D., & Grob, C. S. (2005). Editors' introduction: Ayahuasca use in cross-cultural perspective. *Journal of Psychoactive Drugs, 37*(2), 119–121.

DeArmond, S., Tye, M., Chen, P. Y., Krauss, A., et al. (2006). Age and gender stereotypes: New challenges in a changing workplace and workforce. *Journal of Applied Social Psychology, 36*(9), 2184–2214.

Deaux, K., & Emswiller, T. (1974). Explanation of successful performance on sex-linked tasks: What is skill for the male is luck for the female. *Journal of Personality & Social Psychology, 29,* 80–85.

Deckers, L. (2005). *Motivation: Biological, psychological, and environmental* (2nd ed.). Boston: Allyn & Bacon.

Deckro, G. R., Ballinger, K. M., Hoyt, M., Wilcher, M., et al. (2002). The evaluation of a mind/body intervention to reduce psychological distress and perceived stress in college students. *Journal of American College Health, 50*(6), 281–287.

Deeb, S. S. (2004). Molecular genetics of color-vision deficiencies. *Visual Neuroscience, 21*(3), 191–196.

DeGaetano, G. (2005). The impact of media violence on developing minds and hearts. In S. Olfman (Ed.), *Childhood lost: How American culture is failing our kids.* Westport, CT: Praeger Publishers.

Dein, S., & Littlewood, R. (2005). Apocalyptic suicide: From a pathological to an eschatological interpretation. *International Journal of Social Psychiatry, 51*(3), 198–210.

Deinzer, R., Kleineidam, C., Stiller-Winkler, R., Idel, H., et al. (2000). Prolonged reduction of salivary immunoglobulin A (sIgA) after a major academic exam. *International Journal of Psychophysiology, 37,* 219–232.

Delgado, B. M., & Ford, L. (1998). Parental perceptions of child development among low-income Mexican American families. *Journal of Child & Family Studies, 7*(4), 469–481.

Delpero, W. T., O'Neill, H., Casson, E., & Hovis, J. (2005). Aviation-relevent epidemiology of color vision deficiency. *Aviation, Space, & Environmental Medicine, 76*(2), 127–133.

Demos, J. N. (2005). *Getting started with neurofeedback.* New York: Norton.

Denmark, F. L., Rabinowitz, V. C., & Sechzer, J. A. (2005). *Engendering psychology: Women and gender revisited* (2nd ed.). Boston: Allyn & Bacon.

Denollet, J., & Van Heck, G. L. (2001). Psychological risk factors in heart disease. *Journal of Psychosomatic Research, 51*(3), 465–468.

Derlega, V. J., Winstead, B. A., & Jones, W. H. (2005). *Personality: Contemporary theory and research* (3rd ed.). Belmont, CA: Cengage Learning/Wadsworth.

Deutsch, M. (1993). Educating for a peaceful world. *American Psychologist, 48*(5), 510–517.

Devine, D. J., Clayton, L. D., Dunford, B.B., Seying, R., et al. (2001). Jury decision making: 45 years of empirical research on deliberating groups. *Psychology, Public Policy, & Law, 7*(3), 622–727.

Devine, P. G., Monteith, M. J., Zuerink, J. R., & Elliot, A. J. (1991). Prejudice with and without compunction. *Journal of Personality & Social Psychology, 60*(6), 817–830.

Devlin, B., Daniels, M., & Roeder, K. (1997). The heritability of IQ. *Nature, 388*(6641), 468–471.

Devoto, A., Lucidi, F., Violani, C., & Bertini, M. (1999). Effects of different sleep reductions on daytime sleepiness. *Sleep, 22*(3), 336–343.

Di Forti, M., Lappin, J. M., & Murray, R. M. (2007). Risk factors for schizophrenia: All roads lead to dopamine. *European Neuropsychopharmacology, 17*(Suppl 2), S101–S107.

Di Marzo, V., Goparaju, S. K., Wang, L., Liu, J., et al. (2001). Leptin-regulated endocannabinoids are involved in maintaining food intake. *Nature, 410*(6830), 822–825.

Diamond, L. M. (1998). Development of sexual orientation among adolescent and young adult women. *Developmental Psychology, 34*(5), 1085–1095.

Diano, S., Farr, S. A., Benoit, S. C., McNay, E. C., et al. (2006). Ghrelin controls hippocampal spine synapse density and memory performance. *Nature Neuroscience, 9,* 381–388.

Dickens, W. T., & Flynn, J. R. (2001). Heritability estimates versus large environmental effects: The IQ paradox resolved. *Psychological Review, 108,* 346–369.

Dickerson, F. B., Tenhula, W. N., & Green-Paden, L. D. (2005). The token economy for schizophrenia: Review of the literature and recommendations for future research. *Schizophrenia Research, 75*(2–3), 405–416.

Dickinson, D. K., & Tabors, P. O. (Eds.). (2001). *Beginning literacy with language.* Baltimore: Paul H. Brookes.

Dick-Niederhauser, A., & Silverman, W. K. (2006). Separation anxiety disorder. In J. E. Fisher & W. T. O'Donohue (Eds.), *Practitioner's guide to evidence-based psychotherapy.* New York: Springer.

Dierdorff, E. C., & Wilson, M. A. (2003). A meta-analysis of job analysis reliability. *Journal of Applied Psychology, 88*(4), 635–646.

Dieterich, S. E., Assel, M. A., Swank, P., Smith, K. E., et al. (2006). The impact of early maternal verbal scaffolding and child language abilities on later decoding and reading comprehension skills. *Journal of School Psychology, 43*(6), 481–494.

Dinan, T. G. (2001). Stress, depression and cardiovascular disease. *Stress & Health: Journal of the International Society for the Investigation of Stress, 17*(2), 65–66.

Dingus, T. A., Klauer, S. G., Neale, V. L., Petersen, A., et al. (2006). The 100-Car Naturalistic Driving Study, Phase II—results of the 100-car field experiment. *National Highway Traffic Safety Administration Report No. DOT HS 810 593.* Retrieved May 18, 2007, from http://www-nrd.nhtsa.dot.gov/departments/nrd-13/driver-distraction/PDF/100CarMain.pdf.

Dinkmeyer, D., Sr., McKay, G. D., & Dinkmeyer, D., Jr. (1997). *The parent's handbook.* Circle Pines, MN: American Guidance Service.

Dion, K. L. (2003). Prejudice, racism, and discrimination. In T. Millon & M. J. Lerner (Eds.), *Personality and social psychology: The comprehensive handbook of psychology* (Vol. 5). New York: Wiley.

Dirkzwager, A. J. E., Bramsen, I., & Van Der Ploeg, H. M. (2001). The longitudinal course of posttraumatic stress disorder symptoms among aging military veterans. *Journal of Nervous & Mental Disease, 189*(12), 846–853.

Distin, K. (2006). *Gifted children: A guide for parents and professionals.* London: Jessica Kingsley Publishers.

Dixon, M. J., Smilek, D., & Merikle, P. M. (2004). Not all synaesthetes are created equal: Projector versus associator synaesthetes. *Cognitive, Affective, & Behavioral Neuroscience, 4*(3), 335–343.

Dobelle, W. H. (2000). Artificial vision for the blind by connecting a television camera to the visual cortex. *American Society of Artificial Internal Organs, 46,* 3–9.

Dobson, K. S., Backs-Dermott, G. J., & Dozois, D. J. A. (2000). Cognitive and cognitive-behavioral therapies. In C. R. Snyder & R. E. Ingram (Eds.), *Handbook of psychological change: Psychotherapy processes and practices for the 21st century.* New York: Wiley.

Dodds, P. S., Muhamad, R., & Watts, D. J. (2003). An experimental study of search in global social networks. *Science, 301*(5634), 827–829.

Doidge, N. (1997). Empirical evidence for the efficacy of psychoanalytic psychotherapies and psychoanalysis. *Psychoanalytic Inquiry,* (Suppl.), 102–150.

Dollard, J., & Miller, N. E. (1950). *Personality and psychotherapy: An analysis in terms of learning, thinking and culture.* New York: McGraw-Hill.

Domhoff, W. (2003). *The scientific study of dreams: Neural networks, cognitive development, and content analysis.* Washington, DC: American Psychological Association.

Domingo, R. A., & Goldstein-Alpern, N. (1999). "What dis?" and other toddler-initiated, expressive language-learning strategies. *Infant-Toddler Intervention, 9*(1), 39–60.

Domjan, M. (2006). *The principles of learning and behavior* (5th ed.). Belmont, CA: Cengage Learning/Wadsworth.

Donate-Bartfield, E., & Passman, R. H. (2004). Relations between children's attachments to their mothers and to security blankets. *Journal of Family Psychology, 18*(3), 453–458.

Dooling, D. J., & Lachman, R. (1971). Effects of comprehension on retention of prose. *Journal of Experimental Psychology, 88,* 216–222.

Doran, S. M., Van Dongen, H. P., & Dinges, D. F. (2001). Sustained attention performance during sleep deprivation. *Archives of Italian Biology, 139,* 253–267.

Dorman, M. F., & Wilson, B. S. (2004). The design and function of cochlear implants. *American Scientist, 92*(Sept.–Oct.), 436–445.

Dosher, B. A., & Ma, J. (1998). Output loss or rehearsal loop? *Journal of Experimental Psychology: Learning, Memory, & Cognition, 24*(2), 316–335.

Dougall, A. L., & Baum, A. (2003). Stress, coping, and immune function. In M. Gallagher & R. J. Nelson (Eds.), *Handbook of psychology: Biological psychology* (Vol. 3). New York: John Wiley.

Dougherty, D. D., Baer, L., Cosgrove, G. R., Cassem, E. H., et al. (2002). Prospective long-term follow-up of 44 patients who received cingulotomy for treatment-refractory obsessive-compulsive disorder. *American Journal of Psychiatry, 159*(2), 269–275.

Douvan, E. (1997). Erik Erikson: Critical times, critical theory. *Child Psychiatry & Human Development, 28*(1), 15–21.

Dovidio, J. F., & Gaertner, S. L. (1999). Reducing prejudice: Combating intergroup biases. *Current Directions in Psychological Science, 8*(4), 101–105.

Dovidio, J. F., & Penner, L. A. (2001). Helping and altruism. In M. Hewstone & M. Brewer (Eds.), *Handbook of social psychology.* London: Blackwell.

Dovidio, J. F., Gaertner, S. L., Kawakami, K., & Hodson, G. (2002). Why can't we just get along? *Cultural Diversity and Ethnic Minority Psychology, 8*(2), 88–102.

Dovidio, J. F., Glick, P., & Rudman, L. A. (Eds.). (2005). *On the nature of prejudice: Fifty years after Allport.* Malden, MA: Blackwell.

Dovidio, J. F., Piliavin, J. A., Schroeder, D. A., & Penner, L. A. (2006). *The social psychology of prosocial behavior.* Mahwah, NJ: Erlbaum.

Dowling, K. W. (2005). The effect of lunar phases on domestic violence incident rates. *Forensic Examiner, 14*(4), 13–18.

Dozois, D. J. A., & Dobson, K. S. (2002). Depression. In M. M. Antony & D. H. Barlow (Eds.), *Handbook of assessment and treatment planning for psychological disorders.* New York: Guilford.

Dozois, D. J. A., & Dobson, K. S. (Eds.). (2004). *The prevention of anxiety and depression: Theory, research, and practice.* Washington, DC: American Psychological Association.

Draguns, J. G., Gielen, U. P., & Fish, J. M. (2004). Approaches to culture, healing, and psychotherapy. In U. P. Gielen, J. M. Fish, et al. (Eds.), *Handbook of culture, therapy, and healing.* Mahwah, NJ: Erlbaum.

Drigotas, S. M., Rusbult, C. E., Wieselquist, J., & Whitton, S. W. (1999). Close partner as sculptor of the ideal self: Behavioral affirmation and the Michelangelo phenomenon. *Journal of Personality & Social Psychology, 77*(2), 293–323.

Driver, J. L., & Gottman, J. M. (2004). Daily marital interactions and positive affect during marital conflict among newlywed couples. *Family Process, 43*(3), 301–314.

Drolet, G., Dumont, E. C., Gosselin, I., Kinkead, R., et al. (2001). Role of endogenous opioid system in the regulation of the stress response. *Progress in Neuro-Psychopharmacology & Biological Psychiatry, 25*(4), 729–741.

Drucker, P. (1993). *Post-capitalist society.* New York: HarperCollins.

Druckman, D., & Bjork, R. A. (1994). *Learning, remembering, believing: Enhancing human performance.* Washington, DC: National Academy Press.

DSM-IV-TR: Diagnostic and statistical manual of mental disorders (5th ed.). (2000). Washington, DC: American Psychiatric Association.

Duclos, S. E., & Laird, J. D. (2001). The deliberate control of emotional experience through control of expressions. *Cognition & Emotion, 15,* 27–56.

Duffy, J. F., & Wright, Jr., K. P. (2005). Entrainment of the human circadian system by light. *Journal of Biological Rhythms, 20*(4), 326–338.

Dulewicz, V., & Higgs, M. (2000). Emotional intelligence. *Journal of Managerial Psychology, 15*(4), 341–372.

Duncan, J. (2005). Frontal lobe function and general intelligence: Why it matters. *Cortex, 41*(2), 215–217.

Duncker, K. (1945). On problem solving. *Psychological Monographs, 58*(270).

Durand, V. M., & Barlow, D. H. (2006). *Essentials of abnormal psychology* (4th ed.). Belmont, CA: Cengage Learning/Wadsworth.

Durham, M. D., & Dane, F. C. (1999). Juror knowledge of eyewitness behavior. *Journal of Social Behavior & Personality, 14*(2), 299–308.

Durrant, J. E., & Janson, S. (2005). Legal reform, corporal punishment and child abuse: The case of Sweden. *International Review of Victimology, 12,* 139–158.

Dutta, T., & Mandal, M. K. (2005). The relationship of handedness and accidents: A meta-analytical review of findings. *Psychological Studies, 50*(4), 309–316.

Dutton, D. G., & Aron, A. P. (1974). Some evidence for heightened sexual attraction under conditions of high anxiety. *Journal of Personality & Social Psychology, 30,* 510–517.

Dwyer, W. O., Leeming, F. C., Cobern, M. K., Porter, B. E., et al. (1993). Critical review of behavioral interventions to preserve the environment. *Environment and Behavior, 25*(3), 275–321.

Dyer, K. A. (2001). Dealing with death and dying in medical education and practice. Retrieved May 24, 2007, from http://dying.about.com/gi/dynamic/offsite.htm?zi=1/XJ&sdn=dying&cdn=health&tm=176&f=10&su=p247.2.140.ip_p726.2.152.ip_p284.8.150.ip_&tt=2&bt=0&bts=0&zu=http%3A//www.journeyofhearts.org/jofh/kirstimd/AMSA/mywish.htm.

Dywan, J., & Bowers, K. S. (1983). The use of hypnosis to enhance recall. *Science, 222,* 184–185.

Dzokoto, V. A., & Adams, G. (2005). Understanding genital-shrinking epidemics in West Africa: Koro, juju, or mass psychogenic illness? *Culture, Medicine & Psychiatry, 29*(1), 53–78.

Eagly, A. H. (2000). Gender roles. In A. Kazdin (Ed.), *Encyclopedia of psychology.* Washington, DC: American Psychological Association.

Eagly, A. H. (2001). Social role theory of sex differences and similarities. In J. Worell (Ed.), *Encyclopedia of women and gender.* San Diego: Academic Press.

Eagly, A. H. (2007). Female leadership advantage and disadvantage: Resolving the contradictions. *Psychology of Women Quarterly, 31*(1), 1–12.

Eagly, A. H., & Karau, S. J. (2002). Role congruity theory of prejudice toward female leaders. *Psychological Review, 109*(3), 573–598.

Ebbinghaus, H. (1885). *Memory: A contribution to experimental psychology.* Translated by H. A. Ruger & C. E. Bussenius, 1913. New York: New York Teacher's College, Columbia University.

Eckerman, D. A. (1999). Scheduling reinforcement about once a day. *Behavioural Processes, 45*(1–3), 101–114.

Eddy, K. T., Dutra, L., Bradley, R., & Westen, D. (2004). A multidimensional meta-analysis of psychotherapy and pharmacotherapy for obsessive-compulsive disorder. *Clinical Psychology Review, 24*(8), 1011–1030.

Eichenbaum, H., & Fortin, N. J. (2005). Bridging the gap between brain and behavior: Cognitive and neural mechanisms of episodic memory. *Journal of the Experimental Analysis of Behavior, 84*(3), 619–629.

Eidelson, R. J., & Eidelson, J. I. (2003). Dangerous ideas. *American Psychologist, 58*(3), 182–192.

Eifert, G. H., & Lejuez, C. W. (2000). Aversion therapy. In A. E. Kazdin (Ed.), *Encyclopedia of psychology.* Washington, DC: American Psychological Association.

Eimas, P. D., Quinn, P. C., & Cowan, P. (1994). Development of exclusivity in perceptually based categories of young infants. *Journal of Experimental Child Psychology, 58*(3), 418–431.

Eisenberg, N., Valiente, C., Fabes, R. A., Smith, C. L., et al. (2003). The relations of effortful control and ego control to children's resiliency and social functioning. *Developmental Psychology, 39*(4), 761–776.

Eisler, I., Simic, M., Russell, G. F. M., & Dare, C. (2007). A randomised controlled treatment trial of two forms of family therapy in adolescent anorexia nervosa: A five-year follow-up. *Journal of Child Psychology & Psychiatry, 48*(6), 552–560.

Eisler, J. A., Justice, Jr., J. B., & Neill, D. B. (2004). Individual differences in reward sensitivity: Implications for psychostimulant abuse vulnerability. *North American Journal of Psychology, 6*(3), 527–544.

Ekman, P. (1993). Facial expression and emotion. *American Psychologist, 48*(4), 384–392.

Ekman, P., Levenson, R. W., & Friesen, W. V. (1983). Autonomic nervous system activity distinguishes among emotions. *Science, 223,* 1208–1210.

Elder, P. (2006). *Critical thinking: Learn the tools the best thinkers use.* Englewood Cliffs, NJ: Prentice-Hall.

Eliot, L. (1999). *What's going on in there?* New York: Bantam

Elli, K. A., & Nathan, P. J. (2001). The pharmacology of human working memory. *International Journal of Neuropsychopharmacology, 4*(3), 299–313.

Ellickson, P. L., Martino, S. C., & Collins, R. L. (2004). Marijuana use from adolescence to young adulthood. *Health Psychology, 23*(3), 299–307.

Elliott, M., & Williams, D. (2003). The client experience of counselling and psychotherapy. *Counselling Psychology Review, 18*(1), 34–38.

Elliott, M., Browne, K., & Kilcoyne, J. (1995). Child sexual abuse prevention: What offenders tell us. *Child Abuse & Neglect, 19*(5), 579–594.

Ellis, A. (1979). The practice of rational-emotive therapy. In A. Ellis & J. Whiteley (Eds.), *Theoretical and*

empirical foundations of rational-emotive therapy. Monterey, CA: Brooks/Cole.

Ellis, A. (1995). Changing rational-emotive therapy (RET) to rational emotive behavior therapy (REBT). *Journal of Rational-Emotive & Cognitive Behavior Therapy, 13*(2), 85–89.

Ellis, A. (2004). Why rational emotive behavior therapy is the most comprehensive and effective form of behavior therapy. *Journal of Rational-Emotive & Cognitive Behavior Therapy, 22*(2), 85–92.

Ellis, P. J., West, B. J., Ryan, A. M., & Deshon, R. P. (2002). The use of impression management tactics in structured interviews: A function of question type. *Journal of Applied Psychology, 87,* 1200–1208.

Elovainio, M., Kivimaeki, M., Steen, N., & Kalliomaeki-Levanto, T. (2000). Organizational and individual factors affecting mental health and job satisfaction. *Journal of Occupational Health Psychology, 5*(2) 269–277.

Emmorey, K., Grabowski, T., McCullough, S., Damasio, H., et al. (2003). Neural systems underlying lexical retrieval for sign language. *Neuropsychologia, 41*(1), 85–95.

Emurian, H. H. (2005). Web-based programmed instruction: Evidence of rule-governed learning. *Computers in Human Behavior, 21*(6), 893–915.

Engle, D. E., & Arkowitz, H. (2006). *Ambivalence in psychotherapy: Facilitating readiness to change.* New York: Guilford.

Enns, J. T., & Coren, S. (1995). The box alignment illusion. *Perception & Psychophysics, 57*(8), 1163–1174.

Enns, M. W., Cox, B. J., & Clara, I. P. (2005). Perfectionism and neuroticism: A longitudinal study of specific vulnerability and diathesis-stress models. *Cognitive Therapy & Research, 29*(4), 463–478.

Erickson, C. D., & Al-Timimi, N. R. (2001). Providing mental health services to Arab Americans. *Cultural Diversity & Ethnic Minority Psychology, 7*(4), 308–327.

Ericsson, K. A. (2000). How experts attain and maintain superior performance. *Journal of Aging & Physical Activity, 8*(4), 366–372.

Ericsson, K. A., & Charness, N. (1994). Expert performance. *American Psychologist, 49*(8), 725–747.

Ericsson, K. A., & Chase, W. G. (1982). Exceptional memory. *American Scientist, 70,* 607–615.

Ericsson, K. A., Delaney, P. F., Weaver, G., & Mahadevan, R. (2004). Uncovering the structure of a memorist's superior "basic" memory capacity. *Cognitive Psychology, 49*(3), 191–237.

Erikson, E. H. (1963). *Childhood and society.* New York: Norton.

Erlacher, D., & Schredl, M. (2004). Dreams reflecting waking sport activities: A comparison of sport and psychology students. *International Journal of Sport Psychology, 35*(4), 301–308.

Erlich, P. R., & Erlich, A. H. (1990). The population explosion. *The Amicus Journal,* Winter, 18–29.

Ernst, E. (1994). Is acupuncture effective for pain control? *Journal of Pain & Symptom Management, 9*(2), 72–74.

Eron, L. D. (1987). The development of aggressive behavior from the perspective of a developing behaviorism. *American Psychologist, 42,* 435–442.

Eschholz, S., Chiricos, T., & Gertz, M. (2003). Television and fear of crime: Program types, audience traits, and the mediating effect of perceived neighborhood racial composition. *Social Problems, 50*(3), 395–415.

Espie, C. A. (2002). Insomnia. *Annual Review of Psychology, 53,* 215–243.

Esterling, B. A., L'Abate, L., Murray, E. J., & Pennebaker, J. W. (1999). Empirical foundations for writing in prevention and psychotherapy: Mental and physical health outcomes. *Clinical Psychology Review, 19*(1), 79–96.

Ethier, K. A., Kershaw, T., Niccolai, L., Lewis, J. B., et al. (2003). Adolescent women underestimate their susceptibility to sexually transmitted infections. *Sexually Transmitted Infections, 79,* 408–411.

Evans, G. W. (2006). Child development and the physical environment. *Annual Review of Psychology, 57,* 423–451.

Evans, G. W., Lercher, P., & Kofler, W. W. (2002). Crowding and children's mental health: the role of house type. *Journal of Environmental Psychology, 22,* 221–231.

Evans, G.W., Lepore, S. J., & Schroeder, A. (1996). The role of interior design elements in human responses to crowding. *Journal of Personality & Social Psychology, 70*(1), 41–46.

Evans, G. W., & Wener, R. E. (2007). Crowding and personal space invasion on the train: Please don't make me sit in the middle. *Journal of Environmental Psychology, 27*(1), 90–94.

Everly, G. S. (2002). Thoughts on peer (paraprofessional) support in the provision of mental health services. *International Journal of Emergency Mental Health, 4*(2), 89–92.

Ewen, R. B. (2003). *An introduction to theories of personality* (6th ed.). Mahwah, NJ: Erlbaum.

Ewing, G. (2001). Altruistic, egoistic, and normative effects on curbside recycling. *Environment & Behavior, 33*(6), 733–764.

Eysenck, H. J. (1994). The outcome problem in psychotherapy: What have we learned? *Behaviour Research & Therapy, 32*(5), 477–495.

Eysenck, H. J. (Ed.). (1981). *A model for personality.* New York: Springer-Verlag.

Fabrega, H., Jr. (2004). Culture and the origins of psychopathology. In U. P. Gielen, J. M., Fish, et al. (Eds.), *Handbook of culture, therapy, and healing.* Mahwah, NJ: Erlbaum.

Fagan, J. F., & Holland, C. R. (2007). Racial equality in intelligence: Predictions from a theory of intelligence as processing. *Intelligence, 35*(4), 319–334.

Fahim, C., Stip, E., Mancini-Marïe, A., Mensour, B., et al. (2005). Brain activity during emotionally negative pictures in schizophrenia with and without flat affect: An fMRI study. *Psychiatry Research: Neuroimaging, 140*(1), 1–15.

Fahle, M., & Poggio, T. (Eds.). (2002). *Perceptual learning.* Cambridge, MA: MIT Press.

Fain, G. L. (2003). *Sensory transduction.* Sunderland, MA: Sinauer.

Faith, M. S., Wong, F. Y., & Carpenter, K. M. (1995). Group sensitivity training: Update, meta-analysis, and recommendations. *Journal of Counseling Psychology, 42*(3), 390–399.

Falkowski, C. (2000). *Dangerous drugs.* Center City, MN: Hazelden Information Education.

Farah, M. J. (2004). *Visual agnosia* (2nd ed.). Cambridge, MA: MIT Press.

Farah, M. J. (2006). Prosopagnosia. In M. J. Farah & T. E. Feinberg (Eds.), *Patient-based approaches to cognitive neuroscience* (2nd ed.). Cambridge, MA: MIT Press.

Farrimond, T. (1990). Effect of alcohol on visual constancy values and possible relation to driving performance. *Perceptual & Motor Skills, 70*(1), 291–295.

Farroni, T., Massaccesi, S., Pividori, D., & Johnson, M. H. (2004). Gaze following in newborns. *Infancy, 5*(1), 39–60.

FBI (2005). *Crime in the United States, 2005.* Washington, DC: Federal Bureau of Investigation. Retrieved September 3, 2007, from http://www.fbi.gov/ucr/05cius/.

Feingold, A. (1992). Gender differences in mate selection preferences. *Psychological Bulletin, 111,* 304–341.

Feldhusen, J. F., & Goh, B. E. (1995). Assessing and accessing creativity: An integrative review of theory, research, and development. *Creativity Research Journal, 8*(3), 231–247.

Feldman, D. H. (2004). Piaget's stages: The unfinished symphony of cognitive development. *New*

Ideas in Psychology, 22(3), 175–231.

Feldman, S. (2003). Enforcing social conformity: A theory of authoritarianism. *Political Psychology, 24*(1), 41–47.

Fellous, J.-M., & Ledoux, J. E. (2005). Toward basic principles for emotional processing: What the fearful brain tells the robot. In J.-M. Fellous & M. A. Arbib (Eds.), *Who needs emotions? The brain meets the robot*. New York: Oxford University Press.

Fenn, K. M., Nusbaum, H. C., & Margoliash, D. (2003). Consolidation during sleep of perceptual learning of spoken language. *Nature, 425*(6958), 614–616.

Fenton, G. W. (1998). Neurosurgery for mental disorder. *Irish Journal of Psychological Medicine, 15*(2), 45–48.

Fernald, A. (1989). Intonation and communicative intent in mothers' speech to infants: Is the melody the message? *Child Development, 60*(6), 1497–1510.

Fernald, A., Perfors, A., & Marchman, V. A. (2006). Picking up speed in understanding: Speech processing efficiency and vocabulary growth across the 2nd year. *Developmental Psychology, 42*(1), 98–116.

Féron, F., Perry, C., Cochrane, J., Licina, P., et al. (2005). Autologous olfactory ensheathing cell transplantation in human spinal cord injury. *Brain: A Journal of Neurology, 128*(12), 2951–2960.

Ferrari, J. R., & Scher, S. J. (2000). Toward an understanding of academic and nonacademic tasks procrastinated by students: The use of daily logs. *Psychology in the Schools, 37*(4), 359–366.

Festinger, L. (1957). *A theory of cognitive dissonance*. Stanford, CA: Stanford University Press.

Festinger, L., & Carlsmith, J. M. (1959). Cognitive consequences of forced compliance. *Journal of Abnormal & Social Psychology, 58*, 203–210.

Field, C. E., Nash, H. M., Handwerk, M. L., & Friman, P. C. (2004). A modification of the token economy for nonresponsive youth in family-style residential care. *Behavior Modification, 28*(3), 438–457.

Fields, R. M., & Margolin, J. (2001). *Coping with trauma*. Washington, DC: American Psychological Association.

Figueredo, A. J., Sefcek, J. A., & Jones, D. N. (2006). The ideal romantic partner personality. *Personality & Individual Differences, 41*(3), 431–441.

Fink, M. (2000). Electroshock revisited. *American Scientist, 88*(March–April), 162–167.

Fink, M., & Taylor, M. A. (2003). *Catatonia: A clinician's guide to diagnosis and treatment*. London: Cambridge University Press.

Fiorina, C. (2006). *Tough choices: A memoir*. New York: Penguin.

First, M. B., & Pincus, H. A. (2002). The DSM-IV text revision: Rationale and potential impact on clinical practice. *Psychiatric Services, 53*, 288–292.

Fischer, A. H., Manstead, A. S. R., Rodriquez Mosquera, P. M., & van Vianen, A. E. M. (2004). Gender and culture differences in emotion. *Emotion, 4*(1), 87–94.

Fisher, B. S., Cullen, F. T., & Daigle, L. E. (2005). The discovery of acquaintance rape: The salience of methodological innovation and rigor. *Journal of Interpersonal Violence, 20*(4), 493–500.

Fisher, R. P., & Geiselman, R. E. (1987). Enhancing eyewitness memory with the cognitive interview. In M. M. Gruneberg, P. E. Morris, et al. (Eds.), *Practical aspects of memory: Current research and issues*. Chinchester, UK: Wiley.

Fisher, S. (1973). *The female orgasm*. New York: Basic.

Fisher, S., & Greenberg, R. P. (1996). *Freud scientifically reappraised*. New York: Wiley.

Fiske, S. T. (1993). Social cognition and social perception. *Annual Review of Psychology, 44*, 155–194.

Fiske, S. T., Cuddy, A. J. C., Glick, P., & Xu, J. (2002). A model of (often mixed) stereotype content. *Journal of Personality & Social Psychology, 82*(6), 878–902.

Flanagan, M. B., May, J. G., & Dobie, T. G. (2004). The role of vection, eye movements and postural instability in the etiology of motion sickness. *Journal of Vestibular Research: Equilibrium & Orientation, 14*(4), 335–346.

Flannery, D. J., Rowe, D. C., & Gulley, B. L. (1993). Impact of pubertal status, timing, and age on adolescent sexual experience and delinquency. *Journal of Adolescent Research, 8*(1), 21–40.

Flavell, J. H. (1992). Cognitive development: Past, present, and future. *Developmental Psychology, 28*(6), 998–1005.

Fleming, J. (1974). Field report: The state of the apes. *Psychology Today*, Jan., 46.

Flowe, H. D., & Ebbese, E. B. (2007). The effect of lineup member similarity on recognition accuracy in simultaneous and sequential lineups. *Law & Human Behavior, 31*(1), 33–52.

Fobair, P. (1997). Cancer support groups and group therapies. *Journal of Psychosocial Oncology, 15*(3–4), 123–147.

Fochtmann, L. J. (1995). Intractable sneezing as a conversion symptom. *Psychosomatics, 36*(2), 103–112.

Fogel, S. M., Nader, R., Cote, K. A., & Smith, C. T. (2007). Sleep spindles and learning potential. *Behavioral Neuroscience, 121*(1), 1–10.

Folkman, S., & Moskowitz, J. T. (2004). Coping. *Annual Review of Psychology, 55*, 745–774.

Follett, K., & Hess, T. M. (2002). Aging, cognitive complexity, and the fundamental attribution error. *Journals of Gerontology: Series B: Psychological Sciences and Social Sciences, 57B*(4), 312–323.

Fontaine, K. R., Redden, D. T., Wang, C., Westfall, A. O., et al. (2003). Years of life lost due to obesity. *Journal of the American Medical Association, 289*, 187–193.

Fontenelle, D. H. (1989). *How to live with your children*. Tucson, AZ: Fisher Books.

Foo, P., Warren, W. H., Duchon, A., & Tarr, M. J. (2005). Do humans integrate routes into a cognitive map? Map- versus landmark-based navigation of novel shortcuts. *Journal of Experimental Psychology: Learning, Memory, & Cognition, 31*(2), 195–215.

Foot, M., & Koszycki, D. (2004). Gender differences in anxiety-related traits in patients with panic disorder. *Depression & Anxiety, 20*(3), 123–130.

Forbes, G. B., Adams-Curtis, L. E., & White, K. B. (2004). First- and second-generation measures of sexism, rape myths and related beliefs, and hostility toward women: Their interrelationships and association with college students' experiences with dating aggression and sexual coercion. *Violence Against Women, 10*(3), 236–261.

Ford, D. Y., & Moore, J. L. (2006). Being gifted and adolescent: Issues and needs of students of color. In F. A. Dixon & S. M. Moon (Eds.), *The handbook of secondary gifted education*. Waco, TX: Prufrock Press.

Ford, G. G., Gallagher, S. H., Lacy, B. A., Bridwell, A. M., et al. (1999). Repositioning the home plate umpire to provide enhanced perceptual cues and more accurate ball-strike judgments. *Journal of Sport Behavior, 22*(1), 28–44.

Forney, W. S., Forney, J. C., & Crutsinger, C. (2005). Developmental stages of age and moral reasoning as predictors of juvenile delinquents' behavioral intention to steal clothing. *Family & Consumer Sciences Research Journal, 34*(2), 110–126.

ForsterLee, R., ForsterLee, L., Horowitz, I. A., & King, E. (2006). The effects of defendant race, victim race, and juror gender on evidence processing in a murder trial. *Behavioral Sciences & the Law, 24*(2), 179–198.

Forsyth, D. R. (2006). *Group dynamics* (4th ed.). Belmont, CA: Cengage Learning/Wadsworth.

Forsyth, J. P., & Savsevitz, J. (2002). Behavior therapy: Historical perspective and overview. In M. Hersen & W. H. Sledge (Eds.), *Encyclopedia of psychotherapy*. San Diego: Academic Press.

Fosse, R., Stickgold, R., & Hobson, J. A. (2001). The mind in REM sleep: Reports of emotional experience. *Sleep: Journal of Sleep & Sleep Disorders Research, 24*(8), 947–955.

Foster, C. A., Witcher, B. S., Campbell, W. K., & Green, J. D. (1998). Arousal and attraction. *Journal of Personality & Social Psychology, 74*(1), 86–101.

Foster, G., & Ysseldyke, J. (1976). Expectancy and halo effects as a result of artificially induced teacher bias. *Contemporary Educational Psychology, 1*, 37–45.

Fowers, B. J., & Davidov, B. J. (2006). The virtue of multiculturalism: Personal transformation, character, and openness to the other. *American Psychologist, 61*(6), 581–594.

Fowers, B. J., & Davidov, B. J. (2006). The virtue of multiculturalism: Personal transformation, character, and openness to the other. *American Psychologist, 61*(6), 581–594.

Fowers, B. J., & Richardson, F. C. (1996). Why is multiculturalism good? *American Psychologist, 51*(6), 609–621.

Foxhall, K. (2000). Suddenly, a big impact on criminal justice. *APA Monitor, Jan.*, 36–37.

Frank, J. D., & Frank, J. (2004). Therapeutic components shared by all psychotherapies. In A. Freeman, M. J. Mahoney, et al. (Eds.), *Cognition and psychotherapy* (2nd ed.). New York: Springer.

Franken, R. E. (2007). *Human motivation* (6th ed.). Belmont, CA: Cengage Learning/Wadsworth.

Frankl, V. (1955). *The doctor and the soul*. New York: Knopf.

Franzoi, S. L. (2002). *Social psychology*. New York: McGraw-Hill.

Franzoi, S. L., & Klaiber, J. R. (2007). Body use and reference group impact: With whom do we compare our bodies? *Sex Roles, 56*(3–4), 205–214.

Fraser, C. (2002). Fact and fiction: A clarification of phantom limb phenomena. *British Journal of Occupational Therapy, 65*(6), 256–260.

Frederick, C. J. (1987) Psychic trauma in victims of crime and terrorism. In G. R. VandenBos & B. K. Bryant (Eds.), *Cataclysms, crises, and catastrophes: Psychology in action*. Washington, DC: American Psychological Association.

Fredrickson, B. L. (2003). The value of positive emotions. *American Scientist, 91*, 330–335.

Fredrickson, B. L., & Branigan, C. (2005). Positive emotions broaden the scope of attention and thought-action repertoires. *Cognition & Emotion, 19*(3), 313–332.

Freeman, D., & Garety, P. A. (2004). *Paranoia: The psychology of persecutory delusions.* New York: Routledge.

Freiwald, W. A., & Kanwisher, N. G. (2004). Visual selective attention: Insights from brain imaging and neurophysiology. In M. S. Gazzaniga (Ed.), *The cognitive neurosciences* (3rd ed.). Cambridge, MA: MIT Press.

Freize, I. H. (1987). The female victim. In G. R. VandenBos & B. K. Bryant (Eds.), *Cataclysms, crises, and catastrophes: Psychology in action.* Washington, DC: American Psychological Association.

French, C. C., Fowler, M., McCarthy, K., & Peers, D. (1991). A test of the Barnum effect. *Skeptical Inquirer, 15*(4), 66–72.

French, S. E., Kim, T. E., & Pillado, O. (2006). Ethnic identity, social group membership, and youth violence. In N. G. Guerra & E. P. Smith (Eds.), *Preventing youth violence in a multicultural society.* Washington, DC: American Psychological Association.

Freud, S. (1900). *The interpretation of dreams.* London: Hogarth.

Freud, S. (1949). *An outline of psychoanalysis.* New York: Norton.

Frey, M. C., & Detterman, D. K. (2004). Scholastic assessment or g? The relationship between the scholastic assessment test and general cognitive ability. *Psychological Science, 15*(6), 373–378.

Fried, P. A., & Smith, A. M. (2001). A literature review of the consequences of prenatal marihuana exposure. *Neurotoxicology and Teratology, 23*(1), 1–11.

Friedman, H. S. (2002). *Health psychology* (2nd ed.). Englewood Cliffs, NJ: Prentice-Hall.

Friedman, L. (2006). What is psychoanalysis? *Psychoanalytic Quarterly, 75*(3), 689–713.

Friedman, L. J. (2004). Erik Erikson on generativity: A biographer's perspective. In E. de St. Aubin, D. P. McAdams, et al. (Eds.), *The generative society: Caring for future generations.* Washington, DC: American Psychological Association.

Friedman, M., & Rosenman, R. H. (1983). *Type A behavior and your heart.* New York: Knopf.

Friedman, R. C., Bucci, W., Christian, C., Drucker, P., et al. (1998). Private psychotherapy patients of psychiatrist psychoanalysts. *American Journal of Psychiatry, 155,* 1772–1774.

Fritz, C. O., Morris, P. E., Acton, M., Voelkel, A. R., et al. (2007). Comparing and combining retrieval practice and the keyword mnemonic for foreign vocabulary learning. *Applied Cognitive Psychology, 21*(4), 499–526.

Froufe, M., & Schwartz, C. (2001). Subliminal messages for increasing self-esteem: Placebo effect. *Spanish Journal of Psychology, 4*(1), 19–25.

Frydman, M. (1999). Television, aggressiveness and violence. *International Journal of Adolescent Medicine & Health, 11*(3–4), 335–344.

Fu, J. H., Morris, M. W., Lee, S., Chao, M., et al. (2007). Epistemic motives and cultural conformity: Need for closure, culture, and context as determinants of conflict judgments. *Journal of Personality & Social Psychology, 92*(2), 191–207.

Fukuda, K., & Ishihara, K. (2001). Age-related changes of sleeping pattern during adolescence. *Psychiatry & Clinical Neurosciences, 55*(3), 231–232.

Funder, D. C. (2006). *The personality puzzle* (4th ed.). New York: Norton.

Funk, J. B. (2005). Children's exposure to violent video games and desensitization to violence. *Child and Adolescent Psychiatric Clinics of North America, 14*(3), 387–404.

Fuqua, D. R., & Newman, J. L. (2002). Creating caring organizations. *Consulting Psychology Journal: Practice & Research, 54*(2), 131–140.

Furnham, A., Chamorro-Premuzic, T., & Callahan, I. (2003). Does graphology predict personality and intelligence? *Individual Differences Research, 1*(2), 78–94.

FVPF. (2007). Domestic violence is a serious, widespread social problem in America: The facts. Family Violence Prevention Fund. Retrieved July 29, 2007, from http://www.endabuse.org/resources/facts/.

Gable, S. L., Reis, H. T., Impett, E. A., & Asher, E. R. (2004). What do you do when things go right? *Journal of Personality & Social Psychology, 87*(3), 228–245.

Gable, S. L., Reis, H. T., Impett, E., & Asher, E. R. (2004). What do you do when things go right? The intrapersonal and interpersonal benefits of sharing positive events. *Journal of Personality & Social Psychology, 87,* 228–245.

Gaertner, S. L., Dovidio, J. F., Banker, B. S., Houlette, M., et al. (2000). Reducing intergroup conflict: From superordinate goals to decategorization, recategorization, and mutual differentiation. *Group Dynamics, 4*(1), 98–114.

Galambos, N. L., Barker, E. T., & Tilton-Weaver, L. C. (2003). Who gets caught at maturity gap? A study of pseudomature, immature and mature adolescents. *International Journal of Behavioral Development, 27*(3), 253–263.

Galanter, M., Hayden, F., Castañeda, R, & Franco, H. (2005). Group therapy, self-help groups, and network therapy. In R. J. Frances, S. I. Miller, et al. (Eds.), *Clinical textbook of addictive disorders* (3rd ed.). New York: Guilford.

Galati, D., Scherer, K. R., & Ricci-Bitti, P. E. (1997). Voluntary facial expression of emotion: Comparing congenitally blind with normally sighted encoders. *Journal of Personality & Social Psychology, 73*(6), 1363–1379.

Galea, S., & Resnick, H. (2005). Posttraumatic stress disorder in the general population after mass terrorist incidents: Considerations about the nature of exposure. *CNS Spectrums, 10*(2), 107–115.

Galea, S., Ahern, J., Resnick, H., Kilpatrick, D., et al. (2002). Psychological sequelae of the September 11 terrorist attacks in New York City. *New England Journal of Medicine, 346*(13), 982–987.

Gamache, G. (2004). *Essentials in human factors.* San Mateo, CA: Usernomics.

Ganis, G., Thompson, W. L., & Kosslyn, S. M. (2004). Brain areas underlying visual mental imagery and visual perception: An fMRI study. *Cognitive Brain Research, 20*(2), 226–241.

Ganster, D. C., Fox, M. L., & Dwyer, D. J. (2001). Explaining employees' health care costs: A prospective examination of stressful job demands, personal control, and physiological reactivity. *Journal of Applied Psychology, 86,* 954–964.

Garbarino, S., Beelke, M., Costa, G., Violani, C., et al. (2002). Brain function and effects of shift work: Implications for clinical neuropharmacology. *Neuropsychobiology, 45,* 50–56.

Garbarino, S., Mascialino, B., Penco, M. A., Squarcia, S., et al. (2004). Professional shift-work drivers who adopt prophylactic naps can reduce the risk of car accidents during night work. *Sleep: Journal of Sleep & Sleep Disorders Research, 27*(7), 1295–1302.

García-Junco-Clemente, P., Linares-Clemente, P., & Fernández-Chacón, R. (2005). Active zones for presynaptic plasticity in the brain. *Molecular Psychiatry, 10*(2), 185–200.

Gardner, H. (2003). *Multiple intelligences after twenty years.* Invited Address, American Educational Research Association, April. Retrieved July 3, 2007, from http://www.pz.harvard.edu/PIs/HG_MI_after_20_years.pdf.

Gardner, H. (2004). *Frames of mind* (Tenth-anniversary ed.). New York: Basic.

Gardner, R. A., & Gardner, B. T. (1989). *Teaching sign language to chimpanzees.* Albany, NY: State University of New York Press.

Garland, A. F., & Zigler, E. (1993). Adolescent suicide prevention. *American Psychologist, 48*(2), 169–182.

Garlow, S. J., Purselle, D. C., & Heninger, M. (2007). Cocaine and alcohol use preceding suicide in African American and White adolescents. *Journal of Psychiatric Research, 41*(6), 530–536.

Garnets, L. D. (2002). Sexual orientation in perspective. *Cultural Diversity & Ethnic Minority Psychology, 8*(2), 115–129.

Garnets, L. D., & Kimmel, D. (1991). Lesbian and gay male dimensions in the psychological study of human diversity. *Psychological perspectives on human diversity in America.* Washington, DC: American Psychological Association.

Gastner, M. T., Shalizi, C. R., & Newman, M. E. J. (2005). Maps and cartograms of the 2004 US presidential election results. *Advances in Complex Systems, 8*(1), 117–123.

Gates, A. I. (1958). Recitation as a factor in memorizing. In J. Deese (Ed.), *The psychology of learning.* New York: McGraw-Hill.

Gathchel, R. J., & Oordt, M. S. (2003). Insomnia. In R. J. Gatchel & M. S. Oordt (Eds.), *Clinical health psychology and primary care: Practical advice and clinical guidance for successful collaboration.* Washington, DC: American Psychological Association.

Gayle, H. (2000). An overview of the global HIV/AIDS epidemic, with a focus on the United States. *AIDS, 14*(Suppl 2), S8–S17.

Gazzaniga, M. S. (1970). *The bisected brain.* New York: Plenum.

Gazzaniga, M. S. (2005). Forty-five years of split-brain research and still going strong. *Nature Reviews Neuroscience, 6*(8), 653–659.

Geary, N. (2004). Endocrine controls of eating: CCK, leptin, and ghrelin. *Physiology & Behavior, 81*(5), 719–733.

Gedo, J. E. (2002). The enduring scientific contributions of Sigmund Freud. *Perspectives in Biology & Medicine, 45,* 200–211.

Geehr, J. L., Burke, M. J., & Sulzer, J. L. (1995). Quality circles: The effects of varying degrees of voluntary participation on employee attitudes and program efficacy. *Educational & Psychological Measurement, 55*(1), 124–134.

Gegenfurtner, K. R., & Kiper, D. C. (2003). Color vision. *Annual Review of Neuroscience, 26,* 181–206.

Geiselman, R. E., Fisher, R. P., MacKinnon, D. P., & Holland, H. L. (1986). Eyewitness memory enhancement with the cognitive interview. *American Journal of Psychology, 99,* 385–401.

Geliebter, A., & Aversa, A. (2003). Emotional eating in overweight, normal weight, and underweight individuals. *Eating Behaviors, 3*(4), 341–347.

Genesee, F., Paradis., J., & Crago, M. (2004). *Dual language development and disorders: A handbook on bilingualism and second language learning*. Baltimore: Paul H. Brookes.

George, A. (2006). Living online: The end of privacy? *New Scientist, 2659* (Sept. 18), 50–51.

Georgiades, A., Serwood, A., Gullette, E. C., Babyak, M. A., et al. (2000). Effects of exercise and weight loss on mental stress-induced cardiovascular responses in individuals with high blood pressure. *Hypertension, 36*, 171–176.

Germain, A., Krakow, B., Faucher, B., Zadra, A., et al. (2004). Increased mastery elements associated with imagery rehearsal treatment for nightmares in sexual assault survivors with PTSD. *Dreaming, 14*(4), 195–206.

German, T. P., & Barrett, H. C. (2005). Functional fixedness in a technologically sparse culture. *Psychological Science, 16*(1), 1–5.

German, T. P., & Defeyter, M. A. (2000). Immunity to functional fixedness in young children. *Psychonomic Bulletin & Review, 7*(4), 707–712.

Gersh, R. D. (1982). Learning when not to shoot. *Santa Barbara News Press*, June 20.

Gershoff, E. T. (2002). Corporal punishment by parents and associated child behaviors and experiences: A meta-analytic and theoretical review. *Psychological Bulletin, 128*(4), 539–579.

Gerwood, J. B. (1998). The legacy of Viktor Frankl. *Psychological Reports, 82*(2), 673–674.

Geschwind, N. (1979). Specializations of the human brain. *Scientific American, 241*, 180–199.

Gewirtz, J. C., & Davis, M. (1998). Application of Pavlovian higher-order conditioning to the analysis of the neural substrates of fear conditioning. *Neuropharmacology, 37*(4–5), 453–459.

Giarratano, J. C., & Riley, G. (2005). *Expert systems, principles and programming* (4th ed.). Belmont, CA: Cengage Learning/Wadsworth.

Gibson, E. J., & Walk, R. D. (1960). The "visual cliff." *Scientific American, 202*(4), 67–71.

Gibson, K. R. (2002). Evolution of human intelligence: The roles of brain size and mental construction. *Brain, Behavior & Evolution, 59*(1–2), 10–20.

Gifford, R. (2002). *Environmental psychology: Principles and practice* (3rd ed.). Colville, WA: Optimal Books.

Gilbert, P. (2001). *Overcoming depression*. New York: Oxford University Press.

Giliovich, T., Keltner, D., & Nisbett, R. (2005). *Social psychology*. New York: Norton.

Gillespie, C. F., & Nemeroff, C. B. (2007). Corticotropin-releasing factor and the psychobiology of early-life stress. *Current Directions in Psychological Science, 16*(2), 85–89.

Gilligan, C. (1982). *In a different voice*. Cambridge, MA: Harvard University Press.

Gilligan, C., & Attanucci, J. (1988). Two moral orientations: Gender differences and similarities. *Merrill-Palmer Quarterly, 34*(3), 223–237.

Gilman, S. E., Cochran, S. D., Mays, V. M., Hughes, M., et al. (2001). Risk of psychiatric disorders among individuals reporting same-sex sexual partners in the National Comorbidity Survey. *American Journal of Public Health, 91*(6), 933–939.

Ginet, M., & Py, J. (2001). A technique for enhancing memory in eyewitness testimonies for use by police officers and judicial officials: The cognitive interview. *Travail Humain, 64*(2), 173–191.

Ginott, H. G. (1965). *Between parent and child: New solutions to old problems*. New York: Macmillan.

Ginsberg, D. L. (2006). Fatal agranulocytosis four years after clozapine discontinuation. *Primary Psychiatry, 13*(2), 32–33.

Giuseppe, R. (2005). Virtual reality in psychotherapy: Review. *CyberPsychology & Behavior. Special Use of Virtual Environments in Training and Rehabilitation: International Perspectives, 8*(3), 220–230.

Gladwell, M. (2005). *Blink: The power of thinking without thinking*. New York: Little, Brown.

Gleason, J. B. (2005). *The development of language* (6th ed.). Boston: Allyn & Bacon.

Glisky, M. L., Williams, J. M., & Kihlstrom, J. F. (1996). Internal and external mental imagery perspectives and performance on two tasks. *Journal of Sport Behavior, 19*(1), 3–18.

Global Footprint Network (2006). *Ecological footprint: Overview*. Retrieved August 9, 2007, from http://www.footprintnetwork.org/gfn_sub.php?content=footprint_overview.

Glomb, T. M. (2002). Workplace anger and aggression. *Journal of Occupational Health Psychology, 7*(1), 20–36.

Glover, R. J. (2001). Discriminators of moral orientation: Gender role or personality? *Journal of Adult Development, 8*(1), 1–7.

Gobet, F. (2005). Chunking models of expertise: Implications for education. *Applied Cognitive Psychology, 19*(2), 183–204.

Gobet, F., & Simon, H. A. (1996). Recall of random and distorted chess positions: Implications for the theory of expertise. *Memory & Cognition, 24*(4), 493–503.

Goel, V., & Dolan, R. J. (2004). Differential involvement of left prefrontal cortex in inductive and deductive reasoning. *Cognition, 93*(3), 109–121.

Goel, V., & Grafman, J. (1995). Are the frontal lobes implicated in "planning" functions? Interpreting data from the Tower of Hanoi. *Neuropsychologia, 33*(5), 623–642.

Gogate, L. J., Bahrick, L. E., & Watson, J. D. (2000). A study of multimodal motherese: The role of temporal synchrony between verbal labels and gestures. *Child Development, 71*(4), 878–894.

Goldberg, C. (2001). Of prophets, true believers, and terrorists. *The Dana Forum on Brain Science, 3*(3), 21–24.

Goldberg, R. (2006). *Drugs across the spectrum* (5th ed.). Belmont, CA: Cengage Learning/Wadsworth.

Golden, J. (2005). *Message in a bottle: The making of fetal alcohol syndrome*. Cambridge, MA: Harvard University Press.

Golden, T. D., Veiga, J. F., & Simsek, Z. (2006). Telecommuting's differential impact on work-family conflict: Is there no place like home? *Journal of Applied Psychology, 91*(6), 1340–1350.

Goldenberg, H., & Goldenberg, I. (2004). *Family therapy: An overview* (6th ed.). Pacific Grove, CA: Brooks/Cole.

Goldfried, M. R. (2001). Integrating gay, lesbian, and bisexual issues into mainstream psychology. *American Psychologist, 56*(11), 977–987.

Golding, J. M., Bradshaw, G. S., Dunlap, E. E., & Hodell, E. C. (2007). The impact of mock jury gender composition on deliberations and conviction rates in a child sexual assault trial. *Child Maltreatment, 12*(2), 182–190.

Goldman, H. H. (1998). Deinstitutionalization and community care. *Harvard Review of Psychiatry, 6*(4), 219–222.

Goldstein, E. B. (2007). *Sensation and perception* (7th ed.). Belmont, CA: Cengage Learning/Wadsworth.

Goldstein, E. B. (2008). *Cognitive psychology: Connecting mind, research and everyday experience* (2nd ed.). Belmont, CA: Cengage Learning/Wadsworth.

Goleman, D. (1995). *Emotional intelligence*. New York: Bantam.

Goodall, J. (1990). *Through a window: My thirty years with the chimpanzees of the Gombe*. Boston: Houghton Mifflin.

Goode, E. (1996). Gender and courtship entitlement: Responses to personal ads. *Sex Roles, 34*(3–4), 141–169.

Goodman-Delahunty, J. Greene, E., & Hsiao, W. (1998). Construing motive in videotaped killings: The role of jurors' attitudes toward the death penalty. *Law & Human Behavior, 22*(3), 257–271.

Goodwin, R. D., Fergusson, D. M., & Horwood, L. J. (2005). Childhood abuse and familial violence and the risk of panic attacks and panic disorder in young adulthood. *Psychological Medicine, 35*(6), 881–890.

Goodwin, S. A., & Fiske, S. T. (2001). Power and gender. In R. K. Unger (Ed.), *Handbook of the psychology of women and gender*. New York: Wiley.

Gopnik, A., Meltzoff, A. N., & Kuhl, P. K. (2000). *The scientist in the crib: What early learning tells us about the mind*. New York: HarperCollins.

Gordon, A. K., & Kaplar, M. E. (2002). A new technique for demonstrating the actor-observer bias. *Teaching of Psychology, 29*(4), 301–303.

Gordon, T. (2000). *Parent effectiveness training: The proven program for raising responsible children*. New York: Three Rivers Press.

Gorman, J. M. (1996). *The essential guide to mental health*. New York: St. Martin's Griffin.

Gottlieb, G. (1998). Normally occurring environmental and behavioral influences on gene activity: From central dogma to probabilistic epigenesis. *Psychological Review, 105*(4), 792–802.

Gottman, J. M. (1994). *Why marriages succeed or fail*. New York: Simon & Schuster.

Gottman, J. M., & Krokoff, L. J. (1989). Marital interaction and satisfaction: A longitudinal view. *Journal of Consulting & Clinical Psychology, 57*(1), 47–52.

Gould, D., & Udry, E. (1994). Psychological skills for enhancing performance: Arousal regulation strategies. *Medicine & Science in Sports & Exercise, 26*(4), 478–485.

Gould, E., & Gross, C. G. (2002). Neurogenesis in adult mammals: Some progress and problems. *Journal of Neuroscience, 22*(3), 619–623.

Gould, R. (1975). Growth toward self-tolerance. *Psychology Today*, Feb., 74–78.

Grabe, M. (2006). *Integrating technology for meaningful learning*. Boston: Houghton Mifflin.

Grack, C., & Richman, C. L. (1996). Reducing general and specific heterosexism through cooperative contact. *Journal of Psychology & Human Sexuality, 8*(4), 59–68.

Grande, T., Rudolf, G., Oberbracht, C., & Pauli-Magnus, C. (2003). Progressive changes in patients' lives after psychotherapy. *Psychotherapy Research, 13*(1), 43–58.

Grandner, M. A., & Kripke, D. F. (2004). Self-reported sleep complaints with long and short sleep: A nationally representative sample. *Psychosomatic Medicine, 66,* 239–241.

Granrud, C. E. (2004). Visual metacognition and the development of size constancy. In D. T. Levin (Ed.), *Thinking and seeing: Visual metacognition in adults and children.* Cambridge, MA: MIT Press.

Grant, B. F., & Dawson, D. A. (1997). Age at onset of alcohol use and its association with DSM-IV alcohol abuse and dependence. *Journal of Substance Abuse, 9,* 103.

Grant, B. F., Hasin, D. S., Stinson, F. S., Dawson, D. A., et al. (2006). The epidemiology of DSM-IV panic disorder and agoraphobia in the United States: Results from the National Epidemiologic Survey on Alcohol and Related Conditions. *Journal of Clinical Psychiatry, 67*(3), 363–374.

Grant, I., Gonzalez, R., Carey, C., & Natarajan, L. (2001). Long-term neurocognitive fconsequences of marijuana. In *National Institute on Drug Abuse Workshop on Clinical Consequences of Marijuana,* August 13, Rockville, MD.

Graves, J. L. (2001). *The emperor's new clothes.* Piscataway, NJ: Rutgers University Press.

Gravetter, F. J., & Wallnau, L. B. (2007). *Statistics for the behavioral sciences* (7th ed.). Belmont, CA: Cengage Learning/Wadsworth.

Gray, J. M., & Wilson, M. A. (2007). A detailed analysis of the reliability and validity of the sensation seeking scale in a UK sample. *Personality & Individual Differences, 42*(4), 641–651.

Graziottin, A. (1998). The biological basis of female sexuality. *International Clinical Psychopharmacology, 13*(Suppl 6), S15–S22.

Greenberg, D. L. (2004). President Bush's false "flashbulb" memory of 9/11/01. *Applied Cognitive Psychology, 18*(3), 363–370.

Greene, D., & Lepper, M. R. (1974). How to turn play into work. *Psychology Today,* Sept., 49.

Greenfield, P. M. (1997). You can't take it with you: Why abilities assessments don't cross cultures. *American Psychologist, 52,* 1115–1124.

Greenglass, E. R., Burke, R. J., & Konarski, R. (1998). Components of burnout, resources, and gender-related differences. *Journal of Applied Social Psychology, 28*(12), 1088–1106.

Greenglass, E. R., Burke, R. J., & Moore, K. A. (2003). Reactions to increased workload: Effects on professional efficacy of nurses. *Applied Psychology: An International Review, 52*(4), 580–597.

Greenwald, R. (2006). Eye movement desensitization and reprocess-

ing with traumatized youth. In N. B. Webb (Ed.), *Working with traumatized youth in child welfare: Social work practice with children and families.* New York: Guilford.

Greenwood, J. G., Greenwood, J. J. D., McCullagh, J. F., Beggs, J., et al. (2006). A survey of sidedness in Northern Irish schoolchildren: The interaction of sex, age, and task. *Laterality: Asymmetries of Body, Brain & Cognition, 12*(1), 1–18.

Gregory, R. L. (1990). *Eye and brain: The psychology of seeing.* Princeton, NJ: Princeton University Press.

Gregory, R. L. (2003). Seeing after blindness. *Nature Neuroscience, 6*(9), 909–910.

Grenier, G., & Byers, E. S. (1995). Rapid ejaculation: A review of conceptual, etiological, and treatment issues. *Archives of Sexual Behavior, 24*(4), 447–472.

Griffin, D. R. (1992). *Animal minds.* Chicago: University of Chicago Press.

Griffin, W. A. (2002). Family therapy. In M. Hersen & W. H. Sledge (Eds.), *Encyclopedia of psychotherapy.* San Diego: Academic Press.

Griffin-Fennell, F., & Williams, M. (2006). Examining the complexities of suicidal behavior in the African American community. *Journal of Black Psychology, 32*(3), 303–319.

Grigorenko, E. L. (2005). The inherent complexities of gene-environment interactions. *Journals of Gerontology: Series B: Psychological Sciences & Social Sciences, 60B*(1, Spec. Issue), 53–64.

Grigorenko, E. L., & Sternberg, R. J. (2003). The nature-nurture issue. In A. Slater & G. Bremner (Eds.), *An introduction to developmental psychology.* Malden, MA: Blackwell.

Grobstein, P., & Chow, K. L. (1975). Perceptive field development and individual experience. *Science, 190,* 352–358.

Gross, J. J. (2001). Emotion regulation in adulthood: Timing is everything. *Current Directions in Psychological Science, 10*(6), 214–219.

Grubin, D., & Madsen, L. (2005). Lie detection and the polygraph: A historical review. *Journal of Forensic Psychiatry & Psychology, 16*(2), 357–369.

Grunbaum, J. A., Kann, L., Kinchen, S., & Ross, J., et al. (2004). Youth Risk Behavior Surveillance: United States, 2003. *Centers for Disease Control and Prevention Morbidity and Mortality Weekly Report Surveillance Summary, 53*(SS02), 1–96.

Gruner, C. R., & Tighe, M. R. (1995). Semantic differential measurements of connotations of verbal terms and their doublespeak facsimiles in sentence contexts. *Psy-

chological Reports, 77*(3, Pt. 1), 778.

Grzegorek, J. L., Slaney, R. B., Franze, S., & Rice, K. G. (2004). Self-criticism, dependency, self-esteem, and grade point average satisfaction among clusters of perfectionists and nonperfectionists. *Journal of Counseling Psychology, 51*(2), 192–200.

Guastello, D. D., & Guastello, S. J. (2003). Androgyny, gender role behavior, and emotional intelligence among college students and their parents. *Sex Roles, 49*(11-12), 663–673.

Guéguen, N. (2002). Status, apparel and touch: Their joint effects on compliance to a request. *North American Journal of Psychology, 4*(2), 279–286.

Guéguen, N., & Pascual, A. (2003). Status and people's tolerance towards an ill-mannered person: A field study. *Journal of Mundane Behavior, 4*(1). Retrieved August 4, 2007 from http://www.mundanebehavior.org/issues/v4n1/gueguen-pascual.htm.

Guéguen, N., Pascual, A., & Dagot, L. (2002). Low-ball and compliance to a request: An application in a field setting. *Psychological Reports, 91*(1), 81–84.

Guffey, M. E. (2007). Essentials of business communication (7th ed.). Belmont, CA: Cengage Learning/South-western.

Gullette, D. L., & Lyons, M. A. (2005). Sexual sensation seeking, compulsivity, and HIV risk behaviors in college students. *Journal of Community Health Nursing, 22*(1), 47–60.

Gump, B. B., & Kulik, J. A. (1997). Stress, affiliation, and emotional contagion. *Journal of Personality & Social Psychology, 72*(2), 305–319.

Gündogan, N. Ü., Durmazlar, N., Gümüs, K., Özdemir, P. G., et al. (2005). Projected color slides as a method for mass screening test for color vision deficiency (a preliminary study). *International Journal of Neuroscience, 115*(8), 1105–1117.

Gur, R. E., Cowell, P., Turetsky, B. I., Gallacher, F., et al. (1998). A follow-up magnetic resonance imaging study of schizophrenia. *Archives of General Psychiatry, 55*(2), 145–152.

Gurung, R. (2006). *Health psychology: A cultural approach.* Belmont, CA: Cengage Learning/Wadsworth.

Gustavsson, J. P., Weinryb, R. M., Göransson, S., Pedersen, N. L., et al. (1997). Stability and predictive ability of personality traits across 9 years. *Personality & Individual Differences, 22*(6), 783–791.

Haas, B. W., Omura, K., Constable, R. T., & Canli, T. (2007). Is automatic emotion regulation associ-

ated with agreeableness? A perspective using a social neuroscience approach. *Psychological Science, 18*(2), 130–132.

Haas, L. J., Benedict, J. G., & Kobos, J. C. (1996). Psychotherapy by telephone: Risks and benefits for psychologists and consumers. *Professional Psychology: Research & Practice, 27*(2), 154–160.

Haber, R. N. (1969). Eidetic images; with biographical sketches. *Scientific American, 220*(12), 36–44.

Haber, R. N. (1970). How we remember what we see. *Scientific American, 222*(5), 104–112.

Haber, R. N., & Haber, L. (2000). Eidetic imagery. In A. E. Kazdin, (Ed.), *Encyclopedia of psychology* (Vol. 3). Washington, DC: American Psychological Association.

Haddad, S. (2003). Islam and attitudes toward U.S. policy in the Middle East: Evidence from survey research in Lebanon. *Studies in Conflict & Terrorism, 26*(2), 135–154.

Hadwin, A. F., Kirby, J. R., & Woodhouse, R. A. (1999). Individual differences in notetaking, summarization and learning from lectures. *Alberta Journal of Educational Research, 45*(1), 1–17.

Haenschel, C., Vernon, D. J., Dwivedi, P., Gruzelier, J. H., et al. (2005). Event-related brain potential correlates of human auditory sensory memory-trace formation. *Journal of Neuroscience, 25*(45), 10494–10501.

Hafer, C. L., & Bègue, L. (2005). Experimental research on just-world theory: Problems, developments, and future challenges. *Psychological Bulletin, 131*(1), 128–167.

Haier, R. J., Jung, R. E., Yeo, R. A., Head, K., et al. (2004). Structural brain variation and general intelligence. *NeuroImage, 23,* 425–433.

Haier, R. J., Siegel, B. V., Nuechterlein, K. H., Hazlett, E., et al. (1988). Cortical glucose metabolic rate correlates of abstract reasoning and attention studied with positron emission tomography. *Intelligence, 12,* 199–217.

Haier, R. J., White, N. S., & Alkire, M. T. (2003). Individual differences in general intelligence correlate with brain function during nonreasoning tasks. *Intelligence, 31*(5), 429–441.

Haines, M. M., Stansfeld, S. A., Job, R. F. S., Berglund, B., et al. (2001). Chronic aircraft noise exposure, stress responses, mental health and cognitive performance in school children. *Psychological Medicine, 31*(2), 265–277.

Halbert, J., Crotty, M., & Cameron, I. D. (2002). Evidence for the optimal management of acute and chronic phantom pain. *Clinical Journal of Pain, 18*(2), 84–92.

Hall, C. (1966). *The meaning of dreams.* New York: McGraw-Hill.

Hall, C. (1974). What people dream about. In R. L. Woods & H. B. Greenhouse (Eds.), *The new world of dreams: An anthology.* New York: Macmillan.

Hall, E. T. (1966). *The hidden dimension.* Garden City, NY: Doubleday.

Hall, J. (2006). *What is clinical psychology?* (4th ed.). New York: Oxford University Press.

Hallahan, D. P., & Kauffman, J. M. (2006). *Exceptional learners* (10th ed.). Boston: Allyn & Bacon.

Halpern, D. F. (2001). Sex difference research: Cognitive abilities. In J. Worell (Ed.), *Encyclopedia of women and gender.* New York: Oxford University Press.

Hamilton, V. L., & Sanders, J. (1995). Crimes of obedience and conformity in the workplace. *Journal of Social Issues, 51*(3), 67–88.

Hammer, J. C., Fisher, J. D., Fitzgerald, P., & Fisher, W. A. (1996). When two heads aren't better than one: AIDS risk behavior in college-age couples. *Journal of Applied Social Psychology, 26*(5), 375–397.

Hammer, L. B., Grigsby, T. D., & Woods, S. (1998). The conflicting demands of work, family, and school among students at an urban university. *Journal of Psychology, 132*(2), 220–226.

Hancock, P. A., & Ganey, H. C. N. (2003). From the inverted-U to the extended-U: The evolution of a law of psychology. *Journal of Human Performance in Extreme Environments, 7*(1), 5–14.

Handsfield, H. H. (2001). Resurgent sexually transmitted diseases among men who have sex with men. *Medscape Infectious Disease,* Medscape.com.

Hanley, S. J., & Abell, S. C. (2002). Maslow and relatedness: Creating an interpersonal model of self-actualization. *Journal of Humanistic Psychology, 42*(4), 37–56.

Hansell, J. H. (2007). *Abnormal psychology: The enduring issues* (2nd ed.). New York: Wiley.

Hansen, C. J., Stevens, L. C., & Coast, J. R. (2001). Exercise duration and mood state. *Health Psychology, 20*(4), 267–275.

Hansen, N. B., Lambert, M. J., & Forman, E. M. (2002). The psychotherapy dose-response effect and its implications for treatment delivery services. *Clinical Psychology: Science & Practice, 9*(3), 329–334.

Hanton, S., Mellalieu, S. D., & Hall, R. (2004). Self-confidence and anxiety interpretation: A qualitative investigation. *Psychology of Sport & Exercise, 5*(4), 477–495.

Hardaway, C. A., & Gregory, K. B. (2005). Fatigue and sleep debt in an operational navy squadron. *International Journal of Aviation Psychology, 15*(2), 157–171.

Hardin, G. (1968). The tragedy of the commons. *Science, 162,* 1243–1248.

Hardin, G. (1985). *Filters against folly.* New York: Viking.

Harding, D. J., Fox, C., & Mehta, J. D. (2002). Studying rare events through qualitative case studies. *Sociological Methods & Research, 31*(2), 174–217.

Harding, R. W., Morgan, F. H., Indermaur, D., Ferrante, A. M., et al. (1998). Road rage and the epidemiology of violence. *Studies on Crime & Crime Prevention, 7*(2), 221–238.

Hare, R. D. (2006). Psychopathy: A clinical and forensic overview. *Psychiatric Clinics of North America, 29*(3), 709–724.

Harker, L., & Keltner, D. (2001). Expressions of positive emotion in women's college yearbook pictures and their relationship to personality and life outcomes across adulthood. *Journal of Personality & Social Psychology, 80*(1), 112–124.

Harlow, H. F., & Harlow, M. K. (1962). Social deprivation in monkeys. *Scientific American, 207,* 136–146.

Harlow, J. M. (1868). Recovery from the passage of an iron bar through the head. *Publications of the Massachusetts Medical Society, 2,* 327–347.

Harrigan, J. A. (2005). Proxemics, kinesics, and gaze. In J. A. Harrigan, R. Rosenthal, et al. (Eds.), *The new handbook of methods in nonverbal behavior research.* New York: Oxford University Press.

Harris, C. (2004). The evolution of jealousy. *American Scientist, 92,* 62–71.

Harris, J. A., Rushton, J. P., Hampson, E., & Jackson, D. N. (1996). Salivary testosterone and self-report aggressive and pro-social personality characteristics in men and women. *Aggressive Behavior, 22*(5), 321–331.

Harris, J. C. (2003). Pinel delivering the insane. *Archives of General Psychiatry, 60*(6), 552.

Harris, J. R., & Liebert, R. M. (1991). *The child.* Englewood Cliffs, NJ: Prentice Hall.

Harrison, P. J., & Weinberger, D. R. (2005). Schizophrenia genes, gene expression, and neuropathology: On the matter of their convergence. *Molecular Psychiatry, 10*(1), 40–68.

Hart, B., & Risley, T. R. (1999). *The social world of children learning to talk.* Baltimore: Paul H. Brookes.

Hart, D., & Carlo, G. (2005). Moral development in adolescence. *Journal of Research on Adolescence, 15*(3), 223–233.

Hartgens, F., & Kuipers, H. (2004). Effects of androgenic–anabolic steroids in athletes. *Sports Medicine, 34*(8), 513–554.

Hartlep, K. L., & Forsyth, G. A. (2000). The effect of self-reference on learning and retention. *Teaching of Psychology, 27*(4), 269–271.

Hartmann, P., Reuter, M., & Nyborg, H. (2006). The relationship between date of birth and individual differences in personality and general intelligence: A largescale study. *Personality & Individual Differences, 40*(7), 1349–1362.

Harvey, C. A., Curson, D. A., Pantelis, C., & Taylor, J. (1996). Four behavioural syndromes of schizophrenia. *British Journal of Psychiatry, 168*(5), 562–570.

Harway, M. (Ed.). (2004). *Handbook of couples therapy.* San Francisco: Jossey-Bass.

Hashibe, M., Straif, K., Tashkin, D. P., Morgenstern, H., et al. (2005). Epidemiologic review of marijuana use and cancer risk. *Alcohol, 35*(3), 265–275.

Hashimoto, I., Suzuki, A., Kimura, T., Iguchi Y., et al. (2004). Is there training-dependent reorganization of digit representations in area 3b of string players? *Clinical Neurophysiology, 115*(2), 435–447.

Hauck, F. R., Moore, C. M., Herman, S. M., Donovan, M., et al. (2002). The contribution of prone sleeping position to the racial disparity in sudden infant death syndrome. *Pediatrics, 110,* 772–780.

Hauri, P., & Linde, S. (1990). *No more sleepless nights.* New York: Wiley.

Hayes, C. (1951). *The ape in our house.* New York: Harper & Row.

Hayne, H., & Rovee-Collier, C. (1995). The organization of reactivated memory in infancy. *Child Development, 66*(3), 893–906.

Heath, R. G. (1963). Electrical self-stimulation of the brain in man. *American Journal of Psychiatry, 120,* 571–577.

Hebl, M. R., King, E. G., & Lin, J. (2004). The swimsuit becomes us all: Ethnicity, gender, and vulnerability to self-objectification. *Personality & Social Psychology Bulletin, 30,* 1322–1331.

Hecht, J. (2007). *The happiness myth: Why what we think is right is wrong.* New York: HarperCollins.

Heiby, E. M. (1983). Assessment of frequency of self-reinforcement. *Journal of Personality & Social Psychology, 44,* 1304–1307.

Heilman, M. E., Wallen, A. S., Fuchs, D., & Tamkins, M. M. (2004). Penalties for success: Reactions to women who succeed at male gender-typed tasks. *Journal of Applied Psychology, 89*(3), 416–427.

Heiman, J. R. (2002). Sexual dysfunction: Overview of prevalence, etiological factors, and treatments. *Journal of Sex Research, 39*(1), 73–78.

Heimann, M., & Meltzoff, A. N. (1996). Deferred imitation in 9- and 14-month-old infants. *British Journal of Developmental Psychology, 14*(March), 55–64.

Heinrichs, R. W. (2001). *In search of madness: Schizophrenia and neuroscience.* New York: Oxford University Press.

Heisel, M. J., Flett, G. L., & Hewitt, P. L. (2003). Social hopelessness and college student suicide ideation. *Archives of Suicide Research, 7*(3), 221–235.

Helgeson, V. S. (2005). *The psychology of gender* (2nd ed.). Englewood Cliffs, NJ: Prentice Hall.

Hellerstein, D. J., Rosenthal, R. N., Pinsker, H., Samstag, L. W., et al. (1998). A randomized prospective study comparing supportive and dynamic therapies. *Journal of Psychotherapy Practice & Research, 7*(4), 261–271.

Hellige, J. B. (1993). *Hemispheric asymmetry.* Cambridge, MA: Harvard University Press.

Helson, R., & Srivastava, S. (2002). Creative and wise people. *Personality & Social Psychology Bulletin, 28*(10), 1430–1440.

Helwig, A. A. (1998). Gender-role stereotyping: Testing theory with a longitudinal sample. *Sex Roles, 38*(5–6), 403–423.

Henderson, N. D. (1982). Human behavior genetics. *Annual Review of Psychology, 33,* 403–440.

Hendrick, S. S., & Hendrick, C. (1993). Lovers as friends. *Journal of Social & Personal Relationships, 10*(3), 459–466.

Henman, L. D. (2001). Humor as a coping mechanism. *Humor: International Journal of Humor Research, 14*(1), 83–94.

Henningsen, D. D., Henningsen, M. L. M., Eden, J., & Cruz, M. G. (2006). Examining the symptoms of groupthink and retrospective sensemaking. *Small Group Research, 37*(1), 36–64.

Hepper, P. G., Wells, D. L., & Lynch, C. (2005). Prenatal thumb sucking is related to postnatal handedness. *Neuropsychologia, 43*(3), 313–315.

Hepper, P.G., McCartney, G. R., & Shannon, E. A. (1998). Lateralised behaviour in first trimester human foetuses. *Neuropsychologia, 36*(6), 531–534.

Hergenhahn, B. R. (2005). *An introduction to the history of psychology* (5th ed.). Belmont, CA: Cengage Learning/Wadsworth.

Hergenhahn, B. R., & Olson, M. (2007). *An introduction to theories of personality* (7th ed.). Englewood Cliffs, NJ: Prentice Hall.

Hergenhahn, B. R., & Olson, M. (2005). *Introduction to the theories* of learning (6th ed.). Englewood Cliffs, NJ: Prentice Hall.

Heriot, S. A., & Pritchard, M. (2004). "Reciprocal Inhibition as the Main Basis of Psychotherapeutic Effects" by Joseph Wolpe (1954). *Clinical Child Psychology & Psychiatry, 9*(2), 297–307.

Hermann, B., Seidenberg, M., Sears, L., Hansen, R., et al. (2004). Cerebellar atrophy in temporal lobe epilepsy affects procedural memory. *Neurology, 63*(11), 2129–2131.

Hernstein, R., & Murray, C. (1994). *The bell curve*. New York: Free Press.

Herrmann, D. J., Yoder, C. Y., Gruneberg, M., & Payne, D. G. (2006). *Applied cognitive psychology: A textbook*. Mahwah, NJ: Erlbaum.

Herxheimer, A., & Waterhouse, J. (2003). The prevention and treatment of jet lag. *British Medical Journal, 326*(7384), 296–297.

Herz, R. S. (2001). Ah sweet skunk! *Cerebrum, 3*(4), 31–47.

Hettich, P. I. (2005). *Connect college to career: Student guide to work and life transition*. Belmont, CA: Cengage Learning/Wadsworth.

Higbee, K. L. (1997). Novices, apprentices, and mnemonists: Acquiring expertise with the phonetic mnemonic. *Applied Cognitive Psychology, 11*(2), 147–161.

Higbee, K. L., Clawson, C., DeLano, L., & Campbell, S. (1990). Using the link mnemonic to remember errands. *Psychological Record, 40*(3), 429–436.

Higgins, S. T., Heil, S. H., & Lussier, J. P. (2004). Clinical implications of reinforcement as a determinant of substance use disorders. *Annual Review of Psychology, 55*, 431–461.

Higham, P. A., & Gerrard, C. (2005). Not all errors are created equal: Metacognition and changing answers on multiple-choice tests. *Canadian Journal of Experimental Psychology, 59*(1), 28–34.

Hilgard, E. R. (1968). *The experience of hypnosis*. New York: Harcourt Brace Jovanovich.

Hilgard, E. R. (1977). *Divided consciousness*. New York: Wiley.

Hilgard, E. R. (1994) Neodissociation theory. In S. J. Lynn & J. W. Rhue (Eds.), *Dissociation: Clinical, theoretical and research perspectives*. New York: Guilford.

Hilsenroth, M. J. (2000). Rorschach test. In A. Kazdin (Ed.), *Encyclopedia of psychology*. Washington, DC: American Psychological Association.

Hinkel, E. (Ed.). (2005). *Handbook of research in second language teaching and learning*. Mahwah, NJ: Erlbaum.

Hinterberger, T., Kübler, A., Kaiser, J., Neumann, N., et al. (2003). A brain-computer interface (BCI) for the locked-in: Comparison of different EEG classifications for the thought translation device. *Clinical Neurophysiology, 114*(3), 416–425.

Hintzman, D. L. (2005). Memory strength and recency judgments. *Psychonomic Bulletin & Review,12*(5), 858–864.

Hirstein, W. (2005). *Brain fiction: Self-deception and the riddle of confabulation*. Cambridge, MA: MIT Press.

Hiscock, M., Perachio, N., & Inch, R. (2001). Is there a sex difference in human laterality? *Journal of Clinical & Experimental Neuropsychology, 23*(2), 137–148.

Hite, S. (1976). *The Hite report*. New York: Macmillan.

Hobson, J. A. (2000). Dreams: Physiology. In A. Kazdin (Ed.), *Encyclopedia of psychology*. Washington, DC: American Psychological Association.

Hobson, J. A. (2001). *Consciousness*. New York: Freeman.

Hobson, J. A. (2005). Sleep is of the brain, by the brain and for the brain. *Nature, 437*(7063), 1254–1256.

Hobson, J. A., Pace–Schott, E. F., & Stickgold, R. (2000). Dream science 2000. *Behavioral & Brain Sciences, 23*(6), 1019–1035, 1083–1121.

Hochstenbach, J., Mulder, T., van Limbeek, J., Donders, R., et al. (1998). Cognitive decline following stroke: A comprehensive study of cognitive decline following stroke. *Journal of Clinical & Experimental Neuropsychology, 20*(4), 503–517.

Hodapp, R. M. (1994). Mental retardation. *Encyclopedia of human behavior* (Vol. 3). San Diego: Academic Press.

Hodgson, R., & Miller, P. (1982). *Selfwatching*. New York: Facts on File.

Hofer, B. K., & Yu, S. L. (2003). Teaching self-regulated learning through a "Learning to Learn" course. *Teaching of Psychology, 30*(1), 30–33.

Hoff, E. (2006). How social contexts support and shape language development. *Developmental Review, 26*(1), 55–88.

Hoff, E., & Tian, C. (2005). Socioeconomic status and cultural influences on language. *Journal of Communication Disorders, 38*(4), 271–278.

Hoffart, A. (2005). Interpersonal therapy for social phobia: Theoretical model and review of the evidence. In M. E. Abelian (Ed.), *Focus on psychotherapy research*. Hauppauge, NY: Nova Science Publishers.

Hoffer, A., & Youngren, V. R. (2004). Is free association still at the core of psychoanalysis? *International Journal of Psychoanalysis, 85*(6), 1489–1492.

Hoffman, H. G., Garcia-Palacios, A., Carlin, A., Furness, T. A., et al. (2003). Interfaces that heal: Coupling real and virtual objects to treat spider phobia. *International Journal of Human–Computer Interaction, 16*(2), 283–300.

Hogan, E. H., Hornick, B. A., & Bouchoux, A. (2002). Focus on communications: Communicating the message: Clarifying the controversies about caffeine. *Nutrition Today, 37*, 28–35.

Hogben, D., & Lawson, M. J. (1992). Superiority of the keyword method for backward recall in vocabulary acquisition. *Psychological Reports, 71*(3, Pt. 1), 880–882.

Hoge, C. W., Castro, C. A., Messer, S. C., McGurk, D., et al. (2004). Combat duty in Iraq and Afghanistan, mental health problems, and barriers to care. *New England Journal of Medicine, 351*(1), 13–22.

Hohwy, J., & Rosenberg, R. (2005). Unusual experiences, reality testing and delusions of alien control. *Mind & Language, 20*(2), 141–162.

Holden, C. (1980). Twins reunited. *Science 80,* Nov., 55–59.

Holland, J. L. (1997). *Making vocational choices*. Odessa, FL: Psychological Assessment Resources.

Holmes, J., & Adams, J. W. (2006). Working memory and children's mathematical skills: Implications for mathematical development and mathematics curricula. *Educational Psychology, 26*(3), 339–366.

Holmes, M. (2002). Rethinking the meaning and management of intersexuality. *Sexualities, 5*(2), 159–180.

Holmes, P. S., & Collins, D. J. (2001). The PETTLEP approach to motor imagery: A functional equivalence model for sport psychologists. *Journal of Applied Sport Psychology, 13*(1), 60–83.

Holmes, T. H., & Rahe, R. H. (1967). The social readjustment rating scale. *Journal of Psychosomatic Research, 11*(2), 213–218.

Holstein, M. (1997). Reflections on death and dying. *Academic Medicine, 72*(10), 848–855.

Holtzen, D. W. (2000). Handedness and professional tennis. *International Journal of Neuroscience, 105*(1–4), 101–111.

Holzinger, B., LaBerge, S., & Levitan, L. (2006). Psychophysiological correlates of lucid dreaming. *Dreaming, 16*(2), 88–95.

Horgan, J. (2005). The forgotten era of brain chips. *Scientific American, 293*(4), 66–73.

Horn, J., Nelson, C. E., & Brannick, M. T. (2004). Integrity, conscientiousness, and honesty. *Psychological Reports, 95*(1), 27–38.

Horn, R. R., Williams, A. M., Scot M. A., & Hodges, N. J. (2005). Visual search and coordination changes in response to video and point-light demonstrations without KR. *Journal of Motor Behavior, 37*(4), 265–274.

Horne, R. S. C., Andrew, S., Mitchell, K., Sly, D. J., et al. (2001). Apnoea of prematurity and arousal from sleep. *Early Human Development, 61*(2), 119–133.

Hortman, G. (2003). What do facial expressions convey? *Emotion, 3*(2), 150–166.

Horvath, L. S., Milich, R., Lynam, D., Leukefeld, C., et al. (2004). Sensation seeking and substance use: A cross-lagged panel design. *Individual Differences Research, 2*(3), 175–183.

Hosch, H. M., & Cooper, D. S. (1982). Victimization as a determinant of eyewitness accuracy. *Journal of Applied Psychology, 67*, 649–652.

Hough, L. M., & Oswald, F. L. (2000). Personnel selection. *Annual Review of Psychology, 51*, 631–664.

Howard, A., Pion, G. M., Gottfredson, G. D., Flattau, P. E., et al. (1986). The changing face of American psychology. *American Psychologist, 41*, 1311–1327.

Howard, I. P., & Rogers, B. J. (2001a). *Seeing in depth* (Vol. 1): *Basic mechanisms*. Toronto: Porteous.

Howard, I. P., & Rogers, B. J. (2001b) *Seeing in depth* (Vol. 2): *Depth perception*. Toronto: Porteous.

Howard, J. L., & Ferris, G. R. (1996). The employment interview context. *Journal of Applied Social Psychology, 26*(2), 112–136.

Howell, D. C. (2008). *Fundamental statistics for the behavioral sciences* (6th ed.). Belmont, CA: Cengage Learning/Wadsworth.

Howes, C. (1997). Children's experiences in center-based child care as a function of teacher background and adult:child ratio. *Merrill–Palmer Quarterly, 43*(3), 404–425.

Hsia, Y., & Graham, C. H. (1997). Color blindness. In A. Byrne, D. R. Hilbert, et al. (Eds.), *Readings on color* (Vol. 2): *The science of color*. Cambridge, MA: MIT Press.

Hu, S., Pattatucci, A. M., Patterson, C., Li. L., et al. (1995). Linkage between sexual orientation and chromosome Xq28 in males but not in females. *Nature Genetics 11*(3), 248–256.

Hubble, M.A., Duncan, B. L., & Miller, S. D. (Eds.) (1999). *The heart and soul of change: What works in therapy*. Washington, DC: American Psychological Association.

Hubel D. H., & Wiesel, W. N. (2005). *Brain & visual perception:*

The story of a 25-year collaboration. New York: Oxford University Press.

Hübner, R., & Volberg, G. (2005). The integration of object levels and their content: A theory of global/local processing and related hemispheric differences. *Journal of Experimental Psychology: Human Perception & Performance, 31*(3), 520–541.

Huesmann, L. R., Moise-Titus, J., Podolski, C., & Eron, L. D. (2003). Longitudinal relations between children's exposure to TV violence and their aggressive and violent behavior in young adulthood: 1977–1992. *Developmental Psychology, 39*(2), 201–221.

Hughes, J. N., & Hasbrouck, J. E. (1996). Television violence: Implications for violence prevention. *School Psychology Review, 25*(2), 134–151.

Hughes, J. R., Oliveto, A. H., Liguori, A., Carpenter, J., et al. (1998). Endorsement of DSM-IV dependence criteria among caffeine users. *Drug & Alcohol Dependence, 52*(2), 99–107.

Huijbregts, S. C., Séguin, J. R., Zelazo, P. D., Parent, S., et al. (2006). Interrelations between maternal smoking during pregnancy, birth weight and sociodemographic factors in the prediction of early cognitive abilities. *Infant & Child Development, 15*(6), 593–607.

Human Rights Watch. (2003). *Ill-equipped: U.S. prisons and offenders with mental illness.* New York: Human Rights Watch.

Hunt, R. R., & Ellis, H. C. (2004). *Fundamentals of cognitive psychology* (7th ed.). New York: McGraw-Hill.

Hunter, E. (1998). Adolescent attraction to cults. *Adolescence, 33*(131), 709–714.

Hunter, J. P., Katz, J., & Davis, K. D. (2003). The effect of tactile and visual sensory inputs on phantom limb awareness. *Brain, 126*(3), 579–589.

Hutchinson, S. R. (2004). Survey research. In K. deMarrais & S. D. Lapan (Eds.), *Foundations for research: Methods of inquiry in education and the social sciences. Inquiry and pedagogy across diverse contexts.* Mahwah, NJ: Erlbaum.

Hutchinson, S., Lee, L. H. L., Gaab, N., & Schlaug, G. (2003). Cerebellar volume of musicians. *Cerebral Cortex, 13*(9), 943–949.

Hyde, J. S. (2004). *Half the human experience: The psychology of women* (6th ed.). Boston: Houghton Mifflin.

Hyde, J. S., & DeLamater, J. D. (2006). *Understanding human sexuality* (9th ed.). New York: McGraw-Hill.

Hyman, R. (1996a). Evaluation of the military's twenty-year program on psychic spying. *Skeptical Inquirer, 20*(2), 21–23.

Hyman, R. (1996b). The evidence for psychic functioning: Claims vs. reality. *Skeptical Inquirer, 20*(2), 24–26.

Hysenbegasi, A., Hass, S. L., & Rowland, C. R. (2005). The impact of depression on the academic productivity of university students. *Journal of Mental Health Policy & Economics, 8*(3), 145–151.

Ida, Y., & Mandal, M. K. (2003). Cultural differences in side bias: Evidence from Japan and India. *Laterality: Asymmetries of Body, Brain & Cognition, 8*(2), 121–133.

Ingram, V. (2003). Alzheimer's disease. *American Scientist, 91,* 312–321.

Iosif, A., & Ballon, B. (2005). Bad moon rising: The persistent belief in lunar connections to madness. *Canadian Medical Association Journal, 173*(12), 1498–1500.

Ivanco, T. L., & Racine, R. J. (2000). Long-term potentiation in the pathways between the hippocampus and neocortex in the chronically implanted, freely moving, rat. *Hippocampus, 10,* 143–152.

Iversen, L. (2006). *Speed, ecstasy, ritalin: The science of amphetamines.* New York: Oxford University Press.

Izard, C. E. (1977). *Human emotions.* New York: Plenum.

Izard, C. E. (1990). Facial expressions and the regulation of emotions. *Journal of Personality & Social Psychology, 58*(3), 487–498.

Izard, C. E., Fantauzzo, C. A., Castle, J. M., Haynes, O. M., et al. (1995). The ontogeny and significance of infants' facial expressions in the first 9 months of life. *Developmental Psychology, 31*(6), 997–1013.

Jablonski, N.G., & Chaplin, G. (2000). The evolution of human skin coloration. *Journal of Human Evolution, 39*(1), 57–106.

Jackson, S. L. (2008). *Research methods: A modular approach.* Belmont, CA: Cengage Learning/Wadsworth.

Jackson, T., Fritch, A., Nagasaka, T., & Gunderson, J. (2002). Towards explaining the association between shyness and loneliness. *Social Behavior & Personality, 30*(3), 263–270.

Jackson, T., Towson, S., & Narduzzi, K. (1997). Predictors of shyness. *Social Behavior & Personality, 25*(2), 149–154.

Jacob, A., Prasad, S., Boggild, M., & Chandratre, S. (2004). Charles Bonnet syndrome: Elderly people and visual hallucinations. *British Medical Journal, 328*(7455), 1552–1554.

Jacobs, M. (2003). *Sigmund Freud.* Thousand Oaks, CA: Sage.

Jacobs, M. K., Christensen, A., Snibbe, J. R., Dolezal-Wood, S., et al. (2001). A comparison of computer-based versus traditional individual psychotherapy. *Professional Psychology: Research & Practice, 32*(1), 92–96.

Jacobs, S. R., & Dodd, D. K. (2003). Student burnout as a function of personality, social support, and workload. *Journal of College Student Development, 44*(3), 291–303.

Jacobsen, P. B., Bovbjerg, D. H., Schwartz, M. D., Andrykowski, M. A., et al. (1993). Formation of food aversions in cancer patients receiving repeated infusions of chemotherapy. *Behavior Research & Therapy, 31*(8), 739–748.

Jaffe, J., Beatrice, B., Feldstein, S., Crown, C. L., et al. (2001). Rhythms of dialogue in infancy. *Monographs of the Society for Research in Child Development, 66*(2), vi–131.

Jamison, K. R. (2001). Suicide in the young: An essay. *Cerebrum, 3*(3), 39–42.

Janis, I. L., & Wheeler, D. (1978). Thinking clearly about career choices. *Psychology Today, 11,* 66–78.

Janssen, S. A., & Arntz, A. (2001). Real-life stress and opioid-mediated analgesia in novice parachute jumpers. *Journal of Psychophysiology, 15*(2), 106–113.

Janus, S. S., & Janus, C. L. (1993). *The Janus report.* New York: Wiley.

Jarvin, L., & Sternberg, R. J. (2003). Alfred Binet's contributions to educational psychology. In B. J. Zimmerman & D. H. Schunk (Eds.), *Educational psychology: A century of contributions.* Mahwah, NJ: Erlbaum.

Jawahar, I. M., Stone, T. H., & Kisamore, J. L. (2007). Role conflict and burnout: The direct and moderating effects of political skill and perceived organizational support on burnout dimensions. *International Journal of Stress Management, 14*(2), 142–159.

Jay, T. B. (2003). *Psychology of language.* Englewood Cliffs, NJ: Prentice Hall.

Jeffery, R. W., & Wing R. R. (2001). The effects of an enhanced exercise program on long-term weight loss. *Obesity Research, 9*(3), O193.

Jenkins, J. G., & Dallenbach, K. M. (1924). Obliviscence during sleep and waking. *American Journal of Psychology, 35,* 605–612.

Jerabek, I., & Standing, L. (1992). Imagined test situations produce contextual memory enhancement. *Perceptual & Motor Skills, 75*(2), 400.

Johnson, K. E., & Mervis, C. B. (1997). Effects of varying levels of expertise on the basic level of categorization. *Journal of Experimental Psychology: General, 126*(3), 248–277.

Johnson, K. J., & Fredrickson, B. L. (2005). "We all look the same to me": Positive emotions eliminate the own-race bias in face recognition. *Psychological Science, 16*(11), 875–881.

Johnson, S. (2005). *Everything bad is good for you: How today's popular culture is actually making us smarter.* New York: Riverhead.

Johnson, S. M., & White, G. (1971). Self-observation as an agent of behavioral change. *Behavior Therapy, 2,* 488–497.

Johnson, T. J. (2002). College students' self-reported reasons for why drinking games end. *Addictive Behaviors, 27*(1), 145–153.

Jones, E. E., & Nisbett, R. E. (1971). The actor and observer: Divergent perceptions of the causes of behavior. In E. E. Jones, D. E. Kanouse, et al. (Eds.), *Attribution: Perceiving the causes of behavior.* Morristown, NJ: General Learning Press.

Jones, G. V., & Martin, M. (2001). Confirming the X–linked handedness gene as recessive, not additive. *Psychological Review, 108*(4), 811–813.

Jones, L., & Petruzzi, D. C. (1995). Test anxiety: A review of theory and current treatment. *Journal of College Student Psychotherapy, 10*(1), 3–15.

Jones, M. E., Russell, R. L., & Bryant, F. B. (1998). The structure of rape attitudes for men and women. *Journal of Research in Personality, 32*(3), 331–350.

Jones, M. K., & Menzies, R. G. (1998). Danger ideation reduction therapy (DIRT) for obsessive-compulsive washers. *Behaviour Research & Therapy, 36*(10), 959–970.

Jones, R. N. (2003). Racial bias in the assessment of cognitive functioning of older adults. *Aging & Mental Health, 7*(2), 83–102.

Jones, S. S., & Hong, H.-W. (2001). Onset of voluntary communication: Smiling looks to mother. *Infancy, 2*(3), 353–370.

Jorm, A. F., Korten, A. E., Rodgers, B., Jacomb, P. A., et al. (2002). Sexual orientation and mental health. *British Journal of Psychiatry, 180*(5), 423–427.

Jourard, S. M. (1963). *Personal adjustment.* New York: Macmillan.

Jouvet, M. (1999). *The paradox of sleep.* Cambridge, MA: MIT Press.

Jowett, G. S. (2006). Brainwashing: The Korean POW controversy and the origins of a myth. In G. S. Jowett & V. O'Donnell (Eds.), *Readings in propaganda and persuasion: New and classic essays.* Thousand Oaks, CA, Sage.

Joyce, P., & Sills, C. (2001). *Skills in Gestalt counseling & psychotherapy.* Newbury Park: Sage.

Juliano, L. M., & Griffiths, R. R. (2004). A critical review of caffeine withdrawal: Empirical validation of symptoms and signs, incidence, severity, and associated features. *Psychopharmacology, 176*(1), 1–29.

Julien, R. M. (2005). *A primer of drug action: A comprehensive guide to the actions, uses, and side effects* (10th ed.). New York: Worth.

Jussim, L., & Harber, K. D. (2005). Teacher expectations and self-fulfilling prophecies: Knowns and unknowns, resolved and unresolved controversies. *Personality & Social Psychology Review, 9*(2), 131–155.

Kagan, J. (1971). *Change and continuity in infancy.* New York: Wiley.

Kagan, J. (2004). New insights into temperament. *Cerebrum, 6*(1), 51–66.

Kagan, J. (2005). Personality and temperament: Historical perspectives. In M. Rosenbluth, S. H. Kennedy, et al. (Eds.), *Depression and personality: Conceptual and clinical challenges.* Washington, DC: American Psychiatric Publishing.

Kahneman, D. (2003). A perspective on judgment and choice. *American Psychologist, 58*(9), 697–720.

Kahneman, D., & Tversky, A. (1972). Subjective probability: A judgment of representativeness. *Cognitive Psychology, 3,* 430–454.

Kahneman, D., & Tversky, A. (1973). On the psychology of prediction. *Psychological Review, 80,* 237–251.

Kahneman, D., Krueger, A. B., Schkade, D., Schwarz, N., et al. (2004). A survey method for characterizing daily life experience: The day reconstruction method. *Science, 306*(5702), 1776–1780.

Kahneman, D., Slovic, P., & Tversky, A. (1982). *Judgment under uncertainty: Heuristics and biases.* Cambridge, MA: Cambridge University Press.

Kalat, J. W. (2007). *Biological psychology* (8th ed.). Belmont, CA: Cengage Learning/Wadsworth.

Kalat, J. W., & Shiota, M. N. (2007). *Emotion.* Belmont, CA: Cengage Learning/Wadsworth.

Kallio, S., & Revonsuo, A. (2003). Hypnotic phenomena and altered states of consciousness: A multilevel framework of description and explanation. *Contemporary Hypnosis, 20*(3), 111–164.

Kamimori, G. H., Johnson, D., Thorne, D., & Belenky, G. (2005). Multiple caffeine doses maintain vigilance during early morning operations. *Aviation, Space, & Environmental Medicine, 76*(11), 1046–1050.

Kamin, L. J. (1981). *The intelligence controversy.* New York: Wiley.

Kandel, E. R., Schwartz, J. H., & Jessell, T. M. (2003). *Principles of neuroscience* (5th ed.). New York: McGraw-Hill.

Kaplan, H. S. (1974). *The new sex therapy.* New York: Brunner/Mazel.

Kaplan, P. S. (1998). *The human odyssey.* Pacific Grove, CA: Brooks/Cole.

Kapleau, P. (1966). *The three pillars of Zen.* New York: Harper & Row.

Kapur, S., & Lecrubier, Y. (Eds.). (2003). *Dopamine in the pathophysiology and treatment of schizophrenia: New findings.* Washington, DC: Taylor & Francis.

Karim, A. A., Hinterberger, T., Richter, J, Mellinger, J., et al. (2006). Neural internet: Web surfing with brain potentials for the completely paralyzed. *Neurorehabilitation & Neural Repair, 20*(4), 508–515.

Karon, B. P., & Widener, A. J. (1997). Repressed memories and World War II: Lest we forget! *Professional Psychology: Research & Practice, 28*(4), 338–340.

Kasser, T., & Ryan, R. M. (1993). A dark side of the American dream: Correlates of financial success as a central life aspiration. *Journal of Personality & Social Psychology, 65*(2), 410–422.

Kasser, T., & Ryan, R. M. (1996). Further examining the American dream: Differential correlates of intrinsic and extrinsic goals. *Personality & Social Psychology Bulletin, 22*(3), 280–287.

Kassin, S. M. (2005). On the psychology of confessions: Does innocence put innocents at risk? *American Psychologist, 60*(3), 215–228.

Kassin, S. M., Fein, S., & Markus, H. R. (2008). *Social psychology* (7th ed.). Boston: Houghton Mifflin.

Kassin, S. M., Tubb, V. A., Hosch, H. M., & Memon, A. (2001). On the "general acceptance" of eyewitness testimony research. *American Psychologist, 56*(5), 405–416.

Kataria, S. (2004). A clinical guide to pediatric sleep: Diagnosis and management of sleep problems. *Journal of Developmental & Behavioral Pediatrics, 25*(2), 132–133.

Katz, P. A. (2003). Racists or tolerant multiculturalists? *American Psychologist, 58*(11), 897–909.

Kaufman, A. S. (2000). Intelligence tests and school psychology: Predicting the future by studying the past. *Psychology in the Schools, 37*(1), 7–16.

Kaufman, L., & Kaufman, J. H. (2000). Explaining the moon illusion. *Proceedings of the National Academy of Sciences, 97*(1), 500–505.

Kaufmann, J. (2007). Transfiguration: A narrative analysis of male-to-female transsexual. *International Journal of Qualitative Studies in Education, 20*(1), 1–13.

Kawai, K., Sugimoto, K., Nakashima, K., Miura, H., et al. (2000). Leptin as a modulator of sweet taste sensitivities in mice. *Proceedings: National Academy of Sciences, 97*(20), 11044–11049.

Kawasaki, H., Adolphs, R., Oya, H., Kovach, C. et al. (2005). Analysis of single-unit responses to emotional scenes in human ventromedial prefrontal cortex. *Journal of Cognitive Neuroscience, 17*(10), 1509–1518.

Kearney, C. A., Sims, K. E., Pursell, C. R., & Tillotson, C. A. (2003). Separation anxiety disorder in young children: A longitudinal and family analysis. *Journal of Clinical Child & Adolescent Psychology, 32*(4), 593–598.

Kebbell, M. R., & Wagstaff, G. F. (1998). Hypnotic interviewing: The best way to interview eyewitnesses? *Behavioral Sciences & the Law, 16*(1), 115–129.

Keefe, F. J., Abernethy, A. P., & Campbell, L. C. (2005). Psychological approaches to understanding and treating disease-related pain. *Annual Review of Psychology, 56,* 601–630.

Keel, P. K., & Klump, K. L. (2003). Are eating disorders culture-bound syndromes? Implications for conceptualizing their etiology. *Psychological Bulletin, 129*(5), 747–769.

Keller, M. C., & Young, R. K. (1996). Mate assortment in dating and married couples. *Personality & Individual Differences, 21*(2), 217–221.

Kellermann, A. L., Rivara, F. P., Rushforth, N. B., Banton, J. G., et al. (1993). Gun ownership as a risk factor for homicide in the home. *New England Journal of Medicine, 329*(15), 1084–1091.

Kelley, H. H. (1950). The warm–cold variable in first impressions of persons. *Journal of Personality, 18,* 431–439.

Kelly, I. W. (1999). "Debunking the debunkers": A response to an astrologer's debunking of skeptics. *Skeptical Inquirer,* Nov.-Dec., 37–43.

Kelly, M. P., Strassberg, D. S., & Turner, C. M. (2006). Behavioral assessment of couples' communication in female orgasmic disorder. *Journal of Sex & Marital Therapy, 32*(2), 81–95.

Kempermann, G. (2005). *Adult neurogenesis: Stem cells and neuronal development in the adult brain.* New York: Oxford University Press.

Kendler, K. S., Thornton, L. M., & Prescott, C. A. (2001). Gender differences in the rates of exposure to stressful life events and sensitivity to their depressogenic effects. *American Journal of Psychiatry, 158*(4), 587–593.

Kennaway, D. J., & Wright, H. (2002). Melatonin and circadian rhythms. *Current Topics in Medicinal Chemistry, 2,* 199–209.

Kenneth, M., Carpenter, K. M., & Hasin, D. S. (1998). Reasons for drinking alcohol. *Psychology of Addictive Behaviors, 12*(3), 168–184.

Kenny, P. J., & Markou, A. (2006). Nicotine self-administration acutely activates brain reward systems and induces a long-lasting increase in reward sensitivity. *Neuropsychopharmacology, 31*(6), 1203–1211.

Kerr, N. L., & Bray, R. M. (2005). Simulation, realism, and the study of the jury. In N. Brewer & K. D. Williams, (Eds.), *Psychology and law: An empirical perspective.* New York: Guilford.

Kety, S. S. (1979). Disorders of the human brain. *Scientific American, 241,* 202–214.

Keyes, C. L. M., & Haidt, J. (2003). Introduction: Human flourishing. In C. L. M. Keyes & J. Haidt (Eds.), *Flourishing.* Washington, DC: American Psychological Association.

Keysers, C., Xiao, D.-K., Földiák, P., & Perrett, D. I. (2005). Out of sight but not out of mind: The neurophysiology of iconic memory in the superior temporal sulcus. *Cognitive Neuropsychology, 22*(3–4), 316–332.

Kida, T. E. (2006). *Don't believe everything you think.* Buffalo, NY: Prometheus.

Kiecolt-Glaser, J. K., McGuire, L., Robles, T. F., & Glaser, R. (2002). Emotions, morbidity, and mortality. *Annual Review of Psychology, 53,* 83–107.

Killen, J. D., & Fortmann, S. P. (1997). Craving is associated with smoking relapse. *Experimental and Clinical Psychopharmacology, 5*(2), 137–142.

Kim, J., Singer, R. N., & Radlo, S. J. (1996). Degree of cognitive demands in psychomotor tasks and the effects of the five-step strategy on achievement. *Human Performance, 9*(2), 155–169.

Kim, S. (2000). Bogglers. *Discover,* Dec., 98.

Kim, S. (2002). Participative management and job satisfaction: Lessons for management leadership. *Public Administration Review, 62*(2), 231–241.

Kim-Cohen, J., Moffitt, T. E., Caspi, A., & Taylor, A. (2004). Genetic and environmental processes in young children's resilience and vulnerability to socioeconomic deprivation. *Child Development, 75*(3), 651–668.

King, B. E. (2005). *Human sexuality today* (5th ed.). Englewood Cliffs, NJ: Prentice Hall.

King, H. E. (1961). Psychological effects of excitation in the limbic system. In D. E. Sheer (Ed.), *Electrical stimulation of the brain*. Austin: University of Texas Press.

King, N. J., Muris, P., & Ollendick, T. H. (2005). Childhood fears and phobias: Assessment and treatment. *Child & Adolescent Mental Health, 10*(2), 50–56.

Kingsley, C. H. & Lambert, K. G. (2006). The maternal brain. *Scientific American, 294*(1), 72–79.

Kinnunen, L. H., Moltz, H., Metz, J., & Cooper, M. (2004). Differential brain activation in exclusively homosexual and heterosexual men produced by the selective serotonin reuptake inhibitor, fluoxetine. *Brain Research, 1024*(1–2), 251–254.

Kinsey, A., Pomeroy, W., & Martin, C. (1948). *Sexual behavior in the human male*. Philadelphia: Saunders.

Kinsey, A., Pomeroy, W., & Martin, C. (1953). *Sexual behavior in the human female*. Philadelphia: Saunders.

Kirsch, I., & Lynn, S. J. (1995). The altered state of hypnosis. *American Psychologist, 50*(10), 846–858.

Kirsch, I., & Sapirstein, G. (1998). Listening to Prozac but hearing placebo: A meta-analysis of antidepressant medication. *Prevention & Treatment, 1*, art. 0002a. Retrieved May 18, 2007, from http://journals.apa.org/prevention/volume1/pre0010002a.html.

Kirsch, I., (2005). The flexible observer and neodissociation theory. *Contemporary Hypnosis, 22*(3), 121–122.

Kirsh, S. J. (2005). *Children, adolescents, and media violence: A critical look at the research*. Newbury Park: Sage.

Kirveskari, E., Salmelin, R., & Hari, R. (2006). Neuromagnetic responses to vowels vs. tones reveal hemispheric lateralization. *Clinical Neurophysiology, 117*(3), 643–648.

Kiser, L. J., Heston, J. D., & Paavola, M. (2006). Day treatment centers/Partial hospitalization settings. In T. A. Petti & C. Salguero (Eds.), *Community child & adolescent psychiatry: A manual of clinical practice and consultation*. Washington, DC: American Psychiatric Publishing.

Kisilevsky, B. S., Hains, S. M. J., Jacquet, A.-Y., Granier-Deferre, C., et al. (2004). Maturation of fetal responses to music. *Developmental Science, 7*(5), 550–559.

Kitayama, S., Markus, H. R., & Kurokawa, M. (2000). Culture, emotion, and well-being: Good feelings in Japan and the United States. *Cognition & Emotion, 14*, 93–124.

Kite, M. E., Russo, N. F., Brehm, S. S., Fouad, N. A., et al. (2001). Women psychologists in academe.

American Psychologist, 56(12), 1080–1098.

Klein, B., Richards, J. C., & Austin, D. W. (2006). Efficacy of internet therapy for panic disorder. *Journal of Behavior Therapy & Experimental Psychiatry, 37*(3), 213–238.

Klein, K., & Boals, A. (2001a). The relationship of life event stress and working memory capacity. *Applied Cognitive Psychology, 15*(5), 565–579.

Klein, K., & Boals, A. (2001b). Expressive writing can increase working memory capacity. *Journal of Experimental Psychology: General, 130*(3), 520–533.

Kleinke, C. L., Peterson, T. R., & Rutledge, T. R. (1998). Effects of self-generated facial expressions on mood. *Journal of Personality and Social Psychology, 74*(1), 272–279.

Kleinplatz, P. J. (1996). The erotic encounter. *Journal of Humanistic Psychology, 36*(3), 105–123.

Klohnen, E. C., & Luo, S. (2003). Interpersonal attraction and personality: What is attractive—self similarity, ideal similarity, complementarity or attachment security? *Journal of Personality & Social Psychology, 85*(4), 709–722.

Knaus, W. J., & Ellis, A. (2002). *The procrastination workbook: Your personalized program for breaking free from the patterns that hold you back*. Oakland, CA: New Harbinger Press.

Knight, J. (2005). The truth about lying. *Nature, 428*, 692–694.

Knoops, K. T. B., de Groot, L. C., Kromhout, D., Perrin, A., et al. (2004). Mediterranean diet, lifestyle factors, and 10-year mortality in elderly European men and women. *Journal of the American Medical Association, 292*(12), 1433–1439.

Koch, C. (2004). *The quest for consciousness: A neurobiological approach*. Englewood, CO: Roberts.

Koch, W. H., & Pratarelli, M. E. (2004). Effects of intro/extraversion and sex on social internet use. *North American Journal of Psychology, 6*(3), 371–382.

Kohlberg, L. (1969). The cognitive-developmental approach to socialization. In A. Goslin (Ed.), *Handbook of socialization theory and research*. Chicago: Rand McNally.

Kohlberg, L. (1981). *Essays on moral development* (Vol. 1): *The philosophy of moral development*. San Francisco: Harper.

Kohn, C. S., & Antonuccio, D. O. (2002). Treatment of kleptomania using cognitive and behavioral strategies. *Clinical Case Studies, 1*(1), 25–38.

Köke, A., Schouten J. S., Lamerichs-Geelen. M. J. H., Lipsch J. S. M., et al. (2004). Pain reducing effect of three types of transcutaneous electrical nerve stimulation in

patients with chronic pain: A randomized crossover trial. *Pain, 108*(1–2), 36–42.

Kolb, B. (1990). Recovery from occipital stroke: A self-report and an inquiry into visual processes. *Canadian Journal of Psychology, 44*(2), 130–147.

Kolb, B., & Whishaw, I.Q. (2006). *Introduction to brain and behavior* (2nd ed.). New York: Freeman-Worth.

Kolb, B., Gibb, R., & Gorny, G. (2003). Experience-dependent changes in dendritic arbor and spine density in neocortex vary with age and sex. *Neurobiology of Learning & Memory, 79*(1), 1–10.

Kornhaber, M. L., & Gardner, H. (2006). Multiple intelligences: Developments in implementation and theory. In M. A. Constas & R. J. Sternberg (Eds.), *Translating theory and research into educational practice: Developments in content domains, large-scale reform, and intellectual capacity*. Mahwah, NJ: Erlbaum.

Korol, C., Craig, K. D., & Firestone, P. (2003). Dissociative and somatoform disorders. In P. Firestone & W. L. Marshall (Eds.), *Abnormal psychology: Perspectives* (2nd ed.). Toronto: Prentice Hall.

Koss, M. P. (1993). Rape. *American Psychologist, 48*(10), 1062–1069.

Koss, M. P. (2000). Blame, shame, and community: Justice responses to violence against women. *American Psychologist, 55*(11), 1332–1343.

Kosslyn, S. M. (1983). *Ghosts in the mind's machine*. New York: Norton.

Kosslyn, S. M. (1985). Stalking the mental image. *Psychology Today*, May, 23–28.

Kosslyn, S. M. (2005). Mental images and the brain. *Cognitive Neuropsychology, 22*(3–4), 333–347.

Kosslyn, S. M., Ball, T. M., & Reiser, B. J. (1978). Visual images preserve metric spatial information: Evidence from studies of image scanning. *Journal of Experimental Psychology: Human Perception and Performance, 4*, 47–60.

Kosslyn, S. M., Thompson, W. L., Costantini-Ferrando, M. F., Alpert, N. M., et al. (2000). Hypnotic visual illusion alters color processing in the brain. *American Journal of Psychiatry, 157*(8), 1279–1284.

Kosson, D. S., Suchy, Y., Mayer, A. R., & Libby, J. (2002). Facial affect recognition in criminal psychopaths. *Emotion, 2*(4), 398–411.

Kotkin, M., Daviet, C., & Gurin, J. (1996). The Consumer Reports mental health survey. *American Psychologist, 51*(10), 1080–1082.

Kottler, J. A. (2004). *Introduction to therapeutic counseling*. Belmont,

CA: Cengage Learning/Wadsworth.

Kowert, P. A. (2002). *Groupthink or deadlock: When do leaders learn from their advisors? SUNY series on the presidency*. Albany, NY: State University of New York Press.

Kozart, M. F. (2002). Understanding efficacy in psychotherapy. *American Journal of Orthopsychiatry, 72*(2), 217–231.

Krakow, B., & Krakow, J. K. (2002). *Turning nightmares into dreams*. Albuquerque, NM: New Sleepy-Times.

Krakow, B., & Zadra, A. (2006). Clinical management of chronic nightmares: Imagery rehearsal therapy. *Behavioral Sleep Medicine, 4*(1), 45–70.

Krall, E. A., Garvey, A. J., & Garcia, R. I. (2002). Smoking relapse after 2 years of abstinence: Findings from the VA Normative Aging Study. *Nicotine & Tobacco Research, 4*(1), 95–100.

Krantz, D. S., & McCeney, M. K. (2002). Effects of psychological and social factors on organic disease. *Annual Review of Psychology, 53*, 341–369.

Krishnan, H. A., & Park, D. (2005). A few good women—on top management teams. *Journal of Business Research, 58*, 1712–1720.

Kristof-Brown, A. L., Barrick, M. R., & Franke, M. (2002). Applicant impression management: Dispositional influences and consequences for recruiter perceptions of fit and similarity. *Journal of Management, 28*, 27–46.

Ksir, C. J., Hart, C. L., & Ray, O. S. (2006). *Drugs, society, and human behavior* (11th ed.). New York: McGraw-Hill.

Kübler-Ross, E. (1975). *Death: The final stage of growth*. Englewood Cliffs, NJ: Prentice Hall.

Kubovy, M., & Gepshtein, S. (2003). Grouping in space and in space-time: An exercise in phenomenological psychophysics. In R. Kimchi, M. Behrmann, et al. (Eds.), *Perceptual organization in vision: Behavioral and neural perspectives*. Mahwah, NJ: Erlbaum.

Kuehner, C. (2003). Gender differences in unipolar depression: an update of epidemiological findings and possible explanations. *Acta Psychiatrica Scandinavica, 108*(3), 163–174.

Kuhl, P. K. (2004). Early language acquisition: Cracking the speech code. *Nature Reviews Neuroscience, 5*(11), 831–841.

Kuhn, C. M., & Wilson, W. A. (2001). Our dangerous love affair with Ecstasy. *Cerebrum, 3*(2), 22–33.

Kulik, J., Mahler, H. I. M., & Moore, P. J. (2003). Social comparison affiliation under threat: Effects on recovery from major surgery. In P. Salovey & A. J. Rothman (Eds.), *Social psychology of health: Key readings in social psychology.* New York: Psychology Press.

Kumaran, D., & Maguire, E. A. (2005). The human hippocampus: Cognitive maps or relational memory? *Journal of Neuroscience, 25*(31), 7254–7259.

Kunkel, M. A. (1993). A teaching demonstration involving perceived lunar size. *Teaching of Psychology, 20*(3), 178–180.

Kusseling, F. S., Shapiro, M. F., Greenberg, J. M., & Wenger, N. S. (1996). Understanding why heterosexual adults do not practice safer sex: A comparison of two samples. *AIDS Education & Prevention, 8*(3), 247–257.

Laan, E., Everaerd, W., van Bellen, G., & Hanewald, G. J. F. P. (1994). Women's sexual and emotional responses to male- and female-produced erotica. *Archives of Sexual Behavior, 23*(2), 153–169.

LaBar, K. S., & LeDoux, J. E. (2002). Emotional learning circuits in animals and man. In R. J. Davidson, K. R. Scherer, et al. (Eds.), *Handbook of affective sciences.* New York: Oxford University Press.

Laberge, L., Petit, D., Simard, C., Vitaro, F., et al. (2001). Development of sleep patterns in early adolescence. *Journal of Sleep Research, 10*(1), 59–67.

LaBerge, S. (2000). Lucid dreaming: Evidence and methodology. In F. E. Pace-Schott, M. Solms, et al. (Eds.), *Sleep and dreaming: Scientific advances and reconsiderations.* Cambridge, UK: Cambridge University Press.

Labov, W. (1973). The boundaries of words and their meanings. In C. J. N. Bailey & R. W. Shuy (Eds.), *New ways of analyzing variation in English.* Washington, DC: Georgetown University Press.

LaBrie, R. A., & Shaffer, H. J. (2007). Gambling with adolescent health. *Journal of Adolescent Health, 40*(5), 387–389.

Lacayo, A. (1995). Neurologic and psychiatric complications of cocaine abuse. *Neuropsychiatry, Neuropsychology, & Behavioral Neurology, 8*(1), 53–60.

Lachman, M. E. (2004). Development in midlife. *Annual Review of Psychology, 55,* 305–331.

Lackner, J. R., & DiZio, P. (2005). Vestibular, proprioceptive, and haptic contributions to spatial orientation. *Annual Review of Psychology, 56,* 115–147.

Lamb, M. R., & Yund, E. W. (1996). Spatial frequency and attention. *Perception & Psychophysics, 58*(3), 363–373.

Lambert, M. J. (1999). Are differential treatment effects inflated by researcher therapy allegiance? *Clinical Psychology: Science & Practice, 6*(1), 127–130.

Lambert, M. J., & Cattani-Thompson, K. (1996). Current findings regarding the effectiveness of counseling. *Journal of Counseling & Development, 74*(6), 601–608.

Lambert, M. J., & Ogles, B. M. (2002). The efficacy and effectiveness of psychotherapy. In M. J. Lambert (Ed.), *Handbook of psychotherapy and behavior change* (5th ed.). New York: Wiley.

Lambert, W. E. (1987). The effects of bilingual and bicultural experiences on children's attitudes and social perspectives. In P. Homel, M. Palij, et al. (Eds.), *Childhood bilingualism.* Mahwah, NJ: Erlbaum.

Lance, C. E., LaPointe, J. A., & Stewart, A. M. (1994). A test of the context dependency of three causal models of halo rater error. *Journal of Applied Psychology, 79*(3), 332–340.

Landau, J. D., & Bavaria A. J. (2003). Does deliberate source monitoring reduce students's misconceptions about psychology? *Teaching of Psychology, 30,* 311–314.

Landy, F. J., & Conte, J. M. (2007). *Work in the 21st century: An introduction to industrial and organizational psychology* (2nd ed.). London: Blackwell.

Landy, F. J., Shankster, L. J., & Kohler, S. S. (1994). Personnel selection and placement. *Annual Review of Psychology, 45,* 261–296.

Langer, E. J. (2000). Mindful learning. *Current Directions in Psychological Science, 9*(6), 220–223.

Langleben, D. D., Dattilio, F. M., & Gutheil, T. G. (2006). True lies: Delusions and lie-detection technology. *Journal of Psychiatry & Law, 34*(3), 351–370.

Langleben, D. D., Loughead, J. W., Bilker, W. B., Ruparel, K., et al. (2005). Telling truth from lie in individual subjects with fast event-related fMRI. *Human Brain Mapping, 26*(4), 262–272.

Langleben, D. D., Schroeder, L, Maldjian, J. A., Gur, R. C., et al. (2002). Brain activity during simulated deception: An event-related functional magnetic resonance study. *NeuroImage, 15,* 727–732.

Langone, M. D. (2002). Cults, conversion, science, and harm. *Cultic Studies Review, 1*(2), 178–186.

Lanzetta, J. T., & Englis, B. G. (1989). Expectations of cooperation and competition and their effects on observers' vicarious emotional responses. *Journal of Personality & Social Psychology, 56*(4), 543–554.

Larner, A. J., Moss, J., Rossi, M. L., & Anderson, M. (1994). Congenital insensitivity to pain. *Journal of Neurology, Neurosurgery & Psychiatry, 57*(8), 973–974.

Larsen, R. J., & Buss, D. M. (2005). *Personality psychology* (2nd ed.). New York: McGraw-Hill.

Larsen, R. J., & Kasimatis, M. (1990). Individual differences in entrainment of mood to the weekly calendar. *Journal of Personality & Social Psychology, 58*(1), 164–171.

Larsen, R.J., & Prizmic, Z. (2004). Affect regulation. In R. Baumeister & K. D. Voohs (Eds.), *Handbook of self-regulation: Research, theory, and applications.* New York: Guilford.

Larson, M. E., Houlihan, D., & Goernert, P. N. (1995). Effects of informational feedback on aluminum can recycling. *Behavioral Interventions, 10*(2), 111–117.

Larsson, B., Carlsson, J., Fichtel, Å., & Melin, L. (2005). Relaxation treatment of adolescent headache sufferers: Results from a school-based replication series. *Headache: The Journal of Head & Face Pain, 45*(6), 692–704.

Larsson, J.-O., Larsson, H., & Lichtenstein, P. (2004). Genetic and environmental contributions to stability and change of ADHD symptoms between 8 and 13 years of age: A longitudinal twin study. *Journal of the American Academy of Child & Adolescent Psychiatry, 43*(10), 1267–1275.

Latané, B., Nida, S. A., & Wilson, D. W. (1981). The effects of group size on helping behavior. In J. P. Rushton & R. M. Sorrentino (Eds.), *Altruism and helping behavior: Social, personality and developmental perspectives.* Mahwah, NJ: Erlbaum.

Lattal, K. A., Reilly, M. P., & Kohn, J. P. (1998). Response persistence under ratio and interval reinforcement schedules. *Journal of the Experimental Analysis of Behavior, 70*(2), 165–183.

Laub, J. H., & Sampson, R. J. (2003). *Shared beginnings, divergent lives: Delinquent boys to age 70.* Cambridge, MA: Harvard University Press.

Laumann, E., Michael, R., Michaels, S., & Gagnon, J. (1994). *The social organization of sexuality.* Chicago: University of Chicago Press.

Laurent, G., Stopfer, M., Friedrich, R. W., Rabinovich, M. I., et al. (2001). Odor encoding as an active, dynamical process. *Annual Review of Neuroscience, 24,* 263–297.

Lavie, P. (2001). Sleep–wake as a biological rhythm. *Annual Review of Psychology, 52,* 277–303.

Lawson, H. M., & Leck, K. (2006). Dynamics of Internet dating. *Social Science Computer Review, 24*(2), 189–208.

Lay, C., & Verkuyten, M. (1999). Ethnic identity and its relation to personal self-esteem. *Journal of Social Psychology, 139*(3), 288–299.

Lazar, S. W. (2005). Mindfulness research. In C. K. Germer, R. D. Siegel, et al. (Eds.), *Mindfulness and psychotherapy.* New York: Guilford.

Lazar, S. W., Bush, G., Gollub, R. L., Fricchione, G. L., et al. (2000). Functional brain mapping of the relaxation response and meditation. *Neuroreport, 11*(7), 1581–1585.

Lazarus, R. S. (1991a). Progress on a cognitive–motivational–relational theory of emotion. *American Psychologist, 46*(8), 819–834.

Lazarus, R. S. (1991b). Cognition and motivation in emotion. *American Psychologist, 46*(4), 352–367.

Lazev, A. B., Herzog, T. A., & Brandon, T. H. (1999). Classical conditioning of environmental cues to cigarette smoking. *Experimental and Clinical Psychopharmacology, 7*(1), 56–63.

Leal, M. C., Shin, Y. J., Laborde, M.-L., Calmels, M.-N., et al. (2003). Music perception in adult cochlear implant recipients. *Acta Oto-Laryngologica, 123*(7), 826–835.

Leavens, D. A., & Hopkins, W. D. (1998). Intentional communication by chimpanzees. *Developmental Psychology, 34*(5), 813–822.

LeBlanc, G., & Bearison, D. J. (2004). Teaching and learning as a bi-directional activity: Investigating dyadic interactions between child teachers and child learners. *Cognitive Development, 19*(4), 499–515.

Lederman, S. J., & Klatzky, R. L. (2004). Haptic identification of common objects: Effects of constraining the manual exploration process. *Perception & Psychophysics, 66*(4), 618–628.

Lederman, S. J., Howe, R. D., Klatzky, R. L., & Hamilton, C. (2004). Force variability during surface contact with bare finger or rigid probe. *12th International Symposium on Haptic Interfaces for Virtual Environment and Teleoperator Systems,*154–160.

LeDoux, J. (1996). *The emotional brain: The mysterious underpinnings of emotional life.* New York: Simon & Schuster.

LeDoux, J. (1999). The power of emotions. In R. Conlan (Ed.), *States of mind.* New York: Wiley.

LeDoux, J. E., & Gorman, J. M. (2001). A call to action: Overcoming anxiety through active coping. *American Journal of Psychiatry. 158*(12), 1953–1955.

Lee, J. M., Ku, J. H., Jang, D. P., Kim, D., et al. (2002). Virtual reality system for treatment of the fear of public speaking using image-based rendering and moving pictures. *CyberPsychology & Behavior, 5*(3), 191–195.

Lee, M., Zimbardo, P. G., & Bertholf, M. (1977). Shy murderers. *Psychology Today*, Nov., 69.

Leenaars, A. A., Lester, D., & Wenckstern, S. (2005). Coping with: The art and the research. In R. I. Yufit & D. Lester (Eds.), *Assessment, treatment, and prevention of suicidal behavior*. New York: Wiley.

Leeper, R. W. (1935). A study of a neglected portion of the field of learning: The development of sensory organization. *Pedagogical Seminary & Journal of Genetic Psychology, 46*, 41–75.

Lefcourt, H. M. (2003). Humor as a moderator of life stress in adults. In C. E. Schaefer (Ed.), *Play therapy with adults*. New York: Wiley.

Lefkowitz, E. S., & Zeldow, P. B. (2006). Masculinity and femininity predict optimal mental health: A belated test of the androgyny hypothesis. *Journal of Personality Assessment, 87*(1), 95–101.

Lefrançois, G. R. (2006). *Theories of human learning: What the old woman said* (5th ed.). Belmont, CA: Cengage Learning/Wadsworth.

Lehman, C. M., & DuFrene, D. D. (2008). *Business communication* (15th ed.). Belmont, CA: Cengage Learning/South-western.

Lehman, D. R., Chiu, C., & Schaller, M. (2004). Psychology and culture. *Annual Review of Psychology, 55*, 689–714.

Leichtman, M. (2004). Projective tests: The nature of the task. In M. J. Hilsenroth & D. L. Segal (Eds.), *Comprehensive handbook of psychological assessment* (Vol. 2): *Personality assessment*. New York: Wiley.

Leiter, M. P., & Maslach, C. (2005). *Banishing burnout: Six strategies for improving your relationship with work*. San Francisco: Jossey-Bass.

Lejuez, C. W., Eifert, G. H., Zvolensky, M. J., & Richards, J. B. (2000). Preference between onset predictable and unpredictable administrations of 20% carbon-dioxide-enriched air: Implications for better understanding the etiology and treatment of panic disorder. *Journal of Experimental Psychology: Applied, 6*(4), 349–358.

Lench, H. C. (2004). Anger management: Diagnostic differences and treatment implications. *Journal of Social & Clinical Psychology, 23*(4), 512–531.

Lenton, A. P., & Bryan, A. (2005). An affair to remember: The role of sexual scripts in perceptions of sexual intent. *Personal Relationships, 12*(4), 483–498.

Lenzenweger, M. F., & Gottesman, I. I. (1994). Schizophrenia. In V. S. Ramachandran (Ed.), *Ency-*

clopedia of human behavior. San Diego: Academic Press.

Leor, J., Poole, W. K., & Kloner, R. A. (1996). Sudden cardiac death triggered by earthquake. *The New England Journal of Medicine, 334*(7), 413.

Lepore, F. E. (2002). When seeing is not believing. *Cerebrum, 4*(2), 23–38.

Leslie, K., & Ogilvie, R. (1996). Vestibular dreams: The effect of rocking on dream mentation. *Dreaming: Journal of the Association for the Study of Dreams, 6*(1), 1–16.

Lessow-Hurley, J. (2005). *Foundations of dual language instruction* (4th ed.). Boston: Allyn & Bacon.

Lester, D. (2006). Sexual orientation and suicidal behavior. *Psychological Reports, 99*(3), 923–924.

Lester, D., & Yang, B. (2005). Regional and time-series studies of suicide in nations of the world. *Archives of Suicide Research, 9*(2), 123–133.

Lettvin, J. Y. (1961). Two remarks on the visual system of the frog. In W. Rosenblith (Ed.), *Sensory communication*. Cambridge, MA: MIT Press.

LeUnes, J., & Nation, J. R. (2002). *Sport psychology* (3rd ed.). Belmont, CA: Cengage Learning/Wadsworth.

Levant, R. F. (1996). The new psychology of men. *Professional Psychology: Research & Practice, 27*(3), 259–265.

Levant, R. F. (2001). Men and masculinity. In J. Worell (Ed.), *Encyclopedia of women and gender*. San Diego: Academic Press.

Levant, R. F. (2003). Treating male alexithymia. In L. B. Silverstein & T. J. Goodrich (Eds.), *Feminist family therapy: Empowerment in social context*. Washington, DC: American Psychological Association.

Levant, R. F., Good, G. E., Cook, S. W., O'Neil, J. M., et al. (2006). The Normative Male Alexithymia Scale: Measurement of a gender-linked syndrome. *Psychology of Men & Masculinity, 7*(4), 212–224.

LeVay, S. (1993). *The sexual brain*. Cambridge, MA: MIT Press.

LeVay, S. (2006). *The biology of sexual orientation*. Retrieved July 30, 2007, from http://members.aol.com/slevay/page22.html.

LeVay, S., & Valente, S. M. (2006). *Human sexuality* (2nd ed.). Sunderland, MA: Sinauer Associates.

Levenston, G. K., Patrick, C. J., Bradley, M. M., & Lange, P. J. (2000). The psychopathic observer. *Journal of Abnormal Psychology, 109*, 373–385.

Levesque, M. J., Steciuk, M., & Ledley, C. (2002). Self-disclosure patterns among well-acquainted individuals. *Social Behavior & Personality, 30*(6), 579–592.

Levett, L. M., Danielsen, E. M., Kovera, M. B., & Cutler, B. L. (2005). The psychology of jury and juror decision making. In N. Brewer & K. D. Williams (Eds.), *Psychology and law: An empirical perspective*. New York: Guilford.

Levi, A. M. (1998). Are defendants guilty if they were chosen in a lineup? *Law & Human Behavior, 22*(4), 389–407.

Levin, B. E. (2006). Metabolic sensing neurons and the control of energy homeostasis. *Physiology & Behavior, 89*(4), 486–489.

Levin, R., & Fireman, G. (2002). Nightmare prevalence, nightmare distress, and self-reported psychological disturbance. *Sleep: Journal of Sleep & Sleep Disorders Research, 25*(2), 205–212.

Levine, D. (2000). Virtual attraction: What rocks your boat. *CyberPsychology & Behavior, 3*(4), 565–573.

Levine, M., & Harrison, K. (2004). Media's role in the perpetuation and prevention of negative body image and disordered eating. In J. K. Thompson (Ed.), *Handbook of eating disorders and obesity*. New York: Wiley.

Levine, R. V. (1998). *A geography of time*. New York: Basic.

Levine, R. V. (2003). The kindness of strangers. *American Scientist, 91*(May-June), 226–233.

Levinson, D. J. (1986). A conception of adult development. *American Psychologist, 41*(1), 3–13.

Levinson, D. J., & Levinson, J. D. (1996). *The seasons of a woman's life*. New York: Knopf.

Levitsky, D. A., Nussbaum, M., Halbmaier, C.A., & Mrdjenovic, G. (2003). The Freshman 15: A model for the study of techniques to curb the "epidemic" of obesity. *Society for the Study of Ingestive Behavior: Annual Meeting*, July 15–19, University of Groningen, Haren, The Netherlands.

Levy, D. A. (2003). *Tools of critical thinking: Metathoughts for psychology*. Long Grove, IL: Waveland Press.

Levy, J., & Reid, M. (1976). Cerebral organization. *Science, 194*, 337–339.

Lewchanin, S., & Zubrod, L. A. (2001). Choices in life: A clinical tool for facilitating midlife review. *Journal of Adult Development, 8*(3), 193–196.

Lewis, M. (1995). Self-conscious emotions. *American Scientist, 83*(Jan.–Feb.), 68–78.

Lewis, P. S., Goodman, S. H., & Fandt, P. M. (1995). *Management*. St Paul, MN: West.

Lewy, A. J., Bauer V. K., Cutler, N. L., Sack, R. L., et al. (1998). Morning vs. evening light treatment of patients with winter de-

pression. *Archives of General Psychiatry, 55*(10), 890–896.

Leyendecker, B., Harwood, R. L., Comparini, L., & Yalçinkaya, A. (2005). Socioeconomic status, ethnicity, and parenting. In T. Luster & L. Okagaki (Eds.), *Parenting: An ecological perspective* (2nd ed.). Mahwah, NJ: Erlbaum.

Lichtman, A. H., & Martin, B. R. (2006). Understanding the pharmacology and physiology of cannabis dependence. In R. Roffman & R. S. Stephens (Eds.), *Cannabis dependence. Its nature, consequences and treatment*. New York: Cambridge University Press.

Liddell, S. K. (2003). *Grammar, gesture and meaning in American Sign Language*. Cambridge, UK: Cambridge University Press.

Lidz, C. W., Banks, S., Simon, L., Schubert, C., et al. (2007). Violence and mental illness: A new analytic approach. *Law & Human Behavior, 31*(1), 23–31.

Lieberman, D. A. (2004). *Learning and memory: An integrative approach*. Belmont, CA: Cengage Learning/Wadsworth.

Lievens, F., & Sackett, P. R. (2006). Video-based versus written situational judgment tests: A comparison in terms of predictive validity. *Journal of Applied Psychology, 91*(5), 1181–1188.

Lilienfeld, S. O. (1999). Projective measures of personality and psychopathology. *Skeptical Inquirer*, Sept.-Oct., 32–39.

Lilienfeld, S. O. (2005). Pseudoscience, nonscience, and nonsense in clinical psychology: Dangers and remedies. In K. A. Fowler, J. M. Lohr, et al. (Eds.), *Destructive trends in mental health: The well-intentioned path to harm*. New York: Routledge.

Lilienfeld, S. O., Fowler, K. A., Lohr, J. M., & Lynn, S. (2005). Pseudoscience, nonscience & nonsense in clinical psychology: Dangers and remedies. In R. H. Wright & N. A. Cummings (Eds.), *Destructive trends in mental health: The well-intentioned path to harm*. New York: Routledge.

Lindemann, B. (2000). A taste for umami. *Nature Neuroscience, 3*, 99–100.

Lindemann, B. (2001). Receptors and transduction in taste. *Nature, 413*, 219–225.

Linden, W. (2005). *Stress management: From basic science to better practice*. Thousand Oaks, CA: Sage.

Linderoth, B., & Foreman, R. D. (2006). Mechanisms of spinal cord stimulation in painful syndromes: Role of animal models. *Pain Medicine, 7*(Suppl 1), S14–S26.

Lindsay, E. W., Mize, J., & Pettit, G. S. (1997). Differential pay patterns of mothers and fathers of sons and daughters. *Sex Roles, 37*(9–10), 643–661.

Lipsey, M. W., & Wilson, D. B. (1993). The efficacy of psychological, educational, and behavioral treatment: Confirmation from meta-analysis. *American Psychologist, 48,* 1181–1209.

Liu, X., Matochik, J. A., Cadet, J., & London, E. D. (1998). Smaller volume of prefrontal lobe in polysubstance abusers. *Neuropsychopharmacology, 18*(4), 243–252.

Liu, Y., Gao, J., Liu, H., & Fox, P. T. (2000). The temporal response of the brain after eating revealed by functional MRI. *Nature, 405,* 1058–1062.

Locke, B. D., & Mahalik, J. R. (2005). Examining masculinity norms, problem drinking, and athletic involvement as predictors of sexual aggression in college men. *Journal of Counseling Psychology, 52*(3), 279–283.

Loeber, R., & Hay, D. (1997). Key issues in the development of aggression and violence from childhood to early adulthood. *Annual Review of Psychology, 48,* 371–410.

Loehlin, J. C., McCrae, R. R., Costa, P. T., & John, O. (1998). Heritabilities of common and measure-specific components of the Big Five personality factors. *Journal of Research in Personality, 32*(4), 431–453.

Loftus, E., & Loftus, G. (1980). On the permanence of stored information in the human brain. *American Psychologist, 35,* 409–420.

Loftus, E. F. (2003a). Make-believe memories. *American Psychologist, 58*(11), 867–873.

Loftus, E. F. (2003b). Memory in Canadian courts of law. *Canadian Psychology, 44*(3), 207–212.

Loftus, E. F., & Bernstein, D. M. (2005). Rich false memories: The royal road to success. In A. F. Healy (Ed.), *Experimental cognitive psychology and its applications.* Washington, DC: American Psychological Association.

Loftus, E. F., & Ketcham, K. (1994). *The myth of repressed memory: False memories and allegations of abuse.* New York: St. Martin's Press.

Loftus, E. F., & Palmer, J. C. (1974). Reconstruction of automobile destruction: An example of interaction between language and memory. *Journal of Verbal Learning & Verbal Behavior, 13,* 585–589.

Loftus, G. R., & Mackworth, N. H. (1978). Cognitive determinants of fixation location during picture viewing. *Journal of Experimental Psychology: Human Perception & Performance, 4,* 565–572.

LoLordo, V. M. (2001). Learned helplessness and depression. In M. E. Carroll & J. B. Overmier (Eds.), *Animal research and human health: Advancing human welfare through*

behavioral science. Washington, DC: American Psychological Association.

Long, E. C., & Andrews, D. W. (1990). Perspective taking as a predictor of marital adjustment. *Journal of Personality & Social Psychology, 59*(1), 126–131.

Long, V. O. (1989). Relation of masculinity to self-esteem and self-acceptance in male professionals, college students, and clients. *Journal of Counseling Psychology, 36*(1), 84–87.

López, S. R., & Guarnaccia, P. J. J. (2000). Cultural psychopathology. *Annual Review of Psychology, 51,* 571–598.

Lorenz, K. (1966). *On aggression.* Translated by M. Kerr-Wilson. New York: Harcourt Brace Jovanovich.

Lorenz, K. (1974). *The eight deadly sins of civilized man.* Translated by M. Kerr-Wilson. New York: Harcourt Brace Jovanovich.

Lovaas, O., & Simmons, J. (1969). Manipulation of self-destruction in three retarded children. *Journal of Applied Behavior Analysis, 2,* 143–157.

Low, K. G., & Feissner, J. M. (1998). Seasonal affective disorder in college students: Prevalence and latitude. *Journal of American College Health, 47*(3), 135–137.

Low, S. M. (2001). The edge and the center: Gated communities and the discourse of urban fear. *American Anthropologist, 103*(1), 45–58.

Lucas, F., & Sclafani, A. (1990). Hyperphagia in rats produced by a mixture of fat and sugar. *Physiology & Behavior, 47*(1), 51–55.

Lucas, J. L., & Heady, R. B. (2002). Flextime commuters and their driver stress, feelings of time urgency, and commute satisfaction. *Journal of Business & Psychology, 16*(4), 565–572.

Luce, G. G. (1965). *Current research on sleep and dreams.* Health Service Publication no. 1389. Washington, DC: U.S. Department of Health, Education, and Welfare.

Luchins, D. J., Cooper, A. E., Hanrahan, P., & Rasinski, K. (2004). Psychiatrists' attitudes toward involuntary hospitalization. *Psychiatric Services, 55*(9), 1058–1060.

Ludwig, T. D., Gray, T. W., & Rowell, A. (1998). Increasing recycling in academic buildings. *Journal of Applied Behavior Analysis, 31*(4), 683–686.

Lumley, M. A. (2004). Alexithymia, emotional disclosure, and health: A program of research. *Journal of Personality, 72*(6), 1271–1300.

Lundh, L., Berg, B., Johansson, H., Nilsson, L., et al. (2002). Social anxiety is associated with a negatively distorted perception of one's own voice. *Cognitive Behaviour Therapy, 31*(1), 25–30.

Luppa, M., Heinrich, S., Angermeyer, M. C., König, H.-H., et al. (2007). Cost-of-illness studies of depression: A systematic review. *Journal of Affective Disorders, 98*(1–2), 29–43.

Luria, A. R. (1968). *The mind of a mnemonist.* New York: Basic Books.

Lustig, C., May, C. P., Hasher, L. (2001). Working memory span and the role of proactive interference. *Journal of Experimental Psychology: General, 130*(2), 199–207.

Luyben, P. D., Hipworth, K., & Pappas, T. (2003). Effects of CAI on the academic performance and attitudes of college students. *Teaching of Psychology, 30*(2), 154–158.

Lykken, D. T. (1998). *A tremor in the blood: Uses and abuses of the lie detector.* New York: Plenum.

Lykken, D. T. (2001). Lie detection. In W. E. Craighead & C. B. Nemeroff (Eds.), *The Corsini encyclopedia of psychology and behavioral science* (3rd ed.). New York: Wiley.

Lynch, K. B., Geller, S. R., & Schmidt, M. G. (2004). Multiyear evaluation of the effectiveness of a resilience-based prevention program for young children. *Journal of Primary Prevention, 24*(3), 335–353.

Lynch, T. R., Robins, C. J., Morse, J. Q., & Krause, E. D. (2001). A mediational model relating affect intensity, emotion inhibition, and psychological distress. *Behavior Therapy, 32*(3), 519–536.

Lynn, S. J., & Kirsch, I. (2006). Introduction: Definitions and early history. In S. J. Lynn & I. Kirsch (Eds.), *Essentials of clinical hypnosis: An evidence-based approach.* Washington, DC: American Psychological Association.

Lyons, A. C., & Chamberlain, K. (2006). *Health psychology.* Cambridge, MA: Cambridge University Press.

Lyubomirsky, S., & Tucker, K. L. (1998). Implications of individual differences in subjective happiness for perceiving, interpreting, and thinking about life events. *Motivation & Emotion, 22*(2), 155–186.

Maas, J. (1999). *Power Sleep.* New York: HarperCollins.

Maccoby, E. E. (1990). Gender and relationships: A developmental account. *American Psychologist, 45*(4), 513–520.

Maccoby, E. E., & Jacklin, C. N. (1974). *The psychology of sex differences.* Stanford, CA: Stanford University Press.

Mack, A. (2002). Is the visual world a grand illusion? *Journal of Consciousness Studies, 9*(5–6), 102–110.

Mackintosh, N. J. (2003). Pavlov and associationism. *Spanish Journal of Psychology, 6*(2), 177–184.

Macklin, C. B., & McDaniel, M. A. (2005). The bizarreness effect: Dissociation between item and source memory. *Memory, 13*(7), 682–689.

MacLeod, C. M. (2005). The Stroop task in cognitive research. In A. Wenzel & D. C. Rubin (Eds.), *Cognitive methods and their application to clinical research.* Washington, DC: American Psychological Association.

Macmillan, R. (2001). Violence and the life course. *Annual Review of Sociology, 27,* 1–22.

Maddi, S. R. (2006). Hardiness: The courage to grow from stresses. *Journal of Positive Psychology, 1*(3), 160–168.

Maddock, J. E., Laforge, R. G., Rossi, J. S., & O'Hare, T. (2001). The College Alcohol Problems Scale. *Addictive Behaviors, 26,* 385–398.

Maddock, J., & Glanz, K. (2005). The relationship of proximal normative beliefs and global subjective norms to college students' alcohol consumption. *Addictive Behaviors, 30*(2), 315–323.

Maddox, K. B. (2004). Perspectives on racial phenotypicality bias. *Personality & Social Psychology Review, 8*(4), 383–401.

Maguire, E. A., Frackowiak, R. S. J., & Frith, C. D. (1997). Recalling routes around London: Activation of the hippocampus in taxi drivers. *Journal of Neuroscience, 17*(8), 7103.

Maguire, E. A., Valentine, E. R., Wilding, J. M., & Kapur, N. (2003). Routes to remembering: The brains behind superior memory. *Nature Neuroscience, 6*(1), 90–95.

Mah, K., & Binik, Y. M. (2001). The nature of human orgasm: A critical review of major trends. *Clinical Psychology Review, 21*(6), 823–856.

Mahay, J., & Laumann, E. O. (2004). Meeting and mating over the life course. In E. O. Laumann & R. Michael (Eds.), *The sexual organization of the city.* Chicago: University of Chicago Press.

Maheu, M. M., Pulier, M. L., Wilhelm, F. H., McMenamin, J. P., et al. (2004). *The mental health professional and the new technologies: A handbook for practice today.* Mahwah, NJ: Erlbaum.

Maier, N. R. F. (1949). *Frustration.* New York: McGraw-Hill.

Maier, S. F. (2001). Exposure to the stressor environment prevents the temporal dissipation of behavioral depression/learned helplessness. *Biological Psychiatry, 49*(9), 763–773.

Mailis-Gagnon, A., & Israelson, D. (2005). *Beyond pain: Making the mind-body connection.* Ann Arbor, MI: University of Michigan Press.

Malaspina, D., Reichenberg, A., Weiser, M., Fennig, S., et al.

(2005). Paternal age and intelligence: Implications for age-related genomic changes in male germ cells. *Psychiatric Genetics, 15*(2), 117–125.

Manalo, E. (2002). Uses of mnemonics in educational settings: A brief review of selected research. *Psychologia: An International Journal of Psychology in the Orient, 45*(2), 69–79.

Mandler, J. M., & McDonough, L. (1998). On developing a knowledge base in infancy. *Developmental Psychology, 34*(6), 1274–1288.

Mangan, M. A. (2004). A phenomenology of problematic sexual behavior occurring in sleep. *Archives of Sexual Behavior, 33*(3), 287–293.

Mangels, J. A., Picton, T. W., & Craik, F. I. M. (2001). Attention and successful episodic encoding: An event-related potential study. *Brain Research, 11*, 77–95.

Manschreck, T. C. (1996). Delusional disorder: The recognition and management of paranoia. *Journal of Clinical Psychiatry, 57*(3, Suppl), 32–38.

Mansouri, A., & Adityanjee. (1995). Delusion of pregnancy in males: A case report and literature review. *Psychopathology, 28*(6), 307–311.

Mantyla, T. (1986). Optimizing cue effectiveness: Recall of 600 incidentally learned words. *Journal of Experimental Psychology: Learning, Memory, and Cognition, 12*(1), 66–71.

Marcus, E. (2002). Psychoanalytic psychotherapy and psychoanalysis: An overview. In M. Hersen & W. H. Sledge (Eds.), *Encyclopedia of psychotherapy*. San Diego: Academic Press.

Margolin, G., & Gordis, E. B. (2000). The effects of family and community violence on children. *Annual Review of Psychology, 51*, 445–479.

Markowitz, J. C. (2005). Interpersonal therapy. In J. M. Oldham, A. E. Skodol et al. (Eds.), *The American Psychiatric Publishing textbook of personality disorders*. Washington, DC: American Psychiatric Publishing.

Marks, D. F. (2000). *The psychology of the psychic*. Buffalo, NY: Prometheus.

Markus, H. R., Uchida, Y., Omoregie, H., Townsend, S. S. M., et al. (2006). Going for the gold: Models of agency in Japanese and American contexts. *Psychological Science, 17*(2), 103–112.

Markus, H., & Nurius, P. (1986). Possible selves. *American Psychologist, 41*, 954–969.

Marmarosh, C., Holtz, A., & Schottenbauer, M. (2005). Group cohesiveness, group-derived collective self-esteem, group-derived hope, and the well-being of group therapy members. *Group Dynamics: Theory, Research, & Practice, 9*(1), 32–44.

Marsella, A. J. (1998). Urbanization, mental health, and social deviancy. *American Psychologist, 53*(6), 624–634.

Marshall, R. D., Bryant, R. A., Amsel, L., Suh, E. J., et al. (2007). The psychology of ongoing threat: Relative risk appraisal, the September 11 attacks, and terrorism-related fears. *American Psychologist, 62*(4), 304–316.

Marsiglia, F. F., Kulis, S., Hecht, M. L., & Sills, S. (2004). Ethnicity and ethnic identity as predictors of drug norms and drug use among preadolescents in the US southwest. *Substance Use & Misuse, 39*(7), 1061–1094.

Martens, R., & Trachet, T. (1998). *Making sense of astrology*. Amherst, MA: Prometheus.

Martin, A. J., & Marsh, H. W. (2003). Fear of failure: Friend or foe? *Australian Psychologist, 38*(1), 31–38.

Martin, C. L., & Fabes, R. A. (2001). The stability and consequences of young children's same-sex peer interactions. *Developmental Psychology, 37*(3), 431–446.

Martin, E. K., Taft, C. T., & Resick, P. A. (2007). A review of marital rape. *Aggression & Violent Behavior, 12*(3), 329–347.

Martin, G., & Pear, J. (2003). *Behavior modification* (7th ed.). Englewood Cliffs, NJ: Prentice Hall.

Martin, L. R., Friedman, H. S., & Schwartz, J. E. (2007). Personality and mortality risk across the life span: The importance of conscientiousness as a biopsychosocial attribute. *Health Psychology, 26*(4), 428–436.

Martin, S. (2007). The labyrinth of leadership. *Monitor on Psychology*, July-Aug., 90–91.

Martin, W. L. B., & Freitas, M. B. (2002). Mean mortality among Brazilian left- and right-handers: Modification or selective elimination. *Laterality, 7*(1), 31–44.

Martinez-Gonzalez, M. A., Gual, P., Lahortiga, F., Alonso, Y., et al. (2003). Parental factors, mass media influences, and the onset of eating disorders in a prospective population-based cohort. *Pediatrics, 111*, 315–320.

Martinko, M. J., Douglas, S. C., & Harvey, P. (2006). Understanding and managing workplace aggression. *Organizational Dynamics, 35*(2), 117–130.

Martino, G., & Marks, L. E. (2001). Synesthesia: Strong and weak. *Current Directions in Psychological Science, 10*(2), 61–65

Marx, B. P., Gross, A. M., & Adams, H. E. (1999). The effect of alcohol on the responses of sexually coercive and noncoercive men to an experimental rape analogue. *Sexual Abuse: Journal of Research & Treatment, 11*(2), 131–145.

Mashour, G. A., Walker, E. E., & Martuza, R. L. (2005). Psychosurgery: Past, present, and future. *Brain Research Reviews, 48*(3), 409–419.

Masi, G., Mucci, M., & Millepiedi, S. (2001). Separation anxiety disorder in children and adolescents. *CNS Drugs, 15*(2), 93–104.

Maslach, C., Schaufeli, W. B., & Leiter, M. P. (2001). Job burnout. *Annual Review of Psychology, 52*, 397–422.

Maslow, A. H. (1954). *Motivation and personality*. New York: Harper.

Maslow, A. H. (1967). Self-actualization and beyond. In J. F. T. Bugental (Ed.), *Challenges of humanistic psychology*. New York: McGraw-Hill.

Maslow, A. H. (1969). *The psychology of science*. Chicago: Henry Regnery.

Maslow, A. H. (1970). *Motivation and personality*. New York: Harper & Row.

Maslow, A. H. (1971). *The farther reaches of human nature*. New York: Viking.

Masse, L. C., & Tremblay, R. E. (1997). Behavior of boys in kindergarten and the onset of substance use during adolescence. *Archives of General Psychiatry, 54*(1), 62.

Masten, A. S. (2001). Ordinary magic: Resilience processes in development. *American Psychologist, 56*(3), 227–238.

Masters, W. H., & Johnson, V. E. (1966). *Human sexual response*. Boston: Little, Brown.

Masters, W. H., & Johnson, V. E. (1970). *The pleasure bond: A new look at sexuality and commitment*. Boston: Little, Brown.

Matheny, K. B., Brack, G. L., McCarthy, C. J., Penick, J. M. (1996). The effectiveness of cognitively-based approaches in treating stress-related symptoms. *Psychotherapy, 33*(2), 305–320.

Matossian, M. K. (1982). Ergot and the Salem witchcraft affair. *American Scientist, 70*, 355–357.

Matson, J. L., Sevin, J. A., Fridley D., & Love, S. R. (1990). Increasing spontaneous language in three autistic children. *Journal of Applied Behavior Analysis, 23*(2), 223–227.

Matthews, G., Deary, I. J., & Whiteman, M. C. (2003). *Personality traits* (2nd ed.). New York: Cambridge University Press.

Matthews, P. H., & Matthews, M. S. (2004). Heritage language instruction and giftedness in language minority students: Pathways toward success. *Journal of Secondary Gifted Education, 15*(1), 50–55.

Mayer, J. D. (2005). A tale of two visions: Can a new view of personality help integrate psychology? *American Psychologist, 60*(4), 294–307.

Mayer, J. D., Salovey, P., Caruso, D. R., & Sitarenios, G. (2001). Emotional intelligence as standard intelligence. *Emotion, 1*(3), 232–242.

Mayer, R. E. (1995). *Thinking, problem solving, and cognition*. New York: Freeman.

Mayer, R. E. (2004). Should there be a three-strikes rule against pure discovery learning? *American Psychologist, 59*(1), 14–19.

Mays, V. M., & Cochran, S. D. (2001). Mental health correlates of perceived discrimination among lesbian, gay, and bisexual adults in the United States. *American Journal of Public Health, 91*(11), 1869–1876.

Mazur, J. E. (2006). *Learning and behavior* (6th ed.). Englewood Cliffs, NJ: Prentice Hall.

McAdams, D. P., & Pals, J. L. (2006). A new Big Five: Fundamental principles for an integrative science of personality. *American Psychologist, 61*(3), 204–217.

McAlister, A. L., Ama, E., Barroso, C., Peters, R. J., et al. (2000). Promoting tolerance and moral engagement through peer modeling. *Cultural Diversity & Ethnic Minority Psychology, 6*(4), 363–373.

McBride, W. J., Murphy, J. M., & Ikemoto, S. (1999). Localization of brain reinforcement mechanisms. *Behavioural Brain Research, 101*(2), 129–152.

McCabe, M. P. (1992). A program for the treatment of inhibited sexual desire in males. *Psychotherapy, 29*(2), 288–296.

McCabe, M. P., & Ricciardelli, L. A. (2004). Weight and shape concerns of boys and men. In Thompson, J. K. (Ed.), *Handbook of eating disorders and obesity*. New York: Wiley.

McCall, W. V., Prudic, J., Olfson, M., & Sackeim, H. (2006). Health-related quality of life following ECT in a large community sample. *Journal of Affective Disorders, 90*(2–3), 269–274.

McCarley, R. W. (1998). Dreams: Disguise of forbidden wishes or transparent reflections of a distinct brain state? In R. M. Bilder, F. F. LeFever, et al. (Eds.), *Neuroscience of the mind on the centennial of Freud's Project for a Scientific Psychology*. New York: New York Academy of Sciences.

McCarthy, B. W. (1995). Bridges to sexual desire. *Journal of Sex Education & Therapy, 21*(2), 132–141.

McCarthy, B. W., & Fucito, L. M. (2005). Integrating medication, realistic expectations, and therapeutic interventions in the treatment of male sexual dysfunction. *Journal of Sex & Marital Therapy, 31*(4), 319–328.

McClelland, D. C. (1961). *The achieving society*. New York: Van Nostrand.

McClelland, D. C. (1965). Achievement and entrepreneurship. *Journal of Personality & Social Psychology, 1*, 389–393.

McClelland, D. C. (1975). *Power: The inner experience*. New York: Irvington.

McClelland, D. C. (1994). The knowledge-testing–educational complex strikes back. *American Psychologist, 49*(1), 66–69.

McClelland, D. C., & Cheriff, A. D. (1997). The immunoenhancing effects of humor on secretory IgA and resistance to respiratory infections. *Psychology & Health, 12*(3), 329–344.

McClelland, D. C., & Pilon, D. A. (1983). Sources of adult motives in patterns of parent behavior in early childhood. *Journal of Personality & Social Psychology, 44*, 564–574.

McClelland, J. L., & Rogers, T. T. (2003). The parallel distributed processing approach to semantic cognition. *Nature Reviews Neuroscience, 4*(4), 310–322.

McClelland, L., & Cook, S. W. (1980). Promoting energy conservation in master-metered apartments through group financial incentives. *Journal of Applied & Social Psychology, 10*, 20–31.

McCluskey, U. (2002). The dynamics of attachment and systems-centered group psychotherapy. *Group Dynamics, 6*(2), 131–142.

McCrae, R. R., & Costa, P. T. (2001). A five-factor theory of personality. In L. A. Pervin & O. P. John (Eds.), *Handbook of personality*. New York: Guilford.

McCrae, R. R., & Terracciano, A. (2005). Universal features of personality traits from the observer's perspective: Data from 50 cultures. *Journal of Personality & Social Psychology, 88*(3), 547–561.

McDonald, J. K., Yanchar, S. C., & Osguthorpe, R. (2005). Learning from programmed instruction: Examining implications for modern instructional technology. *Educational Technology Research & Development, 53*(2), 84–98.

McGaugh, J. L. (2004). The amygdala modulates the consolidation of memories of emotionally arousing experiences. *Annual Review of Neuroscience, 27*, 1–28.

McGregor, D. (1960). *The human side of enterprise*. New York: McGraw-Hill.

McGregor, I., McAdams, D. P., & Little, B. R. (2006). Personal projects, life stories, and happiness: On being true to traits. *Journal of Research in Personality, 40*(5), 551–572.

McGuffin, P., Rijsdijk, F., Andrew, M., Sham, P., et al. (2003). The heritability of bipolar affective dis-

order and the genetic relationship to unipolar depression. *Archives of General Psychiatry, 60*(5), 497–502.

McIntosh, W. D., Harlow, T. F., & Martin, L. L. (1995). Linkers and nonlinkers: Goal beliefs as a moderator of the effects of everyday hassles on rumination, depression, and physical complaints. *Journal of Applied Social Psychology, 25*(14), 1231–1244.

McKay, A. (2005). Sexuality and substance use: The impact of tobacco, alcohol, and selected recreational drugs on sexual function. *Canadian Journal of Human Sexuality, 14*(1–2), 47–56.

McKeever, L. (2006). Online plagiarism detection services: Saviour or scourge?. *Assessment & Evaluation in Higher Education, 31*(2), 155–165.

McKeever, W. F. (2000). A new family handedness sample with findings consistent with X-linked transmission. *British Journal of Psychology, 91*(1), 21–39.

McKeever, W. F., Cerone, L. J., Suter, P. J., & Wu, S. M. (2000). Family size, miscarriage-proneness, and handedness. *Laterality, 5*(2), 111–120.

McKenna, M. W., & Ossoff, E. P. (1998). Age differences in children's comprehension of a popular television program. *Child Study Journal, 28*(1), 52–68.

McKenzie, K., Serfaty, M., & Crawford, M. (2003). Suicide in ethnic minority groups. *British Journal of Psychiatry, 183*(2), 100–101.

McKim, W. A. (2003). *Drugs and behavior* (5th ed.). Englewood Cliffs, NJ: Prentice Hall.

McKone, E., Brewer, J. L., MacPherson, S., Rhodes, G., et al. (2007). Familiar other-race faces show normal holistic processing and are robust to perceptual stress. *Perception, 36*(2), 244–248.

McLewin, L. A., & Muller, R. T. (2006). Childhood trauma, imaginary companions, and the development of pathological dissociation. *Aggression & Violent Behavior, 11*(5), 531–545.

McLoyd, V. C., & Smith, J. (2002). Physical discipline and behavior problems in African American, European American, and Hispanic children: Emotional support as a moderator. *Journal of Marriage & Family, 64*(1), 40–53.

McMahon, S., & Koltzenburg, M. (2005). *Wall & Melzacks textbook of pain* (5th ed.). London: Churchill Livingstone.

McNally, R. J., & Clancy, S. A. (2005). Sleep paralysis, sexual abuse, and space alien abduction. *Transcultural Psychiatry, 42*(1), 113–122.

McNally, R. J., Clancy, S. A., & Barrett, H. M. (2004). Forgetting

trauma? In D. Reisberg & P. Hertel (Eds.), *Memory & emotion*. New York: Oxford University Press.

McNamara, D. S., & Scott, J. L. (2001). Working memory capacity and strategy use. *Memory & Cognition, 29*(1), 10–17.

McRobbie, H., & Hajek, P. (2007). Effects of rapid smoking on post-cessation urges to smoke. *Addiction, 102*(3), 483–489.

Mead, M. (1935). *Sex and temperament in three primitive societies*. New York: Morrow.

Medhus, E. (2001). *Child rearing challenges*. Retrieved May 25, 2007, from http://www.drmedhus.com/childchallenges.htm

Mehrabian, A. (2000). Beyond IQ. *Genetic Social, and General Psychology Monographs, 126*, 133–239.

Meier, P. S., Donmall, M. C., McElduff, P., Barrowclough, C., et al. (2006). The role of the early therapeutic alliance in predicting drug treatment dropout. *Drug & Alcohol Dependence, 83*(1), 57–64.

Meltzoff, A. N. (2005). Imitation and other minds: The "Like Me" Hypothesis. In S. Hurley & N. Chater (Eds.), *Perspectives on imitation: From neuroscience to social science* (Vol. 2): *Imitation, human development, and culture*. Cambridge, MA: MIT Press.

Meltzoff, A. N., & Prinz, W. (2002). *The imitative mind: Development, evolution, and brain bases*. Cambridge, MA: Cambridge University Press.

Melzack, R. (1999). From the gate to the neuromatrix. *Pain* (Suppl. 6), S121–S126.

Melzack, R., & Katz, J. (2004). The gate control theory: Reaching for the brain. In T. Hadjistavropoulos & K. D. Craig (Eds.), *Pain: Psychological perspectives*. Mahwah, NJ: Erlbaum.

Melzack, R., & Katz, J. (2006). Pain in the 21st century: The neuromatrix and beyond. In G. Young, A. W. Kane, et al. (Eds.), *Psychological knowledge in court: PTSD, pain, and TBI*. New York: Springer.

Melzack, R., & Wall, P. D. (1996). *The challenge of pain*. Harmondsworth, UK: Penguin.

Mendolia, M. (2002). An index of self-regulation of emotion and the study of repression in social contexts that threaten or do not threaten self-concept. *Emotion, 2*(3), 215–232.

Meneses, G. D., & Beerlipalacio, A. (2005). Recycling behavior: A multidimensional approach. *Environment & Behavior, 37*(6), 837–860.

Menzel, P., Eisert, S., Mann, C. C., & Kennedy, P. (1994). *Material world: A global family portrait*. San Francisco: Sierra Club Books.

Mercer, J. (2006). *Understanding attachment: Parenting, child care, and*

emotional development. Westport, CT: Praeger.

Merritt, J. M., Stickgold, R., Pace-Schott, E., Williams, J., et al. (1994). Emotion profiles in the dreams of men and women. *Consciousness & Cognition, 3*(1), 46–60.

Mesquita, B., & Markus, H. R. (2004). Culture and emotion: Models of agency as sources of cultural variation in emotion. In A. S. R. Manstead, S. R. Antony, et al. (Eds.), *Feelings and emotions: The Amsterdam symposium*. New York: Cambridge University Press.

Messer, S. B., & Kaplan, A. H. (2004). Outcomes and factors related to efficacy of brief psychodynamic therapy. In D. P. Charman (Ed.), *Core processes in brief psychodynamic psychotherapy: Advancing effective practice*. Mahwah, NJ: Erlbaum.

Messick, D. M., & Mackie, D. M. (1989). Intergroup relations. *Annual Review of Psychology, 40*, 45–81.

Messick, D. M., Wilke, H., Brewer, M., Kramer, R. M., et al. (1983). Individual adaptations and structural change as solutions to social dilemmas. *Journal of Personality & Social Psychology, 44*, 294–309.

Meyer, G. J., Finn, S. E., Eyde, L. D., Kay, G. G., et al. (2001). Psychological testing and psychological assessment. *American Psychologist, 56*(2), 128–165.

Meyers, L. (2006). Behind the scenes of the "Dr. Phil" show. *Monitor on Psychology, 37*(9), 63.

Michael, D., & Chen, S. (2006). *Serious games: Games that educate, train, and inform*. Boston, MA: Cengage Learning/Course Technology.

Michalak, E. E., & Lam, R. W. (2002). Seasonal affective disorder: The latitude hypothesis revisited. *Canadian Journal of Psychiatry, 47*(8), 787–788.

Michalko, M. (1998). *Cracking creativity*. Berkeley, CA: Ten Speed Press.

Michel, C., Caldara, R., & Rossion, B. (2006). Same-race faces are perceived more holistically than other-race faces. *Visual Cognition, 14*(1), 55–73.

Michelangelo, I., Stefania, B., Donatella, P., Maria, C. Z., et al. (2006). Electrocortical effects of MDMA are potentiated by acoustic stimulation in rats. *BMC Neuroscience*, DOI :10.1186/1471-2202-7-13. Retrieved May 25, 2007, from http://www.biomedcentral.com/content/pdf/1471-2202-7-13.pdf.

Middaugh, S. J., & Pawlick, K. (2002). Biofeedback and behavioral treatment of persistent pain in the older adult: A review and a study. *Applied Psychophysiology & Biofeedback, 27*(3), 185–202.

Mielke, H. W. (1999). Lead in the inner cities. *American Scientist, 87*(Jan.–Feb.), 62–73.

Mignot, E. (2001). A hundred years of narcolepsy research. *Archives of Italian Biology, 139,* 207–220.

Milgram, S. (1963). Behavioral study of obedience. *Journal of Abnormal and Social Psychology, 67,* 371–378.

Milgram, S. (1965). Some conditions of obedience and disobedience to authority. *Human Relations, 18,* 57–76.

Milgram, S. (1967). The small-world problem. *Psychology Today,* May, 61–67.

Milgram, S. (1970). The experience of living in the cities: A psychological analysis. *Science, 167,* 1461–1468.

Milgram, S. (1974). *Obedience to authority: An experimental view.* New York: Harper & Row.

Milgram, S., Bickman, L., & Berkowitz, L. (1969). Note on the drawing power of crowds of different size. *Journal of Personality & Social Psychology, 13,* 79–82.

Miller, D. T. (2006). *An invitation to social psychology.* Belmont, CA: Cengage Learning/Wadsworth.

Miller, E. K., & Cohen, J. D. (2001). An integrative theory of prefrontal cortex function. *Annual Review of Neuroscience, 24,* 167–202.

Miller, G. A. (1956). The magical number seven, plus or minus two: Some limits on our capacity for processing information. *Psychological Review, 63,* 81–87.

Miller, G. A. (1999). On knowing a word. *Annual Review of Psychology, 50,* 1–19.

Miller, G. E., Cohen, S., & Ritchey, A. K. (2002). Chronic psychological stress and the regulation of proinflammatory cytokines. *Health Psychology, 21*(6), 531–541.

Miller, N. E. (1944). Experimental studies of conflict. In J. McV. Hunt (Ed.), *Personality and the behavior disorders* (Vol. 1). New York: Ronald Press.

Miller, N. E., & Bugelski. R. (1970). The influence of frustration imposed by the in-group on attitudes expressed toward out-groups. In R. I. Evans & R. M. Rozelle (Eds.), *Social psychology in life.* Boston: Allyn & Bacon.

Miller, N., Pedersen, W. C., Earleywine, M., & Pollock, V. E. (2003). A theoretical model of triggered displaced aggression. *Personality & Social Psychology Review, 7*(1), 75–97.

Miller, R., Perlman, D., & Brehm, S. S. (2007). *Intimate relationships* (4th ed.). New York: McGraw-Hill.

Miller, W. R., & Munoz, R. F. (2005). *Controlling your drinking: Tools to make moderation work for you.* New York: Guilford.

Millman, R. B., & Ross, E. J. (2003). Steroid and nutritional supplement use in professional athletes. *American Journal on Addictions, 12*(Suppl 2), S48–S54.

Millon, T. (1981) *Disorders of personality: DSM-III: Axis II.* New York: Wiley.

Milne, R., & Bull, R. (2002). Back to basics: A componential analysis of the original cognitive interview mnemonics with three age groups. *Applied Cognitive Psychology, 16*(7), 743–753.

Milner, B. (1965). Memory disturbance after bilateral hippocampal lesions. In P. Milner & S. Glickman (Eds.), *Cognitive processes and the brain.* Princeton, NJ: Van Nostrand.

Miltenberger, R. G. (2008). *Behavior modification: Principles and procedures* (4th ed.). Belmont, CA: Cengage Learning/Wadsworth.

Miltner, W. H. R., Krieschel, S., Hecht, H., Trippe, R., et al. (2004). Eye movements and behavioral responses to threatening and nonthreatening stimuli during visual search in phobic and non-phobic subjects. *Emotion, 4*(4), 323–339.

Milton, J., & Wiseman, R. (1997). *Guidelines for extrasensory perception research.* Hertfordshire, UK: University of Hertfordshire Press.

Milton, J., & Wiseman, R. (1999b). A meta-analysis of mass-media tests of extrasensory perception. *British Journal of Psychology, 90*(2), 235–240.

Minda, J. P., & Smith, J. D. (2001). Prototypes in category learning. *Journal of Experimental Psychology: Learning, Memory, & Cognition, 27*(3), 775–799.

Minton, H. L. (2000). Psychology and gender at the turn of the century. *American Psychologist, 55*(6), 613–615.

Miotto, K., Darakjian, J., Basch, J., Murray, S., et al. (2001). Gamma-hydroxybutyric acid: Patterns of use, effects and withdrawal. *American Journal on Addictions, 10*(3), 232–241.

Miranda, R., & Kihlstrom, J. F. (2005). Mood congruence in childhood and recent autobiographical memory. *Cognition & Emotion, 19*(7), 981–998.

Mirsky, A. F., & Duncan, C. C. (2005). Pathophysiology of mental illness: A view from the fourth ventricle. *International Journal of Psychophysiology, 58*(2–3), 162–178.

Mirsky, A. F., Bieliauskas, L. M., Van Kammen, D. P., Jonsson, E., et al. (2000). A 39-year followup of the Genain quadruplets. *Schizophrenia Bulletin, 3,* 5–18.

Mischel, W. (2004). Toward an integrative science of the person. *Annual Review of Psychology, 55,* 1–22.

Mischel, W., & Shoda, Y. (1998). Reconciling processing dynamics and personality dispositions. *Annual Review of Psychology, 49,* 229–258.

Mischel, W., Shoda, Y., & Smith, R. E. (2004). *Introduction to personality: Toward an integration* (7th ed.). Hoboken, NJ: Wiley.

Mistlberger, R. E. (2005). Circadian regulation of sleep in mammals: Role of the suprachiasmatic nucleus. *Brain Research Reviews, 49*(3), 429–454.

Mitchell, D. (1987). Firewalking cults: Nothing but hot air. *Laser,* Feb., 7–8.

Mitru, G., Millrood, D.L., & Mateika, J. H. (2002). The impact of sleep on learning and behavior in adolescents. *Teachers College Record, 104*(4), 704–726.

Miyake, A. (2001). Individual differences in working memory. *Journal of Experimental Psychology: General, 130*(2), 163–168.

Moerman, D. E. (2002). The meaning response and the ethics of avoiding placebos. *Evaluation & the Health Professions. Special Recent Advances in Placebo Research, 25*(4), 399–409.

Mogg, K., Bradley, B. P., Hyare, H., & Lee, S. (1998). Selective attention to food-related stimuli in hunger. *Behaviour Research & Therapy, 36*(2), 227–237.

Moghaddam, B. (2002). Stress activation of glutamate neurotransmission in the prefrontal cortex. *Biological Psychiatry, 51*(10), 775–787.

Mohr, D. C., Hart, S. L., Julian, L., Catledge, C., et al. (2005). Telephone-administered psychotherapy for depression. *Archives of General Psychiatry, 62*(9), 1007–1014.

Mokdad, A. H., Marks, J. S., Stroup, D. F., & Gerberding, J. L. (2004). Actual causes of death in the United States, 2000. *Journal of the American Medical Association, 291*(March 10), 1238–1245.

Monahan, J., Steadman, H. J., Silver, E., Appelbaum, P. S., et al. (2001). *Rethinking risk assessment: The MacArthur Study of Mental Disorder and Violence.* New York: Oxford University Press.

Montgomery, P., & Dennis, J. (2004). A systematic review of non-pharmacological therapies for sleep problems in later life. *Sleep Medicine Reviews, 8*(1), 47–62.

Moor, J. (Ed.). (2003). *The Turing test: The elusive standard of artificial intelligence.* London: Kluwer Academic Publishers.

Moore, S. A., & Zoellner, L. A. (2007). Overgeneral autobiographical memory and traumatic events: An evaluative review. *Psychological Bulletin, 133*(3), 419–437.

Moore, T. O. (2001). Testosterone and male behavior: Empirical research with hamsters does not support the use of castration to deter human sexual aggression. *North American Journal of Psychology, 3*(3), 503–520.

Moore-Ede, M. C., Sulzman, F. M., & Fuller, C. A. (1982). *The clocks that time us.* Cambridge, MA: Harvard University Press.

Moran, J. M., Macrae, C. N., Heatherton, T. F., Wyland, C. L. et al. (2006). Neuroanatomical evidence for distinct cognitive and affective components of self. *Journal of Cognitive Neuroscience, 18*(9), 1586–1594.

Moras, K. (2002). Research on psychotherapy. In M. Hersen & W. H. Sledge (Eds.), *Encyclopedia of psychotherapy.* San Diego: Academic Press.

Moreno, J. L. (1953). *Who shall survive?* New York: Beacon.

Morgan, J. P. (Ed.). (2005). *Psychology of aggression.* Hauppauge, NY: Nova Science Publishers.

Morgenstern, J., Labouvie, E., McCrady, B. S., Kahler, C. W., et al. (1997). Affiliation with Alcoholics Anonymous after treatment. *Journal of Consulting & Clinical Psychology, 65*(5), 768–777.

Morisse, D., Batra, L., Hess, L., & Silverman, R. (1996). A demonstration of a token economy for the real world. *Applied & Preventive Psychology, 5*(1), 41–46.

Moritz, A. P., & Zamchech, N. (1946). Sudden and unexpected deaths of young soldiers. *American Medical Association Archives of Pathology, 42,* 459–494.

Morris, T., Spittle, M., & Watt, T. (2005). *Imagery in sport.* Champaign, IL: Human Kinetics.

Morrison, R. G., & Wallace, B. (2001). Imagery vividness, creativity and the visual arts. *Journal of Mental Imagery, 25*(3–4), 135–152.

Morsella, E., & Krauss, R. M. (2004). The role of gestures in spatial working memory and speech. *American Journal of Psychology, 117*(3), 411–424.

Mosher, W. D., Chandra, C., & Jones, J. (2005). *Sexual behavior and selected health measures: Men and women 15–44 years of age, United States, 2002.* Atlanta: Centers for Disease Control. Retrieved August 25, 2006, from http://www.cdc.gov/nchs/data/ad/ad362.pdf.

Most, S. B., Scholl, B. J., Clifford, E. R., & Simons, D. J. (2005). What you see is what you set: Sustained inattentional blindness and the capture of awareness. *Psychological Review, 112*(1), 217–242.

Motivala, S. J., & Irwin, M. R. (2007). Sleep and immunity: Cytokine pathways linking sleep and health outcomes. *Current Directions in Psychological Science, 16*(1), 21–25.

Muchinsky, P. M. (2006). *Psychology applied to work* (8th ed.). Belmont,

CA: Cengage Learning/ Wadsworth.

Mundy, A. (2004). Divided we stand. *American Demographics, 26*(5), 26–31.

Munsey, C. (2006). RxP legislation made historic progress in Hawaii. *APA Monitor*, June, 42.

Murray, B. (2001). A daunting unbelievable experience. *Monitor on Psychology*, Nov., 18.

Murray, J. B. (1995). Evidence for acupuncture's analgesic effectiveness and proposals for the physiological mechanisms involved. *Journal of Psychology, 129*(4), 443–461.

Murray, J. B. (2002). Phencyclidine (PCP): A dangerous drug, but useful in schizophrenia research. *Journal of Psychology, 136*(3), 319–327.

Murray, S. L., Holmes, J. G., & Griffin, D. W. (1996). The self-fulfilling nature of positive illusions in romantic relationships. *Journal of Personality & Social Psychology, 71*(6), 1155–1180.

Murray, S., Holmes, J. G., & Griffin, D. W. (2003). Reflections on the self-fulfilling effects of positive illusions. *Psychological Inquiry, 14*(3–4), 2003, 289–295.

Mussen, P. H., Conger, J. J., Kagan, J., & Geiwitz, J. (1979). *Psychological development: A life span approach*. New York: Harper & Row.

Musso, M., Weiller, C., Kiebel, S., Muller, S. P., et al. (1999). Training-induced brain plasticity in aphasia. *Brain, 122*, 1781–1790.

Mustanski, B. S., Chivers, M. L., & Bailey, J. M. (2002). A critical review of recent biological research on human sexual orientation. *Annual Review of Sex Research, 13*, 89–140.

Myers, H. F., Lesser, I., Rodriguez, N., Mira, C. B., et al. (2002). Ethnic differences in clinical presentation of depression in adult women. *Cultural Diversity & Ethnic Minority Psychology, 8*(2), 138–156.

Myers, L. (2007). The problem with DNA. *Monitor on Psychology*, June, 52–53.

NAFE (2004). Salary survey. *National Association for Female Executives Magazine, 27*(4), 20–21.

Nagel, T. (1974). What is it like to be a bat? *The Philosophical Review, 83*, 435–450.

Nairne, J. S. (2002). Remembering over the short-term. *Annual Review of Psychology, 53*, 53–81.

Naitoh, P., Kelly, T. L., & Englund, C. E. (1989). *Health effects of sleep deprivation*. U.S. Naval Health Research Center Report no. 89-46.

Nakamichi, M. (2004). Tool-use and toolmaking by captive, group-living orangutans (Pongo pygmaeus abelii) at an artificial termite mound. *Behavioural Processes, 65*(1), 87–93.

Nakamura, J., & Csikszentmihalyi, M. (2003). The motivational sources of creativity as viewed from the paradigm of positive psychology. In L. G. Aspinwall & U. M. Staudinger (Eds.), *A psychology of human strengths: Fundamental questions and future directions for a positive psychology*. Washington, DC: American Psychological Association.

National Academy of Sciences. (2002). *The polygraph and lie detection*. Washington, DC: National Academy of Sciences.

National Institute of Child Health and Human Development. (1999). The NICHD Study of Early Child Care: Child outcomes when child care center classes meet recommended standards for quality. *American Journal of Public Health, 89*, 1072–1077.

Nau, S. D., & Lichstein, K. L. (2005). Insomnia: Causes and treatments. In P. R. Carney, J. D. Geyer, et al. (Eds.), *Clinical sleep disorders*. Philadelphia: Lippincott Williams & Wilkins.

Naveh-Benjamin, M., Guez, J., & Sorek, S. (2007). The effects of divided attention on encoding processes in memory: Mapping the locus of interference. *Canadian Journal of Experimental Psychology, 61*(1), 1–12.

NCCDPHP (National Center for Chronic Disease Prevention and Health Promotion). (2004). *Health effects of cigarette smoking*. Retrieved July 19, 2006, from http:// www.cdc.gov/Tobacco/factsheets/ HealthEffectsofCigaretteSmoking_ Factsheet.htm\

Neath, I., & Surprenant, A. (2003). *Human memory* (2nd ed.). Belmont, CA: Cengage Learning/ Wadsworth.

Neave, N., & Wolfson, S. (2003). Testosterone, territoriality, and the "home advantage." *Physiology & Behavior, 78*(2), 269–275.

Needles, D. J., & Abramson, L. Y. (1990). Positive life events, attributional style, and hopefulness: Testing a model of recovery from depression. *Journal of Abnormal Psychology, 99*(2), 156–165.

Nehlig, A. (Ed.). (2004). *Coffee, tea, chocolate, and the brain*. Boca Raton, FL: CRC Press.

Neisser, U., Boodoo, G., Bouchard, T. J., Boykin, A. W., et al. (1996). Intelligence: Knowns and unknowns. *American Psychologist, 51*(2), 77–101.

Nelson, C. A. (1999). How important are the first 3 years of life? *Applied Developmental Science, 3*(4), 235–238.

Nelson, G., & Prilleltensky, I. (Eds.). (2005). *Community psychology: In pursuit of liberation and well-being*. New York: Palgrave MacMillan.

Nelson, T. D. (2005). Ageism: Prejudice against our feared future self. *Journal of Social Issues, 61*(2), 207–221.

Nelson, T. D. (2006). *The psychology of prejudice* (2nd ed.). Needham Heights, MA: Allyn and Bacon.

Nemeroff, C. B., Bremner, J. D., Foa, E. B., Mayberg, H. S., et al. (2006). Posttraumatic stress disorder: A state-of-the-science review. *Journal of Psychiatric Research, 40*(1), 1–21.

Neter, E., & Ben-Shakhar, G. (1989). The predictive validity of graphological inferences: A meta-analytic approach. *Personality & Individual Differences, 10*(7), 737–745.

Neubert, M. J. (1998). The value of feedback and goal setting over goal setting alone and potential moderators of this effect: A meta-analysis. *Human Performance, 11*(4), 321–335.

Neufeld, R. W. J., Carter, J. R., Nicholson, I. R., & Vollick, D. N. (2003). Schizophrenia. In P. Firestone & W. L. Marshall (Eds.), *Abnormal psychology: Perspectives* (2nd ed.). Toronto: Prentice Hall.

Neuman, G. A., & Baydoun, R. (1998). An empirical examination of overt and covert integrity tests. *Journal of Business & Psychology, 13*(1), 65–79.

Neumeister, A. (2004). Neurotransmitter depletion and seasonal affective disorder: Relevance for the biologic effects of light therapy. *Primary Psychiatry. Special Neurotransmitter Depletion, 11*(6), 44–48.

Nevid, J. S., & Greene, B. (2005). *Abnormal psychology in a changing world, media and research update* (5th ed.). Englewood Cliffs, NJ: Prentice Hall.

Newman, A. W., & Thompson, J. W. (2001). The rise and fall of forensic hypnosis in criminal investigation. *Journal of the American Academy of Psychiatry & the Law, 29*(1), 75–84.

Ng, S. H. (2002). Will families support their elders? Answers from across cultures. In T. Nelson (Ed.), *Ageism: Stereotyping and prejudice against older persons*. Cambridge, MA: MIT Press.

Niaura, R., Todaro, J. F., Stroud, L., Spiro, A., et al. (2002). Hostility, the metabolic syndrome, and incident coronary heart disease. *Health Psychology, 21*(6), 588–593.

Nickell, J. (2001). John Edward: Hustling the bereaved. *Skeptical Inquirer*, Nov.-Dec., 19–22.

Nickerson, R. S., & Adams, M. J. (1979). Long-term memory for a common object. *Cognitive Psychology, 11*, 287–307.

NIDA. (2006). *Tobacco addiction*. National Institute on Drug Abuse, NIH Publication Number 06-

4342. Retrieved July 24, 2006, from http://www.nida.nih.gov/ PDF/RRTobacco.pdf.

Niedzwienska, A. (2004). Metamemory knowledge and the accuracy of flashbulb memories. *Memory, 12*(5), 603–613.

Niehaus, D. J. H., Stein, D. J., Koen, L., Lochner, C., et al. (2005). A case of "Ifufunyane": A Xhosa culture-bound syndrome. *Journal of Psychiatric Practice, 11*(6), 411–413.

Niehoff, B. P., Moorman, R. H., Blakely, G., & Fuller, J. (2001). The influence of empowerment and job enrichment on employee loyalty in a downsizing environment. *Group & Organization Management, 26*(1), 93–113.

Nielsen, D. M., & Metha, A. (1994). Parental behavior and adolescent self-esteem in clinical and nonclinical samples. *Adolescence, 29*(115), 525–542.

Nielsen, M., & Dissanayake, C. (2004). Pretend play, mirror self-recognition and imitation: A longitudinal investigation through the second year. *Infant Behavior & Development, 27*(3), 342–365.

NIMH (2003). *In harm's way: Suicide in America*. Bethesda, MD: National Institute of Mental Health. Retrieved July 25, 2007, from http://www.nimh.nih.gov/publicat/ harmsway.cfm.

NIMH (2005). *Getting help: Locate services*. Bethesda, MD: National Institute of Mental Health. Retrieved August 20, 2007, from http://www.nimh.nih.gov/tools/ contactus.cfm.

NIMH. (2006a). *Facts about anxiety disorders*. Bethesda, MD: National Institute of Mental Health. Retrieved July 25, 2007, from http:// www.nimh.nih.gov/publicat/ anxiety.cfm

NIMH. (2006b). *The numbers count: Mental disorders in America*. Bethesda, MD: National Institute of Mental Health. Retrieved July 25, 2007, from http://www.nimh. nih.gov/publicat/numbers.cfm.

Nisbett, R. E. (2005). Heredity, environment, and race differences in IQ: A commentary on Rushton and Jensen (2005). *Psychology, Public Policy, & Law, 11*(2), 302–310.

Njeri, I. (1991). Beyond the melting pot. *Los Angeles Times*, Jan. 13, E1, E8.

Noble, P. (1997). Violence in psychiatric in-patients. *International Review of Psychiatry, 9*(2–3), 207–216.

Noice, H., & Noice, T. (1999). Long-term retention of theatrical roles. *Memory, 7*(3), 357–382.

Noland, J. S., Singer, L. T., Short, E. J., Minnes, S., et al. (2005). Prenatal drug exposure and selective attention in preschoolers.

Neurotoxicology & Teratology, 27(3), 429–438.

Nolen-Hoeksema, S. (2007). *Abnormal psychology* (4th ed.). New York: McGraw-Hill.

Norcross, J. C., Hedges, M., & Prochaska, J. O. (2002). The face of 2010: A Delphi poll on the future of psychotherapy. *Professional Psychology: Research & Practice, 33*(3), 316–322.

Norem, J. K. (2002). *The positive power of negative thinking: Using defensive pessimism to harness anxiety and perform at your peak.* New York: Basic Books.

Nori, G. (1998). Glucagon and the control of meal size. In G. P. Smith (Ed.), *Satiation: From gut to brain.* New York: Oxford University Press.

Norlander, T., Bergman, H., & Archer, T. (1998). Effects of flotation rest on creative problem solving and originality. *Journal of Environmental Psychology, 18*(4), 399–408.

Norlander, T., Bergman, H., & Archer, T. (1999). Primary process in competitive archery performance: Effects of flotation REST. *Journal of Applied Sport Psychology, 11*(2), 194–209.

Norman, D. A. (1994) *Things that make us smart.* Menlo Park, CA: Addison-Wesley.

Norman, K. L., & Panizzi, E. (2006). Levels of automation and user participation in usability testing. *Interacting with Computers, 18*(2), 246–264.

Norris, R. M., & Weinman, J. A. (1996). Psychological change following a long sail training voyage. *Personality & Individual Differences, 21*(2), 189–194.

North, C. S. (1987). *Welcome silence.* New York: Simon & Schuster.

North, C. S., Kienstra, D. M., Osborne, V. A., Dokucu, M. E., et al. (2006). Interrater reliability and coding guide for nonpsychotic formal thought disorder. *Perceptual & Motor Skills, 103*(2), 395–411.

Northcutt, R. G. (2004). Taste buds: Development and evolution. *Brain, Behavior & Evolution, 64*(3), 198–206.

Norton, P. (2003). *Teaching with technology: Designing opportunities to learn.* Belmont, CA: Cengage Learning/Wadsworth.

Nosek, B. A., Greenwald, A. G., & Banaji, M. R. (2005). Understanding and using the implicit association test: II. Method variables and construct validity. *Personality & Social Psychology Bulletin, 31*(2), 166–180.

Nurnberger, J. I., & Zimmerman, J. (1970). Applied analysis of human behaviors: An alternative to conventional motivational inferences and unconscious determination in therapeutic programming. *Behavior Therapy, 1,* 59–69.

Oakley R. (2004). How the mind hurts and heals the body. *American Psychologist, 59*(1), 29–40.

Oakley, D. A., Whitman, L. G., & Halligan, P. W. (2002). Hypnotic imagery as a treatment for phantom limb pain. *Clinical Rehabilitation, 16*(4), 368–377.

Oberauer, K., & Göthe, K. (2006). Dual-task effects in working memory: Interference between two processing tasks, between two memory demands, and between storage and processing. *European Journal of Cognitive Psychology, 18*(4), 493–519.

Obhi, S. S., & Haggard, P. (2004). Free will and free won't. *American Scientist, 92*(July–Aug.), 358–365.

Ochoa, J. G., & Pulido, M. (2005). Parasomnias. In P. R. Carney, J. D. Geyer, et al. (Eds.), *Clinical sleep disorders.* Philadelphia: Lippincott Williams & Wilkins.

O'Conner, T. G., Marvin, R. S., Rutter, M., Olrick, J. T., et al. (2003). Child–parent attachment following early institutional deprivation. *Development & Psychopathology, 15*(1), 19–38.

O'Connor, M. G., Sieggreen, M. A., Bachna, K., Kaplan, B., et al. (2000). Long-term retention of transient news events. *Journal of the International Neuropsychological Society, 6*(1), 44–51.

O'Craven, K. M., & Kanwisher, N. (2000). Mental imagery of faces and places activates corresponding stimulus-specific brain regions. *Journal of Cognitive Neuroscience, 12*(6), 1013–1023.

Ogloff, J. R. P. (2006). Psychopathy/antisocial personality disorder conundrum. *Australian & New Zealand Journal of Psychiatry, 40*(6), 519–528.

Ohayon, M. M., Guilleminault, C., & Priest, R. G. (1999). Night terrors, sleepwalking, and confusional arousals in the general population. *Journal of Clinical Psychiatry, 60*(4), 268–276.

O'Keeffe, C., & Wiseman, R. (2005). Testing alleged mediumship: Methods and results. *British Journal of Psychology, 96*(2), 165–179.

Okiishi, J., Lambert, M. J., Nielsen, S. L., & Ogles, B. M. (2003). Waiting for supershrink: An empirical analysis of therapist effects. *Clinical Psychology & Psychotherapy, 10*(6), 361–373.

Olds, M. E., & Fobes, J. L. (1981). The central basis of motivation: Intracranial self-stimulation studies. *Annual Review of Psychology, 32,* 523–574.

O'Leary, E. (2006). Person-centred gestalt therapy. In E. O'Leary & M. Murphy (Eds.), *New approaches to integration in psychotherapy.* New York: Routledge.

Olio, K. A. (2004). The truth about "false memory syndrome." In P. J. Caplan & L. Cosgrove (Eds.), *Bias in psychiatric diagnosis. A project of the association for women in psychology.* Northvale, NJ: Jason Aronson.

Olson, J. M., & Zanna, M. P. (1993). Attitudes and attitude change. *Annual Review of Psychology, 44,* 117–154.

Olson-Buchanan, J. B., & Drasgow, F. (2006). Multimedia situational judgment tests: The medium creates the message. In J. A. Weekley & R. E. Ployhart (Eds.), *Situational judgment tests: Theory, measurement, and application.* Mahwah, NJ: Erlbaum.

Olszewski, P. K., Li, D., Grace, M. K., Billington, C. J., et al. (2003). Neural basis of orexigenic effects of ghrelin acting within lateral hypothalamus. *Peptides, 24*(4), 597–602.

O'Neill, B. (2003). *Don't believe everything you read online.* BBC News. Retrieved May 18, 2007, from http://newswww.bbc.net.uk/1/hi/magazine/3151595.stm.

O'Neill, P. (2005). The ethics of problem definition. *Canadian Psychology, 46,* 13–20.

Ones, D. S., & Viswesvaran, C. (2001). Integrity tests and other criterion-focused occupational personality scales (COPS) used in personnel selection. *International Journal of Selection & Assessment, 9*(1–2), 31–39.

Ones, D. S., Viswesvaran, C., & Schmidt, F. L. (2003). Personality and absenteeism: A meta-analysis of integrity tests. *European Journal of Personality, 17*(Suppl. 1), S19–S38.

Onwuegbuzie, A. J. (2000). Academic procrastinators and perfectionistic tendencies among graduate students. *Journal of Social Behavior & Personality, 15*(5), 103–109.

Ooki, S. (2005). Genetic and environmental influences on the handedness and footedness in Japanese twin children. *Twin Research & Human Genetics, 8*(6), 649–656.

Oppliger, P. A. (2007). Effects of gender stereotyping on socialization. In R. W. Preiss, B. M. Gayle, et al. (Eds.), *Mass media effects research: Advances through meta-analysis.* Mahwah, NJ: Erlbaum.

Ord, T. J., Martins E. P., Thakur S., Mane K. K., et al. (2005). Trends in animal behaviour research (1968–2002): Ethoinformatics and the mining of library databases. *Animal Behaviour, 69*(6), 1399–1413.

Orleans, C. T. (2000). Promoting the maintenance of health behavior change. *Health Psychology, 19*(Suppl. 1), 76–83.

Orleans, C. T., Gruman, J., & Hollendonner, J. K. (1999). Rating our progress in population health promotion: Report card on six behaviors. *American Journal of Health Promotion, 14*(2), 75–82.

Ormay, T. (2006). Cybertherapy: Psychotherapy on the Internet. *International Journal of Psychotherapy, 10*(2), 51–60.

Ornstein, R., & Ehrlich, P. (1989). *New world new mind.* New York: Simon & Schuster.

Ornstein, S., & Isabella, L. (1990). Age vs. stage models of career attitudes of women: A partial replication and extension. *Journal of Vocational Behavior, 36,* 1–19.

O'Roark, A. M. (2001). Personality assessment, projective methods and a triptych perspective. *Journal of Projective Psychology & Mental Health, 8*(2), 116–126.

Osgood, C. E. (1952). The nature and measurement of meaning. *Psychological Bulletin, 49,* 197–237.

Oskamp, S. (1995). Resource conservation and recycling: Behavior and policy. *Journal of Social Issues, 51*(4), 157–177.

Oskamp, S. (2000). A sustainable future for humanity? *American Psychologist, 55*(5), 496–508.

Oskamp, S. (2002). Summarizing sustainability issues and research approaches. In P. Schmuck & W. P. Schultz (Eds.), *Psychology of sustainable development.* Dordrecht, Netherlands: Kluwer.

Oskamp, S., & Schultz, P. W. (2005). *Attitudes and opinions* (3rd ed.). Mahwah, NJ: Erlbaum.

Oskamp, S., & Schultz, P. W. (2006). Using psychological science to achieve ecological sustainability. In S. I. Donaldson, D. E. Berger, et al. (Eds.), *Applied psychology: New frontiers and rewarding careers.* Mahwah, NJ: Erlbaum.

Oster, H. (2005). The repertoire of infant facial expressions: a ontogenetic perspective. In J. Nadel & D. Muir (Eds.), *Emotional development: Recent research advances.* New York: Oxford University Press.

Overmier, J. B., & LoLordo, V. M. (1998). Learned helplessness. In O'Donohue, W. T. (Ed.), *Learning and behavior therapy.* Boston: Allyn & Bacon.

Oyserman, D., Bybee, D., Terry, K., & Hart-Johnson, T. (2004). Possible selves as roadmaps. *Journal of Research in Personality, 38*(2), 130–149.

Page, K. (1999). The graduate. *Washington Post Magazine, 152*(May 16), 18–20.

Page, M. P. A., Madge, A., Cumming, N., & Norris, D. G. (2007). Speech errors and the phonological similarity effect in short-term memory: Evidence suggesting a common locus. *Journal of Memory & Language, 56*(1), 49–64.

Pagnin, D., de Queiroz, V., Pini, S., & Cassano, G. B. (2004). Efficacy of ECT in depression: A meta-analytic review. *Journal of ECT, 20*(1), 13–20.

Palm, K., & Gibson, P. (1998). Recovered memories of childhood sexual abuse: Clinicians' practices and beliefs. *Professional Psychology: Research & Practice, 29*(3), 257–261.

Palmer, S. E. (1992). Common region: A new principle of perceptual grouping. *Cognitive Psychology, 24*(3), 436–447.

Pals, J. L. (2006). Narrative identity processing of difficult life experiences: Pathways of personality development and positive self-transformation in adulthood. *Journal of Personality, 74*(4), 1079–1110.

Pandey, S. (1999). Role of perceived control in coping with crowding. *Psychological Studies, 44*(3), 86–91.

Panksepp, J., & Pasqualini, M. S. (2005). The search for the fundamental brain/mind sources of affective experience. In J. Nadel & D. Muir (Eds.), *Emotional development: Recent research advances*. New York: Oxford University Press.

Papa, F. J., Aldrich, D., & Schumacker, R. E. (1999). The effects of immediate online feedback upon diagnostic performance. *Academic Medicine, 74*(Suppl. 10), S16–S18.

Papanicolaou, A. C. (Ed.). (2006). *The amnesias: A clinical textbook of memory disorders*. New York: Oxford University Press.

Paquette, D., Carbonneau, R., Dubeau, D., Bigras, M., et al. (2003). Prevalence of father-child rough-and-tumble play and physical aggression in preschool children. *European Journal of Psychology of Education, 18*(2), 171–189.

Paquette, V., Lévesque, J., Mensour, B., Leroux, J.-M., et al. (2003). "Change the mind and you change the brain": Effects of cognitive-behavioral therapy on the neural correlates of spider phobia. *NeuroImage, 18*, 401–409.

Paradis, C. M., Solomon, L. Z., Florer, F., & Thompson, T. (2004). Flashbulb memories of personal events of 9/11 and the day after for a sample of New York City residents. *Psychological Reports, 95*(1), 304–310.

Park, D. C., Smith, A. D., & Cavanaugh, J. C. (1990). Metamemories of memory researchers. *Memory & Cognition, 18*(3), 321–327.

Park, N., Peterson, C., & Seligman, M.E. P. (2004). Strengths of character and well-being. *Journal of Social & Clinical Psychology, 23*(5), 603–619.

Parke, R. D. (2004). Development in the family. *Annual Review of Psychology, 55*, 365–399.

Parker, A., Ngu, H., & Cassaday, H. J. (2001). Odour and Proustian memory. *Applied Cognitive Psychology, 15*(2), 159–171.

Parker, J. D. A. (2005). The relevance of emotional intelligence for clinical psychology. In R. Schulze & R. D. Roberts (Eds.), *Emotional intelligence: An international handbook* (pp. 271–287). Ashland, OH: Hogrefe & Huber.

Pascual, A., & Guéguen, N. (2005). Foot-in-the-door and door-in-the-face: A comparative meta-analytic study. *Psychological Reports, 96*(1), 122–128.

Pasupathi, M., & Staudinger, U. M. (2001). Do advanced moral reasoners also show wisdom? *International Journal of Behavioral Development, 25*(5), 401–415.

Patterson, C. J. (2002). Lesbian and gay parenthood. In M. Bornstein (Ed.), *Handbook of Parenting, 3, 4, 5*. Mahwah, NJ: Erlbaum.

Paulhus, D. L. (1998). Interpersonal and intrapsychic adaptiveness of trait self-enhancement. *Journal of Personality and Social Psychology, 74*(5), 1197–1208.

Paulsson, T., & Parker, A. (2006). The effects of a two-week reflection-intention training program on lucid dream recall. *Dreaming, 16*(1), 22–35.

Pavlidis, I., Eberhardt, N. L., & Levine, J. A. (2002). Seeing through the face of deception. *Nature, 415*(6867), 35.

Pavlov, I. P. (1927). *Conditioned reflexes*. Translated by G. V. Anrep. New York: Dover.

Pearce, C. L., Conger, J. A., & Locke, E. A. (2007). Shared leadership theory. *Leadership Quarterly, 18*(3), 281–288.

Pelton, T. (1983). The shootists. *Science 83, 4*(4), 84–86.

Penfield, W. (1957). Brain's record of past a continuous movie film. *Science News Letter*, April 27, 265.

Penfield, W. (1958). *The excitable cortex in conscious man*. Springfield, IL: Charles C. Thomas.

Pennebaker, J. W. (2004). *Writing to heal: A guided journal for recovering from trauma and emotional upheaval*. Oakland, CA: New Harbinger Press.

Pennebaker, J. W., & Chung, C. K. (2007). Expressive writing, emotional upheavals, and health. In H. S. Friedman & R. C. Silver (Eds.), *Foundations of health psychology*. New York: Oxford University Press.

Peplau, L. A. (2003). Human sexuality: How do men and women differ? *Current Directions in Psychological Science, 12*(2), 37–40.

Perin, C. T. (1943). A quantitative investigation of the delay of reinforcement gradient. *Journal of Experimental Psychology, 32*, 37–51.

Perlman, D., & Cozby, P. C. (1983). *Social psychology*. New York: Holt, Rinehart & Winston.

Perls, F. (1969). *Gestalt therapy verbatim*. Lafayette, CA: Real People.

Perreault, S., & Bourhis, R. Y. (1999). Ethnocentrism, social identification, and discrimination. *Personality & Social Psychology Bulletin, 25*(1), 92–103.

Perry, R. P. (2003). Perceived (academic) control and causal thinking in achievement settings. *Canadian Psychology, 44*(4), 312–331.

Perry, R. P., Hladkyj, S., Pekrun, R. H., & Pelletier, S. T. (2001). Academic control and action control in the achievement of college students: A longitudinal field study. *Journal of Educational Psychology, 93*(4), 776–789.

Pervin, L. A., Cervone, D., & John, O. P. (2005). *Personality: Theory and research* (9th ed.). New York: Wiley.

Pesant, N., & Zadra, A. (2006). Dream content and psychological well-being: A longitudinal study of the continuity hypothesis. *Journal of Clinical Psychology, 62*(1), 111–121.

Pescatello, L. S. (2001). Exercising for health. *Western Journal of Medicine, 174*(2), 114–118.

Peters, W. A. (1971). *A class divided*. Garden City, NY: Doubleday.

Peterson, C., & Chang, E. C. (2003). Optimism and flourishing. In C. L. M. Keyes & J. Haidt (Eds.), *Flourishing*. Washington, DC: American Psychological Association.

Peterson, C., & Seligman, M. E. P. (2004). *Character strengths and virtues*. Washington, DC: American Psychological Association.

Peterson, C., & Vaidya, R. S. (2001). Explanatory style, expectations, and depressive symptoms. *Personality & Individual Differences, 31*(7), 1217–1223.

Peterson, L. R., & Peterson, M. J. (1959). Short-term retention of individual verbal items. *Journal of Experimental Psychology, 58*, 193–198.

Peterson, S. E. (1992). The cognitive functions of underlining as a study technique. *Reading Research & Instruction, 31*(2), 49–56.

Petrie, T. A., & Diehl, N. S. (1995). Sport psychology in the profession of psychology. *Professional Psychology: Research & Practice, 26*(3), 288–291.

Pett, M. A., & Johnson, M. J. M. (2005). Development and psychometric evaluation of the Revised University Student Hassles Scale. *Educational & Psychological Measurement, 65*(6), 984–1010.

Pettigrew, T. F. (1998). Intergroup contact theory. *Annual Review of Psychology, 49*, 65–85.

Peverly, S. T., Brobst, K. E., Graham, M., & Shaw, R. (2003). College adults are not good at self-regulation. *Journal of Educational Psychology, 95*(2), 335–346.

Phillips, D. P., Liu, G. C., Kwok, K., Jarvinen, J., et al. (2001). The *Hound of the Baskervilles* effect: Natural experiment on the influence of psychological stress on timing of death. *British Medical Journal, 323*(7327), 1443–1446

Piaget, J. (1951, original French, 1945). *The psychology of intelligence*. New York: Norton.

Piaget, J. (1952). *The origins of intelligence in children*. New York: International University Press.

Pickel, K. L., French, T. A., & Betts, J. M. (2003). A cross-modal weapon focus effect: The influence of a weapon's presence on memory for auditory information. *Memory, 11*(3), 277–292.

Piek, J. P. (2006). *Infant motor development*. Champaign, Il: Human Kinetics Publishers.

Pierce, W. D., & Cheney, C. D. (2004). *Behavior analysis and learning* (3rd ed.). Mahwah, NJ: Erlbaum.

Pierrehumbert, B., Ramstein, T., Karmaniola, A., Miljkovitch, R., et al. (2002). Quality of child care in the preschool years. *International Journal of Behavioral Development, 26*(5), 385–396.

Pierrel, R., & Sherman, J. G. (1963). Train your pet the Barnabus way. *Brown Alumni Monthly*, Feb., 8–14.

Piliavin, I. M., Rodin, J., & Piliavin, J. A. (1969). Good samaritanism: An underground phenomenon? *Journal of Personality & Social Psychology, 13*, 289–299.

Piliavin, J. A. (2003). Doing well by doing good: Benefits to the benefactor. In C. L. M. Keyes & J. Haidt (Eds.), *Flourishing*. Washington, DC: American Psychological Association.

Pillow, D. R., Zautra, A. J., & Sandler, I. (1996). Major life events and minor stressors: Identifying mediational links in the stress process. *Journal of Personality & Social Psychology, 70*(2), 381–394.

Pinel, J. P. J., Assanand, S., & Lehman, D. R. (2000). Hunger, eating, and ill health. *American Psychologist, 55*(10), 1105–1116.

Pines, A. M., Ben-Ari, A., Utasi, A., & Larson, D. (2002). A cross-cultural investigation of social support and burnout. *European Psychologist, 7*(4), 256–264.

Pinker, S., & Jackendoff, R. (2005). The faculty of language: What's special about it? *Cognition, 95*(2), 201–236.

Pizam, A., Jeong, G.-H., Reichel, A., Van Boemmel, H., et al. (2004). The relationship between risk-taking, sensation-seeking, and the tourist behavior of young adults: A cross-cultural study. *Journal of Travel Research, 42*, 251–260.

Plazzi, G., Vetrugno, R., Provini, F., Montagna, P. (2005). Sleepwalking and other ambulatory behaviours during sleep. *Neurological Sciences, 26*(Suppl 3), S193–S198.

Pliner, P., & Mann, N. (2004). Influence of social norms and palatability on amount consumed and food choice. *Appetite, 42*(2), 227–237.

Plous, S. (2003). *Understanding prejudice and discrimination.* New York: McGraw-Hill.

Plutchik, R. (2003). *Emotions and life.* Washington, DC: American Psychological Assocation.

Poland, J., & Caplan, P. J. (2004). The deep structure of bias in psychiatric diagnosis. In P. J. Caplan & L. Cosgrove (Eds.), *Bias in psychiatric diagnosis. A project of the association for women in psychology.* Lanham, MD: Jason Aronson.

Polemikos, N., & Papaeliou, C. (2000). Sidedness preference as an index of organization of laterality. *Perceptual & Motor Skills, 91*(3, Pt. 2), 1083–1090.

Polivy, J., & Herman, C. P. (2002). Causes of eating disorders. *Annual Review of Psychology, 53,* 187–213.

Pollner, M. (1998). The effects of interviewer gender in mental health interviews. *Journal of Nervous & Mental Disease, 186*(6), 369–373.

Pollock, V. E., Briere, J., Schneider, L., Knop, J., et al. (1990). Childhood antecedents of antisocial behavior. *American Journal of Psychiatry, 147*(10), 1290–1293.

Pomaki, G., Supeli, A., & Verhoeven, C. (2007). Role conflict and health behaviors: Moderating effects on psychological distress and somatic complaints. *Psychology & Health, 22*(3), 317–335.

Pope, H. G., Gruber, A. J., & Yurgelun-Todd, D. (1995). The residual neuropsychological effects of cannabis. *Drug & Alcohol Dependence, 38*(1), 25–34.

Popma, A., Vermeiren, R., Geluk, C., Rinne, T., et al. (2007). Cortisol moderates the relationship between testosterone and aggression in delinquent male adolescents. *Biological Psychiatry, 61*(3), 405–411.

Population Institute (2006). *Population issues.* Washington, DC: Population Institute. Retrieved August 14, 2007, from http://www .populationinstitute.org/ population-issues/.

Porter, K. (2003). *The mental athlete: Inner training for peak performance in all sports.* Champaign, IL: Human Kinetics.

Porter, S., Campbell, M. A., Birt, A. R., & Woodworth, M. T. (2003). "He said, she said": A psychological perspective on historical memory evidence in the courtroom. *Canadian Psychology, 44*(3), 190–206.

Porteus, L. (2004). "Group Think" Led to Iraq WMD Assessment. *Fox News,* July 11. Retrieved August 4, 2007, from http://www.foxnews. com/story/0,2933,125123,00. html.

Posada, G., Jacobs, A., Richmond, M. K., Carbonell, O. A., et al. (2002). Maternal caregiving and infant security in two cultures. *Developmental Psychology, 38*(1), 67–78.

Poulton, R. G., & Andrews, G. (1996). Change in danger cognitions in agoraphobia and social phobia during treatment. *Behaviour Research & Therapy, 34*(5–6), 413–421.

Powell, A. L., & Thelen, M. H. (1996). Emotions and cognitions associated with bingeing and weight control behavior in bulimia. *Journal of Psychosomatic Research, 40*(3), 317–328.

Powell, R. A., Symbaluk, D. G., & Macdonald, S. E. (2005). *Introduction to learning and behavior.* Belmont, CA: Cengage Learning/ Wadsworth.

Preckel, F., Holling, H., & Wiese, M. (2006). Relationship of intelligence and creativity in gifted and non-gifted students: An investigation of threshold theory. *Personality & Individual Differences, 40*(1), 159–170.

Premack, A. J., & Premack, D. (1972). Teaching language to an ape. *Scientific American,* Oct., 92–99.

Premack, D., & Premack, A. J. (1983). *The mind of an ape.* New York: Norton.

Pressley, M. (1987). Are key-word method effects limited to slow presentation rates? An empirically based reply to Hall and Fuson (1986). *Journal of Educational Psychology, 79*(3), 333–335.

Prigerson, H. G., Maciejewski, P. K., & Rosenheck, R. A. (2002). Population attributable fractions of psychiatric disorders and behavioral outcomes associated with combat exposure among US men. *American Journal of Public Health, 92,* 59–63.

Priluck, R., & Till, B. D. (2004). The role of contingency awareness, involvement, and need for cognition in attitude formation. *Journal of the Academy of Marketing Science, 32*(3), 329–344.

Prinstein, M. J., Meade, C. S. & Cohen, G. L. (2003). Adolescent oral sex, peer popularity, and perceptions of best friends' sexual behavior. *Journal of Pediatric Psychology, 28*(4), 243–249.

Prochaska, J. O., & Norcross, J. C. (2007). *Systems of psychotherapy: A transtheoretical analysis* (6th ed.). Belmont, CA: Cengage Learning/ Wadsworth.

Provencher, M. D., Dugas, M. J., & Ladouceur, R. (2004). Efficacy of problem-solving training and cognitive exposure in the treatment of generalized anxiety disorder: A case replication series. *Cognitive & Behavioral Practice, 11*(4), 404–414.

Puca, R. M., & Schmalt, H. (1999). Task enjoyment: A mediator between achievement motives and performance. *Motivation & Emotion, 23*(1), 15–29.

Pychyl, T. A., Lee, J. M., Thibodeau, R., & Blunt, A. (2000). Five days of emotion: An experience sampling study of undergraduate student procrastination. *Journal of Social Behavior & Personality, 15*(5), 239–254.

Quednow, B. B., Jessen, F., Kühn, K.-W., Maier, W., et al. (2006). Memory deficits in abstinent MDMA (ecstasy) users: Neuropsychological evidence of frontal dysfunction. *Journal of Psychopharmacology, 20*(3), 373–384.

Quigley, B. M., & Leonard, K. E. (2000). Alcohol, drugs, and violence. In V. B. Van Hasselt & M. Hersen (Eds.), *Aggression and violence: An introductory text.* Boston: Allyn & Bacon.

Quinn, P. C., & Bhatt, R. S. (1998). Visual pop-out in young infants. *Infant Behavior & Development, 21*(2), 273–288.

Raag, T., & Rackliff, C. L. (1998). Preschoolers' awareness of social expectations of gender: Relationships to toy choices. *Sex Roles, 38*(9–10), 685–700.

Rabius, V., McAlister, A. L., Geiger, A., Huang, P., et al. (2004). Telephone counseling increases cessation rates among young adult smokers. *Health Psychology, 23*(5), 539–541.

Rachman, S. (2004). *Anxiety* (2nd ed.). New York: Routledge.

Rahman, Q., & Wilson, G. D. (2003). Born gay? The psychobiology of human sexual orientation. *Personality & Individual Differences, 34*(8), 1337–1382.

Rainville, P. (2004). Pain & emotions. In D. D. Price & M. C. Bushnell (Eds.), *Psychological methods of pain control: Basic science and clinical perspectives.* Seattle: IASP Press.

Ramachandran, V. S. (1995). 2-D or not 2-D—that is the question. In R. Gregory, J. Harris, et al. (Eds.), *The artful eye.* New York: Oxford University Press.

Ramanaiah, N. V., Detwiler, F. R. J., & Byravan, A. (1995). Sex-role orientation and satisfaction with life. *Psychological Reports, 77*(3, Dec., Pt 2), 1260–1262.

Ramsay, M. C., Reynolds, C. R., & Kamphaus, R. W. (2002). *Essentials of behavioral assessment.* New York: Wiley.

Randi, J. (1983). Science and the chimera. In G. O. Abell & B. Singer (Eds.), *Science and the paranormal.* New York: Scribner's.

Randi, J. (1997). *An encyclopedia of claims, frauds, and hoaxes of the oc-*

cult and supernatural. New York: St. Martin's Press.

Rathus, R., Nevid, J., & Fichner-Rathus, L. (2005). *Human sexuality in a world of diversity* (6th ed.). Boston: Allyn & Bacon.

Rau, H., Bührer, M., & Weitkunat, R. (2003). Biofeedback of R-wave-to-pulse interval normalizes blood pressure. *Applied Psychophysiology and Biofeedback, 28*(1), 37–46.

Rau, P. R. (2005). *Drowsy driver detection and warning system for commercial vehicle drivers: Field operational test design, data analyses, and progress.* National Highway Traffic Safety Administration Paper Number 05-0192. Retrieved July 24, 2006, from http://www-nrd.nhtsa. dot.gov/pdf/nrd-01/esv/esv19/ 05-0192-W.pdf.

Rau, W., & Durand, A. (2000). The academic ethic and college grades: Does hard work help students to "make the grade"? *Sociology of Education, 73*(1), 19–38.

Read, J. (1995). Female sexual dysfunction. *International Review of Psychiatry, 7*(2), 175–182.

Reed, J. D., & Bruce, D. (1982). Longitudinal tracking of difficult memory retrievals. *Cognitive Psychology, 14,* 280–300.

Reed, S. K. (2007). *Cognition: Theory and applications* (7th ed.). Belmont, CA: Cengage Learning/ Wadsworth.

Reevy, G. M., & Maslach, C. (2001). Use of social support: Gender and personality differences. *Sex Roles, 44*(7–8), 437–459.

Regan, P. C., Levin, L., Sprecher, S., Christopher, F. S., et al. (2000). Partner preferences: What characteristics do men and women desire in their short-term sexual and long-term romantic partners? *Journal of Psychology & Human Sexuality, 12*(3), 1–21.

Regev, L. G., Zeiss, A., & Zeiss, R. (2006). Orgasmic disorders. In J. E. Fisher & W. T. O'Donohue (Eds.), *Practitioner's guide to evidence-based psychotherapy.* New York: Springer Science.

Regoeczi, W. C. (2003). When context matters: A multilevel analysis of household and neighbourhood crowding on aggression and withdrawal. *Journal of Environmental Psychology, 23*(4), 457–470.

Reid, M. R., Mackinnon, L. T., & Drummond, P. D. (2001). The effects of stress management on symptoms of upper respiratory tract infection, secretory immunoglobulin A, and mood in young adults. *Journal of Psychosomatic Research, 51*(6), 721–728.

Reid, P. T. (2002). Multicultural psychology. *Cultural Diversity & Ethnic Minority Psychology, 8*(2), 103–114.

Reiff, S., Katkin, E. S., & Friedman, R. (1999). Classical conditioning of the human blood pressure response. *International Journal of Psychophysiology, 34*(2), 135–145.

Reifman, A. S., Larrick, R. P., & Fein, S. (1991). Temper and temperature on the diamond: The heat-aggression relationship in major league baseball. *Personality & Social Psychology Bulletin, 17*(5), 580–585.

Reisner, A. D. (2006). A case of Munchausen Syndrome by proxy with subsequent stalking behavior. *International Journal of Offender Therapy & Comparative Criminology, 50*(3), 245–254.

Reiss, M., Tymnik, G., Koegler, P., Koegler, W., et al. (1999). Laterality of hand, foot, eye, and ear in twins. *Laterality, 4*(3), 287–297.

Reiss, S., & Havercamp, S. M. (2005). Motivation in developmental context: A new method for studying self-actualization. *Journal of Humanistic Psychology, 45*(1), 41–53.

Reissing, E. D., Binik, Y. M., Khalifé, S., Cohen, D., et al. (2004). Vaginal spasm, pain, and behavior: An empirical investigation of the diagnosis of vaginismus. *Archives of Sexual Behavior, 33*(1), 5–17.

Reissing, E. D., Binik, Y. M., Khalifé, S., Cohen, D., et al. (2003). Etiological correlates of vaginismus: Sexual and physical abuse, sexual knowledge sexual self-schema and relationship adjustment. *Journal of Sex & Marital Therapy, 29*(1), 47–59.

Reiterman, T. (1993). Parallel roads led to Jonestown, Waco. *The Los Angeles Times,* April 23, A24.

Reitman, D., Murphy, M. A., Hupp, S. D. A., & O'Callaghan, P. M. (2004). Behavior change and perceptions of change: Evaluating the effectiveness of a token economy. *Child & Family Behavior Therapy, 26*(2), 17–36.

Remland, M. S., Jones, T. S., & Brinkman, H. (1991). Proxemic and haptic behavior in three European countries. *Journal of Nonverbal Behavior, 15*(4), 215–232.

Renner, M. J., & Mackin, R. S. (1998). A life stress instrument for classroom use. *Teaching of Psychology, 25*(1), 46–48.

Rentfrow, P. J., & Gosling, S. D. (2003). The do re mi's of everyday life: The structure and personality correlates of music preferences. *Journal of Personality & Social Psychology, 84*(6), 1236–1256.

Reppucci, N. D., Woolard, J. L., & Fried, C. S. (1999). Social, community, and preventive interventions. *Annual Review of Psychology, 50,* 387–418.

Rescorla, R. A. (1987). A Pavlovian analysis of goal-directed behavior. *American Psychologist, 42,* 119–126.

Rescorla, R. A. (2004). Spontaneous recovery. *Learning & Memory, 11*(5), 501–509.

Restak, R. M. (2001). *The secret life of the brain.* New York: Dana Press.

Rhine, J. B. (1953). *New world of the mind.* New York: Sloane.

Rice, M. E. (1997). Violent offender research and implications for the criminal justice system. *American Psychologist, 52*(4), 414–423.

Richards, J. M., & Gross, J. J. (2000). Emotion regulation and memory: The cognitive costs of keeping one's cool. *Journal of Personality & Social Psychology, 79*(3), 410–424.

Richardson, D. R., & Green, L. R. (1999). Social sanction and threat explanations on gender effects in direct and indirect aggression. *Aggressive Behavior, 25,* 425–434.

Richmond, L. J. (2004). When spirituality goes awry: Students in cults. *Professional School Counseling, 7*(5), 367–375.

Ricketts, M. S., & Galloway, R. E. (1984). Effects of three different one-hour single-session treatments for test anxiety. *Psychological Reports, 54,* 113–119.

Ridenour, T. A., Maldonado-Molina M., Compton, W. M., Spitznagel, E. L., et al. (2005). Factors associated with the transition from abuse to dependence among substance abusers: Implications for a measure of addictive liability. *Drug & Alcohol Dependence, 80*(1), 1–14.

Ridings, C. M., & Gefen, D. (2004). Virtual community attraction: Why people hang out online. *Journal of Computer-Mediated Communication, 10*(1).

Riefer, D. M., Keveri, M. K., & Kramer, D. L. (1995). Name that tune: Eliciting the tip-of-the-tongue experience using auditory stimuli. *Psychological Reports, 77*(3, Pt. 2), 1379–1390.

Rieke, M. L., & Guastello, S. J. (1995). Unresolved issues in honesty and integrity testing. *American Psychologist,* June, 458–459.

Riley, W., Jerome, A., Behar, A., & Zack, S. (2002). Feasibility of computerized scheduled gradual reduction for adolescent smoking cessation. *Substance Use & Misuse, 37*(2), 255–263.

Riquelme, H. (2002). Can people creative in imagery interpret ambiguous figures faster than people less creative in imagery? *Journal of Creative Behavior, 36*(2), 105–116.

Ritter, J. (1998). Uniforms changing the culture of the nation's classrooms. *USA Today,* Oct. 15, 1A, 2A.

Riva, G., & Wiederhold, B. K. (2006). Emerging trends in cybertherapy: Introduction to the special issue. *PsychNology Journal, 4*(2), 121–128.

Rizzolatti, G., & Craighero, L. (2004). The mirror-neuron system.

Annual Review of Neuroscience, 27, 169–192.

Roberti, J. W. (2004). A review of behavioral and biological correlates of sensation seeking. *Journal of Research in Personality, 38,* 256–279.

Roberts, B. W., Walton, K. E., & Viechtbauer, W. (2006). Patterns of mean-level change in personality traits across the life course: a meta-analysis of longitudinal studies. *Psychological Bulletin, 132,* 1–25.

Roberts, D. F., Foehr, U. G., & Rideout, V. (2005). *Generation M: Media in the lives of 8-18 year-olds.* Kaiser Family Foundation. Retrieved June 6, 2007, from http://www.kff.org/entmedia/7251.cfm.

Roberts, R. E., Phinney, J. S., Masse, L. C., Chen, Y. R., et al. (1999). The structure of ethnic identity of young adolescents from diverse ethnocultural groups. *Journal of Early Adolescence, 19*(3), 301–322.

Roberts, W. A. & Roberts, S. (2002). Two tests of the stuck-in-time hypothesis. *Journal of General Psychology, 129*(4), 415–429.

Roberts, W. A. (2002). Are animals stuck in time? *Psychological Bulletin, 128*(3), 473–489.

Robertson, I. S. (2001). *Problem solving.* Hove, UK: Psychology Press.

Robertson, L. C., & Sagiv, N. (2005). *Synesthesia: Perspectives from cognitive neuroscience.* New York: Oxford University Press.

Robins, R. W., Gosling, S. D., & Craik, K. H. (1998). Psychological science at the crossroads. *American Scientist, 86,* (July–Aug.), 310–313.

Robinson, A., & Clinkenbeard, P. R. (1998). Giftedness. *Annual Review of Psychology, 49,* 117–139.

Robinson, B., Frye, E. M., & Bradley, L. J. (1997). Cult affiliation and disaffiliation. *Counseling & Values, 41*(2), 166–173.

Robinson, T. E., & Berridge, K. C. (2003). Addiction. *Annual Review of Psychology, 54,* 25–53.

Robinson, T. N., Wilde, M. L., Navracruz, L. C., Haydel, K. F., et al. (2001). Effects of reducing children's television and video game use on aggressive behavior. *Archives of Pediatrics & Adolescent Medicine, 155*(1), 17–23.

Robinson-Riegler, B., & McDaniel, M. (1994). Further constraints on the bizarreness effect: Elaboration at encoding. *Memory & Cognition, 22*(6), 702–712.

Rock, A. (2004). *The mind at night: The new science of how and why we dream.* New York: Basic Books.

Rodd, Z. A., Bell, R. L., McQueen, V. K., Davids, M. R., et al. (2005). Chronic ethanol drinking by alcohol-preferring rats increases the sensitivity of the posterior ventral tegmental area to the reinforcing effects of ethanol. *Alcoholism:*

Clinical & Experimental Research, 29(3), 358–366.

Roeckelein, J. E. (2004). *Imagery in psychology: A reference guide.* Westport, CT: Praeger.

Roediger, III, H. L., & McDermott, K. B. (1995). Creating false memories: Remembering words not presented on lists. *Journal of Experimental Psychology: Learning, Memory, and Cognition, 21*(4), 803–814.

Roediger, III, H. L., & Amir, N., (2005). Implicit memory tasks: Retention without conscious recollection. In A. Wenzel & D. C. Rubin (Eds.), *Cognitive methods and their application to clinical research.* Washington, DC: American Psychological Association.

Rogers, C. R. (1959). A theory of therapy, personality, and interpersonal relationships, as developed in the client-centered framework. In S. Koch (Ed.), *Psychology: A study of a science* (Vol. 3). New York: McGraw-Hill.

Rogers, C. R. (1961). *On becoming a person: A therapist's view of psychotherapy.* Boston: Houghton Mifflin.

Rogers, S., & Silver, S. M. (2002). Is EMDR an exposure therapy? A review of trauma protocols. *Journal of Clinical Psychology, 58*(1), 43–59.

Rohsenow, D. J., & Smith R. E. (1982). Irrational beliefs as predictors of negative affective states. *Motivation and Emotion, 6,* 299–301.

Roid, G. (2003). *Technical manual: Stanford-Binet Intelligence Scales* (5th ed.). Itasca, IL: Riverside.

Roney, J. R. (2003). Effects of visual exposure to the opposite sex: Cognitive aspects of mate attraction in human males. *Personality & Social Psychology Bulletin, 29,* 393–404.

Roos, P. E., & Cohen, L. H. (1987). Sex roles and social support as moderators of life stress adjustment. *Journal of Personality & Social Psychology, 52,* 576–585.

Rosch, E. (1977). Classification of real-world objects: Origins and representations in cognition. In P. N. Johnson-Laird & P. C. Wason (Eds.), *Thinking: Reading in cognitive science.* Cambridge, UK: Cambridge University Press.

Rosen, G., Hugdahl, K., Ersland, L., Lundervold, A., et al. (2001). Different brain areas activated during imagery of painful and non-painful "finger movements" in a subject with an amputated arm. *Neurocase, 7*(3), 255–260.

Rosenberg, L. B. (1994). The effect of interocular distance upon depth perception when using stereoscopic displays to perform work within virtual and telepresent environments. *USAF AMRL Technical Report (Wright-Patterson),* July, AL/CF-TR-1994-0052.

Rosenberg, S. S., & Lynch, J. E. (2002). Fritz Perls revisited: A micro-assessment of a live clinical session. *Gestalt Review, 6*(3), 184–202.

Rosenhan, D. L. (1973). On being sane in insane places. *Science, 179,* 250–258.

Rosenkranz, M.A., Jackson, D. C., Dalton, K. M., Dolski, I., et al. (2003). Affective style and in vivo immune response: Neurobehavioral mechanisms. *Proceedings of the National Academy of Sciences, 100,* 11148–11152.

Rosenman, R. H., Brand, R. J., Jenkins, C. D., Friedman, M., et al. (1975). Coronary heart disease in the Western Collaborative Group Study: Final follow-up experience of 8 1/2 years. *Journal of the American Medical Association, 233,* 872–877.

Rosenthal, D., & Quinn, O. W. (1977). Quadruplet hallucinations: Phenotypic variations of a schizophrenic genotype. *Archives of General Psychiatry, 34*(7), 817–827.

Rosenthal, R. (1965). *Clever Hans: A case study of scientific method. Introduction to Clever Hans: (The horse of Mr. Von Osten), by O. Pfungst.* New York: Holt, Rinehart & Winston.

Rosenthal, R. (1973). The Pygmalion effect lives. *Psychology Today,* Sept., 56–63.

Rosenthal, R. (1994). Science and ethics in conducting, analyzing, and reporting psychological research. *Psychological Science, 5,* 127–134.

Rosenthal, S. L., Von Ranson, K. M., Cotton, S., Biro, F. M., et al. (2001). Sexual initiation: Predictors and developmental trends. *Sexually Transmitted Diseases, 28*(9), 527–532.

Rosenthal, T. L. (1993). To soothe the savage breast. *Behavior Research & Therapy, 31*(5), 439–462.

Rosenthal, T. L., & Rosenthal, R. (1980). *The vicious cycle of stress reaction.* Renate & Ted Rosenthal, Stress Management Clinic, Department of Psychiatry, University of Tennessee College of Medicine, Memphis, Tennessee.

Rosenzweig, M. R., Breedlove, S. M., & Watson, N. V. (2004). Biological psychology: *An introduction to behavioral and cognitive neuroscience* (4th ed.). Sunderland, MA: Sinauer Associates.

Rosnow, R. L. (2006). *Writing papers in psychology: A student guide to research papers, essays, proposals, posters, and handouts* (7th ed.). Belmont, CA: Cengage Learning/Wadsworth.

Ross, H. E., & Plug, C. (2002). *The mystery of the moon illusion.* New York: Oxford University Press.

Ross, M., Heine, S. J., Wilson, A. E., & Sugimori, S. (2005). Cross-cultural discrepancies in self-appraisals. *Personality & Social Psychology Bulletin, 31*(9), 1175–1188.

Ross, P. E. (2006). The expert mind. *Scientific American, 294*(7), 64–71.

Rothbard, N. P., Phillips, K. W., & Dumas, T. L. (2005). Managing multiple roles: Work-family policies and individuals' desires for segmentation. *Organization Science, 16*(3), 243–258.

Rothschild, B., & Rand, M. (2006). *Help for the helper: The psychophysiology of compassion fatigue and vicarious trauma.* New York: Norton.

Rotter, J. B., & Hochreich, D. J. (1975). *Personality.* Glenview, IL: Scott, Foresman.

Rowe, B. (2007). *College awareness guide: What students need to know to succeed in college.* Englewood Cliffs, NJ: Prentice Hall.

Rowland, D. L. (2007). Sexual health and problems: Erectile dysfunction, premature ejaculation, and male orgasmic disorder. In J. E. Grant & M. N. Potenza (Eds.), *Textbook of men's mental health.* Washington, DC: American Psychiatric Publishing.

Rozin, P., Kabnick, K., Pete, E., Fischler, C., et al. (2003). The ecology of eating: Smaller portion sizes in France than in the United States help explain the French paradox. *Psychological Science, 14*(5), 450–454.

Rubenstein, C. (1983). The modern art of courtly love. *Psychology Today, 17*(7), 43–49.

Rubenstein, C. (2002). What turns you on? *My Generation,* July–Aug., 55–58.

Rubenstein, C., & Tavris, C. (1987). Special survey results: 2600 women reveal the secrets of intimacy. *Redbook, 159,* 147–149.

Rubin, D. C. (1985). The subtle deceiver: Recalling our past. *Psychology Today,* Sept., 38–46.

Rubin, Z. (1973). *Liking and loving: An invitation to social psychology.* New York: Holt.

Rudd, M. D., Joiner, T. E., Jr., & Rajab, M. H. (2001). *Treating suicidal behavior.* New York: Guilford.

Rueckl, J. G., & Galantucci, B. (2005). The locus and time course of long-term morphological priming. *Language & Cognitive Processes, 20*(1), 115–138.

Rummens, J., Beiser, M., & Noh, S. (Eds.). (2003). *Immigration, ethnicity and health.* Toronto: University of Toronto Press.

Runco, M. A. (2003). *Critical creative processes.* Cresskill, NJ: Hampton Press.

Runco, M. A. (2004). Creativity. *Annual Review of Psychology, 55,* 657–687.

Rushton, J. P., & Jensen, A. R. (2005). Thirty years of research on race differences in cognitive ability. *Psychology, Public Policy, & Law, 11,* 235–294.

Russell, S., & Norvig, P. (2003). *Artificial intelligence: A modern approach* (2nd ed.). Englewood Cliffs, NJ: Prentice Hall.

Russo, M. B., Brooks, F. R., Fontenot, J., Dopler, D. M., et al. (1998). Conversion disorder presenting as multiple sclerosis. *Military Medicine, 163*(10), 709–710.

Rutledge, T., & Linden, W. (1998). To eat or not to eat: Affective and physiological mechanisms in the stress–eating relationship. *Journal of Behavioral Medicine, 21*(3), 221–240.

Ruva, C., McEvoy, C., & Bryant, J. B. (2007). Effects of pre-trial publicity and jury deliberation on juror bias and source memory errors. *Applied Cognitive Psychology, 21*(1), 45–67.

Ryan, M. P. (2001). Conceptual models of lecture learning. *Reading Psychology, 22*(4), 289–312.

Ryan, R. M., & Deci, E. L. (2000). Self-determination theory and the facilitation of intrinsic motivation, social development, and well-being. *American Psychologist, 55,* 68–78.

Ryckman, R. M. (2008). *Theories of personality* (9th ed.). Belmont, CA: Cengage Learning/Wadsworth.

Ryff, C. D. (1995). Psychological well-being in adult life. *Current Directions in Psychological Science, 4*(4), 99–104.

Ryff, C. D., & Keyes, C. L. (1995). The structure of psychological well-being revisited. *Journal of Personality & Social Psychology, 69*(4), 719–727.

Ryff, C. D., & Singer, B. (2000). Interpersonal flourishing. *Personality & Social Psychology Review, 4,* 30–44.

Ryff, C. D., Singer, B. H., & Palmersheim, K. A. (2004). Social inequalities in health and well-being: The role of relational and religious protective factors. In O. G. Brim, C. D. Ryff, et al. (Eds.), *How healthy are we? A national study of wellbeing at midlife.* Chicago, IL: University of Chicago Press.

Saadeh, W., Rizzo, C. P., & Roberts, D. G. (2002). Spanking. *Clinical Pediatrics, 41*(2), 87–88.

Sackeim, H. A., Haskett, R. F., Mulsant, B. H., Thase, M. E., et al. (2001). Continuation pharmacotherapy in the prevention of relapse following electroconvulsive therapy. *Journal of the American Medical Association, 285,* 1299–1307.

Sahelian, R. (1998). *5-HTP.* Wakefield, RI: Moyer Bell.

Saksida, L. M., & Wilkie, D. M. (1994). Time-of-day discrimination by pigeons. *Animal Learning & Behavior, 22,* 143–154.

Sales, B. D., & Hafemeister, T. L. (1985). Law and psychology. In E. M. Altmeir & M. E. Meyer (Eds.), *Applied specialties in psychology.* New York: Random House.

Salmela, J. H. (1974). An information processing approach to volleyball. *C.V.A. Technical Journal, 1,* 49–62.

Salmela, J. H. (1975). Psycho-motor task demands of artistic gymnastics. In J. H. Salmela (Ed.), *The advanced study of gymnastics: A textbook.* Springfield, IL: Charles C Thomas.

Salmon, P. (2001). Effects of physical exercise on anxiety, depression, and sensitivity to stress: A unifying theory. *Clinical Psychology Review, 21*(1), 33–61.

Salovey, P., & Mayer, J. (1997). *Emotional development and emotional intelligence.* New York: Basic Books.

Salthouse, T. A. (2004). What and when of cognitive aging. *Current Directions in Psychological Science, 13*(4), 140–144.

SAMHAS (Substance Abuse and Mental Health Services Administration). (2005). *Overview of Findings from the 2004 National Survey on Drug Use and Health.* Rockville, MD: Office of Applied Studies, NSDUH Series H-27, DHHS Publication No. SMA 05-4061. Retrieved June 6, 2007, from http://www.oas.samhsa.gov/nsduh/2k4nsduh/2k4overview/2k4overview.pdf.

Sankofa, B. M., Hurley, E. A., Allen, B. A., & Boykin, A. W. (2005). Cultural expression and black students' attitudes toward high achievers. *Journal of Psychology: Interdisciplinary & Applied, 139*(3), 247–259.

Santrock, J. W. (2007). *Child development* (11th ed.). New York: McGraw-Hill.

Santrock, J. W., & Halonen, J. S. (2007). *Connections to college success.* Belmont, CA: Cengage Learning/Wadsworth.

Sarason, I. G., & Sarason, B. R. (2005). *Abnormal psychology* (11th ed.). Englewood Cliffs, NJ: Prentice Hall.

Sateia, M. J., & Nowell, P. D. (2004). Insomnia. *Lancet, 364*(9449), 1959–1973.

Saunders, T., Driskell, J. E., Johnston, J. H., Salas, E. (1996). The effect of stress inoculation training on anxiety and performance. *Journal of Occupational Health Psychology, 1*(2), 170–186.

Savage-Rumbaugh, S., & Lewin, R. (1996). *Kanzi.* New York: Wiley.

Savage-Rumbaugh, S., Murphy, J., Sevcik, R. A., Brakke, K. E., et al. (1993). Language comprehension in ape and child. *Monographs of the Society for Research in Child Development, Serial No. 233* (Vol. 58, Nos. 3–4).

Savage-Rumbaugh, S., Sevcik, R. A., Brakke, K. E., Rumbaugh, D. M., et al. (1990). Symbols: Their communicative use, comprehension, and combination by bonobos (Pan paniscus). *Advances in Infancy Research, 6,* 221–278.

Savage-Rumbaugh, S., Shanker, S., & Taylor, T. (1998). *Apes, language, and mind.* New York: Oxford University Press.

Sawyer, R. G., & Smith, N. G. (1996). A survey of situational factors at first intercourse among college students. *American Journal of Health Behavior, 20*(4), 208–217.

Saxton, M., Houston-Price, C., & Dawson, N. (2005). The prompt hypothesis: Clarification requests as corrective input for grammatical errors. *Applied Psycholinguistics, 26*(3), 393–414.

Saywitz, K. J., Mannarino, A. P., Berliner, L., & Cohen, J. A. (2000). Treatment for sexually abused children and adolescents. *American Psychologist, 55*(9), 1040–1049.

Schachter, S. (1959). *Psychology of affiliation.* Stanford, CA: Stanford University Press.

Schachter, S., & Wheeler, L. (1962). Epinephrine, chlorpromazine and amusement. *Journal of Abnormal & Social Psychology, 65,* 121–128.

Schacter, D. L. (1996). *Searching for memory: The brain, the mind, and the past.* New York: Basic Books.

Schacter, D. L. (2000). Memory: Memory systems. In A. Kazdin (Ed.), *Encyclopedia of psychology.* Washington, DC: American Psychological Association.

Schacter, D. L. (2001). *The seven sins of memory.* Boston: Houghton Mifflin.

Schacter, D. L., Norman, K. A., & Koutstaal, W. (1998). The cognitive neuroscience of constructive memory. *Annual Review of Psychology, 49,* 289–318.

Schafer, M., & Crichlow, S. (1996). Antecedents of groupthink: A quantitative study. *Journal of Conflict Resolution, 40*(3), 415–435.

Schaie, K. W. (1994). The course of adult intellectual development. *American Psychologist, 49*(4), 304–313.

Schaie, K. W. (2005). *Developmental influences on adult intelligence: The Seattle longitudinal study.* New York: Oxford University Press.

Scheck, B., Neufeld, P., & Dwyer, J. (2000). *Actual innocence.* New York: Doubleday.

Schenck, C. H., & Mahowald, M. W. (2005). Rapid eye movement and non-REM sleep parasomnias. *Primary Psychiatry, 12*(8), 67–74.

Schick, T., & Vaughn, L. (2004). *How to think about weird things: Critical thinking for a new age* (4th ed.). New York: McGraw-Hill.

Schilling, M. A. (2005). A "Small-World" network model of cognitive insight. *Creativity Research Journal, 17*(2–3), 131–154.

Schiraldi, G. R., & Brown, S. L. (2001). Primary prevention for mental health: Results of an exploratory cognitive-behavioral college course. *Journal of Primary Prevention, 22*(1), 55–67.

Schleicher, S. S., & Gilbert, L. A. (2005). Heterosexual dating discourses among college students: Is there still a double standard? *Journal of College Student Psychotherapy, 19*(3), 7–23.

Schlosberg, H. (1954). Three dimensions of emotion. *Psychological Review, 61,* 81–88.

Schmidt, F. L., & Hunter, J. E. (1998). The validity and utility of selection methods in personnel psychology. *Psychological Bulletin, 124*(2), 262–274.

Schmidt, F. L., Ones, D. S., & Hunter, J. E. (1992). Personnel selection. *Annual Review of Psychology, 43,* 627–670.

Schmitt, D. P., & Allik, J. (2005). Simultaneous administration of the Rosenberg Self-Esteem Scale in 53 nations: Exploring the universal and culture-specific features of global self-esteem. *Journal of Personality & Social Psychology, 89*(4), 623–642.

Schmitt, E. (2001). U.S. now more diverse, ethnically and racially. *New York Times,* Apr. 1, A18.

Schmolck, H., Buffalo, E. A., & Squire, L. R. (2000). Memory distortions develop over time. *Psychological Science, 11*(1), 39–45.

Schmuck, P., & Vlek, C. (2003). Psychologists can do much to support sustainable development. *European Psychologist, 8*(2), 66–76.

Schneider, K. J. (2002). Humanistic psychotherapy. In M. Hersen & W. H. Sledge (Eds.), *Encyclopedia of psychotherapy.* San Diego: Academic Press.

Schneider, K. J., Bugental, J. F. T., & Pierson, J. F. (2001). Introduction. *The Handbook of Humanistic Psychology.* Thousand Oaks, CA: Sage.

Schneiderman, N., Antoni, M. H., Saab, P. G., & Ironson, G. (2001). Health psychology: Psychological and biobehavioral aspects of chronic disease management. *Annual Review of Psychology, 52,* 555–580.

Schooler, C. (1998). Environmental complexity and the Flynn effect. In U. Neisser (Ed.), *The rising curve: Long-term gains in IQ and related measures.* Washington, DC: American Psychological Association.

Schopp, L. H., Demiris, G., & Glueckauf, R. L. (2006). Rural backwaters or front-runners? Rural telehealth in the vanguard of psychology practice. *Professional Psychology: Research & Practice, 37*(2), 165–173.

Schouten, S. A. (1994). An overview of quantitatively evaluated studies with mediums and psychics. *Journal of the American Society for Psychical Research, 88*(3), 221–254.

Schreiber, E. H., & Schreiber, D. E. (1999). Use of hypnosis with witnesses of vehicular homicide. *Contemporary Hypnosis, 16*(1), 40–44.

Schreiber, F. R. (1973). *Sybil.* Chicago: Regency.

Schroeder, J. E. (1995). Self-concept, social anxiety, and interpersonal perception skills. *Personality & Individual Differences, 19*(6), 955–958.

Schuel, H., Chang, M. C., Burkman, L. J., Picone, R. P., et al. (1999). Cannabinoid receptors in sperm. In G. Nahas, K. M. Sutin, et al. (Eds.), *Marihuana and medicine.* Totowa, NJ: Humana Press.

Schuetze, P., & Eiden, R. D. (2006). The association between maternal cocaine use during pregnancy and physiological regulation in 4- to 8-week-old infants: An examination of possible mediators and moderators. *Journal of Pediatric Psychology, 31*(1), 15–26.

Schuiling, G. A. (2004). Death in Venice: The homosexuality enigma. *Journal of Psychosomatic Obstetrics & Gynecology, 25*(1), 67–76.

Schultheiss, O. C., Wirth, M. M., & Stanton, S. J. (2004). Effects of affiliation and power motivation arousal on salivary progesterone and testosterone. *Hormones and Behavior, 46*(5), 592–599.

Schultz, D. P., & Schultz, S. E. (2005). *Theories of personality* (8th ed.). Belmont, CA: Cengage Learning/Wadsworth.

Schultz, D. P., & Schultz, S. E. (2006). *Psychology and work today* (9th ed.). Englewood Cliffs, NJ: Prentice Hall.

Schultz, D. P., & Schultz, S. E. (2008). *A history of modern psychology* (9th ed.). Belmont, CA: Cengage Learning/Wadsworth.

Schultz, H. T. (2004). Good and bad movie therapy with good and bad outcomes. *The Amplifier: Official Newsletter of APA Division 46, Media Psychology,* Fall/Winter. Retrieved May 18, 2007, from http://www.apa.org/divisions/div46/Amp%20Winter%2005/for%20Website/ampwinter05.html#therapy.

Schultz, P. W. (1999). Changing behavior with normative feedback interventions. *Basic & Applied Social Psychology, 21*(1), 25–36.

Schum T. R., Kolb, T. M., McAuliffe T. L., Simms, M., et al. (2002). Sequential acquisition of toilet-training skills: A descriptive study of gender and age differences in normal children. *Pediatrics, 3,* e48. Retrieved May 25, 2007, from http://pediatrics.aappublications.org/cgi/content/abstract/109/3/e48.

Schum, T. R., McAuliffe, T. L., Simms, M. D., Walter, J. A., et al. (2001). Factors associated with toilet training in the 1990s. *Ambulatory Pediatrics, 1*(2), 79–86.

Schuster, M. A., Stein, B. D., Jaycox, L. H., Collins, R. L., et al. (2001). A national survey of stress reactions after the September 11, 2001, terrorist attacks. *New England Journal of Medicine, 345*(20), 1507–1512.

Schwartz, B. L. (2002). *Tip-of-the-tongue states: Phenomenology, mechanism, and lexical retrieval.* Mahwah, NJ: Erlbaum.

Schwartz, M. S., & Andrasik, F. (Eds.). (2003). *Biofeedback: A practitioner's guide* (3rd ed.). New York: Guilford.

Sclafani, A., & Springer, D. (1976). Dietary obesity in adult rats: Similarities to hypothalamic and human obesity syndromes. *Psychology & Behavior, 17,* 461–471.

Scoboria, A., Mazzoni, G., Kirsch, I., & Milling, L. S. (2002). Immediate and persisting effects of misleading questions and hypnosis on memory reports. *Journal of Experimental Psychology: Applied, 8*(1), 26–32.

Scott, J. P., & Ginsburg, B. E. (1994). The Seville statement on violence revisited. *American Psychologist, 49*(10), 849–850.

Scott, L., & O'Hara, M. W. (1993). Self-discrepancies in clinically anxious and depressed university students. *Journal of Abnormal Psychology, 102*(2), 282–287.

Scurfield, R. M. (2002). Commentary about the terrorist acts of September 11, 2001: Posttraumatic reactions and related social and policy issues. *Trauma Violence & Abuse, 3*(1), 3–14.

Searcy, W. A., & Nowicki, S. (2005). *The evolution of animal communication: Reliability and deception in signaling systems.* Princeton, NJ: Princeton University Press.

Seckel, A. (2000). *The art of optical illusions.* London: Carlton Books.

Segerdahl, P., Fields, W., & Savage-Rumbaugh, S. (2005). *Kanzi's primal language: The cultural initiation of primates into language.* New York: Palgrave MacMillan.

Segerstrom, S., & Miller, G. E. (2004). Psychological stress and the human immune system: A meta-analytic study of 30 years of inquiry. *Psychological Bulletin, 130*(4), 601–630.

Segraves, R. T., & Segraves, K. B. (1995). Human sexuality and aging. *Journal of Sex Education & Therapy, 21*(2), 88–102.

Segraves, R., & Woodard, T. (2006). Female hypoactive sexual desire disorder: History and current status. *Journal of Sexual Medicine, 3*(3), 408–418.

Segraves, T., & Althof, S. (2002). Psychotherapy and pharmacotherapy for sexual dysfunctions. In P. E. Nathan & J. M. Gorman (Eds.), *A guide to treatments that work* (2nd ed.). New York: Oxford University Press.

Seidler, G. H., & Wagner, F. E. (2006). Comparing the efficacy of EMDR and trauma-focused cognitive-behavioral therapy in the treatment of PTSD: A meta-analytic study. *Psychological Medicine, 36*(11), 1515–1522.

Seidman, B. F. (2001). Medicine wars. *Skeptical Inquirer,* Jan.–Feb., 28–35.

Seitz, A., & Watanabe, T. (2005). A unified model for perceptual learning. *Trends in Cognitive Sciences, 9*(7), 329–334.

Sekuler, R., & Blake, R. (2006). *Perception* (5th ed.). New York: McGraw-Hill.

Seligman, M. E. P. (1972). For helplessness: Can we immunize the weak? In *Readings in psychology today* (2nd ed.). Del Mar, CA: CRM.

Seligman, M. E. P. (1989). *Helplessness.* New York: Freeman.

Seligman, M. E. P. (1989). Research in clinical psychology: Why is there so much depression today? In I. S. Cohen (Ed.), *The G. Stanley Hall lecture series* (Vol. 9). Washington, DC: American Psychological Association.

Seligman, M. E. P. (1994). *What you can change and what you can't.* New York: Knopf.

Seligman, M. E. P. (1995). The effectiveness of psychotherapy. *American Psychologist, 50*(12), 965–974.

Seligman, M. E. P. (1998). Why therapy works. *APA Monitor, 29*(12), 2.

Seligman, M. E. P. (2002). *Authentic happiness.* New York: Free Press.

Seligman, M. E. P. (2003). Positive psychology: Fundamental assumptions. *Source Psychologist, 16*(3), 126–127.

Seligman, M. E. P., & Csikszentmihalyi, M. (2000). Positive psychology: An introduction. *American Psychologist, 55,* 5–14.

Seltzer, R. (2006). Scientific jury selection: Does it work?. *Journal of Applied Social Psychology, 36*(10), 2417–2435.

Selye, H. (1976). *The stress of life.* New York: Knopf.

Senécal, C., Julien, E., & Guay, F. (2003). Role conflict and academic procrastination: A self-determination perspective.

European Journal of Social Psychology, 33(1), 135–145.

Service, R. F. (1994). Will a new type of drug make memory-making easier? *Science, 266,* 218–219.

Sessa, V. I., & London, M. (2006). *Continuous learning in organizations: Individual, group, and organizational perspectives.* Mahwah, NJ: Erlbaum.

Seybolt, D. C., & Wagner, M. K. (1997). Self-reinforcement, gender-role, and sex of participant in prediction of life satisfaction. *Psychological Reports, 81*(2), 519–522.

Seyle, D. C., & Newman, M. L. (2006). A house divided? The psychology of red and blue America. *American Psychologist, 61*(6), 571–580.

Shaffer, D. R. (2002). *Developmental psychology.* Belmont, CA: Cengage Learning/Wadsworth.

Shaffer, J. B., & Galinsky, M. D. (1989). *Models of group therapy.* Englewood Cliffs, NJ: Prentice Hall.

Shafir, E. (1993). Choosing versus rejecting: Why some options are both better and worse than others. *Memory and Cognition, 21,* 546–556.

Shafton, A. (1995). *Dream reader.* Albany, NY: State University of New York Press.

Shakesby, A. C., Anwyl, R., & Rowan, M. J. (2002). Overcoming the effects of stress on synaptic plasticity in the intact hippocampus: Rapid actions of serotonergic and antidepressant agents. *Journal of Neuroscience, 22,* 3638–3644.

Shapiro, C. M., Trajanovic, N. N., & Fedoroff, J. P. (2003). Sexsomnia: A new parasomnia? *Canadian Journal of Psychiatry, 48*(5), 311–317.

Shapiro, D. A., Barkham, M., Stiles, W. B., Hardy, G. E., et al. (2003). Time is of the essence: A selective review of the fall and rise of brief therapy research. *Psychology & Psychotherapy: Theory, Research & Practice, 76*(3), 211–235.

Shapiro, F. (2001). *Eye movement desensitization and reprocessing: Basic principles, protocols and procedures* (2nd ed.). New York: Guilford.

Shapiro, F., & Forrest, M. S. (2004). *EMDR: The breakthrough therapy for overcoming anxiety, stress, and trauma.* New York: Basic Books.

Shapiro, J. M. (2006). A "memory-jamming" theory of advertising. *Social Science Research Network.* Retrieved June 20, 2007, from http://ssrn.com/abstract=903474.

Shapiro, S. L., & Walsh, R. (2006). The meeting of meditative disciplines and Western psychology: A mutually enriching dialogue. *American Psychologist, 61*(3), 227–239.

Sharf, R. S. (2008). *Theories of psychotherapy & counseling: Concepts and cases* (4th ed.). Belmont, CA: Cengage Learning/Wadsworth.

Shaywitz, B. A, Shaywitz, S. E., Pugh, K. R., Constable, R. T., et al. (1995). Sex differences in the functional organization of the brain for language. *Nature, 373*(6515), 607–609.

Shaywitz, S. E., & Gore, J. C. (1995). Sex differences in functional organization of the brain for language. *Nature, 373*(6515), 607.

Sheehy, M., & Cournos, F. (1992). What is mental illness? In F. I. Kass, J. M. Oldham, et al. (Eds.), *The Columbia University College of Physicians and Surgeons complete home guide to mental health.* New York: Sharpe Communications/Henry Holt.

Sheldon, K. M., Ryan, R. M., Rawsthorne, L. J., & Ilardi, B. (1997). Trait self and true self: Cross-role variation in the Big-Five personality traits and its relations with psychological authenticity and subjective well-being. *Journal of Personality & Social Psychology, 73*(6), 1380–1393.

Shen, J., Botly, L. C. P., Chung, S. A., Gibbs, A. L., et al. (2006). Fatigue and shift work. *Journal of Sleep Research, 15*(1), 1–5.

Shepard, R. N. (1975). Form, formation, and transformation of internal representations. In R. L. Solso (Ed.), *Information processing and cognition: The Loyola Symposium.* Mahwah, NJ: Erlbaum.

Sherif, M., Harvey, O. J., White, B. J., Hood, W. R., et al. (1961). *Intergroup conflict and cooperation: The Robbers Cave experiment.* University of Oklahoma, Institute of Group Relations.

Shiffman, S., Scharf, D. M., Shadel, W. G., Gwaltney, C. J., et al. (2006). Analyzing milestones in smoking cessation: Illustration in a nicotine patch trial in adult smokers. *Journal of Consulting & Clinical Psychology, 74*(2), 276–285.

Shires, A., & Miller, D. (1998). A preliminary study comparing psychological factors associated with erectile dysfunction in heterosexual and homosexual men. *Sexual & Marital Therapy, 13*(1), 37–49.

Shneerson, J. M. (2005). *Sleep medicine: A guide to sleep and its disorders* (2nd ed.). London: Blackwell.

Shneidman, E. S. (1987a). At the point of no return. *Psychology Today,* March, 54–58.

Shneidman, E. S. (1987b). Psychological approaches to suicide. In G. R. VandenBos & B. K. Bryant (Eds.), *Cataclysms, crises, and catastrophes: Psychology in action.* Washington, DC: American Psychological Association.

Shore, H. (2003). Personal communication.

Short, S. E., Ross-Stewart, L., & Monsma, E. V. (2006). Onwards with the evolution of imagery research in sport psychology. *Athletic Insight: Online Journal of Sport Psychology, 8*(3), 1–15.

Shurkin, J. N. (1992). *Terman's kids.* Boston: Little, Brown.

Siegel, R. K. (2005). *Intoxication: The universal drive for mind-altering substances.* Rochester, VT: Park Street Press.

Siegler, R. S. (2004). *Children's thinking* (4th ed.). Mahwah, NJ: Erlbaum.

Siegler, R. S., DeLoache, J. S., & Eisenberg, N. (2006). *How children develop* (2nd ed.). New York: Worth.

Siever, L. J., & Koenigsberg, H. W. (2000). The frustrating no-man's land of borderline personality disorder. *Cerebrum, 2*(4), 85–99.

Sigelman, C. K., & Rider, E. A. (2006). *Life-span human development* (5th ed.). Belmont, CA: Cengage Learning/Wadsworth.

Silver, S. M., Rogers, S., Knipe, J., & Colelli, G. (2005). EMDR therapy following the 9/11 terrorist attacks: A community-based intervention project in New York City. *International Journal of Stress Management, 12*(1), 29–42.

Silverstein, B. (1989). Enemy images. *American Psychologist, 44*(6), 903–913.

Simeon, D., Guralnik, O., Knutelska, M., & Schmeidler, J. (2002). Personality factors associated with dissociation: Temperament, defenses, and cognitive schemata. *American Journal of Psychiatry, 159,* 489–491.

Simister, J., & Cooper, C. (2005). Thermal stress in the U.S.A.: Effects on violence and on employee behaviour. *Stress & Health, 21,* 3–15.

Simner, M. L., & Goffin, R. D. (2003). A position statement by the international graphonomics society on the use of graphology in personnel selection testing. *International Journal of Testing, 3*(4), 353–364.

Simon, G. E, Ludman, E. J., Tutty, S., Operskalski, B., et al. (2004). Telephone psychotherapy and telephone care management for primary care patients starting antidepressant treatment. *Journal of the American Medical Association, 292,* 935–942.

Simons, D. J., & Chabris, C. F. (1999). Gorillas in our midst: Sustained inattentional blindness for dynamic events. *Perception, 28,* 1059–1074.

Simons, D. J., & Levin, D. T. (1998). Failure to detect changes to people during a real-world interaction. *Psychonomic Bulletin & Review, 5*(4), 644–649.

Simons, J. S., Dodson, C. S., Bell, D., & Schacter, D. L. (2004). Specific- and partial-source memory: Effects of aging. *Psychology & Aging, 19*(4), 689–694.

Simonton, D. K., & Baumeister, R. F. (2005). Positive psychology at the summit. *Review of General Psychology, 9*(2), 99–102.

Simpson, D. D., Joe, G. W., Fletcher, B. W., Hubbard, R. L, et al. (1999). A national evaluation of treatment outcomes for cocaine dependence. *Archives of General Psychiatry, 57*(6), 507–514.

Singer, M. T. (2003). *Cults in our midst: The continuing fight against their hidden menace* (rev. ed.). San Francisco: Jossey-Bass.

Singer, M. T., & Addis, M. E. (1992). Cults, coercion, and contumely. *Cultic Studies Journal, 9*(2), 163–189.

Singleton, J. L., & Newport, E. L. (2004). When learners surpass their models: The acquisition of American Sign Language from inconsistent input. *Cognitive Psychology, 49*(4), 370–407.

Sinha, R., Garcia, M., Paliwal, P., Kreek, M. J., et al. (2006). Stress-induced cocaine craving and hypothalamic-pituitary-adrenal responses are predictive of cocaine relapse outcomes. *Archives of General Psychiatry, 63*(3), 324–331.

Sipos, A., Rasmussen, F., Harrison, G., Tynelius, P., et al. (2004). Paternal age and schizophrenia: A population based cohort study. *British Medical Journal, 329*(7474), 1070.

Sirkin, M. I. (1990). Cult involvement: A systems approach to assessment and treatment. *Psychotherapy, 27*(1), 116–123.

Skeels, H. M. (1966). Adult status of children with contrasting early life experiences. *Monograph of the Society for Research in Child Development, 31*(3), 105.

Skillsoft (2006). *IT pros more likely to suffer from stress, says new survey.* Retrieved July 17, 2007, from http://www.skillsoft.com/EMEA/news/19-May-06.asp.

Skinner, B. F. (1938). *The behavior of organisms: An experimental analysis.* New York: Appleton-Century-Crofts.

Skipton, L. H. (1997). The many faces of character. *Consulting Psychology Journal: Practice & Research, 49*(4), 235–245.

Skoog, I. (1996). Sex and Swedish 85-year-olds. *British Journal of Clinical Psychology, 334*(17), 1140–1141.

Slaby, A. E., Garfinkel, B. D., & Garfinkel, L. F. (1994). *No one say my pain.* New York: Norton.

Slater, A., Mattock, A., & Brown, E. (1990). Size constancy at birth: Newborn infants' responses to retinal and real size. *Journal of Experimental Child Psychology, 49*(2), 314–322.

Slater, A., Mattock, A., Brown, E., & Bremner, J. G. (1991). Form

perception at birth: Cohen and Younger (1984) revisited. *Journal of Experimental Child Psychology, 51*(3), 395–406.

Slijper, F. M. E., Drop, S. L. S., Molenaar, J. C.; de Muinck, K., et al. (2000). "Long-term psychological evaluation of intersex children": Reply. *Archives of Sexual Behavior, 29*(1), 119–121.

Slot, L. A. B., & Colpaert, F. C. (1999). Recall rendered dependent on an opiate state. *Behavioral Neuroscience, 113*(2), 337–344.

Smedley, A., & Smedley, B. D. (2005). Race as biology is fiction, racism as a social problem is real. *American Psychologist, 60*(1), 16–26.

Smith, A. P. (2005). Caffeine at work. *Human Psychopharmacology: Clinical & Experimental, 20*(6), 441–445.

Smith, A. P., Clark, R., & Gallagher, J. (1999). Breakfast cereal and caffeinated coffee: Effects on working memory, attention, mood and cardiovascular function. *Physiology & Behavior, 67*(1), 9–17.

Smith, C., Carey, S., & Wiser, M. (1985). On differentiation: A case study of the development of the concepts of size, weight, and density. *Cognition, 21*(3), 177–237.

Smith, E., & Delargy, M (2005). Locked-in syndrome. *British Medical Journal, 330*, 406–409.

Smith, J. L., & Cahusac, P. M. B. (2001). Right-sided asymmetry in sensitivity to tickle. *Laterality, 6*(3), 233–238.

Smith, L. F. (2002). The effects of confidence and perception of test-taking skills on performance. *North American Journal of Psychology, 4*(1), 37–50.

Smith, M. L., Cottrell, G. W., Gosselin, F., & Schyns, P. G. (2005). Transmitting and decoding facial expressions. *Psychological Science, 16*(3), 184–189.

Smith, T. W. (1990). *Adult sexual behavior in 1989: Number of partners, frequency, and risk.* Paper presented to the American Association for the Advancement of Science, February 1990, New Orleans.

Smith, T. W., Glazer, K., Ruiz, J. M., & Gallo, L. C. (2004). Hostility, anger, aggressiveness, and coronary heart disease: An interpersonal perspective on personality, emotion, and health. *Journal of Personality, 72*(6), 1217–1270.

Smith, T. W., Ruiz, J. M., & Uchino, B. N. (2004). Mental activation of supportive ties, hostility, and cardiovascular reactivity to laboratory stress in young men and women. *Health Psychology, 23*(5), 476–485.

Smyth, M. M., & Waller, A. (1998). Movement imagery in rock climbing. *Applied Cognitive Psychology, 12*(1), 145–157.

Sobel, E., Shine, D., DiPietro, D., & Rabinowitz, M. (1996). Con-

dom use among HIV/infected patients in South Bronx, New York. *AIDS, 10*(2), 235–236.

Sobolewski, J. M., & Amato, P. R. (2005). Economic hardship in the family of origin and children's psychological well-being in adulthood. *Journal of Marriage & Family, 67*(1), 141–156.

Solomon, J. L., Marshall, P., & Gardner, H. (2005). Crossing boundaries to generative wisdom: An analysis of professional work. In R. J. Sternberg & J. Jordan (Eds.), *A handbook of wisdom: Psychological perspectives.* New York: Cambridge University Press.

Solowij, N., Stephens, R. S., Roffman, R. A., & the Marijuana Treatment Project Research Group. (2002). Cognitive functioning of long-term heavy cannabis users seeking treatment. *Journal of the American Medical Association, 287*, 1123–1131.

Solso, R. L., MacLin, M. K., & MacLin, O. H. (2005). *Cognitive psychology* (7th ed). Boston: Allyn and Bacon.

Somberg, D. R., Stone, G., & Claiborn, C. D. (1993). Informed consent: Therapist's beliefs and practices. *Professional Psychology: Research & Practice, 24*(2), 153–159.

Sommers-Flanagan, J., & Sommers-Flanagan, R. (2002). *Clinical interviewing* (3rd ed.). New York: Wiley.

Soussignan, R. (2002). Duchenne smile, emotional experience, and autonomic reactivity. *Emotion, 2*(1), 52–74.

Soyez, V., & Broekaert, E. (2003). How do substance abusers and their significant others experience the re-entry phase of therapeutic community treatment: a qualitative study. *International Journal of Social Welfare, 12*(3), 211–220.

Spangenberg, J. J., & Lategan, T. P. (1993). Coping, androgyny, and attributional style. *South African Journal of Psychology, 23*(4), 195–203.

Spector, P. E. (2005). *Industrial and organizational psychology: Research and practice* (4th ed.). New York: Wiley.

Spence, S., & David, A. (Eds.). (2004). *Voices in the brain: The cognitive neuropsychiatry of auditory verbal hallucinations.* London: Psychology Press.

Sperry, R. W. (1968). Hemisphere deconnection and unity in conscious awareness. *American Psychologist, 23*, 723–733.

Spiegler, M. D., & Guevremont, D. C. (2003). *Contemporary behavior therapy.* Belmont, CA: Cengage Learning/Wadsworth

Spinella, M. (2005). Compulsive behavior in tobacco users. *Addictive Behaviors, 30*(1), 183–186.

Spiro Wagner, P., & Spiro, C. S. (2005). *Divided minds: Twin sisters and their journey through schizophrenia.* New York, St. Martin's Press, 2005

Sporer, S. L. (2001). Recognizing faces of other ethnic groups. *Psychology, Public Policy, & Law, 7*(1), 36–97.

Sprecher, S. (1998). Insiders' perspectives on reasons for attraction to a close other. *Social Psychology Quarterly, 61*(4), 287–300.

Sprecher, S., & Hatfield, E. (1996). Premarital sexual standards among U.S. college students. *Archives of Sexual Behavior, 25*(3), 261–288.

Springer, S. P., & Deutsch, G. (1998). *Left brain, right brain.* New York: Freeman.

Sprinthall, R. C. (2007). *Basic statistical analysis* (8th ed.). Boston: Allyn & Bacon.

Squire, L. R. (2004). Memory systems of the brain: A brief history and current perspective. *Neurobiology of Learning & Memory, 82*, 171–177.

Squire, L. R., & Kandel, E. R. (2000). *Memory: From mind to molecule.* New York: Worth.

Squire, L. R., & Zola-Morgan, S. (1988). Memory: Brain systems and behavior. *Trends in Neurosciences, 11*(4), 170–175.

Srivastava, S., John, O. P., Gosling, S. D., & Potter, J. (2003). Development of personality in early and middle adulthood: Set like plaster or persistent change? *Journal of Personality & Social Psychology, 84*(5), 1041–1053.

Sroufe, L. A., Egeland, B., Carlson, E., & Collins, W. A. (2005). Placing early attachment experiences in developmental context: The Minnesota Longitudinal Study. In K. E. Grossmann, K. Grossmann, et al. (Eds.), *Attachment from infancy to adulthood: The major longitudinal studies.* New York: Guilford.

Staemmler, F-M. (2004). Dialogue and interpretation in Gestalt therapy: Making sense together. *International Gestalt Journal, 27*(2), 33–57.

Stanovich, K. E. (2007). *How to think straight about psychology* (8th ed.). Boston: Allyn & Bacon.

Stapel, D. A., & Marx, D. M. (2007). Distinctiveness is key: How different types of self-other similarity moderate social comparison effects. *Personality & Social Psychology Bulletin, 33*(3), 439–448.

Staples, S. L. (1996). Human response to environmental noise. *American Psychologist, 51*(2), 143–150.

Steblay, N. M. (1987). Helping behavior in rural and urban environments: A meta-analysis. *Psychological Bulletin, 102*(3), 346–356.

Stein, L. M., & Memon, A. (2006). Testing the efficacy of the cognitive interview in a developing country. *Applied Cognitive Psychology, 20*(5), 597–605.

Stein, M. D., & Friedmann, P. D. (2005). Disturbed sleep and its relationship to alcohol use. *Substance Abuse, 26*(1), 1–13.

Stein, M. T., & Ferber, R. (2001). Recent onset of sleepwalking in early adolescence. *Journal of Development, Behavior, and Pediatrics, 22*, S33–S35.

Steinberg, L. (2001). Adolescent development. *Annual Review of Psychology, 52*, 83–110.

Stemler, S. E., & Sternberg, R. J. (2006). Using situational judgment tests to measure practical intelligence. In J. A. Weekley & R. E. Ployhart (Eds.), *Situational judgment tests: Theory, measurement, and application*. Mahwah, NJ: Erlbaum.

Stephan, W., Berscheid, E., & Walster, E. (1971). Sexual arousal and heterosexual perception. *Journal of Personality & Social Psychology, 20*(1), 93–101.

Stephens, K., Kiger, L., Karnes, F. A., & Whorton, J. E. (1999). Use of nonverbal measures of intelligence in identification of culturally diverse gifted students in rural areas. *Perceptual & Motor Skills, 88*(3, Pt. 1), 793–796.

Stern, P. C. (1992). Psychological dimensions of global environmental change. In M. R. Rosenzweig & L. W. Porter (Eds.), *Annual Review of Psychology, 43*, 269–302.

Stern, S. L., Dhanda, R., & Hazuda, H. P. (2001). Hopelessness predicts mortality in older Mexican and European Americans. *Psychosomatic Medicine, 63*(3), 344–351.

Sternberg, E. M. (2000). *The balance within: The science of connecting health with emotions*. New York: Freeman.

Sternberg, R. J. (2001). What is the common thread of creativity? *American Psychologist, 56*(4), 360–362.

Sternberg, R. J. (2004). Culture and intelligence. *American Psychologist, 59*(5), 325–338.

Sternberg, R. J., & Davidson, J. D. (1982). The mind of the puzzler. *Psychology Today*, June, 37–44.

Sternberg, R. J., & Grigorenko, E. L. (2005). Cultural explorations of the nature of intelligence. In A. F. Healy (Ed.), *Experimental cognitive psychology and its applications*. Washington, DC: American Psychological Association.

Sternberg, R. J., & Grigorenko, E. L. (2006). Cultural intelligence and successful intelligence. *Group & Organization Management, 31*(1), 27–39.

Sternberg, R. J., & Lubart, T. I. (1995). *Defying the crowd*. New York: Free Press.

Sternberg, R. J., Grigorenko, E. L., & Kidd, K. K. (2005). Intelli-

gence, race, and genetics. *American Psychologist, 60*(1), 46–59.

Steuer, F. B., & Hustedt, J. T. (2002). *TV or No TV? A primer on the psychology of television*. Lanham, MD: University Press of America.

Stewart, A. J. & McDermott, C. (2004). Gender in psychology. *Annual Review of Psychology, 55*, 519–544.

Stewart, A. J., & Ostrove, J. M. (1998). Women's personality in middle age. *American Psychologist, 53*(11), 1185–1194.

Stewart, A. J., & Vandewater, E. A. (1999). "If I had it to do over again . . .": Midlife review, midcourse corrections, and women's well-being in midlife. *Journal of Personality & Social Psychology, 76*(2), 270–283.

Stewart-Williams, S. (2004). The placebo puzzle: Putting together the pieces. *Health Psychology, 23*(2), 198–206.

Stickgold, R., & Walker, M. (2004). To sleep, perchance to gain creative insight? *Trends in Cognitive Sciences, 8*(5), 191–192.

Stipek, D. (2001). *Motivation to learn* (4th ed.). Boston: Allyn & Bacon.

Stöber, J. (2004). Dimensions of test anxiety: Relations to ways of coping with pre-exam anxiety and uncertainty. *Anxiety, Stress & Coping: An International Journal, 17*(3), 213–226.

Stockhorst, U., Klosterhalfen, S., & Steingrueber, H. (1998). Conditioned nausea and further side-effects in cancer chemotherapy. *Journal of Psychophysiology, 12*(Supp. 1), 14–33.

Stokes, D. M. (2001). The shrinking filedrawer. *Skeptical Inquirer*, May–June, 22–25.

Stokoe, W. C. (2001). *Language in hand: Why sign came before speech*. Washington, DC: Gallaudet University Press.

Stolerman, I. P., & Jarvis, M. J. (1995). The scientific case that nicotine is addictive. *Psychopharmacology, 117*(1), 2–10.

Stone, J., Perry, Z. W., & Darley, J. M. (1997). "White men can't jump." *Basic and Applied Social Psychology, 19*(3), 291–306.

Stoppard, J. M., & McMullen, L. M. (Eds.). (2003). *Situating sadness: Women and depression in social context*. New York: New York University Press.

Strack, F., Martin, L. L., & Stepper, S. (1988). Inhibiting and facilitating conditions of facial expressions: A non-obtrusive test of the facial feedback hypothesis. *Journal of Personality & Social Psychology, 54*, 768–777.

Straneva, P. A., Maixner, W., Light, K. C., Pedersen, C. A., et al. (2002). Menstrual cycle, beta-endorphins, and pain sensitivity in

premenstrual dysphoric disorder. *Health Psychology, 21*(4), 358–367.

Strange, J. R. (1965). *Abnormal psychology*. New York: McGraw-Hill.

Straub, R. (2006). *Health psychology* (2nd ed.) New York: Worth.

Strayer, D. L., Drews, F. A., & Johnston, W. A. (2003). Cell phone–induced failures of visual attention during simulated driving. *Journal of Experimental Psychology: Applied, 9*(1), 23–32.

Strickler, E. M., & Verbalis, J. G. (1988). Hormones and behavior: The biology of thirst and sodium appetite. *American Scientist*, May–June, 261–267.

Strier, F. (1999). Whither trial consulting? Issues and projections. *Law & Human Behavior, 23*(1), 93–115.

Stroeher, S. K. (1994). Sixteen kindergartners' gender-related views of careers. *Elementary School Journal, 95*(1), 95–103.

Strong, B., & DeVault, C. (1994). *Understanding our sexuality*. St. Paul, MN: West.

Strongman, K. T. (2003). *The psychology of emotion: From everyday life to theory* (5th Ed.). New York: Wiley.

Strote, J., Lee, J. E., & Wechsler, H. (2002). Increasing MDMA use among college students: Results of a national survey. *Journal of Adolescent Health, 30*(1), 64–72.

Sturges, J. W., & Sturges, L. V. (1998). In vivo *systematic desensitization* in a single-session treatment of an 11-year old girl's elevator phobia. *Child & Family Behavior Therapy, 20*(4), 55–62.

Stuss, D. T., & Alexander, M. P. (2000). The anatomical basis of affective behavior, emotion and self-awareness: A specific role of the right frontal lobe. In G. Hatano, N. Okada, et al. (Eds.), *Affective minds: The 13th Toyota conference*. Amsterdam: Elsevier.

Stuss, D. T., & Knight, R. T. (2002). *Principles of frontal lobe function*. New York: Oxford University Press.

Stuss, D. T., & Levine, B. (2002). Adult clinical neuropsychology. *Annual Review of Psychology, 53*, 401–433.

Sue, D., Sue, D. W., & Sue, S. (1996). *Understanding abnormal behavior*. Boston: Houghton Mifflin.

Suedfeld, P., & Steel, G. D. (2000). The environmental psychology of capsule habitats. *Annual Review of Psychology, 51*, 227–253.

Suedfeld, P., & Borrie, R. A. (1999). Health and therapeutic applications of chamber and flotation restricted environmental stimulation therapy (REST). *Psychology & Health, 14*(3), 545–566.

Sugihara, Y., & Warner, J. A. (1999). Endorsements by Mexican-

Americans of the Bem Sex-Role Inventory: Cross-ethnic comparison. *Psychological Reports, 85*(1), 201–211.

Sugimoto, K., & Ninomiya, Y. (2005). Introductory remarks on umami research: Candidate receptors and signal transduction mechanisms on umami. *Chemical Senses, 30*(Suppl. 1), i21–i22, 2005.

Suinn, R. M. (1975). *Fundamentals of behavior pathology* (2nd ed.). New York: Wiley.

Suinn, R. M. (1999). Scaling the summit: Valuing ethnicity. *APA Monitor*, March, 2.

Suinn, R. M. (2001). The terrible twos—Anger and anxiety. *American Psychologist, 56*(1), 27–36.

Suls, J. (1989). Self-awareness and self-identity in adolescence. In J. Worell & F. Danner (Eds.), *The adolescent as decision-maker*. New York: Academic Press.

Sumathipala, A., Siribaddana, S. H., & Bhugra, D. (2004). Culture-bound syndromes: The story of dhat syndrome. *British Journal of Psychiatry, 184*(3), 200–209.

Sumerlin, J. R., & Bundrick, C. M. (1996). Brief Index of Self-Actualization: A measure of Maslow's model. *Journal of Social Behavior & Personality, 11*(2), 253–271.

Sumi, K., & Kanda, K. (2002). Relationship between neurotic perfectionism, depression, anxiety, and psychosomatic symptoms. *Personality & Individual Differences, 32*(5), 817–826.

Sunnafrank, M., Ramirez, A., & Metts, S. (2004). At first sight: Persistent relational effects of get-acquainted conversations. *Journal of Social & Personal Relationships, 21*(3), 361–379.

Sutherland, R. J., Lehmann, H., Spanswick, S. C., Sparks, F. T., et al. (2006). Growth points in research on memory and hippocampus. *Canadian Journal of Experimental Psychology, 60*(2), 166–174.

Suzuki, L., & Aronson, J. (2005). The cultural malleability of intelligence and its impact on the racial/ethnic hierarchy. *Psychology, Public Policy, & Law, 11*, 320–327.

Svartdal, F. (2003). Extinction after partial reinforcement: Predicted vs. judged persistence. *Scandinavian Journal of Psychology, 44*(1), 55–64.

Swaak, J., de Jong, T., & van Joolingen, W. R. (2004). The effects of discovery learning and expository instruction on the acquisition of definitional and intuitive knowledge. *Journal of Computer Assisted Learning, 20*(4), 225–234.

Swann, W. B., Jr., Chang-Schneider, C., & Larsen McClarty, K. (2007). Do people's self-views matter? Self-concept and self-esteem in everyday life. *American Psychologist, 62*(2), 84–94.

Swim, J. K., & Sanna, L. J. (1996). He's skilled, she's lucky: A meta-analysis of observers' attributions for women's and men's successes and failures. *Personality & Social Psychology Bulletin, 22*(5), 507–519.

Synhorst, L. L., Buckley, J. A., Reid, R., Epstein, M. H., et al. (2005). Cross informant agreement of the Behavioral and Emotional Rating Scale–2nd Edition (BERS-2) parent and youth rating scales. *Child & Family Behavior Therapy, 27*(3), 1–11.

Szabo, A. (2003). The acute effects of humor and exercise on mood and anxiety. *Journal of Leisure Research, 35*(2), 152–162.

Takooshian, H., Haber, S., & Lucido, D. J. (1977). Who wouldn't help a lost child? You, maybe. *Psychology Today*, Feb., 67.

Talbott, J. A. (2004). Deinstitutionalization: Avoiding the disasters of the past. *Psychiatric Services, 55*(10), 1112–1115.

Talley, P. F., Strupp, H. H., & Morey, L. C. (1990). Matchmaking in psychotherapy: Patient–therapist dimensions and their impact on outcome. *Journal of Consulting & Clinical Psychology, 58*(2), 182–188.

Tal-Or, N., & Papirman, Y. (2007). The fundamental attribution error in attributing fictional figures' characteristics to the actors. *Media Psychology, 9*(2), 331–345.

Tamis-LeMonda, C. S., Bornstein, M. H., & Baumwell, L. (2001). Maternal responsiveness and children's achievement of language milestones. *Child Development, 72*, 748–767.

Tamis-LeMonda, C. S., Shannon, J. D., Cabrera, N. J., & Lamb, M. E. (2004). Fathers and mothers at play with their 2- and 3-year-olds: Contributions to language and cognitive development. *Child Development, 75*(6), 1806–1820.

Tanner, J. M. (1973). Growing up. *Scientific American*, Sept., 34–43.

Taraban, R., Rynearson, K., & Kerr, M. (2000). College students' academic performance and self-reports of comprehension strategy use. *Reading Psychology, 21*(4), 283–308.

Tardif, T. Z., & Sternberg, R. J. (1988). What do we know about creativity? In R. J. Sternberg (Ed.), *The nature of creativity.* New York: Cambridge University Press.

Taris, T. W., Bakker, A. B., Schaufeli, W. B., Stoffelsen, J., et al. (2005). Job control and burnout across occupations. *Psychological Reports, 97*(3), 955–961.

Taub, E. (2004). Harnessing brain plasticity through behavioral techniques to produce new treatments in neurorehabilitation A*merican Psychologist, 59*(8), 692–704.

Tausig, M., Michello, J., & Subedi, S. (2004). *A sociology of mental illness* (2nd ed.). Englewood Cliffs, NJ: Prentice Hall.

Tavris, C., & Aronson, E. (2007). *Mistakes were made (but not by me): Why we justify foolish beliefs, bad decisions, and hurtful acts.* New York: Harcourt.

Taylor, G. J., & Taylor-Allan, H. L. (2007). Applying emotional intelligence in understanding and treating physical and psychological disorders: What we have learned from alexithymia. In R. Bar-On, M. J. G. Reuven, et al. (Eds.), *Educating people to be emotionally intelligent.* Westport, CT: Praeger.

Taylor, K. (2004). *Brainwashing: The science of thought control.* New York: Oxford University Press.

Taylor, S. E. (2002). Classical conditioning. In M. Hersen & W. H. Sledge (Eds.), *Encyclopedia of psychotherapy.* San Diego: Academic Press.

Taylor, S. E. (2006). *Health psychology* (6th ed.). New York: McGraw-Hill.

Taylor, S. E., Kemeny, M. E., Reed, G. M., Bower, J. E., et al. (2000). Psychological resources, positive illusions, and health. *American Psychologist, 55*(1), 99–109.

Taylor, S. E., Lerner, J. S., Sherman, D. K., Sage, R. M., & McDowell, N. K. (2003). Are self-enhancing cognitions associated with healthy or unhealthy biological profiles? *Journal of Personality & Social Psychology, 85*(4), 605–615.

Taylor-Seehafer, M., & Rew, L. (2000). Risky sexual behavior among adolescent women. *Journal of Social Pediatric Nursing, 5*(1), 15–25.

Tedeschi, J. T., Lindskold, S., & Rosenfeld, P. (1985). *Introduction to social psychology.* St. Paul: West Publishing.

Teen sex: Not for love. (1989). *Psychology Today*, May, 10. They'd kill for $1 million. (1991). *Los Angeles Times*, July 1, A8.

Tenenbaum, G., Bar-Eli, M., & Eyal, N. (1996). Imagery orientation and vividness: Their effect on a motor skill performance. *Journal of Sport Behavior, 19*(1), 32–49.

Terman, L. M., & Merrill, M. A. (1937, revised 1960). *Stanford–Binet Intelligence Scale.* Boston: Houghton Mifflin.

Terman, L. M., & Oden, M. (1959). *The gifted group in mid-life* (Vol. 5): *Genetic studies of genius.* Stanford, CA: Stanford University Press.

Terry, D. J., & Hogg, M. A. (1996). Group norms and the attitude-behavior relationship. *Personality & Social Psychology Bulletin, 22*(8), 776–793.

Thase, M. E. (2006). Major depressive disorder. In F. Andrasik (Ed.),

Comprehensive handbook of personality and psychopathology (Vol. 2): *Adult psychopathology.* New York: Wiley.

The Nature Conservancy (2007). *Carbon calculator.* The Nature Conservancy. Retrieved August 10, 2007, from http://www.nature.org/initiatives/climatechange/calculator/.

Thelen, E. (2000). Infancy: Perception and motor development. In A. Kazdin (Ed.), *Encyclopedia of psychology.* Washington, DC: American Psychological Association.

Thiessen, E. D., Hill, E. A., & Saffran, J. R. (2005). Infant-directed speech facilitates word segmentation. *Infancy, 7*(1), 53–71.

Thomas, E. M. (2004). *Aggressive behaviour outcomes for young children: Change in parenting environment predicts change in behaviour.* Ottawa, ON: Statistics Canada. Retrieved June 6, 2007, from http://www.statcan.ca/cgi-bin/downpub/listpub.cgi?catno=89-599-MIE2004001.

Thompson, C. P., Cowan, T. M., & Frieman, J. (1993). *Memory search by a menorist.* Mahwah, NJ: Erlbaum.

Thompson, R. A., & Nelson, C. A. (2001). Developmental science and the media. *American Psychologist, 56*(1), 5–15.

Thompson, R. F. (2005). In search of memory traces. *Annual Review of Psychology, 56*, 1–23.

Thorpy, M. J. (2006). Cataplexy associated with narcolepsy: Epidemiology, pathophysiology and management. *CNS Drugs, 20*(1), 43–50.

Thorson, J. A., & Powell, F. C. (1990). Meanings of death and intrinsic religiosity. *Journal of Clinical Psychology, 46*(4), 379–391.

Thyen, U., Richter-Appelt, H., Wiesemann, C., Holterhus, P. M., et al. (2005). Deciding on gender in children with intersex conditions: Considerations and controversies. *Treatments in Endocrinology, 4*(1), 1–8.

Tidwell, M. O., Reis, H. T., & Shaver, P. R. (1996). Attachment, attractiveness, and social interaction. *Journal of Personality & Social Psychology, 71*(4), 729–745.

Tierny, J. (1987). Stitches: Good news; Better health linked to sin, sloth. *Hippocrates*, Sept.–Oct., 30–35.

Tijerino, R. (1998). Civil spaces: A critical perspective of defensible space. *Journal of Architectural & Planning Research, 15*(4), 321–337.

Till, B. D., & Priluck, R. L. (2000). Stimulus generalization in classical conditioning: An initial investigation and extension. *Psychology & Marketing, 17*(1), 55–72.

Timmerman, C. K., & Kruepke, K. A. (2006). Computer-assisted in-

struction, media richness, and college student performance. *Communication Education, 55*(1), 73–104.

Timmerman, I. G. H., Emmelkamp, P. M. G., & Sanderman, R. (1998). The effects of a stress-management training program in individuals at risk in the community at large. *Behaviour Research & Therapy, 36*(9), 863–875.

Tipples, J., Atkinson, A. P., & Young, A. W. (2002). The eyebrow frown: A salient social signal. *Emotion, 2*(3), 288–296.

Tobler, N. S., Roona, M. R., Ocshorn, P., Marshall, D. G., et al. (2000). School-based adolescent drug prevention programs: 1998 meta-analysis. *Journal of Primary Prevention, 20*, 275–337.

Tolman, E. C., & Honzik, C. H. (1930). Introduction and removal of reward and maze performance in rats. *University of California Publications in Psychology, 4*, 257–275.

Tolman, E. C., Ritchie, B. F., & Kalish, D. (1946). Studies in spatial learning: II. Place learning versus response learning. *Journal of Experimental Psychology, 36*, 221–229.

Tomasello, M. (2003). *Constructing a language: A usage-based theory of language acquisition.* Cambridge, MA: Harvard University Press.

Toneatto, T. (2002). Cognitive therapy for problem gambling. *Cognitive & Behavioral Practice, 9*(3), 191–199.

Toneatto, T., Sobell, L. C., Sobell, M. B., & Rubel, E. (1999). Natural recovery from cocaine dependence. *Psychology of Addictive Behaviors, 13*(4), 259–268.

Toro, C. T., & Deakin, J. F. W. (2007). Adult neurogenesis and schizophrenia: A window on abnormal early brain development? *Schizophrenia Research, 90*(1–3), 1–14.

Torrey, E. F. (1996). *Out of the shadows.* New York: John Wiley & Sons.

Tourangeau, R. (2004). Survey research and societal change. *Annual Review of Psychology, 55*, 775–801.

Toyota, H., & Kikuchi, Y. (2005). Encoding richness of self-generated elaboration and spacing effects on incidental memory. *Perceptual & Motor Skills, 101*(2), 621–627.

Trainor, L. J., & Desjardins, R. N. (2002). Pitch characteristics of infant-directed speech affect infants' ability to discriminate vowels. *Psychonomic Bulletin & Review, 9*(2), 335–340.

Travis, F., Arenander, A., & DuBois, D. (2004). Psychological and physiological characteristics of a proposed objectreferral/self-referral continuum of selfawareness. *Consciousness & Cognition, 13*, 401–420.

Treffert, D. A., & Christensen, C. D. (2005). Inside the mind of a savant. *Scientific American, 293*(6), 108–113.

Trehub, S. E., Unyk, A. M., & Trainor, L. J. (1993a). Adults identify infant-directed music across cultures. *Infant Behavior & Development, 16*(2), 193–211.

Trehub, S. E., Unyk, A. M., & Trainor, L. J. (1993b). Maternal singing in cross-cultural perspective. *Infant Behavior & Development, 16*(3), 285–295.

Trepel, C., & Racine, R. J. (1999). Blockade and disruption of neocortical long-term potentiation following electroconvulsive shock in the adult, freely moving rat. *Cerebral Cortex, 9*(3), 300–305.

Triandis, H. C., & Suh, E. M. (2002). Cultural influences on personality. *Annual Review of Psychology, 53,* 133–160.

Troll, L. E., & Skaff, M. M. (1997). Perceived continuity of self in very old age. *Psychology & Aging, 12*(1), 162–169.

Truax, S. R. (1983). Active search, mediation, and the manipulation of cue dimensions: Emotion attribution in the false feedback paradigm. *Motivation & Emotion, 7,* 41–60.

Trull, T. (2005). *Clinical psychology* (7th ed.). Belmont, CA: Cengage Learning/Wadsworth.

Tsai, G., & Coyle, J. T. (2002). Glutamatergic mechanisms in schizophrenia. *Annual Review of Pharmacology & Toxicology, 42,* 165–179.

Tsai, W-C., Chen, C.-C., & Chiu, S-F. (2005). Exploring boundaries of the effects of applicant impression management tactics in job interviews. *Journal of Management, 31*(1), 108–125.

Tse, L. (1999). Finding a place to be: Ethnic identity exploration of Asian Americans. *Adolescence, 34*(133), 121–138.

Tugade, M. M., Fredrickson, B. L., & Barrett, L. F. (2004). Psychological resilience and positive emotional granularity: Examining the benefits of positive emotions on coping and health. *Journal of Personality, 72*(6), 1161–1190.

Tulving, E. (1989). Remembering and knowing the past. *American Scientist, 77*(4), 361–367.

Tulving, E. (2002). Episodic memory. *Annual Review of Psychology, 53,* 1–25.

Turiel, E. (2006).Thought, emotions, and social interactional processes in moral development. In M. Killen & J. G. Smetana (Eds.), *Handbook of moral development.* Mahwah, NJ: Erlbaum.

Turkheimer, E., Haley, A., Waldron, M., D'Onofrio, B. M., et al. (2003). Socioeconomic status modifies heritability of IQ in young children. *Psychological Science, 14,* 623–628.

Turner, S. J. M. (1997). The use of the reflective team in a psychodrama therapy group. *International Journal of Action Methods, 50*(1), 17–26.

Tversky, A., & Kahneman, D. (1981). The framing of decisions and the psychology of choice. *Science, 211,* 453–458.

Tversky, A., & Kahneman, D. (1982). Judgments of and by representativeness. In D. Kahneman, P. Slovic, et al (Eds.), *Judgment under uncertainty: Heuristics and biases.* Cambridge, UK: Cambridge University Press.

Twenge, J. M., & Campbell, W. K. (2001). Age and birth cohort differences in self-esteem. *Personality & Social Psychology Review, 5*(4), 321–344.

Tye-Murray, N., Spencer, L., & Woodworth, G. G. (1995). Acquisition of speech by children who have prolonged cochlear implant experience. *Journal of Speech & Hearing Research, 38*(2), 327–337.

Tzeng, M. (1992). The effects of socioeconomic heterogamy and changes on marital dissolution for first marriages. *Journal of Marriage & Family, 54,* 609–619.

U.S. Department of Energy Human Office of Science. (2005). *About the Human Genome Project.* Washington, DC: U.S. Department of Energy. Retrieved May 25, 2007, from http://www.ornl.gov/sci/techresources/Human_Genome/project/about.shtml.

U.S. Department of Labor (2005). *Occupational outlook handbook job interview tips.* Washington, DC: U. S. Department of Labor. Retrieved August 9, 2007, from http://www.bls.gov/oco/oco20045.htm.

UN (2004). *World population to 2300.* New York: United Nations. Retrieved August 9, 2007, from http://www.un.org/esa/population/publications/longrange2/WorldPop2300final.pdf.

UNAIDS (2006). *UNAIDS/WHOAIDS Epidemic Update: December 2006.* New York: United Nations. Retrieved July 27, 2007, from http://www.unaids.org/en/HIV_data/epi2006/default.asp.

Underwood, B. J. (1957). Interference and forgetting. *Psychological Review, 64,* 49–60.

UNESCO. (1990). The Seville statement on violence. *American Psychologist, 45*(10), 1167–1168.

Unsworth, G., & Ward, T. (2001). Video games and aggressive behaviour. *Australian Psychologist, 36*(3), 184–192.

Urbina, S. (2004). *Essentials of psychological testing.* New York: Wiley.

USDHHS (U.S. Department of Health and Human Services). (2004). *The health consequences of smoking: A report of the Surgeon General, executive summary.* Washington, DC: Department of Health and Human Services. Retrieved June 6, 2007, from http://www.cdc.gov/tobacco/data_statistics/sgr/sgr_2004/00_pdfs/executivesummary.pdf.

Uwe P. Gielen, U. P., Fish, J. M., & Draguns, J. G. (Eds.) (2006). *Handbook of culture, therapy, and healing.* Mahwah, NJ: Erlbaum.

Vaillant, G. E. (2002). *Aging well.* Boston: Little, Brown.

Vaillant, G. E. (2005). Alcoholics Anonymous: Cult or cure? *Australian & New Zealand Journal of Psychiatry, 39*(6), 431–436.

Vaillant, G. E., & Mukamal, K. (2001). Successful aging. *American Journal of Psychiatry, 158*(6), 839–847.

Valins, S. (1966). Cognitive effects of false heart-rate feedback. *Journal of Personality & Social Psychology, 4,* 400–408.

Valins, S. (1967). Emotionality and information concerning internal reactions. *Journal of Personality & Social Psychology, 6,* 458–463.

van der Hart, O., Lierens, R., & Goodwin, J. (1996). Jeanne Fery: A sixteenth-century case of dissociative identity disorder. *Journal of Psychohistory, 24*(1), 18–35.

van Deurzen, E., & Kenward, R. (2005). *Dictionary of existential psychotherapy and counselling.* Thousand Oaks, CA: Sage.

van Dierendonck, D., & Te Nijenhuis, J. (2005). Flotation restricted environmental stimulation therapy (REST) as a stress-management tool: A meta-analysis. *Psychology & Health, 20*(3), 405–412.

van Elst, L. T., Valerius, G., Büchert, M., Thiel, T., et al. (2005). Increased prefrontal and hippocampal glutamate concentration in schizophrenia: Evidence from a magnetic resonance spectroscopy study. *Biological Psychiatry, 58*(9), 724–730.

Van Goozen, S. H. M., Cohen-Kettenis, P. T., Gooren, L. J. G., & Frijda, N. H. (1995). Gender differences in behaviour: Activating effects of cross-sex hormones. *Psychoneuroendocrinology, 20*(4), 343–363.

Van Lawick-Goodall, J. (1971). *In the shadow of man.* New York: Houghton Mifflin.

Van Rooij, J. J. F. (1994). Introversion–extraversion: Astrology versus psychology. *Personality & Individual Differences, 16*(6), 985–988.

Van Vugt, M. (2002). Central, individual, or collective control? Social dilemma strategies for natural resource management. *American Behavioral Scientist, 45*(5), 783–800.

Vandell, D. L. (2004). Early child care: The known and the unknown. *Merrill–Palmer Quarterly. 50*(3), 387–414.

Vasa, R. A., Carlino, A. R., & Pine, D. S. (2006). Pharmacotherapy of depressed children and adolescents: Current issues and potential directions. *Biological Psychiatry, 59*(11), 1021–1028.

Velakoulis, D., & Pantelis, C. (1996). What have we learned from functional imaging studies in schizophrenia? *Australian & New Zealand Journal of Psychiatry, 30*(2), 195–209.

Venezia, M., Messinger, D. S., Thorp, D., & Mundy, P. (2004). The development of anticipatory smiling. *Infancy, 6*(3), 397–406.

Vi, P. (2006). A field study investigating the effects of a rebar-tying machine on trunk flexion, tool usability and productivity. *Ergonomics, 49*(14), 1437–1455.

Videon, T. M. (2005). Parent–child relations and children's psychological well-being: Do dads matter? *Journal of Family Issues, 26*(1), 55–78.

Viegener, B. J., Perri, M. G., Nezu, A. M., Renjilian, D. A., et al. (1990). Effects of an intermittent, low-fat, low-calorie diet in the behavioral treatment of obesity. *Behavior Therapy, 21*(4), 499–509.

Viveros, M. P., Llorente, R., Moreno, E., & Marco, E. M. (2005). Behavioural and neuroendocrine effects of cannabinoids in critical developmental periods. *Behavioural Pharmacology, 16*(5–6), 353–362.

Vogel, E. K., Woodman, G. F., & Luck, S. J. (2006). The time course of consolidation in visual working memory. *Journal of Experimental Psychology: Human Perception and Performance, 32*(6), 1436–1451.

Vogler, R. E., & Bartz, W. R. (1992). *Teenagers and alcohol.* Philadelphia: Charles Press.

Vogler, R. E., Weissbach, T. A., Compton, J. V., & Martin, G. T. (1977). Integrated behavior change techniques for problem drinkers in the community. *Journal of Consulting and Clinical Psychology, 45,* 267–279.

Volkow, N. D., Gillespie, H., Mullani, N., & Tancredi, L. (1996). Brain glucose metabolism in chronic marijuana users at baseline and during marijuana intoxication. *Psychiatry Research: Neuroimaging, 67*(1), 29–38.

Volpicelli, J. R., Ulm, R. R., Altenor, A., & Seligman, M. E. P. (1983). Learned mastery in the rat. *Learning and Motivation, 14,* 204–222.

Vygotsky, L. S. (1962). *Thought and language.* Cambridge, MA: MIT Press.

Vygotsky, L. S. (1978). *Mind in society.* Cambridge, MA: Harvard University Press.

Wager, T. D., Rilling, J. K., Smith, E. E., Sokolik, A., et al. (2004). Placebo-induced changes in fMRI in the anticipation and experience of pain. *Science, 303*(Feb. 20), 1162–1166.

Wagstaff, G., Brunas-Wagstaff, J., Cole, J., & Wheatcroft, J. (2004). New directions in forensic hypnosis: Facilitating memory with a focused meditation technique. *Contemporary Hypnosis, 21*(1), 14–27.

Waid, W. M., & Orne, M. T. (1982). The physiological detection of deception. *American Scientist, 70*(July–Aug.), 402–409.

Wainright, J. L., Russell, S. T., & Patterson, C. J. (2004). Psychosocial adjustment, school outcomes, and romantic relationships of adolescents with same-sex parents. *Child Development, 75*(6), 1886–1898.

Wakefield, J. C. (1992). The concept of mental disorder. *American Psychologist, 47*(3), 373–388.

Wald, J., & Taylor, S. (2000). Efficacy of virtual reality exposure therapy to treat driving phobia. *Journal of Behavior Therapy & Experimental Psychiatry, 31*(3–4), 249–257.

Walker, E., Kestler, L. Bollini, A., & Hochman, K. M. (2004). Schizophrenia: Etiology and course. *Annual Review of Psychology, 55,* 401–430.

Walker, I., & Crogan, M. (1998). Academic performance, prejudice, and the Jigsaw classroom. *Journal of Community & Applied Social Psychology, 8*(6), 381–393.

Walker, M. P., & Stickgold, R. (2006). Sleep, memory, and plasticity. *Annual Review of Psychology, 57,* 139–166.

Wallach, M. A., & Kogan, N. (1965). *Modes of thinking in young children.* New York: Holt.

Walster, E. (1971). Passionate love. In B. I. Murstein (Ed.), *Theories of attraction and love.* New York: Springer.

Walton, C. E., Bower, M. L., & Bower, T. G. (1992). Recognition of familiar faces by newborns. *Infant Behavior & Development, 15*(2), 265–269.

Wampold, B. E., Minami T., Tierney, S. C., Baskin, T. W., et al. (2005). The placebo is powerful: Estimating placebo effects in medicine and psychotherapy from randomized clinical trials. *Journal of Clinical Psychology, 61*(7), 835–854.

Wampold, B. E., Mondin, G. W., Moody, M., Stich, E., et al. (1997). A meta-analysis of outcome studies comparing bona fide psychotherapies. *Psychological Bulletin, 122*(3), 203–215.

Wandersman, A., & Florin, P. (2003). Community interventions and effective prevention. *American Psychologist, 58*(6–7), 441–448.

Wang, Q., & Conway, M. A. (2004). The stories we keep: Autobiographical memory in American and Chinese middle-aged adults. *Journal of Personality, 72*(5), 911–938.

Wang, S. S., & Brownell, K. D. (2005). Public policy and obesity: The need to marry science with advocacy. *Psychiatric Clinics of North America, 28*(1), 235–252.

Ward, C., & Rana-Deuba, A. (1999). Acculturation and adaptation revisited. *Journal of Cross-Cultural Psychology, 30*(4), 422–442.

Ward, J. (2006). *The student's guide to cognitive neuroscience.* Hove, UK: Psychology Press.

Ward, L. M. (2004). Wading through the stereotypes: Positive and negative associations between media use and Black adolescents' conceptions of self. *Developmental Psychology, 40,* 284–294.

Wark, G. R., & Krebs, D. L. (1996). Gender and dilemma differences in real-life moral judgment. *Developmental Psychology, 32*(2), 220–230.

Warren, D. J., & Normann, R. A. (2005). Functional reorganization of primary visual cortex induced by electrical stimulation in the cat. *Vision Research, 45,* 551–565.

Waterfield, R. (2002). *Hidden depths: The story of hypnosis.* London: Macmillan.

Watson, D. L., & Tharp, R. G. (2007). *Self-directed behavior* (9th ed.). Belmont, CA: Cengage Learning/Wadsworth.

Watson, J. B. (1913/1994). Psychology as the behaviorist views it. *Psychological Review, 101*(2), 248–253.

Way, I., vanDeusen, K. M., Martin, G., Applegate, B., et al. (2004). Vicarious trauma: A comparison of clinicians who treat survivors of sexual abuse and sexual offenders. *Journal of Interpersonal Violence, 19*(1), 49–71.

Wechsler, H., & Wuethrich, B. (2002). *Dying to drink.* Emmaus, PA: Rodale Books.

Wechsler, H., Lee, J. E., Kuo, M., Seibring, M., et al. (2002). Trends in college binge drinking during a period of increased prevention efforts. *Journal of American College Health, 50*(5), 203–217.

Wedding, D., & Corsini, R. J. (2005). *Case studies in psychotherapy* (4th ed.). Belmont, CA: Cengage Learning/Wadsworth.

Weekley, J. A., & Jones, C. (1997). Video-based situational testing. *Personnel Psychology, 50*(1), 25–49.

Weems, C. F. (1998). The evaluation of heart rate biofeedback using a multi-element design. *Journal of Behavior Therapy & Experimental Psychiatry, 29*(2), 157–162.

Wehr, T. A., Duncan, W. C., Sher, L., Aeschbach, D., et al. (2001). A circadian signal of change of season in patients with seasonal affective disorder. *Archives of General Psychiatry, 58*(12), 1108–1114.

Weinberg, R. A. (1989). Intelligence and IQ. *American Psychologist, 44*(2), 98–104.

Weintraub, M. I. (1983). *Hysterical conversion reactions.* New York: SP Medical & Scientific Books.

Weishaar, M. E. (2006). A cognitive-behavioral approach to suicide risk reduction in crisis intervention. In A. R. Roberts & K. R. Yeager, (Eds.), *Foundations of evidence-based social work practice.* New York: Oxford University Press.

Weisskirch, R. S. (2005). Ethnicity and perceptions relationship to ethnic identity development. *International Journal of Intercultural Relations, 29*(3), 355–366.

Weissman, A. M., Jogerst, G. J., & Dawson, J. D. (2003). Community characteristics associated with child abuse in Iowa. *Child Abuse & Neglect, 27*(10), 1145–1159.

Weiten, W. (1998). Pressure, major life events, and psychological symptoms. *Journal of Social Behavior & Personality, 13*(1), 51–68.

Weitzman, E. R. (2004). Poor mental health, depression, and associations with alcohol consumption, harm, and abuse in a national sample of young adults in college. *Journal of Nervous & Mental Disease, 192*(4), 269–277.

Wells, B. E., & Twenge, J. M. (2005). Changes in young people's sexual behavior and attitudes, 1943–1999: A cross-temporal meta-analysis. *Review of General Psychology, 9*(3), 249–261.

Wells, G. L. (2001). Police lineups: Data, theory, and policy. *Psychology, Public Policy, & Law, 7*(4), 791–801.

Wells, G. L., & Olsen, E. A. (2003). Eyewitness testimony. *Annual Review of Psychology, 54,* 277–295.

Wells, G. L., Memon, A., & Penrod, S. D. (2006). Eyewitness evidence: Improving its probative value. *Psychological Science in the Public Interest, 7*(2), 45–75.

Weltzin, T. E., Weisensel, N., Franczyk, D., Burnett, K., et al. (2005). Eating disorders in men: Update. *Journal of Men's Health & Gender, 2*(2), 186–193.

Werner, C. M., & Makela, E. (1998). Motivations and behaviors that support recycling. *Journal of Environmental Psychology, 18*(4), 373–386.

Wernet, S. P., Follman, C., Magueja, C., & Moore-Chambers, R. (2003). Building bridges and improving racial harmony: An evaluation of the Bridges Across Racial Polarization Program. In J. J. Stretch, E. M. Burkemper, et al. (Eds.), *Practicing social justice.* New York: Haworth Press.

Wertheimer, M. (1959). *Productive thinking.* New York: Harper & Row.

Wesensten, N. J., Belenky, G., Kautz, M. A., Thorne, D. R., et al. (2002). Maintaining alertness and performance during sleep deprivation: Modafinil versus caffeine. *Psychopharmacology, 159*(3), 238–247.

Wessel, I., & Wright, D. B. (Eds.). (2004). *Emotional memory failures.* Hove, UK: Psychology Press.

West, R., & Sohal, T. (2006). "Catastrophic" pathways to smoking cessation: Findings from national survey. *British Medical Journal, 332*(7539), 458–460.

West, T. G. (1991). *In the mind's eye.* Buffalo, NY: Prometheus.

Wethington, E. (2000). Expecting stress: Americans and the "midlife crisis." *Motivation & Emotion, 24*(2), 85–103.

Wethington, E. (2003). Turning points as opportunities for psychological growth. In C. L. M. Keyes & J. Haidt (Eds.), *Flourishing.* Washington, DC: American Psychological Association.

Wethington, E., Kessler, R. C., & Pixley, J. E. (2004). Turning points in adulthood. In O. G. Brim, C. D. Ryff, et al. (Eds.), *How healthy are we?: A national study of well-being at midlife.* Chicago: University of Chicago Press.

Wexler, M. N. (1995). Expanding the groupthink explanation to the study of contemporary cults. *Cultic Studies Journal, 12*(1), 49–71.

Whipple, B. (2000). Beyond the G spot. *Scandinavian Journal of Sexology, 3*(2), 35–42.

Whitaker, B. G. (2007). Internet-based attitude assessment: Does gender affect measurement equivalence? *Computers in Human Behavior, 23*(3), 1183–1194.

White, G. L., & Taytroe, L. (2003). Personal problem-solving using dream incubation: Dreaming, relaxation, or waking cognition? *Dreaming, 13*(4), 193–209.

White, J. (2006). *Intelligence, destiny and education: The ideological roots of intelligence testing.* New York: Brunner-Routledge.

Whitehouse, A. J. O., Maybery, M. T., & Durkin, K. (2006). The development of the picture-superiority effect. *British Journal of Developmental Psychology, 24*(4), 767–773.

Whitley, B. E. (1999). Right-wing authoritarianism, social dominance orientation, and prejudice. *Journal of Personality & Social Psychology, 77*(l), 126–134.

Whitton, E. (2003). *Humanistic approach to psychotherapy.* New York: Wiley.

Whyte, G. (2000). Groupthink. In A. E. Kazdin (Ed.), *Encyclopedia of psychology* (Vol. 4). Washington, DC: American Psychological Association.

Wickett, J. C., Vernon, P. A., & Lee, D. H. (2000). Relationships between factors of intelligence and brain volume. *Personality & Individual Differences, 29*(6), 1095–1122.

Widiger, T. A. (2005). Classification and diagnosis: Historical development and contemporary issues. In J. E. Maddux & B. A. Winstead (Eds.), *Psychopathology: Foundations for a contemporary understanding*. Mahwah, NJ: Erlbaum.

Widner, Jr., R. L., Otani, H., & Winkelman, S. E. (2005). Tip-of-the-tongue experiences are not merely strong feeling-of-knowing experiences. *Journal of General Psychology, 132*(4), 392–407.

Wiederhold, B. K., & Wiederhold, M. D. (2005). Acrophobia. In B. K. Wiederhold & M. D. Wiederhold, *Virtual reality therapy for anxiety disorders: Advances in evaluation and treatment*. Washington: American Psychological Association.

Wiederman, M. W. (2001). Gender differences in sexuality: Perceptions, myths, and realities. *Family Journal-Counseling & Therapy for Couples & Families, 9*(4), 468–471.

Wigfield, A., & Eccles, J. (Eds.). (2002). *Development of achievement motivation*. San Diego: Academic Press.

Wilber, M. K., & Potenza, M. N. (2006). Adolescent gambling: Research and clinical implications. *Psychiatry, 3*(10), 40–46.

Wilder, D. A., Simon, A. F., & Faith, M. (1996). Enhancing the impact of counterstereotypic information. *Journal of Personality & Social Psychology, 71*(2), 276–287.

Wilding, J., & Valentine, E. (1994). Memory champions. *British Journal of Psychology, 85*(2), 231–244.

Wilkinson, D., & Abraham, C. (2004). Constructing an integrated model of the antecedents of adolescent smoking. *British Journal of Health Psychology, 9*(3), 315–333.

Wilkinson, M. (2006). The dreaming mindbrain: A Jungian perspective. *Journal of Analytical Psychology, 51*(1), 43–59.

Williams, G., Cai, X. J., Elliott, J. C., & Harrold, J. A. (2004). Anabolic neuropeptides. *Physiology & Behavior, 81*(2), 211–222.

Williams, N. (2002). The imposition of gender: Psychoanalytic encounters with genital atypicality. *Psychoanalytic Psychology, 19*(3), 455–474.

Williams, R. (1989). *The trusting heart: Great news about Type A behavior*. New York: Random House.

Williams, R. B., Barefoot, J. C., & Schneiderman, N. (2003). Psychosocial risk factors for cardiovascular disease: More than one culprit at work. *JAMA: Journal of the American Medical Association, 290*(16), 2190–2192.

Williams, R. L., & Eggert, A. (2002). Notetaking predictors of test performance. *Teaching of Psychology, 29*(3), 234–236.

Williams, R. L., & Long, J. D. (1991). *Toward a self-managed life style*. Boston: Houghton Mifflin.

Williams, R. L., Agnew, H. W., & Webb, W. B. (1964). Sleep patterns in young adults: An EEG study. *Electroencephalography & Clinical Neurophysiology, 17*, 376–381.

Williamson, D. A., Ravussin, E., Wong, M.-L., Wagner, A., et al. (2005). Microanalysis of eating behavior of three leptin deficient adults treated with leptin therapy. *Appetite, 45*, 75–80.

Willoughby, T., Wood, E., Desmarais, S., Sims, S., et al. (1997). Mechanisms that facilitate the effectiveness of elaboration strategies. *Journal of Educational Psychology, 89*(4), 682–685.

Wilmot, W. W., & Hocker, J. L. (2007). *Interpersonal conflict* (7th ed.). Boston: McGraw-Hill.

Wilson, F. L. (1995). The effects of age, gender, and ethnic/cultural background on moral reasoning. *Journal of Social Behavior & Personality, 10*(1), 67–78.

Wilson, T. D. (2002). *Strangers to ourselves: Discovering the adaptive unconscious*. Cambridge, MA: Harvard University Press.

Winger, G., Woods, J. H., Galuska, C. M., & Wade-Galuska, T. (2005). Behavioral perspectives on the neuroscience of drug addiction. *Journal of the Experimental Analysis of Behavior, 84*(3), 667–681.

Wingood, G. M., DiClemente, R.J., Bernhardt, J. M., Harrington, K., et al. (2003). A prospective study of exposure to rap music videos and African American female adolescents' health. *American Journal of Public Health, 93*, 437–439.

Winner, E. (2003). Creativity and talent. In M. H. Bornstein, L. Davidson, et al. (Eds.), *Well-being: Positive development across the life course*. Mahwah, NJ: Erlbaum.

Winstead, B. A., & Sanchez, J. (2005). Gender and psychopathology. In J. E. Maddux & B. A. Winstead (Eds.), *Psychopathology: Foundations for a contemporary understanding*. Mahwah, NJ: Erlbaum.

Winter, D. D. N., & Koger, S. M. (2004). *The psychology of environmental problems* (2nd ed.). Mahwah, NJ: Erlbaum.

Wise, R. A., & Safer, M. A. (2004). What US judges know and believe about eyewitness testimony. *Applied Cognitive Psychology, 18*(4), 427–443.

Wiseman, R., & Watt, C. (2006). Belief in psychic ability and the misattribution hypothesis: A qualitative review. *British Journal of Psychology, 97*(3), 323–338.

Witelson, S. F. (1991). Neural sexual mosaicism: Sexual differentiation of the human temporo-parietal region for functional asymmetry. *Psychoneuroendocrinology, 16*(1–3), 131–153.

Witelson, S. F., Beresh, H., & Kigar, D. L. (2006). Intelligence and brain size in 100 postmortem brains: Sex, lateralization and age factors. *Brain: A Journal of Neurology, 129*(2), 386–398.

Witherington, D. C., Campos, J. J., Anderson, D. I., Lejeune, L., et al. (2005). Avoidance of heights on the visual cliff in newly walking infants. *Infancy, 7*(3), 285–298.

Withers, N. W., Pulvirenti, L., Koob, G. F., & Gillin, J. C. (1995). Cocaine abuse and dependence. *Journal of Clinical Psychopharmacology, 15*(1), 63–78.

Witt, S. D. (1997). Parental influences on children's socialization to gender roles. *Adolescence, 32*(126), 253–259.

Wixted, J. T. (2004). The psychology and neuroscience of forgetting. *Annual Review of Psychology, 55*, 235–269.

Wixted, J. T. (2005). A theory about why we forget what we once knew. *Current Directions in Psychological Science, 14*(1), 6–9.

Wolfe, J. B. (1936). Effectiveness of token rewards for chimpanzees. *Comparative Psychology Monographs, 12*(5), Whole no. 60.

Wolfe, J. M., Kluender, K. R., Levi, D. M., Bartoshuk, L. M., et al. (2005). *Sensation and perception*. Sunderland, MA: Sinauer Associates.

Wolpe, J. (1974). *The practice of behavior therapy* (2nd ed.). New York: Pergamon.

Wolpin, M., Marston, A., Randolph, C., & Clothier, A. (1992). Individual difference correlates of reported lucid dreaming frequency and control. *Journal of Mental Imagery, 16*(3–4), 231–236.

Wong, C. Y., Sommer, R., & Cook, E. J. (1992). The soft classroom 17 years later. *Journal of Environmental Psychology, 12*(4), 337–343.

Wood, E., & Willoughby, T. (1995). Cognitive strategies for test-taking. In E. Wood, V. Woloshyn, et al. (Eds.), *Cognitive strategy instruction for middle and high schools*. Cambridge, MA: Brookline Books.

Wood, J. M., Nezworski, M. T., Lilienfeld, S. O., & Garb, H. N. (2003). The Rorschach Inkblot test, fortune tellers, and cold reading. *Skeptical Inquirer, 27*(4), 29–33.

Woods, S. C., Schwartz, M. W, Baskin, D. G., & Seeley, R J. (2000). Food intake and the regulation of body weight. *Annual Review of Psychology, 51*, 255–277.

Worthen, J. B., & Marshall, P. H. (1996). Intralist and extralist sources of distinctiveness and the bizarreness effect. *American Journal of Psychology, 109*(2), 239–263.

Worthen, J. B., & Wade, C. E. (1999). Direction of travel and visiting team athletic performance: Support for a circadian dysrhythmia hypothesis. *Journal of Sport Behavior, 22*(2), 279–287.

Wraga, M., Shephard, J. M., Church, J. A., Inati, S., et al. (2005). Imagined rotations of self versus objects: An fMRI study. *Neuropsychologia, 43*(9), 1351–1361.

Wright, T. A., & Bonett, D. G. (2007). Job satisfaction and psychological well-being as nonadditive predictors of workplace turnover. *Journal of Management, 33*(2), 141–160.

Wright, T. A., & Cropanzano, R. (2000). Psychological well-being and job satisfaction as predictors of job performance. *Journal of Occupational Health Psychology, 5*(1), 84–94.

Wrightsman, L. S., & Fulero, S. M. (2005). *Forensic psychology* (2nd ed.). Belmont, CA: Cengage Learning/Wadsworth.

Wu, C. W. H., & Kaas, J. H. (2002). The effects of long-standing limb loss on anatomical reorganization of the somatosensory afferents in the brainstem and spinal cord. *Somatosensory & Motor Research, 19*(2), 153–163.

Wulf, G., McConnel, N., Gärtner, M., & Schwarz, A. (2002). Enhancing the learning of sport skills through external-focus feedback. *Journal of Motor Behavior, 34*(2), 171–182.

Wyatt, J. W., Posey, A., Welker, W., & Seamonds, C. (1984). Natural levels of similarities between identical twins and between unrelated people. *Skeptical Inquirer, 9*, 62–66.

Wynne, C. D. L. (2004). The perils of anthropomorphism. *Nature, 428*(6983), 606.

X Day, S., & Schneider, P. L. (2002). Psychotherapy using distance technology. *Journal of Counseling Psychology, 49*(4), 499–503.

Yahnke, B. H., Sheikh, A. A., & Beckman, H. T. (2003). Imagery and the treatment of phobic disorders. In A. A. Sheikh (Ed.), *Healing images: The role of imagination in health*. Amityville, NY: Baywood Publishing.

Yarmey, A. D. (2003). Eyewitness identification: Guidelines and recommendations for identification procedures in the United States and in Canada. *Canadian Psychology, 44*(3), 181–189.

Yedidia, M. J., & MacGregor, B. (2001). Confronting the prospect of dying. *Journal of Pain & Symptom Management, 22*(4), 807–819.

Yeh, C. J. (2003). Age, acculturation, cultural adjustment, and mental health symptoms of Chinese, Korean, and Japanese immigrant youths. *Cultural Diversity & Ethnic Minority Psychology, 9*(1), 34–48.

Yip, P. S. F., & Thorburn, J. (2004). Marital status and the risk of suicide: Experience from England and Wales, 1982–1996. *Psychological Reports, 94*(2), 401–407.

Yokota, F., & Thompson, K. M. (2000). Violence in G-rated animated films. *Journal of the American Medical Association, 283*(20), 2716.

Yonas, A., Elieff, C. A., & Arterberry, M. E. (2002). Emergence of sensitivity to pictorial depth cues: Charting development in individual infants. *Infant Behavior & Development, 25*(4), 495–514.

Yoshida, M. (1993). Three-dimensional electrophysiological atlas created by computer mapping of clinical responses elicited on stimulation of human subcortical structures. *Stereotactic & Functional Neurosurgery, 60*(1–3), 127–134.

Yost, W. A. (2007). *Fundamentals of hearing: An introduction* (5th ed.). San Diego: Elsevier.

Young, S. M., & Pinsky, D. (2006). Narcissism and celebrity. *Journal of Research in Personality, 40*(5), 463–471.

Zarcadoolas, C., Pleasant, A., & Greer, D. S. (2006). *Advancing health literacy: A framework for understanding and action.* San Francisco: Jossey-Bass.

Zarraga, C., & Bonache, J. (2005). The impact of team atmosphere on knowledge outcomes in self-managed teams. *Organization Studies, 26*(5), 661–681.

Zeisel, J. (2006). *Inquiry by design: Environment/behavior/neuroscience in architecture, interiors, landscape, and planning.* New York: Norton.

Zelezny, L. C. (1999). Educational interventions that improve environmental behaviors: A meta-analysis. *Journal of Environmental Education, 31*(1), 5–14.

Zellner, D. A., Harner, D. E., & Adler, R. L. (1989). Effects of eating abnormalities and gender on perceptions of desirable body shape. *Journal of Abnormal Psychology, 98*(1), 93–96.

Zemishlany, Z., Aizenberg, D., & Weizman, A. (2001). Subjective effects of MDMA ("Ecstasy") on human sexual function. *European Psychiatry, 16*(2), 127–130.

Zentall, T. R. (2002). A cognitive behaviorist approach to the study of animal behavior. *Journal of General Psychology. Special Issue: Animal Behavior, 129*(4), 328–363.

Zentall, T. R. (2005). Animals may not be stuck in time. *Learning and Motivation, 36*(2), 208–225.

Zhang R. L., Zhang Z. G., & Chopp, M. (2005). Neurogenesis in the adult ischemic brain: generation, migration, survival, and restorative therapy. *Neuroscientist, 11*(5), 408–416.

Zimbardo, P. (2007). *The Lucifer Effect: Understanding how good people turn evil.* New York: Random House.

Zimbardo, P. G., Pilkonis, P. A., & Norwood, R. M. (1978). The social disease called shyness. In *Annual editions, personality and adjustment 78/79.* Guilford, CT: Dushkin.

Zohar, D. (1998). An additive model of test anxiety: Role of examspecific expectations. *Journal of Educational Psychology, 90,* 330–340.

Zola, S. M., & Squire, L. R. (2001). Relationship between magnitude of damage to the hippocampus and impaired recognition in monkeys. *Hippocampus, 11,* 92–98.

Zuckerman, M. (1990). The psychophysiology of sensation seeking. *Journal of Personality, 58*(1), 313–345.

Zuckerman, M. (1996). Item revisions in the Sensation Seeking Scale Form V (SSS-V). *EDRA: Environmental Design Research Association, 20*(4), 515.

Zuckerman, M. (2000). Sensation seeking. In A. Kazdin (Ed.), *Encyclopedia of psychology.* Washington, DC: American Psychological Association.

Zuckerman, M. (2002). Genetics of sensation seeking. In J. Benjamin, R. P. Ebstein, et al. (Eds.), *Molecular genetics and the human personality.* Washington, DC: American Psychiatric Publishing.

Zuwerink, J. R., Devine, P. G., Monteith, M. J., & Cook, D. A. (1996). Prejudice toward Blacks: With and without compunction? *Basic & Applied Social Psychology, 18*(2), 131–150.

Credits

Chapter 1. 13: Corbis Images/Jupiterimages **14:** Jeff Greenberg/PhotoEdit **17:** Mireille Vauier/Woodfin Camp/Jupiterimages **17:** Warren Morgan/Corbis **17:** Anne-Marie Weber/Getty Images **17:** Greg Johnston/Lonely Planet Images **16:** Ron Cohn/The Gorilla Foundation **18:** Charles Gupton/Stock Boston **21:** Bettmann/Corbis **21:** Dennis Coon **24:** Dan McCoy/Rainbow **27:** Archives of the History of American Psychology, University of Akron **28:** Archives of the History of American Psychology, University of Akron **28:** Archives of the History of American Psychology, University of Akron **28:** Neena Leen/Life Magazine/Timepix/Getty Images **29:** Archives of the History of American Psychology, University of Akron **30:** Archives of the History of American Psychology, University of Akron **30:** Bettmann/Corbis **31, all:** Archives of the History of American Psychology, University of Akron **33:** Patrick Giardino/Corbis **36:** Universal Studios/The Kobal Collection **44:** Royalty-Free/Corbis **47:** Baron Hugo van Lawick/National Geographic Society **54:** John Nordell/The Image Works

Chapter 2. 53: Arthur Toga, UCLA/Photo Researchers, Inc. **60:** Blend Images/Jupiterimages **64:** CNRI/Photo Researchers, Inc. **66, top:** AJPhoto/Photo Researchers, Inc. **66, bottom:** WDCN/Univ. College London/Photo Researchers, Inc. **67:** Courtesy of Richard Haier, University of California, Irvine **67:** Langleben et al., Human Brain Mapping (2005). Courtesy of Daniel Langleben, University of Pennsylvania **72:** Ronald C. James **75:** Shaywitz et al., 1995 NMR Research/Yale Medical School **83:** Rod Planch/Photo Researchers, Inc. **82:** Getty Images **82:** Amanda Edwards/Getty Images **84:** Brad Mangin/Getty Images **88:** Custom Medical Stock Photo **89:** Bob Daemmrich/The Image Works **83:** Tom McCarthy/PhotoEdit

Chapter 3. 97: Paul Kuroda/Superstock **99:** Biophoto Associates/Photo Researchers, Inc. **100:** Myrleen Ferguson/PhotoEdit **101:** Reprinted by permission of the publisher from *The Postnatal Development of the Human Cerebral Cortex, Vols. I–III* by Jesse LeRoy Conel, Cambridge, Mass.: Harvard University Press, Copyright © 1935, 1975 by the President and Fellows of Harvard College. **101, left:** Petit Format/Photo Researchers, Inc. **101, right:** Ted Wood **102:** Anna Kaufman Moon/Stock Boston **105:** Margaret Miller/Photo Researchers, Inc. **106:** From A.N. Meltzoff & M. K. Moore, "Imitation of facial and manual gestures by human neonates," *Science,* 1977,198, 75–78 **106:** Robert L. Fantz, Copyright © 1961 by Scientific American, Inc. All Rights Reserved **106:** Rubberball Productions/Getty Images **108:** Michael Newman/PhotoEdit **111, left:** Chris Lowe/Index Stock Imagery **111, right:** Michael Newman/PhotoEdit **114:** BananaStock/SuperStock **116:** Jeff Greenberg/PhotoEdit **120:** Gary Conner/Index Stock Imagery **122:** Tony Freeman/PhotoEdit **122:** Farrell Grehan/Index Stock Imagery **123:** FogStock LLC/Index Stock Imagery **135:** Sarah Putnum/Index Stock Imagery **136:** Jeff Greenberg/PhotoEdit **139:** Tony Ranze/AFP/Getty Image **140:** Michael Newman/PhotoEdit **143:** image100/SuperStock

Chapter 4. 149: © 2007 "Pintos" by Bev Doolittle®, courtesy of The Greenwich Workshop, Inc. www.greenwichworkshop.com **157:** Omikron/Photo Researchers, Inc. **159:** Michael Newman/PhotoEdit **161:** Jon L. Barken/Index Stock Imagery **165:** Dr. G. Oran Bredberg/SPL/Photo Researchers, Inc. **167, top:** Richard Costana, *Discover Magazine,* 1993 **167, bottom:** Omikron/Photo Researchers, Inc. **169:** Herve Donnezan/Photo Researchers, Inc. **171:** Roger Ressmeyer/Corbis **173, left:** Yvaral, © 1990, Marilyn Numerisee #420, Courtesy of Circle Gallery **173, right:** Mark Richards/PhotoEdit **176:** E. R. Degginger/Animals Animals **177:** © Shigeo Fukuda, 1985 **179:** Mark Richards/PhotoEdit **180, top:** Bob Western **180, bottom:** © 2008 Magic Eye Inc., www.magiceye.com **182:** Dennis Coon **183:** M. C. Escher's "Convex and Concave" © 2002 Cordon Art B. V. Baarn—Holland. All rights reserved. **184:** Dennis Coon **187:** Art © Estate of Al Held/Licensed by VAGA, NY, NY **189, top:** Superstock, Inc./SuperStock **189, center:** Bob Daemmrich/The Image Works **189, bottom:** Mark McKenna **194:** Susan Van Etten/PhotoEdit **196:** Dennis Coon **198:** AP/Wide World Photo

Chapter 5. 203: Iconica/Getty Images **205:** Joel Gordon **206:** Timothy Ross/The Image Works **208:** Yale Joel/TimePix/Getty Images **210:** Detroit Institute of the Arts/SuperStock **216:** Michael Newman/PhotoEdit **217:** Kactus Foto/SuperStock **221, all:** Dennis Coon **223:** Dennis Coon **231:** National Library of Medicine **233:** The Everett Collection **237:** Creasource Series/Jupiterimages **238:** Reprinted with permission from SCIENCE NEWS, the weekly newsmagazine of science, copyright 1993 **239:** Courtesy of Dr. Lester Grinspoon/Harvard Medical School **240:** Courtesy of the Brant County Health Unit **242:** Courtesy of Maryanne Mott

Chapter 6. 247: David R. Frazier/PhotoEdit **252:** Dennis Coon **259:** Yale Joel/Life Magazine/TimePix/Getty Images **262:** Chimp-O-Mat, Yukes Regional Primate Research Center, Emory University **266:** Christoph Wilhelm/Getty Images **268:** George McCarthy/NPL/Minden Pictures **269:** Carleton Ray/Photo Researchers, Inc. **272:** Jiang Jin/SuperStock **276:** Peter Cade/Getty Images **278:** Bambu Productions/Getty Images **279:** Courtesy of Albert Bandura/Stanford University **280:** Erik S. Lesser/AP/Wide World Photo **282:** Rubberball/SuperStock

Chapter 7. 287: Richard Heinzen/SuperStock **290:** Malcolm Linton/Liaison/Getty Images **293:** From Wilder Penfield, The Excitable Cortex in Conscious Man, 1958. Courtesy of the author and Charles C. Thomas Publisher, Springfield, Illinois **294:** William Fritsch/Jupiterimages **296:** A. Ramey/PhotoEdit **301:** SW Production/Index Stock Imagery **306:** Paul Conklin/PhotoEdit **308:** Andy Reynolds/Getty Images **309:** AP/Wide World Photo **310:** AP/Wide World Photo **312, left:** © Tulving, E. (1989). Remembering and knowing the past. *American Scientist,* 77,(4), 361–367 **312, right:** Jeffrey L. Rotman/Corbis **319:** Gregg Segal/Getty Image **323:** Ulrike Welsch

Chapter 8. 327: Richard Green **328, top:** James D. Wilson/Getty Images **328, bottom:** David Young-Wolff/PhotoEdit **331:** AP/Wide World Photo **333, left:** Dan McCoy/Rainbow **333, right:** Christiana Dittmann/Rainbow **334:** Stan Godlweski/Getty Images **335, left:** Getty Images **335, center:** Archiv/Photo Researchers, Inc. **335, right:** Courtesy of Cray Computer **342:** Dennis Coon **342:** Brian Bailey/Getty Images **345:** Billy Hustace/Getty Images **345:** Guy Edwards/Getty Images **347:** Myrleen Ferguson Cate/PhotoEdit **348:** The Great Ape Trust of Iowa **357:** Time Life Pictures/Getty Images **359:** Hulton Archive/Getty Images **359:** Rainbow **359:** Image Bank/Getty Images

Chapter 9. 371: Camay Sungu/AP/Wide World Photo **373:** David Austen/Woodfin Camp and Associates, Inc. **377:** Coutesy of Neal Miller **378:** Charron Smith Amgen, Inc. John Sholtis, The Rockerfeller University **380, top:** Royalty-Free/Corbis **380, left:** Frederick M. Brown/Getty Images **380, right:** Frazier Harrison/Getty Images **382:** AP/Wide World Photo **383:** Alain Evrard/Photo Researchers, Inc. **386:** Courtesy of Harry F. Harlow, University of Wisconsin Primate Laboratory **387:** Jeffrey L. Rotman/Corbis **389:** Kevin Lamarque/Reuters/Corbis **391:** Reuters/Corbis **392:** Rick Friedman/Corbis **392:** Gregory A. Beaumont/® The Great Arcata to Ferndale World Championship Cross Country Kinetic Sculpture Race **397:** Bob Daemmrich/The Image Works **400:** Gary Conner/PhotoEdit **401, top:** Sergei Karpukhgin/Reuters/Corbis **401, bottom:** Amy Etra/PhotoEdit **403:** Chad Slattery/Getty Images **404:** Dennis Coon **408:** Peter Beavis/Getty Images

Chapter 10. 413: Andre Forget/AP/Wide World Photo **414, left:** Matthew Mendelsohn/Corbis **414, right:** Bill Bachman/PhotoEdit **415:** Courtesy of Pam Wagner **417:** O'Brien Productions/Corbis **424:** Eleanor Bentall/Corbis **428:** "All is Vanity" by Allen Gilbert **429:** Bettmann/Corbis **432:** fotostock/SuperStock **433:** Joel Gordon **434:** David Young-Wolff/PhotoEdit **435:** Laura Dwight/PhotoEdit **440:** Photolibrary/Jupiterimages **444:** Zia Soleil/Getty Image **446:** David McNew/Newsmakers/Getty Images **452:** Digital Vision/Getty Images

Chapter 11. 457: Greg Epperson/Index Stock Imagery **459, left:** Darren Robb/Getty Images **459, right:** Jeffery Allan Salter/Corbis SABA **461:** Reuters/Corbis **464:** Tom Stewart/Corbis **465:** Daniel G. Lavoie/Corbis **466:** Rubberball/Getty Images **467:** Ken Cedeno/Corbis **470, top:** Tony Anderson/Getty Images **470, bottom:**

Name Index

Subject Index

Chapter 1: Introducing Psychology and Research Methods

Chapter Overview

The field of psychology is an exciting one because it helps us understand ourselves and one another, how we think and act, using the scientific method. Psychologists deal with many different aspects of human and animal behavior, and psychology can be applied to any number of careers.

Science in psychology is necessary because critical thinking requires that we test our assumptions rather than basing our beliefs on hunches. Psychologists rely on empirical evidence.

Psychology evolved from Philosophy departments to become a unique discipline. Early psychology explored the nature of the conscious mind, but shifted to focus on behavior, which is more readily observable. Psychological theory is designed to answer the question of why people do what they do, with biological, sociocultural, and psychological evidence providing key explanations.

Individuals who specialize in psychology can either do research to understand behavior, or can engage applying that understanding to people's lives through work in hospitals, schools, workplaces, government, or any number of other settings.

Experiments allow psychologists to answer cause and effect questions by controlling situations and removing personal biases. Because the subject matter involves sentient life, ethical protections of research participants is critical.

Observations provide another method of learning about behavior, in the form of interviews, surveys, or just watching people. Although these methods do not allow clear inferences about causes of behavior, they do allow some understanding of relationships, particularly for things that are impossible or ethically unreasonable to control experimentally.

Psychology is interesting, and so research shows up frequently in popular media. However, there can be mistakes or distortions in reporting, so you should always be careful and think critically when you get information from popular rather than scientific sources.

Learning Objectives

OBJECTIVE 1.1 – Describe reasons for studying psychology and why it is considered both a science and a profession; and define *psychology* and *behavior*, differentiating between *overt* and *covert behaviors*.

OBJECTIVE 1.2 – Describe how the search for empirical evidence sets psychology apart from "common-sense" beliefs and from other fields of study; define the terms *data*, *scientific observation*, and *research method*; and explain why some topics in psychology are difficult to study.

OBJECTIVE 1.3 – Describe each of the following research specialities in psychology:
a. developmental; b. learning; c. personality; d. sensation and perception;
e. comparative; f. biopsychology; g. cognitive; h. gender; i. social; j. cultural;
k. evolutionary, and l. forensic; and explain why and how animals are used in research, defining the term animal model and listing ways in which psychological research may benefit animals.

OBJECTIVE 1.4 – Explain the four goals of psychology.

OBJECTIVE 1.5 – Define the term critical thinking, and describe the four basic principles which form the foundation of critical thinking.

OBJECTIVE 1.6 – Define *pseudo-psychology*; explain how it differs from psychology; describe the pseudo-psychologies of palmistry, phrenology, graphology, and astrology; and explain why they continue to thrive even though they have no scientific basis.

OBJECTIVE 1.7 – Explain the problem with using common-sense as a source of information; list and define the six steps of the scientific method; define the terms *hypothesis*, *operational definition*, and *theory*; explain the importance of publishing; and list and describe the parts of a research report.

OBJECTIVE 1.8 – For each of these schools of psychology — structuralism, functionalism, behaviorism, Gestalt psychology, psychoanalytic, and humanism — answer each of the following questions: a. its founder, b. reasons it was founded, c. its goal or main focus, and d. its impact on modern psychology and/or possible use in psychotherapy.

OBJECTIVE 1.9 – Identify notable events within the history of psychology, and describe the contribution of women to the early history of psychology and their representation in the field then and now.

OBJECTIVE 1.10: Explain the contemporary perspectives in psychology, including the concepts of *eclectic*, *positive psychology*, *cultural diversity*, *cultural relativity*, and *social norms*.

OBJECTIVE 1.11 – Characterize the differences in training, emphasis, and sources of employment among psychologists, psychiatrists, psychoanalysts, counselors, and psychiatric social workers; explain how the media often portrays psychologists; and discuss psychology as a career option, including the various specialities, such as clinical and counseling psychology, the "scientist-practitioner" model, the APA code of ethics, and the types of research (applied or basic) performed.

OBJECTIVE 1.12 – List and describe the three essential variables of the experimental method; and explain the nature and purpose of the control group and the experimental group in an experiment, as well as the purpose of randomly assigning subjects to these two groups.

OBJECTIVE 1.13 – Describe three areas of ethical concern in behavioral research, and list the basic ethical guidelines for psychological researchers.

OBJECTIVE 1.14 – Describe what a placebo is and why it is used in an experiment; explain how the single-blind and double-blind experimental approaches control for the placebo effect and the experimenter effect, respectively; and discuss the self-fulfilling prophecy.

OBJECTIVE 1.15 – Explain the use of non-experimental methods of research.

OBJECTIVE 1.16 – Describe naturalistic observation and its advantages and limitations, including the concepts of *observer effect*, *observer bias*, and *anthropomorphic error*; and define the term *observation record*.

OBJECTIVE 1.17 – Describe a correlational study, its advantages and limitations, how a correlation coefficient is expressed and what it means, and why correlation does NOT demonstrate causation.

OBJECTIVE 1.18 – Briefly describe the clinical method of research, or case study method, including when it is used and its advantages and limitations.

OBJECTIVE 1.19 – Briefly describe the use of the survey method, including its advantages and limitations and the new use of Internet surveys, and define the terms *population*, *representative sample*, *random selection*, *biased sample*, and *courtesy bias*.

OBJECTIVE 1.20 – List the suggestions from the textbook authors that will help you become a more critical reader of psychological information in the popular press.

Language Development Guide

Introduction
(12) *riddle*: puzzling question
(12) *panorama*: wide view
(12) *envy*: be jealous of

Module 1.1
(14) *You can't teach an old dog new tricks*: it is difficult for people to learn new things
(14) *blazing hot*: very hot, as if almost on fire
(14) *hot under the collar*: irritable
(15) *psychotic*: having an extreme behavioral disorder
(15) *yield evidence*: provide information
(15) *vividly*: clearly
(16) *eyewitness testimony*: someone who saw something giving evidence in court
(18) *bystander apathy*: lack of interest or concern among witnesses to an accident or crime
(19) *diffusion of responsibility*: responsibility for action is spread out among those present and is lessened
(19) *boil down*: summarize

Module 1.2
(20) *take it with a grain of salt*: consider, think about it
(20) *probe*: examine, look closely, investigate
(20) *transcend*: go beyond or above, avoid
(22) *compatibility*: match, similarity
(22) *ring of truth*: sounds like it could be true
(22) *nitpicking*: criticizing about small or unimportant things
(22) *frank*: open, honest
(24) *covert*: hidden, secret, unobserved

Module 1.3

(27) *heft*: to get a sense of, to lift something to weigh it
(27,28) *settle*: come to agreement
(28) *overstatement*: exaggeration
(29) *launched*: began
(34) *delusion*: imaginary belief

Module 1.4

(36) *postgraduate* - education beyond a bachelors degree
(36) *moustache and gotee*: facial hair on the upper lip and chin
(36) *spectacles*: glasses
(38) *hang a shingle*: begin or open a professional business
(38) *rebirther*: a person who helps you imagine the experience of your birth
(38) *primal feeling facilitator*: a person who helps you express your anger
(38) *cosmic aura balancer*: a person who tries to align unseen energy forces around the body
(38) *Rolfer*: a person who gives deep tissue massages

Module 1.5

(42) *dunces*: slang for an unintelligent person
(43) *inert:* inactive, powerless

Module 1.6

(48) *surly*: grumpy, irritable
(49) *rampage*: wild, chaotic destructive activity
(49) *quads*: short for quadruplets
(49) *blue-collar workers*: non-professional workers, laborers, factory workers, service workers

Module 1.7

(53) *hoaxes*: untrue stories or cheating schemes
(53) *sixth sense*: an extrasensory perception, such as telepathy or precognition
(53) *debunked*: disproved
(53) *biofeedback*: devices used to measure physical arousal responses, or the training therapy which uses biofeedback equipment to train control over one's arousal level
(53) *sleep-learning devices*: tapes or CDs which play spoken language to you while you are sleeping
(53) *subliminal*: stimuli presented outside of conscious awareness, below or above a perceptual threshold
(53) *testimonials*: statements from individuals about their first-hand experience

Recite and Review

Module 1.1 The Science of Psychology

Survey Question: What is psychology? What are its goals? Pages 14-18, Objectives 1.1, 1.2, 1.3, 1.4
Psychology is the (1) _____ of behavior and mental processes.
Psychologists engage in critical (2) _____ as they gather and analyze empirical (3) _____ to answer questions about behavior.
Some major areas of research in psychology are comparative, learning, (4) _____, perception, personality, biopsychology, motivation and emotion, (5) _____, cognitive, developmental, the psychology of gender, cultural psychology, (6) _____ psychology, and forensic psychology.

Some psychologists are directly interested in (7) _____ behavior. Others study (8) _____ as models of human behavior.

As a science, psychology's goals are to (9) _____, understand, (10) _____, and control behavior.

Module 1.2 Critical Thinking and the Scientific Method in Psychology

Survey Question: What is critical thinking? Pages 20-21, Objective 1.5

Critical thinking is the ability to actively (11)_____, compare, analyze, (12) _____, synthesize, and (13) _____ on information.

To judge the (14) _____ of a claim, it is important to gather evidence (15)_____ the claim and to evaluate the *quality* of the (16)_____.

Survey Question: How does psychology differ from false explanations of behavior? Pages 21-23,
    Objective 1.6

Numerous pseudo-psychologies exist. These (17) _____systems are frequently confused with (18)_____ psychology. Belief in pseudo-psychologies is based in part on (19)_____, the fallacy of positive instances, and the Barnum effect.

Survey Question: Why is the scientific method important to psychologists? Pages 23-25, Objective 1.7

In the scientific method, systematic (20) _____is used to test hypotheses about behavior and mental events.

Important elements of a scientific investigation include observing, defining a problem, proposing a (21)_____, gathering evidence/testing the (21) _____, publishing results, and forming a (22)_____.

Concepts must be (23) _____operationally before they can be studied empirically.

Module 1.3 History and Contemporary Perspectives

Survey Question: How did the field of psychology emerge? Pages 27-31, Objectives 1.8, 1.9

Historically, psychology is an (24) _____of philosophy. Psychology first became a (25)_____ when researchers began to directly study and observe psychological events.

The first psychological laboratory was established in (26) _____by Wilhelm Wundt, who studied conscious (27)_____.

The first (28) _____in psychology was structuralism, a kind of "mental chemistry" based on (29)_____.

Structuralism was followed by (30)_____, behaviorism, and Gestalt psychology.

Survey Question: What are the contemporary perspectives in psychology? Pages 32-34, Objective 1.10

Psychodynamic approaches, such as Freud's (31)_____ theory, emphasize the unconscious origins of (32)_____.

Humanistic psychology accentuates (33)_____ experience, human potentials, and (34)_____.

Three complementary streams of thought in modern psychology are the (35) _____ perspective, including biopsychology and evolutionary psychology; the (36)_____ perspective, including behaviorism, cognitive psychology, the psychodynamic approach, and humanism; and the (37)_____ perspective.

Psychologists have recently begun to formally study positive aspects of human behavior, or (38)_____ psychology.

Most of what we (39)_____, feel, and do is influenced by the social and (40)_____ worlds in which we live.

Module 1.4 Psychologists and Their Specialties

Survey Question: What are the major specialties in psychology? Pages 36-39, Objective 1.11

Although psychologists, psychiatrists, psychoanalysts, and counselors all work in the field of mental health, their training and methods (41) _____ considerably.

Clinical and (42)_____ psychologists, who do psychotherapy, represent only two of dozens of specialties in psychology.

Other representative areas of specialization are industrial, (43)_____, consumer, (44)_____, developmental, engineering, (45)_____, environmental, forensic, community, psychometric, and experimental psychology.

Psychological research may be (46)_____ or applied.

Module 1.5 The Psychology Experiment

Survey Question: How is an experiment performed? Pages 41-44, Objectives 1.12, 1.13, 1.14

(47)_____ involve two or more groups of subjects that differ only with regard to the independent variable.

Effects on the (48)_____ variable are then measured. All other conditions (extraneous variables) are held (49)_____.

Because experiments are set up so the independent variable is the only possible cause of a change in the (50)_____ variable, clear cause-and-effect connections can be (51)_____.

The placebo effect is a problem in some studies, especially in experiments involving (52)_____, but double-blind testing allows us to draw (53)_____ conclusions. The placebo effect is also referred to as the (54)_____.

A related problem is the experimenter effect (a tendency for experimenters to (55)_____ influence the outcome of an experiment). Researcher (56)_____ can create a self-fulfilling prophecy, in which a (57)_____ changes in the direction of the expectation.

Psychological research must be done (58)_____, in order to protect the rights, dignity, and welfare of (59)_____.

Module 1.6 Non-Experimental Research Methods

Survey Question: What other research methods do psychologists use? Pages 46-51, Objectives 1.15, 1.16, 1.17, 1.18, 1.19

Unlike controlled experiments, (60)_____ methods usually cannot demonstrate cause-and-effect relationships.

Naturalistic (61)_____ is a starting place in many investigations.

Two problems with naturalistic observation are the effects of the observer on the observed and (62)_____.

In the correlational method, relationships between (63)_____ traits, responses, or events are measured.

A (64)_____ is computed to gauge the strength of the relationship.

Correlations allow (65)_____, but do not demonstrate cause-and-effect.

(66)_____ and natural clinical tests provide insights into human behavior that can't be gained by other methods.

In the survey method, people in a (67)_____ sample are asked a series of carefully worded questions.

Obtaining a (67)_____ sample of people is crucial when the survey method is used to study large populations.

6

Module 1.7 Psychology in Action: Psychology in the Media
Survey Question: How good is psychological information found in the popular media? Pages 53-55, Objective 1.20

Information in the mass media varies greatly in (68)_____ and accuracy.
It is wise to approach such information with (69)_____ and caution. Critical thinking and (69)_____ about media reports is often necessary to separate (70)_____ from fallacies.
Problems in media reports are often related to (71)_____ or unreliable sources of information, uncontrolled observation, misleading correlations, (72)_____ inferences, over-simplification, use of (73)_____ examples, and unrepeatable results.

Connections

Module 1.1

1. _____ biopsychology	a. mental activities
2. _____ psychology	b. systematic observation
3. _____ personality theorist	c. animal behavior
4. _____ empirical evidence	d. detailed record
5. _____ covert behavior	e. human and animal behavior
6. _____ scientific observation	f. "why" questions
7. _____ comparative psychology	g. brain and behavior
8. _____ description	h. direct observation
9. _____ understanding	i. traits, dynamics, individual differences
10. _____ control	j. influencing behavior

Module 1.2

1. _____ critical thinking	a. general descriptions
2. _____ operational definitions	b. participation is voluntary
3. _____ pseudo-psychology	c. believe flattery
4. _____ Barnum effect	d. method of measurement
5. _____ theory	e. summarize data
6. _____ uncritical acceptance	f. astrology
7. _____ ethical research	g. test assumptions
8. _____ Clever Hans	h. head signals

Module 1.3

1. _____	Alfred Adler	a. father of psychology
2. _____	Wundt	b. psychoanalysis
3. _____	Titchener	c. natural selection
4. _____	James	d. behaviorism
5. _____	Darwin	e. neo-Freudian
6. _____	Skinner	f. functionalism
7. _____	Maslow	g. color vision
8. _____	Freud	h. introspection
9. _____	Pavlov	i. self-actualization
10. _____	Wertheimer	j. Gestalt
11. _____	Ladd-Franklin	k. conditioned responses

Module 1.4

1. _____	ethics	a. internal forces
2. _____	psychiatrist	b. environmental forces
3. _____	psychologist	c. marital consultant
4. _____	social psychologist	d. solves practical problems
5. _____	counseling psychologist	e. information processing
6. _____	school psychologist	f. investigates attitudes and persuasion
7. _____	applied research	g. Ph.D., Psy.D., Ed.D.
8. _____	positive psychology	h. M.D.
9. _____	behavioristic view	i. professional code of conduct
10. _____	psychodynamic view	j. self-image
11. _____	cognitive view	k. optimal behavior
12. _____	humanistic view	l. conducts psychological testing

Module 1.5

1. _____	identify causes of behavior	a. done by using chance
2. _____	independent variable	b. excluded by experimenter
3. _____	dependent variable	c. reference for comparison
4. _____	extraneous variables	d. experimental method
5. _____	control group	e. varied by experimenter
6. _____	random assignment	f. effect on behavior
7. _____	placebos	g. sugar pills

Module 1.6

1. _____	observer effect	a. public polling techniques
2. _____	survey method	b. placebo effect control
3. _____	valid sample	c. representative of population
4. _____	case studies	d. related traits, behaviors
5. _____	single-blind experiment	e. math error
6. _____	correlational study	f. clinical method
7. _____	correlation of +3.5	g. behavioral change due to awareness
8. _____	courtesy bias	h. inaccurate answers

Module 1.7

1. _____ skepticism	a. firewalking
2. _____ no control group	b. urban legends
3. _____ oversimplification	c. easy answer
4. _____ use of single examples	d. testimonial

Check Your Memory

Module 1.1 The Science of Psychology

Survey Question: What is psychology? What are its goals? Pages 14-18, Objectives 1.1, 1.2, 1.3, 1.4

T F   1. Psychology can best be described as a profession, not a science.

T F   2. Psychology is defined as the scientific study of human behavior.

T F   3. Although it is a covert activity, dreaming is a behavior.

T F   4. The term *empirical evidence* refers to the opinion of an acknowledged authority.

T F   5. The term *data* refers to a systematic procedure for answering scientific questions.

T F   6. Naming and classifying are the heart of psychology's second goal, understanding behavior.

T F   7. Cognitive psychologists are interested in researching memory, reasoning, and problem solving.

T F   8. Animal models are used to discover principles that can be applied to animals only.

Module 1.2 Critical Thinking and the Scientific Method in Psychology

Survey Question: What is critical thinking? Pages 20-21, Objective 1.5

T F   9. Critical thinking is the ability to make good use of intuition and mental imagery.

T F   10. Critical thinkers actively evaluate claims, ideas, and propositions.

T F   11. A key element of critical thinking is evaluating the quality of evidence related to a claim.

T F   12. Critical thinkers recognize that the opinions of experts and authorities should be respected without question.

Survey Question: How does psychology differ from false explanations of behavior? Pages 21-23, Objective 1.6

T F   13. Pseudo-scientists test their concepts by gathering data.

T F   14. Phrenologists believe that lines on the hands reveal personality traits.

T F   15. Graphology is only valid if a large enough sample of handwriting is analyzed.

T F   16. Astrological charts consisting of positive traits tend to be perceived as "accurate" or true, even if they are not.

T F   17. The Barnum effect refers to our tendency to remember things that confirm our expectations.

Survey Question: Why is the scientific method important to psychologists? Pages 23-25, Objective 1.7

T F   18. The scientific method involves testing a proposition by systematic observation.

T F   19. An operational definition states the exact hypothesis used to represent a concept.

T F   20. Clever Hans couldn't do math problems when his owner left the room.

T F   21. Operational definitions link concepts with concrete observations.

T F   22. Most research reports begin with an abstract.

T F   23. Jane Goodall's study of chimpanzees made use of the clinical method.

T F   24. Concealing the observer helps reduce the observer effect.

T F   25. Anthropomorphic error refers to attributing animals' behaviors, thoughts, emotions, and motives to humans.

T F   26. A correlation coefficient of +.100 indicates a perfect positive relationship.

T F   27. Strong relationships produce positive correlation coefficients; weak relationships produce negative correlations.

T F   28. Perfect correlations demonstrate that a causal relationship exists.

T F   29. The best way to identify cause-and-effect relationships is to perform a case study.

Module 1.3 History and Contemporary Perspectives

Survey Question: How did the field of psychology emerge? Pages 27-31, Objectives 1.8, 1.9

T F   30. In 1879, Wundt established a lab to study the philosophy of behavior.

T F   31. Wundt used introspection to study conscious experiences.

T F   32. Edward Titchener is best known for promoting functionalism in America.

T F   33. The functionalists were influenced by the ideas of Charles Darwin.

T F   34. Behaviorists define psychology as the study of conscious experience.

T F   35. Watson used Pavlov's concept of conditioned responses to explain most behavior.

T F   36. The "Skinner Box" is used primarily to study learning in animals.

T F   37. Cognitive behaviorism combines thinking and Gestalt principles to explain human behavior.

T F   38. Margaret Washburn was the first woman in America to be awarded a Ph.D. in psychology.

T F   39. Mary Calkins did early research on memory.

T F   40. According to Freud, repressed thoughts are held out of awareness, in the unconscious.

T F   41. Carl Jung and Erik Erikson were two neo-Freudians who firmly believed in Freud's psychodynamic theory.

T F   42. Humanists generally reject the determinism of the behavioristic and psychodynamic approaches.

Survey Question: What are the contemporary perspectives in psychology? Pages 32-34, Objective 1.10

T F   43. The five major perspectives in psychology today are behaviorism, humanism, functionalism, biopsychology, and cognitive psychology.

T F   44. Believing that human's behaviors are controlled by rewards, B.F. Skinner invented the "Skinner box" to study animals' responses.

T F 45. "The whole is greater than the sum of its parts" is a slogan of structuralism.

T F 46. Mary Calkins was the first woman president of the American Psychological Association in 1905.

T F 47. Freud's psychodynamic theory of personality focused on the unconscious thoughts, impulses, and desires with the exception of sex and aggression since they describe negative views of human behavior.

T F 48. Humanism offers a positive, philosophical view of human nature.

T F 49. The cognitive view explains behavior in terms of information processing.

T F 50. Positive psychology focuses on the negative aspects of the self in order to achieve one's happiness and well-being.

T F 51. To understand behavior, psychologists must be aware of the cultural relativity of standards for evaluating behavior.

Module 1.4 Psychologists and Their Specialties

Survey Question: What are the major specialties in psychology? Pages 36-39, Objective 1.11

T F 52. Most psychologists work in private practice.

T F 53. The differences between clinical and counseling psychology are beginning to fade.

T F 54. To enter the profession of psychology today you would need to earn a doctorate degree.

T F 55. The Psy.D. degree emphasizes scientific research skills.

T F 56. More than half of all psychologists specialize in clinical or counseling psychology.

T F 57. Clinical psychologists must be licensed to practice legally.

T F 58. Over 40 percent of all psychologists are employed by the military.

T F 59. Studying ways to improve the memories of eyewitnesses to crimes would be an example of applied research.

Module 1.5 The Psychology Experiment

Survey Question: How is an experiment performed? Pages 41-44, Objectives 1.12, 1.13, 1.14

T F 60. Extraneous variables are those that are varied by the experimenter.

T F 61. Independent variables are suspected causes for differences in behavior.

T F 62. In an experiment to test whether hunger affects memory, hunger is the dependent variable.

T F 63. Independent variables are randomly assigned to the experimental and control groups.

T F 64. A person who takes a drug may be influenced by his or her expectations about the drug's effects.

T F 65. Placebos appear to reduce pain because they cause a release of endogenous dexedrine.

T F 66. In a single-blind experiment, the experimenter remains blind as to whether she or he is administering a drug.

T F 67. Subjects in psychology experiments can be very sensitive to hints about what is expected of them.

T F 68. The use of deception, invasion of privacy, and risk of harming subjects are some areas of ethical concerns in psychology.

T F 69. It is easier and more accessible to use animals in research since guidelines for animals are more lenient than guidelines for humans.

Module 1.6 Non-Experimental Research Methods

Survey Question: What other research methods do psychologists use? Pages 46-51, Objectives 1.15, 1.16, 1.17, 1.18, 1.19

T F   70. Phineas Gage is remembered as the first psychologist to do a case study.

T F   71. Case studies may be inconclusive because they lack formal control groups.

T F   72. The case study of the four Genain sisters who developed schizophrenia by the age of 25 is an example of environmental (nature) influence.

T F   73. Representative samples are often obtained by randomly selecting people to study.

T F   74. Representative sampling is an advantage of web-based research.

T F   75. A tendency to give socially desirable answers to questions can lower the accuracy of surveys.

Module 1.7 Psychology in Action: Psychology in the Media

Survey Question: How good is psychological information found in the popular media? Pages 53-55, Objective 1.20

T F   76. The existence of dermo-optical perception (sixth sense) was confirmed by recent experiments.

T F   77. Psychological courses and services offered for profit may be misrepresented, just as some other products are.

T F   78. At least some psychic ability is necessary to perform as a stage mentalist.

T F   79. Successful fire walking requires neurolinguistic programming.

T F   80. Violent crime rises and falls with lunar cycles.

T F   81. If you see a person crying, you must infer that he or she is sad.

T F   82. Individual cases and specific examples tell us nothing about what is true in general.

Critical Thinking

Module 1.1

1. All sciences are interested in controlling the phenomena they study. True or false?

Module 1.2

2. Can you think of some "commonsense" statements that contradict each other?

3. Try constructing a few "Barnum statements", personality statements that are so general that virtually everyone will think they apply to themselves. Can you string them together to make a "Barnum personality profile"? Can you adapt the same statements to construct a "Barnum horoscope"?

Module 1.3

4. Modern sciences like psychology are built on observations that can be verified by two or more independent observers. Did structuralism meet this standard? Why or why not?

Module 1.4

5. If most psychologists work in applied settings, why is basic research still of great importance?

Module 1.5

6. There is a loophole in the statement, "I've been taking Echinacea tablets, and I haven't had a cold all year. Echinacea is great!" What is the loophole?

7. People who believe strongly in astrology have personality characteristics that actually match, to a degree, those predicted by their astrological signs. Can you explain why this occurs?

Module 1.6

8. Adults who often ate Frosted Flakes cereal as children now have half the cancer rate seen in adults who never ate Frosted Flakes. What do you think explains this strange correlation?

9. A psychologist conducting a survey at a shopping mall (The Gallery of Wretched Excess) flips a coin before stopping passersby. If the coin shows heads, he interviews the person; if it shows tails, he skips that person. Has the psychologist obtained a random sample?

10. Attributing mischievous motives to a car that is not working properly is a thinking error similar to anthropomorphizing. T or F?

Module 1.7

11. Many parents believe that children become "hyperactive" when they eat too much sugar, and some early studies seemed to confirm this connection. However, we now know that eating sugar rarely has any effect on children. Why do you think that sugar appears to cause hyperactivity?

Final Survey and Review

Module 1.1 The Science of Psychology
Survey Question: What is psychology? What are its goals? Objectives 1.1, 1.2, 1.3, 1.4
1. Psychology is the scientific study of _____.
2. Psychologists engage in _____thinking as they gather and analyze _____ evidence to answer questions about behavior.
3. Some major areas of research in psychology are _____, learning, sensation, _____, personality, biopsychology, motivation and emotion, social, _____, developmental, the psychology of gender, cultural psychology, evolutionary psychology, and _____ psychology.
4. Some psychologists are directly interested in animal _____. Others study animals as _____of human behavior.
5. As a science, psychology's goals are to describe, _____, predict, and _____ behavior.

Module 1.2 Critical Thinking and the Scientific Method in Psychology
Survey Question: What is critical thinking? Objective 1.5
6. Critical thinking is the ability to actively evaluate, _____, _____, critique, _____, and reflect on information.
7. To judge the validity of a claim, it is important to _____for and against the claim and to evaluate the _____ of the evidence.

Survey Question: How does psychology differ from false explanations of behavior? Objective 1.6
8. Numerous _____ exist. These false systems are _____confused with valid psychology. Belief in pseudo-psychologies is based in part on uncritical acceptance, the fallacy of, and the Barnum effect.

Survey Question: Why is the scientific method important to psychologists? Objective 1.7
9. In the scientific method, _____observation is used to test hypotheses about _____and mental events.
10. Important elements of a scientific investigation include _____, _____a problem, proposing a hypothesis, gathering evidence/testing the hypothesis, _____, and forming a theory.
11. Concepts must be defined _____ before they can be studied _____.

Module 1.3 History and Contemporary Perspectives
Survey Question: How did the field of psychology emerge? Objectives 1.8, 1.9
12. Historically, psychology is an outgrowth of _____. Psychology first became a science when
_____.
13. The first psychological laboratory was established in Germany by _____, who studied
_____.
14. The first school of thought in psychology was _____, a kind of "mental chemistry" based on introspection.
15. _____was followed by functionalism, _____, and _____ psychology.

Survey Question: What are the contemporary perspectives in psychology? Objective 1.10
16. _____ approaches, such as Freud's psychoanalytic theory, emphasize the _____ origins of behavior.
17. _____ psychology accentuates subjective experience, _____, and personal growth.
18. Three complementary streams of thought in modern psychology are the biological perspective, including _____ and _____ psychology; the psychological perspective, including _____, cognitive psychology, the _____approach, and _____; and the sociocultural perspective.
19. Psychologists have recently begun to _____ positive aspects of human behavior, or positive psychology.
20. Most of what we think, feel, and _____ is influenced by the _____ and cultural worlds in which we live.

Module 1.4 Psychologists and Their Specialties
Survey Question: What are the major specialties in psychology? Objective 1.11
21. Although psychologists, psychiatrists, psychoanalysts, and counselors all work in the field of _____, their _____ differ considerably.
22. _____and counseling psychologists, who do psychotherapy, represent only two of _____ specialties in psychology.
23. Other representative areas of specialization are _____, educational, _____, school, developmental, _____, medical, _____, forensic, community, _____, and experimental psychology.
24. Psychological _____ may be basic or applied.

Module 1.5 The Psychology Experiment

Survey Question: How is an experiment performed? Objectives 1.12, 1.13, 1.14

25. Experiments involve two or more groups of subjects that differ only with regard to the _____ variable.

26. Effects on the dependent variable are then _____. All other conditions (_____ variables) are held constant.

27. Because experiments are set up so the _____ variable is the only possible cause of a change in the _____ variable, clear _____ connections can be identified.

28. The _____ effect is a problem in some studies, especially in experiments involving drugs, but _____ testing allows us to draw valid conclusions. The _____ is also referred to as the *meaning response.*

29. A related problem is _____ (a tendency for experimenters to unconsciously influence the outcome of an experiment). Researcher expectations can create a _____, in which a participant changes in the direction of the expectation.

30. Psychological research must be done ethically, in order to protect the _____ of participants.

Module 1.6 Non-Experimental Research Methods

Survey Question: What other research methods do psychologists use? Objectives 1.15, 1.16, 1.17, 1.18, 1.19

31. Unlike controlled experiments, non-experimental methods usually cannot demonstrate _____ _____.

32. _____ observation is a starting place in many investigations.

33. Two problems with naturalistic observation are _____ and observer bias.

34. In the _____ method, relationships between two traits, responses, or events are measured.

35. A correlation coefficient is computed to gauge the _____ of the relationship. Correlations allow prediction, but do not demonstrate _____.

36. Case studies and _____ provide insights into human behavior that can't be gained by other methods.

37. In the _____ method, people in a representative _____ are asked a series of carefully worded questions.

38. Obtaining a representative _____ of people is crucial when the survey method is used to study large _____.

Module 1.7 Psychology in Action: Psychology in the Media

Survey Question: How good is psychological information found in the popular media? Objective 1.20

39. Information in the mass media varies greatly in quality and _____.

40. It is wise to approach such information with skepticism and _____. Critical thinking and skepticism about media reports is often necessary to separate facts from _____.

41. Problems in media reports are often related to biased or _____ sources of information, uncontrolled observation, _____ correlations, false _____, over-simplification, use of single examples, and _____ results.

Mastery Test

1. Data in psychology are typically gathered to answer questions about
   a. clinical problems
   b. human groups
   c. human cognition
   d. overt or covert behavior

2. Who among the following would most likely study the behavior of gorillas?
   a. developmental psychologist
   b. comparative psychologist
   c. environmental psychologist
   d. forensic psychologist

3. An engineering psychologist helps redesign an airplane to make it safer to fly. The psychologist's work reflects which of psychology's goals?
   a. understanding
   b. control
   c. prediction
   d. description

4. Who among the following placed the greatest emphasis on introspection?
   a. Watson
   b. Wertheimer
   c. Washburn
   d. Wundt

5. Which pair of persons had the most similar ideas?
   a. Titchener — Skinner
   b. James — Darwin
   c. Watson — Rogers
   d. Wertheimer — Maslow

6. The behaviorist definition of psychology clearly places great emphasis on
   a. overt behavior
   b. conscious experience
   c. psychodynamic responses
   d. introspective analysis

7. As a profession, psychology is fully open to men and women, a fact that began with the success of
   a. O'Sullivan-Calkins.
   b. Tyler-James.
   c. Ladd-Franklin.
   d. Neal-Collins.

8. The idea that threatening thoughts are sometimes repressed would be of most interest to a
   a. structuralist.
   b. psychoanalyst.
   c. humanist.
   d. Gestaltist.

9. "A neutral, reductionistic, mechanistic view of human nature." This best describes which viewpoint?
a. psychodynamic
b. cognitive
c. psychoanalytic
d. biopsychological

10. Which of the following professional titles usually requires a doctorate degree?
a. psychologist
b. psychiatric social worker
c. counselor
d. all of the preceding

11. Who among the following is most likely to treat the physical causes of psychological problems?
a. scientist-practitioner
b. psychoanalyst
c. forensic psychologist
d. psychiatrist

12. More than half of all psychologists specialize in what branches of psychology?
a. counseling and comparative
b. applied and counseling
c. psychodynamic and clinical
d. counseling and clinical

13. When critically evaluating claims about behavior it is important to also evaluate
a. the source of anecdotal evidence.
b. the credentials of an authority.
c. the quality of the evidence.
d. the strength of one's intuition.

14. Which of the following pairs is most different?
a. pseudo-psychology — critical thinking
b. graphology — pseudo-psychology
c. palmistry — phrenology
d. psychology — empirical evidence

15. The German anatomy teacher Franz Gall popularized
a. palmistry.
b. phrenology.
c. graphology.
d. astrology.

16. A tendency to believe flattering descriptions of oneself is called
a. the Barnum effect.
b. the astrologer's dilemma.
c. the fallacy of positive instances.
d. uncritical acceptance.

17. Descriptions of personality that contain both sides of several personal dimensions tend to create
    a. an illusion of accuracy.
    b. disbelief and rejection.
    c. the astrologer's dilemma.
    d. a system similar to phrenology.

18. Appreciating an orchestra playing Mozart's fifth symphony more than a musician playing a solo on a clarinet reflects _____ psychology.
    a. Gestalt
    b. cognitive
    c. behavioral
    d. biopsychology

19. If an entire population is surveyed, it becomes unnecessary to obtain a
    a. control group.
    b. random comparison.
    c. random sample.
    d. control variable.

20. Control groups are most often used in
    a. naturalistic observation.
    b. the clinical method.
    c. parascience.
    d. experiments.

21. Concealing the observer can be used to minimize the
    a. observer bias effect.
    b. double-blind effect.
    c. observer effect.
    d. effects of extraneous correlations.

22. A psychologist studying lowland gorillas should be careful to avoid the
    a. anthropomorphic error.
    b. Gestalt fallacy.
    c. psychodynamic fallacy.
    d. fallacy of positive instances.

23. Testing the hypothesis that frustration encourages aggression would require
    a. a field study.
    b. operational definitions.
    c. adult subjects.
    d. perfect correlations.

24. In experiments involving drugs, experimenters remain unaware of who received placebos in a _____ arrangement.
    a. zero-blind
    b. single-blind
    c. double-blind
    d. control-blind

25. The idea that Clever Hans's owner might be signaling him was an informal
    a. research hypothesis.
    b. self-fulfilling prophecy.
    c. operational definition.
    d. dependent variable.

26. In psychology, the _____ variable is a suspected cause of differences in

    _____.
    a. independent, the control group
    b. dependent, the experimenter effect
    c. independent, behavior
    d. dependent, correlations

27. A person who is observed crying may not be sad. This suggests that it is important to distinguish between
    a. individual cases and generalizations.
    b. correlation and causation.
    c. control groups and experimental groups.
    d. observation and inference.

28. In an experiment on the effects of hunger on the reading scores of elementary school children, reading scores are the
    a. control variable.
    b. independent variable.
    c. dependent variable.
    d. reference variable.

29. Which of the following correlation coefficients indicates a perfect relationship?
    a. 1.00
    b. 100.0
    c. −1
    d. both a and c

30. Jane Goodall's studies of chimpanzees in Tanzania are good examples of
    a. field experiments.
    b. experimental control.
    c. correlational studies.
    d. naturalistic observation.

31. To equalize the intelligence of members of the experimental group and the control group in an experiment, you could use
    a. extraneous control.
    b. random assignment.
    c. independent control.
    d. subject replication.

32. Which method would most likely be used to study the effects of tumors in the frontal lobes?
    a. sampling method
    b. correlational method
    c. clinical method
    d. experimental method

33. An in-depth study on the life history of the four Genain sisters, who by the age of 25 had developed schizophrenia, is an example of
    a. survey method.
    b. correlational method.
    c. scientific method.
    d. clinical method.

34. The fact that all four identical Genain sisters developed schizophrenia and were in and out of mental hospitals by the age of 25 suggests that their disorder was influenced by
    a. only environmental conditions.
    b. nature.
    c. heredity.
    d. both a and b.

35. The release of endorphins by the pituitary gland helps explain the
    a. experimenter effect.
    b. placebo effect.
    c. multiple-personality effect.
    d. gender-bias effect.

36. Cause is to effect as _____ variable is to _____ variable.
    a. extraneous, dependent
    b. dependent, independent
    c. independent, extraneous
    d. independent, dependent

37. Which of the following correlations demonstrates a cause-effect relationship?
    a. .980
    b. 1.00
    c. .50
    d. none of the preceding

Chapter 3: Human Development

Chapter Overview

Most of Introductory Psychology deals with normal, adult behavior. In this chapter, Coon discusses how we get to be the way we are, and explores a lifespan of variation, from the very young to the very old.

Heredity and environment are both important in the development of an individual. Genes express periodically and interact with environmental factors to create who you become. Many prenatal environmental factors affect our early development and potential.

Once we are born, we continue to develop, moving from basic reflexes to actively engaging with our world. We mature at different rates, but in an orderly way as we learn and grow.

As we interact with those around us, we develop expectations about relationships, attachments to parents and other caregivers. Early parenting patterns, which vary by gender and culture, can impact emotional and intellectual development.

Intellectual development in early childhood is strongly influenced by development of language, as we gain skills in both vocabulary and interpersonal understanding.

Piaget describes how thought and intellect changes as we mature, and how our cognitive readiness affects how we learn, reason, and play. Vygotsky explains that we can encourage growth in our mental development by challenging ourselves and interacting with those ahead of us.

As we progress through adolescence into young adulthood, we expand our understanding, explore our identities, and are able to progress into more complex and abstract moral reasoning.

Erikson's psychosocial theory expanded developmental thought beyond adolescence, arguing that life is a continual series of events that affect how we change over time. We adjust somewhat in midlife and have to cope with decline and eventually death.

The Psychology In Action section explores what psychologists have discovered about effective parenting. Communication and positive, consistent, developmentally-appropriate discipline are key.

Learning Objectives

OBJECTIVE 3.1 – Define *developmental psychology; and* describe the roles that heredity ("nature") and environment ("nurture") play in a person's development, including the basic mechanisms of heredity, the plasticity of the newborn brain, and the definitions of the following terms: a. chromosome, b. DNA, c. gene, d. dominant trait (gene); e. recessive trait (gene); f. polygenic, and g. the human growth sequence.

OBJECTIVE 3.2 – Distinguish between congenital and genetic problems; describe the relationship between the blood supplies of the mother and her developing child; and discuss the effects of teratogens, such as tobacco, alcohol, and other drugs, on an unborn child.

39

OBJECTIVE 3.3 – Discuss the importance of the sensitive period and the effects of enrichment and deprivation on development; and explain *reciprocal interaction, reaction range, temperament* and the characteristics of easy, difficult, and slow-to-warm-up children; and describe the three factors that combine to determine one's developmental level.

OBJECTIVE 3.4 – Describe the world of the neonate, including their adaptive reflexes and their sensory and intellectual capabilities.

OBJECTIVE 3.5 – Discuss motor development and the concepts of *maturation, cephalocaudal pattern, proximodistal pattern*, and *readiness*, including how readiness is related to walking and toilet training.

OBJECTIVE 3.6 – Describe the course of early emotional development, according to Bridges and Izard, and explain the importance of the social smile.

OBJECTIVE 3.7 – Explain how self-awareness and emotional attachment are related to early social development, define *separation anxiety* and *separation anxiety disorder*, differentiate between the three types of attachment identified by Mary Ainsworth, and describe how these attachments can influence how people relate to others as adults.

OBJECTIVE 3.8 – Describe how parents can promote secure attachments and the characteristics of fathers who have securely attached infants; discuss the effects of day care on the quality of attachment, including the criteria for evaluating child care; and explain the importance of attachment in meeting a child's affectional needs.

OBJECTIVE 3.9 – Describe Baumrind's three major styles of parenting, including characteristics of both parents and children in each style; compare maternal and paternal influences on a child; and describe ethnic differences in parenting.

OBJECTIVE 3.10 – Describe the five stages of language acquisition and discuss children's increasing use of language in combination with their growing independence, including the time period known as the "terrible twos."

OBJECTIVE 3.11 – Discuss the roots of language, including Chomsky's theory and the research of other psycholinguists regarding the role of innate and environmental factors in language acquisition; and explain how parents communicate with infants before the infants can talk, including the concepts of *signals, turn-taking*, and *parentese*.

OBJECTIVE 3.12 – With regard to Piaget's theory of cognitive development:
   a. explain how a child's intelligence and thinking differ from an adult's (include the concept of transformation).
   b. explain the concepts of *assimilation* and *accommodation*.
   c. list (in order) and describe the specific characteristics of each stage.
   d. explain how parents can best guide their child's intellectual development.
   e. evaluate the usefulness of Piaget's theory in light of current brain research, research by learning theorists, and research on infant cognition.

OBJECTIVE 3.13 – Discuss Vygotsky's sociocultural theory; and define the terms zone of proximal development and scaffolding.

OBJECTIVE 3.14 – Differentiate between *adolescence* and *puberty*; describe the advantages and disadvantages of early and late maturation for males and females; and discuss identity formation, including the impact of one's ethnic heritage, and the transition to adulthood and the new status of *emerging adulthood*.

OBJECTIVE 3.15 – Discuss the concept of moral development by describing each of Kohlberg's three levels of moral development, the technique he used to study moral development, the proportion of the population that appears to function at each of his levels, and Gilligan's argument against Kohlberg's system and the current status of this argument.

OBJECTIVE 3.16 – Define the terms *developmental milestones*, *developmental tasks*, and *psychosocial dilemma*; and discuss Erikson's theory involving eight psychosocial dilemmas.

OBJECTIVE 3.17 – Discuss the challenges persons in mid-life to late adulthood experience, including Ryff's elements of well-being, Gould's crisis of questions and crisis of urgency, Levinson's midlife transition period for men and women, midcourse corrections, Schaie's suggestions for staying "mentally sharp," the psychological characteristics of successful aging, ageism in different cultures, and the fluid and crystallized abilities of older workers.

OBJECTIVE 3.18 – Discuss the emotional reactions toward death, including what people fear about death, the definition of a thanatologist, Kubler-Ross' five typical emotional reactions to impending death, and suggestions on how to offer support to a dying person.

OBJECTIVE 3.19 – Regarding effective parenting techniques, briefly discuss
   a. positive parent-child interactions.
   b. characteristics of effective discipline.
   c. characteristics and effects of the child rearing methods of power assertion, withdrawal of love, and management techniques on children's behavior and their self-esteem.
   d. the effects of consistent and inconsistent discipline.
   e. the effects of punishment, including spanking, and guidelines for its use.
   f. the elements of effective communication, according to Haim Ginott.
   g. Thomas Gordon's concepts of I-messages and you-messages.
   h. the use of natural and logical consequences.

Language Development Guide

Introduction
(96) *prune*: wrinkly dried fruit
(96) *pudgy*: fat

Module 3.1
(98) *inborn*: hereditary
(98) *from the womb to the tomb*: from birth to death
(98) *room left over to spare*: extra space
(99) *blooming and pruning*: dendrites growing when used and reducing in complexity and number when unused
(100) *gangsta rapper*: a recording artist/musician
(101) *defects*: flaws, errors

(102) *milder*: softer, more gentle

(102) *vicious cycle:* repeating never-ending sequence

(102) *grim*: harsh

(102) *wonderland*: playground

(103) *a dynamic relationship blossoms*: social bonds form

(103) *elicit*: bring out, cause

Module 3.2

(105) *timetable*: schedule

(105) *adaptive*: useful, functional

(105) *trapeze artists*: high-flying, swinging circus performers

(106) *checkerboards*: grids with boxes of alternating colors

(106) *bull's-eyes*: concentric circles

(106) *scrambled*: mixed-up, rearranged

(107) *wobbly*: unstable

(107) *tune*: correct, fix, improve

(108) *the wet look is in*: joke - referring to damp hair being popular

(108) *abundant:* many

(108) *hardwired:* fixed, determined

(108) *baby buggy*: pram, cart, stroller

Module 3.3

(111) *except perhaps early on Monday morning*: joke - referring to early week sleepiness

(111) *core*: important aspect

(111) *optimal*: ideal, desirable, best

(112) *be a serious handicap*: cause trouble

(112) *resiliency:* ability to recover after problems or difficulties

(112) *plight*: suffering

(112) *adversely affect*: hurt, damage

(112) *beforehand*: already

(112) *menagerie*: wild animal collection

(112) *stockade*: pen for farm animals or a prison

(113) *be emotionally stiff*: unexpressive

(113) *run amok*: crazy, chaotic

(114) *tactile*: touch

(114) *peekaboo*: baby game where parent hides their face behind their hands, and then surprises the child by opening their hands quickly and saying, "peekaboo"

(115) *roots lie in*: ancestors from

(115) *child-rearing*: raising children, parenting

(115) *extended family*: grandparents, aunts, uncles, cousins, in-laws, etc.

Module 3.4

(118) *miraculous*: magical

(118) *mischief*: getting into trouble

(118) *temper tantrum*: anger expressed in uncontrollable behavior - screaming, hitting, crying, etc.

(118) *stubborn*: unwilling to change

(118) *truly entered the world of*: can use

(118) *predisposition*: natural ability or interest

(120) *full flowering*: complete development

(120) *cultivation*: nurturing, care

Module 3.5

(122) *illustrious*: famous

(122) *a dime is worth less than a (larger) nickel*: dimes ($0.10) are smaller in size than nickels ($0.05).

(123) *retaliate*: fight back, seek revenge

(123) *panty, girdle*: women's undergarments

(124) *believing in Santa Claus*: Christmas gift-giver, Saint Nicholas bringing presents down the chimney on Christmas Eve

(124) *Monopoly*: popular board game where players buy properties, charge rent, build hotels, and try to end the game owning everything or having the most money

(124) *underestimated*: error, guessing too low

(126) *master the intellectual tools*: learn

(126) *jigsaw puzzle*: game where you must reassemble a picture that has been divided up into small pieces

(126) *tailored*: fit, made, gave, matched

(127) *unconsciously*: without knowing or being aware of it

Module 3.6

(129) *taking a job*: being hired

(129) *weather*: go through, experience

(129) *clear-cut*: obvious, straightforward

(129) *prestige*: popularity, recognition

(130) *Scarlett Johansson or Orlando Bloom*: attractive young movie actors

(130) *prolong*: lengthen

(132) *arrive at*: make

(132) *comprehensive*: complete, overall, all-inclusive

(132) *moral compass*: personal standard for making ethical decisions

(133) *moral yardstick*: set of ethical rules

Module 3.7

(135) *Rocky Road or Garden Path*: difficult or easy time

(136) *warm/cold parenting*: affectionate, caring or not

(136) *ridiculed*: teased, made fun of

(137) *strife*: difficulty, fighting

(138) *hardy*: emotionally strong

(138) *taking stock*: evaluating, looking over, examining

(138) *infirm*: disabled, handicapped, hospitalized

(138) *silver-haired stars*: successful older people

(139) *obselescence*: being unnecessary, thrown away or discarded, been replaced by something new

(139) *cast aside*: ignore, reject

(140) *homicides*: murders

(140) *futility*: hopelessness

(140) *inevitable*: something you can't escape or avoid

Module 3.8

(143) *smear*: spread

(146) *live the message*: be an example of

Recite and Review

Module 3.1 The Interplay of Heredity and Environment

Survey Question: How do heredity and environment affect development? Pages 98-103, Objectives 3.1, 3.2, 3.3

Developmental psychology is the study of (1)_____ changes in behavior and (2)_____ from birth to death.

Heredity (3)(_____) and environment (4)(_____) are interacting forces that are both necessary for human development. However, (5)_____ can only influence environment.

Newborn brains are highly (6)_____(capable of being altered by experience). Early learning environments can cause new (7)_____to grow ("blooming") and unused (8)_____to be reduced ("pruning").

Hereditary instructions are carried by the (9)_____and genes in each cell of the body. Most characteristics are polygenic and reflect the combined effects of (10)_____and recessive genes.

Prenatal development is influenced by (11)_____factors, such as diseases, drugs, radiation, various teratogens, and the mother's diet, health, and emotions. These factors can shape one's (12)_____, limiting the effects of heredity.

During sensitive periods in development, infants are (13)_____sensitive to specific environmental influences.

Early perceptual, intellectual, or emotional deprivation seriously (14)_____development while deliberate enrichment of the environment has a (15)_____effect on infants.

Temperament is (16)_____. Most infants fall into one of three temperament categories: easy children, (17)_____children, and slow-to-warm-up children.

Infants' heredity affects their temperament, which affects how parents respond to them, which affects how their genes express, a (18)_____.

A child's developmental level reflects (19)_____, environment, and the effects of the child's own (20)_____.

Module 3.2 The Neonate and Early Maturation

Survey Question: What can newborn babies do? Pages 105-107, Objective 3.4

Infant development is strongly influenced by heredity. However, environmental factors such as nutrition, (21)_____, and learning are also important.

The human neonate has a number of (22)_____reflexes, including the grasping, rooting, (23)_____, and Moro reflexes. Neonates begin to learn (24)_____and they appear to be aware of the effects of their actions.

Tests in a (25)_____reveal a number of visual preferences in the newborn. The neonate is drawn to (26)_____lights and circular or (27)_____designs.

Infants prefer human face patterns, especially (28)_____faces. In later infancy, interest in the (29)_____emerges.

Survey Question: What influence does maturation have on early development? Pages 107-109, Objective 3.5

Maturation of the body and nervous system underlies the orderly development of, (30)_____, cognitive abilities, emotions, and (31)_____.

Physical maturation typically is from the head downward (32)(_____), and from the core outward (33)(_____).

The (34)_____of maturation varies from person to person. Also, (35)_____contributes greatly to the development of basic motor skills.

Emotions develop in a (36)_____order, starting with generalized excitement in newborn babies. Three of the basic emotions — (37)_____, (38)_____, and joy — may be unlearned.

Many early skills, such as (39)_____and toilet training, are subject to the principle of readiness.

44

Module 3.3 Social Development in Childhood

Survey Question: Of what significance is a child's emotional bond with parents? Pages 111-112, Objectives 3.6, 3.7

Opportunities for social interaction increase as infants develop (40)_____and they begin to (41)_____seek guidance from adults.

Emotional (42)_____of human infants is a critical early event.

Infant attachment is reflected by (43)_____anxiety. The quality of attachment can be classified as secure, insecure-(44)_____, or insecure-(45)_____.

Secure attachment is fostered by (46)_____ care from parents who are sensitive to a baby's (47)_____and rhythms.

High-quality day care is (48)_____and can even be (49)_____to preschool children. Low-quality care can be (50)_____.

Meeting a baby's (51)_____needs is as important as meeting needs for physical care.

Survey Question: How important are parenting styles? Pages 113-115, Objectives 3.8, 3.9

Studies suggest that parental styles have a substantial impact on emotional and (52)_____development.

Three major parental styles are authoritarian, (53)_____, and authoritative.

(54)_____ parenting appears to benefit children the most.

Whereas mothers typically emphasize (55)_____, fathers tend to function as (56)_____for infants. Both care giving styles contribute to the (57)_____of young children.

The ultimate success of various parenting styles depends on what (58)_____or ethnic community a child will enter.

Parenting styles (59)_____across cultures.

Module 3.4 Language Development in Childhood

Survey Question: How do children acquire language? Pages 118-120, Objectives 3.10, 3.11

Learning to use (60)_____is a cornerstone of early intellectual development.

Language development proceeds from crying, to cooing, then (61)_____, the use of single words, and then to (62)_____speech.

The underlying patterns of telegraphic speech suggest a (63)_____ predisposition to acquire language. This (64)_____tendency is augmented by learning.

Prelanguage communication between parent and child involves shared (65)_____, nonverbal signals, and turn-taking.

Motherese or (66)_____is a simplified, musical style of speaking that parents use to help their children learn language.

Module 3.5 Cognitive Development in Childhood

Survey Question: How do children learn to think? Pages 122-127, Objectives 3.12, 3.13

The intellect of a child is (67)_____abstract than that of an adult. Jean Piaget theorized that intellectual growth occurs through a combination of (68)_____ and accommodation.

Piaget also held that children mature through a fixed series of cognitive stages. The stages and their approximate age ranges are (69)_____(0–2), preoperational (2–7), (70)_____operational (7–11), and formal operations (11–adult).

Caregivers should offer learning opportunities that are (71)_____for a child's level of cognitive development.

Learning principles provide an alternate explanation that assumes cognitive development is (72)_____; it does not occur in stages.

Recent studies of infants under the age of one year suggest that they are (73)_____ of thought well beyond that observed by Piaget.

Lev Vygotsky's (74)_____theory emphasizes that a child's mental abilities are advanced by interactions with (75)_____competent partners. Mental growth takes place in a child's zone of (76)_____development, where a (77)_____person may scaffold the child's progress. As children rely on adults to help them discover new skills and principles they learn (78)_____ beliefs and values.

Module 3.6 Adolescence, Young Adulthood, and Moral Development

Survey Question: Why is development during adolescence and young adulthood especially challenging?
        Pages 129-130, Objective 3.14

(79)_____is a biological event which initiates adolescence, and it can affect social and (80)_____development, particularly when it occurs earlier or later than for one's peers. Transitioning from childhood to adulthood requires the formation of a personal (81)_____; the major life task of adolescence. Identity formation is even more challenging for adolescents of (82)_____descent.

In western industrialized societies the transition into adulthood is further complicated as it is increasingly (83)_____well into the twenties.

Survey Question: How do we develop morals and values? Pages 132-133, Objective 3.15
Lawrence (84)_____identified preconventional, conventional, and (85)_____ levels of moral reasoning.

Most people function at the (86)_____level of morality, but some never get beyond the selfish, preconventional level. (87)_____ people attain the highest, or postconventional level, of moral reasoning.

Module 3.7 Challenges Across the Lifespan

Survey Question: What are the typical tasks and dilemmas through the life span? Pages 135-137,
        Objective 3.16

(88)_____identified a series of challenges that occur across the lifespan. These range from a need to gain (89)_____in infancy, through learning independence, establishing identity and the ability to achieve intimacy and (90)_____, to the need to live with (91)_____in old age.

Survey Question: What issues arise during later adulthood? Pages 137-139, Objective 3.17
Well-being during adulthood consists of six elements: self-acceptance, positive relations with others, (92)_____, environmental mastery, having (93)_____in life, and continued personal growth. (94)_____ people have a midlife crisis, questioning aspects of their life or feeling a renewed sense of (95)_____, but midlife course (96)_____are more common. Even if no crisis occurs, people tend to move through repeated cycles of stability and (97)_____throughout adulthood.

Intellectual declines associated with aging are (98)_____, at least through one's 70s. This is especially true of individuals who (99)_____mentally active.

(100)_____ refers to prejudice, discrimination, and stereotyping on the basis of age. It affects people of all ages but is especially damaging to older people. Most (101)_____is based on stereotypes, myths, and misinformation.

Survey Question: How do people typically react to death? Pages 139-141, Objective 3.18
Death is a natural part of life. There is value in understanding it and accepting it.

Typical emotional reactions to impending death include (102)_____, anger, bargaining, (103)_____, and acceptance, but not necessarily in that order or (104)_____.

Module 3.8 Psychology in Action: Effective Parenting

Survey Question: How do effective parents discipline and communicate with their children? Pages 143-146, Objective 3.18

(105)_____parent-child interactions occur when parents spend enjoyable time
(106)_____their children in a loving and mutually respectful fashion.
Effective parental discipline tends to emphasize child management techniques (especially
(107)_____), rather than power assertion or (108)_____.
Punishment may lead to unintended (109)_____and behavioral consequences, and so should
be used with (110)_____.
(111)_____ is also an important aspect of effective parenting.
Effective parents allow their children to (112)_____their feelings but (113)_____ their
behavior.
Much misbehavior can be managed by use of (114)_____and the application of natural and
(115)_____consequences.

Connections

Module 3.1

1. _____ gene	a. DNA area
2. _____ congenital problems	b. nature
3. _____ heredity	c. nurture
4. _____ sensitive period	d. conception to birth
5. _____ environment	e. radiation, drug or dangerous substance
6. _____ enrichment	f. magnified environmental impact
7. _____ prenatal period	g. personality characteristics
8. _____ teratogen	h. "birth defects"
9. _____ temperament	i. stimulating environment

Module 3.2

1. _____ grasping reflex	a. rapid motor learning
2. _____ rooting reflex	b. palm grip
3. _____ Moro reflex	c. startled embrace
4. _____ neonate	d. food search
5. _____ readiness	e. control of muscles and movement
6. _____ motor development	f. newborn infant
7. _____ familiar faces	g. physical growth
8. _____ maturation	h. preferred pattern

Module 3.3

1. _____ secure attachment	a. social development
2. _____ insecure-avoidant	b. anxious emotional bond
3. _____ separation anxiety	c. positive emotional bond
4. _____ resilience	d. emotional distress
5. _____ social referencing	e. observing reactions of others
6. _____ cooperative play	f. firm and consistent guidance
7. _____ Asian-American families	g. little guidance
	h. playmates
8. _____ paternal influence	i. strict obedience
9. _____ authoritative style	j. interdependence
10. _____ authoritarian style	k. bouncing back after hardship
11. _____ permissive style	l. show of force
12. _____ power assertion	

Module 3.4

1. _____ biological predisposition	a. vowel sounds
	b. vowels and consonants
2. _____ cooing	c. caretaker speech
3. _____ babbling	d. "Mama gone."
4. _____ telegraphic speech	e. hereditary readiness for language
5. _____ turn-taking	f. psycholinguists
6. _____ Noam Chomsky	g. conversational style of communication
7. _____ parentese	

Module 3.5

1. _____ assimilation	a. changing existing mental patterns
2. _____ accommodation	b. egocentricism
3. _____ sensorimotor stage	c. applying mental patterns
4. _____ preoperational stage	d. abstract principles
5. _____ concrete operations	e. conservation
6. _____ formal operations	f. object permanence
7. _____ scaffolding	g. skilled support for learning
8. _____ Piaget	h. stage theory of cognitive development

Module 3.6

1. _____ adolescence	a. moral dilemmas
2. _____ puberty	b. status or role clue
3. _____ social marker	c. social contract/individual principles
4. _____ imaginary audiences	d. good boy or girl/respect for authority
5. _____ emerging adulthood	e. avoiding punishment or seeking pleasure
6. _____ Kohlberg	f. sexual maturation
7. _____ preconventional	g. mid 20s
8. _____ conventional	h. cultural status
9. _____ postconventional	i. imagined viewers
10. _____ identity	j. teen's task

Module 3.7

1. _____ optimal development	a. received praises versus lacking support	
2. _____ trust versus mistrust	b. self-control versus inadequacy	
3. _____ developmental task	c. love versus insecurity	
4. _____ autonomy versus shame and doubt	d. freedom to choose versus criticism	
5. _____ initiative versus guilt	e. mastered developmental tasks	
6. _____ industry versus inferiority	f. skills to be attained	
7. _____ "empty nest"	g. common prejudice	
8. _____ transition period	h. life change	
9. _____ Roger Gould	i. adult development	
10. _____ ageism	j. daily exercise and low-fat diet	
11. _____ increased life expectancy	k. children leave	
12. _____ thanatologist	l. intense sorrow	
13. _____ Elizabeth Kübler-Ross	m. expert on death	
14. _____ bargaining	n. acceptance of loss	
15. _____ grief	o. reactions to dying	
16. _____ resolution	p. reaction to impending death	

Module 3.8

1. _____ withdrawal of love	a. reasonable outcomes defined by parent
2. _____ power assertion	b. coercion or physical punishment
3. _____ self-esteem	c. stable rules of conduct
4. _____ consistency	d. positive evaluation
5. _____ I-message	e. withholding affection
6. _____ natural consequences	f. stating how someone's behavior affects you
7. _____ logical consequences	g. touching a hot stove gets you burned

Check Your Memory

Module 3.1 The Interplay of Heredity and Environment

Survey Question: How do heredity and environment affect development? Pages 98-103, Objectives 3.1, 3.2, 3.3

T F   1. Developmental psychology is the study of progressive changes in behavior and abilities during childhood.

T F   2. Each cell in the human body (except sperm cells and ova) contains 23 chromosomes.

T F   3. The order of organic bases in DNA acts as a genetic code.

T F   4. Two brown-eyed parents cannot have a blue-eyed child.

T F   5. Identical twins have identical genes.

49

T F   6. More children have a slow-to-warm-up temperament than a difficult temperament.

T F   7. The sensitive period during which German measles can damage the fetus occurs near the end of pregnancy.

T F   8. Teratogens are substances capable of causing birth defects.

T F   9. An infant damaged by exposure to X-rays during the prenatal period suffers from a genetic problem.

T F   10. Many drugs can reach the fetus within the intrauterine environment.

T F   11. To prevent fetal alcohol syndrome, the best advice to pregnant women is to get plenty of rest, vitamins, and good nutrition.

T F   12. Prepared childbirth tends to reduce the need for pain medications during birth.

T F   13. Poverty is associated with retarded emotional and intellectual development.

T F   14. In animals, enriched environments can actually increase brain size and weight.

T F   15. Factors that influence developmental levels are heredity, environment, and parental discipline.

Module 3.2 The Neonate and Early Maturation
Survey Question: What can newborn babies do? Pages 105-107, Objective 3.4

T F   16. The Moro reflex helps infants hold on to objects placed in their hands.

T F   17. As early as nine weeks of age, infants can imitate actions a full day after seeing them.

T F   18. Three-day-old infants will pay an equal amount of attention to a person who is gazing at them as well as a person who is not looking at them.

T F   19. Three-day-old infants prefer to look at simple colored backgrounds rather than more complex patterns.

T F   20. After age two, familiar faces begin to hold great interest for infants.

Survey Question: What influence does maturation have on early development? Pages 107-109, Objective 3.5

T F   21. Most infants learn to stand alone before they begin crawling.

T F   22. Motor development follows a top-down, center-outward pattern.

T F   23. Toilet training should begin soon after a child is one year old.

T F   24. Anger and fear are the first two emotions to emerge in infancy.

T F   25. An infant's social smile appears within one month after birth.

Module 3.3 Social Development in Childhood
Survey Question: Of what significance is a child's emotional bond with parents? Pages 111-112, Objectives 3.6, 3.7

T F   26. Most infants have to be 15 weeks old before they can recognize themselves on videotape.

T F   27. Securely attached infants turn away from their mother when she returns after a period of separation.

T F   28. A small number of children per caregiver is desirable in day care settings.

T F 29. Children who spend too much time in poor-quality day care tend to be insecure and aggressive.

T F 30. Responsive parents are sensitive to a child's feelings, need, rhythms, and signals.

T F 31. Fathers typically spend about half their time in caregiving and half playing with the baby.

T F 32. Paternal play tends to be more physically arousing for infants than maternal play is.

T F 33. Since mothers spend more time caring for infants, mothers are more important than fathers.

Survey Question: How important are parenting styles? Pages 113-115, Objectives 3.8, 3.9
T F 34. Authoritarian parents view children as having adult-like responsibilities.

T F 35. Permissive parents basically give their children the message "Do it because I say so."

T F 36. The children of authoritarian parents tend to be independent, assertive, and inquiring.

T F 37. Asian cultures tend to be group-oriented and they emphasize interdependence among individuals.

T F 38. African-American families tend to have strict forms of discipline

T F 39. Hispanic families tend to emphasize family values, loyalty, and social skills.

T F 40. Arab-American families emphasize individual identity and achievement over the welfare of the family.

Module 3.4 Language Development in Childhood
Survey Question: How do children acquire language? Pages 118-120, Objectives 3.10, 3.11
T F 41. The single-word stage begins at about six months of age.

T F 42. "That red ball mine" is an example of telegraphic speech.

T F 43. Noam Chomsky believes that basic language patterns are innate.

T F 44. The "terrible twos" refers to the two-word stage of language development.

T F 45. The "I'm-going-to-get-you" game is an example of prelanguage communication.

T F 46. Parentese is spoken in higher pitched tones with a musical inflection.

T F 47. Motherese or parentese language used by mothers and fathers to talk to their infants does more harm than good to their infants' language development.

Module 3.5 Cognitive Development in Childhood
Survey Question: How do children learn to think? Pages 122-127, Objectives 3.12, 3.13
T F 48. According to Piaget, children first learn to make transformations at about age three.

T F 49. Assimilation refers to modifying existing ideas to fit new situations or demands.

T F 50. Cognitive development during the sensorimotor stage is mostly nonverbal.

T F 51. Reversibility of thoughts and the concept of conservation both appear during the concrete operational stage.

T F 52. Three-year-old children are surprisingly good at understanding what other people are thinking.

T F 53. An understanding of hypothetical possibilities develops during the preoperational stage.

T F 54. Playing peekaboo is a good way to establish the permanence of objects for children in the sensorimotor stage.

T F 55. Contrary to what Piaget observed, infants as young as three months of age show signs of object permanence.

T F 56. Hothousing or the forced teaching of children to learn reading or math is encouraged to accelerate their intellectual development and to prevent apathy.

T F 57. A criticism of Piaget's theory of cognitive development is that he underestimated the impact of cultural influences on children's mental development.

T F 58. Vygotsky's key insight was that children's thinking develops through dialogues with more capable persons.

T F 59. Learning experiences are most helpful when they take place outside of a child's zone of proximal development.

T F 60. Scaffolding is like setting up temporary bridges to help children move into new mental territory.

T F 61. Vygotsky empasized that children use adults to learn about their culture and society.

Module 3.6 Adolescence, Young Adulthood, and Moral Development
Survey Question: Why is development during adolescence and young adulthood especially challenging?
Pages 129-130, Objective 3.14
T F 62. The length of adolescence varies in different cultures.

T F 63. Early maturation tends to enhance self-image for boys.

T F 64. Early-maturing girls tend to date sooner and are more likely to get into trouble.

T F 65. By taking pride in their ethnic heritage, teenagers from different ethnic groups have reduced self-esteem, a negative self-image, and a weakened ethnic identity.

T F 66. "Twixters" are pre-teens who act more mature than they really are.

Survey Question: How do we develop morals and values? Pages 132-133, Objective 3.15
T F 67. Lawrence Kohlberg used moral dilemmas to assess children's levels of moral development.

T F 68. At the preconventional level, moral decisions are guided by the consequences of actions, such as punishment or pleasure.

T F 69. The traditional morality of authority defines moral behavior in the preconventional stage.

T F 70. Most adults function at the conventional level of moral reasoning.

T F 71. All children will achieve Kohlberg's conventional level of moral development, and approximately 80 percent of all adults will achieve the postconventional level of morality.

T F 72. Both men and women may use justice or caring as a basis for making moral judgments.

Module 3.7 Challenges Across the Lifespan
Survey Question: What are the typical tasks and dilemmas through the life span? Pages 135-137,
Objective 3.16
T F 73. Learning to read in childhood and establishing a vocation as an adult are typical life stages.

T F 74. Psychosocial dilemmas occur when a person is in conflict with his or her social world

T F 75. Initiative versus guilt is the first psychosocial dilemma a child faces.

T F 76. Answering the question "Who am I?" is a primary task during adolescence.

T F 77. Generativity is expressed through taking an interest in the next generation.

T F   78. A "midlife crisis" is a virtually universal experience.

T F   79. A crisis of urgency tends to hit people around the age of 30.

T F   80. Maintaining good health is a prominent goal among the elderly.

T F   81. Levinson places the midlife transition in the 40-55 age range.

T F   82. During the midlife transition, women are less likely than men to define success in terms of a key event.

T F   83. Having a sense of purpose in life is one element of well-being during adulthood.

T F   84. Crystallized abilities are the first to decline as a person ages.

T F   85. For many people, successful aging requires a combination of activity and disengagement.

T F   86. Ageism refers to prejudice and discrimination toward the elderly.

T F   87. Few elderly persons become senile or suffer from mental decay.

Survey Question: How do people typically react to death? Pages 139-141, Objective 3.18

T F   88. Most of the deaths portrayed on television are homicides.

T F   89. The "Why me" reaction to impending death is an expression of anger.

T F   90. Trying to be "good" in order to live longer is characteristic of the denial reaction to impending death.

T F   91. It is best to go through all the stages of dying described by Kübler-Ross in the correct order.

T F   92. To help reduce the feeling of isolation, Kirsti Dyer suggests that family members or friends should try to be respectful, genuine, aware of nonverbal cues, or just be there for the dying person.

Module 3.8 Psychology in Action: Effective Parenting

Survey Question: How do effective parents discipline and communicate with their children? Pages 143-146, Objective 3.18

T F   93. As a means of child discipline, power assertion refers to rejecting a child.

T F   94. Severely punished children tend to be defiant and aggressive.

T F   95. Punishment is most effective when it is given immediately after a disapproved act.

T F   96. Spanking, even if it is backed up with a supportive parenting technique, is still emotionally damaging to most children.

T F   97. An authoritarian style of parenting is necessary since encouraging resiliency in children is challenging and difficult for most parents and children.

T F   98. Consistency of child discipline is more important than whether limits on children's behavior are strict or lenient.

T F   99. Encouragement means giving recognition for effort and improvement.

T F   100. Logical consequences should be stated as you-messages.

Critical Thinking

Module 3.1

1. Environmental influences can interact with hereditary programming in an exceedingly direct way. Can you guess what it is?

Module 3.2

2. If you were going to test newborn infants to see if they prefer their own mother's face to that of a stranger, what precautions would you take?

Module 3.3

3. Can you think of another way to tell if infants have self-awareness?

4. Can emotional bonding begin before birth?

5. If power assertion is a poor way to discipline children, why do so many parents use it?

Module 3.4

6. The children of professional parents hear more words per hour than the children of welfare parents, and they also tend to score higher on tests of mental abilities. How else could their higher scores be explained?

Module 3.5

7. Using Piaget's theory as a guide, at what age would you expect a child to recognize that a Styrofoam cup has weight?

Module 3.6

8. Are labels like "adolescent" or "young adult" reflective of heredity or environment?

Module 3.7

9. Trying to make generalizations about development throughout life is complicated by at least one major factor. What do you think it is?

Module 3.8

10. Several Scandinavian countries have made it illegal for parents to spank their own children. Does this infringe on the rights of parents?

Final Survey and Review

Module 3.1 The Interplay of Heredity and Environment
Survey Question: How do heredity and environment affect development? Objectives 3.1, 3.2, 3.3

1. Developmental psychology is the study of progressive changes in _____ and abilities from _____ to _____.

2. _____ (nature) and _____ (nurture) are interacting forces that are both necessary for human development. However, caregivers can only influence _____.

3. Newborn brains are highly plastic (_____). Early learning environments can cause new dendrites to grow ("_____") and unused synapses to be reduced ("_____").

4. Hereditary instructions are carried by the chromosomes and _____ in each cell of the body. Most characteristics are _____ and reflect the combined effects of dominant and recessive genes.

5. Prenatal development is influenced by environmental factors, such as_____, drugs, radiation, various teratogens, and the mother's diet, health, and_____. These factors can shape one's reaction range, limiting the effects of_____.

6. During sensitive periods in development, infants are more sensitive to specific _____influences.

7. Early perceptual, intellectual, or emotional _____seriously retards development while deliberate _____of the environment has a beneficial effect on infants.

8. _____is hereditary. Most infants fall into one of three _____categories: easy children, difficult children, and _____children.

9. Infants' heredity affects their temperament, which affects how _____respond to them, which affects how their _____express, a reciprocal interaction.

10. A child's _____reflects heredity, _____, and the effects of the child's own behavior.

Module 3.2 The Neonate and Early Maturation
Survey Question: What can newborn babies do? Objective 3.4

11. Infant development is strongly influenced by heredity. However, environmental factors such as_____, parenting, and learning are also important.

12. The human _____has a number of adaptive reflexes, including the grasping, _____, sucking, and Moro reflexes. Neonates begin to learn immediately and they appear to be _____ of the effects of their actions.

13. Tests in a looking chamber reveal a number of _____preferences in the newborn. The neonate is drawn to bright _____ and _____or curved designs.

14. _____ prefer human face patterns, especially familiar faces. In _____, interest in the unfamiliar emerges.

Survey Question: What influence does maturation have on early development? Objective 3.5

15. Maturation of the body and nervous system underlies the orderly development of motor skills, _____, _____, and language.

16. Physical maturation typically is from the _____(cephalocaudal), and from the _____(proximodistal).

17. The rate of _____varies from person to person. Also, learning contributes greatly to the development of_____.

18. _____develop in a consistent order, starting with generalized excitement in newborn babies. Three of the basic emotions — fear, anger, and_____ — may be unlearned.

19. Many early skills, such as walking and_____, are subject to the principle of readiness.

Module 3.3 Social Development in Childhood
Survey Question: Of what significance is a child's emotional bond with parents? Objectives 3.6, 3.7

20. Opportunities for _____increase as infants develop self-awareness and they begin to actively seek_____ from adults.

21. Emotional attachment of human infants is a _____early event. Infant attachment is reflected by separation_____. The quality of attachment can be classified as_____, insecure-avoidant, or insecure-ambivalent. _____attachment is fostered by consistent care from parents who are sensitive to a baby's signals and_____.

22. _____day care is not harmful and can even be helpful to preschool children. _____ care can be risky.

23. Meeting a baby's affectional needs is as important as meeting needs for _____care.

Survey Question: How important are parenting styles? Objectives 3.8, 3.9

24. Studies suggest that parental styles have a substantial impact on _____ and intellectual development.

25. Three major parental styles are _____, permissive, and authoritative. Authoritative parenting appears to benefit children the _____.

26. Whereas _____ typically emphasize care giving, _____ tend to function as playmates for infants. Both care giving styles contribute to the competence of _____ children.

27. The ultimate success of various parenting styles depends on what culture or _____ community a child will enter.

28. Parenting styles vary across _____.

Module 3.4 Language Development in Childhood

Survey Question: How do children acquire language? Objectives 3.10, 3.11

29. Learning to use language is a cornerstone of early _____ development.

30. Language development proceeds from crying, to cooing, _____, then babbling, and then to telegraphic speech.

31. The underlying patterns of telegraphic speech suggest a biological _____ to acquire language. This innate tendency is augmented by _____.

32. Prelanguage communication between parent and child involves shared rhythms, nonverbal signals, and _____.

33. _____ or parentese is a simplified, musical style of speaking that parents use to help their children learn language.

Module 3.5 Cognitive Development in Childhood

Survey Question: How do children learn to think? Objectives 3.12, 3.13

34. The intellect of a child is less _____ than that of an adult. Jean Piaget theorized that intellectual growth occurs through a combination of assimilation and _____.

35. Piaget also held that children mature through a fixed series of cognitive stages. The stages and their approximate age ranges are sensorimotor (0–2), _____ (2–7), concrete operational (7–11), and _____ (11–adult).

36. Caregivers should offer _____ that are appropriate for a child's level of cognitive development.

37. Learning principles provide an alternate explanation that assumes cognitive development is continuous; it does not occur in _____.

38. Recent studies of _____ suggest that they are capable of thought well beyond that observed by Piaget.

39. Lev _____'s sociocultural theory emphasizes that a child's mental abilities are advanced by interactions with more _____ partners. Mental growth takes place in a child's _____ of proximal development, where a more skillful person may _____ the child's progress. As children rely on adults to help them discover new skills and principles they learn cultural _____.

Module 3.6 Adolescence, Young Adulthood, and Moral Development

Survey Question: Why is development during adolescence and young adulthood especially challenging?
Objective 3.14

40. Puberty is a _____ event which initiates adolescence, and it can affect _____ and behavioral development, particularly when it occurs earlier or later than for one's peers.

41. Transitioning from childhood to adulthood requires the formation of a personal identity; the major life task of. _____ is even more challenging for adolescents of ethnic descent.

42. In _____ societies the transition into adulthood is further complicated as it is increasingly delayed well into the twenties.

Survey Question: How do we develop morals and values? Objective 3.15
43. Lawrence Kohlberg identified _____, conventional, and _____ levels of moral reasoning.
44. Most people function at the conventional level of morality, but some never get beyond the selfish, _____ level. Only a minority of people attain the highest, or _____ level, of moral reasoning.

Module 3.7 Challenges Across the Lifespan

Survey Question: What are the typical tasks and dilemmas through the life span? Objective 3.16
45. Erik Erikson identified a series of _____ that occur across the lifespan.
46. These range from a need to gain trust in infancy, through learning _____, establishing identity and the ability to achieve _____ and productivity, to the need to live with integrity in _____.

Survey Question: What issues arise during later adulthood? Objective 3.17
47. Well-being during adulthood consists of six elements: self-acceptance, _____, autonomy, environmental mastery, having a purpose in life, and continued _____.
48. Only a minority of people have _____, questioning aspects of their life or feeling a renewed sense of urgency, but midlife course corrections are _____.
49. Even if no crisis occurs, people tend to move through repeated cycles of _____ and transition throughout adulthood.
50. _____ associated with aging are limited, at least through one's 70s. This is especially true of individuals who remain _____ active.
51. Ageism refers to _____, _____, and _____ on the basis of age. It affects people of all ages but is especially damaging to _____ people. Most ageism is based on stereotypes, myths, and misinformation.

Survey Question: How do people typically react to death? Objective 3.18
52. Death is a natural part of life. There is value in understanding it and accepting it. Typical emotional reactions to impending death include denial, _____, bargaining, depression, and _____, but not necessarily _____ or in every case.

Module 3.8 Psychology in Action: Effective Parenting

Survey Question: How do effective parents discipline and communicate with their children? Objective 3.18
53. Positive _____ interactions occur when parents spend enjoyable time encouraging their children in a loving and _____ fashion.
54. Effective parental discipline tends to emphasize _____ techniques (especially communication), rather than _____ or withdrawal of love.
55. _____ may lead to unintended psychological and _____ consequences, and so should be used with caution.
56. Consistency is also an important aspect of _____ parenting.
57. Effective parents allow their children to express _____ but place limits on _____.
58. Much _____ can be managed by use of I-messages and the application of _____ and logical consequences.

Mastery Test

1. The universal patterns of the human growth sequence can be attributed to
   a. recessive genes.
   b. environment.
   c. polygenic imprinting.
   d. heredity.

2. Exaggerated or musical voice inflections are characteristic of
   a. prelanguage turn-taking.
   b. parentese.
   c. telegraphic speech.
   d. prompting and expansion.

3. The emotion most clearly expressed by newborn infants is
   a. joy.
   b. fear.
   c. anger.
   d. excitement.

4. Explaining things abstractly or symbolically to a child becomes most effective during which stage of cognitive development?
   a. postconventional
   b. formal operations
   c. preoperational
   d. post intuitive

5. An infant startled by a loud noise will typically display
   a. a Moro reflex.
   b. a rooting reflex.
   c. a Meltzoff reflex.
   d. an imprinting reflex.

6. If one identical twin has a Y chromosome, the other must have a
   a. recessive chromosome.
   b. sex-linked trait.
   c. dominant chromosome.
   d. Y chromosome.

7. Ideas about Piaget's stages and the cognitive abilities of infants are challenged by infants' reactions to
   a. hypothetical possibilities.
   b. impossible events.
   c. turn-taking.
   d. separation anxiety.

8. The largest percentage of children display what type of temperament?
   a. easy
   b. difficult
   c. slow-to-warm-up
   d. generic

9. Which of the following is a congenital problem?
    a. FAS
    b. sickle-cell anemia
    c. hemophilia
    d. muscular dystrophy

10. A child might begin to question the idea that Santa Claus's sack could carry millions of toys when the child has grasped the concept of
    a. assimilation.
    b. egocentricism.
    c. conservation.
    d. reversibility of permanence.

11. In most areas of development, heredity and environment are
    a. independent.
    b. interacting.
    c. conflicting.
    d. responsible for temperament.

12. By definition, a trait that is controlled by a dominant gene cannot be
    a. eugenic.
    b. hereditary.
    c. carried by DNA.
    d. polygenic.

13. _____ development proceeds head-down and center-outward.
    a. Cognitive
    b. Motor
    c. Prelanguage
    d. Preoperational

14. You could test for _____ by videotaping a child and then letting the child see the video on television.
    a. social referencing
    b. self-awareness
    c. the quality of attachment
    d. the degree of readiness

15. After age two, infants become much more interested in
    a. bonding.
    b. nonverbal communication.
    c. familiar voices.
    d. unfamiliar faces.

16. According to Piaget, one of the major developments during the sensorimotor stage is emergence of the concept of
    a. assimilation.
    b. accommodation.
    c. object permanence.
    d. transformation.

17. Poverty is to deprivation as early childhood stimulation is to
    a. imprinting.
    b. enrichment.
    c. responsiveness.
    d. assimilation.

18. Which principle is most relevant to the timing of toilet training?
    a. readiness
    b. sensitive periods
    c. nonverbal signals
    d. assimilation

19. High self-esteem is most often a product of what style of child discipline?
    a. power assertion
    b. child management
    c. withdrawal of love
    d. the natural consequences method

20. Consonants first enter a child's language when the child begins
    a. babbling.
    b. cooing.
    c. the single-word stage.
    d. turn-taking.

21. Physically arousing play is typically an element of
    a. the zookeeper mother's caregiving style.
    b. paternal influences.
    c. proactive maternal involvement.
    d. secure attachment.

22. Insecure attachment is revealed by
    a. separation anxiety.
    b. seeking to be near the mother after separation.
    c. turning away from the mother after separation.
    d. social referencing.

23. A healthy balance between the rights of parents and their children is characteristic of
    a. authoritarian parenting.
    b. permissive parenting.
    c. authoritative parenting.
    d. consistent parenting.

24. Studies of infant imitation
    a. are conducted in a looking chamber.
    b. confirm that infants mimic adult facial gestures.
    c. show that self-awareness precedes imitation.
    d. are used to assess the quality of infant attachment.

25. Threatening, accusing, bossing, and lecturing children is most characteristic of
    a. PET.
    b. you-messages.
    c. applying natural consequences.
    d. management techniques.

26. According to Vygotsky, children learn important cultural beliefs and values when adults provide _____ to help them gain new ideas and skills.
    a. scaffolding
    b. proactive nurturance
    c. imprinting stimuli
    d. parentese

27. One thing that all forms of effective child discipline have in common is that they
    a. are consistent.
    b. make use of punishment.
    c. involve temporary withdrawal of love.
    d. emphasize you-messages.

28. Children who are securely attached to their parents tend to _____ when they interact with others.
    a. be anxious and remote
    b. be resilient and curious
    c. dislike direct physical contact
    d. lack social skills

29. Which statement correctly states the relationship between sensitive caregiving and secure attachment when applied cross-culturally?
    a. There is no relationship between the two variables in any culture.
    b. A minimal relationship can be found only in the United States.
    c. A relationship between the two variables can be found in all cultures.
    d. A relationship between the two variables can be found in all cultures if both biological parents raised the child.

30. To provide optimal care for children, caregivers
    a. must get involved proactively in educating children.
    b. must respond to children's feelings and needs.
    c. and children temperaments should match closely to each other.
    d. all the preceding

31. The debate on the issue of the effectiveness of spanking suggests that
    a. frequent spanking may lead to an increase in aggression in children.
    b. spanking stops the bad behavior from occurring again in the future.
    c. when coupled with harsh parenting, frequent spanking leads to more problem behaviors.
    d. both a and c

32. Parents who use a(an) _____ form of parenting tend to teach their children to manage and control their emotions and to use positive coping skills.
    a. authoritative
    b. authoritarian
    c. overly permissive
    d. power assertion

33. According to Erikson, a conflict between trust and mistrust is characteristic of
    a. infancy.
    b. adolescence.
    c. marriage.
    d. old age.

34. Identity formation during adolescence is aided by
    a. cognitive development.
    b. attaining the preoperational stage.
    c. emotional bargaining.
    d. you-messages from parents.

35. The thought, "It's all a mistake" would most likely occur as part of which reaction to impending death?
    a. anger
    b. freezing up
    c. denial
    d. bargaining

36. According to Erikson, the first dilemma a newborn infant must resolve is
    a. independence versus dependence.
    b. initiative versus guilt.
    c. trust versus mistrust.
    d. attachment versus confusion.

37. Seeking approval and upholding law, order, and authority are characteristics of what stage of moral development?
    a. preconventional
    b. conventional
    c. postconventional
    d. postformal

38. For both boys and girls, a growth spurt corresponds with
    a. adolescence.
    b. puberty.
    c. cognitive maturation.
    d. less prestige with peers.

39. Autonomy, environmental mastery, a purpose in life, and continued personal growth help maintain well-being in old age. This observation supports the _____ theory of successful aging.
    a. disengagement
    b. reengagement
    c. activity
    d. reactivation

40. Research on well-being suggests that a good life is one that combines happiness and
    a. financial success.
    b. educational achievement.
    c. an introverted personality.
    d. achieving meaningful goals.

41. According to Erikson, developing a sense of integrity is a special challenge in
    a. adolescence.
    b. young adulthood.
    c. middle adulthood.
    d. late adulthood.

42. Grief following bereavement typically begins with _____ and ends with
    _____.
    a. anger, disengagement
    b. dejection, disengagement
    c. isolation, depression
    d. shock, resolution

43. The smallest number of Levinson's subjects experienced midlife as a(an)
    a. last chance.
    b. period of serious decline.
    c. time to start over.
    d. escape from dominance.

44. According to Erikson, a dilemma concerning _____ usually follows one that
    focuses on identity.
    a. trust
    b. industry
    c. initiative
    d. intimacy

45. People who have many positive emotional experiences and relatively few negative experiences
    usually rate high in
    a. generativity.
    b. moral reasoning.
    c. subjective well-being.
    d. crystallized abilities.

46. Skills that rely on fluid abilities could be expected to show declines beginning in
    a. adolescence.
    b. young adulthood.
    c. middle adulthood.
    d. late adulthood.

47. Which of the following is a common myth about old age?
    a. Most elderly persons are isolated and neglected.
    b. A large percentage of the elderly suffer from senility.
    c. A majority of the elderly are dissastified with their lives.
    d. All the preceding are myths.

48. Gould's study of adult development found that a crisis of _____ is common between
    the ages of 35 and 43.
    a. urgency
    b. questions
    c. dominance
    d. stability

49. A period of _____ has been extended from the late teens to the mid 20s because young people are _____.
   a. emerging adulthood, prolonging their identity exploration
   b. emerging adolescence, actively exploring their love and worldviews
   c. puberty, immature and irresponsible
   d. none of the above

50. Kohlberg believed that moral development typically begins _____ and continues into adulthood with ___ percent of adults achieving postconventional morality.
   a. at the onset of puberty, 50
   b. in childhood, 20
   c. in early adolescence, 40
   d. in late adolescence, 80

Chapter 6: Conditioning and Learning

Chapter Overview

Learning gives us the opportunity to move beyond simple, instinctive behaviors, to adapt to a rapidly changing environment. Learning gives us behavioral flexibility.

In classical, or Pavlovian, conditioning, we learn to associate two stimuli. One thing serves as a signal that another thing is soon to come, so we respond in anticipation. Responses with classical conditioning tend to be simple, reflexive behaviors or emotions.

In operant, or instrumental, conditioning, we learn to connect an action with a consequence. Reinforcement causes behaviors to increase; punishment causes behaviors to decrease. Operant behaviors are more complex and more voluntary than we see with classical conditioning learning, and so may require some shaping to build complexity.

Schedules of reinforcement allow us to adjust the learning situation to get the behavior to continue without the learner having to be constantly reminded. Through stimulus control, we can broaden or narrow our focus of what we respond to and when.

Effective punishment is tricky because more aspects of the situation have to be just right in order for learning to occur the way you want it to. Also, unfortunately, punishment can lead to learning undesirable behaviors and attitudes at the same time.

Strict behaviorists believe that conditioning happens automatically, that we respond to our environment without thinking. Cognitive behaviorists allow mental processes in learning; they believe that we actively process our environment and exert more choice in what we respond to.

The end of the chapter describes several ways that conditioning principles can be used to change or manage behaviors in your life.

Learning Objectives

OBJECTIVE 6.1 – Define *learning, response, reinforcement, antecedents, consequences, reflex; and explain* how these terms are related to classical and operant conditioning.

OBJECTIVE 6.2 – Briefly describe the history of classical conditioning and give examples of how classical conditioning takes place, including the example of coping with chemotherapy, utilizing the following terms: a. neutral stimulus (NS); b. conditioned stimulus (CS); c. unconditioned stimulus (UCS); d. unconditioned response (UCR); e. conditioned response (CR).

OBJECTIVE 6.3 – Explain how reinforcement occurs during the acquisition of a classically conditioned response; describe higher-order conditioning; and discuss the informational view of classical conditioning.

OBJECTIVE 6.4 – Describe and give examples of the following concepts as they relate to classical conditioning: a. extinction; b. spontaneous recovery; c. stimulus generalization; and d. stimulus discrimination.

OBJECTIVE 6.5 – Describe the relationship between classical conditioning and reflex responses, explain what a conditioned emotional response (CER) is and how it is it is acquired, and discuss the therapy techniques of desensitization and virtual reality exposure and the concept of vicarious classical conditioning.

OBJECTIVE 6.6 – Briefly describe the history of operant conditioning, including Thorndike's law of effect and the work of B.F. Skinner; contrast the two types of conditioning; and differentiate between the terms reward and reinforcement.

OBJECTIVE 6.7 – Explain operant conditioning in terms of the informational view; define response-contingent reinforcement; and describe the deterimental effect of delaying reinforcement and how response chaining can counteract this effect.

OBJECTIVE 6.8 – Explain why superstitious behavior develops and why it persists; describe the process of shaping; and explain how extinction and spontanous recovery occur in operant conditioning and how reinforcement and extinction are involved in negative attention-seeking behavior.

OBJECTIVE 6.9 – Compare and contrast positive reinforcement, negative reinforcement, and the two types of punishment and give examples of each.

OBJECTIVE 6.10 – Define and give examples of primary reinforcers, secondary reinforcers, tokens, social reinforcers, and feedback (knowledge of results); and explain how conditioning techniques can be applied to energy conservation and learning aids, such as programmed instruction, computer-assisted instruction, and interactive simulations.

OBJECTIVE 6.11 – Compare and contrast the effects of continuous and partial reinforcement; and discuss the following schedules of partial reinforcement: a. fixed ratio (FR); b. variable ratio (VR); c. fixed interval (FI); and d. variable interval (VI), including definitions, examples, the effects of each schedule, and how conditioning studies have shown that animals as well as humans are cognitive time travelers.

OBJECTIVE 6.12 – Explain the concept of stimulus control and describe the processes of generalization and discrimination as they relate to operant conditioning.

OBJECTIVE 6.13 – Explain how punishers can be defined by their effects on behavior; discuss the three factors that influence the effectiveness of punishment; and differentiate the effects of severe punishment from mild punishment.

OBJECTIVE 6.14 –Describe three problems associated with punishment, the effects of punishment on the behavior of children when it is used frequently, and the three basic tools available to control simple learning (reinforcement, nonreinforcement, and punishment); discuss seven guidelines for using punishment; and explain why using punishment can become "habit-forming."

OBJECTIVE 6.15 – Define cognitive learning; describe the concepts of a cognitive map and latent learning; and explain the difference between discovery learning and rote learning.

OBJECTIVE 6.16 – Discuss the factors that determine whether observational learning (modeling) will occur; describe Bandura's Bo-Bo doll experiment; explain why what a parent does may be more important than what a parent says; and briefly describe the general conclusions that can be drawn from studies on the effects of media violence on children and adults.

OBJECTIVE 6.17 – Briefly describe the seven steps in a behavioral self-management program; describe the Premack principle; explain how self-recording can aid a self-management program; and discuss four strategies for changing bad habits.

Language Development Guide

Introduction
(246) *intriguing flaw*: interesting problem
(246) *drop*: lessen
(246) *scalding*: liquid able to cause burns
(246) *flock of*: group, usually refers to birds
(246) *starving to death:* very hungry
(246) *reach into every corner*: are continually present

Module 6.1
(248) *dull*: uninteresting
(248) *unlocking the secrets*: understanding
(248) *triggers*: causes
(249) *snicker*: quietly laugh
(249) *Does the name Pavlov Ring a Bell?*: Is Pavlov familiar to you?
(249) *drooled*: salivated
(249) *tidbit*: small piece
(249) *misplaced affection*: to salivate can sometimes mean to like or want
(250) *squirt*: spray
(251) *chemotherapy*: cancer treatment involving strong chemicals
(251) *hypodermic*: to go under the skin
(252) *poked*: jabbed, stuck, pricked
(252) *buzzer*: noisemaker
(253) *you're in a heap of trouble*: you did a very bad thing
(253) *Wii controller*: remote control for a video game
(253) *bakery*: a store where bread, cookies, and cakes are made
(253) *belittle*: tease or criticize
(253) *bugs:* insects

Module 6.2
(256) *ping-pong*: table tennis
(256) *obnoxious*: annoying
(257) *grooms*: cleans oneself
(257) *depresses*: pushes down
(257) *severely disturbed*: with a behavior disorder
(258) *athletic supporter*: protective undergarment for male athletes

(258) *better safe than sorry*: it is better to do everything possible to bring about a desired result than to fail
(258) *molding*: changing, creating
(259) *fooled*: tricked
(260) *stereo:* music player
(260) *pound on:* hit with the side of your fist
(260) *radar trap*: police hide and wait to catch drivers in the act of speeding
(260) *M&M candy*: small chocolates
(260) *rooted in*: caused by
(260) *double latte*: a strong coffee drink with milk
(261) *sleep with*: have sex with
(262) *mischievous*: a playful trick
(262) *driven and blazing*: strong, intense
(262) *dances*: moves quickly
(262) *furiously*: rapidly, quickly
(262) *excel at*: be the best
(263) *pick-off moves*: strategy in baseball to throw to particular bases to strike players out
(263) *it pays*: it is a good thing

Module 6.3
(266) *ill equipped*: unprepared
(266) *would be well advised to*: should
(266) *lost in the lore of*: now unknown
(266) *mecca*: place to travel to
(266) *payoff*: win money
(266) *Bingo!*: I won! Bingo is a board game where the winner yells Bingo!
(266) *cleaned out*: lose all your money
(267) *cumulative recorder*: machine that measures number of responses over time
(267) *tick marks*: small diagonal lines
(267) *piecework*: per item made
(267) *spurts*: brief but fast
(267) *keen*: exact, expert
(268) *bulldog tenacity*: bulldogs were bred to hold on to an angry bull; so extreme stubbornness, refusal to give up
(269) *mildly*: slightly
(269) *tailgating*: driving too closely behind someone
(270) *contraband*: illegal items

Module 6.4
(272) *reprimands*: scoldings, warnings
(272) *humanely*: ethically
(272) *feared brute*: monster
(272) *sneaks*: steals
(273) *suppress*: reduce, hold in
(273) *drawbacks*: disadvantages
(273) *sidestep*: avoid or escape
(274) *sparing the rod*: part of a Biblical saying, used to suggest that if a child is not physically punished, he or she will behave badly and have a bad character
(274) *over-rely*: use too much
(274) *silence may be golden*: the common saying "silence is golden" means that quiet moments are special and should be enjoyed

Module 6.5
(278) *tedious*: tiring, boring or repetitive work
(278) *tuneup*: minor car maintenance
(278) *cartoon*: drawing
(278) *duplicate*: copy
(279) *so why does everybody love Raymond, anyway?*: joke, reference to the television show title, 'Everybody Loves Raymond'
(279) *lion's share*: majority
(279) *massive dose*: very large amount
(280) *gore*: blood and extreme physical injury
(280) *writhe*: twist and turn
(280) *prone*: likely

Module 6.6
(282) *iPod*: small music player
(282) *fall short:* fail
(283) *cappuccino*: strong coffee drink
(283) *tally*: count, total
(284) *forfeited*: given up, lost
(284) *Ku Klux Klan and American Nazi Party*: extreme racist organizations

Recite and Review

Module 6.1 Learning and Classical Conditioning
Survey Question: What is learning? Pages 248-249, Objective 6.1
Learning is a relatively permanent (1)_____ in behavior due to experience. Learning depends on reinforcement, which (2)_____ the probability that a particular response will occur.
Classical (3) _____ and operant (3) _____ are responsible for basic learning capacity in humans and animals.
In (4)_____ conditioning, a neutral stimulus is followed by an unconditioned stimulus. With repeated pairings, the (5)_____ stimulus begins to elicit a response.
In (6)_____ conditioning, responses that are followed by reinforcement occur more frequently.

Survey Question: How does classical conditioning occur? Pages 249-253, Objectives 6.2, 6.3, 6.4
Classical conditioning, studied by (7)_____, occurs when a neutral stimulus ((8)_____) is associated with an unconditioned stimulus ((9)_____).
The (9)_____ triggers a reflex called the unconditioned response ((10)_____). If the (11)_____ is consistently paired with the (12)_____, it becomes a conditioned stimulus ((13)_____). After conditioning, a (13) _____ is capable of producing a conditioned (learned) response ((14)_____).
When the conditioned stimulus is (15)_____ by the unconditioned stimulus, conditioning is reinforced ((16)_____).
When the CS is repeatedly presented (17)_____, conditioning is extinguished ((18)_____).
In classical conditioning, the CS creates an (19) _____ that the US will follow, which alters behavior.
In (20)_____ conditioning, a well-learned conditioned stimulus is used as if it were an unconditioned stimulus, which leads to further learning.

Through stimulus (21)_____, stimuli similar to the conditioned stimulus will also produce a response. Stimulus (22)_____ occurs when we learn to respond to a particular stimulus, but not to others that are similar.

Survey Question: Does conditioning affect emotions? Pages 253-254, Objective 6.5
Conditioning applies to (23)_____ responses as well as simple reflexes. As a result, conditioned (24)_____ responses (CERs) also occur.
Irrational fears called phobias may begin as (25)_____. Conditioning of emotional responses can occur vicariously ((26)_____) as well as directly.

Module 6.2 Operant Conditioning
Survey Question: How does operant conditioning occur? Pages 256-260, Objectives 6.6, 6.7, 6.8, 6.9
To understand why people behave as they do, it is important to identify how their responses are being (27)_____.
(28)_____ conditioning occurs when a voluntary action is followed by a reinforcer, which (29)_____ the frequency of the response. Operant learning is based on the law of (30)_____.
(31)_____ reinforcement greatly reduces its effectiveness, but long chains of responses may be maintained by a (32)_____ reinforcer.
Superstitious behaviors often become part of response chains because they (33)_____ to be associated with reinforcement.
By rewarding successive approximations to a particular response, behavior can be (34)_____ into desired patterns.
If an operant response is (35)_____, it may extinguish ((36)_____). But after extinction seems complete, it may temporarily (37)_____ (spontaneous recovery).
Both positive reinforcement and negative reinforcement (38)_____ the likelihood that a response will be repeated. Punishment (39)_____ the likelihood that the response will occur again.

Survey Question: Are there different kinds of operant reinforcement? Pages 260-264, Objective 6.10
Operant learning may be based on primary (40)_____ or secondary (40)_____.
(41)_____, or knowledge of results, also aids learning and (42)_____ performance.
(43)_____ breaks learning into a series of small steps and provides immediate feedback. (44)_____ (CAI) does the same, but has the added advantage of providing alternative exercises and information when needed.

Module 6.3 Partial Reinforcement and Stimulus Control
Survey Question: How are we influenced by patterns of reward? Pages 266-270, Objectives 6.11, 6.12
Reward or reinforcement may be given continuously ((45)_____) or on a schedule of (46)_____ reinforcement. (46)_____ reinforcement produces greater resistance to extinction.
Five basic schedules of reinforcement are continuous, (47)_____, variable ratio, fixed interval, and (48)_____. Each schedule produces a different pattern of (49)_____.
Stimuli that (50)_____ a reinforced response tend to control when and where operant responses occur ((51)_____). Two aspects of (51)_____ are generalization and discrimination.
In (52)_____, an operant response tends to occur when stimuli similar to those preceding reinforcement are present.
In (53)_____, responses are given in the presence of discriminative stimuli associated with reinforcement (S+) and withheld in the presence of stimuli associated with (54)_____ (S–).

Module 6.4 Punishment

Survey Question: What does punishment do to behavior? Pages 272-274, Objectives 6.13, 6.14
Punishment (55)_____ responding. Punishment occurs when a response is followed by the onset of an aversive event or by (56)_____ (response cost).
Punishment is most effective when it is immediate, (57)_____, and intense.
Although severe punishment can virtually eliminate a particular behavior, (58)_____ punishment usually only temporarily suppresses responding. (59)_____ must be used to make lasting changes in the behavior of a person or an animal.
Punishment tends to produce (60)_____ and avoidance learning, and it encourages the learning of (61)_____ responses.

Module 6.5 Cognitive Learning and Imitation

Survey Question: What is cognitive learning? Pages 276-278, Objective 6.15
(62)_____ learning involves higher mental processes, such as memory, thinking, problem solving, understanding, knowing, and anticipating.
Even in relatively simple learning situations, animals and people seem to form (63)_____ (internal representations of relationships).
In latent learning, learning remains (64)_____ until a reward or incentive for performance is offered.
Discovery learning emphasizes insight and understanding, in contrast to (65)_____ learning.

Survey Question: Does learning occur by imitation? Pages 278-280, Objective 6.16
Learning can occur by merely (66)_____ and imitating the actions of another person or by noting the (67)_____ of the person's actions.
Observational learning is influenced by the (68)_____ of the model and the success or failure of the model's behavior. Aggression is readily learned and released by (69)_____.
(70)_____ can act as powerful models for observational learning. Televised violence (71)_____ _____ the likelihood of aggression by viewers.

Module 6.6 Psychology in Action: Behavioral Self-Management — A Rewarding Project

Survey Question: How does conditioning apply to practical problems? Pages 282-284, Objective 6.17
By applying (72)_____ conditioning principles, it is possible to change or manage your own behavior.
When managing behavior, self-reinforcement, self-recording, feedback, and (73)_____ are all helpful.
Four strategies that can help change bad habits are reinforcing (74)_____, promoting extinction, breaking response chains, and avoiding (75).

Connections

Module 6.1

1. _____ respondent conditioning	a. before responses
2. _____ instrumental learning	b. Pavlov's CS
3. _____ antecedents	c. after responses
4. _____ meat powder	d. higher-order conditioning
5. _____ spontaneous recovery	e. Pavlovian conditioning
6. _____ bell	f. US missing
7. _____ salivation	g. reinforcement period
8. _____ consequences	h. UR
9. _____ expectancies	i. Pavlov's US
10. _____ CS used as US	j. operant conditioning
11. _____ desensitization	k. CER
12. _____ extinction	l. extinction of fear
13. _____ acquisition	m. informational view
14. _____ phobia	n. incomplete extinction

Module 6.2

1. _____ response cost	a. nonlearned reinforcer
2. _____ negative reinforcement	b. increased responding
3. _____ Skinner	c. decreased responding
4. _____ shaping	d. social reinforcer
5. _____ primary reinforcer	e. Chimp-O-Mat
6. _____ secondary reinforcer	f. approximations
7. _____ punishment	g. educational simulations
8. _____ law of effect	h. feedback
9. _____ tokens	i. Edward Thorndike
10. _____ approval	j. losing privileges
11. _____ KR	k. learned reinforcer
12. _____ CAI	l. conditioning chamber

Module 6.3

1. _____ fixed interval	a. resistance to extinction
2. _____ stimulus control	b. antecedent stimuli
3. _____ continuous reinforcement	c. paper due every two weeks
4. _____ partial reinforcement	d. S+ and S-
5. _____ fixed ratio	e. high response rate
6. _____ variable ratio	f. reinforcement schedule
7. _____ variable interval	g. steady response rate
8. _____ discriminative stimuli	h. reinforce all correct responses

Module 6.4

1. _____ punishment	a. lying to prevent discomfort
2. _____ avoidance learning	b. side effects of punishment
3. _____ escape learning	c. escape and avoidance
4. _____ mild punishment	d. running away
5. _____ fear and aggression	e. weak effect

Module 6.5

1. _____ cognitive map	a. insight
2. _____ observational learning	b. imitation
3. _____ modeling	c. mental image of campus
4. _____ discovery learning	d. learning through repetition
5. _____ rote learning	e. Albert Bandura
6. _____ latent learning	f. hidden learning

Module 6.6

1. _____ baseline	a. what you currently do
2. _____ contracting	b. location where a smoker smokes
3. _____ response chains	c. statement of goals and consequences
4. _____ antecedents	d. routine sequence

Check Your Memory

Module 6.1 Learning and Classical Conditioning
Survey Question: What is learning? Pages 248-249, Objective 6.1

T F 1. Learning to press the buttons on a vending machine is based on operant conditioning.

T F 2. In classical conditioning, the consequences that follow responses become associated with one another.

T F 3. Getting compliments from friends could serve as reinforcement for operant learning.

Survey Question: How does classical conditioning occur? Pages 249-253, Objectives 6.2, 6.3, 6.4

T F 4. Ivan Pavlov studied digestion and operant conditioning in dogs.

T F 5. Pavlov used meat powder to reinforce conditioned salivation to the sound of a bell.

T F 6. During successful conditioning, the NS becomes a CS.

T F 7. During acquisition, the CS is presented repeatedly without the US.

T F 8. The optimal delay between the CS and the US is five to fifteen seconds.

T F 9. Spontaneous recovery occurs when a CS becomes strong enough to be used like a US.

T F 10. Discriminations are learned when generalized responses to stimuli similar to the CS are extinguished.

Survey Question: Does conditioning affect emotions? Pages 253-254, Objective 6.5

T F 11. Narrowing of the pupils in response to bright lights is learned in early infancy.

T F 12. Emotional conditioning involves autonomic nervous system responses.

T F 13. Eye-blink conditioning, a form of operant conditioning, can be used to detect dementia.

T F 14. Stimulus generalization helps convert some CERs into phobias.

T F 15. Pleasant music can be used as a UR to create a CER.

T F 16. To learn a CER vicariously, you would observe the actions of another person and try to imitate them.

Module 6.2 Operant Conditioning

Survey Question: How does operant conditioning occur? Pages 256-260, Objectives 6.6, 6.7, 6.8, 6.9

T F 17. In operant conditioning, learners actively emit responses.

T F 18. Rewards are the same as reinforcers.

T F 19. The Skinner box is primarily used to study classical conditioning.

T F 20. Reinforcement in operant conditioning alters how frequently involuntary responses are elicited.

T F 21. Operant reinforcers are most effective when they are response contingent.

T F 22. Operant learning is most effective if you wait a minute or two after the response is over before reinforcing it.

T F 23. Response chains allow delayed reinforcers to support learning.

T F 24. Superstitious responses appear to be associated with reinforcement, but they are not.

T F 25. Teaching a pigeon to play ping-pong would most likely make use of the principle of response cost.

T F 26. Children who misbehave may be reinforced by attention from parents.

T F 27. Negative reinforcement is a type of punishment that is used to strengthen learning.

T F 28. Pressing a button on the alarm clock to stop the annoying sound is an example of negative reinforcement.

T F 29. Avoiding eating hot sauce because it burns your mouth is an example of punishment.

T F 30. Both response cost and negative reinforcement decrease responding.

Survey Question: Are there different kinds of operant reinforcement? Pages 260-264, Objective 6.10

T F 31. Food, water, grades, and sex are primary reinforcers.

T F 32. ICS is a good example of a secondary reinforcer.

T F 33. Social reinforcers are secondary reinforcers.

T F 34. Attention and approval can be used to shape another person's behavior.

T F 35. The effects of primary reinforcers may quickly decline as the person becomes satiated.

T F 36. The Chimp-O-Mat accepted primary reinforcers and dispensed secondary reinforcers.

T F 37. People are more likely to recycle used materials if they receive weekly feedback about how much they have recycled.

T F 38. CAI is another term for informational feedback.

T F 39. In sports, feedback is most effective when a skilled coach directs attention to important details.

T F 40. The final level of skill and knowledge is almost always higher following CAI than it is with conventional methods.

Module 6.3 Partial Reinforcement and Stimulus Control

Survey Question: How are we influenced by patterns of reward? Pages 266-270, Objectives 6.11, 6.12

T F 41. Continuous reinforcement means that reinforcers are given continuously, regardless of whether or not responses are made.

T F 42. An FR-3 schedule means that each correct response produces three reinforcers.

T F 43. The time interval in FI schedules is measured from the last reinforced response.

T F 44. In business, commissions and profit sharing are examples of FI reinforcement.

T F 45. Antecedent stimuli tend to control when and where previously rewarded responses will occur.

T F 46. Stimulus control refers to noticing an event occurring, performing a behavior, then getting a reward for the behavior.

T F 47. Stimulus generalization is the primary method used to train dogs to detect contraband.

T F 48. S+ represents a discriminative stimulus that precedes a nonreinforced response.

Module 6.4 Punishment

Survey Question: What does punishment do to behavior? Pages 272-274, Objectives 6.13, 6.14

T F 49. Like reinforcement, punishment should be response contingent.

T F 50. Punishment is most effective if it is unpredictable.

T F 51. Speeding tickets are an example of response cost.

T F 52. Mild punishment causes reinforced responses to extinguish more rapidly.

T F 53. Generally, punishment should be the last resort for altering behavior.

T F 54. Punishment does not have to be consistent to extinguish a behavior quickly as long as positive behaviors are reinforced.

T F 55. For humans, avoidance learning is reinforced by a sense of relief.

T F 56. Punishment frequently leads to increases in aggression by the person who is punished.

Module 6.5 Cognitive Learning and Imitation

Survey Question: What is cognitive learning? Pages 276-278, Objective 6.15

T F 57. Cognitive learning involves thinking, memory, and problem solving.

T F 58. Animals learning their way through a maze memorize the correct order of right and left turns to make.

T F 59. Typically, reinforcement must be provided in order to make latent learning visible.

T F 60. In many situations, discovery learning produces better understanding of problems.

T F 61. Rote learning produces skills through insight and understanding.

Survey Question: Does learning occur by imitation? Pages 278-280, Objective 6.16

T F 62. Modeling is another term for discovery learning.

T F 63. After a new response is acquired through modeling, normal reinforcement determines if it will be repeated.

T F 64. Successful observational learning requires two steps: observing and reproducing the behavior.

T F 65. Children imitate aggressive acts performed by other people, but they are not likely to imitate cartoon characters.

T F 66. Violence on television causes children to be more violent.

T F 67. Playing violent video games leads to an increase in aggression.

Module 6.6 Psychology in Action: Behavioral Self-Management — A Rewarding Project
Survey Question: How does conditioning apply to practical problems? Pages 282-284, Objective 6.17

T F 68. Choosing reinforcers is the first step in behavioral self-management.

T F 69. Self-recording can be an effective way to change behavior, even without using specific reinforcers.

T F 70. A prepotent response is one that occurs frequently.

T F 71. To use extinction to break a bad habit, you should remove, avoid, or delay the reinforcement that is supporting the habit.

T F 72. It is necessary to use cues or antecedents when breaking a bad habit.

T F 73. In a behavioral contract, you spell out what response chains you are going to extinguish.

T F 74. Self-regulated learners actively seek feedback in both formal and informal ways.

Critical Thinking

Module 6.1
1. Lately you have been getting a shock of static electricity every time you touch a door handle. Now there is a hesitation in your door-opening movements. Can you analyze this situation in terms of classical conditioning?

Module 6.2
2. How might operant conditioning principles be used to encourage people to pick up litter? (What rewards could be offered, and how might the cost of rewards be kept low?)

Module 6.3
3. A business owner who pays employees an hourly wage wants to increase productivity. How could the owner make more effective use of reinforcement?

4. How could you use conditioning principles to teach a dog or a cat to come when called?

Module 6.4
5. Using the concept of partial reinforcement, can you explain why inconsistent punishment is especially ineffective?

6. Escape and avoidance learning have been applied to encourage automobile seat belt use. Can you explain how?

Module 6.5

7. Draw a map of your school's campus as you picture it now. Draw a map of the campus as you pictured it after your first visit. Why do the maps differ?

8. Children who watch many aggressive programs on television tend to be more aggressive than average. Why doesn't this observation prove that televised aggression causes aggressive behavior?

Module 6.6

9. How does setting daily goals in a behavioral self-management program help maximize the effects of reinforcement?

Final Survey and Review

Module 6.1 Learning and Classical Conditioning

Survey Question: What is learning? Objective 6.1

1. Learning is a _____ permanent change in behavior due to _____. Learning depends on _____, which increases the _____ that a particular response will occur.

2. _____ conditioning and _____ conditioning are responsible for basic learning capacity in humans and animals.

3. In classical conditioning, a _____ stimulus is followed by an _____ stimulus. With repeated pairings, the _____ stimulus begins to _____ a response.

4. In operant conditioning, responses that are followed by _____ occur more _____.

Survey Question: How does classical conditioning occur? Objectives 6.2, 6.3, 6.4

5. _____ conditioning, studied by Pavlov, occurs when a _____(NS) is associated with _____ (US).

6. The US triggers a reflex called the _____(UR). If the NS is consistently paired with the US, it becomes a _____ (CS). After conditioning, a CS is capable of producing a _____(CR).

7. When the conditioned stimulus is followed by the unconditioned stimulus, conditioning is _____ (strengthened).

8. When the CS is repeatedly presented_____, conditioning is _____ (weakened or inhibited).

9. In _____ conditioning, the CS creates an expectancy that the US will _____, which alters behavior.

10. In higher order conditioning, a well-learned _____ stimulus is used as if it were a(n) _____ stimulus, which leads to further learning.

11. Through stimulus generalization, stimuli _____ to the conditioned stimulus will also produce a response. Stimulus discrimination occurs when we learn to respond to a particular stimulus, but _____others that are _____.

Survey Question: Does conditioning affect emotions? Objective 6.5

12. Conditioning applies to visceral or emotional responses as well as _____. As a result, _____(CERs) also occur.

13. Irrational fears called _____ may begin as CERs. Conditioning of emotional responses can occur _____ (secondhand) as well as directly.

118

Module 6.2 Operant Conditioning

Survey Question: How does operant conditioning occur? Objectives 6.6, 6.7, 6.8, 6.9

14. To understand why people _____ as they do, it is important to identify how their _____ are being reinforced.

15. Operant conditioning occurs when a _____ action is followed by a _____, which increases the frequency of the_____. _____ is based on the law of effect.

16. Delaying reinforcement greatly _____ its effectiveness, but _____ of responses may be maintained by a single reinforcer.

17. _____ behaviors often become part of response chains because they appear to be associated with _____.

18. By rewarding _____to a particular response, behavior can be shaped into _____ patterns.

19. If an operant response is not reinforced, it may _____ (disappear). But after _____ seems complete, it may temporarily reappear (_____).

20. Both _____ and _____ increase the likelihood that a response will be repeated.

21. Punishment _____ the likelihood that the response will occur again.

Survey Question: Are there different kinds of operant reinforcement? Objective 6.10

22. Operant learning may be based on _____ reinforcers or _____ reinforcers.

23. Feedback, or_____, also aids _____ and improves performance.

24. Programmed instruction breaks learning into a series of small steps and provides _____. Computer-assisted instruction (CAI) does the same, but has the added advantage of _____ _____ and information when needed.

Module 6.3 Partial Reinforcement and Stimulus Control

Survey Question: How are we influenced by patterns of reward? Objectives 6.11, 6.12

25. Reward or reinforcement may be given _____ (after every response) or on a schedule of _____ reinforcement. _____ reinforcement produces greater resistance to _____.

26. Five basic schedules of reinforcement are _____, fixed ratio, _____, _____ _____, and variable interval. Each schedule produces a different pattern of responding.

27. Stimuli that precede a _____ response tend to control when and where _____ responses occur (stimulus control). Two aspects of _____ are generalization and discrimination.

28. In generalization, an _____ response tends to occur when stimuli _____ to those preceding reinforcement are present.

29. In discrimination, responses are _____ in the presence of _____ stimuli associated with reinforcement (S+) and _____ in the presence of stimuli associated with non-reinforcement (S–).

Module 6.4 Punishment

Survey Question: What does punishment do to behavior? Objectives 6.13, 6.14

30. Punishment decreases _____. Punishment occurs when a response is followed by the _____ of an aversive event or by the _____ of a positive event (response _____).

31. Punishment is most effective when it is _____, consistent, and _____.

32. Although _____ punishment can virtually eliminate a particular behavior, mild punishment usually only _____ responding. Reinforcement must be used to make _____ in the behavior of a person or an animal.

33. Punishment tends to produce escape and _____ learning, and it _____ the learning of aggressive responses.

Module 6.5 Cognitive Learning and Imitation

Survey Question: What is cognitive learning? Objective 6.15

34. Cognitive learning involves higher _____ processes, such as memory, thinking, _____ solving, understanding, knowing, and _____.

35. Even in relatively simple learning situations, animals and people seem to form cognitive maps (_____ _____).

36. In _____ learning, learning remains hidden or unseen until a _____ for performance is offered.

37. _____ learning emphasizes insight and understanding, in contrast to rote learning.

Survey Question: Does learning occur by imitation? Objective 6.16

38. Learning can occur by merely observing and _____ the actions of another person or by _____ the consequences of the person's actions.

39. Observational learning is influenced by the personal characteristics of the model and the _____ of the model's behavior. _____ is readily learned and released by modeling.

40. Television characters can act as _____ for observational learning. Televised violence increases the likelihood of _____ by viewers.

Module 6.6 Psychology in Action: Behavioral Self-Management — A Rewarding Project

Survey Question: How does conditioning apply to practical problems? Objective 6.17

41. By applying operant conditioning principles, it is possible to _____ your own behavior.

42. When _____ behavior, self-reinforcement, _____, _____, and behavioral contracting are all helpful.

43. Four strategies that can help change _____ habits are _____ alternative responses, promoting _____, breaking response chains, and _____ antecedent cues.

Mastery Test

1. Tokens are a good example of
   a. secondary reinforcers.
   b. the effects of ICS on behavior.
   c. noncontingent reinforcers.
   d. generalized reinforcers.

2. The principle of feedback is of particular importance to
   a. CERs.
   b. ICS.
   c. CAI.
   d. higher-order conditioning.

3. As a coffee lover, you have become very efficient at carrying out the steps necessary to make a cup of espresso. Your learning is an example of
    a. response chaining.
    b. spontaneous recovery.
    c. vicarious reinforcement.
    d. secondary reinforcement.

4. To teach a pet dog to use a new dog door, it would be helpful to use
    a. the Premack principle.
    b. shaping.
    c. respondent conditioning.
    d. delayed reinforcement.

5. To test for the presence of classical conditioning, you would omit the
    a. CS.
    b. US.
    c. CR.
    d. S+.

6. Which of the following does not belong with the others?
    a. Thorndike
    b. Skinner
    c. Pavlov
    d. instrumental learning

7. To teach a child to say, "Please," when she asks for things, you should make getting the requested item
    a. the CS.
    b. a token.
    c. a negative reinforcer.
    d. response contingent.

8. Money is to secondary reinforcer as food is to
    a. ICS.
    b. prepotent responses.
    c. primary reinforcer.
    d. negative reinforcer.

9. Whether a model is reinforced has a great impact on
    a. discovery learning.
    b. latent learning.
    c. observational learning.
    d. self-regulated learning.

10. Which of the following circumstances would most likely lead to your having a lucky test pen?
    a. the pen being given to you by your grandfather
    b. accidentally getting a good grade when using the pen
    c. studying with the pen
    d. putting your pen in the same drawer as your lucky basketball socks

11. To shape the behavior of a teacher in one of your classes, you would probably have to rely on
    a. tokens.
    b. primary reinforcers.
    c. negative attention seeking.
    d. social reinforcers.

12. The concept that best explains persistence at gambling is
    a. partial reinforcement.
    b. continuous reinforcement.
    c. fixed interval reinforcement.
    d. fixed ratio reinforcement.

13. Which of the following is NOT a common side effect of mild punishment?
    a. escape learning
    b. avoidance learning
    c. aggression
    d. accelerated extinction

14. With respect to televised violence it can be said that TV violence
    a. causes viewers to be more aggressive.
    b. makes aggression more likely.
    c. has no effect on the majority of viewers.
    d. vicariously lowers aggressive urges.

15. Which of the following types of learning is most related to the consequences of making a response?
    a. Pavlovian conditioning
    b. operant conditioning
    c. classical conditioning
    d. respondent conditioning

16. Which combination would most likely make a CER into a phobia?
    a. CER-discrimination
    b. CER-desensitization
    c. CER-response cost
    d. CER-generalization

17. A loud, unexpected sound causes a startle reflex; thus, a loud sound could be used as a _____ in conditioning.
    a. NS
    b. CR
    c. UR
    d. US

18. Antecedents are to _____ as consequences are to _____.
    a. discriminative stimuli, reinforcers
    b. shaping, response chaining
    c. conditioned stimuli, cognitive maps
    d. punishment, negative reinforcement

19. The use of self-recording to change personal behavior is closely related to the principle of
    a. response chaining.
    b. feedback.
    c. two-factor reinforcement.
    d. stimulus control.

20. _____ typically only temporarily suppresses reinforced responses.
    a. Negative reinforcement
    b. Extinction
    c. Mild punishment
    d. Stimulus generalization

21. In general, the highest rates of responding are associated with
    a. delayed reinforcement.
    b. variable reinforcement.
    c. interval reinforcement.
    d. fixed ratio reinforcement.

22. A child who has learned, through classical conditioning, to fear sitting in a dentist's chair
    becomes frightened when he is placed in a barber's chair. This illustrates the concept of
    a. stimulus generalization.
    b. spontaneous recovery.
    c. higher-order discrimination.
    d. vicarious conditioning.

23. The informational view of learning places emphasis on the creation of mental
    a. expectancies.
    b. reinforcement schedules.
    c. contracts.
    d. antecedents.

24. For some adults, blushing when embarrassed or ashamed is probably a _____ first formed in
    childhood.
    a. conditioned stimulus
    b. CAI
    c. discriminative stimulus
    d. CER

25. Learning to obey traffic signals is related to the phenomenon called
    a. stimulus control.
    b. spontaneous recovery.
    c. avoidance learning.
    d. modeling.

26. To be most effective, punishment should be combined with
    a. response costs.
    b. aversive stimuli.
    c. delayed feedback.
    d. reinforcement.

27. Involuntary responses are to _____ conditioning as voluntary responses are to _____ conditioning.
    a. classical, respondent
    b. classical, operant
    c. operant, classical
    d. operant, instrumental

28. Negative attention seeking by children demonstrates the impact of _____ on behavior.
    a. operant extinction
    b. social reinforcers
    c. response costs
    d. prepotent responses

29. Which consequence increases the probability that a response will be repeated?
    a. punishment
    b. response cost
    c. nonreinforcement
    d. negative reinforcement

30. Which method uses the principles of classical conditioning to detect early development of dementia?
    a. eye blinking
    b. memory task
    c. rote learning
    d. vocabulary test

31. Successive approximations are used in _____ to train animals to perform tricks.
    a. observational conditioning
    b. classical conditioning
    c. shaping
    d. latent learning

32. Putting on a pair of gloves to stop your hands from hurting while working in the cold weather demonstrates
    a. positive reinforcement.
    b. negative reinforcement.
    c. punishment.
    d. response cost.

33. Wanting to do some light reading while his roommate drove, Cody picked up a magazine, and after a few minutes, Cody felt nauseated and had to stop reading. To avoid getting sick in the future, Cody no longer read while riding in a car. This illustrates
    a. positive reinforcement.
    b. negative reinforcement.
    c. punishment.
    d. response cost.

34. Introducing an energy tax to reduce people's tendency to waste energy or polluting the
    environment utilizes _____, a form of operant conditioning.
    a. positive reinforcement
    b. negative reinforcement
    c. punishment
    d. response cost

35. _____ gives students enough freedom and guidance to actively think and gain knowledge.
    a. Guided discovery
    b. Latent discovery
    c. Observational learning
    d. Classical learning

36. Which of the following is the correct sequence when using observational learning?
    a. attention, remembering, reproduction, and rewards
    b. attention, rewards, reproduction, and remembering
    c. rewards, remembering, attention, and reproduction
    d. remembering, rewards, attention, and reproduction

37. Increased aggression and violence among children and adolescents has been attributed to
    a. watching violent TV programs.
    b. playing violent video games.
    c. imitating others' aggressive behaviors.
    d. all the preceding

Chapter 7: Memory

Chapter Overview

The memory chapter is a useful one for students because it offers many suggestions for how to study better and more efficiently. Memory is reconstructive, rather than a pure recording, so our memories are not always as accurate as we might believe.

The three basic types of memories are sensory memory, short-term memory, and long-term memory. While these are not specific structures in the brain, they allow us to talk about what memory does and how it functions, particularly in terms of selecting, storing and retrieving information.

Because memory cannot be directly observed, we have to measure memory through tests of recognition or recall - what you can demonstrate you can remember.

There are many reasons why someone might fail to remember a piece of information at any particular time. Besides not learning it in the first place, and to some extent decay over time, much of forgetting can be because of either lack of proper retrieval cues or because of interference between new and old information.

Thankfully, there are many things we can do to improve our memory, making it more efficient, less prone to error, and to last longer. Your book gives several such suggestions, based on research of how people study and process information.

Learning Objectives

OBJECTIVE 7.1 -- Define *memory;* explain the three processes of memory — encoding, storage, and retrieval; and list the three stages of memory in the Atkinson-Schiffrin model — sensory, short-term, and long-term.

OBJECTIVE 7.2 -- Describe sensory memory, including icons and echoes; and how information is transferred from sensory memory to short-term memory.

OBJECTIVE 7.3 -- Describe short-term memory, including its capacity, how information is encoded, the permanence of short-term memory, its susceptibility to interference, and the concept of working memory.

OBJECTIVE 7.4 -- Describe long-term memory in terms of permanence, capacity, and the basis on which information is stored; define dual memory; and explain how one's culture affects memory.

OBJECTIVE 7.5 -- Explain the "magic number" seven; describe chunking; and explain how the two types of rehearsal affect memory.

OBJECTIVE 7.6 -- Discuss the permanence of memory, including the research done by Penfield and the Loftuses; explain constructive processing, pseudomemories, and how "memory jamming" works in advertising; and describe the effects of hypnosis on memory and how a cognitive interview can improve eyewitness memories.

OBJECTIVE 7.7 -- Briefly describe how long-term memories are organized, including the network model and redintegrative memories.

OBJECTIVE 7.8 -- Differentiate procedural (skill) memory from declarative (fact) memory; and define and give examples of the two kinds of declarative memory (semantic and episodic).

OBJECTIVE 7.9 -- Discuss how memory is tested, including the concepts of *partial memories*, the *tip-of-the-tongue state*, and the *feeling of knowing*; and describe and give examples of each of the following ways of measuring memory: a. recall, including the *serial position effect*; b. recognition, including a comparison to recall and the concept of *distractors;* and c. relearning, including the concept of *savings score*.

OBJECTIVE 7.10 -- Distinguish between explicit and implicit memories; and describe priming.

OBJECTIVE 7.11 -- Explain Ebbinghaus' curve of forgetting; and discuss the following explanations of forgetting: a. encoding failure; b. decay of memory traces; c. disuse, including why this explanation is questioned; d. cue-dependent forgetting; e. state-dependent learning; f. retroactive and proactive interference; and g. repression, including the recovered memory/false memory debate and how repression differs from suppression.

OBJECTIVE 7.12 -- Describe flashbulb memories, retrograde and anterograde amnesia, and the consolidation of memory, including the effects of ECS and the role of the hippocampus; and discuss the research on where in the brain different types of memories are stored, the relationship between learning and transmitter chemicals, and long-term potentiation.

OBJECTIVE 7.13 -- Differentiate the concepts of internal mental images and eidetic imagery; and explain how these abilities are different from having an exceptional memory.

OBJECTIVE 7.14 -- Discuss how each of the following can improve memory: a. knowledge of results (feedback); b. recitation; c. rehearsal; d. selection; e. organization; f. whole versus part learning; g. serial position effect; h. cues; i. overlearning; j. spaced practice; k. sleep; l. hunger; m. extension of memory intervals; n. review; and o. other strategies that aid recall, including the cognitive interview.

OBJECTIVE 7.15 -- Define mnemonic; explain the four basic principles of using mnemonics; and describe three techniques for using mnemonics to remember things in order.

Language Development Guide

Introduction
(286) *Put yourself in Steven's shoes*: imagine you are Steven
(286) *vividly*: clearly
(286) *wiped out*: erased

Module 7.1
(288) *flurry*: rapid burst
(289) *dumped*: lost, thrown away
(289) *scratchpad*: notebook
(289) *from aardvark to zucchini*: from the beginning to the end
(289) *hocked*: sold
(289) *typifies*: describes
(289) *forging along*: working continually
(290) *feat*: achievement
(290) *Maasai*: an African tribe

Module 7.2
(292) *TV*: television
(292) *IBM*: International Business Machines, a computer company
(292) *USN*: United States Navy
(292) *YMCA*: Young Men's Christian Association, an international organization that promotes the spiritual, social, and physical welfare of young men
(292) *stack*: pile
(292) *prolong*: extend
(293) *electrode*: a small electronic that gives or measures electrical activity
(294) *jam*: used in two ways on this page - a fruit spread and a clog or blockage
(295) *overwrite*: replace
(297) *touched off*: begun

Module 7.3
(300) *drew a blank*: could not remember
(300) *World Series*: baseball championship
(301) *It's all Greek to me*: I don't understand
(302) *nutritionist*: expert in healthy diets
(302) *You are what you eat*: healthy eaters are healthy people, unhealthy eaters are not healthy people

Module 7.4
(304) *vexing*: frustrating
(304) *detergent*: soap
(304) *cramming*: intense studying shortly before an exam
(304) *penny*: one cent coin
(305) *switch*: swap, trade, change
(306) *leaky bucket*: a container with a crack or hole
(306) *trivial*: unimportant
(307) *rehashing*: repeating
(308) *moral*: lesson

(308) *mandolin*: a guitar-like stringed musical instrument
(311) *switching station*: where a train changes directions to a different track
(311) *striking*: surprising

Module 7.5
(317) *diabolical*: evil, bad, cruel
(318) *boil down:* reduce
(318) *going blank*: forgetting
(318) *daunting*: difficult
(318) *jog*: assist
(318) *knit*: combine
(318) *bare*: basic
(319) *flash cards*: a study tool, small pieces of paper with a term or question on one side and its definition or answer on the other
(319) *icing on your study cake*: a pleasant extra
(320) *TV dinners:* frozen meals
(320) *Twinkies*: yellow snack cake

Module 7.6
(323) *Van Gogh*: Dutch painter
(323) *dim past*: long ago
(324) *fair trial:* try it out before criticizing it

Recite and Review

Module 7.1 Memory Systems
Survey Question: Is there more than one type of memory? Pages 288-290, Objectives 7.1, 7.2, 7.3, 7.4
Memory systems allow us to encode, (1)_____, and (2)_____ information.
The three stages of memory (sensory memory, (3)_____ memory, and long-term memory) hold information for increasingly (4)_____ periods of time.
The best way to (5)_____ depends, to an extent, on which memory system you are using.
Sensory memories are encoded as (6)_____ memories or echoic memories. Short-term memories tend to be encoded by sound, and long-term memories by (7)_____.

Module 7.2 STM and LTM
Survey Question: What are the features of short-term memory? Pages 292-293, Objective 7.5
Selective (8)_____ determines what information moves from sensory memory, which is exact but very brief, on to (9)_____.
STM has a capacity of about (10)_____ bits of information, but this limit can be extended by (11)_____. Short-term memories are brief and very sensitive to (12)_____ or interference. However, they can be kept (13)_____ by maintenance rehearsal.

Survey Questions: What are the features of long-term memory? Is there more than one type of long-term memory? Pages 293-298, Objectives 7.6, 7.7, 7.8
LTM serves as a (14)_____ storehouse for meaningful information. Elaborative rehearsal helps us form (15)_____, long-term memories.
Long-term memories are relatively (16)_____. LTM seems to have an almost unlimited (17)_____ capacity.

(18)_____ processing tends to alter memories. (19)_____ is an active process. Our memories are frequently lost, altered, revised, or (20)_____.

LTM is highly (21)_____. The (22)_____ of memory networks is the subject of current research.

Redintegrative memories are (23)_____, as one bit of information leads to others, which then serve as cues for further (24)_____.

LTM contains procedural ((25)_____) and declarative ((26)_____) memories.

(27)_____ memories can be semantic or episodic.

Module 7.3 Measuring Memory

Survey Question: How is memory measured? Pages 300-302, Objectives 7.9, 7.10

The tip-of-the-tongue state shows that memory is not an (28)_____ event. Memories may therefore be revealed by recall, recognition, (29)_____, or priming.

In recall, memories are retrieved (30)_____ explicit cues, as in an essay exam. Recall of (31)_____ information often reveals a serial position effect.

A common test of (32)_____ is the multiple-choice question.

In relearning, material that seems to be forgotten is (33)_____, and (34)_____ is revealed by a savings score.

Recall, (35)_____, and relearning mainly measure explicit memories. Other techniques, such as (36)_____, are necessary to reveal implicit memories.

Module 7.4 Forgetting

Survey Question: What causes forgetting? Pages 304-310, Objective 7.11

Herman (37) _____ found that forgetting is most (38)_____ immediately after learning, as shown by the curve of forgetting.

Failure to (39)_____ information is a common cause of "forgetting."

Forgetting in (40)_____ memory and STM probably reflects a weakening (decay) of memory traces. Decay of memory traces may also explain (41)_____ LTM losses.

Forgetting is often based on a lack of memory (42)_____. State-dependent learning is related to the effects of memory (42) _____.

Much (43)_____ in STM and LTM is caused by interference.

In (44)_____ interference, new learning interferes with the ability to remember earlier learning.

(45)_____ interference occurs when old learning interferes with new learning.

Memories can be consciously suppressed and they may be unconsciously (46)_____.

Survey Question: What happens in the brain when memories are formed? Pages 311-312, Objective 7.12

It takes (47)_____ to consolidate memories. Lasting memories are recorded by changes in the activity, (48)_____, and chemistry of brain cells.

In the brain, memory consolidation takes place in the (49)_____. After memories have been consolidated, they appear to be stored in the (50)_____ of the brain.

Module 7.5 Exceptional Memory and Improving Memory

Survey Question: What are "photographic" memories? Pages 315-317, Objective 7.13

Eidetic imagery ((51)_____ memory) occurs when a person is able to project an image onto a blank surface.

Eidetic imagery is (52)_____ found in adults. However, many adults have internal memory (53)_____, which can be very vivid.

Exceptional memory may be based on natural ability or (54)_____. Usually it involves both.

Survey Question: How can I improve my memory? Pages 317-320, Objective 7.14

Excellent memory abilities are based on using strategies and techniques that make learning (55)_____ and that compensate for natural weaknesses in human memory.

Some people have naturally (56)_____ memories, but even they find it beneficial to use (57)_____ _____.

Memory can be improved by using feedback, recitation, and rehearsal, by (58)_____ and organizing information, and by using the progressive part method, spaced practice, (59)_____, and active search strategies.

When you are studying or (60)_____, you should also keep in mind the effects of serial position, sleep, review, cues, and (61)_____.

Module 7.6 Psychology in Action: Mnemonics — Memory Magic

Survey Question: Are there any tricks to help me with my memory? Pages 322-324, Objective 7.15

Memory (62)_____ (mnemonics) greatly improve immediate memory. However, conventional learning tends to create the most (63)_____ memories.

Mnemonic systems use mental (64)_____ and unusual associations to link new information with (65)_____ memories already stored in LTM.

(66)_____ mnemonics tend to rely on mental images and bizarre or exaggerated mental (67)_____.

Connections

Module 7.1

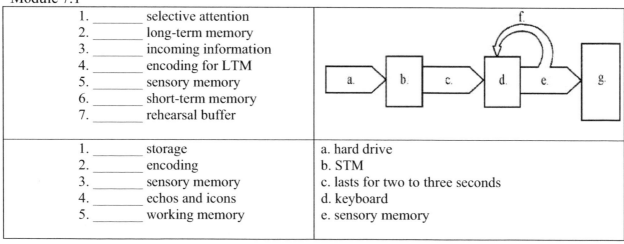

1. _____ selective attention	
2. _____ long-term memory	
3. _____ incoming information	
4. _____ encoding for LTM	
5. _____ sensory memory	
6. _____ short-term memory	
7. _____ rehearsal buffer	

1. _____ storage	a. hard drive
2. _____ encoding	b. STM
3. _____ sensory memory	c. lasts for two to three seconds
4. _____ echos and icons	d. keyboard
5. _____ working memory	e. sensory memory

Module 7.2

1. _____ semantic memory		
2. _____ long-term memory		a
3. _____ procedural memory		↓
4. _____ sensory memory		b
5. _____ episodic memory		↓
6. _____ short-term memory		c
7. _____ declarative memory		d e
		f g

1. _____ chunking	a. magic number
2. _____ skill memory	b. recoding
3. _____ revised memories	c. constructive processing
4. _____ seven information bits	d. network model
5. _____ memory structure	e. procedures

Module 7.3

1. _____ relearning	a. retrieval of facts
2. _____ recall	b. middle items are least recalled
3. _____ recognition memory	c. multiple-choice questions
4. _____ implicit memory	d. conscious memories
5. _____ serial position effect	e. memories that are outside of awareness
6. _____ explicit memory	f. memory test

Module 7.4

1. _____ memory trace	a. disuse of memory
2. _____ amnesia	b. forgetting curve
3. _____ suppression	c. pseudo memory
4. _____ repression	d. engram
5. _____ interference	e. memory loss
6. _____ Ebbinghaus	f. motivated forgetting
7. _____ false memory	g. conscious forgetting
8. _____ hippocampus	h. prevent retrieval of information
9. _____ decay	i. consolidation of memories

Module 7.5

1. _____ exceptional memory		a. highlighting in your text
2. _____ recitation		b. experts
3. _____ selection		c. a stimulus linked with memory
4. _____ rehearsal		d. mental review
5. _____ eidetic imagery		e. study in short periods
6. _____ memory cue		f. summarize out loud
7. _____ spaced practice		g. photographic memory

Module 7.6

1. _____ mnemonics		a. memory strategies
2. _____ acrostics		b. form a story
3. _____ order of events		c. mandible: man dribbling
4. _____ imagery		d. first letters form sentences
5. _____ keyword method		e. insert bloody ear into Van Gogh paintings

Check Your Memory

Module 7.1 Memory Systems

Survey Question: Is there more than one type of memory? Pages 288-290, Objectives 7.1, 7.2, 7.3, 7.4

T F   1. Incoming information must be encoded before it is stored in memory.

T F   2. Sensory memories last for a few minutes or less.

T F   3. A memory that cannot be retrieved has little value.

T F   4. Selective attention influences what information enters STM.

T F   5. Working memory is another name for sensory memory.

T F   6. Errors in long-term memory tend to focus on the sounds of words.

T F   7. Generally, the more you know, the more new information you can store in long-term memory.

T F   8. The type of memory people store is not affected by their cultural values.

Module 7.2 STM and LTM

Survey Question: What are the features of short-term memory? Pages 292-293, Objective 7.5
Survey Questions: What are the features of long-term memory? Is there more than one type of long-term memory? Pages 293-298, Objectives 7.6, 7.7, 7.8

T F   9. For many kinds of information, STM can store an average of five bits of information.

T F   10. Nelson Cowan coined the term "magic number."

T F   11. Chunking recodes information into smaller units that are easier to fit into STM.

T F   12. The more times a short-term memory is rehearsed, the better its chance of being stored in LTM.

T F   13. On average, short-term memories last only about 18 minutes unless they are rehearsed.

T F   14. Maintenance rehearsal keeps memories active in sensory memory.

T F 15. The surface of the brain records the past like a movie, complete with sound track.

T F 16. Long-term memory is *relatively* permanent as we tend to update, change, lose, or revise our old memories.

T F 17. Being confident about a memory tells little about the true accuracy of the memory.

T F 18. False memory refers to having memories that never happened.

T F 19. Eyewitnesses do not provide false testimonies as a result of false memories.

T F 20. In combination with misleading questions, hypnosis increases false memories more than it does true ones.

T F 21. Long-term memories appear to be organized alphabetically for speedy access.

T F 22. Knowing how to swing a golf club is a type of declarative memory.

T F 23. A person lacking declarative memory might still remember how to solve a mechanical puzzle.

T F 24. Semantic memories are almost immune to forgetting.

T F 25. Semantic memories are a type of declarative memory.

T F 26. Episodic memories have no connection to particular times and places.

Module 7.3 Measuring Memory

Survey Question: How is memory measured? Pages 300-302, Objectives 7.9, 7.10

T F 27. Remembering the first sound of a name you are trying to recall is an example of the tip-of-the-tongue state.

T F 28. Tests of recognition require verbatim memory.

T F 29. The serial position effect measures the strength of the feeling of knowing.

T F 30. Recognition tends to be a more sensitive test of memory than recall.

T F 31. False positives and distractors greatly affect the accuracy of relearning tests.

T F 32. Recall, recognition, and relearning are used to measure explicit memories.

T F 33. Priming is used to activate explicit (hidden) memories.

Module 7.4 Forgetting

Survey Question: What causes forgetting? Pages 304-310, Objective 7.11

T F 34. Ebbinghaus chose to learn nonsense syllables so that they would all be the same length.

T F 35. Ebbinghaus's curve of forgetting levels off after two days, showing little further memory loss after that.

T F 36. Ebbinghaus's curve of forgetting only applies to memories of nonsense syllables.

T F 37. The magic card trick demonstrates our ability to focus and pay attention.

T F 38. Decay of memory traces clearly applies to information in STM.

T F 39. Disuse theories of forgetting answer the question: Have I been storing the information in the first place?

T F 40. The presence of memory cues almost always improves memory.

T F 41. Information learned under the influence of a drug may be best remembered when the drugged state occurs again.

T F 42. If you are in a bad mood, you are more likely to remember unpleasant events.

T F 43. Categorizing a person as a member of a group tends to limit the accuracy of memories about the person's appearance.

T F 44. Eyewitnesses are better at identifying members of other ethnic groups since they "look" different.

T F 45. Sleeping tends to interfere with retaining new memories.

T F 46. You learn information A and then information B. If your memory of B is lowered by having first learned A, you have experienced retroactive interference.

T F 47. Interference only applies to the initial stage of learning. Learned information is permanent and can be easily retrieved.

T F 48. Unconsciously forgetting painful memories is called negative transfer.

T F 49. A conscious attempt to put a memory out of mind is called repression.

T F 50. Suggestion and fantasy are elements of many techniques used in attempts to recover repressed memories.

T F 51. Unless a memory can be independently confirmed, there is no way to tell if it is real or not.

T F 52. Flashbulb memories tend to be formed when an event is surprising or emotional.

T F 53. The confidence we have in flashbulb memories is well placed—they are much more accurate than most other memories.

Survey Question: What happens in the brain when memories are formed? Pages 311-312, Objective 7.12
T F 54. Retrograde amnesia is a gap in memories of events preceding a head injury.

T F 55. People with damage to the hippocampus typically cannot remember events that occurred before the damage.

T F 56. In the early 1920s, Karl Lashley found the location of engrams in the brain.

T F 57. Storing memories alters the activity, structure, and chemistry of the brain.

Module 7.5 Exceptional Memory and Improving Memory
Survey Question: What are "photographic" memories? Pages 315-317, Objective 7.13
T F 58. Eidetic images last for 30 seconds or more.

T F 59. About eight percent of all children have eidetic images.

T F 60. Eidetic imagery becomes rare by adulthood.

T F 61. Mr. S (the mnemonist) had virtually unlimited eidetic imagery.

T F 62. Practice in remembering one type of information increases the capacity of STM to store other types of information too.

T F 63. All contestants in the World Memory Championship performed poorly on tasks that prevented the use of learned strategies.

T F   64. Recitation is a good way to generate feedback while studying.

T F   65. Elaborative rehearsal involving "why" questions improves memory.

T F   66. Overlearning is inefficient; you should stop studying at the point of initial mastery of new information.

T F   67. Massed practice is almost always superior to spaced practice.

T F   68. When learning, it helps to gradually extend how long you remember new information before reviewing it again.

T F   69. Recalling events from different viewpoints is part of doing a cognitive interview.

Module 7.6 Psychology in Action: Mnemonics — Memory Magic

Survey Question: Are there any tricks to help me with my memory? Pages 322-324, Objective 7.15

T F   70. Roy G. Biv is a mnemonic for the notes on a musical staff.

T F   71. Many mnemonics make use of mental images or pictures.

T F   72. Mnemonics often link new information to familiar memories.

T F   73. The keyword method is superior to rote learning for memorizing vocabulary words in another language.

Critical Thinking

Module 7.1

1. Why is sensory memory important to filmmakers?

Module 7.2

2. Parents sometimes warn children not to read comic books, fearing that they will learn less in school if they "fill their heads up with junk." Why is this warning unnecessary?

Module 7.3

3. When asked to explain why they may have failed to recall some information, people often claim it must be because the information is no longer in their memory. Why does the existence of implicit memories challenge this explanation?

Module 7.4

4. Based on state-dependent learning, why do you think that music often strongly evokes memories?

5. You must study French, Spanish, psychology, and biology in one evening. What do you think would be the best order in which to study these subjects so as to minimize interference?

6. There may be another way to explain why flashbulb memories are so long lasting. Can you think of one?

Module 7.5

7. Mr. S had great difficulty remembering faces. Can you guess why?

8. What advantages would there be to taking notes as you read a textbook, as opposed to underlining words in the text?

Module 7.6

9. How are elaborative rehearsal and mnemonics alike?

Final Survey and Review

Module 7.1 Memory Systems

Survey Question: Is there more than one type of memory? Objectives 7.1, 7.2, 7.3, 7.4

1. Memory systems allow us to _____, store, and retrieve _____.
2. The three stages of memory (_____, _____, and _____) hold information for increasingly longer periods of time.
3. The _____ way to remember depends, to an extent, on which _____ you are using.
4. _____ memories are encoded as iconic memories or memories. Short-term memories tend to be encoded by_____, and long-term memories by meaning.

Module 7.2 STM and LTM

Survey Question: What are the features of short-term memory? Objective 7.5

5. _____ attention determines what information moves from sensory memory, which is _____ but very _____, on to STM.
6. STM has a _____ of about five to seven bits of information, but this limit can be _____ by chunking. Short-term memories are brief and very _____ to interruption or _____. However, they can be kept alive by _____.

Survey Questions: What are the features of long-term memory? Is there more than one type of long-term memory? Objectives 7.6, 7.7, 7.8

7. LTM serves as a general storehouse for _____. _____rehearsal helps us form lasting, long-term memories.
8. Long-term memories are _____ permanent. LTM seems to have an _____ storage capacity.
9. Constructive processing tends to _____ memories. Remembering is an _____ process. Our memories are frequently lost, _____, _____, or distorted.
10. _____ is highly organized. The structure of memory _____ is the subject of current research.
11. _____ memories are reconstructed, as one bit of information _____, which then serve as cues for further _____.
12. LTM contains _____ (skill) and _____ (fact) memories. Declarative memories can be _____ or _____.

137

Module 7.3 Measuring Memory

Survey Question: How is memory measured? Objectives 7.9, 7.10

13. The _____ state shows that memory is not an all-or-nothing event. Memories may therefore be revealed by recall, _____, relearning, or _____.

14. In recall, memories are retrieved without _____, as in an essay exam. Recall of listed information often reveals a _____ effect.

15. A common test of recognition is the _____ question.

16. In _____, material that seems to be forgotten is learned again, and memory is revealed by a _____.

17. Recall, recognition, and relearning mainly measure _____ memories. Other techniques, such as priming, are necessary to reveal _____ memories.

Module 7.4 Forgetting

Survey Question: What causes forgetting? Objective 7.11

18. Herman Ebbinghaus found that _____ is most rapid _____ after learning, as shown by the _____ of forgetting.

19. Failure to encode information is a common cause of "_____."

20. Forgetting in sensory memory and STM probably reflects a _____(decay) of memory _____. Decay of memory _____ may also explain some _____ losses.

21. Forgetting is often based on a _____ of memory cues. _____ learning is related to the effects of memory cues.

22. Much forgetting in _____ and _____ is caused by interference.

23. In retroactive interference, _____ learning interferes with the ability to remember _____ learning.

24. Proactive interference occurs when _____ learning interferes with _____ learning.

25. Memories can be _____ suppressed and they may be _____ _____ repressed.

Survey Question: What happens in the brain when memories are formed? Objective 7.12

26. It takes time to _____ memories. Lasting memories are recorded by changes in the activity, structure, and chemistry of.

27. In the brain, memory _____ takes place in the hippocampus. After memories have been, they appear to be stored in the cortex of the brain.

Module 7.5 Exceptional Memory and Improving Memory

Survey Question: What are "photographic" memories? Objective 7.13

28. _____ imagery (photographic memory) occurs when a person is able to _____ an image onto a blank surface.

29. _____ imagery is rarely found in adults. However, many _____ have internal memory images, which can be very vivid.

30. Exceptional memory may be based on _____ or learned strategies. Usually it involves both.

Survey Question: How can I improve my memory? Objective 7.14

31. Excellent memory abilities are based on using strategies and techniques that make _____ efficient and that _____ for natural weaknesses in human memory.

32. Some people have naturally superior _____, but even they find it _____ to use memory strategies.

33. Memory can be improved by using _____, recitation, and rehearsal, by selecting and organizing information, and by using the _____ part method, _____ practice, overlearning, and active _____ strategies.

138

34. When you are studying or memorizing, you should also keep in mind the effects of serial position, _____, review, _____, and elaboration.

Module 7.6 Psychology in Action: Mnemonics — Memory Magic
Survey Question: Are there any tricks to help me with my memory? Objective 7.15
35. Memory systems (_____) greatly improve immediate memory. However, _____ learning tends to create the most lasting memories.
36. _____ systems use mental images and _____ to link new information with familiar memories already stored in _____.
37. Effective mnemonics tend to rely on mental _____ and _____ mental associations.

Mastery Test

1. The meaning and importance of information has a strong impact on
   a. sensory memory.
   b. eidetic memory.
   c. long-term memory.
   d. procedural memory.

2. Pseudo-memories are closely related to the effects of
   a. repression.
   b. suppression.
   c. semantic forgetting.
   d. constructive processing.

3. The occurrence of _____ implies that consolidation has been prevented.
   a. retrograde amnesia
   b. hippocampal transfer
   c. suppression
   d. changes in the activities of individual nerve cells

4. Most of the techniques used to recover supposedly repressed memories involve
   a. redintegration and hypnosis.
   b. suggestion and fantasy.
   c. reconstruction and priming.
   d. coercion and fabrication.

5. Most daily memory chores are handled by
   a. sensory memory and LTM.
   b. STM and working memory.
   c. STM and LTM.
   d. STM and declarative memory.

6. Three key processes in memory systems are
   a. storage, organization, recovery.
   b. encoding, attention, reprocessing.
   c. storage, retrieval, encoding.
   d. retrieval, reprocessing, reorganization.

7. Procedural memories are to skills as _____ memories are to facts.
   a. declarative
   b. short-term
   c. redintegrative
   d. eidetic

8. An ability to answer questions about distances on a map you have seen only once implies that some memories are based on
   a. constructive processing.
   b. redintegration.
   c. internal images.
   d. episodic processing.

9. The first potential cause of forgetting that may occur is
   a. engram decay.
   b. disuse.
   c. cue-dependent forgetting.
   d. encoding failure.

10. The persistence of icons and echoes is the basis for
    a. sensory memory.
    b. short-term memory.
    c. long-term memory.
    d. working memory.

11. Priming is most often used to reveal
    a. semantic memories.
    b. episodic memories.
    c. implicit memories.
    d. eidetic memories.

12. "Projection" onto an external surface is most characteristic of
    a. sensory memories.
    b. eidetic images.
    c. flashbulb memories.
    d. mnemonic images.

13. Chunking helps especially to extend the capacity of
    a. sensory memory.
    b. STM.
    c. LTM.
    d. declarative memory.

14. There is presently no way to tell if a "recovered" memory is true or false unless independent _____ exists.
    a. evidence
    b. amnesia
    c. elaboration
    d. consolidation

15. Taking an essay test inevitably requires a person to use
    a. recall.
    b. recognition.
    c. relearning.
    d. priming.

16. A savings score is used in what memory task?
    a. recall
    b. recognition
    c. relearning
    d. priming

17. _____ rehearsal helps link new information to existing memories by
    concentrating on meaning.
    a. Redintegrative
    b. Constructive
    c. Maintenance
    d. Elaborative

18. Middle items are neither held in STM nor moved to LTM. This statement explains the
    a. feeling of knowing.
    b. serial position effect.
    c. tip-of-the-tongue state.
    d. semantic forgetting curve.

19. According to the curve of forgetting, the greatest decline in the amount recalled occurs during the
    _____ after learning.
    a. first hour
    b. second day
    c. third to sixth days
    d. retroactive period

20. Work with brain stimulation, truth serums, and hypnosis suggests that long-term memories are
    a. stored in the hippocampus.
    b. relatively permanent.
    c. unaffected by later input.
    d. always redintegrative.

21. Which of the following is most likely to improve the accuracy of memory?
    a. hypnosis
    b. constructive processing
    c. the serial position effect
    d. memory cues

22. To qualify as repression, forgetting must be
    a. retroactive.
    b. proactive.
    c. unconscious.
    d. explicit.

23. Which of the following typically is NOT a good way to improve memory?
   a. massed practice
   b. overlearning
   c. rehearsal
   d. recall strategies

24. A witness to a crime is questioned in ways that re-create the context of the crime and that provide many memory cues. It appears that she is undergoing
   a. retroactive priming.
   b. the progressive part method.
   c. retroactive consolidation.
   d. a cognitive interview.

25. One thing that is clearly true about flashbulb memories is that
   a. they are unusually accurate.
   b. we place great confidence in them.
   c. they apply primarily to public tragedies.
   d. they are recovered by using visualization and hypnosis.

26. One common mnemonic strategy is the
   a. serial position technique.
   b. feeling of knowing tactic.
   c. network procedure.
   d. keyword method.

27. A perspective that helps explain redintegrative memories is
   a. the feeling of knowing model.
   b. recoding and chunking.
   c. the network model.
   d. mnemonic models.

28. Which of the following is NOT considered a part of long-term memory?
   a. echoic memory
   b. semantic memory
   c. episodic memory
   d. declarative memory

29. You are very thirsty. Suddenly you remember a time years ago when you became very thirsty while hiking. This suggests that your memory is
   a. proactive.
   b. state dependent.
   c. still not consolidated.
   d. eidetic.

30. After memorizing five lists of words, you recall less of the last list than a person who only memorized list number five. This observation is explained by
   a. reactive processing.
   b. reconstructive processing.
   c. proactive interference.
   d. retroactive interference.

31. Who coined the term "magic number" seven (plus or minus two)?
    a. George Miller
    b. Nelson Cowan
    c. Herman Ebbinghaus
    d. Karl Lashley

32. When shown a picture of their third-grade class, a group of college students claimed to recall putting goo in the teacher's desk, an event that never took place, by simply filling in gaps with related childhood events. This is best explained by
    a. encoding failure.
    b. retroactive interference.
    c. retrograde amnesia.
    d. constructive processing.

33. People from the United States tend to recall memories that focus on what they did in a particular event while people from China tend to recall memories that focus on their interactions with family members and friends. Recalling different memories of similar events is the result of
    a. cultural influence.
    b. effective use of mnemonic strategy.
    c. highly developed cognition.
    d. none of the above

34. False memory is likely to occur if hypnosis is used in conjunction with
    a. a medical doctor conducting the procedure.
    b. the presence of a loved one.
    c. misleading questions.
    d. both a and b

35. To reduce false identification from eyewitnesses, police should
    a. have witnesses view all the pictures of people at one time.
    b. have witnesses view pictures of people one at a time.
    c. use hypnosis since it has proven to be a reliable source data gathering.
    d. not use eyewitness testimonies since they are not reliable.

36. Which of the following is NOT a recommendation for how to improve your memory?
    a. highlight only the important concepts in your text
    b. continue studying after you have learned the material
    c. eat breakfast
    d. pull an "all-nighter" right before the test

37. A card dealer asks you to silently pick out a card from the six cards laid out in front of you and to memorize it. Without knowing the card you picked, he takes your card away and presents to you the other five cards. To perform this trick properly, the dealer hopes that
    a. you failed to encode the other five cards as you memorize the card you picked.
    b. you do have eidetic memory.
    c. you believe that he can read your mind.
    d. the serial position effect does influence your memory.

Chapter 8: Intelligence, Cognition, Language, and Creativity

Chapter Overview

This chapter explores a number of issues related to cognition, how we think.

Intelligence is a characteristic or set of abilities which describes how one processes information. Tests of intelligence allow individuals to be grouped according to their demonstrated level of ability. Some measures result in a single score, other tests give scores on several different types of abilities. The application section at the end of the chapter examines the issue of cultural and racial bias in intelligence testing.

We can explore the nature of thought by studying our mental pictures, our classification and organization of different ideas and categories, and our development and use of language.

Thought can also be examined by studying the way we solve, or fail to solve, problems. Your book offers several methods for generating possible solutions.

Creativity can lead to better problem solving. Intuition and emotions can also help, but can often lead to poor choices, errors, or biases in thought.

Learning Objectives

OBJECTIVE 8.1 — Describe what it means to have autism and to also be a savant.

OBJECTIVE 8.2 — Describe Binet's role in intelligence testing; give a general definition of intelligence; and explain the g-factor, what an operational definition of intelligence is, and how other cultures view intelligence.

OBJECTIVE 8.3 — Describe the development of the original Stanford-Binet and the five cognitive factors measured by the *Stanford-Binet Intelligence Scales, Fifth Edition* (SB5).

OBJECTIVE 8.4 — Define mental age and chronological age; use examples to show how they are used to compute an intelligence quotient (IQ); differentiate between this IQ (MA/CA x 100) and deviation IQs; and explain how percentiles are interpreted.

OBJECTIVE 8.5 — Distinguish the Wechsler tests from the Stanford-Binet tests and between group and individual tests; and describe the distribution of IQ scores observed in the general population.

OBJECTIVE 8.6 — Differentiate between the terms gifted and genius; describe Terman's study of the gifted, including how the successful ones differed from the less successful ones as adults; explain the relationship between IQ and school grades and IQ and "real world" success; and list early signs of giftedness.

OBJECTIVE 8.7 — Define intellectually disabled and state the dividing line between normal intelligence and an intellectual disability; describe the levels of intellectual disability; and differentiate between familial and organic intellectual disability.

OBJECTIVE 8.8 — Explain why psychologists are developing broader definitions of intelligence; and describe Howard Gardner's theory of multiple intelligences.

OBJECTIVE 8.9 — Define the term artificial intelligence (AI); explain what AI is based on; list its advantages and limitations; and describe how computer simulations and expert systems are being used.

OBJECTIVE 8.10 — Describe the studies that provide evidence for the hereditary view and for the environmental view of intelligence, including the twin studies, the adoption studies, Skeels' study, IQ gains in Westernized nations, and the effects of video games, the Internet, and television.

OBJECTIVE 8.11 — Define and give examples of cognition; and list and define the three basic units of thought.

OBJECTIVE 8.12 — Describe mental imagery and its properties, synesthesia, and the process of "reverse vision"; explain how both stored and created images may be used to solve problems, including how the size of a mental image may be important; and describe how kinesthetic imagery aids thinking.

OBJECTIVE 8.13 — Define the terms concept, concept formation, conceptual rule, and prototype; explain how children and adults learn concepts; differentiate among the three types of concepts (conjunctive, relational, and disjunctive) and between denotative and connotative meanings, including how connotative meanings can be measured; and discuss problems associated with the use of faulty concepts, such as social stereotypes and all-or-nothing thinking.

OBJECTIVE 8.14 — Explain how language aids thought; define semantics; and discuss bilingual education, including the concepts of additive and subtractive bilingualism and two-way bilingual education.

OBJECTIVE 8.15 — Briefly explain the following three requirements of a language and their related concepts: a. symbols (phonemes and morphemes); b. grammar (syntax and transformation rules); c. productivity; describe the characteristics of gestural languages; and discuss the extent to which chimpanzees have been taught to use language.

OBJECTIVE 8.16 — Define and explain how each of the following strategies are related to problem-solving: a. mechanical solutions, including trial-and-error and rote; b. algorithms; c. solutions by understanding, including general solution and functional solutions; d. random search strategy; e. heuristics, including the differences in experts and novices and the role of automatic processing; and f. insight, including selective encoding, selective combination, and selective comparison and the influence of cultures on selective comparison.

OBJECTIVE 8.17 — Explain and give examples of how fixation and functional fixedness block problem-solving; and describe the four common barriers to creative thinking.

OBJECTIVE 8.18 — Describe and give examples of the four kinds of thought (inductive, deductive, logical, and illogical); define the creative processes of fluency, flexibility, and originality; differentiate between convergent and divergent thinking; explain how creativity can be measured and why creativity is more than divergent thinking; discuss the five stages of creative problem-solving and the typical characteristics of creative persons; and list Csikszentmihalyi's recommendations for developing one's creativity.

OBJECTIVE 8.19 — Define intuition; describe the process of "thin-slicing"; explain the following three common intuitive thinking errors: a. representativeness (include representativeness heuristic); b. emotion; c. underlying odds (base rate); d. framing; and include a brief description of what it means to have wisdom.

OBJECTIVE 8.20 — Describe how IQ tests may be unfair to certain groups and what a culture-fair test is; explain how group differences in IQ scores are related to cultural and environmental differences rather than race; and list the advantages and disadvantages of standardized testing in schools.

Language Development Guide

Module 8.1
(328) *astounded*: surprised
(331) *aptitudes*: ability, likely future success
(333) *persevere*: to last, survive, hold on
(333) *spot*: identify
(333) *precocious*: early, advanced
(334) *adaptive*: useful for survival, health, or effective functioning
(334) *defective*: flawed, broken, damaged
(334) *impoverished*: below standard, lacking, poor
(334) *intricate*: with small or complex detail
(334) *pursuits*: jobs, interests
(335) *prospect*: possibility
(335) *stymied*: thrown off, distracted, prevented from a solution
(336) *demystified*: understood, explained
(336) *reared*: raised, parented
(337) *reflects*: shows, reveals

Module 8.2
(340) *frenzied*: busy
(340) *placid*: calm, relaxed
(341) *oversize*: large, expand
(342) *kneading*: folding, pressing
(342) *whatchamacallit*: what you may call it; used when the exact name for something cannot be remembered
(342) *fanciers*: experts, people who enjoy
(343) *dust mop*: a broom of strings or ropes

(343) *punk*: music marked by extreme and often offensive expressions of social discontent

(343) *hip-hop*: popular urban youth culture, closely associated with rap music and with the style and fashions of African-American inner-city residents

(343) *fusion*: music that blends jazz music and rock rhythms

(343) *salsa*: Latin-American music

(343) *metal*: energetic rock music with loud electric guitars and drums

(343) *country*: and western music, often slow ballads with guitars and musicians wearing cowboy hats

(343) *rap*: characterized by lyrics that are spoken rather than sung

(343) *vase*: container for flowers

(343) *muddle*: confuse

(344) *nudist*: person who prefers to live life without wearing clothes

(344) *censor*: job to find and remove objectionable or bad or damaging content

(344) *nitpicky*: too detail-focused; from finding and removing baby lice from hair

(344) *vague*: unclear, subtle

(345) *cause a rash*: result in many

(346) *sink or swim*: try and either succeed or fail

(346) *grasp*: understanding

(346) *in short*: to summarize

(346) *poses no threat*: does not damage

(346) *eroding*: damaging

(346) *"We hold these truths..."*: quote from the U.S. Declaration of Independence, 1776

(346) *mime*: acting without words

(346) *spatial*: relating to space or location

(347) *remnant*: piece

(347) *sucker*: a general term referring to someone or something

(347) *dismal*: very bad

(347) *belch*: burp

(348) *spontaneous*: original, by oneself without instruction

(348) *wet*: urinated

(348) *pygmy*: very small

(348) *prompt*: cue, signal

(349) *On the other hand*: instead

(349) *unravel the mysteries*: help understanding

Module 8.3

(351) *commonplace*: simple, easy

(351) *nonpoisonous*: safe

(351) *leftovers*: uneaten meal portions

(351) *rote*: memorization through repetition, without thought

(351) *Rubik's Cube*: 9x9x9 piece cube with different colors on each face; parts of the object are rotated so that the colors are all in the wrong place

(352) *"Genius is one percent inspiration and ninety-nine percent perspiration"*: what appears to be intelligence is usually the result of a lot of hard work or effort

(353) *hourglass*: a time instrument where sand falls from one glass ball to another

(353) *overcoat*: a long coat for the rain, generally would go over a suit jacket

(353) *C-clamp*: a tool for holding pieces of wood together while glue sets

(354) *wedged*: squeezed, fit

(354) *hung up*: delayed, slowed

(354) *dime*: 10 cent coin

(354) *screwdriver*: tool for tightening or loosening screws

(354) *mount*: hang

(355) *preconceptions*: biases, previous knowledge or beliefs
(355) *precariously*: unstable, likely to fall
(355) *taboos*: restrictions imposed by social custom

Module 8.4
(357) *the course of human history:* over time
(357) *elusive*: able to hide or escape
(358) *brings...to bear*: uses
(359) *saturate themselves*: use
(359) *depicted*: shown, drawn
(359) *Legend has it:* there was a story
(360) *eccentric*: strangely playful
(360) *introverted*: shy, unsocial, interested in one's own mental life
(360) *neurotic*: emotionally unstable or anxious
(360) *inept*: failure, awkward, unskilled
(360) *cultivate*: nurture, use, encourage
(360) *outlandish*: different, strange, weird
(361) *in the face of:* when at the same time we are
(361) *flawed*: containing errors or mistakes
(361) *pitfall*: hidden danger or difficulty
(362) *custody*: legal home and care, right to primary parenting
(362) *disqualify*: throw out, eliminate from consideration
(362) *channel us down a narrow path:* restrict our list of choices
(363) *short-circuit*: disrupt, break

Module 8.5
(366) *lie at the heart of*: are important to
(367) *arbitrary*: made carelessly
(367) *ambiguous*: can be understood in many ways
(367) *are a double-edged sword*: have advantages and disadvantages

Recite and Review

Module 8.1 Intelligence
*Survey Question: How is human intelligence defined and measured? Pages 328-331, Objectives 8.1, 8.2,
        8.3, 8.4, 8.5*
Intelligence refers to the (1)_____ capacity (or g-factor) to act purposefully, think
(2)_____, and deal effectively with the environment. In practice, intelligence is operationally
defined by (3)_____.
The first intelligence test was assembled by (4)_____. A modern version of
(4)_____'s test is the *Stanford-Binet Intelligence Scale.*
Intelligence is expressed as an intelligence (5)_____ (IQ), defined as mental age divided by
chronological age and then multiplied by (6)_____. The (7)_____ of IQ scores
approximates a normal curve.
Another major intelligence test is the (8)_____ (WAIS). The
WAIS measures both verbal and (9)_____ intelligence. Group
(10)_____ tests are also available.

Survey Question: How much does intelligence vary from person to person? Pages 332-334, Objectives 8.6, 8.7

People with IQs in the gifted or "genius" range of (11)_____ tend to be superior in many respects. However, by criteria other than IQ, many children can be considered (12)_____ in one way or another.

The term *intellectually disabled* is applied to those whose IQ falls (13)_____ or who lack various adaptive behaviors. About (14)_____ percent of the cases of intellectual disability are organic. The remaining cases are of (15)_____ cause. Many of these cases are thought to reflect (16)_____ intellectual disability.

Survey Question: What are some controversies in the study of intelligence? Pages 334-337, Objectives 8.8, 8.9, 8.10

Many psychologists have begun to forge new, (17)_____ definitions of intelligence. Howard (18)_____'s theory of multiple intelligences is a good example.

Artificial intelligence refers to any (19)_____ system that can perform tasks that require intelligence when done by (20)_____. Two principal areas of artificial intelligence research on particular human skills are computer simulations and (21)_____.

(22)_____ is partially determined by heredity. However, environment is also important, as revealed by IQ (23)_____ induced by education and stimulating environments.

Module 8.2 Imagery, Concepts, and Language

Survey Question: What is the nature of thought? Page 340, Objective 8.11

Thinking is an (24)_____ representation of external stimuli or situations.

Three basic units of thought are images, (25)_____, and language (or symbols).

Survey Question: In what ways are images related to thinking? Pages 340-342, Objective 8.12

Images may be retrieved from memory or (26)_____ to solve problems.

Images can be (27)_____, they can be rotated in space, and their size may change.

Kinesthetic images are used to represent (28)_____ and actions. Kinesthetic sensations help structure the flow of (29)_____ for many people.

Survey Question: How do we learn concepts? Pages 342-344, Objective 8.13

A (30)_____ is a generalized idea of a class of objects or events.

Concept formation may be based on positive and negative instances or (31)_____.

Concept identification frequently makes use of prototypes, or (32)_____ models.

Concepts may be conjunctive ("(33)_____" concepts), disjunctive ("(34)_____" concepts), or relational.

The denotative meaning of a word or concept is its (35)_____ definition. Connotative meaning is (36)_____.

Survey Question: What is the role of language in thinking? Pages 344-349, Objectives 8.14, 8.15

Language encodes events as (37)_____, for easy mental manipulation. The study of (38)_____ in language is called *semantics*.

Bilingualism is a (39)_____ ability. (40)_____ bilingual education allows children to develop additive bilingualism while in school.

Language carries meaning by combining a set of symbols according to a set of (41)_____ (grammar), which includes (41)_____ about word (42)_____ (syntax).

True languages are productive and can be used to (43)_____.

Complex (44)_____ systems, such as American Sign Language, are true languages.

(45)_____ have been taught American Sign Language and similar systems. This suggests to some that (45)_____ are capable of very basic language use. Others question this conclusion.

Module 8.3 Problem Solving

Survey Question: What do we know about problem solving? Pages 351-355, Objectives 8.16, 8.17
The solution to a problem may be arrived at (46)_____ (by trial and error or by rote application of rules), but (47)_____ solutions are often inefficient.
Solutions by (48)_____ usually begin with discovery of the general properties of an answer, followed by a (49)_____ solution.
Problem solving is aided by heuristics, which (50)_____ the search for solutions.
(51)_____ problem solving is based on learned mental heuristics and highly organized knowledge.
When understanding leads to a (52)_____ solution, insight has occurred. Three elements of insight are selective encoding, selective (53)_____, and selective comparison.
Insight can be (54)_____ by fixations. Functional fixedness is a common fixation, but emotional blocks, (55)_____ values, learned conventions, and perceptual (56)_____ are also problems.

Module 8.4 Creative Thinking and Intuition

Survey Question: What is creative thinking? Pages 357-360, Objective 8.18
To be creative, a solution must be practical and sensible as well as (57)_____. Creative thinking requires (58)_____ thought, characterized by fluency, flexibility, and originality. Tests of creativity measure these qualities.
Five stages often seen in creative problem solving are orientation, (59)_____, incubation, illumination, and (60)_____. Not all creative thinking fits this pattern.
Studies suggest that the creative personality has a number of characteristics, most of which (61)_____ popular stereotypes. There is (62)_____ correlation between IQ and creativity.
Some (63)_____ thinking skills can be learned.

Survey Question: How accurate is intuition? Pages 360-363, Objective 8.19
Intuitive thinking often leads to (64)_____. Wrong conclusions may be drawn when an answer seems (65)_____ representative of what we already believe is true.
(66)_____ also lead to intuitive thinking and poor choices.
Another problem is ignoring the base rate (or (67)_____) of an event.
Clear thinking is usually aided by (68)_____ or framing a problem in broad terms.

Module 8.5 Psychology in Action: Culture, Race, IQ, and You

Survey Question: Are IQ tests fair to all cultural and racial groups? Pages 365-367, Objective 8.20
Traditional IQ tests often suffer from a degree of cultural (69)_____. For this and other reasons, it is wise to remember that IQ is merely an (70)_____ of intelligence and that intelligence is (71)_____ defined by most tests.
IQ is related to achievement in (72)_____, but many other factors are also important. Outside (72)_____, the connection between IQ and achievement is (73)_____.
The use of standard IQ tests for educational (74)_____ of students (especially into special education classes) has been prohibited by law in some (75)_____.

Connections

Module 8.1

1. _____ Binet	a. same genes
2. _____ average intelligence	b. relative standing
3. _____ identical twins	c. IQ of 140
4. _____ IQ	d. Wechsler test
5. _____ deviation IQ	e. first intelligence test
6. _____ IQ of 115	f. "people smart" and "nature smart"
7. _____ gifted people	g. SAT
8. _____ developmentally disabled	h. bell shape
9. _____ group test	i. 84th percentile
10. _____ WAIS	j. MA/CA x 100
11. _____ normal curve	k. IQ below 70
12. _____ multiple intelligence	l. IQ of 100

Module 8.2

1. _____ cognition	a. 3-D images
2. _____ language	b. remembered perceptions
3. _____ social stereotypes	c. images created by the brain
4. _____ mental rotation	d. mental class
5. _____ reverse vision	e. implicit actions
6. _____ stored images	f. thinking
7. _____ kinesthetic imagery	g. ideal or model
8. _____ concept	h. semantic differential
9. _____ prototype	i. faulty, oversimplified concepts
10. _____ connotative meaning	j. symbols and rules

1. _____ word meanings	a. meaningful unit
2. _____ morpheme	b. ASL
3. _____ phoneme	c. semantics
4. _____ "hidden" grammar	d. lexigrams
5. _____ Washoe	e. language sound
6. _____ if-then statement	f. conditional relationship
7. _____ Kanzi	g. transformation rules

Module 8.3

1. _____ expert versus novice	a. mechanical solution
2. _____ AI	b. thinking strategy
3. _____ insight	c. element of insight
4. _____ trial-and-error	d. knowledge plus rules
5. _____ random search strategy	e. a clear, sudden solution
6. _____ heuristic	f. trial-and-error
7. _____ understanding	g. Deep Blue
8. _____ selective comparison	h. acquired strategies
9. _____ fixation	i. blind to alternatives
10. _____ expert system	j. deep comprehension

Module 8.4

1. _____	fluency	a.	preconceived concept
2. _____	flexibility	b.	many types of solutions
3. _____	originality	c.	one correct answer
4. _____	logical	d.	follow explicit rule
5. _____	convergent thinking	e.	moment of insight
6. _____	Anagrams Test	f.	underlying odds
7. _____	mental set	g.	quick and impulsive thought
8. _____	illumination	h.	many solutions
9. _____	base rate	i.	measures divergent thinking
10. _____	intuition	j.	novelty of solutions

Module 8.5

1. _____	Dove Test	a.	pattern recognition
2. _____	high-stakes testing	b.	college admission or employment
3. _____	culture-fair testing	c.	book learning
4. _____	practical intelligence	d.	common sense
5. _____	analytical intelligence	e.	African-American slant

Check Your Memory

Module 8.1 Intelligence

Survey Question: How is human intelligence defined and measured? Pages 328-331, Objectives 8.1, 8.2, 8.3, 8.4, 8.5

T F   1. Alfred Binet's first test was designed to measure mechanical aptitude.

T F   2. Lewis Terman helped write the Stanford-Binet intelligence test.

T F   3. The Stanford-Binet intelligence test measures three intelligence factors: knowledge, quantitative reasoning, and visual-spatial processing.

T F   4. The Stanford-Binet intelligence test does include a memory task (repeating a series of digits) to determine a person's ability to use his/her short-term memory.

T F   5. Mental age refers to average mental ability for a person of a given age.

T F   6. Mental age can't be higher than chronological age.

T F   7. An IQ will be greater than 100 when CA is larger than MA.

T F   8. Average intelligence is defined as an IQ from 90 to 109.

T F   9. Modern IQ tests give scores as deviation IQs.

T F   10. Being placed in the 84th percentile means that 16 percent of your peers received IQ scores higher than you and 84 percent have IQ scores lower than you.

T F   11. The WISC is designed to test adult performance intelligence.

T F   12. The Stanford-Binet, Wechsler's, and the SAT are all group intelligence tests.

T F   13. In a normal curve, a majority of scores are found near the average.

Survey Question: How much does intelligence vary from person to person? Pages 332-334, Objectives 8.6, 8.7

T F   14. An IQ above 130 is described as "bright normal."

T F   15. The correlation between IQ scores and school grades is .5.

T F   16. Research has shown that men do score higher on the Stanford-Binet Intelligence Scale than women, which proves that men are smarter than women.

T F   17. Only 12 people out of 100 score above 130 on IQ tests.

T F   18. Gifted children tend to get average IQ scores by the time they reach adulthood.

T F   19. Gifted persons are more susceptible to mental illness.

T F   20. Talking in complete sentences at age two is regarded as a sign of giftedness.

T F   21. Howard Gardner suggests that each of us has eight different types of intelligence such as being "people smart," "word smart," etc.

T F   22. The moderately retarded can usually learn routine self-help skills.

Survey Question: What are some controversies in the study of intelligence? Pages 334-337, Objectives 8.8, 8.9, 8.10

T F   23. The IQs of identical twins are more alike than those of fraternal twins.

T F   24. Adult intelligence is approximately 50 percent hereditary.

T F   25. The environmental influence on twins does include development inside their mother's womb before birth.

T F   26. Herrnstein and Murray, in their book, *The Bell Curve*, suggested that racial group differences in IQ were due to environmental influences, not genes.

T F   27. AI is frequently based on a set of rules applied to a body of information.

T F   28. Computer simulations are used to test models of human cognition.

T F   29. Deep Blue, an artificial computer program, has "fooled" people into believing that it is human, therefore, it is considered intelligent.

Module 8.2 Imagery, Concepts, and Language

Survey Question: What is the nature of thought? Page 340, Objective 8.11

T F   30. Cognition refers to the process of encoding, storing, and retrieving information.

T F   31. Images, concepts, and language may be used to mentally represent problems.

T F   32. Images are generalized ideas of a class of related objects or events.

T F   33. Blindfolded chess players mainly use concepts to represent chess problems and solutions.

Survey Question: In what ways are images related to thinking? Pages 340-342, Objective 8.12

T F   34. Images are used to make decisions, change feelings, and to improve memory.

T F   35. Mental images may be used to improve memory and skilled actions.

T F   36. The visual cortex is activated when a person has a mental image.

T F   37. The more the image of a shape has to be rotated in space, the longer it takes to tell if it matches another view of the same shape.

T F   38. People who have good imaging abilities tend to score high on tests of creativity.

T F   39. The smaller a mental image is, the harder it is to identify its details.

T F   40. People with good kinesthetic imagery tend to learn sports skills faster than average.

Survey Question: How do we learn concepts? Pages 342-344, Objective 8.13

T F   41. Concept formation is typically based on examples and rules.

T F   42. Prototypes are very strong negative instances of a concept.

T F   43. "Greater than" and "lopsided" are relational concepts.

T F   44. The semantic differential is used to rate the objective meanings of words and concepts.

T F   45. Social stereotypes are accurate, oversimplified concepts people use to form mental images of groups of people.

Survey Question: What is the role of language in thinking? Pages 344-349, Objectives 8.14, 8.15

T F   46. Encoding is the study of the meanings of language.

T F   47. The Stroop interference test shows that thought is greatly influenced by language.

T F   48. People can easily name the color of the word without the meaning of the word interfering with their thought processing.

T F   49. Morphemes are the basic speech sounds of a language.

T F   50. Syntax is a part of grammar.

T F   51. Noam Chomsky believes that a child who says, "I drinked my juice," has applied the semantic differential to a simple, core sentence.

T F   52. ASL has 600,000 root signs.

T F   53. True languages are productive, thus ASL is not a true language.

T F   54. If one is fluent in ASL, one can sign and understand other gestural languages such as Yiddish Sign.

T F   55. Animal communication can be described as productive.

T F   56. Chimpanzees have never learned to speak even a single word.

T F   57. One of Sarah chimpanzee's outstanding achievements was mastery of sentences involving transformational rules.

T F   58. Some "language" use by chimpanzees appears to be no more than simple operant responses.

T F   59. Only a minority of the things that language-trained chimps "say" have anything to do with food.

T F   60. Language-trained chimps have been known to hold conversations when no humans were present.

T F   61. Kanzi's use of grammar is on a par with that of a two-year-old child.

Module 8.3 Problem Solving

Survey Question: What do we know about problem solving? Pages 351-355, Objectives 8.16, 8.17

T F   62. Except for the simplest problems, mechanical solutions are typically best left to computers.

T F   63. An algorithm is a learned set of rules (grammar) for language.

T F   64. Karl Duncker's famous tumor problem could only be solved by trial-and-error.

T F   65. In solutions by understanding, functional solutions are usually discovered by use of a random search strategy.

T F   66. Working backward from the desired goal to the starting point can be a useful heuristic.

T F   67. In problem solving, rapid insights are more likely to be correct than those that develop slowly.

T F   68. Selective encoding refers to bringing together seemingly unrelated bits of useful information.

T F   69. An advantage of selective comparison is our ability to solve problems in all cultures.

T F   70. Functional fixedness is an inability to see new uses for familiar objects.

T F   71. Learned barriers in functional fixedness refer to our habits causing us to not identify other important elements of a problem.

T F   72. Much human expertise is based on acquired strategies for solving problems.

T F   73. Chess experts have an exceptional ability to remember the positions of chess pieces placed at random on a chessboard.

Module 8.4 Creative Thinking and Intuition

Survey Question: What is creative thinking? Pages 357-360, Objective 8.18

T F   74. In inductive thinking, a general rule is inferred from specific examples.

T F   75. Fluency and flexibility are measures of convergent thinking.

T F   76. Creative thinkers typically apply reasoning and critical thinking to novel ideas after they produce them.

T F   77. Creative ideas combine originality with feasibility.

T F   78. Creative problem solving temporarily stops during the incubation period.

T F   79. Creative people have an openness to experience, and they have a wide range of knowledge and interests.

T F   80. An IQ score of 120 or above means that a person is creative.

T F   81. Most creative people like Vincent Van Gogh and Edgar Allan Poe tend to become insane later in life.

Survey Question: How accurate is intuition? Pages 360-363, Objective 8.19

T F   82. Intuition is a quick, impulsive insight into the true nature of a problem and its solution.

T F   83. The probability of two events occurring together is lower than the probability of either one occurring alone.

T F   84. The representativeness heuristic is the strategy of stating problems in broad terms.

T F   85. Being logical, most people do not let their emotions interfere when making important decisions.

T F   86. Framing refers to the way in which a problem is stated or structured.

T F   87. People who are intelligent are also wise because they live their lives with openness and tolerance.

T F   88. Creative problem solving involves defining problems as narrowly as possible.

T F   89. It is wise to allow time for incubation if you are seeking a creative solution to a problem.

T F   90. Edward de Bono suggests that digging deeper with logic is a good way to increase your creativity.

T F   91. People seeking creative solutions should avoid taking risks; doing so just leads to dead ends.

T F   92. Delaying evaluation during the early stages of creative problem solving tends to lead to poor thinking.

T F   93. The cross-stimulation effect is an important part of brainstorming in groups.

Module 8.5 Psychology in Action: Culture, Race, IQ, and You

Survey Question: Are IQ tests fair to all cultural and racial groups? Pages 365-367, Objective 8.20

T F   94. The Stanford-Binet, Wechsler's, and the SAT are all culture-fair tests.

T F   95. Whites score lower than blacks on Dove's Counterbalance Intelligence Test.

T F   96. Sternberg considered "street smarts" to be a different form of intelligence than "book smarts."

Critical Thinking

Module 8.1

1. Is it ever accurate to describe a machine as "intelligent"?

2. Some people treat IQ as if it were a fixed number, permanently stamped on the forehead of each child. Why is this view in error?

Module 8.2

3. A Democrat and a Republican are asked to rate the word *democratic* on the semantic differential. Under what conditions would their ratings be most alike?

4. Chimpanzees and other apes are intelligent and entertaining animals. If you were doing language research with a chimp, what major problem would you have to guard against?

Module 8.3

5. Do you think that it is true that "a problem clearly defined is a problem half solved"?

6. Sea otters select suitably sized rocks and use them to hammer shellfish loose for eating. They then use the rock to open the shell. Does this qualify as thinking?

Module 8.4

7. A coin is flipped four times with one of the following results: *(a)* H T T H, *(b)* T T T T, *(c)* H H H H, *(d)* H H T H. Which sequence would most likely precede getting a head on the fifth coin flip?

Module 8.5

8. Assume that a test of memory for words is translated from English to Spanish. Would the Spanish version of the test be equal in difficulty to the English version?

Final Survey and Review

Module 8.1 Intelligence

Survey Question: How is human intelligence defined and measured? Objectives 8.1, 8.2, 8.3, 8.4, 8.5

1. Intelligence refers to the general capacity (or _____) to act _____, think rationally, and deal _____ with the environment. In practice, intelligence is _____ by intelligence tests.

2. The first _____ was assembled by Alfred Binet. A modern version of Binet's test is the _____.

3. Intelligence is expressed as an intelligence quotient (IQ), defined as _____ age divided by _____ age and then multiplied by 100. The distribution of IQ scores approximates _____.

4. Another _____ intelligence test is the *Wechsler Adult Intelligence Scale* (WAIS). The WAIS measures both _____ and performance intelligence. _____ intelligence tests are also available.

Survey Question: How much does intelligence vary from person to person? Objectives 8.6, 8.7

5. People with IQs in the _____ range of above 140 tend to be superior in many respects. However, by criteria other than IQ, _____ children can be considered gifted or talented in one way or another.

6. The term _____ is applied to those whose IQ falls below 70 or who lack various _____ behaviors. About 50 percent of the cases of intellectual disability are _____. The remaining cases are of undetermined cause. _____ of these cases are thought to _____ familial intellectual disability.

Survey Question: What are some controversies in the study of intelligence? Objectives 8.8, 8.9, 8.10

7. Many psychologists have begun to forge new, broader definitions of _____. Howard Gardner's theory of _____ is a good example.

8. _____ refers to any artificial system that can perform _____ that require intelligence when done by people. Two principal areas of artificial intelligence research on particular human skills _____ and expert systems.

9. Intelligence is partially determined by _____. However, _____ is also important, as revealed by IQ increases induced by _____ and stimulating _____.

Module 8.2 Imagery, Concepts, and Language

Survey Question: What is the nature of thought? Objective 8.11

10. Thinking is an internal representation of _____ or situations.

11. Three basic units of thought are _____, _____, and _____ (or symbols).

Survey Question: In what ways are images related to thinking? Objective 8.12

12. Images may be _____ or created to solve problems.

13. Images can be three-dimensional, they can be _____ in space, and their _____ may change.

14. _____ images are used to represent movements and actions. _____ sensations help structure the _____ of thoughts for many people.

Survey Question: How do we learn concepts? Objective 8.13

15. A concept is a _____ idea of a class of objects or _____.

16. Concept formation may be based on _____ or rule learning.

17. Concept identification frequently makes use of _____, or ideal models.

18. Concepts may be _____ ("and" concepts), _____ ("either/or" concepts), or _____.

19. The _____ meaning of a word or concept is its dictionary definition. _____ meaning is personal or emotional.

Survey Question: What is the role of language in thinking? Objectives 8.14, 8.15

20. Language _____ events as symbols, for easy mental manipulation. The study of meaning in language is called _____.

21. _____ is a valuable ability. Two-way bilingual education allows children to develop _____ _____ while in school.

22. Language carries meaning by combining a set of _____ according to a set of rules (_____), which includes rules about word order (_____).

23. True languages are _____ and can be used to generate new ideas or possibilities.

24. Complex gestural systems, such as _____, are true languages.

25. Chimpanzees and other primates have been taught _____ and similar systems. This suggests to some that primates are capable of _____ language use. Others question this conclusion.

Module 8.3 Problem Solving

Survey Question: What do we know about problem solving? Objectives 8.16, 8.17

26. The solution to a problem may be arrived at mechanically (by trial and error or by _____), but mechanical solutions are often _____.

27. Solutions by understanding usually begin with discovery of the _____ of an answer, followed by a functional solution.

28. Problem solving is aided by _____, which narrow the search for solutions.

29. Expert problem solving is based on learned _____ and highly organized knowledge.

30. When understanding leads to a rapid solution, _____ has occurred. Three elements of _____ are selective encoding, selective combination, and selective _____.

31. Insight can be blocked by _____. Functional fixedness is a common _____, but emotional _____, cultural values, learned _____, and perceptual habits are also problems.

Module 8.4 Creative Thinking and Intuition

Survey Question: What is creative thinking? Objective 8.18

32. To be creative, a solution must be _____ and _____ as well as original. Creative thinking requires divergent thought, characterized by _____, _____, and originality. Tests of creativity measure these qualities.

33. Five stages often seen in creative problem solving are _____, preparation, _____, illumination, and verification. _____ creative thinking fits this pattern.

34. Studies suggest that the _____ has a number of characteristics, most of which contradict popular stereotypes. There is only a very small correlation between _____ and creativity.

35. Some creative thinking skills can be _____.

Survey Question: How accurate is intuition? Objective 8.19

36. _____ thinking often leads to errors. Wrong conclusions may be drawn when an answer seems highly _____ of what we already believe is true.

37. Emotions also lead to _____ thinking and _____ choices.

38. Another problem is ignoring the _____ (or underlying probability) of an event.

39. Clear thinking is usually aided by stating or _____ a problem in broad terms.

Module 8.5 Psychology in Action: Culture, Race, IQ, and You
Survey Question: Are IQ tests fair to all cultural and racial groups? Objective 8.20

40. Traditional IQ tests often suffer from a degree of _____ bias. For this and other reasons, it is wise to remember that IQ is _____ an index of intelligence and that _____ is narrowly defined by most tests.

41. IQ is related to _____ in school, but many other factors are also important. Outside school, the connection between IQ and _____ is even weaker.

42. The use of _____ IQ tests for educational placement of students (especially into _____ _____ classes) has been _____ by law in some states.

Mastery Test

1. The mark of a true language is that it must be
   a. spoken.
   b. productive.
   c. based on spatial grammar and syntax.
   d. capable of encoding conditional relationships.

2. Computer simulations and expert systems are two major applications of
   a. AI.
   b. ASL.
   c. brainstorming.
   d. problem framing.

3. Failure to wear automobile seat belts is an example of which intuitive thinking error?
   a. allowing too much time for incubation
   b. framing a problem broadly
   c. ignoring base rates
   d. recognition that two events occurring together are more likely than either one alone

4. One thing that images, concepts, and symbols all have in common is that they are
   a. morphemes.
   b. internal representations.
   c. based on reverse vision.
   d. translated into micromovements.

5. To decide if a container is a cup, bowl, or vase, most people compare it to
   a. a prototype.
   b. its connotative meaning.
   c. a series of negative instances.
   d. a series of relevant phonemes.

6. During problem solving, being "cold," "warm," or "very warm" is closely associated with
   a. insight.
   b. fixation.
   c. automatic processing.
   d. rote problem solving.

7. The Anagrams Test measures
    a. mental sets.
    b. inductive thinking.
    c. logical reasoning.
    d. divergent thinking.

8. "Either-or" concepts are
    a. conjunctive.
    b. disjunctive.
    c. relational.
    d. prototypical.

9. Which term does not belong with the others?
    a. selective comparison
    b. functional fixedness
    c. learned conventions
    d. emotional blocks

10. Separate collections of verbal and performance subtests are a feature of the
    a. WAIS.
    b. Gardner-8.
    c. CQT.
    d. Stanford-Binet.

11. Mental retardation is formally defined by deficiencies in
    a. aptitudes and self-help skills.
    b. intelligence and scholastic aptitudes.
    c. language and spatial thinking.
    d. IQ and adaptive behaviors.

12. A 12-year-old child, with an IQ of 100, must have an MA of
    a. 100.
    b. 12.
    c. 10.
    d. 15.

13. The difference between prime beef and dead cow is primarily a matter of
    a. syntax.
    b. conjunctive meaning.
    c. semantics.
    d. the productive nature of language.

14. Culture-fair tests attempt to measure intelligence without being affected by a person's
    a. verbal skills.
    b. cultural background.
    c. educational level.
    d. all the preceding

15. Which of the listed terms does NOT correctly complete this sentence: Insight involves selective
_____.
    a. encoding
    b. combination
    c. comparison
    d. fixation

16. Which of the following is LEAST likely to predict that a person is creative?
    a. high IQ
    b. a preference for complexity
    c. fluency in combining ideas
    d. use of mental images

17. "Try working backward from the desired goal to the starting point or current state." This advice
    describes a
    a. syllogism.
    b. heuristic.
    c. prototype.
    d. dimension of the semantic differential.

18. Language allows events to be _____ into _____.
    a. translated, concepts
    b. fixated, codes
    c. rearranged, lexigrams
    d. encoded, symbols

19. "A triangle must be a closed shape with three sides made of straight lines." This statement is
    an example of a
    a. prototype.
    b. positive instance.
    c. conceptual rule.
    d. disjunctive concept.

20. Fluency, flexibility, and originality are all measures of
    a. inductive thinking.
    b. selective comparison.
    c. intuitive framing.
    d. divergent thinking.

21. The form of imagery that is especially important in music, sports, dance, and martial arts is
    a. kinesthetic imagery.
    b. semantic imagery.
    c. prototypical imagery.
    d. conjunctive imagery.

22. Among animals trained to use language, Kanzi has been unusually accurate at
    a. using proper syntax.
    b. substituting gestures for lexigrams.
    c. expressing conditional relationships.
    d. forming chains of operant responses.

23. The largest number of people are found in which IQ range?
    a. 80-89
    b. 90-109
    c. 110-119
    d. below 70

24. Looking for analogies and delaying evaluation are helpful strategies for increasing
    a. divergent thinking.
    b. convergent thinking.
    c. functional fixedness.
    d. concept formation.

25. Comparing two three-dimensional shapes to see if they match is easiest if only a small amount of _____ is required.
    a. conceptual recoding
    b. mental rotation
    c. concept formation
    d. kinesthetic transformation

26. The good-bad dimension on the semantic differential is closely related to a concept's
    a. disjunctive meaning.
    b. conjunctive meaning.
    c. connotative meaning.
    d. denotative meaning.

27. According to Noam Chomsky, surface sentences are created by applying _____ to simple sentences.
    a. encoding grammars
    b. transformation rules
    c. conditional prototypes
    d. selective conjunctions

28. The occurrence of an insight corresponds to which stage of creative thinking?
    a. verification
    b. incubation
    c. illumination
    d. fixation

29. The _____ has demonstrated that people can quickly identify the color of a word if the word's meaning is similar to the word's color. This suggests that the meaning of words do influence our thoughts.
    a. memory task
    b. Stroop test
    c. Stanford-Binet Intelligence Scale
    d. American Sign Language

30. When one divides a number into another, step-by-step without the aid of a calculator, one is using a(an) _____ to find a solution.
    a. algorithm
    b. conceptual rule
    c. prototype
    d. Anagrams Test

31. Most American students were unable to solve a problem of how a chief can collect taxes without a scale to balance the right amount of gold coins each villager owes, whereas most Chinese students were able to since most Chinese students were familiar with a traditional story about weighing an elephant that is too big to be on a scale. This example illustrates which nature of insight?
    a. selective encoding
    b. selective combination
    c. selective comparison
    d. selective intuition

32. Which of the five Stanford-Binet Intelligence Scales measures how well people can imagine and correctly determine their location by following written instructions?
    a. fluid reasoning
    b. visual-spatial processing
    c. knowledge
    d. working memory

33. Winnie took an IQ test and she is ranked in the 97th percentile. Without knowing her actual IQ score, you can assume that
    a. she is smarter than 97 percent of the people who took the test.
    b. she and 97 percent of the others who took the test have the same IQ scores.
    c. she is smarter than 3 percent of the people who took the test.
    d. 97 percent of the people who took the test are smarter than Winnie.

34. The argument that people from different regions and cultures are taught to understand the world differently by using different kinds of knowledge and mental abilities suggests that a _____ is necessary to measure intelligence accurately.
    a. Stanford-Binet Intelligence Scale
    b. culture-fair test
    c. SAT
    d. WAIS

35. The performance gap on intelligence test scores between men and women can be traced back to
    a. heredity.
    b. women being told they cannot outperform men.
    c. women too busy taking care of their family to maintain their physical skills.
    d. availability of resources allocated to men versus women.

36. People who choose political candidates because they like them have fallen prey to which form of intuitive thinking error?
    a. representativeness
    b. emotions
    c. underlying odds
    d. framing

Chapter 9: Motivation and Emotion

Chapter Overview

Motivation theories answer the question, "why do we do what we do?" We are usually motivated by an internal push, and external pull, or a combination of the two.

Basic motivations involve survival needs (such as hunger, thirst, or, evolutionarily, sex) and physical motivators for pleasure (such as sex) or the avoidance of pain. Therefore, motivation researchers look for brain areas, neurotransmitters, and social or environmental triggers for these sorts of behaviors.

Other researchers examine more complex motivations, such as the need for stimulation (excitement, variety), achievement (or competition), and personal, professional, or mental improvement and growth. These motivations rely on something more than tissue deficits or other bodily needs, but focus more on abstract or cognitive functions. Maslow's Hierarchy of Needs is one example of this type of motivation theory.

The second part of the chapter deals with the study of emotions; how they are experienced in the body and brain, as well as how they are communicated with (or hidden from) other people.

Emotional expression varies by culture, gender, and personal preference.

The text describes several of the major theories, which describe the complex relationship between bodily sensation, mental states, and conscious awareness of the experience of an emotion.

The last section in the chapter explores the concept of "emotional intelligence," which involves the ability to manage one's own emotions as well as the ability to perceive and understand the emotions of others.

Learning Objectives

OBJECTIVE 9.1 — Define *motivation;* explain the factors that influence one's motivation and emotions; describe the condition known as *alexithymia;* and explain the need reduction model and how the incentive value of a goal can affect motivation.

OBJECTIVE 9.2 — Describe and give an example of each of the three types of motives; and define homeostasis.

OBJECTIVE 9.3 — Describe how circadian rhythms affect energy levels, motivation, and performance; and explain how and why shift work and jet lag may adversely affect a person and how to minimize the effects of shifting one's rhythms.

OBJECTIVE 9.4 — Discuss why hunger cannot be fully explained by the contractions of an empty stomach and describe the relationship of each of the following to hunger: a. blood sugar; b. liver; c. hypothalamus: 1) feeding system (lateral hypothalamus), 2) satiety system (ventromedial hypothalamus), 3) blood sugar regulator (paraventricular nucleus); d. GLP-1.

OBJECTIVE 9.5 — Describe how a taste aversion develops; and explain how each of the following is related to overeating and obesity: a. a person's set point; b. the release of leptin; c. external eating cues; d. variety and taste, e. emotions, f. cultural factors, and g. dietary content.

OBJECTIVE 9.6 — Explain the paradox of "yo-yo" dieting; and describe what is meant by behavioral dieting and how these techniques can enable you to control your weight.

OBJECTIVE 9.7 — Describe the essential features of the eating disorders of anorexia nervosa and bulimia nervosa; explain what seems to cause them in men and women; and what treatments are available.

OBJECTIVE 9.8 — Name the brain structure that appears to control thirst; and differentiate between extracellular and intracellular thirst.

OBJECTIVE 9.9 — Explain how the drive to avoid pain and the sex drive differ from other primary drives; describe how the sex drive in humans differs from that of lower animals and how alcohol and various other drugs affect one's sex drive; and define the term aphrodisiac.

OBJECTIVE 9.10 — Discuss the importance of the stimulus drives; describe the arousal theory, the characteristics of high and low sensation-seekers, the inverted-U function, and the Yerkes-Dodson law; and explain how one can cope with test anxiety.

OBJECTIVE 9.11 — Describe social motives and explain how they are acquired; define the need for achievement (nAch) and differentiate it from the need for power; relate this need for achievement to risk taking; explain the influences of drive and determination in the success of high achievers; and list seven steps to enhance self-confidence.

OBJECTIVE 9.12 — List (in order) the needs found in Maslow's hierarchy of motives; distinguish between basic needs and growth needs; explain why Maslow's lower (physiological) needs are considered prepotent; and define and give examples of meta-needs.

OBJECTIVE 9.13 — Distinguish between intrinsic and extrinsic motivation, and explain how each type of motivation may affect a person's interest in work, leisure activities, and creativity.

OBJECTIVE 9.14 — Define emotion and mood, explain how emotions aid survival; describe the three elements of emotions; list Plutchiks' eight primary emotions and how they combine to make more complex emotions; and explain how a person can experience two opposite emotions simultaneously.

OBJECTIVE 9.15 — Describe the role of the sympathetic and parasympathetic branches of the ANS in emotional arousal; explain how the parasympathetic rebound may be involved in cases of sudden death; discuss the use and limitations of the lie detector (polygraph); and describe the proposed airport security techniques for detecting lies.

OBJECTIVE 9.16 — Discuss Darwin's view of human emotion and which facial expressions appear to be universal and most recognizeable; describe cultural and gender differences in emotional expression; and discuss kinesics, including the emotional messages conveyed by facial expressions and body language.

OBJECTIVE 9.17 — Describe and give examples of the following theories of emotion: a. James-Lange theory; b. Cannon-Bard theory; c. Schachter's cognitive theory; d. the effects of attribution on emotion; e. the facial feedback hypothesis, including the dangers of suppressing emotions; f. emotional appraisal; and g. the contemporary model of emotion.

OBJECTIVE 9.18 — Describe the concept of emotional intelligence and its five skills; and discuss the benefits of positive emotions.

Language Development Guide

Introduction
(370) *empathize*: be sensitive to, emotionally understand

Module 9.1
(372) *vigorously*: hard, energetic
(372) *deficiency*: lack, absence
(372) *fasting*: intentionally going without food
(372) *pie lust*: desire, wanting food
(372) *bare*: empty
(372) *manipulation*: doing things, changing one's surroundings
(372) *blogging*: writing a web log or internet diary
(373) *X Games*: competition for extreme sports like skateboarding or stunt bicycling or rollerblading
(373) *rest room*: bathroom
(373) *equilibrium*: balance
(373) *thermostat*: a control for room temperature, turning on and off the furnace or air conditioning
(374) *resychronize*: get back into a normal rhythm
(374) *burned the midnight oil*: stay up late at night to work or study
(375) *destination*: where you are going

Module 9.2
(376) *instructive*: something you can learn from
(376) *contractions*: muscles get suddenly tighter and possibly painful
(376) *hunger pangs*: extreme feeling of hunger
(376) *inflated conclusion*: joke; inflated could mean filled with air, or in this context, an exaggeration
(377) *satiety*: signal that you are full, that you have eaten enough
(377) *munchies*: a craving for food
(378) *spare tire is well-inflated:* joke; normal reference is an extra wheel in your car has air in it - in this context a reference to extra fat around one's stomach or waist
(378) *stigma*: rejected or criticized by society, perceived as a negative characteristic, mark or sign of shame

(379) *Frosh 15*: slang for a 15 pound weight gain occurring during the first year of college

(379) *cheese Danish*: a sweet baked pastry

(379) *fad diet*: a food plan that is popular for a short time

(379) *grapefruit*: citrus fruit; one fad diet was to eat only grapefruits to lose weight

(379) *delicacy*: a special and often expensive food

(379) *barbaric*: cruel and primitive

(379) *pampered*: nurtured with extra special care, treated very well

(380) *bouncing* between feast and famine: sometimes eating a lot and sometimes not eating

(380) *battle of the bulge*: slang for the struggle against being fat

(380) *malnutrition*: bad or unbalanced diet, perhaps not enough food

(380) *debilitating*: harmful

(381) *overhaul*: make major changes

(381) *super-size me*: advertising slogan, to ask for extra large servings

(381) *bouillon*: juices, drippings from meat

(381) *gorge*: eat a lot

(381) *laxatives*: medicines that cause diarrhea

(381) *bingeing*: consuming a lot of something at one time

(381) *purging*: causing oneself to vomit

(382) *excessive exercise*: exercising much more than you need to for basic health, such as walking for four hours a day when thirty minutes is recommended

(382) *wasting away:* getting thinner and thinner

(382) *pole vaulting:* an Olympic sport to use a long rod to propel oneself over a high bar

(382) *ridding themselves:* getting rid of

(383) *nomadic*: people who travel, who have no permanent home

(383) *Gatorade*: a drink taken especially after exercise to help restore minerals lost through perspiration

(383) *cutting*: body mutilation involving slashing one's own skin

(383) *agonize*: hurt

(383) *devotees*: people who enjoy or worship

(383) *body art*: tattoos and other permanent body decoration

(384) *receptive*: willing to mate

(384) *Candy is dandy, but liquor is quicker*: romance can be seductive, but a woman's defenses can be lowered more rapidly by serving her alcohol

Module 9.3

(386) *skydiving*: sport of parachuting out of a plane

(386) *surfing the web:* going online, exploring on the Internet

(387) *cage diving*: going under water in a safety cage to watch sharks feeding

(387) *bungee jumping*: sport of jumping off a bridge with an elastic cord tied around one's ankles

(387) *white-water rafting:* traveling on an inflatable boat down a fast and rocky river

(387) *sharp*: intelligent

(387) *below par:* poorly

(387) *bearing down on you*: coming at you

(388) *antidote*: cure

(388) *status*: importance, rank, privilege

(388) *affiliation*: being with people, having friends

(389) *prestige*: fame

(389) *beanbag*: small cloth sealed pocket with beans or other pellets, used as a substitute for a ball in some tossing games

(390) *prodigies*: highly talented children

(390) *eminent*: famous or important

(390) *regard it as a sign*: recognize

(390) *pyramid*: structure or three-dimensional shape made of triangles
(391) *syndrome of decay*: decline
(391) *vitality*: energy
(391) *drudgery*: dull and tiring work
(391) *lavishly*: richly, excessively
(392) *bribed*: paid for favors
(392) *faking it:* acting a lie

Module 9.4
(394) *telltale signs*: indicators
(394) *choking*: performing badly when normally you perform well
(394) *butterflies*: nervousness
(394) *contorts*: twists
(395) *ticklish*: sensitive to touch
(395) *Bushman*: plains tribe
(395) *prowler*: a person moving about secretly, as in search of things to steal
(396) *backwoods midwife*: a person in a remote area who can assist with delivering a baby
(397) *baseline*: standard measurement for normal
(397) *unqualified*: definite
(397) *misgivings*: reservations, hesitations, regrets

Module 9.5
(400) *bare their teeth*: show teeth, snarl in threatening or menacing way
(400) *scheming*: being tricky or evil
(401) *Westerns*: cowboy films
(401) *curtail*: hold back
(401) *blunted*: made less sharp or strong
(402) *lean toward*: can mean either posture or preference
(402) *abrupt*: sudden
(403) *slapstick*: humor involving injury to others, such as falling down or getting hit with something
(403) *slides*: pictures
(403) *budding romance:* relationship in its early stages
(403) *on the sly*: in secret
(403) *suspension bridge*: bridge hanging on wires
(403) *chasm*: deep hole or crack in the earth
(403) *farfetched*: difficult to believe
(403) *ingenious*: creative, intelligent
(404) *case of love at first fright*: play on the saying, "Love at first sight", meaning developing romantic feelings instantly
(404) *crosswise*: sideways, horizontally
(405) *snarling*: growling
(405) *lunges*: jumps or dives, moves suddenly toward
(406) *cuts you off*: moves suddenly into the road lane closely in front of you, often causing you to have to slow down
(406) *wear-and-tear*: damage over time

Module 9.6
(408) *stifle*: hold in
(408) *mesh well:* fit, match
(408) *sabotage*: damage, undermine, disrupt

(408) *tuned in to:* aware of, notice
(408) *pinpoint:* identify
(408) *amplify or restrain:* make larger or smaller, enhance or hold back
(409) *impel:* cause, encourage
(409) *save their skins:* survive
(409) *expelling:* getting rid of, spitting out
(409) *buffers:* protections
(409) *roast:* a party for a person where jokes or embarrassing stories are told about them

Recite and Review

Module 9.1 Overview of Motivation

Survey Question: What is motivation? Page 372, Objective 9.1
(1) _____ initiate, sustain, and direct activities. Many motives involve the following sequence:
(2)_____, drive, (3)_____, and goal attainment (need reduction).
Behavior can be activated either by needs ((4)_____) or by goals ((5)_____).
The (6)_____ of a goal and its ability to (7)_____ action are related to its incentive value.

Survey Question: Are there different types of motives? Pages 372-375, Objectives 9.2, 9.3
Three basic categories of motives are (8)_____ motives, stimulus motives, and
(9)_____ motives.
Most (10)_____ motives operate to maintain homeostasis.
(11)_____ are closely tied to sleep, activity, and energy cycles.
(12)_____ and (13)_____ can seriously disrupt motivation, sleep, and bodily rhythms.

Module 9.2 Hunger, Thirst, Pain, and Sex

Survey Question: What causes hunger? Overeating? Eating disorders? Pages 376-382, Objectives 9.4, 9.5, 9.6, 9.7
Hunger is influenced by a complex interplay between fullness of the stomach, (14)_____ levels, metabolism in the liver, and (15)_____ stores in the body.
The most direct control of eating comes from the (16)_____, which is sensitive to both neural and chemical messages that affect eating.
Other factors influencing hunger are the body's (17)_____, external eating cues, the attractiveness and variety of diet, (18)_____, learned taste preferences and aversions, and
(19)_____ values.
Obesity is the result of internal and external influences, (20)_____, emotions, genetics, and
(21)_____ .
(22)_____ is based on techniques that change eating patterns and exercise habits.
(23)_____ nervosa and (24)_____ nervosa are two prominent eating disorders.
Both tend to involve conflicts about (25)_____, self-control, and anxiety.

Survey Question: Is there more than one type of thirst? In what ways are pain avoidance and the sex drive unusual? Pages 383-384, Objectives 9.8, 9.9

Like hunger, thirst and other basic motives are primarily under the central control of the (26)_____. (27)_____ may be either intracellular or extracellular.

Pain avoidance is (28)_____ as opposed to cyclic. Pain avoidance and pain tolerance are partially (29)_____.

The sex drive is (30)_____ because it is non-homeostatic.

Module 9.3 Arousal, Achievement, and Growth Needs

Survey Question: How does arousal relate to motivation? Pages 386-388, Objective 9.10

Many activities are related to needs for (31)_____ and our efforts to maintain desired levels of (32)_____.

Drives for stimulation are partially explained by (33)_____ theory, which states that people seek to maintain ideal levels of (34)_____. People vary in their desired level of (35)_____, as measured by the Sensation-Seeking Scale.

(36)_____ performance usually occurs at moderate levels of arousal, as described by an inverted U function. The (37)_____ law further states that the ideal arousal level is higher for simple tasks and lower for complex tasks.

Survey Question: What are social motives? Why are they important? Pages 388-390, Objective 9.11

(38)_____ motives, which are learned, account for much of the diversity of human motivation.

One prominent social motive is the (39)_____ (nAch). High nAch is correlated with moderate risk taking and (40)_____ in many situations.

Self-confidence greatly affects (41)_____ in everyday life.

Survey Question: Are some motives more basic than others? Pages 390-392, Objectives 9.12, 9.13

(42)_____'s hierarchy of motives categorizes needs as either basic or growth oriented. Lower needs are assumed to be prepotent ((43)_____) over higher needs. Self-actualization, the (44)_____ and most fragile need, is reflected in meta-needs.

(45)_____ are closely related to intrinsic motivation. In some situations, external rewards can (46)_____ intrinsic motivation, enjoyment, and creativity.

Module 9.4 Emotion and Physiological Arousal

Survey Question: What happens during emotion? Pages 394-395, Objective 9.14

Emotions can be (47)_____, but overall they help us to adapt and survive. An emotion consists of (48)_____ changes, adaptive behavior, emotional expressions, and emotional (49)_____.

The (50)_____ emotions of fear, surprise, sadness, disgust, anger, anticipation, joy, and acceptance can be mixed to produce (51)_____ emotional experiences.

Bodily changes that occur during emotion are caused by the (52)_____ adrenaline and by activity in the (53)_____ nervous system (ANS).

The sympathetic branch of the ANS is primarily responsible for (54)_____ the body, the parasympathetic branch for (55)_____ it.

Survey Question: Can "lie detectors" really detect lies? Pages 395-398, Objective 9.15

The (56)_____, or "lie detector," measures emotional arousal (rather than lying) by monitoring heart rate, blood pressure, breathing rate, and the galvanic skin response (GSR).

Under some circumstances, the accuracy of the lie detector can be quite (57)_____.

Module 9.5 Emotional Expression and Theories of Emotion

Survey Question: How accurately are emotions expressed by the face and "body language"? Pages 400-402, Objective 9.16

Basic (58)_____ of fear, anger, disgust, sadness, and happiness are universal.
Contempt, (59)_____, and interest may be, too.
Body gestures and movements ((60)_____) express (61)_____
rather than specific universal messages.
(62)_____ reveal pleasantness versus unpleasantness, attention versus rejection, and a
person's degree of emotional activation. (63)_____ expresses relaxation or tension
and liking or disliking.

Survey Question: How do psychologists explain emotions? Pages 402-406, Objective 9.17

The (64)_____ theory says that emotional experience follows bodily reactions. In
contrast, the (65)_____ theory says that bodily reactions and emotional experiences occur
at the same time.
(66)_____ cognitive theory emphasizes that labeling bodily arousal can determine what
emotion you feel. Emotions are also influenced by attribution
((67)_____).
The (68)_____ hypothesis holds that facial expressions help define the emotions we
feel.
Contemporary views of emotion emphasize the effects of (69)_____. Also, our
feelings and actions (70)_____ as each element of emotion interacts with others. One of the
best ways to manage emotion is to (71)_____ your emotional appraisal of a situation.

Module 9.6 Psychology in Action

Survey Question: What does it mean to have "emotional intelligence"? Pages 408-409, Objective 9.18

(72)_____ is the ability to consciously make your emotions work for you in a wide
variety of life circumstances.
Important elements of emotional intelligence include (73)_____, empathy, an ability to
(74)_____ emotions, understanding emotion, and knowing how to use emotions to enhance
thinking, decision-making, and (75)_____.
(76)_____ emotions are valuable because they tend to broaden our focus and they encourage
personal growth and (77)_____.

Connections

Module 9.1

1. _____ incentive value	a. internal deficiency
2. _____ motivational model	b. goal desirability
3. _____ need	c. learned goals
4. _____ homeostasis	d. need reduction
5. _____ secondary motives	e. steady state

Module 9.2

1. _____ ventromedial hypothalamus 2. _____ lateral hypothalamus 3. _____ paraventricular nucleus	
1. _____ extracellular thirst 2. _____ satiety system 3. _____ taste aversion 4. _____ set point 5. _____ hunger and satiety 6. _____ body mass index 7. _____ weight cycling 8. _____ changes eating habits 9. _____ feeding system 10. _____ estrus	a. weight/height2 x 703 b. classical condition c. result from diarrhea d. thermostat for fat level e. lateral hypothalamus f. estrogen levels g. yo-yo dieting h. paraventricular nucleus i. ventromedial hypothalamus j. behavioral dieting

Module 9.3

1. _____ safety and security 2. _____ basic needs 3. _____ love and belonging 4. _____ self-actualization 5. _____ physiological needs 6. _____ esteem and self-esteem 7. _____ growth needs	
1. _____ safety and security 2. _____ heightened physiological arousal 3. _____ nAch 4. _____ SSS 5. _____ moderate risk takers 6. _____ meta-needs 7. _____ extrinsic motivation	a. standards of excellence b. self-actualization c. sensation seekers d. impaired test performance e. high in nAch f. hierarchy of needs g. external rewards

Module 9.4

1. _____	adrenaline	a. eight primary emotions
2. _____	parasympathetic rebound	b. arousal-producing hormone
3. _____	Robert Plutchik	c. "Did you murder Hensley?"
4. _____	irrelevant questions	d. nonemotional questions
5. _____	polygraph	e. prolonged mild emotion
6. _____	sympathetic branch	f. fight or flight
7. _____	relevant questions	g. intense emotional overreaction
8. _____	mood	h. lie detection

Module 9.5

1. _____	anxiety	a. arousal + label then emotions
2. _____	sadness	b. bodily arousal then emotions
3. _____	authentic happiness	c. mixing 2+ facial emotions
4. _____	James-Lange theory	d. appraisal of loss
5. _____	body language	e. appraisal of threat
6. _____	facial blend	f. kinesics
7. _____	self-awareness	g. emotional skills
8. _____	Schachter's cognitive theory	h. in tune with own feelings
9. _____	emotional intelligence	i. emphasize natural strengths

Module 9.6

1. _____	emotional intelligence	a. amplify or restrain
2. _____	self-awareness	b. reading others' emotion
3. _____	self-control	c. competence and ability to use emotion
4. _____	empathy	d. recognize and label how you feel

Check Your Memory

Module 9.1 Overview of Motivation

Survey Question: What is motivation? Are there different types of motives? Pages 372-375, Objectives 9.1, 9.2, 9.3

T F   1. The terms *need* and *drive* are used interchangeably to describe motivation.

T F   2. Incentive value refers to the "pull" of valued goals.

T F   3. Primary motives are based on needs that must be met for survival.

T F   4. Much of the time, homeostasis is maintained by automatic reactions within the body.

Module 9.2 Hunger, Thirst, Pain, and Sex

Survey Question: What causes hunger? Overeating? Eating disorders? Pages 376-382, Objectives 9.4, 9.5, 9.6, 9.7

T F   5. Cutting the sensory nerves from the stomach abolishes hunger.

T F   6. Lowered levels of glucose in the blood can cause hunger.

T F   7. The body's hunger center is found in the thalamus.

T F   8. The paraventricular nucleus is sensitive to neuropeptide Y.

T F   9. Both glucagon-like peptide 1 (GLP-1) and leptin act as stop signals that inhibit eating.

T F   10. BMI is an estimation of body fat.

T F   11. Dieting speeds up the body's metabolic rate.

T F   12. Exercise makes people hungry and tends to disrupt dieting and weight loss.

T F   13. External cues have little impact on one's tendency to overeat.

T F   14. The fast-food industry promotes healthy and tasty products that have contributed to the problem of obesity.

T F   15. "Yo-yo dieting" refers to repeatedly losing and gaining weight through the process of bingeing and purging.

T F   16. Behavioral dieting changes habits without reducing the number of calories consumed.

T F   17. People who diet intensely every other day lose as much weight as those who diet moderately every day.

T F   18. Charting daily progress is a basic behavioral dieting technique.

T F   19. The incentive value of foods is largely determined by cultural values.

T F   20. Taste aversions may be learned after longer time delays than in other forms of classical conditioning.

T F   21. Taste aversions tend to promote nutritional imbalance.

T F   22. Many victims of anorexia nervosa overestimate their body size.

T F   23. Overtime anorexics lose their appetite and do not feel hungry.

T F   24. Treatment for anorexia begins with counseling.

Survey Question: Is there more than one type of thirst? In what ways are pain avoidance and the sex drive unusual? Pages 383-384, Objectives 9.8, 9.9

T F   25. Bleeding, vomiting, or sweating can cause extracellular thirst.

T F   26. Intracellular thirst is best satisfied by a slightly salty liquid.

T F   27. Tolerance for pain is largely unaffected by learning.

T F   28. Getting drunk decreases sexual desire, arousal, pleasure, and performance.

Module 9.3 Arousal, Achievement, and Growth Needs

Survey Question: How does arousal relate to motivation? Pages 386-388, Objective 9.10

T F   29. It is uncomfortable to experience both very high and very low levels of arousal.

T F   30. Disinhibition and boredom susceptibility are characteristics of sensation-seeking persons.

T F 31. For nearly all activities, the best performance occurs at high levels of arousal.

T F 32. Test anxiety is a combination of arousal and excessive worry.

T F 33. Being overprepared is a common cause of test anxiety.

Survey Question: What are social motives? Why are they important? Pages 388-390, Objective 9.11
T F 34. The need for achievement refers to a desire to have impact on other people.

T F 35. Subliminal self-help audiotapes such as "Improve Study Habits" and "Passing Exams" are effective. That is why each year consumers spend millions of dollars on them.

T F 36. People high in nAch generally prefer "long shots" or "sure things."

T F 37. Benjamin Bloom found that high achievement is based as much on hard work as it is on talent.

T F 38. Subliminal motivational tapes are no more effective than placebo tapes that lack any "hidden messages."

T F 39. For many activities, self-confidence is one of the most important sources of motivation.

Survey Question: Are some motives more basic than others? Pages 390-392, Objectives 9.12, 9.13
T F 40. Maslow's hierarchy of needs places self-esteem at the top of the pyramid.

T F 41. Maslow believed that needs for safety and security are more prepotent than needs for love and belonging.

T F 42. Meta-needs are the most basic needs in Maslow's hierarchy.

T F 43. Maslow believed that most people are motivated to seek esteem, love and security rather than self-actualization.

T F 44. Intrinsic motivation occurs when obvious external rewards are provided for engaging in an activity.

T F 45. People are more likely to be creative when they are intrinsically motivated.

T F 46. Happy, positive moods are as equally adaptive as negative moods in influencing creativity, efficiency, and helpfulness to others.

Module 9.4 Emotion and Physiological Arousal
Survey Question: What happens during emotion? Pages 394-395, Objective 9.14
T F 47. Emotions help people survive by bonding with each other as they socialize and work together.

T F 48. Most physiological changes during emotion are related to the release of adrenaline into the brain.

T F 49. Robert Plutchik's theory lists contempt as a primary emotion.

T F 50. For most students, elevated moods tend to occur on Saturdays and Tuesdays.

T F 51. Positive emotions are processed mainly in the left hemisphere of the brain.

T F 52. The sympathetic branch of the ANS is under voluntary controls and the parasympathetic branch is involuntary.

T F 53. The parasympathetic branch of the ANS slows the heart and lowers blood pressure.

T F 54. Most sudden deaths due to strong emotion are associated with the traumatic disruption of a close relationship.

Survey Question: Can "lie detectors" really detect lies? Pages 395-398, Objective 9.15

T F   55. The polygraph measures the body's unique physical responses to lying.

T F   56. Only a guilty person should react emotionally to irrelevant questions.

T F   57. Control questions used in polygraph exams are designed to make almost everyone anxious.

T F   58. The lie detector's most common error is to label innocent persons guilty.

T F   59. Gestures such as rubbing hands, twisting hair, and biting lips are consistently related to lying.

Module 9.5 Emotional Expression and Theories of Emotion

Survey Question: How accurately are emotions expressed by the face and "body language"? Pages 400-402, Objective 9.16

T F   60. Children born deaf and blind express emotions with their faces in about the same way as other people do.

T F   61. People from Asian cultures are more likely to express anger in public than people from Western cultures.

T F   62. In Western cultures, men tend to be more emotionally expressive than women.

T F   63. The "A-okay" hand gesture means "everything is fine" around the world.

T F   64. Facial blends mix two or more basic expressions.

T F   65. Liking is expressed in body language by leaning back and relaxing the extremities.

Survey Question: How do psychologists explain emotions? Pages 402-406, Objective 9.17

T F   66. The James-Lange theory of emotion says that we see a bear, feel fear, are aroused, and then run.

T F   67. The Cannon-Bard theory states that emotion and bodily arousal occur at the same time.

T F   68. According to Schachter's cognitive theory, arousal must be labeled in order to become an emotion.

T F   69. Attribution theory predicts that people are most likely to "love" someone who does not agitate, anger, and frustrate them.

T F   70. Making facial expressions can actually cause emotions to occur and alter physiological activities in the body.

T F   71. Emotional appraisal refers to deciding if your own facial expressions are appropriate for the situation you are in.

T F   72. Moving toward a desired goal is associated with the emotion of happiness.

T F   73. Emotional intelligence refers to the ability to use primarily the right cerebral hemisphere to process emotional events.

Module 9.6 Psychology in Action

Survey Question: What does it mean to have "emotional intelligence"? Pages 408-409, Objective 9.18

T F   74. People who excel in life tend to be emotionally intelligent.

T F   75. People who are empathetic are keenly tuned in to their own feelings.

T F   76. People who are emotionally intelligent know what causes them to feel various emotions.

T F   77. Negative emotions can be valuable because they impart useful information to us.

176

T F   78. Positive emotions produce urges to be creative, to explore, and to seek new experiences.

T F   79. Martin Seligman believes that to be genuinely happy, people must cultivate their own natural strengths.

T F   80. A first step toward becoming emotionally intelligent is to pay attention to and value your feelings and emotional reactions.

Critical Thinking

Module 9.1

1. Many people mistakenly believe that they suffer from "hypoglycemia" (low blood sugar), which is often blamed for fatigue, difficulty concentrating, irritability, and other symptoms. Why is it unlikely that many people actually have hypoglycemia?

Module 9.2

2. Kim, who is overweight, is highly sensitive to external eating cues. How might her wristwatch contribute to her overeating?

Module 9.3

3. Many U.S. college freshmen say that "being well-off financially" is an essential life goal and that "making more money" was a very important factor in their decision to attend college. Which meta-needs are fulfilled by "making more money"?

Module 9.4

4. Can you explain why people "cursed" by shamans or "witch doctors" sometimes actually die?

Module 9.5

5. People with high spinal injuries may feel almost no signs of physiological arousal from their bodies. Nevertheless they still feel emotion, which can be intense at times. What theory of emotion does this observation contradict?

Module 9.6

6. You are angry because a friend borrowed money from you and hasn't repaid it. What would be an emotionally intelligent response to this situation?

Final Survey and Review

Module 9.1 Overview of Motivation

Survey Question: What is motivation? Objective 9.1

1. Motives _____, sustain, and _____ activities. Many motives involve the following sequence: need, _____, goal, and goal _____ (need reduction).

2. Behavior can be activated either by _____ (push) or by _____ (pull).

3. The attractiveness of a goal and its _____ to initiate action are related to its _____ value.

Survey Question: Are there different types of motives? Objectives 9.2, 9.3

4. Three basic categories of motives are primary motives, _____, and secondary motives.

5. Most primary motives operate to maintain _____.

6. Circadian rhythms are closely tied to _____, _____, and _____ cycles. Time zone travel and shift work can seriously disrupt _____, _____, and bodily rhythms.

Module 9.2 Hunger, Thirst, Pain, and Sex

Survey Question: What causes hunger? Overeating? Eating disorders? Objectives 9.4, 9.5, 9.6, 9.7

7. Hunger is influenced by a complex interplay between _____ of the stomach, blood sugar levels, metabolism in the _____, and fat stores in the_____.

8. The most direct _____ of eating comes from the hypothalamus, which is sensitive to both _____ and _____ messages that affect eating.

9. Other factors influencing hunger are the body's set point, _____ eating cues, the _____ and _____ of diet, emotions, learned taste preferences and _____, and cultural values.

10. Obesity is the result of internal and external influences, diet, _____, _____, and exercise.

11. Behavioral dieting is based on techniques that change _____ patterns and _____ habits.

12. Anorexia nervosa and bulimia nervosa are two prominent _____. Both tend to involve conflicts about self-image, _____, and anxiety.

Survey Question: Is there more than one type of thirst? In what ways are pain avoidance and the sex drive unusual? Objectives 9.8, 9.9

13. Like hunger, _____ are primarily under the central control of the hypothalamus. Thirst may be either _____ or _____.

14. Pain _____ is episodic as opposed to cyclic. Pain _____ and pain _____ are partially learned.

15. The sex drive is unusual because it is _____.

Module 9.3 Arousal, Achievement, and Growth Needs

Survey Question: How does arousal relate to motivation? Objective 9.10

16. Many activities are related to _____ for stimulation and our efforts to maintain _____ of arousal.

17. Drives for stimulation are partially explained by arousal theory, which states that people seek to _____ _____ of bodily arousal. People vary in their desired level of arousal or stimulation, as measured by the _____.

18. Optimal performance usually occurs at _____ levels of arousal, as described by an _____ function. The Yerkes-Dodson law further states that the ideal arousal level is _____ for simple tasks and _____ for complex tasks.

Survey Question: What are social motives? Why are they important? Objective 9.11

19. Social motives, which are _____, account for much of the diversity of human motivation.

20. One prominent _____ is the need for achievement (nAch). High nAch is correlated with _____ risk taking and success in many situations.

21. _____ greatly affects motivation in everyday life.

Survey Question: Are some motives more basic than others? Objectives 9.12, 9.13

22. Maslow's hierarchy of motives categorizes needs as either _____ or _____ oriented. Lower needs are assumed to be _____ (dominant) over higher needs. Self-actualization, the highest and most _____ need, is reflected in _____.

23. Meta-needs are closely related to _____ motivation. In some situations, _____ can undermine _____ motivation, enjoyment, and _____.

Module 9.4 Emotion and Physiological Arousal

Survey Question: What happens during emotion? Objective 9.14

24. Emotions can be disruptive, but overall they help us to _____ and _____. An emotion consists of physiological changes, _____ behavior, emotional _____, and emotional feelings.

25. The primary emotions of fear, _____, sadness, _____, anger, anticipation, joy, and _____ can be mixed to produce more complex emotional experiences.

26. _____ changes that occur during emotion are caused by the hormone _____ and by _____ in the autonomic nervous system (ANS).

27. The _____ branch of the ANS is primarily responsible for arousing the body, the _____ branch for quieting it.

Survey Question: Can "lie detectors" really detect lies? Objective 9.15

28. The polygraph, or "lie detector," measures _____ (rather than lying) by monitoring heart rate, blood pressure, breathing rate, and the _____ (GSR).

29. Under some circumstances, the _____ of the lie detector can be quite low.

Module 9.5 Emotional Expression and Theories of Emotion

Survey Question: How accurately are emotions expressed by the face and "body language"? Objective 9.16

30. Basic facial expressions of fear, _____, disgust, _____, and happiness are universal. _____, surprise, and interest may be, too.

31. Body _____ and movements (body language) express general emotional tone rather than _____ _____ messages.

32. Facial expressions reveal _____ versus _____, _____ versus _____, and a person's degree of emotional activation. Body positioning expresses _____ or _____ and liking or disliking.

Survey Question: How do psychologists explain emotions? Objective 9.17

33. The James-Lange theory says that _____ follows _____. In contrast, the Cannon-Bard theory says that _____ and _____ occur at the same time.

34. Schachter's cognitive theory emphasizes that _____ can determine what emotion you feel. Emotions are also influenced by _____ (ascribing arousal to a particular source).

35. The facial feedback hypothesis holds that facial expressions help _____ the emotions we feel.

36. Contemporary views of emotion _____ the effects of cognitive appraisals. Also, our feelings and actions change as each element of emotion _____ with others. One of the best ways to manage emotion is to change your emotional _____ of a situation.

Module 9.6 Psychology in Action

Survey Question: What does it mean to have "emotional intelligence"? Objective 9.18

37. Emotional intelligence is the ability to _____ make your emotions _____ in a wide variety of life circumstances.

38. Important elements of emotional intelligence include self-awareness, _____, an ability to manage emotions, _____ emotion, and knowing how to use emotions to _____ thinking, decision-making, and relationships.

39. Positive emotions are _____ because they tend to _____ our focus and they _____ personal growth and social connection.

Mastery Test

1. Which of the following is NOT one of the signs of emotional arousal recorded by a polygraph?
   a. heart rate
   b. pupil dilation
   c. blood pressure
   d. breathing rate

2. Plain water is most satisfying when a person has _____ thirst.
   a. intracellular
   b. hypothalamic
   c. extracellular
   d. homeostatic

3. We have a biological tendency to associate an upset stomach with foods eaten earlier. This is the basis for the development of
   a. taste aversions.
   b. yo-yo dieting.
   c. bulimia.
   d. frequent weight cycling.

4. Strong external rewards tend to undermine
   a. extrinsic motivation.
   b. intrinsic motivation.
   c. prepotent motivation.
   d. stimulus motivation.

5. Activity in the ANS is directly responsible for which element of emotion?
   a. emotional feelings
   b. emotional expressions
   c. physiological changes
   d. misattributions

6. Empathy is a major element of
   a. nAch.
   b. intrinsic motivation.
   c. emotional intelligence.
   d. the sensation-seeking personality.

7. Motivation refers to the ways in which activities are initiated, sustained, and
    a. acquired.
    b. valued.
    c. directed.
    d. aroused.

8. The psychological state or feeling we call thirst corresponds to which element of motivation?
    a. need
    b. drive
    c. deprivation
    d. incentive value

9. People who score high on the SSS generally prefer
    a. low levels of arousal.
    b. moderate levels of arousal.
    c. high levels of arousal.
    d. the middle of the V function.

10. Which facial expression is NOT recognized by people of all cultures?
    a. anger
    b. disgust
    c. optimism
    d. fear

11. Learning to weaken eating cues is useful in
    a. self-selection feeding.
    b. yo-yo dieting.
    c. rapid weight cycling.
    d. behavioral dieting.

12. People who score high on tests of the need for achievement tend to be
    a. motivated by power and prestige.
    b. moderate risk takers.
    c. sensation seekers.
    d. attracted to long shots.

13. Which theory holds that emotional feelings, arousal, and behavior are generated simultaneously in the brain?
    a. James-Lange
    b. Cannon-Bard
    c. cognitive
    d. attribution

14. Compared with people in North America, people in Asian cultures are less likely to express which emotion?
    a. anger
    b. jealousy
    c. curiosity
    d. fear

15. Binge eating is most associated with
    a. bulimia nervosa.
    b. bait shyness.
    c. low levels of NPY.
    d. anorexia nervosa.

16. Goals that are desirable are high in
    a. need reduction.
    b. incentive value.
    c. homeostatic valence.
    d. motivational "push".

17. _____ is to pain avoidance as _____ is to the sex drive.
    a. Nonhomeostatic, episodic
    b. Episodic, nonhomeostatic
    c. Nonhomeostatic, cyclic
    d. Cyclic, nonhomeostatic

18. A specialist in kinesics could be expected to be most interested in
    a. facial blends.
    b. circadian rhythms.
    c. sensation seeking.
    d. primary motives.

19. Coping statements are a way to directly correct which part of test anxiety?
    a. overpreparation
    b. underarousal
    c. excessive worry
    d. compulsive rehearsal

20. Drives for exploration and activity are categorized as
    a. primary motives
    b. secondary motives
    c. stimulus motives
    d. extrinsic motives

21. Sudden death following a period of intense fear may occur when _____ slows the heart to a stop.
    a. a sympathetic overload
    b. adrenaline poisoning
    c. opponent-process feedback
    d. a parasympathetic rebound

22. People who enjoy skydiving and ski jumping are very likely high in
    a. parasympathetic arousal.
    b. extrinsic motivation.
    c. their desires to meet meta-needs.
    d. the trait of sensation seeking.

23. You could induce eating in a laboratory rat by activating the
    a. lateral hypothalamus.
    b. corpus callosum.
    c. rat's set point.
    d. ventromedial hypothalamus.

24. People think cartoons are funnier if they see them while holding a pen crosswise in their teeth. This observation supports
    a. the James-Lange theory.
    b. the Cannon-Bard theory.
    c. Schachter's cognitive theory.
    d. the facial feedback hypothesis.

25. Basic biological motives are closely related to
    a. nAch.
    b. homeostasis.
    c. activity in the thalamus.
    d. levels of melatonin in the body.

26. Self-actualization is to _____ needs as safety and security are to _____ needs.
    a. growth, basic
    b. basic, meta-
    c. prepotent, basic
    d. meta-, extrinsic

27. Which of the following is NOT a core element of emotion?
    a. physiological changes
    b. emotional expressions
    c. emotional feelings
    d. misattributions

28. The effects of a "supermarket diet" on eating are related to the effects of _____ on eating.
    a. anxiety
    b. metabolic rates
    c. incentive value
    d. stomach distention

29. According to the Yerkes-Dodson law, optimum performance occurs at _____ levels of arousal for simple tasks and _____ levels of arousal for complex tasks.
    a. higher, lower
    b. lower, higher
    c. minimum, high
    d. average, high

30. Contemporary models of emotion place greater emphasis on _____, or the way situations are evaluated.
   a. appraisal
   b. attribution
   c. feedback
   d. emotional tone

31. Which statement correctly explains why there is an obesity problem in the United States?
   a. The all-you-can-eat dining halls and restaurants temp people to overeat.
   b. Although the food industry has made dinner easier to cook and buy, the food is high in fat and sugar.
   c. Overeating during large meals increases one's body set point.
   d. All the preceding

32. Although in some parts of the world, eating monkey eyes is considered a delicacy, to Americans it is not. This difference in preference is largely influenced by
   a. cultural values.
   b. primary motives.
   c. the availability of taste buds.
   d. overdeveloped hypothalamus.

33. Bev placed herself on a strict diet of eating no other fruits except for grapefruit. Eventually, she began to crave other fruits and could not stand seeing, smelling, or tasting another grapefruit. One explanation for Bev's strong dislike of grapefruit is her body was trying to avoid nutritional imbalance by producing
   a. positive reinforcement.
   b. a taste aversion.
   c. shaping.
   d. purging.

34. The causes of anorexia have been attributed to
   a. unrealistic comparison of body image to others.
   b. seeking control.
   c. distorted body image.
   d. all the preceding

35. Variables that aid our survival include _____ moods, which help us make better decisions and be more helpful, efficient, and creative. The ability to understand and display _____ expressions such as anger helps us communicate with others.
   a. primary, universal
   b. negative, natural
   c. positive, facial
   d. natural, primary

36. The National Academy of Sciences has concluded that polygraph tests should not be used to screen _____ since the test tends to label honest people dishonest.
   a. immigrants
   b. employees
   c. government officials
   d. mentally disturbed people

37. According to Martin Seligman, to be genuinely happy, one must
   a. optimize one's natural strengths.
   b. focus on fixing one's weaknesses.
   c. strengthen negative emotions to better understand positive emotions.
   d. balance both negative and positive emotions.

Chapter 10: Personality

Chapter Overview

Personality is how psychologists describe the pattern of behaviors that makes you uniquely you. Each of the major psychological perspectives has developed a theory for what personality is and where it comes from.

One way to think about your personality is as a collection of traits. Some traits might help predict your behavior in only certain situations; other, more central ones, might predict your actions in a majority of circumstances. Theorists have debated about the number of traits necessary to accurately describe a person; the popular view today is that there are five key dimensions.

Psychodynamic theorists explore unconscious motives, often formed in early childhood. Freud began this movement, and is most well-known, but there are other psychodynamic theorist who borrowed parts of Freud's theory and rejected other parts.

Behaviorists believe that personality is learned just like any other behavior, through conditioning or social learning from one's environment and circumstances.

Humanistic theorists, such as Rogers, believe that the personality, or "self," is based on the motivation to feel good about oneself and to improve in the process of achieving one's goals. Self-worth and self discovery are important aspects of personality.

Personality can be measured in a number of ways: through interviews, observations of behaviors, self-reports, or projective tests.

The last section in this chapter explores shyness as an example of a personality characteristic.

Learning Objectives

OBJECTIVE 10.1 — Define the term *personality* and explain how personality differs from character and temperament.

OBJECTIVE 10.2 — Explain what a *personality trait* is and discuss the stability of personality traits; define *behavioral genetics* and describe the findings of the twin studies regarding the contribution of heredity and environment; and explain how some of the "amazing similarities" between twins can be explained, including the *fallacy of positive instances*.

OBJECTIVE 10.3 — Define the term *personality type;* describe the characteristics of introverts and extroverts; and explain the advantages and disadvantages of using types to classify personalities.

OBJECTIVE 10.4 — Explain the terms *self-concept* and *self-esteem* and how they affect behavior and personal adjustment; and explain the differences in how Eastern and Western cultures view self-esteem.

OBJECTIVE 10.5 — Define the term *personality theory*; describe Eysenck's dimensions of personality that were first recognized by the early Greeks (Fig. 10.2) ; explain the best way to judge a theory; and compare and contrast the trait theories, psychoanalytic theory, behavioristic and social learning theories, and the humanistic theory (Table 10.1).

OBJECTIVE 10.6 — Explain how each of the trait theories describes personality and which theory is currently the most influenential: a. Rentfrow and Gosling's musical personalities; b. Gordon Allport; c. Raymond Cattell; d. the Five-Factor Model of Personality; and discuss unhealthy perfectionism and what is meant by *trait-situation interaction*.

OBJECTIVE 10.7 — Discuss Freud's view of personality development, including the three parts of the personality; b. neurotic and moral anxiety; c. the three levels of awareness; d. the psychosexual stages and fixations; and e. the positive and negative aspects of Freud's theory.

OBJECTIVE 10.8 — Describe how behavioral theorists view personality; and explain how strict behaviorists differ from social learning theorists by discussing the behavioral concepts of *situational determinants, habit, drive, cue, response, and reward* and the social learning concepts of *psychological situation, expectancy, reinforcement value, self-efficacy*, and *self-reinforc*ement.

OBJECTIVE 10.9 — Explain why Freud and the behaviorists both considered the first six years of life important to personality development; define social reinforcement; describe Dollard and Miller's critical situations in development; and discuss the role of imitation and identification in personality development and how Western cultures encourage boys to engage in instrumental behaviors and girls, in expressive behaviors.

OBJECTIVE 10.10 — Briefly explain how humanism differs from the Freudian and behaviorist viewpoints of personality; discuss Maslow's concept of self-actualization, the characteristics of self-actualizers, and ways to promote self-actualization; and describe the six human strengths that contribute to well-being and life satisfaction.

OBJECTIVE 10.11 — Discuss Rogers' views of a fully functioning individual; define his concepts of the *self, self-image, incongruence, being authentic, ideal self, conditions of worth, organismic valuing, positive self-regard*, and *unconditional positive regard*; and explain how *possible selves* and the *narrative approach* can help to direct our future behavior.

OBJECTIVE 10.12 — Discuss the following assessment techniques in terms of purpose, method, advantages, and limitations: a. structured and unstructured interviews, including the problem of the *halo effect*; b. direct observation using rating scales, behavioral assessment, and/or situational testing; c. personality questionnaires, including the definitions of test *reliability* and *validity* and an overview of the MMPI-2; d. honesty tests; e. projective tests, including an overview of the Rorschach and the TAT; and f. a test battery.

OBJECTIVE 10.13 — Describe the personality characteristics of sudden murderers, and explain how their characteristics differ from those of habitually violent persons.

OBJECTIVE 10.14 — Discuss the characeristics of shyness; its causes; why shyness involves public self-consciousness rather than private self-consciousness; the key difference in shy and not-shy persons; how shyness is maintained by four self-defeating beliefs; and how shyness can be treated by replacing these unproductive beliefs and learning social skills.

Language Development Guide

Introduction

(412) *brain-jarring rut*: large trench in the road

(412) *dilapidated*: in disrepair, run down

(412) *hooting and whooping*: happy screams

(412) *lumberjack, lumberjill*: person who cuts down trees

(412) *zaniest*: most crazy or silly

Module 10.1

(414) *Do you know any good characters?:* Do you know anyone with an entertaining personality?

(414) *keep your bearings*: stay organized

(415) *preposterous*: ridiculous

(415) *eerie*: in this case, remarkable; usually used to mean scary, creepy, spooky, unsettling

(415) *span many years*: last a long time

(416) *tics*: twitches or spasms, habits

(416) *wired in*: established, permanent

(416) *techno geek*: someone skilled with computers and other technology

(417) *maladaptive*: damaging, harmful

(417) *think you're hot*: hold a high opinion of yourself, be egotistical

(417) *bestowed*: given, awarded

(417) *dazzling array*: variety, several

(418) *bask in the glow*: enjoy, celebrate

(418) *hotshot*: celebrity

(418) *pumped up by:* encouraged by

(418) *downplay*: ignore, minimize, reduce the importance of

(418) *a sort of lens*: a method, a perspective

(418) *fared differently:* some have performed well, some have performed poorly

Module 10.2

(421) *face-to-face:* in person, directly

(422) *reflective*: causing someone to think

(423) *space capsule*: small vehicle, pod, ship, for traveling off of the planet

(424) *is a recipe for*: leads to, causes

(425) *off-color jokes*: humor that is rude or offensive, disrespectful, racist or sexist

(425) *boisterous*: excited and happy

Module 10.3

(427) *Id came to me in a dream:* play on the words, "it came to me in a dream", meaning you had a vision - joke comes from the use of Freud's concept of the Id, and the importance of dreams in understanding the unconscious

(428) *in a nutshell*: briefly, to summarize

(428) *Go for it!:* give it a try, do it

(429) *push-ups:* a form of exercise

(430) *hang-up*: problem, barrier

(430) *overindulgence*: doing too much of something

(430) *Biting sarcasm*: cruel humor

(430) *forte*: strength or specialty; also, in music, means loud

(430) *obstinate*: stubborn, unwilling to change

(430) *Oedipus*: (ED-eh-puss), character in a Greek tragedy who mistakenly fell in love with his mother and killed his father

(430) *Electra*: (eh-LECK-truh), character in a Greek tragedy who kills her mother

(430) *dormant*: asleep or withdrawn, appearing dead

(430) *offshoot*: extension, variation

Module 10.4

(432) *Data of Star Trek:* an android character on a television show, a computer made to look and act human

(432) *mud pies:* playing with wet dirt

(432) *blender*: kitchen appliance used for cutting and mixing

(432) *checkout line*: queue, row of people waiting in a store to pay for their purchases

(433) *menacing*: looking dangerous

(433) *face a fact*: notice, admit

(433) *or an accident*: unintended

(433) *has paid off:* has been successful

(434) *ask him or her out*: invite on a date

(434) *snowboard*: mountain winter sport using a single, wide panel instead of skis

(434) *counterpart*: alternative

(434) *good to yourself*: treat yourself well

(435) *crushing frustrations*: strong disappointments

(435) *aghast*: horrified

Module 10.5

(438) *mule*: mix of a horse and a donkey

(438) *encourage our potentials to blossom:* like growing a flower, to grow and develop toward our goals and hopes

(438) *spontaneous*: unplanned

(439) *wry*: ironic humor

(439) *prodding*: soft push, nudge

(439) *shortcomings*: mistakes or flaws

(439) *shouldering responsibility*: accepting, taking charge of

(440) *proponents*: supporters

(440) *prudence*: carefulness

(440) *gratitude*: thankfulness

(440) *ample*: lots, much

(440) *authentic*: real, true

(441) *carefree*: not worried about appearances

(441) *party animal:* person who prefers socializing to working or studying

(441) *conscientious*: responsible, organized

(441) *bookworm*: person who enjoys reading

(442) *enterprising*: innovative, hard-working

(442) *grossly obese*: very fat

Module 10.6

(444) *yardsticks*: measuring tool

(444) *caught off-guard*: seen when they do not expect it

(444) *probe*: examine, explore, study

(444) *contemplated*: thought about

(444) *geek*: intelligent but awkward person

(444) *ski bum*: someone who would rather ski than work or study

(445) *bus depots*: places to get tickets to ride a bus

(445) *taverns*: bars, pubs, saloons

(445) *disturbed*: mentally ill

(446) *American Idol*: real people compete to see who is the best singer

(446) *Survivor*: real people are stranded on an island without supplies and compete for prizes and vote to eliminate one another from the game

(446) *The Amazing Race*: pairs of people are given limited money and have to travel around the world completing tasks faster than the other teams

(446) *hold fire*: do not shoot

(447) *satirize*: make fun of, make a joke about

(447) *gag items*: funny joke statements, fake test

(448) *brushes with the law*: being arrested, illegal actions

(448) *sole*: only

(448) *inkblot*: pattern made by putting a pool of ink on a page and then folding the page

(448) *dagger*: knife

(450) *upsetting*: emotional

(450) *habitual violence*: many cases of past violent behavior

(450) *belittlement*: causing to feel unimportant or bad or foolish

Module 10.7

(452) *retreat*: run away

(452) *animation*: excitement, movement

(452) *novel*: new

(452) *see through them*: discover their deception

(453) *stage fright*: fear such as an actor feels when standing before an audience, fear of needing to perform well or be the center of attention in public

(453) *broken the ice*: became acquainted, begun to talk

Recite and Review

Module 10.1 Overview of Personality

Survey Question: How do psychologists use the term personality? What core concepts make up the psychology of personality? Pages 414-419, Objectives 10.2, 10.2, 10.3, 10.4, 10.5

(1)_____ refers to a person's unique pattern of thinking, emotion, and behavior.

(2) _____ is personality evaluated, or the possession of desirable qualities.

(3) _____ refers to the hereditary aspects of one's emotional nature.

(4) _____ are lasting personal qualities that are inferred from behavior.

Behavioral genetics and studies of (5) _____ how that heredity contributes significantly to

(6)_____.

Personality (7)_____ group people into categories on the basis of shared traits.

Behavior is influenced by (8)_____ and self-esteem.

Personality theories combine interrelated (9)_____, ideas, and principles to explain personality.

Four main types of (10)_____ are trait, psychodynamic, behavioristic and social learning, and humanistic.

Module 10.2 Trait Theories

Survey Question: Are some personality traits more basic or important than others? Pages 421-425, Objective 10.6

(11)_____ theories identify lasting and consistent personal characteristics.

(12)_____ made distinctions between common traits and individual traits and among cardinal, central, and secondary traits.

(13)_____ theory attributes visible surface traits to the existence of 16 underlying source traits.

The (14)_____ model identifies the following five universal dimensions of personality: extroversion, agreeableness, conscientiousness, neuroticism, and openness to experience.

Traits and situations (15)_____ to determine how we behave.

Module 10.3 Psychoanalytic Theory

Survey Question: How do psychodynamic theories explain personality? Pages 427-431, Objective 10.7

Psychodynamic theories emphasize (16)_____ (and often unconscious) forces and mental activities.

According to (17)_____'s psychoanalytic theory, personality consists of three mental systems: the id, the ego, and the (18)_____.

(19)_____, derived from the life instincts, is the primary source of (20)_____ within the personality.

Internal (21)_____ may cause neurotic anxiety or moral anxiety and lead to the use of (22)_____ mechanisms.

Personal awareness operates on three levels: (23)_____, preconscious, and unconscious.

According to Freud, personality development occurs in four psychosexual stages: (24)_____, anal, phallic, and (25)_____.

(26)_____ at any stage of psychosexual development can leave a lasting imprint on adult personality.

Module 10.4 Behavioral and Social Learning Theories

Survey Question: What do behaviorists and social learning theorists emphasize in personality? Pages 432-436, Objectives 10.8, 10.9

(27)_____ theories of personality emphasize (28)_____, conditioning, and the situational determinants of behavior.

Learning theorists (29)_____ and (30)_____ consider habits the basic core of personality.

(31)_____ express the combined effects of drive, cue, response, and reward.

To explain personality, (32)_____ theory combines learning with thinking, expectations, and other mental processes.

Social learning theory is exemplified by (33)_____'s concepts of the psychological situation, expectancies, and reinforcement value.

The behavioristic view of personality development holds that social (34)_____ in four situations is critical: feeding, (35)_____ training, sex training, and (36)_____ training.

Identification and (37) are of particular importance in learning to be "male" or "female."

Module 10.5 Humanistic Theories

Survey Question: How do humanistic theories differ from other perspectives? ? Pages 438-442, Objectives 10.10, 10.11

Humanistic theories stress subjective experience, (38)_____, self-actualization, and (39)_____ models of human nature.

(40)_____'s study of self-actualizers showed that they share traits that range from efficient perceptions of reality to frequent (41)_____ experiences.

(42)_____ is best viewed as an ongoing process of personal growth, rather than a (43)_____.

(44)_____ psychologists have identified six human strengths that contribute to well-being and life satisfaction: wisdom and knowledge, (45)_____, humanity, (46)_____, temperance, and transcendence.

(47)_____ viewed the self as an entity that emerges from personal (48)_____. (49)_____ functioning occurs when there is a good match between your true self, your self-image, and your (50)_____ self.

The (51)_____ person has an unrealistic self-image and/or a (52)_____ between the self-image and the ideal self. The (53)_____ or fully functioning person is flexible and open to experiences and (54)_____.

In the development of personality, humanists are interested in the emergence of a self-image and in (55)_____ _____.

As parents apply (56)_____ to children's behavior, thoughts, and feelings, children begin to (57)_____. Internalized conditions of worth then contribute to (58)_____.

(59)_____ self-regard is nurtured by organismic valuing and by receiving (60)_____ _____.

Module 10.6 Personality Assessment

Survey Question: How do psychologists measure personality? Pages 444-450, Objectives 10.12, 10.13

Personality is typically assessed with interviews, direct observation, (61)_____, and projective tests.

Structured and (62)_____ interviews provide much information, but they are subject to interviewer bias, misperceptions, and the (63)_____ effect.

(64)_____, sometimes involving situational tests, behavioral assessment, or (65)_____ scales, allows psychologists to evaluate a person's actual behavior.

To have any value, (66)_____ must be reliable and valid.

Personality questionnaires, such as the Minnesota Multiphasic Personality Inventory-2 (MMPI-2), are objective and (67)_____, but their (68)_____is open to question.

(69)_____ tests ask a person to project thoughts or feelings to an ambiguous stimulus or unstructured situation.

The Rorschach Technique, or (70)_____ test, is a well-known projective technique. A second is the (71) _____(TAT).

Projective tests are (72)_____ in validity and objectivity. Nevertheless, they are considered (73)_____ by many clinicians.

Accurate measures of personality often require the use of a test (74)_____ (collection of assessment devices and interviews).

Module 10.7 Psychology in Action

Survey Question: What causes shyness? What can be done about it? Pages 452-454, Objective 10.14

Shyness typically involves (75)_____, evaluation fears, self-defeating thoughts, public self-consciousness, and a lack of (76)_____.

Shyness is marked by heightened (77)_____ and a tendency to regard one's shyness as a (78)_____.

Shyness can be (79)_____ by replacing self-defeating beliefs with more supportive thoughts and by learning (80)_____.

Connections

Module 10.1

1. _____ character	a. heart attack risk
2. _____ trait	b. positive evaluation
3. _____ Type A	c. personality judged
4. _____ temperament	d. reserved, internally-focused
5. _____ extrovert	e. hereditary personality
6. _____ self-esteem	f. your perception of who you are
7. _____ self-concept	g. bold, outgoing
8. _____ introvert	h. lasting personal quality

Module 10.2

1. _____ cardinal traits	a. basic underlying dimensions
2. _____ conscientiousness	b. individual definition
3. _____ source traits	c. everything you do relates
4. _____ factor analysis	d. core traits that describe an individual
5. _____ individual traits	e. source traits
6. _____ neuroticism	f. culturally typical
7. _____ behavior genetics	g. emotional stability
8. _____ central traits	h. universal dimensions
9. _____ trait situation	i. statistical grouping
10. _____ 16 PF	j. hard-working, organized
11. _____ common traits	k. twin studies
12. _____ Big Five	l. interaction

Module 10.3

1. _____ Thanatos	a. mouth
2. _____ Eros	b. pride
3. _____ conscience	c. genitals
4. _____ ego ideal	d. female conflict
5. _____ oral stage	e. male conflict
6. _____ anal stage	f. death instinct
7. _____ phallic stage	g. elimination
8. _____ id	h. life instinct
9. _____ Oedipus complex	i. guilt
10. _____ Electra complex	j. pleasure principle
11. _____ conscious	k. mental contents you are aware of

Module 10.4

1. _____	self-efficacy	a. anticipation
2. _____	reward	b. belief in one's capability
3. _____	expectancy	c. learned behavior pattern
4. _____	situational determinants	d. positive reinforcer
5. _____	habits	e. external causes
6. _____	social learning	f. cognitive behaviorism

Module 10.5

1. _____	unconditional positive regard	a. self-image = ideal self
2. _____	Rogers	b. unshakable love
3. _____	Maslow	c. private perceptions of reality
4. _____	congruence	d. fully functioning person
5. _____	subjective experience	e. self-actualization

Module 10.6

1. _____	validity scale	a. Rorschach
2. _____	social anxiety	b. integrity at work
3. _____	MMPI	c. interview problem
4. _____	inkblot	d. personality questionnaire
5. _____	private self-consciousness	e. faking good
6. _____	situational test	f. Shoot Don't Shoot
7. _____	public self-consciousness	g. view self as social object
8. _____	honesty test	h. focus on inner feelings
9. _____	self-defeating bias	i. distortion in thinking
10. _____	halo effect	j. evaluation fears

Module 10.7

1. _____	social skills	a. attention to inner thoughts
2. _____	private self-consciousness	b. self-blame
3. _____	social anxiety	c. will be made fun of or embarrassed
4. _____	public self-consciousness	d. good at interacting with others
5. _____	evaluation fears	e. awareness of self as object
6. _____	self-defeating bias	f. nervous around others

Check Your Memory

Module 10.1 Overview of Personality

Survey Question: How do psychologists use the term personality? What core concepts make up the psychology of personality? Pages 414-419, Objectives 10.2, 10.2, 10.3, 10.4, 10.5

T F 1. The term *personality* refers to charisma or personal style.

T F 2. Personality is a person's relatively stable pattern of attitudes.

T F   3. Character refers to the inherited "raw material" from which personality is formed.

T F   4. A person with genuine high self-esteem has a tendency to accurately appraise his/her own strengths and weaknesses.

T F   5. In Asian cultures, self-esteem is strongly tied to personal achievement rather than group success.

T F   6. Traits are stable or lasting qualities of personality, displayed in most situations.

T F   7. Personality traits typically become quite stable by age 30 with the exception of conscientiousness and agreeability.

T F   8. Paranoid, dependent, and antisocial personalities are regarded as personality types.

T F   9. Two major dimensions of Eysenck's personality theory are stable-unstable and calm-moody.

T F   10. Trait theories of personality stress subjective experience and personal growth.

Module 10.2 Trait Theories
Survey Question: Are some personality traits more basic or important than others? Pages 421-425, Objective 10.6

T F   11. Extroverted students tend to study in noisy areas of the library.

T F   12. Peter Rentfrow and Samuel Gosling found that one's preference to music is linked to personality characteristics.

T F   13. People who are cheerful, conventional, extroverted, and reliable tend to prefer blues, jazz, and classical music.

T F   14. Nearly all of a person's activities can be traced to one or two common traits.

T F   15. Roughly seven central traits are needed, on the average, to describe an individual's personality.

T F   16. Allport used factor analysis to identify central traits.

T F   17. The 16 PF is designed to measure surface traits.

T F   18. Judging from scores on the 16 PF, airline pilots have traits that are similar to creative artists.

T F   19. As one of the Big Five factors, neuroticism refers to having negative, upsetting emotions.

T F   20. The expression of personality traits tends to be influenced by external situations.

T F   21. Similarities between reunited identical twins show that personality is mostly shaped by genetics.

T F   22. Studies of identical twins show that personality traits are approximately 70 percent hereditary.

T F   23. Some of the coincidences shared by identical twins appear to be based on the fallacy of positive instances.

T F   24. Unrelated people can share amazingly similar personality characteristics due to their age, gender, and living conditions.

Module 10.3 Psychoanalytic Theory
Survey Question: How do psychodynamic theories explain personality? Pages 427-431, Objective 10.7

T F   25. Freud described the id, ego, and superego as "little people" that manage the human psyche.

T F   26. The id is totally unconscious.

T F   27. The ego is guided by the pleasure principle.

T F   28. The superego is the source of feelings of guilt and pride.

T F 29. Threats of punishment from the Thanatos cause moral anxiety.

T F 30. Oral-dependent persons are gullible.

T F 31. Vanity and narcissism are traits of the anal-retentive personality.

T F 32. According to Freud, boys experience the Oedipus complex and girls experience the Electra complex.

T F 33. The genital stage occurs between the ages of three and six, just before latency.

T F 34. Boys are more likely to develop a strong conscience if their fathers are affectionate and accepting.

T F 35. Freud regarded latency as the most important stage of psychosexual development.

T F 36. Erik Erikson's psychosocial stages were derived, in part, from Freud's psychosexual stages.

Module 10.4 Behavioral and Social Learning Theories
Survey Question: What do behaviorists and social learning theorists emphasize in personality? Pages 432-436, Objectives 10.8, 10.9

T F 37. Behaviorists view personality as a collection of learned behavior patterns.

T F 38. Behaviorists attribute our actions to prior learning and specific situations.

T F 39. Behaviors are influenced by an interaction between the situation and previously gained knowledge.

T F 40. Knowing the consistent ways people respond to certain situations allows us to predict their personality characteristics.

T F 41. According to Dollard and Miller, habits are acquired through observational learning.

T F 42. Cues are signals from the environment that guide responses.

T F 43. An expectancy refers to the anticipation that making a response will lead to reinforcement.

T F 44. Self-reinforcement is highly related to one's self-esteem.

T F 45. People who are depressed tend to engage in a high rate of self-reinforcement to make themselves feel better.

T F 46. Social reinforcement is based on attention and approval from others.

T F 47. In elementary school, misbehaving boys typically get more attention from teachers than girls.

Module 10.5 Humanistic Theories
Survey Question: How do humanistic theories differ from other perspectives? Pages 438-442, Objectives 10.10, 10.11

T F 48. Humanists believe that humans are capable of free choice.

T F 49. To investigate self-actualization, Maslow studied eminent men and women exclusively.

T F 50. Self-actualizers usually try to avoid task centering.

T F 51. Personal autonomy is a characteristic of the self-actualizing person.

T F 52. People who live happy and meaningful lives are people who possess the traits characteristic of a self-actualizer and express such human strengths as courage, justice, and temperance.

T F 53. Information inconsistent with one's self-image is described as incongruent.

T F 54. Images of our possible selves are derived from our hopes, fears, fantasies, and goals.

T F 55. Poor self-knowledge is associated with high self-esteem because people do not have to think about their own faults.

T F 56. Congruence represents a close correspondence between self-image, the ideal self, and the true self.

T F 57. Images of possible selves typically cause feelings of incongruence.

T F 58. Rogers believed that organismic valuing is healthier than trying to meet someone else's conditions of worth.

Module 10.6 Personality Assessment
Survey Question: How do psychologists measure personality? Pages 444-450, Objectives 10.12, 10.13

T F 59. Planned questions are used in a structured interview.

T F 60. The halo effect may involve either a positive or a negative impression.

T F 61. Personality questionnaires are used to do behavioral assessments.

T F 62. Judgmental firearms training is a type of honesty test.

T F 63. Items on the MMPI-2 were selected for their ability to identify persons with psychiatric problems.

T F 64. The validity scale of the MMPI-2 is used to rate Type A behavior.

T F 65. The psychasthenia scale of the MMPI-2 detects the presence of phobias and compulsive actions.

T F 66. It is very easy to fake responses to a projective test.

T F 67. The TAT is a situational test.

T F 68. Habitually violent prison inmates are aggressive and overcontrolled.

Module 10.7 Psychology in Action
Survey Question: What causes shyness? What can be done about it? Pages 452-454, Objective 10.14

T F 69. Shyness is closely related to private self-consciousness.

T F 70. Non-shy persons believe that external situations cause their occasional feelings of shyness.

T F 71. The odds of meeting someone interested in socializing are about the same wherever you are.

T F 72. Open-ended questions help keep conversations going.

Critical Thinking

Module 10.1

1. In what way would memory contribute to the formation of an accurate or inaccurate self-image?

Module 10.2

2. Are situations equally powerful in their impact on behavior?

Module 10.3

3. Many adults would find it embarrassing or humiliating to drink from a baby bottle. Can you explain why?

Module 10.4

4. Rotter's concept of *reinforcement value* is closely related to a motivational principle discussed in Module 9.1. Can you name it?

Module 10.5

5. What role would "possible selves" have in the choice of a college major?

Module 10.6

6. Can you think of one more reason why personality traits may not be accurately revealed by interviews?

7. Projective testing would be of greatest interest to which type of personality theorist?

Module 10.7

8. Shyness is a trait of Vonda's personality. Like most shy people, Vonda is most likely to feel shy in unfamiliar social settings. Vonda's shy behavior demonstrates that the expression of traits is governed by what concept?

Final Survey and Review

Module 10.1 Overview of Personality

Survey Question: How do psychologists use the term personality? What core concepts make up the psychology of personality? Objectives 10.2, 10.2, 10.3, 10.4, 10.5

1. Personality refers to a person's unique pattern of _____, _____, and _____.
2. Character is personality _____, or the possession of _____ qualities.
3. Temperament refers to the _____ aspects of one's _____ nature.
4. Traits are lasting personal _____ that are inferred from _____.
5. _____ and studies of identical twins show that heredity _____ to personality traits.
6. Personality types group people into _____ on the basis of _____.
7. Behavior is influenced by self-concept and _____.
8. Personality theories _____ interrelated assumptions, ideas, and principles to explain personality.
9. Four main types of personality theories are _____, psychodynamic, _____ and social learning, and _____.

Module 10.2 Trait Theories

Survey Question: Are some personality traits more basic or important than others? Objective 10.6

10. Trait theories identify _____ and consistent personal _____.
11. Allport made distinctions between _____ traits and individual traits and among _____, central, and _____ traits.
12. Cattell's theory attributes visible _____ traits to the existence of 16 underlying _____ traits.
13. The five-factor model identifies the following five universal dimensions of personality: extroversion, _____, conscientiousness, _____, and openness to experience.
14. _____ and _____ interact to determine how we behave.

Module 10.3 Psychoanalytic Theory

Survey Question: How do psychodynamic theories explain personality? Objective 10.7

15. Psychodynamic theories emphasize internal (and often _____) forces and mental activities.

16. According to Sigmund Freud's psychoanalytic theory, personality consists of three mental systems: the _____, the _____, and the superego.

17. Libido, derived from the _____ instincts, is the primary _____ of energy within the personality.

18. Internal conflicts may cause _____ anxiety or _____ anxiety and lead to the use of ego-defense mechanisms.

19. _____ operates on three levels: conscious, _____, and unconscious.

20. According to Freud, personality development occurs in four _____ stages: oral, _____, _____, and genital.

21. Fixation at any stage of _____ development can _____ adult personality.

Module 10.4 Behavioral and Social Learning Theories

Survey Question: What do behaviorists and social learning theorists emphasize in personality? Objectives 10.8, 10.9

22. Behavioral theories of personality emphasize learning, _____, and the _____ determinants of behavior.

23. Learning theorists John Dollard and Neal Miller consider _____ the basic core of personality.

24. Habits express the combined effects of _____, _____, _____, and_____.

25. To explain personality, social learning theory combines learning with _____, _____, and other mental processes.

26. Social learning theory is exemplified by Julian Rotter's concepts of the psychological _____, _____, and reinforcement _____.

27. The behavioristic view of personality development holds that social reinforcement in four situations is critical: _____, toilet or cleanliness training, _____ training, and anger or aggression training.

28. _____ and imitation are of particular importance in learning to be "male" or "female."

Module 10.5 Humanistic Theories

Survey Question: How do humanistic theories differ from other perspectives? ? Objectives 10.10, 10.11

29. Humanistic theories stress _____, free choice, self-_____, and positive models of _____.

30. Abraham Maslow's study of _____ showed that they share traits that range from efficient perceptions of _____ to frequent peak experiences.

31. Self-actualization is best viewed as _____, rather than a final destination.

32. Positive psychologists have identified six human _____that contribute to well-being and life satisfaction: _____ and knowledge, courage, humanity, justice, _____, and _____.

33. Carl Rogers viewed the _____ as an entity that emerges from personal experience. Optimal functioning occurs when there is _____ between your true self, your _____, and your ideal self.

34. The incongruent person has an _____ self-image and/or a mismatch between the _____ and the _____. The congruent or _____ person is flexible and open to experiences and feelings.

35. In the development of personality, humanists are interested in _____ and in self-evaluations.

36. As _____ apply conditions of worth to _____'s behavior, thoughts, and feelings, _____ begin to do the same. _____ conditions of worth then contribute to incongruence.

37. Positive self-regard is nurtured by _____ and by receiving unconditional positive regard.

Module 10.6 Personality Assessment

Survey Question: How do psychologists measure personality? Objectives 10.12, 10.13

38. Personality is typically assessed with _____, direct _____, questionnaires, and _____ tests.

39. Structured and unstructured interviews provide _____, but they are subject to interviewer _____, _____, and the halo effect.

40. Direct observation, sometimes involving _____ tests, _____ assessment, or rating scales, allows psychologists to evaluate a person's _____ behavior.

41. To have any _____, personality measures must be reliable and _____.

42. Personality questionnaires, such as the _____(MMPI-2), are objective and reliable, but their validity is open to question.

43. Projective tests ask a person to project thoughts or feelings to an _____ stimulus or _____ situation.

44. The _____ Technique, or inkblot test, is a well-known projective technique. A second is the Thematic _____ Test (TAT).

45. Projective tests are low in _____ and_____. Nevertheless, they are considered useful by many _____.

46. _____ measures of personality often require the use of a test battery (collection of _____ _____ and _____).

Module 10.7 Psychology in Action

Survey Question: What causes shyness? What can be done about it?, Objective 10.14

47. Shyness typically involves social anxiety, _____ fears, self-_____ thoughts, _____ self-consciousness, and a lack of social skills.

48. Shyness is marked by _____ public self-consciousness and a _____ to regard one's shyness as a lasting trait.

49. Shyness can be reduced by _____ self-defeating beliefs with _____ thoughts and by _____ social skills.

Mastery Test

1. The hereditary aspects of a person's emotional nature define his or her
   a. character.
   b. personality.
   c. cardinal traits.
   d. temperament.

2. Two parts of the psyche that operate on all three levels of awareness are the
   a. id and ego.
   b. ego and superego.
   c. id and superego.
   d. id and ego ideal.

3. The four critical situations Miller and Dollard consider important in the development of personality are feeding, toilet training,
   a. sex, and aggression.
   b. cleanliness, and language.
   c. attachment, and imitation.
   d. and social learning.

4. Scales that rate a person's tendencies for depression, hysteria, paranoia, and mania are found on the
   a. MMPI-2.
   b. Rorschach.
   c. TAT.
   d. 16 PF.

5. In the five-factor model, people who score high on openness to experience are
   a. intelligent.
   b. extroverted.
   c. choleric.
   d. a personality type.

6. Maslow used the term _____ to describe the tendency to make full use of personal potentials.
   a. full functionality
   b. self-potentiation
   c. ego-idealization
   d. self-actualization

7. Studies of reunited identical twins support the idea that
   a. personality traits are 70 percent hereditary.
   b. fixations influence the expression of personality traits.
   c. personality traits are altered by selective mating and placement in families of comparable status.
   d. personality is shaped as much or more by environment as by heredity.

8. A person's perception of his or her own personality is the core of
   a. temperament.
   b. source traits.
   c. self-concept.
   d. trait-situation interactions.

9. Which of the following concepts is NOT part of Dollard and Miller's behavioral model of personality?
   a. drive
   b. expectancy
   c. cue
   d. reward

10. The terms *structured* and *unstructured* apply most to
    a. the halo effect.
    b. interviews.
    c. questionnaires.
    d. honesty tests.

11. Behavioral theorists account for the existence of a conscience with the concept of
    a. traits of honesty and integrity.
    b. the superego.
    c. self-reinforcement.
    d. conditions of worth.

12. Feelings of pride come from the _____, a part of the _____.
    a. libido, conscience
    b. ego ideal, superego
    c. reality principle, superego
    d. superego, ego

13. Which of the following is a disadvantage of assigning personality types?
    a. Types are not reliable or valid.
    b. Types are often based on stereotypes rather than scientific research.
    c. Types label people who have several key traits in common.
    d. Types tend to oversimplify personality.

14. Freud believed that boys identify with their fathers in order to resolve the _____ complex.
    a. Animus
    b. Electra
    c. Oedipus
    d. Persona

15. Maslow regarded peak experiences as temporary moments of
    a. task centering.
    b. congruent selfhood.
    c. self-actualization.
    d. organismic valuing.

16. Ambiguous stimuli are used primarily in the
    a. MMPI-2.
    b. Shoot Don't Shoot Test.
    c. Rorschach.
    d. 16 PF.

17. A person who is generally extroverted is more outgoing in some situations than in others. This observation supports the concept of
    a. trait-situation interactions.
    b. behavioral genetic determinants.
    c. situational fixations.
    d. possible selves.

18. Allport's concept of central traits is most closely related to Cattell's
    a. surface traits.
    b. source traits.
    c. secondary traits.
    d. cardinal traits.

19. According to Freud, tendencies to be orderly, obstinate, and stingy are formed during the
    _____ stage.
    a. genital
    b. anal
    c. oral
    d. phallic

20. Which of the following is NOT part of Carl Rogers's view of personality?
    a. possible selves
    b. organismic valuing
    c. conditions of worth
    d. congruence

21. Rating scales are primarily used in which approach to personality assessment?
    a. projective testing
    b. direct observation
    c. questionnaires
    d. the TAT technique

22. Which theory of personality places the greatest emphasis on the effects of the environment?
    a. trait
    b. psychodynamic
    c. behavioristic
    d. humanistic

23. Freudian psychosexual stages occur in the order _____.
    a. oral, anal, genital, phallic
    b. oral, phallic, anal, genital
    c. genital, oral, anal, phallic
    d. oral, anal, phallic, genital

24. Rogers described mismatches between one's self-image and reality as a state of
    a. moral anxiety.
    b. incongruence.
    c. basic anxiety.
    d. negative symbolization.

25. All but one of the following are major elements of shyness; which does not apply?
    a. private self-consciousness
    b. social anxiety
    c. self-defeating thoughts
    d. belief that shyness is a lasting trait

26. People who all grew up in the same culture would be most likely to have the same _____ traits.
    a. cardinal
    b. common
    c. secondary
    d. source

27. A trait profile is used to report the results of
    a. the 16 PF.
    b. situational tests.
    c. the TAT.
    d. the inkblot test.

28. Expectancies and the psychological situation are concepts important to
    a. the five-factor model.
    b. development of the superego.
    c. social learning theory.
    d. Maslow.

29. In Asian cultures, _____ tends to be more strongly related to group membership and the success of the group.
    a. temperament
    b. character
    c. self-esteem
    d. moral anxiety

30. An emphasis on the situational determinants of actions is a key feature of _____ theories of personality.
    a. psychodynamic
    b. projective
    c. learning
    d. humanist

31. Which two personality characteristics continue to increase as people age?
    a. creativity and organization
    b. conscientiousness and agreeability
    c. affection and trust
    d. irritability and disorganization

32. People who prefer hip-hop, soul, and electronic music tend to
    a. be talkative and forgiving.
    b. value aesthetic experiences.
    c. be conservative.
    d. enjoy taking risks.

33. Jill was invited to go snowboarding, an activity she has not done before. Jill believes she has the ability to learn snowboarding and keep up with her friends because she is a fast learner. Bandura would say that Jill is high in
   a. self-actualizing.
   b. organismic valuing.
   c. congruence.
   d. self-efficacy.

34. _____ psychologists believe that one's well-being and life satisfaction are influenced by six personality traits, including courage, temperance, and transcendence.
   a. Behavioral
   b. Positive
   c. Psychodynamic
   d. Learning

Chapter 12: Psychological Disorders

Chapter Overview

Abnormal psychology studies people with mental or emotional disturbances. The DSM is used to classify mental disorders. This chapter describes the common or well-known disorders.

Personality disorders are patterns of behavior that are long-standing and affect people across situation. They sometimes look like milder forms of other disorders.

Anxiety disorders (fears), dissociative disorders (memory loss), and somatoform disorders (fake body symptoms) all seem to result from failure to cope effectively with scary situations.

Schizophrenia and other psychotic disorders are characterized by distortions of perception and thought. Many of these disorders appear to have biological causes.

Depression and bipolar disorder are common mood disorders. They seem to be partially biochemical and partially cognitive in origin. Your text gives several good suggestions for how to help a friend who is suicidal.

There are many other disorders as well, some of which are covered in other chapters.

Learning Objectives

OBJECTIVE 12.1 — Indicate the magnitude of mental health problems in the U.S. and Canada; define *psychopathology*; describe the following ways of viewing normality: a. subjective discomfort; b. statistical abnormality; c. social nonconformity; d. situational context; and e. cultural relativity; give examples of how race, gender, and social class continue to affect the diagnosis of various disorders; and indicate the two core features of abnormal behavior.

OBJECTIVE 12.2 —Explain how the DSM-IV-TR is used; define mental disorder; and briefly describe each of the following categories of mental disorders: a. psychotic disorders; b. organic mental disorders; c. mood disorders; d. anxiety disorders; e. somatoform disorders; f. dissociative disorders, g. personality disorders, h. sexual and gender identity disorders, and i. substance related disorders.

OBJECTIVE 12.3 — Define the term neurosis and explain why it was droppped from use; describe examples of culture-bound syndromes from around the world; list the four general risk factors that contribute to psychopathology; define insanity and explain how it is established in court; and describe the "medical student's disease."

OBJECTIVE 12.4 — Describe the ten different types of personality disorders (Table 12.3); and include an indepth discussion of the distinctive characteristics and causes of the antisocial personality.

OBJECTIVE 12.5 — Define anxiety and describe the characteristics of anxiety-related disorders; explain why the term nervous breakdown has no formal meaning and how it may be related to adjustment disorders; and describe an adjustment disorder, including its characteristics, causes, treatment, and how it differs from anxiety disorders.

OBJECTIVE 12.6 — Describethe following anxiety disorders: a. generalized anxiety disorder; b. panic disorder (without agoraphobia); c. panic disorder (with agoraphobia); d. agoraphobia (without panic); e. specific phobia; f. social phobia; g. obsessive-compulsive disorder; h. acute stress disorder; and i. post-traumatic stress disorder.

OBJECTIVE 12.7 — Discuss the following dissociative disorders: a. dissociative amnesia; b. dissociative fugue; and c. dissociative identity disorder.

OBJECTIVE 12.8 — Discuss the following somatoform disorders: a. hypochondriasis; b. somatization disorder;   c. pain disorder; and d. conversion disorder, including "glove anesthesia; describe the related disorders known as Munchausen syndrome and Munchausen by proxy; and define the term comorbid.

OBJECTIVE 12.9 — Describe the heritability of anxiety-based disorders; and explain how each of the major perspectives in psychology view the causes of anxiety disorders: a. psychodynamic, b. humanistic (Rogers); c. existential; d. behavioral, including the terms avoidance learning and anxiety reduction hypothesis; and e. the cognitive view.

OBJECTIVE 12.10 —Discuss the major features of psychotic disorders, including the different types of delusions and hallucinations; list the warning signs of psychotic disorders and major mood disorders, and describe the various types of organic psychoses, including poisionings and dementia.

OBJECTIVE 12.11 — List the main feature of delusional disorders; describe the five types of delusional disorders, including the most common delusional disorder, paranoid psychosis; and explain how it differs from schizophrenia.

OBJECTIVE 12.12 — Discuss schizophrenia, including its frequency, symptoms, and the problems with selective attention; list and describe the four major subtypes of schizophrenia, and explain the general relationship between psychosis and violence.

OBJECTIVE 12.13 — Discuss the following causes of schizophrenia: a. the environment, including the prenatal environment, birth complications, early psychological trauma, disturbed family environment, and deviant communication patterns; b. heredity, including inherited potential and genetic mutations; c. brain chemistry, including the roles of dopamine and glutamate; and d. brain structure and activity, including information gained through CT, MRI, and PET scans; and explain the stress-vulnerability model.

OBJECTIVE 12.14 — Discuss mood disorders, including the following: a. the incidence; b. the two general types; c. characteristics of the moderate mood disorders of dysthymic and cyclothymic disorders; d. the characteristics of the three major mood disorders: major depression, bipolar I and bipolar II; and e. how major mood disorders differ from moderate mood disorders, including the definition of the term endogenous.

OBJECTIVE 12.15 — Discuss the following causes of depression: a. brain chemicals; b. psychoanalytic theory; c. behavioral theory; d. cognitive theory; e. the social and environmental stresses that cause women to experience depression more than men, including postpartum depression; f. the role of heredity; and g. the time or season of the year, including the cause, symptoms, and treatment of seasonal affective disorder (SAD).

OBJECTIVE 12.16 — Describe Rosenhan's pseudo-patient study and his observations regarding psychiatric labeling; and discuss the dangers of psychiatric labeling, including the social stigma, and give a general description of the treatment and prognosis for various mental disorders.

OBJECTIVE 12.17 — Discuss the following aspects of suicide: a. factors that affect suicide rates, including sex, ethnicity, age, and marital status; b. the immediate causes of suicide; c. warning signs; d. common characteristics of suicidal thoughts and feelings; e. how to help someone who is suicidal; and f. crisis intervention.

Language Development Guide

Introduction
(496) *plagued*: constantly bothered, harassed
(496) *incapacitated*: unable to function
(496) *cracked*: broken, slang for insane

Module 12.1
(498) *flagrantly*: clearly, openly
(498) *reclusive*: in hiding, secret
(498) *eccentric*: weird, strange, odd
(498) "*That guy is really wacko...go postal*": slang expressions for crazy, insane
(498) *arbitrary*: without clear rules or process
(499) *virtuous*: very good, moral

Module 12.2
(507) *gouging*: poking, prying, digging
(508) *flamboyant*: showy, colorful
(508) *bizarre*: unusual, strange
(511) *jingle*: song in a radio or television advertisement, used as a memory aid
(514) *high strung*: alert, anxious, responds quickly, "wound too tight"
(515) *crushing*: powerful, strong

Module 12.3
(518) *striking*: dramatic, obvious
(519) *garbled*: mixed up, difficult to understand
(519) *word salad*: using real words and perhaps some kinds of grammar but not making any sense; scrambled language
(519) *soldered*: joined by melted metal
(519) *lead-glazed*: with melted lead-based paint
(520) *maligned*: reputation damaged

(520) *far-fetched*: difficult to believe

(520) *crank letter*: note written by a crazy person, or as a joke or harassment

(525) *alleviate*: heal, relieve

(526) *fissuring*: cracks, in this case in the brain

Module 12.4

(529) elated: very happy

(531) cabin fever: extreme irritability and restlessness resulting from living in isolation or within a confined indoor area for a long period

Module 12.5

(536) intolerable: difficult

(536) infeasible: will not work, ineffective

(536) anguish: extreme pain or suffering

Recite and Review

Module 12.1 Normality and Psychopathology

Survey Question: How is normality defined, and what are the major psychological disorders? Pages 498-505, Objectives 12.1, 12.2, 12.3

(1)_____ refers to maladaptive behavior and to the scientific study of mental disorders. Factors that typically affect judgments of abnormality include subjective (2)_____, statistical (3)_____, non-conformity, context, and (4)_____.

Two key elements of mental disorder are that abnormal behavior is (5)_____ and that it involves a loss of self-control.

Judgments of (6)_____ are relative, but (7)_____ clearly exist and they need to be classified, explained, and treated.

A widely used system for classifying mental disorders is found in the (8)_____ (DSM).

Major mental problems include psychotic disorders, organic disorders, (9)_____ disorders, (10)_____ disorders, somatoform disorders, dissociative disorders, personality disorders, (11)_____ or gender identity disorders, and (12)_____ -related disorders.

(13) _____ is a legal term defining whether a person may be held responsible for his or her actions. (14) _____ is determined in court on the basis of testimony by expert witnesses.

Module 12.2 Personality Disorders and Anxiety-Based Disorders

Survey Question: What is a personality disorder? Pages 507-509, Objective 12.4

Personality disorders are persistent, maladaptive (15)_____ patterns.

Sociopathy is a common (16)_____ disorder. Antisocial persons lack a (17)_____ and they are emotionally cold, (18)_____ , shallow, and dishonest.

Survey Question: What problems result when a person suffers high levels of anxiety? Pages 509-514, Objectives 12.5, 12.6, 12.7, 12.8

Anxiety disorders, dissociative disorders, and somatoform disorders are characterized by high levels of (19)_____, rigid defense mechanisms, and self-defeating (20) _____ patterns.

In an (21) _____ disorder, ordinary stresses push people beyond their ability to cope with life.

Anxiety disorders include generalized anxiety disorder, (22) _____ disorder (with or without agoraphobia), agoraphobia, specific (23) _____, social phobia, obsessive-compulsive disorder, (24)_____ stress disorder, and acute stress disorder.

High levels of anxiety also underlie the unhealthy distortions in behavior that occur in (25)_____ disorders and (26) _____ disorders.

(25) _____ disorders may take the form of amnesia, fugue, or multiple identities.

(26) _____ disorders center on physical complaints that mimic disease or disability. Four examples of (26) _____ disorders are hypochondriasis, somatization disorder, (26)_____ pain disorder, and conversion disorders.

Survey Question: How do psychologists explain anxiety-based disorders? Pages 514-516, Objective 12.9

Understanding anxiety-based disorders requires a (27) _____ of biological, psychodynamic, humanistic-existential, behavioral, and cognitive perspectives.

Module 12.3 Psychosis, Delusional Disorders, and Schizophrenia

Survey Question: What are the general characteristics of psychotic disorders? Pages 518-520, Objective 12.10

Psychosis is a (28) _____ in contact with reality that is marked by delusions, (29)_____, sensory changes, disturbed (30) _____, disturbed communication, and personality disintegration.

An (31) _____ psychosis is based on known injuries or diseases of the brain.

Some common causes of (31) _____ psychosis are poisoning, drug abuse, and dementia (especially (32) _____ disease).

Survey Question: What is the nature of a delusional disorder? Pages 520-521, Objective 12.11

Delusional disorders are almost totally based on the presence of delusions of (33) _____, persecution, infidelity, romantic attraction, or (34) _____. The most common delusional disorder is (35) _____ psychosis.

Survey Question: What forms does schizophrenia take? What causes it? Pages 521-527, Objectives 12.12, 12.13

Schizophrenia involves delusions, hallucinations, (36) _____ difficulties, and a split between (37) _____ and emotion.

(38) _____ schizophrenia is marked by extreme personality disintegration and silly, bizarre, or obscene behavior.

(39) _____ schizophrenia is associated with stupor, mutism, and odd postures. Sometimes violent and agitated behavior also occurs.

In (40) _____ schizophrenia (the most common type), outlandish delusions of grandeur and persecution are coupled with psychotic symptoms and personality breakdown.

Current explanations of schizophrenia emphasize a combination of (41) _____ injuries, early trauma, environmental (42) _____, inherited susceptibility, and abnormalities in the brain.

Heredity is a (43) _____ factor in schizophrenia.

Recent (44) _____ studies have focused on the brain transmitter dopamine and its receptor sites.

The dominant explanation of (45) _____, and other problems as well, is the stress-vulnerability model.

Module 12.4 Mood Disorders

Survey Question: What are mood disorders? What causes depression? Pages 529-533, Objectives 12.14, 12.15, 12.16

Mood disorders primarily involve disturbances of mood or (46) _____, producing manic or (47)_____ states. (48)_____ mood disorders may include psychotic features.

In a dysthymic disorder, depression is long lasting, though (49) _____. In a cyclothymic disorder, people suffer from long-lasting, though (49) _____, (50) _____ between depression and elation.

(51) _____ disorders combine mania and depression. In a (52) _____ disorder the person swings between severe mania and severe depression. In a (53) _____ disorder the person is mostly depressed, but has had periods of mild mania.

A (54) _____ disorder involves extreme sadness and despondency but no signs of mania.

Major mood disorders are partially explained by genetic vulnerability and changes in (55) _____. Other important factors are (56) _____, anger, learned helplessness, (57) _____, and self-defeating thinking patterns.

Many women experience a brief period of depression, called (58) _____, shortly after giving birth. Some women suffer from a more (59) _____ and (60) _____ condition called postpartum depression.

(61) _____ (SAD), which occurs during the winter months, is another common form of depression. SAD is typically (62) _____ with phototherapy.

Module 12.5 Psychology in Action

Survey Question: Why do people commit suicide? Can suicide be prevented? Pages 535-537, Objective 12.17

Suicide is a relatively frequent (63) _____ that can, in many cases, be prevented.

Suicide is (64) _____ related to such factors as age, sex, and marital status.

In individual cases, the (65) _____ for suicide is best identified by a desire to escape, unbearable psychological pain, and (66) _____ psychological needs.

People contemplating suicide (67) _____ their options until death seems like the only way out.

The impulse to attempt suicide is usually (68) _____. Efforts to (69) _____ suicide are worthwhile.

Connections

Module 12.1

1. _____	DSM-IV-TR	a. culturally recognized disorder
2. _____	drapetomania	b. physical symptoms
3. _____	mood disorder	c. legal problem
4. _____	somatoform disorder	d. outdated term
5. _____	insanity	e. sexual deviation
6. _____	organic disorder	f. diagnostic manual
7. _____	neurosis	g. fear of germs
8. _____	paraphilia	h. brain pathology
9. _____	amok	i. mania or depression

Module 12.2

1. _____	dependent personality	a. self-importance
2. _____	histrionic personality	b. rigid routines
3. _____	narcissistic personality	c. submissiveness
4. _____	antisocial personality	d. little emotion
5. _____	obsessive-compulsive	e. attention seeking
6. _____	schizoid personality	f. unstable self-image
7. _____	avoidant personality	g. odd, disturbed thinking
8. _____	borderline personality	h. suspiciousness
9. _____	paranoid personality	i. fear of social situations
10. _____	schizotypal personality	j. no conscience

1. _____	adjustment disorder	a. afraid to leave the house
2. _____	generalized anxiety	b. fears being observed
3. _____	panic disorder	c. conversion disorder
4. _____	agoraphobia	d. one month after extreme stress
5. _____	specific phobia	e. dissociation
6. _____	social phobia	f. within weeks after extreme stress
7. _____	PTSD	g. sudden attacks of fear
8. _____	acute stress disorder	h. normal life stress
9. _____	glove anesthesia	i. chronic worry
10. _____	fugue	j. fears objects or activities

Module 12.3

1. _____	psychosis	a. retreat from reality
2. _____	catatonic type	b. incoherence, bizarre thinking
3. _____	paranoid type	c. false belief
4. _____	disorganized type	d. genetics of schizophrenia
5. _____	psychological trauma	e. grandeur or persecution
6. _____	twin studies	f. chemical messenger
7. _____	hallucinations	g. risk factor for schizophrenia
8. _____	dopamine	h. dementia
9. _____	delusion	i. imaginary sensations
10. _____	Alzheimer's disease	j. stuporous or agitated

Module 12.4

1. _____ bipolar I	a. produced from within
2. _____ social stigma	b. winter depression
3. _____ bipolar II	c. depression after childbirth
4. _____ endogenous	d. light treatment
5. _____ suicide	e. leads to prejudice
6. _____ postpartum depression	f. desire to end all pains
7. _____ phototherapy	g. depression and hypomania
8. _____ SAD	h. severe mania and depression

Module 12.5

1. _____ males	a. associated with low suicide rate
2. _____ Native Americans	b. more completed suicides
3. _____ cause of suicide	c. highest suicide rate
4. _____ marriage	d. alcohol use
5. _____ withdrawal	e. warning sign

Check Your Memory

Module 12.1 Normality and Psychopathology

Survey Question: How is normality defined, and what are the major psychological disorders? Pages 498-505, Objectives 12.1, 12.2, 12.3

T F   1. Psychopathology refers to the study of mental disorders and to disorders themselves.

T F   2. One out of every 10 persons will require mental hospitalization during his or her lifetime.

T F   3. Statistical definitions do not automatically tell us where to draw the line between normality and abnormality.

T F   4. To understand how social norms define normality, a person could perform a mild abnormal behavior in public to observe the public's reaction.

T F   5. Cultural relativity refers to making personal judgments about another culture's practices.

T F   6. All cultures classify people as abnormal if they fail to communicate with others.

T F   7. Drapetomania, childhood masturbation, and nymphomania are considered mental disorders listed in the DSM-IV-TR.

T F   8. Gender is a common source of bias in judging normality.

T F   9. Being a persistent danger to oneself or others is regarded as a clear sign of disturbed psychological functioning.

T F   10. Poverty, abusive parents, low intelligence, and head injuries are risk factors for mental disorder.

T F   11. "Organic mental disorders" is one of the major categories in DSM-IV-TR.

T F   12. Koro, locura, and zar are brain diseases that cause psychosis.

T F   13. Neurosis is a legal term, not a type of mental disorder.

Module 12.2 Personality Disorders and Anxiety-Based Disorders

Survey Question: What is a personality disorder? Pages 507-509, Objective 12.4

T F   14. The "emotional storms" experienced by people with borderline personality disorder is a normal process about which they and their friends have a clear understanding.

T F   15. Histrionic persons are preoccupied with their own self-importance.

T F   16. Personality disorders usually appear suddenly in early adulthood.

T F   17. The schizoid person shows little emotion and is uninterested in relationships with others.

T F   18. "Psychopath" is another term for the borderline personality.

T F   19. Sociopaths usually have a childhood history of emotional deprivation, neglect, and abuse.

T F   20. Antisocial behavior typically declines somewhat after age.

T F   21. Antisocial personality disorders are often treated successfully with drugs.

Survey Question: What problems result when a person suffers high levels of anxiety? Pages 509-514, Objectives 12.5, 12.6, 12.7, 12.8

T F   22. Anxiety is an emotional response to an ambiguous threat.

T F   23. Adjustment disorders occur when severe stresses outside the normal range of human experience push people to their breaking points.

T F   24. Sudden, unexpected episodes of intense panic are a key feature of generalized anxiety disorder.

T F   25. A person who fears he or she will have a panic attack in public places or unfamiliar situations suffers from acrophobia.

T F   26. Arachnophobia, claustrophobia, and pathophobia are all specific phobias.

T F   27. Many people who have an obsessive-compulsive disorder are checkers or cleaners.

T F   28. PTSD is a psychological disturbance lasting more than a month after exposure to severe stress.

T F   29. Multiple personality is a dissociative disorder.

T F   30. Multiple personality is the most common form of schizophrenia.

T F   31. Depersonalization and fusion are the goals of therapy for dissociative identity disorders.

T F   32. The word "somatoform" means "body form."

T F   33. An unusual lack of concern about the appearance of a sudden disability is a sign of a conversion reaction.

Survey Question: How do psychologists explain anxiety-based disorders? Pages 514-516, Objective 12.9

T F   34. Anxiety disorders appear to be partly hereditary.

T F   35. The psychodynamic approach characterizes anxiety disorders as a product of id impulses that threaten a loss of control.

T F   36. Carl Rogers interpreted emotional disorders as the result of a loss of meaning in one's life.

T F   37. Disordered behavior is paradoxical because it makes the person more anxious and unhappy in the long run.

T F   38. The cognitive view attributes anxiety disorders to distorted thinking that leads to avoidance learning.

Module 12.3 Psychosis, Delusional Disorders, and Schizophrenia

Survey Question: What are the general characteristics of psychotic disorders? Pages 518-520, Objective 12.10

T F   39. The most common psychotic delusion is hearing voices.

T F   40. People with depressive delusions believe that they are depressed but that they do not need therapy.

T F   41. Even a person who displays flat affect may continue to privately feel strong emotion.

T F   42. Severe brain injuries or diseases sometimes cause psychoses.

T F   43. Children must eat leaded paint flakes before they are at risk for lead poisoning.

T F   44. Roughly 80 percent of all cases of Alzheimer's disease are genetic.

Survey Question: What is the nature of a delusional disorder? Pages 520-521, Objective 12.11

T F   45. In delusional disorders, people have auditory hallucinations of grandeur or persecution.

T F   46. Delusions of persecution are a key symptom of paranoid psychosis.

T F   47. A person who believes that his body is diseased and rotting has an erotomanic type of delusional disorder.

T F   48. Delusional disorders are common and are easily treated with drugs.

Survey Question: What forms does schizophrenia take? What causes it? Pages 521-527, Objectives 12.12, 12.13

T F   49. One person out of 100 will become schizophrenic.

T F   50. Schizophrenia is the most common dissociative psychosis.

T F   51. Silliness, laughter, and bizarre behavior are common in disorganized schizophrenia.

T F   52. Periods of immobility and odd posturing are characteristic of paranoid schizophrenia.

T F   53. At various times, patients may shift from one type of schizophrenia to another.

T F   54. Exposure to influenza during pregnancy produces children who are more likely to become schizophrenic later in life.

T F   55. If one identical twin is schizophrenic, the other twin has a 46 percent chance of also becoming schizophrenic.

T F   56. Excess amounts of the neurotransmitter substance PCP are suspected as a cause of schizophrenia.

T F   57. The brains of schizophrenics tend to be more responsive to dopamine and glutamate than the brains of normal persons.

T F   58. PET scans show that activity in the frontal lobes of schizophrenics tends to be abnormally low.

T F   59. At least three schizophrenic patients out of four are completely recovered 10 years after being diagnosed.

T F   60. The stress-vulnerability model suggests that psychotic disorders are caused by a combination of environment and heredity.

Module 12.4 Mood Disorders

Survey Question: What are mood disorders? What causes depression? Pages 529-533, Objectives 12.14, 12.15, 12.16

T F   61. The two most basic types of mood disorder are bipolar I and bipolar II.

T F   62. In bipolar disorders, people experience both mania and depression.

T F   63. If a person is moderately depressed for at least two weeks, a dysthymic disorder exists.

T F   64. A cyclothymic disorder is characterized by moderate levels of depression and manic behavior.

T F   65. Endogenous depression appears to be generated from within, with little connection to external events.

T F   66. Behavioral theories of depression emphasize the concept of learned helplessness.

T F   67. Overall, women are twice as likely as men to become depressed.

T F   68. Having limited education, experiencing high levels of stress, not being married, and feeling hopeless are some characteristics that increase a woman's chance of being depressed.

T F   69. Research indicates that heredity does not play a role in major mood disorder.

T F   70. Postpartum depression typically lasts from about two months to a year after giving birth.

T F   71. SAD is most likely to occur during the winter in countries located near the equator.

T F   72. Phototherapy is used to treat SAD successfully 80 percent of the time.

T F   73. Labeling a person with a disorder when they do not have one does not harm them in any way.

T F   74. People who have been successfully treated for a mental disorder are no longer a threat to society and, therefore, are not stigmatized like criminals.

Module 12.5 Psychology in Action

Survey Question: Why do people commit suicide? Can suicide be prevented? Pages 535-537, Objective 12.17

T F   75. The greatest number of suicides during a single day takes place at New Year's.

T F   76. More men than women complete suicide.

T F   77. Suicide rates steadily decline after young adulthood.

T F   78. Most suicides involve despair, anger, and guilt.

T F   79. People who threaten suicide rarely actually attempt it—they're just crying wolf.

T F   80. Only a minority of people who attempt suicide really want to die.

T F   81. The risk of attempted suicide is high if a person has a concrete, workable plan for doing it.

Critical Thinking

Module 12.1

1. Brian, a fan of grunge rock, occasionally wears a skirt in public. Does Brian's cross-dressing indicate that he has a mental disorder?

2. Many states began to restrict use of the insanity defense after John Hinkley, Jr., who tried to murder former U.S. President Ronald Reagan, was acquitted by reason of insanity. What does this trend reveal about insanity?

Module 12.2

3. Many of the physical complaints associated with anxiety disorders are closely related to activity of what part of the nervous system?

4. How could someone get away with Munchausen syndrome by proxy? Wouldn't doctors figure out that something was fishy with Ben long before he had 40 surgeries for a faked sinus disorder (see "Sick of Being Sick")?

Module 12.3

5. Researchers have found nearly double the normal number of dopamine receptor sites in the brains of schizophrenics. Why might that be important?

6. Enlarged surface fissures and ventricles are frequently found in the brains of chronic schizophrenics. Why is it a mistake to conclude that such features cause schizophrenia?

Module 12.4

7. How might relationships contribute to the higher rates of depression experienced by women?

Module 12.5

8. If you follow the history of popular music, see if you can answer this question: What two major risk factors contributed to the 1994 suicide of Kurt Cobain, lead singer for the rock group Nirvana?

Final Survey and Review

Module 12.1 Normality and Psychopathology

Survey Question: How is normality defined, and what are the major psychological disorders? Objectives 12.1, 12.2, 12.3

1. Psychopathology refers to _____ behavior and to the scientific study of _____.

2. Factors that typically affect judgments of abnormality include _____ discomfort, _____ abnormality, non-conformity, _____, and culture.

3. Two key elements of mental disorder are that abnormal behavior is maladaptive and that it involves a _____.

4. Judgments of normality are _____, but psychological disorders clearly exist and they need to be _____, explained, and _____.

5. A widely used _____ is found in the *Diagnostic and Statistical Manual of Mental Disorders* (DSM).

6. Major mental problems include _____ disorders, _____ disorders, mood disorders, anxiety disorders, _____ disorders, _____ disorders, personality disorders, sexual or gender identity disorders, and substance-related disorders.

7. Insanity is a _____ term defining whether a person may be held _____ for his or her actions. Sanity is determined in court on the basis of _____ by expert witnesses.

Module 12.2 Personality Disorders and Anxiety-Based Disorders

Survey Question: What is a personality disorder? Objective 12.4

8. Personality disorders are _____, maladaptive personality patterns.

9. _____ is a common personality disorder. _____ persons lack a conscience, and they are emotionally cold, manipulative, _____, and _____.

Survey Question: What problems result when a person suffers high levels of anxiety? Objectives 12.5, 12.6, 12.7, 12.8

10. Anxiety disorders, _____ disorders, and somatoform disorders are characterized by high levels of anxiety, _____ defense mechanisms, and _____ behavior patterns.

11. In an adjustment disorder, _____ push people beyond their ability to _____.

12. Anxiety disorders include _____ anxiety disorder, panic disorder (with or without _____), _____, specific phobias, social phobia, _____ disorder, posttraumatic stress disorder, and _____ stress disorder.

13. High levels of _____ also underlie the unhealthy distortions in behavior that occur in dissociative disorders and somatoform disorders.

14. Dissociative disorders may take the form of amnesia, _____, or multiple _____.

15. Somatoform disorders center on physical complaints that _____ disease or disability. Four examples of somatoform disorders are hypochondriasis, _____ disorder, somatoform pain disorder, and _____ disorders.

Survey Question: How do psychologists explain anxiety based disorders? Objective 12.9

16. Understanding anxiety-based disorders requires a combination of biological, _____, humanistic-_____, behavioral, and cognitive perspectives.

Module 12.3 Psychosis, Delusional Disorders, and Schizophrenia

Survey Question: What are the general characteristics of psychotic disorders? Objective 12.10

17. Psychosis is a break in contact with _____ that is marked by delusions, hallucinations, _____ changes, disturbed emotions, disturbed _____, and personality _____.

18. An organic psychosis is based on known_____ or _____ of the brain.

19. Some common causes of organic psychosis are poisoning, _____, and _____ (especially Alzheimer's disease).

Survey Question: What is the nature of a delusional disorder? Objective 12.11

20. Delusional disorders are _____ based on the presence of delusions of grandeur, _____, _____, romantic attraction, or physical disease. The most common delusional disorder is paranoid _____.

Survey Question: What forms does schizophrenia take? What causes it? Objectives 12.12, 12.13

21. Schizophrenia involves delusions, _____, communication difficulties, and a split between thought and _____.

22. Disorganized schizophrenia is marked by extreme _____ disintegration and silly, bizarre, or _____ behavior.

23. Catatonic schizophrenia is associated with _____, mutism, and odd postures. Sometimes _____ and agitated behavior also occurs.

24. In paranoid schizophrenia (the most _____ type), outlandish delusions of grandeur and _____ are coupled with psychotic symptoms and _____ breakdown.

25. Current explanations of schizophrenia emphasize a combination of prenatal injuries, _____, environmental stress, inherited _____, and abnormalities in the _____.

26. _____ is a major factor in schizophrenia.

27. Recent biochemical studies have focused on the brain transmitter _____ and its receptor sites.

28. The dominant explanation of schizophrenia, and other problems as well, is the _____ model.

Module 12.4 Mood Disorders

Survey Question: What are mood disorders? What causes depression? Objectives 12.14, 12.15, 12.16

29. _____ disorders primarily involve disturbances of mood or emotion, producing _____ or depressive states. Severe mood disorders may include _____ features.

30. In a _____ disorder, depression is long lasting, though moderate. In a _____ disorder, people suffer from long-lasting, though moderate, swings between depression and elation.

31. Bipolar disorders combine _____ and _____. In a bipolar I disorder the person swings between severe _____ and severe _____. In a bipolar II disorder the person is mostly _____, but has had periods of mild _____.

32. A major depressive disorder involves extreme _____ and _____ but no signs of _____.

33. Major mood disorders are partially explained by genetic _____ and changes in brain chemistry. Other important factors are loss, anger, _____, stress, and _____ thinking patterns.

34. _____ women experience a brief period of depression, called the maternity blues, shortly after giving birth. _____ women suffer from a more serious and lasting condition called _____ depression.

35. Seasonal affective disorder (SAD), which occurs during _____, is another common form of depression. SAD is typically treated with _____.

Module 12.5 Psychology in Action

Survey Question: Why do people commit suicide? Can suicide be prevented? Objective 12.17

36. Suicide is a relatively _____ cause of death that can, in many cases, be _____.

37. Suicide is statistically related to such factors as _____, _____, and _____ status.

38. In individual cases, the potential for suicide is best identified by a desire to _____, unbearable _____, and frustrated psychological _____.

39. People contemplating suicide narrow their options until death seems like _____.

40. The impulse to _____ suicide is usually temporary. Efforts to prevent suicide are _____.

Mastery Test

1. The difference between an acute stress disorder and PTSD is
   a. how long the disturbance lasts.
   b. the severity of the stress.
   c. whether the anxiety is free-floating.
   d. whether dissociative behavior is observed.

2. A person is at greatest risk of becoming schizophrenic if he or she has
   a. schizophrenic parents.
   b. a schizophrenic fraternal twin.
   c. a schizophrenic mother.
   d. a schizophrenic sibling.

3. A core feature of all abnormal behavior is that it is
   a. statistically extreme.
   b. associated with subjective discomfort.
   c. ultimately maladaptive.
   d. marked by a loss of contact with reality.

4. Excess amounts of dopamine in the brain, or high sensitivity to dopamine, provide one major explanation for the problem known as
   a. PTSD.
   b. schizophrenia.
   c. major depression.
   d. SAD.

5. The descriptions acro, claustro, and pyro refer to
   a. common obsessions.
   b. specific phobias.
   c. free-floating anxieties.
   d. hypochondriasis.

6. Glove anesthesia strongly implies the existence of a(an)_____ disorder.
   a. organic
   b. depersonalization
   c. somatization
   d. conversion

7. In the stress-vulnerability model of psychosis, vulnerability is primarily attributed to
   a. heredity.
   b. exposure to influenza.
   c. psychological trauma.
   d. disturbed family life.

8. A patient believes that she has a mysterious disease that is causing her body to rot away. What type of symptom is she suffering from?
   a. bipolar
   b. delusion
   c. neurosis
   d. cyclothymic

9. Phototherapy is used primarily to treat
   a. postseasonal depression.
   b. SAD.
   c. catatonic depression.
   d. affective psychoses.

10. Psychopathology is defined as an inability to behave in ways that
   a. foster personal growth and happiness.
   b. match social norms.
   c. lead to personal achievement.
   d. do not cause anxiety.

11. Which of the following is NOT characteristic of suicidal thinking?
   a. desires to escape
   b. psychological pain
   c. frustrated needs
   d. too many options

12. Fear of using the restroom in public is
   a. a social phobia.
   b. an acute stress disorder.
   c. a panic disorder.
   d. an adjustment disorder.

13. A person who displays personality disintegration, waxy flexibility, and delusions of persecution
       suffers from_____ schizophrenia.
   a. disorganized
   b. catatonic
   c. paranoid
   d. undifferentiated

14. You find yourself in an unfamiliar town and you can't remember your name or address. It is likely
    that you are suffering from
   a. paraphilia.
   b. Alzheimer's disease.
   c. a borderline personality disorder.
   d. a dissociative disorder.

15. A major problem with statistical definitions of abnormality is
   a. calculating the normal curve.
   b. choosing dividing lines.
   c. that they do not apply to groups of people.
   d. that they do not take norms into account.

16. DSM-IV-TR primarily describes and classifies _____ disorders.
   a. mental
   b. organic
   c. psychotic
   d. cognitive

17. A person who is a frequent checker may have which disorder?
    a. agoraphobia
    b. somatization
    c. free-floating fugue
    d. obsessive-compulsive

18. The most direct explanation for the anxiety-reducing properties of self-defeating behavior is found in
    a. an overwhelmed ego.
    b. avoidance learning.
    c. the loss of meaning in one's life.
    d. the concept of existential anxiety.

19. A person with a(an) _____ personality disorder might be described as charming by people who don't know the person well.
    a. avoidant
    b. schizoid
    c. antisocial
    d. dependent

20. One of the most powerful situational contexts for judging the normality of behavior is
    a. culture.
    b. gender.
    c. statistical norms.
    d. private discomfort.

21. A person who is manic most likely suffers from a(an) _____ disorder.
    a. anxiety
    b. somatoform
    c. organic
    d. mood

22. The principal problem in paranoid psychosis is
    a. delusions.
    b. hallucinations.
    c. disturbed emotions.
    d. personality disintegration.

23. A problem that may occur with or without agoraphobia is
    a. dissociative disorder.
    b. somatoform disorder.
    c. panic disorder.
    d. obsessive-compulsive disorder.

24. Hearing voices that do not exist is an almost sure sign of a _____ disorder.
    a. psychotic
    b. dissociative
    c. personality
    d. delusional

25. A conversion reaction is a type of _____ disorder.
    a. somatoform
    b. dissociative
    c. obsessive-compulsive
    d. postpartum

26. The existence, in the past, of disorders such as drapetomania and nymphomania suggests that judging normality is greatly affected by
    a. gender.
    b. cultural disapproval.
    c. levels of functioning.
    d. subjective discomfort.

27. Which of the following terms does NOT belong with the others?
    a. neurosis
    b. somatoform disorder
    c. personality disorder
    d. dissociative disorder

28. Threats to one's self-image are a key element in the_____ approach to understanding anxiety and disordered functioning.
    a. Freudian
    b. humanistic
    c. existential
    d. behavioral

29. Which of the following is NOT classified as an anxiety disorder?
    a. adjustment disorder
    b. panic disorder
    c. agoraphobia
    d. obsessive-compulsive disorder

30. Cyclothymic disorder is most closely related to
    a. reactive depression.
    b. major depressive disorder.
    c. bipolar disorder.
    d. SAD.

31. Pretending to possess a delusional disorder (schizophrenia) by walking around campus on a sunny day with a raincoat on and holding an open umbrella over one's head and, when inside, continuing to hold the open umbrella over one's head is a way to
    a. understand how social norms define normality.
    b. determine how normality is defined.
    c. test cultural relativism.
    d. all the preceding

32. A person who sometimes is friendly, charming, impulsive, moody, extremely sensitive to ordinary criticisms, and suicidal has the _____ personality disorder.
   a. dependent
   b. borderline
   c. dissociative
   d. narcissistic

33. A person who is "blind" to signs that would disgust others, and who is charming, lacks a conscience, and feels no guilt, shame, fear, loyalty, or love has the _____ personality disorder.
   a. histrionic
   b. schizoid
   c. avoidant
   d. antisocial

34. Which of the following is NOT a type of delusion?
   a. avoidant
   b. depressive
   c. reference
   d. influence

35. Which of the following statement is true of delusional disorders?
   a. The disorders are common and easily treated.
   b. The main feature is a deeply held false belief.
   c. Symptoms include perceiving sensations that do not exist (e.g., seeing insects crawling under their skin).
   d. The disorder is genetically linked.

36. Which of the following is NOT a cause of schizophrenia?
   a. Malnutrition during pregnancy and exposure to influenza.
   b. Females are more vulnerable to developing schizophrenic disorder.
   c. Psychological trauma during childhood increases the risk.
   d. Sensitivity to neurotransmitters dopamine and glutamate.

37. Knowing that Lloyd is suffering from bipolar disorder and currently is undergoing treatment, Joan assumes that he will relapse sooner or later and, therefore, refuses to hire him as a delivery person. Joan's reaction and response to Lloyd's application reflects the impact of
   a. labeling a person with a disorder rather than identifying the problem.
   b. prejudice and discrimination.
   c. stigmatism.
   d. all the preceding

Chapter 13: Therapies

Chapter Overview

Each of the major theoretical perspectives in psychology has provided a method of fixing problems, or providing therapy.

Psychoanalysis, originally developed by Freud, helps the patient gain insight into their behavior by exploring unconscious thoughts and childhood issues.

Humanistic therapies focus on insight through self-discovery rather than the therapist providing the answers. Client-centered therapy, existential therapy, and gestalt therapy are each examples of this perspective.

Effective therapy is usually done in person, or by technology with the ability to see faces, but other technology-based distance therapies have been tried.

Behavior therapy is focused more on solutions than on causes. There are several effective methods based on the principles of classical or operant conditioning. There are also several behavioral methods that focus on correcting irrational thought and beliefs.

Group therapy and skills training incorporate social learning into treatment. Family and marital therapy focus on improving interpersonal relationships.

Medical therapies treat the physical causes or symptoms of mental illness. Drugs are most common, but surgery and electric shock are also sometimes used.

Treatment effectiveness can be measured by the client, the therapist, or the client's family and friends. All of the therapies are effective, at least for some people or some situations. Ultimately, one should seek the form of therapy that is right for you and/or the problem.

Learning Objectives

OBJECTIVE 13.1 — Define *psychotherapy*; describe the following aspects of various therapies: a. individual therapy, b. group therapy, c. insight therapy, d. action therapy, e. directive therapy, f. non-directive therapy, g. time-limited therapy, h. supportive therapy, and i. positive therapy; discuss what a person can expect the outcomes of therapy to be; and list the elements of positive mental health.

OBJECTIVE 13.2 — Briefly describe the history of the treatment of psychological problems, including trepanning, demonology, exorcism, ergotism, and the work of Philippe Pinel.

OBJECTIVE 13.3 — Discuss the development of psychoanalysis and its four basic techniques: a. free association; b. dream analysis, including the terms latent content, manifest content, and dream symbols; c. analysis of resistance; and d. transference; and discuss today's brief psychodyanamic therapy, including interpersonal psychotherapy (IPT), why this brief therapy took the place of traditional psychoanalysis, and the concept of spontaneous remissions.

OBJECTIVE 13.4 — Explain how the insight therapy of humanistic approaches differs from insight gained through traditional psychoanalysis; and describe the core features of the following humanistic approaches and compare them to each other: a. Rogers' client-centered therapy; b. existential therapy, including Frankl's logotherapy; and c. Perls' Gestalt therapy.

OBJECTIVE 13.5 — Discuss the advantages and disadvantages of media (TV and talk-radio) psychologists, telephone therapists, and internet therapy; describe the APA recommendation regarding these therapies; and explain how videoconferencing can solve some of the problems of these long-distance therapies.

OBJECTIVE 13.6 — Describe behavior therapy and behavior modification; and discuss aversion therapy, including its relationship to classical conditioning, the procedures of rapid smoking and response-contingent shocks, and the justification for its use.

OBJECTIVE 13.7 — Discuss the behavioral approach of desensitization, including: a. the hierarchy; b. reciprocal inhibition; c. the problems desensitization is used to treat; d. how systematic desensitization is performed; e. how to achieve relaxation using the tension-release method, f. vicarious desensitization, g. desensitization by imagining fear stimuli, h. virtual reality exposure, and i. eye movement desensitization and reprocessing (EMDR).

OBJECTIVE 13.8 — List and briefly describe the seven operant principles most frequently used by behavior therapists; explain how nonreinforcement (non-reward) and time out can be used to bring about extinction of a maladaptive behavior; and describe a token economy.

OBJECTIVE 13.9 — Explain how cognitive therapies differ from behavioral therapies; describe the three thinking errors that Beck said underlie depression and what can be done to correct such thinking; discuss Ellis' rational-emotive behavior therapy (REBT), including the A-B-C of the therapy, the ten most common irrational beliefs, and the three core ideas that Ellis' said served as the basis for most of these irrational beliefs; and explain how cognitive distortions can lead to a gambling addiction.

OBJECTIVE 13.10 — List the advantages of group therapy; and briefly describe each of the following group therapies: a. psychodrama, including role-playing, role reversal, and the mirror technique; b. family therapy; c. sensitivity groups; d. encounter groups, and e. large group awareness training; and explain the therapy placebo effect.

OBJECTIVE 13.11 — Discuss the effectiveness of therapy; the four core features and goals of all psychotherapies; the strengths of each type of psychotherapy (Table 13.2); how psychotherapy will likely look in the future; the nine basic counseling skills and helping behaviors that can be used by anyone to comfort a person in distress; and the skills necessary to be a culturally skilled therapist.

OBJECTIVE 13.12 — Discuss the three types of somatic therapy: a. pharmacotherapy, including the three major types of drugs, examples of each type (see Table 13.4), the benefits and limitations of drug therapy, and the concept of risk-benefit ratio; b. electoconvulsive therapy (ECT), including how it is performed and what most experts believe regarding this therapy; and c. psychosurgery, including the prefrontal lobotomy and deep lesioning techniques.

OBJECTIVE 13.13 — Describe the role of hospitalization and partial hospitalization in the treatment of psychological disorders; explain what deinstitutionalization is and how halfway houses have attempted to help in easing the patient's return to the community; and discuss the roles of the community mental health centers and the work of paraprofessionals within these centers.

OBJECTIVE 13.14 — Describe the following behavioral procedures that can be applied to solve everyday problems: a. covert sensitzation, b. thought stopping, c. covert reinforcement, and d. self-directed desensitization.

OBJECTIVE 13.15 — Explain how a person can find professional help by discussing each of the following topics: a. indicators that signal the need for professional help; b. sources for locating a therapist (see Table 13.5); c. deciding on the type of therapist, such as a psychiatrist, psychologist, counselor, social worker, peer counselor, or self-help group; d. finding out about the therapist's qualifications; and e. evaluating a therapist, including danger signals to watch for in therapy.

Language Development Guide

Introduction
(540) *absenteeism*: missing school or work

Module 13.1
(542) *depicted*: shown, described, perceived
(542) *major overhaul*: redone from the beginning, making totally new
(543) *bored/boring*: drilled or poked
(543) *exorcism*: religious rite to remove demons
(544) *granddaddy*: either foundation, beginning, or most important or well known
(544) *stemming from*: beginning in, growing out of
(544) *self-censorship*: preventing oneself
(545) *roadblocks*: barriers, sources of frustration

Module 13.2
(548) *picture*: imagine
(548) *hysterical misery into common unhappiness*: not made happy but less sad than you were
(548) *phony fronts*: masks, fake images or false impressions
(549) *mortality*: reality of death
(549) *impair*: damage, slow, injure, prevent
(549) *paradoxically*: in a surprising conflict or contradiction
(550) *let the consumer beware*: the buyer has to make sure they aren't cheated

Module 13.3

(553) *covert sensitization*: hidden method of reacting more strongly to something

(554) *be a candidate for*: try

(556) *molestations*: sexual touching, usually of children

Module 13.4

(558) *ward*: wing or residential area of a hospital

(561) *total zero*: unimportant, worthless

(561) *dwelling on:* thinking repeatedly about

(561) *dumped*: abandoned, left by a romantic partner

(562) *lost his shirt*: lost all his money

(562) *Texas Hold 'Em*: form of poker, a card game involving gambling

(562) *rotten*: bad

(563) *full-scale*: complete, large, frequent

Module 13.5

(564) *reenacts*: pretends, acts out

(565) *confrontation*: facing flaws, exposing problems

(565) *versatility*: able to be used for many purposes or in many places

(566) *alliance*: partnership

(567) *distilled*: extracted or taken from

(568) *heart wrenching*: emotional

(569) *gossip*: to share personal information or secrets about someone to someone else

(569) *slant*: bias

(571) *proponents*: people in favor of

(571) *vegetables*: alive but inactive, comatose

(571) *stupor*: unresponsive

(572) *bleak*: hopeless, depressing

(573) *bright spot*: positive, a hopeful thing

Module 13.6

(575) *indulging*: doing for pleasure

(576) *curb*: slow, reduce, or stop

(576) *toned down*: made less strong

(576) *maggots*: fly larvae

(576) *put yourself down*: be self-critical or insulting

(576) *diaphragm*: muscle below the lungs that helps breathing

(578) *reputable*: known to be good

(579) *referral*: sent to someone else

(579) *belittling*: made to feel small or unimportant or stupid

Recite and Review

Module 13.1 Psychotherapy and Psychoanalysis

Survey Question: How do psychotherapies differ? Page 542, Objective 13.1

Psychotherapy facilitates positive (1) _____ in personality, behavior, or adjustment.
Psychotherapies may be classified as insight, (2) _____, directive, (3) _____,
supportive, or (4) _____ therapies, or combinations of these.
Therapies may be conducted either (5) _____ or (6) _____, and they may be time
limited.

Survey Question: How did psychotherapy originate? Pages 542-544, Objective 13.2

Early approaches to mental illness were dominated by (7) _____ and moral condemnation.
(8) _____ attributed mental disturbance to supernatural forces, such as demonic possession,
and prescribed exorcism as the cure.
In some instances, the actual cause of (9) _____ may have been ergot poisoning.
More humane treatment began in 1793 with the work of (10) _____ in Paris.

Survey Question: Is Freudian psychoanalysis still used? Pages 544-546, Objective 13.3

As the first true psychotherapy, (11) _____ gave rise to modern psychodynamic therapies.
Psychoanalysis seeks to reveal (12) _____ thoughts, emotions, and conflicts.
The psychoanalyst uses free association, (13) _____ analysis, and analysis of resistance and
(14) _____ to reveal health-producing insights.
Some critics argue that (15) _____ receives credit for spontaneous remissions of symptoms.
However, psychoanalysis is (16) _____ for many patients.
Brief psychodynamic therapy, which relies on psychoanalytic theory but is (17) _____, is as
effective as other major therapies. One example is interpersonal (18) _____.

Module 13.2 Insight Therapies

Survey Question: What are the major humanistic therapies? Pages 548-550, Objective 13.4

Client-centered (or (19) _____) therapy is non-directive, based on insights gained from
conscious thoughts and feelings, and is dedicated to creating an atmosphere of (20) _____.
(21) _____, empathy, authenticity, and reflection are combined to give the
(22) _____ a chance to solve (23) _____ problems.
(24) _____ therapies focus on the end result of the choices one makes in life. Clients are
encouraged through (25) _____ and encounter to exercise free will and to
(26) _____ for their choices.
(27) _____ therapy emphasizes immediate awareness of thoughts and feelings. Its goal is to
rebuild thinking, feeling, and acting into (28) _____, and to help clients break through
emotional (29) _____.

Survey Question: Can therapy be conducted at a distance? Pages 550-551, Objective 13.5

Media psychologists, telephone counselors, and cybertherapists may, on occasion, do
(30) _____. However, each has (31) _____, and the effectiveness of telephone
counseling and cybertherapy has (32) _____.
Therapy by videoconferencing shows (33) _____ as a way to provide mental health services at
a distance.

Module 13.3 Behavior Therapy

Survey Question: What is behavior therapy? How is behavior therapy used to treat phobias, fears, and anxieties? Pages 553-556, Objectives 13.6, 13.7

(34) _____ therapists use the learning principles of classical or operant conditioning to directly change human behavior.

In (35) _____ therapy, classical conditioning is used to associate maladaptive behavior (such as smoking or drinking) with pain or other aversive events in order to inhibit (36) undesirable responses.

In (36) _____, exposure to fear stimuli, adaptation, and reciprocal inhibition are used to break the link between (37) _____ and particular situations.

Typical steps in desensitization are: Construct a fear hierarchy, learn to produce (38) _____, and perform items on the hierarchy (from least to most disturbing).

Desensitization may be carried out in (39) _____, or it may be done by (40) _____ feared stimuli or by watching (41) _____ perform the feared responses.

In some cases, (42) _____ exposure can be used to present fear stimuli in a controlled manner.

A technique called (43) _____ desensitization and reprocessing (EMDR) shows promise as a treatment for traumatic memories and stress disorders. At present, however, EMDR is highly (44)_____.

Module 13.4 Operant Therapies and Cognitive Therapies

Survey Question: What role does reinforcement play in behavior therapy? Pages 558-559, Objective 13.8

(45) _____ makes use of operant principles, such as positive reinforcement, non-reinforcement, extinction, punishment, shaping, stimulus·control, and (46) _____. These principles are used to extinguish undesirable responses and to promote (47) _____ behavior.

Non-reward can (48) _____ troublesome behaviors. Often this is done by simply identifying and eliminating reinforcers, particularly (49) _____ and (50) _____.

To apply (51) _____ and operant shaping, tokens are often used to (52) _____ selected target behaviors.

Full-scale use of tokens in an institutional setting produces a (53)_____. Toward the end of a (53)_____ program, patients are shifted to social rewards such as recognition and (54)_____.

Survey Question: Can therapy change thoughts and emotions? Pages 560-562, Objective 13.9

(55) _____ therapy emphasizes changing thought patterns that underlie emotional or behavioral problems. Its goals are to correct distorted (56) _____ and/or teach improved coping skills.

Irrational beliefs are the core of many (57) _____ thinking patterns. Changing such beliefs can have a (58) _____ impact on emotions and behavior.

In a variation of cognitive therapy called (59) _____ therapy (REBT), clients learn to recognize and challenge their irrational beliefs.

Module 13.5 Group Therapy, Helping Skills, and Medical Therapies

Survey Question: Can psychotherapy be done with groups of people? Pages 564-565, Objective 13.10

(60) _____ therapy may be an extension of individual methods or it may be based on special techniques developed for groups. (61) _____ therapy is especially good for relationship problems.

In (62) _____, individuals enact roles and incidents resembling real-life problems. In (63)_____ therapy, the family group is treated as a unit.

(64) _____ and encounter groups encourage positive personality change. Large-group (65)_____ training attempts to do the same, but the benefits of such programs are questionable.

Survey Question: What do various therapies have in common? Pages 565-569, Objective 13.11
Effective psychotherapies are based on the therapeutic (66) _____, a protected setting, catharsis, insights, new perspectives, and a chance to practice (67) _____.

All of the following are helping skills that can be learned: active listening, (68) _____, reflection, open-ended (69) _____, support, (70) _____, patience, genuineness, and paraphrasing.

The culturally skilled counselor must be able to establish (71) _____ with a person from a different cultural background, and (72) _____ traditional theories and techniques to meet the needs of clients from non-European ethnic groups.

Survey Question: How do psychiatrists treat psychological disorders? Pages 569-573, Objectives 13.12, 13.13
Medical approaches to (73) _____ disorders, such as drugs, surgery, and hospitalization, are similar to medical treatments for (74) _____ ailments.

Three somatic approaches to treatment are pharmacotherapy, (75) _____ therapy (ECT), and psychosurgery.

Community mental health centers seek to (76) _____ or minimize mental hospitalization. They also seek to prevent mental health problems through (77) _____, consultation, and crisis intervention.

Module 13.6 Psychology in Action

Survey Question: How are behavioral principles applied to everyday problems? Pages 575-577, Objective 13.14
Some personal problems can be successfully treated using (78) _____ techniques, such as covert reinforcement, covert sensitization, thought stopping, and self-directed desensitization.

In (79) _____, aversive images are used to discourage unwanted behavior.

(80) _____ uses mild punishment to prevent upsetting thoughts.

(81) _____ is a way to encourage desired responses by mental rehearsal.

(82) _____ pairs relaxation with a hierarchy of upsetting images in order to lessen fears.

Survey Question: How could a person find professional help? Pages 577-579, Objective 13.15
(83) _____ should know how to obtain high-quality mental health care in his or her community.

Various psychotherapies are (84) _____ successful, but some therapists are (85) _____ than others. If you need help, it is worth the effort required to find a (86) _____, highly recommended therapist.

In most communities, a competent and reputable therapist can be located with (87) _____ or through a referral.

Connections

Module 13.1

1. _____ positive therapy	a. tainted rye
2. _____ trepanning	b. old relationships
3. _____ exorcism	c. hysteria
4. _____ ergotism	d. waiting list control
5. _____ Pinel	e. Bicêtre
6. _____ free association	f. latent content
7. _____ Freud	g. possession
8. _____ dream analysis	h. enhanced personal strength
9. _____ transference	i. release of evil spirits
10. _____ spontaneous remission	j. saying anything on mind

Module 13.2

1. _____ telephone therapy	a. reflection
2. _____ authenticity	b. client centered
3. _____ unconditional positive regard	c. no facades
4. _____ rephrasing	d. being in the world
5. _____ distance therapy	e. lack visual cues
6. _____ existentialist	f. telehealth
7. _____ Rogers	g. whole experiences
8. _____ Gestalt therapy	h. unshakable personal acceptance
9. _____ cybertherapy	i. may not be trained professionals

Module 13.3

1. _____ behavior modification	a. unlearned reaction
2. _____ unconditional response	b. easing post-traumatic stress
3. _____ vicarious desensitization	c. secondhand learning
4. _____ desensitization	d. applied behavior analysis
5. _____ EMDR	e. aversion therapy
6. _____ rapid smoking	f. fear hierarchy

Module 13.4

1. _____ overgeneralization	a. operant extinction
2. _____ cognitive therapy	b. token economy
3. _____ time-out	c. Aaron Beck
4. _____ REBT	d. thinking error
5. _____ target behaviors	e. irrational beliefs

Module 13.5

1. _____ psychodrama		a. public education
2. _____ family therapy		b. enhanced self-awareness
3. _____ sensitivity group		c. emotional release
4. _____ encounter group		d. systems approach
5. _____ media psychologist		e. role reversals
6. _____ therapeutic alliance		f. caring relationship
7. _____ catharsis		g. intense interactions

Module 13.6

1. _____ covert sensitization		a. shouting to yourself
2. _____ covert reinforcement		b. prescriptions
3. _____ thought stopping		c. PhD, not MD
4. _____ peer counselors		d. positive imagery
5. _____ self-help group		e. shared problems
6. _____ psychologist		f. nonprofessionals
7. _____ psychiatrist		g. aversive imagery

Check Your Memory

Module 13.1 Psychotherapy and Psychoanalysis

Survey Question: How do psychotherapies differ? Page 542, Objective 13.1

T F   1. A goal of positive therapy is to "fix" a person's weaknesses to enhance their personal strength.

T F   2. A particular psychotherapy could be both insight and action oriented.

T F   3. With the help of psychotherapy, chances of improvement are fairly good for phobias and low self-esteem.

T F   4. Psychotherapy is sometimes used to encourage personal growth for people who are already functioning well.

T F   5. Personal autonomy, a sense of identity, and feelings of personal worth are elements of mental health.

Survey Question: How did psychotherapy originate? Pages 542-544, Objective 13.2

T F   6. Trepanning was really an excuse to kill people since none of the patients survived.

T F   7. Exorcism sometimes took the form of physical torture.

T F   8. Trepanning was the most common treatment for ergotism.

T F   9. Pinel was the first person to successfully treat ergotism.

T F   10. The problem Freud called hysteria is now called a somatoform disorder.

Survey Question: Is Freudian psychoanalysis still used? Pages 544-546, Objective 13.3

T F 11. During free association, patients try to remember the earliest events in their lives.

T F 12. Freud called transference the royal road to the unconscious.

T F 13. Using dream analysis, a therapist seeks to uncover the latent content or symbolic meaning of a person's dreams.

T F 14. The manifest content of a dream is its surface or visible meaning.

T F 15. In an analysis of resistance, the psychoanalyst tries to understand a client's resistance to forming satisfying relationships.

T F 16. Therapists use direct interviewing as part of brief psychodynamic therapy.

T F 17. If members of a waiting list control group improve at the same rate as people in therapy, it demonstrates that the therapy is effective.

Module 13.2 Insight Therapies

Survey Question: What are the major humanistic therapies? Pages 548-550, Objective 13.4

T F 18. Through client-centered therapy, Carl Rogers sought to explore unconscious thoughts and feelings.

T F 19. The client-centered therapist does not hesitate to react with shock, dismay, or disapproval to a client's inappropriate thoughts or feelings.

T F 20. In a sense, the person-centered therapist acts as a psychological mirror for clients.

T F 21. Existential therapy emphasizes our ability to freely make choices.

T F 22. According to the existentialists, our choices must be courageous.

T F 23. Existential therapy emphasizes the integration of fragmented experiences into connected wholes.

T F 24. Fritz Perls was an originator of telehealth.

T F 25. Gestalt therapy may be done individually or in a group.

T F 26. Gestalt therapists urge clients to intellectualize their feelings.

Survey Question: Can therapy be conducted at a distance? Pages 550-551, Objective 13.5

T F 27. The APA suggests that media psychologists should discuss only problems of a general nature.

T F 28. Under certain conditions, telephone therapy can be as successful as face-to-face therapy.

T F 29. The problem with doing therapy by videoconferencing is that facial expressions are not available to the therapist or the client.

Module 13.3 Behavior Therapy

Survey Question: What is behavior therapy? How is behavior therapy used to treat phobias, fears, and anxieties? Pages 553-556, Objectives 13.6, 13.7

T F 30. Behavior modification, or applied behavior analysis, uses classical and operant conditioning to directly alter human behavior.

T F 31. Aversion therapy is based primarily on operant conditioning.

T F 32. For many children, the sight of a hypodermic needle becomes a conditioned stimulus for fear because it is often followed by pain.

T F   33. Rapid smoking creates an aversion because people must hyperventilate to smoke at the prescribed rate.

T F   34. About one-half of all people who quit smoking begin again.

T F   35. In aversion therapy for alcohol abuse, the delivery of shock must appear to be response-contingent to be most effective.

T F   36. Poor generalization of conditioned aversions to situations outside of therapy can be a problem.

T F   37. During desensitization, the steps of a hierarchy are used to produce deep relaxation.

T F   38. Relaxation is the key ingredient of reciprocal inhibition.

T F   39. Clients typically begin with the most disturbing item in a desensitization hierarchy.

T F   40. Desensitization is most effective when people are directly exposed to feared stimuli.

T F   41. The tension-release method is used to produce deep relaxation.

T F   42. Live or filmed models are used in vicarious desensitization.

T F   43. During eye-movement desensitization, clients concentrate on pleasant, calming images.

T F   44. According to REBT, you would hold an irrational belief if you believe that you should depend on others who are stronger than you.

Module 13.4 Operant Therapies and Cognitive Therapies
Survey Question: What role does reinforcement play in behavior therapy? Pages 558-559, Objective 13.8
T F   45. Operant punishment is basically the same thing as nonreinforcement.

T F   46. Shaping involves reinforcing ever-closer approximations to a desired response.

T F   47. An undesirable response can be extinguished by reversing stimulus control.

T F   48. Misbehavior tends to decrease when others ignore it.

T F   49. To be effective, tokens must be tangible rewards, such as slips of paper or poker chips.

T F   50. The value of tokens is based on the fact that they can be exchanged for other reinforcers.

T F   51. A goal of token economies is to eventually switch patients to social reinforcers.

Survey Question: Can therapy change thoughts and emotions? Pages 560-562, Objective 13.9
T F   52. Cognitive therapy is especially successful in treating depression.

T F   53. Depressed persons tend to magnify the importance of events.

T F   54. Cognitive therapy is as effective as drugs for treating many cases of depression.

T F   55. Stress inoculation is a form of rational-emotive behavior therapy.

T F   56. The A in the ABC analysis of REBT stands for anticipation.

T F   57. The C in the ABC analysis of REBT stands for consequence.

Module 13.5 Group Therapy, Helping Skills, and Medical Therapies
Survey Question: Can psychotherapy be done with groups of people? Pages 564-565, Objective 13.10
T F   58. The mirror technique is the principal method used in family therapy.

T F   59. Family therapists try to meet with the entire family unit during each session of therapy.

T F   60. A trust walk is a typical sensitivity group exercise.

T F   61. Large group awareness training has been known to create emotional crises where none existed before.

Survey Question: What do various therapies have in common? Pages 565-569, Objective 13.11

T F   62. Half of all people who begin psychotherapy feel better after eight sessions.

T F   63. Emotional rapport is a key feature of the therapeutic alliance.

T F   64. Therapy gives clients a chance to practice new behaviors.

T F   65. An increase in short-term therapy, telephone counseling, and self-help groups in the future is likely the result of the high cost of mental health services.

T F   66. Competent counselors do not hesitate to criticize clients, place blame when it is deserved, and probe painful topics.

T F   67. Why don't you . . . Yes, but . . . is a common game used to avoid taking responsibility in therapy.

T F   68. Closed questions tend to be most helpful in counseling another person.

T F   69. Cultural barriers to effective counseling include differences in language, social class, and nonverbal communication.

T F   70. A necessary step toward becoming a culturally skilled counselor is to adopt the culture of your clients as your own.

Survey Question: How do psychiatrists treat psychological disorders? Pages 569-573, Objectives 13.12, 13.13

T F   71. Major mental disorders are primarily treated with psychotherapy.

T F   72. When used for long periods of time, major tranquilizers can cause a neurological disorder.

T F   73. Two percent of all patients taking Clozaril suffer from a serious blood disease.

T F   74. ECT treatments are usually given in a series of 20 to 30 sessions, occurring once a day.

T F   75. ECT is most effective when used to treat depression.

T F   76. To reduce a relapse, antidepressant drugs are recommended for patients with depression following ECT treatment.

T F   77. The prefrontal lobotomy is the most commonly performed type of psychosurgery today.

T F   78. In the approach known as partial hospitalization, patients live at home.

T F   79. Admitting a person to a mental institution is the first step to treating the disorder.

T F   80. Deinstitutionalization increased the number of homeless persons living in many communities.

T F   81. Most halfway houses are located on the grounds of mental hospitals.

T F   82. Crisis intervention is typically one of the services provided by community mental health centers.

T F   83. Most people prefer to seek help from a professional doctor over a paraprofessional because of their approachability.

Module 13.6 Psychology in Action

Survey Question: How are behavioral principles applied to everyday problems? Pages 575-577, Objective 13.14

T F   84. To do covert sensitization, you must first learn relaxation exercises.

T F   85. Disgusting images are used in thought stopping.

T F   86. Covert reinforcement should be visualized before performing steps in a fear hierarchy.

Survey Question: How could a person find professional help? Pages 577-579, Objective 13.15

T F   87. Approximately 50 percent of all American households had someone who received mental health treatment.

T F   88. Significant changes in your work, relationships, or use of drugs or alcohol can be signs that you should seek professional help.

T F   89. Marital problems are the most common reason for seeing a mental health professional.

T F   90. For some problems, paraprofessional counselors and self-help groups are as effective as professional psychotherapy.

T F   91. All major types of psychotherapy are about equally successful.

T F   92. All therapists are equally qualified and successful at treating mental disorders.

Critical Thinking

Module 13.1

1. Waiting-list control groups help separate the effects of therapy from improvement related to the mere passage of time. What other type of control group might be needed to learn if therapy is truly beneficial?

Module 13.2

2. How might using the term *patient* affect the relationship between an individual and a therapist?

Module 13.3

3. Alcoholics who take a drug called Antabuse become ill after drinking alcohol. Why, then, don't they develop an aversion to drinking?

4. A natural form of desensitization often takes place in hospitals. Can you guess what it is?

Module 13.4

5. In Aaron Beck's terms, a belief such as "I must perform well or I am a rotten person" involves two thinking errors. These are:

Module 13.5

6. In your opinion, do psychologists have a duty to protect others who may be harmed by their clients? For example, if a patient has homicidal fantasies about his ex-wife, should she be informed?

7. Residents of Berkeley, California, once voted on a referendum to ban the use of ECT within city limits. Do you think that the use of certain psychiatric treatments should be controlled by law?

Module 13.6

8. Would it be acceptable for a therapist to urge a client to break all ties with a troublesome family member?

Final Survey and Review

Module 13.1 Psychotherapy and Psychoanalysis

Survey Question: How do psychotherapies differ? Objective 13.1

1. Psychotherapy facilitates positive changes in _____, behavior, or _____.

2. Psychotherapies may be classified as _____, action, _____, non-directive, _____, or positive therapies, or combinations of these.

3. Therapies may be conducted either individually or in groups, and they may be _____.

Survey Question: How did psychotherapy originate? Objective 13.2

4. Early approaches to mental illness were dominated by superstition and _____.

5. Demonology attributed mental disturbance to _____, such as demonic _____, and prescribed _____ as the cure.

6. In some instances, the actual cause of bizarre behavior may have been _____.

7. More _____ treatment began in 1793 with the work of Philippe Pinel in _____.

Survey Question: Is Freudian psychoanalysis still used? Objective 13.3

8. As the first true psychotherapy, Freud's psychoanalysis gave rise to modern _____ therapies.

9. Psychoanalysis seeks to reveal unconscious _____, emotions, and _____.

10. The psychoanalyst uses free _____, dream analysis, and analysis of _____ and transference to reveal health-producing _____.

11. Some critics argue that traditional psychoanalysis receives credit for _____ of symptoms. However, psychoanalysis is _____ for many patients.

12. Brief _____ therapy, which relies on _____ theory but is brief and focused, is as effective as other major therapies. One example is _____ psychotherapy.

Module 13.2 Insight Therapies

Survey Question: What are the major humanistic therapies? Objective 13.4

13. _____ (or person-centered) therapy is _____, based on insights gained from _____ thoughts and feelings, and is dedicated to creating an atmosphere of growth.

14. Unconditional positive regard, empathy, _____, and _____ are combined to give the client a chance to solve his or her own problems.

15. Existential therapies focus on the end result of the _____ one makes in life. Clients are encouraged through confrontation and _____ to exercise _____ and to take responsibility for their choices.

16. Gestalt therapy emphasizes _____ of thoughts and feelings. Its goal is to rebuild thinking, feeling, and _____ into connected wholes, and to help clients break through _____ blockages.

Survey Question: Can therapy be conducted at a distance? Objective 13.5

17. Media psychologists, _____ counselors, and _____ may, on occasion, do some good. However, each has drawbacks, and the effectiveness of _____ counseling and _____ has not been unambiguously established.

18. Therapy by _____ shows more promise as a way to provide mental health services at a distance.

Module 13.3 Behavior Therapy

Survey Question: What is behavior therapy? How is behavior therapy used to treat phobias, fears, and anxieties? Objectives 13.6, 13.7

19. Behavior therapists use the learning principles of _____ or _____ conditioning to directly change human behavior.

20. In aversion therapy, _____ conditioning is used to associate _____ behavior (such as smoking or drinking) with pain or other aversive events in order to _____ undesirable responses.

21. In desensitization, _____ to fear stimuli, adaptation, and _____ _____ are used to break the link between fear and particular situations.

22. Typical steps in desensitization are: Construct a fear _____, learn to produce total relaxation, and perform items on the hierarchy (from _____ to _____ disturbing).

23. Desensitization may be _____ in real settings or it may be done by vividly imagining _____ or by watching models _____.

24. In some cases, virtual reality exposure can be used to present _____ in a _____ manner.

25. A technique called eye movement _____ and _____ (EMDR) shows promise as a treatment for _____ _____ and _____ disorders. At present, however, EMDR is _____ controversial.

Module 13.4 Operant Therapies and Cognitive Therapies

Survey Question: What role does reinforcement play in behavior therapy? Objective 13.8

26. Behavior modification makes use of _____ principles, such as positive reinforcement, non-reinforcement, _____, punishment, _____, stimulus _____, and time out. These principles are used to extinguish _____ and to _____ constructive behavior.

27. Non-reward can extinguish _____. Often this is done by simply _____ and _____ reinforcers, particularly attention and social approval.

28. To apply positive reinforcement and _____ shaping, _____ are often used to reinforce selected target behaviors.

29. Full-scale use of _____ in an _____ setting produces a token economy. Toward the end of a token economy program, patients are shifted to _____, such as recognition and approval.

Survey Question: Can therapy change thoughts and emotions? Objective 13.9

30. Cognitive therapy emphasizes changing _____ that underlie emotional or behavioral problems. Its goals are to correct _____ thinking and/or teach improved _____ skills.

31. Irrational _____ are the core of many maladaptive _____ patterns. Changing such beliefs can have a positive impact on _____ and _____.

32. In a variation of cognitive therapy called rational-emotive _____ therapy (REBT), clients learn to recognize and challenge their _____.

Module 13.5 Group Therapy, Helping Skills, and Medical Therapies

Survey Question: Can psychotherapy be done with groups of people? Objective 13.10

33. Group therapy may be an extension of _____ methods or it may be based on special techniques developed for groups. Group therapy is especially good for _____.

34. In psychodrama, individuals enact _____ and incidents resembling _____. In family therapy, the family group is treated as _____.

35. Sensitivity and _____ groups encourage positive _____ change. Large-group awareness training attempts to do the same, but the _____ of such programs are questionable.

Survey Question: What do various therapies have in common? Objective 13.11

36. Effective psychotherapies are based on the _____ alliance, a protected setting, _____, insights, new perspectives, and a chance to _____.

37. All of the following are helping skills that can be learned: _____ listening, acceptance, reflection, _____ questioning, support, respect, patience, genuineness, and _____.

38. The _____ counselor must be able to establish rapport with a person from a different cultural background and adapt _____ theories and techniques to meet the needs of clients from _____ groups.

Survey Question: How do psychiatrists treat psychological disorders? Objectives 13.12, 13.13

39. Medical approaches to mental disorders, such as _____, _____, and hospitalization, are similar to _____ treatments for physical ailments.

40. Three somatic approaches to treatment are _____, electroconvulsive therapy (ECT), and

_____.

41. _____ seek to avoid or minimize mental hospitalization. They also seek to prevent mental health problems through education, _____, and _____ intervention.

Module 13.6 Psychology in Action

Survey Question: How are behavioral principles applied to everyday problems? Objective 13.14

42. Some _____ can be successfully treated using self-management techniques, such as covert _____, covert sensitization, thought stopping, and _____ desensitization.

43. In covert sensitization, _____ are used to discourage unwanted behavior.

44. Thought stopping uses _____ to prevent upsetting thoughts.

45. Covert reinforcement is a way to encourage desired responses by _____.

46. Desensitization pairs _____ with a hierarchy of _____ in order to lessen fears.

Survey Question: How could a person find professional help? Objective 13.15

47. Everyone should know how to obtain _____ in his or her community.

48. Various psychotherapies are about equally _____, but some _____ are more effective than others. If you need help, it is worth the effort required to find a well qualified, highly _____ therapist.

49. In most communities, a competent and _____ therapist can be located with public sources of information or through _____.

Mastery Test

1. To demonstrate that spontaneous remissions are occurring, you could use a
    a. patient-defined hierarchy.
    b. waiting list control group.
    c. target behavior group.
    d. short-term dynamic correlation.

2. In desensitization, relaxation is induced to block fear, a process known as
    a. systematic adaptation.
    b. vicarious opposition.
    c. stimulus control.
    d. reciprocal inhibition.

3. Role reversals and the mirror technique are methods of
   a. psychodrama.
   b. person-centered therapy.
   c. family therapy.
   d. brief psychodynamic therapy.

4. One thing that both trepanning and exorcism have in common is that both were used
   a. to treat ergotism.
   b. by Pinel in the Bicêtre Asylum.
   c. to remove spirits.
   d. to treat cases of hysteria.

5. Unconditional positive regard is a concept particularly associated with
   a. Beck.
   b. Frankl.
   c. Perls.
   d. Rogers.

6. Many of the claimed benefits of large group awareness trainings appear to represent a therapy
   a. remission.
   b. education.
   c. placebo.
   d. transference.

7. Personal change is LEAST likely to be the goal of
   a. supportive therapy.
   b. action therapy.
   c. desensitization.
   d. humanistic therapy.

8. Inducing seizures is a standard part of using
   a. Gestalt therapy.
   b. antidepressants.
   c. ECT.
   d. cybertherapy.

9. Which counseling behavior does not belong with the others listed here?
   a. paraphrasing
   b. judging
   c. reflecting
   d. active listening

10. In psychoanalysis, the process most directly opposite to free association is
    a. resistance.
    b. transference.
    c. symbolization.
    d. remission.

11. Identification of target behaviors is an important step in designing
    a. a desensitization hierarchy.
    b. activating stimuli.
    c. token economies.
    d. encounter groups.

12. A person who wants to lose weight looks at a dessert and visualizes maggots crawling all over it. The person is obviously using
    a. systematic adaptation.
    b. covert sensitization.
    c. stress inoculation.
    d. systematic desensitization.

13. Which of the following is NOT a humanistic therapy?
    a. client-centered
    b. Gestalt
    c. existential
    d. cognitive

14. Not many emergency room doctors drive without using their seat belts. This observation helps explain the effectiveness of
    a. systematic desensitization.
    b. aversion therapy.
    c. covert reinforcement.
    d. the mirror technique.

15. Telephone counselors have little chance of using which element of effective psychotherapy?
    a. empathy
    b. nondirective reflection
    c. the therapeutic alliance
    d. accepting the person's frame of reference

16. Which of the following is a self-management technique?
    a. thought stopping
    b. vicarious reality exposure
    c. REBT
    d. EMDR

17. A good example of a nondirective insight therapy is _____ therapy.
    a. client-centered
    b. Gestalt
    c. psychoanalytic
    d. brief psychodynamic

18. Which statement about psychotherapy is true?
    a. Most therapists are equally successful.
    b. Most techniques are equally successful.
    c. Therapists and clients need not agree about the goals of therapy.
    d. Effective therapists instruct their clients not to discuss their therapy with anyone else.

19. Analysis of resistances and transferences is a standard feature of
    a. client-centered therapy.
    b. Gestalt therapy.
    c. REBT.
    d. psychoanalysis.

20. Both classical and operant conditioning are the basis for
    a. desensitization.
    b. token economies.
    c. behavior therapy.
    d. aversion therapy.

21. Rational-emotive behavior therapy is best described by which three characteristics?
    a. insight, nondirective, individual
    b. insight, supportive, individual
    c. action, supportive, group
    d. action, directive, individual

22. Deep lesioning is a form of
    a. ECT.
    b. psychosurgery.
    c. pharmacotherapy.
    d. PET.

23. Identifying and removing rewards is a behavioral technique designed to bring about
    a. operant shaping.
    b. extinction.
    c. respondent aversion.
    d. token inhibition.

24. Culturally skilled counselors must be aware of their own cultural backgrounds as well as
    a. the percentage of ethnic populations in the community.
    b. that of their clients.
    c. the importance of maintaining confidentiality.
    d. the life goals of minorities.

25. A behavioral therapist would treat acrophobia with
    a. desensitization.
    b. aversion therapy.
    c. covert sensitization.
    d. cybertherapy.

26. Which technique most closely relates to the idea of nondirective therapy?
    a. confrontation
    b. dream analysis
    c. role reversal
    d. reflection

27. Fifty percent of psychotherapy patients say they feel better after the first _____ sessions.
    a. 4
    b. 8
    c. 12
    d. 20

28. Overgeneralization is a thinking error that contributes to
    a. depression.
    b. somatization.
    c. phobias.
    d. emotional reprocessing.

29. Death, freedom, and meaning are special concerns of
    a. REBT.
    b. cognitive therapy.
    c. existential therapy.
    d. psychodrama.

30. An intense awareness of present experience and breaking through emotional impasses is key to
    a. action therapy.
    b. Gestalt therapy.
    c. time-limited therapy.
    d. REBT.

31. The ABCs of REBT stand for _____, _____, _____.
    a. anticipation, behavior, conduct
    b. action, behavior, conflict
    c. activating experience, belief, consequence
    d. anticipation, belief, congruent experience

32. Which of the following in NOT a "distance therapy"?
    a. REBT
    b. telephone therapy
    c. cybertherapy
    d. telehealth

33. Virtual reality exposure is a type of
    a. psychodrama.
    b. ECT therapy.
    c. cognitive therapy.
    d. desensitization.

34. ECT is most often used to treat
    a. psychosis.
    b. anxiety.
    c. hysteria.
    d. depression.

35. Which of the following is most often associated with community mental health programs?
    a. pharmacotherapy
    b. covert reinforcement
    c. crisis intervention
    d. REBT

36. Which therapy's main purpose is to enhance people's personal strengths rather than try to fix their weakness?
    a. supportive
    b. positive
    c. insight
    d. directive

37. An element of positive mental health that therapists seek to promote is
    a. dependency on therapist.
    b. a sense of identity.
    c. personal autonomy and independence.
    d. both b and c

38. Which theory relies on dream analysis to uncover the unconscious roots of neurosis?
    a. existential
    b. psychoanalytic
    c. client-centered
    d. telehealth

39. _____ has been one of the most successful behavioral therapies for reducing fears, anxieties, and psychological pains.
    a. Vicarious desensitization
    b. Virtual reality exposure
    c. Eye-movement desensitization
    d. Desensitization

40. Research suggests that mental hospitals in our society are being replaced by
    a. a full-time live-in nurse.
    b. placing them in jail.
    c. medicating the mentally ill until they reach 65 years old.
    d. allowing the mentally ill to take care of themselves.

41. "There is always a perfect solution to human problems and it is awful if this solution is not found" is a typical _____ statement.
    a. irrational belief
    b. self-awareness
    c. health-promoting
    d. response-contingent

42. Experts predict that the shift from traditional forms of psychotherapy to short-term, solution-focused, telephone, and self-help group therapy is a reflection of
    a. the lack of time available in people's busy lives to seek mental health services.
    b. fewer people needing mental health services.
    c. societal pressures to reduce costs in mental health services.
    d. people being afraid to reveal their mental illness.

Chapter 15: Social Behavior

Chapter Overview

Social Psychology is a combination of several social sciences, exploring our relationships with others and how those relationships affect our behavior.

One area of research is attraction and interpersonal relationships. Friendship and romantic relationships involve a complex combination of personal and interpersonal factors.

As part of a group, we often look to others to see what to do. Roles, norms, and status within and between groups shape our actions, beliefs, and attributions.

Social influence is exerting social pressure to change the behavior of others. This could be subtle, as in some cases of conformity, in the form of a request (compliance), or a direct command (obedience). Our personal sense of control is constantly balancing against the power of the situation.

When the situation is weak, we tend to act in accordance with our attitudes. However, our behavior can be changed through external social influence or because of attitude change (persuasion).

Although stereotypes can be positive or negative, accurate or inaccurate, when stereotypes result in negative judgments and differential treatment there is prejudice and discrimination. Prejudice seems to be partially based on personality and part on social conflicts and inequalities. Prejudice can be intercultural or between groups within a society.

In addition to trying to reduce prejudice, social psychologists are also trying to reduce societal and interpersonal aggression and increase prosocial or helping behaviors. Many biological, psychological, and social variables have been identified that influence these behaviors.

Learning Objectives

OBJECTIVE 15.1 — Define *social psychology*; discuss our need to afflilate, including a description of Schachter's classic experiment on afflliation; and describe the social comparison theory, including how meaningful evaluations take place.

OBJECTIVE 15.2 — Define interpersonal attraction; describe how the following factors influence interpersonal attraction: a. physical proximity; b. physical attractiveness, including the halo effect; c. competence; and d. similarity, including homogamy; and discuss the effects of varying degrees of self-disclosure on interpersonal relationships.

OBJECTIVE 15.3 — Discuss Rubin's studies of romantic love, including the differences between loving and liking, the differences between male and female friendships, and the concept of mutual absorption; and describe the field of evolutionary psychology and how this field of study explains the different mate selection preferences of males and females.

OBJECTIVE 15.4 — Discuss the following dimensions of being in a social group: a. social roles, including ascribed roles, achieved roles, and role conflict; b. group structure; c. group cohesiveness, d. in-groups and out-groups; e. status; and f. group norms.

OBJECTIVE 15.5 — Discuss the process of attribution, including the difference between external and internal causes; explain the fundamental attribution error and the actor-observer bias; and describe gender differences in attributing success.

OBJECTIVE 15.6 — Define social influence; explain the three major forms of social influence; describe Asch's experiment on conformity and the personal characteristics that make some people more susceptible to group pressures; explain how groupthink may contribute to poor decision-making and list ways to prevent it; and describe how the following factors affect conformity: a. group sanctions, b. the importance of the group, c. the number of group members, d. the unanimity of the group, and e. the power of an ally.

OBJECTIVE 15.7 — Explain how compliance differs from conformity; discuss the following methods of gaining compliance: a. foot-in-the-door; b. door-in-the-face; and c. low-ball technique; and describe how knowing these strategies can protect a person from being manipulated.

OBJECTIVE 15.8 — Describe Milgram's study of obedience; discuss how each of the following factors affected the degree of obedience in Milgram's follow-up experiments: a. prestige of the authority, b. distance between the teacher and the learner, c. distance from the authority, and d. group support; and give examples of "crimes of obedience" in world events and everyday life.

OBJECTIVE 15.9 — Discuss the following aspects of assertiveness training: a. the three basic rights, including the concept of self-assertion; b. a comparison of assertive, non-assertive, and aggressive behaviors (Table 15.2); and c. assertiveness training, including the importance of practice, using rehearsal and role-playing, the principle of overlearning, and the *broken record* technique.

OBJECTIVE 15.10 — Define attitude; describe the belief, emotional, and action components of an attitude; list and give examples of six ways in which attitudes are acquired; and explain three reasons why people may exhibit discrepancies between attitudes and behavior, and how conviction affects attitudes.

OBJECTIVE 15.11 — Explain the difference between membership groups and reference groups, including how one's point of reference affects attitude change; and define persuasion and explain how the characteristics of the communicator, audience, and message affect attitude change.

OBJECTIVE 15.12 — Explain cognitive dissonance theory; list five strategies for reducing dissonance (Table 15.3); and describe how the amount of justification affects the amount of dissonance felt and why people are especially likely to experience dissonance after causing an event that they wish hadn't happened.

OBJECTIVE 15.13 — Differentiate between brainwashing and other persuasive techniques; describe the techniques used in brainwashing; indicate how permanent the attitude changes brought about by brainwashing are; and describe how cults are able to recruit, convert, and retain their members and how cult leaders differ from true spiritual leaders.

OBJECTIVE 15.14 — Differentiate between the concepts of prejudice and discrimination; describe how prejudice may be a form of scapegoating; distinguish between the two sources of prejudice, personal and group prejudices; and explain how prejudice can be considered a general personality characteristic by discussing the following: a. the authoritarian personality, b. ethnocentrism, c. the use of the F-scale to measure authoritarian beliefs, and d. how authoritarian beliefs are learned as children.

OBJECTIVE 15.15 — Describe the shared beliefs that tend to trigger intergroup conflict; explain the characterisitcs of social stereotypes and how they can amplify the conflict between groups; describe symbolic prejudice; and explain how some elements of prejudice appear to be unconscious.

OBJECTIVE 15.16 — Describe Jane Elliot's experiment in which prejudice was caused by status inequalities; explain how reducing the complex American society into two oversimplified stereotypes, "red and blue states," has led to an increase in between-group prejudice; and describe how more frequent equal-status contact between groups in conflict could reduce prejudice and stereotyping.

OBJECTIVE 15.17 — Describe the summer camp experiment in which superordinate goals were used to help reduce the conflict between the two groups; and explain how superordinate goals can be applied to reduce global conflict and to reduce prejudices within ordinary classrooms through the jigsaw classrooms and their goal of mutual interdependence.

OBJECTIVE 15.18 — Define aggression; and discuss the role of each of the following in aggressive behavior: a. instincts and why psychologists question this theory; b. biology, including physical factors and the effects of drugs and alcohol; c. the frustration-aggression hypothesis; d. aversive stimuli, including the activation of internal and external aggressive cues and the weapons effect; and e. social learning theory.

OBJECTIVE 15.19 — Explain how television can teach new antisocial actions, serve as a disinhibiting factor, cause desensitization to violence, increase aggressive thoughts, and make one more prone to aggress when faced with frustrating stiuations or cues; and list seven ways in which parents can buffer the impact of television on children's behavior.

OBJECTIVE 15.20 — Define prosocial behavior; describe the Kitty Genovese case in terms of bystander apathy; explain how the presence of other people can influence bystanders' willingness to help; describe four conditions that need to exist before bystanders are likely to give help; discuss factors, such as heightened and emotional arousal and the empathy-helping relationship, that make one more likely to help; describe how one can "de-victimize" oneself and be more likely to receive help; and give examples of some "everyday heroes."

OBJECTIVE 15.21 — Define the term multiculturalism; discuss eight ways by which a person can become more tolerant; and explain how a person can develop cultural awareness.

Language Development Guide

Introduction
(620) *intermediaries*: people in between
(620) *tapestry*: colorful woven rug

Module 15.1
(622) *deprived of*: without
(622) *alleviate*: remove, heal, relieve
(622) *misery loves company*: people who are unhappy prefer to be with other people who are also unhappy
(622) *hip-hop*: urban music style
(622) *How did you do?*: How well did you perform?
(623) *birds of a feather flock together*: people want to be with others who have similar characteristics or personalities
(623) *familiarity breeds contempt*: the more one knows about a person, the less one likes that person
(623) *opposites attract*: people are curious about people who are different
(623) *absence makes the heart grow fonder*: people in a relationship have stronger love after being separated for a period of time
(623) *folklore*: traditional customs, stories, or sayings of a people
(623) *one and only*: each person has a perfect partner in the world, a "soul-mate" or best match
(623) *made in heaven*: perfect, ideal
(623) *witty*: having humor
(624) *close to the vest*: careful, without revealing too much
(625) *freer*: more free, open, able
(625) *angle*: perspective, set of beliefs
(625) *gazing*: looking intensely
(625) *idealize*: believe someone else is perfect
(626) *trophy wives*: a marriage to gain prestige and admiration, a wealthy but perhaps older or unattractive man with a much younger and much more attractive woman
(627) *inevitable*: will definitely occur

Module 15.2
(628) *attained*: earned
(628) *streamline*: make more easy or effortless
(628) *coordinated*: match, be similar
(628) *bestows*: awards, gives
(628) *croissant*: a small moon-shaped bread
(629) *preoccupation*: concern, interest, fascination
(629) *littering*: dropping garbage
(629) *trash*: destroy, leave dirty or messy
(629) *shreds*: pieces
(629) *Sousa*: an American music composer
(630) *Ye Old Double Standard*: the old double standard; the idea that there is one set of rules for women and a different set of rules for men
(630) *haunt*: constant bad presence
(631) *lethal*: deadly
(631) *flange*: a raised edge of a wheel
(631) *Thou shalt conform*: joke, worded to sound like one of the biblical Ten Commandments, an absolute rule

(631) *erred*: made a mistake or error

(631) *disastrous*: very bad

(631) *sanctions*: punishments involving rejection, isolation, exclusion

(632) *yielding*: giving up

(632) *mean*: angry, scary, grumpy

(632) *ally*: friend

(632) *dissenting*: not agreeing with the majority

Module 15.3

(634) *cappuccino*: strong coffee drink

(634) *notorious*: well-known

(634) *lowball*: undercutting, deceptively below everyone else's

(634) *bump the price up*: increase the price

(635) *grumble*: talk about how unhappy you are

(636) *going up the scale*: giving stronger shocks

(636) *chillingly*: anxiously, with fear or uncertain discomfort

(637) *sanctioned massacres*: lots of killing that is supposedly acceptable or allowable

(637) *chilling proportions*: an uncomfortable amount

(638) *misguided*: bad, uninformed, poor, incorrect

(638) *exclusively*: only

(638) *pent-up*: held in, saved

(638) *irresponsible*: lazy, can't be trusted

(638) *flustered*: confused, anxious

Module 15.4

(641) *affirmative action*: rules to reduce discrimination, particularly based on sex or race

(641) *death penalty*: using execution as a punishment for crime

(641) *doomsday group*: a group who believes that the end of the world is coming soon

(641) *bitter*: harsh

(641) *predisposes*: prepares

(641) *gun control*: laws reducing the sale or ownership of guns

(641) *orient*: make familiar

(641) *take an unduly dim view*: dislike

(642) *coaxed*: gently urged

(642) *channeled*: directed, focused

(642) *steady diet*: constant exposure

(643) *stick to:* continue believing in

(643) *blitz*: bombardment, attack

(644) *lure*: trap, draw in

(644) *barge*: large car

(644) *gas-guzzler*: a car or truck that uses a lot of gasoline

(645) *POW*: prisoner of war

(645) *lulled*: made sleepy

(645) *rigid*: stiff, inflexible, harsh, strict

(645) *authoritarian*: with a strong and commanding leader

(645) *mores*: norms, ethical rules

Module 15.5

(648) *prevalent*: common

(648) *depiction*: being shown

(648) *anti-Semitism*: prejudice against Jews

(648) *black-and-white thinking*: all or nothing, only option being good or bad, simplified into only two choices or sides

(649) *fascism*: tendency toward strong autocratic or dictatorial control

(649) *bigotry*: prejudice

(649) *foster*: encourage, cause

(649) *jarring strife*: conflict

(649) *exploited*: used unfairly

(649) *amplified*: made stronger

(649) *blue-collar*: manufacturing, industrial, lower income or education

(649) *rednecks*: white working class or poor rural person

(650) *demeaning*: negative

(650) *stolid*: unemotional

(650) *pugnacious*: gets into fights

(650) *mercenary*: doing things only for money

(651) *eradicate*: erase, remove, eliminate

(651) *wanton*: careless

(651) *slurs*: insults

(651) *thinly veiled*: only slightly hidden or disguised

(651) *mingling*: interacting

(651) *viciousness*: cruelty

(652) *equal footing*: fair basis

(652) *staked out:* claimed

(652) *baited*: tried to bring into conflict

(652) *raided*: attacked and stole items or created a mess

(653) *gang colors*: particular colors, usually of clothing that identify members of particular groups of youths

(653) *staged*: created

(653) *we're all in the same boat*: we will succeed together or all fail

(653) *jigsaw puzzle*: a puzzle consisting of small irregularly cut pieces that are to be fit together to form a picture

(654) *debases*: hurts

Module 15.6

(656) *revulsion*: strong dislike

(656) *pressing*: urgent

(656) *staggering*: large, unbelievable

(656) *offer sad testimony*: show bad things

(656) *lunge*: jump at

(656) *bare its throat*: lifting one's head, revealing the neck; to show vulnerability

(656) *the Arapesh, the Senoi, the Navajo, the Eskimo*: Arapesh and Senoi are tribes in Malaysia, the Navajo a Native American tribe, the Eskimo a tribe in Alaska and northern Canada

(657) *threshold*: limit, starting point

(657) *nipped*: bitten

(657) *spectators*: watchers

(658) *trappings*: tools, clothing, gear, appearances

(658) *pipe bombing*: homemade explosive devices

(658) *bean balls*: in baseball, pitches thrown to hit another player in the head

(658) *an almost nonstop parade*: many

(658) *mugging*: street robbery

(658) *gross*: disgusting

(659) *aggression begets aggression*: fighting causes revenge and more fighting

(659) *spiral of aggression*: in revenge, each response to aggression increases in intensity

(659) *pulling the plug*: discontinuing

(660) *apathetic*: complacent, not doing

(661) *coolly*: without emotion

(661) *fake each other out*: send misleading messages

(661) *confidentiality*: privacy

(661) *passed out*: unconscious

(661) *keyed-up*: anxious or active

(661) *plight*: bad situation

(662) *Peace Corp*: group that sends workers to Third World countries to provide aid

(662) *Doctors of the World*: physicians that volunteer to travel to other countries to provide free medical care

Module 15.7

(664) *tossed salad*: metaphor for multiculturalism where people are mixed together but maintain their individual identity

(664) *melting pot*: metaphor for multiculturalism like a soup or molten metals, where materials are blended together to create something new

(664) *fall prey to*: be tricked

(665) *degrade*: insult, reduce, demean/

(665) *emulating*: copying

(665) *puts a premium on*: values, emphasizes

(665) *vanquish*: eliminate, erase, destroy

(666) *Confucian-steeped*: where the writings of Confucius are common and well-known

(666) *friction*: conflict, difficulty

(666) *kosher*: Jewish food purity practices

Recite and Review

Module 15.1 Affiliation, Friendship, and Love

Survey Questions: Why do people affiliate? What factors influence interpersonal attraction? Pages 622-627, Objectives 15.1, 15.2, 15.3

(1) _____ studies how we behave, think, and feel in social situations.

We are attracted to other people for reasons that are fairly (2) _____.

Affiliation is tied to needs for (3) _____, support, (4) _____, and information. Also, affiliation can (5) _____ anxiety.

(6) _____ theory holds that we affiliate to evaluate our actions, feelings, and abilities.

Interpersonal attraction is increased by proximity, (7) _____ contact, (8) _____, and similarity.

Mate selection is characterized by a (9) _____ of similarity on (10) _____ dimensions.

(11) _____ follows a reciprocity norm: Low levels of (11) _____ are met with low levels in return; moderate (11) _____ elicits more personal replies.

In comparison with liking, (12) _____ involves higher levels of emotional arousal and it is accompanied by mutual absorption between (13) _____.

(14) _____ psychologists attribute human mating patterns to the reproductive challenges men and women faced during the course of evolution.

Module 15.2 Groups, Social Influence, and Conformity

Survey Question: How does group membership affect our behavior? Pages 628-630, Objectives 15.4, 15.5

To understand social behavior we must know what (15) _____ people play, their status, the (16)_____ they follow, and the attributions they make.

Social roles are particular (17) _____ patterns associated with (18) _____ positions.

(19) _____ within groups is associated with special privileges and respect.

Norms are (20) _____ enforced (formally or informally) by groups.

We (21) _____ behavior to various causes. These (22) _____, in turn, affect how we act.

The (23) _____ is to think that internal causes explain the actions of other people. In contrast, we tend to attribute (24) _____ to external causes.

Survey Question: What have social psychologists learned about conformity? Pages 630-632, Objective 15.6

(25)_____ refers to alterations in behavior brought about by the behavior of others.

The famous (26) _____ experiments demonstrated that people are likely to conform when they face social pressure from other group members.

(27)_____ refers to compulsive conformity in group decision making.

Module 15.3 Compliance, Obedience, and Self-Assertion

Survey Question: What have psychologists learned about compliance, obedience, and self-assertion? Pages 634-639, Objectives 15.7, 15.8, 15.9

Three strategies for gaining compliance are the (28) _____ technique, the door-in-the-face approach, and the low-ball technique.

Most people have a strong tendency to (29) _____ legitimate authority. Usually this is desirable, but it can be damaging when (30) _____ is used in misguided or unscrupulous ways.

Obedience to authority in Milgram's studies decreased when the "teacher" and "learner" were (31) _____, when the authority was absent, and when (32) _____ refused to obey.

(33)_____ helps people meet their needs without resorting to aggressive behavior.

Module 15.4 Attitudes and Persuasion

Survey Question: How are attitudes acquired and changed? Pages 641-642, Objective 15.10

Attitudes are made up of a belief component, an (34) _____ component, and an action component.

Attitudes (35) _____ are most likely to affect our behavior.

Attitudes may be formed by direct contact, (36) _____ with others, child-rearing practices, group pressures, (37) _____ influences, reference group membership, the (38) _____, and chance conditioning.

Survey Question: Under what conditions is persuasion most effective? Pages 643-645, Objectives 15.11, 15.12

Effective (39) _____ must take into account characteristics of the communicator, the message, and the audience.

In general, a (40) _____ and believable communicator who repeats a credible message that arouses (41)_____ in the audience and states clear-cut (42) _____ will be persuasive.

(43)_____ theory explains many aspects of attitude change.

(44)_____ is a form of forced attitude change. It depends on (45)_____ of the target person's environment.

Three steps in brainwashing are unfreezing, changing, and (46)_____ attitudes and beliefs.

Many cults recruit (47)_____ with high-pressure indoctrination techniques.

Module 15.5 Prejudice and Intergroup Conflict

Survey Question: What causes prejudice and intergroup conflict? Pages 648-654, Objectives 15.14,
        15.15, 15.16, 15.17

(48)_____ is a negative attitude held toward members of various out-groups.

One theory attributes prejudice to (49)_____.

Prejudices may be held for personal reasons ((50)_____) or simply through adherence to group norms ((51) _____).

Prejudiced individuals tend to have an (52) _____ personality.

(53)_____ gives rise to hostility and the formation of social stereotypes.

Status (54)_____ tend to build prejudice.

Equal-status (55)_____, mutual interdependence, and superordinate (56)_____ tend to reduce prejudice.

On a smaller scale, (57)_____ classrooms have been shown to combat prejudice.

Module 15.6 Aggression and Prosocial Behavior

Survey Question: How do psychologists explain human aggression? Pages 656-660, Objectives 15.18,
        15.19

(58)_____ is a fact of life, but humans are not inevitably aggressive. The same factors that help explain aggression can form the basis for (59)_____ it.

(60)_____ explanations of aggression attribute it to inherited instincts.

(61)_____ explanations of aggression emphasize brain mechanisms and physical factors that lower the threshold for aggression.

According to the (62) _____ hypothesis, frustration and aggression are closely linked.

(63)_____ is only one of many aversive stimuli that can arouse a person and make aggression more likely.

Aggression is especially likely to occur when (64)_____ are present.

(65)_____ theory has focused attention on the role of aggressive models in the development of aggressive behavior.

Survey Question: Why are bystanders so often unwilling to help in an emergency? Pages 660-662,
        Objective 15.20

Four decision points that must be passed before a person gives help are: (66)_____, defining an emergency, taking (67)_____, and selecting a course of action.

Helping is encouraged by general arousal, (68)_____ arousal, being in a good mood,
(69)_____ effort or risk, and perceived (70)_____ between the victim and the helper.

(71)_____ behavior is most likely to occur when people feel sympathy or empathy for a person in need.

For several reasons, (72)_____ tends to encourage others to help, too.

Module 15.7 Psychology in Action

*Survey Question: What can be done to avoid prejudice and promote social harmony? Pages 664-666,
        Objective 15.21*

(73)_____ is a recognition and acceptance of human diversity.

Multicultural (74)_____ can be attained through conscious efforts to be more tolerant of others.

Greater (75)_____ can be encouraged by neutralizing stereotypes with individuating

information; by looking for commonalities with others; and by avoiding the effects of

(76)_____ beliefs, self-fulfilling prophecies, and (77)_____ competition.

Cultural (78)_____ is a key element in promoting greater social harmony.

Connections

Module 15.1

1. _____ competency	a. comparing ourselves to others	
2. _____ reciprocity	b. return in kind	
3. _____ proximity	c. a person's proficiency	
4. _____ interpersonal attraction	d. affinity to others	
5. _____ social comparison	e. desire to associate	
6. _____ need to affiliate	f. nearness	

Module 15.2

1. _____ achieved role	a. privilege and importance
2. _____ ascribed role	b. rule or standard
3. _____ attribution	c. assigned role
4. _____ norm	d. matching behavior
5. _____ social comparison	e. relating self to others
6. _____ conformity	f. rewards and punishments
7. _____ status	g. voluntary role
8. _____ group sanctions	h. social inference

Module 15.3

1. _____ assertiveness	a. self-assertion technique
2. _____ broken record	b. salesperson's tactic
3. _____ obedience	c. honest expression
4. _____ compliance	d. following authority
5. _____ foot-in-the-door	e. yielding to requests

Module 15.4

1. _____ brainwashing	a. change attitude with arguments
2. _____ attitude	b. coincidence
3. _____ reference group	c. belief + emotion + action
4. _____ chance conditioning	d. uncomfortable clash
5. _____ persuasion	e. standard for social comparison
6. _____ dissonance	f. thought reform

Module 15.5

1. _____ scapegoat	a. aggression target
2. _____ stereotype	b. above all others
3. _____ superordinate	c. group centered
4. _____ symbolic prejudice	d. unequal treatment
5. _____ discrimination	e. oversimplified image
6. _____ authoritarianism	f. F Scale
7. _____ ethnocentric	g. modern bias

Module 15.6

1. _____ bystander apathy	a. altruistic behavior
2. _____ desensitization	b. reduced emotional sensitivity
3. _____ prosocial	c. remove inhibition
4. _____ disinhibition	d. feeling someone's anguish
5. _____ weapons effect	e. aggression cue
6. _____ empathic arousal	f. Kitty Genovese
7. _____ aggression	g. intent to harm

Module 15.7

1. _____ just world beliefs	a. "tossed salad"
2. _____ self-fulfilling prophesy	b. rivalry for limited resources
3. _____ social competition	c. people respond to you the way you expect
4. _____ multiculturalism	d. people get what they deserve

Check Your Memory

Module 15.1 Affiliation, Friendship, and Love

Survey Questions: Why do people affiliate? What factors influence interpersonal attraction? Pages 622-627, Objectives 15.1, 15.2, 15.3

T F   1. The Stanford prison experiment investigated the impact of the roles of prisoner and guard.

T F   2. The need to affiliate is a basic human characteristic.

T F   3. People who are frightened prefer to be with others who are in similar circumstances.

T F   4. Interpersonal attraction to someone takes weeks to develop.

T F   5. Social comparisons are used to confirm objective evaluations and measurements.

T F   6. Useful social comparisons are usually made with persons similar to ourselves.

T F   7. Nearness has a powerful impact on forming friendships.

T F   8. Homogamy, marrying someone who is like oneself, does not apply to unmarried couples.

T F   9. Physical proximity leads us to think of people as competent and therefore worth knowing.

T F   10. The halo effect is the tendency to generalize a positive or negative first impression to other personal characteristics.

T F 11. Physical attractiveness is closely associated with intelligence, talents, and abilities.

T F 12. The risk of divorce is higher than average for couples who have large differences in age and education.

T F 13. In choosing mates, women rank physical attractiveness as the most important feature.

T F 14. Self-disclosure is a major step toward friendship.

T F 15. Overdisclosure tends to elicit maximum self-disclosure from others.

T F 16. Self-disclosure through an Internet chat room can lead to genuine, face-to-face friendship.

T F 17. The statement "I find it easy to ignore _____'s faults" is an item on the Liking Scale.

T F 18. Where their mates are concerned, men tend to be more jealous over a loss of emotional commitment than they are over sexual infidelities.

Module 15.2 Groups, Social Influence, and Conformity

Survey Question: How does group membership affect our behavior? Pages 628-630, Objectives 15.4, 15.5

T F 19. Son, husband, and teacher are achieved roles.

T F 20. Persons of higher status tend to receive special treatment and privileges.

T F 21. A group could have a high degree of structure but low cohesiveness.

T F 22. Group cohesion refers to the dimensions that define a group such as ethnicity, age, or religion.

T F 23. "Us and them" refers to members of the in-group perceiving themselves as one unit and everyone else as the out-group.

T F 24. The more trash that is visible in public places, the more likely people are to litter.

T F 25. If someone always salts her food before eating, it implies that her behavior has an external cause.

T F 26. Attributing the actions of others to external causes is the most common attributional error.

T F 27. Good performances by women are more often attributed to luck than skill.

Survey Question: What have social psychologists learned about conformity? Pages 630-632, Objective 15.6

T F 28. Conformity situations occur when a person becomes aware of differences between his or her own behavior and that of a group.

T F 29. Most subjects in the Asch conformity experiments suspected that they were being deceived in some way.

T F 30. Seventy-five percent of Asch's subjects yielded to the group at least once.

T F 31. People who are anxious are more likely to conform to group pressure.

T F 32. Groupthink is more likely to occur when people emphasize the task at hand rather than the bonds between group members.

T F 33. Rejection, ridicule, and disapproval are group norms that tend to enforce conformity.

T F 34. A unanimous majority of three is more powerful than a majority of eight with one person dissenting.

Module 15.3 Compliance, Obedience, and Self-Assertion

Survey Question: What have psychologists learned about compliance, obedience, and self-assertion?
   Pages 634-639, Objectives 15.7, 15.8, 15.9

T F   35. Milgram's famous shock experiment was done to study compliance and conformity.

T F   36. Over half of Milgram's "teachers" went all the way to the maximum shock level.

T F   37. Being face-to-face with the learner had no effect on the number of subjects who obeyed in the Milgram experiments.

T F   38. People are less likely to obey an unjust authority if they have seen others disobey.

T F   39. The foot-in-the-door effect is a way to gain compliance from another person.

T F   40. The low-ball technique involves changing the terms that a person has agreed to so that they are less desirable from the person's point of view.

T F   41. Using the door-in-the-face strategy is an effective way to even the odds with salespeople for using the low-ball technique.

T F   42. Many people have difficulty asserting themselves because they have learned to be obedient and good.

T F   43. Self-assertion involves the rights to request, reject, and retaliate.

T F   44. In order to be assertive, you should never admit that you were wrong.

Module 15.4 Attitudes and Persuasion

Survey Question: How are attitudes acquired and changed? Pages 641-642, Objective 15.10

T F   45. Attitudes predict and direct future actions. *true*

T F   46. What you think about the object of an attitude makes up its belief component. *true*

T F   47. Attitudes are only composed of our positive or negative opinions of others. They do not include a behavioral component. *false*

T F   48. If both parents belong to the same political party, their child probably will too. *true*

T F   49. A person who deviates from the majority opinion in a group tends to be excluded from conversation. *true*

T F   50. Heavy TV viewers feel safer than average because they spend so much time in security at home. *false*

T F   51. An attitude held with conviction is more likely to be acted upon. *true*

Survey Question: Under what conditions is persuasion most effective? Pages 643-645, Objectives 15.11, 15.12

T F   52. Our attitudes are more likely to match those held by members of our reference groups than our membership groups. *true*

T F   53. Persuasion refers to a deliberate attempt to change a person's reference groups. *false*

T F   54. Persuasion is less effective if the message appeals to the emotions. *false*

T F   55. For a poorly informed audience, persuasion is more effective if only one side of the argument is presented. *true*

T F   56. A persuasive message should not be repeated; doing so just weakens its impact. *false*

T F   57. Acting contrary to one's attitudes or self-image causes cognitive dissonance. *true*

T F 58. Public commitment to an attitude or belief makes it more difficult to change. *true*

T F 59. The greater the reward or justification for acting contrary to one's beliefs, the greater the cognitive dissonance felt. *false*

T F 60. Dissonance is especially likely to be felt when a person causes an undesired event to occur. *true*

Survey Questions: Is brainwashing actually possible? How are people converted to cult membership? Pages 645-646, Objective 15.13

T F 61. Roughly 16 percent of American POWs in the Korean War signed false confessions. *true*

T F 62. True brainwashing requires a captive audience. *true*

T F 63. In brainwashing, the target person is housed with other people who hold the same attitudes and beliefs that he or she does. *false*

T F 64. In most cases, the effects of brainwashing are very resistant to further change. *false*

T F 65. Cult leaders, like David Koresh, use brainwashing as a technique to persuade people to conform. *true*

T F 66. A cult is a group in which the belief system is more important than the leader who espouses it. *false*

T F 67. Cults play on emotions and discourage critical thinking. *true*

T F 68. Cult members are typically isolated from former reference groups. *true*

Module 15.5 Prejudice and Intergroup Conflict

Survey Question: What causes prejudice and intergroup conflict? Pages 648-654, Objectives 15.14, 15.15, 15.16, 15.17

T F 69. Sexism is a type of prejudice. *true*

T F 70. The term racial profiling refers to giving preferential treatment to some students seeking admission to college. *false*

T F 71. Scapegoating is a prime example of discrimination. *false*

T F 72. A person who views members of another group as competitors for jobs displays group prejudice. *false*

T F 73. Authoritarian persons tend to be prejudiced against all out-groups. *true*

T F 74. The F in F Scale stands for fanatic. *false*

T F 75. An authoritarian would agree that people can be divided into the weak and the strong. *true*

T F 76. Social stereotypes can be positive as well as negative. *true*

T F 77. Symbolic prejudice is the most obvious and socially unacceptable form of bigotry. *false*

T F 78. Children as young as age three have begun to show signs of racial bias. *true*

T F 79. Beliefs in superiority, injustice, and distrust are common variables that tend to promote conflict among members of the in-group. *false*

T F 80. Symbolic prejudice occurs when people understand the causes of prejudice and do not discriminate against minorities. *false*

T F 81. The key to creating prejudice in Jane Elliot's experiment was her use of scapegoating to cause group conflict. *false*

T F 82. Equal-status contact tends to reduce prejudice and stereotypes. *true*

T F 83. Superordinate groups help people of opposing groups to see themselves as members of a single larger group. *true*

Module 15.6 Aggression and Prosocial Behavior

Survey Question: How do psychologists explain human aggression? Pages 656-660, Objectives 15.18, 15.19

T F 84. Ethologists argue that humans learn to be aggressive by observing aggressive behavior in lower animals. *false*

T F 85. Specific areas of the brain are capable of initiating or ending aggression. *true*

T F 86. Intoxication tends to raise the threshold for aggression, making it more likely. *true false*

T F 87. Higher levels of the hormone testosterone are associated with more aggressive behavior by both men and women. *true*

T F 88. The frustration-aggression hypothesis says that being aggressive is frustrating. *false*

T F 89. People exposed to aversive stimuli tend to become less sensitive to aggression cues. *false*

T F 90. Murders are less likely to occur in homes where guns are kept. *false*

T F 91. Social learning theorists assume that instinctive patterns of human aggression are modified by learning. *true*

T F 92. American Quakers have adopted a nonviolent way of life as a way to inhibit aggression. *true*

T F 93. According to Eron, children learn aggression from direct contact with other children and not from indirect contact from TV programs. *false*

T F 94. To discourage violence, parents should get themselves and their children involved in community-related activities. *true*

T F 95. Aggressive crimes in TV dramas occur at a much higher rate than they do in real life. *true*

Survey Question: Why are bystanders so often unwilling to help in an emergency? Pages 660-662, Objective 15.20

T F 96. In the Kitty Genovese murder, no one called the police until after the attack was over. *true false*

T F 97. In an emergency, the more potential helpers present, the more likely a person is to get help. *false*

T F 98. The first step in giving help is to define the situation as an emergency. *false*

T F 99. Emotional arousal, especially empathic arousal, lowers the likelihood that one person will help another. *false*

T F 100. You are more likely to help a person who seems similar to yourself. *true*

T F 101. In many emergency situations it can be more effective to shout "Fire!" rather than "Help!" *true*

Module 15.7 Psychology in Action

Survey Question: What can be done to avoid prejudice and promote social harmony? Pages 664-666, Objective 15.21

T F 102. Multiculturalism is an attempt to blend multiple ethnic backgrounds into one universal culture.

T F 103. A study conducted in Canada found that increasing interaction among different groups only increases negative stereotypes of both groups.

T F 104. Members of major groups in the United States rated themselves better than other groups to enhance their self-esteem.

T F 105. The emotional component of prejudicial attitudes may remain even after a person intellectually renounces prejudice.

T F   106. Both prejudiced and unprejudiced people are equally aware of social stereotypes.

T F   107. Individuating information forces us to focus mainly on the labels attached to a person.

T F   108. From a scientific point of view, race is a matter of social labeling, not a biological reality.

T F   109. People who hold just-world beliefs assume that people generally get what they deserve.

T F   110. Each ethnic group has strengths that members of other groups could benefit from emulating.

T F   111. The statement "Don't judge somebody until you know them. The color of their skin doesn't matter" is an example of a way to promote understanding in an ethnically diverse group of people.

Critical Thinking

Module 15.1
1. How has the Internet altered the effects of proximity on interpersonal attraction?

Module 15.2
2. Would it be possible to be completely non-conforming (that is, to not conform to some group norm)?

Module 15.3
3. Modern warfare allows killing to take place impersonally and at a distance. How does this relate to Milgram's experiments?

Module 15.4
4. Students entering a college gym are asked to sign a banner promoting water conservation. Later, the students shower at the gym. What effect would you expect signing the banner to have on how long students stay in the showers?

5. Cognitive dissonance theory predicts that false confessions obtained during brainwashing are not likely to bring about lasting changes in attitudes. Why?

Module 15.5
6. In court trials, defense lawyers sometimes try to identify and eliminate prospective jurors who have authoritarian personality traits. Can you guess why?

Module 15.6
7. If media violence contributes to aggressive behavior in our society, do you think it is possible that media could also promote prosocial behavior?

Module 15.7
8. Why is it valuable to learn the terms by which members of various groups prefer to be addressed (for example, Mexican-American, Latino/Latina, Hispanic, or Chicano/Chicana)?

Final Survey and Review

Module 15.1 Affiliation, Friendship, and Love

Survey Questions: Why do people affiliate? What factors influence interpersonal attraction? Objectives 15.1, 15.2, 15.3

1. Social psychology studies how we behave, think, and feel in _____.
2. We are _____ to other people for reasons that are _____.
3. Affiliation is tied to needs for approval, _____, friendship, and _____. Also, affiliation can reduce _____.
4. Social comparison theory holds that we affiliate to _____ our actions, feelings, and abilities.
5. Interpersonal attraction is increased by _____, frequent _____, beauty, and _____.
6. _____ is characterized by a large degree of similarity on many dimensions.
7. Self-disclosure follows a _____ norm: Low levels of self-disclosure are met with _____ levels in return; moderate self-disclosure elicits _____ replies.
8. In comparison with liking, romantic love involves higher levels of _____ and it is accompanied by _____ between lovers.
9. Evolutionary psychologists attribute human mating patterns to the _____ men and women faced during the _____ of evolution.

Module 15.2 Groups, Social Influence, and Conformity

Survey Question: How does group membership affect our behavior? Objectives 15.4, 15.5

10. To understand social behavior we must know what roles people play, their _____, the norms they follow, and the _____ they make.
11. Social roles are particular behavior patterns associated with _____.
12. Higher status within groups is associated with _____ and _____.
13. Norms are standards of _____ enforced (_____ or _____) by groups.
14. We attribute behavior to various _____. These attributions, in turn, affect _____.
15. The fundamental attributional error is to think that _____ causes explain the actions of other people. In contrast, we tend to attribute our own behavior to _____ causes.

Survey Question: What have social psychologists learned about conformity? Objective 15.6

16. Social influence refers to _____ in behavior brought about by the_____ of others.
17. The famous Asch experiments demonstrated that people are likely to conform when they face _____ from other group members.
18. Groupthink refers to _____ conformity in group _____.

Module 15.3 Compliance, Obedience, and Self-Assertion

Survey Question: What have psychologists learned about compliance, obedience, and self-assertion? Objectives 15.7, 15.8, 15.9

19. Three strategies for gaining compliance are the foot-in-the-door technique, the _____ approach, and the _____ technique.
20. Most people have a_____ tendency to obey legitimate authority. Usually this is _____, but it can be _____ when social power is used in misguided or _____ ways.
21. Obedience to authority in _____'s studies decreased when the "teacher" and "learner" were close to one another, when the authority was _____, and when others _____.
22. Self-assertion helps people _____ their needs _____ resorting to aggressive behavior.

Module 15.4 Attitudes and Persuasion

Survey Question: How are attitudes acquired and changed? Objective 15.10

23. Attitudes are made up of a _____ component, an emotional component, and an _____ component.

24. Attitudes held with conviction are most likely to _____.

25. Attitudes may be formed by _____ contact, interaction with others, _____ practices, group pressures, peer group influences, _____ membership, the mass media, and chance conditioning.

Survey Question: Under what conditions is persuasion most effective? Objectives 15.11, 15.12

26. Effective persuasion must take into account characteristics of the _____, the _____, and the _____.

27. In general, a likable and believable communicator who _____ a credible message that arouses emotion in the _____ and states _____ will be persuasive.

28. Cognitive dissonance theory explains many aspects of _____.

Survey Questions: Is brainwashing actually possible? How are people converted to cult membership? Objective 15.13

29. Brainwashing is a form of _____ attitude change. It depends on control of the _____'s environment.

30. Three steps in brainwashing are unfreezing, changing, and refreezing _____ and _____.

31. Many cults recruit new members with _____ techniques.

Module 15.5 Prejudice and Intergroup Conflict

Survey Question: What causes prejudice and intergroup conflict? Objectives 15.14, 15.15, 15.16, 15.17

32. Prejudice is a _____ held toward members of _____.

33. One theory attributes _____ to scapegoating.

34. Prejudices may be held for _____ (personal prejudice) or simply through adherence to _____ (group prejudice).

35. Prejudiced individuals tend to have an authoritarian _____.

36. Intergroup conflict gives rise to _____ and the formation of _____.

37. _____ inequalities tend to build prejudice.

38. _____ contact, mutual _____, and _____ goals tend to reduce prejudice.

39. On a smaller scale, jigsaw classrooms have been shown to _____ prejudice.

Module 15.6 Aggression and Prosocial Behavior

Survey Question: How do psychologists explain human aggression? Pages 656-660, Objectives 15.18, 15.19

40. Aggression is_____, but humans are _____ aggressive. _____ factors that help explain aggression can form the basis for preventing it.

41. Ethological explanations of aggression attribute it to _____.

42. Biological explanations of aggression emphasize _____ and _____ that lower the threshold for aggression.

43. According to the frustration-aggression hypothesis, _____ and _____ are closely linked.

44. Frustration is only one of many _____ that can _____ a person and make _____ more likely.

Chapter 1: Introducing Psychology and Research Methods

Solutions

Recite and Review

Module 1.1
1. scientific study
2. thinking
3. evidence
4. sensation
5. social
6. evolutionary
7. animal
8. animals
9. describe
10. predict

Module 1.2
11. evaluate
12. critique
13. reflect
14. validity
15. for and against
16. evidence
17. false
18. valid
19. uncritical acceptance
20. observation
21. hypothesis
22. theory
23. defined

Module 1.3
24. outgrowth
25. science
26. Germany
27. experience
28. school of thought
29. introspection
30. functionalism
31. psychoanalytic
32. behavior
33. subjective
34. personal growth
35. biological
36. psychological
37. sociocultural
38. positive
39. think
40. cultural

Module 1.4
41. differ
42. counseling
43. educational
44. school
45. medical
46. basic

Module 1.5
47. Experiments
48. dependent

49. constant
50. dependent
51. identified
52. drugs
53. valid
54. meaning response
55. unconsciously
56. expectations
57. participant
58. ethically
59. participants

Module 1.6
60. non-experimental
61. observation
62. observer bias
63. two
64. correlation coefficient
65. prediction
66. Case studies
67. representative

Module 1.7
68. quality
69. skepticism
70. facts
71. biased
72. false
73. single

Connections

Module 1.1
1. g
2. e
3. i

Module 1.2
1. g
2. d
3. f
4. a
5. e
6. c
7. b
8. h

Module 1.3
1. e
2. a
3. h
4. f
5. c
6. d
7. i
8. b
9. k
10. j

4. h
5. a
6. b
7. c
11. g

Module 1.4
1. i
2. h
3. g
4. f
5. c
6. l
7. d
8. k
9. b
10. a
11. e
12. j

Module 1.5
1. d
2. e
3. f
4. b
5. c

8. d
9. f
10. j

6. a
7. g

Module 1.6
1. g
2. a
3. c
4. f
5. b
6. d
7. e
8. h

Module 1.7
1. b
2. a
3. c
4. d

Check Your Memory

Module 1.1
1. F
2. F
3. T
4. F
5. F
6. F
7. T
8. F

Module 1.2
9. F
10. T
11. T
12. F
13. F
14. F

15. F
16. T
17. F
18. T
19. F
20. F
21. T
22. T
23. F
24. T
25. F
26. F
27. F
28. F
29. F

Module 1.3
30. F

31. T
32. F
33. T
34. F
35. T
36. T
37. F
38. T
39. T
40. T
41. F
42. T
43. F
44. T
45. F
46. T
47. F
48. T

49. T
50. F
51. T

Module 1.4
52. F
53. T
54. F
55. F
56. T
57. T
58. F
59. T

Module 1.5
60. F
61. T
62. F
63. F
64. T
65. F
66. F
67. T
68. T
69. F

Module 1.6
70. F
71. T

72. F
73. T
74. F
75. T

Module 1.7
76. F
77. T
78. F
79. F
80. F
81. F
82. T

Critical Thinking

Module 1.1
1. False. Astronomy and archaeology are examples of sciences that do not share psychology's fourth goal.

Module 1.2
2. There are many examples. Here are a few more to add to the ones you thought of: "Where there's smoke there's fire" versus "You can't judge a book by looking at its cover." "He (or she) who hesitates is lost" versus "Haste makes waste." "Birds of a feather flock together" versus "Opposites attract."
3. The term "Barnum statement" comes from Levy (2003), who offers the following examples: You are afraid of being hurt. You are trying to find a balance between autonomy and closeness. You don't like being overly dependent. You just want to be understood.

Module 1.3
4. No, it did not. The downfall of structuralism was that each observer examined the contents of his or her own mind, which is something that no other person can observe.

Module 1.4
5. Because practitioners benefit from basic psychological research in the same way that physicians benefit from basic research in biology. Discoveries in basic science form the knowledge base that leads to useful applications.

Module 1.5
6. The statement implies that Echinacea prevented colds. However, not getting a cold could just be a coincidence. A controlled experiment with a group given Echinacea and a control group not taking Echinacea would be needed to learn if Echinacea actually has any effect on susceptibility to colds.
7. Belief in astrology can create a self-fulfilling prophecy in which people alter their behaviors and self-concepts to match their astrological signs (van Rooij, 1994).

Module 1.6
8. The correlation is related to an age bias in the group of people studied. Older adults have higher cancer rates than younger adults, and Frosted Flakes weren't available during the childhoods of older people. Thus, Frosted Flakes appear to be related to cancer, when age is the real connection (Tierny, 1987).
9. The psychologist's coin flips *might* produce a reasonably good sample of people *at the mall*. The real problem is that people who go to the mall may be mostly from one part of town, from upper income groups, or from some other nonrepresentative group. The psychologist's sample is likely to be seriously flawed.
10. True. It appears to be difficult for humans to resist thinking of other species and even machines in human terms.

Module 1.7

11. This is another case of mistaking correlation for causation. Children who are hyperactive may eat more sugar (and other foods) to fuel their frenetic activity levels.

Final Survey and Review

Module 1.1

1. behavior and mental processes
2. critical empirical
3. comparative perception cognitive forensic
4. behavior models
5. understand control

Module 1.2

6. compare analyze synthesize
7. gather evidence quality
8. pseudo-psychologies frequently positive instances
9. systematic behavior
10. observing defining publishing results
11. operationally empirically

Module 1.3

12. philosophy researchers began to directly study and observe psychological events
13. Wilhelm Wundt conscious experience
14. structuralism
15. Structuralism behaviorism Gestalt
16. Psychodynamic unconscious
17. Humanistic human potentials
18. biopsychology evolutionary behaviorism psychodynamic humanism
19. formally study
20. do social

Module 1.4

21. mental health training and methods
22. Clinical dozens of
23. industrial consumer engineering environmental psychometric
24. research

Module 1.5

25. independent
26. measured extraneous
27. independent dependent cause-and-effect
28. placebo double-blind placebo effect
29. the experimenter effect self-fulfilling prophecy
30. rights, dignity, and welfare

Module 1.6

31. cause-and-effect relationships
32. Naturalistic
33. the effects of the observer on the observed
34. correlational
35. strength cause-and-effect
36. natural clinical tests
37. survey sample
38. sample populations

Module 1.7

39. accuracy
40. caution fallacies
41. unreliable misleading inferences unrepeatable

Mastery Test

1. D, (p. 14 , Objective 1.1)
2. B, (p. 16, Objective 1.3)
3. B, (p. 17, Objective 1.4)
4. D, (p. 27, Objective 1.8)
5. B, (p. 28, Objective 1.8)
6. A, (p. 28, Objective 1.8)
7. C, (p. 31, Objective 1.9)
8. B, (p. 30, Objective 1.8)
9. D, (p. 32, Objective 1.10)
10. A, (p. 36, Objective 1.11)
11. D, (p. 36, Objective 1.11)
12. D, (p. 38, Objective 1.11)
13. C, (p. 20, Objective 1.5)
14. A, (p. 21, Objective 1.6)
15. B, (p. 21, Objective 1.6)
16. D, (p. 22, Objective 1.6)
17. A, (p. 23, Objective 1.6)
18. A, (p. 29, Objective 1.8)
19. C, (p. 49, Objective 1.19)
20. D, (p. 41, Objective 1.12)

21. C, (p. 46, Objective 1.16)
22. A, (p. 47, Objective 1.16)
23. B, (p. 24, Objective 1.7)
24. C, (p. 44, Objective 1.14)
25. A, (p. 24, Objective 1.7)
26. C, (p. 41, Objective 1.12)
27. D, (p. 54, Objective 1.20)
28. C, (p. 41 Objective 1.12)
29. D, (p. 47, Objective 1.17)

30. D, (p. 46, Objective 1.16)
31. B, (p. 42, Objective 1.12)
32. C, (p. 48, Objective 1.18)
33. D, (p. 49, Objective 1.18)
34. C, (p. 49, Objective 1.18)
35. B, (p. 43, Objective 1.14)
36. D, (p. 41, Objective 1.12)
37. D, (p. 48, Objective 1.17)

Chapter 3: Human Development Solutions

Recite and Review

Module 3.1
1. progressive
2. abilities
3. nature
4. nurture
5. caregivers
6. plastic
7. dendrites
8. synapses
9. chromosomes
10. dominant
11. environmental
12. reaction range
13. more
14. retards
15. beneficial
16. hereditary
17. difficult
18. reciprocal interaction
19. heredity
20. behavior

Module 3.2
21. parenting
22. adaptive
23. sucking
24. immediately
25. looking chamber
26. bright
27. curved
28. familiar
29. unfamiliar
30. motor skills
31. language
32. cephalocaudal
33. proximodistal
34. rate
35. learning
36. consistent
37. fear
38. anger
39. walking

Module 3.3
40. self-awareness
41. actively
42. attachment
43. separation
44. avoidant
45. ambivalent
46. consistent
47. signals
48. not harmful
49. helpful
50. risky
51. affectional
52. intellectual
53. permissive
54. Authoritative
55. care giving
56. playmates
57. competence
58. culture
59. vary

Module 3.4
60. language
61. babbling
62. telegraphic
63. biological
64. innate
65. rhythms
66. parentese

Module 3.5
67. less
68. assimilation
69. sensorimotor
70. concrete
71. appropriate
72. continuous
73. capable
74. sociocultural
75. more
76. proximal
77. more skillful
78. cultural

Module 3.6
79. Puberty
80. behavioral
81. identity
82. ethnic
83. delayed
84. Kohlberg
85. postconventional
86. conventional
87. Only a minority of

Module 3.7
88. Erik Erikson
89. trust
90. productivity
91. integrity
92. autonomy
93. a purpose
94. Only a minority of
95. urgency
96. corrections
97. transition
98. limited
99. remain
100. Ageism
101. ageism

102. denial
103. depression
104. in every case

Module 3.8
105. Positive

106. encouraging
107. communication
108. withdrawal of love
109. psychological
110. caution
111. Consistency

112. express
113. place limits on
114. I-messages
115. logical

Connections

Module 3.1
1. a
2. h
3. b
4. f
5. c
6. i
7. d
8. e
9. g

Module 3.2
1. b
2. d
3. c
4. f
5. a
6. e
7. h
8. g

Module 3.3
1. c
2. b
3. d
4. k
5. e
6. a
7. j
8. h
9. f

10. i
11. g
12. l

Module 3.4
1. e
2. a
3. b
4. d
5. g
6. f
7. c

Module 3.5
1. c
2. a
3. f
4. b
5. e
6. d
7. g
8. h

Module 3.6
1. h
2. f
3. b
4. i
5. g
6. a
7. e

8. d
9. c
10. j

Module 3.7
1. e
2. c
3. f
4. b
5. d
6. a
7. k
8. h
9. i
10. g
11. j
12. m
13. o
14. p
15. l
16. n

Module 3.8
1. e
2. b
3. d
4. c
5. f
6. g
7. a

Check Your Memory

Module 3.1
1. F
2. F
3. T
4. F
5. T
6. T
7. F
8. T
9. F

10. T
11. F
12. T
13. T
14. T
15. F

Module 3.2
16. F
17. F

18. F
19. F
20. F
21. F
22. T
23. F
24. F
25. F

Module 3.3
26. F

27. F
28. T
29. T
30. T
31. F
32. T
33. F
34. T
35. F
36. F
37. T
38. T
39. T
40. F

Module 3.4
41. F
42. F
43. T
44. F
45. T
46. T
47. F

Module 3.5
48. F
49. F
50. T
51. T

52. F
53. F
54. T
55. T
56. F
57. T
58. T
59. F
60. T
61. T

Module 3.6
62. T
63. T
64. T
65. F
66. F
67. T
68. T
69. F
70. T
71. F
72. T

Module 3.7
73. F
74. T
75. F
76. T

77. T
78. F
79. F
80. T
81. F
82. T
83. T
84. F
85. T
86. F
87. T
88. T
89. T
90. F
91. F
92. T

Module 3.8
93. F
94. T
95. T
96. F
97. F
98. T
99. T
100. F

Critical Thinking

Module 3.1
1. Environmental conditions sometimes turn specific genes on or off, thus directly affecting the expression of genetic tendencies (Gottlieb, 1998).

Module 3.2
2. In one study of the preferences of newborns, the hair color and complexion of strangers was matched to that of the mothers. Also, only the mother's or stranger's face was visible during testing. And finally, a scent was used to mask olfactory (smell) cues so that an infant's preference could not be based on the mother's familiar odor (Bushnell, Sai, & Mullin, 1989).

Module 3.3
3. Another successful method is to secretly rub a spot of rouge on an infant's nose. The child is then placed in front of a mirror. The question is, will the child touch the red spot, showing recognition of the mirror image as his or her own? The probability that a child will do so jumps dramatically during the second year.
4. It certainly can for parents. When a pregnant woman begins to feel fetal movements she becomes aware that a baby is coming to life inside of her. Likewise, prospective parents who hear a fetal heartbeat at the doctor's office or see an ultrasound image of the fetus begin to become emotionally attached to the unborn child (Santrock, 2007).
5. Most parents discipline their children in the same ways that they themselves were disciplined. Parenting is a responsibility of tremendous importance, for which most people receive almost no training.

Module 3.4

6. Children in professional homes receive many educational benefits that are less common in welfare homes. Yet, even when such differences are taken into account, brighter children tend to come from richer language environments (Hart & Risley, 1999).

Module 3.5

7. Seventy-five percent of 4- to 6-year-olds say that a Styrofoam cup has no weight after lifting it! Most children judge weight intuitively (by the way an object feels) until they begin to move into the concrete operational stage (Smith, Carey, & Wiser, 1985).

Module 3.6

8. Environment, rather than heredity, is the better answer. Even better, the meanings of terms like "adolescence" or "adult" vary considerably from culture to culture indicating that it is really a matter of definition (Côté, 2006).

Module 3.7

9. Different *cohorts* (groups of people born in the same year) live in different historical times. People born in various decades may have very different life experiences. This makes it difficult to identify universal patterns (Stewart & Ostrove, 1998).

Module 3.8

10. Such laws are based on the view that it should be illegal to physically assault any person, regardless of their age. Although parents may believe they have a "right" to spank their children, it can be argued that children need special protection because they are small, powerless, and dependent (Durrant & Janson, 2005).

Final Survey and Review

Module 3.1

1. behavior birth death
2. Heredity environment environment
3. capable of being altered by experience blooming pruning
4. chromosomes genes polygenic
5. diseases emotions heredity
6. environmental
7. deprivation enrichment
8. Temperament temperament slow-to-warm-up
9. parents genes
10. developmental level environment

Module 3.2

11. nutrition
12. neonate adaptive rooting aware
13. visual lights circular
14. Infants later infancy
15. cognitive abilities emotions
16. head downward core outward
17. maturation basic motor skills
18. Emotions joy
19. toilet training

Module 3.3

20. social interaction guidance

21. critical anxiety secure Secure rhythms
22. High-quality Low-quality
23. physical
24. emotional
25. authoritarian most
26. mothers fathers young
27. ethnic
28. cultures

Module 3.4

29. intellectual
30. the use of single words
31. predisposition learning
32. turn-taking
33. Motherese

Module 3.5

34. abstract accommodation
35. preoperational formal operations
36. learning opportunities
37. stages
38. infants under the age of one year
39. Vygotsky competent proximal zone scaffold beliefs and values

Module 3.6

40. biological social
41. adolescence Identity formation
42. western industrialized
43. preconventional postconventional
44. preconventional postconventional

Module 3.7

45. challenges
46. independence intimacy old age
47. positive relations with others personal growth
48. a midlife crisis more common
49. stability

50. Intellectual declines mentally
51. prejudice discrimination stereotyping older
52. anger acceptance in that order

Module 3.8

53. Parent-child mutually respectful
54. child management power assertion
55. Punishment behavioral
56. effective
57. their feelings their behavior
58. misbehavior natural

Mastery Test

1. D, (p. 99, Objective 3.1)
2. B, (p. 120, Objective 3.11)
3. D, (p. 108, Objective 3.6)
4. B, (p. 124, Objective 3.12)
5. A, (p. 105, Objective 3.4)
6. D, (p. 99, Objective 3.1)
7. B, (p. 125, Objective 3.12)
8. A, (p. 103, Objective 3.3)
9. A, (p. 100, Objective 3.2)
10. C, (p. 124, Objective 3.12)
11. B, (p. 98, Objective 3.1)
12. D, (p. 99, Objective 3.1)
13. B, (p. 107, Objective 3.5)
14. B, (p. 111, Objective 3.6)
15. D, (p. 107, Objective 3.6)
16. C, (p. 123, Objective 3.12)
17. B, (p. 102, Objective 3.3)
18. A, (p. 108, Objective 3.5)
19. B, (p. 144, Objective 3.19)
20. A, (p. 118, Objective 3.4)
21. B, (p. 114, Objective 3.8)
22. C, (p. 112, Objective 3.8)
23. C, (p. 111, Objective 3.9)
24. B, (p. 108, Objective 3.7)
25. B, (p. 145, Objective 3.19)

26. A, (p. 126, Objective 3.13)
27. A, (p. 144, Objective 3.19)
28. B, (p. 112, Objective 3.7)
29. C, (p. 115, Objective 3.8)
30. D, (p. 112, Objective 3.8)
31. D, (p. 144, Objective 3.19)
32. A, (p. 113, Objective 3.9)
33. A, (p. 135, Objective 3.16)
34. A, (p. 129, Objective 3.14)
35. C, (p. 140, Objective 3.18)
36. C, (p. 135, Objective 3.16)
37. B, (p. 132, Objective 3.15)
38. B, (p. 129, Objective 3.14)
39. C, (p. 137, Objective 3.17)
40. D, (p. 137, Objective 3.17)
41. D, (p. 137, Objective 3.16)
42. D, (p. 140, Objective 3.18)
43. C, (p. 138, Objective 3.17)
44. D, (p. 136, Objective 3.16)
45. C, (p. 139, Objective 3.17)
46. B, (p. 139, Objective 3.17)
47. D, (p. 138, Objective 3.17)
48. A, (p. 138, Objective 3.17)
49. A, (p. 131, Objective 3.14)
50. B, (p. 137, Objective 3.15)

Chapter 6: Conditioning and Learning Solutions

Recite and Review

Module 6.1
1. change
2. increases
3. conditioning
4. classical
5. neutral
6. operant
7. Pavlov
8. NS
9. US
10. UR
11. NS
12. US
13. CS
14. CR
15. followed
16. strengthened
17. alone
18. weakened or inhibited
19. expectancy
20. higher order
21. generalization
22. discrimination
23. visceral or emotional
24. emotional
25. CERs
26. secondhand

Module 6.2
27. reinforced
28. Operant
29. increases
30. effect

31. Delaying
32. single
33. appear
34. shaped
35. not reinforced
36. disappear
37. reappear
38. increase
39. decreases
40. reinforcers
41. Feedback
42. improves
43. Programmed instruction
44. Computer-assisted instruction

Module 6.3
45. after every response
46. partial
47. fixed ratio
48. variable interval
49. responding
50. precede
51. stimulus control
52. generalization
53. discrimination
54. non-reinforcement

Module 6.4
55. decreases
56. the removal of a positive event
57. consistent

58. mild
59. Reinforcement
60. escape
61. aggressive

Module 6.5
62. Cognitive
63. cognitive maps
64. hidden or unseen
65. rote
66. observing
67. consequences
68. personal characteristics
69. modeling
70. Television characters
71. increases

Module 6.6
72. operant
73. behavioral contracting
74. alternative responses
75. antecedent cues

Connections

Module 6.1
1. e
2. j
3. a
4. i
5. n
6. b
7. h
8. c
9. m
10. d
11. l
12. f
13. g
14. k

Module 6.2
1. j
2. b
3. k
4. f
5. a

6. l
7. c
8. i
9. e
10. d
11. h
12. g

Module 6.3
1. f
2. b
3. h
4. a
5. e
6. c
7. g
8. d

Module 6.4
1. c
2. a
3. d

4. e
5. b

Module 6.5
1. c
2. e
3. b
4. a
5. d
6. f

Module 6.6
1. a
2. c
3. d
4. b

Check Your Memory

Module 6.1
1. T
2. F
3. T
4. F
5. T
6. T
7. F
8. F
9. F
10. T
11. F
12. T
13. F
14. T
15. F
16. F

Module 6.2
17. T
18. F
19. F
20. F
21. T
22. F

23. T
24. T
25. F
26. T
27. F
28. T
29. T
30. F
31. F
32. F
33. T
34. T
35. T
36. F
37. T
38. F
39. T
40. F

Module 6.3
41. F
42. F
43. T
44. F

45. T
46. T
47. F
48. F

Module 6.4
49. T
50. F
51. T
52. F
53. T
54. F
55. T
56. T

Module 6.5
57. T
58. F
59. T
60. T
61. F
62. F
63. T

64. F
65. F
66. F
67. T

Module 6.6
68. F
69. T
70. T
71. T

72. F
73. F
74. T

Critical Thinking

Module 6.1
1. Door handles have become conditioned stimuli that elicit the reflex withdrawal and muscle tensing that normally follows getting a shock. This conditioned response has also generalized to other handles.

Module 6.2
2. A strategy that has been used with some success is to hold drawings for various prizes, such as movie or concert passes. Each time a person turns in a specific amount of litter, he or she receives one chance (a token) to enter in the drawing. Giving refunds for cans and bottles is another way to reinforce recycling of litter.

Module 6.3
3. Continuing to use fixed interval rewards (hourly wage or salary) would guarantee a basic level of income for employees. To reward extra effort, the owner could add some fixed ratio reinforcement (such as incentives, bonuses, commissions, or profit sharing) to employees' pay.
4. An excellent way to train a pet to come when you call is to give a distinctive call or whistle each time you feed the animal. This makes the signal a secondary reinforcer and a discriminative stimulus for reward (food). Of course, it also helps to directly reinforce an animal with praise, petting, or food for coming when called.

Module 6.4
5. An inconsistently punished response will continue to be reinforced on a partial schedule, which makes it even more resistant to extinction.
6. Many automobiles have an unpleasant buzzer that sounds if the ignition key is turned before the driver's seat belt is fastened. Most drivers quickly learn to fasten the belt to stop the annoying sound. This is an example of escape conditioning. Avoidance conditioning is evident when a driver learns to buckle up before the buzzer sounds.

Module 6.5
7. Your cognitive map of the campus has undoubtedly become more accurate and intricate over time as you have added details to it. Your drawings should reflect this change.
8. Because the observation is based on a correlation. Children who are already aggressive may choose to watch more aggressive programs, rather than being made aggressive by them. It took experimental studies to verify that televised aggression promotes aggression by viewers.

Module 6.6
9. Daily performance goals and rewards reduce the delay of reinforcement, which maximizes its impact.

Final Survey and Review

Module 6.1
1. relatively experience reinforcement probability
2. Classical operant
3. neutral unconditioned neutral elicit
4. reinforcement frequently
5. Classical neutral stimulus an unconditioned stimulus
6. unconditioned response conditioned stimulus conditioned response
7. reinforced
8. alone extinguished
9. classical follow
10. conditioned unconditioned
11. similar not to similar
12. simple reflexes conditioned emotional responses
13. phobias vicariously

Module 6.2

14. behave responses
15. voluntary reinforcer response Operant learning
16. reduces long chains
17. Superstitious reinforcement
18. successive approximations desired
19. extinguish extinction spontaneous recovery
20. positive reinforcement negative reinforcement
21. decreases
22. primary secondary
23. knowledge of results learning
24. immediate feedback providing alternative exercises

Module 6.3

25. continuously partial Partial extinction
26. continuous variable ratio fixed interval
27. reinforced operant stimulus control
28. operant similar
29. given discriminative withheld

Module 6.4

30. responding onset removal cost
31. immediate intense
32. severe temporarily suppresses lasting changes
33. avoidance encourages

Module 6.5

34. mental problem anticipating
35. internal representations of relationships
36. latent reward or incentive
37. Discovery
38. imitating noting
39. success or failure Aggression
40. powerful models aggression

Module 6.6

41. change or manage
42. managing self-recording feedback
43. bad reinforcing extinction avoiding

Mastery Test

1. A, (p. 261, Objective 6.10)
2. C, (p. 263, Objective 6.10)
3. A, (p. 258, Objective 6.7)
4. B, (p. 258, Objective 6.8)
5. B, (p. 249, Objective 6.2)
6. C, (p. 256-257, Objective 6.6)
7. D, (p. 257, Objective 6.7)
8. C, (p. 260, Objective 6.10)
9. C, (p. 278, Objective 6.16)
10. B (p. 258, Objective 6.8)
11. D, (p. 262, Objective 6.10)
12. A, (p. 266, Objective 6.11)
13. D, (p. 273, Objective 6.14)
14. B, (p. 280, Objective 6.16)
15. B, (p. 248, Objective 6.1)
16. D, (p. 253, Objective 6.5)
17. D, (p. 249, Objective 6.2)
18. A, (p. 269, Objective 6.12)
19. B, (p. 283, Objective 6.17)
20. C, (p. 272, Objective 6.13)
21. D, (p. 267, Objective 6.11)
22. A, (p. 252, Objective 6.4)
23. A, (p. 251, Objective 6.3)
24. D, (p. 253, Objective 6.5)
25. A, (p. 268, Objective 6.12)
26. D, (p. 274, Objective 6.14)
27. B, (p. 256, Objective 6.6)
28. B, (p. 262, Objective 6.10)
29. D, (p. 259, Objective 6.6)
30. A, (p. 248, Objective 6.1)
31. C, (p. 258, Objective 6.8)
32. B, (p. 259, Objective 6.9)
33. C, (p. 260, Objective 6.9)
34. D, (p. 260, Objective 6.9)
35. A, (p. 277, Objective 6.15)
36. A, (p. 278, Objective 6.16)
37. D, (p. 279, Objective 6.16)

Chapter 7: Memory

Solutions

Recite and Review

Module 7.1
1. store
2. retrieve
3. short-term
4. longer
5. remember
6. iconic
7. meaning

Module 7.2
8. attention
9. STM
10. 5 to 7
11. chunking
12. interruption
13. alive
14. general
15. lasting
16. permanent
17. storage
18. Constructive
19. Remembering
20. distorted
21. organized
22. structure
23. reconstructed
24. recall

25. skill
26. fact
27. Declarative

Module 7.3
28. all-or-nothing
29. relearning
30. without
31. listed
32. recognition
33. learned again
34. memory
35. recognition
36. priming

Module 7.4
37. Ebbinghaus
38. rapid
39. encode
40. sensory
41. some
42. cues
43. forgetting
44. retroactive
45. Proactive
46. repressed
47. time

48. structure
49. hippocampus
50. cortex

Module 7.5
51. photographic
52. rarely
53. images
54. learned strategies
55. efficient
56. superior
57. memory strategies
58. selecting
59. overlearning
60. memorizing
61. elaboration

Module 7.6
62. systems
63. lasting
64. images
65. familiar
66. Effective
67. associations

Connections

Module 7.1
1. c
2. g
3. a
4. e

5. b
6. d
7. f
1. a
2. d

3. c
4. e
5. b

Module 7.2
1. f or g
2. c
3. d
4. a
5. f or g
6. b
7. e
1. b
2. e
3. c
4. a
5. d

Module 7.3
1. f

2. a
3. c
4. e
5. b
6. d

Module 7.4
1. d
2. e
3. g
4. f
5. h
6. b
7. c
8. i
9. a

Module 7.5
1. b
2. f
3. a
4. d
5. g
6. c
7. e

Module 7.6
1. a
2. d
3. b
4. e
5. c

Check Your Memory

Module 7.1
1. T
2. F
3. T
4. T
5. F
6. F
7. T
8. F

Module 7.2
9. T
10. F
11. F
12. T
13. F
14. F
15. F
16. T
17. T
18. T
19. F
20. T
21. F
22. F
23. T
24. T
25. T
26. F

Module 7.3
27. T
28. F
29. F
30. T
31. F
32. T
33. F

Module 7.4
34. F
35. T
36. F
37. F
38. T
39. F
40. T
41. T
42. T
43. T
44. F
45. F
46. F
47. F
48. F
49. F
50. T
51. T
52. T

53. F
54. T
55. F
56. F
57. T

Module 7.5
58. T
59. T
60. T
61. F
62. F
63. F
64. T
65. T
66. F
67. F
68. T
69. T

Module 7.6
70. F
71. T
72. T
73. T

Critical Thinking

Module 7.1
1. Without sensory memory, a movie would look like a series of still pictures. The split-second persistence of visual images helps blend one motion-picture frame into the next.

Module 7.2
2. Because the more information you have in long-term memory, the greater the possibilities for linking new information to it. Generally, the more you know, the more you can learn, even if some of what you know is "junk."

Module 7.3
3. It is possible to have an implicit memory that cannot be consciously recalled. Memories like these (*available* in memory even though they are not consciously *accessible)* show that failing to recall something does not mean it is no longer in memory (Allik, 2000). The *feeling of knowing* is related. Have you ever left an examination unable to recall the correct answer to a question *knowing* that you know the answer? That's because the answer was available but not accessible at the time of the exam.

Module 7.4
4. Music tends to affect the mood that a person is in, and moods tend to affect memory (Miranda & Kihlstrom, 2005).
5. Any order that separates French from Spanish and psychology from biology would work (for instance: French, psychology, Spanish, biology).
6. Memories of emotionally significant events may be unusually strong because such memories are rehearsed more frequently. People usually mentally review emotionally charged events many times.

Module 7.5
7. Mr. S's memory was so specific that faces seemed different and unfamiliar if he saw them from a new angle or if a face had a different expression on it than when Mr. S last saw it.
8. Note-taking is a form of recitation, it encourages elaborative rehearsal, facilitates the organization and selection of important ideas, and your notes can be used for review.

Module 7.6
9. Both attempt to relate new information to information stored in LTM that is familiar or already easy to retrieve.

Final Survey and Review

Module 7.1
1. encode information
2. sensory memory short-term memory long-term memory
3. best memory system
4. Sensory echoic sound

Module 7.2
5. Selective exact brief
6. capacity extended sensitive interference maintenance rehearsal
7. meaningful information Elaborative

8. relatively almost unlimited
9. alter active altered revised
10. LTM networks
11. Redintegrative leads to others recall
12. procedural declarative semantic episodic

Module 7.3
13. tip-of-the-tongue recognition priming
14. explicit cues serial position
15. multiple-choice
16. relearning savings score
17. explicit implicit

Module 7.4

18. forgetting immediately curve
19. forgetting
20. weakening traces traces LTM
21. lack State-dependent
22. STM LTM
23. new earlier
24. old new
25. consciously unconsciously
26. consolidate brain cells
27. consolidation consolidated

Module 7.5

28. Eidetic project
29. Eidetic adults
30. natural ability
31. learning compensate
32. memories beneficial
33. feedback progressive spaced search
34. sleep cues

Module 7.6

35. mnemonics conventional
36. Mnemonic unusual associations LTM
37. images bizarre or exaggerated

Mastery Test

1. C, (p. 289, Objective 7.1)
2. D, (p. 295, Objective 7.6)
3. A, (p. 311, Objective 7.12)
4. B, (p. 309, Objective 7.11)
5. C, (p. 289, Objective 7.1)
6. C, (p. 288, Objective 7.1)
7. A, (p. 297, Objective 7.8)
8. C, (p. 315, Objective 7.13)
9. D, (p. 304, Objective 7.11)
10. A, (p. 298, Objective 7.2)
11. C, (p. 302, Objective 7.10)
12. B, (p. 315, Objective 7.13)
13. B, (p. 292, Objective 7.5)
14. A, (p. 309, Objective 7.11)
15. A, (p. 300, Objective 7.9)
16. C, (p. 302, Objective 7.9)
17. D, (p. 293, Objective 7.5)
18. B, (p. 300, Objective 7.9)
19. A, (p. 304, Objective 7.11)

20. B, (p. 295, Objective 7.6)
21. D, (p. 295, Objective 7.6)
22. C, (p. 310, Objective 7.11)
23. A, (p. 319, Objective 7.14)
24. D, (p. 295, Objective 7.6)
25. B, (p. 310, Objective 7.12)
26. D, (p. 322, Objective 7.15)
27. C, (p. 296, Objective 7.7)
28. A, (p. 288, Objective 7.2)
29. B, (p. 307, Objective 7.11)
30. C, (p. 308, Objective 7.11)
31. A, (p. 292, Objective 7.5)
32. D, (p. 294, Objective 7.6)
33. A, (p. 290, Objective 7.4)
34. C, (p. 295, Objective 7.6)
35. B, (p. 295, Objective 7.6)
36. D, (p. 319, Objective 7.14)
37. A, (p. 305, Objective 7.11)

Chapter 8: Intelligence, Cognition, Language and Creativity

Solutions

Recite and Review

Module 8.1
1. general
2. rationally
3. intelligence tests
4. Alfred Binet
5. quotient
6. 100
7. distribution
8. *Wechsler Adult Intelligence Scale*
9. performance
10. intelligence
11. above 140
12. gifted or talented
13. below 70
14. 50
15. undetermined
16. familial
17. broader
18. Gardner
19. artificial
20. people
21. expert systems
22. Intelligence
23. increases

Module 8.2
24. internal
25. concepts
26. created

27. three-dimensional
28. movements
29. thoughts
30. concept
31. rule learning
32. ideal
33. and
34. either/or
35. dictionary
36. personal or emotional
37. symbols
38. meaning
39. valuable
40. Two-way
41. rules
42. order
43. generate new ideas or possibilities
44. gestural
45. Chimpanzees and other primates

Module 8.3
46. mechanically
47. mechanical
48. understanding
49. functional
50. narrow
51. Expert
52. rapid

53. combination
54. blocked
55. cultural
56. habits

Module 8.4
57. original
58. divergent
59. preparation
60. verification
61. contradict
62. only a very small
63. creative
64. errors
65. highly
66. Emotions
67. underlying probability
68. stating

Module 8.5
69. bias
70. index
71. narrowly
72. school
73. even weaker
74. placement
75. states

Connections

Module 8.1
1. e
2. l
3. a
4. j
5. b
6. i
7. c
8. k
9. g
10. d
11. h
12. f

Module 8.2
1. f
2. j
3. i
4. a
5. c
6. b
7. e
8. d

9. g
10. h
1. c
2. a
3. e
4. g
5. b
6. f
7. d

Module 8.3
1. h
2. g
3. e
4. a
5. f
6. b
7. j
8. c
9. i
10. d

Module 8.4
1. h
2. b
3. j
4. d
5. c
6. i
7. a
8. e
9. f
10. g

Module 8.5
1. e
2. b
3. a
4. d
5. c

Check Your Memory

Module 8.1
1. F
2. T
3. F
4. T
5. T
6. F
7. F
8. T
9. T
10. T
11. F
12. F
13. T
14. F
15. T
16. F
17. F
18. F
19. F
20. T
21. F
22. F
23. T
24. T

25. T
26. F
27. T
28. T
29. F

Module 8.2
30. F
31. T
32. F
33. F
34. T
35. T
36. T
37. T
38. T
39. T
40. T
41. T
42. F
43. T
44. F
45. F
46. F
47. T

48. F
49. F
50. T
51. F
52. F
53. F
54. F
55. F
56. F
57. F
58. T
59. T
60. T
61. T

Module 8.3
62. T
63. F
64. F
65. F
66. T
67. T
68. F
69. F

70. T	79. T	90. F
71. F	80. F	91. F
72. T	81. F	92. F
73. F	82. F	93. T
	83. T	

Module 8.4

74. T
75. F
76. T
77. T
78. F

84. F	**Module 8.5**
85. F	94. F
86. T	95. T
87. F	96. T
88. F	
89. T	

Critical Thinking

Module 8.1

1. Rule-driven expert systems may appear "intelligent" within a narrow range of problem solving. However, they are "stone stupid" at everything else. This is usually not what we have in mind when discussing human intelligence.
2. Because one's IQ depends on the intelligence test used to measure it: Change the test and you will change the score. Also, heredity establishes a range of possibilities; it does not automatically preordain a person's intellectual capacities.

Module 8.2

3. If they both assume the word refers to a form of government, not a political party or a candidate.
4. The problem of anthropomorphizing (ascribing human characteristics to animals) is especially difficult to avoid when researchers spend many hours "conversing" with chimps.

Module 8.3

5. Although this might be an overstatement, it is true that clearly defining a starting point and the desired goal can serve as a heuristic in problem solving.
6. Psychologist Donald Griffin (1992) believes it does because thinking is implied by actions that appear to be planned with an awareness of likely results.

Module 8.4

7. The chance of getting a head on the fifth flip is the same in each case. Each time you flip a coin, the chance of getting a head is 50 percent, no matter what happened before. However, many people intuitively think that *b* is the answer because a head is "overdue," or that *c* is correct because the coin is "on a roll" for heads.

Module 8.5

8. Probably not, because the Spanish words might be longer or shorter than the same words in English. The Spanish words might also sound more or less alike than words on the original test. Translating an intelligence test into another language can subtly change the meaning and difficulty of test items.

Final Survey and Review

Module 8.1

1. g-factor purposefully effectively operationally defined
2. intelligence test *Stanford-Binet Intelligence Scale*
3. mental chronological a normal curve
4. major verbal Group
5. gifted or "genius" many
6. intellectually disabled adaptive organic Many reflect
7. intelligence multiple intelligences
8. Artificial intelligence tasks are computer simulations
9. heredity environment education environments

Module 8.2

10. external stimuli
11. images concepts language
12. retrieved from memory
13. rotated size
14. Kinesthetic Kinesthetic flow
15. generalized events
16. positive and negative instances
17. prototypes
18. conjunctive disjunctive relational
19. denotative Connotative
20. encodes semantics
21. Bilingualism additive bilingualism
22. symbols grammar syntax

23. productive
24. American Sign Language
25. American Sign Language very basic

Module 8.3

26. rote application of rules inefficient
27. general properties
28. heuristics
29. mental heuristics
30. insight insight comparison
31. fixations fixation blocks conventions

Module 8.4

32. practical sensible fluency flexibility
33. orientation incubation Not all
34. creative personality IQ
35. learned
36. Intuitive representative
37. intuitive poor
38. base rate
39. framing

Module 8.5

40. cultural merely intelligence
41. achievement achievement
42. standard special education prohibited

Mastery Test

1. B, (p. 346, Objective 8.15)
2. A, (p. 336, Objective 8.9)
3. C, (p. 362, Objective 8.19)
4. B, (p. 340, Objective 8.11)
5. A, (p. 343, Objective 8.13)
6. A, (p. 352, Objective 8.16)
7. D, (p. 358, Objective 8.18)
8. B, (p. 343, Objective 8.13)
9. A, (p. 355, Objective 8.17)
10. A, (p. 331, Objective 8.5)
11. D, (p. 333-334, Objective 8.7)
12. B, (p. 330, Objective 8.4)
13. C, (p. 345, Objective 8.14)
14. D, (p. 366, Objective 8.20)
15. D, (p. 353, Objective 8.16)
16. A, (p. 358, Objective 8.18)
17. B, (p. 352, Objective 8.16)
18. D, (p. 344, Objective 8.14)

19. C, (p. 343, Objective 8.13)
20. D, (p. 357, Objective 8.18)
21. A, (p. 342, Objective 8.12)
22. A, (p. 348, Objective 8.15)
23. B, (p. 331, Objective 8.5)
24. A, (p. 357, Objective 8.18)
25. B, (p. 341, Objective 8.12)
26. C, (p. 344, Objective 8.13)
27. B, (p. 346, Objective 8.15)
28. C, (p. 359, Objective 8.18)
29. B, (p. 345, Objective 8.14)
30. A, (p. 351, Objective 8.16)
31. C, (p. 353, Objective 8.16)
32. B, (p. 330, Objective 8.3)
33. A, (p. 331, Objective 8.4)
34. B, (p. 366, Objective 8.20)
35. D, (p. 337, Objective 8.10)
36. B, (p. 362, Objective 8.19)

Chapter 9: Motivation and Emotion Solutions

Recite and Review

Module 9.1
1. Motives
2. need
3. goal
4. push
5. pull
6. attractiveness
7. initiate
8. primary
9. secondary
10. primary
11. Circadian rhythms
12. Time zone travel
13. shift work

Module 9.2
14. blood sugar
15. fat
16. hypothalamus
17. set point
18. emotions
19. cultural
20. diet
21. exercise
22. Behavioral dieting
23. Anorexia
24. bulimia
25. self-image
26. hypothalamus
27. Thirst

28. episodic
29. learned
30. unusual

Module 9.3
31. stimulation
32. arousal
33. arousal
34. bodily arousal
35. arousal or stimulation
36. Optimal
37. Yerkes-Dodson
38. Social
39. need for achievement
40. success
41. motivation
42. Maslow
43. dominant
44. highest
45. Meta-needs
46. undermine

Module 9.4
47. disruptive
48. physiological
49. feelings
50. primary
51. more complex
52. hormone
53. autonomic

54. arousing
55. quieting
56. polygraph
57. low

Module 9.5
58. facial expressions
59. surprise
60. body language
61. general emotional tone
62. Facial expressions
63. Body positioning
64. James-Lange
65. Cannon-Bard
66. Schachter's
67. ascribing arousal to a particular source
68. facial feedback
69. cognitive appraisals
70. change
71. change

Module 9.6
72. Emotional intelligence
73. self-awareness
74. manage
75. relationships
76. Positive
77. social connection

Connections

Module 9.1
1. b
2. d
3. a
4. e
5. c

Module 9.2
1. b
2. a
3. c
1. c
2. i
3. b
4. d
5. h
6. a
7. g
8. j
9. e
10. f

Module 9.3
1. d
2. g
3. c
4. a
5. e
6. b
7. f
1. f
2. d
3. a
4. c
5. e
6. b
7. g

Module 9.4
1. b
2. g
3. a
4. d
5. h

6. f
7. c
8. e

Module 9.5
1. e
2. d
3. i
4. b
5. f
6. c
7. h
8. a
9. g

Module 9.6
1. c
2. d
3. a
4. b

Check Your Memory

Module 9.1
1. F
2. T
3. T
4. T

Module 9.2
5. F
6. T
7. F
8. T
9. T
10. T
11. F
12. F
13. F
14. F
15. F
16. F
17. T
18. T
19. T
20. T
21. F
22. T
23. F

24. F
25. T
26. F
27. F
28. T

Module 9.3
29. T
30. T
31. F
32. T
33. F
34. F
35. F
36. F
37. T
38. T
39. T
40. F
41. T
42. F
43. T
44. F
45. T
46. F

Module 9.4
47. T
48. F
49. F
50. F
51. T
52. F
53. T
54. T
55. F
56. F
57. T
58. T
59. F

Module 9.5
60. T
61. F
62. F
63. F
64. T
65. F
66. F
67. T
68. T
69. F

371

70. T
71. F
72. T
73. F

Module 9.6
74. T
75. F
76. T

77. T
78. T
79. T
80. T

Critical Thinking

Module 9.1

1. Because of homeostasis: Blood sugar is normally maintained within narrow bounds. While blood sugar levels fluctuate enough to affect hunger, true hypoglycemia is an infrequent medical problem.

Module 9.2

2. The time of day can influence eating, especially for externally-cued eaters, who tend to get hungry at mealtimes, irrespective of their internal needs for food.

Module 9.3

3. None of them.

Module 9.4

4. In cultures where there is deep belief in magic or voodoo, a person who thinks that she or he has been cursed may become uncontrollably emotional. After several days of intense terror, a parasympathetic rebound is likely. If the rebound is severe enough, it can lead to physical collapse and "voodoo death".

Module 9.5

5. The James-Lange theory and Schachter's cognitive theory. The facial feedback hypothesis also helps explain the observation.

Module 9.6

6. There's no single right answer to this question. However, rather than being angry it might be better to reflect on whether friendship or money is more important in life. If you appreciate your friend's virtues, accept that no one is perfect, and reappraise the loan as a gift; you could save a valued relationship and reduce your anger at the same time.

Final Survey and Review

Module 9.1

1. initiate direct drive attainment
2. needs goals
3. ability incentive
4. stimulus motives
5. homeostasis
6. sleep activity energy motivation sleep

Module 9.2

7. fullness liver body
8. control neural chemical
9. external attractiveness variety aversions
10. emotions genetics
11. eating exercise
12. eating disorders self-control

13. thirst and other basic motives intracellular extracellular
14. avoidance avoidance tolerance
15. non-homeostatic

Module 9.3

16. needs desired levels
17. maintain ideal levels Sensation-Seeking Scale
18. moderate inverted U higher lower
19. learned
20. social motive moderate
21. Self-confidence
22. basic growth prepotent fragile meta-needs
23. intrinsic external rewards intrinsic creativity

Module 9.4

24. adapt survive adaptive expressions
25. surprise disgust acceptance
26. Bodily adrenaline activity
27. sympathetic parasympathetic
28. emotional arousal galvanic skin response
29. accuracy

Module 9.5

30. anger sadness Contempt
31. gestures specific universal

32. pleasantness unpleasantness attention rejection relaxation tension
33. emotional experience bodily reactions bodily reactions emotional experiences
34. labeling bodily arousal attribution
35. define
36. emphasize interacts appraisal

Module 9.6

37. consciously work for you
38. empathy understanding enhance
39. valuable broaden encourage

Mastery Test

1. B, (p. 397, Objective 9.15)
2. A, (p. 383, Objective 9.8)
3. A, (p. 379, Objective 9.5)
4. B, (p. 391, Objective 9.13)
5. C, (p. 394, Objective 9.14)
6. C, (p. 408, Objective 9.18)
7. C, (p. 372, Objective 9.1)
8. B, (p. 372, Objective 9.1)
9. C, (p. 387, Objective 9.10)
10. C, (p. 400, Objective 9.16)
11. D, (p. 381, Objective 9.6)
12. B, (p. 389, Objective 9.11)
13. B, (p. 402, Objective 9.17)
14. A, (p. 401, Objective 9.16)
15. A, (p. 381, Objective 9.7)
16. B, (p. 372, Objective 9.1)
17. B, (p. 383, Objective 9.9)
18. A, (p. 401-402, Objective 9.16)
19. C, (p. 388, Objective 9.10)

20. C, (p. 372, Objective 9.2)
21. D, (p. 396, Objective 9.15)
22. D, (p. 386, Objective 9.10)
23. A, (p. 377, Objective 9.4)
24. D, (p. 404, Objective 9.17)
25. B, (p. 373, Objective 9.2)
26. A, (p. 390, Objective 9.12)
27. D, (p. 394, Objective 9.14)
28. C, (p. 379, Objective 9.5)
29. A, (p. 387, Objective 9.10)
30. A, (p. 405-406, Objective 9.17)
31. D, (p. 379, Objective 9.5)
32. A, (p. 379, Objective 9.5)
33. B, (p. 379, Objective 9.5)
34. D, (p. 382, Objective 9.7)
35. C, (p. 409, Objective 9.18)
36. B, (p. 398, Objective 9.15)
37. A, (p. 409, Objective 9.18)

Chapter 10: Personality

Solutions

Recite and Review

Module 10.1
1. Personality
2. Character
3. Temperament
4. Traits
5. identical twins
6. personality traits
7. types
8. self-concept
9. assumptions
10. personality theories

Module 10.2
11. Trait
12. Allport
13. Cattell's
14. five-factor
15. interact

Module 10.3
16. internal
17. Sigmund Freud
18. superego
19. Libido
20. energy
21. conflicts
22. ego-defense
23. conscious
24. oral
25. genital
26. Fixation

Module 10.4
27. Behavioral
28. learning
29. John Dollard
30. Neal Miller
31. Habits
32. social learning
33. Julian Rotter
34. reinforcement
35. toilet or cleanliness
36. anger or aggression
37. imitation

Module 10.5
38. free choice
39. positive
40. Abraham Maslow
41. peak
42. Self-actualization
43. final destination
44. Positive
45. courage
46. justice
47. Carl Rogers
48. experience
49. Optimal
50. ideal
51. incongruent
52. mismatch
53. congruent
54. feelings
55. self-evaluations

56. conditions of worth
57. do the same
58. incongruence
59. Positive
60. unconditional positive regard

Module 10.6
61. questionnaires
62. unstructured
63. halo
64. Direct observation
65. rating
66. personality measures
67. reliable
68. validity
69. Projective
70. inkblot
71. Thematic Apperception Test
72. low
73. useful
74. battery

Module 10.7
75. social anxiety
76. social skills
77. public self-consciousness
78. lasting trait
79. reduced
80. social skills

Connections

Module 10.1
1. c
2. h
3. a
4. e
5. g
6. b
7. f
8. d

Module 10.2
1. c
2. j
3. a
4. i
5. b
6. g
7. k
8. d
9. l
10. e
11. f
12. h

Module 10.3
1. f
2. h
3. i
4. b
5. a
6. g
7. c
8. j
9. e
10. d
11. k

Module 10.4
1. b
2. d
3. a
4. e
5. c
6. f

Module 10.5
1. b
2. d
3. e
4. a
5. c

Module 10.6
1. e
2. j
3. d
4. a
5. h
6. f
7. a
8. b
9. i
10. c

Module 10.7
1. d
2. a
3. f
4. e
5. c
6. b

Check Your Memory

Module 10.1
1. F
2. F
3. F
4. T
5. F
6. T
7. T
8. T
9. F
10. F

Module 10.2
11. T
12. T
13. F
14. F
15. T
16. F
17. F
18. F
19. T
20. T
21. F
22. F
23. T
24. T

Module 10.3
25. F
26. T
27. F
28. T
29. F
30. T
31. F
32. T
33. F
34. T
35. F
36. T

Module 10.4
37. T
38. T
39. T
40. T
41. F
42. T
43. T
44. T
45. F
46. T
47. T

Module 10.5
48. T
49. F
50. F
51. T
52. T
53. T
54. T

55. F	61. F	**Module 10.7**
56. T	62. F	69. F
57. F	63. T	70. T
58. T	64. F	71. F
	65. T	72. T
Module 10.6	66. F	
59. T	67. F	
60. T	68. F	

Critical Thinking

Module 10.1

1. As discussed in Chapter 7, memory is highly selective, and long-term memories are often distorted by recent information. Such properties add to the moldability of self-concept.

Module 10.2

2. No. Circumstances can have a strong or weak influence. In some situations, almost everyone will act the same, no matter what their personality traits may be. In other situations, traits may be of greater importance.

Module 10.3

3. A psychoanalytic theorist would say that it is because the bottle rekindles oral conflicts and feelings of vulnerability and dependence.

Module 10.4

4. Incentive value.

Module 10.5

5. Career decisions almost always involve, in part, picturing oneself occupying various occupational roles.

Module 10.6

6. Because of trait-situation interactions, a person may not behave in a normal fashion while being evaluated in an interview.
7. Psychodynamic: Because projective testing is designed to uncover unconscious thoughts, feelings, and conflicts.

Module 10.7

8. trait-situation interactions (again)

Final Survey and Review

Module 10.1

1. thinking emotion behavior
2. evaluated desirable
3. hereditary emotional
4. qualities behavior
5. Behavioral genetics contributes significantly
6. categories shared traits
7. self-esteem
8. combine
9. trait behavioristic humanistic

Module 10.2

10. lasting characteristics
11. common cardinal secondary
12. surface source
13. agreeableness neuroticism
14. Traits situations

Module 10.3

15. unconscious
16. id ego
17. life source

18. neurotic moral
19. Personal awareness preconscious
20. psychosexual anal phallic
21. psychosexual leave a lasting imprint on

Module 10.4
22. conditioning situational
23. habits
24. drive cue response reward
25. thinking expectations
26. situation expectancies value
27. feeding sex
28. Identification

Module 10.5
29. subjective experience actualization human nature
30. self-actualizers reality
31. an ongoing process of personal growth
32. strengths wisdom temperance transcendence
33. self a good match self-image
34. unrealistic self-image ideal self fully functioning

35. the emergence of a self-image
36. parents children children Internalized
37. organismic valuing

Module 10.6
38. interviews observation projective
39. much information bias misperceptions
40. situational behavioral actual
41. value valid
42. Minnesota Multiphasic Personality Inventory-2
43. ambiguous unstructured
44. Rorschach Apperception
45. validity objectivity clinicians
46. Accurate assessment devices interviews

Module 10.7
47. evaluation defeating public
48. heightened tendency
49. replacing more supportive learning

Mastery Test

1. D, (p. 414, Objective 10.1)
2. B, (p. 428, Objective 10.7)
3. A, (p. 433, Objective 10.9)
4. A, (p. 418, Objective 10.12)
5. A, (p. 423, Objective 10.6)
6. D, (p. 438, Objective 10.10)
7. D, (p. 415, Objective 10.2)
8. C, (p. 417, Objective 10.4)
9. B, (p. 433, Objective 10.9)
10. B, (p. 444, Objective 10.12)
11. C, (p. 434, Objective 10.8)
12. B, (p. 428, Objective 10.7)
13. D, (p. 416, Objective 10.3)
14. C, (p. 430, Objective 10.7)
15. C, (p. 439, Objective 10.10)
16. B, (p. 448, Objective 10.12)
17. A, (p. 425, Objective 10.6)

18. C, (p. 422, Objective 10.6)
19. B, (p. 430, Objective 10.7)
20. A, (p. 440, Objective 10.11)
21. B, (p. 445, Objective 10.12)
22. C, (p. 418, Objective 10.5)
23. D, (p. 430, Objective 10.7)
24. B, (p. 440, Objective 10.11)
25. A, (p. 452, Objective 10.14)
26. B, (p. 421, Objective 10.6)
27. A, (p. 422, Objective 10.6)
28. C, (p. 433, Objective 10.8)
29. C, (p. 417, Objective 10.4)
30. C, (p. 418, Objective 10.5)
31. B, (p. 415, Objective 10.2)
32. A, (p. 422, Objective 10.6)
33. D, (p. 434, Objective 10.8)
34. B, (p. 440, Objective 10.10)

Chapter 12: Psychological Disorders Solutions

Recite and Review

Module 12.1
1. Psychopathology
2. discomfort
3. abnormality
4. culture
5. maladaptive
6. normality
7. psychological disorders
8. *Diagnostic and Statistical Manual of Mental Disorders*
9. mood
10. anxiety
11. sexual
12. substance
13. Insanity
14. Sanity

Module 12.2
15. personality
16. personality
17. conscience
18. manipulative
19. anxiety
20. behavior
21. adjustment
22. panic
23. phobias
24. posttraumatic
25. dissociative
26. somatoform
27. combination

Module 12.3
28. break
29. hallucinations
30. emotions
31. organic
32. Alzheimer's
33. grandeur
34. physical disease
35. paranoid
36. communication
37. thought
38. Disorganized
39. Catatonic
40. paranoid
41. prenatal
42. stress
43. major
44. biochemical
45. schizophrenia

Module 12.4
46. emotion
47. depressive
48. Severe
49. moderate
50. swings
51. Bipolar
52. bipolar I
53. bipolar II
54. major depressive
55. brain chemistry
56. loss
57. stress
58. the maternity blues
59. serious
60. lasting
61. Seasonal affective disorder
62. treated

Module 12.5
63. cause of death
64. statistically
65. potential
66. frustrated
67. narrow
68. temporary
69. prevent

Connections

Module 12.1
1. f
2. a
3. i
4. b
5. c
6. h
7. d
8. e
9. g

Module 12.2
1. c
2. e
3. a
4. j
5. b
6. d
7. i
8. f
9. h
10. g
1. h

2. i
3. g
4. a
5. j
6. b
7. d
8. f
9. c
10. e

Module 12.3
1. a
2. j
3. e
4. b
5. g
6. d
7. i
8. f
9. c
10. h

Module 12.4
1. h
2. e
3. g
4. a
5. f
6. c
7. d
8. b

Module 12.5
1. b
2. c
3. d
4. a
5. e

Check Your Memory

Module 12.1
1. T
2. F
3. T
4. T
5. F
6. T
7. F
8. T
9. T
10. T
11. F
12. F
13. F

Module 12.2
14. F
15. F
16. F
17. T
18. F
19. T
20. F

21. F
22. T
23. F
24. F
25. F
26. T
27. T
28. T
29. T
30. F
31. F
32. T
33. T
34. T
35. T
36. F
37. T
38. F

Module 12.3
39. F
40. F
41. T

42. T
43. F
44. F
45. F
46. T
47. F
48. F
49. T
50. F
51. T
52. F
53. T
54. T
55. T
56. F
57. T
58. T
59. F
60. T

Module 12.4
61. F
62. T
63. F

64. T
65. T
66. T
67. T
68. T
69. F
70. T
71. F
72. T

73. F
74. F

Module 12.5
75. T
76. T
77. F
78. T

79. F
80. T
81. T

Critical Thinking

Module 12.1

1. Probably not. Undoubtedly, Brian's cross-dressing is socially disapproved by many people. Nevertheless, to be classified as a mental disorder it must cause him to feel disabling shame, guilt, depression, or anxiety. The cultural relativity of behavior like Brian's is revealed by the fact that it is fashionable and acceptable for women to wear men's clothing.

2. It emphasizes that insanity is a legal concept, not a psychiatric diagnosis. Laws reflect community standards. When those standards change, lawmakers may seek to alter definitions of legal responsibility.

Module 12.2

3. The autonomic nervous system (ANS), especially the sympathetic branch of the ANS.

4 No one doctor tolerates false symptoms for long. Once a doctor refuses further treatment, the Munchausen sufferer will move on to another. Also, sometimes more than one doctor is being seen at one time.

Module 12.3

5. Because of the extra receptors, schizophrenics may get psychedelic effects from normal levels of dopamine in the brain.

6. Because correlation does not confirm causation. Structural brain abnormalities are merely *correlated* with schizophrenia. They could be additional symptoms, rather than causes, of the disorder.

Module 12.4

7. Women tend to be more focused on relationships than men are. When listing the stresses in their lives, depressed women consistently report higher rates of relationship problems, such as loss of a friend, spouse, or lover; problems getting along with others; and illnesses suffered by people they care about. Depressed men tend to mention issues such as job loss, legal problems, or work problems (Kendler, Thornton, & Prescott, (2001).

Module 12.5

8. Drug or alcohol abuse and availability of a firearm.

Final Survey and Review

Module 12.1

1. maladaptive mental disorders
2. subjective statistical context
3. loss of self-control
4. relative classified treated
5. system for classifying mental disorders
6. psychotic organic somatoform dissociative
7. legal responsible testimony

Module 12.2

8. persistent
9. Sociopathy Antisocial shallow dishonest
10. dissociative rigid self-defeating
11. ordinary stresses cope with life
12. generalized agoraphobia agoraphobia obsessive-compulsive acute
13. anxiety
14. fugue identities
15. mimic somatization conversion
16. psychodynamic existential

Module 12.3

17. reality sensory communication disintegration
18. injuries diseases
19. drug abuse dementia
20. almost totally persecution infidelity psychosis

21. hallucinations emotion
22. personality obscene
23. stupor violent
24. common persecution personality
25. early trauma susceptibility brain
26. Heredity
27. dopamine
28. stress-vulnerability

Module 12.4

29. Mood manic psychotic
30. dysthymic cyclothymic
31. mania depression mania depression depressed mania
32. sadness despondency mania
33. vulnerability learned helplessness self-defeating
34. Many Some postpartum
35. the winter months phototherapy

Module 12.5

36. frequent prevented
37. age sex marital
38. escape psychological pain needs
39. the only way out
40. attempt worthwhile

Mastery Test

1. A, (p. 512, Objective 12.6)
2. A, (p. 524, Objective 12.13)
3. C, (p. 499, Objective 12.1)
4. B, (p. 525, Objective 12.13)
5. B, (p. 510, Objective 12.6)
6. D, (p. 514, Objective 12.8)
7. A, (p. 527, Objective 12.13)
8. B, (p. 520, Objective 12.11)
9. B, (p. 532, Objective 12.15)
10. A, (p. 498, Objective 12.1)
11. D, (pp. 536-537, Objective 12.17)
12. A, (p. 511, Objective 12.6)
13. D, (p. 524, Objective 12.12)
14. D, (p. 512, Objective 12.7)
15. B, (p. 498, Objective 12.1)
16. A, (p. 500, Objective 12.2)
17. D, (p. 511, Objective 12.6)
18. B, (p. 515, Objective 12.9)
19. C, (p. 507, Objective 12.4)

20. A, (p. 499, Objective 12.1)
21. D, (p. 502, Objective 12.2)
22. A, (p. 520, Objective 12.10)
23. C, (p. 510, Objective 12.6)
24. A, (p. 518, Objective 12.10)
25. A, (p. 514, Objective 12.8)
26. B, (p. 499, Objective 12.1)
27. A, (p. 503, Objective 12.3)
28. B, (p. 515, Objective 12.9)
29. A, (p. 509, Objective 12.5)
30. C, (p. 529, Objective 12.14)
31. D, (p. 498, Objective 12.1)
32. B, (p. 507, Objective 12.4)
33. D, (p. 507, Objective 12.4)
34. A, (p. 518, Objective 12.10)
35. B, (p. 520, Objective 12.11)
36. B, (pp. 524-526, Objective 12.13)
37. D, (p. 532, Objective 12.16)

Chapter 13: Therapies

Solutions

Recite and Review

Module 13.1
1. changes
2. action
3. non-directive
4. positive
5. individually
6. in groups
7. superstition
8. Demonology
9. bizarre behavior
10. Philippe Pinel
11. Freud's psychoanalysis
12. unconscious
13. dream
14. transference
15. traditional psychoanalysis
16. successful
17. brief and focused
18. psychotherapy

Module 13.2
19. person-centered
20. growth
21. Unconditional positive regard
22. client
23. his or her own
24. Existential
25. confrontation
26. take responsibility
27. Gestalt
28. connected wholes
29. blockages
30. some good

31. drawbacks
32. not been unambiguously established
33. more promise

Module 13.3
34. Behavior
35. aversion
36. desensitization
37. fear
38. total relaxation
39. real settings
40. vividly imagining
41. models
42. virtual reality
43. eye movement
44. controversial

Module 13.4
45. Behavior modification
46. time out
47. constructive
48. extinguish
49. attention
50. social approval
51. positive reinforcement
52. reinforce
53. token economy
54. approval
55. Cognitive
56. thinking
57. maladaptive
58. positive
59. rational-emotive behavior

Module 13.5
60. Group
61. Group
62. psychodrama
63. family
64. Sensitivity
65. awareness
66. alliance
67. new behaviors
68. acceptance
69. questioning
70. respect
71. rapport
72. adapt
73. mental
74. physical
75. electroconvulsive
76. avoid
77. education

Module 13.6
78. self-management
79. covert sensitization
80. Thought stopping
81. Covert reinforcement
82. Desensitization
83. Everyone
84. about equally
85. more effective
86. well qualified
87. public sources of information

Connections

Module 13.1
1. h
2. i
3. g
4. a
5. e
6. j
7. c
8. f
9. b
10. d

Module 13.2
1. e
2. c
3. h
4. a
5. f
6. d

7. b
8. g
9. i

Module 13.3
1. d
2. a
3. c
4. f
5. b
6. e

Module 13.4
1. d
2. c
3. a
4. e
5. b

Module 13.5
1. e
2. d
3. b
4. g
5. a
6. f
7. c

Module 13.6
1. g
2. d
3. a
4. f
5. e
6. c
7. b

Check Your Memory

Module 13.1
1. F
2. T
3. T
4. T
5. T
6. F
7. T
8. F
9. F
10. T
11. F
12. F
13. T
14. F
15. F
16. T
17. F

Module 13.2
18. F
19. F
20. T
21. T
22. T
23. F
24. F
25. T
26. F

27. T
28. T
29. F

Module 13.3
30. T
31. F
32. T
33. F
34. T
35. T
36. T
37. F
38. T
39. F
40. T
41. T
42. T
43. F
44. T

Module 13.4
45. F
46. T
47. F
48. T
49. F
50. T

51. T
52. T
53. T
54. T
55. F
56. F
57. T

Module 13.5
58. F
59. F
60. T
61. T
62. T
63. T
64. T
65. T
66. F
67. T
68. F
69. T
70. F
71. F
72. T
73. T
74. F
75. T
76. T
77. F
78. T

79. F	**Module 13.6**	89. F
80. T	84. F	90. T
81. F	85. F	91. T
82. T	86. F	92. F
83. F	87. T	
	88. T	

Critical Thinking

Module 13.1

1. Placebo therapy is sometimes used to assess the benefits of real therapy. Placebo therapy superficially resembles the real thing, but lacks key elements that are thought to be therapeutic.

Module 13.2

2. The terms *doctor* and *patient* imply a large gap in status and authority between the individual and his or her therapist. Client-centered therapy attempts to narrow this gap by making the person the final authority concerning solutions to his or her problems. Also, the word *patient* implies that a person is "sick" and needs to be "cured." Many regard this as an inappropriate way to think about human problems.

Module 13.3

3. Committed alcoholics may actually "drink through it" and learn to tolerate the nauseating effects.
4. Doctors and nurses learn to relax and remain calm at the sight of blood because of their frequent exposure to it.

Module 13.4

5. Overgeneralization and all-or-nothing thinking.

Module 13.5

6. According to the law, there is a duty to protect others where a therapist could, with little effort, prevent serious harm. However, this duty can conflict with a client's rights to confidentiality and with client-therapist trust. Therapists often must make difficult choices in such situations.
7. The question of who can prescribe drugs, do surgery, and administer ECT *is* controlled by law. However, psychiatrists strongly object to residents, city councils, or government agencies making *medical* decisions.

Module 13.6

8. Such decisions must be made by clients themselves. Therapists can help clients evaluate important decisions and feelings about significant persons in their lives. However, actively urging a client to sever a relationship borders on unethical behavior.

Final Survey and Review

Module 13.1

1. personality adjustment
2. insight directive supportive
3. time limited
4. moral condemnation
5. supernatural forces possession exorcism
6. ergot poisoning
7. humane Paris
8. psychodynamic
9. thoughts conflicts
10. association resistance insights
11. spontaneous remissions successful
12. psychodynamic psychoanalytic interpersonal

Module 13.2
13. Client-centered non-directive conscious
14. authenticity reflection
15. choices encounter free will
16. immediate awareness acting emotional
17. telephone cybertherapists telephone cybertherapy
18. videoconferencing

Module 13.3
19. classical operant
20. classical maladaptive inhibit
21. exposure reciprocal inhibition
22. hierarchy least most
23. carried out feared stimuli perform the feared responses
24. fear stimuli controlled
25. desensitization reprocessing traumatic memories stress highly

Module 13.4
26. operant extinction shaping control undesirable responses promote
27. troublesome behaviors identifying eliminating
28. operant tokens
29. tokens institutional social rewards

30. thought patterns distorted coping
31. beliefs thinking emotions behavior
32. behavior irrational beliefs

Module 13.5
33. individual relationship problems
34. roles real-life problems a unit
35. encounter personality benefits
36. therapeutic catharsis practice new behaviors
37. active open-ended paraphrasing
38. culturally skilled traditional non-European ethnic
39. drugs surgery medical
40. pharmacotherapy psychosurgery
41. Community mental health centers consultation crisis

Module 13.6
42. personal problems reinforcement self-directed
43. aversive images
44. mild punishment
45. mental rehearsal
46. relaxation upsetting images
47. high-quality mental health care
48. successful therapists recommended
49. reputable a referral

Mastery Test
1. B, (pp. 545-546, Objective 13.3)
2. D, (p. 554, Objective 13.7)
3. A, (p. 564, Objective 13.10)
4. C, (p. 543, Objective 13.2)
5. D, (p. 548, Objective 13.4)
6. C, (p. 565, Objective 13.10)
7. A, (p. 542, Objective 13.1)
8. C, (p. 570, Objective 13.12)
9. B, (p. 567-569, Objective 13.11)
10. A, (p. 545, Objective 13.3)
11. C, (p. 559, Objective 13.8)
12. B, (p. 575, Objective 13.14)
13. D, (p. 548, Objective 13.4)
14. B, (p. 553, Objective 13.6)
15. C, (p. 550, Objective 13.5)
16. A, (p. 576, Objective 13.14)
17. A, (p. 548, Objective 13.1)
18. B, (p. 579, Objective 13.15)
19. D, (p. 545, Objective 13.3)
20. C, (p. 553, Objective 13.6)
21. D, (p. 561, Objective 13.1)
22. B, (p. 571, Objective 13.12)
23. B, (p. 558, Objective 13.8)
24. B, (p. 569, Objective 13.11)
25. A, (p. 554, Objective 13.7)
26. D, (p. 548, Objective 13.4)
27. B, (p. 566, Objective 13.11)
28. A, (p. 560, Objective 13.9)
29. C, (p. 548, Objective 13.4)
30. B, (p. 549, Objective 13.4)
31. C, (p. 561, Objective 13.9)
32. A, (p. 550, Objective 13.5)
33. D, (p. 556, Objective 13.7)
34. D, (p. 570, Objective 13.12)
35. C, (p. 573, Objective 13.13)
36. B, (p. 542, Objective 13.1)
37. D, (p. 542, Objective 13.1)
38. B, (p. 544, Objective 13.3)
39. D, (p. 554, Objective 13.7)
40. B, (p. 572, Objective 13.13)
41. A, (p. 562, Objective 13.9)
42. C, (p. 572, Objective 13.13)

27. D, (p. 623, Objective 15.2)
28. D, (p. 628, Objective 15.4)
29. B, (p. 642, Objective 15.10)
30. A, (p. 632, Objective 15.6)
31. A, (p. 648, Objective 15.14)
32. C, (p. 643, Objective 15.11)
33. B, (p. 628, Objective 15.4)
34. A, (p. 628, Objective 15.4)

35. A, (p. 645, Objective 15.13)
36. D, (p. 634, Objective 15.7)
37. C, (p. 638, Objective 15.9)
38. C, (p. 649, Objective 15.15)
39. D, (p. 651, Objective 15.15)
40. A, (p. 658, Objective 15.18)
41. A, (p. 658, Objective 15.18)
42. C, (p.652, Objective 15.16)

Chapter 1

MODULE 1.1

The Science of Psychology

Psychology is the scientific study of behavior and mental processes. Psychologists seek empirical evidence based on scientific observation.

Psychology
Scientific study of
- Behavior
- Mental processes

Behaviors
- Eating
- Sleeping
- Talking
- Walking

Mental Processes
- Thoughts
- Memories
- Emotions
- Dreams

Four Goals of Psychology

1. Describe
What is happening?

2. Understand
Why is it happening?

3. Predict
When will it happen?

4. Control
Can it be changed?

MODULE 1.2

Critical Thinking and the Scientific Method in Psychology

The Scientific Method

1. Observe
Computer game designers have varying levels of stress.

2. Define the Problem
In what ways are high stress and low stress game designers different?
High control vs. Low control?

3. Propose the Hypothesis
Game designers who have *more control* over difficult tasks will report *less* stress.

4. Gather the Evidence and Test the Hypothesis
Ramdomly assign subjects into two groups:
1. Forced pace (low control) = high stress
2. Self pace (high control) = low stress

5. Publish Results
Write and publish a scholarly article. Describe the research question, the methods, the results, and the conclusions.

6. Build Theories
Use the results from this and other experiments to create a theory that explains why having control over a task reduces stress.

History and Contemporary Perspectives

Psychology began as a branch of philosophy, which includes the study of knowledge, reality, and human nature. Psychology developed as a science when the scientific method began to be applied.

Modern Psychological Perspectives

Biological
Based on biological principles
- Brain processes
- Evolution
- Genetics
- Neuroscience

Careers
Biopsychologists
Evolutionary psychologists

Psychological
Based on psychological principles
- Objective observation
- Mental processes
- Humanistic view
- Psychodynamic view

Careers
Cognitive psychologists
Psychodynamic psychologists

Sociocultural
Based on social and cultural principles
- Multiculturalism
- Universal behaviors
- Cultural relativity
- Social norms

Careers
Crosscultural psychologists

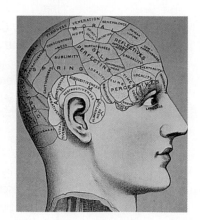

Psychologists and Their Specialties

Myths

Psychologists are all shrinks.

Psychologists are more disturbed than their patients.

Most psychologists are therapists in private practice.

Psychologists, psychiatrists, social workers, counselors . . . what's the difference?

Facts

"Shrinks" are psychiatrists, not psychologists. Psychologists hold master's or doctorate degrees. Psychologists are trained in psychological
- Methods
- Knowledge
- Theories

Psychologists are often inaccurately portrayed in the media.
Psychologists are responsible and hardworking.
Psychologists follow an ethical code and must respect people's privacy, dignity, confidentiality, and welfare.

ONLY 16 percent of psychologists work in clinical settings. Most psychologists work in varied settings:
- Teaching
- Research
- Administer psychological tests
- Serving as consultants

Clinical psychologists have a Ph.D or Psy.D. and treat mental disorders through psychotherapy.
Counseling psychologists have a master's degree and treat milder problems at school or work.
Psychiatrists are medical doctors (M.D.s), and also treat mental disorders, often through drug therapy.
Psychiatric social workers have an M.S.W and assist both psychologists and psychiatrists as part of a team.

The Psychology Experiment

The Psychology Experiment

1. Directly vary a condition, called the independent variable
2. Create two or more groups of subjects (using random assignment)
3. Record whether
   the **independent variable (IV)**
   causes an effect on
   the **dependent variable (DV)**

Group 1
Experimental Group
- Receives the IV
- All other conditions are kept the same

Group 2
Control Group
- Does not receive the IV
- All other conditions are kept the same

Compare the Results
Did the results of the experimental group differ significantly from the control?
  If yes, then the IV caused the differences (reject the null hypothesis).
  If no, then the IV had no effect (accept the null hypothesis).

Notes

_____

_____

_____

_____

_____

_____

_____

Nonexperimental Research Methods

Naturalistic Observation
Observing behavior in natural settings

Clinical Method/Case Studies
Studying psychological problems in clinical settings

Surveys
Using questionnaires to poll large groups

Correlation Studies
Studying the relationships between events

Psychology in Action: Psychology in the Media
How to tell fact from fiction.

Suggestion 1
Be skeptical.

Suggestion 5
Observation or interference?

Suggestion 2
How credible is the source?

Suggestion 6
Oversimplification?

Suggestion 3
Was there a control group?

Suggestion 7
Overgeneralization?

Suggestion 4
Correlation or causation?

1. Information gained through direct observation is known as
   a. empirical evidence.
   b. overt behaviors.
   c. covert behaviors.
   d. scientific observation.

2. If you are studying issues such as how people deal with death and dying, you may be considered a(n) _____ psychologist.
   a. social
   b. forensic
   c. developmental
   d. evolutionary

3. Psychology's goals include all of the following except
   a. control.
   b. observe.
   c. describe.
   d. predict.

4. Ray observes that more batters are hit by pitched balls on hot days than on cold days. His explanation for this is that the heat makes the pitchers more aggressive. This explanation is an example of a(n)
   a. theory.
   b. fallacy.
   c. hypothesis.
   d. assumption.

5. If Ray then specifies that "hot" means above 90° F, we would say he has _____ "hot."
   a. operationally defined
   b. systematically defined
   c. inappropriately defined
   d. explicitly defined

6. _____ is often referred to as the father of psychology.
   a. Dennis Coon
   b. Jean Piaget
   c. Edward Titchener
   d. Wilhelm Wundt

7. If you were interested in exploring those thoughts, feelings, and emotions that lie outside one's awareness, you might be considered a student of _____ psychology.
   a. Gestalt
   b. psychoanalytic
   c. cognitive behavioral
   d. humanistic

8. The slogan "Be all that you can be" is an example of
   a. self-actualization.
   b. self-evaluation.
   c. self-concept.
   d. self-esteem.

9. _____ is best described as the study of human strengths, virtues, and optimal behavior.
   a. The psychological perspective
   b. The biological perspective
   c. Positive psychology
   d. The sociocultural perspective

10. Joshua works with children who demonstrate difficulties in successfully adjusting to kindergarten. It is most probable that Joshua is a _____ psychologist.
    a. clinical
    b. counseling
    c. psychoanalytic
    d. social

11. In an experiment on the effects of caffeine on college student test performance, caffeine would be considered the
    a. independent variable.
    b. dependent variable.
    c. extraneous variable.
    d. conditioned response.

12. Your friend visits a local mental health clinic where he receives psychotherapy and a prescription for an antidepressant. Your friend has probably seen a
    a. counselor.
    b. psychiatric social worker.
    c. psychiatrist.
    d. psychologist.

13. Issues such as competency levels and a client's right to confidentiality and privacy are examples of _____ standards or guidelines.
    a. ethical
    b. moral
    c. legal
    d. psychological

14. _____ means that a participant has an equal chance of being in either the experimental group or the control group.
    a. Placebo effect
    b. Self-fulfilling prophecy
    c. Random assignment
    d. Representative sampling

15. If you are approached at the mall and answer questions regarding your buying preferences, you have probably just participated in a(n)
    a. naturalistic observation.
    b. survey.
    c. experiment.
    d. correlational study.

16. Dr. Walinski is attempting to prove a cause-and-effect relationship between the viewing of violent media and subsequent increases in aggressive behaviors. The research method he will most likely utilize in this attempt would be a(n)
    a. experiment.
    b. survey.
    c. clinical study.
    d. random sample.

17. In an attempt to reduce the _____, you install cameras to covertly record the behaviors of students who are riding on the school bus.
    a. observer bias
    b. anthropomorphic error
    c. experimenter effect
    d. placebo effect

18. Which of the following correlation coefficients indicates the strongest relationship between two variables?
    a. 20.75
    b. 0
    c. 10.64
    d. 10.23

19. While researching a topic on the Internet for your introductory psychology course, the text recommends that you do the following:
    a. Take into account the source of the information.
    b. Be skeptical.
    c. Both (a) and (b).
    d. Neither (a) nor (b).

20. A professor believes that most students who sit at the back of the classroom are unmotivated and apathetic towards their studies. This belief is confirmed at the end of the semester as the majority of the back-row students are given a below-average grade. This outcome could be due to which of the following?
    a. observer effect
    b. self-fulfilling prophecy
    c. double-blind approach
    d. None of the above.

Chapter 2

Neurons and the Nervous System

The nervous system is divided into two major systems, then subdivided into more sections, each with their corresponding duties and responsibilities.

Central Nervous System

The central nervous system (CNS) consists of
- The brain (the central "computer" of the nervous system)
- The spinal cord (connecting the brain to other parts of the body).

Peripheral Nervous System

The peripheral nervous system (PNS) carries information to and from the CNS.

Autonomic Nervous System

The autonomic nervous system (ANS) serves the
- Internal organs
- Glands of the body

Somatic Nervous System

The somatic nervous system (SNS) carries messages to and from
- Sense organs
- Skeletal muscles

Sympathetic Branch

Emergency system that prepares the body for *fight or flight*.

Parasympathetic Branch

- Quiets the body and returns it to low levels of arousal
- Keeps vital life processes at moderate levels

The Neuron and Its Parts

The neuron is the *basic nerve cell* of the nervous system.
- It carries and processes information throughout the nervous system.
- 100 billion neurons join to form neural networks in our brain.
- Neural networks produce intelligence and consciousness.

Dendrites

- Receive messages from other neurons

Soma (Cell Body)

- Receives messages
- Contains cell nucleus
- Sends nerve impulses

Axon

- Thin fiber
- Transmits nerve impulses (action potential)

Axon Terminals

- Send messages to other neurons through chemicals called *neurotransmitters*

Brain Research

Methods for Studying Brain Structures

CT Scan
X-rays from numerous angles form one image

MRI Scan
The body is placed in a magnetic field. The image is processed by computer, yielding a 3-D model of the brain. An MRI is more detailed than a CT scan.

Methods for Studying Brain Functions

Ablation and Deep Lesioning
Involves surgical removal or damage to brain parts.

ESB
Electrical stimulation of the brain.

EEG
Uses electrodes to record neural impulses.

PET Scan
Positron emission tomography produces great images of activity.

fMRI
Provides images of activity throughout the brain.

MODULE 2.3

Hemispheres and Lobes of the Cerebral Cortex

The cerebrum can be subdivided into both association cortex areas and the four lobes of the cerebral cortex.

Cerebrum
Two large hemispheres (the cerebrum) cover the upper part of the brain. Generally, each side of the brain controls functions on the opposing side of the body.

Association Cortex
The *association cortex*, the larger portion of the cortex, combines and processes information from the senses.

Brain Damage
Damage to association cortex can result in loss of function such as *aphasia*, impaired ability to use language.

Lobes of Cerebral Cortex
Large sections of the cerebral cortex are subdivided into lobes. Lobes perform *specific functions*.

Occipital Lobes
The occipital lobes at the rear of the brain process primary *visual information*.

Temporal Lobes
The temporal lobes located low on each side of the brain process *auditory information and language*.

Parietal Lobes
The parietal lobes register *body sensations* including touch, temperature, pressure, and other somatic sensations.

Frontal Lobes
Higher mental abilities, reasoning, and planning take place in the frontal lobes.

Brain Damage
Damage depends on the specific brain lobe that was affected.

Subcortex and Endocrine System

The cerebrum is not the only area that controls behavior.

Subcortex

Life-sustaining functions are controlled by subcortex structures.

Endocrine System

Glands in the endocrine system disperse *hormones* throughout the body, where they affect internal activities and behaviors. Linked to brain through the *hypothalamus*.

Forebrain

Includes cerebral cortex

- *Hypothalmus* controls basic motives such as sex, eating, drinking, and sleep, and links the brain to the endocrine system.
- *Thalamus* acts as a switching station for sensory messages.

Limbic System

Primitive core of the brain.
- *Amygdala* is the brain's fear and emotional system.
- *Hippocampus* helps form lasting memories.

Midbrain

Connector

Hindbrain

Controls vital life functions

Reticular Formation and RAS

- *Reticular formation* influences attention and reflexes and prioritizes messages throughout the brain.
- *Reticular activating system (RAS)* stimulates the cortex, keeping it active and alert.

Hindbrain

Controls vital life functions
- *Medulla* controls breathing, heart rate, swallowing, etc.
- *Pons* is involved in sleep/arousal.
- *Cerebellum* controls muscular coordination, muscle tone, and posture.

Pituitary Gland

- Regulates growth by releasing *growth hormone*.
- "Master Gland" of the endocrine system.

Pineal Gland

Controls body rhythms and sleep cycles by releasing *melatonin*.

Thyroid Gland

Controls metabolism.

Adrenal Gland

- Releases catecholamines and corticoids involved in fight-or-flight responses and stress.
- Secondary source of sex hormones.

Psychology in Action: Handedness—Are You Dexterous or Sinister?

Right-Handers

- *Brain Dominance*
  - 97% Left brain
  - 3% Right brain
- *Advantages*
  - Right-handed world
  - Longer lifespan

Left-Handers

- *Brain Dominance*
  - 68% Left brain
  - 19% Right brain
  - 12% Both sides
- *Advantages*
  - Superiority in art
  - Less lateralization
  - Less language loss after brain injury
  - Better math skills

Notes

1. The processing of information occurs in our
   a. brain.
   b. spinal cord.
   c. peripheral nervous system.
   d. sympathetic nervous system.

2. The _____ gap is the microscopic space between two neurons.
   a. somatic
   c. synaptic
   b. axonic
   d. dendritic

3. _____ are chemicals that alter activity within neurons and carry messages from one neuron to another.
   a. Neuropeptides
   c. Neural regulators
   b. Neurotransmitters
   d. Neural receptors

4. Kelli suffers from multiple sclerosis. If we examine a neuron from her brain, we may find degeneration of her
   a. soma.
   c. nerves.
   b. axon terminals.
   d. myelin.

5. While watching a scary movie, Caleb hears a sudden and unexpected noise. It is probable that such a situation would activate his _____ system.
   a. central nervous
   c. parasympathetic
   b. sympathetic
   d. somatic nervous

6. Which imaging technique utilizes strong magnetic fields to identify structures of the brain and the functions they control?
   a. CT scan
   c. EEG
   b. fMRI scan
   d. PET scan

7. Identify (of those listed) the least intrusive technique for brain study.
   a. deep lesioning
   c. EEG
   b. ablation
   d. electrical stimulation

8. _____ are large bundles of axons and dendrites.
   a. Nerves
   c. Neurogenesis
   b. Neurons
   d. Neurotoxins

9. Although only 3 millimeters thick, the _____ contains 70% of the neurons for the central nervous system.
   a. cerebrum
   c. cerebral cortex
   b. corpus callosum
   d. white matter

10. Approximately 95% of all people use their left hemisphere for language. This is an example of
    a. spatial neglect.
    b. corticalization.
    c. cerebral development.
    d. hemispheric specialization.

11. Body sensations, such as pressure, temperature and touch, are processed predominantly in the _____ lobe.
    a. temporal
    c. frontal
    b. parietal
    d. occipital

12. Damage to the _____ could result in disruption of reflexes and vital life functions.
    a. pons
    c. cerebellum
    b. medulla
    d. prefrontal lobe

13. Laurie kept pinching her arm to keep herself from falling asleep while driving. In doing so, Laurie was arousing her cortex by way of the
    a. reticular activating system.
    b. endocrine system.
    c. parasympathetic nervous system.
    d. central nervous system.

14. Tyron threw his golf club after missing his putt. What part of his brain was involved in this expression of frustration and anger?
    a. limbic system
    c. reticular formation
    b. endocrine system
    d. Broca's region

15. Chemicals that are carried throughout the body, affecting both internal activities and visible behavior, are called
    a. neurotransmitters.
    c. hormones.
    b. neuropeptides.
    d. GABA.

16. _____ might be released in someone watching a scary movie, whereas getting angry at the person who is talking during the movie would instead result in the release of _____
    _____.
    a. Epinephrine; norepinephrine
    b. Norepinephrine; epinephrine
    c. Testosterone; melatonin
    d. Melatonin; testosterone

17. Whether one is right or left handed is influenced by
    a. genetics.
    c. birth traumas.
    b. social pressures.
    d. All of the above.

18. The specialization of abilities to the right or left hemispheres of the brain is referred to as
    a. plasticity.
    c. neurogenesis.
    b. lateralization.
    d. action potential.

19. What are the short, branchlike structures of a neuron that receive signals from receptors or other neurons?
    a. axons
    c. dendrites
    b. somas
    d. cell membranes

20. Which of these activities most likely involves activation of the parasympathetic division?
    a. reading a newspaper article about stress
    b. taking an introductory psychology practice test
    c. resting after a stressful meeting
    d. getting oneself motivated to go exercise

Chapter 3

MODULE 3.1

The Interplay of Heredity and Environment

Nature or nurture?

Heredity (Nature)

Environment (Nurture)

What did you inherit from your parents?
Genetics
- Genetic transmission of physical and psychological characteristics
- Dominant or recessive
- Polygenic control

Examples:
- Eye color
- Genetic disorders, such as hemophilia, MS

How were you raised?
Environment
- External conditions that affect a person
- Prenatal influences
- Sensitive periods
- Enriched or deprived environments

Examples:
- Congenital problems
- Fetal alcohol syndrome
- Poverty

Both
Reciprocal Influences

Example:
Temperament (genetic)   Parent-child bond (nurture)

MODULE 3.2

The Neonate and Early Maturation

Infant reflexes

Grasping Reflex
Babies grasp tightly when an object is placed in their palms.

Rooting Reflex
Babies reflexively turn their heads when touched on the cheek.

Sucking Reflex
Babies reflexively suck to obtain food when touched on the lips.

Moro Reflex
Babies make a hugging motion when slartled by a loud noise.

Notes

_____

_____

_____

_____

_____

_____

_____

Social Development in Childhood

Attachment
The close emotional bond that babies form with their primary caregivers.

Secure Attachment
Children with secure attachment show stable and positive emotional bonds.
- They are upset by their mother's absence.
- They seek closeness upon her return.

Insecure Attachment

Avoidant
Children with avoidant attachment have anxious emotional bonds. They turn away from their mother upon return.

Ambivalent
Children with ambivalent attachment have anxious emotional bonds. They show mixed feelings: they seek closeness and resist contact.

Language Development in Childhood

Birth
Use crying to get attention

6-8 Weeks Old
Begin cooing, repeating vowels "oo" or "ah"

6-8 Months Old
Begin babbling, mixing consonants with vowels such as "dadadada" or "bababa"

1 Year Old
Begin responding to real words, say "Mama" or "Dada"

18 Months-2 Years Old
Use 100 words or more, first in single-word stage, then two-word stage: use telegraphic speech

Notes

_____

_____

_____

_____

_____

_____

_____

Cognitive Development in Childhood

Piaget's stages.

Sensorimotor Stage (0-2 Years)

- Involves motor and sensory coordination
- Object permanence emerges
- Child's conceptions become more stable

Preoperational Stage (2-7 Years)

- Symbolic thinking and language strengthen
- Child's thinking is very intuitive
- Child is egocentric

Concrete Operational Stage (7-11 Years)

- Conservation and reversibility emerge
- Child's thinking is more logical, yet very concrete

Formal Operations Stage (11 Years and Up)

- Abstract thinking emerges
- Metacognition emerges: thinking about thinking
- Full adult intellectual ability is attained
    Inductive and deductive thought
    Scientific thought
    Knowledge, experience, and wisdom

Adolescence, Young Adulthood, and Moral Development

Kohlberg's Levels of Moral Development

Preconventional Level

Moral thinking guided by consequences of actions: punishment, rewards, or mutual benefit.

Conventional Level

Moral thinking guided by desire to please others or to follow accepted authority, rules, and values.

Postconventional Level

Moral thinking guided by self-chosen ethical principles that are general, comprehensive, and universal.

Notes

Challenges Across the Lifespan

Erikson's Stages of Psychosocial Dilemma

0–1 Year: Trust vs. Mistrust
Loved, touched, nurtured

1–3 Years: Autonomy vs. Shame and Doubt
Independence is encouraged

3–5 Years: Initiative vs. Guilt
Makes plans and is allowed to carry them out

6–12 Years: Industry vs. Inferiority
Able to succeed in school

Adolescence: Identity vs. Role Confusion
Able to build a stable identity

Young Adulthood: Intimacy vs. Isolation
Able to share meaningful relationships

Middle Adulthood: Generativity vs. Stagnation
Desires to guide the next generation

Late Adulthood: Integrity vs. Despair
Able to view life with acceptance and satisfaction

Psychology in Action: Effective Parenting—Raising Healthy Children

Power Assertion
Using physical punishment or a show of force, such as taking away toys or privileges

Associated with fear, hatred of parents, and a lack of spontaneity and warmth Child has *low self-esteem.*

Withdrawal of Love
Refusing to speak to a child, threatening to leave, rejecting the child, or otherwise acting as if the child is temporarily unlovable

Produces "model" children, yet they are often anxious, insecure, and dependent on adults for approval. Child has *low self-esteem.*

Child Management Techniques
- Combining praise, recognition, approval, rules, and reasoning to encourage desirable behavior.
- Parent uses communication that is fair but loving and authoritative yet sensitive. This allows the child to move freely within consistent, well-defined boundaries for acceptable behavior.
- Must be carefully adjusted to child's level of understanding, because younger children don't always see the connection between rules, explanations, and their own behavior.

Produces socialized children who love and trust their parents. Children feel free to express their deepest feelings. Children move freely within consistent, well-defined boundaries for acceptable behavior. Child has *high self-esteem.*

1. Developmental psychology is the study of progressive changes in behavior and abilities in an individual, from _____ to death.
   a. birth
   b. conception
   c. infancy
   d. childhood

2. Dr. Worthington believes people who are intelligent have become so because of their life experiences. Dr. Jakway believes people are more or less intelligent because of genetic factors. What developmental psychology debate is illustrated by their disagreement?
   a. nature versus nurture
   b. correlation versus causation
   c. psychology versus philosophy
   d. cognitive psychology versus biological psychology

3. The typical human cell (excluding sex cells) contains how many chromosomes?
   a. 46 pairs
   b. 23
   c. 46
   d. Each cell has a varying number of chromosomes.

4. A trait controlled by a dominant gene
   a. will be expressed even if the instructions of the corresponding gene in the other half of the pair are different.
   b. may or may not be expressed. depending upon whether environmental conditions facilitate or prevent the expression of the trait.
   c. is always a positive, beneficial trait.
   d. will be expressed only if the instructions of the corresponding gene in the other half of the pair are the same.

5. Anything capable of directly causing birth defects (like alcohol) is known as a
   a. congenital problem.
   b. genetic disorder.
   c. teratogen.
   d. sensitive period.

6. An infant's home would be considered _____ if it is deliberately made more stimulating.
   a. beneficial
   b. detrimental
   c. depressing
   d. enriching

7. Core is to apple as _____ is to personality.
   a. reaction range
   b. temperament
   c. reciprocal series
   d. environment

8. _____ determines one's developmental level.
   a. Heredity
   b. Environment
   c. Behavior
   d. All of the above.

9. Which of the following is not one of the three categories for temperament?
   a. slow to warm up
   b. disorganized
   c. difficult
   d. easy

10. How might you elicit the grasping reflex in a neonate?
    a. Stroke his or her cheek lightly.
    b. Place a bottle in the child's mouth.
    c. Loudly clap your hands.
    d. Place your finger in the palm of the neonate's hand.

11. The physical growth and development of the body, brain, and nervous system is known as
    a. maturation.
    b. cephalocaudal development.
    c. proximodistal development.
    d. augmentation.

12. As discussed in the text regarding human development, although _____ may vary, _____ will typically remain the same.
    a. order; rate
    b. intelligence; motor skills
    c. rate; order
    d. motor skills; intelligence

13. At 10 months of age, Elizabeth displays mild anxiety when her mother leaves the room. This may be a direct sign that _____ _____ has occurred.
    a. social referencing
    b. social development
    c. an insecure attachment
    d. a secure attachment

14. Which Baumrind parenting style utilizes high levels of firm and consistent guidance along with increased amounts of warmth and love?
    a. authoritarian
    b. authoritative
    c. overly permissive
    d. None of the above.

15. While talking to his infant daughter, Doug raises his voice and begins to speak in short, simple sentences. His change in speech is known as an example of
    a. receptive language.
    b. expressive language.
    c. parentese.
    d. infant inflections.

16. _____ is the culturally defined period between childhood and adulthood.
    a. Puberty
    b. Adolescence
    c. Young adulthood
    d. Child-adult transition

17. Your niece sees an airplane flying overhead and states, "Look at the birdie!" This is an example of Piagetian process of
    a. assimilation.
    b. accommodation.
    c. inductive thought.
    d. deductive thought.

18. Mary Ainsworth identified all of the following classifications of attachment except
    a. securely attached.
    b. insecure-deteriorated.
    c. insecure-avoidant.
    d. insecure-ambivalent.

19. Dennis states that during emergencies, he believes it is "OK" to speed. His identification of this self-chosen moral principle may be considered an example of moral reasoning at the
    a. preconventional level.
    b. conventional level.
    c. postconventional level.
    d. concrete level.

20. What factor is generally considered to be an essential aspect of an infant's first psychosocial task (Erikson)?
    a. learning to control body sensations or developing shame if unsuccessful and not sensitively treated by caregivers
    b. becoming aware of pleasurable sensations and sharing these sensations with others
    c. receiving encouragement, guidance, and reinforcement from caregivers and developing a sense of independence or autonomy
    d. being treated lovingly and predictably by caregivers and learning to trust

Chapter 4

Sensation and Perception

Sensory Systems and Selective Attention

Vision
How do we see?

Data Reduction
Through psychophysics, physical energy is measured and related to dimensions of the resulting sensations.

Sensory Adaptation
Sensory receptors respond less to unchanging stimuli.

Sensory Analysis
Sensory information is divided by perceptual features.

Sensory Coding
Sensory information is converted into neural messages understood by the brain.

Normal Vision
Various wavelengths of light make up the visible spectrum.

Short Wavelengths
- 400 nanometers
- Purple or violet sensations

Long Wavelengths
- 700 nanometers
- Blue, green, yellow, orange, and red

Visual Problems
- The shape of the eye affects the ability to focus:
- Hyperopia (farsightedness)
- Myopia (nearsightedness)
- Astigmatism (multiple focal points)
- Presbyopia (farsightedness due to aging)
- The sensitivity of the eye affects the ability to produce color sensation; color blindness

Eye Structure
The eye is like a camera relying on a lens and light receptors.

Cornea
Clear membrane that bends light inward

Lens
Focuses images on the retina

Retina
Has a layer of photoreceptors

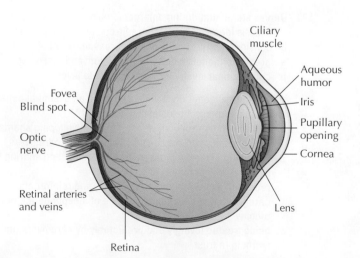

Ciliary muscle
Aqueous humor
Iris
Pupillary opening
Cornea
Lens
Retina
Retinal arteries and veins
Optic nerve
Blind spot
Fovea

Hearing, the Chemical Senses, and the Somesthetic Senses

Hearing, smell, and taste help keep us safe and add pleasure to our lives.

Hearing
A series of invisible waves of *compression* and *rarefaction* in the air provide the stimulus for sound.

How We Hear
1. First, the visible part of the ear concentrates sound waves and funnels them to the eardrum.
2. Second, a series of actions result in nerve impulses to the brain.

Deafness
Deafness comes in two main forms:
1. *Conduction deafness* happens when sounds are carried ineffectively from eardrum to inner ear.
2. *Nerve deafness* involves damage to the hair cells or the auditory nerve.

The Chemical Senses: Smell and Taste
Olfaction (smell) and gustation (taste) are responsive to chemical molecules.

Smell
At least 10,000 different odors can be detected based on which receptors are activated and where they are located.

The number of activated cells indicates how strong an odor is.

Taste and Flavors
Four (possibly five) basic tastes combine with sensations of texture, temperature, smell, and pain to provide us the many different flavors.

Perceptual Constancies and Perceptual Grouping

Perceptual constancies help us to interpret sensory information that is constantly changing.

Size Constancy
The perceived size of an object remains stable, even though the size of its retinal image changes.

Shape Constancy
The perceived shape of an object remains stable, even though the shape of its retinal image changes.

Brightness Constancy
Brightness of an object appears stable even though the lighting conditions change.

Depth Perception

The ability to see three-dimensional space and judge distances is vital to many daily functions.

Binocular Cues

Convergence
When looking at something that is 50 feet or less in distance, the eyes must turn in (converge) to focus on the object.

Retinal Disparity
Because the eyes are spaced 2.5 inches apart, each eye receives a slightly different view of the world.

Monocular Cues

Accommodation
When looking at something within 4 feet of each eye, the lens bends in order to focus on nearby objects.

Pictorial Cues
We perceive depth on two-dimensional surfaces such as paintings and photos by use of pictorial cues:
- Linear perspective
- Relative size
- Height in picture plane
- Light and shadow
- Overlap
- Texture gradients
- Aerial perspective
- Relative motion

Perception and Objectivity

Learning, expectations, and motives can alter our perception of the world.

Perceptual Learning
Learning can affect how we process sensory information. We may learn to focus on just one part of a group of stimuli.

Perceptual Habits
Learning may create ingrained patterns of organization and attention (perceptual habits).

Illusions
Illusions are distorted perceptions of stimuli that actually exist. Perceptual learning contributes to illusions.

Lack of Objectivity
Perception is not always objective. A variety of factors may influence what we perceive.

Attention
Attention is key to perception. Failure to pay attention to stimuli can result in not perceiving important events.

Motives and Attention
Your motives may make you focus on, or ignore, stimuli.

Hallucinations
Hallucinations are sensory (sight, sound, smell, taste, or touch) perceptions that have no external reality.

Perceptual Expectancies
Expectancies prepare you to perceive what you expect to perceive. Suggestion may play a large part in expectancies.

Extrasensory Perception

The purported ability to perceive events in ways outside the normal senses is a topic that fascinates many people.

Telepathy
The ability to read someone else's mind.

Clairvoyance
The ability to perceive events or information without regard to distance or physical barriers.

Precognition
The ability to perceive or predict future events.

Psychokinesis
The ability to influence inanimate objects by willpower.

Psychology in Action: Becoming a Better Eyewitness to Life

Tips for becoming a better eyewitness to life.

Remember that perceptions are constructions of reality.

Break perceptual habits and interrupt habituation.

Shift adaptation levels and broaden frames of reference by seeking out-of-the-ordinary experiences.

Beware of perceptual sets.

Be aware of the ways in which motives and emotions influence perceptions.

Make a habit of engaging in reality testing.

Pay attention.

1. You turn on the radio in your car; however, it is turned down so low that you cannot hear it. Someone utilizing the approach of psychophysics would say that the sound had not reached
   a. minimum threshold.
   b. absolute threshold.
   c. sensory adaptation.
   d. sensory identification.

2. You answer your phone and immediately recognize the voice of your best friend. What process is involved in this recognition?
   a. olfaction
   b. perception
   c. adaptation
   d. sensation

3. The cornea, or the lens, of Josh's eye is misshapen, resulting in part of his vision being focused and part being fuzzy. This problem is commonly referred to as
   a. hyperopia.
   b. myopia.
   c. presbyopia.
   d. astigmatism.

4. The physical height of a sound wave corresponds to what we would typically refer to as
   a. frequency.
   b. loudness.
   c. pitch.
   d. range.

5. As you move from a darkened movie theater into the bright theater lobby, your eye transitions from using its _____ to _____.
   a. cones; rods
   b. photo receptors; bars
   c. rods; cones
   d. cones; visual receptors

6. What type of hearing loss cannot be compensated for with the use of a hearing aid?
   a. conductive hearing loss
   b. innate hearing loss
   c. sensorineural hearing loss
   d. natural hearing loss

7. After reading information about the sense of taste, your friend asks you, "How, if there are only (up to) five different tastes that can be sensed, can there be so many flavors?" You correctly respond that
   a. additional information like texture and smell enhances taste.
   b. there are actually more than five tastes.
   c. the gustatory cortex fills in any missing information, resulting in additional flavors being perceived.
   d. None of the above.

8. What are the five taste sensations described in your text?
   a. rich, sweet, salty, bitter, sour
   b. bitter, sweet, hot, cool, salty
   c. brothy, buttery, sweet, sour, bitter
   d. sweet, salty, sour, bitter, umami

9. Gustation and olfaction are similar in that they both
   a. require the sensing of chemicals.
   b. would be hard to live without.
   c. involve perception but not sensation.
   d. All of the above.

10. Receptors in muscles and joints that detect body position and movement are referred to as the _____ sense.
    a. gustatory
    b. kinesthetic
    c. vestibular
    d. lock and key

11. Which of the following statements about depth perception are true?
    a. It may develop as early as 2 weeks of age.
    b. It is, at a basic level, inborn.
    c. It is partly learned through experience.
    d. All of the above.

12. Analyzing information starting with small features and building upward to a complete perception is known as
    a. top-down processing.
    b. lateral processing.
    c. bottom-up processing.
    d. puzzle theory processing.

13. After you watch a horror movie, you begin to notice sounds both inside and outside the house that seem to be unusual. This change in perception may be due to what your text refers to as a perceptual
    a. disturbance.
    b. expectancy.
    c. sensory experience.
    d. hallucination.

14. An illusion
    a. is the same as a hallucination.
    b. typically accompanies many mental illnesses.
    c. is a perceptual misjudgment.
    d. is the perception of a sensation without the presence of any external energy.

15. The four basic forms of ESP include all of the following except
    a. clairvoyance.
    b. telepathy.
    c. psychokinesis.
    d. psychosurgery.

16. _____ is the decreased response to unchanging and predictable stimuli.
    a. Habituation
    b. Dishabituation
    c. Perceptual deprivation
    d. Sensory illusion

17. According to the text, all of the following could improve one's ability to be a better eyewitness except
    a. breaking perceptual habits and interrupting habituation.
    b. learning to regularly question your own perceptions.
    c. regularly testing reality.
    d. being wary of looking at facial expressions or making eye contact with others.

18. What is the theory of color vision based on three cone types: red, green, and blue?
    a. trichromatic theory
    b. opponent-process theory
    c. cone-color theory
    d. primary color theory

19. _____ explains motion sickness that one might experience as the result of a mismatch between information from vision (playing a video game in which you are riding a rollercoaster) and the vestibular system and kinesthetic senses (actually sitting still).
    a. Gate control theory
    b. Sensory conflict theory
    c. Lock and key theory
    d. Perceptual divergence theory

20. Voluntarily focusing on one thing while excluding other sensory messages is an example of
    a. selective attention.
    b. alternating concentration.
    c. discriminating awareness.
    d. selective exclusion.

Chapter 5

Altered States and Sleep

Changes in the *quality* and *pattern* of mental activity are known as altered states of consciousness (ASC).

Consciousness

Consciousness consists of all the sensations, perceptions, memories, and feelings you are aware of at any instant.

Altered States of Consciousness

Changes occur in the *quality* and *pattern* of mental activity.

Waking Consciousness

A state of clear and organized alertness.

Sleep

Sleep is an innate biological rhythm that can never be entirely ignored.

Other Altered States

Examples include: drug-induced altered states, long-distance running, listening to music, meditation, hypnosis.

Stages of Sleep

As we sleep, we cycle in and out of four NREM sleep stages + REM

Stage 1 NREM: *Light sleep*—heart rate slows, breathing becomes irregular, muscles relax; EEG shows small, irregular waves

Stage 2 NREM: Sleep deepens, body temperature drops; EEG shows *sleep spindles*

Stage 3 NREM: New large and slow brain waves appear; EEG begins to show *delta waves*

Stage 4 NREM: *Deep sleep*—reached within 1 hour; EEG shows almost pure *delta waves*

REM: Rapid eye movement sleep is associated with dreaming.

Sleep Needs and Patterns

Individuals have varying needs for sleep. Averages range from 5 hours to 11 hours.

Sleep Deprivation

Going without sleep can result in:

- Hallucinations (and other reality distortions)
- Inability to perform required tasks
- Poor moods
- Accidents

Sleep Disturbances and Dreaming

Sleep disturbances are a serious risk to health and happiness. Sleep clinics treat thousands of people each year for sleep disorders or complaints.

Common Sleep Problems

Many factors contribute to our poor sleep quality in North America. Sleep problems are nearing epidemic rates. Thousands of people each year suffer from sleep disorders.

Insomnia
- Difficulty sleeping
- Frequent nighttime awakenings
- Waking too early
- Affects work, health, and relationships

Sleepwalking and Sleeptalking
- Usually take place during stage 3 and stage 4 sleep
- Somnabulists do many activities
- Sleeptalkers may not make sense

Nightmares and Night Terrors
- Nightmares are bad dreams (REM)
- Night terrors cause total panic, hallucinations, and high physiological arousal (NREM)

Narcolepsy
- Sudden irresistible sleep attacks
- May last a few minutes to 1/2 hour
- Victim sleeps while standing, talking, or even driving

Sleep Apnea
- Breathing stops for periods of 20 seconds to 2 minutes
- Causes the person to gulp for air

Sudden Infant Death Syndrome (SIDS)
- Also known as "crib death"
- Affects 1 of 500 babies per year
- Baby stops breathing after apnea

Dreams

Most people dream four or five times a night. Dreams are not always remembered.

REM Sleep Revisited
REM sleep is associated with normal dreaming. In children, REM may stimulate the developing brain. In adults, REM may prevent sensory deprivation and help to process emotional events.

Activation-Synthesis Hypothesis
The activation-synthesis hypothesis argues that several parts of the brain are activated during REM sleep, and the cortex of the brain synthesizes this activity into stories and visual images.

Dream Theories
Most theorists agree that dreams reflect our waking thoughts, fantasies, and emotions.

Psychodynamic Dream Theory
Freud's psychodynamic dream theory emphasized internal conflicts and unconscious forces disguised as dream symbols.

Hypnosis, Meditation, and Sensory Deprivation

Other altered states of consciousness (ASCs) play a role in human behavior.

Hypnosis

People are hypnotized by many different methods that encourage *focused attention, relaxation, easy acceptance* of suggestions, and use of *vivid imagination*.

Meditation

In general, meditation focuses attention and interrupts the typical flow of thoughts, worries, and analysis. Benefits include lower heart rate, blood pressure, muscle tension, and other signs of stress.

Sensory Deprivation

Limited or monotonous stimulation may produce bizarre sensations, distorted perceptions, and dangerous lapses in attention. Under proper conditions, sensory deprivation may help break long-standing habits.

Psychoactive Drugs

Psychoactive drugs affect attention, judgment, memory, time sense, self-control, emotion, or perception.

Effects on the Brain

Drugs may imitate or alter neurotransmitters.
- Some drugs increase neurotransmission (stimulants).
- Other drugs slow or block stimulation (depressants).

Addiction

Addictive drugs stimulate the brain's reward circuitry.

Stimulants
("Uppers")
- Amphetamines
- Cocaine
- Caffeine
- Nicotine

Depressants
("Downers")
- Barbiturates
- GHB
- Tranquilizers
- Alcohol

Hallucinogens
- Marijuana
- Hashish
- LSD
- PCP

Physical Dependence
Physical dependence (addiction) exists when a person compulsively uses a drug to maintain bodily comfort.

Withdrawal Symptoms
When physical illness follows removal of a drug

Drug Tolerance
Reduced response to a drug

Psychological Dependence
Persons who develop a psychological dependence feel that a drug is necessary to maintain feelings of comfort or well-being.

Psychology in Action: Exploring and Using Dreams

Freud identified four dream processes, or mental filters, that disguise the meanings of dreams.

Condensation
Combines several people, objects, or events into a single dream image.

Displacement
May cause important emotions or actions of a dream to be redirected toward safe or seemingly unimportant images.

Symbolization
Dreams are often expressed in images that are symbolic rather than literal.

Secondary Elaboration
The tendency to make a dream more logical and to add details when remembering it.

Notes

_____

_____

_____

_____

_____

_____

_____

1. Psychologists refer to _____ as all the sensations, perceptions, memories, and feelings that you are aware of at any given moment.
   a. unconscious
   b. preconscience
   c. conscience
   d. consciousness

2. All of the following would be considered altered states of consciousness except
   a. sleep.
   b. severe states of dehydration.
   c. intoxication.
   d. watching your favorite football team play in the Super Bowl.

3. REM sleep refers to
   a. sleep periods in which a person's eyes move rapidly.
   b. sleep periods ranging from stage 1 to stage 4.
   c. sleep periods in which night terrors might occur.
   d. sleep periods in which only 10% of all dreaming occurs.

4. A _____ is a brief shift in brain activity to the pattern normally recorded during sleep.
   a. microsleep
   b. deprivation
   c. hypersomnia
   d. daydream

5. Tony is experiencing sleep deprivation. Due to this deprivation, Tony may
   a. experience sensory illusions or hallucinations.
   b. have trouble paying attention to routine activities.
   c. be at greater risk for being in a car accident.
   d. All of the above.

6. While you are awake, an EEG registers _____ waves in your brain. However, while you are asleep your brain produces _____ _____ waves.
   a. alpha; beta
   b. beta; alpha
   c. alpha; delta
   d. delta; alpha

7. Just as you are drifting off to sleep the muscles in your leg twitch, causing you to wake up. This twitch is referred to as a
   a. hypnic jerk.
   b. sleep spindle.
   c. stage 1 spasm.
   d. dream shudder.

8. Insomnia includes
   a. trouble falling asleep.
   b. trouble staying asleep.
   c. waking up to early.
   d. All of the above.

9. In order to try to sleep, you instead try to keep your eyes open as long as possible. This behavioral remedy for insomnia is referred to as
   a. systematic relaxation.
   b. paradoxical intention.
   c. stimulus control.
   d. sleep contradiction.

10. Nightmare is to night terror as:
    a. REM is to NREM.
    b. bad is to worse.
    c. awake is to asleep.
    d. narcolepsy is to cataplexy.

11. An individual who suffers from sleep apnea will experience
    a. interrupted breathing while asleep.
    b. recurrent nightmares.
    c. increased REM sleep.
    d. reduced sleepiness during the day.

12. SIDS
    a. is seen in babies with a strong arousal reflex.
    b. is an acronym for serious inhalation deficit syndrome.
    c. annually affects approximately 1 out of every 500 babies.
    d. is less likely to affect babies who are open-mouth breathers.

13. _____ is defined by your text as an altered state of consciousness, characterized by narrowed attention and an increased openness to suggestion.
    a. Meditation
    b. Hypnosis
    c. Auto suggestion
    d. Dissociation

14. If you focus on the golf ball intently while taking exactly two practice swings before teeing off, you may be engaging in
    a. concentrative meditation.
    b. auto suggestion.
    c. mindfulness meditation.
    d. the use of a mantra.

15. Which of the following often characterize(s) addiction?
    a. drug withdrawal
    b. drug discomfort
    c. drug tolerance
    d. Both a and c.

16. Which of the following is not one of Freud's four identified dream processes?
    a. condensation
    b. recitation
    c. symbolization
    d. displacement

17. Larry stated that when he dreams, he sometimes realizes that he is in fact dreaming and then decides to do extraordinary things such as flying like Superman. This awareness during dreaming is called a _____ dream.
    a. lucid
    b. logical
    c. coherent
    d. cognent

18. Images in dreams that serve as visible signs of hidden ideas, desires, impulses, emotions, relationships, and so forth are called
    a. manifest images.
    b. latent symbols.
    c. dream images.
    d. dream symbols.

19. Which of the following is considered a depressant?
    a. cocaine
    b. alcohol
    c. caffeine
    d. nicotine

20. _____ is defined as downing five or more drinks (four for women) in a short time.
    a. Alcoholism
    b. Binge drinking
    c. Intoxication
    d. Alcohol dependence

MODULE 6.1

Learning and Classical Conditioning

Psychology is the scientific study of behavior and mental processes. Psychologists seek empirical evidence based on scientific observation.

Various Types of Learning

Learning is a relatively permanent change in behavior due to experience. Learning can result from classical, operant, or observational conditioning.

Classical Conditioning

- Classical conditioning is based on what happens before a response is made (antecedents).
- It involves passive behaviors.
- A neutral stimulus (NS) is paired repeatedly with an unconditioned stimulus (US) (unlearned) that leads to an unconditioned response (UR).
- Learning happens when the neutral stimulus is able to elicit the same response, now called the conditioned response (CR).

Operant Conditioning

- Operant conditioning is based on what happens after a response is made (consequences).
- It involves active behaviors as the learner operates on the environment.
- A response is made that is followed by either a reinforcing or punishing consequence.
- Learning happens when an event that follows a response increases the probability of repetition of the response.

Generalization

After conditioning, a stimulus that is similar to the original NS may cause the conditioned response.

Discrimination

Stimulus discrimination occurs when similar stimuli evoke different responses.

Extinction and Spontaneous Recovery

- Removing the US causes the CR to cease (extinction of the response).
- The CR may reappear in response to a generalized stimulus (spontaneous recovery of the response).

Conditioned Emotional Responses

- Conditioned responses may not be just reflexes.
- Responses may be emotional.
- Phobias (learned fears) are conditioned emotional responses (CERs).

Vicarious Conditioning

- Observing what happens to others may cause a conditioned response (vicarious classical conditioning).
- Vicarious conditioning involves learning from watching the reinforcement or punishment of others.

Operant Conditioning

Behaviors and consequences play a role in operant conditioning. Responses are voluntary (unlike classical conditioning) because we learn to expect that a certain response will lead to a certain effect (consequence). Consequences can be either reinforcing or punishing.

Reinforcement

An operant reinforcer is a consequence that *increases* the chance that the behavior will be repeated.

Positive Reinforcement

- Occurs when a response leads to the addition of a pleasant or desirable consequence.
- Increases responses.

Negative Reinforcement

- Occurs when a response leads to the removal of an unpleasant or undesirable event.
- Like positive reinforcement, negative reinforcement increases responses.

Punishment

Punishment is an aversive consequence that *decreases* the chance that the behavior will be repeated.

Punishment by Application

- Occurs when a response leads to the addition of an unpleasant or undesirable consequence.
- Decreases responses.

Punishment by Removal

- Occurs when a response leads to the removal of a pleasant or desirable event (negative reinforcement).
- Like punishment by application, it decreases responses.

Partial Reinforcement and Stimulus Control

Schedules of Partial Reinforcement

Partial reinforcement can be given in a variety of patterns. Reinforcement patterns can be either based on ratios or intervals.

Ratio Schedules
Based on number of responses

Interval Schedules
Based on time elapsed

Fixed Ratio (FR)
Reinforcement is given after a set number of responses. FR produces high response rates.

Variable Ratio (VR)
Reinforcement is given after a varied number of responses. VR is highly resistant to extinction.

Fixed Interval (FI)
Reinforcement is given after a fixed amount of time has elapsed between correct responses. The number of responses makes no difference in reinforcement.

Variable Interval (VI)
Reinforcement is given after a varied amount of time has passed between responses. Slow, steady response rates are produced.

Punishment

Punishment is frequently used to control behavior.

Variables Affecting Punishment

Behaviors are performed because there is some expectancy of reinforcement. The task of punishment is to overcome the reinforcement value.

Timing

Punishment should be given as the response is made or immediately after the response. This allows the learner to associate the behavior to the consequence.

Consistency

Punishment should be given each time an undesirable behavior occurs. Partially punishing a behavior will not speed extinction.

Intensity

Severe punishment may stop a behavior immediately and forever. The danger is in being too severe. Mild punishments may only have a temporary effect.

Side Effects of Punishment

As punishment increases in severity, so do the drawbacks.

Aversive

Punishment is painful or uncomfortable. Through classical conditioning, it can cause fear or resentment toward the person doing the punishing.

Escape and Avoidance

It is natural to try to avoid an aversive stimulus. Children may avoid parents and/or lie to parents to escape punishment.

Aggression

Aggression is a common response to frustration. Punishment can be very frustrating.

Cognitive Learning and Imitation

Cognitive Learning

Learning that involves higher mental processes, such as memory, thinking, problem solving, understanding, knowing, and anticipating.

Latent Learning

Learning remains hidden or unseen until a reward or incentive for performance is offered.

Discovery Learning

Learning emphasizes insight and understanding, in contrast to rote learning.

Observational Learning

Learning is influenced by observing and imitating the actions of another person or learning from the consequences of their actions.

Using Punishment Wisely

Punishment should not be used at all when other means to discourage behavior are available. Positive reinforcement for not misbehaving is more effective than punishment.

Apply punishment during, or immediately after, misbehavior.

Be consistent.

Use the minimum punishment necessary to suppress behavior.

Avoid harsh punishment.

Don't rely exclusively on punishment.

Expect anger from a punished person.

Punish with kindness and respect.

Psychology in Action: Behavioral Self-Management—A Rewarding Project

By applying learning principles to one's life, many behaviors can be improved.

Applying Operant Conditioning

By applying operant conditioning principles, it is possible to change or manage your own behavior.

1. Choose a Target Behavior
Identify the activity you want to change.

2. Record a Baseline
Record how much time you currently spend performing the target activity or count the number of desired or undesired responses you make each day.

3. Establish Goals
Remember the principle of shaping, and set realistic goals for gradual improvement on each successive week. Also, set daily goals that add up to the weekly goal.

4. Choose Reinforcers
Establish daily and weekly rewards for your accomplishments.

5. Record Your Progress
Keep accurate records of the amount of time spend each day on the desired activity or the number of times you make the desired response.

6. Reward Successes
If you meet your daily goal, collect your reward. If you fall short, be honest with yourself and skip the reward. Do the same for weekly goals.

7. Adjust Your Plan as You Learn More About Your Behavior
Overall progress will reinforce your attempts at self-management.

Breaking Bad Habits

Here are additional strategies that can help break bad habits.

Reinforce Alternative Responses
Try to get the same reinforcement with a new response.

Promote Extinction
Try to discover what is reinforcing an unwanted response and remove, avoid, or delay the reinforcement.

Break Response Chains
Break up response chains that precede an undesired behavior. Scramble the chain of events that leads to an undesired response.

Avoid Antecedent Cues
Try to avoid, narrow down, or remove stimuli that elicit the bad habit.

Try Behavioral Contracting
If all else fails, try behavioral contracting.
- First, state the specific problem behavior you want to control, or a goal you want to achieve.
- Second, state the rewards you will receive, privileges you will forfeit, or punishments you must accept.
- Third, sign the contract and have a person you trust also sign.
- Follow through.

1. Which term describes a relatively permanent change in behavior or the potential to make a response that occurs as a result of experience?
   a. learning
   b. conditioning
   c. perception
   d. understanding

2. Caleb gets paid $5 each week for mowing the lawn. If the money Caleb gets paid each week makes it more likely that he will mow the lawn again the following week, behavioral psychologists would refer to the money as a(n)
   a. allowance.
   b. bribe.
   c. reward.
   d. reinforcement.

3. Events that precede an experience are called _____, whereas those that follow a response are known as _____.
   a. punishments; reinforcements
   b. consequences; antecedents
   c. reinforcements; punishments
   d. antecedents; consequences

4. What must be paired together for classical conditioning to occur?
   a. neutral stimulus and conditioned stimulus
   b. neutral stimulus and unconditioned stimulus
   c. conditioned response and unconditioned response
   d. unconditioned stimulus and conditioned response

5. If you have the goal of teaching someone to respond reflexively to a stimulus that currently evokes no response, you will most likely utilize a(n) _____ approach.
   a. operant conditioning
   b. classical conditioning
   c. instrumental learning
   d. observational learning

6. While growing up, Susan often observed her mother have a panic attack in the presence of mice. As an adult, Susan now responds with intense anxiety at even the thought of a mouse. This learning of an emotional response would be considered an example of
   a. vicarious learning.
   b. indirect conditioning.
   c. instrumental conditioning.
   d. operant learning.

7. Stimulus _____ occurs when we learn to respond to a particular stimulus but not to others that are similar.
   a. identification
   b. extinction
   c. generalization
   d. discrimination

8. Edward L. Thorndike referred to the probability of a response being altered by the effect it has as
   a. classical conditioning.
   b. the theory of consequences.
   c. the law of effect.
   d. the state of affairs.

9. The text describes operant reinforcement as being most effective when it _____ a correct response.
   a. rapidly follows
   b. rapidly precedes
   c. is delayed, following
   d. is prematurely given, preceding

10. Behaviors that are repeated because they appear to produce reinforcement (even though they are actually unrelated) are often referred to as _____ behaviors.
    a. correlational
    b. superstitious
    c. consequential
    d. substantial

11. The process of reinforcing successive approximations is called
    a. shaping.
    b. molding.
    c. cognitive mapping.
    d. delayed gratification.

12. One way to differentiate operant conditioning from classical conditioning is to decide if the
    a. response is voluntary or reflexive in nature.
    b. stimulus is conditioned or unconditioned.
    c. response is pleasant or unpleasant.
    d. antecedent comes before or after the response.

13. Giving a child a spanking is an example of
    a. a negative reinforcement.
    b. a punishment.
    c. an antecedent.
    d. vicarious learning.

14. Magnolia took an aspirin, which subsequently relieved her headache. This relief is an example of a
    a. punishment.
    b. positive reinforcement.
    c. stimulus generalization.
    d. negative reinforcement.

15. Cookies and a glass of milk would be considered a _____ reinforcer.
    a. secondary
    b. primary
    c. token
    d. social

16. Ty gets paid at his job every 2 weeks, whereas Jevon gets paid for every car he sells. Ty's schedule of reinforcement is _____ _____, and Jevon's is _____.
    a. fixed interval; variable ratio
    b. fixed ratio; variable interval
    c. variable interval; variable ratio
    d. fixed interval; fixed ratio

17. The text describes all of the following drawbacks with punishment except
    a. avoidance learning.
    b. increased effectiveness in toilet training.
    c. escape learning.
    d. increasing aggression.

18. _____ refers to understanding, knowing, anticipating, or otherwise making use of information-rich higher mental processes.
    a. Observational learning
    b. Latent learning
    c. Cognitive learning
    d. Discovery learning

19. In creating your plan for how you will move through campus to get to your next class, it is likely you will use a
    a. cognitive route.
    b. created image.
    c. symbol representation.
    d. cognitive map.

20. Tracy was asked to label the keys on a blank computer keyboard. She initially stated that she would not be able to do it. However, upon being offered $50 if she could do it successfully, Tracy was able to complete the task. This is an example of _____ learning.
    a. passive
    b. manifest
    c. latent
    d. unintended

Memory Systems

Psychologists have identified three stages of memory.

Sensory Memory

Sensory memory registers incoming information from the environment through our senses just long enough to move it to the next stage.

Iconic Memory

An exact copy of what you see (icon).

Echoic Memory

An exact copy of what you hear (echo).

Short-Term Memory

Holds small amounts of information in conscious awareness to be moved to the next stage.

Limited Capacity of Information

Holds ONLY small amounts of information.

Sensitive to Interruption and Interference

Difficult to do more than one task at a time.

Working Memory

Combines with other mental processes to "think."

Long-Term Memory

Acts as a lasting, nearly limitless, storehouse for knowledge. LTM is stored on basis of meaning and importance.

Unlimited Capacity of Information

Holds nearly limitless amounts of information.

Stored on the Basis of Meaning

New information must be linked to previous knowledge.

Notes

STM and LTM

Knowing the characteristics of STM and LTM can help make good use of your memory.

Short-Term Memory

STM *capacity* is typically about 7 bits of information (plus or minus 2). STM *duration* is typically about 12 to 18 seconds.

Chunking

By reorganizing information into *chunks* we can make better use of our short-term memory.

Rehearsal

Rehearsal (repetition) of information in STM stops it from being lost forever.

Maintenance Rehearsal

Lengthens the duration of STM.

Elaborative Rehearsal

Makes information more meaningful. Links new information to memories that are already in LTM.

Long-Term Memory

LTM acts as a lasting, nearly limitless storehouse of memory. LTM is stored on basis of meaning and importance.

Permanence

Experts believe that long-term memories are only relatively permanent.

Constructing Memories

Memories are often updated, changed, lost, or revised. These processes may result in including false information.

Organizing Memories

Information in LTM may be arranged hierarchically according to rules, images, categories, symbols, similarity, or meaning.

Redintegrative Memories

Redintegration occurs when entire past experiences are reconstructed from one small recollection.

Skill Memory and Fact Memory

Long-term memories fall into at least two categories: *procedural* (skill) memory and *declarative* (fact) memory.

Notes

_____

_____

_____

_____

_____

_____

_____

Measuring Memory

Our memories may be revealed through various means.

Implicit and Explicit Memories

Memories from past experiences that are consciously brought to mind are *explicit*. Memories outside of awareness are *implicit*.

Explicit

Recall
A direct retrieval of facts or information involves *recall*.
Example: Essay exam

Recognition
In recognition memory, previously learned material is correctly identified.
Example: Multiple-choice exam

Relearning
Information learned once can be relearned with a "savings" in time or effort.

Implicit

Priming
Priming involves the activation of memories that lie outside of awareness.
Example: Riding a bike

Proactive
When prior learning inhibits recall of new learning.

Retroactive
When new learning inhibits recall of old learning.

Forgetting

Knowing how we "lose" memories helps us retain them. Why do we forget?

Encoding Failure

In many cases we "forget" because the memory was never formed (encoded) in the first place.

Repression

Through repression, memories are held out of consciousness.

Memory Decay

Memory traces (changes in nerve cells or brain activity) decay (fade) over time.

Suppression

Suppression is an active, conscious attempt to put something out of mind.

Cue-Dependent Forgetting

Memories may be "forgotten" because *memory cues* (stimuli associated with a memory) are missing.

State-Dependent Learning

The *bodily state* that exists during learning can be a strong cue for later memory. For example, if you learn a list of words while in a happy mood, you will recall those words better when you are happy again.

Interference

Interference refers to the tendency for new memories to impair retrieval of older memories (and the reverse).

Exceptional Memory and Improving Memory

Memory skills *can* be developed. The following are tips for building better memories.

Knowledge of Results
Feedback allows you to check your progress.

Spaced Practice
Alternate short study sessions with brief rest periods.

Selection
Memory chores will be more manageable if you select one or two important terms or ideas to focus on.

Whole vs. Part Learning
The amount of material to be learned may dictate whether it is more efficiently leaned as a whole or in parts.

Recitation
Recitation (summarizing aloud) forces you to practice retrieving information.

Organization
Difficult information can be organized into "chunks" for better retention.

Rehearsal
The more you mentally review (rehearse) information as you read, the better you will remember it.

Overlearning
Overlearning is the best insurance against going blank on a test.

Memory Cues
The best memory cues are the stimuli that were present during encoding.

Notes

1. Memory includes all of the following processes except
   a. storage.
   b. encoding.
   c. bypassing.
   d. retrieving.

2. Which term describes a fleeting flurry of auditory activity that lasts for a few seconds or less?
   a. logo
   b. echo
   c. icon
   d. image

3. _____ attention is required in order to move information from sensory memory to short-term memory.
   a. Special
   b. Sustained
   c. Alternating
   d. Selective

4. In order for information to be stored for an extended period, it must pass into or through all of the following stages except
   a. sensory memory.
   b. short-term memory.
   c. long-term memory.
   d. episodic memory.

5. Most often, short-term memories are stored
   a. phonetically.
   b. mentally.
   c. with the sense of smell.
   d. as images.

6. Information that is transferred from short-term memory to long-term memory must either be _____ or _____.
   a. important; meaningful
   b. limited; general
   c. insightful; understood
   d. emphasized; memorized

7. _____ are made up of bits of information grouped into larger units.
   a. Information bits
   b. Rehearsing information
   c. Information chunks
   d. Information clusters

8. By repeating the phone number silently to himself, Shawn was able to prolong the memory. This is an example of
   a. chunking.
   b. episodic memory.
   c. elaborative memory.
   d. maintenance rehearsal.

9. When gaps in memory are filled in by logic, guessing, or new information, _____ has occurred.
   a. constructive processing
   b. elaborative memory
   c. confabulation
   d. redintegration

10. _____ is a technique created by Edward Geiselman and Ron Fisher and is used by law enforcement for jogging the memory of eyewitnesses and increasing the accuracy of the memories being recalled.
    a. Hypnosis
    b. Shaping
    c. Behavioral interview
    d. Cognitive interview

11. As you look through your old high school yearbook, you are flooded with memories. This process is known as
    a. redintegration.
    b. constructive processing.
    c. cognitive processing.
    d. memory networking.

12. Declarative memory can be divided into _____ and _____ memories.
    a. sensory; procedural
    b. short-term; long-term
    c. procedural; semantic
    d. semantic; episodic

13. _____ is the feeling that a memory is available, but not quite retrievable.
    a. Drew-a-blank
    b. Tip-of-the-tongue
    c. Feeling-of-knowing
    d. Interference

14. What do psychologists call it when you can remember the first and last items of your grocery list, but have problems with the items in the middle of the list?
    a. rote memory effect
    b. interference
    c. amnesia
    d. serial position effect

15. A memory that can be consciously brought to mind is referred to in the text as a(n)
    a. implicit memory.
    b. explicit memory.
    c. voluntary memory.
    d. intentional memory.

16. What did Ebbinghaus' curve of forgetting imply?
    a. Forgetting is slow at first and is then followed by a rapid decline.
    b. Forgetting is rapid at first and is then followed by a slow decline.
    c. Forgetting is a constant and does not change with time.
    d. Everyone forgets at different rates.

17. A multiple-choice question is a common test of
    a. identification.
    b. recall.
    c. recognition.
    d. detection.

18. Remembering where you where and what you were doing on the second Tuesday of September, 2001, only after being told it was September 11 (9/11), is an example of
    a. state-dependent learning.
    b. cue-dependent learning.
    c. recitation.
    d. date-dependent recall.

19. Suppression is to repression as _____ is to _____.
    a. unconscious; conscious
    b. recognition; recall
    c. conscious; unconscious
    d. recall; recognition

20. Following his car accident (in which he hit his head on the steering wheel), Jacob was unable to remember what he was doing *before* the accident. This gap in memory is an example of
    a. anterograde amnesia.
    b. proactive interference.
    c. retrograde amnesia.
    d. retroactive interference.

Intelligence

In general, intelligence is the global capacity to act purposefully, to think rationally, and to deal effectively with the environment.

Intelligence Tests

Stanford-Binet Intelligence Scales, 5th ed.
Provides a score for fluid reasoning, knowledge, quantitative reasoning, visual-spatial processing, and working memory.

Wechsler Scales
Provides a performance score (nonverbal) and a verbal score (language or symbol oriented).

Intelligence Quotients

Mental Age
Dividing *mental age* (the level a person answers age-related questions) by *chronological age* and multiplying by 100 gives an IQ.

Mental Giftedness
Individuals who score above 130 on IQ tests are often identified as "gifted." Gifted children typically (although not always) are successful as adults.

IQ and Environment
Most experts agree that improving social conditions and providing a stimulating environment can raise intelligence.

Deviation IQ
Measuring how high or how low a person scores *relative to his or her own age group* gives a different form of IQ.

Intellectual Disability
Mental abilities far below average are identified as *intellectually disabled*.

Causes of Intellectual Disability
Fetal damage, birth injuries, metabolic disorders, and genetic abnormalities may cause intellectual difficulties.

Notes

_____

_____

_____

_____

_____

_____

_____

Imagery, Concepts, and Language

Cognition refers to mentally processing information. Abstract thinking is possible through *mental images*, *concepts*, and *language*.

Mental Images

Images are picture-like mental representations.

Most of us use images to think, remember, and solve problems.

Kinesthetic Imagery

Kinesthetic images are created from muscular sensations and help us think about movements and actions.

Concepts

Concepts are ideas that represent categories of objects or events.

Forming Concepts

Concept formation is the process of classifying the world into meaningful categories.

Meaning

Concepts have both
- an exact (denotative) meaning
- an emotional or personal (connotative) meaning.

Types of Concepts

Conjunctive concepts require two or more features.

Relational concepts are based on how an object relates to something else.

Disjunctive concepts have a least one of several possible features.

Language

Language consists of words or symbols and rules for combining them.

Structure of Language

Language requires:
1. *Grammar*—rules for making sounds into words and sentences
2. *Syntax*—rules for word order

Gestural Languages

Language is not limited to speech. Sign languages are true languages.

Look at    **Stare**

Problem Solving

Problem solving can be commonplace or highly significant.

Mechanical Solutions

Mechanical solutions are achieved by trial and error or by rote application of rules.

Least efficient.

Solutions by Understanding

Understanding (deep comprehension of a problem) is necessary in some cases.

Heuristics

Strategies for identifying and evaluating problem solutions (*heuristics*) typically involve a "rule of thumb" that reduces the number of alternatives to be considered.

More efficient.

Insightful Solutions

When understanding leads to a rapid solution, *insight* has taken place.

Nature of Insight

- *Selective encoding* is focusing on relevant information.
- *Selective combination* is bringing together apparently unrelated bits of useful information.
- *Selective comparison* is comparing new problems with old, solved problems which are the keys to insight.

Most efficient.

Barriers to Problem Solving

Common barriers to problem solving include:
- Functional fixedness
- Emotional barriers
- Cultural barriers
- Learned barriers
- Perceptual barriers

Notes

_____

_____

_____

_____

_____

_____

_____

Creative Thinking and Intuition

Original ideas in art, medicine, music, and science have changed the course of human history.

Divergent vs. Convergent Thinking

Routine problem solving involves *convergent thinking*, which results in a single solution. Creative thinking involves *divergent thinking*, which results in multiple solutions.

Creative Thinking

Creative thinking involves:

- *Fluency* (number of suggestions made)
- *Flexibility* (number of times a shift is made to another set of possible solutions)
- *Originality* (how unusual an idea is)

Stages of Creative Thought

Five stages often seen in creative problem solving are:

- *Orientation*
- *Preparation*
- *Incubation*
- *Illumination*
- *Verification*

The Creative Personality

Thinking styles and personality characteristics have more to do with creativity than intelligence alone.

Creative Characteristics

Characteristics of creative thinking include:

- A wide range of knowledge and interests
- An openness to a variety of experiences
- Taking pleasure from symbolic thinking
- Independence
- A preference for complexity

Intuition

Intuition is quick, impulsive thought that lacks formal logic or clear reasoning.

Pitfalls of Intuition

Errors in intuitive thought include disregarding or *failing to recognize probability, emotional involvement,* and *how the problem is worded* (framed).

Psychology in Action: Culture, Race, IQ, and YOU

Cultural values, knowledge, language patterns, and traditions can greatly affect performance on tests designed for western cultures.

High-Stakes Testing

Widespread reliance on standardized testing raises questions about the relative good and harm that they do.

Positive Effects

1. Tests can open opportunities.
2. Test scores may be more fair and objective than subjective judgments made by individuals.
3. Test do accurately predict academic performance.

Culture-Fair Tests

Designed to minimize the importance of skills and knowledge that may be more common in some cultures than in others.

Negative Effects

1. Tests can close opportunities and exclude people of obvious ability.
2. Tests often contain poorly written or ambiguous questions.
3. Tests are often biased.
4. Most standardized tests do not test critical thinking, creativity, or problem solving.

Culture-Biased Tests

Fail to minimize the importance of skills and knowledge that may be more common in some cultures than in others.

1. _____ is the global capacity to act purposely, to think rationally, and to deal effectively with the environment.
   a. IQ
   b. Mental age
   c. Intelligence
   d. G factor

2. An operational definition of intelligence is based on
   a. the theoretical perspective of the clinician.
   b. the mental and psychological age of the person.
   c. the procedures used to measure intelligence.
   d. the general core of intelligence.

3. In order to estimate Sally's intelligence, we would need to know both her _____ and _____.
   a. mental age; test score
   b. developmental level; family history
   c. chronological age; mental age
   d. cultural background; emotional functioning

4. If an individual's chronological age is the same as his or her mental age, what would the IQ be?
   a. 100
   b. 125
   c. above average
   d. None of the above; more information is needed.

5. What do the Wechsler tests provide?
   a. verbal IQ
   b. full-scale IQ
   c. performance IQ
   d. All of the above.

6. In Gardner's theory of multiple intelligence, he identified all of the following types of intelligence except
   a. music.
   b. logic and math.
   c. interpersonal.
   d. common sense.

7. _____ usually refers to computer programs capable of doing things that require intelligence when done by people.
   a. Artificial intelligence
   b. Synthetic intelligence
   c. Cybernetics
   d. Software intellect

8. _____ refers to mentally processing information.
   a. Judgment
   b. Wisdom
   c. Cognition
   d. Maintenance rehearsal

9. The basic units of thought include all of the following except
   a. concepts.
   b. cognitions.
   c. languages.
   d. images.

10. Language allows events to be _____ into _____ for mental manipulation.
    a. encoded; symbols
    b. divided; parts
    c. separated; groupings
    d. programmed; neurons

11. Concept formation is based on experience with _____ and _____ instances.
    a. new; old
    b. created; stored
    c. familiar; novel
    d. positive; negative

12. A concept's _____ meaning is its exact or dictionary definition.
    a. faulty
    b. connotative
    c. denotative
    d. semantic

13. Doug attempted to find the correct key for the lock by using each key on the key ring. This is an example of a(n) _____ solution.
    a. understanding
    b. hypothetical
    c. functional
    d. mechanical

14. A(n) _____ is a "rule of thumb" that reduces the number of possible solutions.
    a. mnemonic
    b. algorithm
    c. heuristic
    d. general solution

15. Coach Ray explained that in order for the team to win, they simply needed to score more points than the other team. This is an example of a(n) _____ solution.
    a. functional
    b. general
    c. simple
    d. intentional

16. A sudden mental reorganization that makes the solution obvious is known as
    a. understanding.
    b. insight.
    c. enlightenment.
    d. perception.

17. If you are too inhibited to offer an answer in class because you are afraid of looking foolish, you may be experiencing a(n) _____ barrier to problem solving.
    a. emotional
    b. cultural
    c. learned
    d. perceptual

18. You would be involved in _____ thinking if you were trying to come up with as many solutions as possible.
    a. convergent
    b. inductive
    c. divergent
    d. deductive

19. If Malika is attempting to gather all the pertinent information available in order to creatively solve a problem, we categorize her as being in the _____ stage.
    a. orientation
    b. preparation
    c. incubation
    d. verification

20. The text states that when we tend to give a choice greater weight if it seems to be representative of what we already know, we are experiencing
    a. the representativeness heuristic.
    b. intuition.
    c. functional fixedness.
    d. wisdom.

Overview of Motivation

Motivation refers to the ways in which our actions are *initiated*, *sustained*, *directed*, and *terminated*.

A Model of Motivation

Needs (internal deficiencies) cause a *drive* (an energized motivational state), which prompts responses (an action or series of actions) to attain goals (the target of motivated behavior). Needs push. Behaviors can be activated by either needs or goals. Goals pull. There are three categories of motives:

Primary Motives

Primary motives are based on biological needs for food, water, air, etc. to ensure survival of the individual.

Homeostasis

An attempt to maintain a "steady state," a state of balance with regard to the primary motives, is referred to as *homeostasis*.

Stimulus Motives

Our needs for stimulation and information appear to be innate, but not strictly necessary for survival.

Examples:
- Activity
- Curiosity
- Exploration
- Manipulation
- Physical Contact

Secondary Motives

Secondary motives are based on *learned* needs, drives, and goals.

Examples:
- Power
- Affiliation
- Approval
- Status
- Security
- Achievement

Notes

_____

_____

_____

_____

_____

_____

Hunger, Thirst, Pain, and Sex

Hunger

Both internal and external factors direct hunger. The brain receives internal signals from the stomach, intestines, hormones, and liver. The brain also detects external eating cues, such as sight and availability of food.

Hypothalamus

Plays a critical role in determining if hunger begins and stops.

Set Point

The weight you maintain when you are making no effort to gain or lose weight.

Eating Disorders

Anorexia nervosa (self-starvation) and bulimia (excessive eating/purging) are health-, even life-threatening.

Diet

The *types* and *amounts* of food you regularly eat define your diet. Some diets encourage overeating.

Behavioral Dieting

Overhauling eating habits with an approach called *behavioral dieting* can assist weight loss.

Two Types of Thirst

1. Thirst develops when there is a loss of fluid volume *between* body cells (extracellular thirst).
2. Thirst develops when there is a loss of fluid from *within* body cells (intracellular thirst).

Pain

Pain is an episodic drive that prompts us to avoid damage to the body. Pain avoidance is at least partially learned.

Sex

Because sex is not necessary for *individual survival*, many psychologists do not consider it to be a true primary motive. It is *nonhomeostatic*.

Notes

_____

_____

_____

_____

_____

_____

_____

Arousal, Achievement, and Growth Needs

Arousal: Stimulus Drives

Stimulus drives reflect our need for *information, exploration, manipulation,* and *sensory input.*

Arousal Theory

According to arousal theory, people attempt to maintain ideal levels of bodily arousal. We seek excitement or quiet when levels are too high or too low.

Sensation Seekers

People's needs for stimulation vary. Sensation seeking is a trait of people who prefer high levels of stimulation.

Achievement: Learned Motives

Social *(learned)* motives are acquired as part of growing up in a society or culture.

Need for Achievement

A need for achievement (nAch) is a desire to meet an internal standard of excellence.

Characteristics of Achievers

People with high nAch are moderate risk takers. They avoid goals that are too difficult or too easy.

Power

A need for power is a desire to have impact or control over others.

Growth: Growth Needs

Maslow's hierarchy of human needs places growth needs (self-actualization) at the top.

Intrinsic and Extrinsic Motivation

To act without any obvious external rewards is to be *intrinsically motivated.* When obvious external factors prompt our action, we are *extrinsically* motivated.

Creativity

People are more likely to be creative when they are intrinsically motivated.

Notes

Emotion and Physiological Arousal

Emotion is characterized by *physiological arousal*, *subjective feelings* (private, internal experience), and *changes in behavior* (facial expressions, gestures, or posture).

Physiology and Emotion
Reactions to threats are innate, caused by arousal of the autonomic nervous system (ANS).

Sympathetic
The sympathetic branch of the ANS activates the body for emergency action—that is, flight or fight.

Lie Detectors
Lie detectors detect *physiological arousal* caused by lying. Results are not always accurate.

Parasympathetic
The parasympathetic branch of the ANS reverses emotional arousal.

Sudden Death
An overreaction to intense emotion is called a *parasympathetic rebound*. If it is too severe, it can cause death.

Suppressing Emotions
Emotions may be suppressed when necessary.

Primary Emotions
Eight primary emotions (*fear, surprise, sadness, disgust, anger, anticipation, joy, and trust*) have been identified.

Moods
Low-intensity emotional states can last for many hours, or even days.

Brain and Emotion
With the way the brain processes emotions, it is possible to have two emotions at the same time.

Right Hemisphere
Negative emotions are processed here.

Left Hemisphere
Positive emotions are processed here.

Emotional Expression and Theories of Emotion

Next to our own feelings, the expressions of others are the most familiar aspect of emotion.

Emotional Expression
Psychologists believe that emotional expressions evolved to communicate our feelings to others, which aided in survival.

Facial Expressions
The facial expressions of *fear, anger, disgust, sadness*, and *happiness* are recognized around the world.

Body Language
Much communication takes place through facial and bodily expressions of emotion.

Gender and Emotion
Private experiences of emotion appear not to be gender based.

Culture and Emotion
Culture may influence behavioral expressions of emotion.

Theories of Emotion
Theories of emotion vary. Each may offer a part of the truth.

James-Lange
Emotional feelings follow bodily arousal in this theory.

Cannon-Bard
Emotional feelings and arousal occur at the same time here.

Schachter
Mental factors enter into emotion. Interpretation of the arousal (including facial expression) determines the emotion we experience.

Contemporary Model
In modern theory, an *appraisal* is made of an emotional stimulus causing ANS arousal and innate emotional expressions. At the same time, adaptive behaviors are enacted.

1. _____ refers to the ways in which our actions are initiated, sustained, directed, and terminated.
   a. Need
   b. Emotion
   c. Motivation
   d. Learning

2. A goal's appeal beyond its ability to fulfill the need is known as
   a. additional value.
   b. stimulus value.
   c. motivational value.
   d. incentive value.

3. Which of the following is the correct sequence of the model of motivation?
   a. drive-need-response-goal attainment
   b. need-drive-response-goal attainment
   c. need-drive-goal attainment-response
   d. drive-need-goal attainment-response

4. The psychological expression known as "hunger" corresponds to which aspect of motivation?
   a. need
   b. drive
   c. goal
   d. goal attainment

5. _____ motives, such as curiosity and exploration, express our needs for stimulation and information.
   a. Stimulus
   b. Secondary
   c. Primary
   d. None of the above.

6. The body's optimal level of functioning, or its "steady state," is known as
   a. equilibrium incentives.
   b. circadian rhythms.
   c. homeostasis.
   d. learning.

7. After eating a hotdog while watching a baseball game, Caleb became nauseous. Caleb no longer likes hotdogs. This is an example of a(n)
   a. operant conditioning.
   b. taste aversion.
   c. prototype.
   d. yo-yo dieting.

8. Which of the following would not be recommended as a means of behavioral dieting?
   a. exercising
   b. counting calories
   c. keeping a "diet diary"
   d. strengthening your eating cues

9. Which of the following is the eating disorder characterized by extremely low weight?
   a. obesity
   b. anorexia
   c. bulimia
   d. None of the above.

10. Thirst that results from bleeding or sweating is known as _____ thirst.
    a. extracellular
    b. intracellular
    c. intercellular
    d. primary

11. Which of the following describes the inverted U hypothesis?
    a. You will not perform well at very low levels of arousal.
    b. You will not perform well at very high levels of arousal.
    c. There is an optimum level of arousal for peak performance.
    d. All of the above.

12. Which of the following are true according to the arousal theory?
    a. There are ideal levels of activation for various activities.
    b. People become uncomfortable when arousal is too low or too high.

c. Most adults vary their activities to keep arousal at moderate levels.
d. All of these are true.

13. The Yekes-Dodson law states that
    a. if a task is complex, arousal should be high.
    b. if a task is simple, arousal should low.
    c. if a task is complex, arousal should low.
    d. there is no relationship between task complexity and appropriate arousal levels.

14. In order for Josh to avoid test anxiety, he may be encouraged to do all of the following except
    a. increase preparation.
    b. learn self-relaxation skills.
    c. rehearse coping skills.
    d. ignore any troubling or disturbing thoughts.

15. _____ is a desire to meet an internal standard of excellence.
    a. Need for achievement
    b. Need for success
    c. Craving for accomplishment
    d. Need for power

16. Which of the following is the correct order of Maslow's hierarchy of needs, from the bottom of the pyramid to the top of the pyramid?
    a. physiological, safety, esteem, love and belonging, self-actualization
    b. self-actualization, esteem, safety, love and belonging, physiological
    c. physiological, safety, love and belonging, esteem, self-actualization
    d. physiological, esteem, love and belonging, safety, self-actualization

17. If Laurie bakes cakes simply because she enjoys it, we would say this activity is one of _____ motivation.
    a. secondary
    b. primary
    c. intrinsic
    d. extrinsic

18. Which of the following characterizes emotion?
    a. subjective feelings
    b. changes in facial expressions
    c. physiological arousal
    d. All of the above.

19. According to the _____ theory, emotional feelings and bodily arousal occur at the same time.
    a. Cannon-Bard
    b. James-Lang
    c. Schachter's cognitive
    d. Spencer-Sweet

20. Which of the following is not considered an element of emotional intelligence?
    a. self-awareness
    b. apathy
    c. managing emotions
    d. emotional flexibility

Overview of Personality

Personality refers to the consistency in who you are, have been, and will become.

Personality

Personality refers to a person's unique pattern of thinking, behaving, and expressing feelings.

Personality

Personality is the special blend of talents, values, hopes, loves, hates, and habits that make us each unique.

Personality Types

A *personality type* refers to people who have several traits in common (e.g., introverts vs. extroverts).

Personality Traits

Traits are stable qualities a person shows in most situations.
1. Traits are inferred from behavior.
2. Once identified, they can be used to predict future behavior.
3. Trait consistencies can span many years.

Personality Theories

Personality theories are systems of concepts, assumptions, ideas, and principles used to explain personality.

Trait Theories

Trait theories attempt to discover what traits make up personality.

Psychodynamic Theories

These theories focus on inner working of personality, especially internal conflicts.

Behavioral and Social Learning Theories

These theories place importance on the external environment and the effects of conditioning and learning.

Humanistic Theories

Humanistic theories stress private, subjective experience, and personal growth.

Personality Is Not

Character

Character and personality are not the same. *Character* implies an evaluation of personality.

Temperament

Temperament refers to the "raw material" from which personalities are formed—that is, the hereditary aspects of personality.

Self-Concept

Self-concept consists of your ideas, perceptions, and feelings about yourself. It includes your sense of self-esteem.

Permanently "Wired In"

Personality slowly matures during old age as people become more conscientious and agreeable.

Trait Theories

The dominant approach to the study of personality is the trait approach. Trait theories attempt to analyze, classify, and interrelate traits.

Common Traits

Characteristics shared by most members of a culture (e.g., Competitiveness is a fairly common trait in America).

Central and Cardinal Traits

Central traits are basic building blocks of personality. *Cardinal traits* are so basic that all their activities can be traced back to the trait.

Source Traits

Source traits are the deeper characteristics or dimensions of the personality.

Individual Traits

Describe a person's unique qualities (e.g., Your American friend is low in competitiveness).

Secondary Traits

Secondary traits are more superficial qualities such as preferences, opinions, and tastes that may change.

Surface Traits

Surface traits are the more visible features of the personality.

The Big-Five Factors

1. *Extroversion:* Level of extroversion vs. introversion.
2. *Agreeableness:* How friendly, nurturing, and caring a person is.
3. *Conscientious:* Level of self-discipline, responsibility, and achievement orientation.
4. *Neuroticism:* How anxious, irritable, and unhappy a person is.
5. *Openness to experience:* How intelligent and open to new ideas a person is.

Psychoanalytic Theory

Freud evolved a theory of personality that discussed the structure of personality, levels of awareness, and the stages of personality development.

Structure of Personality

Freud's model portrays personality as a dynamic system directed by three mental structures.

Id
The id operates on the pleasure principle and is made up of innate biological instincts and urges.

Ego
The ego directs the id's energies and focuses on the reality principle.

Superego
The superego acts as a judge or censor for the thoughts and actions of the ego.

Levels of Awareness

Personal awareness operates on three levels: the conscious, preconscious, and unconscious.

Conscious
The id operates on the pleasure principle and is made up of innate biological instincts and urges.

Preconscious
The id operates on the pleasure principle and is made up of innate biological instincts and urges.

Unconscious
The unconscious holds repressed memories and emotions, plus the instinctual drives of the id.

Personality Development

Personality development occurs in four psychosexual stages: *oral, anal, phallic,* and *genital.*

Freud's Psychosexual Stages

Oral Stage
During the first year of life, most pleasure comes from stimulation of the mouth.

Anal Stage
Between ages 1 and 3, a child can gain approval or express rebellion/aggression by "holding on" or "letting go" during toilet training.

Phallic Stage
Phallic fixations develop between ages 3 and 6. Adult traits of phallic personality are vanity, exhibitionism, sensitive pride, and narcissism.

Genital Stage
The genital stage begins at puberty; it is marked by an upswing in sexual energies; and ends with a mature capacity for love and the realization of full adult sexuality.

Notes

_____

_____

_____

_____

_____

_____

_____

Behavioral and Social Learning Theories

Behavioral and social learning theories are based on scientific research (unlike psychodynamic theories).

Behavioral

Learning theories emphasize that personality is a collection of learned behavior patterns.

View of Personality Development

Personality is acquired through:

- Classical and operant conditioning
- Observational learning
- Reinforcement
- Extinction
- Generalization and discrimination

Personality Structure

Habits make up the structure of personality. Habits are governed by:

- Drives
- Cues
- Responses
- Rewards

Social Learning

Social learning theory is often called *cognitive behaviorism*. It focuses on the social situation, expectancy, and reinforcement value to explain personality.

View of Personality Development

Personality is acquired through:

- Learning principles
- Modeling
- Thought patterns
- Perceptions and expectations
- Beliefs and goals
- Emotions and social relationships

Psychological Situation

How we interpret or define a situation.

Expectancy

Whether or not our response will be reinforced may determine how we act.

Reinforcement Value

Different reinforcements have different values.

Humanistic Theories

Humanistic theories pay special attention to the fuller use of human potentials. Humanism focuses on human experience, problems, potentials, and ideals. It emphasizes an inherently good view of human nature, freedom of choice, and subjective experiences.

Abraham Maslow

Maslow's theory of *self-actualization* emphasized people who were living rich, creative, and satisfying lives.

Self-Actualization

Self-actualization is the process of fully developing personal potentials. It is characterized by a continuous search for personal fulfillment.

Characteristics of Self-Actualizers

Self-actualizers feel safe, nonanxious, accepted, loved, loving, and alive.

Carl Rogers' Theory

Carl Rogers emphasized the *self*.

Self-Image

Attempts to maintain *congruence* between our *self-image* and our *actions* explain many behaviors.

View of Development

Children develop conditions of *worth*, positive *self-regard*, and *organismic valuing* when they are given unconditional positive regard from others.

Positive Psychology

Positive psychologists have identified six human strengths contributing to well-being: wisdom and knowledge, courage, humanity, justice, temperance, transcendence.

Personality Assessment

Measuring personality can help predict how people will behave at work, school, and therapy. Psychologists use a variety of methods to measure personality.

Interviews

Interviews may be either:
1. *Unstructured* (with topics discussed as they arise)
2. *Structured* (with a planned series of questions).

Direct Observation

Direct observation may provide information about personality.

Situational Testing

Simulated real-life situations allow for observation of reactions (such as frustration, anger, or boredom).

Personality Questionnaires

Questionnaires are more objective than interviews or observation.

Projective Tests

Projective tests use ambiguous stimuli to uncover hidden or unconscious wishes, thoughts, and needs.

Advantages and Limitations

An interview allows tone of *voice* and *body language* to be observed. However, *preconceptions* or *deceit* may influence the interviewer.

Rating Scales

Rating scales (lists of personality traits or behaviors) can be used to overcome observer misperceptions.

Rorshach Inkblot Test

The Rorshach test, one of the best-known projective tests, uses descriptions of standard inkblots to detect emotional disturbances.

Limitations of Projective Testing

Projective tests are considered to be the least valid tests of personality because the scorer has to interpret the responses.

Notes

_____

_____

_____

_____

_____

_____

_____

1. _____ refers to a person's unique pattern of thinking, emotions, and behavior.
   a. Temperament
   b. Personality
   c. Character
   d. Charisma

2. You are told by a friend that they want you to meet someone they know who is nice, honest, outgoing, and friendly. As described in the text, they are most accurately describing to you the person's
   a. character.
   b. personality.
   c. inherent value.
   d. temperament.

3. A personality _____ refers to people who have several traits in common.
   a. illness
   b. trait
   c. combination
   d. type

4. Which people might describe themselves as stupid, worthless, or a failure?
   a. People with high self-esteem.
   b. People with moderate self-esteem.
   c. People with low self-esteem.
   d. All of these people.

5. Your psychology instructor asks you to write a paper that answers the question, "Who am I?" The most likely title for this paper would be
   a. My Self-Concept.
   b. Personality and Me.
   c. My Self-Esteem.
   d. none of the above.

6. _____ theories focus on the inner workings of personality, especially internal conflicts and struggles.
   a. Cognitive
   b. Behavioral
   c. Psychodynamic
   d. Trait

7. Which of the following is not one of the Big Five personality factors identified in the text?
   a. Curiosity
   b. Agreeableness
   c. Extroversion
   d. Neuroticism

8. Traits shared by most members of a culture are referred to as _____ traits.
   a. type
   b. cardinal
   c. individualistic
   d. common

9. According to Freud, which part of the personality acts as the negotiator or decision maker?
   a. Id
   b. Ego
   c. Superego
   d. Conscious self

10. According to the text, the _____ mind contains material that can be easily brought to awareness.
    a. conscious
    b. unconscious
    c. subconscious
    d. preconscious

11. Identify the correct order of Freud's psychosexual stages.
    a. Anal, oral, phallic, genital
    b. Oral, anal, genital, phallic
    c. Oral, anal, phallic, genital
    d. Phallic, anal, oral, genital

12. _____ theories emphasize that personality is acquired through classical and operant conditioning, observational learning, reinforcement, extinction, generalization, and discrimination.
    a. Psychodynamic
    b. Trait
    c. Behavioral
    d. Humanistic

13. Habits are governed by all of the following elements of learning, except
    a. goal.
    b. drive.
    c. cue.
    d. response.

14. What did Albert Bandura call the capacity for producing a desired result?
    a. Self-esteem
    b. Self-efficacy
    c. Self-reinforcement
    d. Self-concept

15. Which of the following is not one of Dollard and Miller's four critical situations?
    a. Feeding
    b. Sex training
    c. Social inclusion
    d. Toilet training

16. Jacob states that someday he hopes to be just like his dad: funny, brave, tough, and caring. This might be referred to as Jacob's _____.
    a. self-actualization
    b. perfect self
    c. ideal self
    d. potential personality

17. Chris tells his daughters that he will always accept them and love them, regardless of what they do or don't do. Chris's daughters have received what Rogers would refer to as
    a. authoritative parenting.
    b. unconditional positive regard.
    c. self-actualization.
    d. unrestricted valuing.

18. In which of the following is information regarding one's personality gathered by asking a planned series of questions?
    a. Structured interview
    b. Unstructured interview
    c. Situational test
    d. All of the above

19. One of the best-known and most widely used objective personality tests is the
    a. Guilford-Zimmerman Temperament Survey.
    b. 16 PF.
    c. MMPI - 2.
    d. California Psychological Inventory.

20. The Rorschach Inkblot Test is an example of a(n) _____ personality test.
    a. projective
    b. objective
    c. subjective
    d. predictive

Health Psychology

Health psychology aims to use behavioral principles to prevent illness and promote health.

- Health-promoting behaviors: Some diseases can be treated or prevented by making relatively minor but very specific changes in behavior.

- Community health: Community programs that educate larger numbers of people often offer services such as screenings, advice, and even treatment.

- Early prevention: Often, learning how to not start a risky behavior can do much to prevent the development of a disease.

Stress, Frustration, and Conflict

Although a natural part of life, stress can be a major behavioral risk factor if it is prolonged or severe. Stress is the mental and physical condition that occurs when we adapt to the environment.

Appraising Stressors
Ultimately, stress depends on how we perceive a situation. Do we view it as a *thrill or a threat*?

Conflict
Conflict occurs when contradictory choices must be made.

Frustration
Frustration occurs when obstacles prevent us from reaching desired goals.

Primary and Secondary Appraisal
We need to assess the situation:
1. *Primary Appraisal*
   Is the situation relevant to us?
2. *Secondary Appraisal*
   What can we do about it if it is?

Coping with Threat
If we appraise a situation as a threat, we can use:
1. *Problem*-focused coping
   or
2. *Emotion*-focused coping

When Is Stress a Pain?
Stressors (events that challenge or threaten) may be unpredictable or there may be a time limit (*pressure*).
This is known as distress.

Stress Elements
Intense, repeated, or *uncontrolled* stressors related to pressure will magnify stress.

Types of Conflict
The five major types of conflict are:
- *Approach-approach*
- *Avoidance-avoidance*
- *Approach-avoidance*
- *Double approach-avoidance*
- *Multiple approach-avoidance*

Coping with Conflict
1. Don't be hasty when making important decisions.
2. Try out important decisions partially when possible.
3. Look for workable compromises.
4. When all else fails, make a decision and live with it.

Obstacles
External frustrations are represented by conditions outside the individual. *Personal frustrations* stem from personal characteristics.

Reactions to Frustration
Reactions to frustration include *persistence, more vigorous responding, circumvention, direct aggression, displaced aggression,* and *escape/withdrawal.*

Coping with Frustration
1. Identify the source of frustration.
2. Is the source something that can be changed?
3. If the source can be changed or removed, are the efforts worth it?
Distinguish between *real* barriers and *imagined* barriers.

Defenses, Helplessness, and Depression

We react to threatening experiences and anxiety in various ways.

Psychological Defense Mechanisms

A psychological defense mechanism is any mental process used to avoid, deny, or distort sources of threat or anxiety, especially threats to one's self-image.

Denial

Protecting oneself from an unpleasant reality by refusing to accept it or believe it.

Repression

Protecting oneself by repressing threatening thoughts and impulses.

Reaction Formation

Repressing impulses by exaggerating opposite behavior.

Regression

Any return to earlier, less demanding situations or habits.

Projection

An unconscious process that protects us from the anxiety we would feel if we were to discern our faults.

Rationalization

Justifying personal actions by giving "rational" but false reasons for them.

Compensation

Going to unusual lengths to overcome a weakness or excel in other areas.

Sublimation

Working off frustrated desires through socially acceptable activities.

Learned Helplessness

Learned helplessness is an acquired inability to overcome obstacles and avoid aversive stimuli. Occurs when events appear to be *uncontrollable*.

Hope

Hope and a feeling of control are essential to overcoming learned helplessness or depression.

Depression

Depression is a widespread emotional problem. Learned helplessness and depression share many similarities.

Recognizing Depression

Depression is marked by feelings of despondency, powerlessness, and overwhelming hopelessness.

Notes

_____

_____

_____

_____

_____

_____

_____

Stress and Health

Psychologists have established that stress has many effects on our health by reducing the body's natural defenses against disease.

Life Events and Stress

Life events, both major and minor, can impact our health in a many ways.

Social Readjustment Rating Scale (SRRS)

Life changes (good and bad) can increase risk of accidents or illness. Life change units (LCUs) from the SRRS rank the importance of events to the changes in health 1 or 2 years later.

Hazzards and Hassles

Frequent, severe *hassles (microstressors)* predict day-to-day health.

Psychosomatic Disorders

Psychosomatic disorders are real disorders where psychological factors contribute to bodily damage.

NOT Hypochondriasis!

People suffering from psychosomatic disorders face asthma, migraine headaches, or high blood pressure, NOT imagined diseases.

Most Common Problems

Gastrointestinal and respiratory problems are the most frequently reported psychosomatic problems.

Personality Types

Personality, genetic differences, organ weakness, and learned reactions to stress can all enter into the stress picture.

Cardiac Personality

Among other characteristics, Type A personalities are *chronically angry* and are also at risk for heart attacks.

Hardy Personality

The hardy personality shares many of the same characteristics as the Type A but does not become ill as often.

Stress, Illness, and the Immune System

Prolonged stress can weaken the immune system, thus creating opportunity for serious health risks.

Psychoneuroimmunology

This specialty studies the links among behavior, stress, disease, and the immune system.

Boosting Immune System

Various psychological approaches, such as support groups, relaxation exercises, guided imagery, and stress management training, can boost immune system functioning.

Stress Management

Stress management is the use of behavioral strategies to reduce stress and improve coping skills.

Ways to Manage Bodily Reactions to Stress

Exercise
Any full-body exercise can be effective for managing stress. Choose vigorous yet enjoyable activities and do them daily!

Meditation
Meditation is often recommended for quieting the body and promoting relaxation. Meditation is one of the most effective ways to relax.

Progressive Relaxation
By tightening all the muscles in a given area of your body, then voluntarily relaxing them, you are engaging in progressive relaxation.

Guided Imagery
In guided imagery, you visualize images that are calming, relaxing, or beneficial in other ways.

Ways to Minimize Ineffective Behavior When You Are Stressed Out

Slow Down
Stress can be self-generated, so try to do things at a slower pace.

Get Organized
Disorganization causes stress . . . so get organized! Set priorities and keep it simple (KIS).

Balance Work and Relaxation
Damaging stress often comes from letting one element, such as work or school, get blown out of proportion.

Accept Your Limits
Set gradual, achievable goals and realistic limits on what you try to do on any given day. Learn to say: NO!

Write About Your Feelings
Several studies have found that writing about your thoughts and feelings allows you to better cope with stress, experience fewer illnesses, and get better grades!

Notes

_____

_____

_____

_____

_____

_____

_____

1. Health psychology uses behavioral principles to prevent _____ and promote _____.
   a. problems, communication
   b. illness, health
   c. mental illness, psychotropic medications
   d. All of the above.

2. Strokes and lung cancer are just two examples of _____ diseases.
   a. lifestyle
   b. personality
   c. behavioral medicine
   d. contagious

3. _____are actions that increase the chances of disease, injury, or early death.
   a. Cognitive variables
   b. Health-complicating events
   c. Combination health threats
   d. Behavioral risk factors

4. Mitch is an anxious and irritable individual who has poor eating and sleeping habits, which leave him frequently ill. Mitch might be described as having a _____ personality.
   a. health-compromised
   b. hardy
   c. resilient
   d. disease-prone

5. The "Just Say No" campaign for preventing drug use would be considered a _____.
   a. refusal skills training program
   b. psychodynamic training program
   c. life skills training program
   d. resistance prevention program

6. _____ is the mental and physical condition that occurs when we adjust or adapt to the environment.
   a. Anxiety
   b. Stress
   c. Trauma
   d. Apprehension

7. If a person is under prolonged stress for an extended period, he or she may experience the
   a. general adaptation syndrome.
   b. rejuvenation effect.
   c. autonomic rebound.
   d. anxiety response disorder.

8. If Brad decided that after graduation, he wanted to find a job studying the links among behavior, stress, disease, and the immune system, he would probably be looking into the field of
   a. medical psychology.
   b. neuropsychology.
   c. eating disorders.
   d. psychoneuroimmunology.

9. Stress is typically considered more damaging when it is
   a. unpredictable yet controllable.
   b. predictable but not controllable.
   c. predictable and controllable.
   d. neither predictable nor controllable.

10. A(n) _____ appraisal is one in which you decide if a situation is relevant or irrelevant, positive or threatening.
    a. initial
    b. secondary
    c. essential
    d. primary

11. When she heard the bad news, Emily concentrated on not crying in front of her children. This might be considered what kind of coping?
    a. Behavior focused
    b. Solution focused
    c. Problem focused
    d. Emotion focused

12. When Connor got caught in traffic on his way to take his final exam, he experienced an _____ frustration.
    a. academic
    b. inherent
    c. internal
    d. external

13. Reactions to frustration include all of the following except
    a. less vigorous responding.
    b. persistence.
    c. scapegoating.
    d. displaced aggression.

14. Having to choose between writing your term paper or going to your friend's birthday party would be described by the text as an example of
    a. anxiety.
    b. stress.
    c. frustration.
    d. conflict.

15. In the _____ conflict, one must choose between two pleasant or desirable options.
    a. avoidance-avoidance
    b. approach-avoidance
    c. approach-approach
    d. double approach-avoidance

16. Ty stated, in defense of his getting caught shoplifting, that the store had probably overcharged him on numerous occasions and therefore owed him the items taken. This would be an example of which defense mechanism?
    a. Rationalization
    b. Denial
    c. Projection
    d. Regression

17. _____ is an acquired inability to overcome obstacles and avoid aversive stimuli.
    a. Learned hopelessness
    b. Learned helplessness
    c. Educated-actualization
    d. Dysfunctional cognition

18. What do you call someone who believes he has a serious disease or illness even though there is no medical evidence of its presence?
    a. College student during finals week
    b. Malingerer
    c. Hypochondriac
    d. All of the above

19. Friedman and Rosenman (1983) classified people who have a _____ risk of cardiac problems as Type A personalities.
    a. low
    b. medium
    c. high
    d. no

20. Which of the following is not one of the three goals for reducing hostility as described by the text?
    a. Learn to be kinder.
    b. Reduce feelings of anger.
    c. Stop mistrusting the motives of others.
    d. Learn to use humor more readily.

Normality and Psychopathology

Determining if a person's behavior is abnormal can be difficult.

Classifying Mental Disorders

A *mental disorder* is a serious impairment in psychological functioning. The *Diagnostic and Statistical Manual of Mental Disorders* (DSM-IV-TR, 2000) helps correctly identify mental disorders.

Normality—What Is Normal?

The term *psychopathology* refers to both the scientific study of mental, emotional, and behavioral disorders and also the disorders themselves.

Abnormality

It is possible to vary from the norm in a variety of ways. Depending on the context in which the variation occurs, it may be seen as psychopathology.

Major Mental Disorders

Major mental problems include *psychotic, organic, mood, anxiety, somatoform, dissociative, personality, sexual or gender identity,* and *substance-related* disorders.

Subjective Discomfort

A sense of *subjective discomfort* (private feelings of pain, unhappiness, or emotional distress) or a lack of discomfort when it would be appropriate may be a sign of psychopathology.

Disordered Behavior

Two core features are key to abnormality:
- The behavior is *maladaptive* (prevents day-to-day normal coping).
- There is a *loss of control* over the behavior.

Social Noncomformity

Social nonconformity may be a sign of mental disorder. However, the context of the nonconformity is important.

Statistical Abnormality

Statistical abnormality refers to scoring very high or low on some dimension, such as intelligence, anxiety, or depression.

Insanity

Insanity is a legal term referring to an inability to manage one's affairs or see the consequences of one's actions.

Notes

_____

_____

_____

_____

_____

_____

_____

Personality and Anxiety-Based Disorders

Personality and anxiety disorders can make life very difficult and be very debilitating.

Personality Disorders

Maladaptive personality patterns are referred to as *personality disorders*.

Antisocial Personality

An antisocial personality is one (*sometimes called a sociopath*) who lacks a conscience, is impulsive, selfish, dishonest, emotionally shallow, and manipulative.

Sociopaths . . . Dangerous?

Sociopaths or psychopaths are poorly socialized and seem to be incapable of feeling guilt, shame, fear, loyalty, or love. Many are delinquents or criminals who may be a threat to the public.

Common Behaviors

Sociopaths have been found to be "blind" to the signs of disgust in others. This may add to their capacity for cruelty and their ability to coldly use others and cheat their way through life.

Causes

People with antisocial personalities were typically emotionally deprived, neglected, and abused as children.

Stress and Dissociative Disorders

Stress disorders occur when people experience stresses outside the range of normal human experience. Dissociative disorders show amnesia, fugue, or multiple identities.

Acute Stress Disorder

Acute stress disorder occurs when traumatic events (combat, rape, etc.) lead to reactions that last LESS than a month after the event.

Posttraumatic Stress Disorder

Posttraumatic stress disorder occurs when violent, traumatic events (combat, rape, etc.) lead to reactions that last MORE than a month. Symptoms include insomnia, nightmares, wariness, and reliving of the traumatic event.

Dissociative Disorders

Dissociations are often triggered by highly traumatic events the individual wishes to flee. Dissociative disorders may take the form of amnesia, fugue, and dissociative identity disorder (commonly known as multiple personalities).

Causes

Traumatic events, such as floods, earthquakes, and horrible accidents, can lead to the stress disorders. Highly traumatic events, such as prolonged and extreme abuse, are common to the dissociative disorders.

Anxiety-Based Disorders

Anxiety refers to feelings of apprehension, dread, or uneasiness. In anxiety disorders, these feelings are extreme, out of control, and self-defeating.

Panic Disorder

Panic disorder causes people to feel sudden, intense, unexpected panic (may occur with or without agoraphobia–fear of embarrassment in unfamiliar situations).

Phobias

Phobias involve fear and avoidance of particular objects, activities, or situations.

Obsessive-Compulsive Disorder

Obsessive-compulsive disorder involves preoccupation with distressing thoughts and a need to perform certain behaviors.

Somatoform Disorders

Somatoform disorders center on physical complaints that mimic disease or disability.

Causes

In most anxiety disorders, distress seems greatly out of proportion to a person's circumstances. It may also underlie the dissociative and somatoform disorders, where maladaptive behavior serves to reduce anxiety and discomfort.

Psychosis, Delusional Disorders, and Schizophrenia

Psychotic disorders are among the most serious of all mental problems.

Psychosis

Psychosis is a loss of contact with reality. Hallucinations and delusions, disturbed thought and emotions, and personality disorganization are common.

Delusions

False beliefs (against all contrary evidence) about yourself or others are *delusions*.

Hallucinations

When you have imaginary sensations (seeing, smelling, tasting, or hearing things that are not there) you are having *hallucinations*.

Organic Psychosis

Psychosis may occur because of brain injury or disease (old age, stroke, Alzheimer's disease, etc.).

Paranoid Psychosis

Paranoid psychosis is a common delusional disorder. Treatment is rare because the individual resists treatment as part of the "conspiracy."

Delusional Disorders

People with delusional disorders have an unmistakable break with reality that may involve paranoia, jealousy, delusions of grandeur, or personal capabilities. The main feature of the delusional disorders is the presence of deeply held false beliefs.

Erotomanic Type

Erotomanic types have erotic delusions that they are loved by another person, especially by someone famous or of higher status.

Grandiose Type

People with this disorder suffer from the delusion that they have some great, unrecognized talent, knowledge, or insight.

Jealous Type

People with this type of delusion have an all-consuming, but unfounded, belief that their spouse or lover is unfaithful.

Persecutory Type

Persecutory types have delusions of persecution, such as being conspired against, cheated on, spied on, followed, poisoned, maligned, or harassed.

Somatic Type

People with somatic type delusions believe that their body is diseased, rotting, or infested with insects or parasites, or that parts of their body are defective.

Schizophrenia

The most common form of psychosis is schizophrenia. Delusions, hallucinations, inappropriate emotions, and thinking abnormalities are all found in schizophrenia.

Major Subtypes

Schizophrenics may develop one of four subtypes:
- *Disorganized*
- *Catatonic*
- *Paranoid*
- *Undifferentiated*

Causes of Schizophrenia

Possible causes of schizophrenia include *environment* (including teratogens), *heredity*, and *brain chemistry*.

Notes

_____

_____

_____

_____

_____

_____

_____

Mood Disorders

Mood disorders, major disturbances in emotion, are the most common disorders of all. Brain chemistry, learned behaviors, stress, genetics, and culture have been cited as possible causes of mood disorders.

Depressive Disorder

Exaggerated, prolonged, or unreasonable sadness and despondency are signs of *depressive disorders*.

Major Depressive Disorder

When the person suffers a steep emotional depression.

Dysthymic Disorder

When the person suffers a mild depression for at least 2 years.

Bipolar Disorders

Exaggerated, prolonged, or unreasonable sadness and despondency that alternate with manic episodes of varying degree, are signs of the bipolar disorders.

Bipolar I Disorder

People who experience both extreme mania and deep depression suffer from *bipolar I disorder*.

Bipolar II Disorder

In *bipolar II* disorder the person is mostly sad and guilt ridden but has had at least one mildly manic episode.

Notes

_____

_____

_____

_____

_____

_____

_____

Psychology in Action: Suicide—Lives on the Brink

Why do people commit suicide?

Mental Disorders

A diagnosable mental disorder, such as depression or substance abuse, is a factor in 90 percent of all suicides.

Substance Abuse

Drug and alcohol abuse impairs judgment and moods.

Anger and Aggression

Antisocial, impulsive, or aggressive behaviors are major risk factors for suicide.

Prior Suicide Attempts

A previous attempt, or family history of suicidal behavior are risk factors.

Feelings of Social Rejection

Shame, humiliation, failure and isolation are all risk factors.

Availability of a Firearm

Combined with other risk factors, simply having access to a firearm can be lethal.

Feelings of Hopelessness

When combined with an extremely negative self-image, feelings of hopelessness can indicate a very HIGH risk of suicide.

1. _____ refers to the scientific study of mental, emotional, and behavioral disorders.
   a. Abnormal psychology   c. Psychopathy
   b. Psychopathology   d. Behaviorism

2. Upon what criteria might someone with red hair be considered abnormal?
   a. Personal distress
   b. Social nonconformity
   c. Statistical abnormality
   d. Interference with daily functioning

3. In the United States, psychological problems are classified using what manual?
   a. DSM-IV-TR
   b. ICM-10
   c. 16 PF
   d. No manual is necessary; only clinical opinion is required.

4. A person with a significant impairment in psychological functioning might be diagnosed with a
   a. psychological disease.   c. mental disorder.
   b. brain illness.   d. psychotic issue.

5. Due to his drug use, Chad now has impaired memory, an altered personality, and fluctuating moods. Chad would be diagnosed with a(n)
   a. organic mental disorder.
   b. impaired brain disease.
   c. mood disorder.
   d. stress-related illness.

6. _____ is a word that has been replaced by the term *anxiety*.
   a. Neurosis   c. Trauma
   b. Stress   d. Nervous

7. Tara's sexual identity does not match her gender and therefore results in personal discomfort. Tara may be diagnosed with a
   a. paraphilia.
   b. sexual confusion disorder.
   c. gender-identity disorder.
   d. mood disorder.

8. Temporary psychological amnesia, fugue and multiple personality are classified as _____ disorders.
   a. dissociative   c. psychotic
   b. anxiety   d. somatoform

9. Which of the following factors contribute to psychopathology?
   a. Family factors
   b. Social factors
   c. Psychological factors
   d. All of the above can contribute to psychopathology.

10. Being *insane* refers to
   a. any psychiatric diagnosis.
   b. a legal declaration indicating an inability to manage one's own affairs or foresee the consequences of their actions.
   c. the psychiatric diagnosis indicating that an individual is suffering from a severe and persistent mental illness.
   d. a requirement for involuntary hospitalization.

11. A person who has trouble forming close relationships because he is emotionally shallow, dishonest, and manipulative may be diagnosed with
   a. major depression.
   b. acute stress.
   c. antisocial personality disorder.
   d. mental retardation.

12. If Glenda suffers from chronic anxiety and stays in her home because she is afraid of having another panic attack in public, a psychologist might consider her to have the diagnosis of
   a. panic attack with agoraphobia.
   b. acute anxiety.
   c. social phobia.
   d. adjustment disorder.

13. A _____ is an intense, irrational fear.
   a. stimulus   c. obsession
   b. phobia   d. generalized anxiety

14. In obsessive-compulsive disorder, the obsession is the _____, whereas the compulsion is the _____.
   a. thought; behavior
   b. control; thought
   c. consequence; antecedent
   d. stimulus; control

15. A person who suffers from more than one disorder at a time would be considered to have _____ illnesses.
   a. stress-related   c. recurrent
   b. dissociative   d. comorbid

16. In a somatoform illness (such as conversion disorder), people convert _____ conflicts into ones that resemble _____ _____ problems.
   a. group; personal
   b. physical; medical
   c. emotional; physical
   d. psychological; emotional

17. The term _____ refers to internal motives, conflicts, unconscious forces, and other dynamics of mental life.
   a. cognitive   c. humanistic
   b. psychodynamic   d. organic

18. Which of the following is not one of the subtypes of schizophrenia?
   a. Catatonic   c. Organic
   b. Disorganized   d. Undifferentiated

19. If your friend has been mildly depressed for more than 2 years, he may be suffering from which mood disorder?
   a. Dysthymia   c. Major depression
   b. Cyclothymia   d. Bipolar disorder

20. Which of the following is not one of the major risk factors for suicide, as listed in the text?
   a. Increased socialization
   b. Alcohol or drug abuse
   c. Severe anxiety
   d. A history of suicide attempts

Psychotherapy and Psychoanalysis

Psychotherapy refers to any psychological technique that can bring about positive changes in personality, behavior, or personal adjustment.

Psychotherapy

Origins of Therapy

History includes many examples of attempts to deal with mental problems. Humane treatment of the mentally ill began in Paris in 1793.

Primitive Methods

Early treatments for mental problems such as *trepanning* or *demonology* give good reasons to appreciate modern therapies.

Dimensions of Modern Therapy

Therapies may be:

Individual	or	Group
Insight	or	Action oriented
Directive	or	Nondirective
Time limited	or	Open ended
Supportive	or	Positive

Myths

Not all therapies work equally well for all problems. Therapies do not change a person's history.

Freud's Theory of Psychoanalysis

The main goal of psychoanalysis is to reduce internal conflicts that lead to emotional suffering.

Freud's Theory of Psychoanalysis

Freud created the first true psychotherapy 100 years ago. His theory stressed neurosis and hysteria as effects of:

- Repressed memories
- Motives
- Conflicts

Techniques

Freud relied on these techniques:

- Free association
- Dream analysis
- Analysis of resistance
- Analysis of transference

to uncover the unconscious roots of what he termed *neurosis*.

Psychoanalysis Today

The expense and length of treatment have made psychoanalysis a relatively rare treatment today.

Brief Psychodynamic Therapy

A more direct style of therapy uses direct questioning to reveal unconscious conflicts. Modern therapists also provoke emotional reactions that will lower defenses and provide insights.

Notes

_____

_____

_____

_____

_____

_____

_____

Insight Therapies

Insight therapists help clients gain a deeper understanding of their thoughts, emotions, and behavior.

Humanistic Therapies

Humanistic therapies generally assume that it is possible for people to live rich, rewarding lives by using their full potentials.

Psychotherapy at a Distance

Various forms of psychological services are being offered over the phone, Internet, teleconferences, radio, and television. The value of therapy offered by telephone counselors and Internet therapists remains questionable. The best advice being offered is to discuss the problem with a psychologist or counselor in one's own community.

Client-Centered Therapy

Client-centered therapy is *nondirective*, allowing the patient to direct the therapy session. The intent is to gain *insight* while discussing conscious thoughts and feelings.

Existential Therapy

Existential therapy is an insight therapy that focuses on the problems of existence, such as meaning, choice, and responsibility. Making choices, and personal responsibility are keystones of this therapy.

Gestalt Therapy

Gestalt therapy is directive and based on the idea that perception is disjointed and incomplete in maladjusted persons. Integration of fragmented experiences into a whole (a Gestalt) is the focus.

Goals

Client-centered therapy seeks to uncover a "true self" hidden behind a screen of defenses.

Goals

Existential therapy emphasizes free will, the human ability to make choices, and that you can *choose to become* the person you want to be.

Goals

Gestalt therapy helps people rebuild thinking, feeling, and acting into connected wholes.

Behavior Therapy

Behavior therapists use *learning principles* to make constructive changes in behavior patterns. *Behavior modification* refers to any use of classical or operant conditioning to directly alter human behavior.

Healing by Learning

Behavior therapists assume that people have learned their phobias, fears, and anxieties. *Relearning responses* can make changes in a person's quality of life. Aversion therapy and desensitization are based on *classical conditioning*.

Aversion Therapy

In aversion therapy, an individual learns to associate a strong aversion to an undesirable habit.

Desensitization

Desensitization efforts focus on undoing conditioned emotional responses by blocking out the fear.

Performing Aversive Therapy

Aversive therapy can be accomplished by pairing the undesirable habit, such as smoking or drinking, immediately with a negative stimulus, such as shock or pain.

Performing Desensitization

Desensitization can be accomplished through three steps: construction of a hierarchy, relaxation, and performance of least disturbing items on the list.

Uses for Aversive Therapy

Aversive therapy can be used for undesirable habits such as smoking, drinking, gambling, drug addictions (marijuana, cocaine), and stuttering.

Uses for Desensitization

Desensitization is primarily used to help people unlearn phobias or strong anxieties. Vicarious desensitization uses the power of observational learning. Virtual reality exposure facilitates exposure to feared stimuli without the associated risks.

Operant and Cognitive Therapies

Operant and cognitive therapies take contrasting approaches to human problems.

Operant Therapies

Operant therapies are based on the *consequences of behaviors* (operant conditioning).

Operant Principles

Positive Reinforcement
Responses that are followed by reward tend to occur more frequently.

Nonreinforcement
A response that is not followed by a reward will occur less frequently.

Extinction
A response that is not followed by a reward many times will eventually go away.

Punishment
A response that is followed by discomfort or an undesirable effect will be suppressed.

Shaping
Successive approximations of a desired behavior are rewarded.

Therapy Example

Reinforcement and Token Economies
By using tokens (symbolic rewards that can be exchanged for real rewards), a therapist can immediately reward positive behaviors.

Stimulus Control
Control of the stimuli in a situation can lead to a response.

Time Out
The individual is rewarded from a situation in which reinforcement is occurring. This is a variation of nonreinforcement.

Cognitive Therapy

In general, cognitive therapy helps change thinking patterns that lead to troublesome emotions or behaviors.

Cognitive Principles

Rational-Emotive Behavior Therapy (REBT)
Rational-emotive behavior therapy attempts to do away with irrational beliefs that cause many emotional problems. REBT is very directive.

Core Irrational Beliefs
- I must perform well and be approved of by significant others.
- You must treat me fairly.
- Conditions must be the way I want them to be.

Therapy Example

Cognitive Therapy for Depression
Cognitive therapists attempt to change the maladaptive thoughts, beliefs, and feelings that lead to depression or similar problems.

Beck's Basics
Aaron Beck believes depressed persons see themselves, the world, and the future in negative terms. Beck believes depression is a result of three major distortions in thinking:
- Selective perception
- Overgeneralization
- All-or-nothing thinking

Group Therapy, Therapy Skills, and Medical Therapies

Successful therapy is carried out in other important ways.

Group Therapy

Group therapy is often as effective as individual therapy, and it has some advantages.

Psychodrama

Psychodrama (acting out personal conflicts and feelings in the presence of others) allows a person to gain insights that can be transferred to real-life situations.

Family Therapy

In family therapy, husband, wife, and children must work individually and as a group to resolve the problems of each family member.

Group Awareness Training

Encounter groups and sensitivity training groups are often used to improve employee relationships. The claimed benefits may result from a therapy placebo effect.

Psychotherapy

Some general helping skills can be distilled from the various therapy approaches.

Core Features of Psychotherapy

All therapies have four core elements:
1. A caring relationship between client and therapist (therapeutic alliance).
2. Therapy offers a protected setting for catharsis.
3. All therapies offer some extent of explanation for the client's suffering.
4. Clients have a new perspective about themselves and their situations.

Basic Counseling Skills

- Listen actively.
- Clarify the problem.
- Focus on feelings.
- Avoid giving advice.
- Accept the person's frame of reference.
- Reflect thoughts and feelings.
- Use silence in between responses.
- Ask open-ended questions.
- Maintain confidentiality.

Medical Therapies

Major mental disorders (major depressive disorders, schizophrenia, etc.) are most often treated medically.

Drug Therapies

Drugs have shortened hospital stays and improved the chances that people will recover from major psychological disorders.

Electroshock

Electroconvulsive therapy (ECT) involves administering an electric current to the brain in order to end severe depression and suicidal behavior.

Psychosurgery

Psychosurgery (any surgical alteration of the brain) is a technique with both supporters and detractors.

Psychology in Action: Self-Management and Seeking Professional Help

Self-Management Techniques

Some personal problems can be successfully treated using self-management techniques.

Covert Reinforcement

The use of positive imagery to reinforce desired behavior.

Covert Sensitization

The use of aversive imagery to discourage unwanted behavior.

Thought Stopping

The use of mild punishment to prevent upsetting thoughts.

Self-Directed Desensitization

Pairing relaxation with a hierarchy of upsetting images to lessen fears.

Seeking Professional Help

Seek help if you have psychological discomfort, changes in behavior, suicidal thoughts, or if friends suggest that you may need help. Seek out a mental health association or call a crisis hotline; psychologists are also listed in the phone book. The choice between a psychiatrist and a psychologist can be arbitrary.

1. _____ is any psychological technique used to facilitate positive changes in a person's personality, behavior, or adjustment.
   a. Pharmacotherapy
   b. Directive therapy
   c. Psychotherapy
   d. Positive therapy

2. _____ therapy is any psychotherapy whose goal is to lead clients to a deeper understanding of their thoughts, emotions, and behavior.
   a. Insight
   b. Supportive
   c. Directive
   d. Cognitive

3. _____ created the first recognized psychotherapy.
   a. Albert Bandura
   b. Wilhelm Wundt
   c. Sigmund Freud
   d. Abraham Maslow

4. In dream analysis, the _____ content is to the hidden meaning of the dream.
   a. latent
   b. manifest
   c. indirect
   d. reciprocal

5. _____ is the tendency to assign feelings to a therapist that match those the patient had for important persons in his or her past.
   a. Redesigned assignment
   b. Counter-transference
   c. Transference
   d. Resistance

6. Carl Rogers believed all of the following were essential conditions of therapy, except
   a. empathy.
   b. authenticity.
   c. conditional regard.
   d. reflection.

7. _____ therapy helps people rebuild thinking, feeling, and acting into connected wholes.
   a. Gestalt
   b. Existential
   c. Psychoanalytic
   d. Behavioral

8. The use of classical or operant conditioning to alter behavior is known as _____.
   a. behavioral desensitization
   b. behavior modification
   c. action-oriented therapy
   d. psychoanalysis

9. When an alcoholic takes a medication that results in her getting nauseous following the ingestion of alcohol, she is experiencing a(n) _____ therapy.
   a. physiological
   b. cognitive
   c. aversion
   d. reality

10. By watching his father pet dogs without fear, Carl's fear of dogs gradually began to decrease. This learning is an example of
    a. operant conditioning.
    b. vicarious desensitization.
    c. aversion therapy.
    d. systematic desensitization.

11. Using the therapeutic technique of _____, you might be asked to play the part of someone else in order to increase your understanding of that person.
    a. empathic acting
    b. mirroring
    c. psychodrama
    d. role reversal

12. Which of the following is not considered one of the basic counseling skills discussed in the text?
    a. Accepting the person's frame of reference
    b. Problem clarification
    c. Passive listening
    d. Avoiding giving advice

13. The use of drugs to treat mental illnesses is known as:
    a. pharmacotherapy.
    b. medical therapy.
    c. biopsychotherapy.
    d. psychotherapy.

14. The use of electrical currents to induce seizure activity in the brain to alleviate the symptoms of depression is known as
    a. PET.
    b. psychosurgery.
    c. neuroelectrotherapy.
    d. ECT.

15. _____ is the most extreme medical treatment.
    a. Psychopharmacology
    b. MRI
    c. Psychosurgery
    d. Biofeedback

16. Within a(n) _____ treatment program, patients spend their day at the hospital but go home at night.
    a. inpatient hospitalization
    b. temporary hospitalization
    c. partial hospitalization
    d. sunlight therapy

17. A community mental health (CMH) center is a treatment option typically
    a. serving the upper class or "private pay" clients.
    b. offering a wide range of mental health and psychiatric services.
    c. providing long-term treatment and inpatient care.
    d. utilizing a psychoanalytic approach.

18. Whenever Doug begins to think of himself as a failure, he snaps a rubber band worn around his wrist. This technique is known as
    a. overt desensitization.
    b. covert sensitization.
    c. aversive behaviorism.
    d. thought stopping.

19. _____ offer mutual support and a chance for discussion to members who share a common type of problem.
    a. Paraprofessional groups
    b. Self-help groups
    c. Maintenance groups
    d. Conversation groups

20. Trepanning involves
    a. the use of electric shock in order to induce a convulsion within the patient's brain.
    b. rewarding close approximations of a desired behavior.
    c. the use of psychiatric medications to treat mental illnesses.
    d. boring a hole in a person's head to "release evil spirits" or relieve pressure.

MODULE 14.1

Sex, Gender, and Androgyny

Sex and gender have a tremendous impact on relationships, personal identity, and health. In sexual development, being male or female is both biological *(sex)* and psychological *(gender)*.

Biological Dimensions of Sex

When classifying a person as male or female, we must take into account many factors:

- Genetic sex (chromosomes)
- Gonadal sex (ovaries or testes)
- Hormonal sex (proportion of androgens or estrogens)
- Genital sex (clitoris, vagina, penis, and scrotum)
- Gender identity (one's subjective sense of maleness or femaleness)

Prenatal Sexual Development

Genetic sex is determined at conception with the combination of XX or XY chromosomes.

Female or Male?

Males differ in both primary (sexual and reproductive organs) and secondary (superficial physical features that appear at puberty) sexual characteristics.

Sex Hormones

Sex differences are related to the proportion of estrogens (female hormones) and androgens (male hormones) found in both male and female bodies.

Psychological Origins of Male-Female Differences

Most human sex-linked behaviors are influenced much more by learning than by biological causes. Most male-female performance gaps can be traced to social differences in power and opportunity.

Gender Identity

Your personal, private sense of being female or male is your gender identity. It begins with how you are labeled at birth.

Gender Role Socialization

Gender roles (culturally favored patterns of behavior expected of each sex) have as big an influence on sexual behavior as any other factor.

Psychological Androgyny

Androgyny refers to the presence of both "masculine" and "feminine" traits in a single person. Androgynous individuals are very adaptable.

Sexual Behavior and Sexual Orientation

Sexuality is a natural part of being human. Sexual orientation is a very basic dimension of sexuality.

Sexual Arousal

Human sexual arousal is complex. Although direct stimulation of the body's erogenous zones (produces arousal), there is a large cognitive element.

Sexual Orientation

Sexual orientation refers to the degree to which you are emotionally and erotically attracted to members of the same sex, opposite sex, or both sexes. A combination of biological and social factors is most likely involved in sexual orientation.

Sexual Scripts

Sexual scripts are unspoken mental plans that guide our sexual behavior. Sexual scripts determine when and where we are likely to express sexual feelings, and with whom.

Sex Drive

The strength of one's motivation to engage in sexual behavior (sex drive) is influenced by attitudes toward sex, sexual experience, how long since sexual activity, and physical factors.

Erogenous Zones

Human erogenous zones include the genitals, mouth, breasts, ears, anus, and to a lesser degree, the entire surface of the body. Beyond just physical contact, human sexual arousal obviously includes a large mental element.

Scripts and Plots

A "script" defines a plot, dialogue, and actions that should take place. Sexual scripts provide a "plot" for the order of events in lovemaking, and they outline "approved" actions, motives, and outcomes.

Masturbation

Masturbation is a basic sexual behavior that is engaged in large percentages of both men and women. Typically, the only negative effects are feelings of fear, guilt, or anxiety that arise from being taught to think of masturbation as "bad" or "wrong."

Heterosexuality

Heterosexual people are romantically attracted to members of the opposite sex.

Homosexuality

Homosexual people are attracted to people whose sex matches their own.

Bisexuality

Bisexual people are attracted to both men and women.

Notes

Sexual Response, Attitudes, and Behavior

An understanding of human sexual response contributes to healthy sexuality.

Human Sexual Response

Sexual responses of both men and women follow four phases (excitement, plateau, orgasm, and resolution).

Excitement Phase
First level of sexual response, indicated by initial signs of sexual arousal.

Plateau Phase
Second level of sexual response, during which physical arousal intensifies.

Orgasm
A climax and release of sexual excitement.

Resolution
The final phase of sexual response, involving a return to lower levels of sexual tension and arousal.

Atypical Sexual Behavior

Public standards and private behavior are often at odds. True sexual deviations are compulsive and destructive.

Exhibitionism
Generally, the goal of an exhibitionist is to shock and alarm the victim.

Paraphilias
Sexual deviations (paraphilias) typically cause feelings of guilt, anxiety, or discomfort for one or both participants.

Child Molestation
The effects of molestation vary. How long it lasts, the type of molestation, and the parents' reactions impact on how severe the emotional harm is.

The Crime of Rape
A recent dramatic increase in date rape (by a forced intercourse in the context of a date has occurred).

Rape Myths
Often a rapist justifies the act by citing one of several widely held beliefs (rape myths).

Forcible Rape
Date rape is coercive but not necessarily violent. Forcible rape is now viewed more as a crime of violence than sex alone.

STDs and Safer Sex

Sexually transmitted diseases (STDs) particularly HIV, are behavioral risk factors. Yet many sexually active people continue to take unnecessary risks with their health by not following safer sex practices.

Chlamydia

Gonorrhea

Hepatitis B

Herpes

HPV (genital warts)

Syphilis

HIV/AIDS

Psychology in Action: Sexual Problems—When Pleasure Fades

Sexual dysfunctions/disorders are far more common than many people realize. Most people who seek sexual counseling have one or more of the following types of problems:

Desire Disorders

Hypoactive Sexual Desire
This condition is characterized by persistent loss of desire plus the person is troubled by it.

Sexual Aversion
This describes a person who is repelled by sex and seeks to avoid it.

Treatment
Treatments include drug therapy, behavioral methods, and counseling.

Arousal Disorders

Male Erectile Disorder
Men with this disorder cannot maintain an erection for lovemaking.

Female Sexual Arousal Disorder
Women who respond with little or no physical arousal to sexual stimulation.

Treatment
Treatment includes behavioral methods and counseling.

Orgasmic Disorders

Female and Male Orgasmic Disorder
This condition describes a person with the persistent inability to reach orgasm during lovemaking.

Premature Ejaculation
Ejaculation is premature if it consistently occurs before the man and his partner want it to occur.

Treatment
Treatment includes behavioral methods, such as the squeeze technique.

Sexual Pain Disorders

Dyspareunia
Dyspareunia involves pain in the genitals before, during. or after sexual intercourse.

Vaginismus
In this condition, muscle spasms of the vagina prevent intercourse.

Treatment
Treatment includes behavioral methods, such as progressive relaxation and counseling.

Practice Exam

1. What term refers to all the psychological and social traits associated with being male or female?
   a. Gender
   b. Sex
   c. Sexual category
   d. None of the above.

2. If Donn's biological sex conflicts with his preferred psychological and social gender role, he might be considered a
   a. transvestite.
   b. transsexual.
   c. homosexual.
   d. androgynous.

3. The vagina, ovaries, testes, and penis are all considered _____ _____ sex characteristics.
   a. secondary
   b. fundamental
   c. initial
   d. primary

4. The onset of menstruation in females is referred to as
   a. ovulation.
   b. menopause.
   c. menarche.
   d. a sex difference.

5. Estrogens is to androgens as _____ is to _____.
   a. small; large
   b. female; male
   c. young; old
   d. primary; secondary

6. The text defines classifying someone as male or female as taking into account all of the following except
   a. genetic sex.
   b. genital sex.
   c. gonadal sex.
   d. gender sex.

7. Which of the following combinations of chromosomes would result in male development?
   a. XX
   b. XY
   c. YY
   d. None of the above

8. Being taught by one's culture that hunting is something that men should do is an example of
   a. gender discrimination.
   b. gender stereotyping.
   c. action-oriented learning.
   d. gender role socialization.

9. Oversimplified beliefs about what men and women are actually like are known as
   a. sexual identities.
   b. cognitive gender distortions.
   c. gender role stereotypes.
   d. sex generated roles.

10. If Sally encourages her children to show their emotions, we would say that they are being encouraged in _____ behaviors.
    a. expressive
    b. instrumental
    c. aversive
    d. empathic

11. Tamara describes herself as having both masculine and feminine interests. Because of this, she might be considered as having a high level of
    a. confusion.
    b. androgyny.
    c. reversed role interests.
    d. gender stability.

12. _____ zones are areas of the body that can be directly stimulated for sexual arousal.
    a. Erogenous
    b. Arousal
    c. Stimulation
    d. Sexual orientation

13. Which of the following terms best describes someone who is attracted to both men and women?
    a. Omnisexual
    b. Heterosexual
    c. Homosexual
    d. Bisexual

14. As discussed in the text, rates for teen premarital intercourse have evidenced _____ between 1988 and 2002.
    a. a decrease
    b. an increase
    c. no change
    d. little activity

15. Forced intercourse that occurs in the context of a date or other voluntary encounter is the definition of
    a. acquaintance rape.
    b. date violence.
    c. voluntary rape.
    d. rape stereotyping.

16. Which of the following is not true of STDs?
    a. Many people who carry an STD may not know it.
    b. Sexually active people run a high risk of contracting a STD.
    c. Gonorrhea, herpes, genital warts, and syphilis are examples of STDs.
    d. It is difficult to have an STD infection and not know it.

17. A person experiencing _____ feels fear, anxiety, or disgust about engaging in sex.
    a. a paraphilia
    b. erotic distaste
    c. sexual aversion
    d. erectile dysfunction

18. *Sensate focus* directs attention to _____ sensations of pleasure and builds _____ skills
    a. erotic; interpersonal
    b. natural; communication
    c. aversive; tolerance
    d. sexual; socialization

19. Which of the following is not one of the ways, identified by Bryan Strong and Christine DeVault (1994), to avoid intimacy?
    a. Never argue.
    b. Never compromise.
    c. Turn off the television.
    d. Take care of your own need first.

20. Barry McCarthy identified all of the following elements necessary for a continuing healthy sexual relationship except
    a. sexual anticipation.
    b. valuing one's sexuality.
    c. believing you don't deserve sexual satisfaction.
    d. valuing intimacy.

Chapter 15

Affiliation, Friendship, and Love

Humans are social animals who need contact with family and friends.

Affiliation

The need to affiliate (associate with other people) is based on basic human desires for approval, support, friendship, and information.

Social Comparison Theory

Group membership fills our need for social comparison (comparing our own actions, feelings, opinions, or abilities with those of others). This theory holds that we affiliate to evaluate our actions, feelings, and abilities.

Interpersonal Attraction

Most voluntary social relationships are based on interpersonal attraction. All affect the degree to which we are attracted to others.

- Physical proximity
- Physical attractiveness
- Similarity
- Competence

Factors that Influence Interpersonal Attraction

Self-Disclosure

We find out about similarity by disclosing information about ourselves and finding out information about others. Self-disclosure at a moderate pace builds trust and reciprocity.

Loving and Liking

Romantic love is based on interpersonal attraction with high levels of emotional arousal, sexual desire, and mutual absorption. Liking is affection without passion or deep commitment.

Sex, Evolution, and Mate Selection

Evolutionary psychologists believe that evolution left an imprint on men and women that influences everything from sexual attraction and infidelity to jealousy and divorce.

Groups, Social Influence, and Conformity

To understand social behavior we must know what roles people play, their status, the norms they follow, and the attributions they make.

Group Structure, Cohesion, and Norms

We all belong to many overlapping social groups in which we occupy a position in the structure of the group. Groups have *structure* (a network of roles, communication, and power), *cohesiveness* (a desire to remain in the group), and *norms* (an accepted standard for behavior). Group membership affects our behavior.

Social Influence

Social psychologists are very interested in social influence (changes in behavior induced by the actions of others).

Social Roles

Our social roles are patterns of behavior expected of persons in various social positions.

Norms

Social behavior is affected by group norms. Norms are widely accepted standards for appropriate behavior.

Status

A person's social position within groups determines his or her status, or level of social power and importance. Higher status bestows special privileges and respect.

Attributions

We attribute people's behavior to various causes. We infer causes from circumstances.

Conformity

Group pressure can cause us to conform to the group norm. Nonconformity may be met with group sanctions.

Groupthink

Groupthink is an urge by decision makers to maintain each other's approval, even if critical thinking has to be suspended.

Compliance, Obedience and Self-Assertion

Compliance and obedience to authority are normal parts of social life.

Compliance

Compliance refers to situations in which a person bends to the requests of someone else who has little or no authority.

Obedience

Obedience is a special type of conformity to the demands of an authority. Stanley Milgram, social psychologist, conducted a classic study on obedience.

Self-Assertion

Self-assertion helps people meet their needs without resorting to aggressive behavior. Self-assertion is a direct, honest expression of feelings and desires. Assertion techniques emphasize firmness, not attack.

Low-Ball

The low-ball technique involves getting agreement to a small request and then changing the requirement to a larger situation.

Foot-in-Door

A person who agrees to a small request is more likely to comply with a larger demand later.

Door-in-Face

A person who turns down a large request is more likely to agree to a later, smaller request.

Milgram's Experiment

In Milgram's study, subjects were told to shock a man with a heart condition who was screaming and asking to be released. Sixty-five percent of his subjects "shocked" the man to the extreme, as long as there was a "legitimate authority" to obey.

Milgram's Follow-Up

Milgram found his initial findings disturbing. Consequently, he changed the variables of the study and found lower obedience rates as the distance from the learner and the authority changed.

Implications

Milgram suggested that when directions come from an authority, people rationalize that they are not personally responsible for their actions. Fortunately, he also found the presence of dissenters could free the others to disobey.

Attitudes and Persuasion

Attitudes are intimately woven into our actions and views of the world.

Attitudes

An attitude is a mixture of belief and emotion that predisposes us to respond to other people, objects, or groups in a positive or negative way.

Persuasion

Persuasion is any deliberate attempt to change attitudes or beliefs through information and arguments. Persuasion can be enhanced by a variety of known techniques.

Forming Attitudes

Attitudes may come from direct contact, interaction with others, group membership, child rearing, the mass media, or chance conditioning.

Brainwashing

Brainwashing (forced attitude change) requires a captive audience that can be made to feel totally helpless and dependent on the captor.

Changing Attitudes

Attitudes are fairly stable, but may change if the reference group (the group used for social comparison) changes.

Cults

Cults employ high-pressure techniques similar to brainwashing to gain control of cult members.

Attitudes and Behavior

Some attitudes may not be acted upon because of the consequences of the behavior (public reaction), or old habits, or lack of conviction.

Cognitive Dissonance Theory

This theory states that contradicting or clashing thoughts cause discomfort. Efforts to resolve the inconsistency may result in attitude change.

Prejudice and Intergroup Conflict

Prejudice, marked by suspicion, fear, or hatred, breaks people apart. Unfortunately, it is an all-too-common part of daily life.

Prejudice

Prejudice is a *negative emotional attitude* held toward members of a specific social group. Prejudices may be reflected in the policies of organizations and may be referred to as *racism, sexism, ageism,* or *heterosexism,* depending on the group affected.

Origins of Prejudice

Prejudice may lead to discrimination (the behavioral element of the attitude).

Reducing Prejudice

Any of these methods can be used to reduce prejudice and increase tolerance.

Scapegoating
Here, a person or a group is blamed for the actions of others or for conditions not of their making, also known as displaced aggression.

Personal Prejudice
This occurs when members of another ethnic group are perceived as a threat to one's own interests.

Group Prejudice
This occurs when a person conforms to group norms.

Prejudiced Personality
Prejudice can be a general personality characteristic (authoritarian, ethnocentric, and concerned with power).

Intergroup Conflict
Shared beliefs concerning *superiority, injustice, vulnerability,* and *distrust* are common triggers for hostility between groups.

Combating Prejudice
Research has shown that prejudice can be reduced by the following methods:

Equal-Status Contact
When social groups interact on an equal footing, without obvious differences in power or status.

Superordinate Goals
The establishment of goals that override other lesser goals, forcing cooperation among members of both groups, reduces prejudice.

Mutual Interdependence
Having to depend on one another to meet each person's goals can lessen prejudice.

Jigsaw Classrooms
When each student is given a "piece" of the information needed to complete a project or prepare for a test, students from different social groups display less prejudice.

Aggression and Prosocial Behavior

Reducing violence and increasing prosocial behavior are pressing issues.

Aggression

Aggression refers to any action carried out with the intention of harming another person.

Instincts

The idea that humans are naturally aggressive is rejected by many psychologists.

Biology

Aggression may have some biological roots in brain areas.

Frustration

Frustration may lead to aggression; however, frustration can also lead to other behaviors.

Aversive Stimuli

Aversive stimuli, which are unpleasant, can heighten hostility and aggression.

Social Learning

Aggression may be learned in a social situation or demonstrated by aggressive models (including television).

Prosocial Behavior

Prosocial behaviors include actions that are constructive, altruistic, or helpful to others.

Bystander Intervention

For bystander intervention to occur a bystander must: notice the need, interpret an emergency, decide to take responsibility, and select a course of action.

Who Helps?

When we see a person in trouble, it tends to cause heightened arousal. Potential helpers may feel empathetic arousal, and there is a strong empathy-helping relationship.

Psychology in Action: Multiculturalism—Living with Diversity

How can tolerance be encouraged?

Break the Prejudice Habit

Value openness to the other, the ability to genuinely appreciate those who differ from us culturally.

Beware of Stereotyping

Make the effort to tear down stereotypes, emphasize fairness and equality, and get to know people from various ethnic and cultural groups.

Seek Individuating Information

Seek information that helps us see a person as an individual, rather than as a member of a group.

Don't Fall Prey to Just-World Beliefs

Believing that the world is sufficiently just so that people generally get what they deserve can directly increase prejudiced thinking.

Be Aware of Self-Fulfilling Prophecies

Beware of having expectations that prompt people to act in ways that make the expectations come true.

Remember, Different Does Not Mean Inferior

It is not necessary to degrade other groups in order to feel positive about one's own group identity.

Understand That Race Is a Social Construction

Race is an illusion based on superficial physical differences and learned ethnic identities.

Look for Commonalities

Overcome the need to demean, defeat, and vanquish others. Try to cooperate with others so as to share their joys and suffer their sorrows.

Set an Example for Others

Act in a tolerant fashion so you can serve as a model of tolerance for others.

1. _____ is the scientific study of how individuals behave, think, and feel in social situations
   a. Social psychology
   b. Sociology
   c. Psychology
   d. Intrapersonal psychology

2. Although Mia was not happy, initially, with her midterm grade, when she found out that all her friends' grades were lower she began to feel better about her grade. A social psychologist would accurately refer to this change in belief as a result of social
   a. association.
   b. assessment.
   c. comparison.
   d. relativity.

3. Physical proximity promotes attraction due to increases in
   a. similarity of interests.
   b. frequency of contact.
   c. initial contact.
   d. social interaction.

4. The process of disclosing private thoughts and feelings and revealing yourself to others is referred to as
   a. interpersonal release.
   b. mutual absorption.
   c. romantic love.
   d. self-disclosure.

5. "Husband" and "psychologist" would be examples of _____ roles.
   a. ascribed
   b. achieved
   c. conflicted
   d. primary

6. What is the term for the degree of attraction among group members or the strength of their desire to remain in the group?
   a. Group cohesiveness
   b. Group structure
   c. Intergroup appeal
   d. None of the above.

7. Devon considers himself a big Detroit Lions fan and identifies with other Lions fans. He also despises the Chicago Bears and cannot understand why anyone would want to be a fan of that team. For Devon, other Detroit Lions fans would be considered a(n) _____, whereas Chicago Bears fans would be a(n) _____.
   a. out-group, in-group
   b. social support, social threat
   c. benefit, detriment
   d. in-group, out-group

8. Allison always stands during the playing of the national anthem. This standard for appropriate behavior would be considered by social psychologists a
   a. standard.
   b. norm.
   c. social rule.
   d. value set.

9. Dennis gets "cut off" on the highway while driving to class. His first belief is that the person driving the other car was rude and self-absorbed. He does not consider the situational influences that may have affected the driver's actions. Dennis has committed
   a. self-serving biasing.
   b. the fundamental attribution error.
   c. actor-observer bias.
   d. cognitive reversal.

10. "Because we have always been in agreement in the past, I hope we will be able to agree this time as well" is a statement one might hear if _____ is occurring.
    a. obedience
    b. group bias
    c. attribution
    d. groupthink

11. John was asked by the salesman to "simply take the car for a drive around the block." This request would be considered an example of the _____ effect.
    a. foot-in-the-door
    b. door-in-the-face
    c. low-ball
    d. door-to-door

12. Stanley Milgram's experiments, in which a subject gave varying degrees of shocks to a "learner," demonstrated the effects of the situation on the subject's
    a. obedience.
    b. understanding.
    c. stress levels.
    d. acceptance.

13. The three basic rights of assertiveness training include all of the following except
    a. the right to request.
    b. the right to refuse.
    c. the right to restitution.
    d. the right to right a wrong.

14. _____, as defined by the text, involves hurting another person or achieving one's goals at the expense of another.
    a. Violence
    b. Hostility
    c. Assertion
    d. Aggression

15. _____ is any deliberate attempt to change attitudes or beliefs through information and arguments.
    a. Persuasion
    b. Conformity
    c. Compliance
    d. Obedience

16. Glenna bought a new car even though she had already decided that she would only buy a used car. Because of this contradiction in her thoughts and behaviors, she is now experiencing increased anxiety. This anxiety may be a result of what social psychologists refer to as
    a. a personal neurosis.
    b. behavioral conflict.
    c. cognitive dissonance.
    d. groupthink.

17. Prejudice is to discrimination as _____ is to _____.
    a. secondary; primary
    b. attitude; behavior
    c. primary; secondary
    d. behavior; attitude

18. _____ simplify(ies) people by putting them into categories.
    a. Social labeling
    b. Cultural blindness
    c. Biases
    d. Stereotypes

19. Darley and Latané believe that in order for people to help someone else, they must
    a. notice that something is happening.
    b. define the event as an emergency.
    c. take responsibility.
    d. do all of the above.

20. Because Todd believed that he could not pass the final exam, he did very little to prepare for it. His eventual failure on the exam could be considered an example of a
    a. self-fulfilling prophecy.
    b. self-serving bias.
    c. just-world effect.
    d. social competition.

Chapter 16

Applied Psychology

Industrial/Organizational Psychology

Industrial/organizational (I/O) psychologists study the behavior of people at work.

Theories of Leadership
Two basic leadership theories are often found in the workplace.

Organizational Culture
Culture refers to a blend of customs, beliefs, values, attitudes, and rituals that give each organization its unique "flavor."

Personnel Psychology
Personnel psychologists are concerned with testing, selection, placement, and promotion of employees.

Theory X Leaders
Use scientific management.

Emphasis on work efficiency.

Task orientation

Assume workers must be goaded or guided into being productive.

Low Job Satisfaction
Low job satisfaction is linked with high absenteeism, low morale, and high employee turnover, which leads to higher training costs and inefficiency.

Theory Y Leaders
Use shared leadership and management by objectives.

Emphasis on human relations at work.

People orientation

Assume workers enjoy autonomy, responsibility, industry, creativity, and challenging work.

High Job Satisfaction
High job satisfaction is linked with better cooperation, better performance, greater willingness to help others, more creative problem solving, and less absenteeism.

Organizational Citizenship
Workers who are helpful, conscientious, courteous, and avoid pettiness and gossip, are highly valued by their leaders.

Job Analysis
Job analysis (a detailed description of the skills, knowledge, and activities required by a job) is the first step in personnel selection.

Selection Procedures
Once desirable skills and traits are known, the next step is to find people who have these abilities. Biodata, interviews, and psychological tests may be used.

Four Coping Styles for Dissatisfied Workers
Four basic coping styles these workers are common for workers with extreme job dissatisfaction.
- The vigilant style: The most effective style, these workers evaluate information objectively and make decisions by reviewing alternatives.
- The complacent style: Workers with this style let chance direct their careers with no planning.
- The defensive-avoidant style: Defensive-avoidant workers procrastinate due to indecision, rationalize, and make excuses for inaction and indecision.
- The hypervigilant style: Hypervigilant workers panic when forced to make career decisions.

Environmental Psychology

Environmental psychology is a specialty concerned with the relationship between environments and human behavior. Environmental psychologists are interested in both physical environments and social environments.

Social Environments and Behavioral Settings

Social environments are defined by groups of people, such as a dance, business meeting, or party. Behavioral settings are smaller areas within an environment whose use is well defined.

Personal Space

Personal space is our individual envelope which we regard as private. The systematic study of rules for use of personal space is called *proxemics*.

Spatial Norms

In North America, social distances are:

- Intimate (0-18 inches)
- Personal (18 inches to 4 feet)
- Social (4-12 feet)
- Public (12 feet plus)

Territoriality

Personal space extends to our "territory, the area we consider ours." Note how students "claim" a seat in classrooms.

Physical Environments

Physical environments are natural or constructed.

Stressful Environments

Overcrowding, traffic congestion, high-noise areas, toxic environments, and declining resources all contribute to stress-laden environments.

Crowding

Crowding refers to the subjective feelings of being over-stimulated by social inputs or loss of privacy.

Noise

Noise pollution, annoying and intrusive noise, is a major source of environmental stress.

Toxic Environments

Human activities drastically change the natural environment. Examples include deforestation, burning fossil fuels, and chemical usage.

Environmental Problem Solving

Environmental psychologists are working on ways to educate and motivate people to act in ways that create healthier environments.

- Reduce, reuse, recycle
- Educate
- Provide money rewards
- Remove barriers
- Use persuasion
- Seek public commitment
- Encourage goal setting
- Give feedback
- Revise attitudes

The Psychology of Law and Sports

Psychology can be seen in action at courthouses and sporting events.

Psychology and Law

The psychology of law is the study of the behavioral dimensions of the legal system.

Jury Behavior

Psychologists use mock juries to help understand what determines how real juries vote.

Jury Problems

Research shows jurors:
- are not able to put aside biases and values.
- are not good at separating evidence from other information.
- are influenced by inadmissible evidence.
- are not able to suspend judgment until all evidence is presented.

Jury Selection

Many attorneys use psychologists to assist in scientific jury selection using social science principles.

Death-Qualified Juries

Members of a death-qualified jury must favor the death penalty (or at least be indifferent to it). Such juries have a higher than average conviction rate.

Sports Psychology

Sports psychology is the study of the behavioral dimensions of sports performance.

Task Analysis

By doing a task analysis, sports skills can be broken into subparts in order to identify key elements and teach them to the competitor. Focus is on motor skill refinement.

Positive Psychology

During peak performance, physical, mental, and emotional states are in harmony and are optimal. Psychologists are seeking to identify conditions that facilitate peak performance.

Notes

_____

_____

_____

_____

_____

_____

_____

Psychology in Action: Human Factors Psychology—Who's the Boss Here?

Human factors psychology helps create machines that are more user friendly. The goal of human factors psychology, also known as *ergonomics*, is to design machines and work environments so they are compatible with our sensory and motor capacities.

Usability Testing
Usability testing involves the measurement of ease with which people can learn to use a machine.

Use of Natural Design
Natural design makes use of perceptual signals that people understand naturally.

Human-Computer Interaction
HCI involves using human factors methods to design computers and software.

Using Tools Effectively
When using tools, one should understand the task first, then attempt to understand the tool. Beware of satisficing.

Notes

1. _____ refers to the use of psychological principles and research methods to solve practical problems.
   a. Practical psychology
   b. Social psychology
   c. Organizational psychology
   d. Applied psychology

2. Chad's job is to assist companies in identifying ways in which their workers could become more efficient. Chad would most accurately be identified as a(n) _____ psychologist.
   a. professional
   b. organizational
   c. social
   d. clinical

3. The idea that "happy workers are productive workers" demonstrates the importance of _____.
   a. psychological efficiency
   b. work efficiency
   c. morale efficiency
   d. work humor efficiency

4. Joy is considered a people person and typically assumes that her employees prefer independence and are willing to accept personal responsibility in their jobs. Joy would most likely be considered a _____ leader.
   a. Theory Y
   b. Theory X
   c. personable
   d. scientific

5. A group of employees who work together toward a shared goal are referred to as a(n)
   a. objective-managed team.
   b. shared-leadership team.
   c. self-managed team.
   d. participative-managed team.

6. _____ is the degree to which a person is pleased with his or her work.
   a. Work contentment
   b. Job enrichment
   c. Employment appeal
   d. Job satisfaction

7. In his job at the factory, Steve works 10 hours per day but only 4 days per week. This practice is known as
   a. practice management.
   b. flex time.
   c. a compressed work week.
   d. work condensation.

8. Which of the following is not one of the four coping styles described by Wheeler and Janis?
   a. Hypervigilant
   b. Vigilante
   c. Defensive-avoidant
   d. Complacent

9. _____ psychology is concerned with testing, selection, placement, and promotion of employees.
   a. Personnel
   b. Personality
   c. Person-centered
   d. Personal

10. The use of an employee's past behavior to predict future behavior is the idea behind _____.
    a. biopsychosocial data collection
    b. profiling
    c. attrition theory
    d. biodata

11. Which of the following is not one of the recommendations made by the U.S. Department of Labor for surviving a job interview?
    a. Consider possible questions and outline your specific answers.
    b. Do not chew gum.
    c. Be on time.
    d. Avoid the use of slang terms.

12. The *Kuder Occupational Interest Survey* and the *Strong-Campbell Interest Inventory* are examples of what kind of test?
    a. Employment aptitude tests
    b. Vocational interest tests
    c. Computerized tests
    d. Occupational interest inventories

13. *Proxemics* is the systematic study of rules for the use of
    a. verbal communication.
    b. personality tests.
    c. public speaking.
    d. personal space.

14. What did Stanley Milgram identify as a result of overcrowding and high-density populations?
    a. Hostile motivation
    b. Cognitive overload
    c. Attentional overload
    d. Intentional excess

15. The volume of greenhouse gases each individual's consumption adds to the atmosphere is referred to as the
    a. carbon footprint.
    b. carbon neutral lifestyle.
    c. carbon debit.
    d. carbon meter.

16. The text identifies all of the following responses for lightening the environmental impact of our "throw-away" society, except
    a. recycling materials.
    b. reproducing attitudes.
    c. reducing consumption.
    d. reusing products.

17. In order to understand the possible behaviors one might observe within a jury setting, psychologist employ the use of _____.
    a. mock juries
    b. scientific juries
    c. replicated juries
    d. simulated juries

18. What attitude must a death-qualified juror typically have toward the death penalty?
    a. Against
    b. In favor of
    c. Unaware of
    d. All of the above are possible.

19. _____ is the study of the behavioral dimensions of sports performance.
    a. Game theory
    b. Aerobic empiricism
    c. Exercise science
    d. Sports psychology

20. Driving a car, putting a golf ball, playing drums, and even typing your research paper are all examples of
    a. motor skills.
    b. motor abilities.
    c. motor programs.
    d. motor competition.

MODULE A.1

Descriptive Statistics

Descriptive statistics summarize numbers so they become more meaningful and easier to communicate to others.

Graphical Statistics

Summarizing data pictorially (graphically) helps us to envision the results.

Z-Score

A z-score is a number that tells how many standard deviations above or below the mean a score is.

Normal Curve

A normal distribution curve is often found when recording chance events shows that some outcomes have a high probability and occur very often, whereas others occur less often.

Measures of Central Tendency

Central tendency measures include the following:

- *Mean*—the average of all scores.
- *Median*—the middle score.
- *Mode*—the score that occurs most often.

Measures of Variability

Variability measures include the following:

- *Range*—the difference between the highest and lowest scores.
- *Standard deviation*—how much scores deviate from the mean of a group of scores.

MODULE A.2

Inferential Statistics

Inferential statistics are techniques that allow us to make inferences, to generalize from samples and draw conclusions.

Samples and Population

Samples (smaller cross sections of a population) allow us to make inferences about the whole population.

Representative and Random

Samples are most valid when they truly reflect the membership and characteristics of the larger population.

Significant Differences

Tests of *statistical significance* provide an estimate of how often experimental results could have occurred by chance alone.

Correlation

Correlations tell us about the relationship between two variables. Knowledge about one factor allows us to make *predictions* concerning the other factor.

Correlation vs. Causation

It is important to understand that correlation does not demonstrate causation.

1. Summary is to conclusion as _____ is to
   _____.
   a. validity; reliability
   b. descriptive; inferential
   c. reliability; validity
   d. inferential; descriptive

2. All of the following are examples of graphical statistics except
   a. frequency distribution.
   b. frequency polygon.
   c. inferential polygram.
   d. histogram.

3. In his attempt to identify the central tendency of test scores
   within his classroom, what could Larry calculate?
   a. Mode
   b. Median
   c. Mean
   d. All of the above.

4. A standard deviation is considered a measure of _____.
   a. variability
   b. reliability
   c. validity
   d. central tendency

5. The distribution of many naturally occurring characteristics is
   often represented by
   a. an inverted U.
   b. a z-line.
   c. a normal curve.
   d. None of the above.

6. _____ statistics allow us to generalize behaviors
   of a relatively small group of individuals to that of a larger group.
   a. Simplified
   b. Deductive
   c. Inferential
   d. Descriptive

7. If for every additional bowl of Wheatios cereal eaten each day,
   your cholesterol dropped 5 points, we would conclude
   a. that a perfect positive correlational relationship exists.
   b. that it is by mere chance and no relationship exists.
   c. that a causal relationship exists.
   d. that a perfect negative correlational relationship exists.

8. Tests of _____ provide an estimate of how often
   experimental results could have occurred by chance alone.
   a. representative transference.
   b. correlational coefficients
   c. random assignment
   d. statistical significance

9. If Tashana has a score on her exam of 130, with the average
   score for the class being 120 and a standard deviation of 10, her
   z-score would be _____.
   a. +1.0
   b. +0.1
   c. −1.0
   d. −0.1

10. In order for a representative sample to be considered _____,
    each member of the population must have an equal chance of
    being involved in the sample.
    a. causal
    b. co-relating
    c. significant
    d. random

ANSWERS TO PRACTICE EXAMS

Chapter 1: Introducing Psychology and Research Methods

1. a	5. a	9. c	13. a	17. c
2. c	6. d	10. b	14. c	18. a
3. b	7. b	11. a	15. b	19. c
4. c	8. a	12. c	16. a	20. b

Chapter 2: Brain and Behavior

1. a	5. b	9. c	13. a	17. d
2. c	6. b	10. d	14. a	18. b
3. b	7. c	11. b	15. c	19. c
4. d	8. a	12. b	16. a	20. c

Chapter 3: Human Development

1. b	5. c	9. c	13. d	17. a
2. a	6. d	10. d	14. b	18. b
3. c	7. b	11. a	15. c	19. c
4. a	8. d	12. c	16. b	20. d

Chapter 4: Sensation and Perception

1. b	5. c	9. a	13. b	17. d
2. b	6. c	10. b	14. c	18. a
3. d	7. a	11. d	15. d	19. b
4. b	8. d	12. c	16. a	20. a

Chapter 5: States of Consciousness

1. d	5. d	9. b	13. b	17. a
2. d	6. b	10. a	14. a	18. b
3. a	7. a	11. a	15. d	19. b
4. a	8. d	12. c	16. b	20. b

Chapter 6: Conditioning and Learning

1. a	5. b	9. a	13. b	17. b
2. d	6. a	10. b	14. d	18. c
3. d	7. d	11. a	15. b	19. d
4. b	8. c	12. a	16. d	20. c

Chapter 7: Memory

1. c	5. a	9. a	13. b	17. c
2. b	6. a	10. d	14. d	18. b
3. d	7. c	11. a	15. b	19. c
4. d	8. d	12. d	16. b	20. c

Chapter 8: Intelligence, Cognition, Language, and Creativity

1. c	5. d	9. b	13. d	17. a
2. c	6. d	10. a	14. c	18. c
3. c	7. a	11. d	15. b	19. b
4. a	8. c	12. c	16. b	20. a

Chapter 9: Motivation and Emotion

1. c	5. a	9. b	13. c	17. c
2. d	6. c	10. a	14. d	18. d
3. b	7. b	11. d	15. a	19. a
4. b	8. d	12. d	16. c	20. b

Chapter 10: Personality

1. b	5. a	9. b	13. a	17. b
2. a	6. c	10. d	14. b	18. a
3. d	7. a	11. c	15. c	19. c
4. c	8. d	12. c	16. c	20. a

Chapter 11: Health, Stress, and Coping

1. b	5. a	9. d	13. a	17. b
2. a	6. b	10. d	14. d	18. c
3. d	7. a	11. d	15. c	19. c
4. d	8. d	12. c	16. a	20. d

Chapter 12: Psychological Disorders

1. b	5. a	9. d	13. b	17. b
2. c	6. a	10. b	14. a	18. c
3. a	7. c	11. c	15. d	19. a
4. c	8. a	12. a	16. c	20. a

Chapter 13: Therapies

1. c	5. c	9. c	13. a	17. b
2. a	6. c	10. b	14. d	18. c
3. c	7. a	11. d	15. c	19. b
4. a	8. b	12. c	16. c	20. d

Chapter 14: Gender and Sexuality

1. a	5. b	9. c	13. d	17. c
2. b	6. d	10. a	14. a	18. b
3. d	7. b	11. b	15. a	19. c
4. c	8. d	12. a	16. d	20. c

Chapter 15: Social Behavior

1. a	5. b	9. b	13. c	17. b
2. c	6. a	10. d	14. a	18. d
3. b	7. d	11. a	15. a	19. d
4. d	8. b	12. a	16. c	20. a

Chapter 16: Applied Psychology

1. d	5. c	9. a	13. d	17. a
2. b	6. d	10. d	14. c	18. b
3. a	7. c	11. a	15. a	19. d
4. a	8. b	12. b	16. b	20. a

Appendix: Behavioral Statistics

1. b	5. c	9. a
2. c	6. c	10. d
3. d	7. d	
4. a	8. d	